Place-of-Service Codes for Professional Clai

Listed below are place-of-service codes and descriptions. These codes should be use entity where service(s) were rendered. Check with individual payers (eg, Medicare, N reimbursement policies regarding these codes. If you would like to comment on a code(s) or description(s), your request to posinfo@cms.hhs.gov.

Place of Service Code(s)	Place of Service Name	Place of Service Description
01	Pharmacy	A facility or location where drugs and other medically related items and services are sold, dispensed, or otherwise provided directly to patients. (effective 10/1/05)
02	Unassigned	N/A
03	School	A facility whose primary purpose is education.
04	Homeless shelter	A facility or location whose primary purpose is to provide temporary housing to homeless individuals (eg, emergency shelters, individual or family shelters).
05	Indian Health Service freestanding facility	A facility or location, owned and operated by the Indian Health Service, that provides diagnostic, therapeutic (surgical and nonsurgical), and rehabilitation services to American Indians and Alaska Natives who do not require hospitalization.
06	Indian Health Service provider-based facility	A facility or location, owned and operated by the Indian Health Service, that provides diagnostic, therapeutic (surgical and nonsurgical), and rehabilitation services rendered by, or under the supervision of, physicians to American Indians and Alaska Natives admitted as inpatients or outpatients.
07	Tribal 638 freestanding facility	A facility or location owned and operated by a federally recognized American Indian or Alaska Native tribe or tribal organization under a 638 agreement that provides diagnostic, therapeutic (surgical and nonsurgical), and rehabilitation services to tribal members who do not require hospitalization.
08	Tribal 638 provider-based facility	A facility or location owned and operated by a federally recognized American Indian or Alaska Native tribe or tribal organization under a 638 agreement that provides diagnostic, therapeutic (surgical and nonsurgical), and rehabilitation services to tribal members admitted as inpatients or outpatients.
9-10	Unassigned	N/A
11	Office	Location, other than a hospital, skilled nursing facility, military treatment facility, community health center, state or local public health clinic, or intermediate care facility, where the health professional routinely provides health examinations, diagnosis, and treatment of illness or injury on an ambulatory basis.
12	Home	Location, other than a hospital or other facility, where the patient receives care in a private residence.
13	Assisted living facility	Congregate residential facility with self-contained living units providing assessment of each resident's needs and on-site support 24 hours a day, seven days a week, with the capacity to deliver or arrange for services including some health care and other services. (effective 10/1/03)
14	Group home	A residence, with shared living areas, where clients receive supervision and other services such as social and/or behavioral services, custodial service, and minimal services (eg, medication administration) (effective 4/1/04)
15	Mobile unit	A facility or unit that moves from place to place and is equipped to provide preventive, screening, diagnostic, and/or treatment services.
16	Temporary lodging	A short-term accommodation such as a hotel, camp ground, hostel, cruise ship, or resort where the patient receives care, and which is not identified by any other POS code. (effective 4/1/08)
17-19	Unassigned	N/A
20	Urgent care facility	Location, distinct from a hospital emergency department, an office, or a clinic, whose purpose is to diagnose and treat illness or injury for unscheduled, ambulatory patients seeking immediate medical attention.
21	Inpatient hospital	A facility, other than psychiatric, that primarily provides diagnostic, therapeutic (both surgical and nonsurgical), and rehabilitation services by, or under, the supervision of physicians to patients admitted for a variety of medical conditions..
22	Outpatient hospital	A portion of a hospital that provides diagnostic, therapeutic (both surgical and nonsurgical), and rehabilitation services to sick or injured persons who do not require hospitalization or institutionalization.
23	Emergency room— hospital	A portion of a hospital where emergency diagnosis and treatment of illness or injury is provided.
24	Ambulatory surgical center	A freestanding facility, other than a physician's office, where surgical and diagnostic services are provided on an ambulatory basis.
25	Birthing center	A facility, other than a hospital's maternity facilities or a physician's office, that provides a setting for labor, delivery, and immediate postpartum care as well as immediate care of newborn infants.
26	Military treatment facility	A medical facility operated by one or more of the uniformed services. Military treatment facility also refers to certain former US Public Health Service facilities now designated as uniformed service treatment facilities.
27-30	Unassigned	N/A
31	Skilled nursing facility	A facility that primarily provides inpatient skilled nursing care and related services to patients who require medical, nursing, or rehabilitative services but does not provide the level of care or treatment available in a hospital.

32	Nursing facility	A facility that primarily provides to residents skilled nursing care and related services for the rehabilitation of injured, disabled, or sick persons, or, on a regular basis, health-related care services above the level of custodial care to other than mentally retarded individuals.
33	Custodial care facility	A facility that provides room, board, and other personal assistance services, generally on a long-term basis, and does not include a medical component.
34	Hospice	A facility, other than a patient's home, in which palliative and supportive care for terminally ill patients and their families are provided.
35-40	Unassigned	N/A
41	Ambulance—land	A land vehicle specifically designed, equipped, and staffed for lifesaving and transporting the sick or injured.
42	Ambulance—air or water	An air or water vehicle specifically designed, equipped, and staffed for lifesaving and transporting the sick or injured.
43-48	Unassigned	N/A
49	Independent clinic	A location, not part of a hospital and not described by any other place-of-service code, that is organized and operated to provide preventive, diagnostic, therapeutic, rehabilitative, or palliative services to outpatients only. (effective 10/1/03)
50	Federally qualified health center	A facility located in a medically underserved area that provides Medicare beneficiaries preventive primary medical care under the general direction of a physician.
51	Inpatient psychiatric facility	A facility that provides inpatient psychiatric services for the diagnosis and treatment of mental illness on a 24-hour basis, by or under the supervision of a physician.
52	Psychiatric facility—partial hospitalization	A facility for the diagnosis and treatment of mental illness that provides a planned therapeutic program for patients who do not require full-time hospitalization but who need broader programs than are possible from outpatient visits to a hospital-based or hospital-affiliated facility.
53	Community mental health center	A facility that provides the following services: outpatient services, including specialized outpatient services for children, the elderly, individuals who are chronically ill, and residents of the community mental health center's mental health services area who have been discharged from inpatient treatment at a mental health facility; 24-hour-a-day emergency care services; day treatment, other partial hospitalization services, or psychosocial rehabilitation services; screening for patients being considered for admission to state mental health facilities to determine the appropriateness of such admission; and consultation and education services.
54	Intermediate care facility/mentally retarded	A facility that primarily provides health-related care and services above the level of custodial care to mentally retarded individuals but does not provide the level of care or treatment available in a hospital or skilled nursing facility.
55	Residential substance abuse treatment facility	A facility that provides treatment for substance (alcohol and drug) abuse to live-in residents who do not require acute medical care. Services include individual and group therapy and counseling, family counseling, laboratory tests, drugs and supplies, psychological testing, and room and board.
56	Psychiatric residential treatment center	A facility or distinct part of a facility for psychiatric care that provides a total 24-hour therapeutically planned and professionally staffed group living and learning environment.
57	Nonresidential substance abuse treatment facility	A location that provides treatment for substance (alcohol and drug) abuse on an ambulatory basis. Services include individual and group therapy and counseling, family counseling, laboratory tests, drugs and supplies, and psychological testing. (effective 10/1/03)
58-59	Unassigned	N/A
60	Mass immunization center	A location where providers administer pneumococcal pneumonia and influenza virus vaccinations and submit these services as electronic media claims or paper claims or by using the roster billing method. This generally takes place in a mass immunization setting, such as a public health center, pharmacy, or mall but may include a physician office setting.
61	Comprehensive inpatient rehabilitation facility	A facility that provides comprehensive rehabilitation services under the supervision of a physician to inpatients with physical disabilities. Services include physical therapy, occupational therapy, speech pathology, social or psychological services, and orthotics and prosthetics services.
62	Comprehensive outpatient rehabilitation facility	A facility that provides comprehensive rehabilitation services under the supervision of a physician to outpatients with physical disabilities. Services include physical therapy, occupational therapy, and speech pathology services.
63-64	Unassigned	N/A
65	End-stage renal disease treatment facility	A facility, other than a hospital, that provides dialysis treatment, maintenance, and/or training to patients or caregivers on an ambulatory or home-care basis.
66-70	Unassigned	N/A
71	Public health clinic	A facility maintained by either state or local health departments that provides ambulatory primary medical care under the general direction of a physician. (effective 10/1/03)
72	Rural health clinic	A certified facility located in a rural, medically underserved area that provides ambulatory primary medical care under the general direction of a physician.
73-80	Unassigned	N/A
81	Independent laboratory	A laboratory certified to perform diagnostic and/or clinical tests independent of an institution or a physician's office.
82-98	Unassigned	N/A
99	Other place of service	Other place of service not identified above.

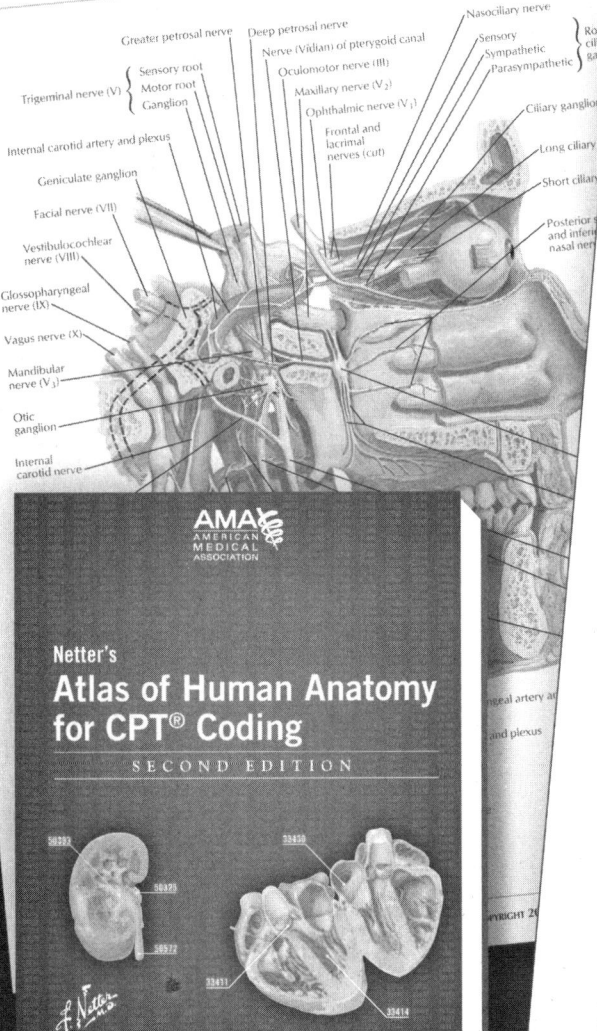

current procedural terminology

cpt® 2010

Standard Edition

Michelle Abraham, BS
Michael Beebe
Joyce A. Dalton
Desiree D. Evans, AAS
Rejina L. Glenn
Gloria Green, BA
DeHandro Hayden, BS

Elizabeth Lumakovska, MPA, RHIT
Janette Meggs, RHIA
Marie L. Mindeman, BA, RHIT
Karen E. O'Hara, BS, CCS-P
Mary R. O'Heron, RHIA, CCS-P
Danielle Pavloski, BS, RHIT, CCS-P
Marjorie C. Rallins, DPM

Dan Reyes
Desiree Rozell, MPA
Lianne Stancik, RHIT
Peggy Thompson, MS, RHIA, CCS
Susan Tracy, MA, RHIT
Ada Walker, CCA
Arletrice Watkins, MHA, RHIA

AMA
AMERICAN
MEDICAL
ASSOCIATION

Standard ISBN: 978-1-60359-118-8
ISSN: 0276-8283

Foreword

Current Procedural Terminology (CPT®), Fourth Edition, is a listing of descriptive terms and identifying codes for reporting medical services and procedures performed by physicians. The purpose of the terminology is to provide a uniform language that will accurately describe medical, surgical, and diagnostic services, and will thereby provide an effective means for reliable nationwide communication among physicians, patients, and third parties. *CPT 2010* is the most recent revision of a work that first appeared in 1966.

CPT descriptive terms and identifying codes currently serve a wide variety of important functions in the field of medical nomenclature. The CPT codebook is useful for administrative management purposes such as claims processing and for the development of guidelines for medical care review. The uniform language is also applicable to medical education and outcomes, health services, and quality research by providing a useful basis for local, regional, and national utilization comparisons. The CPT codebook is the most widely accepted nomenclature for the reporting of physician procedures and services under government and private health insurance programs. In 2000, the CPT code set was designated by the Department of Health and Human Services as the national coding standard for physician and other health care professional services and procedures under the Health Insurance Portability and Accountability Act (HIPAA). This means that for all financial and administrative health care transactions sent electronically, the CPT code set will need to be used.

The changes that appear in this revision have been prepared by the CPT Editorial Panel with the assistance of physicians representing all specialties of medicine, and with important contributions from many third-party payers and governmental agencies.

The American Medical Association trusts that this revision will continue the usefulness of its predecessors in identifying, describing, and coding medical, surgical, and diagnostic services.

Michael D. Maves, MD, MBA
Executive Vice President, CEO

Acknowledgments

Publication of the annual CPT codebook represents many challenges and opportunities. From reconciling the many differences of opinion about the best way to describe a procedure, to the last details on placement of a semicolon, many individuals and organizations devote their energies and expertise to the preparation of this revision.

The editorial staff wishes to express sincere thanks to the many national medical specialty societies, health insurance organizations and agencies, and individual physicians and other health professionals who have made contributions.

Thanks are due to Robert A. Musacchio, PhD, Sr VP, American Medical Association; Claudia Bonnell, Blue Cross and Blue Shield Association; Nelly Leon-Chisen, American Hospital Association; Jeannette Thornton, America's Health Insurance Plans; and Sue Bowman, RHIA, American Health Information Management Association, for their invaluable assistance for enhancing the CPT code set.

For their assistance in development of the CPT Category II codes:

Ronald A. Gabel, MD	Phil Renner, MBA
Darryl T. Gray, MD, ScD	Sam J. W. Romeo, MD, MBA
Robert S. Haskey, MD	Paul M. Schyve, MD
Susan M. Nedza, MD	Sharon Sprenger, RHIA, PHQ, MPA
Gregory Pawlson, MD, MPH	Sally Turbyville, MA
Sylvia Publ, RHIA, MBA	

We recognize the following people for efforts in working with the Physician Consortium for Performance Improvement and other quality measurement organizations:

Mark Antman, DDS, MBA	Shannon Sims, MD, PhD
Heidi Bossley, MSN, MBA	Beth Tapper, MA, MPH
Joseph Gave, MPH	Sheila Teasdale, MMed Sci FBCS
Kendra Hanley, MS	Samantha Tierney, MPH
Erin Kaleba, MPH	E. ChynaWilcoxson, BS
Karen S. Kmetik, PhD	Temaka Williams, MPH, MBA

AMA CPT Editorial Panel

Chair
William T. Thorwarth, Jr, MD, FACR*

Vice-Chair
Peter A. Hollmann, MD*

Albert E. Bothe, Jr, MD, FACS†
Joel F. Bradley, Jr, MD
Kenneth P. Brin, MD, PhD
Boyd R. Buser, DO, FACOFP
Patrick J. Cafferty, MPAS, PA-C*
Jeffrey W. Cozzens, MD, FACS
Richard Duszak, Jr, MD, FACR†
David A. Ellington, MD†
Helene M. Fearon, PT
Robert Haskey, MD
M. Bradford Henley, MD, MBA
Joseph V. Messer, MD, MACC†
Andrea H. McGuire, MD, MBA
Antonio E. Puente, PhD†
Kenneth B. Simon, MD, MBA*
Stanley W. Stead, MD, MBA*
Mark S. Synovec, MD
J. Martin Tucker, MD*
Richard W. Waguespack, MD

Secretary
Marie L. Mindeman, BA, RHIT

*Member of the CPT Executive Committee
†New Panel Member June 2008 and November 2008
‡New Advisors

AMA CPT Advisory Committee

Academy of Pharmaceutical Physicians and Investigators
Grant P. Bagley, MD
American Academy of Allergy, Asthma and Immunology
Donald W. Aaronson, MD
American Academy of Child & Adolescent Psychiatry
David I. Berland, MD
American Academy of Dermatology
Dirk M. Elston, MD
American Academy of Facial Plastic and Reconstructive Surgery
Edward H. Farrior, MD, FACS
American Academy of Family Physicians
Robert J. Carr, Jr, MD‡
American Academy of Neurology
Marc Nuwer, MD, PhD
American Academy of Ophthalmology
Michael X. Repka, MD
American Academy of Orthopaedic Surgeons
Richard J. Friedman, MD, FACSC
American Academy of Otolaryngic Allergy
Paul T. Fass, MD, FACS
American Academy of Otolaryngology-Head and Neck Surgery
Joseph E. Leonard, MD, FACS
American Academy of Pain Medicine
Eduardo M. Fraifeld, MD
American Academy of Pediatrics
Richard A. Molteni, MD
American Academy of Physical Medicine and Rehabilitation
Francis P. Lagattuta, MD
American Academy of Sleep Medicine
Samuel A. Fleishman, MD
American Association for Clinical Chemistry
Robert L. Murray, JD, PhD
American Association for Thoracic Surgery
Kirk R. Kanter, MD

American Association of Clinical Endocrinologists
Eric A. Orzek, MD, FACP, FACE
American Association of Hip and Knee Surgeons
Richard Iorio, MD
American Association of Neurological Surgeons
R. Patrick Jacob, MD
American Association of Neuromuscular and Electrodiagnostic Medicine
Kyle W. Ruffing, MD
American Association of Public Health Physicians
Arvind K. Goyal, MD, MPH, FAAFP, FACPM
American Clinical Neurophysiology Society
Marc Nuwer, MD, PhD
American College of Allergy, Asthma, and Immunology
Gary N. Gross, MD
American College of Cardiology
Robert N. Piana, MD, FACC‡
American College of Chest Physicians
Steve G. Peters, MD
American College of Emergency Physicians
Kenneth L. DeHart, MD, FACEP
American College of Gastroenterology
Daniel C. DeMarco, MD, FACG‡
American College of Medical Genetics
David B. Flannery, MD
American College of Medical Quality
Joel Grossman, MD
American College of Nuclear Physicians
Gary L. Dillehay, MD, FACNP, FACR
American College of Obstetricians and Gynecologists
Jordan G. Pritzker, MD, MBA, FACOG
American College of Occupational and Environmental Medicine
Lee S. Glass, MD
American College of Physicians
R. Scott Hanson, MD, MPH
American College of Preventive Medicine
Ryung Suh, MD, MPP, MBA, MPH
American College of Radiation Oncology
Carl C. Van Wey, MD‡
American College of Radiology
Daniel Picus, MD, FACR, RCC‡
American College of Rheumatology
Robert J. Lloyd, MD
American College of Surgeons
Linda M. Barney, MD, FACS‡
American Dental Association
Anthony M. Spina, DDS, MD‡
American Gastroenterological Association
Joel V. Brill, MD, AGAF, FASGE, FACG, CHCQM
American Geriatric Society
Robert A. Zorowitz, MD, MBA
American Institute of Ultrasound in Medicine
Harvey L. Nisenbaum, MD
American Medical Directors Association
Dennis L. Stone, MD, MBA
American Medical Group Association
David E. Hooper, MD
American Orthopaedic Association
Blair C. Filler, MD
American Orthopaedic Foot and Ankle Society
Walter J. Pedowitz, MD
American Osteopathic Association
Judith A. O'Connell, DO, FAAO
American Psychiatric Association
David K. Nace, MD
American Roentgen Ray Society
Mark D. Alson, MD

American Society for Aesthetic Plastic Surgery, Inc.
Paul R. Weiss, MD
American Society for Clinical Pathology
Lee H. Hilborne, MD, MPH, FASCP
American Society for Dermatologic Surgery
Pamela K. Phillips, MD
American Society for Gastrointestinal Endoscopy
Glenn D. Littenberg, MD
American Society for Reproductive Medicine
John T. Queenan, Jr, MD
American Society for Surgery of the Hand
Daniel J. Nagle, MD
American Society for Radiation Oncology
Michael L. Steinberg, MD, FACR
American Society of Abdominal Surgeons
Louis F. Alfano, Jr, MD
American Society of Anesthesiologists
Doug G. Merrill, MD
American Society of Bariatric Physicians
Mary C. Vernon, MD
American Society of Cataract and Refractive Surgery
Stephen S. Lane, MD
American Society of Clinical Oncology
William C. Penley, MD
American Society of Colon and Rectal Surgeons
Guy R. Orangio, MD, FACS, FASCRS
American Society of Cytopathology
Patricia A. Gregg, MD, FACP
American Society of General Surgeons
Charles Drueck III, MD, FACS
American Society of Hematology
Samuel M. Silver, MD, PhD, FACP, FAHA
American Society of Neuroimaging
Mircea A. Morariu, Jr, MD
American Society of Neuroradiology
C. Douglas Phillips, MD, FACR
American Society of Ophthalmic Plastic and Reconstructive Surgery
L. Neal Freeman, MD, MBA, CCS-P, FACS
American Society of Plastic Surgeons
Raymond V. Janevicius, MD
American Thoracic Society
Stephen P. Hoffmann, MD
American Urological Association
Jeffrey A. Dann, MD, MBA
College of American Pathologists
James P. Almas, MD, FCAP
Congress of Neurological Surgeons
Joseph S. Cheng, MD‡
Contact Lens Association of Ophthalmologists
Charles B. Slonim, MD, FACS
Infectious Disease Society of America
Steven K. Schmitt, MD‡
National Association of Medical Examiners
Paul A. Raslavicus, MD
North American Spine Society
William Mitchell, MD
Radiological Society of North America
Timothy A. Crummy, MD
Renal Physicians Association
Richard J. Hamburger, MD
Society for Investigative Dermatology
Stephen P. Stone, MD
Society for Vascular Surgery
Sean Roddy, MD
Society of American Gastrointestinal Endoscopic Surgeons
Paresh C. Shah, MD

Society of Critical Care Medicine
George A. Sample, MD, FCCP
Society of Interventional Radiology
Katharine L. Krol, MD
Society of Nuclear Medicine
Kenneth A. McKusick, MD
Society of Thoracic Surgeons
Cameron D. Wright, MD
The Endocrine Society
Richard A. Guthrie, MD
United States and Canadian Academy of Pathology
David S. Wilkinson, MD, PhD

AMA Health Care Professionals Advisory Committee (HCPAC)

William T. Thorwarth, Jr, MD, Co-Chair
AMA CPT Editorial Panel
Patrick J. Cafferty, MPAS, PA-C, Co-Chair
AMA CPT Editorial Panel
American Academy of Physician Assistants
Terry E. Carlisle, PA-C, MPAS
American Association of Naturopathic Physicians
Wendell B. Milliman, ND
American Association for Respiratory Care
Susan Rinaldo-Gallo, Med, RRT
American Chiropractic Association
Craig S. Little, DC
American Dietetic Association
Keith Thomas-Ayoob, EdD, RD, FADA, CSP
American Massage Therapy Association
Susan B. Rosen
American Nurses Association
Julie E. Chicoine, JD, RN, CPC‡
American Occupational Therapy Association
Leslie F. Davidson, MS, Ed, OTR/L
American Optometric Association
Douglas C. Morrow, OD
American Physical Therapy Association
Paul A. Rockar, Jr, PT, MS
American Podiatric Medical Association
Michael J. King, DPM
American Speech Hearing Association
R. Wayne Holland, EdD, CCC-SLP
National Athletic Trainers' Association
J. David Jones, MSHA, MS, ATC
National Association of Social Workers
Mirean Coleman, LICSW
National Society of Genetic Counselors
Debra L. Doyle, MS, CGC
Pharmacist Services Technical Advisory Coalition
Daniel E. Buffington, PharmD, MBA

Contents

Introduction

Current Procedural Terminology (CPT®), Fourth Edition, is a set of codes, descriptions, and guidelines intended to describe procedures and services performed by physicians and other health care providers. Each procedure or service is identified with a five-digit code. The use of CPT codes simplifies the reporting of services.

Inclusion of a descriptor and its associated five-digit code number in the CPT codebook is based on whether the procedure is consistent with contemporary medical practice and is performed by many practitioners in clinical practice in multiple locations. Inclusion in the CPT codebook does not represent endorsement by the American Medical Association (AMA) of any particular diagnostic or therapeutic procedure. Inclusion or exclusion of a procedure does not imply any health insurance coverage or reimbursement policy

The CPT code set is published annually in the late summer or early fall as both electronic data files and books. The release of CPT data files on the Internet typically precedes the book by several weeks. In any case, January 1 is the effective date for use of the update of the CPT code set. The interval between the release of the update and the effective date is considered the implementation period and is intended to allow physicians and other providers, payers, and vendors to incorporate CPT changes into their systems. The exceptions to this schedule of release and effective dates are CPT Category III and vaccine product codes, which are released twice a year on January 1 or July 1 with effective dates for use six months later, and CPT Category II codes. Changes to the CPT code set are meant to be applied prospectively from the effective date.

The main body of the material is listed in six sections. Each section is divided into subsections with anatomic, procedural, condition, or descriptor subheadings. The procedures and services with their identifying codes are presented in numeric order with one exception—the entire **Evaluation and Management** section (99201-99499) appears at the beginning of the listed procedures. These items are used by most physicians in reporting a significant portion of their services.

Section Numbers and Their Sequences

Evaluation and Management 99201-99499
Anesthesiology 00100-01999, 99100-99140
Surgery 10021-69990
Radiology (Including Nuclear Medicine
    and Diagnostic Ultrasound) 70010-79999
Pathology and Laboratory 80048-89356
Medicine
    (except Anesthesiology)   90281-99199, 99500-99602

The first and last code numbers and the subsection name of the items appear at the top margin of most pages (eg, "11010-11306 Surgery/Integumentary System"). The continuous pagination of the CPT codebook is found on the lower margin of each page along with explanation of any code symbols that are found on that page.

Instructions for Use of the CPT Codebook

Select the name of the procedure or service that accurately identifies the service performed. Do not select a CPT code that merely approximates the service provided. If no such specific code exists, then report the service using the appropriate unlisted procedure or service code. In surgery, it may be an operation; in medicine, a diagnostic or therapeutic procedure; in radiology, a radiograph. Other additional procedures performed or pertinent special services are also listed. When necessary, any modifying or extenuating circumstances are added. Any service or procedure should be adequately documented in the medical record.

It is important to recognize that the listing of a service or procedure and its code number in a specific section of this book does not restrict its use to a specific specialty group. Any procedure or service in any section of this book may be used to designate the services rendered by any qualified physician or other qualified health care professional.

Instructions, typically included as parenthetical notes with selected codes, indicate that a code should not be reported with another code or codes. These instructions are intended to prevent errors of significant probability and are not all inclusive. For example, the code with such instructions may be a component of another code and therefore it would be incorrect to report both codes even when the component service is performed. These instructions are not intended as a listing of all possible code combinations that should not be reported, nor to indicate all possible code combinations that are appropriately reported. When reporting codes for services provided, it is important to assure the accuracy and quality of coding through verification of the intent of the code by use of the related guidelines, parenthetical instructions, and coding resources, including *CPT Assistant* and other publications resulting from collaborative efforts of the American Medical Association with medical specialty societies (ie, *Clinical Examples in Radiology*).

Format of the Terminology

The CPT code set has been developed as stand-alone descriptions of medical procedures. However, some of the procedures in the CPT codebook are not printed in their entirety but refer back to a common portion of the procedure listed in a preceding entry. This is evident when an entry is followed by one or more indentations. This is done in an effort to conserve space.

Example

25100   Arthrotomy, wrist joint; with biopsy

25105   with synovectomy

Note that the common part of code 25100 (the part before the semicolon) should be considered part of code 25105. Therefore, the full procedure represented by code 25105 should read:

25105   Arthrotomy, wrist joint; with synovectomy

Requests to Update the CPT Nomenclature

The effectiveness of the CPT nomenclature depends on constant updating to reflect changes in medical practice. This can only be accomplished through the interest and timely suggestions of practicing physicians, medical specialty societies, state medical associations, and other organizations and agencies. Accordingly, the AMA welcomes correspondence, inquiries, and suggestions concerning old and new procedures, as well as other matters such as codes and indices.

To submit a suggestion to add, delete, or revise procedures contained in the CPT codebook, please contact:

CPT Editorial Research & Development
American Medical Association
515 North State Street
Chicago, Illinois 60654

Coding change request forms are available at the AMA's CPT web site: www.ama-assn.org/ama/pub/category/3866.html.

All proposed changes of the CPT codebook will be considered by the CPT Editorial Panel with consultation of appropriate medical specialty societies.

Guidelines

Specific guidelines are presented at the beginning of each of the six sections. These guidelines define items that are necessary to appropriately interpret and report the procedures and services contained in that section. For example, in the **Medicine** section, specific instructions are provided for handling unlisted services or procedures, special reports, and supplies and materials provided. Guidelines also provide explanations regarding terms that apply only to a particular section. For instance, **Radiology Guidelines** provide a definition of the unique term, "radiological supervision and interpretation." While in **Anesthesia,** a discussion of reporting time is included.

Add-on Codes

Some of the listed procedures are commonly carried out in addition to the primary procedure performed. These additional or supplemental procedures are designated as add-on codes with the symbol **+** and they are listed in **Appendix D** of the CPT codebook. Add-on codes in *CPT 2010* can be readily identified by specific descriptor nomenclature that includes phrases such as "each additional" or "(List separately in addition to primary procedure)."

The add-on code concept in *CPT 2010* applies only to add-on procedures or services performed by the same physician. Add-on codes describe additional intra-service work associated with the primary procedure (eg, additional digit[s], lesion[s], neurorrhaphy[s], vertebral segment[s], tendon[s], joint[s]).

Add-on codes are always performed in addition to the primary service or procedure and must never be reported as a stand-alone code. All add-on codes found in the CPT codebook are exempt from the multiple procedure concept (see the modifier 51 definition in **Appendix A**)..

Modifiers

A modifier provides the means to report or indicate that a service or procedure that has been performed has been altered by some specific circumstance but not changed in its definition or code. Modifiers also enable health care professionals to effectively respond to payment policy requirements established by other entities. The judicious application of modifiers obviates the necessity for separate procedure listings that may describe the modifying circumstance. Modifiers may be used to indicate to the recipient of a report that:

- A service or procedure had both a professional and technical component.
- A service or procedure was performed by more than one physician and/or in more than one location.
- A service or procedure was increased or reduced.
- Only part of a service was performed.
- An adjunctive service was performed.
- A bilateral procedure was performed.
- A service or procedure was provided more than once.
- Unusual events occurred.

Example

A physician providing diagnostic or therapeutic radiology services, ultrasound, or nuclear medicine services in a hospital would add modifier 26 to report the professional component.

73090 with modifier 26 = Professional component only for an X-ray of the forearm

Example

Two surgeons may be required to manage a specific surgical problem. When two surgeons work together as primary surgeons performing distinct part(s) of a procedure, each surgeon should report his/her distinct operative work by adding modifier 62 to the procedure code and any associated code(s) for that procedure as long as both surgeons continue to work together as primary surgeons. Each surgeon should report the co-surgery once using the same procedure code. Modifier 62 would be applicable. For instance, a neurological surgeon and an otolaryngologist are working as co-surgeons in performing transphenoidal excision of a pituitary neoplasm.

The first surgeon would report:

61548 62 = Hypophysectomy or excision of pituitary tumor, transnasal or transseptal approach, nonstereotactic + two surgeons modifier

AND the second surgeon would report:

61548 62 = Hypophysectomy or excision of pituitary tumor, transnasal or transseptal approach, nonstereotactic + two surgeons modifier

If additional procedure(s) (including add-on procedure[s]) are performed during the same surgical session, separate code(s) may also be reported with modifier 62 added. It should be noted that if a co-surgeon acts as an assistant in the performance of additional procedure(s) during the same surgical session, those services may be reported using separate procedure code(s) with modifier 80 or modifier 82 added, as appropriate. A complete listing of modifiers is found in **Appendix A.**

Place of Service and Facility Reporting

Some codes have specified places of service (eg, evaluation and management codes are specific to a setting). Other services and procedures may have instructions specific to the place of service (eg, therapeutic, prophylactic, and diagnostic injections and infusions). The CPT code set is designated for reporting physician and qualified health care professional services. It is also the designated code set for reporting services by organizational or facility providers (eg, hospitals) in specific circumstances. Facilities are entities that may report services in addition to the physician or qualified health care professional for the same service. For example, a physician may report a procedure performed in the outpatient department of the hospital and the hospital may report the same procedure. The CPT codebook uses the term *facility* to describe such providers and the term *nonfacility* to describe services where no facility reporting may occur. Services provided in the home by an agency are facility services. Services provided in the home by a physician or qualified health care professional who is not a representative of the agency are nonfacility services.

Unlisted Procedure or Service

It is recognized that there may be services or procedures performed by physicians or other qualified health care professionals that are not found in the CPT codebook. Therefore, a number of specific code numbers have been designated for reporting unlisted procedures. When an unlisted procedure number is used, the service or procedure should be described (see specific section guidelines). Each of these unlisted procedural code numbers (with the appropriate accompanying topical entry) relates to a specific section of the book and is presented in the guidelines of that section.

In some cases alternative coding and procedural nomenclature as contained in other code sets may allow appropriate reporting of a more specific code. CPT references to use an unlisted procedure code do not preclude the reporting of an appropriate code that may be found in other code sets.

Results, Testing, Interpretation, and Report

Results are the technical component of a service. Testing leads to results; results lead to interpretation. Reports are the work product of the interpretation of test results. Certain procedures or services described in CPT involve a technical component (eg, tests) which produce "results" (eg, data, images, slides). For clinical use, some of these results require interpretation. Some CPT descriptors specifically require interpretation and reporting to report that code.

Special Report

A service that is rarely provided, unusual, variable, or new may require a special report. Pertinent information should include an adequate definition or description of the nature, extent, and need for the procedure and the time, effort, and equipment necessary to provide the service.

Code Symbols

A summary listing of additions, deletions, and revisions applicable to the CPT codebook is found in **Appendix B.** New procedure numbers added to the CPT codebook are identified throughout the text with the symbol ● placed before the code number. In instances where a code revision has resulted in a substantially altered procedure descriptor, the symbol ▲ is placed before the code number. The symbols ► ◄ are used to indicate new and revised text other than the procedure descriptors. These symbols indicate CPT Editorial Panel actions. The AMA reserves the right to correct typographical errors and make stylistic improvements.

CPT add-on codes are annotated by the symbol ✛ and are listed in **Appendix D.** The symbol ⊘ is used to identify codes that are exempt from the use of modifier 51 but have not been designated as CPT add-on procedures or services. A list of codes exempt from modifier 51 usage is included in **Appendix E.** The symbol ⊙ is used to identify codes that include moderate sedation (see **Appendix G**). The symbol ⚡ is used to identify codes for vaccines that are pending FDA approval (see **Appendix K**).

Resequenced codes that are not placed numerically are identified with the # symbol, and a reference placed numerically (eg, **Code is out of numerical sequence. See...**) as a navigational alert to direct the user to the location of the out-of-sequence code (see **Appendix N**). Resequencing is utilized to allow placement of related concepts in appropriate locations within the families of codes regardless of the availability of numbers for sequential numerical placement.

Alphabetical Reference Index

This codebook features an expanded alphabetical index that includes listings by procedure and anatomic site. Procedures and services commonly known by their eponyms or other designations are also included.

CPT 2010 in Electronic Formats

CPT 2010 procedure codes and descriptions are available on CD-ROM as data files and electronic software. Data files are available in ASCII and EBCDIC formats and can be imported into any billing and claims reporting software that accepts a text (.TXT) file format. *CPT 2010 Electronic Professional* software, with *Netter's Atlas of Human Anatomy for CPT Coding,* provides access to the entire *CPT 2010 Professional Edition* codebook on your desktop. Easy-to-use and fully searchable, this invaluable software contains all of the favorite *CPT Professional* features plus CPT codes and quick linking access between CPT codes, guidelines, modifiers, appendices, index, and more. For more information call (800) 621-8335 or visit *www.amabookstore.com.*

References to AMA Resources

Subscriptions to *CPT Assistant* and *Clinical Examples in Radiology* can be purchased by calling the AMA's Unified Service Center at (800) 621-8335. Individual back issues are available for purchase and immediate download at *www.amabookstore.com.*

An archive software product with every issue of *CPT Assistant* is also available. *CPT Assistant Archives 1990-2009* provides convenient access to 20 years of *CPT Assistant* newsletter articles on your desktop. Search past issues of the AMA's authoritative coding newsletter by keyword, phrase, CPT code number, newsletter issue, article index, or codebook table of contents. This product offers simple search capabilities and a complete historical CPT code list from 1990-2008 that references when a code was added, deleted, and/or revised. Call (800) 621-8335 or visit *www.amabookstore.com* for more information.

Current and past editions of *CPT Changes: An Insider's View* can be purchased by calling the AMA's Unified Service Center at (800) 621-8335 or visiting *www.amabookstore.com.*

Additionally, an archives software product with all content from past and present editions of *CPT Changes: An Insider's View* is available. *CPT Changes Archives 2000-2010* provides access to current and historical CPT code and guideline changes on your computer desktop. Search by keyword, phrase, CPT code number, edition, and CPT codebook table of contents. For more information, call (800) 621-8335 or visit *www.amabookstore.com.*

Illustrated Anatomical and Procedural Review

It is essential that coders have a thorough understanding of medical terminology and anatomy to code accurately. The following section reviewing the basics of vocabulary and anatomy can be used as a quick reference to help you with your coding. It is not intended as a replacement for up-to-date medical dictionaries and anatomy texts, which are essential tools for accurate coding.

Prefixes, Suffixes, and Roots

Although medical terminology may seem complex, many medical terms can be broken into component parts, which makes them easier to understand. Many of these terms are derived from Latin or Greek words, but some include the names of physicians.

Prefixes are word parts that appear at the beginning of a word and modify its meaning; suffixes are found at the end of words. By learning what various prefixes and suffixes mean, it is possible to decipher the meaning of a word quickly. The following lists are a quick reference for some common prefixes and suffixes.

Numbers

Prefix	Meaning	Example
mono-, uni-	one	monocyte, unilateral
bi-	two	bilateral
tri-	three	triad
quadr-	four	quadriplegia
hex-, sex-	six	hexose
diplo-	double	diplopia

Surgical Procedures

Suffix	Meaning	Example
-centesis	puncture a cavity to remove fluid	amniocentesis
-ectomy	surgical removal (excision)	appendectomy
-ostomy	a new permanent opening	colostomy
-otomy	cutting into (incision)	tracheotomy
-orrhaphy	surgical repair/suture	herniorrhaphy
-opexy	surgical fixation	nephropexy
-oplasty	surgical repair	rhinoplasty
-otripsy	crushing, destroying	lithotripsy

Conditions

Prefix	Meaning	Example
ambi-	both	ambidextrous
aniso-	unequal	anisocoria
dys-	bad, painful, difficult	dysphoria
eu-	good, normal	euthanasia
hetero-	different	heterogeneous
homo-	same	homogeneous
hyper-	excessive, above	hypergastric
hypo-	deficient, below	hypogastric
iso-	equal, same	isotonic
mal-	bad, poor	malaise
megalo-	large	megalocardia

Conditions (continued)

Suffix	Meaning	Example
-algia	pain	neuralgia
-asthenia	weakness	myasthenia
-emia	blood	anemia
-iasis	condition of	amebiasis
-itis	inflammation	appendicitis
-lysis	destruction, break down	hemolysis
-lytic	destroy, break down	hemolytic
-oid	like	lipoid
-oma	tumor	carcinoma
-opathy	disease of	arthropathy
-orrhagia	hemorrhage	menorrhagia
-orrhea	flow or discharge	amenorrhea
-osis	abnormal condition of	tuberculosis
-paresis	weakness	hemiparesis
-plasia	growth	hyperplasia
-plegia	paralysis	paraplegia
-pnea	breathing	apnea

Directions and Positions

Prefix	Meaning	Example
ab-	away from	abduction
ad-	toward	adduction
ecto, exo-	outside	ectopic, exocrine
endo-	within	endoscope
epi-	upon	epigastric
infra-	below, under	infrastructure
ipsi-	same	ipsilateral
meso-	middle	mesopexy
meta-	after, beyond, transformation	metastasis
peri-	surrounding	pericardium
retro-	behind, back	retroversion
trans-	across, through	transvaginal

Word	Meaning
anterior or ventral	at or near the front surface of the body
posterior or dorsal	at or near the back surface of the body
superior	above
inferior	below
lateral	side

Directions and Positions (continued)

Word	Meaning
distal	farthest from center
proximal	nearest to center
medial	middle
supine	face up or palm up
prone	face down or palm down
sagittal	vertical body plane, divides the body into equal right and left sides
transverse	horizontal body plane, divides the body into top and bottom sections
coronal	vertical body plane, divides the body into front and back sections

Additional References

For best coding results, you will need to use other reference materials in addition to your coding books. These references include a medical dictionary and one or more anatomy books that can be purchased from the American Medical Association by calling 800 621-8335.

Medical Dictionaries

Stedman's CPT® Dictionary, 2nd ed.
Chicago, IL: American Medical Association, 2009.
OP300609

Merriam-Webster's Medical Desk Dictionary.
Springfield, Mass: Merriam Webster.
OP941493

Stedman's Medical Dictionary. 27th ed.
Baltimore, Md: Williams & Wilkins; 2000.
OP982900

Anatomy References

Kirschner, CG. *Netter's Atlas of Anatomy for CPT® Coding, 2nd ed.*
Chicago, Ill: American Medical Association; 2005
OP490609

Kirschner, CG. *Netter's Atlas of Human Anatomy for CPT® and ICD-9-CM Coding Series: Musculoskeletal.*
Chicago, Ill: American Medical Association
OP492206

Netter, FH. *Atlas of Human Anatomy.* 3rd ed.
East Hanover, NJ: Novartis; 2003.
OP936798

Lists of Illustrations

To further aid coders in properly assigning CPT codes, the codebook contains a number of anatomical and procedural illustrations.

Anatomical Illustrations

Figure 1A
Body Planes — 3/4 View

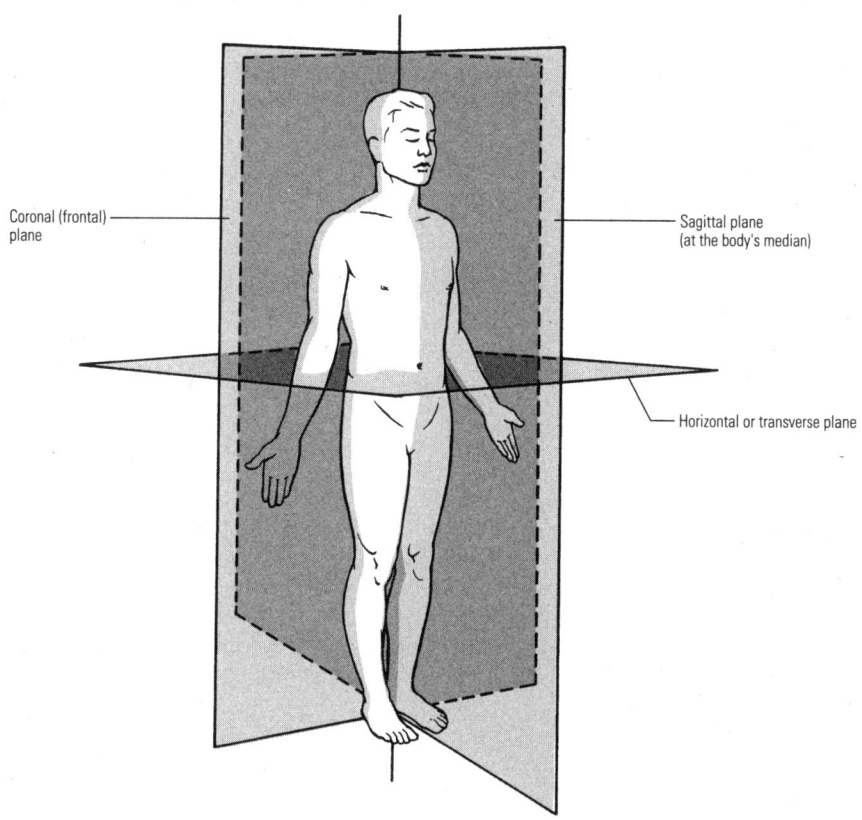

Coronal (frontal) plane

Sagittal plane (at the body's median)

Horizontal or transverse plane

Figure 1B
Body Aspects — Side View

Figure 1C
Body Planes — Front View

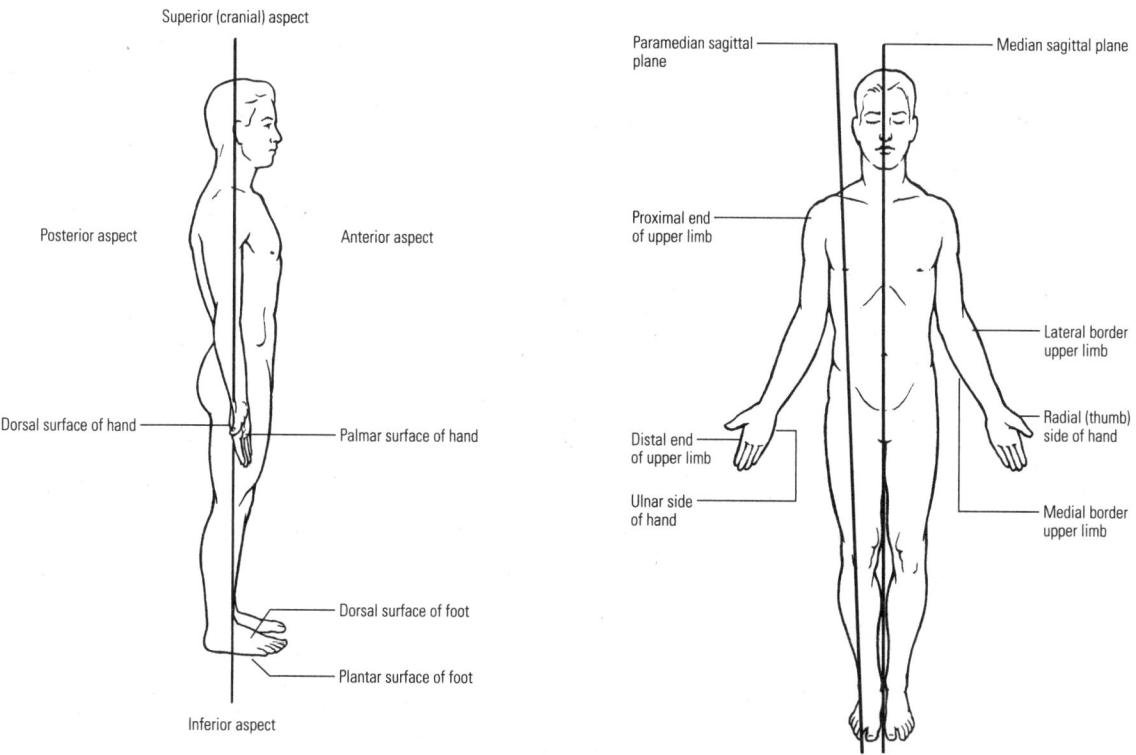

Superior (cranial) aspect

Posterior aspect

Anterior aspect

Dorsal surface of hand

Palmar surface of hand

Dorsal surface of foot

Plantar surface of foot

Inferior aspect

Paramedian sagittal plane

Median sagittal plane

Proximal end of upper limb

Lateral border upper limb

Radial (thumb) side of hand

Distal end of upper limb

Ulnar side of hand

Medial border upper limb

Figure 2
Structure of Skin

Hair shaft

Hair root

Epidermis

Sebaceous gland

Dermis

Nerve endings

Hair bulb

Subcutaneous tissue

Sweat gland

Cutaneous nerve

Blood vessels

Figure 3
Skeletal System

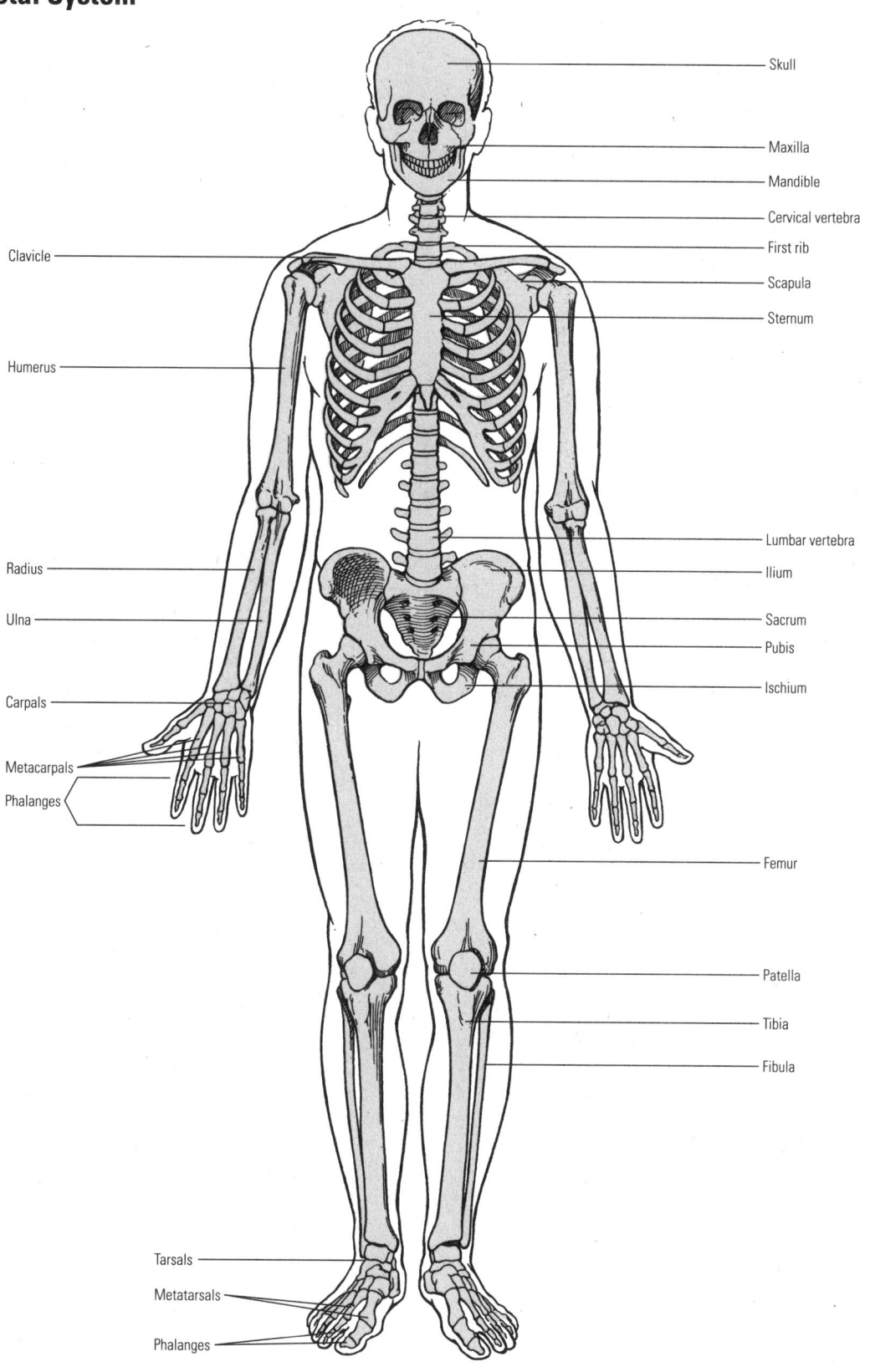

Skull
Maxilla
Mandible
Cervical vertebra
First rib
Scapula
Sternum

Clavicle

Humerus

Radius

Ulna

Carpals

Metacarpals

Phalanges

Lumbar vertebra
Ilium
Sacrum
Pubis
Ischium

Femur

Patella

Tibia

Fibula

Tarsals

Metatarsals

Phalanges

Figure 4
Skull

Parietal bone

Temporal bone

Sphenoid bone

Zygomatic bone

Maxilla

Mandible

Frontal bone

Nasal bone

Frontal bone

Nasal bone

Zygomatic bone

Maxilla bone

Mandible

Parietal bone

Occipital bone

Temporal bone

Temporomandibular joint

Figure 5A
Muscular System — Front

Sternocleidomastoid m.
Omohyoid m.
Sternohyoid m.
Trapezius m.
Deltoid m.
Pectoralis major m.
Latissimus dorsi m.
Serratas anterior m.
Oblique external m.
Rectus abdominus m.

Biceps m.
Brachialus m.
Brachioradialus m.
Pronator teres m.
Flexor carpi radialus m.
Palmaris longus m.
Flexor digitorum superficialus m.
Flexor carpi ulnaris m.

Pectineus m.
Adductor longus m.
Adductor magnus m.
Gracilis m.
Sartorius m.
Rectus femoris m.
Vastus medialis m.
Vastus lateralis m.
} Quadriceps

Peroneus longus m.
Tibialis anterior m.
Gastrocnemius m.
Extensor digitorum longus m.
Soleus m.

Figure 5B
Muscular System — Back

Trapezius m.
Deltoid m.
Infraspinatus m.
Teres minor m.
Teres major m.
Triceps m.
Latissimus dorsi m.
Anconeus m.
Extensor carpi radialis longus m.
Flexor carpi ulnaris m.
Extensor carpi radialis brevis m.
Extensor digitorum m.
Extensor carpi ulnaris m.
Abductor pollicis longus m.
Extensor pollicis brevis m.

Gluteus medius m.
Gluteus maximus m.
Adductor magnus m.
Biceps femoris m.
Semitendinosus m.
Gracilis m.
Semimembranosus m.
Vastus lateralis m.
Sartorius m.
Gastrocnemius m.
Peroneus longus m.
Flexor hallicis longus m.

Figure 6A
Thoracic Vertebra—Superior View

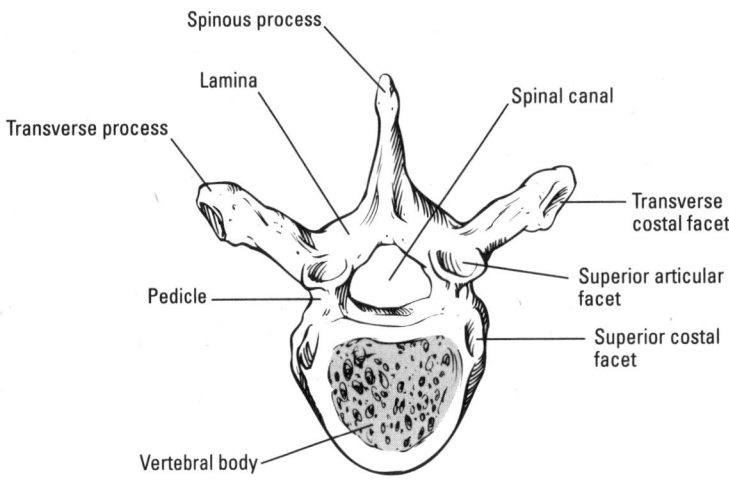

Figure 6B
Lumbar Vertebra—Superior View

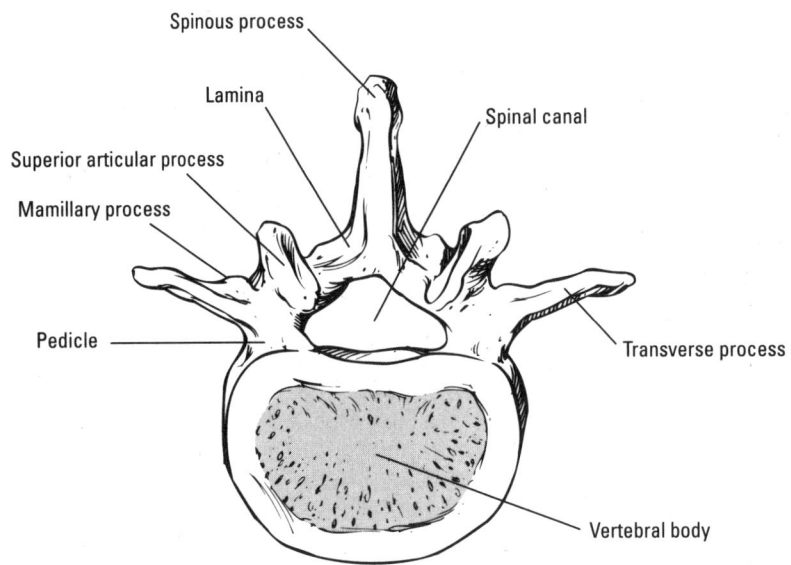

Figure 7
Lumbar Vertebrae—Lateral View

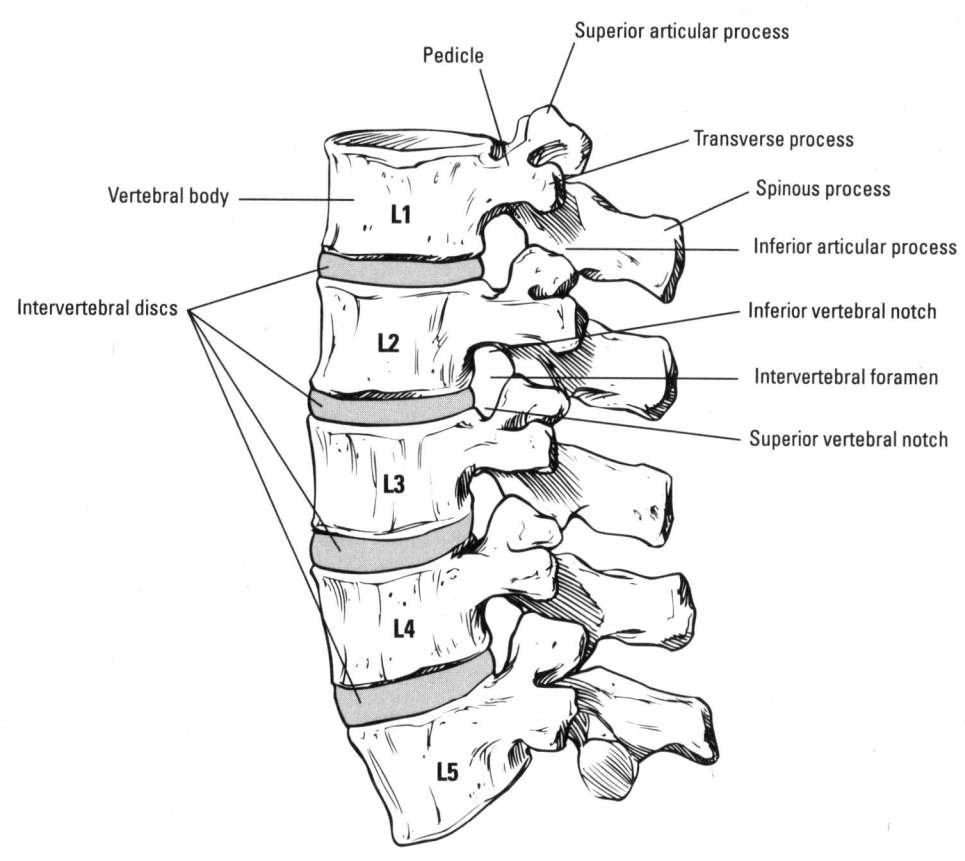

Figure 8
Bones, Muscles, and Tendons of Hand

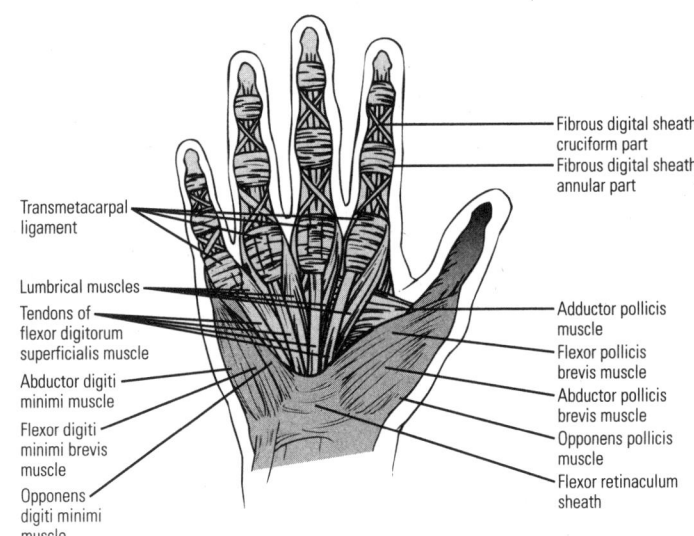

Phalanges

Metacarpal bones

Carpal bones

Ulna

Radius

Transmetacarpal ligament

Lumbrical muscles

Tendons of flexor digitorum superficialis muscle

Abductor digiti minimi muscle

Flexor digiti minimi brevis muscle

Opponens digiti minimi muscle

Fibrous digital sheath, cruciform part

Fibrous digital sheath, annular part

Adductor pollicis muscle

Flexor pollicis brevis muscle

Abductor pollicis brevis muscle

Opponens pollicis muscle

Flexor retinaculum sheath

Figure 9
Bones and Muscles of Foot

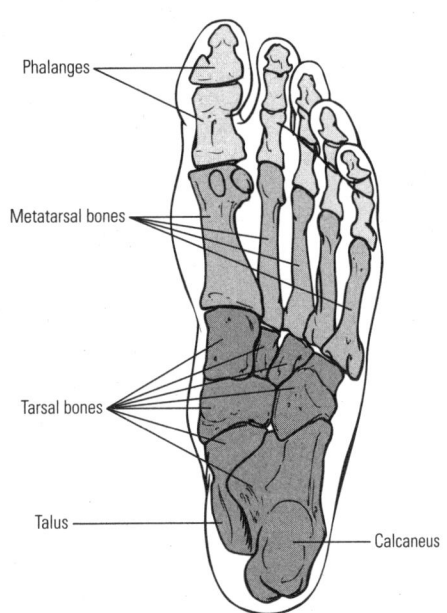

Phalanges

Metatarsal bones

Tarsal bones

Talus

Calcaneus

Tendon of flexor hallucis longus muscle

Flexor hallucis brevis muscle

Abductor hallucis muscle

Lumbrical muscles

Flexor digitorum brevis muscle

Flexor digiti minimi brevis muscle

Abductor digiti minimi muscle

Figure 10
Paranasal Sinuses

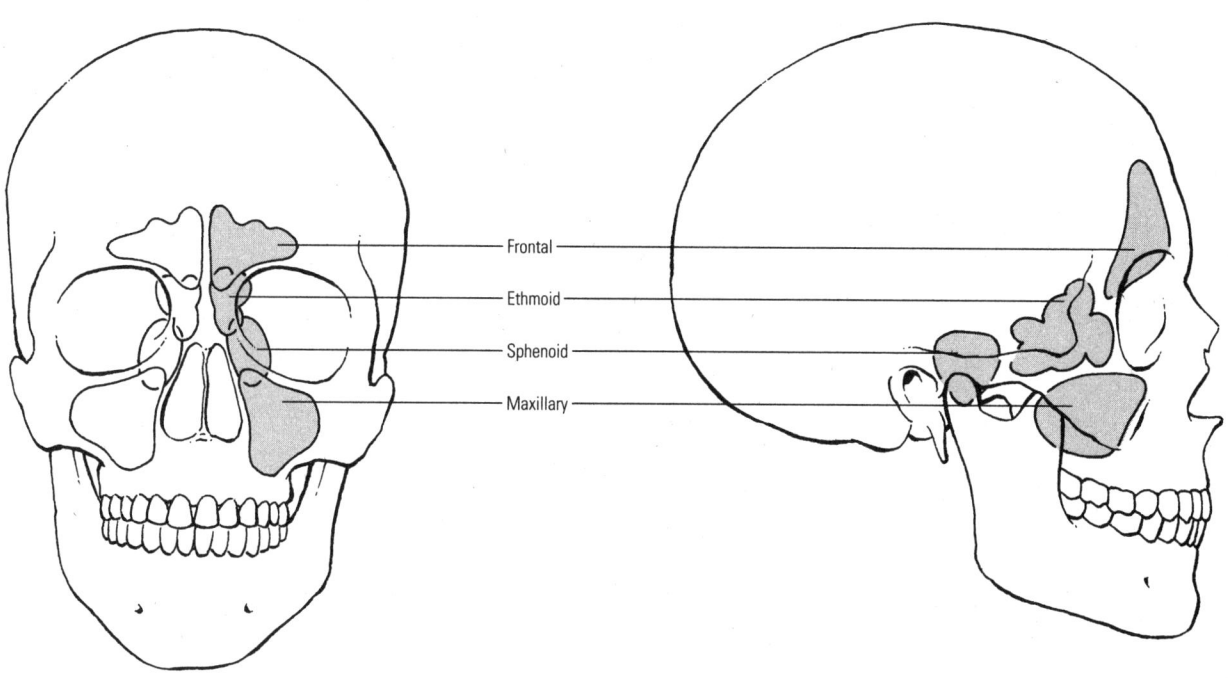

Frontal

Ethmoid

Sphenoid

Maxillary

Figure 11
Respiratory System

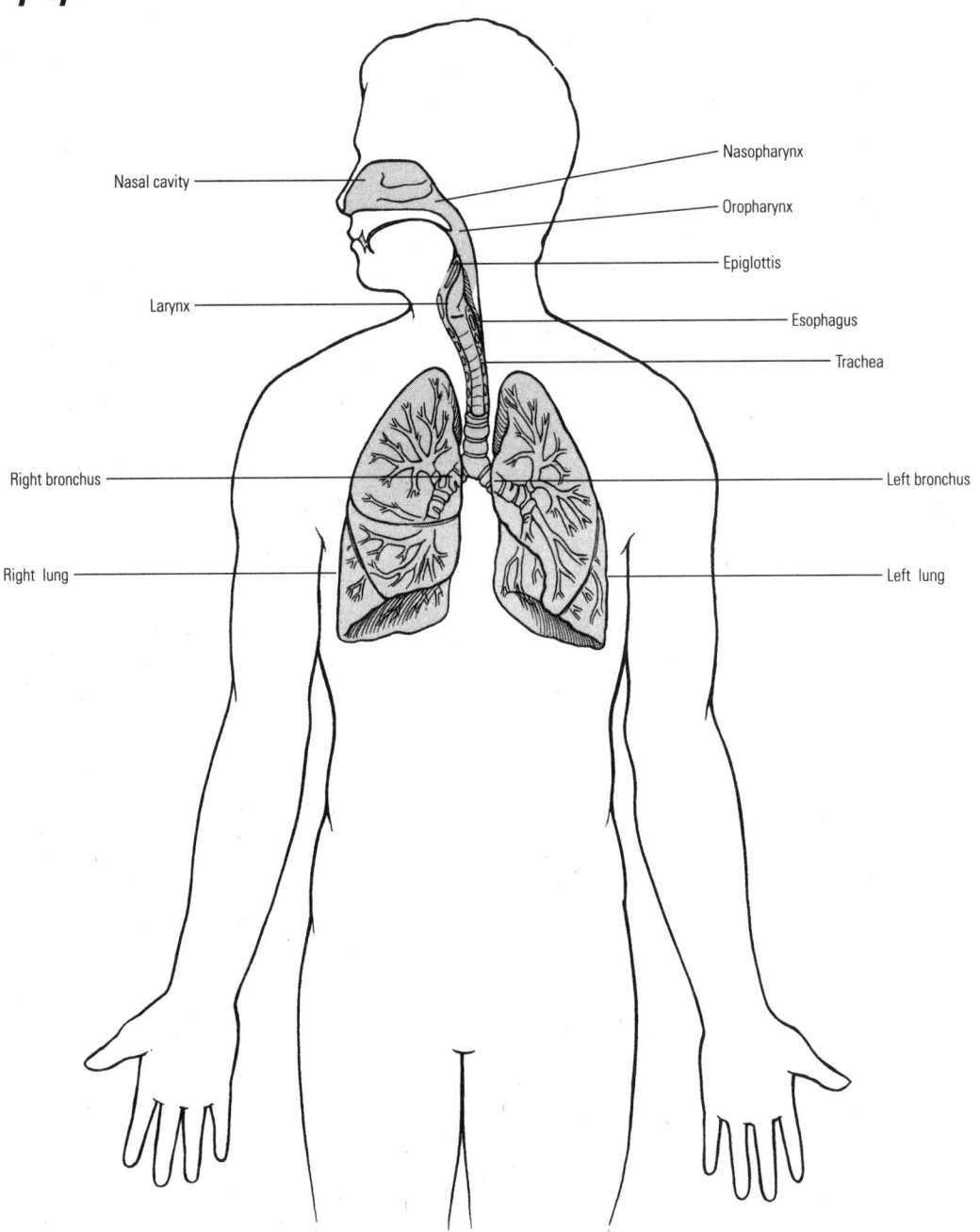

Nasal cavity

Larynx

Right bronchus

Right lung

Nasopharynx

Oropharynx

Epiglottis

Esophagus

Trachea

Left bronchus

Left lung

Figure 12
Circulatory System — Arteries

Superficial temporal a.
Posterior auricular a.
Common carotid a.
Subclavian a.
Brachiocephalic trunk
Axillary a.
Deep brachial a.
Brachial a.
Aorta
Radial a.
Interosseous a.
Ulnar a.
Deep palmar arch
Superficial palmar arch
Descending genicular a.

External carotid a.
Internal carotid a.
Vertebral a.
Aorta and arch
Pulmonary a.
Cardiac a.
Thoracic aorta
Celiac trunk
Superior mesenteric a.
Renal a.
Gonadal a.
Inferior mesenteric a.
Common iliac a.
External iliac a.
Internal iliac a.
Deep femoral a.
Femoral a.
Popliteal a.
Anterior tibial a.
Peroneal a.
Posterior tibial a.

Figure 13
Cardiac Anatomy

Superior vena cava
Right pulmonary artery
Pulmonary valve
Location of sinoatrial node
Location of atrioventricular node
Right atrium
Tricuspid valve
Right ventricle
Inferior vena cava

Aorta
Pulmonary artery
Left atrium
Aortic valve
Mitral valve
Left ventricle
Ventricular septum
Descending thoracic aorta

Figure 14
**Circulatory System —
Veins**

Superficial
temporal v.

Facial v.

External jugular v.

Internal jugular v.

Subclavian v.

Brachiocephalic v.

Superior vena cava

Axillary v.

Brachial v.

Cephalic v.

Hepatic v.

Basilic v.

Median cubital v.

Renal v.

Gonadal v.

Inferior vena cava

Medial antebrachial v.

Common iliac v.

Internal iliac v.

External iliac v.

Superficial venous
palmar arch

Deep femoral v.

Femoral v.

Great saphenous v.

Popliteal v.

Small saphenous v.

Anterior tibial v.

Posterior tibial v.

Dorsal venous arch

Figure 15
Lymphatic System

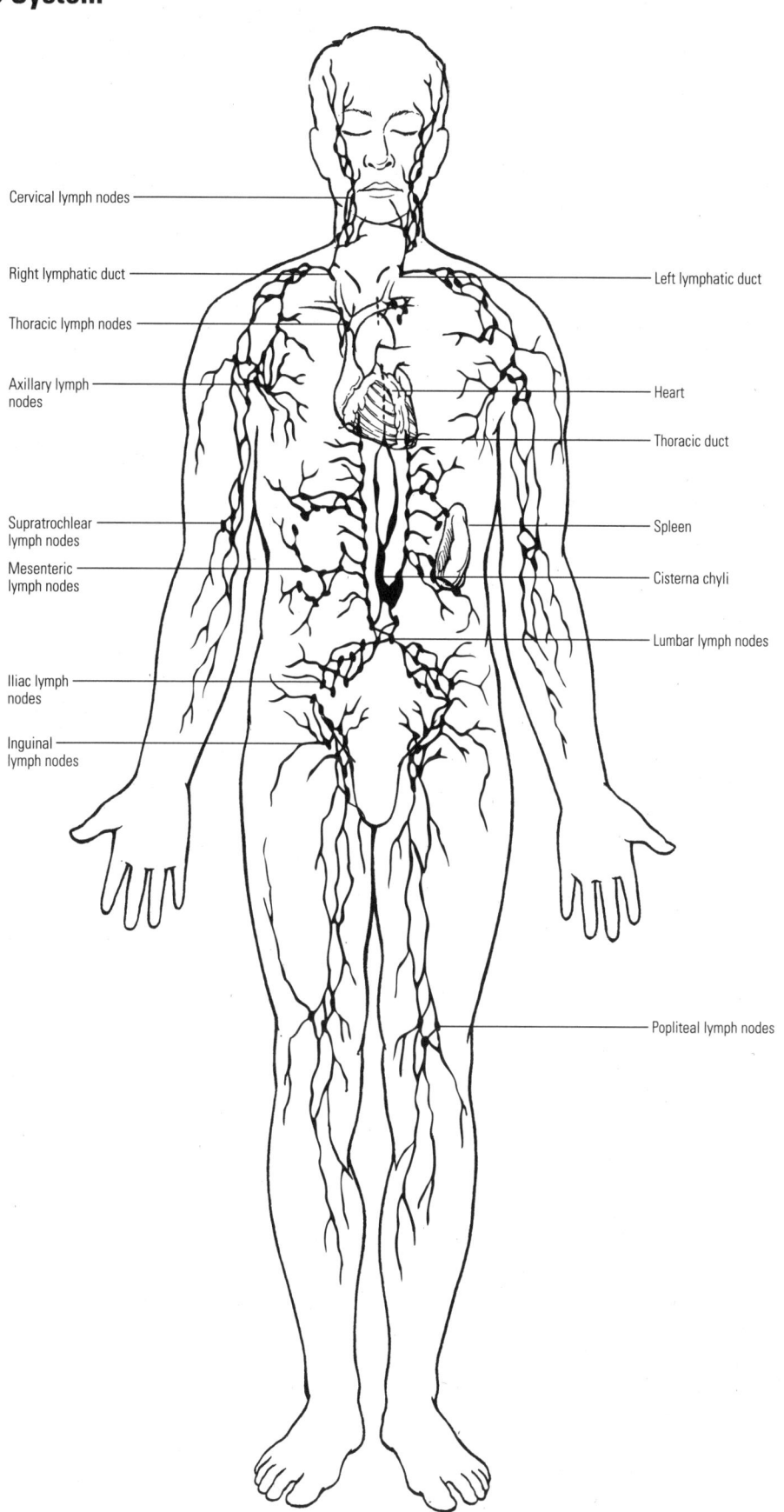

Cervical lymph nodes

Right lymphatic duct

Thoracic lymph nodes

Axillary lymph nodes

Supratrochlear lymph nodes

Mesenteric lymph nodes

Iliac lymph nodes

Inguinal lymph nodes

Left lymphatic duct

Heart

Thoracic duct

Spleen

Cisterna chyli

Lumbar lymph nodes

Popliteal lymph nodes

Figure 16
Digestive System

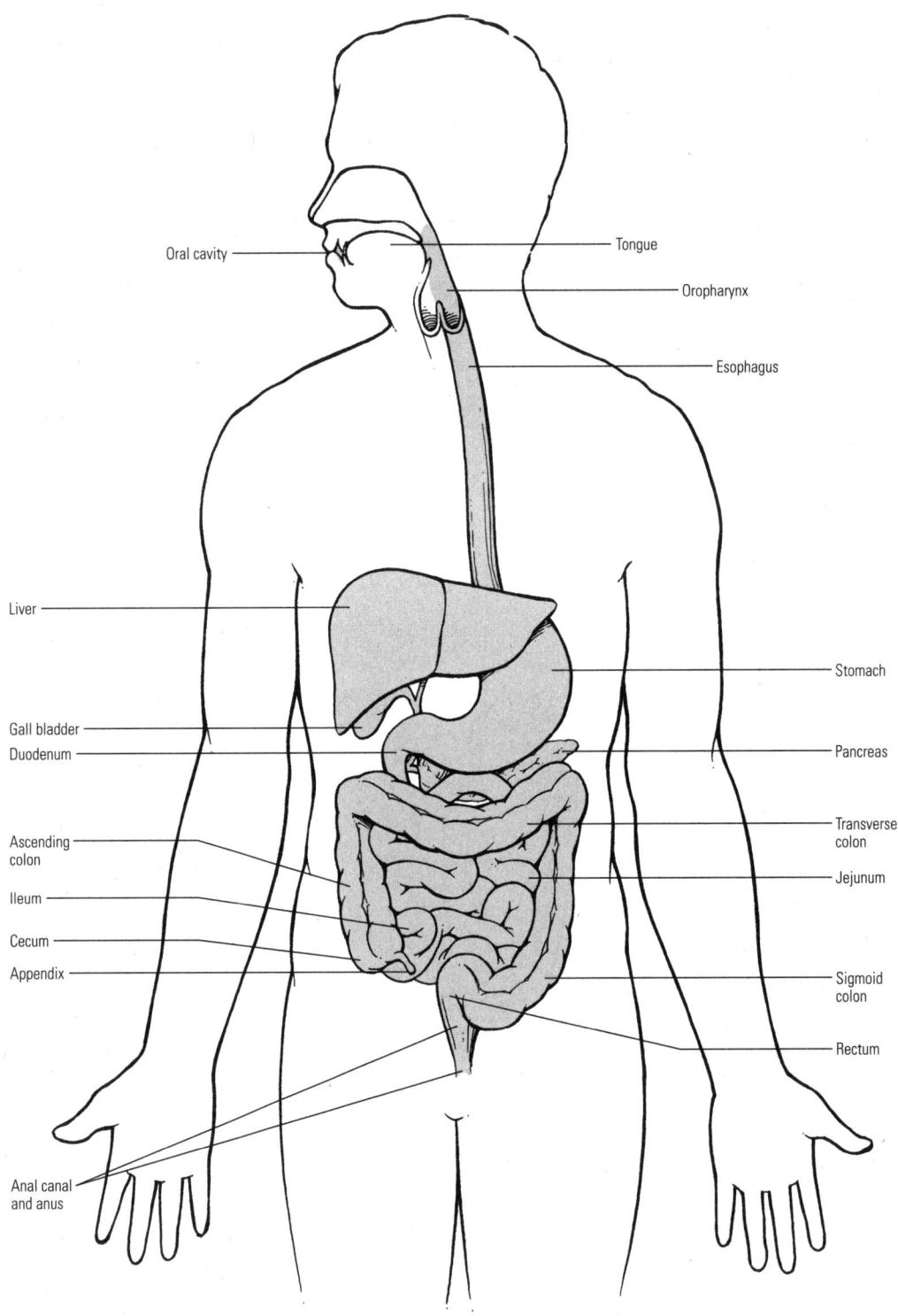

Oral cavity

Tongue

Oropharynx

Esophagus

Liver

Stomach

Gall bladder

Pancreas

Duodenum

Ascending colon

Transverse colon

Ileum

Jejunum

Cecum

Appendix

Sigmoid colon

Rectum

Anal canal and anus

Figure 17
Urinary System

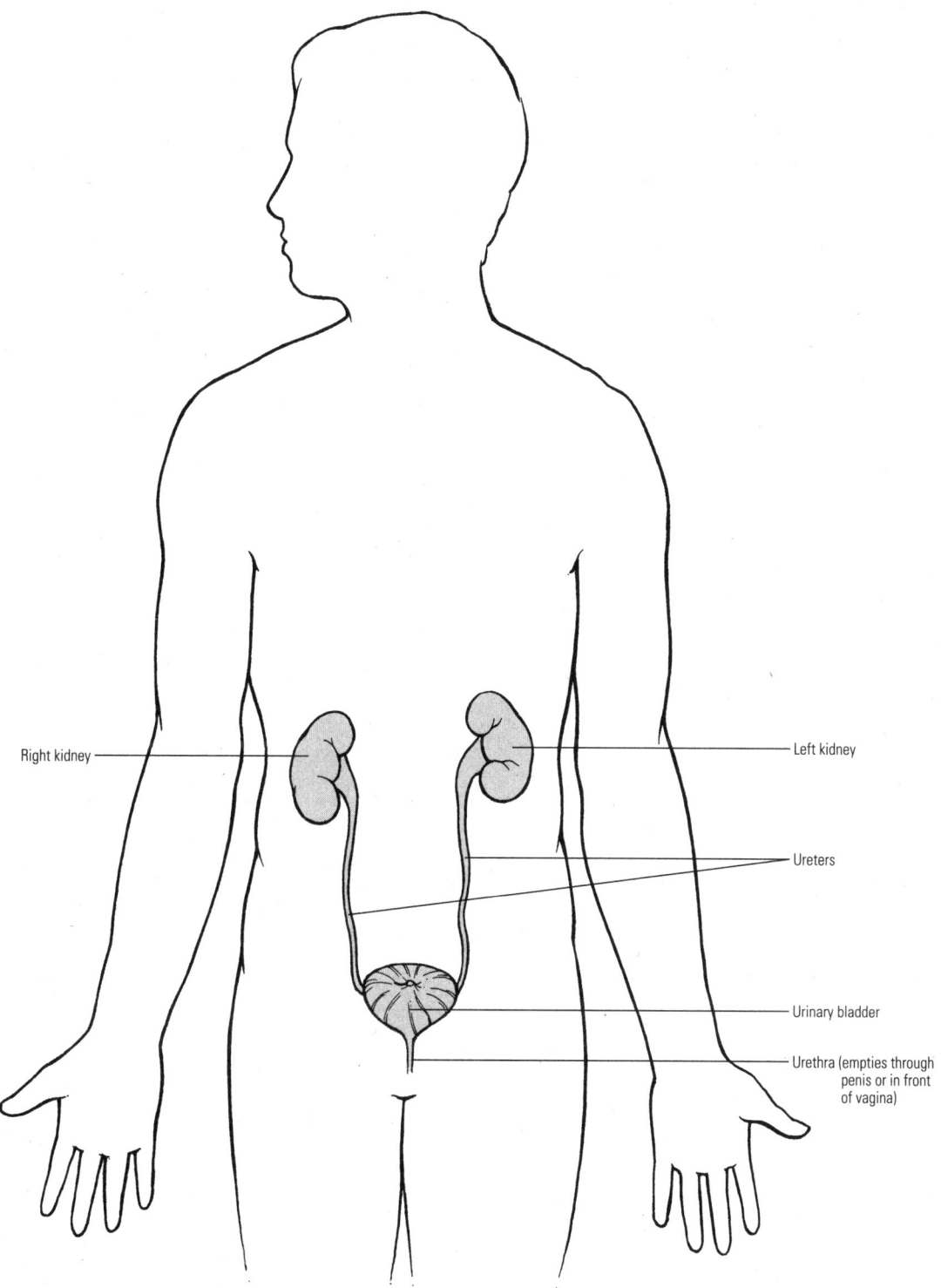

Right kidney

Left kidney

Ureters

Urinary bladder

Urethra (empties through
penis or in front
of vagina)

Figure 18
Male Genital System

Deferent duct

Urinary bladder and cavity

Corpus cavernosa

Corpus spongiosum

Penis

Glans penis

Prepuce

Seminal vesicle

Ejaculatory duct

Prostate gland

Spermatic cord and deferent duct

Epididymus

Testes

Scrotum

Figure 19
Female Genital System

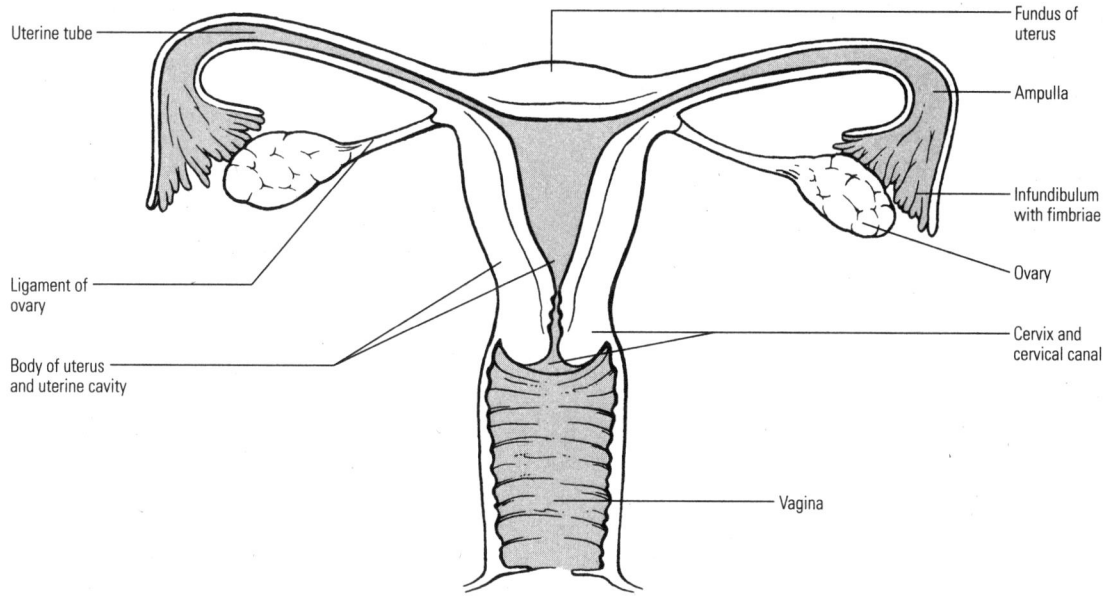

Uterine tube

Fundus of
uterus

Ampulla

Infundibulum
with fimbriae

Ovary

Ligament of
ovary

Cervix and
cervical canal

Body of uterus
and uterine cavity

Vagina

Figure 20
Nervous System

Brain

Cerebellum

Spinal cord

Brachial plexus

Musculocutaneous n.

Radial n.

Intercostal nerves
(with ribs)

Subcostal nerve
(12th thoracic)

Lumbar plexus

Median n.

Iliohypogastric n.

Ilioinguinal n.

Deep branch of radial n.

Lat. femoral cutaneous n.

Genitofemoral n.

Superficial branch of radial n.

Obturator n.

Sacral plexus

Femoral n.

Pudendal n.

Sciatic n.

Ulnar n.

Muscular branches
of femoral n.

Saphenous n.

Tibial n.

Common peroneal n.

Deep peroneal n.

Superficial peroneal n.

Figure 21A
Brain Anatomy

- Frontal lobes
- Longitudinal fissure
- Parietal lobes
- Occipital lobes
- Frontal lobe
- Parietal lobe
- Occipital lobe
- Temporal lobe
- Cerebellum

Figure 21B
Sagittal Section of Brain and Brain Stem

- Cerebrum
- Corpus collosum
- Ventricles
- Thalamus
- Hypothalamus
- Mid brain
- Pituitary gland
- Cerebellum
- Pons
- Brain stem
- Medulla

Figure 22
Eyeball

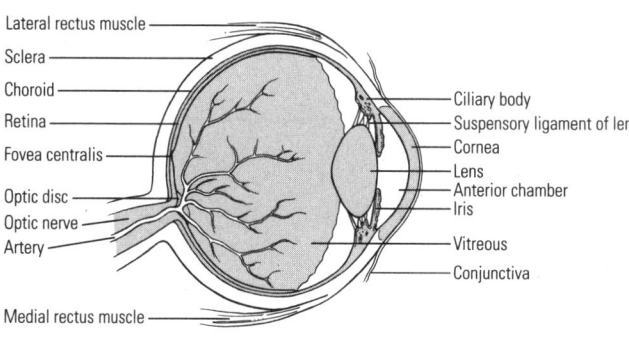

- Lateral rectus muscle
- Sclera
- Choroid
- Retina
- Fovea centralis
- Optic disc
- Optic nerve
- Artery
- Medial rectus muscle
- Ciliary body
- Suspensory ligament of lens
- Cornea
- Lens
- Anterior chamber
- Iris
- Vitreous
- Conjunctiva

Transverse (horizontal) section of eyeball

Figure 23
Ear

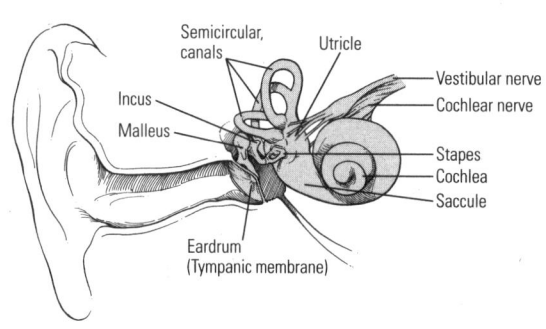

- Semicircular, canals
- Utricle
- Incus
- Vestibular nerve
- Cochlear nerve
- Malleus
- Stapes
- Cochlea
- Saccule
- Eardrum (Tympanic membrane)

Figure 24
Endocrine System

Evaluation and Management (E/M) Services Guidelines

In addition to the information presented in the Introduction, several other items unique to this section are defined or identified here.

Classification of Evaluation and Management (E/M) Services

The E/M section is divided into broad categories such as office visits, hospital visits, and consultations. Most of the categories are further divided into two or more subcategories of E/M services. For example, there are two subcategories of office visits (new patient and established patient) and there are two subcategories of hospital visits (initial and subsequent). The subcategories of E/M services are further classified into levels of E/M services that are identified by specific codes. This classification is important because the nature of physician work varies by type of service, place of service, and the patient's status.

The basic format of the levels of E/M services is the same for most categories. First, a unique code number is listed. Second, the place and/or type of service is specified, eg, office consultation. Third, the content of the service is defined, eg, comprehensive history and comprehensive examination. (See "Levels of E/M Services," page 3, for details on the content of E/M services.) Fourth, the nature of the presenting problem(s) usually associated with a given level is described. Fifth, the time typically required to provide the service is specified. (A detailed discussion of time is provided on page 4.)

Definitions of Commonly Used Terms

Certain key words and phrases are used throughout the E/M section. The following definitions are intended to reduce the potential for differing interpretations and to increase the consistency of reporting by physicians in differing specialties. E/M services may also be reported by other qualified health care professionals who are authorized to perform such services within the scope of their practice.

New and Established Patient

Solely for the purposes of distinguishing between new and established patients, **professional services** are those face-to-face services rendered by a physician and reported by a specific CPT code(s). A new patient is one who has not received any professional services from the physician or another physician of the same specialty who belongs to the same group practice, within the past three years.

An established patient is one who has received professional services from the physician or another physician of the same specialty who belongs to the same group practice, within the past three years.

In the instance where a physician is on call for or covering for another physician, the patient's encounter will be classified as it would have been by the physician who is not available.

No distinction is made between new and established patients in the emergency department. E/M services in the emergency department category may be reported for any new or established patient who presents for treatment in the emergency department.

The decision tree on page 2 is provided to aid in determining whether to report the E/M service provided as a new or an established patient encounter.

Chief Complaint

A chief complaint is a concise statement describing the symptom, problem, condition, diagnosis, or other factor that is the reason for the encounter, usually stated in the patient's words.

►Concurrent Care and Transfer of Care◄

►Concurrent care is the provision of similar services (eg, hospital visits) to the same patient by more than one physician on the same day. When concurrent care is provided, no special reporting is required. Transfer of care is the process whereby a physician who is providing management for some or all of a patient's problems relinquishes this responsibility to another physician who explicitly agrees to accept this responsibility and who, from the initial encounter, is not providing consultative services. The physician transferring care is then no longer providing care for these problems though he or she may continue providing care for other conditions when appropriate. Consultation codes should not be reported by the physician who has agreed to accept transfer of care before an initial evaluation but are appropriate to report if the decision to accept transfer of care cannot be made until after the initial consultation evaluation, regardless of site of service.◄

Evaluation and Management Guidelines

Decision Tree for New vs Established Patients

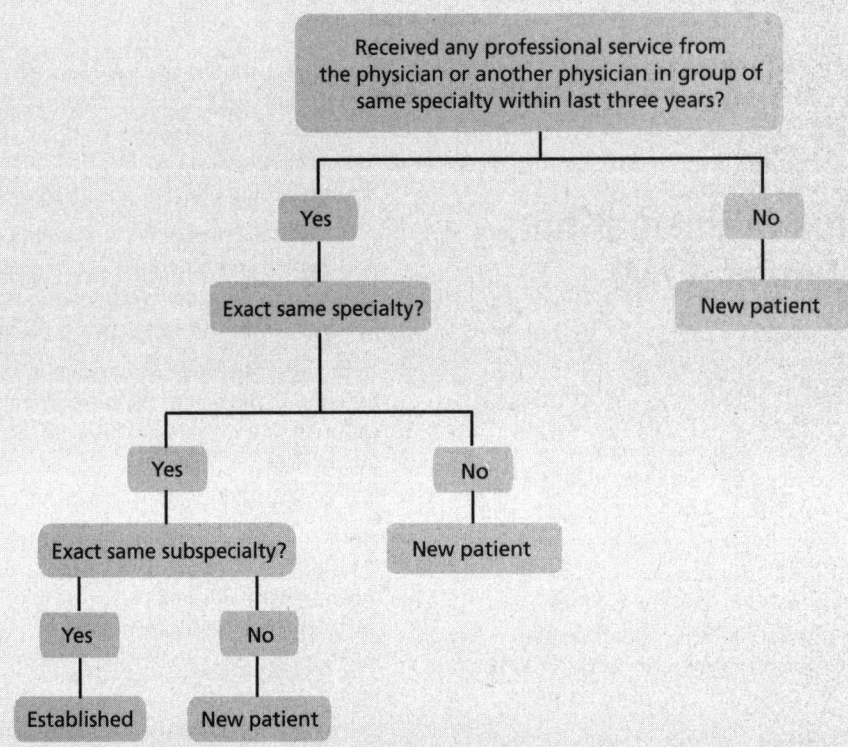

Counseling

Counseling is a discussion with a patient and/or family concerning one or more of the following areas:

- Diagnostic results, impressions, and/or recommended diagnostic studies
- Prognosis
- Risks and benefits of management (treatment) options
- Instructions for management (treatment) and/or follow-up
- Importance of compliance with chosen management (treatment) options
- Risk factor reduction
- Patient and family education

(For psychotherapy, see 90804-90857)

Family History

A review of medical events in the patient's family that includes significant information about:

- The health status or cause of death of parents, siblings, and children
- Specific diseases related to problems identified in the Chief Complaint or History of the Present Illness, and/or System Review
- Diseases of family members that may be hereditary or place the patient at risk

History of Present Illness

A chronological description of the development of the patient's present illness from the first sign and/or symptom to the present. This includes a description of location, quality, severity, timing, context, modifying factors, and associated signs and symptoms significantly related to the presenting problem(s).

Levels of E/M Services

Within each category or subcategory of E/M service, there are three to five levels of E/M services available for reporting purposes. Levels of E/M services are **not** interchangeable among the different categories or subcategories of service. For example, the first level of E/M services in the subcategory of office visit, new patient, does not have the same definition as the first level of E/M services in the subcategory of office visit, established patient.

The levels of E/M services include examinations, evaluations, treatments, conferences with or concerning patients, preventive pediatric and adult health supervision, and similar medical services, such as the determination of the need and/or location for appropriate care. Medical screening includes the history, examination, and medical decision-making required to determine the need and/or location for appropriate care and treatment of the patient (eg, office and other outpatient setting,

emergency department, nursing facility). The levels of E/M services encompass the wide variations in skill, effort, time, responsibility, and medical knowledge required for the prevention or diagnosis and treatment of illness or injury and the promotion of optimal health. Each level of E/M services may be used by all physicians.

The descriptors for the levels of E/M services recognize seven components, six of which are used in defining the levels of E/M services. These components are:

- History
- Examination
- Medical decision making
- Counseling
- Coordination of care
- Nature of presenting problem
- Time

The first three of these components (history, examination, and medical decision making) are considered the **key** components in selecting a level of E/M services. (See "Determine the Extent of History Obtained," page 11.)

The next three components (counseling, coordination of care, and the nature of the presenting problem) are considered **contributory** factors in the majority of encounters. Although the first two of these contributory factors are important E/M services, it is not required that these services be provided at every patient encounter.

Coordination of care with other providers or agencies without a patient encounter on that day is reported using the case management codes.

The final component, time, is discussed in detail on page 8.

Any specifically identifiable procedure (ie, identified with a specific CPT code) performed on or subsequent to the date of initial or subsequent E/M services should be reported separately.

The actual performance and/or interpretation of diagnostic tests/studies ordered during a patient encounter are not included in the levels of E/M services. Physician performance of diagnostic tests/studies for which specific CPT codes are available may be reported separately, in addition to the appropriate E/M code. The physician's interpretation of the results of diagnostic tests/studies (ie, professional component) with preparation of a separate distinctly identifiable signed written report may also be reported separately, using the appropriate CPT code with modifier 26 appended.

The physician may need to indicate that on the day a procedure or service identified by a CPT code was performed, the patient's condition required a significant separately identifiable E/M service above and beyond other services provided or beyond the usual preservice and postservice care associated with the procedure that was performed. The E/M service may be caused or prompted by the symptoms or condition for which the procedure and/or service was provided. This circumstance may be reported by adding modifier 25 to the appropriate level of E/M service. As such, different diagnoses are not required for reporting of the procedure and the E/M services on the same date.

Nature of Presenting Problem

A presenting problem is a disease, condition, illness, injury, symptom, sign, finding, complaint, or other reason for encounter, with or without a diagnosis being established at the time of the encounter. The E/M codes recognize five types of presenting problems that are defined as follows:

Minimal: A problem that may not require the presence of the physician, but service is provided under the physician's supervision.

Self-limited or minor: A problem that runs a definite and prescribed course, is transient in nature, and is not likely to permanently alter health status OR has a good prognosis with management/compliance.

Low severity: A problem where the risk of morbidity without treatment is low; there is little to no risk of mortality without treatment; full recovery without functional impairment is expected.

Moderate severity: A problem where the risk of morbidity without treatment is moderate; there is moderate risk of mortality without treatment; uncertain prognosis OR increased probability of prolonged functional impairment.

High severity: A problem where the risk of morbidity without treatment is high to extreme; there is a moderate to high risk of mortality without treatment OR high probability of severe, prolonged functional impairment.

Past History

A review of the patient's past experiences with illnesses, injuries, and treatments that includes significant information about:

- Prior major illnesses and injuries
- Prior operations
- Prior hospitalizations
- Current medications
- Allergies (eg, drug, food)
- Age appropriate immunization status
- Age appropriate feeding/dietary status

Social History

An age appropriate review of past and current activities that includes significant information about:

- Marital status and/or living arrangements

- Current employment
- Occupational history
- Use of drugs, alcohol, and tobacco
- Level of education
- Sexual history
- Other relevant social factors

System Review (Review of Systems)

An inventory of body systems obtained through a series of questions seeking to identify signs and/or symptoms that the patient may be experiencing or has experienced. For the purposes of the CPT codebook the following elements of a system review have been identified:

- Constitutional symptoms (fever, weight loss, etc)
- Eyes
- Ears, nose, mouth, throat
- Cardiovascular
- Respiratory
- Gastrointestinal
- Genitourinary
- Musculoskeletal
- Integumentary (skin and/or breast)
- Neurological
- Psychiatric
- Endocrine
- Hematologic/lymphatic
- Allergic/immunologic

The review of systems helps define the problem, clarify the differential diagnosis, identify needed testing, or serves as baseline data on other systems that might be affected by any possible management options.

Time

The inclusion of time in the definitions of levels of E/M services has been implicit in prior editions of the CPT codebook. The inclusion of time as an explicit factor beginning in *CPT 1992* is done to assist physicians in selecting the most appropriate level of E/M services. It should be recognized that the specific times expressed in the visit code descriptors are averages and, therefore, represent a range of times that may be higher or lower depending on actual clinical circumstances.

Time is **not** a descriptive component for the emergency department levels of E/M services because emergency department services are typically provided on a variable intensity basis, often involving multiple encounters with several patients over an extended period of time. Therefore, it is often difficult for physicians to provide accurate estimates of the time spent face-to-face with the patient.

Studies to establish levels of E/M services employed surveys of practicing physicians to obtain data on the amount of time and work associated with typical E/M services. Since "work" is not easily quantifiable, the codes must rely on other objective, verifiable measures that correlate with physicians' estimates of their "work." It has been demonstrated that physicians' estimations of **intraservice** time (as explained on the next page), both within and across specialties, is a variable that is predictive of the "work" of E/M services. This same research has shown there is a strong relationship between intraservice time and total time for E/M services. Intraservice time, rather than total time, was chosen for inclusion with the codes because of its relative ease of measurement and because of its direct correlation with measurements of the total amount of time and work associated with typical E/M services.

Intraservice times are defined as **face-to-face** time for office and other outpatient visits and as **unit/floor** time for hospital and other inpatient visits. This distinction is necessary because most of the work of typical office visits takes place during the face-to-face time with the patient, while most of the work of typical hospital visits takes place during the time spent on the patient's floor or unit.

Face-to-face time (office and other outpatient visits and office consultations): For coding purposes, face-to-face time for these services is defined as only that time that the physician spends face-to-face with the patient and/or family. This includes the time in which the physician performs such tasks as obtaining a history, performing an examination, and counseling the patient.

Physicians also spend time doing work before or after the face-to-face time with the patient, performing such tasks as reviewing records and tests, arranging for further services, and communicating further with other professionals and the patient through written reports and telephone contact.

This **non-face-to-face** time for office services—also called pre- and postencounter time—is not included in the time component described in the E/M codes. However, the pre- and post-face-to-face work associated with an encounter was included in calculating the total work of typical services in physician surveys.

Thus, the face-to-face time associated with the services described by any E/M code is a valid proxy for the total work done before, during, and after the visit.

▶ *Unit/floor time (hospital observation services, inpatient hospital care, initial inpatient hospital consultations, nursing facility):* For reporting purposes, intraservice time for these services is defined as unit/floor time, which includes the time that the physician is present on the patient's hospital unit and at the bedside rendering services for that patient. This includes the time in which the physician establishes and/or reviews the patient's chart, examines the patient, writes notes, and

communicates with other professionals and the patient's family.◀

In the hospital, pre- and post-time includes time spent off the patient's floor performing such tasks as reviewing pathology and radiology findings in another part of the hospital.

This pre- and postvisit time is not included in the time component described in these codes. However, the pre- and postwork performed during the time spent off the floor or unit was included in calculating the total work of typical services in physician surveys.

Thus, the unit/floor time associated with the services described by any code is a valid proxy for the total work done before, during, and after the visit.

Unlisted Service

An E/M service may be provided that is not listed in this section of the CPT codebook. When reporting such a service, the appropriate unlisted code may be used to indicate the service, identifying it by "Special Report," as discussed in the following paragraph. The "Unlisted Services" and accompanying codes for the E/M section are as follows:

99429   **Unlisted preventive** medicine service

99499   **Unlisted evaluation and management** service

Special Report

An unlisted service or one that is unusual, variable, or new may require a special report demonstrating the medical appropriateness of the service. Pertinent information should include an adequate definition or description of the nature, extent, and need for the procedure and the time, effort, and equipment necessary to provide the service. Additional items that may be included are complexity of symptoms, final diagnosis, pertinent physical findings, diagnostic and therapeutic procedures, concurrent problems, and follow-up care.

Clinical Examples

Clinical examples of the codes for E/M services are provided to assist physicians in understanding the meaning of the descriptors and selecting the correct code. The clinical examples are listed in Appendix C. Each example was developed by physicians in the specialties shown.

The same problem, when seen by physicians in different specialties, may involve different amounts of work. Therefore, the appropriate level of encounter should be reported using the descriptors rather than the examples.

The examples have been tested for validity and approved by the CPT Editorial Panel. Physicians were given the examples and asked to assign a code or assess the amount of time and work involved. Only examples that were rated consistently have been included in Appendix C.

Instructions for Selecting a Level of E/M Service

▶Identify the category and subcategory of service codes available for reporting E/M services shown in the subsection opener (pages 1-3).◀

Review the Reporting Instructions for the Selected Category or Subcategory

Most of the categories and many of the subcategories of service have special guidelines or instructions unique to that category or subcategory. Where these are indicated, eg, "Inpatient Hospital Care," special instructions will be presented preceding the levels of E/M services.

Review the Level of E/M Service Descriptors and Examples in the Selected Category or Subcategory

The descriptors for the levels of E/M services recognize seven components, six of which are used in defining the levels of E/M services. These components are:

- History
- Examination
- Medical decision making
- Counseling
- Coordination of care
- Nature of presenting problem
- Time

The first three of these components (ie, history, examination, and medical decision making) should be considered the **key** components in selecting the level of E/M services. An exception to this rule is in the case of visits that consist predominantly of counseling or coordination of care (see numbered paragraph 3, page 8).

The nature of the presenting problem and time are provided in some levels to assist the physician in determining the appropriate level of E/M service.

Determine the Extent of History Obtained

The extent of the history is dependent upon clinical judgment and on the nature of the presenting problems(s). The levels of E/M services recognize four types of history that are defined as follows:

Problem focused: Chief complaint; brief history of present illness or problem.

Expanded problem focused: Chief complaint; brief history of present illness; problem pertinent system review.

Detailed: Chief complaint; extended history of present illness; problem pertinent system review extended to include a review of a limited number of additional systems; **pertinent** past, family, and/or social history **directly related to the patient's problems.**

Comprehensive: Chief complaint; extended history of present illness; review of systems that is directly related to the problem(s) identified in the history of the present illness plus a review of all additional body systems; **complete** past, family, and social history.

The comprehensive history obtained as part of the preventive medicine E/M service is not problem-oriented and does not involve a chief complaint or present illness. It does, however, include a comprehensive system review and comprehensive or interval past, family, and social history as well as a comprehensive assessment/history of pertinent risk factors.

Determine the Extent of Examination Performed

The extent of the examination performed is dependent on clinical judgment and on the nature of the presenting problem(s). The levels of E/M services recognize four types of examination that are defined as follows:

Problem focused: A limited examination of the affected body area or organ system.

Expanded problem focused: A limited examination of the affected body area or organ system and other symptomatic or related organ system(s).

Detailed: An extended examination of the affected body area(s) and other symptomatic or related organ system(s).

Comprehensive: A general multisystem examination or a complete examination of a single organ system. **Note:** The comprehensive examination performed as part of the preventive medicine E/M service is multisystem, but its extent is based on age and risk factors identified.

For the purposes of these CPT definitions, the following body areas are recognized:

- Head, including the face
- Neck
- Chest, including breasts and axilla
- Abdomen
- Genitalia, groin, buttocks
- Back
- Each extremity

Table 1

Complexity of Medical Decision Making

Number of Diagnoses or Management Options	Amount and/or Complexity of Data to be Reviewed	Risk of Complications and/or Morbidity or Mortality	Type of Decision Making
minimal	minimal or none	minimal	**straightforward**
limited	limited	low	**low complexity**
multiple	moderate	moderate	**moderate complexity**
extensive	extensive	high	**high complexity**

For the purposes of these CPT definitions, the following organ systems are recognized:

- Eyes
- Ears, nose, mouth, and throat
- Cardiovascular
- Respiratory
- Gastrointestinal
- Genitourinary
- Musculoskeletal
- Skin
- Neurologic
- Psychiatric
- Hematologic/lymphatic/immunologic

Determine the Complexity of Medical Decision Making

Medical decision making refers to the complexity of establishing a diagnosis and/or selecting a management option as measured by:

- The number of possible diagnoses and/or the number of management options that must be considered
- The amount and/or complexity of medical records, diagnostic tests, and/or other information that must be obtained, reviewed, and analyzed
- The risk of significant complications, morbidity, and/or mortality, as well as comorbidities, associated with the patient's presenting problems(s), the diagnostic procedure(s), and/or the possible management options

Four types of medical decision making are recognized: straightforward, low complexity, moderate complexity, and high complexity. To qualify for a given type of decision making, two of the three elements in Table 1 must be met or exceeded.

Comorbidities/underlying diseases, in and of themselves, are not considered in selecting a level of E/M services *unless* their presence significantly increases the complexity of the medical decision making.

Select the Appropriate Level of E/M Services Based on the Following

1. For the following categories/subcategories, **all of the key components,** ie, history, examination, and medical decision making, must meet or exceed the stated requirements to qualify for a particular level of E/M service: office, new patient; hospital observation services; initial hospital care; office consultations; initial inpatient consultations; emergency department services; initial nursing facility care; domiciliary care, new patient; and home, new patient.

2. For the following categories/subcategories, **two of the three key components** (ie, history, examination, and medical decision making) must meet or exceed the stated requirements to qualify for a particular level of E/M services: office, established patient; subsequent hospital care; subsequent nursing facility care; domiciliary care, established patient; and home, established patient.

3. When counseling and/or coordination of care dominates (more than 50%) the physician/patient and/or family encounter (face-to-face time in the office or other outpatient setting or floor/unit time in the hospital or nursing facility), then **time** may be considered the key or controlling factor to qualify for a particular level of E/M services. This includes time spent with parties who have assumed responsibility for the care of the patient or decision making whether or not they are family members (eg, foster parents, person acting in loco parentis, legal guardian). The extent of counseling and/or coordination of care must be documented in the medical record.

Notes

⊙=Moderate sedation ✚=Add-on code ⟋=FDA approval pending #=Resequenced code

Evaluation and Management

Office or Other Outpatient Services

The following codes are used to report evaluation and management services provided in the physician's office or in an outpatient or other ambulatory facility. A patient is considered an outpatient until inpatient admission to a health care facility occurs.

To report services provided to a patient who is admitted to a hospital or nursing facility in the course of an encounter in the office or other ambulatory facility, see the notes for initial hospital inpatient care (page 12) or initial nursing facility care (page 20).

For services provided by physicians in the emergency department, see 99281-99285.

For observation care, see 99217-99220.

For observation or inpatient care services (including admission and discharge services), see 99234-99236.

New Patient

99201   **Office or other outpatient visit** for the evaluation and management of a new patient, which requires these 3 key components:

- **A problem focused history;**
- **A problem focused examination;**
- **Straightforward medical decision making.**

Counseling and/or coordination of care with other providers or agencies are provided consistent with the nature of the problem(s) and the patient's and/or family's needs.

Usually, the presenting problem(s) are self limited or minor. Physicians typically spend 10 minutes face-to-face with the patient and/or family.

99202   **Office or other outpatient visit** for the evaluation and management of a new patient, which requires these 3 key components:

- **An expanded problem focused history;**
- **An expanded problem focused examination;**
- **Straightforward medical decision making.**

Counseling and/or coordination of care with other providers or agencies are provided consistent with the nature of the problem(s) and the patient's and/or family's needs.

Usually, the presenting problem(s) are of low to moderate severity. Physicians typically spend 20 minutes face-to-face with the patient and/or family.

99203   **Office or other outpatient visit** for the evaluation and management of a new patient, which requires these 3 key components:

- **A detailed history;**
- **A detailed examination;**
- **Medical decision making of low complexity.**

Counseling and/or coordination of care with other providers or agencies are provided consistent with the nature of the problem(s) and the patient's and/or family's needs.

Usually, the presenting problem(s) are of moderate severity. Physicians typically spend 30 minutes face-to-face with the patient and/or family.

99204   **Office or other outpatient visit** for the evaluation and management of a new patient, which requires these 3 key components:

- **A comprehensive history;**
- **A comprehensive examination;**
- **Medical decision making of moderate complexity.**

Counseling and/or coordination of care with other providers or agencies are provided consistent with the nature of the problem(s) and the patient's and/or family's needs.

Usually, the presenting problem(s) are of moderate to high severity. Physicians typically spend 45 minutes face-to-face with the patient and/or family.

99205   **Office or other outpatient visit** for the evaluation and management of a new patient, which requires these 3 key components:

- **A comprehensive history;**
- **A comprehensive examination;**
- **Medical decision making of high complexity.**

Counseling and/or coordination of care with other providers or agencies are provided consistent with the nature of the problem(s) and the patient's and/or family's needs.

Usually, the presenting problem(s) are of moderate to high severity. Physicians typically spend 60 minutes face-to-face with the patient and/or family.

Established Patient

99211   **Office or other outpatient visit** for the evaluation and management of an established patient, that may not require the presence of a physician. Usually, the presenting problem(s) are minimal. Typically, 5 minutes are spent performing or supervising these services.

99212 **Office or other outpatient visit** for the evaluation and management of an established patient, which requires at least 2 of these 3 key components:

- **A problem focused history;**
- **A problem focused examination;**
- **Straightforward medical decision making.**

Counseling and/or coordination of care with other providers or agencies are provided consistent with the nature of the problem(s) and the patient's and/or family's needs.

Usually, the presenting problem(s) are self limited or minor. Physicians typically spend 10 minutes face-to-face with the patient and/or family.

99213 **Office or other outpatient visit** for the evaluation and management of an established patient, which requires at least 2 of these 3 key components:

- **An expanded problem focused history;**
- **An expanded problem focused examination;**
- **Medical decision making of low complexity.**

Counseling and coordination of care with other providers or agencies are provided consistent with the nature of the problem(s) and the patient's and/or family's needs.

Usually, the presenting problem(s) are of low to moderate severity. Physicians typically spend 15 minutes face-to-face with the patient and/or family.

99214 **Office or other outpatient visit** for the evaluation and management of an established patient, which requires at least 2 of these 3 key components:

- **A detailed history;**
- **A detailed examination;**
- **Medical decision making of moderate complexity.**

Counseling and/or coordination of care with other providers or agencies are provided consistent with the nature of the problem(s) and the patient's and/or family's needs.

Usually, the presenting problem(s) are of moderate to high severity. Physicians typically spend 25 minutes face-to-face with the patient and/or family.

99215 **Office or other outpatient visit** for the evaluation and management of an established patient, which requires at least 2 of these 3 key components:

- **A comprehensive history;**
- **A comprehensive examination;**
- **Medical decision making of high complexity.**

Counseling and/or coordination of care with other providers or agencies are provided consistent with the nature of the problem(s) and the patient's and/or family's needs.

Usually, the presenting problem(s) are of moderate to high severity. Physicians typically spend 40 minutes face-to-face with the patient and/or family.

Hospital Observation Services

The following codes are used to report evaluation and management services provided to patients designated/admitted as "observation status" in a hospital. It is not necessary that the patient be located in an observation area designated by the hospital.

If such an area does exist in a hospital (as a separate unit in the hospital, in the emergency department, etc.), these codes are to be utilized if the patient is placed in such an area.

For definitions of key components and commonly used terms, please see **Evaluation and Management Services Guidelines.**

Typical times have not yet been established for this category of services.

Observation Care Discharge Services

Observation care discharge of a patient from "observation status" includes final examination of the patient, discussion of the hospital stay, instructions for continuing care, and preparation of discharge records. For observation or inpatient hospital care including the admission and discharge of the patient on the same date, see codes 99234-99236 as appropriate.

99217 **Observation care discharge** day management (This code is to be utilized by the physician to report all services provided to a patient on discharge from "observation status" if the discharge is on other than the initial date of "observation status." To report services to a patient designated as "observation status" or "inpatient status" and discharged on the same date, use the codes for Observation or Inpatient Care Services [including Admission and Discharge Services, 99234-99236 as appropriate.])

Initial Observation Care

New or Established Patient

The following codes are used to report the encounter(s) by the supervising physician with the patient when designated as "observation status." This refers to the initiation of observation status, supervision of the care plan for observation and performance of periodic reassessments. For observation encounters by other physicians, see Office or Other Outpatient Consultation codes (99241-99245).

To report services provided to a patient who is admitted to the hospital after receiving hospital observation care services on the same date, see the notes for initial hospital inpatient care (page 12). For a patient admitted to the hospital on a date subsequent to the date of observation status, the hospital admission would be reported with the appropriate Initial Hospital Care code (99221-99223). For a patient admitted and discharged from observation or inpatient status on the same date, the services should be reported with codes 99234-99236 as appropriate. Do not report observation discharge (99217) in conjunction with a hospital admission.

When "observation status" is initiated in the course of an encounter in another site of service (eg, hospital emergency department, physician's office, nursing facility) all evaluation and management services provided by the supervising physician in conjunction with initiating "observation status" are considered part of the initial observation care when performed on the same date. The observation care level of service reported by the supervising physician should include the services related to initiating "observation status" provided in the other sites of service as well as in the observation setting.

Evaluation and management services on the same date provided in sites that are related to initiating "observation status" should **not** be reported separately.

These codes may not be utilized for post-operative recovery if the procedure is considered part of the surgical "package." These codes apply to all evaluation and management services that are provided on the same date of initiating "observation status."

99218   **Initial observation care,** per day, for the evaluation and management of a patient which requires these 3 key components:

- **A detailed or comprehensive history;**
- **A detailed or comprehensive examination; and**
- **Medical decision making that is straightforward or of low complexity.**

Counseling and/or coordination of care with other providers or agencies are provided consistent with the nature of the problem(s) and the patient's and/or family's needs.

Usually, the problem(s) requiring admission to "observation status" are of low severity.

99219   **Initial observation care,** per day, for the evaluation and management of a patient, which requires these 3 key components:

- **A comprehensive history;**
- **A comprehensive examination; and**
- **Medical decision making of moderate complexity.**

Counseling and/or coordination of care with other providers or agencies are provided consistent with the nature of the problem(s) and the patient's and/or family's needs.

Usually, the problem(s) requiring admission to "observation status" are of moderate severity.

99220   **Initial observation care,** per day, for the evaluation and management of a patient, which requires these 3 key components:

- **A comprehensive history;**
- **A comprehensive examination; and**
- **Medical decision making of high complexity.**

Counseling and/or coordination of care with other providers or agencies are provided consistent with the nature of the problem(s) and the patient's and/or family's needs.

Usually, the problem(s) requiring admission to "observation status" are of high severity.

Hospital Inpatient Services

The following codes are used to report evaluation and management services provided to hospital inpatients. Hospital inpatient services include those services provided to patients in a "partial hospital" setting. These codes are to be used to report these partial hospitalization services. See also psychiatry notes in the full text of the CPT codebook.

For definitions of key components and commonly used terms, please see **Evaluation and Management Services Guidelines.** For Hospital Observation Services, see 99218-99220. For a patient admitted and discharged from observation or inpatient status on the same date, the services should be reported with codes 99234-99236 as appropriate.

Initial Hospital Care

New or Established Patient

The following codes are used to report the first hospital inpatient encounter with the patient by the admitting physician.

For initial inpatient encounters by physicians other than the admitting physician, see initial inpatient consultation codes (99251-99255) or subsequent hospital care codes (99231-99233) as appropriate.

For admission services for the neonate (28 days of age or younger) requiring intensive observation, frequent interventions, and other intensive care services, see 99477.

When the patient is admitted to the hospital as an inpatient in the course of an encounter in another site of service (eg, hospital emergency department, observation status in a hospital, physician's office, nursing facility) all evaluation and management services provided by that physician in conjunction with that admission are considered part of the initial hospital care when

Evaluation and Management

Evaluation and Management

performed on the same date as the admission. The inpatient care level of service reported by the admitting physician should include the services related to the admission he/she provided in the other sites of service as well as in the inpatient setting.

Evaluation and management services on the same date provided in sites that are related to the admission "observation status" should **not** be reported separately. For a patient admitted and discharged from observation or inpatient status on the same date, the services should be reported with codes 99234-99236 as appropriate.

99221 Initial hospital care, per day, for the evaluation and management of a patient, which requires these 3 key components:

- **A detailed or comprehensive history;**
- **A detailed or comprehensive examination; and**
- **Medical decision making that is straightforward or of low complexity.**

Counseling and/or coordination of care with other providers or agencies are provided consistent with the nature of the problem(s) and the patient's and/or family's needs.

Usually, the problem(s) requiring admission are of low severity. Physicians typically spend 30 minutes at the bedside and on the patient's hospital floor or unit.

99222 Initial hospital care, per day, for the evaluation and management of a patient, which requires these 3 key components:

- **A comprehensive history;**
- **A comprehensive examination; and**
- **Medical decision making of moderate complexity.**

Counseling and/or coordination of care with other providers or agencies are provided consistent with the nature of the problem(s) and the patient's and/or family's needs.

Usually, the problem(s) requiring admission are of moderate severity. Physicians typically spend 50 minutes at the bedside and on the patient's hospital floor or unit.

99223 Initial hospital care, per day, for the evaluation and management of a patient, which requires these 3 key components:

- **A comprehensive history;**
- **A comprehensive examination; and**
- **Medical decision making of high complexity.**

Counseling and/or coordination of care with other providers or agencies are provided consistent with the nature of the problem(s) and the patient's and/or family's needs.

Usually, the problem(s) requiring admission are of high severity. Physicians typically spend 70 minutes at the bedside and on the patient's hospital floor or unit.

Subsequent Hospital Care

All levels of subsequent hospital care include reviewing the medical record and reviewing the results of diagnostic studies and changes in the patient's status (ie, changes in history, physical condition and response to management) since the last assessment by the physician.

99231 Subsequent hospital care, per day, for the evaluation and management of a patient, which requires at least 2 of these 3 key components:

- **A problem focused interval history;**
- **A problem focused examination;**
- **Medical decision making that is straightforward or of low complexity.**

Counseling and/or coordination of care with other providers or agencies are provided consistent with the nature of the problem(s) and the patient's and/or family's needs.

Usually, the patient is stable, recovering or improving. Physicians typically spend 15 minutes at the bedside and on the patient's hospital floor or unit.

99232 Subsequent hospital care, per day, for the evaluation and management of a patient, which requires at least 2 of these 3 key components:

- **An expanded problem focused interval history;**
- **An expanded problem focused examination;**
- **Medical decision making of moderate complexity.**

Counseling and/or coordination of care with other providers or agencies are provided consistent with the nature of the problem(s) and the patient's and/or family's needs.

Usually, the patient is responding inadequately to therapy or has developed a minor complication. Physicians typically spend 25 minutes at the bedside and on the patient's hospital floor or unit.

99233 Subsequent hospital care, per day, for the evaluation and management of a patient, which requires at least 2 of these 3 key components:

- **A detailed interval history;**
- **A detailed examination;**
- **Medical decision making of high complexity.**

Counseling and/or coordination of care with other providers or agencies are provided consistent with the nature of the problem(s) and the patient's and/or family's needs.

Usually, the patient is unstable or has developed a significant complication or a significant new problem. Physicians typically spend 35 minutes at the bedside and on the patient's hospital floor or unit.

Observation or Inpatient Care Services (Including Admission and Discharge Services)

The following codes are used to report observation or inpatient hospital care services provided to patients admitted and discharged on the same date of service. When a patient is admitted to the hospital from observation status on the same date, the physician should report only the initial hospital care code. The initial hospital care code reported by the admitting physician should include the services related to the observation status services he/she provided on the same date of inpatient admission.

When "observation status" is initiated in the course of an encounter in another site of service (eg, hospital emergency department, physician's office, nursing facility) all evaluation and management services provided by the supervising physician in conjunction with initiating "observation status" are considered part of the initial observation care when performed on the same date. The observation care level of service should include the services related to initiating "observation status" provided in the other sites of service as well as in the observation setting when provided by the same physician.

For patients admitted to observation or inpatient care and discharged on a different date, see codes 99218-99220 and 99217, or 99221-99223 and 99238, 99239.

99234   **Observation or inpatient hospital care,** for the evaluation and management of a patient including admission and discharge on the same date, which requires these 3 key components:

- **A detailed or comprehensive history;**
- **A detailed or comprehensive examination; and**
- **Medical decision making that is straightforward or of low complexity.**

Counseling and/or coordination of care with other providers or agencies are provided consistent with the nature of the problem(s) and the patient's and/or family's needs.

Usually the presenting problem(s) requiring admission are of low severity.

99235   **Observation or inpatient hospital care,** for the evaluation and management of a patient including admission and discharge on the same date, which requires these 3 key components:

- **A comprehensive history;**
- **A comprehensive examination; and**
- **Medical decision making of moderate complexity.**

Counseling and/or coordination of care with other providers or agencies are provided consistent with the nature of the problem(s) and the patient's and/or family's needs.

Usually the presenting problem(s) requiring admission are of moderate severity.

99236   **Observation or inpatient hospital care,** for the evaluation and management of a patient including admission and discharge on the same date, which requires these 3 key components:

- **A comprehensive history;**
- **A comprehensive examination; and**
- **Medical decision making of high complexity.**

Counseling and/or coordination of care with other providers or agencies are provided consistent with the nature of the problem(s) and the patient's and/or family's needs.

Usually the presenting problem(s) requiring admission are of high severity.

Hospital Discharge Services

The hospital discharge day management codes are to be used to report the total duration of time spent by a physician for final hospital discharge of a patient. The codes include, as appropriate, final examination of the patient, discussion of the hospital stay, even if the time spent by the physician on that date is not continuous, instructions for continuing care to all relevant caregivers, and preparation of discharge records, prescriptions and referral forms. For a patient admitted and discharged from observation or inpatient status on the same date, the services should be reported with codes 99234-99236 as appropriate.

99238   **Hospital discharge day management;** 30 minutes or less

99239   more than 30 minutes

(These codes are to be utilized by the physician to report all services provided to a patient on the date of discharge, if other than the initial date of inpatient status. To report services to a patient who is admitted as an inpatient and discharged on the same date, see codes 99234-99236 for observation or inpatient hospital care including the admission and discharge of the patient on the same date. To report concurrent care services provided by a physician[s] other than the attending physician, use subsequent hospital care codes [99231-99233] on the day of discharge.)

(For Observation Care Discharge, use 99217)

(For observation or inpatient hospital care including the admission and discharge of the patient on the same date, see 99234-99236)

(For Nursing Facility Care Discharge, see 99315, 99316)

(For discharge services provided to newborns admitted and discharged on the same date, use 99463)

Evaluation and Management

Consultations

►A consultation is a type of evaluation and management service provided by a physician at the request of another physician or appropriate source to either recommend care for a specific condition or problem or to determine whether to accept responsibility for ongoing management of the patient's entire care or for the care of a specific condition or problem.◄

A physician consultant may initiate diagnostic and/or therapeutic services at the same or subsequent visit.

►A "consultation" initiated by a patient and/or family, and not requested by a physician or other appropriate source (eg, physician assistant, nurse practitioner, doctor of chiropractic, physical therapist, occupational therapist, speech-language pathologist, psychologist, social worker, lawyer, or insurance company), is not reported using the consultation codes but may be reported using the office visit, home service, or domiciliary/rest home care codes as appropriate.

The written or verbal request for consult may be made by a physician or other appropriate source and documented in the patient's medical record by either the consulting or requesting physician or appropriate source. The consultant's opinion and any services that were ordered or performed must also be documented in the patient's medical record and communicated by written report to the requesting physician or other appropriate source.◄

If a consultation is mandated (eg, by a third-party payer) modifier 32 should also be reported.

Any specifically identifiable procedure (ie, identified with a specific CPT code) performed on or subsequent to the date of the initial consultation should be reported separately.

If subsequent to the completion of a consultation the consultant assumes responsibility for management of a portion or all of the patient's condition(s), the appropriate **Evaluation and Management** services code for the site of service should be reported. In the hospital or nursing facility setting, the consulting physician should use the appropriate inpatient consultation code for the initial encounter and then subsequent hospital or nursing facility care codes. In the office setting, the physician should use the appropriate office or other outpatient consultation codes and then the established patient office or other outpatient services codes.

►To report services provided to a patient who is admitted to a hospital or nursing facility in the course of an encounter in the office or other ambulatory facility, see the notes for Initial Hospital Inpatient Care (page 16) or Initial Nursing Facility Care (page 24).◄

For definitions of key components and commonly used terms, please see **Evaluation and Management Services Guidelines.**

Office or Other Outpatient Consultations

New or Established Patient

►The following codes are used to report consultations provided in the physician's office or in an outpatient or other ambulatory facility, including hospital observation services, home services, domiciliary, rest home, or emergency department (see the preceding consultation definition above). Follow-up visits in the consultant's office or other outpatient facility that are initiated by the physician consultant or patient are reported using the appropriate codes for established patients, office visits (99211-99215), domiciliary, rest home (99334-99337), or home (99347-99350). If an additional request for an opinion or advice regarding the same or a new problem is received from another physician or other appropriate source and documented in the medical record, the office consultation codes may be used again. Services that constitute transfer of care (ie, are provided for the management of the patient's entire care or for the care of a specific condition or problem) are reported with the appropriate new or established patient codes for office or other outpatient visits, domiciliary, rest home services, or home services.◄

99241 **Office consultation** for a new or established patient, which requires these 3 key components:

- **A problem focused history;**
- **A problem focused examination; and**
- **Straightforward medical decision making.**

Counseling and/or coordination of care with other providers or agencies are provided consistent with the nature of the problem(s) and the patient's and/or family's needs.

Usually, the presenting problem(s) are self limited or minor. Physicians typically spend 15 minutes face-to-face with the patient and/or family.

99242 **Office consultation** for a new or established patient, which requires these 3 key components:

- **An expanded problem focused history;**
- **An expanded problem focused examination; and**
- **Straightforward medical decision making.**

Counseling and/or coordination of care with other providers or agencies are provided consistent with the nature of the problem(s) and the patient's and/or family's needs.

Usually, the presenting problem(s) are of low severity. Physicians typically spend 30 minutes face-to-face with the patient and/or family.

99243   **Office consultation** for a new or established patient, which requires these 3 key components:

- **A detailed history;**
- **A detailed examination; and**
- **Medical decision making of low complexity.**

Counseling and/or coordination of care with other providers or agencies are provided consistent with the nature of the problem(s) and the patient's and/or family's needs.

Usually, the presenting problem(s) are of moderate severity. Physicians typically spend 40 minutes face-to-face with the patient and/or family.

99244   **Office consultation** for a new or established patient, which requires these 3 key components:

- **A comprehensive history;**
- **A comprehensive examination; and**
- **Medical decision making of moderate complexity.**

Counseling and/or coordination of care with other providers or agencies are provided consistent with the nature of the problem(s) and the patient's and/or family's needs.

Usually, the presenting problem(s) are of moderate to high severity. Physicians typically spend 60 minutes face-to-face with the patient and/or family.

99245   **Office consultation** for a new or established patient, which requires these 3 key components:

- **A comprehensive history;**
- **A comprehensive examination; and**
- **Medical decision making of high complexity.**

Counseling and/or coordination of care with other providers or agencies are provided consistent with the nature of the problem(s) and the patient's and/or family's needs.

Usually, the presenting problem(s) are of moderate to high severity. Physicians typically spend 80 minutes face-to-face with the patient and/or family.

Inpatient Consultations

New or Established Patient

▶The following codes are used to report physician consultations provided to hospital inpatients, residents of nursing facilities, or patients in a partial hospital setting. Only one consultation should be reported by a consultant per admission. Subsequent services during the same admission are reported using subsequent hospital care codes (99231-99233) or subsequent nursing facility care codes (99307-99310), including services to complete the initial consultation, monitor progress, revise

recommendations, or address a new problem. Use subsequent hospital care codes (99231-99233) or subsequent nursing facility care codes (99307-99310) to report transfer of care services (see page 25, Concurrent Care and Transfer of Care definitions).

When an inpatient consultation is performed on a date that a patient is admitted to a hospital or nursing facility, all evaluation and management services provided by the consultant related to the admission are reported with the inpatient consultation service code (99251-99255). If a patient is admitted after an outpatient consultation (office, emergency department, etc), and the patient is not seen on the unit on the date of admission, only report the outpatient consultation code (99241-99245). If the patient is seen by the consultant on the unit on the date of admission, report all evaluation and management services provided by the consultant related to the admission with either the inpatient consultation code (99251-99255) or with the initial inpatient admission service code (99221-99223). Do not report both an outpatient consultation and inpatient consultation for services related to the same inpatient stay. When transfer of care services are provided on a date subsequent to the outpatient consultation, use the subsequent hospital care codes (99231-99233) or subsequent nursing facility care codes (99307-99310).◀

99251   **Inpatient consultation** for a new or established patient, which requires these 3 key components:

- **A problem focused history;**
- **A problem focused examination; and**
- **Straightforward medical decision making.**

Counseling and/or coordination of care with other providers or agencies are provided consistent with the nature of the problem(s) and the patient's and/or family's needs.

Usually, the presenting problem(s) are self limited or minor. Physicians typically spend 20 minutes at the bedside and on the patient's hospital floor or unit.

99252   **Inpatient consultation** for a new or established patient, which requires these 3 key components:

- **An expanded problem focused history;**
- **An expanded problem focused examination; and**
- **Straightforward medical decision making.**

Counseling and/or coordination of care with other providers or agencies are provided consistent with the nature of the problem(s) and the patient's and/or family's needs.

Usually, the presenting problem(s) are of low severity. Physicians typically spend 40 minutes at the bedside and on the patient's hospital floor or unit.

Evaluation and Management

Evaluation and Management

99253 **Inpatient consultation** for a new or established patient, which requires these 3 key components:

- **A detailed history;**
- **A detailed examination; and**
- **Medical decision making of low complexity.**

Counseling and/or coordination of care with other providers or agencies are provided consistent with the nature of the problem(s) and the patient's and/or family's needs.

Usually, the presenting problem(s) are of moderate severity. Physicians typically spend 55 minutes at the bedside and on the patient's hospital floor or unit.

99254 **Inpatient consultation** for a new or established patient, which requires these 3 key components:

- **A comprehensive history;**
- **A comprehensive examination; and**
- **Medical decision making of moderate complexity.**

Counseling and/or coordination of care with other providers or agencies are provided consistent with the nature of the problem(s) and the patient's and/or family's needs.

Usually, the presenting problem(s) are of moderate to high severity. Physicians typically spend 80 minutes at the bedside and on the patient's hospital floor or unit.

99255 **Inpatient consultation** for a new or established patient, which requires these 3 key components:

- **A comprehensive history;**
- **A comprehensive examination; and**
- **Medical decision making of high complexity.**

Counseling and/or coordination of care with other providers or agencies are provided consistent with the nature of the problem(s) and the patient's and/or family's needs.

Usually, the presenting problem(s) are of moderate to high severity. Physicians typically spend 110 minutes at the bedside and on the patient's hospital floor or unit.

Emergency Department Services

New or Established Patient

The following codes are used to report evaluation and management services provided in the emergency department. No distinction is made between new and established patients in the emergency department.

An emergency department is defined as an organized hospital-based facility for the provision of unscheduled episodic services to patients who present for immediate medical attention. The facility must be available 24 hours a day.

For critical care services provided in the emergency department, see Critical Care notes and 99291, 99292.

For evaluation and management services provided to a patient in an observation area of a hospital, see 99217-99220.

For observation or inpatient care services (including admission and discharge services), see 99234-99236.

99281 **Emergency department visit** for the evaluation and management of a patient, which requires these 3 key components:

- **A problem focused history;**
- **A problem focused examination; and**
- **Straightforward medical decision making.**

Counseling and/or coordination of care with other providers or agencies are provided consistent with the nature of the problem(s) and the patient's and/or family's needs.

Usually, the presenting problem(s) are self limited or minor.

99282 **Emergency department visit** for the evaluation and management of a patient, which requires these 3 key components:

- **An expanded problem focused history;**
- **An expanded problem focused examination; and**
- **Medical decision making of low complexity.**

Counseling and/or coordination of care with other providers or agencies are provided consistent with the nature of the problem(s) and the patient's and/or family's needs.

Usually, the presenting problem(s) are of low to moderate severity.

99283 **Emergency department visit** for the evaluation and management of a patient, which requires these 3 key components:

- **An expanded problem focused history;**
- **An expanded problem focused examination; and**
- **Medical decision making of moderate complexity.**

Counseling and/or coordination of care with other providers or agencies are provided consistent with the nature of the problem(s) and the patient's and/or family's needs.

Usually, the presenting problem(s) are of moderate severity.

99284 **Emergency department visit** for the evaluation and management of a patient, which requires these 3 key components:

- **A detailed history;**
- **A detailed examination; and**
- **Medical decision making of moderate complexity.**

Counseling and/or coordination of care with other providers or agencies are provided consistent with the nature of the problem(s) and the patient's and/or family's needs.

Usually, the presenting problem(s) are of high severity, and require urgent evaluation by the physician but do not pose an immediate significant threat to life or physiologic function.

99285   **Emergency department visit** for the evaluation and management of a patient, which requires these 3 key components within the constraints imposed by the urgency of the patient's clinical condition and/or mental status:

- **A comprehensive history;**
- **A comprehensive examination; and**
- **Medical decision making of high complexity.**

Counseling and/or coordination of care with other providers or agencies are provided consistent with the nature of the problem(s) and the patient's and/or family's needs.

Usually, the presenting problem(s) are of high severity and pose an immediate significant threat to life or physiologic function.

Other Emergency Services

In physician directed emergency care, advanced life support, the physician is located in a hospital emergency or critical care department, and is in two-way voice communication with ambulance or rescue personnel outside the hospital. The physician directs the performance of necessary medical procedures, including but not limited to: telemetry of cardiac rhythm; cardiac and/or pulmonary resuscitation; endotracheal or esophageal obturator airway intubation; administration of intravenous fluids and/or administration of intramuscular, intratracheal or subcutaneous drugs; and/or electrical conversion of arrhythmia.

99288   **Physician direction of** emergency medical systems (EMS) emergency care, advanced life support

(99289 has been deleted. To report, use 99466)

(99290 has been deleted. To report, use 99467)

Critical Care Services

Critical care is the direct delivery by a physician(s) of medical care for a critically ill or critically injured patient. A critical illness or injury acutely impairs one or more vital organ systems such that there is a high probability of imminent or life threatening deterioration in the patient's condition. Critical care involves high complexity decision making to assess, manipulate, and support vital system function(s) to treat single or multiple vital organ system failure and/or to prevent further life threatening

deterioration of the patient's condition. Examples of vital organ system failure include, but are not limited to: central nervous system failure, circulatory failure, shock, renal, hepatic, metabolic, and/or respiratory failure. Although critical care typically requires interpretation of multiple physiologic parameters and/or application of advanced technology(s), critical care may be provided in life threatening situations when these elements are not present. Critical care may be provided on multiple days, even if no changes are made in the treatment rendered to the patient, provided that the patient's condition continues to require the level of physician attention described above.

Providing medical care to a critically ill, injured, or post-operative patient qualifies as a critical care service only if both the illness or injury and the treatment being provided meet the above requirements. Critical care is usually, but not always, given in a critical care area, such as the coronary care unit, intensive care unit, pediatric intensive care unit, respiratory care unit, or the emergency care facility.

Inpatient critical care services provided to infants 29 days through 71 months of age are reported with pediatric critical care codes 99471-99476. The pediatric critical care codes are reported as long as the infant/young child qualifies for critical care services during the hospital stay through 71 months of age. Inpatient critical care services provided to neonates (28 days of age or younger) are reported with the neonatal critical care codes 99468 and 99469. The neonatal critical care codes are reported as long as the neonate qualifies for critical care services during the hospital stay through the 28th postnatal day. The reporting of the pediatric and neonatal critical care services is not based on time or the type of unit (eg, pediatric or neonatal critical care unit) and it is not dependent upon the type of provider delivering the care. To report critical care services provided in the outpatient setting (eg, emergency department or office), for neonates and pediatric patients up through 71 months of age, see the critical care codes 99291, 99292. If the same physician provides critical care services for a neonatal or pediatric patient in both the outpatient and inpatient settings on the same day, report only the appropriate neonatal or pediatric critical care code 99468-99472 for all critical care services provided on that day. Also report 99291-99292 for neonatal or pediatric critical care services provided by the physician providing critical care at one facility but transferring the patient to another facility. Critical care services provided by a second physician of a different specialty not reporting a per day neonatal or pediatric critical care code can be reported with codes 99291-99292. For additional instructions on reporting these services, see the Neonatal and Pediatric Critical Care section and codes 99468-99476.

Services for a patient who is not critically ill but happens to be in a critical care unit are reported using other appropriate E/M codes.

Evaluation and Management

Critical care and other E/M services may be provided to the same patient on the same date by the same physician.

The following services are included in reporting critical care when performed during the critical period by the physician(s) providing critical care: the interpretation of cardiac output measurements (93561, 93562), chest X-rays (71010, 71015, 71020), pulse oximetry (94760, 94761, 94762), blood gases, and information data stored in computers (eg, ECGs, blood pressures, hematologic data [99090]); gastric intubation (43752, 91105); temporary transcutaneous pacing (92953); ventilatory management (94002-94004, 94660, 94662); and vascular access procedures (36000, 36410, 36415, 36591, 36600). Any services performed that are not included in this listing should be reported separately.

Codes 99291, 99292 should be reported for the physician's attendance during the transport of critically ill or critically injured patients older than 24 months of age to or from a facility or hospital. For physician transport services of critically ill or critically injured pediatric patients 24 months of age or younger, see 99466, 99467.

The critical care codes 99291 and 99292 are used to report the total duration of time spent by a physician providing critical care services to a critically ill or critically injured patient, even if the time spent by the physician on that date is not continuous. For any given period of time spent providing critical care services, the physician must devote his or her full attention to the patient and, therefore, cannot provide services to any other patient during the same period of time.

Time spent with the individual patient should be recorded in the patient's record. The time that can be reported as critical care is the time spent engaged in work directly related to the individual patient's care whether that time was spent at the immediate bedside or elsewhere on the floor or unit. For example, time spent on the unit or at the nursing station on the floor reviewing test results or imaging studies, discussing the critically ill patient's care with other medical staff or documenting critical care services in the medical record would be reported as critical care, even though it does not occur at the bedside. Also, when the patient is unable or lacks capacity to participate in discussions, time spent on the floor or unit with family members or surrogate decision makers obtaining a medical history, reviewing the patient's condition or prognosis, or discussing treatment or limitation(s) of treatment may be reported as critical care, provided that the conversation bears directly on the management of the patient.

Time spent in activities that occur outside of the unit or off the floor (eg, telephone calls whether taken at home, in the office, or elsewhere in the hospital) may not be reported as critical care since the physician is not immediately available to the patient. Time spent in activities that do not directly contribute to the treatment of the patient may not be reported as critical care, even if they are performed in the critical care unit (eg, participation in administrative meetings or telephone calls to discuss other patients). Time spent performing separately reportable procedures or services should not be included in the time reported as critical care time. No physician may report remote real-time interactive video-conferenced critical care services (0188T, 0189T) for the period in which any physician reports 99291-99292.

Code 99291 is used to report the first 30-74 minutes of critical care on a given date. It should be used only once per date even if the time spent by the physician is not continuous on that date. Critical care of less than 30 minutes total duration on a given date should be reported with the appropriate E/M code.

Code 99292 is used to report additional block(s) of time, of up to 30 minutes each beyond the first 74 minutes. (See the following table.)

The following examples illustrate the correct reporting of critical care services:

Total Duration of Critical Care	Codes
less than 30 minutes	appropriate E/M codes
30-74 minutes (30 minutes - 1 hr. 14 min.)	99291 X 1
75-104 minutes (1 hr. 15 min. - 1 hr. 44 min.)	99291 X 1 AND 99292 X 1
105-134 minutes (1 hr. 45 min. - 2 hr. 14 min.)	99291 X 1 AND 99292 X 2
135 - 164 minutes (2 hr. 15 min. - 2 hr. 44 min.)	99291 X 1 AND 99292 X 3
165 - 194 minutes (2 hr. 45 min. - 3 hr. 14 min.)	99291 X 1 AND 99292 X 4
195 minutes or longer (3 hr. 15 min. - etc.)	99291 and 99292 as appropriate (see illustrated reporting examples above)

99291   **Critical care, evaluation and management** of the critically ill or critically injured patient; first 30-74 minutes

+ 99292   each additional 30 minutes (List separately in addition to code for primary service)

(Use 99292 in conjunction with 99291)

(99293 has been deleted. To report, use 99471)

(99294 has been deleted. To report, use 99472)

(99295 has been deleted. To report, use 99468)

(99296 has been deleted. To report, use 99469)

(99298 has been deleted. To report, use 99478)

(99299 has been deleted. To report, use 99479)

(99300 has been deleted. To report, use 99480)

Nursing Facility Services

The following codes are used to report evaluation and management services to patients in nursing facilities (formerly called skilled nursing facilities [SNFs], intermediate care facilities [ICFs], or long-term care facilities [LTCFs]).

These codes should also be used to report evaluation and management services provided to a patient in a psychiatric residential treatment center (a facility or a distinct part of a facility for psychiatric care, which provides a 24-hour therapeutically planned and professionally staffed group living and learning environment). If procedures such as medical psychotherapy are provided in addition to evaluation and management services, these should be reported in addition to the evaluation and management services provided.

Nursing facilities that provide convalescent, rehabilitative, or long term care are required to conduct comprehensive, accurate, standardized, and reproducible assessments of each resident's functional capacity using a Resident Assessment Instrument (RAI). All RAIs include the Minimum Data Set (MDS), Resident Assessment Protocols (RAPs), and utilization guidelines. The MDS is the primary screening and assessment tool; the RAPs trigger the identification of potential problems and provide guidelines for follow-up assessments.

Physicians have a central role in assuring that all residents receive thorough assessments and that medical plans of care are instituted or revised to enhance or maintain the residents' physical and psychosocial functioning. This role includes providing input in the development of the MDS and a multi-disciplinary plan of care, as required by regulations pertaining to the care of nursing facility residents.

Two major subcategories of nursing facility services are recognized: Initial Nursing Facility Care and Subsequent Nursing Facility Care. Both subcategories apply to new or established patients.

For definitions of key components and commonly used terms, please see **Evaluation and Management Services Guidelines.**

> (For care plan oversight services provided to nursing facility residents, see 99379-99380)

Initial Nursing Facility Care

New or Established Patient

When the patient is admitted to the nursing facility in the course of an encounter in another site of service (eg, hospital emergency department, physician's office), all evaluation and management services provided by that physician in conjunction with that admission are considered part of the initial nursing facility care when performed on the same date as the admission or readmission. The nursing facility care level of service reported by the admitting physician should include the services related to the admission he/she provided in the other sites of service as well as in the nursing facility setting.

Hospital discharge or observation discharge services performed on the same date of nursing facility admission or readmission may be reported separately. For a patient discharged from inpatient status on the same date of nursing facility admission or readmission, the hospital discharge services should be reported with codes 99238, 99239 as appropriate. For a patient discharged from observation status on the same date of nursing facility admission or readmission, the observation care discharge services should be reported with code 99217. For a patient admitted and discharged from observation or inpatient status on the same date, see codes 99234-99236.

(For nursing facility care discharge, see 99315, 99316)

▲ **99304**   Initial nursing facility care, per day, for the evaluation and management of a patient, which requires these 3 key components:

- **A detailed or comprehensive history;**
- **A detailed or comprehensive examination; and**
- **Medical decision making that is straightforward or of low complexity.**

Counseling and/or coordination of care with other providers or agencies are provided consistent with the nature of the problem(s) and the patient's and/or family's needs.

Usually, the problem(s) requiring admission are of low severity. Physicians typically spend 25 minutes at the bedside and on the patient's facility floor or unit.

▲ **99305**   Initial nursing facility care, per day, for the evaluation and management of a patient, which requires these 3 key components:

- **A comprehensive history;**
- **A comprehensive examination; and**
- **Medical decision making of moderate complexity.**

Counseling and/or coordination of care with other providers or agencies are provided consistent with the nature of the problem(s) and the patient's and/or family's needs.

Evaluation and Management

Usually, the problem(s) requiring admission are of moderate severity. Physicians typically spend 35 minutes at the bedside and on the patient's facility floor or unit.

▲ 99306   Initial nursing facility care, per day, for the evaluation and management of a patient, which requires these 3 key components:

- **A comprehensive history;**
- **A comprehensive examination; and**
- **Medical decision making of high complexity.**

Counseling and/or coordination of care with other providers or agencies are provided consistent with the nature of the problem(s) and the patient's and/or family's needs.

Usually, the problem(s) requiring admission are of high severity. Physicians typically spend 45 minutes at the bedside and on the patient's facility floor or unit.

Subsequent Nursing Facility Care

All levels of subsequent nursing facility care include reviewing the medical record and reviewing the results of diagnostic studies and changes in the patient's status (ie, changes in history, physical condition, and response to management) since the last assessment by the physician.

▲ 99307   Subsequent nursing facility care, per day, for the evaluation and management of a patient, which requires at least 2 of these 3 key components:

- **A problem focused interval history;**
- **A problem focused examination;**
- **Straightforward medical decision making.**

Counseling and/or coordination of care with other providers or agencies are provided consistent with the nature of the problem(s) and the patient's and/or family's needs.

Usually, the patient is stable, recovering, or improving. Physicians typically spend 10 minutes at the bedside and on the patient's facility floor or unit.

▲ 99308   Subsequent nursing facility care, per day, for the evaluation and management of a patient, which requires at least 2 of these 3 key components:

- **An expanded problem focused interval history;**
- **An expanded problem focused examination;**
- **Medical decision making of low complexity.**

Counseling and/or coordination of care with other providers or agencies are provided consistent with the nature of the problem(s) and the patient's and/or family's needs.

Usually, the patient is responding inadequately to therapy or has developed a minor complication. Physicians typically spend 15 minutes at the bedside and on the patient's facility floor or unit.

▲ 99309   Subsequent nursing facility care, per day, for the evaluation and management of a patient, which requires at least 2 of these 3 key components:

- **A detailed interval history;**
- **A detailed examination;**
- **Medical decision making of moderate complexity.**

Counseling and/or coordination of care with other providers or agencies are provided consistent with the nature of the problem(s) and the patient's and/or family's needs.

Usually, the patient has developed a significant complication or a significant new problem. Physicians typically spend 25 minutes at the bedside and on the patient's facility floor or unit.

▲ 99310   Subsequent nursing facility care, per day, for the evaluation and management of a patient, which requires at least 2 of these 3 key components:

- **A comprehensive interval history;**
- **A comprehensive examination;**
- **Medical decision making of high complexity.**

Counseling and/or coordination of care with other providers or agencies are provided consistent with the nature of the problem(s) and the patient's and/or family's needs.

The patient may be unstable or may have developed a significant new problem requiring immediate physician attention. Physicians typically spend 35 minutes at the bedside and on the patient's facility floor or unit.

Nursing Facility Discharge Services

The nursing facility discharge day management codes are to be used to report the total duration of time spent by a physician for the final nursing facility discharge of a patient. The codes include, as appropriate, final examination of the patient, discussion of the nursing facility stay, even if the time spent by the physician on that date is not continuous. Instructions are given for continuing care to all relevant caregivers, and preparation of discharge records, prescriptions and referral forms.

99315   Nursing facility discharge day management; 30 minutes or less

99316   more than 30 minutes

Other Nursing Facility Services

▲ 99318   Evaluation and management of a patient involving an annual nursing facility assessment, which requires these 3 key components:

- **A detailed interval history;**
- **A comprehensive examination; and**
- **Medical decision making that is of low to moderate complexity.**

Counseling and/or coordination of care with other providers or agencies are provided consistent with the nature of the problem(s) and the patient's and/or family's needs.

Usually, the patient is stable, recovering, or improving. Physicians typically spend 30 minutes at the bedside and on the patient's facility floor or unit.

(Do not report 99318 on the same date of service as nursing facility services codes 99304-99316)

Domiciliary, Rest Home (eg, Boarding Home), or Custodial Care Services

The following codes are used to report evaluation and management services in a facility which provides room, board and other personal assistance services, generally on a long-term basis. They also are used to report evaluation and management services in an assisted living facility.

The facility's services do not include a medical component.

For definitions of key components and commonly used terms, please see **Evaluation and Management Services Guidelines**.

(For care plan oversight services provided to a patient in a domiciliary facility under the care of a home health agency, see 99374-99375)

(For care plan oversight services provided to a patient in a domiciliary facility under the individual supervision of a physician, see 99339, 99340)

New Patient

99324   Domiciliary or rest home visit for the evaluation and management of a new patient, which requires these 3 key components:

- **A problem focused history;**
- **A problem focused examination; and**
- **Straightforward medical decision making.**

Counseling and/or coordination of care with other providers or agencies are provided consistent with the nature of the problem(s) and the patient's and/or family's needs.

Usually, the presenting problem(s) are of low severity. Physicians typically spend 20 minutes with the patient and/or family or caregiver.

99325   Domiciliary or rest home visit for the evaluation and management of a new patient, which requires these 3 key components:

- **An expanded problem focused history;**
- **An expanded problem focused examination; and**
- **Medical decision making of low complexity.**

Counseling and/or coordination of care with other providers or agencies are provided consistent with the nature of the problem(s) and the patient's and/or family's needs.

Usually, the presenting problem(s) are of moderate severity. Physicians typically spend 30 minutes with the patient and/or family or caregiver.

99326   Domiciliary or rest home visit for the evaluation and management of a new patient, which requires these 3 key components:

- **A detailed history;**
- **A detailed examination; and**
- **Medical decision making of moderate complexity.**

Counseling and/or coordination of care with other providers or agencies are provided consistent with the nature of the problem(s) and the patient's and/or family's needs.

Usually, the presenting problem(s) are of moderate to high severity. Physicians typically spend 45 minutes with the patient and/or family or caregiver.

99327   Domiciliary or rest home visit for the evaluation and management of a new patient, which requires these 3 key components:

- **A comprehensive history;**
- **A comprehensive examination; and**
- **Medical decision making of moderate complexity.**

Counseling and/or coordination of care with other providers or agencies are provided consistent with the nature of the problem(s) and the patient's and/or family's needs.

Usually, the presenting problem(s) are of high severity. Physicians typically spend 60 minutes with the patient and/or family or caregiver.

99328   Domiciliary or rest home visit for the evaluation and management of a new patient, which requires these 3 key components:

- **A comprehensive history;**
- **A comprehensive examination; and**
- **Medical decision making of high complexity.**

Counseling and/or coordination of care with other providers or agencies are provided consistent with the nature of the problem(s) and the patient's and/or family's needs.

Usually, the patient is unstable or has developed a significant new problem requiring immediate physician attention. Physicians typically spend 75 minutes with the patient and/or family or caregiver.

Evaluation and Management

Established Patient

99334   Domiciliary or rest home visit for the evaluation and management of an established patient, which requires at least 2 of these 3 key components:

- **A problem focused interval history;**
- **A problem focused examination;**
- **Straightforward medical decision making.**

Counseling and/or coordination of care with other providers or agencies are provided consistent with the nature of the problem(s) and the patient's and/or family's needs.

Usually, the presenting problem(s) are self-limited or minor. Physicians typically spend 15 minutes with the patient and/or family or caregiver.

99335   Domiciliary or rest home visit for the evaluation and management of an established patient, which requires at least 2 of these 3 key components:

- **An expanded problem focused interval history;**
- **An expanded problem focused examination;**
- **Medical decision making of low complexity.**

Counseling and/or coordination of care with other providers or agencies are provided consistent with the nature of the problem(s) and the patient's and/or family's needs.

Usually, the presenting problem(s) are of low to moderate severity. Physicians typically spend 25 minutes with the patient and/or family or caregiver.

99336   Domiciliary or rest home visit for the evaluation and management of an established patient, which requires at least 2 of these 3 key components:

- **A detailed interval history;**
- **A detailed examination;**
- **Medical decision making of moderate complexity.**

Counseling and/or coordination of care with other providers or agencies are provided consistent with the nature of the problem(s) and the patient's and/or family's needs.

Usually, the presenting problem(s) are of moderate to high severity. Physicians typically spend 40 minutes with the patient and/or family or caregiver.

99337   Domiciliary or rest home visit for the evaluation and management of an established patient, which requires at least 2 of these 3 key components:

- **A comprehensive interval history;**
- **A comprehensive examination;**
- **Medical decision making of moderate to high complexity.**

Counseling and/or coordination of care with other providers or agencies are provided consistent with the nature of the problem(s) and the patient's and/or family's needs.

Usually, the presenting problem(s) are of moderate to high severity. The patient may be unstable or may have developed a significant new problem requiring immediate physician attention. Physicians typically spend 60 minutes with the patient and/or family or caregiver.

Domiciliary, Rest Home (eg, Assisted Living Facility), or Home Care Plan Oversight Services

(For instructions on the use of 99339, 99340, see introductory notes for 99374-99380)

(For care plan oversight services for patients under the care of a home health agency, hospice, or nursing facility, see 99374-99380)

(Do not report 99339, 99340 for time reported with 98966-98969, 99441-99444)

99339   Individual physician supervision of a patient (patient not present) in home, domiciliary or rest home (eg, assisted living facility) requiring complex and multidisciplinary care modalities involving regular physician development and/or revision of care plans, review of subsequent reports of patient status, review of related laboratory and other studies, communication (including telephone calls) for purposes of assessment or care decisions with health care professional(s), family member(s), surrogate decision maker(s) (eg, legal guardian) and/or key caregiver(s) involved in patient's care, integration of new information into the medical treatment plan and/or adjustment of medical therapy, within a calendar month; 15-29 minutes

99340   30 minutes or more

(Do not report 99339, 99340 for patients under the care of a home health agency, enrolled in a hospice program, or for nursing facility residents)

Home Services

The following codes are used to report evaluation and management services provided in a private residence.

For definitions of key components and commonly used terms, please see **Evaluation and Management Services Guidelines.**

(For care plan oversight services provided to a patient in the home under the care of a home health agency, see 99374-99375)

(For care plan oversight services provided to a patient in the home under the individual supervision of a physician, see 99339, 99340)

New Patient

99341 **Home visit** for the evaluation and management of a new patient, which requires these 3 key components:

- **A problem focused history;**
- **A problem focused examination; and**
- **Straightforward medical decision making.**

Counseling and/or coordination of care with other providers or agencies are provided consistent with the nature of the problem(s) and the patient's and/or family's needs.

Usually, the presenting problem(s) are of low severity. Physicians typically spend 20 minutes face-to-face with the patient and/or family.

99342 **Home visit** for the evaluation and management of a new patient, which requires these 3 key components:

- **An expanded problem focused history;**
- **An expanded problem focused examination; and**
- **Medical decision making of low complexity.**

Counseling and/or coordination of care with other providers or agencies are provided consistent with the nature of the problem(s) and the patient's and/or family's needs.

Usually, the presenting problem(s) are of moderate severity. Physicians typically spend 30 minutes face-to-face with the patient and/or family.

99343 **Home visit** for the evaluation and management of a new patient, which requires these 3 key components:

- **A detailed history;**
- **A detailed examination; and**
- **Medical decision making of moderate complexity.**

Counseling and/or coordination of care with other providers or agencies are provided consistent with the nature of the problem(s) and the patient's and/or family's needs.

Usually, the presenting problem(s) are of moderate to high severity. Physicians typically spend 45 minutes face-to-face with the patient and/or family.

99344 **Home visit** for the evaluation and management of a new patient, which requires these 3 key components:

- **A comprehensive history;**
- **A comprehensive examination; and**
- **Medical decision making of moderate complexity.**

Counseling and/or coordination of care with other providers or agencies are provided consistent with the nature of the problem(s) and the patient's and/or family's needs.

Usually, the presenting problem(s) are of high severity. Physicians typically spend 60 minutes face-to-face with the patient and/or family.

99345 **Home visit** for the evaluation and management of a new patient, which requires these 3 key components:

- **A comprehensive history;**
- **A comprehensive examination; and**
- **Medical decision making of high complexity.**

Counseling and/or coordination of care with other providers or agencies are provided consistent with the nature of the problem(s) and the patient's and/or family's needs.

Usually, the patient is unstable or has developed a significant new problem requiring immediate physician attention. Physicians typically spend 75 minutes face-to-face with the patient and/or family.

Established Patient

99347 **Home visit** for the evaluation and management of an established patient, which requires at least 2 of these 3 key components:

- **A problem focused interval history;**
- **A problem focused examination;**
- **Straightforward medical decision making.**

Counseling and/or coordination of care with other providers or agencies are provided consistent with the nature of the problem(s) and the patient's and/or family's needs.

Usually, the presenting problem(s) are self limited or minor. Physicians typically spend 15 minutes face-to-face with the patient and/or family.

99348 **Home visit** for the evaluation and management of an established patient, which requires at least 2 of these 3 key components:

- **An expanded problem focused interval history;**
- **An expanded problem focused examination;**
- **Medical decision making of low complexity.**

Counseling and/or coordination of care with other providers or agencies are provided consistent with the nature of the problem(s) and the patient's and/or family's needs.

Usually, the presenting problem(s) are of low to moderate severity. Physicians typically spend 25 minutes face-to-face with the patient and/or family.

99349 **Home visit** for the evaluation and management of an established patient, which requires at least 2 of these 3 key components:

- **A detailed interval history;**
- **A detailed examination;**
- **Medical decision making of moderate complexity.**

Counseling and/or coordination of care with other providers or agencies are provided consistent with the nature of the problem(s) and the patient's and/or family's needs.

Evaluation and Management

Usually, the presenting problem(s) are moderate to high severity. Physicians typically spend 40 minutes face-to-face with the patient and/or family.

99350   **Home visit** for the evaluation and management of an established patient, which requires at least 2 of these 3 key components:

- **A comprehensive interval history;**
- **A comprehensive examination;**
- **Medical decision making of moderate to high complexity.**

Counseling and/or coordination of care with other providers or agencies are provided consistent with the nature of the problem(s) and the patient's and/or family's needs.

Usually, the presenting problem(s) are of moderate to high severity. The patient may be unstable or may have developed a significant new problem requiring immediate physician attention. Physicians typically spend 60 minutes face-to-face with the patient and/or family.

Prolonged Services

Prolonged Physician Service With Direct (Face-To-Face) Patient Contact

Codes 99354-99357 are used when a physician provides prolonged service involving direct (face-to-face) patient contact that is beyond the usual service in either the inpatient or outpatient setting. This service is reported in addition to the designated evaluation and management services at any level and any other physician services provided at the same session as evaluation and management services. Appropriate codes should be selected for supplies provided or procedures performed in the care of the patient during this period.

Codes 99354-99355 are used to report the total duration of face-to-face time spent by a physician on a given date providing prolonged service, even if the time spent by the physician on that date is not continuous. Codes 99356-99357 are used to report the total duration of unit time spent by a physician on a given date providing prolonged service to a patient, even if the time spent by the physician on that date is not continuous.

Code 99354 or 99356 is used to report the first hour of prolonged service on a given date, depending on the place of service.

Either code should be used only once per date, even if the time spent by the physician is not continuous on that date. Prolonged service of less than 30 minutes total duration on a given date is not separately reported because the work involved is included in the total work of the evaluation and management codes.

Code 99355 or 99357 is used to report each additional 30 minutes beyond the first hour, depending on the place of service. Either code may also be used to report the final 15-30 minutes of prolonged service on a given date. Prolonged service of less than 15 minutes beyond the first hour or less than 15 minutes beyond the final 30 minutes is not reported separately.

The use of the time based add-on codes requires that the primary evaluation and management service have a typical or specified time published in the CPT codebook.

The following examples illustrate the correct reporting of prolonged physician service with direct patient contact in the office setting:

Total Duration of Prolonged Services	Code(s)
less than 30 minutes (less than 30 minutes)	Not reported separately
30-74 minutes (30 minutes - 1 hr. 14 min.)	99354 X 1
75-104 minutes (1 hr. 15 min. - 1 hr. 44 min.)	99354 X 1 AND 99355 X 1
105 or more (1 hr. 45 min. or more) 30 minutes	99354 X 1 AND 99355 X 2 or more for each additional

+ 99354   Prolonged physician service in the office or other outpatient setting requiring direct (face-to-face) patient contact beyond the usual service; first hour (List separately in addition to code for office or other outpatient **Evaluation and Management** service)

(Use 99354 in conjunction with 99201-99215, 99241-99245, 99324-99337, 99341-99350, 90809, 90815)

+ 99355   each additional 30 minutes (List separately in addition to code for prolonged physician service)

(Use 99355 in conjunction with 99354)

+ 99356   Prolonged physician service in the inpatient setting, requiring unit/floor time beyond the usual service; first hour (List separately in addition to code for inpatient **Evaluation and Management** service)

(Use 99356 in conjunction with 99221-99233, 99251-99255, 99304-99310, 90822, 90829)

+ 99357   each additional 30 minutes (List separately in addition to code for prolonged physician service)

(Use 99357 in conjunction with 99356)

Prolonged Physician Service Without Direct (Face-To-Face) Patient Contact

▶Codes 99358 and 99359 are used when a physician provides prolonged service not involving direct (face-to-face) care that is beyond the usual non-face-to-face component of physician service time.

This service is to be reported in relation to other physician services, including evaluation and management services at any level. This prolonged service may be reported on a different date than the primary service to which it is related. For example, extensive record review may relate to a previous evaluation and management service performed earlier and commences upon receipt of past records. However, it must relate to a service or patient where direct (face-to-face) patient care has occurred or will occur and relate to ongoing patient management. A typical time for the primary service need not be established within CPT code set.

Codes 99358 and 99359 are used to report the total duration of non-face-to-face time spent by a physician on a given date providing prolonged service, even if the time spent by the physician on that date is not continuous. Code 99358 is used to report the first hour of prolonged service on a given date regardless of the place of service. It should be used only once per date.◀

Prolonged service of less than 30 minutes total duration on a given date is not separately reported.

Code 99359 is used to report each additional 30 minutes beyond the first hour regardless of the place of service. It may also be used to report the final 15 to 30 minutes of prolonged service on a given date.

Prolonged service of less than 15 minutes beyond the first hour or less than 15 minutes beyond the final 30 minutes is not reported separately.

▶Do not report 99358-99359 for time spent in medical team conferences, on-line medical evaluations, care plan oversight services, anticoagulation management, or other non-face-to-face services that have more specific codes and no upper time limit in the CPT code set. Codes 99358-99359 may be reported when related to other non-face-to-face services codes that have a published maximum time (eg, telephone services).◀

▲ **99358**   **Prolonged evaluation and management service** before and/or after direct (face-to-face) patient care; first hour

+▲ **99359**   each additional 30 minutes (List separately in addition to code for prolonged physician service)

(Use 99359 in conjunction with 99358)

Physician Standby Services

Code 99360 is used to report physician standby service that is requested by another physician and that involves prolonged physician attendance without direct (face-to-face) patient contact. The physician may not be providing care or services to other patients during this period. This code is not used to report time spent proctoring another physician. It is also not used if the period of standby ends with the performance of a procedure subject to a "surgical" package by the physician who was on standby.

Code 99360 is used to report the total duration of time spent by a physician on a given date on standby. Standby service of less than 30 minutes total duration on a given date is not reported separately.

Second and subsequent periods of standby beyond the first 30 minutes may be reported only if a full 30 minutes of standby was provided for each unit of service reported.

99360   **Physician standby service,** requiring prolonged physician attendance, each 30 minutes (eg, operative standby, standby for frozen section, for cesarean/high risk delivery, for monitoring EEG)

(For hospital mandated on call services, see 99026, 99027)

(99360 may be reported in addition to 99460, 99465 as appropriate)

(Do not report 99360 in conjunction with 99464)

Case Management Services

Case management is a process in which a physician or another qualified health care professional is responsible for direct care of a patient and, additionally, for coordinating, managing access to, initiating, and/or supervising other health care services needed by the patient.

(99361, 99362 have been deleted. To report, see 99366-99368)

Anticoagulant Management

Anticoagulant services are intended to describe the outpatient management of warfarin therapy, including ordering, review, and interpretation of International Normalized Ratio (INR) testing, communication with patient, and dosage adjustments as appropriate.

When reporting these services, the work of anticoagulant management may not be used as a basis for reporting an evaluation and management (E/M) service or care plan oversight time during the reporting period. Do not report these services with 98966-98969, 99441-99444 when telephone or on-line services address anticoagulation with warfarin management. If a significant, separately identifiable E/M service is performed, report the appropriate E/M service code using modifier 25.

Evaluation and Management

These services are outpatient services only. When anticoagulation therapy is initiated or continued in the inpatient or observation setting, a new period begins after discharge and is reported with 99364. Do not report 99363-99364 with 99217-99239, 99291-99292, 99304-99318, 99471-99480 or other code(s) for physician review, interpretation, and patient management of home INR testing for a patient with mechanical heart valve(s).

Any period less than 60 continuous outpatient days is not reported. If less than the specified minimum number of services per period are performed, do not report the anticoagulant management services (99363-99364).

99363   Anticoagulant management for an outpatient taking warfarin, physician review and interpretation of International Normalized Ratio (INR) testing, patient instructions, dosage adjustment (as needed), and ordering of additional tests; initial 90 days of therapy (must include a minimum of 8 INR measurements)

99364   each subsequent 90 days of therapy (must include a minimum of 3 INR measurements)

Medical Team Conferences

Medical team conferences include face-to-face participation by a minimum of three qualified health care professionals from different specialties or disciplines (each of whom provide direct care to the patient), with or without the presence of the patient, family member(s), community agencies, surrogate decision maker(s) (eg, legal guardian), and/or caregiver(s). The participants are actively involved in the development, revision, coordination, and implementation of health care services needed by the patient. Reporting participants shall have performed face-to-face evaluations or treatments of the patient, independent of any team conference, within the previous 60 days.

Physicians may report their time spent in a team conference with the patient and/or family present using evaluation and management (E/M) codes (and time as the key controlling factor for code selection when counseling and/or coordination of care dominates the service). These introductory guidelines do not apply to services reported using E/M codes (see E/M services guidelines). However, the physician must be directly involved with the patient, providing face-to-face services outside of the conference visit with other providers or agencies.

Reporting participants shall document their participation in the team conference as well as their contributed information and subsequent treatment recommendations.

No more than one individual from the same specialty may report 99366-99368 at the same encounter.

Individuals should not report 99366-99368 when their participation in the medical team conference is part of a facility or organizational service contractually provided by the organizational or facility provider.

The team conference starts at the beginning of the review of an individual patient and ends at the conclusion of the review. Time related to record keeping and report generation is not reported. The reporting participant shall be present for all time reported. The time reported is not limited to the time that the participant is communicating to the other team members or patient and/or family. Time reported for medical team conferences may not be used in the determination of time for other services such as care plan oversight (99374-99380), home, domiciliary, or rest home care plan oversight (99339-99340), prolonged services (99354-99359), psychotherapy, or any E/M service. For team conferences where the patient is present for any part of the duration of the conference, nonphysician qualified health care professionals report the team conference face-to-face code 99366.

Medical Team Conference, Direct (Face-to-Face) Contact With Patient and/or Family

99366   **Medical team conference** with interdisciplinary team of health care professionals, face-to-face with patient and/or family, 30 minutes or more, participation by nonphysician qualified health care professional

(Team conference services of less than 30 minutes duration are not reported separately)

(For team conference services by a physician with patient and/or family present, see Evaluation and Management services)

Medical Team Conference, Without Direct (Face-to-Face) Contact With Patient and/or Family

99367   **Medical team conference** with interdisciplinary team of health care professionals, patient and/or family not present, 30 minutes or more; participation by physician

99368   participation by nonphysician qualified health care professional

(Team conference services of less than 30 minutes duration are not reported separately)

(99371-99373 have been deleted. To report telephone evaluation and management services, see 99441-99443)

Care Plan Oversight Services

Care plan oversight services are reported separately from codes for office/outpatient, hospital, home, nursing facility or domiciliary, or non-face-to-face services. The complexity and approximate physician time of the care plan oversight services provided within a 30-day period determine code selection. Only one physician may report services for a given period of time, to reflect that physician's sole or predominant supervisory role with a particular patient. These codes should not be reported for supervision of patients in nursing facilities or under the care of home health agencies unless they require recurrent supervision of therapy.

The work involved in providing very low intensity or infrequent supervision services is included in the pre- and post-encounter work for home, office/outpatient and nursing facility or domiciliary visit codes.

(For care plan oversight services of patients in the home, domiciliary, or rest home (eg, assisted living facility) under the individual supervision of a physician, see 99339, 99340)

(Do not report 99374-99380 for time reported with 98966-98969, 99441-99444)

99374   **Physician supervision** of a patient under care of home health agency (patient not present) in home, domiciliary or equivalent environment (eg, Alzheimer's facility) requiring complex and multidisciplinary care modalities involving regular physician development and/or revision of care plans, review of subsequent reports of patient status, review of related laboratory and other studies, communication (including telephone calls) for purposes of assessment or care decisions with health care professional(s), family member(s), surrogate decision maker(s) (eg, legal guardian) and/or key caregiver(s) involved in patient's care, integration of new information into the medical treatment plan and/or adjustment of medical therapy, within a calendar month; 15-29 minutes

99375   30 minutes or more

99377   **Physician supervision** of a hospice patient (patient not present) requiring complex and multidisciplinary care modalities involving regular physician development and/or revision of care plans, review of subsequent reports of patient status, review of related laboratory and other studies, communication (including telephone calls) for purposes of assessment or care decisions with health care professional(s), family member(s), surrogate decision maker(s) (eg, legal guardian) and/or key caregiver(s) involved in patient's care, integration of new information into the medical treatment plan and/or adjustment of medical therapy, within a calendar month; 15-29 minutes

99378   30 minutes or more

99379   **Physician supervision** of a nursing facility patient (patient not present) requiring complex and multidisciplinary care modalities involving regular physician development and/or revision of care plans, review of subsequent reports of patient status, review of related laboratory and other studies, communication (including telephone calls) for purposes of assessment or care decisions with health care professional(s), family member(s), surrogate decision maker(s) (eg, legal guardian) and/or key caregiver(s) involved in patient's care, integration of new information into the medical treatment plan and/or adjustment of medical therapy, within a calendar month; 15-29 minutes

99380   30 minutes or more

Preventive Medicine Services

The following codes are used to report the preventive medicine evaluation and management of infants, children, adolescents, and adults.

The extent and focus of the services will largely depend on the age of the patient.

If an abnormality is encountered or a preexisting problem is addressed in the process of performing this preventive medicine evaluation and management service, and if the problem or abnormality is significant enough to require additional work to perform the key components of a problem-oriented E/M service, then the appropriate Office/Outpatient code 99201-99215 should also be reported. Modifier 25 should be added to the Office/Outpatient code to indicate that a significant, separately identifiable evaluation and management service was provided by the same physician on the same day as the preventive medicine service. The appropriate preventive medicine service is additionally reported.

An insignificant or trivial problem/abnormality that is encountered in the process of performing the preventive medicine evaluation and management service and which does not require additional work and the performance of the key components of a problem-oriented E/M service should not be reported.

The "comprehensive" nature of the Preventive Medicine Services codes 99381-99397 reflects an age and gender appropriate history/exam and is **not** synonymous with the "comprehensive" examination required in Evaluation and Management codes 99201-99350.

Codes 99381-99397 include counseling/anticipatory guidance/risk factor reduction interventions which are provided at the time of the initial or periodic comprehensive preventive medicine examination. (Refer to codes 99401-99412 for reporting those counseling/anticipatory guidance/risk factor reduction interventions that are provided at an encounter separate from the preventive medicine examination.)

Vaccine/toxoid products, immunization administrations, ancillary studies involving laboratory, radiology, other procedures, or screening tests (eg, vision, hearing, developmental) identified with a specific CPT code are reported separately. For immunization administration and vaccine risk/benefit counseling, see 90465-90474. For vaccine/toxoid products, see 90476-90749.

New Patient

99381   **Initial comprehensive preventive medicine**
evaluation and management of an individual including an
age and gender appropriate history, examination,
counseling/anticipatory guidance/risk factor reduction
interventions, and the ordering of laboratory/diagnostic
procedures, new patient; infant (age younger than 1 year)

99382   early childhood (age 1 through 4 years)

99383   late childhood (age 5 through 11 years)

99384   adolescent (age 12 through 17 years)

99385   18-39 years

99386   40-64 years

99387   65 years and older

Established Patient

99391   **Periodic comprehensive preventive medicine**
reevaluation and management of an individual including
an age and gender appropriate history, examination,
counseling/anticipatory guidance/risk factor reduction
interventions, and the ordering of laboratory/diagnostic
procedures, established patient; infant (age younger than
1 year)

99392   early childhood (age 1 through 4 years)

99393   late childhood (age 5 through 11 years)

99394   adolescent (age 12 through 17 years)

99395   18-39 years

99396   40-64 years

99397   65 years and older

Counseling Risk Factor Reduction and Behavior Change Intervention

New or Established Patient

These codes are used to report services provided face-to-face by a physician or other qualified health care professional for the purpose of promoting health and preventing illness or injury. They are distinct from evaluation and management (E/M) services that may be reported separately when performed. Risk factor reduction services are used for persons without a specific illness for which the counseling might otherwise be used as part of treatment.

Preventive medicine counseling and risk factor reduction interventions will vary with age and should address such issues as family problems, diet and exercise, substance use, sexual practices, injury prevention, dental health, and diagnostic and laboratory test results available at the time of the encounter.

Behavior change interventions are for persons who have a behavior that is often considered an illness itself, such as tobacco use and addiction, substance abuse/misuse, or obesity. Behavior change services may be reported when performed as part of the treatment of condition(s) related to or potentially exacerbated by the behavior or when performed to change the harmful behavior that has not yet resulted in illness. Any E/M services reported on the same day must be distinct, and time spent providing these services may not be used as a basis for the E/M code selection. Behavior change services involve specific validated interventions of assessing readiness for change and barriers to change, advising a change in behavior, assisting by providing specific suggested actions and motivational counseling, and arranging for services and follow-up.

For counseling groups of patients with symptoms or established illness, use 99078.

Health and Behavior Assessment/Intervention services (96150-96155) should not be reported on the same day.

Preventive Medicine, Individual Counseling

99401   **Preventive medicine counseling** and/or risk factor
reduction intervention(s) provided to an individual
(separate procedure); approximately 15 minutes

99402   approximately 30 minutes

99403   approximately 45 minutes

99404   approximately 60 minutes

Behavior Change Interventions, Individual

99406   Smoking and tobacco use cessation counseling visit;
intermediate, greater than 3 minutes up to 10 minutes

99407   intensive, greater than 10 minutes

(Do not report 99407 in conjunction with 99406)

99408   Alcohol and/or substance (other than tobacco) abuse
structured screening (eg, AUDIT, DAST), and brief
intervention (SBI) services; 15 to 30 minutes

(Do not report services of less than 15 minutes with
99408)

99409   greater than 30 minutes

(Do not report 99409 in conjunction with 99408)

(Do not report 99408, 99409 in conjunction with 99420)

(Use 99408, 99409 only for initial screening and brief
intervention)

Preventive Medicine, Group Counseling

99411   **Preventive medicine counseling** and/or risk factor reduction intervention(s) provided to individuals in a group setting (separate procedure); approximately 30 minutes

99412   approximately 60 minutes

Other Preventive Medicine Services

99420   **Administration and interpretation** of health risk assessment instrument (eg, health hazard appraisal)

99429   **Unlisted preventive** medicine service

(99431 has been deleted. To report, use 99460)

(99432 has been deleted. To report, use 99461)

(99433 has been deleted. To report, use 99462)

(99435 has been deleted. To report, use 99463)

(99436 has been deleted. To report, use 99464)

(99440 has been deleted. To report, use 99465)

Non-Face-to-Face Physician Services

Telephone Services

Telephone services are non-face-to-face evaluation and management (E/M) services provided by a physician to a patient using the telephone. These codes are used to report episodes of care by the physician initiated by an established patient or guardian of an established patient. If the telephone service ends with a decision to see the patient within 24 hours or next available urgent visit appointment, the code is not reported; rather the encounter is considered part of the preservice work of the subsequent E/M service, procedure, and visit. Likewise if the telephone call refers to an E/M service performed and reported by the physician within the previous seven days (either physician requested or unsolicited patient follow-up) or within the postoperative period of the previously completed procedure, then the service(s) are considered part of that previous E/M service or procedure. (Do not report 99441-99443 if reporting 99441-99444 performed in the previous seven days.)

(For telephone services provided by a qualified nonphysician health care professional, see 98966-98968)

99441   Telephone evaluation and management service provided by a physician to an established patient, parent, or guardian not originating from a related E/M service provided within the previous 7 days nor leading to an E/M service or procedure within the next 24 hours or soonest available appointment; 5-10 minutes of medical discussion

99442   11-20 minutes of medical discussion

99443   21-30 minutes of medical discussion

(Do not report 99441-99443 when using 99339-99340, 99374-99380 for the same call[s])

(Do not report 99441-99443 for anticoagulation management when reporting 99363-99364)

On-Line Medical Evaluation

An on-line electronic medical evaluation is a non-face-to-face evaluation and management (E/M) service by a physician to a patient using Internet resources in response to a patient's on-line inquiry. Reportable services involve the physician's personal timely response to the patient's inquiry and must involve permanent storage (electronic or hard copy) of the encounter. This service is reported only once for the same episode of care during a seven-day period, although multiple physicians could report their exchange with the same patient. If the on-line medical evaluation refers to an E/M service previously performed and reported by the physician within the previous seven days (either physician requested or unsolicited patient follow-up) or within the postoperative period of the previously completed procedure, then the service(s) are considered covered by the previous E/M service or procedure. A reportable service encompasses the sum of communication (eg, related telephone calls, prescription provision, laboratory orders) pertaining to the on-line patient encounter.

(For an on-line medical evaluation provided by a qualified nonphysician health care professional, use 98969)

99444   Online evaluation and management service provided by a physician to an established patient, guardian, or health care provider not originating from a related E/M service provided within the previous 7 days, using the Internet or similar electronic communications network

(Do not report 99444 when using 99339-99340, 99374-99380 for the same communication[s])

(Do not report 99444 for anticoagulation management when reporting 99363, 99364)

Special Evaluation and Management Services

The following codes are used to report evaluations performed to establish baseline information prior to life or disability insurance certificates being issued. This service is performed in the office or other setting, and applies to both new and established patients. When using these codes, no active management of the problem(s) is undertaken during the encounter.

If other evaluation and management services and/or procedures are performed on the same date, the appropriate E/M or procedure code(s) should be reported in addition to these codes.

Basic Life and/or Disability Evaluation Services

99450   **Basic life** and/or disability examination that includes:

- Measurement of height, weight, and blood pressure;
- Completion of a medical history following a life insurance pro forma;
- Collection of blood sample and/or urinalysis complying with "chain of custody" protocols; and
- Completion of necessary documentation/certificates.

Work Related or Medical Disability Evaluation Services

99455   **Work related** or medical disability examination by the treating physician that includes:

- Completion of a medical history commensurate with the patient's condition;
- Performance of an examination commensurate with the patient's condition;
- Formulation of a diagnosis, assessment of capabilities and stability, and calculation of impairment;
- Development of future medical treatment plan; and
- Completion of necessary documentation/certificates and report.

99456   **Work related** or medical disability examination by other than the treating physician that includes:

- Completion of a medical history commensurate with the patient's condition;
- Performance of an examination commensurate with the patient's condition;
- Formulation of a diagnosis, assessment of capabilities and stability, and calculation of impairment;
- Development of future medical treatment plan; and
- Completion of necessary documentation/certificates and report.

(Do not report 99455, 99456 in conjunction with 99080 for the completion of Workman's Compensation forms)

Newborn Care Services

The following codes are used to report the services provided to newborns (birth through the first 28 days) in several different settings. Use of the normal newborn codes is limited to the initial care of the newborn in the first days after birth prior to home discharge.

Evaluation and Management (E/M) services for the newborn include maternal and/or fetal and newborn history, newborn physical examination(s), ordering of diagnostic tests and treatments, meetings with the family, and documentation in the medical record.

When delivery room attendance services (99464) or delivery room resuscitation services (99465) are required, report these in addition to normal newborn services Evaluation and Management codes.

For E/M services provided to newborns who are other than normal, see codes for hospital inpatient services (99221-99233) and neonatal intensive and critical care services (99466-99469, 99477-99480). When normal newborn services are provided by the same physician on the same date that the newborn later becomes ill and receives additional intensive or critical care services, report the appropriate E/M code with modifier 25 for these services in addition to the normal newborn code.

Procedures (eg, 54150, newborn circumcision) are not included with the normal newborn codes, and when performed, should be reported in addition to the newborn services.

When newborns are seen in follow-up after the date of discharge in the office or outpatient setting, see 99201-99215, 99381, 99391 as appropriate.

99460   Initial hospital or birthing center care, per day, for evaluation and management of normal newborn infant

99461   Initial care, per day, for evaluation and management of normal newborn infant seen in other than hospital or birthing center

99462   Subsequent hospital care, per day, for evaluation and management of normal newborn

99463   Initial hospital or birthing center care, per day, for evaluation and management of normal newborn infant admitted and discharged on the same date

(For newborn hospital discharge services provided on a date subsequent to the admission date, see 99238, 99239)

Delivery/Birthing Room Attendance and Resuscitation Services

99464   Attendance at delivery (when requested by the delivering physician) and initial stabilization of newborn

(99464 may be reported in conjunction with 99460, 99468, 99477)

(Do not report 99464 in conjunction with 99465)

99465   Delivery/birthing room resuscitation, provision of positive pressure ventilation and/or chest compressions in the presence of acute inadequate ventilation and/or cardiac output

▶(99465 may be reported in conjunction with 99460, 99468, 99477)◀

(Do not report 99465 in conjunction with 99464)

(Procedures that are performed as a necessary part of the resuscitation [eg, intubation, vascular lines] are reported separately in addition to 99465. In order to report these procedures, they must be performed as a necessary component of the resuscitation and not as a convenience before admission to the neonatal intensive care unit)

Inpatient Neonatal Intensive Care Services and Pediatric and Neonatal Critical Care Services

Pediatric Critical Care Patient Transport

The following codes (99466, 99467) are used to report the physical attendance and direct face-to-face care by a physician during the interfacility transport of a critically ill or critically injured pediatric patient 24 months of age or younger. For the purpose of reporting codes 99466 and 99467, face-to-face care begins when the physician assumes primary responsibility of the pediatric patient at the referring hospital/facility, and ends when the receiving hospital/facility accepts responsibility for the pediatric patient's care. Only the time the physician spends in direct face-to-face contact with the patient during the transport should be reported. Pediatric patient transport services involving less than 30 minutes of face-to-face physician care should not be reported using codes 99466, 99467. Procedure(s) or service(s) performed by other members of the transporting team may not be reported by the supervising physician.

For the definition of the critically ill or critically injured pediatric patient and the list of services included in critical care, see the **Neonatal and Pediatric Critical Care Services** section. Any services performed, which are not listed, may be reported separately.

The direction of emergency care to transporting staff by a physician located in a hospital or other facility by two-way communication is not considered direct face-to-face care and should not be reported with 99466, 99467. Physician-directed emergency care through outside voice communication to transporting staff personnel is reported with 99288.

Emergency department services (99281-99285), initial hospital care (99221-99223), critical care (99291,

99292), initial date neonatal intensive (99477) or critical care (99468) are only reported after the patient has been admitted to the emergency department, the inpatient floor, or the critical care unit of the receiving facility. If inpatient critical care services are reported in the referring facility prior to transfer to the receiving hospital, use the critical care codes (99291, 99292).

Code 99466 is used to report the first 30 to 74 minutes of direct face-to-face time with the transport pediatric patient and should be reported only once on a given date. Code 99467 is used to report each additional 30 minutes provided on a given date. Face-to-face services of less than 30 minutes should not be reported with these codes.

99466   **Critical care** services delivered by a physician, face-to-face, during an interfacility transport of critically ill or critically injured pediatric patient, 24 months of age or younger; first 30-74 minutes of hands-on care during transport

+ **99467**   each additional 30 minutes (List separately in addition to code for primary service)

(Use 99467 in conjunction with 99466)

(Critical care of less than 30 minutes total duration should be reported with the appropriate E/M code)

Inpatient Neonatal and Pediatric Critical Care

The same definitions for critical care services apply for the adult, child, and neonate.

Codes 99468, 99469 are used to report services provided by a physician directing the inpatient care of a critically ill neonate or infant 28 days of age or younger. They represent care starting with the date of admission (99468) and subsequent day(s) (99469) that the neonate remains critical. These codes may be reported only by a single physician and only once per day, per patient.

The initial day neonatal critical care code (99468) can be used in addition to 99464 or 99465 as appropriate, when the physician is present for the delivery (99464) or resuscitation (99465) is required. Other procedures performed as a necessary part of the resuscitation (eg, endotracheal intubation [31500]) are also reported separately when performed as part of the pre-admission delivery room care. In order to report these procedures separately, they must be performed as a necessary component of the resuscitation and not simply as a convenience before admission to the neonatal intensive care unit.

Codes 99471-99476 are used to report services provided by a physician directing the inpatient care of a critically ill infant or young child from 29 days of postnatal age through five years of age. They represent care starting with the date of admission (99471, 99475) and subsequent day(s) (99472, 99476) the infant or child remains critical. These codes may be reported only by a single physician and only once per day, per patient in a

Evaluation and Management

given setting. Service for the critically ill or critically injured child older than five years of age would be reported with critical care codes (99291, 99292).

The pediatric and neonatal critical care codes include those procedures listed for the critical care codes (99291, 99292). In addition, the following procedures are also included (and not separately reported) in the pediatric and neonatal critical care service codes (99468-99472, 99475, 99476), the intensive care services codes (99477-99480), and the pediatric critical care patient transport codes (99466, 99467):

Invasive or non-invasive electronic monitoring of vital signs

Vascular access procedures

Peripheral vessel catheterization (36000)

Other arterial catheters (36140, 36620)

Umbilical venous catheters (36510)

Central vessel catheterization (36555)

Vascular access procedures (36400, 36405, 36406)

▶Vascular punctures (36420, 36600)◀

Umbilical arterial catheters (36660)

Airway and ventilation management

Endotracheal intubation (31500)

Ventilatory management (94002-94004)

Bedside pulmonary function testing (94375)

Surfactant administration (94610)

Continuous positive airway pressure (CPAP) (94660)

Monitoring or interpretation of blood gases or oxygen saturation (94760-94762)

Transfusion of blood components (36430, 36440)

Oral or nasogastric tube placement (43752)

Suprapubic bladder aspiration (51100)

Bladder catheterization (51701, 51702)

Lumbar puncture (62270)

Any services performed which are not listed above may be reported separately.

When a neonate or infant is not critically ill but requires intensive observation, frequent interventions, and other intensive care services, the Continuing Intensive Care Services codes (99477-99480) should be used to report these services.

To report critical care services provided in the outpatient setting (eg, emergency department or office) for neonates and pediatric patients of any age, see the Critical Care codes 99291, 99292. If the same physician provides critical care services for a neonatal or pediatric patient in both the outpatient and inpatient settings on the same day, report only the appropriate Neonatal or Pediatric Critical Care codes 99468-99476 for all critical care

services provided on that day. Critical care services provided by a second physician of a different specialty not reporting a per-day neonatal or pediatric critical care code can be reported with 99291, 99292.

When critical care services are provided to neonates or pediatric patients less than five years of age at two separate institutions by a physician from a different group on the same date of service, the physician from the referring institution should report their critical care services with the critical care codes (99291, 99292) and the receiving institution should report the appropriate global admission code (99468, 99471, 99475, 99476) for the same date of service.

Critical care services to a pediatric patient six years of age or older are reported with the critical care codes 99291, 99292.

Critical care services to a neonate or pediatric patient provided in an outpatient environment are reported with the critical care codes 99291, 99292.

Critical care services provided by a second physician of a different specialty not reporting a 24-hour global code can be reported with the critical care codes 99291, 99292.

No physician may report remote real-time videoconferenced critical care (0188T, 0189T) when neonatal or pediatric intensive or critical care services (99468-99476) are reported.

99468   **Initial inpatient neonatal critical care,** per day, for the evaluation and management of a critically ill neonate, 28 days of age or younger

99469   **Subsequent inpatient neonatal critical care,** per day, for the evaluation and management of a critically ill neonate, 28 days of age or younger

99471   **Initial inpatient pediatric critical care,** per day, for the evaluation and management of a critically ill infant or young child, 29 days through 24 months of age

99472   **Subsequent inpatient pediatric critical care,** per day, for the evaluation and management of a critically ill infant or young child, 29 days through 24 months of age

99475   **Initial inpatient pediatric critical care,** per day, for the evaluation and management of a critically ill infant or young child, 2 through 5 years of age

99476   **Subsequent inpatient pediatric critical care,** per day, for the evaluation and management of a critically ill infant or young child, 2 through 5 years of age

Initial and Continuing Intensive Care Services

Code 99477 represents the initial day of inpatient care for the child who is not critically ill but requires intensive observation, frequent interventions, and other intensive care services. Codes 99478-99480 are used to report subsequent day services provided by a physician directing the continuing intensive care of the low birth weight

(LBW 1500-2500 grams) present body weight infant, very low birth weight (VLBW less than 1500 grams) present body weight infant, or normal (2501-5000 grams) present body weight newborn who does not meet the definition of critically ill but continues to require intensive observation, frequent interventions, and other intensive care services. These services are for infants and neonates who are not critically ill but continue to require intensive cardiac and respiratory monitoring, continuous and/or frequent vital sign monitoring, heat maintenance, enteral and/or parenteral nutritional adjustments, laboratory and oxygen monitoring, and constant observation by the health care team under direct physician supervision. Codes 99477-99480 may be reported by only one physician and only once per day, per patient. These codes include the same procedures that are outlined in the **Pediatric Critical Care Services** section and these services should not be separately reported.

For the subsequent care of the sick neonate younger than 28 days of age but more than 5000 grams who does not require intensive or critical care services, use codes 99231-99233.

99477   **Initial hospital care,** per day, for the evaluation and management of the neonate, 28 days of age or younger, who requires intensive observation, frequent interventions, and other intensive care services

(For the initiation of inpatient care of the normal newborn, use 99460)

(For the initiation of care of the critically ill neonate, use 99468)

(For initiation of inpatient hospital care of the ill neonate not requiring intensive observation, frequent interventions, and other intensive care services, see 99221-99223)

99478   **Subsequent intensive care,** per day, for the evaluation and management of the recovering very low birth weight infant (present body weight less than 1500 grams)

99479   **Subsequent intensive care,** per day, for the evaluation and management of the recovering low birth weight infant (present body weight of 1500-2500 grams)

99480   **Subsequent intensive care,** per day, for the evaluation and management of the recovering infant (present body weight of 2501-5000 grams)

Other Evaluation and Management Services

99499   **Unlisted evaluation and management** service

Notes

Anesthesia Guidelines

Services involving administration of anesthesia are reported by the use of the anesthesia five-digit procedure code (00100-01999) plus modifier codes (defined under "Anesthesia Modifiers" later in these Guidelines).

The reporting of anesthesia services is appropriate by or under the responsible supervision of a physician. These services may include but are not limited to general, regional, supplementation of local anesthesia, or other supportive services in order to afford the patient the anesthesia care deemed optimal by the anesthesiologist during any procedure. These services include the usual preoperative and postoperative visits, the anesthesia care during the procedure, the administration of fluids and/or blood and the usual monitoring services (eg, ECG, temperature, blood pressure, oximetry, capnography, and mass spectrometry). Unusual forms of monitoring (eg, intra-arterial, central venous, and Swan-Ganz) are not included.

Items used by all physicians in reporting their services are presented in the **Introduction.** Some of the commonalities are repeated in this section for the convenience of those physicians referring to this section on **Anesthesia.** Other definitions and items unique to anesthesia are also listed.

To report moderate (conscious) sedation provided by a physician also performing the service for which conscious sedation is being provided, see codes 99143-99145.

For the procedures listed in Appendix G, when a second physician other than the health care professional performing the diagnostic or therapeutic services provides moderate (conscious) sedation in the facility setting (eg, hospital, outpatient hospital/ambulatory surgery center, skilled nursing facility), the second physician reports the associated moderate sedation procedure/service 99148-99150; when these services are performed by the second physician in the nonfacility setting (eg, physician office, freestanding imaging center), codes 99148-99150 would not be reported. Moderate sedation does not include minimal sedation (anxiolysis), deep sedation, or monitored anesthesia care (00100-01999).

To report regional or general anesthesia provided by a physician also performing the services for which the anesthesia is being provided, see modifier 47 in Appendix A.

Time Reporting

Time for anesthesia procedures may be reported as is customary in the local area. Anesthesia time begins when the anesthesiologist begins to prepare the patient for the induction of anesthesia in the operating room (or in an equivalent area) and ends when the anesthesiologist is no longer in personal attendance, that is, when the patient may be safely placed under postoperative supervision.

Physician's Services

Physician's services rendered in the office, home, or hospital; consultation; and other medical services are listed in the section titled **Evaluation and Management Services** (99201-99499 series) found on page 1. "Special Services and Reporting" (99000-99091 series) are listed in the **Medicine** section.

Materials Supplied by Physician

Supplies and materials provided by the physician (eg, sterile trays, drugs) over and above those usually included with the office visit or other services rendered may be listed separately. Drugs, tray supplies, and materials provided should be listed and identified with 99070 or the appropriate supply code.

Separate or Multiple Procedures

When multiple surgical procedures are performed during a single anesthetic administration, the anesthesia code representing the most complex procedure is reported. The time reported is the combined total for all procedures.

Special Report

▶A service that is rarely provided, unusual, variable, or new may require a special report. Pertinent information should include an adequate definition or description of the nature, extent, and need for the procedure and the time, effort, and equipment necessary to provide the service.◀

Anesthesia Modifiers

All anesthesia services are reported by use of the anesthesia five-digit procedure code (00100-01999) plus the addition of a physical status modifier. The use of other optional modifiers may be appropriate.

Physical Status Modifiers

Physical Status modifiers are represented by the initial letter 'P' followed by a single digit from 1 to 6 as defined in the following list:

P1: A normal healthy patient

P2: A patient with mild systemic disease

P3: A patient with severe systemic disease

P4: A patient with severe systemic disease that is a constant threat to life

P5: A moribund patient who is not expected to survive without the operation

P6: A declared brain-dead patient whose organs are being removed for donor purposes

These six levels are consistent with the American Society of Anesthesiologists (ASA) ranking of patient physical status. Physical status is included in the CPT codebook to distinguish among various levels of complexity of the anesthesia service provided.

Example: 00100-P1

Qualifying Circumstances

More than one qualifying circumstance may be selected.

Many anesthesia services are provided under particularly difficult circumstances, depending on factors such as extraordinary condition of patient, notable operative conditions, and/or unusual risk factors. This section includes a list of important qualifying circumstances that significantly affect the character of the anesthesia service provided. These procedures would not be reported alone but would be reported as additional procedure numbers qualifying an anesthesia procedure or service.

+ 99100 Anesthesia for patient of extreme age, younger than 1 year and older than 70 (List separately in addition to code for primary anesthesia procedure)

(For procedure performed on infants younger than 1 year of age at time of surgery, see 00326, 00561, 00834, 00836)

+ 99116 Anesthesia complicated by utilization of total body hypothermia (List separately in addition to code for primary anesthesia procedure)

+ 99135 Anesthesia complicated by utilization of controlled hypotension (List separately in addition to code for primary anesthesia procedure)

+ 99140 Anesthesia complicated by emergency conditions (specify) (List separately in addition to code for primary anesthesia procedure)

(An emergency is defined as existing when delay in treatment of the patient would lead to a significant increase in the threat to life or body part.)

Anesthesia

Head

00100   Anesthesia for procedures on salivary glands, including biopsy

00102   Anesthesia for procedures involving plastic repair of cleft lip

00103   Anesthesia for reconstructive procedures of eyelid (eg, blepharoplasty, ptosis surgery)

00104   Anesthesia for electroconvulsive therapy

00120   Anesthesia for procedures on external, middle, and inner ear including biopsy; not otherwise specified

00124   otoscopy

00126   tympanotomy

00140   Anesthesia for procedures on eye; not otherwise specified

00142   lens surgery

00144   corneal transplant

00145   vitreoretinal surgery

00147   iridectomy

00148   ophthalmoscopy

00160   Anesthesia for procedures on nose and accessory sinuses; not otherwise specified

00162   radical surgery

00164   biopsy, soft tissue

00170   Anesthesia for intraoral procedures, including biopsy; not otherwise specified

00172   repair of cleft palate

00174   excision of retropharyngeal tumor

00176   radical surgery

00190   Anesthesia for procedures on facial bones or skull; not otherwise specified

00192   radical surgery (including prognathism)

00210   Anesthesia for intracranial procedures; not otherwise specified

00211   craniotomy or craniectomy for evacuation of hematoma

00212   subdural taps

00214   burr holes, including ventriculography

00215   cranioplasty or elevation of depressed skull fracture, extradural (simple or compound)

00216   vascular procedures

00218   procedures in sitting position

00220   cerebrospinal fluid shunting procedures

00222   electrocoagulation of intracranial nerve

Neck

00300   Anesthesia for all procedures on the integumentary system, muscles and nerves of head, neck, and posterior trunk, not otherwise specified

00320   Anesthesia for all procedures on esophagus, thyroid, larynx, trachea and lymphatic system of neck; not otherwise specified, age 1 year or older

00322   needle biopsy of thyroid

(For procedures on cervical spine and cord, see 00600, 00604, 00670)

00326   Anesthesia for all procedures on the larynx and trachea in children younger than 1 year of age

(Do not report 00326 in conjunction with 99100)

00350   Anesthesia for procedures on major vessels of neck; not otherwise specified

00352   simple ligation

(For arteriography, use 01916)

Thorax (Chest Wall and Shoulder Girdle)

00400   Anesthesia for procedures on the integumentary system on the extremities, anterior trunk and perineum; not otherwise specified

00402   reconstructive procedures on breast (eg, reduction or augmentation mammoplasty, muscle flaps)

00404   radical or modified radical procedures on breast

00406   radical or modified radical procedures on breast with internal mammary node dissection

00410   electrical conversion of arrhythmias

00450   Anesthesia for procedures on clavicle and scapula; not otherwise specified

00452   radical surgery

00454   biopsy of clavicle

00470   Anesthesia for partial rib resection; not otherwise specified

00472   thoracoplasty (any type)

00474   radical procedures (eg, pectus excavatum)

Anesthesia

Intrathoracic

00500   Anesthesia for all procedures on esophagus

00520   Anesthesia for closed chest procedures; (including bronchoscopy) not otherwise specified

00522   needle biopsy of pleura

00524   pneumocentesis

00528   mediastinoscopy and diagnostic thoracoscopy not utilizing 1 lung ventilation

(For tracheobronchial reconstruction, use 00539)

00529   mediastinoscopy and diagnostic thoracoscopy utilizing 1 lung ventilation

00530   Anesthesia for permanent transvenous pacemaker insertion

00532   Anesthesia for access to central venous circulation

00534   Anesthesia for transvenous insertion or replacement of pacing cardioverter-defibrillator

(For transthoracic approach, use 00560)

00537   Anesthesia for cardiac electrophysiologic procedures including radiofrequency ablation

00539   Anesthesia for tracheobronchial reconstruction

00540   Anesthesia for thoracotomy procedures involving lungs, pleura, diaphragm, and mediastinum (including surgical thoracoscopy); not otherwise specified

00541   utilizing 1 lung ventilation

(For thoracic spine and cord anesthesia procedures via an anterior transthoracic approach, see 00625-00626)

00542   decortication

00546   pulmonary resection with thoracoplasty

00548   intrathoracic procedures on the trachea and bronchi

00550   Anesthesia for sternal debridement

00560   Anesthesia for procedures on heart, pericardial sac, and great vessels of chest; without pump oxygenator

00561   with pump oxygenator, younger than 1 year of age

(Do not report 00561 in conjunction with 99100, 99116, and 99135)

00562   with pump oxygenator, age 1 year or older, for all non-coronary bypass procedures (eg, valve procedures) or for re-operation for coronary bypass more than 1 month after original operation

00563   with pump oxygenator with hypothermic circulatory arrest

00566   Anesthesia for direct coronary artery bypass grafting; without pump oxygenator

00567   with pump oxygenator

00580   Anesthesia for heart transplant or heart/lung transplant

Spine and Spinal Cord

00600   Anesthesia for procedures on cervical spine and cord; not otherwise specified

(For percutaneous image-guided spine and spinal cord anesthesia procedures, see 01935, 01936)

00604   procedures with patient in the sitting position

00620   Anesthesia for procedures on thoracic spine and cord; not otherwise specified

00622   thoracolumbar sympathectomy

00625   Anesthesia for procedures on the thoracic spine and cord, via an anterior transthoracic approach; not utilizing 1 lung ventilation

00626   utilizing 1 lung ventilation

(For anesthesia for thoracotomy procedures other than spinal, see 00540-00541)

00630   Anesthesia for procedures in lumbar region; not otherwise specified

00632   lumbar sympathectomy

00634   chemonucleolysis

00635   diagnostic or therapeutic lumbar puncture

00640   Anesthesia for manipulation of the spine or for closed procedures on the cervical, thoracic or lumbar spine

00670   Anesthesia for extensive spine and spinal cord procedures (eg, spinal instrumentation or vascular procedures)

Upper Abdomen

00700   Anesthesia for procedures on upper anterior abdominal wall; not otherwise specified

00702   percutaneous liver biopsy

00730   Anesthesia for procedures on upper posterior abdominal wall

00740   Anesthesia for upper gastrointestinal endoscopic procedures, endoscope introduced proximal to duodenum

00750   Anesthesia for hernia repairs in upper abdomen; not otherwise specified

00752   lumbar and ventral (incisional) hernias and/or wound dehiscence

00754   omphalocele

00756   transabdominal repair of diaphragmatic hernia

00770   Anesthesia for all procedures on major abdominal blood vessels

00790   Anesthesia for intraperitoneal procedures in upper abdomen including laparoscopy; not otherwise specified

00792   partial hepatectomy or management of liver hemorrhage (excluding liver biopsy)

00794	pancreatectomy, partial or total (eg, Whipple procedure)
00796	liver transplant (recipient)
	(For harvesting of liver, use 01990)
00797	gastric restrictive procedure for morbid obesity

Lower Abdomen

00800 Anesthesia for procedures on lower anterior abdominal wall; not otherwise specified

00802   panniculectomy

00810 Anesthesia for lower intestinal endoscopic procedures, endoscope introduced distal to duodenum

00820 Anesthesia for procedures on lower posterior abdominal wall

00830 Anesthesia for hernia repairs in lower abdomen; not otherwise specified

00832   ventral and incisional hernias

(For hernia repairs in the infant 1 year of age or younger, see 00834, 00836)

00834 Anesthesia for hernia repairs in the lower abdomen not otherwise specified, younger than 1 year of age

(Do not report 00834 in conjunction with 99100)

00836 Anesthesia for hernia repairs in the lower abdomen not otherwise specified, infants younger than 37 weeks gestational age at birth and younger than 50 weeks gestational age at time of surgery

(Do not report 00836 in conjunction with 99100)

00840 Anesthesia for intraperitoneal procedures in lower abdomen including laparoscopy; not otherwise specified

00842   amniocentesis

00844   abdominoperineal resection

00846   radical hysterectomy

00848   pelvic exenteration

00851   tubal ligation/transection

00860 Anesthesia for extraperitoneal procedures in lower abdomen, including urinary tract; not otherwise specified

00862   renal procedures, including upper one-third of ureter, or donor nephrectomy

00864   total cystectomy

00865   radical prostatectomy (suprapubic, retropubic)

00866   adrenalectomy

00868   renal transplant (recipient)

(For donor nephrectomy, use 00862)

(For harvesting kidney from brain-dead patient, use 01990)

00870   cystolithotomy

00872 Anesthesia for lithotripsy, extracorporeal shock wave; with water bath

00873   without water bath

00880 Anesthesia for procedures on major lower abdominal vessels; not otherwise specified

00882   inferior vena cava ligation

Perineum

(For perineal procedures on integumentary system, muscles and nerves, see 00300, 00400)

00902 Anesthesia for; anorectal procedure

00904   radical perineal procedure

00906   vulvectomy

00908   perineal prostatectomy

00910 Anesthesia for transurethral procedures (including urethrocystoscopy); not otherwise specified

00912   transurethral resection of bladder tumor(s)

00914   transurethral resection of prostate

00916   post-transurethral resection bleeding

00918   with fragmentation, manipulation and/or removal of ureteral calculus

00920 Anesthesia for procedures on male genitalia (including open urethral procedures); not otherwise specified

00921   vasectomy, unilateral or bilateral

00922   seminal vesicles

00924   undescended testis, unilateral or bilateral

00926   radical orchiectomy, inguinal

00928   radical orchiectomy, abdominal

00930   orchiopexy, unilateral or bilateral

00932   complete amputation of penis

00934   radical amputation of penis with bilateral inguinal lymphadenectomy

00936   radical amputation of penis with bilateral inguinal and iliac lymphadenectomy

00938   insertion of penile prosthesis (perineal approach)

00940 Anesthesia for vaginal procedures (including biopsy of labia, vagina, cervix or endometrium); not otherwise specified

00942   colpotomy, vaginectomy, colporrhaphy, and open urethral procedures

00944   vaginal hysterectomy

00948   cervical cerclage

Anesthesia

Anesthesia

| 00950 | culdoscopy |
| 00952 | hysteroscopy and/or hysterosalpingography |

Pelvis (Except Hip)

01112	Anesthesia for bone marrow aspiration and/or biopsy, anterior or posterior iliac crest
01120	Anesthesia for procedures on bony pelvis
01130	Anesthesia for body cast application or revision
01140	Anesthesia for interpelviabdominal (hindquarter) amputation
01150	Anesthesia for radical procedures for tumor of pelvis, except hindquarter amputation
01160	Anesthesia for closed procedures involving symphysis pubis or sacroiliac joint
01170	Anesthesia for open procedures involving symphysis pubis or sacroiliac joint
01173	Anesthesia for open repair of fracture disruption of pelvis or column fracture involving acetabulum
01180	Anesthesia for obturator neurectomy; extrapelvic
01190	intrapelvic

Upper Leg (Except Knee)

01200	Anesthesia for all closed procedures involving hip joint
01202	Anesthesia for arthroscopic procedures of hip joint
01210	Anesthesia for open procedures involving hip joint; not otherwise specified
01212	hip disarticulation
01214	total hip arthroplasty
01215	revision of total hip arthroplasty
01220	Anesthesia for all closed procedures involving upper two-thirds of femur
01230	Anesthesia for open procedures involving upper two-thirds of femur; not otherwise specified
01232	amputation
01234	radical resection
01250	Anesthesia for all procedures on nerves, muscles, tendons, fascia, and bursae of upper leg
01260	Anesthesia for all procedures involving veins of upper leg, including exploration
01270	Anesthesia for procedures involving arteries of upper leg, including bypass graft; not otherwise specified
01272	femoral artery ligation
01274	femoral artery embolectomy

Knee and Popliteal Area

01320	Anesthesia for all procedures on nerves, muscles, tendons, fascia, and bursae of knee and/or popliteal area
01340	Anesthesia for all closed procedures on lower one-third of femur
01360	Anesthesia for all open procedures on lower one-third of femur
01380	Anesthesia for all closed procedures on knee joint
01382	Anesthesia for diagnostic arthroscopic procedures of knee joint
01390	Anesthesia for all closed procedures on upper ends of tibia, fibula, and/or patella
01392	Anesthesia for all open procedures on upper ends of tibia, fibula, and/or patella
01400	Anesthesia for open or surgical arthroscopic procedures on knee joint; not otherwise specified
01402	total knee arthroplasty
01404	disarticulation at knee
01420	Anesthesia for all cast applications, removal, or repair involving knee joint
01430	Anesthesia for procedures on veins of knee and popliteal area; not otherwise specified
01432	arteriovenous fistula
01440	Anesthesia for procedures on arteries of knee and popliteal area; not otherwise specified
01442	popliteal thromboendarterectomy, with or without patch graft
01444	popliteal excision and graft or repair for occlusion or aneurysm

Lower Leg (Below Knee, Includes Ankle and Foot)

01462	Anesthesia for all closed procedures on lower leg, ankle, and foot
01464	Anesthesia for arthroscopic procedures of ankle and/or foot
01470	Anesthesia for procedures on nerves, muscles, tendons, and fascia of lower leg, ankle, and foot; not otherwise specified
01472	repair of ruptured Achilles tendon, with or without graft
01474	gastrocnemius recession (eg, Strayer procedure)
01480	Anesthesia for open procedures on bones of lower leg, ankle, and foot; not otherwise specified
01482	radical resection (including below knee amputation)
01484	osteotomy or osteoplasty of tibia and/or fibula

01486   total ankle replacement

01490   Anesthesia for lower leg cast application, removal, or repair

01500   Anesthesia for procedures on arteries of lower leg, including bypass graft; not otherwise specified

01502   embolectomy, direct or with catheter

01520   Anesthesia for procedures on veins of lower leg; not otherwise specified

01522   venous thrombectomy, direct or with catheter

Shoulder and Axilla

Includes humeral head and neck, sternoclavicular joint, acromioclavicular joint, and shoulder joint.

01610   Anesthesia for all procedures on nerves, muscles, tendons, fascia, and bursae of shoulder and axilla

01620   Anesthesia for all closed procedures on humeral head and neck, sternoclavicular joint, acromioclavicular joint, and shoulder joint

01622   Anesthesia for diagnostic arthroscopic procedures of shoulder joint

01630   Anesthesia for open or surgical arthroscopic procedures on humeral head and neck, sternoclavicular joint, acromioclavicular joint, and shoulder joint; not otherwise specified

▶(01632 has been deleted. To report, see 01630, 01638)◀

01634   shoulder disarticulation

01636   interthoracoscapular (forequarter) amputation

01638   total shoulder replacement

01650   Anesthesia for procedures on arteries of shoulder and axilla; not otherwise specified

01652   axillary-brachial aneurysm

01654   bypass graft

01656   axillary-femoral bypass graft

01670   Anesthesia for all procedures on veins of shoulder and axilla

01680   Anesthesia for shoulder cast application, removal or repair; not otherwise specified

01682   shoulder spica

Upper Arm and Elbow

01710   Anesthesia for procedures on nerves, muscles, tendons, fascia, and bursae of upper arm and elbow; not otherwise specified

01712   tenotomy, elbow to shoulder, open

01714   tenoplasty, elbow to shoulder

01716   tenodesis, rupture of long tendon of biceps

01730   Anesthesia for all closed procedures on humerus and elbow

01732   Anesthesia for diagnostic arthroscopic procedures of elbow joint

01740   Anesthesia for open or surgical arthroscopic procedures of the elbow; not otherwise specified

01742   osteotomy of humerus

01744   repair of nonunion or malunion of humerus

01756   radical procedures

01758   excision of cyst or tumor of humerus

01760   total elbow replacement

01770   Anesthesia for procedures on arteries of upper arm and elbow; not otherwise specified

01772   embolectomy

01780   Anesthesia for procedures on veins of upper arm and elbow; not otherwise specified

01782   phleborrhaphy

Forearm, Wrist, and Hand

01810   Anesthesia for all procedures on nerves, muscles, tendons, fascia, and bursae of forearm, wrist, and hand

01820   Anesthesia for all closed procedures on radius, ulna, wrist, or hand bones

01829   Anesthesia for diagnostic arthroscopic procedures on the wrist

01830   Anesthesia for open or surgical arthroscopic/endoscopic procedures on distal radius, distal ulna, wrist, or hand joints; not otherwise specified

01832   total wrist replacement

01840   Anesthesia for procedures on arteries of forearm, wrist, and hand; not otherwise specified

01842   embolectomy

01844   Anesthesia for vascular shunt, or shunt revision, any type (eg, dialysis)

01850   Anesthesia for procedures on veins of forearm, wrist, and hand; not otherwise specified

01852   phleborrhaphy

01860   Anesthesia for forearm, wrist, or hand cast application, removal, or repair

Anesthesia

Radiological Procedures

(01905 has been deleted. To report, see 01935, 01936)

01916   Anesthesia for diagnostic arteriography/venography

(Do not report 01916 in conjunction with therapeutic codes 01924-01926, 01930-01933)

01920   Anesthesia for cardiac catheterization including coronary angiography and ventriculography (not to include Swan-Ganz catheter)

01922   Anesthesia for non-invasive imaging or radiation therapy

01924   Anesthesia for therapeutic interventional radiological procedures involving the arterial system; not otherwise specified

01925   carotid or coronary

01926   intracranial, intracardiac, or aortic

01930   Anesthesia for therapeutic interventional radiological procedures involving the venous/lymphatic system (not to include access to the central circulation); not otherwise specified

01931   intrahepatic or portal circulation (eg, transvenous intrahepatic portosystemic shunt[s] [TIPS])

01932   intrathoracic or jugular

01933   intracranial

01935   Anesthesia for percutaneous image guided procedures on the spine and spinal cord; diagnostic

01936   therapeutic

Burn Excisions or Debridement

01951   Anesthesia for second- and third-degree burn excision or debridement with or without skin grafting, any site, for total body surface area (TBSA) treated during anesthesia and surgery; less than 4% total body surface area

01952   between 4% and 9% of total body surface area

+ 01953   each additional 9% total body surface area or part thereof (List separately in addition to code for primary procedure)

(Use 01953 in conjunction with 01952)

Obstetric

01958   Anesthesia for external cephalic version procedure

01960   Anesthesia for vaginal delivery only

01961   Anesthesia for cesarean delivery only

01962   Anesthesia for urgent hysterectomy following delivery

01963   Anesthesia for cesarean hysterectomy without any labor analgesia/anesthesia care

01965   Anesthesia for incomplete or missed abortion procedures

01966   Anesthesia for induced abortion procedures

01967   Neuraxial labor analgesia/anesthesia for planned vaginal delivery (this includes any repeat subarachnoid needle placement and drug injection and/or any necessary replacement of an epidural catheter during labor)

+ 01968   Anesthesia for cesarean delivery following neuraxial labor analgesia/anesthesia (List separately in addition to code for primary procedure performed)

(Use 01968 in conjunction with 01967)

+ 01969   Anesthesia for cesarean hysterectomy following neuraxial labor analgesia/anesthesia (List separately in addition to code for primary procedure performed)

(Use 01969 in conjunction with 01967)

Other Procedures

01990   Physiological support for harvesting of organ(s) from brain-dead patient

01991   Anesthesia for diagnostic or therapeutic nerve blocks and injections (when block or injection is performed by a different provider); other than the prone position

01992   prone position

(Do not report 01991 or 01992 in conjunction with 99143-99150)

►(When regional intravenous administration of local anesthetic agent or other medication in the upper or lower extremity is used as the anesthetic for a surgical procedure, report the appropriate anesthesia code. To report a Bier block for pain management, use 64999)◄

(For intra-arterial or intravenous therapy for pain management, see 96373, 96374)

01996   Daily hospital management of epidural or subarachnoid continuous drug administration

(Report code 01996 for daily hospital management of continuous epidural or subarachnoid drug administration performed after insertion of an epidural or subarachnoid catheter)

01999   Unlisted anesthesia procedure(s)

Surgery Guidelines

Items used by all physicians in reporting their services are presented in the **Introduction.** Some of the commonalities are repeated here for the convenience of those physicians referring to this section on **Surgery.** Other definitions and items unique to Surgery are also listed.

Physicians' Services

Physicians' services rendered in the office, home, or hospital, consultations, and other medical services are listed in the section entitled **Evaluation and Management Services** (99201-99499) found in the front of the book, beginning on page 9. "Special Services and Reports" (99000 series) is presented in the **Medicine** section.

CPT Surgical Package Definition

The services provided by the physician to any patient by their very nature are variable. The CPT codes that represent a readily identifiable surgical procedure thereby include, on a procedure-by-procedure basis, a variety of services. In defining the specific services "included" in a given CPT surgical code, the following services are always included in addition to the operation per se:

- Local infiltration, metacarpal/metatarsal/digital block or topical anesthesia

- Subsequent to the decision for surgery, one related Evaluation and Management (E/M) encounter on the date immediately prior to or on the date of procedure (including history and physical)

- Immediate postoperative care, including dictating operative notes, talking with the family and other physicians

- Writing orders

- Evaluating the patient in the postanesthesia recovery area

- Typical postoperative follow-up care

Follow-Up Care for Diagnostic Procedures

Follow-up care for diagnostic procedures (eg, endoscopy, arthroscopy, injection procedures for radiography) includes only that care related to recovery from the diagnostic procedure itself. Care of the condition for which the diagnostic procedure was performed or of other concomitant conditions is not included and may be listed separately.

Follow-Up Care for Therapeutic Surgical Procedures

Follow-up care for therapeutic surgical procedures includes only that care which is usually a part of the surgical service. Complications, exacerbations, recurrence, or the presence of other diseases or injuries requiring additional services should be separately reported.

Materials Supplied by Physician

Supplies and materials provided by the physician (eg, sterile trays/drugs), over and above those usually included with the procedure(s) rendered are reported separately. List drugs, trays, supplies, and materials provided. Identify as 99070 or specific supply code.

Reporting More Than One Procedure/Service

When a physician performs more than one procedure/service on the same date, same session or during a post-operative period (subject to the "surgical package" concept), several CPT modifiers may apply (see Appendix A for definition).

Separate Procedure

Some of the procedures or services listed in the CPT codebook that are commonly carried out as an integral component of a total service or procedure have been identified by the inclusion of the term "separate procedure." The codes designated as "separate procedure" should not be reported in addition to the code for the total procedure or service of which it is considered an integral component.

However, when a procedure or service that is designated as a "separate procedure" is carried out independently or considered to be unrelated or distinct from other procedures/services provided at that time, it may be reported by itself, or in addition to other procedures/services by appending modifier 59 to the specific "separate procedure" code to indicate that the procedure is not considered to be a component of another procedure, but is a distinct, independent procedure. This may represent a different session, different procedure or surgery, different site or organ system, separate incision/excision, separate lesion, or separate injury (or area of injury in extensive injuries).

Unlisted Service or Procedure

A service or procedure may be provided that is not listed in this edition of the CPT codebook. When reporting such a service, the appropriate "Unlisted Procedure" code may be used to indicate the service, identifying it by "Special Report" as discussed in the section below. The "Unlisted Procedures" and accompanying codes for **Surgery** are as follows:

15999 Unlisted procedure, excision pressure ulcer

17999 Unlisted procedure, skin, mucous membrane and subcutaneous tissue

19499 Unlisted procedure, breast

20999 Unlisted procedure, musculoskeletal system, general

21089 Unlisted maxillofacial prosthetic procedure

21299 Unlisted craniofacial and maxillofacial procedure

21499 Unlisted musculoskeletal procedure, head

21899 Unlisted procedure, neck or thorax

22899 Unlisted procedure, spine

22999 Unlisted procedure, abdomen, musculoskeletal system

23929 Unlisted procedure, shoulder

24999 Unlisted procedure, humerus or elbow

25999 Unlisted procedure, forearm or wrist

26989 Unlisted procedure, hands or fingers

27299 Unlisted procedure, pelvis or hip joint

27599 Unlisted procedure, femur or knee

27899 Unlisted procedure, leg or ankle

28899 Unlisted procedure, foot or toes

29799 Unlisted procedure, casting or strapping

29999 Unlisted procedure, arthroscopy

30999 Unlisted procedure, nose

31299 Unlisted procedure, accessory sinuses

31599 Unlisted procedure, larynx

31899 Unlisted procedure, trachea, bronchi

32999 Unlisted procedure, lungs and pleura

33999 Unlisted procedure, cardiac surgery

36299 Unlisted procedure, vascular injection

37501 Unlisted vascular endoscopy procedure

37799 Unlisted procedure, vascular surgery

38129 Unlisted laparoscopy procedure, spleen

38589 Unlisted laparoscopy procedure, lymphatic system

38999 Unlisted procedure, hemic or lymphatic system

39499 Unlisted procedure, mediastinum

39599 Unlisted procedure, diaphragm

40799 Unlisted procedure, lips

40899 Unlisted procedure, vestibule of mouth

41599 Unlisted procedure, tongue, floor of mouth

41899 Unlisted procedure, dentoalveolar structures

42299 Unlisted procedure, palate, uvula

42699 Unlisted procedure, salivary glands or ducts

42999 Unlisted procedure, pharynx, adenoids, or tonsils

43289 Unlisted laparoscopy procedure, esophagus

43499 Unlisted procedure, esophagus

43659 Unlisted laparoscopy procedure, stomach

43999 Unlisted procedure, stomach

44238 Unlisted laparoscopy procedure, intestine (except rectum)

44799 Unlisted procedure, intestine

44899 Unlisted procedure, Meckel's diverticulum and the mesentery

44979 Unlisted laparoscopy procedure, appendix

45499 Unlisted laparoscopy procedure, rectum

45999 Unlisted procedure, rectum

46999 Unlisted procedure, anus

47379 Unlisted laparoscopic procedure, liver

47399 Unlisted procedure, liver

47579 Unlisted laparoscopy procedure, biliary tract

47999 Unlisted procedure, biliary tract

48999 Unlisted procedure, pancreas

49329 Unlisted laparoscopy procedure, abdomen, peritoneum and omentum

49659 Unlisted laparoscopy procedure, hernioplasty, herniorrhaphy, herniotomy

49999	Unlisted procedure, abdomen, peritoneum and omentum
50549	Unlisted laparoscopy procedure, renal
50949	Unlisted laparoscopy procedure, ureter
51999	Unlisted laparoscopy procedure, bladder
53899	Unlisted procedure, urinary system
54699	Unlisted laparoscopy procedure, testis
55559	Unlisted laparoscopy procedure, spermatic cord
55899	Unlisted procedure, male genital system
58578	Unlisted laparoscopy procedure, uterus
58579	Unlisted hysteroscopy procedure, uterus
58679	Unlisted laparoscopy procedure, oviduct, ovary
58999	Unlisted procedure, female genital system (nonobstetrical)
▲ **59897**	Unlisted fetal invasive procedure, including ultrasound guidance, when performed
59898	Unlisted laparoscopy procedure, maternity care and delivery
59899	Unlisted procedure, maternity care and delivery
60659	Unlisted laparoscopy procedure, endocrine system
60699	Unlisted procedure, endocrine system
64999	Unlisted procedure, nervous system
66999	Unlisted procedure, anterior segment of eye
67299	Unlisted procedure, posterior segment
67399	Unlisted procedure, ocular muscle
67599	Unlisted procedure, orbit
67999	Unlisted procedure, eyelids
68399	Unlisted procedure, conjunctiva
68899	Unlisted procedure, lacrimal system
69399	Unlisted procedure, external ear
69799	Unlisted procedure, middle ear
69949	Unlisted procedure, inner ear
69979	Unlisted procedure, temporal bone, middle fossa approach

Special Report

▶A service that is rarely provided, unusual, variable, or new may require a special report. Pertinent information should include an adequate definition or description of the nature, extent, and need for the procedure, and the time, effort, and equipment necessary to provide the service.◀

Surgical Destruction

Surgical destruction is a part of a surgical procedure and different methods of destruction are not ordinarily listed separately unless the technique substantially alters the standard management of a problem or condition. Exceptions under special circumstances are provided for by separate code numbers.

Surgery Guidelines

Notes

⊙=Moderate sedation   ✚=Add-on code   ✗=FDA approval pending   #=Resequenced code

Surgery

General

10021   Fine needle aspiration; without imaging guidance

10022   with imaging guidance

▶(For placement of percutaneous localization clip during breast biopsy, use 19295)◀

(For radiological supervision and interpretation, see 76942, 77002, 77012, 77021)

(For percutaneous needle biopsy other than fine needle aspiration, see 20206 for muscle, 32400 for pleura, 32405 for lung or mediastinum, 42400 for salivary gland, 47000, 47001 for liver, 48102 for pancreas, 49180 for abdominal or retroperitoneal mass, 60100 for thyroid, 62267 for nucleus pulposus, intervertebral disc, or paravertebral tissue, 62269 for spinal cord)

(For evaluation of fine needle aspirate, see 88172, 88173)

Integumentary System

Skin, Subcutaneous, and Accessory Structures

Incision and Drainage

(For excision, see 11400, et seq)

10040   Acne surgery (eg, marsupialization, opening or removal of multiple milia, comedones, cysts, pustules)

10060   Incision and drainage of abscess (eg, carbuncle, suppurative hidradenitis, cutaneous or subcutaneous abscess, cyst, furuncle, or paronychia); simple or single

10061   complicated or multiple

10080   Incision and drainage of pilonidal cyst; simple

10081   complicated

(For excision of pilonidal cyst, see 11770-11772)

10120   Incision and removal of foreign body, subcutaneous tissues; simple

10121   complicated

(To report wound exploration due to penetrating trauma without laparotomy or thoracotomy, see 20100-20103, as appropriate)

(To report debridement associated with open fracture(s) and/or dislocation(s), use 11010-11012, as appropriate)

10140   Incision and drainage of hematoma, seroma or fluid collection

(If imaging guidance is performed, see 76942, 77012, 77021)

10160   Puncture aspiration of abscess, hematoma, bulla, or cyst

(If imaging guidance is performed, see 76942, 77012, 77021)

10180   Incision and drainage, complex, postoperative wound infection

(For secondary closure of surgical wound, see 12020, 12021, 13160)

Excision—Debridement

(For dermabrasions, see 15780-15783)

(For nail debridement, see 11720-11721)

(For burn(s), see 16000-16035)

11000   Debridement of extensive eczematous or infected skin; up to 10% of body surface

(For abdominal wall or genitalia debridement for necrotizing soft tissue infection, see 11004-11006)

+ 11001   each additional 10% of the body surface, or part thereof (List separately in addition to code for primary procedure)

(Use 11001 in conjunction with 11000)

11004   Debridement of skin, subcutaneous tissue, muscle and fascia for necrotizing soft tissue infection; external genitalia and perineum

11005   abdominal wall, with or without fascial closure

11006   external genitalia, perineum and abdominal wall, with or without fascial closure

+ 11008   Removal of prosthetic material or mesh, abdominal wall for infection (eg, for chronic or recurrent mesh infection or necrotizing soft tissue infection) (List separately in addition to code for primary procedure)

(Use 11008 in conjunction with 10180, 11004-11006)

(Do not report 11008 in conjunction with 11000-11001, 11010-11044)

(Report skin grafts or flaps separately when performed for closure at the same session as 11004-11008)

(When insertion of mesh is used for closure, use 49568)

(If orchiectomy is performed, use 54520)

(If testicular transplantation is performed, use 54680)

Surgery: Integumentary System

Surgery: Integumentary System

11010 Debridement including removal of foreign material associated with open fracture(s) and/or dislocation(s); skin and subcutaneous tissues

11011 skin, subcutaneous tissue, muscle fascia, and muscle

11012 skin, subcutaneous tissue, muscle fascia, muscle, and bone

11040 Debridement; skin, partial thickness

11041 skin, full thickness

11042 skin, and subcutaneous tissue

11043 skin, subcutaneous tissue, and muscle

11044 skin, subcutaneous tissue, muscle, and bone

(Do not report 11040-11044 in conjunction with 97597-97602)

Paring or Cutting

(To report destruction, see 17000-17004)

11055 Paring or cutting of benign hyperkeratotic lesion (eg, corn or callus); single lesion

11056 2 to 4 lesions

11057 more than 4 lesions

Biopsy

During certain surgical procedures in the integumentary system, such as excision, destruction, or shave removals, the removed tissue is often submitted for pathologic examination. The obtaining of tissue for pathology during the course of these procedures is a routine component of such procedures. This obtaining of tissue is not considered a separate biopsy procedure and is not separately reported. The use of a biopsy procedure code (eg, 11100, 11101) indicates that the procedure to obtain tissue for pathologic examination was performed independently, or was unrelated or distinct from other procedures/services provided at that time. Such biopsies are not considered components of other procedures when performed on different lesions or different sites on the same date, and are to be reported separately.

(For biopsy of conjunctiva, use 68100; eyelid, use 67810)

11100 Biopsy of skin, subcutaneous tissue and/or mucous membrane (including simple closure), unless otherwise listed; single lesion

+ 11101 each separate/additional lesion (List separately in addition to code for primary procedure)

(Use 11101 in conjunction with 11100)

Removal of Skin Tags

Removal by scissoring or any sharp method, ligature strangulation, electrosurgical destruction or combination of treatment modalities, including chemical destruction or electrocauterization of wound, with or without local anesthesia.

11200 Removal of skin tags, multiple fibrocutaneous tags, any area; up to and including 15 lesions

+ 11201 each additional 10 lesions, or part thereof (List separately in addition to code for primary procedure)

(Use 11201 in conjunction with 11200)

Shaving of Epidermal or Dermal Lesions

Shaving is the sharp removal by transverse incision or horizontal slicing to remove epidermal and dermal lesions without a full-thickness dermal excision. This includes local anesthesia, chemical or electrocauterization of the wound. The wound does not require suture closure.

11300 Shaving of epidermal or dermal lesion, single lesion, trunk, arms or legs; lesion diameter 0.5 cm or less

11301 lesion diameter 0.6 to 1.0 cm

11302 lesion diameter 1.1 to 2.0 cm

11303 lesion diameter over 2.0 cm

11305 Shaving of epidermal or dermal lesion, single lesion, scalp, neck, hands, feet, genitalia; lesion diameter 0.5 cm or less

11306 lesion diameter 0.6 to 1.0 cm

11307 lesion diameter 1.1 to 2.0 cm

11308 lesion diameter over 2.0 cm

11310 Shaving of epidermal or dermal lesion, single lesion, face, ears, eyelids, nose, lips, mucous membrane; lesion diameter 0.5 cm or less

11311 lesion diameter 0.6 to 1.0 cm

11312 lesion diameter 1.1 to 2.0 cm

11313 lesion diameter over 2.0 cm

Excision—Benign Lesions

Excision (including simple closure) of benign lesions of skin (eg, neoplasm, cicatricial, fibrous, inflammatory, congenital, cystic lesions), includes local anesthesia. See appropriate size and area below. For shave removal, see 11300 et seq, and for electrosurgical and other methods see 17000 et seq.

Excision is defined as full-thickness (through the dermis) removal of a lesion, including margins, and includes simple (non-layered) closure when performed. Report separately each benign lesion excised. Code selection is determined by measuring the greatest clinical diameter of the apparent lesion plus that margin required for complete excision (lesion diameter plus the most narrow margins required equals the excised diameter). The margins refer to the most narrow margin required to adequately excise the lesion, based on the physician's judgment. The measurement of lesion plus margin is made prior to excision. The excised diameter is the same whether the surgical defect is repaired in a linear fashion, or reconstructed (eg, with a skin graft).

►The closure of defects created by incision, excision, or trauma may require intermediate or complex closure. Repair by intermediate or complex closure should be reported separately. For excision of benign lesions requiring more than simple closure, ie, requiring intermediate or complex closure, report 11400-11446 in addition to appropriate intermediate (12031-12057) or complex closure (13100-13153) codes. For reconstructive closure, see 15002-15261, 15570-15770. For excision performed in conjunction with adjacent tissue transfer, report only the adjacent tissue transfer code (14000-14302). Excision of lesion (11400–11446) is not separately reportable with adjacent tissue transfer. See page 58 for the definition of *intermediate* or *complex* closure.◄

11400   Excision, benign lesion including margins, except skin tag (unless listed elsewhere), trunk, arms or legs; excised diameter 0.5 cm or less

11401   excised diameter 0.6 to 1.0 cm

11402   excised diameter 1.1 to 2.0 cm

11403   excised diameter 2.1 to 3.0 cm

11404   excised diameter 3.1 to 4.0 cm

11406   excised diameter over 4.0 cm

(For unusual or complicated excision, add modifier 22)

11420   Excision, benign lesion including margins, except skin tag (unless listed elsewhere), scalp, neck, hands, feet, genitalia; excised diameter 0.5 cm or less

11421   excised diameter 0.6 to 1.0 cm

11422   excised diameter 1.1 to 2.0 cm

11423   excised diameter 2.1 to 3.0 cm

11424   excised diameter 3.1 to 4.0 cm

11426   excised diameter over 4.0 cm

(For unusual or complicated excision, add modifier 22)

11440   Excision, other benign lesion including margins, except skin tag (unless listed elsewhere), face, ears, eyelids, nose, lips, mucous membrane; excised diameter 0.5 cm or less

11441   excised diameter 0.6 to 1.0 cm

11442   excised diameter 1.1 to 2.0 cm

11443   excised diameter 2.1 to 3.0 cm

11444   excised diameter 3.1 to 4.0 cm

11446   excised diameter over 4.0 cm

(For unusual or complicated excision, add modifier 22)

(For eyelids involving more than skin, see also 67800 et seq)

11450   Excision of skin and subcutaneous tissue for hidradenitis, axillary; with simple or intermediate repair

11451   with complex repair

11462   Excision of skin and subcutaneous tissue for hidradenitis, inguinal; with simple or intermediate repair

11463   with complex repair

11470   Excision of skin and subcutaneous tissue for hidradenitis, perianal, perineal, or umbilical; with simple or intermediate repair

11471   with complex repair

(When skin graft or flap is used for closure, use appropriate procedure code in addition)

(For bilateral procedure, add modifier 50)

Excision—Malignant Lesions

Excision (including simple closure) of malignant lesions of skin (eg, basal cell carcinoma, squamous cell carcinoma, melanoma) includes local anesthesia. (See appropriate size and body area below.) For destruction of malignant lesions of skin, see destruction codes 17260-17286.

Excision is defined as full-thickness (through the dermis) removal of a lesion including margins, and includes simple (non-layered) closure when performed. Report separately each malignant lesion excised. Code selection is determined by measuring the greatest clinical diameter of the apparent lesion plus that margin required for complete excision (lesion diameter plus the most narrow margins required equals the excised diameter). The margins refer to the most narrow margin required to adequately excise the lesion, based on the physician's judgment. The measurement of lesion plus margin is made prior to excision. The excised diameter is the same whether the surgical defect is repaired in a linear fashion, or reconstructed (eg, with a skin graft).

►The closure of defects created by incision, excision, or trauma may require intermediate or complex closure. Repair by intermediate or complex closure should be reported separately. For excision of malignant lesions requiring more than simple closure, ie, requiring intermediate or complex closure, report 11600-11646 in addition to appropriate intermediate (12031-12057) or complex closure (13100-13153) codes. For reconstructive closure, see 15002-15261, 15570-15770. For excision performed in conjunction with adjacent tissue transfer, report only the adjacent tissue transfer code (14000-14302). Excision of lesion (11600–11646) is not separately reportable with adjacent tissue transfer. See page 58 for the definition of *intermediate* or *complex* closure.◄

When frozen section pathology shows the margins of excision were not adequate, an additional excision may be necessary for complete tumor removal. Use only one code to report the additional excision and re-excision(s) based on the final widest excised diameter required for complete tumor removal at the same operative session. To report a re-excision procedure performed to widen margins at a subsequent operative session, see codes 11600-11646, as appropriate. Append modifier 58 if the re-excision procedure is performed during the postoperative period of the primary excision procedure.

11600	Excision, malignant lesion including margins, trunk, arms, or legs; excised diameter 0.5 cm or less
11601	excised diameter 0.6 to 1.0 cm
11602	excised diameter 1.1 to 2.0 cm
11603	excised diameter 2.1 to 3.0 cm
11604	excised diameter 3.1 to 4.0 cm
11606	excised diameter over 4.0 cm
11620	Excision, malignant lesion including margins, scalp, neck, hands, feet, genitalia; excised diameter 0.5 cm or less
11621	excised diameter 0.6 to 1.0 cm
11622	excised diameter 1.1 to 2.0 cm
11623	excised diameter 2.1 to 3.0 cm
11624	excised diameter 3.1 to 4.0 cm
11626	excised diameter over 4.0 cm
11640	Excision, malignant lesion including margins, face, ears, eyelids, nose, lips; excised diameter 0.5 cm or less
11641	excised diameter 0.6 to 1.0 cm
11642	excised diameter 1.1 to 2.0 cm
11643	excised diameter 2.1 to 3.0 cm
11644	excised diameter 3.1 to 4.0 cm
11646	excised diameter over 4.0 cm

(For eyelids involving more than skin, see also 67800 et seq)

Nails

(For drainage of paronychia or onychia, see 10060, 10061)

11719	Trimming of nondystrophic nails, any number
11720	Debridement of nail(s) by any method(s); 1 to 5
11721	6 or more
11730	Avulsion of nail plate, partial or complete, simple; single
✚ 11732	each additional nail plate (List separately in addition to code for primary procedure)

(Use 11732 in conjunction with 11730)

11740	Evacuation of subungual hematoma
11750	Excision of nail and nail matrix, partial or complete (eg, ingrown or deformed nail), for permanent removal;
11752	with amputation of tuft of distal phalanx

(For skin graft, if used, use 15050)

11755	Biopsy of nail unit (eg, plate, bed, matrix, hyponychium, proximal and lateral nail folds) (separate procedure)
11760	Repair of nail bed
11762	Reconstruction of nail bed with graft
11765	Wedge excision of skin of nail fold (eg, for ingrown toenail)

Pilonidal Cyst

11770	Excision of pilonidal cyst or sinus; simple
11771	extensive
11772	complicated

(For incision of pilonidal cyst, see 10080, 10081)

Introduction

11900	Injection, intralesional; up to and including 7 lesions
11901	more than 7 lesions

(11900, 11901 are not to be used for preoperative local anesthetic injection)

(For veins, see 36470, 36471)

(For intralesional chemotherapy administration, see 96405, 96406)

11920	Tattooing, intradermal introduction of insoluble opaque pigments to correct color defects of skin, including micropigmentation; 6.0 sq cm or less
11921	6.1 to 20.0 sq cm
✚ 11922	each additional 20.0 sq cm, or part thereof (List separately in addition to code for primary procedure)

(Use 11922 in conjunction with 11921)

11950	Subcutaneous injection of filling material (eg, collagen); 1 cc or less
11951	1.1 to 5.0 cc
11952	5.1 to 10.0 cc
11954	over 10.0 cc
11960	Insertion of tissue expander(s) for other than breast, including subsequent expansion

(For breast reconstruction with tissue expander(s), use 19357)

Surgery: Integumentary System

11970   Replacement of tissue expander with permanent prosthesis

11971   Removal of tissue expander(s) without insertion of prosthesis

11975   Insertion, implantable contraceptive capsules

11976   Removal, implantable contraceptive capsules

11977   Removal with reinsertion, implantable contraceptive capsules

11980   Subcutaneous hormone pellet implantation (implantation of estradiol and/or testosterone pellets beneath the skin)

11981   Insertion, non-biodegradable drug delivery implant

11982   Removal, non-biodegradable drug delivery implant

11983   Removal with reinsertion, non-biodegradable drug delivery implant

Repair (Closure)

Use the codes in this section to designate wound closure utilizing sutures, staples, or tissue adhesives (eg, 2-cyanoacrylate), either singly or in combination with each other, or in combination with adhesive strips. Wound closure utilizing adhesive strips as the sole repair material should be coded using the appropriate E/M code.

Definitions

The repair of wounds may be classified as Simple, Intermediate, or Complex.

Simple repair is used when the wound is superficial; eg, involving primarily epidermis or dermis, or subcutaneous tissues without significant involvement of deeper structures, and requires simple one layer closure. This includes local anesthesia and chemical or electrocauterization of wounds not closed.

Intermediate repair includes the repair of wounds that, in addition to the above, require layered closure of one or more of the deeper layers of subcutaneous tissue and superficial (non-muscle) fascia, in addition to the skin (epidermal and dermal) closure. Single-layer closure of heavily contaminated wounds that have required extensive cleaning or removal of particulate matter also constitutes intermediate repair.

Complex repair includes the repair of wounds requiring more than layered closure, viz., scar revision, debridement (eg, traumatic lacerations or avulsions), extensive undermining, stents or retention sutures. Necessary preparation includes creation of a defect for repairs (eg, excision of a scar requiring a complex repair) or the debridement of complicated lacerations or avulsions. Complex repair does not include excision of benign (11400-11446) or malignant (11600-11646) lesions.

Instructions for listing services at time of wound repair:

1. The repaired wound(s) should be measured and recorded in centimeters, whether curved, angular, or stellate.

2. When multiple wounds are repaired, add together the lengths of those in the same classification (see above) and from all anatomic sites that are grouped together into the same code descriptor. For example, add together the lengths of intermediate repairs to the trunk and extremities. Do not add lengths of repairs from different groupings of anatomic sites (eg, face and extremities). Also, do not add together lengths of different classifications (eg, intermediate and complex repairs).

When more than one classification of wounds is repaired, list the more complicated as the primary procedure and the less complicated as the secondary procedure, using modifier 51.

3. Decontamination and/or debridement: Debridement is considered a separate procedure only when gross contamination requires prolonged cleansing, when appreciable amounts of devitalized or contaminated tissue are removed, or when debridement is carried out separately without immediate primary closure. (For extensive debridement of soft tissue and/or bone, see 11040-11044.)

(For extensive debridement of soft tissue and/or bone, not associated with open fracture(s) and/or dislocation(s) resulting from penetrating and/or blunt trauma, see 11040-11044.)

(For extensive debridement of subcutaneous tissue, muscle fascia, muscle, and/or bone associated with open fracture(s) and/or dislocation(s), see 11010-11012.)

4. Involvement of nerves, blood vessels and tendons: Report under appropriate system (Nervous, Cardiovascular, Musculoskeletal) for repair of these structures. The repair of these associated wounds is included in the primary procedure unless it qualifies as a complex wound, in which case modifier 51 applies.

Simple ligation of vessels in an open wound is considered as part of any wound closure.

Simple "exploration" of nerves, blood vessels or tendons exposed in an open wound is also considered part of the essential treatment of the wound and is not a separate procedure unless appreciable dissection is required. If the wound requires enlargement, extension of dissection (to determine penetration), debridement, removal of foreign body(s), ligation or coagulation of minor subcutaneous and/or muscular blood vessel(s) of the subcutaneous tissue, muscle fascia, and/or muscle, not requiring thoracotomy or laparotomy, use codes 20100-20103, as appropriate.

Repair—Simple

Sum of lengths of repairs for each group of anatomic sites.

12001   Simple repair of superficial wounds of scalp, neck, axillae, external genitalia, trunk and/or extremities (including hands and feet); 2.5 cm or less

12002	2.6 cm to 7.5 cm
12004	7.6 cm to 12.5 cm
12005	12.6 cm to 20.0 cm
12006	20.1 cm to 30.0 cm
12007	over 30.0 cm
12011	Simple repair of superficial wounds of face, ears, eyelids, nose, lips and/or mucous membranes; 2.5 cm or less
12013	2.6 cm to 5.0 cm
12014	5.1 cm to 7.5 cm
12015	7.6 cm to 12.5 cm
12016	12.6 cm to 20.0 cm
12017	20.1 cm to 30.0 cm
12018	over 30.0 cm
12020	Treatment of superficial wound dehiscence; simple closure
12021	with packing

(For extensive or complicated secondary wound closure, use 13160)

Repair—Intermediate

Sum of lengths of repairs for each group of anatomic sites.

12031	Repair, intermediate, wounds of scalp, axillae, trunk and/or extremities (excluding hands and feet); 2.5 cm or less
12032	2.6 cm to 7.5 cm
12034	7.6 cm to 12.5 cm
12035	12.6 cm to 20.0 cm
12036	20.1 cm to 30.0 cm
12037	over 30.0 cm
12041	Repair, intermediate, wounds of neck, hands, feet and/or external genitalia; 2.5 cm or less
12042	2.6 cm to 7.5 cm
12044	7.6 cm to 12.5 cm
12045	12.6 cm to 20.0 cm
12046	20.1 cm to 30.0 cm
12047	over 30.0 cm
12051	Repair, intermediate, wounds of face, ears, eyelids, nose, lips and/or mucous membranes; 2.5 cm or less
12052	2.6 cm to 5.0 cm
12053	5.1 cm to 7.5 cm
12054	7.6 cm to 12.5 cm

12055	12.6 cm to 20.0 cm
12056	20.1 cm to 30.0 cm
12057	over 30.0 cm

Repair—Complex

Reconstructive procedures, complicated wound closure.

Sum of lengths of repairs for each group of anatomic sites.

(For full thickness repair of lip or eyelid, see respective anatomical subsections)

13100	Repair, complex, trunk; 1.1 cm to 2.5 cm

(For 1.0 cm or less, see simple or intermediate repairs)

13101	2.6 cm to 7.5 cm
+ 13102	each additional 5 cm or less (List separately in addition to code for primary procedure)

(Use 13102 in conjunction with 13101)

13120	Repair, complex, scalp, arms, and/or legs; 1.1 cm to 2.5 cm

(For 1.0 cm or less, see simple or intermediate repairs)

13121	2.6 cm to 7.5 cm
+ 13122	each additional 5 cm or less (List separately in addition to code for primary procedure)

(Use 13122 in conjunction with 13121)

13131	Repair, complex, forehead, cheeks, chin, mouth, neck, axillae, genitalia, hands and/or feet; 1.1 cm to 2.5 cm

(For 1.0 cm or less, see simple or intermediate repairs)

13132	2.6 cm to 7.5 cm
+ 13133	each additional 5 cm or less (List separately in addition to code for primary procedure)

(Use 13133 in conjunction with 13132)

13150	Repair, complex, eyelids, nose, ears and/or lips; 1.0 cm or less

(See also 40650-40654, 67961-67975)

13151	1.1 cm to 2.5 cm
13152	2.6 cm to 7.5 cm
+ 13153	each additional 5 cm or less (List separately in addition to code for primary procedure)

(Use 13153 in conjunction with 13152)

13160	Secondary closure of surgical wound or dehiscence, extensive or complicated

(For packing or simple secondary wound closure, see 12020, 12021)

Adjacent Tissue Transfer or Rearrangement

For full thickness repair of lip or eyelid, see respective anatomical subsections.

▶Codes 14000-14302 are used for excision (including lesion) and/or repair by adjacent tissue transfer or rearrangement (eg, Z-plasty, W-plasty, V-Y plasty, rotation flap, random island flap, advancement flap). When applied in repairing lacerations, the procedures listed must be performed by the surgeon to accomplish the repair. They do not apply to direct closure or rearrangement of traumatic wounds incidentally resulting in these configurations. Undermining alone of adjacent tissues to achieve closure, without additional incisions, does not constitute adjacent tissue transfer, see complex repair codes 13100-13160. The excision of a benign lesion (11400-11446) or a malignant lesion (11600-11646) is not separately reportable with codes 14000-14302.◀

Skin graft necessary to close secondary defect is considered an additional procedure. For purposes of code selection, the term "defect" includes the primary and secondary defects. The primary defect resulting from the excision and the secondary defect resulting from flap design to perform the reconstruction are measured together to determine the code.

14000   Adjacent tissue transfer or rearrangement, trunk; defect 10 sq cm or less

14001   defect 10.1 sq cm to 30.0 sq cm

14020   Adjacent tissue transfer or rearrangement, scalp, arms and/or legs; defect 10 sq cm or less

14021   defect 10.1 sq cm to 30.0 sq cm

14040   Adjacent tissue transfer or rearrangement, forehead, cheeks, chin, mouth, neck, axillae, genitalia, hands and/or feet; defect 10 sq cm or less

14041   defect 10.1 sq cm to 30.0 sq cm

14060   Adjacent tissue transfer or rearrangement, eyelids, nose, ears and/or lips; defect 10 sq cm or less

14061   defect 10.1 sq cm to 30.0 sq cm

(For eyelid, full thickness, see 67961 et seq)

▶(14300 has been deleted. To report, see 14301, 14302)◀

● **14301**   Adjacent tissue transfer or rearrangement, any area; defect 30.1 sq cm to 60.0 sq cm

+● **14302**   each additional 30.0 sq cm, or part thereof (List separately in addition to code for primary procedure)

▶(Use 14302 in conjunction with 14301)◀

14350   Filleted finger or toe flap, including preparation of recipient site

Skin Replacement Surgery and Skin Substitutes

Identify by size and location of the defect (recipient area) and the type of graft or skin substitute; includes simple debridement of granulation tissue or recent avulsion.

When a primary procedure such as orbitectomy, radical mastectomy, or deep tumor removal requires skin graft for definitive closure, see appropriate anatomical subsection for primary procedure and this section for skin graft or skin substitute.

Use codes 15002-15005 for initial wound recipient site preparation.

Use codes 15100-15261 for autologous skin grafts. For autologous tissue-cultured epidermal grafts, use codes 15150-15157. For harvesting of autologous keratinocytes and dermal tissue for tissue-cultured skin grafts, use code 15040. Procedures are coded by recipient site. Use codes 15170-15176 for acellular dermal replacement.

Repair of donor site requiring skin graft or local flaps is to be added as an additional procedure.

Codes 15002-15005 describe burn and wound preparation or incisional or excisional release of scar contracture resulting in an open wound requiring a skin graft. Codes 15100-15431 describe the application of skin replacements and skin substitutes. The following definition should be applied to those codes that reference "100 sq cm or 1% of body area of infants and children" when determining the involvement of body size: The measurement of 100 sq cm is applicable to adults and children age 10 and older; percentages of body surface area apply to infants and children younger than the age of 10.

These codes are not intended to be reported for simple graft application alone or application stabilized with dressings (eg, by simple gauze wrap). The skin substitute/graft is anchored using the surgeon's choice of fixation. When services are performed in the office, the supply of the skin substitute/graft should be reported separately. Routine dressing supplies are not reported separately. When square centimeters are indicated, this refers to 1 sq cm up to the stated amount. Add-on codes begin with the next sq cm (eg, 130 sq cm would be coded using a code for the first 100 sq cm and an add-on code for the next 30 sq cm). Use modifier 58 for staged application procedure(s).

(For microvascular flaps, see 15756-15758)

Surgical Preparation

15002   Surgical preparation or creation of recipient site by excision of open wounds, burn eschar, or scar (including subcutaneous tissues), or incisional release of scar contracture, trunk, arms, legs; first 100 sq cm or 1% of body area of infants and children

+ 15003 each additional 100 sq cm, or part thereof, or each additional 1% of body area of infants and children (List separately in addition to code for primary procedure)

(Use 15003 in conjunction with 15002)

15004 Surgical preparation or creation of recipient site by excision of open wounds, burn eschar, or scar (including subcutaneous tissues), or incisional release of scar contracture, face, scalp, eyelids, mouth, neck, ears, orbits, genitalia, hands, feet and/or multiple digits; first 100 sq cm or 1% of body area of infants and children

+ 15005 each additional 100 sq cm, or part thereof, or each additional 1% of body area of infants and children (List separately in addition to code for primary procedure)

(Use 15005 in conjunction with 15004)

(Report 15002-15005 in conjunction with code for appropriate skin grafts or replacements [15050-15261, 15330-15336]. List the graft or replacement separately by its procedure number when the graft, immediate or delayed, is applied)

(For excision of benign lesions, see 11400-11471)

(For excision of malignant lesions, see 11600-11646)

(For excision to prepare or create recipient site with dressings or materials not listed in 15040-15431, use 15002-15005 only)

(For excision with immediate skin grafting, use 15002-15005 in conjunction with 15050-15261)

(For excision with immediate allograft skin placement, use 15002-15005 in conjunction with 15300-15336 and 15360-15366)

(For excision with immediate xenogeneic dermis placement, use 15002-15005 in conjunction with 15400-15421)

Grafts

Autograft/Tissue Cultured Autograft

15040 Harvest of skin for tissue cultured skin autograft, 100 sq cm or less

15050 Pinch graft, single or multiple, to cover small ulcer, tip of digit, or other minimal open area (except on face), up to defect size 2 cm diameter

15100 Split-thickness autograft, trunk, arms, legs; first 100 sq cm or less, or 1% of body area of infants and children (except 15050)

+ 15101 each additional 100 sq cm, or each additional 1% of body area of infants and children, or part thereof (List separately in addition to code for primary procedure)

(Use 15101 in conjunction with 15100)

15110 Epidermal autograft, trunk, arms, legs; first 100 sq cm or less, or 1% of body area of infants and children

+ 15111 each additional 100 sq cm, or each additional 1% of body area of infants and children, or part thereof (List separately in addition to code for primary procedure)

(Use 15111 in conjunction with 15110)

15115 Epidermal autograft, face, scalp, eyelids, mouth, neck, ears, orbits, genitalia, hands, feet, and/or multiple digits; first 100 sq cm or less, or 1% of body area of infants and children

+ 15116 each additional 100 sq cm, or each additional 1% of body area of infants and children, or part thereof (List separately in addition to code for primary procedure)

(Use 15116 in conjunction with 15115)

15120 Split-thickness autograft, face, scalp, eyelids, mouth, neck, ears, orbits, genitalia, hands, feet, and/or multiple digits; first 100 sq cm or less, or 1% of body area of infants and children (except 15050)

+ 15121 each additional 100 sq cm, or each additional 1% of body area of infants and children, or part thereof (List separately in addition to code for primary procedure)

(Use 15121 in conjunction with 15120)

(For eyelids, see also 67961 et seq)

15130 Dermal autograft, trunk, arms, legs; first 100 sq cm or less, or 1% of body area of infants and children

+ 15131 each additional 100 sq cm, or each additional 1% of body area of infants and children, or part thereof (List separately in addition to code for primary procedure)

(Use 15131 in conjunction with 15130)

15135 Dermal autograft, face, scalp, eyelids, mouth, neck, ears, orbits, genitalia, hands, feet, and/or multiple digits; first 100 sq cm or less, or 1% of body area of infants and children

+ 15136 each additional 100 sq cm, or each additional 1% of body area of infants and children, or part thereof (List separately in addition to code for primary procedure)

(Use 15136 in conjunction with 15135)

15150 Tissue cultured epidermal autograft, trunk, arms, legs; first 25 sq cm or less

+ 15151 additional 1 sq cm to 75 sq cm (List separately in addition to code for primary procedure)

(Do not report 15151 more than once per session)

(Use 15151 in conjunction with 15150)

+ 15152 each additional 100 sq cm, or each additional 1% of body area of infants and children, or part thereof (List separately in addition to code for primary procedure)

(Use 15152 in conjunction with 15151)

15155 Tissue cultured epidermal autograft, face, scalp, eyelids, mouth, neck, ears, orbits, genitalia, hands, feet, and/or multiple digits; first 25 sq cm or less

+ 15156 additional 1 sq cm to 75 sq cm (List separately in addition to code for primary procedure)

(Do not report 15156 more than once per session)

(Use 15156 in conjunction with 15155)

+ **15157**   each additional 100 sq cm, or each additional 1% of body area of infants and children, or part thereof (List separately in addition to code for primary procedure)

(Use 15157 in conjunction with 15156)

Acellular Dermal Replacement

15170   Acellular dermal replacement, trunk, arms, legs; first 100 sq cm or less, or 1% of body area of infants and children

+ **15171**   each additional 100 sq cm, or each additional 1% of body area of infants and children, or part thereof (List separately in addition to code for primary procedure)

(Use 15171 in conjunction with 15170)

15175   Acellular dermal replacement, face, scalp, eyelids, mouth, neck, ears, orbits, genitalia, hands, feet, and/or multiple digits; first 100 sq cm or less, or 1% of body area of infants and children

+ **15176**   each additional 100 sq cm, or each additional 1% of body area of infants and children, or part thereof (List separately in addition to code for primary procedure)

(Use 15176 in conjunction with 15175)

15200   Full thickness graft, free, including direct closure of donor site, trunk; 20 sq cm or less

+ **15201**   each additional 20 sq cm, or part thereof (List separately in addition to code for primary procedure)

(Use 15201 in conjunction with 15200)

15220   Full thickness graft, free, including direct closure of donor site, scalp, arms, and/or legs; 20 sq cm or less

+ **15221**   each additional 20 sq cm, or part thereof (List separately in addition to code for primary procedure)

(Use 15221 in conjunction with 15220)

15240   Full thickness graft, free, including direct closure of donor site, forehead, cheeks, chin, mouth, neck, axillae, genitalia, hands, and/or feet; 20 sq cm or less

(For finger tip graft, use 15050)

(For repair of syndactyly, fingers, see 26560-26562)

+ **15241**   each additional 20 sq cm, or part thereof (List separately in addition to code for primary procedure)

(Use 15241 in conjunction with 15240)

15260   Full thickness graft, free, including direct closure of donor site, nose, ears, eyelids, and/or lips; 20 sq cm or less

+ **15261**   each additional 20 sq cm, or part thereof (List separately in addition to code for primary procedure)

(Use 15261 in conjunction with 15260)

(For eyelids, see also 67961 et seq)

(Repair of donor site requiring skin graft or local flaps, to be added as additional separate procedure)

Allograft/Tissue Cultured Allogeneic Skin Substitute

Application of a non-autologous human skin graft (ie, homograft) from a donor to a part of the recipient's body to resurface an area damaged by burns, traumatic injury, soft tissue infection and/or tissue necrosis or surgery.

15300   Allograft skin for temporary wound closure, trunk, arms, legs; first 100 sq cm or less, or 1% of body area of infants and children

+ **15301**   each additional 100 sq cm, or each additional 1% of body area of infants and children, or part thereof (List separately in addition to code for primary procedure)

(Use 15301 in conjunction with 15300)

15320   Allograft skin for temporary wound closure, face, scalp, eyelids, mouth, neck, ears, orbits, genitalia, hands, feet, and/or multiple digits; first 100 sq cm or less, or 1% of body area of infants and children

+ **15321**   each additional 100 sq cm, or each additional 1% of body area of infants and children, or part thereof (List separately in addition to code for primary procedure)

(Use 15321 in conjunction with 15320)

15330   Acellular dermal allograft, trunk, arms, legs; first 100 sq cm or less, or 1% of body area of infants and children

+ **15331**   each additional 100 sq cm, or each additional 1% of body area of infants and children, or part thereof (List separately in addition to code for primary procedure)

(Use 15331 in conjunction with 15330)

15335   Acellular dermal allograft, face, scalp, eyelids, mouth, neck, ears, orbits, genitalia, hands, feet, and/or multiple digits; first 100 sq cm or less, or 1% of body area of infants and children

+ **15336**   each additional 100 sq cm, or each additional 1% of body area of infants and children, or part thereof (List separately in addition to code for primary procedure)

(Use 15336 in conjunction with 15335)

15340   Tissue cultured allogeneic skin substitute; first 25 sq cm or less

+ **15341**   each additional 25 sq cm, or part thereof (List separately in addition to code for primary procedure)

(Use 15341 in conjunction with 15340)

(Do not report 15340, 15341 in conjunction with 11040-11042, 15002-15005)

15360   Tissue cultured allogeneic dermal substitute, trunk, arms, legs; first 100 sq cm or less, or 1% of body area of infants and children

+ **15361**   each additional 100 sq cm, or each additional 1% of body area of infants and children, or part thereof (List separately in addition to code for primary procedure)

(Use 15361 in conjunction with 15360)

Surgery: Integumentary System

▲=Revised code   ●=New code   ▶ ◀=Contains new or revised text   ⊘=Modifier 51 exempt

15365   Tissue cultured allogeneic dermal substitute, face, scalp, eyelids, mouth, neck, ears, orbits, genitalia, hands, feet, and/or multiple digits; first 100 sq cm or less, or 1% of body area of infants and children

+ 15366   each additional 100 sq cm, or each additional 1% of body area of infants and children, or part thereof (List separately in addition to code for primary procedure)

(Use 15366 in conjunction with 15365)

Xenograft

Application of a non-human skin graft or biologic wound dressing (eg, porcine tissue or pigskin) to a part of the recipient's body following debridement of the burn wound or area of traumatic injury, soft tissue infection and/or tissue necrosis, or surgery.

15400   Xenograft, skin (dermal), for temporary wound closure, trunk, arms, legs; first 100 sq cm or less, or 1% of body area of infants and children

+ 15401   each additional 100 sq cm, or each additional 1% of body area of infants and children, or part thereof (List separately in addition to code for primary procedure)

(Use 15401 in conjunction with 15400)

15420   Xenograft skin (dermal), for temporary wound closure, face, scalp, eyelids, mouth, neck, ears, orbits, genitalia, hands, feet, and/or multiple digits; first 100 sq cm or less, or 1% of body area of infants and children

+ 15421   each additional 100 sq cm, or each additional 1% of body area of infants and children, or part thereof (List separately in addition to code for primary procedure)

(Use 15421 in conjunction with 15420)

15430   Acellular xenograft implant; first 100 sq cm or less, or 1% of body area of infants and children

+ 15431   each additional 100 sq cm, or each additional 1% of body area of infants and children, or part thereof (List separately in addition to code for primary procedure)

(Use 15431 in conjunction with 15430)

(Do not report 15430, 15431 in conjunction with 11040-11042, 15002-15005, 0170T)

Flaps (Skin and/or Deep Tissues)

The regions listed refer to the recipient area (not the donor site) when a flap is being attached in a transfer or to a final site.

The regions listed refer to a donor site when a tube is formed for later transfer or when a "delay" of flap occurs prior to the transfer.

Procedures 15570-15738 do not include extensive immobilization (eg, large plaster casts and other immobilizing devices are considered additional separate procedures).

A repair of a donor site requiring a skin graft or local flaps is considered an additional separate procedure.

(For microvascular flaps, see 15756-15758)

(For flaps without inclusion of a vascular pedicle, see 15570-15576)

►(For adjacent tissue transfer flaps, see 14000-14302)◄

15570   Formation of direct or tubed pedicle, with or without transfer; trunk

15572   scalp, arms, or legs

15574   forehead, cheeks, chin, mouth, neck, axillae, genitalia, hands or feet

15576   eyelids, nose, ears, lips, or intraoral

15600   Delay of flap or sectioning of flap (division and inset); at trunk

15610   at scalp, arms, or legs

15620   at forehead, cheeks, chin, neck, axillae, genitalia, hands, or feet

15630   at eyelids, nose, ears, or lips

15650   Transfer, intermediate, of any pedicle flap (eg, abdomen to wrist, Walking tube), any location

(For eyelids, nose, ears, or lips, see also anatomical area)

►(For revision, defatting or rearranging of transferred pedicle flap or skin graft, see 13100-14302)◄

(Procedures 15732-15738 are described by donor site of the muscle, myocutaneous, or fasciocutaneous flap)

15731   Forehead flap with preservation of vascular pedicle (eg, axial pattern flap, paramedian forehead flap)

(For muscle, myocutaneous, or fasciocutaneous flap of the head or neck, use 15732)

15732   Muscle, myocutaneous, or fasciocutaneous flap; head and neck (eg, temporalis, masseter muscle, sternocleidomastoid, levator scapulae)

(For forehead flap with preservation of vascular pedicle, use 15731)

15734   trunk

15736   upper extremity

15738   lower extremity

Other Flaps and Grafts

►Code 15740 describes a cutaneous flap, transposed into a nearby but not immediately adjacent defect, with a pedicle that incorporates an axial vessel into its design. The flap is typically transferred through a tunnel underneath the skin and sutured into its new position. The donor site is closed directly.

Neurovascular pedicle procedures are reported with 15750. This code includes not only skin but also a functional motor or sensory nerve(s). The flap serves to reinnervate a damaged portion of the body dependent on touch or movement (eg, thumb).◄

Repair of donor site requiring skin graft or local flaps should be reported as an additional procedure.

15740   Flap; island pedicle

15750   neurovascular pedicle

►(For random island flaps, V-Y subcutaneous flaps and other flaps from adjacent areas, see 14000-14302)◄

15756   Free muscle or myocutaneous flap with microvascular anastomosis

(Do not report code 69990 in addition to code 15756)

15757   Free skin flap with microvascular anastomosis

(Do not report code 69990 in addition to code 15757)

15758   Free fascial flap with microvascular anastomosis

(Do not report code 69990 in addition to code 15758)

15760   Graft; composite (eg, full thickness of external ear or nasal ala), including primary closure, donor area

15770   derma-fat-fascia

15775   Punch graft for hair transplant; 1 to 15 punch grafts

15776   more than 15 punch grafts

(For strip transplant, use 15220)

Other Procedures

15780   Dermabrasion; total face (eg, for acne scarring, fine wrinkling, rhytids, general keratosis)

15781   segmental, face

15782   regional, other than face

15783   superficial, any site (eg, tattoo removal)

15786   Abrasion; single lesion (eg, keratosis, scar)

+ **15787**   each additional 4 lesions or less (List separately in addition to code for primary procedure)

(Use 15787 in conjunction with 15786)

15788   Chemical peel, facial; epidermal

15789   dermal

15792   Chemical peel, nonfacial; epidermal

15793   dermal

15819   Cervicoplasty

15820   Blepharoplasty, lower eyelid;

15821   with extensive herniated fat pad

15822   Blepharoplasty, upper eyelid;

15823   with excessive skin weighting down lid

(For bilateral blepharoplasty, add modifier 50)

15824   Rhytidectomy; forehead

(For repair of brow ptosis, use 67900)

15825   neck with platysmal tightening (platysmal flap, P-flap)

15826   glabellar frown lines

15828   cheek, chin, and neck

15829   superficial musculoaponeurotic system (SMAS) flap

(For bilateral rhytidectomy, add modifier 50)

15830   Excision, excessive skin and subcutaneous tissue (includes lipectomy); abdomen, infraumbilical panniculectomy

►(Do not report 15830 in conjunction with 12031, 12032, 12034, 12035, 12036, 12037, 13100, 13101, 13102, 14000-14001, 14302)◄

15832   thigh

15833   leg

15834   hip

15835   buttock

15836   arm

15837   forearm or hand

15838   submental fat pad

15839   other area

(For bilateral procedure, add modifier 50)

15840   Graft for facial nerve paralysis; free fascia graft (including obtaining fascia)

(For bilateral procedure, add modifier 50)

15841   free muscle graft (including obtaining graft)

15842   free muscle flap by microsurgical technique

(Do not report code 69990 in addition to code 15842)

15845   regional muscle transfer

(For intravenous fluorescein examination of blood flow in graft or flap, use 15860)

(For nerve transfers, decompression, or repair, see 64831-64876, 64905, 64907, 69720, 69725, 69740, 69745, 69955)

+ **15847**   Excision, excessive skin and subcutaneous tissue (includes lipectomy), abdomen (eg, abdominoplasty) (includes umbilical transposition and fascial plication) (List separately in addition to code for primary procedure)

(Use 15847 in conjunction with 15830)

(For abdominal wall hernia repair, see 49491-49587)

(To report other abdominoplasty, use 17999)

15850   Removal of sutures under anesthesia (other than local), same surgeon

Surgery: Integumentary System

15851 Removal of sutures under anesthesia (other than local), other surgeon

15852 Dressing change (for other than burns) under anesthesia (other than local)

15860 Intravenous injection of agent (eg, fluorescein) to test vascular flow in flap or graft

15876 Suction assisted lipectomy; head and neck

15877 trunk

15878 upper extremity

15879 lower extremity

Pressure Ulcers (Decubitus Ulcers)

15920 Excision, coccygeal pressure ulcer, with coccygectomy; with primary suture

15922 with flap closure

15931 Excision, sacral pressure ulcer, with primary suture;

15933 with ostectomy

15934 Excision, sacral pressure ulcer, with skin flap closure;

15935 with ostectomy

15936 Excision, sacral pressure ulcer, in preparation for muscle or myocutaneous flap or skin graft closure;

15937 with ostectomy

(For repair of defect using muscle or myocutaneous flap, use code(s) 15734 and/or 15738 in addition to 15936, 15937. For repair of defect using split skin graft, use codes 15100 and/or 15101 in addition to 15936, 15937)

15940 Excision, ischial pressure ulcer, with primary suture;

15941 with ostectomy (ischiectomy)

15944 Excision, ischial pressure ulcer, with skin flap closure;

15945 with ostectomy

15946 Excision, ischial pressure ulcer, with ostectomy, in preparation for muscle or myocutaneous flap or skin graft closure

(For repair of defect using muscle or myocutaneous flap, use code(s) 15734 and/or 15738 in addition to 15946. For repair of defect using split skin graft, use codes 15100 and/or 15101 in addition to 15946)

15950 Excision, trochanteric pressure ulcer, with primary suture;

15951 with ostectomy

15952 Excision, trochanteric pressure ulcer, with skin flap closure;

15953 with ostectomy

15956 Excision, trochanteric pressure ulcer, in preparation for muscle or myocutaneous flap or skin graft closure;

15958 with ostectomy

(For repair of defect using muscle or myocutaneous flap, use code(s) 15734 and/or 15738 in addition to 15956, 15958. For repair of defect using split skin graft, use codes 15100 and/or 15101 in addition to 15956, 15958)

15999 Unlisted procedure, excision pressure ulcer

(For free skin graft to close ulcer or donor site, see 15002 et seq)

Burns, Local Treatment

Procedures 16000-16036 refer to local treatment of burned surface only. Codes 16020-16030 include the application of materials (eg, dressings) not described in codes 15100-15431.

List percentage of body surface involved and depth of burn.

For necessary related medical services (eg, hospital visits, detention) in management of burned patients, see appropriate services in **Evaluation and Management** and **Medicine** sections.

For the application of skin grafts or skin substitutes, see codes 15100-15650.

16000 Initial treatment, first degree burn, when no more than local treatment is required

16020 Dressings and/or debridement of partial-thickness burns, initial or subsequent; small (less than 5% total body surface area)

16025 medium (eg, whole face or whole extremity, or 5% to 10% total body surface area)

16030 large (eg, more than 1 extremity, or greater than 10% total body surface area)

16035 Escharotomy; initial incision

+ 16036 each additional incision (List separately in addition to code for primary procedure)

(Use 16036 in conjunction with 16035)

(For debridement, curettement of burn wound, see 16020-16030)

Destruction

Destruction means the ablation of benign, premalignant or malignant tissues by any method, with or without curettement, including local anesthesia, and not usually requiring closure.

Any method includes electrosurgery, cryosurgery, laser and chemical treatment. Lesions include condylomata, papillomata, molluscum contagiosum, herpetic lesions, warts (ie, common, plantar, flat), milia, or other benign, premalignant (eg, actinic keratoses), or malignant lesions.

(For destruction of lesion(s) in specific anatomic sites, see 40820, 46900-46917, 46924, 54050-54057, 54065, 56501, 56515, 57061, 57065, 67850, 68135)

►(For laser treatment for inflammatory skin disease, see 96920-96922)◄

(For paring or cutting of benign hyperkeratotic lesions (eg, corns or calluses), see 11055-11057)

(For sharp removal or electrosurgical destruction of skin tags and fibrocutaneous tags, see 11200, 11201)

(For cryotherapy of acne, use 17340)

(For initiation or follow-up care of topical chemotherapy (eg, 5-FU or similar agents), see appropriate office visits)

(For shaving of epidermal or dermal lesions, see 11300-11313)

Destruction, Benign or Premalignant Lesions

17000	Destruction (eg, laser surgery, electrosurgery, cryosurgery, chemosurgery, surgical curettement), premalignant lesions (eg, actinic keratoses); first lesion
+ 17003	second through 14 lesions, each (List separately in addition to code for first lesion)

(Use 17003 in conjunction with 17000)

(For destruction of common or plantar warts, see 17110, 17111)

⊘ **17004**	Destruction (eg, laser surgery, electrosurgery, cryosurgery, chemosurgery, surgical curettement), premalignant lesions (eg, actinic keratoses), 15 or more lesions

(Do not report 17004 in conjunction with 17000-17003)

17106	Destruction of cutaneous vascular proliferative lesions (eg, laser technique); less than 10 sq cm
17107	10.0 to 50.0 sq cm
17108	over 50.0 sq cm
17110	Destruction (eg, laser surgery, electrosurgery, cryosurgery, chemosurgery, surgical curettement), of benign lesions other than skin tags or cutaneous vascular proliferative lesions; up to 14 lesions
17111	15 or more lesions
17250	Chemical cauterization of granulation tissue (proud flesh, sinus or fistula)

(17250 is not to be used with removal or excision codes for the same lesion)

Destruction, Malignant Lesions, Any Method

17260	Destruction, malignant lesion (eg, laser surgery, electrosurgery, cryosurgery, chemosurgery, surgical curettement), trunk, arms or legs; lesion diameter 0.5 cm or less

17261	lesion diameter 0.6 to 1.0 cm
17262	lesion diameter 1.1 to 2.0 cm
17263	lesion diameter 2.1 to 3.0 cm
17264	lesion diameter 3.1 to 4.0 cm
17266	lesion diameter over 4.0 cm
17270	Destruction, malignant lesion (eg, laser surgery, electrosurgery, cryosurgery, chemosurgery, surgical curettement), scalp, neck, hands, feet, genitalia; lesion diameter 0.5 cm or less
17271	lesion diameter 0.6 to 1.0 cm
17272	lesion diameter 1.1 to 2.0 cm
17273	lesion diameter 2.1 to 3.0 cm
17274	lesion diameter 3.1 to 4.0 cm
17276	lesion diameter over 4.0 cm
17280	Destruction, malignant lesion (eg, laser surgery, electrosurgery, cryosurgery, chemosurgery, surgical curettement), face, ears, eyelids, nose, lips, mucous membrane; lesion diameter 0.5 cm or less
17281	lesion diameter 0.6 to 1.0 cm
17282	lesion diameter 1.1 to 2.0 cm
17283	lesion diameter 2.1 to 3.0 cm
17284	lesion diameter 3.1 to 4.0 cm
17286	lesion diameter over 4.0 cm

Mohs Micrographic Surgery

Mohs micrographic surgery is a technique for the removal of complex or ill-defined skin cancer with histologic examination of 100% of the surgical margins. It requires a single physician to act in two integrated but separate and distinct capacities: surgeon and pathologist. If either of these responsibilities is delegated to another physician who reports the services separately, these codes should not be reported. The Mohs surgeon removes the tumor tissue and maps and divides the tumor specimen into pieces, and each piece is embedded into an individual tissue block for histopathologic examination. Thus a tissue block in Mohs surgery is defined as an individual tissue piece embedded in a mounting medium for sectioning.

If repair is performed, use separate repair, flap, or graft codes. If a biopsy of a suspected skin cancer is performed on the same day as Mohs surgery because there was no prior pathology confirmation of a diagnosis, then report diagnostic skin biopsy (11100, 11101) and frozen section pathology (88331) with modifier 59 to distinguish from the subsequent definitive surgical procedure of Mohs surgery.

(If additional special pathology procedures, stains or immunostains are required, use 88311-88314, 88342)

Surgery: Integumentary System

(Do not report 88314 in conjunction with 17311-17315 for routine frozen section stain (eg, hematoxylin and eosin, toluidine blue) performed during Mohs surgery. When a nonroutine histochemical stain on frozen tissue is utilized, report 88314 with modifier 59)

(Do not report 88302-88309 on the same specimen as part of the Mohs surgery)

17311 Mohs micrographic technique, including removal of all gross tumor, surgical excision of tissue specimens, mapping, color coding of specimens, microscopic examination of specimens by the surgeon, and histopathologic preparation including routine stain(s) (eg, hematoxylin and eosin, toluidine blue), head, neck, hands, feet, genitalia, or any location with surgery directly involving muscle, cartilage, bone, tendon, major nerves, or vessels; first stage, up to 5 tissue blocks

+ 17312 each additional stage after the first stage, up to 5 tissue blocks (List separately in addition to code for primary procedure)

(Use 17312 in conjunction with 17311)

17313 Mohs micrographic technique, including removal of all gross tumor, surgical excision of tissue specimens, mapping, color coding of specimens, microscopic examination of specimens by the surgeon, and histopathologic preparation including routine stain(s) (eg, hematoxylin and eosin, toluidine blue), of the trunk, arms, or legs; first stage, up to 5 tissue blocks

+ 17314 each additional stage after the first stage, up to 5 tissue blocks (List separately in addition to code for primary procedure)

(Use 17314 in conjunction with 17313)

+ 17315 Mohs micrographic technique, including removal of all gross tumor, surgical excision of tissue specimens, mapping, color coding of specimens, microscopic examination of specimens by the surgeon, and histopathologic preparation including routine stain(s) (eg, hematoxylin and eosin, toluidine blue), each additional block after the first 5 tissue blocks, any stage (List separately in addition to code for primary procedure)

(Use 17315 in conjunction with 17311-17314)

Other Procedures

17340 Cryotherapy (CO_2 slush, liquid N_2) for acne

17360 Chemical exfoliation for acne (eg, acne paste, acid)

17380 Electrolysis epilation, each 30 minutes

(For actinotherapy, use 96900)

17999 Unlisted procedure, skin, mucous membrane and subcutaneous tissue

Breast

Incision

19000 Puncture aspiration of cyst of breast;

+ 19001 each additional cyst (List separately in addition to code for primary procedure)

(Use 19001 in conjunction with 19000)

(If imaging guidance is performed, see 76942, 77021, 77031, 77032)

19020 Mastotomy with exploration or drainage of abscess, deep

19030 Injection procedure only for mammary ductogram or galactogram

(For radiological supervision and interpretation, see 77053, 77054)

Excision

Excisional breast surgery includes certain biopsy procedures, the removal of cysts or other benign or malignant tumors or lesions, and the surgical treatment of breast and chest wall malignancies. Biopsy procedures may be percutaneous or open, and they involve the removal of differing amounts of tissue for diagnosis.

Breast biopsies are reported using codes 19100-19103. The open excision of breast lesions (eg, lesions of the breast ducts, cysts, benign or malignant tumors), without specific attention to adequate surgical margins, with or without the preoperative placement of radiological markers, is reported using codes 19110-19126. Partial mastectomy procedures (eg, lumpectomy, tylectomy, quadrantectomy, or segmentectomy) describe open excisions of breast tissue with specific attention to adequate surgical margins.

Partial mastectomy procedures are reported using codes 19301 or 19302 as appropriate. Documentation for partial mastectomy procedures includes attention to the removal of adequate surgical margins surrounding the breast mass or lesion.

Total mastectomy procedures include simple mastectomy, complete mastectomy, subcutaneous mastectomy, modified radical mastectomy, radical mastectomy, and more extended procedures (eg, Urban type operation). Total mastectomy procedures are reported using codes 19303-19307 as appropriate.

Excisions or resections of chest wall tumors including ribs, with or without reconstruction, with or without mediastinal lymphadenectomy, are reported using codes 19260, 19271, or 19272. Codes 19260-19272 are not restricted to breast tumors and are used to report resections of chest wall tumors originating from any chest wall component. (For excision of lung or pleura, see 32310 et seq)

(To report bilateral procedure, report modifier 50 with the procedure code)

19100 Biopsy of breast; percutaneous, needle core, not using imaging guidance (separate procedure)

(For fine needle aspiration, use 10021)

(For image guided breast biopsy, see 19102, 19103, 10022)

19101 open, incisional

19102 percutaneous, needle core, using imaging guidance

(For placement of percutaneous localization clip, use 19295)

19103 percutaneous, automated vacuum assisted or rotating biopsy device, using imaging guidance

(For imaging guidance performed in conjunction with 19102, 19103, see 76942, 77012, 77021, 77031, 77032)

(For placement of percutaneous localization clip, use 19295)

19105 Ablation, cryosurgical, of fibroadenoma, including ultrasound guidance, each fibroadenoma

(Do not report 19105 in conjunction with 76940, 76942)

(For adjacent lesions treated with 1 cryoprobe insertion, report once)

19110 Nipple exploration, with or without excision of a solitary lactiferous duct or a papilloma lactiferous duct

19112 Excision of lactiferous duct fistula

19120 Excision of cyst, fibroadenoma, or other benign or malignant tumor, aberrant breast tissue, duct lesion, nipple or areolar lesion (except 19300), open, male or female, 1 or more lesions

19125 Excision of breast lesion identified by preoperative placement of radiological marker, open; single lesion

+ 19126 each additional lesion separately identified by a preoperative radiological marker (List separately in addition to code for primary procedure)

(Use 19126 in conjunction with 19125)

19260 Excision of chest wall tumor including ribs

19271 Excision of chest wall tumor involving ribs, with plastic reconstruction; without mediastinal lymphadenectomy

19272 with mediastinal lymphadenectomy

(Do not report 19260, 19271, 19272 in conjunction with 32100, 32422, 32503, 32504, 32551)

Introduction

19290 Preoperative placement of needle localization wire, breast;

+ 19291 each additional lesion (List separately in addition to code for primary procedure)

(Use 19291 in conjunction with 19290)

(For radiological supervision and interpretation, see 76942, 77031, 77032)

+▲ 19295 Image guided placement, metallic localization clip, percutaneous, during breast biopsy/aspiration (List separately in addition to code for primary procedure)

►(Use 19295 in conjunction with 10022, 19102, 19103)◄

19296 Placement of radiotherapy afterloading expandable catheter (single or multichannel) into the breast for interstitial radioelement application following partial mastectomy, includes imaging guidance; on date separate from partial mastectomy

+ 19297 concurrent with partial mastectomy (List separately in addition to code for primary procedure)

(Use 19297 in conjunction with 19301 or 19302)

⊙ 19298 Placement of radiotherapy afterloading brachytherapy catheters (multiple tube and button type) into the breast for interstitial radioelement application following (at the time of or subsequent to) partial mastectomy, includes imaging guidance

Mastectomy Procedures

19300 Mastectomy for gynecomastia

19301 Mastectomy, partial (eg, lumpectomy, tylectomy, quadrantectomy, segmentectomy);

19302 with axillary lymphadenectomy

(For placement of radiotherapy afterloading balloon/brachytherapy catheters, see 19296-19298)

19303 Mastectomy, simple, complete

(For immediate or delayed insertion of implant, see 19340, 19342)

(For gynecomastia, use 19300)

19304 Mastectomy, subcutaneous

(For immediate or delayed insertion of implant, see 19340, 19342)

19305 Mastectomy, radical, including pectoral muscles, axillary lymph nodes

(For immediate or delayed insertion of implant, see 19340, 19342)

19306 Mastectomy, radical, including pectoral muscles, axillary and internal mammary lymph nodes (Urban type operation)

(For immediate or delayed insertion of implant, see 19340, 19342)

19307 Mastectomy, modified radical, including axillary lymph nodes, with or without pectoralis minor muscle, but excluding pectoralis major muscle

(For immediate or delayed insertion of implant, see 19340, 19342)

Repair and/or Reconstruction

(To report bilateral procedure, report modifier 50 with the procedure code)

19316 Mastopexy

19318 Reduction mammaplasty

19324 Mammaplasty, augmentation; without prosthetic implant

19325 with prosthetic implant

(For flap or graft, use also appropriate number)

19328 Removal of intact mammary implant

19330 Removal of mammary implant material

19340 Immediate insertion of breast prosthesis following mastopexy, mastectomy or in reconstruction

19342 Delayed insertion of breast prosthesis following mastopexy, mastectomy or in reconstruction

(For supply of implant, use 99070)

(For preparation of custom breast implant, use 19396)

19350 Nipple/areola reconstruction

19355 Correction of inverted nipples

19357 Breast reconstruction, immediate or delayed, with tissue expander, including subsequent expansion

19361 Breast reconstruction with latissimus dorsi flap, without prosthetic implant

(For insertion of prosthesis, use also 19340)

19364 Breast reconstruction with free flap

(Do not report code 69990 in addition to code 19364)

(19364 includes harvesting of the flap, microvascular transfer, closure of the donor site, and inset shaping the flap into a breast)

19366 Breast reconstruction with other technique

(For operating microscope, use 69990)

(For insertion of prosthesis, use also 19340 or 19342)

19367 Breast reconstruction with transverse rectus abdominis myocutaneous flap (TRAM), single pedicle, including closure of donor site;

19368 with microvascular anastomosis (supercharging)

(Do not report code 69990 in addition to code 19368)

19369 Breast reconstruction with transverse rectus abdominis myocutaneous flap (TRAM), double pedicle, including closure of donor site

19370 Open periprosthetic capsulotomy, breast

19371 Periprosthetic capsulectomy, breast

19380 Revision of reconstructed breast

19396 Preparation of moulage for custom breast implant

Other Procedures

19499 Unlisted procedure, breast

Musculoskeletal System

Cast and strapping procedures appear at the end of this section.

The services listed below include the application and removal of the first cast or traction device only. Subsequent replacement of cast and/or traction device may require an additional listing.

Definitions

The terms "closed treatment," "open treatment," and "percutaneous skeletal fixation" have been carefully chosen to accurately reflect current orthopaedic procedural treatments.

Closed treatment specifically means that the fracture site is not surgically opened (exposed to the external environment and directly visualized). This terminology is used to describe procedures that treat fractures by three methods: (1) without manipulation; (2) with manipulation; or (3) with or without traction.

Open treatment is used when the fractured bone is either: (1) surgically opened (exposed to the external environment) and the fracture (bone ends) visualized and internal fixation may be used; or (2) the fractured bone is opened remote from the fracture site in order to insert an intramedullary nail across the fracture site (the fracture site is not opened and visualized).

Percutaneous skeletal fixation describes fracture treatment which is neither open nor closed. In this procedure, the fracture fragments are not visualized, but fixation (eg, pins) is placed across the fracture site, usually under X-ray imaging.

The type of fracture (eg, open, compound, closed) does not have any coding correlation with the type of treatment (eg, closed, open, or percutaneous) provided.

The codes for treatment of fractures and joint injuries (dislocations) are categorized by the type of manipulation (reduction) and stabilization (fixation or immobilization). These codes can apply to either open (compound) or closed fractures or joint injuries.

Skeletal traction is the application of a force (distracting or traction force) to a limb segment through a wire, pin, screw, or clamp that is attached (eg, penetrates) to bone.

Skin traction is the application of a force (longitudinal) to a limb using felt or strapping applied directly to skin only.

External fixation is the usage of skeletal pins plus an attaching mechanism/device used for temporary or definitive treatment of acute or chronic bony deformity.

Codes for obtaining autogenous bone grafts, cartilage, tendon, fascia lata grafts or other tissues through separate incisions are to be used only when the graft is not already listed as part of the basic procedure.

Re-reduction of a fracture and/or dislocation performed by the primary physician may be identified by the addition of the modifier 76 to the usual procedure number to indicate "Repeat Procedure or Service by Same Physician." (See Appendix A guidelines.)

Codes for external fixation are to be used only when external fixation is not already listed as part of the basic procedure.

All codes for suction irrigation have been deleted. To report, list only the primary surgical procedure performed (eg, sequestrectomy, deep incision).

Manipulation is used throughout the musculoskeletal fracture and dislocation subsections to specifically mean the attempted reduction or restoration of a fracture or joint dislocation to its normal anatomic alignment by the application of manually applied forces.

►*Excision of subcutaneous soft tissue tumors* (including simple or intermediate repair) involves the simple or marginal resection of tumors confined to subcutaneous tissue below the skin but above the deep fascia. These tumors are usually benign and are resected without removing a significant amount of surrounding normal tissue. Code selection is based on the location and size of the tumor. Code selection is determined by measuring the greatest diameter of the tumor plus that margin required for complete excision of the tumor. The margins refer to the most narrow margin required to adequately excise the tumor, based on the physician's judgment. The measurement of the tumor plus margin is made at the time of the excision. Appreciable vessel exploration and/or neuroplasty should be reported separately. Extensive undermining or other techniques to close a defect created by skin excision may require a complex repair which should be reported separately. Dissection or elevation of tissue planes to permit resection of the tumor is included in the excision.

Excision of fascial or subfascial soft tissue tumors (including simple or intermediate repair) involves the resection of tumors confined to the tissue within or below the deep fascia, but not involving the bone. These tumors are usually benign, are often intramuscular, and are resected without removing a significant amount of surrounding normal tissue. Code selection is based on size and location of the tumor. Code selection is determined by measuring the greatest diameter of the tumor plus that margin required for complete excision of the tumor. The margins refer to the most narrow margin required to adequately excise the tumor, based on the physician's judgment. The measurement of the tumor plus margin is made at the time of the excision. Appreciable vessel exploration and/or neuroplasty should be reported separately. Extensive undermining or other techniques to close a defect created by skin excision may require a complex repair which should be reported separately. Dissection or elevation of tissue planes to permit resection of the tumor is included in the excision.

Digital (ie, fingers and toes) subfascial tumors are defined as those tumors involving the tendons, tendon sheaths, or joints of the digit. Tumors which simply abut but do not breach the tendon, tendon sheath, or joint capsule are considered subcutaneous soft tissue tumors.

Radical resection of soft tissue tumors (including simple or intermediate repair) involves the resection of the tumor with wide margins of normal tissue. Appreciable vessel exploration and/or neuroplasty repair or reconstruction (eg, adjacent tissue transfer[s], flap[s]) should be reported separately. Extensive undermining or other techniques to close a defect created by skin excision may require a complex repair which should be reported separately. Dissection or elevation of tissue planes to permit resection of the tumor is included in the excision. Although these tumors may be confined to a specific layer (eg, subcutaneous, subfascial), radical resection may involve removal of tissue from one or more layers. Radical resection of soft tissue tumors is most commonly used for malignant tumors or very aggressive benign tumors. Code selection is based on size and location of the tumor. Code selection is determined by measuring the greatest diameter of the tumor plus that margin required for complete excision of the tumor. The margins refer to the most narrow margin required to adequately excise the tumor, based on the physician's judgment. The measurement of the tumor plus margin is made at the time of the excision. For radical resection of tumors of cutaneous origin, (eg, melanoma) see 11600-11646.

Radical resection of bone tumors (including simple or intermediate repair) involves the resection of the tumor with wide margins of normal tissue. Appreciable vessel exploration and/or neuroplasty and complex bone repair or reconstruction (eg, adjacent tissue transfer[s], flap[s]) should be reported separately. Extensive undermining or other techniques to close a defect created by skin excision may require a complex repair which should be reported separately. Dissection or elevation of tissue planes to permit resection of the tumor is included in the excision. It may require removal of the entire bone if tumor growth is extensive (eg, clavicle). Radical resection of bone tumors is usually performed for malignant tumors or very aggressive benign tumors. If surrounding soft tissue is removed during these procedures, the radical resection of soft tissue tumor codes should not be reported separately. Code selection is based solely on the location of the tumor, **not** on the size of the tumor or whether the tumor is benign or malignant, primary or metastatic. ◄

General

Incision

20000	Incision of soft tissue abscess (eg, secondary to osteomyelitis); superficial
20005	deep or complicated

Wound Exploration—Trauma (eg, Penetrating Gunshot, Stab Wound)

20100-20103 relate to wound(s) resulting from penetrating trauma. These codes describe surgical exploration and enlargement of the wound, extension of dissection (to determine penetration), debridement, removal of foreign body(s), ligation or coagulation of minor subcutaneous and/or muscular blood vessel(s), of the subcutaneous tissue, muscle fascia, and/or muscle, not requiring thoracotomy or laparotomy. If a repair is done to major structure(s) or major blood vessel(s) requiring thoracotomy or laparotomy, then those specific code(s) would supersede the use of codes 20100-20103. To report simple, intermediate, or complex repair of wound(s) that do not require enlargement of the wound, extension of dissection, etc, as stated above, use specific Repair code(s) in the **Integumentary System** section.

20100	Exploration of penetrating wound (separate procedure); neck
20101	chest
20102	abdomen/flank/back
20103	extremity

Excision

20150	Excision of epiphyseal bar, with or without autogenous soft tissue graft obtained through same fascial incision
	(For aspiration of bone marrow, use 38220)
20200	Biopsy, muscle; superficial
20205	deep
20206	Biopsy, muscle, percutaneous needle
	(If imaging guidance is performed, see 76942, 77012, 77021)
	(For fine needle aspiration, use 10021 or 10022)
	(For evaluation of fine needle aspirate, see 88172-88173)
	(For excision of muscle tumor, deep, see specific anatomic section)
20220	Biopsy, bone, trocar, or needle; superficial (eg, ilium, sternum, spinous process, ribs)
20225	deep (eg, vertebral body, femur)
	(For bone marrow biopsy, use 38221)
	(For radiologic supervision and interpretation, see 77002, 77012, 77021)
20240	Biopsy, bone, open; superficial (eg, ilium, sternum, spinous process, ribs, trochanter of femur)
20245	deep (eg, humerus, ischium, femur)
20250	Biopsy, vertebral body, open; thoracic

Surgery: Musculoskeletal System

20251   lumbar or cervical

(For sequestrectomy, osteomyelitis or drainage of bone abscess, see anatomical area)

Introduction or Removal

(For injection procedure for arthrography, see anatomical area)

20500   Injection of sinus tract; therapeutic (separate procedure)

20501   diagnostic (sinogram)

(For radiological supervision and interpretation, use 76080)

(For contrast injection[s] and radiological assessment of gastrostomy, duodenostomy, jejunostomy, gastro-jejunostomy, or cecostomy [or other colonic] tube including fluoroscopic imaging guidance, use 49465)

20520   Removal of foreign body in muscle or tendon sheath; simple

20525   deep or complicated

20526   Injection, therapeutic (eg, local anesthetic, corticosteroid), carpal tunnel

20550   Injection(s); single tendon sheath, or ligament, aponeurosis (eg, plantar "fascia")

(For injection of Morton's neuroma, see 64455, 64632)

20551   single tendon origin/insertion

20552   Injection(s); single or multiple trigger point(s), 1 or 2 muscle(s)

20553   single or multiple trigger point(s), 3 or more muscle(s)

(If imaging guidance is performed, see 76942, 77002, 77021)

20555   Placement of needles or catheters into muscle and/or soft tissue for subsequent interstitial radioelement application (at the time of or subsequent to the procedure)

(For placement of devices into the breast for interstitial radioelement application, see 19296-19298)

(For placement of needles, catheters, or devices into muscle or soft tissue of the head and neck, for interstitial radioelement application, use 41019)

(For placement of needles or catheters for interstitial radioelement application into prostate, use 55875)

(For placement of needles or catheters into the pelvic organs or genitalia [except prostate] for interstitial radioelement application, use 55920)

▶(For interstitial radioelement application, see 77776-77778, 77785-77787)◀

(For imaging guidance, see 76942, 77002, 77012, 77021)

20600   Arthrocentesis, aspiration and/or injection; small joint or bursa (eg, fingers, toes)

20605   intermediate joint or bursa (eg, temporomandibular, acromioclavicular, wrist, elbow or ankle, olecranon bursa)

20610   major joint or bursa (eg, shoulder, hip, knee joint, subacromial bursa)

(If imaging guidance is performed, see 76942, 77002, 77012, 77021)

20612   Aspiration and/or injection of ganglion cyst(s) any location

(To report multiple ganglion cyst aspirations/injections, use 20612 and append modifier 59)

20615   Aspiration and injection for treatment of bone cyst

20650   Insertion of wire or pin with application of skeletal traction, including removal (separate procedure)

20660   Application of cranial tongs, caliper, or stereotactic frame, including removal (separate procedure)

20661   Application of halo, including removal; cranial

20662   pelvic

20663   femoral

20664   Application of halo, including removal, cranial, 6 or more pins placed, for thin skull osteology (eg, pediatric patients, hydrocephalus, osteogenesis imperfecta), requiring general anesthesia

20665   Removal of tongs or halo applied by another physician

20670   Removal of implant; superficial (eg, buried wire, pin or rod) (separate procedure)

20680   deep (eg, buried wire, pin, screw, metal band, nail, rod or plate)

20690   Application of a uniplane (pins or wires in 1 plane), unilateral, external fixation system

20692   Application of a multiplane (pins or wires in more than 1 plane), unilateral, external fixation system (eg, Ilizarov, Monticelli type)

20693   Adjustment or revision of external fixation system requiring anesthesia (eg, new pin[s] or wire[s] and/or new ring[s] or bar[s])

20694   Removal, under anesthesia, of external fixation system

20696   Application of multiplane (pins or wires in more than 1 plane), unilateral, external fixation with stereotactic computer-assisted adjustment (eg, spatial frame), including imaging; initial and subsequent alignment(s), assessment(s), and computation(s) of adjustment schedule(s)

(Do not report 20696 in conjunction with 20692, 20697)

⊘ **20697**   exchange (ie, removal and replacement) of strut, each

(Do not report 20697 in conjunction with 20692, 20696)

Surgery: Musculoskeletal System

Replantation

20802   Replantation, arm (includes surgical neck of humerus through elbow joint), complete amputation

(To report replantation of incomplete arm amputation, see specific code[s] for repair of bone[s], ligament[s], tendon[s], nerve[s], or blood vessel[s] with modifier 52)

20805   Replantation, forearm (includes radius and ulna to radial carpal joint), complete amputation

(To report replantation of incomplete forearm amputation, see specific code[s] for repair of bone[s], ligament[s], tendon[s], nerve[s], or blood vessel[s] with modifier 52)

20808   Replantation, hand (includes hand through metacarpophalangeal joints), complete amputation

(To report replantation of incomplete hand amputation, see specific code[s] for repair of bone[s], ligament[s], tendon[s], nerve[s], or blood vessel[s] with modifier 52)

20816   Replantation, digit, excluding thumb (includes metacarpophalangeal joint to insertion of flexor sublimis tendon), complete amputation

(To report replantation of incomplete digit amputation, excluding thumb, see specific code[s] for repair of bone[s], ligament[s], tendon[s], nerve[s], or blood vessel[s] with modifier 52)

20822   Replantation, digit, excluding thumb (includes distal tip to sublimis tendon insertion), complete amputation

(To report replantation of incomplete digit amputation, excluding thumb, see specific code[s] for repair of bone[s], ligament[s], tendon[s], nerve[s], or blood vessel[s] with modifier 52)

20824   Replantation, thumb (includes carpometacarpal joint to MP joint), complete amputation

(To report replantation of incomplete thumb amputation, see specific code[s] for repair of bone[s], ligament[s], tendon[s], nerve[s], or blood vessel[s] with modifier 52)

20827   Replantation, thumb (includes distal tip to MP joint), complete amputation

(To report replantation of incomplete thumb amputation, see specific code[s] for repair of bone[s], ligament[s], tendon[s], nerve[s], or blood vessel[s] with modifier 52)

(To report replantation of complete leg amputation, see specific code[s] for repair of bone[s], ligament[s], tendon[s], nerve[s], or blood vessel[s] with modifier 52)

(To report replantation of incomplete leg amputation, see specific code[s] for repair of bone[s], ligament[s], tendon[s], nerve[s], or blood vessel[s] with modifier 52)

20838   Replantation, foot, complete amputation

(To report replantation of incomplete foot amputation, see specific code[s] for repair of bone[s], ligament[s], tendon[s], nerve[s], or blood vessel[s] with modifier 52)

Grafts (or Implants)

Codes for obtaining autogenous bone, cartilage, tendon, fascia lata grafts, or other tissues through separate skin/fascial incisions should be reported separately unless the code descriptor references the harvesting of the graft or implant (eg, includes obtaining graft).

Do not append modifier 62 to bone graft codes 20900-20938.

(For spinal surgery bone graft[s] see codes 20930-20938)

20900   Bone graft, any donor area; minor or small (eg, dowel or button)

20902   major or large

20910   Cartilage graft; costochondral

20912   nasal septum

(For ear cartilage, use 21235)

20920   Fascia lata graft; by stripper

20922   by incision and area exposure, complex or sheet

20924   Tendon graft, from a distance (eg, palmaris, toe extensor, plantaris)

20926   Tissue grafts, other (eg, paratenon, fat, dermis)

+ 20930   Allograft for spine surgery only; morselized (List separately in addition to code for primary procedure)

(Use 20930 in conjunction with 22319, 22532, 22533, 22548-22558, 22590-22612, 22630, 22800-22812, 0195T, 0196T)

+ 20931   structural (List separately in addition to code for primary procedure)

(Use 20931 in conjunction with 22319, 22532-22533, 22548-22558, 22590-22612, 22630, 22800-22812)

+ 20936   Autograft for spine surgery only (includes harvesting the graft); local (eg, ribs, spinous process, or laminar fragments) obtained from same incision (List separately in addition to code for primary procedure)

(Use 20936 in conjunction with 22319, 22532, 22533, 22548-22558, 22590-22612, 22630, 22800-22812, 0195T, 0196T)

+ 20937   morselized (through separate skin or fascial incision) (List separately in addition to code for primary procedure)

(Use 20937 in conjunction with 22319, 22532, 22533, 22548-22558, 22590-22612, 22630, 22800-22812, 0195T, 0196T)

+ 20938   structural, bicortical or tricortical (through separate skin or fascial incision) (List separately in addition to code for primary procedure)

(Use 20938 in conjunction with 22319, 22532, 22533, 22548-22558, 22590-22612, 22630, 22800-22812)

(For needle aspiration of bone marrow for the purpose of bone grafting, use 38220)

Other Procedures

20950 Monitoring of interstitial fluid pressure (includes insertion of device, eg, wick catheter technique, needle manometer technique) in detection of muscle compartment syndrome

20955 Bone graft with microvascular anastomosis; fibula

20956   iliac crest

20957   metatarsal

20962   other than fibula, iliac crest, or metatarsal

(Do not report code 69990 in addition to codes 20955-20962)

20969 Free osteocutaneous flap with microvascular anastomosis; other than iliac crest, metatarsal, or great toe

20970   iliac crest

20972   metatarsal

20973   great toe with web space

(Do not report code 69990 in addition to codes 20969-20973)

(For great toe, wrap-around procedure, use 26551)

⊘ **20974** Electrical stimulation to aid bone healing; noninvasive (nonoperative)

⊘ **20975**   invasive (operative)

20979 Low intensity ultrasound stimulation to aid bone healing, noninvasive (nonoperative)

⊙ **20982** Ablation, bone tumor(s) (eg, osteoid osteoma, metastasis) radiofrequency, percutaneous, including computed tomographic guidance

(Do not report 20982 in conjunction with 77013)

+ **20985** Computer-assisted surgical navigational procedure for musculoskeletal procedures, image-less (List separately in addition to code for primary procedure)

(Do not report 20985 in conjunction with 61795)

(20986, 20987 have been deleted)

(For computer-assisted navigational procedures with image guidance based on pre-operative and intraoperatively obtained images, see 0054T, 0055T)

20999 Unlisted procedure, musculoskeletal system, general

Head

Skull, facial bones, and temporomandibular joint.

Incision

(For drainage of superficial abscess and hematoma, use 20000)

(For removal of embedded foreign body from dentoalveolar structure, see 41805, 41806)

21010 Arthrotomy, temporomandibular joint

(To report bilateral procedure, report 21010 with modifier 50)

Excision

● **21011** Excision, tumor, soft tissue of face or scalp, subcutaneous; less than 2 cm

● **21012**   2 cm or greater

● **21013** Excision, tumor, soft tissue of face and scalp, subfascial (eg, subgaleal, intramuscular); less than 2 cm

● **21014**   2 cm or greater

▲ **21015** Radical resection of tumor (eg, malignant neoplasm), soft tissue of face or scalp; less than 2 cm

(To report excision of skull tumor for osteomyelitis, use 61501)

● **21016**   2 cm or greater

21025 Excision of bone (eg, for osteomyelitis or bone abscess); mandible

21026   facial bone(s)

21029 Removal by contouring of benign tumor of facial bone (eg, fibrous dysplasia)

21030 Excision of benign tumor or cyst of maxilla or zygoma by enucleation and curettage

21031 Excision of torus mandibularis

21032 Excision of maxillary torus palatinus

21034 Excision of malignant tumor of maxilla or zygoma

21040 Excision of benign tumor or cyst of mandible, by enucleation and/or curettage

(For enucleation and/or curettage of benign cysts or tumors of mandible not requiring osteotomy, use 21040)

(For excision of benign tumor or cyst of mandible requiring osteotomy, see 21046-21047)

21044 Excision of malignant tumor of mandible;

21045   radical resection

(For bone graft, use 21215)

21046 Excision of benign tumor or cyst of mandible; requiring intra-oral osteotomy (eg, locally aggressive or destructive lesion(s))

21047   requiring extra-oral osteotomy and partial mandibulectomy (eg, locally aggressive or destructive lesion(s))

21048 Excision of benign tumor or cyst of maxilla; requiring intra-oral osteotomy (eg, locally aggressive or destructive lesion(s))

21049   requiring extra-oral osteotomy and partial maxillectomy (eg, locally aggressive or destructive lesion(s))

21050   Condylectomy, temporomandibular joint (separate procedure)

(For bilateral procedures, report 21050 with modifier 50)

21060   Meniscectomy, partial or complete, temporomandibular joint (separate procedure)

(For bilateral procedures, report 21060 with modifier 50)

21070   Coronoidectomy (separate procedure)

(For bilateral procedures, report 21070 with modifier 50)

Manipulation

21073   Manipulation of temporomandibular joint(s) (TMJ), therapeutic, requiring an anesthesia service (ie, general or monitored anesthesia care)

(For TMJ manipulation without an anesthesia service [ie, general or monitored anesthesia care], see 97140, 98925-98929, 98943)

(For closed treatment of temporomandibular dislocation, see 21480, 21485)

Head Prosthesis

Codes 21076-21089 describe professional services for the rehabilitation of patients with oral, facial, or other anatomical deficiencies by means of prostheses such as an artificial eye, ear, or nose or intraoral obturator to close a cleft. Codes 21076-21089 should only be used when the physician actually designs and prepares the prosthesis (ie, not prepared by an outside laboratory).

(For application or removal of caliper or tongs, see 20660, 20665)

21076   Impression and custom preparation; surgical obturator prosthesis

21077   orbital prosthesis

21079   interim obturator prosthesis

21080   definitive obturator prosthesis

21081   mandibular resection prosthesis

21082   palatal augmentation prosthesis

21083   palatal lift prosthesis

21084   speech aid prosthesis

21085   oral surgical splint

21086   auricular prosthesis

21087   nasal prosthesis

21088   facial prosthesis

Other Procedures

21089   Unlisted maxillofacial prosthetic procedure

Introduction or Removal

21100   Application of halo type appliance for maxillofacial fixation, includes removal (separate procedure)

21110   Application of interdental fixation device for conditions other than fracture or dislocation, includes removal

(For removal of interdental fixation by another physician, see 20670-20680)

21116   Injection procedure for temporomandibular joint arthrography

(For radiological supervision and interpretation, use 70332. Do not report 77002 in conjunction with 70332)

Repair, Revision, and/or Reconstruction

(For cranioplasty, see 21179, 21180 and 62116, 62120, 62140-62147)

21120   Genioplasty; augmentation (autograft, allograft, prosthetic material)

21121   sliding osteotomy, single piece

21122   sliding osteotomies, 2 or more osteotomies (eg, wedge excision or bone wedge reversal for asymmetrical chin)

21123   sliding, augmentation with interpositional bone grafts (includes obtaining autografts)

21125   Augmentation, mandibular body or angle; prosthetic material

21127   with bone graft, onlay or interpositional (includes obtaining autograft)

21137   Reduction forehead; contouring only

21138   contouring and application of prosthetic material or bone graft (includes obtaining autograft)

21139   contouring and setback of anterior frontal sinus wall

21141   Reconstruction midface, LeFort I; single piece, segment movement in any direction (eg, for Long Face Syndrome), without bone graft

21142   2 pieces, segment movement in any direction, without bone graft

21143   3 or more pieces, segment movement in any direction, without bone graft

21145   single piece, segment movement in any direction, requiring bone grafts (includes obtaining autografts)

21146   2 pieces, segment movement in any direction, requiring bone grafts (includes obtaining autografts) (eg, ungrafted unilateral alveolar cleft)

21147   3 or more pieces, segment movement in any direction, requiring bone grafts (includes obtaining autografts) (eg, ungrafted bilateral alveolar cleft or multiple osteotomies)

21150   Reconstruction midface, LeFort II; anterior intrusion (eg, Treacher-Collins Syndrome)

21151   any direction, requiring bone grafts (includes obtaining autografts)

21154   Reconstruction midface, LeFort III (extracranial), any type, requiring bone grafts (includes obtaining autografts); without LeFort I

21155   with LeFort I

21159   Reconstruction midface, LeFort III (extra and intracranial) with forehead advancement (eg, mono bloc), requiring bone grafts (includes obtaining autografts); without LeFort I

21160   with LeFort I

21172   Reconstruction superior-lateral orbital rim and lower forehead, advancement or alteration, with or without grafts (includes obtaining autografts)

(For frontal or parietal craniotomy performed for craniosynostosis, use 61556)

21175   Reconstruction, bifrontal, superior-lateral orbital rims and lower forehead, advancement or alteration (eg, plagiocephaly, trigonocephaly, brachycephaly), with or without grafts (includes obtaining autografts)

(For bifrontal craniotomy performed for craniosynostosis, use 61557)

21179   Reconstruction, entire or majority of forehead and/or supraorbital rims; with grafts (allograft or prosthetic material)

21180   with autograft (includes obtaining grafts)

(For extensive craniectomy for multiple suture craniosynostosis, use only 61558 or 61559)

21181   Reconstruction by contouring of benign tumor of cranial bones (eg, fibrous dysplasia), extracranial

21182   Reconstruction of orbital walls, rims, forehead, nasoethmoid complex following intra- and extracranial excision of benign tumor of cranial bone (eg, fibrous dysplasia), with multiple autografts (includes obtaining grafts); total area of bone grafting less than 40 sq cm

21183   total area of bone grafting greater than 40 sq cm but less than 80 sq cm

21184   total area of bone grafting greater than 80 sq cm

(For excision of benign tumor of cranial bones, see 61563, 61564)

21188   Reconstruction midface, osteotomies (other than LeFort type) and bone grafts (includes obtaining autografts)

21193   Reconstruction of mandibular rami, horizontal, vertical, C, or L osteotomy; without bone graft

21194   with bone graft (includes obtaining graft)

21195   Reconstruction of mandibular rami and/or body, sagittal split; without internal rigid fixation

21196   with internal rigid fixation

21198   Osteotomy, mandible, segmental;

21199   with genioglossus advancement

(To report total osteotomy of the maxilla, see 21141-21160)

21206   Osteotomy, maxilla, segmental (eg, Wassmund or Schuchard)

21208   Osteoplasty, facial bones; augmentation (autograft, allograft, or prosthetic implant)

21209   reduction

21210   Graft, bone; nasal, maxillary or malar areas (includes obtaining graft)

(For cleft palate repair, see 42200-42225)

21215   mandible (includes obtaining graft)

21230   Graft; rib cartilage, autogenous, to face, chin, nose or ear (includes obtaining graft)

21235   ear cartilage, autogenous, to nose or ear (includes obtaining graft)

(To report graft augmentation of facial bones, use 21208)

21240   Arthroplasty, temporomandibular joint, with or without autograft (includes obtaining graft)

21242   Arthroplasty, temporomandibular joint, with allograft

21243   Arthroplasty, temporomandibular joint, with prosthetic joint replacement

21244   Reconstruction of mandible, extraoral, with transosteal bone plate (eg, mandibular staple bone plate)

21245   Reconstruction of mandible or maxilla, subperiosteal implant; partial

21246   complete

21247   Reconstruction of mandibular condyle with bone and cartilage autografts (includes obtaining grafts) (eg, for hemifacial microsomia)

21248   Reconstruction of mandible or maxilla, endosteal implant (eg, blade, cylinder); partial

21249   complete

(To report midface reconstruction, see 21141-21160)

21255   Reconstruction of zygomatic arch and glenoid fossa with bone and cartilage (includes obtaining autografts)

21256   Reconstruction of orbit with osteotomies (extracranial) and with bone grafts (includes obtaining autografts) (eg, micro-ophthalmia)

21260   Periorbital osteotomies for orbital hypertelorism, with bone grafts; extracranial approach

21261   combined intra- and extracranial approach

21263   with forehead advancement

21267   Orbital repositioning, periorbital osteotomies, unilateral, with bone grafts; extracranial approach

21268   combined intra- and extracranial approach

Surgery: Musculoskeletal System

21270   Malar augmentation, prosthetic material

(For malar augmentation with bone graft, use 21210)

21275   Secondary revision of orbitocraniofacial reconstruction

21280   Medial canthopexy (separate procedure)

(For medial canthoplasty, use 67950)

21282   Lateral canthopexy

21295   Reduction of masseter muscle and bone (eg, for treatment of benign masseteric hypertrophy); extraoral approach

21296   intraoral approach

Other Procedures

21299   Unlisted craniofacial and maxillofacial procedure

Fracture and/or Dislocation

(For operative repair of skull fracture, see 62000-62010)

(To report closed treatment of skull fracture, use the appropriate Evaluation and Management code)

21310   Closed treatment of nasal bone fracture without manipulation

21315   Closed treatment of nasal bone fracture; without stabilization

21320   with stabilization

21325   Open treatment of nasal fracture; uncomplicated

21330   complicated, with internal and/or external skeletal fixation

21335   with concomitant open treatment of fractured septum

21336   Open treatment of nasal septal fracture, with or without stabilization

21337   Closed treatment of nasal septal fracture, with or without stabilization

21338   Open treatment of nasoethmoid fracture; without external fixation

21339   with external fixation

21340   Percutaneous treatment of nasoethmoid complex fracture, with splint, wire or headcap fixation, including repair of canthal ligaments and/or the nasolacrimal apparatus

21343   Open treatment of depressed frontal sinus fracture

21344   Open treatment of complicated (eg, comminuted or involving posterior wall) frontal sinus fracture, via coronal or multiple approaches

21345   Closed treatment of nasomaxillary complex fracture (LeFort II type), with interdental wire fixation or fixation of denture or splint

21346   Open treatment of nasomaxillary complex fracture (LeFort II type); with wiring and/or local fixation

21347   requiring multiple open approaches

21348   with bone grafting (includes obtaining graft)

21355   Percutaneous treatment of fracture of malar area, including zygomatic arch and malar tripod, with manipulation

21356   Open treatment of depressed zygomatic arch fracture (eg, Gillies approach)

21360   Open treatment of depressed malar fracture, including zygomatic arch and malar tripod

21365   Open treatment of complicated (eg, comminuted or involving cranial nerve foramina) fracture(s) of malar area, including zygomatic arch and malar tripod; with internal fixation and multiple surgical approaches

21366   with bone grafting (includes obtaining graft)

21385   Open treatment of orbital floor blowout fracture; transantral approach (Caldwell-Luc type operation)

21386   periorbital approach

21387   combined approach

21390   periorbital approach, with alloplastic or other implant

21395   periorbital approach with bone graft (includes obtaining graft)

21400   Closed treatment of fracture of orbit, except blowout; without manipulation

21401   with manipulation

21406   Open treatment of fracture of orbit, except blowout; without implant

21407   with implant

21408   with bone grafting (includes obtaining graft)

21421   Closed treatment of palatal or maxillary fracture (LeFort I type), with interdental wire fixation or fixation of denture or splint

21422   Open treatment of palatal or maxillary fracture (LeFort I type);

21423   complicated (comminuted or involving cranial nerve foramina), multiple approaches

21431   Closed treatment of craniofacial separation (LeFort III type) using interdental wire fixation of denture or splint

21432   Open treatment of craniofacial separation (LeFort III type); with wiring and/or internal fixation

21433   complicated (eg, comminuted or involving cranial nerve foramina), multiple surgical approaches

21435   complicated, utilizing internal and/or external fixation techniques (eg, head cap, halo device, and/or intermaxillary fixation)

(For removal of internal or external fixation device, use 20670)

21436   complicated, multiple surgical approaches, internal fixation, with bone grafting (includes obtaining graft)

21440   Closed treatment of mandibular or maxillary alveolar ridge fracture (separate procedure)

21445   Open treatment of mandibular or maxillary alveolar ridge fracture (separate procedure)

21450   Closed treatment of mandibular fracture; without manipulation

21451   with manipulation

21452   Percutaneous treatment of mandibular fracture, with external fixation

21453   Closed treatment of mandibular fracture with interdental fixation

21454   Open treatment of mandibular fracture with external fixation

21461   Open treatment of mandibular fracture; without interdental fixation

21462   with interdental fixation

21465   Open treatment of mandibular condylar fracture

21470   Open treatment of complicated mandibular fracture by multiple surgical approaches including internal fixation, interdental fixation, and/or wiring of dentures or splints

21480   Closed treatment of temporomandibular dislocation; initial or subsequent

21485   complicated (eg, recurrent requiring intermaxillary fixation or splinting), initial or subsequent

21490   Open treatment of temporomandibular dislocation

(For interdental wire fixation, use 21497)

21495   Open treatment of hyoid fracture

(For laryngoplasty with open reduction of fracture, use 31584)

(To report treatment of closed fracture of larynx, use the applicable Evaluation and Management codes)

21497   Interdental wiring, for condition other than fracture

Other Procedures

21499   Unlisted musculoskeletal procedure, head

(For unlisted craniofacial or maxillofacial procedure, use 21299)

Neck (Soft Tissues) and Thorax

(For cervical spine and back, see 21920 et seq)

(For injection of fracture site or trigger point, use 20550)

Incision

(For incision and drainage of abscess or hematoma, superficial, see 10060, 10140)

21501   Incision and drainage, deep abscess or hematoma, soft tissues of neck or thorax;

(For posterior spine subfascial incision and drainage, see 22010-22015)

21502   with partial rib ostectomy

21510   Incision, deep, with opening of bone cortex (eg, for osteomyelitis or bone abscess), thorax

Excision

(For bone biopsy, see 20220-20251)

21550   Biopsy, soft tissue of neck or thorax

(For needle biopsy of soft tissue, use 20206)

21552   ►Code is out of numerical sequence. See 21550-21632◄

21554   ►Code is out of numerical sequence. See 21550-21632◄

▲ **21555**   Excision, tumor, soft tissue of neck or anterior thorax, subcutaneous; less than 3 cm

#● **21552**   3 cm or greater

▲ **21556**   Excision, tumor, soft tissue of neck or anterior thorax, subfascial (eg, intramuscular); less than 5 cm

#● **21554**   5 cm or greater

▲ **21557**   Radical resection of tumor (eg, malignant neoplasm), soft tissue of neck or anterior thorax; less than 5 cm

● **21558**   5 cm or greater

21600   Excision of rib, partial

(For radical resection of chest wall and rib cage for tumor, use 19260)

(For radical debridement of chest wall and rib cage for injury, see 11040-11044)

21610   Costotransversectomy (separate procedure)

21615   Excision first and/or cervical rib;

21616   with sympathectomy

21620   Ostectomy of sternum, partial

21627   Sternal debridement

(For debridement and closure, use 21750)

21630   Radical resection of sternum;

21632   with mediastinal lymphadenectomy

Repair, Revision, and/or Reconstruction

(For superficial wound, see **Integumentary System** section under Repair—Simple)

21685   Hyoid myotomy and suspension

21700 Division of scalenus anticus; without resection of cervical rib

21705 with resection of cervical rib

21720 Division of sternocleidomastoid for torticollis, open operation; without cast application

(For transection of spinal accessory and cervical nerves, see 63191, 64722)

21725 with cast application

21740 Reconstructive repair of pectus excavatum or carinatum; open

21742 minimally invasive approach (Nuss procedure), without thoracoscopy

21743 minimally invasive approach (Nuss procedure), with thoracoscopy

21750 Closure of median sternotomy separation with or without debridement (separate procedure)

Fracture and/or Dislocation

21800 Closed treatment of rib fracture, uncomplicated, each

21805 Open treatment of rib fracture without fixation, each

21810 Treatment of rib fracture requiring external fixation (flail chest)

21820 Closed treatment of sternum fracture

21825 Open treatment of sternum fracture with or without skeletal fixation

(For sternoclavicular dislocation, see 23520-23532)

Other Procedures

21899 Unlisted procedure, neck or thorax

Back and Flank

Excision

21920 Biopsy, soft tissue of back or flank; superficial

21925 deep

(For needle biopsy of soft tissue, use 20206)

▲ **21930** Excision, tumor, soft tissue of back or flank, subcutaneous; less than 3 cm

● **21931** 3 cm or greater

● **21932** Excision, tumor, soft tissue of back or flank, subfascial (eg, intramuscular); less than 5 cm

● **21933** 5 cm or greater

▲ **21935** Radical resection of tumor (eg, malignant neoplasm), soft tissue of back or flank; less than 5 cm

● **21936** 5 cm or greater

Spine (Vertebral Column)

Cervical, thoracic, and lumbar spine.

Within the spine section, bone grafting procedures are reported separately and in addition to arthrodesis. For bone grafts in other Musculoskeletal sections, see specific code(s) descriptor(s) and/or accompanying guidelines.

To report bone grafts performed after arthrodesis, see 20930-20938. Do not append modifier 62 to bone graft codes 20900-20938.

Example:

Posterior arthrodesis of L5-S1 for degenerative disc disease utilizing morselized autogenous iliac bone graft harvested through a separate fascial incision.

Report as 22612 and 20937.

Within the spine section, instrumentation is reported separately and in addition to arthrodesis. To report instrumentation procedures performed with definitive vertebral procedure(s), see 22840-22855. Instrumentation procedure codes 22840-22848 and 22851 are reported in addition to the definitive procedure(s). Modifier 62 may not be appended to the definitive or add-on spinal instrumentation procedure code(s) 22840-22848 and 22850-22852.

Example:

Posterior arthrodesis of L4-S1, utilizing morselized autogenous iliac bone graft harvested through separate fascial incision, and pedicle screw fixation.

Report as 22612, 22614, 22842, and 20937.

Vertebral procedures are sometimes followed by arthrodesis and in addition may include bone grafts and instrumentation.

When arthrodesis is performed in addition to another procedure, the arthrodesis should be reported in addition to the original procedure with modifier 51 (multiple procedures). Examples are after osteotomy, fracture care, vertebral corpectomy, and laminectomy. Bone grafts and instrumentation are never performed without arthrodesis.

Example:

Treatment of a burst fracture of L2 by corpectomy followed by arthrodesis of L1-L3, utilizing anterior instrumentation L1-L3 and structural allograft.

Report as 63090, 22558-51, 22585, 22845, and 20931.

When two surgeons work together as primary surgeons performing distinct part(s) of a single reportable procedure, each surgeon should report his/her distinct operative work by appending modifier 62 to the single definitive procedure code. If additional procedure(s) (including add-on procedure[s]) are performed during the same surgical session, separate code(s) may be reported by each co-surgeon, with modifier 62 appended (see Appendix A).

Example:

A 42-year-old male with a history of posttraumatic degenerative disc disease at L3-4 and L4-5 (internal disc disruption) underwent surgical repair. Surgeon A performed an anterior exposure of the spine with mobilization of the great vessels. Surgeon B performed anterior (minimal) discectomy and fusion at L3-4 and L4-5 using anterior interbody technique.

Report surgeon A: 22558 append modifier 62, 22585 append modifier 62
Report surgeon B: 22558 append modifier 62, 22585 append modifier 62, 20931

(Do not append modifier 62 to bone graft code 20931)

(For injection procedure for myelography, use 62284)

(For injection procedure for discography, see 62290, 62291)

(For injection procedure, chemonucleolysis, single or multiple levels, use 62292)

►(For injection procedure for facet joints, see 64490-64495, 64622-64627)◄

(For needle or trocar biopsy, see 20220-20225)

Incision

22010   Incision and drainage, open, of deep abscess (subfascial), posterior spine; cervical, thoracic, or cervicothoracic

22015   lumbar, sacral, or lumbosacral

(Do not report 22015 in conjunction with 22010)

(Do not report 22015 in conjunction with instrumentation removal, 10180, 22850, 22852)

(For incision and drainage of abscess or hematoma, superficial, see 10060, 10140)

Excision

For the following codes, when two surgeons work together as primary surgeons performing distinct part(s) of partial vertebral body excision, each surgeon should report his/her distinct operative work by appending modifier 62 to the procedure code. In this situation, modifier 62 may be appended to the procedure code(s) 22100-22102, 22110-22114 and, as appropriate, to the associated additional vertebral segment add-on code(s) 22103, 22116 as long as both surgeons continue to work together as primary surgeons.

(For bone biopsy, see 20220-20251)

(To report soft tissue biopsy of back or flank, see 21920-21925)

(For needle biopsy of soft tissue, use 20206)

(To report excision of soft tissue tumor of back or flank, use 21930)

22100   Partial excision of posterior vertebral component (eg, spinous process, lamina or facet) for intrinsic bony lesion, single vertebral segment; cervical

22101   thoracic

22102   lumbar

(For insertion of posterior spinous process distraction devices, see 0171T, 0172T)

+ 22103   each additional segment (List separately in addition to code for primary procedure)

(Use 22103 in conjunction with 22100, 22101, 22102)

22110   Partial excision of vertebral body, for intrinsic bony lesion, without decompression of spinal cord or nerve root(s), single vertebral segment; cervical

22112   thoracic

22114   lumbar

+ 22116   each additional vertebral segment (List separately in addition to code for primary procedure)

(Use 22116 in conjunction with 22110, 22112, 22114)

(For complete or near complete resection of vertebral body, see vertebral corpectomy, 63081-63091)

(For spinal reconstruction with bone graft (autograft, allograft) and/or methylmethacrylate of cervical vertebral body, use 63081 and 22554 and 20931 or 20938)

(For spinal reconstruction with bone graft (autograft, allograft) and/or methylmethacrylate of thoracic vertebral body, use 63085 or 63087 and 22556 and 20931 or 20938)

(For spinal reconstruction with bone graft (autograft, allograft) and/or methylmethacrylate of lumbar vertebral body, use 63087 or 63090 and 22558 and 20931 or 20938)

(For spinal reconstruction following vertebral body resection, use 63082 or 63086 or 63088 or 63091, and 22585)

(For harvest of bone autograft for vertebral reconstruction, see 20931 or 20938)

(For cervical spinal reconstruction with prosthetic replacement of resected vertebral bodies, see codes 63081 and 22554 and 20931 or 20938 and 22851)

(For thoracic spinal reconstruction with prosthetic replacement of resected vertebral bodies, see codes 63085 or 63087 and 22556 and 20931 or 20938 and 22851)

(For lumbar spinal reconstruction with prosthetic replacement of resected vertebral bodies, see codes 63087 or 63090 and 22558, and 20931 or 20938 and 22851)

(For osteotomy of spine, see 22210-22226)

Osteotomy

To report arthrodesis, see codes 22590-22632. (Report in addition to code[s] for the definitive procedure with modifier 51.)

To report instrumentation procedures, see 22840-22855. (Report in addition to code[s] for the definitive procedure[s].) Do not append modifier 62 to spinal instrumentation codes 22840-22848 and 22850-22852.

To report bone graft procedures, see 20930-20938. (Report in addition to code[s] for the definitive procedure[s].) Do not append modifier 62 to bone graft codes 20900-20938.

For the following codes, when two surgeons work together as primary surgeons performing distinct part(s) of an anterior spine osteotomy, each surgeon should report his/her distinct operative work by appending modifier 62 to the procedure code. In this situation, modifier 62 may be appended to the procedure code(s) 22210-22214, 22220-22224 and, as appropriate, to associated additional segment add-on code(s) 22216, 22226 as long as both surgeons continue to work together as primary surgeons.

Spinal osteotomy procedures are reported when a portion(s) of the vertebral segment(s) is cut and removed in preparation for re-aligning the spine as part of a spinal deformity correction. For excision of an intrinsic lesion of the vertebra without deformity correction, see 22100-22116. For decompression of the spinal cord and/or nerve roots, see 63001-63308.

The three columns are defined as anterior (anterior two-thirds of the vertebral body), middle (posterior third of the vertebral body and the pedicle), and posterior (articular facets, lamina, and spinous process).

22206 Osteotomy of spine, posterior or posterolateral approach, 3 columns, 1 vertebral segment (eg, pedicle/vertebral body subtraction); thoracic

(Do not report 22206 in conjunction with 22207)

22207 lumbar

(Do not report 22207 in conjunction with 22206)

+ 22208 each additional vertebral segment (List separately in addition to code for primary procedure)

(Use 22208 in conjunction with 22206, 22207)

(Do not report 22206, 22207, 22208 in conjunction with 22210-22226, 22830, 63001-63048, 63055-63066, 63075-63091, 63101-63103, when performed at the same level)

22210 Osteotomy of spine, posterior or posterolateral approach, 1 vertebral segment; cervical

22212 thoracic

22214 lumbar

+ 22216 each additional vertebral segment (List separately in addition to primary procedure)

(Use 22216 in conjunction with 22210, 22212, 22214)

22220 Osteotomy of spine, including discectomy, anterior approach, single vertebral segment; cervical

22222 thoracic

22224 lumbar

+ 22226 each additional vertebral segment (List separately in addition to code for primary procedure)

(Use 22226 in conjunction with 22220, 22222, 22224)

(For vertebral corpectomy, see 63081-63091)

Fracture and/or Dislocation

To report arthrodesis, see codes 22590-22632. (Report in addition to code[s] for the definitive procedure with modifier 51.)

To report instrumentation procedures, see 22840-22855. (Report in addition to code[s] for the definitive procedure[s].) Do not append modifier 62 to spinal instrumentation codes 22840-22848 and 22850-22852.

To report bone graft procedures, see 20930-20938. (Report in addition to code[s] for the definitive procedure[s].) Do not append modifier 62 to bone graft codes 20900-20938.

For the following codes, when two surgeons work together as primary surgeons performing distinct part(s) of open fracture and/or dislocation procedure(s), each surgeon should report his/her distinct operative work by appending modifier 62 to the procedure code. In this situation, modifier 62 may be appended to the procedure code(s) 22318-22327 and, as appropriate, the associated additional fracture vertebrae or dislocated segment add-on code 22328 as long as both surgeons continue to work together as primary surgeons.

22305 Closed treatment of vertebral process fracture(s)

22310 Closed treatment of vertebral body fracture(s), without manipulation, requiring and including casting or bracing

22315 Closed treatment of vertebral fracture(s) and/or dislocation(s) requiring casting or bracing, with and including casting and/or bracing, with or without anesthesia, by manipulation or traction

(For spinal subluxation, use 97140)

22318 Open treatment and/or reduction of odontoid fracture(s) and or dislocation(s) (including os odontoideum), anterior approach, including placement of internal fixation; without grafting

Surgery: Musculoskeletal System

22319   with grafting

22325   Open treatment and/or reduction of vertebral fracture(s) and/or dislocation(s), posterior approach, 1 fractured vertebra or dislocated segment; lumbar

22326   cervical

22327   thoracic

+ 22328   each additional fractured vertebra or dislocated segment (List separately in addition to code for primary procedure)

(Use 22328 in conjunction with 22325-22327)

(For treatment of vertebral fracture by the anterior approach, see corpectomy 63081-63091, and appropriate arthrodesis, bone graft and instrument codes)

(For decompression of spine following fracture, see 63001-63091; for arthrodesis of spine following fracture, see 22548-22632)

Manipulation

(For spinal manipulation without anesthesia, use 97140)

22505   Manipulation of spine requiring anesthesia, any region

Vertebral Body, Embolization or Injection

⊙▲ **22520**   Percutaneous vertebroplasty, 1 vertebral body, unilateral or bilateral injection; thoracic

⊙▲ **22521**   lumbar

+ 22522   each additional thoracic or lumbar vertebral body (List separately in addition to code for primary procedure)

(Use 22522 in conjunction with 22520, 22521 as appropriate)

(For radiological supervision and interpretation, see 72291, 72292)

22523   Percutaneous vertebral augmentation, including cavity creation (fracture reduction and bone biopsy included when performed) using mechanical device, 1 vertebral body, unilateral or bilateral cannulation (eg, kyphoplasty); thoracic

22524   lumbar

+ 22525   each additional thoracic or lumbar vertebral body (List separately in addition to code for primary procedure)

(Do not report 22525 in conjunction with 20225 when performed at the same level as 22523-22525)

(Use 22525 in conjunction with 22523, 22524)

(For radiological supervision and interpretation, see 72291, 72292)

⊙ **22526**   Percutaneous intradiscal electrothermal annuloplasty, unilateral or bilateral including fluoroscopic guidance; single level

⊙**+ 22527**   1 or more additional levels (List separately in addition to code for primary procedure)

(Do not report codes 22526, 22527 in conjunction with 77002, 77003)

►(For percutaneous intradiscal annuloplasty using method other than electrothermal, use 22899)◄

Arthrodesis

Arthrodesis may be performed in the absence of other procedures and therefore when it is combined with another definitive procedure (eg, osteotomy, fracture care, vertebral corpectomy or laminectomy), modifier 51 is appropriate. However, arthrodesis codes 22585, 22614, and 22632 are considered add-on procedure codes and should not be used with modifier 51.

To report instrumentation procedures, see 22840-22855. (Codes 22840-22848, 22851 are reported in conjunction with code[s] for the definitive procedure[s]. When instrumentation reinsertion or removal is reported in conjunction with other definitive procedures including arthrodesis, decompression, and exploration of fusion, append modifier 51 to 22849, 22850, 22852, and 22855.) To report exploration of fusion, use 22830. (When exploration is reported in conjunction with other definitive procedures, including arthrodesis and decompression, append modifier 51 to 22830.) Do not append modifier 62 to spinal instrumentation codes 22840-22848 and 22850-22852.

To report bone graft procedures, see 20930-20938. (Report in addition to code[s] for the definitive procedure[s].) Do not append modifier 62 to bone graft codes 20900-20938.

Lateral Extracavitary Approach Technique

22532   Arthrodesis, lateral extracavitary technique, including minimal discectomy to prepare interspace (other than for decompression); thoracic

22533   lumbar

+ 22534   thoracic or lumbar, each additional vertebral segment (List separately in addition to code for primary procedure)

(Use 22534 in conjunction with 22532 and 22533)

Anterior or Anterolateral Approach Technique

Procedure codes 22554-22558 are for SINGLE interspace; for additional interspaces, use 22585. A vertebral interspace is the non-bony compartment between two adjacent vertebral bodies, which contains the intervertebral disc, and includes the nucleus pulposus, annulus fibrosus, and two cartilagenous endplates.

For the following codes, when two surgeons work together as primary surgeons performing distinct part(s) of an anterior interbody arthrodesis, each surgeon should report his/her distinct operative work by appending modifier 62 to the procedure code. In this situation, modifier 62 may be appended to the procedure code(s) 22548-22558 and, as appropriate, to the associated additional interspace add-on code 22585 as long as both surgeons continue to work together as primary surgeons.

22548 Arthrodesis, anterior transoral or extraoral technique, clivus-C1-C2 (atlas-axis), with or without excision of odontoid process

(For intervertebral disc excision by laminotomy or laminectomy, see 63020-63042)

22554 Arthrodesis, anterior interbody technique, including minimal discectomy to prepare interspace (other than for decompression); cervical below C2

22556 thoracic

22558 lumbar

+ 22585 each additional interspace (List separately in addition to code for primary procedure)

(Use 22585 in conjunction with 22554, 22556, 22558)

Posterior, Posterolateral or Lateral Transverse Process Technique

To report instrumentation procedures, see 22840-22855. (Report in addition to code[s] for the definitive procedure[s].) Do not append modifier 62 to spinal instrumentation codes 22840-22848 and 22850-22852.

To report bone graft procedures, see 20930-20938. (Report in addition to code[s] for the definitive procedure[s].) Do not append modifier 62 to bone graft codes 20900-20938.

A vertebral segment describes the basic constituent part into which the spine may be divided. It represents a single complete vertebral bone with its associated articular processes and laminae. A vertebral interspace is the non-bony compartment between two adjacent vertebral bodies which contains the intervertebral disc, and includes the nucleus pulposus, annulus fibrosus, and two cartilagenous endplates.

22590 Arthrodesis, posterior technique, craniocervical (occiput-C2)

22595 Arthrodesis, posterior technique, atlas-axis (C1-C2)

22600 Arthrodesis, posterior or posterolateral technique, single level; cervical below C2 segment

22610 thoracic (with or without lateral transverse technique)

22612 lumbar (with or without lateral transverse technique)

+ 22614 each additional vertebral segment (List separately in addition to code for primary procedure)

(Use 22614 in conjunction with 22600, 22610, 22612)

22630 Arthrodesis, posterior interbody technique, including laminectomy and/or discectomy to prepare interspace (other than for decompression), single interspace; lumbar

+ 22632 each additional interspace (List separately in addition to code for primary procedure)

(Use 22632 in conjunction with 22630)

Spine Deformity (eg, Scoliosis, Kyphosis)

To report instrumentation procedures, see 22840-22855. (Report in addition to code[s] for the definitive procedure[s].) Do not append modifier 62 to spinal instrumentation codes 22840-22848 and 22850-22852.

To report bone graft procedures, see 20930-20938. (Report in addition to code[s] for the definitive procedure[s].) Do not append modifier 62 to bone graft codes 20900-20938.

A vertebral segment describes the basic constituent part into which the spine may be divided. It represents a single complete vertebral bone with its associated articular processes and laminae.

For the following codes, when two surgeons work together as primary surgeons performing distinct part(s) of an arthrodesis for spinal deformity, each surgeon should report his/her distinct operative work by appending modifier 62 to the procedure code. In this situation, modifier 62 may be appended to procedure code(s) 22800-22819 as long as both surgeons continue to work together as primary surgeons.

22800 Arthrodesis, posterior, for spinal deformity, with or without cast; up to 6 vertebral segments

22802 7 to 12 vertebral segments

22804 13 or more vertebral segments

22808 Arthrodesis, anterior, for spinal deformity, with or without cast; 2 to 3 vertebral segments

22810 4 to 7 vertebral segments

22812 8 or more vertebral segments

22818 Kyphectomy, circumferential exposure of spine and resection of vertebral segment(s) (including body and posterior elements); single or 2 segments

22819 3 or more segments

(To report arthrodesis, see 22800-22804 and add modifier 51)

Exploration

To report instrumentation procedures, see 22840-22855. (Codes 22840-22848 and 22851 are reported in conjunction with code[s] for the definitive procedure[s]. When instrumentation reinsertion or removal is reported in conjunction with other definitive procedures including arthrodesis, decompression, and exploration of fusion, append modifier 51 to 22849, 22850, 22852 and 22855.) Code 22849 should not be reported with 22850, 22852, and 22855 at the same spinal levels. To report exploration of fusion, see 22830. (When exploration is reported in conjunction with other definitive procedures, including arthrodesis and decompression, append modifier 51 to 22830.)

(To report bone graft procedures, see 20930-20938)

22830   Exploration of spinal fusion

Spinal Instrumentation

Segmental instrumentation is defined as fixation at each end of the construct and at least one additional interposed bony attachment.

Non-segmental instrumentation is defined as fixation at each end of the construct and may span several vertebral segments without attachment to the intervening segments.

Insertion of spinal instrumentation is reported separately and in addition to arthrodesis. Instrumentation procedure codes 22840-22848 and 22851 are reported in addition to the definitive procedure(s). Do not append modifier 62 to spinal instrumentation codes 22840-22848 and 22850-22852.

To report bone graft procedures, see 20930-20938. (Report in addition to code[s] for definitive procedure[s].) Do not append modifier 62 to bone graft codes 20900-20938.

A vertebral segment describes the basic constituent part into which the spine may be divided. It represents a single complete vertebral bone with its associated articular processes and laminae. A vertebral interspace is the non-bony compartment between two adjacent vertebral bodies, which contains the intervertebral disc, and includes the nucleus pulposus, annulus fibrosus, and two cartilagenous endplates.

Codes 22849, 22850, 22852, and 22855 are subject to modifier 51 if reported with other definitive procedure(s), including arthrodesis, decompression, and exploration of fusion. Code 22849 should not be reported with 22850, 22852, and 22855 at the same spinal levels.

+ **22840**   Posterior non-segmental instrumentation (eg, Harrington rod technique, pedicle fixation across 1 interspace, atlantoaxial transarticular screw fixation, sublaminar wiring at C1, facet screw fixation) (List separately in addition to code for primary procedure)

(Use 22840 in conjunction with 22100-22102, 22110-22114, 22206, 22207, 22210-22214, 22220-22224, 22305-22327, 22532, 22533, 22548-22558, 22590-22612, 22630, 22800-22812, 63001-63030, 63040-63042, 63045-63047, 63050-63056, 63064, 63075, 63077, 63081, 63085, 63087, 63090, 63101, 63102, 63170-63290, 63300-63307)

(For insertion of posterior spinous process distraction devices, see 0171T, 0172T)

+ **22841**   Internal spinal fixation by wiring of spinous processes (List separately in addition to code for primary procedure)

(Use 22841 in conjunction with 22100-22102, 22110-22114, 22206, 22207, 22210-22214, 22220-22224, 22305-22327, 22532, 22533, 22548-22558, 22590-22612, 22630, 22800-22812, 63001-63030, 63040-63042, 63045-63047, 63050-63056, 63064, 63075, 63077, 63081, 63085, 63087, 63090, 63101, 63102, 63170-63290, 63300-63307)

+ **22842**   Posterior segmental instrumentation (eg, pedicle fixation, dual rods with multiple hooks and sublaminar wires); 3 to 6 vertebral segments (List separately in addition to code for primary procedure)

(Use 22842 in conjunction with 22100-22102, 22110-22114, 22206, 22207, 22210-22214, 22220-22224, 22305-22327, 22532, 22533, 22548-22558, 22590-22612, 22630, 22800-22812, 63001-63030, 63040-63042, 63045-63047, 63050-63056, 63064, 63075, 63077, 63081, 63085, 63087, 63090, 63101, 63102, 63170-63290, 63300-63307)

+ **22843**   7 to 12 vertebral segments (List separately in addition to code for primary procedure)

(Use 22843 in conjunction with 22100-22102, 22110-22114, 22206, 22207, 22210-22214, 22220-22224, 22305-22327, 22532, 22533, 22548-22558, 22590-22612, 22630, 22800-22812, 63001-63030, 63040-63042, 63045-63047, 63050-63056, 63064, 63075, 63077, 63081, 63085, 63087, 63090, 63101, 63102, 63170-63290, 63300-63307)

+ **22844**   13 or more vertebral segments (List separately in addition to code for primary procedure)

(Use 22844 in conjunction with 22100-22102, 22110-22114, 22206, 22207, 22210-22214, 22220-22224, 22305-22327, 22532, 22533, 22548-22558, 22590-22612, 22630, 22800-22812, 63001-63030, 63040-63042, 63045-63047, 63050-63056, 63064, 63075, 63077, 63081, 63085, 63087, 63090, 63101, 63102, 63170-63290, 63300-63307)

+ **22845**   Anterior instrumentation; 2 to 3 vertebral segments (List separately in addition to code for primary procedure)

(Use 22845 in conjunction with 22100-22102, 22110-22114, 22206, 22207, 22210-22214, 22220-22224, 22305-22327, 22532, 22533, 22548-22558, 22590-22612, 22630, 22800-22812, 63001-63030, 63040-63042, 63045-63047, 63050-63056, 63064, 63075, 63077, 63081, 63085, 63087, 63090, 63101, 63102, 63170-63290, 63300-63307)

+ **22846**   4 to 7 vertebral segments (List separately in addition to code for primary procedure)

Surgery: Musculoskeletal System

(Use 22846 in conjunction with 22100-22102, 22110-22114, 22206, 22207, 22210-22214, 22220-22224, 22305-22327, 22532, 22533, 22548-22558, 22590-22612, 22630, 22800-22812, 63001-63030, 63040-63042, 63045-63047, 63050-63056, 63064, 63075, 63077, 63081, 63085, 63087, 63090, 63101, 63102, 63170-63290, 63300-63307)

+ **22847**   8 or more vertebral segments (List separately in addition to code for primary procedure)

(Use 22847 in conjunction with 22100-22102, 22110-22114, 22206, 22207, 22210-22214, 22220-22224, 22305-22327, 22532, 22533, 22548-22558, 22590-22612, 22630, 22800-22812, 63001-63030, 63040-63042, 63045-63047, 63050-63056, 63064, 63075, 63077, 63081, 63085, 63087, 63090, 63101, 63102, 63170-63290, 63300-63307)

+ **22848**   Pelvic fixation (attachment of caudal end of instrumentation to pelvic bony structures) other than sacrum (List separately in addition to code for primary procedure)

(Use 22848 in conjunction with 22100-22102, 22110-22114, 22206, 22207, 22210-22214, 22220-22224, 22305-22327, 22532, 22533, 22548-22558, 22590-22612, 22630, 22800-22812, 63001-63030, 63040-63042, 63045-63047, 63050-63056, 63064, 63075, 63077, 63081, 63085, 63087, 63090, 63101, 63102, 63170-63290, 63300-63307)

22849   Reinsertion of spinal fixation device

22850   Removal of posterior nonsegmental instrumentation (eg, Harrington rod)

+ **22851**   Application of intervertebral biomechanical device(s) (eg, synthetic cage(s), threaded bone dowel(s), methylmethacrylate) to vertebral defect or interspace (List separately in addition to code for primary procedure)

(Use 22851 in conjunction with 22100-22102, 22110-22114, 22206, 22207, 22210-22214, 22220-22224, 22305-22327, 22532, 22533, 22548-22558, 22590-22612, 22630, 22800-22812, 63001-63030, 63040-63042, 63045-63047, 63050-63056, 63064, 63075, 63077, 63081, 63085, 63087, 63090, 63101, 63102, 63170-63290, 63300-63307)

(For insertion of posterior spinous process distraction devices, see 0171T, 0172T)

22852   Removal of posterior segmental instrumentation

22855   Removal of anterior instrumentation

22856   Total disc arthroplasty (artificial disc), anterior approach, including discectomy with end plate preparation (includes osteophytectomy for nerve root or spinal cord decompression and microdissection), single interspace, cervical

(Do not report 22856 in conjunction with 22554, 22845, 22851, 63075 when performed at the same level)

(Do not report 22856 in conjunction with 69990)

(For additional interspace cervical total disc arthroplasty, use 0092T)

22857   Total disc arthroplasty (artificial disc), anterior approach, including discectomy to prepare interspace (other than for decompression), single interspace, lumbar

(Do not report 22857 in conjunction with 22558, 22845, 22851, 49010 when performed at the same level)

(For additional interspace, use Category III code 0163T)

22861   Revision including replacement of total disc arthroplasty (artificial disc), anterior approach, single interspace; cervical

(Do not report 22861 in conjunction with 22845, 22851, 22864, 63075 when performed at the same level)

(Do not report 22861 in conjunction with 69990)

(For additional interspace revision of cervical total disc arthroplasty, use 0098T)

22862   lumbar

(Do not report 22862 in conjunction with 22558, 22845, 22851, 22865, 49010 when performed at the same level)

(For additional interspace, use Category III code 0165T)

22864   Removal of total disc arthroplasty (artificial disc), anterior approach, single interspace; cervical

(Do not report 22864 in conjunction with 22861, 69990)

(For additional interspace removal of cervical total disc arthroplasty, use 0095T)

22865   lumbar

(Do not report 22865 in conjunction with 49010)

(For additional interspace, see Category III code 0164T)

(22856-22865 include fluoroscopy when performed)

(For decompression, see 63001-63048)

Other Procedures

22899   Unlisted procedure, spine

Abdomen

Excision

▲ **22900**   Excision, tumor, soft tissue of abdominal wall, subfascial (eg, intramuscular); less than 5 cm

● **22901**   5 cm or greater

● **22902**   Excision, tumor, soft tissue of abdominal wall, subcutaneous; less than 3 cm

● **22903**   3 cm or greater

● **22904**   Radical resection of tumor (eg, malignant neoplasm), soft tissue of abdominal wall; less than 5 cm

● **22905**   5 cm or greater

Other Procedures

22999   Unlisted procedure, abdomen, musculoskeletal system

Shoulder

The area known as the shoulder is made up of the clavicle, scapula, humerus head and neck, sternoclavicular joint, acromioclavicular joint, and shoulder joint.

Incision

23000   Removal of subdeltoid calcareous deposits, open

(For arthroscopic removal of bursal deposits, use 29999)

23020   Capsular contracture release (eg, Sever type procedure)

(For incision and drainage procedures, superficial, see 10040-10160)

23030   Incision and drainage, shoulder area; deep abscess or hematoma

23031   infected bursa

23035   Incision, bone cortex (eg, osteomyelitis or bone abscess), shoulder area

23040   Arthrotomy, glenohumeral joint, including exploration, drainage, or removal of foreign body

23044   Arthrotomy, acromioclavicular, sternoclavicular joint, including exploration, drainage, or removal of foreign body

Excision

23065   Biopsy, soft tissue of shoulder area; superficial

23066   deep

(For needle biopsy of soft tissue, use 20206)

23071   ▶Code is out of numerical sequence. See 23065-23220◀

23073   ▶Code is out of numerical sequence. See 23065-23220◀

▲ **23075**   Excision, tumor, soft tissue of shoulder area, subcutaneous; less than 3 cm

#● **23071**   3 cm or greater

▲ **23076**   Excision, tumor, soft tissue of shoulder area, subfascial (eg, intramuscular); less than 5 cm

#● **23073**   5 cm or greater

▲ **23077**   Radical resection of tumor (eg, malignant neoplasm), soft tissue of shoulder area; less than 5 cm

● **23078**   5 cm or greater

23100   Arthrotomy, glenohumeral joint, including biopsy

23101   Arthrotomy, acromioclavicular joint or sternoclavicular joint, including biopsy and/or excision of torn cartilage

23105   Arthrotomy; glenohumeral joint, with synovectomy, with or without biopsy

23106   sternoclavicular joint, with synovectomy, with or without biopsy

23107   Arthrotomy, glenohumeral joint, with joint exploration, with or without removal of loose or foreign body

23120   Claviculectomy; partial

(For arthroscopic procedure, use 29824)

23125   total

23130   Acromioplasty or acromionectomy, partial, with or without coracoacromial ligament release

23140   Excision or curettage of bone cyst or benign tumor of clavicle or scapula;

23145   with autograft (includes obtaining graft)

23146   with allograft

23150   Excision or curettage of bone cyst or benign tumor of proximal humerus;

23155   with autograft (includes obtaining graft)

23156   with allograft

23170   Sequestrectomy (eg, for osteomyelitis or bone abscess), clavicle

23172   Sequestrectomy (eg, for osteomyelitis or bone abscess), scapula

23174   Sequestrectomy (eg, for osteomyelitis or bone abscess), humeral head to surgical neck

23180   Partial excision (craterization, saucerization, or diaphysectomy) bone (eg, osteomyelitis), clavicle

23182   Partial excision (craterization, saucerization, or diaphysectomy) bone (eg, osteomyelitis), scapula

23184   Partial excision (craterization, saucerization, or diaphysectomy) bone (eg, osteomyelitis), proximal humerus

23190   Ostectomy of scapula, partial (eg, superior medial angle)

23195   Resection, humeral head

(For replacement with implant, use 23470)

▲ **23200**   Radical resection of tumor; clavicle

▲ **23210**   scapula

▲ **23220**   Radical resection of tumor, proximal humerus

▶(23221, 23222 have been deleted)◀

Introduction or Removal

(For arthrocentesis or needling of bursa, use 20610)

(For K-wire or pin insertion or removal, see 20650, 20670, 20680)

23330   Removal of foreign body, shoulder; subcutaneous

23331   deep (eg, Neer hemiarthroplasty removal)

23332   complicated (eg, total shoulder)

Surgery: Musculoskeletal System

23350 Injection procedure for shoulder arthrography or enhanced CT/MRI shoulder arthrography

(For radiographic arthrography, radiological supervision and interpretation, use 73040. Fluoroscopy [77002] is inclusive of radiographic arthrography)

(When fluoroscopic guided injection is performed for enhanced CT arthrography, use 23350, 77002, and 73201 or 73202)

(When fluoroscopic guided injection is performed for enhanced MR arthrography, use 23350, 77002, and 73222 or 73223)

(For enhanced CT or enhanced MRI arthrography, use 77002 and either 73201, 73202, 73222, or 73223)

(To report biopsy of the shoulder and joint, see 29805-29826)

Repair, Revision, and/or Reconstruction

23395 Muscle transfer, any type, shoulder or upper arm; single

23397 multiple

23400 Scapulopexy (eg, Sprengels deformity or for paralysis)

23405 Tenotomy, shoulder area; single tendon

23406 multiple tendons through same incision

23410 Repair of ruptured musculotendinous cuff (eg, rotator cuff) open; acute

23412 chronic

(For arthroscopic procedure, use 29827)

23415 Coracoacromial ligament release, with or without acromioplasty

(For arthroscopic procedure, use 29826)

23420 Reconstruction of complete shoulder (rotator) cuff avulsion, chronic (includes acromioplasty)

23430 Tenodesis of long tendon of biceps

(For arthroscopic biceps tenodesis, use 29828)

23440 Resection or transplantation of long tendon of biceps

23450 Capsulorrhaphy, anterior; Putti-Platt procedure or Magnuson type operation

(To report arthroscopic thermal capsulorrhaphy, use 29999)

23455 with labral repair (eg, Bankart procedure)

(For arthroscopic procedure, use 29806)

23460 Capsulorrhaphy, anterior, any type; with bone block

23462 with coracoid process transfer

(To report open thermal capsulorrhaphy, use 23929)

23465 Capsulorrhaphy, glenohumeral joint, posterior, with or without bone block

(For sternoclavicular and acromioclavicular reconstruction, see 23530, 23550)

23466 Capsulorrhaphy, glenohumeral joint, any type multi-directional instability

23470 Arthroplasty, glenohumeral joint; hemiarthroplasty

23472 total shoulder (glenoid and proximal humeral replacement (eg, total shoulder))

(For removal of total shoulder implants, see 23331, 23332)

(For osteotomy, proximal humerus, use 24400)

23480 Osteotomy, clavicle, with or without internal fixation;

23485 with bone graft for nonunion or malunion (includes obtaining graft and/or necessary fixation)

23490 Prophylactic treatment (nailing, pinning, plating or wiring) with or without methylmethacrylate; clavicle

23491 proximal humerus

Fracture and/or Dislocation

23500 Closed treatment of clavicular fracture; without manipulation

23505 with manipulation

23515 Open treatment of clavicular fracture, includes internal fixation, when performed

23520 Closed treatment of sternoclavicular dislocation; without manipulation

23525 with manipulation

23530 Open treatment of sternoclavicular dislocation, acute or chronic;

23532 with fascial graft (includes obtaining graft)

23540 Closed treatment of acromioclavicular dislocation; without manipulation

23545 with manipulation

23550 Open treatment of acromioclavicular dislocation, acute or chronic;

23552 with fascial graft (includes obtaining graft)

23570 Closed treatment of scapular fracture; without manipulation

23575 with manipulation, with or without skeletal traction (with or without shoulder joint involvement)

23585 Open treatment of scapular fracture (body, glenoid or acromion) includes internal fixation, when performed

23600 Closed treatment of proximal humeral (surgical or anatomical neck) fracture; without manipulation

23605 with manipulation, with or without skeletal traction

23615 Open treatment of proximal humeral (surgical or anatomical neck) fracture, includes internal fixation, when performed, includes repair of tuberosity(s), when performed;

23616 with proximal humeral prosthetic replacement

23620	Closed treatment of greater humeral tuberosity fracture; without manipulation
23625	with manipulation
23630	Open treatment of greater humeral tuberosity fracture, includes internal fixation, when performed
23650	Closed treatment of shoulder dislocation, with manipulation; without anesthesia
23655	requiring anesthesia
23660	Open treatment of acute shoulder dislocation

(Repairs for recurrent dislocations, see 23450-23466)

23665	Closed treatment of shoulder dislocation, with fracture of greater humeral tuberosity, with manipulation
23670	Open treatment of shoulder dislocation, with fracture of greater humeral tuberosity, includes internal fixation, when performed
23675	Closed treatment of shoulder dislocation, with surgical or anatomical neck fracture, with manipulation
23680	Open treatment of shoulder dislocation, with surgical or anatomical neck fracture, includes internal fixation, when performed

Manipulation

23700	Manipulation under anesthesia, shoulder joint, including application of fixation apparatus (dislocation excluded)

Arthrodesis

23800	Arthrodesis, glenohumeral joint;
23802	with autogenous graft (includes obtaining graft)

Amputation

23900	Interthoracoscapular amputation (forequarter)
23920	Disarticulation of shoulder;
23921	secondary closure or scar revision

Other Procedures

23929	Unlisted procedure, shoulder

Humerus (Upper Arm) and Elbow

The elbow area includes the head and neck of the radius and olecranon process.

Incision

(For incision and drainage procedures, superficial, see 10040-10160)

23930	Incision and drainage, upper arm or elbow area; deep abscess or hematoma

23931	bursa
23935	Incision, deep, with opening of bone cortex (eg, for osteomyelitis or bone abscess), humerus or elbow
24000	Arthrotomy, elbow, including exploration, drainage, or removal of foreign body
24006	Arthrotomy of the elbow, with capsular excision for capsular release (separate procedure)

Excision

24065	Biopsy, soft tissue of upper arm or elbow area; superficial
24066	deep (subfascial or intramuscular)

(For needle biopsy of soft tissue, use 20206)

24071	►Code is out of numerical sequence. See 24065-24155◄
24073	►Code is out of numerical sequence. See 24065-24155◄
▲ 24075	Excision, tumor, soft tissue of upper arm or elbow area, subcutaneous; less than 3 cm
#● 24071	3 cm or greater
▲ 24076	Excision, tumor, soft tissue of upper arm or elbow area, subfascial (eg, intramuscular); less than 5 cm
#● 24073	5 cm or greater
▲ 24077	Radical resection of tumor (eg, malignant neoplasm), soft tissue of upper arm or elbow area; less than 5 cm
● 24079	5 cm or greater
24100	Arthrotomy, elbow; with synovial biopsy only
24101	with joint exploration, with or without biopsy, with or without removal of loose or foreign body
24102	with synovectomy
24105	Excision, olecranon bursa
24110	Excision or curettage of bone cyst or benign tumor, humerus;
24115	with autograft (includes obtaining graft)
24116	with allograft
24120	Excision or curettage of bone cyst or benign tumor of head or neck of radius or olecranon process;
24125	with autograft (includes obtaining graft)
24126	with allograft
24130	Excision, radial head

(For replacement with implant, use 24366)

24134	Sequestrectomy (eg, for osteomyelitis or bone abscess), shaft or distal humerus
24136	Sequestrectomy (eg, for osteomyelitis or bone abscess), radial head or neck
24138	Sequestrectomy (eg, for osteomyelitis or bone abscess), olecranon process

Surgery: Musculoskeletal System

Surgery: Musculoskeletal System

24140 Partial excision (craterization, saucerization, or diaphysectomy) bone (eg, osteomyelitis), humerus

24145 Partial excision (craterization, saucerization, or diaphysectomy) bone (eg, osteomyelitis), radial head or neck

24147 Partial excision (craterization, saucerization, or diaphysectomy) bone (eg, osteomyelitis), olecranon process

24149 Radical resection of capsule, soft tissue, and heterotopic bone, elbow, with contracture release (separate procedure)

(For capsular and soft tissue release only, use 24006)

▲ **24150** Radical resection of tumor, shaft or distal humerus

►(24151 has been deleted)◄

▲ **24152** Radical resection of tumor, radial head or neck

►(24153 has been deleted)◄

24155 Resection of elbow joint (arthrectomy)

Introduction or Removal

(For K-wire or pin insertion or removal, see 20650, 20670, 20680)

(For arthrocentesis or needling of bursa or joint, use 20605)

24160 Implant removal; elbow joint

24164   radial head

24200 Removal of foreign body, upper arm or elbow area; subcutaneous

24201   deep (subfascial or intramuscular)

24220 Injection procedure for elbow arthrography

(For radiological supervision and interpretation, use 73085. Do not report 77002 in conjunction with 73085)

(For injection for tennis elbow, use 20550)

Repair, Revision, and/or Reconstruction

24300 Manipulation, elbow, under anesthesia

(For application of external fixation, see 20690 or 20692)

24301 Muscle or tendon transfer, any type, upper arm or elbow, single (excluding 24320-24331)

24305 Tendon lengthening, upper arm or elbow, each tendon

24310 Tenotomy, open, elbow to shoulder, each tendon

24320 Tenoplasty, with muscle transfer, with or without free graft, elbow to shoulder, single (Seddon-Brookes type procedure)

24330 Flexor-plasty, elbow (eg, Steindler type advancement);

24331   with extensor advancement

24332 Tenolysis, triceps

24340 Tenodesis of biceps tendon at elbow (separate procedure)

24341 Repair, tendon or muscle, upper arm or elbow, each tendon or muscle, primary or secondary (excludes rotator cuff)

24342 Reinsertion of ruptured biceps or triceps tendon, distal, with or without tendon graft

24343 Repair lateral collateral ligament, elbow, with local tissue

24344 Reconstruction lateral collateral ligament, elbow, with tendon graft (includes harvesting of graft)

24345 Repair medial collateral ligament, elbow, with local tissue

24346 Reconstruction medial collateral ligament, elbow, with tendon graft (includes harvesting of graft)

(24350-24356 have been deleted. To report, see 24357-24359)

24357 Tenotomy, elbow, lateral or medial (eg, epicondylitis, tennis elbow, golfer's elbow); percutaneous

24358   debridement, soft tissue and/or bone, open

24359   debridement, soft tissue and/or bone, open with tendon repair or reattachment

(Do not report 24357-24359 in conjunction with 29837, 29838)

24360 Arthroplasty, elbow; with membrane (eg, fascial)

24361   with distal humeral prosthetic replacement

24362   with implant and fascia lata ligament reconstruction

24363   with distal humerus and proximal ulnar prosthetic replacement (eg, total elbow)

24365 Arthroplasty, radial head;

24366   with implant

24400 Osteotomy, humerus, with or without internal fixation

24410 Multiple osteotomies with realignment on intramedullary rod, humeral shaft (Sofield type procedure)

24420 Osteoplasty, humerus (eg, shortening or lengthening) (excluding 64876)

24430 Repair of nonunion or malunion, humerus; without graft (eg, compression technique)

24435   with iliac or other autograft (includes obtaining graft)

(For proximal radius and/or ulna, see 25400-25420)

24470 Hemiepiphyseal arrest (eg, cubitus varus or valgus, distal humerus)

24495 Decompression fasciotomy, forearm, with brachial artery exploration

24498 Prophylactic treatment (nailing, pinning, plating or wiring), with or without methylmethacrylate, humeral shaft

---

Fracture and/or Dislocation

24500   Closed treatment of humeral shaft fracture; without manipulation

24505   with manipulation, with or without skeletal traction

24515   Open treatment of humeral shaft fracture with plate/screws, with or without cerclage

24516   Treatment of humeral shaft fracture, with insertion of intramedullary implant, with or without cerclage and/or locking screws

24530   Closed treatment of supracondylar or transcondylar humeral fracture, with or without intercondylar extension; without manipulation

24535   with manipulation, with or without skin or skeletal traction

24538   Percutaneous skeletal fixation of supracondylar or transcondylar humeral fracture, with or without intercondylar extension

24545   Open treatment of humeral supracondylar or transcondylar fracture, includes internal fixation, when performed; without intercondylar extension

24546   with intercondylar extension

24560   Closed treatment of humeral epicondylar fracture, medial or lateral; without manipulation

24565   with manipulation

24566   Percutaneous skeletal fixation of humeral epicondylar fracture, medial or lateral, with manipulation

24575   Open treatment of humeral epicondylar fracture, medial or lateral, includes internal fixation, when performed

24576   Closed treatment of humeral condylar fracture, medial or lateral; without manipulation

24577   with manipulation

24579   Open treatment of humeral condylar fracture, medial or lateral, includes internal fixation, when performed

(To report closed treatment of fractures without manipulation, see 24530, 24560, 24576, 24650, 24670)

(To report closed treatment of fractures with manipulation, see 24535, 24565, 24577, 24675)

24582   Percutaneous skeletal fixation of humeral condylar fracture, medial or lateral, with manipulation

24586   Open treatment of periarticular fracture and/or dislocation of the elbow (fracture distal humerus and proximal ulna and/or proximal radius);

24587   with implant arthroplasty

(See also 24361)

24600   Treatment of closed elbow dislocation; without anesthesia

24605   requiring anesthesia

24615   Open treatment of acute or chronic elbow dislocation

24620   Closed treatment of Monteggia type of fracture dislocation at elbow (fracture proximal end of ulna with dislocation of radial head), with manipulation

24635   Open treatment of Monteggia type of fracture dislocation at elbow (fracture proximal end of ulna with dislocation of radial head), includes internal fixation, when performed

24640   Closed treatment of radial head subluxation in child, nursemaid elbow, with manipulation

24650   Closed treatment of radial head or neck fracture; without manipulation

24655   with manipulation

24665   Open treatment of radial head or neck fracture, includes internal fixation or radial head excision, when performed;

24666   with radial head prosthetic replacement

24670   Closed treatment of ulnar fracture, proximal end (eg, olecranon or coronoid process[es]); without manipulation

24675   with manipulation

24685   Open treatment of ulnar fracture, proximal end (eg, olecranon or coronoid process[es]), includes internal fixation, when performed

(Do not report 24685 in conjunction with 24100-24102)

Arthrodesis

24800   Arthrodesis, elbow joint; local

24802   with autogenous graft (includes obtaining graft)

Amputation

24900   Amputation, arm through humerus; with primary closure

24920   open, circular (guillotine)

24925   secondary closure or scar revision

24930   re-amputation

24931   with implant

24935   Stump elongation, upper extremity

24940   Cineplasty, upper extremity, complete procedure

Other Procedures

24999   Unlisted procedure, humerus or elbow

Forearm and Wrist

Radius, ulna, carpal bones, and joints.

Incision

25000   Incision, extensor tendon sheath, wrist (eg, deQuervains disease)

(For decompression median nerve or for carpal tunnel syndrome, use 64721)

Surgery: Musculoskeletal System

25001	Incision, flexor tendon sheath, wrist (eg, flexor carpi radialis)
25020	Decompression fasciotomy, forearm and/or wrist, flexor OR extensor compartment; without debridement of nonviable muscle and/or nerve
25023	with debridement of nonviable muscle and/or nerve

(For decompression fasciotomy with brachial artery exploration, use 24495)

(For incision and drainage procedures, superficial, see 10060-10160)

(For debridement, see also 11000-11044)

25024	Decompression fasciotomy, forearm and/or wrist, flexor AND extensor compartment; without debridement of nonviable muscle and/or nerve
25025	with debridement of nonviable muscle and/or nerve
25028	Incision and drainage, forearm and/or wrist; deep abscess or hematoma
25031	bursa
25035	Incision, deep, bone cortex, forearm and/or wrist (eg, osteomyelitis or bone abscess)
25040	Arthrotomy, radiocarpal or midcarpal joint, with exploration, drainage, or removal of foreign body

Excision

25065	Biopsy, soft tissue of forearm and/or wrist; superficial
25066	deep (subfascial or intramuscular)

(For needle biopsy of soft tissue, use 20206)

25071	►Code is out of numerical sequence. See 25065-25240◄
25073	►Code is out of numerical sequence. See 25065-25240◄
▲ 25075	Excision, tumor, soft tissue of forearm and/or wrist area, subcutaneous; less than 3 cm
#● 25071	3 cm or greater
▲ 25076	Excision, tumor, soft tissue of forearm and/or wrist area, subfascial (eg, intramuscular); less than 3 cm
#● 25073	3 cm or greater
▲ 25077	Radical resection of tumor (eg, malignant neoplasm), soft tissue of forearm and/or wrist area; less than 3 cm
● 25078	3 cm or greater
25085	Capsulotomy, wrist (eg, contracture)
25100	Arthrotomy, wrist joint; with biopsy
25101	with joint exploration, with or without biopsy, with or without removal of loose or foreign body
25105	with synovectomy

25107	Arthrotomy, distal radioulnar joint including repair of triangular cartilage, complex
25109	Excision of tendon, forearm and/or wrist, flexor or extensor, each
25110	Excision, lesion of tendon sheath, forearm and/or wrist
25111	Excision of ganglion, wrist (dorsal or volar); primary
25112	recurrent

(For hand or finger, use 26160)

25115	Radical excision of bursa, synovia of wrist, or forearm tendon sheaths (eg, tenosynovitis, fungus, Tbc, or other granulomas, rheumatoid arthritis); flexors
25116	extensors, with or without transposition of dorsal retinaculum

(For finger synovectomies, use 26145)

25118	Synovectomy, extensor tendon sheath, wrist, single compartment;
25119	with resection of distal ulna
25120	Excision or curettage of bone cyst or benign tumor of radius or ulna (excluding head or neck of radius and olecranon process);

(For head or neck of radius or olecranon process, see 24120-24126)

25125	with autograft (includes obtaining graft)
25126	with allograft
25130	Excision or curettage of bone cyst or benign tumor of carpal bones;
25135	with autograft (includes obtaining graft)
25136	with allograft
25145	Sequestrectomy (eg, for osteomyelitis or bone abscess), forearm and/or wrist
25150	Partial excision (craterization, saucerization, or diaphysectomy) of bone (eg, for osteomyelitis); ulna
25151	radius

(For head or neck of radius or olecranon process, see 24145, 24147)

▲ 25170	Radical resection of tumor, radius or ulna
25210	Carpectomy; 1 bone

(For carpectomy with implant, see 25441-25445)

25215	all bones of proximal row
25230	Radial styloidectomy (separate procedure)
25240	Excision distal ulna partial or complete (eg, Darrach type or matched resection)

(For implant replacement, distal ulna, use 25442)

(For obtaining fascia for interposition, see 20920, 20922)

Introduction or Removal

(For K-wire, pin or rod insertion or removal, see 20650, 20670, 20680)

25246   Injection procedure for wrist arthrography

(For radiological supervision and interpretation, use 73115. Do not report 77002 in conjunction with 73115)

(For foreign body removal, superficial use 20520)

25248   Exploration with removal of deep foreign body, forearm or wrist

25250   Removal of wrist prosthesis; (separate procedure)

25251   complicated, including total wrist

25259   Manipulation, wrist, under anesthesia

(For application of external fixation, see 20690 or 20692)

Repair, Revision, and/or Reconstruction

25260   Repair, tendon or muscle, flexor, forearm and/or wrist; primary, single, each tendon or muscle

25263   secondary, single, each tendon or muscle

25265   secondary, with free graft (includes obtaining graft), each tendon or muscle

25270   Repair, tendon or muscle, extensor, forearm and/or wrist; primary, single, each tendon or muscle

25272   secondary, single, each tendon or muscle

25274   secondary, with free graft (includes obtaining graft), each tendon or muscle

25275   Repair, tendon sheath, extensor, forearm and/or wrist, with free graft (includes obtaining graft) (eg, for extensor carpi ulnaris subluxation)

25280   Lengthening or shortening of flexor or extensor tendon, forearm and/or wrist, single, each tendon

25290   Tenotomy, open, flexor or extensor tendon, forearm and/or wrist, single, each tendon

25295   Tenolysis, flexor or extensor tendon, forearm and/or wrist, single, each tendon

25300   Tenodesis at wrist; flexors of fingers

25301   extensors of fingers

25310   Tendon transplantation or transfer, flexor or extensor, forearm and/or wrist, single; each tendon

25312   with tendon graft(s) (includes obtaining graft), each tendon

25315   Flexor origin slide (eg, for cerebral palsy, Volkmann contracture), forearm and/or wrist;

25316   with tendon(s) transfer

25320   Capsulorrhaphy or reconstruction, wrist, open (eg, capsulodesis, ligament repair, tendon transfer or graft) (includes synovectomy, capsulotomy and open reduction) for carpal instability

25332   Arthroplasty, wrist, with or without interposition, with or without external or internal fixation

(For obtaining fascia for interposition, see 20920, 20922)

(For prosthetic replacement arthroplasty, see 25441-25446)

25335   Centralization of wrist on ulna (eg, radial club hand)

25337   Reconstruction for stabilization of unstable distal ulna or distal radioulnar joint, secondary by soft tissue stabilization (eg, tendon transfer, tendon graft or weave, or tenodesis) with or without open reduction of distal radioulnar joint

(For harvesting of fascia lata graft, see 20920, 20922)

25350   Osteotomy, radius; distal third

25355   middle or proximal third

25360   Osteotomy; ulna

25365   radius AND ulna

25370   Multiple osteotomies, with realignment on intramedullary rod (Sofield type procedure); radius OR ulna

25375   radius AND ulna

25390   Osteoplasty, radius OR ulna; shortening

25391   lengthening with autograft

25392   Osteoplasty, radius AND ulna; shortening (excluding 64876)

25393   lengthening with autograft

25394   Osteoplasty, carpal bone, shortening

25400   Repair of nonunion or malunion, radius OR ulna; without graft (eg, compression technique)

25405   with autograft (includes obtaining graft)

25415   Repair of nonunion or malunion, radius AND ulna; without graft (eg, compression technique)

25420   with autograft (includes obtaining graft)

25425   Repair of defect with autograft; radius OR ulna

25426   radius AND ulna

25430   Insertion of vascular pedicle into carpal bone (eg, Hori procedure)

25431   Repair of nonunion of carpal bone (excluding carpal scaphoid (navicular)) (includes obtaining graft and necessary fixation), each bone

25440   Repair of nonunion, scaphoid carpal (navicular) bone, with or without radial styloidectomy (includes obtaining graft and necessary fixation)

25441   Arthroplasty with prosthetic replacement; distal radius

25442   distal ulna

25443   scaphoid carpal (navicular)

25444   lunate

25445   trapezium

25446   distal radius and partial or entire carpus (total wrist)

25447   Arthroplasty, interposition, intercarpal or carpometacarpal joints

(For wrist arthroplasty, use 25332)

25449   Revision of arthroplasty, including removal of implant, wrist joint

25450   Epiphyseal arrest by epiphysiodesis or stapling; distal radius OR ulna

25455   distal radius AND ulna

25490   Prophylactic treatment (nailing, pinning, plating or wiring) with or without methylmethacrylate; radius

25491   ulna

25492   radius AND ulna

Fracture and/or Dislocation

(For application of external fixation in addition to internal fixation, use 20690 and the appropriate internal fixation code)

25500   Closed treatment of radial shaft fracture; without manipulation

25505   with manipulation

25515   Open treatment of radial shaft fracture, includes internal fixation, when performed

25520   Closed treatment of radial shaft fracture and closed treatment of dislocation of distal radioulnar joint (Galeazzi fracture/dislocation)

25525   Open treatment of radial shaft fracture, includes internal fixation, when performed, and closed treatment of distal radioulnar joint dislocation (Galeazzi fracture/dislocation), includes percutaneous skeletal fixation, when performed

25526   Open treatment of radial shaft fracture, includes internal fixation, when performed, and open treatment of distal radioulnar joint dislocation (Galeazzi fracture/dislocation), includes internal fixation, when performed, includes repair of triangular fibrocartilage complex

25530   Closed treatment of ulnar shaft fracture; without manipulation

25535   with manipulation

25545   Open treatment of ulnar shaft fracture, includes internal fixation, when performed

25560   Closed treatment of radial and ulnar shaft fractures; without manipulation

25565   with manipulation

25574   Open treatment of radial AND ulnar shaft fractures, with internal fixation, when performed; of radius OR ulna

25575   of radius AND ulna

25600   Closed treatment of distal radial fracture (eg, Colles or Smith type) or epiphyseal separation, includes closed treatment of fracture of ulnar styloid, when performed; without manipulation

25605   with manipulation

(Do not report 25600, 25605 in conjunction with 25650)

25606   Percutaneous skeletal fixation of distal radial fracture or epiphyseal separation

(Do not report 25606 in conjunction with 25650)

(For percutaneous treatment of ulnar styloid fracture, use 25651)

(For open treatment of ulnar styloid fracture, use 25652)

25607   Open treatment of distal radial extra-articular fracture or epiphyseal separation, with internal fixation

(Do not report 25607 in conjunction with 25650)

(For percutaneous treatment of ulnar styloid fracture, use 25651)

(For open treatment of ulnar styloid fracture, use 25652)

25608   Open treatment of distal radial intra-articular fracture or epiphyseal separation; with internal fixation of 2 fragments

(Do not report 25608 in conjunction with 25609)

25609   with internal fixation of 3 or more fragments

(Do not report 25608, 25609 in conjunction with 25650)

(For percutaneous treatment of ulnar styloid fracture, use 25651)

(For open treatment of ulnar styloid fracture, use 25652)

25622   Closed treatment of carpal scaphoid (navicular) fracture; without manipulation

25624   with manipulation

25628   Open treatment of carpal scaphoid (navicular) fracture, includes internal fixation, when performed

25630   Closed treatment of carpal bone fracture (excluding carpal scaphoid [navicular]); without manipulation, each bone

25635   with manipulation, each bone

25645   Open treatment of carpal bone fracture (other than carpal scaphoid [navicular]), each bone

25650   Closed treatment of ulnar styloid fracture

(Do not report 25650 in conjunction with 25600, 25605, 25607-25609)

25651   Percutaneous skeletal fixation of ulnar styloid fracture

25652   Open treatment of ulnar styloid fracture

25660   Closed treatment of radiocarpal or intercarpal dislocation, 1 or more bones, with manipulation

25670   Open treatment of radiocarpal or intercarpal dislocation, 1 or more bones

25671 Percutaneous skeletal fixation of distal radioulnar dislocation

25675 Closed treatment of distal radioulnar dislocation with manipulation

25676 Open treatment of distal radioulnar dislocation, acute or chronic

25680 Closed treatment of trans-scaphoperilunar type of fracture dislocation, with manipulation

25685 Open treatment of trans-scaphoperilunar type of fracture dislocation

25690 Closed treatment of lunate dislocation, with manipulation

25695 Open treatment of lunate dislocation

Arthrodesis

25800 Arthrodesis, wrist; complete, without bone graft (includes radiocarpal and/or intercarpal and/or carpometacarpal joints)

25805 with sliding graft

25810 with iliac or other autograft (includes obtaining graft)

25820 Arthrodesis, wrist; limited, without bone graft (eg, intercarpal or radiocarpal)

25825 with autograft (includes obtaining graft)

25830 Arthrodesis, distal radioulnar joint with segmental resection of ulna, with or without bone graft (eg, Sauve-Kapandji procedure)

Amputation

25900 Amputation, forearm, through radius and ulna;

25905 open, circular (guillotine)

25907 secondary closure or scar revision

25909 re-amputation

25915 Krukenberg procedure

25920 Disarticulation through wrist;

25922 secondary closure or scar revision

25924 re-amputation

25927 Transmetacarpal amputation;

25929 secondary closure or scar revision

25931 re-amputation

Other Procedures

25999 Unlisted procedure, forearm or wrist

Hand and Fingers

Incision

26010 Drainage of finger abscess; simple

26011 complicated (eg, felon)

26020 Drainage of tendon sheath, digit and/or palm, each

26025 Drainage of palmar bursa; single, bursa

26030 multiple bursa

26034 Incision, bone cortex, hand or finger (eg, osteomyelitis or bone abscess)

26035 Decompression fingers and/or hand, injection injury (eg, grease gun)

26037 Decompressive fasciotomy, hand (excludes 26035)

(For injection injury, use 26035)

26040 Fasciotomy, palmar (eg, Dupuytren's contracture); percutaneous

26045 open, partial

(For fasciectomy, see 26121-26125)

26055 Tendon sheath incision (eg, for trigger finger)

26060 Tenotomy, percutaneous, single, each digit

26070 Arthrotomy, with exploration, drainage, or removal of loose or foreign body; carpometacarpal joint

26075 metacarpophalangeal joint, each

26080 interphalangeal joint, each

Excision

26100 Arthrotomy with biopsy; carpometacarpal joint, each

26105 metacarpophalangeal joint, each

26110 interphalangeal joint, each

26111 ▶Code is out of numerical sequence. See 26100-26262◀

26113 ▶Code is out of numerical sequence. See 26100-26262◀

▲ **26115** Excision, tumor or vascular malformation, soft tissue of hand or finger, subcutaneous; less than 1.5 cm

#● **26111** 1.5 cm or greater

▲ **26116** Excision, tumor, soft tissue, or vascular malformation, of hand or finger, subfascial (eg, intramuscular); less than 1.5 cm

#● **26113** 1.5 cm or greater

▲ **26117** Radical resection of tumor (eg, malignant neoplasm), soft tissue of hand or finger; less than 3 cm

● **26118** 3 cm or greater

Surgery: Musculoskeletal System

26121 Fasciectomy, palm only, with or without Z-plasty, other local tissue rearrangement, or skin grafting (includes obtaining graft)

26123 Fasciectomy, partial palmar with release of single digit including proximal interphalangeal joint, with or without Z-plasty, other local tissue rearrangement, or skin grafting (includes obtaining graft);

+ 26125 each additional digit (List separately in addition to code for primary procedure)

(Use 26125 in conjunction with 26123)

(For fasciotomy, see 26040, 26045)

26130 Synovectomy, carpometacarpal joint

26135 Synovectomy, metacarpophalangeal joint including intrinsic release and extensor hood reconstruction, each digit

26140 Synovectomy, proximal interphalangeal joint, including extensor reconstruction, each interphalangeal joint

26145 Synovectomy, tendon sheath, radical (tenosynovectomy), flexor tendon, palm and/or finger, each tendon

(For tendon sheath synovectomies at wrist, see 25115, 25116)

26160 Excision of lesion of tendon sheath or joint capsule (eg, cyst, mucous cyst, or ganglion), hand or finger

(For wrist ganglion, see 25111, 25112)

(For trigger digit, use 26055)

26170 Excision of tendon, palm, flexor or extensor, single, each tendon

(Do not report 26170 in conjunction with 26390, 26415)

26180 Excision of tendon, finger, flexor or extensor, each tendon

(Do not report 26180 in conjunction with 26390, 26415)

26185 Sesamoidectomy, thumb or finger (separate procedure)

26200 Excision or curettage of bone cyst or benign tumor of metacarpal;

26205 with autograft (includes obtaining graft)

26210 Excision or curettage of bone cyst or benign tumor of proximal, middle, or distal phalanx of finger;

26215 with autograft (includes obtaining graft)

26230 Partial excision (craterization, saucerization, or diaphysectomy) bone (eg, osteomyelitis); metacarpal

26235 proximal or middle phalanx of finger

26236 distal phalanx of finger

▲ **26250** Radical resection of tumor, metacarpal

►(26255 has been deleted)◄

▲ **26260** Radical resection of tumor, proximal or middle phalanx of finger

►(26261 has been deleted)◄

▲ **26262** Radical resection of tumor, distal phalanx of finger

Introduction or Removal

26320 Removal of implant from finger or hand

(For removal of foreign body in hand or finger, see 20520, 20525)

Repair, Revision, and/or Reconstruction

26340 Manipulation, finger joint, under anesthesia, each joint

(For application of external fixation, see 20690 or 20692)

26350 Repair or advancement, flexor tendon, not in zone 2 digital flexor tendon sheath (eg, no man's land); primary or secondary without free graft, each tendon

26352 secondary with free graft (includes obtaining graft), each tendon

26356 Repair or advancement, flexor tendon, in zone 2 digital flexor tendon sheath (eg, no man's land); primary, without free graft, each tendon

26357 secondary, without free graft, each tendon

26358 secondary, with free graft (includes obtaining graft), each tendon

26370 Repair or advancement of profundus tendon, with intact superficialis tendon; primary, each tendon

26372 secondary with free graft (includes obtaining graft), each tendon

26373 secondary without free graft, each tendon

26390 Excision flexor tendon, with implantation of synthetic rod for delayed tendon graft, hand or finger, each rod

26392 Removal of synthetic rod and insertion of flexor tendon graft, hand or finger (includes obtaining graft), each rod

26410 Repair, extensor tendon, hand, primary or secondary; without free graft, each tendon

26412 with free graft (includes obtaining graft), each tendon

26415 Excision of extensor tendon, with implantation of synthetic rod for delayed tendon graft, hand or finger, each rod

26416 Removal of synthetic rod and insertion of extensor tendon graft (includes obtaining graft), hand or finger, each rod

26418 Repair, extensor tendon, finger, primary or secondary; without free graft, each tendon

26420 with free graft (includes obtaining graft) each tendon

26426 Repair of extensor tendon, central slip, secondary (eg, boutonniere deformity); using local tissue(s), including lateral band(s), each finger

26428 with free graft (includes obtaining graft), each finger

26432 Closed treatment of distal extensor tendon insertion, with or without percutaneous pinning (eg, mallet finger)

26433 Repair of extensor tendon, distal insertion, primary or secondary; without graft (eg, mallet finger)

⊙=Moderate sedation ✚=Add-on code 𝒩=FDA approval pending #=Resequenced code

26434   with free graft (includes obtaining graft)

            (For tenovaginotomy for trigger finger, use 26055)

26437   Realignment of extensor tendon, hand, each tendon

26440   Tenolysis, flexor tendon; palm OR finger, each tendon

26442   palm AND finger, each tendon

26445   Tenolysis, extensor tendon, hand OR finger, each tendon

26449   Tenolysis, complex, extensor tendon, finger, including forearm, each tendon

26450   Tenotomy, flexor, palm, open, each tendon

26455   Tenotomy, flexor, finger, open, each tendon

26460   Tenotomy, extensor, hand or finger, open, each tendon

26471   Tenodesis; of proximal interphalangeal joint, each joint

26474   of distal joint, each joint

26476   Lengthening of tendon, extensor, hand or finger, each tendon

26477   Shortening of tendon, extensor, hand or finger, each tendon

26478   Lengthening of tendon, flexor, hand or finger, each tendon

26479   Shortening of tendon, flexor, hand or finger, each tendon

26480   Transfer or transplant of tendon, carpometacarpal area or dorsum of hand; without free graft, each tendon

26483   with free tendon graft (includes obtaining graft), each tendon

26485   Transfer or transplant of tendon, palmar; without free tendon graft, each tendon

26489   with free tendon graft (includes obtaining graft), each tendon

26490   Opponensplasty; superficialis tendon transfer type, each tendon

26492   tendon transfer with graft (includes obtaining graft), each tendon

26494   hypothenar muscle transfer

26496   other methods

            (For thumb fusion in opposition, use 26820)

26497   Transfer of tendon to restore intrinsic function; ring and small finger

26498   all 4 fingers

26499   Correction claw finger, other methods

26500   Reconstruction of tendon pulley, each tendon; with local tissues (separate procedure)

26502   with tendon or fascial graft (includes obtaining graft) (separate procedure)

26508   Release of thenar muscle(s) (eg, thumb contracture)

26510   Cross intrinsic transfer, each tendon

26516   Capsulodesis, metacarpophalangeal joint; single digit

26517   2 digits

26518   3 or 4 digits

26520   Capsulectomy or capsulotomy; metacarpophalangeal joint, each joint

26525   interphalangeal joint, each joint

            (To report carpometacarpal joint arthroplasty, use 25447)

26530   Arthroplasty, metacarpophalangeal joint; each joint

26531   with prosthetic implant, each joint

26535   Arthroplasty, interphalangeal joint; each joint

26536   with prosthetic implant, each joint

26540   Repair of collateral ligament, metacarpophalangeal or interphalangeal joint

26541   Reconstruction, collateral ligament, metacarpophalangeal joint, single; with tendon or fascial graft (includes obtaining graft)

26542   with local tissue (eg, adductor advancement)

26545   Reconstruction, collateral ligament, interphalangeal joint, single, including graft, each joint

26546   Repair non-union, metacarpal or phalanx (includes obtaining bone graft with or without external or internal fixation)

26548   Repair and reconstruction, finger, volar plate, interphalangeal joint

26550   Pollicization of a digit

26551   Transfer, toe-to-hand with microvascular anastomosis; great toe wrap-around with bone graft

            (For great toe with web space, use 20973)

26553   other than great toe, single

26554   other than great toe, double

            (Do not report code 69990 in addition to codes 26551-26554)

26555   Transfer, finger to another position without microvascular anastomosis

26556   Transfer, free toe joint, with microvascular anastomosis

            (Do not report code 69990 in addition to code 26556)

            (To report great toe-to-hand transfer, use 20973)

26560   Repair of syndactyly (web finger) each web space; with skin flaps

26561   with skin flaps and grafts

26562   complex (eg, involving bone, nails)

26565   Osteotomy; metacarpal, each

26567   phalanx of finger, each

26568   Osteoplasty, lengthening, metacarpal or phalanx

Surgery: Musculoskeletal System

26580   Repair cleft hand

26587   Reconstruction of polydactylous digit, soft tissue and bone

(For excision of polydactylous digit, soft tissue only, use 11200)

26590   Repair macrodactylia, each digit

26591   Repair, intrinsic muscles of hand, each muscle

26593   Release, intrinsic muscles of hand, each muscle

26596   Excision of constricting ring of finger, with multiple Z-plasties

(To report release of scar contracture or graft repairs see 11041-11042, 14040-14041, or 15120, 15240)

Fracture and/or Dislocation

26600   Closed treatment of metacarpal fracture, single; without manipulation, each bone

26605   with manipulation, each bone

26607   Closed treatment of metacarpal fracture, with manipulation, with external fixation, each bone

26608   Percutaneous skeletal fixation of metacarpal fracture, each bone

26615   Open treatment of metacarpal fracture, single, includes internal fixation, when performed, each bone

26641   Closed treatment of carpometacarpal dislocation, thumb, with manipulation

26645   Closed treatment of carpometacarpal fracture dislocation, thumb (Bennett fracture), with manipulation

26650   Percutaneous skeletal fixation of carpometacarpal fracture dislocation, thumb (Bennett fracture), with manipulation

26665   Open treatment of carpometacarpal fracture dislocation, thumb (Bennett fracture), includes internal fixation, when performed

26670   Closed treatment of carpometacarpal dislocation, other than thumb, with manipulation, each joint; without anesthesia

26675   requiring anesthesia

26676   Percutaneous skeletal fixation of carpometacarpal dislocation, other than thumb, with manipulation, each joint

26685   Open treatment of carpometacarpal dislocation, other than thumb; includes internal fixation, when performed, each joint

26686   complex, multiple, or delayed reduction

26700   Closed treatment of metacarpophalangeal dislocation, single, with manipulation; without anesthesia

26705   requiring anesthesia

26706   Percutaneous skeletal fixation of metacarpophalangeal dislocation, single, with manipulation

26715   Open treatment of metacarpophalangeal dislocation, single, includes internal fixation, when performed

26720   Closed treatment of phalangeal shaft fracture, proximal or middle phalanx, finger or thumb; without manipulation, each

26725   with manipulation, with or without skin or skeletal traction, each

26727   Percutaneous skeletal fixation of unstable phalangeal shaft fracture, proximal or middle phalanx, finger or thumb, with manipulation, each

26735   Open treatment of phalangeal shaft fracture, proximal or middle phalanx, finger or thumb, includes internal fixation, when performed, each

26740   Closed treatment of articular fracture, involving metacarpophalangeal or interphalangeal joint; without manipulation, each

26742   with manipulation, each

26746   Open treatment of articular fracture, involving metacarpophalangeal or interphalangeal joint, includes internal fixation, when performed, each

26750   Closed treatment of distal phalangeal fracture, finger or thumb; without manipulation, each

26755   with manipulation, each

26756   Percutaneous skeletal fixation of distal phalangeal fracture, finger or thumb, each

26765   Open treatment of distal phalangeal fracture, finger or thumb, includes internal fixation, when performed, each

26770   Closed treatment of interphalangeal joint dislocation, single, with manipulation; without anesthesia

26775   requiring anesthesia

26776   Percutaneous skeletal fixation of interphalangeal joint dislocation, single, with manipulation

26785   Open treatment of interphalangeal joint dislocation, includes internal fixation, when performed, single

Arthrodesis

26820   Fusion in opposition, thumb, with autogenous graft (includes obtaining graft)

26841   Arthrodesis, carpometacarpal joint, thumb, with or without internal fixation;

26842   with autograft (includes obtaining graft)

26843   Arthrodesis, carpometacarpal joint, digit, other than thumb, each;

26844   with autograft (includes obtaining graft)

26850   Arthrodesis, metacarpophalangeal joint, with or without internal fixation;

26852   with autograft (includes obtaining graft)

26860   Arthrodesis, interphalangeal joint, with or without internal fixation;

+ 26861   each additional interphalangeal joint (List separately in addition to code for primary procedure)

(Use 26861 in conjunction with 26860)

26862   with autograft (includes obtaining graft)

+ 26863   with autograft (includes obtaining graft), each additional joint (List separately in addition to code for primary procedure)

(Use 26863 in conjunction with 26862)

Amputation

(For hand through metacarpal bones, use 25927)

26910   Amputation, metacarpal, with finger or thumb (ray amputation), single, with or without interosseous transfer

(For repositioning, see 26550, 26555)

26951   Amputation, finger or thumb, primary or secondary, any joint or phalanx, single, including neurectomies; with direct closure

26952   with local advancement flaps (V-Y, hood)

(For repair of soft tissue defect requiring split or full thickness graft or other pedicle flaps, see 15050-15758)

Other Procedures

26989   Unlisted procedure, hands or fingers

Pelvis and Hip Joint

Including head and neck of femur.

Incision

(For incision and drainage procedures, superficial, see 10040-10160)

26990   Incision and drainage, pelvis or hip joint area; deep abscess or hematoma

26991   infected bursa

26992   Incision, bone cortex, pelvis and/or hip joint (eg, osteomyelitis or bone abscess)

27000   Tenotomy, adductor of hip, percutaneous (separate procedure)

27001   Tenotomy, adductor of hip, open

(To report bilateral procedure, report 27001 with modifier 50)

27003   Tenotomy, adductor, subcutaneous, open, with obturator neurectomy

(To report bilateral procedure, report 27003 with modifier 50)

27005   Tenotomy, hip flexor(s), open (separate procedure)

27006   Tenotomy, abductors and/or extensor(s) of hip, open (separate procedure)

27025   Fasciotomy, hip or thigh, any type

(To report bilateral procedure, report 27025 with modifier 50)

27027   Decompression fasciotomy(ies), pelvic (buttock) compartment(s) (eg, gluteus medius-minimus, gluteus maximus, iliopsoas, and/or tensor fascia lata muscle), unilateral

(To report bilateral procedure, report 27027 with modifier 50)

27030   Arthrotomy, hip, with drainage (eg, infection)

27033   Arthrotomy, hip, including exploration or removal of loose or foreign body

27035   Denervation, hip joint, intrapelvic or extrapelvic intra-articular branches of sciatic, femoral, or obturator nerves

(For obturator neurectomy, see 64763, 64766)

27036   Capsulectomy or capsulotomy, hip, with or without excision of heterotopic bone, with release of hip flexor muscles (ie, gluteus medius, gluteus minimus, tensor fascia latae, rectus femoris, sartorius, iliopsoas)

Excision

27040   Biopsy, soft tissue of pelvis and hip area; superficial

27041   deep, subfascial or intramuscular

(For needle biopsy of soft tissue, use 20206)

27043   ▶Code is out of numerical sequence. See 27040-27080◀

27045   ▶Code is out of numerical sequence. See 27040-27080◀

▲ **27047**   Excision, tumor, soft tissue of pelvis and hip area, subcutaneous; less than 3 cm

#● **27043**   3 cm or greater

▲ **27048**   Excision, tumor, soft tissue of pelvis and hip area, subfascial (eg, intramuscular); less than 5 cm

#● **27045**   5 cm or greater

▲ **27049**   Radical resection of tumor (eg, malignant neoplasm), soft tissue of pelvis and hip area; less than 5 cm

#● **27059**   5 cm or greater

27050   Arthrotomy, with biopsy; sacroiliac joint

27052   hip joint

27054   Arthrotomy with synovectomy, hip joint

27057   Decompression fasciotomy(ies), pelvic (buttock) compartment(s) (eg, gluteus medius-minimus, gluteus maximus, iliopsoas, and/or tensor fascia lata muscle) with debridement of nonviable muscle, unilateral

(To report bilateral procedure, report 27057 with modifier 50)

27059   ▶Code is out of numerical sequence. See 27040-27080◀

Surgery: Musculoskeletal System

Surgery: Musculoskeletal System

27060 Excision; ischial bursa

27062 trochanteric bursa or calcification

(For arthrocentesis or needling of bursa, use 20610)

27065 Excision of bone cyst or benign tumor; superficial (wing of ilium, symphysis pubis, or greater trochanter of femur) with or without autograft

27066 deep, with or without autograft

27067 with autograft requiring separate incision

27070 Partial excision (craterization, saucerization) (eg, osteomyelitis or bone abscess); superficial (eg, wing of ilium, symphysis pubis, or greater trochanter of femur)

27071 deep (subfascial or intramuscular)

▲ **27075** Radical resection of tumor; wing of ilium, 1 pubic or ischial ramus or symphysis pubis

▲ **27076** ilium, including acetabulum, both pubic rami, or ischium and acetabulum

▲ **27077** innominate bone, total

▲ **27078** ischial tuberosity and greater trochanter of femur

►(27079 has been deleted)◄

27080 Coccygectomy, primary

(For pressure (decubitus) ulcer, see 15920, 15922 and 15931-15958)

Introduction or Removal

27086 Removal of foreign body, pelvis or hip; subcutaneous tissue

27087 deep (subfascial or intramuscular)

27090 Removal of hip prosthesis; (separate procedure)

27091 complicated, including total hip prosthesis, methylmethacrylate with or without insertion of spacer

27093 Injection procedure for hip arthrography; without anesthesia

(For radiological supervision and interpretation, use 73525. Do not report 77002 in conjunction with 73525)

27095 with anesthesia

(For radiological supervision and interpretation, use 73525. Do not report 77002 in conjunction with 73525)

27096 Injection procedure for sacroiliac joint, arthrography and/or anesthetic/steroid

(27096 is to be used only with imaging confirmation of intra-articular needle positioning)

(For radiological supervision and interpretation of sacroiliac joint arthrography, use 73542)

(For fluoroscopic guidance without formal arthrography, use 77003)

(Code 27096 is a unilateral procedure. For bilateral procedure, use modifier 50)

Repair, Revision, and/or Reconstruction

27097 Release or recession, hamstring, proximal

27098 Transfer, adductor to ischium

27100 Transfer external oblique muscle to greater trochanter including fascial or tendon extension (graft)

27105 Transfer paraspinal muscle to hip (includes fascial or tendon extension graft)

27110 Transfer iliopsoas; to greater trochanter of femur

27111 to femoral neck

27120 Acetabuloplasty; (eg, Whitman, Colonna, Haygroves, or cup type)

27122 resection, femoral head (eg, Girdlestone procedure)

27125 Hemiarthroplasty, hip, partial (eg, femoral stem prosthesis, bipolar arthroplasty)

(For prosthetic replacement following fracture of the hip, use 27236)

27130 Arthroplasty, acetabular and proximal femoral prosthetic replacement (total hip arthroplasty), with or without autograft or allograft

27132 Conversion of previous hip surgery to total hip arthroplasty, with or without autograft or allograft

27134 Revision of total hip arthroplasty; both components, with or without autograft or allograft

27137 acetabular component only, with or without autograft or allograft

27138 femoral component only, with or without allograft

27140 Osteotomy and transfer of greater trochanter of femur (separate procedure)

27146 Osteotomy, iliac, acetabular or innominate bone;

27147 with open reduction of hip

27151 with femoral osteotomy

27156 with femoral osteotomy and with open reduction of hip

27158 Osteotomy, pelvis, bilateral (eg, congenital malformation)

27161 Osteotomy, femoral neck (separate procedure)

27165 Osteotomy, intertrochanteric or subtrochanteric including internal or external fixation and/or cast

27170 Bone graft, femoral head, neck, intertrochanteric or subtrochanteric area (includes obtaining bone graft)

27175 Treatment of slipped femoral epiphysis; by traction, without reduction

27176 by single or multiple pinning, in situ

27177 Open treatment of slipped femoral epiphysis; single or multiple pinning or bone graft (includes obtaining graft)

27178 closed manipulation with single or multiple pinning

27179 osteoplasty of femoral neck (Heyman type procedure)

27181   osteotomy and internal fixation

27185   Epiphyseal arrest by epiphysiodesis or stapling, greater trochanter of femur

27187   Prophylactic treatment (nailing, pinning, plating or wiring) with or without methylmethacrylate, femoral neck and proximal femur

Fracture and/or Dislocation

27193   Closed treatment of pelvic ring fracture, dislocation, diastasis or subluxation; without manipulation

27194   with manipulation, requiring more than local anesthesia

27200   Closed treatment of coccygeal fracture

27202   Open treatment of coccygeal fracture

27215   Open treatment of iliac spine(s), tuberosity avulsion, or iliac wing fracture(s), unilateral, for pelvic bone fracture patterns that do not disrupt the pelvic ring, includes internal fixation, when performed

(To report bilateral procedure, report 27215 with modifier 50)

27216   Percutaneous skeletal fixation of posterior pelvic bone fracture and/or dislocation, for fracture patterns that disrupt the pelvic ring, unilateral (includes ipsilateral ilium, sacroiliac joint and/or sacrum)

(To report bilateral procedure, report 27216 with modifier 50)

27217   Open treatment of anterior pelvic bone fracture and/or dislocation for fracture patterns that disrupt the pelvic ring, unilateral, includes internal fixation, when performed (includes pubic symphysis and/or ipsilateral superior/inferior rami)

(To report bilateral procedure, report 27217 with modifier 50)

27218   Open treatment of posterior pelvic bone fracture and/or dislocation, for fracture patterns that disrupt the pelvic ring, unilateral, includes internal fixation, when performed (includes ipsilateral ilium, sacroiliac joint and/or sacrum)

(To report bilateral procedure, report 27218 with modifier 50)

27220   Closed treatment of acetabulum (hip socket) fracture(s); without manipulation

27222   with manipulation, with or without skeletal traction

27226   Open treatment of posterior or anterior acetabular wall fracture, with internal fixation

27227   Open treatment of acetabular fracture(s) involving anterior or posterior (one) column, or a fracture running transversely across the acetabulum, with internal fixation

27228   Open treatment of acetabular fracture(s) involving anterior and posterior (two) columns, includes T-fracture and both column fracture with complete articular detachment, or single column or transverse fracture with associated acetabular wall fracture, with internal fixation

27230   Closed treatment of femoral fracture, proximal end, neck; without manipulation

27232   with manipulation, with or without skeletal traction

27235   Percutaneous skeletal fixation of femoral fracture, proximal end, neck

27236   Open treatment of femoral fracture, proximal end, neck, internal fixation or prosthetic replacement

27238   Closed treatment of intertrochanteric, peritrochanteric, or subtrochanteric femoral fracture; without manipulation

27240   with manipulation, with or without skin or skeletal traction

27244   Treatment of intertrochanteric, peritrochanteric, or subtrochanteric femoral fracture; with plate/screw type implant, with or without cerclage

27245   with intramedullary implant, with or without interlocking screws and/or cerclage

27246   Closed treatment of greater trochanteric fracture, without manipulation

27248   Open treatment of greater trochanteric fracture, includes internal fixation, when performed

27250   Closed treatment of hip dislocation, traumatic; without anesthesia

27252   requiring anesthesia

27253   Open treatment of hip dislocation, traumatic, without internal fixation

27254   Open treatment of hip dislocation, traumatic, with acetabular wall and femoral head fracture, with or without internal or external fixation

(For treatment of acetabular fracture with fixation, see 27226, 27227)

27256   Treatment of spontaneous hip dislocation (developmental, including congenital or pathological), by abduction, splint or traction; without anesthesia, without manipulation

27257   with manipulation, requiring anesthesia

27258   Open treatment of spontaneous hip dislocation (developmental, including congenital or pathological), replacement of femoral head in acetabulum (including tenotomy, etc);

27259   with femoral shaft shortening

27265   Closed treatment of post hip arthroplasty dislocation; without anesthesia

27266   requiring regional or general anesthesia

27267   Closed treatment of femoral fracture, proximal end, head; without manipulation

27268   with manipulation

27269   Open treatment of femoral fracture, proximal end, head, includes internal fixation, when performed

(Do not report 27269 in conjunction with 27033, 27253)

Manipulation

27275   Manipulation, hip joint, requiring general anesthesia

Arthrodesis

27280   Arthrodesis, sacroiliac joint (including obtaining graft)

(To report bilateral procedure, report 27280 with modifier 50)

27282   Arthrodesis, symphysis pubis (including obtaining graft)

27284   Arthrodesis, hip joint (including obtaining graft);

27286   with subtrochanteric osteotomy

Amputation

27290   Interpelviabdominal amputation (hindquarter amputation)

27295   Disarticulation of hip

Other Procedures

27299   Unlisted procedure, pelvis or hip joint

Femur (Thigh Region) and Knee Joint

Including tibial plateaus.

Incision

(For incision and drainage of abscess or hematoma, superficial, see 10040-10160)

27301   Incision and drainage, deep abscess, bursa, or hematoma, thigh or knee region

27303   Incision, deep, with opening of bone cortex, femur or knee (eg, osteomyelitis or bone abscess)

27305   Fasciotomy, iliotibial (tenotomy), open

(For combined Ober-Yount fasciotomy, use 27025)

27306   Tenotomy, percutaneous, adductor or hamstring; single tendon (separate procedure)

27307   multiple tendons

27310   Arthrotomy, knee, with exploration, drainage, or removal of foreign body (eg, infection)

Excision

27323   Biopsy, soft tissue of thigh or knee area; superficial

27324   deep (subfascial or intramuscular)

(For needle biopsy of soft tissue, use 20206)

27325   Neurectomy, hamstring muscle

27326   Neurectomy, popliteal (gastrocnemius)

▲ **27327**   Excision, tumor, soft tissue of thigh or knee area, subcutaneous; less than 3 cm

#● **27337**   3 cm or greater

▲ **27328**   Excision, tumor, soft tissue of thigh or knee area, subfascial (eg, intramuscular); less than 5 cm

#● **27339**   5 cm or greater

27329   ►Code is out of numerical sequence. See 27323-27365◄

27330   Arthrotomy, knee; with synovial biopsy only

27331   including joint exploration, biopsy, or removal of loose or foreign bodies

27332   Arthrotomy, with excision of semilunar cartilage (meniscectomy) knee; medial OR lateral

27333   medial AND lateral

27334   Arthrotomy, with synovectomy, knee; anterior OR posterior

27335   anterior AND posterior including popliteal area

27337   ►Code is out of numerical sequence. See 27323-27365◄

27339   ►Code is out of numerical sequence. See 27323-27365◄

27340   Excision, prepatellar bursa

27345   Excision of synovial cyst of popliteal space (eg, Baker's cyst)

27347   Excision of lesion of meniscus or capsule (eg, cyst, ganglion), knee

27350   Patellectomy or hemipatellectomy

27355   Excision or curettage of bone cyst or benign tumor of femur;

27356   with allograft

27357   with autograft (includes obtaining graft)

+ **27358**   with internal fixation (List in addition to code for primary procedure)

(Use 27358 in conjunction with 27355, 27356, or 27357)

27360   Partial excision (craterization, saucerization, or diaphysectomy) bone, femur, proximal tibia and/or fibula (eg, osteomyelitis or bone abscess)

#▲ **27329**   Radical resection of tumor (eg, malignant neoplasm), soft tissue of thigh or knee area; less than 5 cm

● **27364**   5 cm or greater

▲ **27365**   Radical resection of tumor, femur or knee

►(For radical resection of tumor, soft tissue of thigh or knee area, see 27329, 27364)◄

Introduction or Removal

27370   Injection procedure for knee arthrography

(For radiological supervision and interpretation, use 73580. Do not report 77002 in conjunction with 73580)

27372   Removal of foreign body, deep, thigh region or knee area

(For removal of knee prosthesis including "total knee," use 27488)

(For surgical arthroscopic knee procedures, see 29870-29887)

Repair, Revision, and/or Reconstruction

27380   Suture of infrapatellar tendon; primary

27381   secondary reconstruction, including fascial or tendon graft

27385   Suture of quadriceps or hamstring muscle rupture; primary

27386   secondary reconstruction, including fascial or tendon graft

27390   Tenotomy, open, hamstring, knee to hip; single tendon

27391   multiple tendons, 1 leg

27392   multiple tendons, bilateral

27393   Lengthening of hamstring tendon; single tendon

27394   multiple tendons, 1 leg

27395   multiple tendons, bilateral

27396   Transplant or transfer (with muscle redirection or rerouting), thigh (eg, extensor to flexor); single tendon

27397   multiple tendons

27400   Transfer, tendon or muscle, hamstrings to femur (eg, Egger's type procedure)

27403   Arthrotomy with meniscus repair, knee

(For arthroscopic repair, use 29882)

27405   Repair, primary, torn ligament and/or capsule, knee; collateral

27407   cruciate

(For cruciate ligament reconstruction, use 27427)

27409   collateral and cruciate ligaments

(For ligament reconstruction, see 27427-27429)

27412   Autologous chondrocyte implantation, knee

(Do not report 27412 in conjunction with 20926, 27331, 27570)

(For harvesting of chondrocytes, use 29870)

27415   Osteochondral allograft, knee, open

(For arthroscopic implant of osteochondral allograft, use 29867)

(Do not report 27415 in conjunction with 27416)

27416   Osteochondral autograft(s), knee, open (eg, mosaicplasty) (includes harvesting of autograft[s])

(Do not report 27416 in conjunction with 27415, 29870, 29871, 29875, 29884 when performed at the same session and/or 29874, 29877, 29879, 29885-29887 when performed in the same compartment)

(For arthroscopic osteochondral autograft of knee, use 29866)

27418   Anterior tibial tubercleplasty (eg, Maquet type procedure)

27420   Reconstruction of dislocating patella; (eg, Hauser type procedure)

27422   with extensor realignment and/or muscle advancement or release (eg, Campbell, Goldwaite type procedure)

27424   with patellectomy

27425   Lateral retinacular release, open

(For arthroscopic lateral release, use 29873)

27427   Ligamentous reconstruction (augmentation), knee; extra-articular

27428   intra-articular (open)

27429   intra-articular (open) and extra-articular

(For primary repair of ligament(s) performed in conjunction with reconstruction, report 27405, 27407 or 27409 in conjunction with 27427, 27428 or 27429)

27430   Quadricepsplasty (eg, Bennett or Thompson type)

27435   Capsulotomy, posterior capsular release, knee

27437   Arthroplasty, patella; without prosthesis

27438   with prosthesis

27440   Arthroplasty, knee, tibial plateau;

27441   with debridement and partial synovectomy

27442   Arthroplasty, femoral condyles or tibial plateau(s), knee;

27443   with debridement and partial synovectomy

27445   Arthroplasty, knee, hinge prosthesis (eg, Walldius type)

27446   Arthroplasty, knee, condyle and plateau; medial OR lateral compartment

27447   medial AND lateral compartments with or without patella resurfacing (total knee arthroplasty)

(For revision of total knee arthroplasty, use 27487)

(For removal of total knee prosthesis, use 27488)

27448   Osteotomy, femur, shaft or supracondylar; without fixation

(To report bilateral procedure, report 27448 with modifier 50)

27450   with fixation

(To report bilateral procedure, report 27450 with modifier 50)

27454 Osteotomy, multiple, with realignment on intramedullary rod, femoral shaft (eg, Sofield type procedure)

27455 Osteotomy, proximal tibia, including fibular excision or osteotomy (includes correction of genu varus [bowleg] or genu valgus [knock-knee]); before epiphyseal closure

(To report bilateral procedure, report 27455 with modifier 50)

27457   after epiphyseal closure

(To report bilateral procedure, report 27457 with modifier 50)

27465 Osteoplasty, femur; shortening (excluding 64876)

27466   lengthening

27468   combined, lengthening and shortening with femoral segment transfer

27470 Repair, nonunion or malunion, femur, distal to head and neck; without graft (eg, compression technique)

27472   with iliac or other autogenous bone graft (includes obtaining graft)

27475 Arrest, epiphyseal, any method (eg, epiphysiodesis); distal femur

27477   tibia and fibula, proximal

27479   combined distal femur, proximal tibia and fibula

27485 Arrest, hemiepiphyseal, distal femur or proximal tibia or fibula (eg, genu varus or valgus)

27486 Revision of total knee arthroplasty, with or without allograft; 1 component

27487   femoral and entire tibial component

27488 Removal of prosthesis, including total knee prosthesis, methylmethacrylate with or without insertion of spacer, knee

27495 Prophylactic treatment (nailing, pinning, plating, or wiring) with or without methylmethacrylate, femur

27496 Decompression fasciotomy, thigh and/or knee, 1 compartment (flexor or extensor or adductor);

27497   with debridement of nonviable muscle and/or nerve

27498 Decompression fasciotomy, thigh and/or knee, multiple compartments;

27499   with debridement of nonviable muscle and/or nerve

Fracture and/or Dislocation

(For arthroscopic treatment of intercondylar spine[s] and tuberosity fracture[s] of the knee, see 29850, 29851)

(For arthroscopic treatment of tibial fracture, see 29855, 29856)

27500 Closed treatment of femoral shaft fracture, without manipulation

27501 Closed treatment of supracondylar or transcondylar femoral fracture with or without intercondylar extension, without manipulation

27502 Closed treatment of femoral shaft fracture, with manipulation, with or without skin or skeletal traction

27503 Closed treatment of supracondylar or transcondylar femoral fracture with or without intercondylar extension, with manipulation, with or without skin or skeletal traction

27506 Open treatment of femoral shaft fracture, with or without external fixation, with insertion of intramedullary implant, with or without cerclage and/or locking screws

27507 Open treatment of femoral shaft fracture with plate/screws, with or without cerclage

27508 Closed treatment of femoral fracture, distal end, medial or lateral condyle, without manipulation

27509 Percutaneous skeletal fixation of femoral fracture, distal end, medial or lateral condyle, or supracondylar or transcondylar, with or without intercondylar extension, or distal femoral epiphyseal separation

27510 Closed treatment of femoral fracture, distal end, medial or lateral condyle, with manipulation

27511 Open treatment of femoral supracondylar or transcondylar fracture without intercondylar extension, includes internal fixation, when performed

27513 Open treatment of femoral supracondylar or transcondylar fracture with intercondylar extension, includes internal fixation, when performed

27514 Open treatment of femoral fracture, distal end, medial or lateral condyle, includes internal fixation, when performed

27516 Closed treatment of distal femoral epiphyseal separation; without manipulation

27517   with manipulation, with or without skin or skeletal traction

27519 Open treatment of distal femoral epiphyseal separation, includes internal fixation, when performed

27520 Closed treatment of patellar fracture, without manipulation

27524 Open treatment of patellar fracture, with internal fixation and/or partial or complete patellectomy and soft tissue repair

27530 Closed treatment of tibial fracture, proximal (plateau); without manipulation

27532   with or without manipulation, with skeletal traction

(For arthroscopic treatment, see 29855, 29856)

27535 Open treatment of tibial fracture, proximal (plateau); unicondylar, includes internal fixation, when performed

27536   bicondylar, with or without internal fixation

(For arthroscopic treatment, see 29855, 29856)

27538   Closed treatment of intercondylar spine(s) and/or tuberosity fracture(s) of knee, with or without manipulation

(For arthroscopic treatment, see 29850, 29851)

27540   Open treatment of intercondylar spine(s) and/or tuberosity fracture(s) of the knee, includes internal fixation, when performed

27550   Closed treatment of knee dislocation; without anesthesia

27552   requiring anesthesia

27556   Open treatment of knee dislocation, includes internal fixation, when performed; without primary ligamentous repair or augmentation/reconstruction

27557   with primary ligamentous repair

27558   with primary ligamentous repair, with augmentation/reconstruction

27560   Closed treatment of patellar dislocation; without anesthesia

(For recurrent dislocation, see 27420-27424)

27562   requiring anesthesia

27566   Open treatment of patellar dislocation, with or without partial or total patellectomy

Manipulation

27570   Manipulation of knee joint under general anesthesia (includes application of traction or other fixation devices)

Arthrodesis

27580   Arthrodesis, knee, any technique

Amputation

27590   Amputation, thigh, through femur, any level;

27591   immediate fitting technique including first cast

27592   open, circular (guillotine)

27594   secondary closure or scar revision

27596   re-amputation

27598   Disarticulation at knee

Other Procedures

27599   Unlisted procedure, femur or knee

Leg (Tibia and Fibula) and Ankle Joint

Incision

27600   Decompression fasciotomy, leg; anterior and/or lateral compartments only

27601   posterior compartment(s) only

27602   anterior and/or lateral, and posterior compartment(s)

(For incision and drainage procedures, superficial, see 10040-10160)

(For decompression fasciotomy with debridement, see 27892-27894)

27603   Incision and drainage, leg or ankle; deep abscess or hematoma

27604   infected bursa

27605   Tenotomy, percutaneous, Achilles tendon (separate procedure); local anesthesia

27606   general anesthesia

27607   Incision (eg, osteomyelitis or bone abscess), leg or ankle

27610   Arthrotomy, ankle, including exploration, drainage, or removal of foreign body

27612   Arthrotomy, posterior capsular release, ankle, with or without Achilles tendon lengthening

(See also 27685)

Excision

27613   Biopsy, soft tissue of leg or ankle area; superficial

27614   deep (subfascial or intramuscular)

(For needle biopsy of soft tissue, use 20206)

▲ **27615**   Radical resection of tumor (eg, malignant neoplasm), soft tissue of leg or ankle area; less than 5 cm

● **27616**   5 cm or greater

▲ **27618**   Excision, tumor, soft tissue of leg or ankle area, subcutaneous; less than 3 cm

#● **27632**   3 cm or greater

▲ **27619**   Excision, tumor, soft tissue of leg or ankle area, subfascial (eg, intramuscular); less than 5 cm

#● **27634**   5 cm or greater

27620   Arthrotomy, ankle, with joint exploration, with or without biopsy, with or without removal of loose or foreign body

27625   Arthrotomy, with synovectomy, ankle;

27626   including tenosynovectomy

27630   Excision of lesion of tendon sheath or capsule (eg, cyst or ganglion), leg and/or ankle

27632   ►Code is out of numerical sequence. See 27613-27647◄

27634   ►Code is out of numerical sequence. See 27613-27647◄

27635   Excision or curettage of bone cyst or benign tumor, tibia or fibula;

27637   with autograft (includes obtaining graft)

27638   with allograft

▲ 27640   Partial excision (craterization, saucerization, or diaphysectomy), bone (eg, osteomyelitis); tibia

▶(For exostosis excision, use 27635)◀

▲ 27641   fibula

▶(For exostosis excision, use 27635)◀

▲ 27645   Radical resection of tumor; tibia

▲ 27646   fibula

▲ 27647   talus or calcaneus

Introduction or Removal

27648   Injection procedure for ankle arthrography

(For radiological supervision and interpretation, use 73615. Do not report 77002 in conjunction with 73615)

(For ankle arthroscopy, see 29894-29898)

Repair, Revision, and/or Reconstruction

27650   Repair, primary, open or percutaneous, ruptured Achilles tendon;

27652   with graft (includes obtaining graft)

27654   Repair, secondary, Achilles tendon, with or without graft

27656   Repair, fascial defect of leg

27658   Repair, flexor tendon, leg; primary, without graft, each tendon

27659   secondary, with or without graft, each tendon

27664   Repair, extensor tendon, leg; primary, without graft, each tendon

27665   secondary, with or without graft, each tendon

27675   Repair, dislocating peroneal tendons; without fibular osteotomy

27676   with fibular osteotomy

27680   Tenolysis, flexor or extensor tendon, leg and/or ankle; single, each tendon

27681   multiple tendons (through separate incision(s))

27685   Lengthening or shortening of tendon, leg or ankle; single tendon (separate procedure)

27686   multiple tendons (through same incision), each

27687   Gastrocnemius recession (eg, Strayer procedure)

(Toe extensors are considered as a group to be a single tendon when transplanted into midfoot)

27690   Transfer or transplant of single tendon (with muscle redirection or rerouting); superficial (eg, anterior tibial extensors into midfoot)

27691   deep (eg, anterior tibial or posterior tibial through interosseous space, flexor digitorum longus, flexor hallucis longus, or peroneal tendon to midfoot or hindfoot)

+ 27692   each additional tendon (List separately in addition to code for primary procedure)

(Use 27692 in conjunction with 27690, 27691)

27695   Repair, primary, disrupted ligament, ankle; collateral

27696   both collateral ligaments

27698   Repair, secondary, disrupted ligament, ankle, collateral (eg, Watson-Jones procedure)

27700   Arthroplasty, ankle;

27702   with implant (total ankle)

27703   revision, total ankle

27704   Removal of ankle implant

27705   Osteotomy; tibia

27707   fibula

27709   tibia and fibula

27712   multiple, with realignment on intramedullary rod (eg, Sofield type procedure)

(For osteotomy to correct genu varus [bowleg] or genu valgus [knock-knee], see 27455-27457)

27715   Osteoplasty, tibia and fibula, lengthening or shortening

27720   Repair of nonunion or malunion, tibia; without graft, (eg, compression technique)

27722   with sliding graft

27724   with iliac or other autograft (includes obtaining graft)

27725   by synostosis, with fibula, any method

27726   Repair of fibula nonunion and/or malunion with internal fixation

(Do not report 27726 in conjunction with 27707)

27727   Repair of congenital pseudarthrosis, tibia

27730   Arrest, epiphyseal (epiphysiodesis), open; distal tibia

27732   distal fibula

27734   distal tibia and fibula

27740   Arrest, epiphyseal (epiphysiodesis), any method, combined, proximal and distal tibia and fibula;

27742   and distal femur

(For epiphyseal arrest of proximal tibia and fibula, use 27477)

27745   Prophylactic treatment (nailing, pinning, plating or wiring) with or without methylmethacrylate, tibia

Fracture and/or Dislocation

27750   Closed treatment of tibial shaft fracture (with or without fibular fracture); without manipulation

27752   with manipulation, with or without skeletal traction

27756   Percutaneous skeletal fixation of tibial shaft fracture (with or without fibular fracture) (eg, pins or screws)

27758   Open treatment of tibial shaft fracture (with or without fibular fracture), with plate/screws, with or without cerclage

27759   Treatment of tibial shaft fracture (with or without fibular fracture) by intramedullary implant, with or without interlocking screws and/or cerclage

27760   Closed treatment of medial malleolus fracture; without manipulation

27762   with manipulation, with or without skin or skeletal traction

27766   Open treatment of medial malleolus fracture, includes internal fixation, when performed

27767   Closed treatment of posterior malleolus fracture; without manipulation

27768   with manipulation

27769   Open treatment of posterior malleolus fracture, includes internal fixation, when performed

          (Do not report 27767-27769 in conjunction with 27808-27823)

27780   Closed treatment of proximal fibula or shaft fracture; without manipulation

27781   with manipulation

27784   Open treatment of proximal fibula or shaft fracture, includes internal fixation, when performed

27786   Closed treatment of distal fibular fracture (lateral malleolus); without manipulation

27788   with manipulation

27792   Open treatment of distal fibular fracture (lateral malleolus), includes internal fixation, when performed

          (For treatment of tibia and fibula shaft fractures, see 27750-27759)

27808   Closed treatment of bimalleolar ankle fracture (eg, lateral and medial malleoli, or lateral and posterior malleoli or medial and posterior malleoli); without manipulation

27810   with manipulation

27814   Open treatment of bimalleolar ankle fracture (eg, lateral and medial malleoli, or lateral and posterior malleoli, or medial and posterior malleoli), includes internal fixation, when performed

27816   Closed treatment of trimalleolar ankle fracture; without manipulation

27818   with manipulation

27822   Open treatment of trimalleolar ankle fracture, includes internal fixation, when performed, medial and/or lateral malleolus; without fixation of posterior lip

27823   with fixation of posterior lip

27824   Closed treatment of fracture of weight bearing articular portion of distal tibia (eg, pilon or tibial plafond), with or without anesthesia; without manipulation

27825   with skeletal traction and/or requiring manipulation

27826   Open treatment of fracture of weight bearing articular surface/portion of distal tibia (eg, pilon or tibial plafond), with internal fixation, when performed; of fibula only

27827   of tibia only

27828   of both tibia and fibula

27829   Open treatment of distal tibiofibular joint (syndesmosis) disruption, includes internal fixation, when performed

27830   Closed treatment of proximal tibiofibular joint dislocation; without anesthesia

27831   requiring anesthesia

27832   Open treatment of proximal tibiofibular joint dislocation, includes internal fixation, when performed, or with excision of proximal fibula

27840   Closed treatment of ankle dislocation; without anesthesia

27842   requiring anesthesia, with or without percutaneous skeletal fixation

27846   Open treatment of ankle dislocation, with or without percutaneous skeletal fixation; without repair or internal fixation

27848   with repair or internal or external fixation

          (For surgical or diagnostic arthroscopic procedures, see 29894-29898)

Manipulation

27860   Manipulation of ankle under general anesthesia (includes application of traction or other fixation apparatus)

Arthrodesis

27870   Arthrodesis, ankle, open

          (For arthroscopic ankle arthrodesis, use 29899)

27871   Arthrodesis, tibiofibular joint, proximal or distal

Amputation

27880   Amputation, leg, through tibia and fibula;

27881   with immediate fitting technique including application of first cast

27882   open, circular (guillotine)

27884   secondary closure or scar revision

27886   re-amputation

27888   Amputation, ankle, through malleoli of tibia and fibula (eg, Syme, Pirogoff type procedures), with plastic closure and resection of nerves

27889   Ankle disarticulation

Other Procedures

27892 Decompression fasciotomy, leg; anterior and/or lateral compartments only, with debridement of nonviable muscle and/or nerve

(For decompression fasciotomy of the leg without debridement, use 27600)

27893 posterior compartment(s) only, with debridement of nonviable muscle and/or nerve

(For decompression fasciotomy of the leg without debridement, use 27601)

27894 anterior and/or lateral, and posterior compartment(s), with debridement of nonviable muscle and/or nerve

(For decompression fasciotomy of the leg without debridement, use 27602)

27899 Unlisted procedure, leg or ankle

Foot and Toes

Incision

(For incision and drainage procedures, superficial, see 10040-10160)

28001 Incision and drainage, bursa, foot

28002 Incision and drainage below fascia, with or without tendon sheath involvement, foot; single bursal space

28003 multiple areas

28005 Incision, bone cortex (eg, osteomyelitis or bone abscess), foot

28008 Fasciotomy, foot and/or toe

(See also 28060, 28062, 28250)

28010 Tenotomy, percutaneous, toe; single tendon

28011 multiple tendons

(For open tenotomy, see 28230-28234)

28020 Arthrotomy, including exploration, drainage, or removal of loose or foreign body; intertarsal or tarsometatarsal joint

28022 metatarsophalangeal joint

28024 interphalangeal joint

28035 Release, tarsal tunnel (posterior tibial nerve decompression)

(For other nerve entrapments, see 64704, 64722)

Excision

28039 ►Code is out of numerical sequence. See 28043-28175◄

28041 ►Code is out of numerical sequence. See 28043-28175◄

▲ **28043** Excision, tumor, soft tissue of foot or toe, subcutaneous; less than 1.5 cm

#● **28039** 1.5 cm or greater

▲ **28045** Excision, tumor, soft tissue of foot or toe, subfascial (eg, intramuscular); less than 1.5 cm

#● **28041** 1.5 cm or greater

▲ **28046** Radical resection of tumor (eg, malignant neoplasm), soft tissue of foot or toe; less than 3 cm

● **28047** 3 cm or greater

28050 Arthrotomy with biopsy; intertarsal or tarsometatarsal joint

28052 metatarsophalangeal joint

28054 interphalangeal joint

28055 Neurectomy, intrinsic musculature of foot

28060 Fasciectomy, plantar fascia; partial (separate procedure)

28062 radical (separate procedure)

(For plantar fasciotomy, see 28008, 28250)

28070 Synovectomy; intertarsal or tarsometatarsal joint, each

28072 metatarsophalangeal joint, each

28080 Excision, interdigital (Morton) neuroma, single, each

28086 Synovectomy, tendon sheath, foot; flexor

28088 extensor

28090 Excision of lesion, tendon, tendon sheath, or capsule (including synovectomy) (eg, cyst or ganglion); foot

28092 toe(s), each

28100 Excision or curettage of bone cyst or benign tumor, talus or calcaneus;

28102 with iliac or other autograft (includes obtaining graft)

28103 with allograft

28104 Excision or curettage of bone cyst or benign tumor, tarsal or metatarsal, except talus or calcaneus;

28106 with iliac or other autograft (includes obtaining graft)

28107 with allograft

28108 Excision or curettage of bone cyst or benign tumor, phalanges of foot

(For ostectomy, partial (eg, hallux valgus, Silver type procedure), use 28290)

28110 Ostectomy, partial excision, fifth metatarsal head (bunionette) (separate procedure)

28111 Ostectomy, complete excision; first metatarsal head

28112 other metatarsal head (second, third or fourth)

28113 fifth metatarsal head

28114 all metatarsal heads, with partial proximal phalangectomy, excluding first metatarsal (eg, Clayton type procedure)

28116 Ostectomy, excision of tarsal coalition

28118 Ostectomy, calcaneus;

28119   for spur, with or without plantar fascial release

28120 Partial excision (craterization, saucerization, sequestrectomy, or diaphysectomy) bone (eg, osteomyelitis or bossing); talus or calcaneus

28122   tarsal or metatarsal bone, except talus or calcaneus

(For partial excision of talus or calcaneus, use 28120)

(For cheilectomy for hallux rigidus, use 28289)

28124   phalanx of toe

28126 Resection, partial or complete, phalangeal base, each toe

28130 Talectomy (astragalectomy)

(For calcanectomy, use 28118)

28140 Metatarsectomy

28150 Phalangectomy, toe, each toe

28153 Resection, condyle(s), distal end of phalanx, each toe

28160 Hemiphalangectomy or interphalangeal joint excision, toe, proximal end of phalanx, each

▲ **28171** Radical resection of tumor; tarsal (except talus or calcaneus)

▲ **28173**   metatarsal

▲ **28175**   phalanx of toe

(For talus or calcaneus, use 27647)

Introduction or Removal

28190 Removal of foreign body, foot; subcutaneous

28192   deep

28193   complicated

Repair, Revision, and/or Reconstruction

28200 Repair, tendon, flexor, foot; primary or secondary, without free graft, each tendon

28202   secondary with free graft, each tendon (includes obtaining graft)

28208 Repair, tendon, extensor, foot; primary or secondary, each tendon

28210   secondary with free graft, each tendon (includes obtaining graft)

28220 Tenolysis, flexor, foot; single tendon

28222   multiple tendons

28225 Tenolysis, extensor, foot; single tendon

28226   multiple tendons

28230 Tenotomy, open, tendon flexor; foot, single or multiple tendon(s) (separate procedure)

28232   toe, single tendon (separate procedure)

28234 Tenotomy, open, extensor, foot or toe, each tendon

(For tendon transfer to midfoot or hindfoot, see 27690, 27691)

28238 Reconstruction (advancement), posterior tibial tendon with excision of accessory tarsal navicular bone (eg, Kidner type procedure)

(For subcutaneous tenotomy, see 28010, 28011)

(For transfer or transplant of tendon with muscle redirection or rerouting, see 27690-27692)

(For extensor hallucis longus transfer with great toe IP fusion (Jones procedure), use 28760)

28240 Tenotomy, lengthening, or release, abductor hallucis muscle

28250 Division of plantar fascia and muscle (eg, Steindler stripping) (separate procedure)

28260 Capsulotomy, midfoot; medial release only (separate procedure)

28261   with tendon lengthening

28262   extensive, including posterior talotibial capsulotomy and tendon(s) lengthening (eg, resistant clubfoot deformity)

28264 Capsulotomy, midtarsal (eg, Heyman type procedure)

28270 Capsulotomy; metatarsophalangeal joint, with or without tenorrhaphy, each joint (separate procedure)

28272   interphalangeal joint, each joint (separate procedure)

28280 Syndactylization, toes (eg, webbing or Kelikian type procedure)

28285 Correction, hammertoe (eg, interphalangeal fusion, partial or total phalangectomy)

28286 Correction, cock-up fifth toe, with plastic skin closure (eg, Ruiz-Mora type procedure)

28288 Ostectomy, partial, exostectomy or condylectomy, metatarsal head, each metatarsal head

28289 Hallux rigidus correction with cheilectomy, debridement and capsular release of the first metatarsophalangeal joint

28290 Correction, hallux valgus (bunion), with or without sesamoidectomy; simple exostectomy (eg, Silver type procedure)

28292   Keller, McBride, or Mayo type procedure

28293   resection of joint with implant

28294   with tendon transplants (eg, Joplin type procedure)

28296   with metatarsal osteotomy (eg, Mitchell, Chevron, or concentric type procedures)

28297   Lapidus-type procedure

28298   by phalanx osteotomy

28299   by double osteotomy

28300   Osteotomy; calcaneus (eg, Dwyer or Chambers type procedure), with or without internal fixation

28302   talus

28304   Osteotomy, tarsal bones, other than calcaneus or talus;

28305   with autograft (includes obtaining graft) (eg, Fowler type)

28306   Osteotomy, with or without lengthening, shortening or angular correction, metatarsal; first metatarsal

28307   first metatarsal with autograft (other than first toe)

28308   other than first metatarsal, each

28309   multiple (eg, Swanson type cavus foot procedure)

28310   Osteotomy, shortening, angular or rotational correction; proximal phalanx, first toe (separate procedure)

28312   other phalanges, any toe

28313   Reconstruction, angular deformity of toe, soft tissue procedures only (eg, overlapping second toe, fifth toe, curly toes)

28315   Sesamoidectomy, first toe (separate procedure)

28320   Repair, nonunion or malunion; tarsal bones

28322   metatarsal, with or without bone graft (includes obtaining graft)

28340   Reconstruction, toe, macrodactyly; soft tissue resection

28341   requiring bone resection

28344   Reconstruction, toe(s); polydactyly

28345   syndactyly, with or without skin graft(s), each web

28360   Reconstruction, cleft foot

Fracture and/or Dislocation

28400   Closed treatment of calcaneal fracture; without manipulation

28405   with manipulation

28406   Percutaneous skeletal fixation of calcaneal fracture, with manipulation

28415   Open treatment of calcaneal fracture, includes internal fixation, when performed;

28420   with primary iliac or other autogenous bone graft (includes obtaining graft)

28430   Closed treatment of talus fracture; without manipulation

28435   with manipulation

28436   Percutaneous skeletal fixation of talus fracture, with manipulation

28445   Open treatment of talus fracture, includes internal fixation, when performed

28446   Open osteochondral autograft, talus (includes obtaining graft[s])

(Do not report 28446 in conjunction with 27705, 27707)

(For arthroscopic osteochondral talus graft, use 29892)

(For open osteochondral allograft or repairs with industrial grafts, use 28899)

28450   Treatment of tarsal bone fracture (except talus and calcaneus); without manipulation, each

28455   with manipulation, each

28456   Percutaneous skeletal fixation of tarsal bone fracture (except talus and calcaneus), with manipulation, each

28465   Open treatment of tarsal bone fracture (except talus and calcaneus), includes internal fixation, when performed, each

28470   Closed treatment of metatarsal fracture; without manipulation, each

28475   with manipulation, each

28476   Percutaneous skeletal fixation of metatarsal fracture, with manipulation, each

28485   Open treatment of metatarsal fracture, includes internal fixation, when performed, each

28490   Closed treatment of fracture great toe, phalanx or phalanges; without manipulation

28495   with manipulation

28496   Percutaneous skeletal fixation of fracture great toe, phalanx or phalanges, with manipulation

28505   Open treatment of fracture, great toe, phalanx or phalanges, includes internal fixation, when performed

28510   Closed treatment of fracture, phalanx or phalanges, other than great toe; without manipulation, each

28515   with manipulation, each

28525   Open treatment of fracture, phalanx or phalanges, other than great toe, includes internal fixation, when performed, each

28530   Closed treatment of sesamoid fracture

28531   Open treatment of sesamoid fracture, with or without internal fixation

28540   Closed treatment of tarsal bone dislocation, other than talotarsal; without anesthesia

28545   requiring anesthesia

28546   Percutaneous skeletal fixation of tarsal bone dislocation, other than talotarsal, with manipulation

28555   Open treatment of tarsal bone dislocation, includes internal fixation, when performed

28570   Closed treatment of talotarsal joint dislocation; without anesthesia

28575   requiring anesthesia

28576   Percutaneous skeletal fixation of talotarsal joint dislocation, with manipulation

28585   Open treatment of talotarsal joint dislocation, includes internal fixation, when performed

28600   Closed treatment of tarsometatarsal joint dislocation; without anesthesia

28605   requiring anesthesia

28606   Percutaneous skeletal fixation of tarsometatarsal joint dislocation, with manipulation

28615   Open treatment of tarsometatarsal joint dislocation, includes internal fixation, when performed

28630   Closed treatment of metatarsophalangeal joint dislocation; without anesthesia

28635   requiring anesthesia

28636   Percutaneous skeletal fixation of metatarsophalangeal joint dislocation, with manipulation

28645   Open treatment of metatarsophalangeal joint dislocation, includes internal fixation, when performed

28660   Closed treatment of interphalangeal joint dislocation; without anesthesia

28665   requiring anesthesia

28666   Percutaneous skeletal fixation of interphalangeal joint dislocation, with manipulation

28675   Open treatment of interphalangeal joint dislocation, includes internal fixation, when performed

Arthrodesis

28705   Arthrodesis; pantalar

28715   triple

28725   subtalar

28730   Arthrodesis, midtarsal or tarsometatarsal, multiple or transverse;

28735   with osteotomy (eg, flatfoot correction)

28737   Arthrodesis, with tendon lengthening and advancement, midtarsal, tarsal navicular-cuneiform (eg, Miller type procedure)

28740   Arthrodesis, midtarsal or tarsometatarsal, single joint

28750   Arthrodesis, great toe; metatarsophalangeal joint

28755   interphalangeal joint

28760   Arthrodesis, with extensor hallucis longus transfer to first metatarsal neck, great toe, interphalangeal joint (eg, Jones type procedure)

(For hammertoe operation or interphalangeal fusion, use 28285)

Amputation

28800   Amputation, foot; midtarsal (eg, Chopart type procedure)

28805   transmetatarsal

28810   Amputation, metatarsal, with toe, single

28820   Amputation, toe; metatarsophalangeal joint

28825   interphalangeal joint

(For amputation of tuft of distal phalanx, use 11752)

Other Procedures

28890   Extracorporeal shock wave, high energy, performed by a physician, requiring anesthesia other than local, including ultrasound guidance, involving the plantar fascia

(For extracorporeal shock wave therapy involving musculoskeletal system not otherwise specified, see Category III codes 0019T, 0101T, 0102T)

28899   Unlisted procedure, foot or toes

Application of Casts and Strapping

The listed procedures apply when the cast application or strapping is a replacement procedure used during or after the period of follow-up care, or when the cast application or strapping is an initial service performed without a restorative treatment or procedure(s) to stabilize or protect a fracture, injury, or dislocation and/or to afford comfort to a patient. Restorative treatment or procedure(s) rendered by another physician following the application of the initial cast/splint/strap may be reported with a treatment of fracture and/or dislocation code.

A physician who applies the initial cast, strap or splint and also assumes all of the subsequent fracture, dislocation, or injury care cannot use the application of casts and strapping codes as an initial service, since the first cast/splint or strap application is included in the treatment of fracture and/or dislocation codes. (See notes under Musculoskeletal System, page 75.) A temporary cast/splint/strap is not considered to be part of the preoperative care, and the use of the modifier 56 is not applicable. Additional evaluation and management services are reportable only if significant identifiable further services are provided at the time of the cast application or strapping.

If cast application or strapping is provided as an initial service (eg, casting of a sprained ankle or knee) in which no other procedure or treatment (eg, surgical repair, reduction of a fracture, or joint dislocation) is performed or is expected to be performed by a physician rendering the initial care only, use the casting, strapping and/or supply code (99070) in addition to an evaluation and management code as appropriate.

Listed procedures include removal of cast or strapping.

(For orthotics management and training, see 97760-97762)

Surgery: Musculoskeletal System

Body and Upper Extremity

Casts

29000	Application of halo type body cast (see 20661-20663 for insertion)
29010	Application of Risser jacket, localizer, body; only
29015	including head
29020	Application of turnbuckle jacket, body; only
29025	including head
29035	Application of body cast, shoulder to hips;
29040	including head, Minerva type
29044	including 1 thigh
29046	including both thighs
29049	Application, cast; figure-of-eight
29055	shoulder spica
29058	plaster Velpeau
29065	shoulder to hand (long arm)
29075	elbow to finger (short arm)
29085	hand and lower forearm (gauntlet)
29086	finger (eg, contracture)

Splints

29105	Application of long arm splint (shoulder to hand)
29125	Application of short arm splint (forearm to hand); static
29126	dynamic
29130	Application of finger splint; static
29131	dynamic

Strapping—Any Age

29200	Strapping; thorax
	▶(29220 has been deleted)◀
	▶(To report low back strapping, use 29799)◀
29240	shoulder (eg, Velpeau)
29260	elbow or wrist
29280	hand or finger

Lower Extremity

Casts

29305	Application of hip spica cast; 1 leg
29325	1 and one-half spica or both legs
	(For hip spica (body) cast, including thighs only, use 29046)
29345	Application of long leg cast (thigh to toes);
29355	walker or ambulatory type
29358	Application of long leg cast brace
29365	Application of cylinder cast (thigh to ankle)
29405	Application of short leg cast (below knee to toes);
29425	walking or ambulatory type
29435	Application of patellar tendon bearing (PTB) cast
29440	Adding walker to previously applied cast
29445	Application of rigid total contact leg cast
29450	Application of clubfoot cast with molding or manipulation, long or short leg
	(To report bilateral procedure, use 29450 with modifier 50)

Splints

29505	Application of long leg splint (thigh to ankle or toes)
29515	Application of short leg splint (calf to foot)

Strapping—Any Age

29520	Strapping; hip
29530	knee
29540	ankle and/or foot
	▶(Do not report 29540 in conjunction with 29581)◀
29550	toes
29580	Unna boot
	▶(Do not report 29580 in conjunction with 29581)◀
● **29581**	Application of multi-layer venous wound compression system, below knee
	▶(Do not report 29581 in conjunction with 29540, 29580)◀
29590	Denis-Browne splint strapping

Surgery: Musculoskeletal System

Removal or Repair

Codes for cast removals should be employed only for casts applied by another physician.

29700   Removal or bivalving; gauntlet, boot or body cast

29705   full arm or full leg cast

29710   shoulder or hip spica, Minerva, or Risser jacket, etc.

29715   turnbuckle jacket

29720   Repair of spica, body cast or jacket

29730   Windowing of cast

29740   Wedging of cast (except clubfoot casts)

29750   Wedging of clubfoot cast

           (To report bilateral procedure, use 29750 with modifier 50)

Other Procedures

29799   Unlisted procedure, casting or strapping

Endoscopy/Arthroscopy

Surgical endoscopy/arthroscopy always includes a diagnostic endoscopy/arthroscopy.

When arthroscopy is performed in conjunction with arthrotomy, add modifier 51.

29800   Arthroscopy, temporomandibular joint, diagnostic, with or without synovial biopsy (separate procedure)

29804   Arthroscopy, temporomandibular joint, surgical

           (For open procedure, use 21010)

29805   Arthroscopy, shoulder, diagnostic, with or without synovial biopsy (separate procedure)

           (For open procedure, see 23065-23066, 23100-23101)

29806   Arthroscopy, shoulder, surgical; capsulorrhaphy

           (For open procedure, see 23450-23466)

           (To report thermal capsulorrhaphy, use 29999)

29807   repair of SLAP lesion

29819   with removal of loose body or foreign body

           (For open procedure, see 23040-23044, 23107)

29820   synovectomy, partial

           (For open procedure, see 23105)

29821   synovectomy, complete

           (For open procedure, see 23105)

29822   debridement, limited

           (For open procedure, see specific open shoulder procedure performed)

29823   debridement, extensive

           (For open procedure, see specific open shoulder procedure performed)

29824   distal claviculectomy including distal articular surface (Mumford procedure)

           (For open procedure, use 23120)

29825   with lysis and resection of adhesions, with or without manipulation

           (For open procedure, see specific open shoulder procedure performed)

29826   decompression of subacromial space with partial acromioplasty, with or without coracoacromial release

           (For open procedure, use 23130 or 23415)

29827   with rotator cuff repair

           (For open or mini-open rotator cuff repair, use 23412)

           (When arthroscopic subacromial decompression is performed at the same setting, use 29826 and append modifier 51)

           (When arthroscopic distal clavicle resection is performed at the same setting, use 29824 and append modifier 51)

29828   biceps tenodesis

           (Do not report 29828 in conjunction with 29805, 29820, 29822)

           (For open biceps tenodesis, use 23430)

29830   Arthroscopy, elbow, diagnostic, with or without synovial biopsy (separate procedure)

29834   Arthroscopy, elbow, surgical; with removal of loose body or foreign body

29835   synovectomy, partial

29836   synovectomy, complete

29837   debridement, limited

29838   debridement, extensive

29840   Arthroscopy, wrist, diagnostic, with or without synovial biopsy (separate procedure)

29843   Arthroscopy, wrist, surgical; for infection, lavage and drainage

29844   synovectomy, partial

29845   synovectomy, complete

29846   excision and/or repair of triangular fibrocartilage and/or joint debridement

29847   internal fixation for fracture or instability

29848   Endoscopy, wrist, surgical, with release of transverse carpal ligament

           (For open procedure, use 64721)

Surgery: Musculoskeletal System

29850 Arthroscopically aided treatment of intercondylar spine(s) and/or tuberosity fracture(s) of the knee, with or without manipulation; without internal or external fixation (includes arthroscopy)

29851 with internal or external fixation (includes arthroscopy)

(For bone graft, use 20900, 20902)

29855 Arthroscopically aided treatment of tibial fracture, proximal (plateau); unicondylar, includes internal fixation, when performed (includes arthroscopy)

29856 bicondylar, includes internal fixation, when performed (includes arthroscopy)

(For bone graft, use 20900, 20902)

29860 Arthroscopy, hip, diagnostic with or without synovial biopsy (separate procedure)

29861 Arthroscopy, hip, surgical; with removal of loose body or foreign body

29862 with debridement/shaving of articular cartilage (chondroplasty), abrasion arthroplasty, and/or resection of labrum

29863 with synovectomy

29866 Arthroscopy, knee, surgical; osteochondral autograft(s) (eg, mosaicplasty) (includes harvesting of the autograft[s])

(Do not report 29866 in conjunction with 29870, 29871, 29875, 29884 when performed at the same session and/or 29874, 29877, 29879, 29885-29887 when performed in the same compartment)

(For open osteochondral autograft of knee, use 27416)

29867 osteochondral allograft (eg, mosaicplasty)

(Do not report 29867 in conjunction with 27570, 29870, 29871, 29875, 29884 when performed at the same session and/or 29874, 29877, 29879, 29885-29887 when performed in the same compartment)

(Do not report 29867 in conjunction with 27415)

29868 meniscal transplantation (includes arthrotomy for meniscal insertion), medial or lateral

(Do not report 29868 in conjunction with 29870, 29871, 29875, 29880, 29883, 29884 when performed at the same session or 29874, 29877, 29881, 29882 when performed in the same compartment)

29870 Arthroscopy, knee, diagnostic, with or without synovial biopsy (separate procedure)

(For open autologous chondrocyte implantation of the knee, use 27412)

29871 Arthroscopy, knee, surgical; for infection, lavage and drainage

(For implantation of osteochondral graft for treatment of articular surface defect, see 27412, 27415, 29866, 29867)

29873 with lateral release

(For open lateral release, use 27425)

29874 for removal of loose body or foreign body (eg, osteochondritis dissecans fragmentation, chondral fragmentation)

29875 synovectomy, limited (eg, plica or shelf resection) (separate procedure)

29876 synovectomy, major, 2 or more compartments (eg, medial or lateral)

29877 debridement/shaving of articular cartilage (chondroplasty)

29879 abrasion arthroplasty (includes chondroplasty where necessary) or multiple drilling or microfracture

29880 with meniscectomy (medial AND lateral, including any meniscal shaving)

29881 with meniscectomy (medial OR lateral, including any meniscal shaving)

29882 with meniscus repair (medial OR lateral)

29883 with meniscus repair (medial AND lateral)

(For meniscal transplantation, medial or lateral, knee, use 29868)

29884 with lysis of adhesions, with or without manipulation (separate procedure)

29885 drilling for osteochondritis dissecans with bone grafting, with or without internal fixation (including debridement of base of lesion)

29886 drilling for intact osteochondritis dissecans lesion

29887 drilling for intact osteochondritis dissecans lesion with internal fixation

29888 Arthroscopically aided anterior cruciate ligament repair/augmentation or reconstruction

29889 Arthroscopically aided posterior cruciate ligament repair/augmentation or reconstruction

(Procedures 29888 and 29889 should not be used with reconstruction procedures 27427-27429)

29891 Arthroscopy, ankle, surgical, excision of osteochondral defect of talus and/or tibia, including drilling of the defect

29892 Arthroscopically aided repair of large osteochondritis dissecans lesion, talar dome fracture, or tibial plafond fracture, with or without internal fixation (includes arthroscopy)

29893 Endoscopic plantar fasciotomy

29894 Arthroscopy, ankle (tibiotalar and fibulotalar joints), surgical; with removal of loose body or foreign body

29895 synovectomy, partial

29897 debridement, limited

29898 debridement, extensive

⊙=Moderate sedation   ✦=Add-on code   ✎=FDA approval pending   #=Resequenced code

29899   with ankle arthrodesis

          (For open ankle arthrodesis, use 27870)

29900   Arthroscopy, metacarpophalangeal joint, diagnostic, includes synovial biopsy

          (Do not report 29900 with 29901, 29902)

29901   Arthroscopy, metacarpophalangeal joint, surgical; with debridement

29902   with reduction of displaced ulnar collateral ligament (eg, Stenar lesion)

29904   Arthroscopy, subtalar joint, surgical; with removal of loose body or foreign body

29905   with synovectomy

29906   with debridement

29907   with subtalar arthrodesis

29999   Unlisted procedure, arthroscopy

Surgery: Musculoskeletal System

Notes

⊙=Moderate sedation ✚=Add-on code ⚡=FDA approval pending #=Resequenced code

Respiratory System

Nose

Incision

30000   Drainage abscess or hematoma, nasal, internal approach

(For external approach, see 10060, 10140)

30020   Drainage abscess or hematoma, nasal septum

(For lateral rhinotomy, see specific application (eg, 30118, 30320))

Excision

30100   Biopsy, intranasal

(For biopsy skin of nose, see 11100, 11101)

30110   Excision, nasal polyp(s), simple

(30110 would normally be completed in an office setting)

(To report bilateral procedure, use 30110 with modifier 50)

30115   Excision, nasal polyp(s), extensive

(30115 would normally require the facilities available in a hospital setting)

(To report bilateral procedure, use 30115 with modifier 50)

30117   Excision or destruction (eg, laser), intranasal lesion; internal approach

30118   external approach (lateral rhinotomy)

30120   Excision or surgical planing of skin of nose for rhinophyma

30124   Excision dermoid cyst, nose; simple, skin, subcutaneous

30125   complex, under bone or cartilage

30130   Excision inferior turbinate, partial or complete, any method

(For excision of superior or middle turbinate, use 30999)

30140   Submucous resection inferior turbinate, partial or complete, any method

(Do not report 30130 or 30140 in conjunction with 30801, 30802, 30930)

(For submucous resection of superior or middle turbinate, use 30999)

(For endoscopic resection of concha bullosa of middle turbinate, use 31240)

(For submucous resection of nasal septum, use 30520)

30150   Rhinectomy; partial

30160   total

▶(For closure and/or reconstruction, primary or delayed, see **Integumentary System,** 13150-13160, 14060-14302, 15120, 15121, 15260, 15261, 15760, 20900-20912)◀

Introduction

30200   Injection into turbinate(s), therapeutic

30210   Displacement therapy (Proetz type)

30220   Insertion, nasal septal prosthesis (button)

Removal of Foreign Body

30300   Removal foreign body, intranasal; office type procedure

30310   requiring general anesthesia

30320   by lateral rhinotomy

Repair

(For obtaining tissues for graft, see 20900-20926, 21210)

30400   Rhinoplasty, primary; lateral and alar cartilages and/or elevation of nasal tip

(For columellar reconstruction, see 13150 et seq)

30410   complete, external parts including bony pyramid, lateral and alar cartilages, and/or elevation of nasal tip

30420   including major septal repair

30430   Rhinoplasty, secondary; minor revision (small amount of nasal tip work)

30435   intermediate revision (bony work with osteotomies)

30450   major revision (nasal tip work and osteotomies)

30460   Rhinoplasty for nasal deformity secondary to congenital cleft lip and/or palate, including columellar lengthening; tip only

30462   tip, septum, osteotomies

30465   Repair of nasal vestibular stenosis (eg, spreader grafting, lateral nasal wall reconstruction)

(30465 excludes obtaining graft. For graft procedure, see 20900-20926, 21210)

(30465 is used to report a bilateral procedure. For unilateral procedure, use modifier 52)

30520   Septoplasty or submucous resection, with or without cartilage scoring, contouring or replacement with graft

(For submucous resection of turbinates, use 30140)

30540   Repair choanal atresia; intranasal

30545   transpalatine

(Do not report modifier 63 in conjunction with 30540, 30545)

30560   Lysis intranasal synechia

30580   Repair fistula; oromaxillary (combine with 31030 if antrotomy is included)

30600   oronasal

30620   Septal or other intranasal dermatoplasty (does not include obtaining graft)

30630   Repair nasal septal perforations

Destruction

▲ **30801**   Ablation, soft tissue of inferior turbinates, unilateral or bilateral, any method (eg, electrocautery, radiofrequency ablation, or tissue volume reduction); superficial

►(For ablation of superior or middle turbinates, use 30999)◄

▲ **30802**   intramural (ie, submucosal)

►(Do not report 30801 in conjunction with 30802)◄

(Do not report 30801, 30802, 30930 in conjunction with 30130 or 30140)

(For cautery performed for control of nasal hemorrhage, see 30901-30906)

Other Procedures

30901   Control nasal hemorrhage, anterior, simple (limited cautery and/or packing) any method

(To report bilateral procedure, use 30901 with modifier 50)

30903   Control nasal hemorrhage, anterior, complex (extensive cautery and/or packing) any method

(To report bilateral procedure, use 30903 with modifier 50)

30905   Control nasal hemorrhage, posterior, with posterior nasal packs and/or cautery, any method; initial

30906   subsequent

30915   Ligation arteries; ethmoidal

30920   internal maxillary artery, transantral

(For ligation external carotid artery, use 37600)

30930   Fracture nasal inferior turbinate(s), therapeutic

(Do not report 30801, 30802, 30930 in conjunction with 30130 or 30140)

(For fracture of superior or middle turbinate(s), use 30999)

30999   Unlisted procedure, nose

Accessory Sinuses

Incision

31000   Lavage by cannulation; maxillary sinus (antrum puncture or natural ostium)

(To report bilateral procedure, use 31000 with modifier 50)

31002   sphenoid sinus

31020   Sinusotomy, maxillary (antrotomy); intranasal

(To report bilateral procedure, use 31020 with modifier 50)

31030   radical (Caldwell-Luc) without removal of antrochoanal polyps

(To report bilateral procedure, use 31030 with modifier 50)

31032   radical (Caldwell-Luc) with removal of antrochoanal polyps

(To report bilateral procedure, use 31032 with modifier 50)

31040   Pterygomaxillary fossa surgery, any approach

(For transantral ligation of internal maxillary artery, use 30920)

31050   Sinusotomy, sphenoid, with or without biopsy;

31051   with mucosal stripping or removal of polyp(s)

31070   Sinusotomy frontal; external, simple (trephine operation)

(For frontal intranasal sinusotomy, use 31276)

31075   transorbital, unilateral (for mucocele or osteoma, Lynch type)

31080   obliterative without osteoplastic flap, brow incision (includes ablation)

31081   obliterative, without osteoplastic flap, coronal incision (includes ablation)

31084   obliterative, with osteoplastic flap, brow incision

31085   obliterative, with osteoplastic flap, coronal incision

31086   nonobliterative, with osteoplastic flap, brow incision

31087   nonobliterative, with osteoplastic flap, coronal incision

31090   Sinusotomy, unilateral, 3 or more paranasal sinuses (frontal, maxillary, ethmoid, sphenoid)

Excision

31200   Ethmoidectomy; intranasal, anterior

31201   intranasal, total

31205   extranasal, total

31225   Maxillectomy; without orbital exenteration

31230   with orbital exenteration (en bloc)

(For orbital exenteration only, see 65110 et seq)

(For skin grafts, see 15120 et seq)

Endoscopy

A surgical sinus endoscopy includes a sinusotomy (when appropriate) and diagnostic endoscopy.

Codes 31231-31294 are used to report unilateral procedures unless otherwise specified.

The codes 31231-31235 for diagnostic evaluation refer to employing a nasal/sinus endoscope to inspect the interior of the nasal cavity and the middle and superior meatus, the turbinates, and the spheno-ethmoid recess. Any time a diagnostic evaluation is performed all these areas would be inspected and a separate code is not reported for each area.

31231   Nasal endoscopy, diagnostic, unilateral or bilateral (separate procedure)

31233   Nasal/sinus endoscopy, diagnostic with maxillary sinusoscopy (via inferior meatus or canine fossa puncture)

31235   Nasal/sinus endoscopy, diagnostic with sphenoid sinusoscopy (via puncture of sphenoidal face or cannulation of ostium)

31237   Nasal/sinus endoscopy, surgical; with biopsy, polypectomy or debridement (separate procedure)

31238   with control of nasal hemorrhage

31239   with dacryocystorhinostomy

31240   with concha bullosa resection

(For endoscopic osteomeatal complex [OMC] resection with antrostomy and/or anterior ethmoidectomy, with or without removal of polyp[s], use 31254 and 31256)

(For endoscopic osteomeatal complex [OMC] resection with antrostomy, removal of antral mucosal disease, and/or anterior ethmoidectomy, with or without removal of polyp[s], use 31254 and 31267)

(For endoscopic frontal sinus exploration, osteomeatal complex [OMC] resection and/or anterior ethmoidectomy, with or without removal of polyp[s], use 31254 and 31276)

(For endoscopic frontal sinus exploration, osteomeatal complex [OMC] resection, antrostomy, and/or anterior ethmoidectomy, with or without removal of polyp[s], use 31254, 31256, and 31276)

(For endoscopic nasal diagnostic endoscopy, see 31231-31235)

(For endoscopic osteomeatal complex [OMC] resection, frontal sinus exploration, antrostomy, removal of antral mucosal disease, and/or anterior ethmoidectomy, with or without removal of polyp[s], use 31254, 31267, and 31276)

31254   Nasal/sinus endoscopy, surgical; with ethmoidectomy, partial (anterior)

31255   with ethmoidectomy, total (anterior and posterior)

31256   Nasal/sinus endoscopy, surgical, with maxillary antrostomy;

(For endoscopic anterior and posterior ethmoidectomy [APE] and antrostomy, with or without removal of polyp[s], use 31255 and 31256)

(For endoscopic anterior and posterior ethmoidectomy [APE], antrostomy and removal of antral mucosal disease, with or without removal of polyp[s], use 31255 and 31267)

(For endoscopic anterior and posterior ethmoidectomy [APE], and frontal sinus exploration, with or without removal of polyp[s], use 31255 and 31276)

31267   with removal of tissue from maxillary sinus

(For endoscopic anterior and posterior ethmoidectomy [APE], and frontal sinus exploration and antrostomy, with or without removal of polyp[s], use 31255, 31256, and 31276)

(For endoscopic anterior and posterior ethmoidectomy [APE], frontal sinus exploration, antrostomy, and removal of antral mucosal disease, with or without removal of polyp[s], use 31255, 31267, and 31276)

31276   Nasal/sinus endoscopy, surgical with frontal sinus exploration, with or without removal of tissue from frontal sinus

(For endoscopic anterior and posterior ethmoidectomy and sphenoidotomy [APS], with or without removal of polyp[s], use 31255, 31287 or 31288)

(For endoscopic anterior and posterior ethmoidectomy and sphenoidotomy [APS], and antrostomy, with or without removal of polyp[s], use 31255, 31256, and 31287 or 31288)

(For endoscopic anterior and posterior ethmoidectomy and sphenoidotomy [APS], antrostomy and removal of antral mucosal disease, with or without removal of polyp[s], use 31255, 31267, and 31287 or 31288)

(For endoscopic anterior and posterior ethmoidectomy and sphenoidotomy [APS], and frontal sinus exploration with or without removal of polyp[s], use 31255, 31287 or 31288, and 31276)

(For endoscopic anterior and posterior ethmoidectomy and sphenoidotomy [APS], with or without removal of polyp[s], with frontal sinus exploration and antrostomy, use 31255, 31256, 31287 or 31288, and 31276)

(For unilateral endoscopy of 2 or more sinuses, see 31231-31235)

(For endoscopic anterior and posterior ethmoidectomy and sphenoidotomy [APS], frontal sinus exploration, antrostomy and removal of antral mucosal disease, with or without removal of polyp[s], see 31255, 31267, 31287 or 31288 and 31276)

31287 Nasal/sinus endoscopy, surgical, with sphenoidotomy;

31288   with removal of tissue from the sphenoid sinus

31290 Nasal/sinus endoscopy, surgical, with repair of cerebrospinal fluid leak; ethmoid region

31291   sphenoid region

31292 Nasal/sinus endoscopy, surgical; with medial or inferior orbital wall decompression

31293   with medial orbital wall and inferior orbital wall decompression

31294   with optic nerve decompression

Other Procedures

(For hypophysectomy, transantral or transeptal approach, use 61548)

(For transcranial hypophysectomy, use 61546)

31299 Unlisted procedure, accessory sinuses

Larynx

Excision

31300 Laryngotomy (thyrotomy, laryngofissure); with removal of tumor or laryngocele, cordectomy

31320   diagnostic

31360 Laryngectomy; total, without radical neck dissection

31365   total, with radical neck dissection

31367   subtotal supraglottic, without radical neck dissection

31368   subtotal supraglottic, with radical neck dissection

31370 Partial laryngectomy (hemilaryngectomy); horizontal

31375   laterovertical

31380   anterovertical

31382   antero-latero-vertical

31390 Pharyngolaryngectomy, with radical neck dissection; without reconstruction

31395   with reconstruction

31400 Arytenoidectomy or arytenoidopexy, external approach

(For endoscopic arytenoidectomy, use 31560)

31420 Epiglottidectomy

Introduction

⊘ **31500** Intubation, endotracheal, emergency procedure

(For injection procedure for segmental bronchography, use 31656)

31502 Tracheotomy tube change prior to establishment of fistula tract

Endoscopy

For endoscopic procedures, code appropriate endoscopy of each anatomic site examined. If using operating microscope, telescope, or both, use the applicable code only once per operative session.

31505 Laryngoscopy, indirect; diagnostic (separate procedure)

31510   with biopsy

31511   with removal of foreign body

31512   with removal of lesion

31513   with vocal cord injection

31515 Laryngoscopy direct, with or without tracheoscopy; for aspiration

31520   diagnostic, newborn

(Do not report modifier 63 in conjunction with 31520)

31525   diagnostic, except newborn

31526   diagnostic, with operating microscope or telescope

(Do not report code 69990 in addition to code 31526)

31527   with insertion of obturator

31528   with dilation, initial

31529   with dilation, subsequent

31530 Laryngoscopy, direct, operative, with foreign body removal;

31531   with operating microscope or telescope

(Do not report code 69990 in addition to code 31531)

31535 Laryngoscopy, direct, operative, with biopsy;

31536   with operating microscope or telescope

(Do not report code 69990 in addition to code 31536)

31540 Laryngoscopy, direct, operative, with excision of tumor and/or stripping of vocal cords or epiglottis;

31541   with operating microscope or telescope

(Do not report code 69990 in addition to code 31541)

31545 Laryngoscopy, direct, operative, with operating microscope or telescope, with submucosal removal of non-neoplastic lesion(s) of vocal cord; reconstruction with local tissue flap(s)

31546   reconstruction with graft(s) (includes obtaining autograft)

(Do not report 31546 in addition to 20926 for graft harvest)

(For reconstruction of vocal cord with allograft, use 31599)

(Do not report 31545 or 31546 in conjunction with 31540, 31541, 69990)

31560 Laryngoscopy, direct, operative, with arytenoidectomy;

31561   with operating microscope or telescope

           (Do not report code 69990 in addition to code 31561)

31570   Laryngoscopy, direct, with injection into vocal cord(s), therapeutic;

31571   with operating microscope or telescope

           (Do not report code 69990 in addition to code 31571)

31575   °Laryngoscopy, flexible fiberoptic; diagnostic

31576   with biopsy

31577   with removal of foreign body

31578   with removal of lesion

           (To report flexible fiberoptic endoscopic evaluation of swallowing, see 92612-92613)

           (To report flexible fiberoptic endoscopic evaluation with sensory testing, see 92614-92615)

           (To report flexible fiberoptic endoscopic evaluation of swallowing with sensory testing, see 92616-92617)

           (For flexible fiberoptic laryngoscopy as part of flexible fiberoptic endoscopic evaluation of swallowing and/or laryngeal sensory testing by cine or video recording, see 92612-92617)

31579   Laryngoscopy, flexible or rigid fiberoptic, with stroboscopy

Repair

31580   Laryngoplasty; for laryngeal web, 2-stage, with keel insertion and removal

31582   for laryngeal stenosis, with graft or core mold, including tracheotomy

31584   with open reduction of fracture

31587   Laryngoplasty, cricoid split

31588   Laryngoplasty, not otherwise specified (eg, for burns, reconstruction after partial laryngectomy)

31590   Laryngeal reinnervation by neuromuscular pedicle

Destruction

31595   Section recurrent laryngeal nerve, therapeutic (separate procedure), unilateral

Other Procedures

31599   Unlisted procedure, larynx

Trachea and Bronchi

Incision

31600   Tracheostomy, planned (separate procedure);

31601   younger than 2 years

31603   Tracheostomy, emergency procedure; transtracheal

31605   cricothyroid membrane

31610   Tracheostomy, fenestration procedure with skin flaps

           (For endotracheal intubation, use 31500)

           (For tracheal aspiration under direct vision, use 31515)

31611   Construction of tracheoesophageal fistula and subsequent insertion of an alaryngeal speech prosthesis (eg, voice button, Blom-Singer prosthesis)

31612   Tracheal puncture, percutaneous with transtracheal aspiration and/or injection

31613   Tracheostoma revision; simple, without flap rotation

31614   complex, with flap rotation

Endoscopy

For endoscopy procedures, code appropriate endoscopy of each anatomic site examined. Surgical bronchoscopy always includes diagnostic bronchoscopy when performed by the same physician. Codes 31622-31646 include fluoroscopic guidance, when performed.

           (For tracheoscopy, see laryngoscopy codes 31515-31578)

⊙ **31615**   Tracheobronchoscopy through established tracheostomy incision

⊙+ **31620**   Endobronchial ultrasound (EBUS) during bronchoscopic diagnostic or therapeutic intervention(s) (List separately in addition to code for primary procedure[s])

           (Use 31620 in conjunction with 31622-31646)

⊙▲ **31622**   Bronchoscopy, rigid or flexible, including fluoroscopic guidance, when performed; diagnostic, with cell washing, when performed (separate procedure)

⊙ **31623**   with brushing or protected brushings

⊙ **31624**   with bronchial alveolar lavage

⊙ **31625**   with bronchial or endobronchial biopsy(s), single or multiple sites

⊙● **31626**   with placement of fiducial markers, single or multiple

           ▶(Report supply of device separately)◀

⊙+● **31627**   with computer-assisted, image-guided navigation (List separately in addition to code for primary procedure[s])

           ▶(31627 includes 3D reconstruction. Do not report 31627 in conjunction with 76376, 76377)◀

           ▶(Use 31627 in conjunction with 31615, 31622-31631, 31635, 31636, 31638-31643)◀

⊙ **31628**   with transbronchial lung biopsy(s), single lobe

           (31628 should be reported only once regardless of how many transbronchial lung biopsies are performed in a lobe)

           (To report transbronchial lung biopsies performed on additional lobe, use 31632)

Surgery: Respiratory System

⊙ **31629**   with transbronchial needle aspiration biopsy(s), trachea, main stem and/or lobar bronchus(i)

(31629 should be reported only once for upper airway biopsies regardless of how many transbronchial needle aspiration biopsies are performed in the upper airway or in a lobe)

(To report transbronchial needle aspiration biopsies performed on additional lobe(s), use 31633)

31630   with tracheal/bronchial dilation or closed reduction of fracture

31631   with placement of tracheal stent(s) (includes tracheal/bronchial dilation as required)

(For placement of bronchial stent, see 31636, 31637)

(For revision of tracheal/bronchial stent, use 31638)

+ **31632**   with transbronchial lung biopsy(s), each additional lobe (List separately in addition to code for primary procedure)

(Use 31632 in conjunction with 31628)

(31632 should be reported only once regardless of how many transbronchial lung biopsies are performed in a lobe)

+ **31633**   with transbronchial needle aspiration biopsy(s), each additional lobe (List separately in addition to code for primary procedure)

(Use 31633 in conjunction with 31629)

(31633 should be reported only once regardless of how many transbronchial needle aspiration biopsies are performed in the trachea or the additional lobe)

⊙ **31635**   with removal of foreign body

31636   with placement of bronchial stent(s) (includes tracheal/bronchial dilation as required), initial bronchus

+ **31637**   each additional major bronchus stented (List separately in addition to code for primary procedure)

(Use 31637 in conjunction with 31636)

31638   with revision of tracheal or bronchial stent inserted at previous session (includes tracheal/bronchial dilation as required)

31640   with excision of tumor

▲ **31641**   with destruction of tumor or relief of stenosis by any method other than excision (eg, laser therapy, cryotherapy)

(For bronchoscopic photodynamic therapy, report 31641 in addition to 96570, 96571 as appropriate)

▲ **31643**   with placement of catheter(s) for intracavitary radioelement application

(For intracavitary radioelement application, see 77761-77763, 77785-77787)

⊙▲ **31645**   with therapeutic aspiration of tracheobronchial tree, initial (eg, drainage of lung abscess)

⊙▲ **31646**   with therapeutic aspiration of tracheobronchial tree, subsequent

(For catheter aspiration of tracheobronchial tree at bedside, use 31725)

⊙▲ **31656**   with injection of contrast material for segmental bronchography (fiberscope only)

(For radiological supervision and interpretation, see 71040, 71060)

Introduction

(For endotracheal intubation, use 31500)

(For tracheal aspiration under direct vision, see 31515)

31715   Transtracheal injection for bronchography

(For radiological supervision and interpretation, see 71040, 71060)

(For prolonged services, see 99354-99360)

31717   Catheterization with bronchial brush biopsy

31720   Catheter aspiration (separate procedure); nasotracheal

⊙ **31725**   tracheobronchial with fiberscope, bedside

31730   Transtracheal (percutaneous) introduction of needle wire dilator/stent or indwelling tube for oxygen therapy

Excision, Repair

31750   Tracheoplasty; cervical

31755   tracheopharyngeal fistulization, each stage

31760   intrathoracic

31766   Carinal reconstruction

31770   Bronchoplasty; graft repair

31775   excision stenosis and anastomosis

(For lobectomy and bronchoplasty, use 32501)

31780   Excision tracheal stenosis and anastomosis; cervical

31781   cervicothoracic

31785   Excision of tracheal tumor or carcinoma; cervical

31786   thoracic

31800   Suture of tracheal wound or injury; cervical

31805   intrathoracic

31820   Surgical closure tracheostomy or fistula; without plastic repair

31825   with plastic repair

(For repair tracheoesophageal fistula, see 43305, 43312)

31830   Revision of tracheostomy scar

Other Procedures

31899   Unlisted procedure, trachea, bronchi

Lungs and Pleura

Incision

(32000 has been deleted. To report, use 32421)

(32002 has been deleted. To report, use 32422)

(32005 has been deleted. To report, use 32560)

(32019 has been deleted. To report, use 32550)

(32020 has been deleted. To report, use 32551)

32035   Thoracostomy; with rib resection for empyema

32036   with open flap drainage for empyema

32095   Thoracotomy, limited, for biopsy of lung or pleura

(To report wound exploration due to penetrating trauma without thoractomy, use 20102)

32100   Thoracotomy, major; with exploration and biopsy

(Do not report 32100 in conjunction with 19260, 19271, 19272, 32503, 32504)

32110   with control of traumatic hemorrhage and/or repair of lung tear

32120   for postoperative complications

32124   with open intrapleural pneumonolysis

32140   with cyst(s) removal, with or without a pleural procedure

32141   with excision-plication of bullae, with or without any pleural procedure

(For lung volume reduction, use 32491)

32150   with removal of intrapleural foreign body or fibrin deposit

32151   with removal of intrapulmonary foreign body

32160   with cardiac massage

(For segmental or other resections of lung, see 32480-32504)

32200   Pneumonostomy; with open drainage of abscess or cyst

⊙ **32201**   with percutaneous drainage of abscess or cyst

(For radiological supervision and interpretation, use 75989)

32215   Pleural scarification for repeat pneumothorax

32220   Decortication, pulmonary (separate procedure); total

32225   partial

Excision

32310   Pleurectomy, parietal (separate procedure)

32320   Decortication and parietal pleurectomy

32400   Biopsy, pleura; percutaneous needle

(If imaging guidance is performed, see 76942, 77002, 77012, 77021)

(For fine needle aspiration, use 10021 or 10022)

(For evaluation of fine needle aspirate, see 88172, 88173)

32402   open

32405   Biopsy, lung or mediastinum, percutaneous needle

(For radiological supervision and interpretation, see 76942, 77002, 77012, 77021)

(For fine needle aspiration, use 10022)

(For evaluation of fine needle aspirate, see 88172, 88173)

Removal

32420   Pneumocentesis, puncture of lung for aspiration

32421   Thoracentesis, puncture of pleural cavity for aspiration, initial or subsequent

(If imaging guidance is performed, see 76942, 77002, 77012)

(For total lung lavage, use 32997)

32422   Thoracentesis with insertion of tube, includes water seal (eg, for pneumothorax), when performed (separate procedure)

(Do not report 32422 in conjunction with 19260, 19271, 19272, 32503, 32504)

(If imaging guidance is performed, see 76942, 77002, 77012)

32440   Removal of lung, total pneumonectomy;

32442   with resection of segment of trachea followed by broncho-tracheal anastomosis (sleeve pneumonectomy)

32445   extrapleural

(For extrapleural pneumonectomy, with empyemectomy, use 32445 and 32540)

(If lung resection is performed with chest wall tumor resection, report the appropriate chest wall tumor resection code, 19260-19272, in addition to lung resection code 32440-32445)

32480   Removal of lung, other than total pneumonectomy; single lobe (lobectomy)

32482   2 lobes (bilobectomy)

32484   single segment (segmentectomy)

(For removal of lung with bronchoplasty, use 32501)

32486   with circumferential resection of segment of bronchus followed by broncho-bronchial anastomosis (sleeve lobectomy)

32488   all remaining lung following previous removal of a portion of lung (completion pneumonectomy)

(For total or segmental lobectomy, with concomitant decortication, use 32320 and the appropriate removal of lung code)

32491   excision-plication of emphysematous lung(s) (bullous or non-bullous) for lung volume reduction, sternal split or transthoracic approach, with or without any pleural procedure

32500   wedge resection, single or multiple

(If lung resection is performed with chest wall tumor resection, report the appropriate chest wall tumor resection code, 19260-19272, in addition to lung resection code 32480-32500)

+ 32501   Resection and repair of portion of bronchus (bronchoplasty) when performed at time of lobectomy or segmentectomy (List separately in addition to code for primary procedure)

(Use 32501 in conjunction with 32480, 32482, 32484)

(32501 is to be used when a portion of the bronchus to preserved lung is removed and requires plastic closure to preserve function of that preserved lung. It is not to be used for closure for the proximal end of a resected bronchus)

32503   Resection of apical lung tumor (eg, Pancoast tumor), including chest wall resection, rib(s) resection(s), neurovascular dissection, when performed; without chest wall reconstruction(s)

32504   with chest wall reconstruction

(Do not report 32503, 32504 in conjunction with 19260, 19271, 19272, 32100, 32422, 32551)

(For performance of lung resection in conjunction with chest wall resection, see 19260, 19271, 19272 and 32480-32500, 32503, 32504)

32540   Extrapleural enucleation of empyema (empyemectomy)

(For extrapleural enucleation of empyema (empyemectomy) with lobectomy, use 32540 and the appropriate removal of lung code)

►Introduction and Removal◄

⊙ **32550**   Insertion of indwelling tunneled pleural catheter with cuff

(Do not report 32550 in conjunction with 32421, 32422)

(If imaging guidance is performed, use 75989)

⊙ **32551**   Tube thoracostomy, includes water seal (eg, for abscess, hemothorax, empyema), when performed (separate procedure)

(Do not report 32551 in conjunction with 19260, 19271, 19272, 32503, 32504)

(If imaging guidance is performed, use 75989)

● **32552**   Removal of indwelling tunneled pleural catheter with cuff

⊙● **32553** Placement of interstitial device(s) for radiation therapy guidance (eg, fiducial markers, dosimeter), percutaneous, intra-thoracic, single or multiple

►(Report supply of device separately)◄

►(For imaging guidance, see 76942, 77002, 77012, 77021)◄

►(For percutaneous placement of interstitial device[s] for intra-abdominal, intrapelvic, and/or retroperitoneal radiation therapy guidance, use 49411)◄

Destruction

►The instillation of a fibrinolytic agent may be performed multiple times per day over the course of several days. Code 32561 should be reported only once on the initial day treatment. Code 32562 should be reported only once on each subsequent day of treatment.◄

▲ **32560** Instillation, via chest tube/catheter, agent for pleurodesis (eg, talc for recurrent or persistent pneumothorax)

►(For chest tube insertion, use 32551)◄

● **32561**   Instillation(s), via chest tube/catheter, agent for fibrinolysis (eg, fibrinolytic agent for break up of multiloculated effusion); initial day

►(For chest tube insertion, use 32551)◄

● **32562**   subsequent day

►(For chest tube insertion, use 32551)◄

Endoscopy

Surgical thoracoscopy always includes diagnostic thoracoscopy.

For endoscopic procedures, code appropriate endoscopy of each anatomic site examined.

32601   Thoracoscopy, diagnostic (separate procedure); lungs and pleural space, without biopsy

32602   lungs and pleural space, with biopsy

32603   pericardial sac, without biopsy

32604   pericardial sac, with biopsy

32605   mediastinal space, without biopsy

32606   mediastinal space, with biopsy

(Surgical thoracoscopy always includes diagnostic thoracoscopy)

32650   Thoracoscopy, surgical; with pleurodesis (eg, mechanical or chemical)

32651   with partial pulmonary decortication

32652   with total pulmonary decortication, including intrapleural pneumonolysis

32653	with removal of intrapleural foreign body or fibrin deposit
32654	with control of traumatic hemorrhage
32655	with excision-plication of bullae, including any pleural procedure
32656	with parietal pleurectomy
32657	with wedge resection of lung, single or multiple
32658	with removal of clot or foreign body from pericardial sac
32659	with creation of pericardial window or partial resection of pericardial sac for drainage
32660	with total pericardiectomy
32661	with excision of pericardial cyst, tumor, or mass
32662	with excision of mediastinal cyst, tumor, or mass
32663	with lobectomy, total or segmental
32664	with thoracic sympathectomy
32665	with esophagomyotomy (Heller type)

(For exploratory thoracoscopy, and exploratory thoracoscopy with biopsy, see 32601-32606)

Repair

32800	Repair lung hernia through chest wall
32810	Closure of chest wall following open flap drainage for empyema (Clagett type procedure)
32815	Open closure of major bronchial fistula
32820	Major reconstruction, chest wall (posttraumatic)

Lung Transplantation

Lung allotransplantation involves three distinct components of physician work:

1. **Cadaver donor pneumonectomy(s)**, which include(s) harvesting the allograft and cold preservation of the allograft (perfusing with cold preservation solution and cold maintenance) (use 32850).

2. **Backbench work**:

Preparation of a cadaver donor single lung allograft prior to transplantation, including dissection of the allograft from surrounding soft tissues to prepare the pulmonary venous/atrial cuff, pulmonary artery, and bronchus unilaterally (use 32855).

Preparation of a cadaver donor double lung allograft prior to transplantation, including dissection of the allograft from surrounding soft tissues to prepare the pulmonary venous/atrial cuff, pulmonary artery, and bronchus bilaterally (use 32856).

3. **Recipient lung allotransplantation**, which includes transplantation of a single or double lung allograft and care of the recipient (see 32851-32854).

32850	Donor pneumonectomy(s) (including cold preservation), from cadaver donor
32851	Lung transplant, single; without cardiopulmonary bypass
32852	with cardiopulmonary bypass
32853	Lung transplant, double (bilateral sequential or en bloc); without cardiopulmonary bypass
32854	with cardiopulmonary bypass
32855	Backbench standard preparation of cadaver donor lung allograft prior to transplantation, including dissection of allograft from surrounding soft tissues to prepare pulmonary venous/atrial cuff, pulmonary artery, and bronchus; unilateral
32856	bilateral

(For repair or resection procedures on the donor lung, see 32491, 32500, 35216, or 35276)

Surgical Collapse Therapy; Thoracoplasty

(See also 32503, 32504)

32900	Resection of ribs, extrapleural, all stages
32905	Thoracoplasty, Schede type or extrapleural (all stages);
32906	with closure of bronchopleural fistula

(For open closure of major bronchial fistula, use 32815)

(For resection of first rib for thoracic outlet compression, see 21615, 21616)

32940	Pneumonolysis, extraperiosteal, including filling or packing procedures
32960	Pneumothorax, therapeutic, intrapleural injection of air

Other Procedures

32997	Total lung lavage (unilateral)

(For bronchoscopic bronchial alveolar lavage, use 31624)

32998	Ablation therapy for reduction or eradication of 1 or more pulmonary tumor(s) including pleura or chest wall when involved by tumor extension, percutaneous, radiofrequency, unilateral

(For imaging guidance and monitoring, see 76940, 77013, 77022)

32999	Unlisted procedure, lungs and pleura

Surgery: Respiratory System

Notes

⊙=Moderate sedation ✛=Add-on code ✂=FDA approval pending #=Resequenced code

Cardiovascular System

Selective vascular catheterizations should be coded to include introduction and all lesser order selective catheterizations used in the approach (eg, the description for a selective right middle cerebral artery catheterization includes the introduction and placement catheterization of the right common and internal carotid arteries).

Additional second and/or third order arterial catheterizations within the same family of arteries supplied by a single first order artery should be expressed by 36218 or 36248. Additional first order or higher catheterizations in vascular families supplied by a first order vessel different from a previously selected and coded family should be separately coded using the conventions described above.

> (For monitoring, operation of pump and other nonsurgical services, see 99190-99192, 99291, 99292, 99354-99360)
>
> (For other medical or laboratory related services, see appropriate section)
>
> (For radiological supervision and interpretation, see 75600-75978)

Heart and Pericardium

Pericardium

⊙ **33010**   Pericardiocentesis; initial

> (For radiological supervision and interpretation, use 76930)

⊙ **33011**   subsequent

> (For radiological supervision and interpretation, use 76930)

33015   Tube pericardiostomy

33020   Pericardiotomy for removal of clot or foreign body (primary procedure)

33025   Creation of pericardial window or partial resection for drainage

33030   Pericardiectomy, subtotal or complete; without cardiopulmonary bypass

33031   with cardiopulmonary bypass

33050   Excision of pericardial cyst or tumor

Cardiac Tumor

33120   Excision of intracardiac tumor, resection with cardiopulmonary bypass

33130   Resection of external cardiac tumor

Transmyocardial Revascularization

33140   Transmyocardial laser revascularization, by thoracotomy; (separate procedure)

+ 33141   performed at the time of other open cardiac procedure(s) (List separately in addition to code for primary procedure)

> (Use 33141 in conjunction with 33400-33496, 33510-33536, 33542)

Pacemaker or Pacing Cardioverter-Defibrillator

A pacemaker system includes a pulse generator containing electronics, a battery, and one or more electrodes (leads). Pulse generators are placed in a subcutaneous "pocket" created in either a subclavicular site or underneath the abdominal muscles just below the ribcage. Electrodes may be inserted through a vein (transvenous) or they may be placed on the surface of the heart (epicardial). The epicardial location of electrodes requires a thoracotomy for electrode insertion.

A single chamber pacemaker system includes a pulse generator and one electrode inserted in either the atrium or ventricle. A dual chamber pacemaker system includes a pulse generator and one electrode inserted in the right atrium and one electrode inserted in the right ventricle. In certain circumstances, an additional electrode may be required to achieve pacing of the left ventricle (bi-ventricular pacing). In this event, transvenous (cardiac vein) placement of the electrode should be separately reported using code 33224 or 33225. Epicardial placement of the electrode should be separately reported using 33202-33203.

Like a pacemaker system, a pacing cardioverter-defibrillator system includes a pulse generator and electrodes, although pacing cardioverter-defibrillators may require multiple leads, even when only a single chamber is being paced. A pacing cardioverter-defibrillator system may be inserted in a single chamber (pacing in the ventricle) or in dual chambers (pacing in atrium and ventricle). These devices use a combination of antitachycardia pacing, low-energy cardioversion or defibrillating shocks to treat ventricular tachycardia or ventricular fibrillation.

Pacing cardioverter-defibrillator pulse generators may be implanted in a subcutaneous infraclavicular pocket or in an abdominal pocket. Removal of a pacing cardioverter-defibrillator pulse generator requires opening of the existing subcutaneous pocket and disconnection of the pulse generator from its electrode(s). A thoracotomy (or laparotomy in the case of abdominally placed pulse generators) is not required to remove the pulse generator.

Surgery: Cardiovascular System

The electrodes (leads) of a pacing cardioverter-defibrillator system are positioned in the heart via the venous system (transvenously), in most circumstances. In certain circumstances, an additional electrode may be required to achieve pacing of the left ventricle (bi-ventricular pacing). In this event, transvenous (cardiac vein) placement of the electrode should be separately reported using code 33224 or 33225. Epicardial placement of the electrode should be separately reported using 33202-33203.

Electrode positioning on the epicardial surface of the heart requires thoracotomy, or thoracoscopic placement of the leads. Removal of electrode(s) may first be attempted by transvenous extraction (code 33244). However, if transvenous extraction is unsuccessful, a thoracotomy may be required to remove the electrodes (code 33243). Use codes 33212, 33213, 33240 as appropriate in addition to the thoracotomy or endoscopic epicardial lead placement codes to report the insertion of the generator if done by the same physician during the same session.

When the "battery" of a pacemaker or pacing cardioverter-defibrillator is changed, it is actually the pulse generator that is changed. Replacement of a pulse generator should be reported with a code for removal of the pulse generator and another code for insertion of a pulse generator.

Repositioning of a pacemaker electrode, pacing cardioverter-defibrillator electrode(s), or a left ventricular pacing electrode is reported using 33215 or 33226, as appropriate. Replacement of a pacemaker electrode, pacing cardioverter-defibrillator electrode(s), or a left ventricular pacing electrode is reported using 33206-33208, 33210-33213, or 33224, as appropriate.

(For electronic, telephonic analysis of internal pacemaker system, see 93279, 93280, 93288, 93293, 93294)

(For radiological supervision and interpretation with insertion of pacemaker, use 71090)

33202   Insertion of epicardial electrode(s); open incision (eg, thoracotomy, median sternotomy, subxiphoid approach)

33203   endoscopic approach (eg, thoracoscopy, pericardioscopy)

(When epicardial lead placement is performed by the same physician at the same session as insertion of the generator, report 33202, 33203 in conjunction with 33212, 33213, as appropriate)

⊙ 33206   Insertion or replacement of permanent pacemaker with transvenous electrode(s); atrial

⊙ 33207   ventricular

⊙ 33208   atrial and ventricular

(Codes 33206-33208 include subcutaneous insertion of the pulse generator and transvenous placement of electrode[s])

⊙ 33210   Insertion or replacement of temporary transvenous single chamber cardiac electrode or pacemaker catheter (separate procedure)

⊙ 33211   Insertion or replacement of temporary transvenous dual chamber pacing electrodes (separate procedure)

⊙ 33212   Insertion or replacement of pacemaker pulse generator only; single chamber, atrial or ventricular

⊙ 33213   dual chamber

(Use 33212, 33213, as appropriate, in conjunction with the epicardial lead placement codes 33202, 33203 to report the insertion of the generator when done by the same physician during the same session)

⊙ 33214   Upgrade of implanted pacemaker system, conversion of single chamber system to dual chamber system (includes removal of previously placed pulse generator, testing of existing lead, insertion of new lead, insertion of new pulse generator)

(When epicardial electrode placement is performed, report 33214 in conjunction with 33202, 33203)

33215   Repositioning of previously implanted transvenous pacemaker or pacing cardioverter-defibrillator (right atrial or right ventricular) electrode

⊙▲ 33216   Insertion of a single transvenous electrode, permanent pacemaker or cardioverter-defibrillator

⊙▲ 33217   Insertion of 2 transvenous electrodes, permanent pacemaker or cardioverter-defibrillator

(Do not report 33216-33217 in conjunction with 33214)

▶(For insertion or replacement of a cardiac venous system lead, see 33224, 33225)◄

⊙ 33218   Repair of single transvenous electrode for a single chamber, permanent pacemaker or single chamber pacing cardioverter-defibrillator

(For atrial or ventricular single chamber repair of pacemaker electrode[s] with replacement of pulse generator, see 33212 or 33213 and 33218 or 33220)

⊙ 33220   Repair of 2 transvenous electrodes for a dual chamber permanent pacemaker or dual chamber pacing cardioverter-defibrillator

⊙ 33222   Revision or relocation of skin pocket for pacemaker

⊙▲ 33223   Revision of skin pocket for cardioverter-defibrillator

33224   Insertion of pacing electrode, cardiac venous system, for left ventricular pacing, with attachment to previously placed pacemaker or pacing cardioverter-defibrillator pulse generator (including revision of pocket, removal, insertion, and/or replacement of generator)

(When epicardial electrode placement is performed, report 33224 in conjunction with 33202, 33203)

+ 33225 Insertion of pacing electrode, cardiac venous system, for left ventricular pacing, at time of insertion of pacing cardioverter-defibrillator or pacemaker pulse generator (including upgrade to dual chamber system) (List separately in addition to code for primary procedure)

(Use 33225 in conjunction with 33206, 33207, 33208, 33212, 33213, 33214, 33216, 33217, 33222, 33233, 33234, 33235, 33240, 33249)

33226 Repositioning of previously implanted cardiac venous system (left ventricular) electrode (including removal, insertion and/or replacement of generator)

⊙ **33233** Removal of permanent pacemaker pulse generator

⊙ **33234** Removal of transvenous pacemaker electrode(s); single lead system, atrial or ventricular

⊙ **33235**   dual lead system

33236 Removal of permanent epicardial pacemaker and electrodes by thoracotomy; single lead system, atrial or ventricular

33237   dual lead system

33238 Removal of permanent transvenous electrode(s) by thoracotomy

⊙ **33240** Insertion of single or dual chamber pacing cardioverter-defibrillator pulse generator

(Use 33240, as appropriate, in addition to the epicardial lead placement codes to report the insertion of the generator when done by the same physician during the same session)

⊙ **33241** Subcutaneous removal of single or dual chamber pacing cardioverter-defibrillator pulse generator

(For removal of electrode[s] by thoracotomy, use 33243 in conjunction with 33241)

(For removal of electrode[s] by transvenous extraction, use 33244 in conjunction with 33241)

(For removal and reinsertion of a pacing cardioverter-defibrillator system (pulse generator and electrodes), report 33241 and 33243 or 33244 and 33249)

(For repair of implantable cardioverter-defibrillator pulse generator and/or leads, see 33218, 33220)

33243 Removal of single or dual chamber pacing cardioverter-defibrillator electrode(s); by thoracotomy

⊙ **33244**   by transvenous extraction

(For subcutaneous removal of the pulse generator, use 33241 in conjunction with 33243 or 33244)

⊙ **33249** Insertion or repositioning of electrode lead(s) for single or dual chamber pacing cardioverter-defibrillator and insertion of pulse generator

(For removal and reinsertion of a pacing cardioverter-defibrillator system (pulse generator and electrodes), report 33241 and 33243 or 33244 and 33249)

(For insertion of implantable cardioverter-defibrillator lead(s), without thoracotomy, use 33216)

Electrophysiologic Operative Procedures

This family of codes describes the surgical treatment of supraventricular dysrhythmias. Tissue ablation, disruption, and reconstruction can be accomplished by many methods including surgical incision or through the use of a variety of energy sources (eg, radiofrequency, cryotherapy, microwave, ultrasound, laser). If excision or isolation of the left atrial appendage by any method, including stapling, oversewing, ligation, or plication, is performed in conjunction with any of the atrial tissue ablation and reconstruction (maze) procedures (33254-33259, 33265-33266), it is considered part of the procedure. Codes 33254-33256 are only to be reported when there is no concurrently performed procedure that requires median sternotomy or cardiopulmonary bypass. The appropriate atrial tissue ablation add-on code, 33257, 33258, 33259 should be reported in addition to an open cardiac procedure requiring sternotomy or cardiopulmonary bypass if performed concurrently.

Definitions

Limited operative ablation and reconstruction includes:

Surgical isolation of triggers of supraventricular dysrhythmias by operative ablation that isolates the pulmonary veins or other anatomically defined triggers in the left or right atrium.

Extensive operative ablation and reconstruction includes:

1. The services included in *"limited"*

2. Additional ablation of atrial tissue to eliminate sustained supraventricular dysrhythmias. This must include operative ablation that involves either the right atrium, the atrial septum, or left atrium in continuity with the atrioventricular annulus.

Incision

33250 Operative ablation of supraventricular arrhythmogenic focus or pathway (eg, Wolff-Parkinson-White, atrioventricular node re-entry), tract(s) and/or focus (foci); without cardiopulmonary bypass

(For intraoperative pacing and mapping by a separate provider, use 93631)

33251   with cardiopulmonary bypass

33254 Operative tissue ablation and reconstruction of atria, limited (eg, modified maze procedure)

33255 Operative tissue ablation and reconstruction of atria, extensive (eg, maze procedure); without cardiopulmonary bypass

33256   with cardiopulmonary bypass

(Do not report 33254-33256 in conjunction with 32100, 32551, 33120, 33130, 33210, 33211, 33400-33507, 33510-33523, 33533-33548, 33600-33853, 33860-33864, 33910-33920)

Surgery: Cardiovascular System

Surgery: Cardiovascular System

+ 33257 Operative tissue ablation and reconstruction of atria, performed at the time of other cardiac procedure(s), limited (eg, modified maze procedure) (List separately in addition to code for primary procedure)

(Use 33257 in conjunction with 33120-33130, 33250-33251, 33261, 33300-33335, 33400-33496, 33500-33507, 33510-33516, 33533-33548, 33600-33619, 33641-33697, 33702-33732, 33735-33767, 33770-33814, 33840-33877, 33910-33922, 33925-33926, 33935, 33945, 33975-33980)

+ 33258 Operative tissue ablation and reconstruction of atria, performed at the time of other cardiac procedure(s), extensive (eg, maze procedure), without cardiopulmonary bypass (List separately in addition to code for primary procedure)

(Use 33258 in conjunction with 33130, 33250, 33300, 33310, 33320, 33321, 33330, 33332, 33401, 33414-33417, 33420, 33470-33472, 33501-33503, 33510-33516, 33533-33536, 33690, 33735, 33737, 33800-33813, 33840-33852, 33915, 33925 when the procedure is performed without cardiopulmonary bypass)

+ 33259 Operative tissue ablation and reconstruction of atria, performed at the time of other cardiac procedure(s), extensive (eg, maze procedure), with cardiopulmonary bypass (List separately in addition to code for primary procedure)

(Use 33259 in conjunction with 33120, 33251, 33261, 33305, 33315, 33322, 33335, 33400, 33403-33413, 33422-33468, 33474-33478, 33496, 33500, 33504-33507, 33510-33516, 33533-33548, 33600-33688, 33692-33722, 33730, 33732, 33736, 33750-33767, 33770-33781, 33786-33788, 33814, 33853, 33860-33877, 33910, 33916-33922, 33926, 33935, 33945, 33975-33980 when the procedure is performed with cardiopulmonary bypass)

(Do not report 33257, 33258 and 33259 in conjunction with 32551, 33210, 33211, 33254-33256, 33265, 33266)

33261 Operative ablation of ventricular arrhythmogenic focus with cardiopulmonary bypass

Endoscopy

33265 Endoscopy, surgical; operative tissue ablation and reconstruction of atria, limited (eg, modified maze procedure), without cardiopulmonary bypass

33266 operative tissue ablation and reconstruction of atria, extensive (eg, maze procedure), without cardiopulmonary bypass

(Do not report 33265-33266 in conjunction with 32551, 33210, 33211)

Patient-Activated Event Recorder

33282 Implantation of patient-activated cardiac event recorder

(Initial implantation includes programming. For subsequent electronic analysis and/or reprogramming, use 93285, 93291, 93298)

33284 Removal of an implantable, patient-activated cardiac event recorder

Wounds of the Heart and Great Vessels

33300 Repair of cardiac wound; without bypass

33305 with cardiopulmonary bypass

33310 Cardiotomy, exploratory (includes removal of foreign body, atrial or ventricular thrombus); without bypass

33315 with cardiopulmonary bypass

(Do not report removal of thrombus [33310-33315] in conjunction with other cardiac procedures unless a separate incision in the heart is required to remove the atrial or ventricular thrombus)

(If removal of thrombus with cardiopulmonary bypass [33315] is reported in conjunction with 33120, 33130, 33420-33430, 33460-33468, 33496, 33542, 33545, 33641-33647, 33670, 33681, 33975-33980 which requires a separate heart incision, report 33315 with modifier 59)

33320 Suture repair of aorta or great vessels; without shunt or cardiopulmonary bypass

33321 with shunt bypass

33322 with cardiopulmonary bypass

33330 Insertion of graft, aorta or great vessels; without shunt, or cardiopulmonary bypass

33332 with shunt bypass

33335 with cardiopulmonary bypass

Cardiac Valves

(For multiple valve procedures, see 33400-33478 and add modifier 51 to the secondary valve procedure code)

Aortic Valve

33400 Valvuloplasty, aortic valve; open, with cardiopulmonary bypass

33401 open, with inflow occlusion

33403 using transventricular dilation, with cardiopulmonary bypass

(Do not report modifier 63 in conjunction with 33401, 33403)

33404 Construction of apical-aortic conduit

33405 Replacement, aortic valve, with cardiopulmonary bypass; with prosthetic valve other than homograft or stentless valve

33406 with allograft valve (freehand)

(For aortic valve valvotomy, [commissurotomy] with inflow occlusion, use 33401)

(For aortic valve valvotomy, [commissurotomy] with cardiopulmonary bypass, use 33403)

33410 with stentless tissue valve

33411 Replacement, aortic valve; with aortic annulus enlargement, noncoronary cusp

33412 with transventricular aortic annulus enlargement (Konno procedure)

33413 by translocation of autologous pulmonary valve with allograft replacement of pulmonary valve (Ross procedure)

33414 Repair of left ventricular outflow tract obstruction by patch enlargement of the outflow tract

33415 Resection or incision of subvalvular tissue for discrete subvalvular aortic stenosis

33416 Ventriculomyotomy (-myectomy) for idiopathic hypertrophic subaortic stenosis (eg, asymmetric septal hypertrophy)

33417 Aortoplasty (gusset) for supravalvular stenosis

Mitral Valve

33420 Valvotomy, mitral valve; closed heart

33422 open heart, with cardiopulmonary bypass

33425 Valvuloplasty, mitral valve, with cardiopulmonary bypass;

33426 with prosthetic ring

33427 radical reconstruction, with or without ring

33430 Replacement, mitral valve, with cardiopulmonary bypass

Tricuspid Valve

33460 Valvectomy, tricuspid valve, with cardiopulmonary bypass

33463 Valvuloplasty, tricuspid valve; without ring insertion

33464 with ring insertion

33465 Replacement, tricuspid valve, with cardiopulmonary bypass

33468 Tricuspid valve repositioning and plication for Ebstein anomaly

Pulmonary Valve

33470 Valvotomy, pulmonary valve, closed heart; transventricular

(Do not report modifier 63 in conjunction with 33470)

33471 via pulmonary artery

(To report percutaneous valvuloplasty of pulmonary valve, use 92990)

33472 Valvotomy, pulmonary valve, open heart; with inflow occlusion

(Do not report modifier 63 in conjunction with 33472)

33474 with cardiopulmonary bypass

33475 Replacement, pulmonary valve

33476 Right ventricular resection for infundibular stenosis, with or without commissurotomy

33478 Outflow tract augmentation (gusset), with or without commissurotomy or infundibular resection

(Use 33478 in conjunction with 33768 when a cavopulmonary anastomosis to a second superior vena cava is performed)

Other Valvular Procedures

33496 Repair of non-structural prosthetic valve dysfunction with cardiopulmonary bypass (separate procedure)

(For reoperation, use 33530 in addition to 33496)

Coronary Artery Anomalies

Basic procedures include endarterectomy or angioplasty.

33500 Repair of coronary arteriovenous or arteriocardiac chamber fistula; with cardiopulmonary bypass

33501 without cardiopulmonary bypass

33502 Repair of anomalous coronary artery from pulmonary artery origin; by ligation

33503 by graft, without cardiopulmonary bypass

(Do not report modifier 63 in conjunction with 33502, 33503)

33504 by graft, with cardiopulmonary bypass

33505 with construction of intrapulmonary artery tunnel (Takeuchi procedure)

33506 by translocation from pulmonary artery to aorta

(Do not report modifier 63 in conjunction with 33505, 33506)

33507 Repair of anomalous (eg, intramural) aortic origin of coronary artery by unroofing or translocation

Endoscopy

Surgical vascular endoscopy always includes diagnostic endoscopy.

+ 33508 Endoscopy, surgical, including video-assisted harvest of vein(s) for coronary artery bypass procedure (List separately in addition to code for primary procedure)

(Use 33508 in conjunction with 33510-33523)

(For open harvest of upper extremity vein procedure, use 35500)

▲=Revised code   ●=New code   ▶ ◀=Contains new or revised text   ⊘=Modifier 51 exempt   American Medical Association   **123**

Venous Grafting Only for Coronary Artery Bypass

The following codes are used to report coronary artery bypass procedures using venous grafts only. These codes should NOT be used to report the performance of coronary artery bypass procedures using arterial grafts and venous grafts during the same procedure. See 33517-33523 and 33533-33536 for reporting combined arterial-venous grafts.

Procurement of the saphenous vein graft is included in the description of the work for 33510-33516 and should not be reported as a separate service or co-surgery. To report harvesting of an upper extremity vein, use 35500 in addition to the bypass procedure. To report harvesting of a femoropopliteal vein segment, report 35572 in addition to the bypass procedure. When surgical assistant performs graft procurement, add modifier 80 to 33510-33516.

33510	Coronary artery bypass, vein only; single coronary venous graft
33511	2 coronary venous grafts
33512	3 coronary venous grafts
33513	4 coronary venous grafts
33514	5 coronary venous grafts
33516	6 or more coronary venous grafts

Combined Arterial-Venous Grafting for Coronary Bypass

The following codes are used to report coronary artery bypass procedures using venous grafts and arterial grafts during the same procedure. These codes may NOT be used alone.

To report combined arterial-venous grafts it is necessary to report two codes: (1) the appropriate combined arterial-venous graft code (33517-33523); and (2) the appropriate arterial graft code (33533-33536).

Procurement of the saphenous vein graft is included in the description of the work for 33517-33523 and should not be reported as a separate service or co-surgery. Procurement of the artery for grafting is included in the description of the work for 33533-33536 and should not be reported as a separate service or co-surgery, except when an upper extremity artery (eg, radial artery) is procured. To report harvesting of an upper extremity artery, use 35600 in addition to the bypass procedure. To report harvesting of an upper extremity vein, use 35500 in addition to the bypass procedure. To report harvesting of a femoropopliteal vein segment, report 35572 in addition to the bypass procedure. When surgical assistant performs arterial and/or venous graft procurement, add modifier 80 to 33517-33523, 33533-33536, as appropriate.

+ 33517   Coronary artery bypass, using venous graft(s) and arterial graft(s); single vein graft (List separately in addition to code for primary procedure)

(Use 33517 in conjunction with 33533-33536)

+ 33518   2 venous grafts (List separately in addition to code for primary procedure)

(Use 33518 in conjunction with 33533-33536)

+ 33519   3 venous grafts (List separately in addition to code for primary procedure)

(Use 33519 in conjunction with 33533-33536)

+ 33521   4 venous grafts (List separately in addition to code for primary procedure)

(Use 33521 in conjunction with 33533-33536)

+ 33522   5 venous grafts (List separately in addition to code for primary procedure)

(Use 33522 in conjunction with 33533-33536)

+ 33523   6 or more venous grafts (List separately in addition to code for primary procedure)

(Use 33523 in conjunction with 33533-33536)

+ 33530   Reoperation, coronary artery bypass procedure or valve procedure, more than 1 month after original operation (List separately in addition to code for primary procedure)

(Use 33530 in conjunction with 33400-33496; 33510-33536, 33863)

Arterial Grafting for Coronary Artery Bypass

The following codes are used to report coronary artery bypass procedures using either arterial grafts only or a combination of arterial-venous grafts. The codes include the use of the internal mammary artery, gastroepiploic artery, epigastric artery, radial artery, and arterial conduits procured from other sites.

To report combined arterial-venous grafts it is necessary to report two codes: (1) the appropriate arterial graft code (33533-33536); and (2) the appropriate combined arterial-venous graft code (33517-33523).

Procurement of the artery for grafting is included in the description of the work for 33533-33536 and should not be reported as a separate service or co-surgery, except when an upper extremity artery (eg, radial artery) is procured. To report harvesting of an upper extremity artery, use 35600 in addition to the bypass procedure. To report harvesting of an upper extremity vein, use 35500 in addition to the bypass procedure. To report harvesting of a femoropopliteal vein segment, report 35572 in addition to the bypass procedure. When surgical assistant performs arterial and/or venous graft procurement, add modifier 80 to 33517-33523, 33533-33536, as appropriate.

33533   Coronary artery bypass, using arterial graft(s); single arterial graft

33534   2 coronary arterial grafts

33535   3 coronary arterial grafts

33536   4 or more coronary arterial grafts

33542   Myocardial resection (eg, ventricular aneurysmectomy)

33545   Repair of postinfarction ventricular septal defect, with or without myocardial resection

33548   Surgical ventricular restoration procedure, includes prosthetic patch, when performed (eg, ventricular remodeling, SVR, SAVER, Dor procedures)

(Do not report 33548 in conjunction with 32551, 33210, 33211, 33310, 33315)

(For Batista procedure or pachopexy, use 33999)

Coronary Endarterectomy

+ **33572**   Coronary endarterectomy, open, any method, of left anterior descending, circumflex, or right coronary artery performed in conjunction with coronary artery bypass graft procedure, each vessel (List separately in addition to primary procedure)

(Use 33572 in conjunction with 33510-33516, 33533-33536)

Single Ventricle and Other Complex Cardiac Anomalies

33600   Closure of atrioventricular valve (mitral or tricuspid) by suture or patch

33602   Closure of semilunar valve (aortic or pulmonary) by suture or patch

33606   Anastomosis of pulmonary artery to aorta (Damus-Kaye-Stansel procedure)

33608   Repair of complex cardiac anomaly other than pulmonary atresia with ventricular septal defect by construction or replacement of conduit from right or left ventricle to pulmonary artery

(For repair of pulmonary artery arborization anomalies by unifocalization, see 33925-33926)

33610   Repair of complex cardiac anomalies (eg, single ventricle with subaortic obstruction) by surgical enlargement of ventricular septal defect

(Do not report modifier 63 in conjunction with 33610)

33611   Repair of double outlet right ventricle with intraventricular tunnel repair;

(Do not report modifier 63 in conjunction with 33611)

33612   with repair of right ventricular outflow tract obstruction

33615   Repair of complex cardiac anomalies (eg, tricuspid atresia) by closure of atrial septal defect and anastomosis of atria or vena cava to pulmonary artery (simple Fontan procedure)

33617   Repair of complex cardiac anomalies (eg, single ventricle) by modified Fontan procedure

(Use 33617 in conjunction with 33768 when a cavopulmonary anastomosis to a second superior vena cava is performed)

33619   Repair of single ventricle with aortic outflow obstruction and aortic arch hypoplasia (hypoplastic left heart syndrome) (eg, Norwood procedure)

(Do not report modifier 63 in conjunction with 33619)

Septal Defect

33641   Repair atrial septal defect, secundum, with cardiopulmonary bypass, with or without patch

33645   Direct or patch closure, sinus venosus, with or without anomalous pulmonary venous drainage

(Do not report 33645 in conjunction with 33724, 33726)

33647   Repair of atrial septal defect and ventricular septal defect, with direct or patch closure

(Do not report modifier 63 in conjunction with 33647)

(For repair of tricuspid atresia (eg, Fontan, Gago procedures), use 33615)

33660   Repair of incomplete or partial atrioventricular canal (ostium primum atrial septal defect), with or without atrioventricular valve repair

33665   Repair of intermediate or transitional atrioventricular canal, with or without atrioventricular valve repair

33670   Repair of complete atrioventricular canal, with or without prosthetic valve

(Do not report modifier 63 in conjunction with 33670)

33675   Closure of multiple ventricular septal defects;

33676   with pulmonary valvotomy or infundibular resection (acyanotic)

33677   with removal of pulmonary artery band, with or without gusset

(Do not report 33675-33677 in conjunction with 32100, 32422, 32551, 33210, 33681, 33684, 33688)

(For transmyocardial closure, see Category III codes 0166T and 0167T)

(For percutaneous closure, use 93581)

33681   Closure of single ventricular septal defect, with or without patch;

33684   with pulmonary valvotomy or infundibular resection (acyanotic)

Surgery: Cardiovascular System

33688   with removal of pulmonary artery band, with or without gusset

(For pulmonary vein repair requiring creation of atrial septal defect, use 33724)

33690   Banding of pulmonary artery

(Do not report modifier 63 in conjunction with 33690)

33692   Complete repair tetralogy of Fallot without pulmonary atresia;

33694   with transannular patch

(Do not report modifier 63 in conjunction with 33694)

(For ligation and takedown of a systemic-to-pulmonary artery shunt, performed in conjunction with a congenital heart procedure; see 33924)

33697   Complete repair tetralogy of Fallot with pulmonary atresia including construction of conduit from right ventricle to pulmonary artery and closure of ventricular septal defect

(For ligation and takedown of a systemic-to-pulmonary artery shunt, performed in conjunction with a congenital heart procedure; see 33924)

Sinus of Valsalva

33702   Repair sinus of Valsalva fistula, with cardiopulmonary bypass;

33710   with repair of ventricular septal defect

33720   Repair sinus of Valsalva aneurysm, with cardiopulmonary bypass

33722   Closure of aortico-left ventricular tunnel

Venous Anomalies

33724   Repair of isolated partial anomalous pulmonary venous return (eg, Scimitar Syndrome)

(Do not report 33724 in conjunction with 32551, 33210, 33211)

33726   Repair of pulmonary venous stenosis

(Do not report 33726 in conjunction with 32551, 33210, 33211)

33730   Complete repair of anomalous pulmonary venous return (supracardiac, intracardiac, or infracardiac types)

(Do not report modifier 63 in conjunction with 33730)

(For partial anomalous pulmonary venous return, use 33724; for repair of pulmonary venous stenosis, use 33726)

33732   Repair of cor triatriatum or supravalvular mitral ring by resection of left atrial membrane

(Do not report modifier 63 in conjunction with 33732)

Shunting Procedures

33735   Atrial septectomy or septostomy; closed heart (Blalock-Hanlon type operation)

33736   open heart with cardiopulmonary bypass

(Do not report modifier 63 in conjunction with 33735, 33736)

33737   open heart, with inflow occlusion

(For transvenous method cardiac catheterization balloon atrial septectomy or septostomy (Rashkind type), use 92992)

(For blade method cardiac catheterization atrial septectomy or septostomy (Sang-Park septostomy), use 92993)

33750   Shunt; subclavian to pulmonary artery (Blalock-Taussig type operation)

33755   ascending aorta to pulmonary artery (Waterston type operation)

33762   descending aorta to pulmonary artery (Potts-Smith type operation)

(Do not report modifier 63 in conjunction with 33750, 33755, 33762)

33764   central, with prosthetic graft

33766   superior vena cava to pulmonary artery for flow to 1 lung (classical Glenn procedure)

33767   superior vena cava to pulmonary artery for flow to both lungs (bidirectional Glenn procedure)

+ 33768   Anastomosis, cavopulmonary, second superior vena cava (List separately in addition to primary procedure)

(Use 33768 in conjunction with 33478, 33617, 33767)

(Do not report 33768 in conjunction with 32551, 33210, 33211)

Transposition of the Great Vessels

33770   Repair of transposition of the great arteries with ventricular septal defect and subpulmonary stenosis; without surgical enlargement of ventricular septal defect

33771   with surgical enlargement of ventricular septal defect

33774   Repair of transposition of the great arteries, atrial baffle procedure (eg, Mustard or Senning type) with cardiopulmonary bypass;

33775   with removal of pulmonary band

33776   with closure of ventricular septal defect

33777   with repair of subpulmonic obstruction

33778   Repair of transposition of the great arteries, aortic pulmonary artery reconstruction (eg, Jatene type);

(Do not report modifier 63 in conjunction with 33778)

33779   with removal of pulmonary band

Surgery: Cardiovascular System

33780   with closure of ventricular septal defect

33781   with repair of subpulmonic obstruction

● **33782**   Aortic root translocation with ventricular septal defect and pulmonary stenosis repair (ie, Nikaidoh procedure); without coronary ostium reimplantation

▶(Do not report 33782 in conjunction with 33412, 33413, 33608, 33681, 33770, 33771, 33778, 33780, 33920)◀

● **33783**   with reimplantation of 1 or both coronary ostia

Truncus Arteriosus

33786   Total repair, truncus arteriosus (Rastelli type operation)

(Do not report modifier 63 in conjunction with 33786)

33788   Reimplantation of an anomalous pulmonary artery

(For pulmonary artery band, use 33690)

Aortic Anomalies

33800   Aortic suspension (aortopexy) for tracheal decompression (eg, for tracheomalacia) (separate procedure)

33802   Division of aberrant vessel (vascular ring);

33803   with reanastomosis

33813   Obliteration of aortopulmonary septal defect; without cardiopulmonary bypass

33814   with cardiopulmonary bypass

33820   Repair of patent ductus arteriosus; by ligation

33822   by division, younger than 18 years

33824   by division, 18 years and older

33840   Excision of coarctation of aorta, with or without associated patent ductus arteriosus; with direct anastomosis

33845   with graft

33851   repair using either left subclavian artery or prosthetic material as gusset for enlargement

33852   Repair of hypoplastic or interrupted aortic arch using autogenous or prosthetic material; without cardiopulmonary bypass

33853   with cardiopulmonary bypass

(For repair of hypoplastic left heart syndrome (eg, Norwood type), via excision of coarctation of aorta, use 33619)

Thoracic Aortic Aneurysm

33860   Ascending aorta graft, with cardiopulmonary bypass, with or without valve suspension;

33861   with coronary reconstruction

33863   with aortic root replacement using composite prosthesis and coronary reconstruction

(For graft of ascending aorta, with cardiopulmonary bypass and valve replacement, with or without coronary implant or valve suspension; use 33860 or 33861 and 33405 or 33406)

33864   Ascending aorta graft, with cardiopulmonary bypass with valve suspension, with coronary reconstruction and valve-sparing aortic annulus remodeling (eg, David Procedure, Yacoub Procedure)

(Do not report 33864 in conjunction with 32551, 33210, 33211, 33400, 33860-33863)

33870   Transverse arch graft, with cardiopulmonary bypass

33875   Descending thoracic aorta graft, with or without bypass

33877   Repair of thoracoabdominal aortic aneurysm with graft, with or without cardiopulmonary bypass

Endovascular Repair of Descending Thoracic Aorta

Codes 33880-33891 represent a family of procedures to report placement of an endovascular graft for repair of the descending thoracic aorta. These codes include all device introduction, manipulation, positioning, and deployment. All balloon angioplasty and/or stent deployment within the target treatment zone for the endoprosthesis, either before or after endograft deployment, are not separately reportable. Open arterial exposure and associated closure of the arteriotomy sites (eg, 34812, 34820, 34833, 34834), introduction of guidewires and catheters (eg, 36140, 36200-36218), and extensive repair or replacement of an artery (eg, 35226, 35286) should be additionally reported. Transposition of subclavian artery to carotid, and carotid-carotid bypass performed in conjunction with endovascular repair of the descending thoracic aorta (eg, 33889, 33891) should be separately reported. The primary codes, 33880 and 33881, include placement of all distal extensions, if required, in the distal thoracic aorta, while proximal extensions, if needed, are reported separately.

For fluoroscopic guidance in conjunction with endovascular repair of the thoracic aorta, see codes 75956-75959 as appropriate. Codes 75956 and 75957 include all angiography of the thoracic aorta and its branches for diagnostic imaging prior to deployment of the primary endovascular devices (including all routine components of modular devices), fluoroscopic guidance in the delivery of the endovascular components, and intraprocedural arterial angiography (eg, confirm position, detect endoleak, evaluate runoff). Code 75958 includes the analogous services for placement of each proximal thoracic endovascular extension. Code 75959 includes the analogous services for placement of a distal thoracic endovascular extension(s) placed during a procedure after the primary repair.

Surgery: Cardiovascular System

Other interventional procedures performed at the time of endovascular repair of the descending thoracic aorta should be additionally reported (eg, innominate, carotid, subclavian, visceral, or iliac artery transluminal angioplasty or stenting, arterial embolization, intravascular ultrasound) when performed before or after deployment of the aortic prostheses.

(For transcatheter placement of wireless physiologic sensor in aneurysmal sac, use 34806)

(For analysis, interpretation, and report of implanted wireless pressure sensor in aneurysmal sac, use 93982)

33880   Endovascular repair of descending thoracic aorta (eg, aneurysm, pseudoaneurysm, dissection, penetrating ulcer, intramural hematoma, or traumatic disruption); involving coverage of left subclavian artery origin, initial endoprosthesis plus descending thoracic aortic extension(s), if required, to level of celiac artery origin

(For radiological supervision and interpretation, use 75956 in conjunction with 33880)

33881   not involving coverage of left subclavian artery origin, initial endoprosthesis plus descending thoracic aortic extension(s), if required, to level of celiac artery origin

(For radiological supervision and interpretation, use 75957 in conjunction with 33881)

33883   Placement of proximal extension prosthesis for endovascular repair of descending thoracic aorta (eg, aneurysm, pseudoaneurysm, dissection, penetrating ulcer, intramural hematoma, or traumatic disruption); initial extension

(For radiological supervision and interpretation, use 75958 in conjunction with 33883)

(Do not report 33881, 33883 when extension placement converts repair to cover left subclavian origin. Use only 33880)

+ 33884   each additional proximal extension (List separately in addition to code for primary procedure)

(Use 33884 in conjunction with 33883)

(For radiological supervision and interpretation, use 75958 in conjunction with 33884)

33886   Placement of distal extension prosthesis(s) delayed after endovascular repair of descending thoracic aorta

(Do not report 33886 in conjunction with 33880, 33881)

(Report 33886 once, regardless of number of modules deployed)

(For radiological supervision and interpretation, use 75959 in conjunction with 33886)

33889   Open subclavian to carotid artery transposition performed in conjunction with endovascular repair of descending thoracic aorta, by neck incision, unilateral

(Do not report 33889 in conjunction with 35694)

33891   Bypass graft, with other than vein, transcervical retropharyngeal carotid-carotid, performed in conjunction with endovascular repair of descending thoracic aorta, by neck incision

(Do not report 33891 in conjunction with 35509, 35601)

Pulmonary Artery

33910   Pulmonary artery embolectomy; with cardiopulmonary bypass

33915   without cardiopulmonary bypass

33916   Pulmonary endarterectomy, with or without embolectomy, with cardiopulmonary bypass

33917   Repair of pulmonary artery stenosis by reconstruction with patch or graft

33920   Repair of pulmonary atresia with ventricular septal defect, by construction or replacement of conduit from right or left ventricle to pulmonary artery

(For repair of other complex cardiac anomalies by construction or replacement of right or left ventricle to pulmonary artery conduit, use 33608)

33922   Transection of pulmonary artery with cardiopulmonary bypass

(Do not report modifier 63 in conjunction with 33922)

+ 33924   Ligation and takedown of a systemic-to-pulmonary artery shunt, performed in conjunction with a congenital heart procedure (List separately in addition to code for primary procedure)

(Use 33924 in conjunction with 33470-33475, 33600-33619, 33684-33688, 33692-33697, 33735-33767, 33770-33781, 33786, 33920-33922)

33925   Repair of pulmonary artery arborization anomalies by unifocalization; without cardiopulmonary bypass

33926   with cardiopulmonary bypass

Heart/Lung Transplantation

Heart with or without lung allotransplantation involves three distinct components of physician work:

1. *Cadaver donor cardiectomy with or without pneumonectomy*, which includes harvesting the allograft and cold preservation of the allograft (perfusing with cold preservation solution and cold maintenance) (see 33930, 33940).

2. *Backbench work*:

   Preparation of a cadaver donor heart and lung allograft prior to transplantation, including dissection of the allograft from surrounding soft tissues to prepare the aorta, superior vena cava, inferior vena cava, and trachea for implantation (use 33933).

Preparation of a cadaver donor heart allograft prior to transplantation, including dissection of the allograft from surrounding soft tissues to prepare aorta, superior vena cava, inferior vena cava, pulmonary artery, and left atrium for implantation (use 33944).

3. ***Recipient heart with or without lung allotransplantation***, which includes transplantation of allograft and care of the recipient (see 33935, 33945).

(For implantation of a total replacement heart system (artificial heart) with recipient cardiectomy or heart replacement system components, see Category III codes 0051T-0053T)

33930   Donor cardiectomy-pneumonectomy (including cold preservation)

33933   Backbench standard preparation of cadaver donor heart/lung allograft prior to transplantation, including dissection of allograft from surrounding soft tissues to prepare aorta, superior vena cava, inferior vena cava, and trachea for implantation

33935   Heart-lung transplant with recipient cardiectomy-pneumonectomy

33940   Donor cardiectomy (including cold preservation)

33944   Backbench standard preparation of cadaver donor heart allograft prior to transplantation, including dissection of allograft from surrounding soft tissues to prepare aorta, superior vena cava, inferior vena cava, pulmonary artery, and left atrium for implantation

(For repair or resection procedures on the donor heart, see 33300, 33310, 33320, 33400, 33463, 33464, 33510, 33641, 35216, 35276 or 35685)

33945   Heart transplant, with or without recipient cardiectomy

Cardiac Assist

▶The insertion of a ventricular assist device (VAD) can be performed via percutaneous (0048T) or transthoracic (33975, 33976, 33979) approach. The location of the ventricular assist device may be intracorporeal or extracorporeal.

Removal of a ventricular assist device (33977, 33978, 33980, 0050T) includes removal of the entire device, including the cannulas.

Replacement of a ventricular assist device pump includes the removal of the pump and insertion of a new pump, connection, de-airing, and initiation of the new pump.

Replacement of the entire ventricular assist device system, ie, pump(s) and cannulas, is reported using the insertion codes. Removal of the ventricular assist device system being replaced is not separately reported.◀

▶(For implantation or removal of ventricular assist device, extracorporeal, percutaneous transseptal access, see 0048T, 0050T. For replacement of a ventricular assist device, extracorporeal, percutaneous transseptal access, use 33999)◀

33960   Prolonged extracorporeal circulation for cardiopulmonary insufficiency; initial 24 hours

+ 33961   each additional 24 hours (List separately in addition to code for primary procedure)

(Do not report modifier 63 in conjunction with 33960, 33961)

(Use 33961 in conjunction with 33960)

(For insertion of cannula for prolonged extracorporeal circulation, use 36822)

33967   Insertion of intra-aortic balloon assist device, percutaneous

33968   Removal of intra-aortic balloon assist device, percutaneous

33970   Insertion of intra-aortic balloon assist device through the femoral artery, open approach

33971   Removal of intra-aortic balloon assist device including repair of femoral artery, with or without graft

33973   Insertion of intra-aortic balloon assist device through the ascending aorta

33974   Removal of intra-aortic balloon assist device from the ascending aorta, including repair of the ascending aorta, with or without graft

33975   Insertion of ventricular assist device; extracorporeal, single ventricle

33976   extracorporeal, biventricular

33977   Removal of ventricular assist device; extracorporeal, single ventricle

33978   extracorporeal, biventricular

33979   Insertion of ventricular assist device, implantable intracorporeal, single ventricle

33980   Removal of ventricular assist device, implantable intracorporeal, single ventricle

● **33981**   Replacement of extracorporeal ventricular assist device, single or biventricular, pump(s), single or each pump

● **33982**   Replacement of ventricular assist device pump(s); implantable intracorporeal, single ventricle, without cardiopulmonary bypass

● **33983**   implantable intracorporeal, single ventricle, with cardiopulmonary bypass

Other Procedures

33999   Unlisted procedure, cardiac surgery

Surgery: Cardiovascular System

Arteries and Veins

Primary vascular procedure listings include establishing both inflow and outflow by whatever procedures necessary. Also included is that portion of the operative arteriogram performed by the surgeon, as indicated. Sympathectomy, when done, is included in the listed aortic procedures. For unlisted vascular procedure, use 37799.

Embolectomy/Thrombectomy

Arterial, With or Without Catheter

34001 Embolectomy or thrombectomy, with or without catheter; carotid, subclavian or innominate artery, by neck incision

34051 innominate, subclavian artery, by thoracic incision

34101 axillary, brachial, innominate, subclavian artery, by arm incision

34111 radial or ulnar artery, by arm incision

34151 renal, celiac, mesentery, aortoiliac artery, by abdominal incision

34201 femoropopliteal, aortoiliac artery, by leg incision

34203 popliteal-tibio-peroneal artery, by leg incision

Venous, Direct or With Catheter

34401 Thrombectomy, direct or with catheter; vena cava, iliac vein, by abdominal incision

34421 vena cava, iliac, femoropopliteal vein, by leg incision

34451 vena cava, iliac, femoropopliteal vein, by abdominal and leg incision

34471 subclavian vein, by neck incision

34490 axillary and subclavian vein, by arm incision

Venous Reconstruction

34501 Valvuloplasty, femoral vein

34502 Reconstruction of vena cava, any method

34510 Venous valve transposition, any vein donor

34520 Cross-over vein graft to venous system

34530 Saphenopopliteal vein anastomosis

Endovascular Repair of Abdominal Aortic Aneurysm

Codes 34800-34826 represent a family of component procedures to report placement of an endovascular graft for abdominal aortic aneurysm repair. These codes describe open femoral or iliac artery exposure, device manipulation and deployment, and closure of the arteriotomy sites. Balloon angioplasty and/or stent deployment within the target treatment zone for the endoprosthesis, either before or after endograft deployment, are not separately reportable. Introduction of guidewires and catheters should be reported separately (eg, 36200, 36245-36248, 36140). Extensive repair or replacement of an artery should be additionally reported (eg, 35226 or 35286).

For fluoroscopic guidance in conjunction with endovascular aneurysm repair, see code 75952 or 75953, as appropriate. Code 75952 includes angiography of the aorta and its branches for diagnostic imaging prior to deployment of the endovascular device (including all routine components of modular devices), fluoroscopic guidance in the delivery of the endovascular components, and intraprocedural arterial angiography (eg, confirm position, detect endoleak, evaluate runoff). Code 75953 includes the analogous services for placement of additional extension prostheses (not for routine components of modular devices).

Other interventional procedures performed at the time of endovascular abdominal aortic aneurysm repair should be additionally reported (eg, renal transluminal angioplasty, arterial embolization, intravascular ultrasound, balloon angioplasty or stenting of native artery[s] outside the endoprosthesis target zone, when done before or after deployment of graft).

(For transcatheter placement of wireless physiologic sensor in aneurysmal sac, use 34806)

(For analysis, interpretation and report of implanted wireless pressure sensor in aneurysmal sac, use 93982)

34800 Endovascular repair of infrarenal abdominal aortic aneurysm or dissection; using aorto-aortic tube prosthesis

34802 using modular bifurcated prosthesis (1 docking limb)

34803 using modular bifurcated prosthesis (2 docking limbs)

(For endovascular repair of abdominal aortic aneurysm or dissection involving visceral vessels using a fenestrated modular bifurcated prosthesis (2 docking limbs), use Category III codes 0078T, 0079T)

34804 using unibody bifurcated prosthesis

34805 using aorto-uniiliac or aorto-unifemoral prosthesis

+ 34806 Transcatheter placement of wireless physiologic sensor in aneurysmal sac during endovascular repair, including radiological supervision and interpretation, instrument calibration, and collection of pressure data (List separately in addition to code for primary procedure)

(Use 34806 in conjunction with 33880, 33881, 33886, 34800-34805, 34825, 34900)

(Do not report 34806 in conjunction with 93982)

+ 34808 Endovascular placement of iliac artery occlusion device (List separately in addition to code for primary procedure)

(Use 34808 in conjunction with 34800, 34805, 34813, 34825, 34826)

(For radiological supervision and interpretation, use 75952 in conjunction with 34800-34808)

(For open arterial exposure, report 34812, 34820, 34833, 34834 as appropriate, in addition to 34800-34808)

34812 Open femoral artery exposure for delivery of endovascular prosthesis, by groin incision, unilateral

(For bilateral procedure, use modifier 50)

+ 34813 Placement of femoral-femoral prosthetic graft during endovascular aortic aneurysm repair (List separately in addition to code for primary procedure)

(Use 34813 in conjunction with 34812)

(For femoral artery grafting, see 35521, 35533, 35539, 35540, 35551-35558, 35566, 35621, 35646, 35651-35661, 35666, 35700)

34820 Open iliac artery exposure for delivery of endovascular prosthesis or iliac occlusion during endovascular therapy, by abdominal or retroperitoneal incision, unilateral

(For bilateral procedure, use modifier 50)

34825 Placement of proximal or distal extension prosthesis for endovascular repair of infrarenal abdominal aortic or iliac aneurysm, false aneurysm, or dissection; initial vessel

+ 34826 each additional vessel (List separately in addition to code for primary procedure)

(Use 34826 in conjunction with 34825)

(Use 34825, 34826 in addition to 34800-34808, 34900 as appropriate)

(For staged procedure, use modifier 58)

(For radiological supervision and interpretation, use 75953)

34830 Open repair of infrarenal aortic aneurysm or dissection, plus repair of associated arterial trauma, following unsuccessful endovascular repair; tube prosthesis

34831 aorto-bi-iliac prosthesis

34832 aorto-bifemoral prosthesis

34833 Open iliac artery exposure with creation of conduit for delivery of aortic or iliac endovascular prosthesis, by abdominal or retroperitoneal incision, unilateral

(For bilateral procedure, use modifier 50)

(Do not report 34833 in addition to 34820)

34834 Open brachial artery exposure to assist in the deployment of aortic or iliac endovascular prosthesis by arm incision, unilateral

(For bilateral procedure, use modifier 50)

Endovascular Repair of Iliac Aneurysm

Code 34900 represents a procedure to report introduction, positioning, and deployment of an endovascular graft for treatment of aneurysm, pseudoaneurysm, or arteriovenous malformation or trauma of the iliac artery (common, hypogastric, external). All balloon angioplasty and/or stent deployments within the target treatment zone for the endoprosthesis, either before or after endograft deployment, are included in the work of 34900 and are not separately reportable. Open femoral or iliac artery exposure (eg, 34812, 34820), introduction of guidewires and catheters (eg, 36200, 36215-36218), and extensive repair or replacement of an artery (eg, 35206-35286) should be additionally reported.

For fluoroscopic guidance in conjunction with endovascular iliac aneurysm repair, see code 75954. Code 75954 includes angiography of the aorta and iliac arteries for diagnostic imaging prior to deployment of the endovascular device (including all routine components), fluoroscopic guidance in the delivery of the endovascular components, and intraprocedural arterial angiography to confirm appropriate position of the graft, detect endoleaks, and evaluate the status of the runoff vessels (eg, evaluation for dissection, stenosis, thrombosis, distal embolization, or iatrogenic injury).

Other interventional procedures performed at the time of endovascular iliac aneurysm repair should be additionally reported (eg, transluminal angioplasty outside the aneurysm target zone, arterial embolization, intravascular ultrasound).

34900 Endovascular graft placement for repair of iliac artery (eg, aneurysm, pseudoaneurysm, arteriovenous malformation, trauma)

(For radiological supervision and interpretation, use 75954)

(For placement of extension prosthesis during endovascular iliac artery repair, use 34825)

(For bilateral procedure, use modifier 50)

Surgery: Cardiovascular System

Direct Repair of Aneurysm or Excision (Partial or Total) and Graft Insertion for Aneurysm, Pseudoaneurysm, Ruptured Aneurysm, and Associated Occlusive Disease

Procedures 35001-35152 include preparation of artery for anastomosis including endarterectomy.

(For direct repairs associated with occlusive disease only, see 35201-35286)

(For intracranial aneurysm, see 61700 et seq)

(For endovascular repair of abdominal aortic aneurysm, see 34800-34826)

(For endovascular repair of iliac artery aneurysm, see 34900)

(For thoracic aortic aneurysm, see 33860-33875)

(For endovascular repair of descending thoracic aorta, involving coverage of left subclavian artery origin, use 33880)

35001 Direct repair of aneurysm, pseudoaneurysm, or excision (partial or total) and graft insertion, with or without patch graft; for aneurysm and associated occlusive disease, carotid, subclavian artery, by neck incision

35002 for ruptured aneurysm, carotid, subclavian artery, by neck incision

35005 for aneurysm, pseudoaneurysm, and associated occlusive disease, vertebral artery

35011 for aneurysm and associated occlusive disease, axillary-brachial artery, by arm incision

35013 for ruptured aneurysm, axillary-brachial artery, by arm incision

35021 for aneurysm, pseudoaneurysm, and associated occlusive disease, innominate, subclavian artery, by thoracic incision

35022 for ruptured aneurysm, innominate, subclavian artery, by thoracic incision

35045 for aneurysm, pseudoaneurysm, and associated occlusive disease, radial or ulnar artery

35081 for aneurysm, pseudoaneurysm, and associated occlusive disease, abdominal aorta

35082 for ruptured aneurysm, abdominal aorta

35091 for aneurysm, pseudoaneurysm, and associated occlusive disease, abdominal aorta involving visceral vessels (mesenteric, celiac, renal)

35092 for ruptured aneurysm, abdominal aorta involving visceral vessels (mesenteric, celiac, renal)

35102 for aneurysm, pseudoaneurysm, and associated occlusive disease, abdominal aorta involving iliac vessels (common, hypogastric, external)

35103 for ruptured aneurysm, abdominal aorta involving iliac vessels (common, hypogastric, external)

35111 for aneurysm, pseudoaneurysm, and associated occlusive disease, splenic artery

35112 for ruptured aneurysm, splenic artery

35121 for aneurysm, pseudoaneurysm, and associated occlusive disease, hepatic, celiac, renal, or mesenteric artery

35122 for ruptured aneurysm, hepatic, celiac, renal, or mesenteric artery

35131 for aneurysm, pseudoaneurysm, and associated occlusive disease, iliac artery (common, hypogastric, external)

35132 for ruptured aneurysm, iliac artery (common, hypogastric, external)

35141 for aneurysm, pseudoaneurysm, and associated occlusive disease, common femoral artery (profunda femoris, superficial femoral)

35142 for ruptured aneurysm, common femoral artery (profunda femoris, superficial femoral)

35151 for aneurysm, pseudoaneurysm, and associated occlusive disease, popliteal artery

35152 for ruptured aneurysm, popliteal artery

Repair Arteriovenous Fistula

35180 Repair, congenital arteriovenous fistula; head and neck

35182 thorax and abdomen

35184 extremities

35188 Repair, acquired or traumatic arteriovenous fistula; head and neck

35189 thorax and abdomen

35190 extremities

Repair Blood Vessel Other Than for Fistula, With or Without Patch Angioplasty

(For AV fistula repair, see 35180-35190)

35201 Repair blood vessel, direct; neck

35206 upper extremity

35207 hand, finger

35211 intrathoracic, with bypass

35216 intrathoracic, without bypass

35221 intra-abdominal

35226 lower extremity

35231 Repair blood vessel with vein graft; neck

35236 upper extremity

35241	intrathoracic, with bypass
35246	intrathoracic, without bypass
35251	intra-abdominal
35256	lower extremity
35261	Repair blood vessel with graft other than vein; neck
35266	upper extremity
35271	intrathoracic, with bypass
35276	intrathoracic, without bypass
35281	intra-abdominal
35286	lower extremity

Thromboendarterectomy

(For coronary artery, see 33510-33536 and 33572)

(35301-35372 include harvest of saphenous or upper extremity vein when performed)

35301	Thromboendarterectomy, including patch graft, if performed; carotid, vertebral, subclavian, by neck incision
35302	superficial femoral artery
35303	popliteal artery

(Do not report 35302, 35303 in conjunction with 35483, 35500)

35304	tibioperoneal trunk artery
35305	tibial or peroneal artery, initial vessel
+ 35306	each additional tibial or peroneal artery (List separately in addition to code for primary procedure)

(Use 35306 in conjunction with 35305)

(Do not report 35304, 35305, 35306 in conjunction with 35485, 35500)

35311	subclavian, innominate, by thoracic incision
35321	axillary-brachial
35331	abdominal aorta
35341	mesenteric, celiac, or renal
35351	iliac
35355	iliofemoral
35361	combined aortoiliac
35363	combined aortoiliofemoral
35371	common femoral
35372	deep (profunda) femoral
+ 35390	Reoperation, carotid, thromboendarterectomy, more than 1 month after original operation (List separately in addition to code for primary procedure)

(Use 35390 in conjunction with 35301)

Angioscopy

+ 35400	Angioscopy (non-coronary vessels or grafts) during therapeutic intervention (List separately in addition to code for primary procedure)

Transluminal Angioplasty

If done as part of another operation, use modifier 51 or use modifier 52.

(For radiological supervision and interpretation, see 75962-75968 and 75978)

Open

35450	Transluminal balloon angioplasty, open; renal or other visceral artery
35452	aortic
35454	iliac
35456	femoral-popliteal
35458	brachiocephalic trunk or branches, each vessel
35459	tibioperoneal trunk and branches
35460	venous

Percutaneous

Codes for catheter placement and the radiologic supervision and interpretation should also be reported, in addition to the code(s) for the therapeutic aspect of the procedure.

⊙ 35470	Transluminal balloon angioplasty, percutaneous; tibioperoneal trunk or branches, each vessel
⊙ 35471	renal or visceral artery
⊙ 35472	aortic
⊙ 35473	iliac
⊙ 35474	femoral-popliteal
⊙ 35475	brachiocephalic trunk or branches, each vessel
⊙ 35476	venous

(For radiological supervision and interpretation, use 75978)

Transluminal Atherectomy

If done as part of another operation, use modifier 51 or use modifier 52.

(For radiological supervision and interpretation, see 75992-75996)

Open

35480	Transluminal peripheral atherectomy, open; renal or other visceral artery

Surgery: Cardiovascular System

35481	aortic
35482	iliac
35483	femoral-popliteal
35484	brachiocephalic trunk or branches, each vessel
35485	tibioperoneal trunk and branches

Percutaneous

Codes for catheter placement and the radiologic supervision and interpretation should also be reported, in addition to the code(s) for the therapeutic aspect of the procedure.

35490	Transluminal peripheral atherectomy, percutaneous; renal or other visceral artery
35491	aortic
35492	iliac
35493	femoral-popliteal
35494	brachiocephalic trunk or branches, each vessel
35495	tibioperoneal trunk and branches

Bypass Graft

Vein

Procurement of the saphenous vein graft is included in the description of the work for 35501-35587 and should not be reported as a separate service or co-surgery. To report harvesting of an upper extremity vein, use 35500 in addition to the bypass procedure. To report harvesting of a femoropopliteal vein segment, use 35572 in addition to the bypass procedure. To report harvesting and construction of an autogenous composite graft of two segments from two distant locations, report 35682 in addition to the bypass procedure, for autogenous composite of three or more segments from distant sites, report 35683.

+ 35500	Harvest of upper extremity vein, 1 segment, for lower extremity or coronary artery bypass procedure (List separately in addition to code for primary procedure)
	(Use 35500 in conjunction with 33510-33536, 35556, 35566, 35571, 35583-35587)
	(For harvest of more than one vein segment, see 35682, 35683)
	(For endoscopic procedure, use 33508)
35501	Bypass graft, with vein; common carotid-ipsilateral internal carotid
35506	carotid-subclavian or subclavian-carotid
35508	carotid-vertebral
35509	carotid-contralateral carotid
35510	carotid-brachial

35511	subclavian-subclavian
35512	subclavian-brachial
35515	subclavian-vertebral
35516	subclavian-axillary
35518	axillary-axillary
35521	axillary-femoral
	(For bypass graft performed with synthetic graft, use 35621)
35522	axillary-brachial
35523	brachial-ulnar or -radial
	(Do not report 35523 in conjunction with 35206, 35500, 35525, 36838)
	(For bypass graft performed with synthetic conduit, use 37799)
35525	brachial-brachial
35526	aortosubclavian or carotid
	(For bypass graft performed with synthetic graft, use 35626)
35531	aortoceliac or aortomesenteric
35533	axillary-femoral-femoral
	(For bypass graft performed with synthetic graft, use 35654)
35535	hepatorenal
	(Do not report 35535 in conjunction with 35221, 35251, 35281, 35500, 35536, 35560, 35631, 35636)
35536	splenorenal
35537	aortoiliac
	(For bypass graft performed with synthetic graft, use 35637)
	(Do not report 35537 in conjunction with 35538)
35538	aortobi-iliac
	(For bypass graft performed with synthetic graft, use 35638)
	(Do not report 35538 in conjunction with 35537)
35539	aortofemoral
	(For bypass graft performed with synthetic graft, use 35647)
	(Do not report 35539 in conjunction with 35540)
35540	aortobifemoral
	(For bypass graft performed with synthetic graft, use 35646)
	(Do not report 35540 in conjunction with 35539)
35548	aortoiliofemoral, unilateral
	(For bypass graft performed with synthetic graft, use 37799)

35549	aortoiliofemoral, bilateral

(For bypass graft performed with synthetic graft, use 37799)

35551	aortofemoral-popliteal
35556	femoral-popliteal
35558	femoral-femoral
35560	aortorenal
35563	ilioiliac
35565	iliofemoral
35566	femoral-anterior tibial, posterior tibial, peroneal artery or other distal vessels
35570	tibial-tibial, peroneal-tibial, or tibial/peroneal trunk-tibial

(Do not report 35570 in conjunction with 35256, 35286)

35571	popliteal-tibial, -peroneal artery or other distal vessels
+ 35572	Harvest of femoropopliteal vein, 1 segment, for vascular reconstruction procedure (eg, aortic, vena caval, coronary, peripheral artery) (List separately in addition to code for primary procedure)

(Use 35572 in conjunction with 33510-33516, 33517-33523, 33533-33536, 34502, 34520, 35001, 35002, 35011-35022, 35102, 35103, 35121-35152, 35231-35256, 35501-35587, 35879-35907)

(For bilateral procedure, use modifier 50)

In-Situ Vein

(To report aortobifemoral bypass using synthetic conduit, and femoral-popliteal bypass with vein conduit in-situ, use 35646 and 35583. To report aorto[uni]femoral bypass with synthetic conduit, and femoral-popliteal bypass with vein conduit in-situ, use 35647 and 35583. To report aortofemoral bypass using vein conduit, and femoral-popliteal bypass with vein conduit in-situ, use 35539 and 35583)

35583	In-situ vein bypass; femoral-popliteal
35585	femoral-anterior tibial, posterior tibial, or peroneal artery
35587	popliteal-tibial, peroneal

Other Than Vein

(For arterial transposition and/or reimplantation, see 35691-35695)

+ 35600	Harvest of upper extremity artery, 1 segment, for coronary artery bypass procedure (List separately in addition to code for primary procedure)

(Use 35600 in conjunction with 33533–33536)

35601	Bypass graft, with other than vein; common carotid-ipsilateral internal carotid

35606	carotid-subclavian

(For open transcervical common carotid-common carotid bypass performed in conjunction with endovascular repair of descending thoracic aorta, use 33891)

(For open subclavian to carotid artery transposition performed in conjunction with endovascular thoracic aneurysm repair by neck incision, use 33889)

35612	subclavian-subclavian
35616	subclavian-axillary
35621	axillary-femoral
35623	axillary-popliteal or -tibial
35626	aortosubclavian or carotid
35631	aortoceliac, aortomesenteric, aortorenal
35632	ilio-celiac

(Do not report 35632 in conjunction with 35221, 35251, 35281, 35531, 35631)

35633	ilio-mesenteric

(Do not report 35633 in conjunction with 35221, 35251, 35281, 35531, 35631)

35634	iliorenal

(Do not report 35634 in conjunction with 35221, 35251, 35281, 35560, 35536, 35631)

35636	splenorenal (splenic to renal arterial anastomosis)
35637	aortoiliac

(Do not report 35637 in conjunction with 35638, 35646)

35638	aortobi-iliac

(Do not report 35638 in conjunction with 35637, 35646)

(For open placement of aortobi-iliac prosthesis following unsuccessful endovascular repair, use 34831)

35642	carotid-vertebral
35645	subclavian-vertebral
35646	aortobifemoral

(For bypass graft performed with vein graft, use 35540)

(For open placement of aortobifemoral prosthesis following unsuccessful endovascular repair, use 34832)

35647	aortofemoral

(For bypass graft performed with vein graft, use 35539)

35650	axillary-axillary
35651	aortofemoral-popliteal
35654	axillary-femoral-femoral
35656	femoral-popliteal
35661	femoral-femoral
35663	ilioiliac
35665	iliofemoral

Surgery: Cardiovascular System

35666   femoral-anterior tibial, posterior tibial, or peroneal artery

35671   popliteal-tibial or -peroneal artery

Composite Grafts

Codes 35682-35683 are used to report harvest and anastomosis of multiple vein segments from distant sites for use as arterial bypass graft conduits. These codes are intended for use when the two or more vein segments are harvested from a limb other than that undergoing bypass. Add-on codes 35682 and 35683 may be reported in addition to codes 35556, 35566, 35571, 35583-35587, as appropriate.

+ 35681   Bypass graft; composite, prosthetic and vein (List separately in addition to code for primary procedure)

            (Do not report 35681 in addition to 35682, 35683)

+ 35682   autogenous composite, 2 segments of veins from 2 locations (List separately in addition to code for primary procedure)

            (Do not report 35682 in addition to 35681, 35683)

+ 35683   autogenous composite, 3 or more segments of vein from 2 or more locations (List separately in addition to code for primary procedure)

            (Do not report 35683 in addition to 35681, 35682)

Adjuvant Techniques

Adjuvant (additional) technique(s) may be required at the time a bypass graft is created to improve patency of the lower extremity autogenous or synthetic bypass graft (eg, femoral-popliteal, femoral-tibial, or popliteal-tibial arteries). Code 35685 should be reported in addition to the primary synthetic bypass graft procedure, when an interposition of venous tissue (vein patch or cuff) is placed at the anastomosis between the synthetic bypass conduit and the involved artery (includes harvest).

Code 35686 should be reported in addition to the primary bypass graft procedure, when autogenous vein is used to create a fistula between the tibial or peroneal artery and vein at or beyond the distal bypass anastomosis site of the involved artery.

            (For composite graft(s), see 35681-35683)

+ 35685   Placement of vein patch or cuff at distal anastomosis of bypass graft, synthetic conduit (List separately in addition to code for primary procedure)

            (Use 35685 in conjunction with 35656, 35666, or 35671)

+ 35686   Creation of distal arteriovenous fistula during lower extremity bypass surgery (non-hemodialysis) (List separately in addition to code for primary procedure)

            (Use 35686 in conjunction with 35556, 35566, 35571, 35583-35587, 35623, 35656, 35666, 35671)

Arterial Transposition

35691   Transposition and/or reimplantation; vertebral to carotid artery

35693   vertebral to subclavian artery

35694   subclavian to carotid artery

            (For open subclavian to carotid artery transposition performed in conjunction with endovascular repair of descending thoracic aorta, use 33889)

35695   carotid to subclavian artery

+ 35697   Reimplantation, visceral artery to infrarenal aortic prosthesis, each artery (List separately in addition to code for primary procedure)

            (Do not report 35697 in conjunction with 33877)

Excision, Exploration, Repair, Revision

+ 35700   Reoperation, femoral-popliteal or femoral (popliteal)-anterior tibial, posterior tibial, peroneal artery, or other distal vessels, more than 1 month after original operation (List separately in addition to code for primary procedure)

            (Use 35700 in conjunction with 35556, 35566, 35571, 35583, 35585, 35587, 35656, 35666, 35671)

35701   Exploration (not followed by surgical repair), with or without lysis of artery; carotid artery

35721   femoral artery

35741   popliteal artery

35761   other vessels

35800   Exploration for postoperative hemorrhage, thrombosis or infection; neck

35820   chest

35840   abdomen

35860   extremity

35870   Repair of graft-enteric fistula

35875   Thrombectomy of arterial or venous graft (other than hemodialysis graft or fistula);

35876   with revision of arterial or venous graft

            (For thrombectomy of hemodialysis graft or fistula, see 36831, 36833)

Codes 35879 and 35881 describe open revision of graft-threatening stenoses of lower extremity arterial bypass graft(s) (previously constructed with autogenous vein conduit) using vein patch angioplasty or segmental vein interposition techniques. For thrombectomy with revision of any non-coronary arterial or venous graft, including those of the lower extremity, (other than hemodialysis graft or fistula), use 35876. For direct repair (other than for fistula) of a lower extremity blood vessel (with or without patch angioplasty), use 35226. For repair (other than for fistula) of a lower extremity blood vessel using a vein graft, use 35256.

Surgery: Cardiovascular System

35879   Revision, lower extremity arterial bypass, without thrombectomy, open; with vein patch angioplasty

35881   with segmental vein interposition

(For revision of femoral anastomosis of synthetic arterial bypass graft, see 35883, 35884)

(For excision of infected graft, see 35901-35907 and appropriate revascularization code)

35883   Revision, femoral anastomosis of synthetic arterial bypass graft in groin, open; with nonautogenous patch graft (eg, Dacron, ePTFE, bovine pericardium)

(For bilateral procedure, use modifier 50)

(Do not report 35883 in conjunction with 35700, 35875, 35876, 35884)

35884   with autogenous vein patch graft

(For bilateral procedure, use modifier 50)

(Do not report 35884 in conjunction with 35700, 35875, 35876, 35883)

35901   Excision of infected graft; neck

35903   extremity

35905   thorax

35907   abdomen

Vascular Injection Procedures

Listed services for injection procedures include necessary local anesthesia, introduction of needles or catheter, injection of contrast media with or without automatic power injection, and/or necessary pre- and postinjection care specifically related to the injection procedure.

Catheters, drugs, and contrast media are not included in the listed service for the injection procedures.

Selective vascular catheterization should be coded to include introduction and all lesser order selective catheterization used in the approach (eg, the description for a selective right middle cerebral artery catheterization includes the introduction and placement catheterization of the right common and internal carotid arteries).

Additional second and/or third order arterial catheterization within the same family of arteries or veins supplied by a single first order vessel should be expressed by 36012, 36218, or 36248.

Additional first order or higher catheterization in vascular families supplied by a first order vessel different from a previously selected and coded family should be separately coded using the conventions described above.

(For radiological supervision and interpretation, see **Radiology**)

(For injection procedures in conjunction with cardiac catheterization, see 93541-93545)

(For chemotherapy of malignant disease, see 96401-96549)

Intravenous

An intracatheter is a sheathed combination of needle and short catheter.

36000   Introduction of needle or intracatheter, vein

36002   Injection procedures (eg, thrombin) for percutaneous treatment of extremity pseudoaneurysm

(For imaging guidance, see 76942, 77002, 77012, 77021)

(For ultrasound guided compression repair of pseudoaneurysms, use 76936)

(Do not report 36002 for vascular sealant of an arteriotomy site)

36005   Injection procedure for extremity venography (including introduction of needle or intracatheter)

(For radiological supervision and interpretation, see 75820, 75822)

36010   Introduction of catheter, superior or inferior vena cava

36011   Selective catheter placement, venous system; first order branch (eg, renal vein, jugular vein)

36012   second order, or more selective, branch (eg, left adrenal vein, petrosal sinus)

36013   Introduction of catheter, right heart or main pulmonary artery

36014   Selective catheter placement, left or right pulmonary artery

36015   Selective catheter placement, segmental or subsegmental pulmonary artery

(For insertion of flow directed catheter (eg, Swan-Ganz), use 93503)

(For venous catheterization for selective organ blood sampling, use 36500)

Intra-Arterial—Intra-Aortic

(For radiological supervision and interpretation, see **Radiology**)

36100   Introduction of needle or intracatheter, carotid or vertebral artery

(For bilateral procedure, report 36100 with modifier 50)

36120   Introduction of needle or intracatheter; retrograde brachial artery

36140   extremity artery

(For insertion of arteriovenous cannula, see 36810-36821)

▶(36145 has been deleted. To report see 36147, 36148)◀

Surgery: Cardiovascular System

Surgery: Cardiovascular System

⊙● **36147** Introduction of needle and/or catheter, arteriovenous shunt created for dialysis (graft/fistula); initial access with complete radiological evaluation of dialysis access, including fluoroscopy, image documentation and report (includes access of shunt, injection[s] of contrast, and all necessary imaging from the arterial anastomosis and adjacent artery through entire venous outflow including the inferior or superior vena cava)

▶(If 36147 indicates the need for a therapeutic intervention requiring a second catheterization of the shunt, use 36148)◀

▶(Do not report 36147 in conjunction with 75791)◀

⊙+● **36148** additional access for therapeutic intervention (List separately in addition to code for primary procedure)

▶(Use 36148 in conjunction with 36147)◀

36160 Introduction of needle or intracatheter, aortic, translumbar

36200 Introduction of catheter, aorta

36215 Selective catheter placement, arterial system; each first order thoracic or brachiocephalic branch, within a vascular family

(For catheter placement for coronary angiography, use 93508)

36216 initial second order thoracic or brachiocephalic branch, within a vascular family

36217 initial third order or more selective thoracic or brachiocephalic branch, within a vascular family

+ **36218** additional second order, third order, and beyond, thoracic or brachiocephalic branch, within a vascular family (List in addition to code for initial second or third order vessel as appropriate)

(Use 36218 in conjunction with 36216, 36217)

▶(For angiography, see 36147, 75600-75774, 75791)◀

(For angioplasty, see 35470-35475)

(For transcatheter therapies, see 37200-37208, 61624, 61626)

(When coronary artery, arterial conduit (eg, internal mammary, inferior epigastric or free radical artery) or venous bypass graft angiography is performed in conjunction with cardiac catheterization, see the appropriate cardiac catheterization, injection procedure, and imaging supervision code(s) (93501-93556) in the **Medicine** section of the CPT codebook. When coronary artery, arterial coronary conduit or venous bypass graft angiography is performed without concomitant left heart cardiac catheterization, use 93508. When internal mammary artery angiography only is performed without a concomitant left heart cardiac catheterization, use 36216 or 36217 as appropriate.)

36245 Selective catheter placement, arterial system; each first order abdominal, pelvic, or lower extremity artery branch, within a vascular family

36246 initial second order abdominal, pelvic, or lower extremity artery branch, within a vascular family

36247 initial third order or more selective abdominal, pelvic, or lower extremity artery branch, within a vascular family

+ **36248** additional second order, third order, and beyond, abdominal, pelvic, or lower extremity artery branch, within a vascular family (List in addition to code for initial second or third order vessel as appropriate)

(Use 36248 in conjunction with 36246, 36247)

36260 Insertion of implantable intra-arterial infusion pump (eg, for chemotherapy of liver)

36261 Revision of implanted intra-arterial infusion pump

36262 Removal of implanted intra-arterial infusion pump

36299 Unlisted procedure, vascular injection

Venous

Venipuncture, needle or catheter for diagnostic study or intravenous therapy, percutaneous. These codes are also used to report the therapy as specified. For collection of a specimen from an established catheter, use 36592. For collection of a specimen from a completely implantable venous access device, use 36591.

36400 Venipuncture, younger than age 3 years, necessitating physician's skill, not to be used for routine venipuncture; femoral or jugular vein

36405 scalp vein

36406 other vein

36410 Venipuncture, age 3 years or older, necessitating physician's skill (separate procedure), for diagnostic or therapeutic purposes (not to be used for routine venipuncture)

36415 Collection of venous blood by venipuncture

(Do not report modifier 63 in conjunction with 36415)

36416 Collection of capillary blood specimen (eg, finger, heel, ear stick)

36420 Venipuncture, cutdown; younger than age 1 year

(Do not report modifier 63 in conjunction with 36420)

36425 age 1 or over

36430 Transfusion, blood or blood components

36440 Push transfusion, blood, 2 years or younger

36450 Exchange transfusion, blood; newborn

(Do not report modifier 63 in conjunction with 36450)

36455 other than newborn

36460 Transfusion, intrauterine, fetal

(Do not report modifier 63 in conjunction with 36460)

(For radiological supervision and interpretation, use 76941)

36468 Single or multiple injections of sclerosing solutions, spider veins (telangiectasia); limb or trunk

36469   face

36470 Injection of sclerosing solution; single vein

36471   multiple veins, same leg

36475 Endovenous ablation therapy of incompetent vein, extremity, inclusive of all imaging guidance and monitoring, percutaneous, radiofrequency; first vein treated

+ 36476   second and subsequent veins treated in a single extremity, each through separate access sites (List separately in addition to code for primary procedure)

(Use 36476 in conjunction with 36475)

(Do not report 36475, 36476 in conjunction with 36000-36005, 36410, 36425, 36478, 36479, 37204, 75894, 76000, 76001, 76937, 76942, 76998, 77022, 93970, 93971)

36478 Endovenous ablation therapy of incompetent vein, extremity, inclusive of all imaging guidance and monitoring, percutaneous, laser; first vein treated

+ 36479   second and subsequent veins treated in a single extremity, each through separate access sites (List separately in addition to code for primary procedure)

(Use 36479 in conjunction with 36478)

(Do not report 36478, 36479 in conjunction with 36000-36005, 36410, 36425, 36475, 36476, 37204, 75894, 76000, 76001, 76937, 76942, 76998, 77022, 93970, 93971)

⊙▲ **36481** Percutaneous portal vein catheterization by any method

(For radiological supervision and interpretation, see 75885, 75887)

36500 Venous catheterization for selective organ blood sampling

(For catheterization in superior or inferior vena cava, use 36010)

(For radiological supervision and interpretation, use 75893)

36510 Catheterization of umbilical vein for diagnosis or therapy, newborn

(Do not report modifier 63 in conjunction with 36510)

36511 Therapeutic apheresis; for white blood cells

36512   for red blood cells

36513   for platelets

36514   for plasma pheresis

36515   with extracorporeal immunoadsorption and plasma reinfusion

36516   with extracorporeal selective adsorption or selective filtration and plasma reinfusion

(For physician evaluation, use modifier 26)

36522 Photopheresis, extracorporeal

(36540 has been deleted. To report, use 36591)

(36550 has been deleted. To report, use 36593)

Central Venous Access Procedures

To qualify as a central venous access catheter or device, the tip of the catheter/device must terminate in the subclavian, brachiocephalic (innominate) or iliac veins, the superior or inferior vena cava, or the right atrium. The venous access device may be either centrally inserted (jugular, subclavian, femoral vein or inferior vena cava catheter entry site) or peripherally inserted (eg, basilic or cephalic vein). The device may be accessed for use either via exposed catheter (external to the skin), via a subcutaneous port or via a subcutaneous pump.

The procedures involving these types of devices fall into five categories:

1. *Insertion* (placement of catheter through a newly established venous access)

2. *Repair* (fixing device without replacement of either catheter or port/pump, other than pharmacologic or mechanical correction of intracatheter or pericatheter occlusion [see 36595 or 36596])

3. *Partial replacement* of only the catheter component associated with a port/pump device, but not entire device

4. *Complete replacement* of entire device via same venous access site (complete exchange)

5. *Removal* of entire device.

There is no coding distinction between venous access achieved percutaneously versus by cutdown or based on catheter size.

For the repair, partial (catheter only) replacement, complete replacement, or removal of both catheters (placed from separate venous access sites) of a multi-catheter device, with or without subcutaneous ports/pumps, use the appropriate code describing the service with a frequency of two.

If an existing central venous access device is removed and a new one placed via a separate venous access site, appropriate codes for both procedures (removal of old, if code exists, and insertion of new device) should be reported.

When imaging is used for these procedures, either for gaining access to the venous entry site or for manipulating the catheter into final central position, use 76937, 77001.

(For refilling and maintenance of an implantable pump or reservoir for intravenous or intra-arterial drug delivery, use 96522)

Surgery: Cardiovascular System

The Central Venous Access Procedures Table

	Non-tunneled	Tunneled Without Port or Pump	Central Tunneled	Tunneled With Port	Tunneled With Pump	Peripheral	<5 years	>5 years
Insertion								
Catheter	36555						36555	
	36556							36556
		36557	36557				36557	
		36558	36558					36558
	36568					36568	36568	
	36569					36569		36569
Device			36560	36560			36560	
			36561	36561				36561
			36563		36563			36563
		36565	36565					36565
			36566	36566				
	36570 (w port)			36570 (w port)		36570 (w port)	36570 (w port)	
				36571 (w port)		36571 (w port)		36571 (w port)
Repair								
Catheter	36575	36575	36575			36575		
Device			36576	36576	36576	36576		
Partial Replacement- Central Venous Access Device (Catheter only)								
			36578	36578	36578	36578	36578	36578
Central Replacement								
Catheter	36580							
		36581	36581					
	36854 (w/o port or pump)			36585 (w port)		36584 (w/o port or pump)		
Device			36582	36582				
			36583		36583			
						36585 (w port)		
Removal								
Catheter		36589						
Device			36590	36590	36590	36590		
Removal of Obstructive Material from Device								
	36595 (pericatheter) 36596 (intraluminal)	36595 (pericatheter) 36596 (intraluminal)	36595 (pericatheter) 36596 (intraluminal)	36595 (pericatheter) 36596 (intraluminal)	36595 (pericatheter) 36596 (intraluminal)	36595 (pericatheter) 36596 (intraluminal)		
Repositioning of Catheter								
36597	36597	36597	36597	36597	36597	36597	36597	36597

Surgery: Cardiovascular System

Insertion of Central Venous Access Device

⊙ **36555**　Insertion of non-tunneled centrally inserted central venous catheter; younger than 5 years of age

(For peripherally inserted non-tunneled central venous catheter, younger than 5 years of age, use 36568)

36556　age 5 years or older

(For peripherally inserted non-tunneled central venous catheter, age 5 years or older, use 36569)

⊙ **36557**　Insertion of tunneled centrally inserted central venous catheter, without subcutaneous port or pump; younger than 5 years of age

⊙ **36558**　age 5 years or older

(For peripherally inserted central venous catheter with port, 5 years or older, use 36571)

⊙ **36560**　Insertion of tunneled centrally inserted central venous access device, with subcutaneous port; younger than 5 years of age

(For peripherally inserted central venous access device with subcutaneous port, younger than 5 years of age, use 36570)

⊙ **36561**　age 5 years or older

(For peripherally inserted central venous catheter with subcutaneous port, 5 years or older, use 36571)

⊙ **36563**　Insertion of tunneled centrally inserted central venous access device with subcutaneous pump

⊙ **36565**　Insertion of tunneled centrally inserted central venous access device, requiring 2 catheters via 2 separate venous access sites; without subcutaneous port or pump (eg, Tesio type catheter)

⊙ **36566**　with subcutaneous port(s)

⊙ **36568**　Insertion of peripherally inserted central venous catheter (PICC), without subcutaneous port or pump; younger than 5 years of age

(For placement of centrally inserted non-tunneled central venous catheter, without subcutaneous port or pump, younger than 5 years of age, use 36555)

36569　age 5 years or older

(For placement of centrally inserted non-tunneled central venous catheter, without subcutaneous port or pump, age 5 years or older, use 36556)

⊙ **36570**　Insertion of peripherally inserted central venous access device, with subcutaneous port; younger than 5 years of age

(For insertion of tunneled centrally inserted central venous access device with subcutaneous port, younger than 5 years of age, use 36560)

⊙ **36571**　age 5 years or older

(For insertion of tunneled centrally inserted central venous access device with subcutaneous port, age 5 years or older, use 36561)

Repair of Central Venous Access Device

(For mechanical removal of pericatheter obstructive material, use 36595)

(For mechanical removal of intracatheter obstructive material, use 36596)

36575　Repair of tunneled or non-tunneled central venous access catheter, without subcutaneous port or pump, central or peripheral insertion site

⊙ **36576**　Repair of central venous access device, with subcutaneous port or pump, central or peripheral insertion site

Partial Replacement of Central Venous Access Device (Catheter Only)

⊙ **36578**　Replacement, catheter only, of central venous access device, with subcutaneous port or pump, central or peripheral insertion site

(For complete replacement of entire device through same venous access, use 36582 or 36583)

Complete Replacement of Central Venous Access Device Through Same Venous Access Site

36580　Replacement, complete, of a non-tunneled centrally inserted central venous catheter, without subcutaneous port or pump, through same venous access

⊙ **36581**　Replacement, complete, of a tunneled centrally inserted central venous catheter, without subcutaneous port or pump, through same venous access

⊙ **36582**　Replacement, complete, of a tunneled centrally inserted central venous access device, with subcutaneous port, through same venous access

⊙ **36583**　Replacement, complete, of a tunneled centrally inserted central venous access device, with subcutaneous pump, through same venous access

36584　Replacement, complete, of a peripherally inserted central venous catheter (PICC), without subcutaneous port or pump, through same venous access

⊙ **36585**　Replacement, complete, of a peripherally inserted central venous access device, with subcutaneous port, through same venous access

Removal of Central Venous Access Device

36589　Removal of tunneled central venous catheter, without subcutaneous port or pump

Surgery: Cardiovascular System

⊙ **36590**   Removal of tunneled central venous access device, with subcutaneous port or pump, central or peripheral insertion

(Do not report 36589 or 36590 for removal of non-tunneled central venous catheters)

Other Central Venous Access Procedures

36591   Collection of blood specimen from a completely implantable venous access device

(Do not report 36591 in conjunction with any other service)

(For collection of venous blood specimen by venipuncture, use 36415)

(For collection of capillary blood specimen, use 36416)

36592   Collection of blood specimen using established central or peripheral catheter, venous, not otherwise specified

(For blood collection from an established arterial catheter, use 37799)

(Do not report 36592 in conjunction with any other service)

36593   Declotting by thrombolytic agent of implanted vascular access device or catheter

36595   Mechanical removal of pericatheter obstructive material (eg, fibrin sheath) from central venous device via separate venous access

(Do not report 36595 in conjunction with 36593)

(For venous catheterization, see 36010-36012)

(For radiological supervision and interpretation, use 75901)

36596   Mechanical removal of intraluminal (intracatheter) obstructive material from central venous device through device lumen

(Do not report 36596 in conjunction with 36593)

(For venous catheterization, see 36010-36012)

(For radiological supervision and interpretation, use 75902)

36597   Repositioning of previously placed central venous catheter under fluoroscopic guidance

(For fluoroscopic guidance, use 76000)

36598   Contrast injection(s) for radiologic evaluation of existing central venous access device, including fluoroscopy, image documentation and report

(Do not report 36598 in conjunction with 76000)

(Do not report 36598 in conjunction with 36595, 36596)

(For complete diagnostic studies, see 75820, 75825, 75827)

Arterial

36600   Arterial puncture, withdrawal of blood for diagnosis

⊘ **36620**   Arterial catheterization or cannulation for sampling, monitoring or transfusion (separate procedure); percutaneous

36625   cutdown

36640   Arterial catheterization for prolonged infusion therapy (chemotherapy), cutdown

(See also 96420-96425)

(For arterial catheterization for occlusion therapy, see 75894)

36660   Catheterization, umbilical artery, newborn, for diagnosis or therapy

(Do not report modifier 63 in conjunction with 36660)

Intraosseous

36680   Placement of needle for intraosseous infusion

Hemodialysis Access, Intervascular Cannulation for Extracorporeal Circulation, or Shunt Insertion

36800   Insertion of cannula for hemodialysis, other purpose (separate procedure); vein to vein

36810   arteriovenous, external (Scribner type)

36815   arteriovenous, external revision, or closure

36818   Arteriovenous anastomosis, open; by upper arm cephalic vein transposition

(Do not report 36818 in conjunction with 36819, 36820, 36821, 36830 during a unilateral upper extremity procedure. For bilateral upper extremity open arteriovenous anastomoses performed at the same operative session, use modifier 50 or 59 as appropriate)

36819   by upper arm basilic vein transposition

(Do not report 36819 in conjunction with 36818, 36820, 36821, 36830 during a unilateral upper extremity procedure. For bilateral upper extremity open arteriovenous anastomoses performed at the same operative session, use modifier 50 or 59 as appropriate)

36820   by forearm vein transposition

36821   direct, any site (eg, Cimino type) (separate procedure)

36822   Insertion of cannula(s) for prolonged extracorporeal circulation for cardiopulmonary insufficiency (ECMO) (separate procedure)

(For maintenance of prolonged extracorporeal circulation, see 33960, 33961)

36823   Insertion of arterial and venous cannula(s) for isolated extracorporeal circulation including regional chemotherapy perfusion to an extremity, with or without hyperthermia, with removal of cannula(s) and repair of arteriotomy and venotomy sites

(36823 includes chemotherapy perfusion supported by a membrane oxygenator/perfusion pump. Do not report 96409-96425 in conjunction with 36823)

36825   Creation of arteriovenous fistula by other than direct arteriovenous anastomosis (separate procedure); autogenous graft

(For direct arteriovenous anastomosis, use 36821)

36830   nonautogenous graft (eg, biological collagen, thermoplastic graft)

(For direct arteriovenous anastomosis, use 36821)

36831   Thrombectomy, open, arteriovenous fistula without revision, autogenous or nonautogenous dialysis graft (separate procedure)

36832   Revision, open, arteriovenous fistula; without thrombectomy, autogenous or nonautogenous dialysis graft (separate procedure)

36833   with thrombectomy, autogenous or nonautogenous dialysis graft (separate procedure)

►(36834 has been deleted. To report an arteriovenous access fistula or graft revision, use 36832)◄

36835   Insertion of Thomas shunt (separate procedure)

36838   Distal revascularization and interval ligation (DRIL), upper extremity hemodialysis access (steal syndrome)

(Do not report 36838 in conjunction with 35512, 35522, 35523, 36832, 37607, 37618)

36860   External cannula declotting (separate procedure); without balloon catheter

36861   with balloon catheter

(If imaging guidance is performed, use 76000)

⊙ **36870**   Thrombectomy, percutaneous, arteriovenous fistula, autogenous or nonautogenous graft (includes mechanical thrombus extraction and intra-graft thrombolysis)

(Do not report 36870 in conjunction with 36593)

►(For catheterization, see 36147, 36148)◄

►(For radiological supervision and interpretation, see 36147, 75791)◄

Portal Decompression Procedures

37140   Venous anastomosis, open; portocaval

(For peritoneal-venous shunt, use 49425)

37145   renoportal

37160   caval-mesenteric

37180   splenorenal, proximal

37181   splenorenal, distal (selective decompression of esophagogastric varices, any technique)

(For percutaneous procedure, use 37182)

37182   Insertion of transvenous intrahepatic portosystemic shunt(s) (TIPS) (includes venous access, hepatic and portal vein catheterization, portography with hemodynamic evaluation, intrahepatic tract formation/dilatation, stent placement and all associated imaging guidance and documentation)

(Do not report 75885 or 75887 in conjunction with 37182)

(For open procedure, use 37140)

⊙▲ **37183**   Revision of transvenous intrahepatic portosystemic shunt(s) (TIPS) (includes venous access, hepatic and portal vein catheterization, portography with hemodynamic evaluation, intrahepatic tract recanulization/dilatation, stent placement and all associated imaging guidance and documentation)

(Do not report 75885 or 75887 in conjunction with 37183)

►(For repair of arteriovenous aneurysm, use 36832)◄

Transcatheter Procedures

Codes for catheter placement and the radiologic supervision and interpretation should also be reported, in addition to the code(s) for the therapeutic aspect of the procedure.

Mechanical Thrombectomy

Code(s) for catheter placement(s), diagnostic studies, and other percutaneous interventions (eg, transluminal balloon angioplasty, stent placement) provided are separately reportable.

Codes 37184-37188 specifically include intraprocedural fluoroscopic radiological supervision and interpretation services for guidance of the procedure.

Intraprocedural injection(s) of a thrombolytic agent is an included service and not separately reportable in conjunction with mechanical thrombectomy. However, subsequent or prior continuous infusion of a thrombolytic is not an included service and is separately reportable (see 37201, 75896, 75898).

For coronary mechanical thrombectomy, use 92973.

For mechanical thrombectomy for dialysis fistula, use 36870.

Arterial Mechanical Thrombectomy

Arterial mechanical thrombectomy may be performed as a "primary" transcatheter procedure with pretreatment planning, performance of the procedure, and postprocedure evaluation focused on providing this service. Typically, the diagnosis of thrombus has been made prior to the procedure, and a mechanical thrombectomy is planned preoperatively. Primary mechanical thrombectomy is reported per vascular family using 37184 for the initial vessel treated and 37185 for second or all subsequent vessel(s) within the same vascular family. To report mechanical thrombectomy of an additional vascular family treated through a separate access site, use modifier 51 in conjunction with 37184-37185.

Primary mechanical thrombectomy may precede or follow another percutaneous intervention. Most commonly primary mechanical thrombectomy will precede another percutaneous intervention with the decision regarding the need for other services not made until after mechanical thrombectomy has been performed. Occasionally, the performance of primary mechanical thrombectomy may follow another percutaneous intervention.

Do **NOT** report 37184-37185 for mechanical thrombectomy performed for the retrieval of short segments of thrombus or embolus evident during other percutaneous interventional procedures. See 37186 for these procedures.

Arterial mechanical thrombectomy is considered a "secondary" transcatheter procedure for removal or retrieval of short segments of thrombus or embolus when performed either before or after another percutaneous intervention (eg, percutaneous transluminal balloon angioplasty, stent placement). Secondary mechanical thrombectomy is reported using 37186. Do **NOT** report 37186 in conjunction with 37184-37185.

Venous Mechanical Thrombectomy

Use 37187 to report the initial application of venous mechanical thrombectomy. To report bilateral venous mechanical thrombectomy performed through a separate access site(s), use modifier 50 in conjunction with 37187. For repeat treatment on a subsequent day during a course of thrombolytic therapy, use 37188.

Arterial Mechanical Thrombectomy

⊙ **37184** Primary percutaneous transluminal mechanical thrombectomy, noncoronary, arterial or arterial bypass graft, including fluoroscopic guidance and intraprocedural pharmacological thrombolytic injection(s); initial vessel

(Do not report 37184 in conjunction with 76000, 76001, 96374, 99143-99150)

⊙+ **37185** second and all subsequent vessel(s) within the same vascular family (List separately in addition to code for primary mechanical thrombectomy procedure)

(Do not report 37185 in conjunction with 76000, 76001, 96375)

⊙+ **37186** Secondary percutaneous transluminal thrombectomy (eg, nonprimary mechanical, snare basket, suction technique), noncoronary, arterial or arterial bypass graft, including fluoroscopic guidance and intraprocedural pharmacological thrombolytic injections, provided in conjunction with another percutaneous intervention other than primary mechanical thrombectomy (List separately in addition to code for primary procedure)

(Do not report 37186 in conjunction with 76000, 76001, 96375)

Venous Mechanical Thrombectomy

⊙ **37187** Percutaneous transluminal mechanical thrombectomy, vein(s), including intraprocedural pharmacological thrombolytic injections and fluoroscopic guidance

(Do not report 37187 in conjunction with 76000, 76001, 96375)

⊙ **37188** Percutaneous transluminal mechanical thrombectomy, vein(s), including intraprocedural pharmacological thrombolytic injections and fluoroscopic guidance, repeat treatment on subsequent day during course of thrombolytic therapy

(Do not report 37188 in conjunction with 76000, 76001, 96375)

Other Procedures

37195 Thrombolysis, cerebral, by intravenous infusion

37200 Transcatheter biopsy

(For radiological supervision and interpretation, use 75970)

37201 Transcatheter therapy, infusion for thrombolysis other than coronary

(For radiological supervision and interpretation, use 75896)

37202 Transcatheter therapy, infusion other than for thrombolysis, any type (eg, spasmolytic, vasoconstrictive)

(For thrombolysis of coronary vessels, see 92975, 92977)

(For radiological supervision and interpretation, use 75896)

⊙ **37203** Transcatheter retrieval, percutaneous, of intravascular foreign body (eg, fractured venous or arterial catheter)

(For radiological supervision and interpretation, use 75961)

37204 Transcatheter occlusion or embolization (eg, for tumor destruction, to achieve hemostasis, to occlude a vascular malformation), percutaneous, any method, non-central nervous system, non-head or neck

(See also 61624, 61626)

(For radiological supervision and interpretation, use 75894)

(For uterine fibroid embolization [uterine artery embolization performed to treat uterine fibroids], use 37210)

(For obstetrical and gynecologic embolization procedures other than uterine fibroid embolization [eg, embolization to treat obstetrical or postpartum hemorrhage], use 37204)

37205   Transcatheter placement of an intravascular stent(s) (except coronary, carotid, and vertebral vessel), percutaneous; initial vessel

(For radiological supervision and interpretation, use 75960)

(For coronary stent placement, see 92980, 92981; intracranial, use 61635)

+ 37206   each additional vessel (List separately in addition to code for primary procedure)

(Use 37206 in conjunction with 37205)

(For transcatheter placement of intravascular cervical carotid artery stent(s), see 37215, 37216)

(For transcatheter placement of extracranial vertebral or intrathoracic carotid artery stent(s), see Category III codes 0075T, 0076T)

(For radiological supervision and interpretation, use 75960)

37207   Transcatheter placement of an intravascular stent(s) (non-coronary vessel), open; initial vessel

+ 37208   each additional vessel (List separately in addition to code for primary procedure)

(Use 37208 in conjunction with 37207)

(For radiological supervision and interpretation, use 75960)

(For catheterizations, see 36215-36248)

(For transcatheter placement of intracoronary stent(s), see 92980, 92981)

37209   Exchange of a previously placed intravascular catheter during thrombolytic therapy

(For radiological supervision and interpretation, use 75900)

⊙ **37210**   Uterine fibroid embolization (UFE, embolization of the uterine arteries to treat uterine fibroids, leiomyomata), percutaneous approach inclusive of vascular access, vessel selection, embolization, and all radiological supervision and interpretation, intraprocedural roadmapping, and imaging guidance necessary to complete the procedure

(37210 includes all catheterizations and intraprocedural imaging required for a UFE procedure to confirm the presence of previously known fibroids and to roadmap vascular anatomy to enable appropriate therapy)

(Do not report 37210 in conjunction with 36200, 36245-36248, 37204, 75894, 75898)

(For all other non-central nervous system (CNS) embolization procedures, use 37204)

⊙ **37215**   Transcatheter placement of intravascular stent(s), cervical carotid artery, percutaneous; with distal embolic protection

⊙ **37216**   without distal embolic protection

(37215 and 37216 include all ipsilateral selective carotid catheterization, all diagnostic imaging for ipsilateral, cervical and cerebral carotid arteriography, and all related radiological supervision and interpretation. When ipsilateral carotid arteriogram (including imaging and selective catheterization) confirms the need for carotid stenting, 37215 and 37216 are inclusive of these services. If carotid stenting is not indicated, then the appropriate codes for carotid catheterization and imaging should be reported in lieu of 37215 and 37216)

(Do not report 37215, 37216 in conjunction with 75671, 75680)

(For transcatheter placement of extracranial vertebral or intrathoracic carotid artery stent(s), see Category III codes 0075T, 0076T)

(For percutaneous transcatheter placement of intravascular stents other than coronary, carotid, or vertebral, see 37205, 37206)

Intravascular Ultrasound Services

Intravascular ultrasound services include all transducer manipulations and repositioning within the specific vessel being examined, both before and after therapeutic intervention (eg, stent placement).

Vascular access for intravascular ultrasound performed during a therapeutic intervention is not reported separately.

+ 37250   Intravascular ultrasound (non-coronary vessel) during diagnostic evaluation and/or therapeutic intervention; initial vessel (List separately in addition to code for primary procedure)

+ 37251   each additional vessel (List separately in addition to code for primary procedure)

(Use 37251 in conjunction with 37250)

(For catheterizations, see 36215-36248)

(For transcatheter therapies, see 37200-37208, 61624, 61626)

(For radiological supervision and interpretation see 75945, 75946)

Surgery: Cardiovascular System

Endoscopy

Surgical vascular endoscopy always includes diagnostic endoscopy.

37500   Vascular endoscopy, surgical, with ligation of perforator veins, subfascial (SEPS)

(For open procedure, use 37760)

37501   Unlisted vascular endoscopy procedure

Ligation

(For phleborraphy and arteriorraphy, see 35201-35286)

37565   Ligation, internal jugular vein

37600   Ligation; external carotid artery

37605   internal or common carotid artery

37606   internal or common carotid artery, with gradual occlusion, as with Selverstone or Crutchfield clamp

(For transcatheter permanent arterial occlusion or embolization, see 61624-61626)

(For endovascular temporary arterial balloon occlusion, use 61623)

(For ligation treatment of intracranial aneurysm, use 61703)

37607   Ligation or banding of angioaccess arteriovenous fistula

37609   Ligation or biopsy, temporal artery

37615   Ligation, major artery (eg, post-traumatic, rupture); neck

37616   chest

37617   abdomen

37618   extremity

37620   Interruption, partial or complete, of inferior vena cava by suture, ligation, plication, clip, extravascular, intravascular (umbrella device)

(For radiological supervision and interpretation, use 75940)

37650   Ligation of femoral vein

(For bilateral procedure, report 37650 with modifier 50)

37660   Ligation of common iliac vein

37700   Ligation and division of long saphenous vein at saphenofemoral junction, or distal interruptions

(Do not report 37700 in conjunction with 37718, 37722)

(For bilateral procedure, report 37700 with modifier 50)

37718   Ligation, division, and stripping, short saphenous vein

(For bilateral procedure, use modifier 50)

(Do not report 37718 in conjunction with 37735, 37780)

37722   Ligation, division, and stripping, long (greater) saphenous veins from saphenofemoral junction to knee or below

(For ligation and stripping of the short saphenous vein, use 37718)

(For bilateral procedure, report 37722 with modifier 50)

(Do not report 37722 in conjunction with 37700, 37735)

(For ligation, division, and stripping of the greater saphenous vein, use 37722. For ligation, division, and stripping of the short saphenous vein, use 37718)

37735   Ligation and division and complete stripping of long or short saphenous veins with radical excision of ulcer and skin graft and/or interruption of communicating veins of lower leg, with excision of deep fascia

(Do not report 37735 in conjunction with 37700, 37718, 37722, 37780)

(For bilateral procedure, report 37735 with modifier 50)

▲ **37760**   Ligation of perforator veins, subfascial, radical (Linton type), including skin graft, when performed, open,1 leg

(For endoscopic procedure, use 37500)

● **37761**   Ligation of perforator vein(s), subfascial, open, including ultrasound guidance, when performed, 1 leg

▶(For bilateral procedure, report 37761 with modifier 50)◀

▶(Do not report 37760, 37761 in conjunction with 76937, 76942, 76998, 93971)◀

▶(For endoscopic ligation of subfascial perforator veins, use 37500)◀

37765   Stab phlebectomy of varicose veins, 1 extremity; 10-20 stab incisions

(For less than 10 incisions, use 37799)

(For more than 20 incisions, use 37766)

37766   more than 20 incisions

37780   Ligation and division of short saphenous vein at saphenopopliteal junction (separate procedure)

(For bilateral procedure, report 37780 with modifier 50)

37785   Ligation, division, and/or excision of varicose vein cluster(s), 1 leg

(For bilateral procedure, report 37785 with modifier 50)

Other Procedures

37788   Penile revascularization, artery, with or without vein graft

37790   Penile venous occlusive procedure

37799   Unlisted procedure, vascular surgery

Hemic and Lymphatic Systems

Spleen

Excision

38100   Splenectomy; total (separate procedure)

38101   partial (separate procedure)

+ **38102**   total, en bloc for extensive disease, in conjunction with other procedure (List in addition to code for primary procedure)

Repair

38115   Repair of ruptured spleen (splenorrhaphy) with or without partial splenectomy

Laparoscopy

Surgical laparoscopy always includes diagnostic laparoscopy. To report a diagnostic laparoscopy (peritoneoscopy) (separate procedure), use 49320.

38120   Laparoscopy, surgical, splenectomy

38129   Unlisted laparoscopy procedure, spleen

Introduction

38200   Injection procedure for splenoportography

          (For radiological supervision and interpretation, use 75810)

General

Bone Marrow or Stem Cell Services/Procedures

Codes 38207-38215 describe various steps used to preserve, prepare and purify bone marrow/stem cells prior to transplantation or reinfusion. Each code may be reported only once per day regardless of the quantity of bone marrow/stem cells manipulated.

38204   Management of recipient hematopoietic progenitor cell donor search and cell acquisition

38205   Blood-derived hematopoietic progenitor cell harvesting for transplantation, per collection; allogenic

38206   autologous

38207   Transplant preparation of hematopoietic progenitor cells; cryopreservation and storage

          (For diagnostic cryopreservation and storage, see 88240)

38208   thawing of previously frozen harvest, without washing

          (For diagnostic thawing and expansion of frozen cells, see 88241)

38209   thawing of previously frozen harvest, with washing

38210   specific cell depletion within harvest, T-cell depletion

38211   tumor cell depletion

38212   red blood cell removal

38213   platelet depletion

38214   plasma (volume) depletion

38215   cell concentration in plasma, mononuclear, or buffy coat layer

          (Do not report 38207-38215 in conjunction with 88182, 88184-88189)

38220   Bone marrow; aspiration only

38221   biopsy, needle or trocar

          (For bone marrow biopsy interpretation, use 88305)

38230   Bone marrow harvesting for transplantation

          (For autologous and allogenic blood-derived peripheral stem cell harvesting for transplantation, see 38205-38206)

38240   Bone marrow or blood-derived peripheral stem cell transplantation; allogenic

38241   autologous

38242   allogeneic donor lymphocyte infusions

          (For bone marrow aspiration, use 38220)

          (For modification, treatment, and processing of bone marrow or blood-derived stem cell specimens for transplantation, use 38210-38213)

          ►(For cryopreservation, freezing, and storage of blood-derived stem cells for transplantation, use 38207)◄

          ►(For thawing and expansion of blood-derived stem cells for transplantation, see 38208, 38209)◄

          (For compatibility studies, see 86812-86822)

Lymph Nodes and Lymphatic Channels

Incision

38300   Drainage of lymph node abscess or lymphadenitis; simple

38305   extensive

38308   Lymphangiotomy or other operations on lymphatic channels

38380   Suture and/or ligation of thoracic duct; cervical approach

38381   thoracic approach

38382   abdominal approach

Surgery: Cardiovascular System

Excision

(For injection for sentinel node identification, use 38792)

38500   Biopsy or excision of lymph node(s); open, superficial

(Do not report 38500 with 38700-38780)

38505   by needle, superficial (eg, cervical, inguinal, axillary)

(If imaging guidance is performed, see 76942, 77012, 77021)

(For fine needle aspiration, use 10021 or 10022)

(For evaluation of fine needle aspirate, see 88172, 88173)

38510   open, deep cervical node(s)

38520   open, deep cervical node(s) with excision scalene fat pad

38525   open, deep axillary node(s)

38530   open, internal mammary node(s)

(Do not report 38530 with 38720-38746)

(For percutaneous needle biopsy, retroperitoneal lymph node or mass, use 49180. For fine needle aspiration, use 10022)

38542   Dissection, deep jugular node(s)

(For radical cervical neck dissection, use 38720)

38550   Excision of cystic hygroma, axillary or cervical; without deep neurovascular dissection

38555   with deep neurovascular dissection

Limited Lymphadenectomy for Staging

38562   Limited lymphadenectomy for staging (separate procedure); pelvic and para-aortic

(When combined with prostatectomy, use 55812 or 55842)

(When combined with insertion of radioactive substance into prostate, use 55862)

38564   retroperitoneal (aortic and/or splenic)

Laparoscopy

Surgical laparoscopy always includes diagnostic laparoscopy. To report a diagnostic laparoscopy (peritoneoscopy) (separate procedure), use 49320.

38570   Laparoscopy, surgical; with retroperitoneal lymph node sampling (biopsy), single or multiple

38571   with bilateral total pelvic lymphadenectomy

38572   with bilateral total pelvic lymphadenectomy and peri-aortic lymph node sampling (biopsy), single or multiple

(For drainage of lymphocele to peritoneal cavity, use 49323)

38589   Unlisted laparoscopy procedure, lymphatic system

Radical Lymphadenectomy (Radical Resection of Lymph Nodes)

(For limited pelvic and retroperitoneal lymphadenectomies, see 38562, 38564)

38700   Suprahyoid lymphadenectomy

(For bilateral procedure, report 38700 with modifier 50)

38720   Cervical lymphadenectomy (complete)

(For bilateral procedure, report 38720 with modifier 50)

38724   Cervical lymphadenectomy (modified radical neck dissection)

38740   Axillary lymphadenectomy; superficial

38745   complete

+ 38746   Thoracic lymphadenectomy, regional, including mediastinal and peritracheal nodes (List separately in addition to code for primary procedure)

+ 38747   Abdominal lymphadenectomy, regional, including celiac, gastric, portal, peripancreatic, with or without para-aortic and vena caval nodes (List separately in addition to code for primary procedure)

38760   Inguinofemoral lymphadenectomy, superficial, including Cloquets node (separate procedure)

(For bilateral procedure, report 38760 with modifier 50)

38765   Inguinofemoral lymphadenectomy, superficial, in continuity with pelvic lymphadenectomy, including external iliac, hypogastric, and obturator nodes (separate procedure)

(For bilateral procedure, report 38765 with modifier 50)

38770   Pelvic lymphadenectomy, including external iliac, hypogastric, and obturator nodes (separate procedure)

(For bilateral procedure, report 38770 with modifier 50)

38780   Retroperitoneal transabdominal lymphadenectomy, extensive, including pelvic, aortic, and renal nodes (separate procedure)

(For excision and repair of lymphedematous skin and subcutaneous tissue, see 15004-15005, 15570-15650)

Introduction

38790   Injection procedure; lymphangiography

(For bilateral procedure, report 38790 with modifier 50)

(For radiological supervision and interpretation, see 75801-75807)

38792   for identification of sentinel node

(For excision of sentinel node, see 38500-38542)

(For nuclear medicine lymphatics and lymph gland imaging, use 78195)

38794   Cannulation, thoracic duct

Other Procedures

38999   Unlisted procedure, hemic or lymphatic system

Mediastinum and Diaphragm

Mediastinum

Incision

39000   Mediastinotomy with exploration, drainage, removal of foreign body, or biopsy; cervical approach

39010   transthoracic approach, including either transthoracic or median sternotomy

Excision

39200   Excision of mediastinal cyst

39220   Excision of mediastinal tumor

(For substernal thyroidectomy, use 60270)

(For thymectomy, use 60520)

Endoscopy

39400   Mediastinoscopy, with or without biopsy

Other Procedures

39499   Unlisted procedure, mediastinum

Diaphragm

Repair

(For transabdominal repair of diaphragmatic [esophageal hiatal] hernia, see 43324, 43325)

39501   Repair, laceration of diaphragm, any approach

39502   Repair, paraesophageal hiatus hernia, transabdominal, with or without fundoplasty, vagotomy, and/or pyloroplasty, except neonatal

▶(For laparoscopic paraesophageal hernia repair, see 43281, 43282)◀

39503   Repair, neonatal diaphragmatic hernia, with or without chest tube insertion and with or without creation of ventral hernia

(Do not report modifier 63 in conjunction with 39503)

39520   Repair, diaphragmatic hernia (esophageal hiatal); transthoracic

▶(For laparoscopic paraesophageal hernia repair, see 43281, 43282)◀

39530   combined, thoracoabdominal

39531   combined, thoracoabdominal, with dilation of stricture (with or without gastroplasty)

39540   Repair, diaphragmatic hernia (other than neonatal), traumatic; acute

39541   chronic

39545   Imbrication of diaphragm for eventration, transthoracic or transabdominal, paralytic or nonparalytic

39560   Resection, diaphragm; with simple repair (eg, primary suture)

39561   with complex repair (eg, prosthetic material, local muscle flap)

Other Procedures

39599   Unlisted procedure, diaphragm

Surgery: Cardiovascular System

Notes

⊙=Moderate sedation   ✚=Add-on code   ✗=FDA approval pending   #=Resequenced code

Digestive System

Lips

(For procedures on skin of lips, see 10040 et seq)

Excision

40490   Biopsy of lip

40500   Vermilionectomy (lip shave), with mucosal advancement

40510   Excision of lip; transverse wedge excision with primary closure

40520   V-excision with primary direct linear closure

(For excision of mucous lesions, see 40810-40816)

40525   full thickness, reconstruction with local flap (eg, Estlander or fan)

40527   full thickness, reconstruction with cross lip flap (Abbe-Estlander)

40530   Resection of lip, more than one-fourth, without reconstruction

(For reconstruction, see 13131 et seq)

Repair (Cheiloplasty)

40650   Repair lip, full thickness; vermilion only

40652   up to half vertical height

40654   over one-half vertical height, or complex

40700   Plastic repair of cleft lip/nasal deformity; primary, partial or complete, unilateral

40701   primary bilateral, 1-stage procedure

40702   primary bilateral, 1 of 2 stages

40720   secondary, by recreation of defect and reclosure

(For bilateral procedure, report 40720 with modifier 50)

(To report rhinoplasty only for nasal deformity secondary to congenital cleft lip, see 30460, 30462)

(For repair of cleft lip, with cross lip pedicle flap (Abbe-Estlander type), use 40527)

40761   with cross lip pedicle flap (Abbe-Estlander type), including sectioning and inserting of pedicle

(For repair cleft palate, see 42200 et seq)

(For other reconstructive procedures, see 14060, 14061, 15120-15261, 15574, 15576, 15630)

Other Procedures

40799   Unlisted procedure, lips

Vestibule of Mouth

The vestibule is the part of the oral cavity outside the dentoalveolar structures; it includes the mucosal and submucosal tissue of lips and cheeks.

Incision

40800   Drainage of abscess, cyst, hematoma, vestibule of mouth; simple

40801   complicated

40804   Removal of embedded foreign body, vestibule of mouth; simple

40805   complicated

40806   Incision of labial frenum (frenotomy)

Excision, Destruction

40808   Biopsy, vestibule of mouth

40810   Excision of lesion of mucosa and submucosa, vestibule of mouth; without repair

40812   with simple repair

40814   with complex repair

40816   complex, with excision of underlying muscle

40818   Excision of mucosa of vestibule of mouth as donor graft

40819   Excision of frenum, labial or buccal (frenumectomy, frenulectomy, frenectomy)

40820   Destruction of lesion or scar of vestibule of mouth by physical methods (eg, laser, thermal, cryo, chemical)

Repair

40830   Closure of laceration, vestibule of mouth; 2.5 cm or less

40831   over 2.5 cm or complex

40840   Vestibuloplasty; anterior

40842   posterior, unilateral

40843   posterior, bilateral

40844   entire arch

40845   complex (including ridge extension, muscle repositioning)

(For skin grafts, see 15002 et seq)

Other Procedures

40899   Unlisted procedure, vestibule of mouth

Surgery: Digestive System

Tongue and Floor of Mouth

Incision

41000 Intraoral incision and drainage of abscess, cyst, or hematoma of tongue or floor of mouth; lingual

41005   sublingual, superficial

41006   sublingual, deep, supramylohyoid

41007   submental space

41008   submandibular space

41009   masticator space

41010 Incision of lingual frenum (frenotomy)

41015 Extraoral incision and drainage of abscess, cyst, or hematoma of floor of mouth; sublingual

41016   submental

41017   submandibular

41018   masticator space

(For frenoplasty, use 41520)

41019 Placement of needles, catheters, or other device(s) into the head and/or neck region (percutaneous, transoral, or transnasal) for subsequent interstitial radioelement application

(For imaging guidance, see 76942, 77002, 77012, 77021)

(For stereotactic insertion of intracranial brachytherapy radiation sources, use 61770)

(For interstitial radioelement application, see 77776-77787)

Excision

41100 Biopsy of tongue; anterior two-thirds

41105   posterior one-third

41108 Biopsy of floor of mouth

41110 Excision of lesion of tongue without closure

41112 Excision of lesion of tongue with closure; anterior two-thirds

41113   posterior one-third

41114   with local tongue flap

(List 41114 in addition to code 41112 or 41113)

41115 Excision of lingual frenum (frenectomy)

41116 Excision, lesion of floor of mouth

41120 Glossectomy; less than one-half tongue

41130   hemiglossectomy

41135   partial, with unilateral radical neck dissection

41140   complete or total, with or without tracheostomy, without radical neck dissection

41145   complete or total, with or without tracheostomy, with unilateral radical neck dissection

41150 composite procedure with resection floor of mouth and mandibular resection, without radical neck dissection

41153 composite procedure with resection floor of mouth, with suprahyoid neck dissection

41155 composite procedure with resection floor of mouth, mandibular resection, and radical neck dissection (Commando type)

Repair

41250 Repair of laceration 2.5 cm or less; floor of mouth and/or anterior two-thirds of tongue

41251   posterior one-third of tongue

41252 Repair of laceration of tongue, floor of mouth, over 2.6 cm or complex

Other Procedures

41500 Fixation of tongue, mechanical, other than suture (eg, K-wire)

41510 Suture of tongue to lip for micrognathia (Douglas type procedure)

41512 Tongue base suspension, permanent suture technique

(For fixation of tongue, mechanical, other than suture, use 41500)

(For suture of tongue to lip for micrognathia, use 41510)

41520 Frenoplasty (surgical revision of frenum, eg, with Z-plasty)

(For frenotomy, see 40806, 41010)

41530 Submucosal ablation of the tongue base, radiofrequency, 1 or more sites, per session

41599 Unlisted procedure, tongue, floor of mouth

Dentoalveolar Structures

Incision

41800 Drainage of abscess, cyst, hematoma from dentoalveolar structures

41805 Removal of embedded foreign body from dentoalveolar structures; soft tissues

41806   bone

Excision, Destruction

41820 Gingivectomy, excision gingiva, each quadrant

41821 Operculectomy, excision pericoronal tissues

41822 Excision of fibrous tuberosities, dentoalveolar structures

---

41823   Excision of osseous tuberosities, dentoalveolar structures

41825   Excision of lesion or tumor (except listed above), dentoalveolar structures; without repair

41826   with simple repair

41827   with complex repair

      (For nonexcisional destruction, use 41850)

41828   Excision of hyperplastic alveolar mucosa, each quadrant (specify)

41830   Alveolectomy, including curettage of osteitis or sequestrectomy

41850   Destruction of lesion (except excision), dentoalveolar structures

Other Procedures

41870   Periodontal mucosal grafting

41872   Gingivoplasty, each quadrant (specify)

41874   Alveoloplasty, each quadrant (specify)

      (For closure of lacerations, see 40830, 40831)

      (For segmental osteotomy, use 21206)

      (For reduction of fractures, see 21421-21490)

41899   Unlisted procedure, dentoalveolar structures

Palate and Uvula

Incision

42000   Drainage of abscess of palate, uvula

Excision, Destruction

42100   Biopsy of palate, uvula

42104   Excision, lesion of palate, uvula; without closure

42106   with simple primary closure

42107   with local flap closure

      ▶(For skin graft, see 14040-14302)◀

      (For mucosal graft, use 40818)

42120   Resection of palate or extensive resection of lesion

      ▶(For reconstruction of palate with extraoral tissue, see 14040-14302, 15050, 15120, 15240, 15576)◀

42140   Uvulectomy, excision of uvula

42145   Palatopharyngoplasty (eg, uvulopalatopharyngoplasty, uvulopharyngoplasty)

      (For removal of exostosis of the bony palate, see 21031, 21032)

42160   Destruction of lesion, palate or uvula (thermal, cryo or chemical)

Repair

42180   Repair, laceration of palate; up to 2 cm

42182   over 2 cm or complex

42200   Palatoplasty for cleft palate, soft and/or hard palate only

42205   Palatoplasty for cleft palate, with closure of alveolar ridge; soft tissue only

42210   with bone graft to alveolar ridge (includes obtaining graft)

42215   Palatoplasty for cleft palate; major revision

42220   secondary lengthening procedure

42225   attachment pharyngeal flap

42226   Lengthening of palate, and pharyngeal flap

42227   Lengthening of palate, with island flap

42235   Repair of anterior palate, including vomer flap

      (For repair of oronasal fistula, use 30600)

42260   Repair of nasolabial fistula

      (For repair of cleft lip, see 40700 et seq)

42280   Maxillary impression for palatal prosthesis

42281   Insertion of pin-retained palatal prosthesis

Other Procedures

42299   Unlisted procedure, palate, uvula

Salivary Gland and Ducts

Incision

42300   Drainage of abscess; parotid, simple

42305   parotid, complicated

42310   Drainage of abscess; submaxillary or sublingual, intraoral

42320   submaxillary, external

42330   Sialolithotomy; submandibular (submaxillary), sublingual or parotid, uncomplicated, intraoral

42335   submandibular (submaxillary), complicated, intraoral

42340   parotid, extraoral or complicated intraoral

Excision

42400   Biopsy of salivary gland; needle

      (For fine needle aspiration, see 10021, 10022)

      (For evaluation of fine needle aspirate, see 88172, 88173)

      (If imaging guidance is performed, see 76942, 77002, 77012, 77021)

Surgery: Digestive System

42405   incisional

(If imaging guidance is performed, see 76942, 77002, 77012, 77021)

42408   Excision of sublingual salivary cyst (ranula)

42409   Marsupialization of sublingual salivary cyst (ranula)

42410   Excision of parotid tumor or parotid gland; lateral lobe, without nerve dissection

42415   lateral lobe, with dissection and preservation of facial nerve

42420   total, with dissection and preservation of facial nerve

42425   total, en bloc removal with sacrifice of facial nerve

42426   total, with unilateral radical neck dissection

(For suture or grafting of facial nerve, see 64864, 64865, 69740, 69745)

42440   Excision of submandibular (submaxillary) gland

42450   Excision of sublingual gland

Repair

42500   Plastic repair of salivary duct, sialodochoplasty; primary or simple

42505   secondary or complicated

42507   Parotid duct diversion, bilateral (Wilke type procedure);

42508   with excision of 1 submandibular gland

42509   with excision of both submandibular glands

42510   with ligation of both submandibular (Wharton's) ducts

Other Procedures

42550   Injection procedure for sialography

(For radiological supervision and interpretation, use 70390)

42600   Closure salivary fistula

42650   Dilation salivary duct

42660   Dilation and catheterization of salivary duct, with or without injection

42665   Ligation salivary duct, intraoral

42699   Unlisted procedure, salivary glands or ducts

Pharynx, Adenoids, and Tonsils

Incision

42700   Incision and drainage abscess; peritonsillar

42720   retropharyngeal or parapharyngeal, intraoral approach

42725   retropharyngeal or parapharyngeal, external approach

Excision, Destruction

42800   Biopsy; oropharynx

42802   hypopharynx

42804   nasopharynx, visible lesion, simple

42806   nasopharynx, survey for unknown primary lesion

(For laryngoscopic biopsy, see 31510, 31535, 31536)

42808   Excision or destruction of lesion of pharynx, any method

42809   Removal of foreign body from pharynx

42810   Excision branchial cleft cyst or vestige, confined to skin and subcutaneous tissues

42815   Excision branchial cleft cyst, vestige, or fistula, extending beneath subcutaneous tissues and/or into pharynx

42820   Tonsillectomy and adenoidectomy; younger than age 12

42821   age 12 or over

42825   Tonsillectomy, primary or secondary; younger than age 12

42826   age 12 or over

42830   Adenoidectomy, primary; younger than age 12

42831   age 12 or over

42835   Adenoidectomy, secondary; younger than age 12

42836   age 12 or over

42842   Radical resection of tonsil, tonsillar pillars, and/or retromolar trigone; without closure

42844   closure with local flap (eg, tongue, buccal)

42845   closure with other flap

(For closure with other flap(s), use appropriate number for flap(s))

(When combined with radical neck dissection, use also 38720)

42860   Excision of tonsil tags

42870   Excision or destruction lingual tonsil, any method (separate procedure)

(For resection of the nasopharynx [eg, juvenile angiofibroma] by bicoronal and/or transzygomatic approach, see 61586 and 61600)

42890   Limited pharyngectomy

42892   Resection of lateral pharyngeal wall or pyriform sinus, direct closure by advancement of lateral and posterior pharyngeal walls

(When combined with radical neck dissection, use also 38720)

Surgery: Digestive System

▲ **42894**   Resection of pharyngeal wall requiring closure with myocutaneous or fasciocutaneous flap or free muscle, skin, or fascial flap with microvascular anastamosis

(When combined with radical neck dissection, use also 38720)

(For limited pharyngectomy with radical neck dissection, use 38720 with 42890)

▶(For flap used for reconstruction, see 15732, 15734, 15756, 15757, 15758)◀

Repair

42900   Suture pharynx for wound or injury

42950   Pharyngoplasty (plastic or reconstructive operation on pharynx)

(For pharyngeal flap, use 42225)

42953   Pharyngoesophageal repair

(For closure with myocutaneous or other flap, use appropriate number in addition)

Other Procedures

42955   Pharyngostomy (fistulization of pharynx, external for feeding)

42960   Control oropharyngeal hemorrhage, primary or secondary (eg, post-tonsillectomy); simple

42961   complicated, requiring hospitalization

42962   with secondary surgical intervention

42970   Control of nasopharyngeal hemorrhage, primary or secondary (eg, postadenoidectomy); simple, with posterior nasal packs, with or without anterior packs and/or cautery

42971   complicated, requiring hospitalization

42972   with secondary surgical intervention

42999   Unlisted procedure, pharynx, adenoids, or tonsils

Esophagus

Incision

(For esophageal intubation with laparotomy, use 43510)

43020   Esophagotomy, cervical approach, with removal of foreign body

43030   Cricopharyngeal myotomy

43045   Esophagotomy, thoracic approach, with removal of foreign body

Excision

(For gastrointestinal reconstruction for previous esophagectomy, see 43360, 43361)

43100   Excision of lesion, esophagus, with primary repair; cervical approach

43101   thoracic or abdominal approach

(For wide excision of malignant lesion of cervical esophagus, with total laryngectomy without radical neck dissection, see 43107, 43116, 43124, and 31360)

(For wide excision of malignant lesion of cervical esophagus, with total laryngectomy with radical neck dissection, see 43107, 43116, 43124, and 31365)

43107   Total or near total esophagectomy, without thoracotomy; with pharyngogastrostomy or cervical esophagogastrostomy, with or without pyloroplasty (transhiatal)

43108   with colon interposition or small intestine reconstruction, including intestine mobilization, preparation and anastomosis(es)

43112   Total or near total esophagectomy, with thoracotomy; with pharyngogastrostomy or cervical esophagogastrostomy, with or without pyloroplasty

43113   with colon interposition or small intestine reconstruction, including intestine mobilization, preparation, and anastomosis(es)

43116   Partial esophagectomy, cervical, with free intestinal graft, including microvascular anastomosis, obtaining the graft and intestinal reconstruction

(Do not report 43116 in conjunction with 69990)

(Report 43116 with the modifier 52 appended if intestinal or free jejunal graft with microvascular anastomosis is performed by another physician)

(For free jejunal graft with microvascular anastomosis performed by another physician, use 43496)

43117   Partial esophagectomy, distal two-thirds, with thoracotomy and separate abdominal incision, with or without proximal gastrectomy; with thoracic esophagogastrostomy, with or without pyloroplasty (Ivor Lewis)

43118   with colon interposition or small intestine reconstruction, including intestine mobilization, preparation, and anastomosis(es)

(For total esophagectomy with gastropharyngostomy, see 43107, 43124)

(For esophagogastrectomy (lower third) and vagotomy, use 43122)

43121   Partial esophagectomy, distal two-thirds, with thoracotomy only, with or without proximal gastrectomy, with thoracic esophagogastrostomy, with or without pyloroplasty

43122   Partial esophagectomy, thoracoabdominal or abdominal approach, with or without proximal gastrectomy; with esophagogastrostomy, with or without pyloroplasty

43123   with colon interposition or small intestine reconstruction, including intestine mobilization, preparation, and anastomosis(es)

43124   Total or partial esophagectomy, without reconstruction (any approach), with cervical esophagostomy

43130   Diverticulectomy of hypopharynx or esophagus, with or without myotomy; cervical approach

43135   thoracic approach

Endoscopy

For endoscopic procedures, code appropriate endoscopy of each anatomic site examined.

Surgical endoscopy always includes diagnostic endoscopy.

⊙ 43200   Esophagoscopy, rigid or flexible; diagnostic, with or without collection of specimen(s) by brushing or washing (separate procedure)

⊙ 43201   with directed submucosal injection(s), any substance

(For injection sclerosis of esophageal varices, use 43204)

⊙ 43202   with biopsy, single or multiple

⊙ 43204   with injection sclerosis of esophageal varices

⊙ 43205   with band ligation of esophageal varices

⊙ 43215   with removal of foreign body

(For radiological supervision and interpretation, use 74235)

⊙ 43216   with removal of tumor(s), polyp(s), or other lesion(s) by hot biopsy forceps or bipolar cautery

⊙ 43217   with removal of tumor(s), polyp(s), or other lesion(s) by snare technique

⊙ 43219   with insertion of plastic tube or stent

⊙ 43220   with balloon dilation (less than 30 mm diameter)

(If imaging guidance is performed, use 74360)

(For endoscopic dilation with balloon 30 mm diameter or larger, use 43458)

(For dilation without visualization, use 43450-43453)

(For diagnostic fiberoptic esophagogastroscopy, use 43200, 43235)

(For fiberoptic esophagogastroscopy with biopsy or collection of specimen, use 43200, 43202, 43235, 43239)

(For fiberoptic esophagogastroscopy with removal of foreign body, use 43215, 43247)

(For fiberoptic esophagogastroscopy with removal of polyp(s), use 43217, 43251)

⊙ 43226   with insertion of guide wire followed by dilation over guide wire

(For radiological supervision and interpretation, use 74360)

⊙ 43227   with control of bleeding (eg, injection, bipolar cautery, unipolar cautery, laser, heater probe, stapler, plasma coagulator)

⊙ 43228   with ablation of tumor(s), polyp(s), or other lesion(s), not amenable to removal by hot biopsy forceps, bipolar cautery or snare technique

(For esophagoscopic photodynamic therapy, report 43228 in addition to 96570, 96571 as appropriate)

⊙ 43231   with endoscopic ultrasound examination

(Do not report 43231 in conjunction with 76975)

⊙ 43232   with transendoscopic ultrasound-guided intramural or transmural fine needle aspiration/biopsy(s)

(Do not report 43232 in conjunction with 76942, 76975)

(For interpretation of specimen, see 88172-88173)

⊙ 43234   Upper gastrointestinal endoscopy, simple primary examination (eg, with small diameter flexible endoscope) (separate procedure)

⊙ 43235   Upper gastrointestinal endoscopy including esophagus, stomach, and either the duodenum and/or jejunum as appropriate; diagnostic, with or without collection of specimen(s) by brushing or washing (separate procedure)

⊙ 43236   with directed submucosal injection(s), any substance

(For injection sclerosis of esophageal and/or gastric varices, use 43243)

⊙ 43237   with endoscopic ultrasound examination limited to the esophagus

(Do not report 43237 in conjunction with 76942, 76975)

⊙ 43238   with transendoscopic ultrasound-guided intramural or transmural fine needle aspiration/biopsy(s), esophagus (includes endoscopic ultrasound examination limited to the esophagus)

(Do not report 43238 in conjunction with 76942 or 76975)

⊙ 43239   with biopsy, single or multiple

⊙ 43240   with transmural drainage of pseudocyst

⊙ 43241   with transendoscopic intraluminal tube or catheter placement

⊙ 43242   with transendoscopic ultrasound-guided intramural or transmural fine needle aspiration/biopsy(s) (includes endoscopic ultrasound examination of the esophagus, stomach, and either the duodenum and/or jejunum as appropriate)

(Do not report 43242 in conjunction with 76942, 76975)

(For transendoscopic fine needle aspiration/biopsy limited to esophagus, use 43238)

(For interpretation of specimen, see 88172-88173)

⊙ **43243**   with injection sclerosis of esophageal and/or gastric varices

⊙ **43244**   with band ligation of esophageal and/or gastric varices

⊙ **43245**   with dilation of gastric outlet for obstruction (eg, balloon, guide wire, bougie)

(Do not report 43245 in conjunction with 43256)

⊙ **43246**   with directed placement of percutaneous gastrostomy tube

(For nonendoscopic percutaneous placement of gastrostomy tube, see 49440)

⊙ **43247**   with removal of foreign body

(For radiological supervision and interpretation, use 74235)

⊙ **43248**   with insertion of guide wire followed by dilation of esophagus over guide wire

⊙ **43249**   with balloon dilation of esophagus (less than 30 mm diameter)

⊙ **43250**   with removal of tumor(s), polyp(s), or other lesion(s) by hot biopsy forceps or bipolar cautery

⊙ **43251**   with removal of tumor(s), polyp(s), or other lesion(s) by snare technique

● **43255**   with control of bleeding, any method

⊙ **43256**   with transendoscopic stent placement (includes predilation)

⊙ **43257**   with delivery of thermal energy to the muscle of lower esophageal sphincter and/or gastric cardia, for treatment of gastroesophageal reflux disease

⊙ **43258**   with ablation of tumor(s), polyp(s), or other lesion(s) not amenable to removal by hot biopsy forceps, bipolar cautery or snare technique

(For injection sclerosis of esophageal varices, use 43204, 43243)

⊙ **43259**   with endoscopic ultrasound examination, including the esophagus, stomach, and either the duodenum and/or jejunum as appropriate

(Do not report 43259 in conjunction with 76975)

⊙ **43260**   Endoscopic retrograde cholangiopancreatography (ERCP); diagnostic, with or without collection of specimen(s) by brushing or washing (separate procedure)

(For radiological supervision and interpretation, see 74328, 74329, 74330)

⊙ **43261**   with biopsy, single or multiple

(For radiological supervision and interpretation, see 74328, 74329, 74330)

⊙ **43262**   with sphincterotomy/papillotomy

(For radiological supervision and interpretation, see 74328, 74329, 74330)

⊙ **43263**   with pressure measurement of sphincter of Oddi (pancreatic duct or common bile duct)

(For radiological supervision and interpretation, see 74328, 74329, 74330)

⊙ **43264**   with endoscopic retrograde removal of calculus/calculi from biliary and/or pancreatic ducts

(When done with sphincterotomy, also use 43262)

(For radiological supervision and interpretation, see 74328, 74329, 74330)

⊙ **43265**   with endoscopic retrograde destruction, lithotripsy of calculus/calculi, any method

(When done with sphincterotomy, also use 43262)

(For radiological supervision and interpretation, see 74328, 74329, 74330)

⊙ **43267**   with endoscopic retrograde insertion of nasobiliary or nasopancreatic drainage tube

(When done with sphincterotomy, also use 43262)

(For radiological supervision and interpretation, see 74328, 74329, 74330)

⊙ **43268**   with endoscopic retrograde insertion of tube or stent into bile or pancreatic duct

(When done with sphincterotomy, also use 43262)

(For radiological supervision and interpretation, see 74328, 74329, 74330)

⊙ **43269**   with endoscopic retrograde removal of foreign body and/or change of tube or stent

(When done with sphincterotomy, also use 43262)

(For radiological supervision and interpretation, see 74328, 74329, 74330)

⊙ **43271**   with endoscopic retrograde balloon dilation of ampulla, biliary and/or pancreatic duct(s)

(When done with sphincterotomy, also use 43262)

(For radiological supervision and interpretation, see 74328, 74329, 74330)

⊙ **43272**   with ablation of tumor(s), polyp(s), or other lesion(s) not amenable to removal by hot biopsy forceps, bipolar cautery or snare technique

(For radiological supervision and interpretation, see 74328, 74329, 74330)

⊙+ **43273**   Endoscopic cannulation of papilla with direct visualization of common bile duct(s) and/or pancreatic duct(s) (List separately in addition to code(s) for primary procedure)

▶(Use 43273 in conjunction with 43260-43265, 43267-43272)◀

Laparoscopy

Surgical laparoscopy always includes diagnostic laparoscopy. To report a diagnostic laparoscopy (peritoneoscopy) (separate procedure), use 49320.

43279   Laparoscopy, surgical, esophagomyotomy (Heller type), with fundoplasty, when performed

(For open approach, see 43330, 43331)

(Do not report 43279 in conjunction with 43280)

43280   Laparoscopy, surgical, esophagogastric fundoplasty (eg, Nissen, Toupet procedures)

(Do not report 43280 in conjunction with 43279)

(For open approach, use 43324)

● **43281**   Laparoscopy, surgical, repair of paraesophageal hernia, includes fundoplasty, when performed; without implantation of mesh

● **43282**   with implantation of mesh

▶(For transthoracic paraesophageal hernia repair, use 39520. For transabdominal paraesophageal hernia repair, use 39502)◀

▶(Do not report 43281, 43282 in conjunction with 43280, 43450, 43453, 43456, 43458, 49568)◀

43289   Unlisted laparoscopy procedure, esophagus

Repair

43300   Esophagoplasty (plastic repair or reconstruction), cervical approach; without repair of tracheoesophageal fistula

43305   with repair of tracheoesophageal fistula

43310   Esophagoplasty (plastic repair or reconstruction), thoracic approach; without repair of tracheoesophageal fistula

43312   with repair of tracheoesophageal fistula

43313   Esophagoplasty for congenital defect (plastic repair or reconstruction), thoracic approach; without repair of congenital tracheoesophageal fistula

43314   with repair of congenital tracheoesophageal fistula

(Do not report modifier 63 in conjunction with 43313, 43314)

43320   Esophagogastrostomy (cardioplasty), with or without vagotomy and pyloroplasty, transabdominal or transthoracic approach

43324   Esophagogastric fundoplasty (eg, Nissen, Belsey IV, Hill procedures)

(For laparoscopic procedure, use 43280)

43325   Esophagogastric fundoplasty; with fundic patch (Thal-Nissen procedure)

(For cricopharyngeal myotomy, use 43030)

43326   with gastroplasty (eg, Collis)

43330   Esophagomyotomy (Heller type); abdominal approach

(For laparoscopic esophagomyotomy procedure, use 43279)

43331   thoracic approach

(For thoracoscopic esophagomyotomy, use 32665)

43340   Esophagojejunostomy (without total gastrectomy); abdominal approach

43341   thoracic approach

43350   Esophagostomy, fistulization of esophagus, external; abdominal approach

43351   thoracic approach

43352   cervical approach

43360   Gastrointestinal reconstruction for previous esophagectomy, for obstructing esophageal lesion or fistula, or for previous esophageal exclusion; with stomach, with or without pyloroplasty

43361   with colon interposition or small intestine reconstruction, including intestine mobilization, preparation, and anastomosis(es)

43400   Ligation, direct, esophageal varices

43401   Transection of esophagus with repair, for esophageal varices

43405   Ligation or stapling at gastroesophageal junction for pre-existing esophageal perforation

43410   Suture of esophageal wound or injury; cervical approach

43415   transthoracic or transabdominal approach

43420   Closure of esophagostomy or fistula; cervical approach

43425   transthoracic or transabdominal approach

(For repair of esophageal hiatal hernia, see 39520 et seq)

Manipulation

(For associated esophagogram, use 74220)

43450   Dilation of esophagus, by unguided sound or bougie, single or multiple passes

(For radiological supervision and interpretation, use 74360)

⊙ **43453**   Dilation of esophagus, over guide wire

(For dilation with direct visualization, use 43220)

(For dilation of esophagus, by balloon or dilator, see 43220, 43458, and 74360)

(For radiological supervision and interpretation, use 74360)

⊙ **43456**   Dilation of esophagus, by balloon or dilator, retrograde

(For radiological supervision and interpretation, use 74360)

Surgery: Digestive System

⊙ **43458**   Dilation of esophagus with balloon (30 mm diameter or larger) for achalasia

(For dilation with balloon less than 30 mm diameter, use 43220)

(For radiological supervision and interpretation, use 74360)

43460   Esophagogastric tamponade, with balloon (Sengstaken type)

(For removal of esophageal foreign body by balloon catheter, see 43215, 43247, 74235)

Other Procedures

43496   Free jejunum transfer with microvascular anastomosis

(Do not report code 69990 in addition to code 43496)

43499   Unlisted procedure, esophagus

Stomach

Incision

43500   Gastrotomy; with exploration or foreign body removal

43501   with suture repair of bleeding ulcer

43502   with suture repair of pre-existing esophagogastric laceration (eg, Mallory-Weiss)

43510   with esophageal dilation and insertion of permanent intraluminal tube (eg, Celestin or Mousseaux-Barbin)

43520   Pyloromyotomy, cutting of pyloric muscle (Fredet-Ramstedt type operation)

(Do not report modifier 63 in conjunction with 43520)

Excision

43600   Biopsy of stomach; by capsule, tube, peroral (1 or more specimens)

43605   by laparotomy

43610   Excision, local; ulcer or benign tumor of stomach

43611   malignant tumor of stomach

43620   Gastrectomy, total; with esophagoenterostomy

43621   with Roux-en-Y reconstruction

43622   with formation of intestinal pouch, any type

43631   Gastrectomy, partial, distal; with gastroduodenostomy

43632   with gastrojejunostomy

43633   with Roux-en-Y reconstruction

43634   with formation of intestinal pouch

+ **43635**   Vagotomy when performed with partial distal gastrectomy (List separately in addition to code[s] for primary procedure)

(Use 43635 in conjunction with 43631, 43632, 43633, 43634)

43640   Vagotomy including pyloroplasty, with or without gastrostomy; truncal or selective

(For pyloroplasty, use 43800)

(For vagotomy, see 64752-64760)

43641   parietal cell (highly selective)

(For upper gastrointestinal endoscopy, see 43234-43259)

Laparoscopy

Surgical laparoscopy always includes diagnostic laparoscopy. To report a diagnostic laparoscopy (peritoneoscopy) (separate procedure), use 49320.

(For upper gastrointestinal endoscopy including esophagus, stomach, and either the duodenum and/or jejunum, see 43235-43259)

43644   Laparoscopy, surgical, gastric restrictive procedure; with gastric bypass and Roux-en-Y gastroenterostomy (roux limb 150 cm or less)

(Do not report 43644 in conjunction with 43846, 49320)

(Esophagogastroduodenoscopy [EGD] performed for a separate condition should be reported with modifier 59)

(For greater than 150 cm, use 43645)

(For open procedure, use 43846)

43645   with gastric bypass and small intestine reconstruction to limit absorption

(Do not report 43645 in conjunction with 49320, 43847)

43647   Laparoscopy, surgical; implantation or replacement of gastric neurostimulator electrodes, antrum

43648   revision or removal of gastric neurostimulator electrodes, antrum

(For open approach, see 43881, 43882)

(For insertion of gastric neurostimulator pulse generator, use 64590)

(For revision or removal of gastric neurostimulator pulse generator, use 64595)

(For electronic analysis and programming of gastric neurostimulator pulse generator, see 95980-95982)

(For laparoscopic implantation, revision, or removal of gastric neurostimulator electrodes, lesser curvature [morbid obesity], see Category III codes 0155T, 0156T)

▶(For electronic analysis and programming of gastric neurostimulator, see 95980-95982)◀

Surgery: Digestive System

Surgery: Digestive System

43651   Laparoscopy, surgical; transection of vagus nerves, truncal

43652   transection of vagus nerves, selective or highly selective

43653   gastrostomy, without construction of gastric tube (eg, Stamm procedure) (separate procedure)

43659   Unlisted laparoscopy procedure, stomach

Introduction

(43750 has been deleted. To report percutaneous gastrostomy tube insertion, use 43246)

43752   Naso- or oro-gastric tube placement, requiring physician's skill and fluoroscopic guidance (includes fluoroscopy, image documentation and report)

(For percutaneous placement of gastrostomy tube, use 49440)

(For enteric tube placement, see 44500, 74340)

(Do not report 43752 in conjunction with critical care codes 99291-99292, neonatal critical care codes 99468, 99469, pediatric critical care codes 99471, 99472 or low birth weight intensive care service codes 99478, 99479)

43760   Change of gastrostomy tube, percutaneous, without imaging or endoscopic guidance

▶(To report fluoroscopically guided replacement of gastrostomy tube, use 49450)◀

(For endoscopic placement of gastrostomy tube, use 43246)

▲ 43761   Repositioning of a naso- or oro-gastric feeding tube, through the duodenum for enteric nutrition

(If imaging guidance is performed, use 76000)

(For endoscopic conversion of a gastrostomy tube to jejunostomy tube, use 44373)

(For placement of a long gastrointestinal tube into the duodenum, use 44500)

(Do not report 43761 in conjunction with 44500, 49446)

Bariatric Surgery

Bariatric surgical procedures may involve the stomach, duodenum, jejunum, and/or the ileum.

Laparoscopy

Surgical laparoscopy always includes diagnostic laparoscopy. To report a diagnostic laparoscopy (separate procedure), use 49320.

Typical postoperative follow-up care (see Surgery Guidelines, CPT Surgical Package Definition) after gastric restriction using the adjustable gastric restrictive device includes subsequent restrictive device adjustment(s) through the postoperative period for the

typical patient. Adjustment consists of changing the gastric restrictive device component diameter by injection or aspiration of fluid through the subcutaneous port component.

43770   Laparoscopy, surgical, gastric restrictive procedure; placement of adjustable gastric restrictive device (eg, gastric band and subcutaneous port components)

(For individual component placement, report 43770 with modifier 52)

43771   revision of adjustable gastric restrictive device component only

43772   removal of adjustable gastric restrictive device component only

43773   removal and replacement of adjustable gastric restrictive device component only

(Do not report 43773 in conjunction with 43772)

43774   removal of adjustable gastric restrictive device and subcutaneous port components

(For removal and replacement of both gastric band and subcutaneous port components, use 43659)

● 43775   longitudinal gastrectomy (ie, sleeve gastrectomy)

▶(For open gastric restrictive procedure, without gastric bypass, for morbid obesity, other than vertical-banded gastroplasty, use 43843)◀

Other Procedures

43800   Pyloroplasty

(For pyloroplasty and vagotomy, use 43640)

43810   Gastroduodenostomy

43820   Gastrojejunostomy; without vagotomy

43825   with vagotomy, any type

43830   Gastrostomy, open; without construction of gastric tube (eg, Stamm procedure) (separate procedure)

43831   neonatal, for feeding

(For change of gastrostomy tube, use 43760)

(Do not report modifier 63 in conjunction with 43831)

43832   with construction of gastric tube (eg, Janeway procedure)

(For percutaneous endoscopic gastrostomy, use 43246)

43840   Gastrorrhaphy, suture of perforated duodenal or gastric ulcer, wound, or injury

43842   Gastric restrictive procedure, without gastric bypass, for morbid obesity; vertical-banded gastroplasty

43843   other than vertical-banded gastroplasty

▶(For laparoscopic longitudinal gastrectomy [ie, sleeve gastrectomy], use 43775)◀

43845   Gastric restrictive procedure with partial gastrectomy, pylorus-preserving duodenoileostomy and ileoileostomy (50 to 100 cm common channel) to limit absorption (biliopancreatic diversion with duodenal switch)

(Do not report 43845 in conjunction with 43633, 43847, 44130, 49000)

43846   Gastric restrictive procedure, with gastric bypass for morbid obesity; with short limb (150 cm or less) Roux-en-Y gastroenterostomy

(For greater than 150 cm, use 43847)

(For laparoscopic procedure, use 43644)

43847   with small intestine reconstruction to limit absorption

43848   Revision, open, of gastric restrictive procedure for morbid obesity, other than adjustable gastric restrictive device (separate procedure)

(For laparoscopic adjustable gastric restrictive procedures, see 43770-43774)

(For gastric restrictive port procedures, see 43886-43888)

43850   Revision of gastroduodenal anastomosis (gastroduodenostomy) with reconstruction; without vagotomy

43855   with vagotomy

43860   Revision of gastrojejunal anastomosis (gastrojejunostomy) with reconstruction, with or without partial gastrectomy or intestine resection; without vagotomy

43865   with vagotomy

43870   Closure of gastrostomy, surgical

43880   Closure of gastrocolic fistula

43881   Implantation or replacement of gastric neurostimulator electrodes, antrum, open

43882   Revision or removal of gastric neurostimulator electrodes, antrum, open

(For laparoscopic approach, see 43647, 43648)

(For insertion of gastric neurostimulator pulse generator, use 64590)

(For revision or removal of gastric neurostimulator pulse generator, use 64595)

(For electronic analysis and programming of gastric neurostimulator pulse generator, see 95980-95982)

(For open implantation, revision, or removal of gastric neurostimulator electrodes, lesser curvature [morbid obesity], see Category III codes 0157T, 0158T)

(For electronic analysis and programming of gastric neurostimulator, lesser curvature, use Category III code 0162T)

43886   Gastric restrictive procedure, open; revision of subcutaneous port component only

43887   removal of subcutaneous port component only

43888   removal and replacement of subcutaneous port component only

(Do not report 43888 in conjunction with 43774, 43887)

(For laparoscopic removal of both gastric restrictive device and subcutaneous port components, use 43774)

(For removal and replacement of both gastric restrictive device and subcutaneous port components, use 43659)

43999   Unlisted procedure, stomach

Intestines (Except Rectum)

Incision

44005   Enterolysis (freeing of intestinal adhesion) (separate procedure)

(Do not report 44005 in addition to 45136)

(For laparoscopic approach, use 44180)

44010   Duodenotomy, for exploration, biopsy(s), or foreign body removal

+ 44015   Tube or needle catheter jejunostomy for enteral alimentation, intraoperative, any method (List separately in addition to primary procedure)

44020   Enterotomy, small intestine, other than duodenum; for exploration, biopsy(s), or foreign body removal

44021   for decompression (eg, Baker tube)

44025   Colotomy, for exploration, biopsy(s), or foreign body removal

(For exteriorization of intestine (Mikulicz resection with crushing of spur), see 44602-44605)

44050   Reduction of volvulus, intussusception, internal hernia, by laparotomy

44055   Correction of malrotation by lysis of duodenal bands and/or reduction of midgut volvulus (eg, Ladd procedure)

(Do not report modifier 63 in conjunction with 44055)

Excision

Intestinal allotransplantation involves three distinct components of physician work:

1. ***Cadaver donor enterectomy***, which includes harvesting the intestine graft and cold preservation of the graft (perfusing with cold preservation solution and cold maintenance) (use 44132). ***Living donor enterectomy***, which includes harvesting the intestine graft, cold preservation of the graft (perfusing with cold preservation solution and cold maintenance), and care of the donor (use 44133).

2. ***Backbench work***:

Standard preparation of an intestine allograft prior to transplantation includes mobilization and fashioning of the superior mesenteric artery and vein (see 44715).

Surgery: Digestive System

Surgery: Digestive System

Additional reconstruction of an intestine allograft prior to transplantation may include venous and/or arterial anastomosis(es) (see 44720-44721).

3. ***Recipient intestinal allotransplantation with or without recipient enterectomy***, which includes transplantation of allograft and care of the recipient (see 44135, 44136).

44100   Biopsy of intestine by capsule, tube, peroral (1 or more specimens)

44110   Excision of 1 or more lesions of small or large intestine not requiring anastomosis, exteriorization, or fistulization; single enterotomy

44111   multiple enterotomies

44120   Enterectomy, resection of small intestine; single resection and anastomosis

(Do not report 44120 in addition to 45136)

+ 44121   each additional resection and anastomosis (List separately in addition to code for primary procedure)

(Use 44121 in conjunction with 44120)

44125   with enterostomy

44126   Enterectomy, resection of small intestine for congenital atresia, single resection and anastomosis of proximal segment of intestine; without tapering

44127   with tapering

+ 44128   each additional resection and anastomosis (List separately in addition to code for primary procedure)

(Use 44128 in conjunction with 44126, 44127)

(Do not report modifier 63 in conjunction with 44126, 44127, 44128)

44130   Enteroenterostomy, anastomosis of intestine, with or without cutaneous enterostomy (separate procedure)

44132   Donor enterectomy (including cold preservation), open; from cadaver donor

44133   partial, from living donor

(For backbench intestinal graft preparation or reconstruction, see 44715, 44720, 44721)

44135   Intestinal allotransplantation; from cadaver donor

44136   from living donor

44137   Removal of transplanted intestinal allograft, complete

(For partial removal of transplant allograft, see 44120, 44121, 44140)

+ 44139   Mobilization (take-down) of splenic flexure performed in conjunction with partial colectomy (List separately in addition to primary procedure)

(Use 44139 in conjunction with 44140-44147)

44140   Colectomy, partial; with anastomosis

(For laparoscopic procedure, use 44204)

44141   with skin level cecostomy or colostomy

44143   with end colostomy and closure of distal segment (Hartmann type procedure)

(For laparoscopic procedure, use 44206)

44144   with resection, with colostomy or ileostomy and creation of mucofistula

44145   with coloproctostomy (low pelvic anastomosis)

(For laparoscopic procedure, use 44207)

44146   with coloproctostomy (low pelvic anastomosis), with colostomy

(For laparoscopic procedure, use 44208)

44147   abdominal and transanal approach

44150   Colectomy, total, abdominal, without proctectomy; with ileostomy or ileoproctostomy

(For laparoscopic procedure, use 44210)

44151   with continent ileostomy

44155   Colectomy, total, abdominal, with proctectomy; with ileostomy

(For laparoscopic procedure, use 44212)

44156   with continent ileostomy

44157   with ileoanal anastomosis, includes loop ileostomy, and rectal mucosectomy, when performed

44158   with ileoanal anastomosis, creation of ileal reservoir (S or J), includes loop ileostomy, and rectal mucosectomy, when performed

(For laparoscopic procedure, use 44211)

44160   Colectomy, partial, with removal of terminal ileum with ileocolostomy

(For laparoscopic procedure, use 44205)

Laparoscopy

Surgical laparoscopy always includes diagnostic laparoscopy. To report a diagnostic laparoscopy (peritoneoscopy) (separate procedure), use 49320.

Incision

44180   Laparoscopy, surgical, enterolysis (freeing of intestinal adhesion) (separate procedure)

(For laparoscopy with salpingolysis, ovariolysis, use 58660)

Enterostomy—External Fistulization of Intestines

44186   Laparoscopy, surgical; jejunostomy (eg, for decompression or feeding)

44187   ileostomy or jejunostomy, non-tube

(For open procedure, use 44310)

44188   Laparoscopy, surgical, colostomy or skin level cecostomy

(For open procedure, use 44320)

(Do not report 44188 in conjunction with 44970)

Excision

44202   Laparoscopy, surgical; enterectomy, resection of small intestine, single resection and anastomosis

+ 44203   each additional small intestine resection and anastomosis (List separately in addition to code for primary procedure)

(Use 44203 in conjunction with 44202)

(For open procedure, see 44120, 44121)

44204   colectomy, partial, with anastomosis

(For open procedure, use 44140)

44205   colectomy, partial, with removal of terminal ileum with ileocolostomy

(For open procedure, use 44160)

44206   colectomy, partial, with end colostomy and closure of distal segment (Hartmann type procedure)

(For open procedure, use 44143)

44207   colectomy, partial, with anastomosis, with coloproctostomy (low pelvic anastomosis)

(For open procedure, use 44145)

44208   colectomy, partial, with anastomosis, with coloproctostomy (low pelvic anastomosis) with colostomy

(For open procedure, use 44146)

44210   colectomy, total, abdominal, without proctectomy, with ileostomy or ileoproctostomy

(For open procedure, use 44150)

44211   colectomy, total, abdominal, with proctectomy, with ileoanal anastomosis, creation of ileal reservoir (S or J), with loop ileostomy, includes rectal mucosectomy, when performed

(For open procedure, see 44157, 44158)

44212   colectomy, total, abdominal, with proctectomy, with ileostomy

(For open procedure, use 44155)

+ 44213   Laparoscopy, surgical, mobilization (take-down) of splenic flexure performed in conjunction with partial colectomy (List separately in addition to primary procedure)

(Use 44213 in conjunction with 44204-44208)

(For open procedure, use 44139)

Repair

44227   Laparoscopy, surgical, closure of enterostomy, large or small intestine, with resection and anastomosis

(For open procedure, see 44625, 44626)

Other Procedures

44238   Unlisted laparoscopy procedure, intestine (except rectum)

Enterostomy—External Fistulization of Intestines

44300   Placement, enterostomy or cecostomy, tube open (eg, for feeding or decompression) (separate procedure)

(For percutaneous placement of duodenostomy, jejunostomy, gastro-jejunostomy or cecostomy [or other colonic] tube including fluoroscopic imaging guidance, see 49441-49442)

44310   Ileostomy or jejunostomy, non-tube

(For laparoscopic procedure, use 44187)

(Do not report 44310 in conjunction with 44144, 44150-44151, 44155, 44156, 45113, 45119, 45136)

44312   Revision of ileostomy; simple (release of superficial scar) (separate procedure)

44314   complicated (reconstruction in-depth) (separate procedure)

44316   Continent ileostomy (Kock procedure) (separate procedure)

(For fiberoptic evaluation, use 44385)

44320   Colostomy or skin level cecostomy;

(For laparoscopic procedure, use 44188)

(Do not report 44320 in conjunction with 44141, 44144, 44146, 44605, 45110, 45119, 45126, 45563, 45805, 45825, 50810, 51597, 57307, or 58240)

44322   with multiple biopsies (eg, for congenital megacolon) (separate procedure)

44340   Revision of colostomy; simple (release of superficial scar) (separate procedure)

44345   complicated (reconstruction in-depth) (separate procedure)

44346   with repair of paracolostomy hernia (separate procedure)

▲=Revised code   ●=New code   ►◄=Contains new or revised text   ⊘=Modifier 51 exempt

Endoscopy, Small Intestine and Stomal

Surgical endoscopy always includes diagnostic endoscopy.

(For upper gastrointestinal endoscopy, see 43234-43258)

⊙ **44360** Small intestinal endoscopy, enteroscopy beyond second portion of duodenum, not including ileum; diagnostic, with or without collection of specimen(s) by brushing or washing (separate procedure)

⊙ **44361**   with biopsy, single or multiple

⊙ **44363**   with removal of foreign body

⊙ **44364**   with removal of tumor(s), polyp(s), or other lesion(s) by snare technique

⊙ **44365**   with removal of tumor(s), polyp(s), or other lesion(s) by hot biopsy forceps or bipolar cautery

⊙ **44366**   with control of bleeding (eg, injection, bipolar cautery, unipolar cautery, laser, heater probe, stapler, plasma coagulator)

⊙ **44369**   with ablation of tumor(s), polyp(s), or other lesion(s) not amenable to removal by hot biopsy forceps, bipolar cautery or snare technique

⊙ **44370**   with transendoscopic stent placement (includes predilation)

⊙ **44372**   with placement of percutaneous jejunostomy tube

⊙ **44373**   with conversion of percutaneous gastrostomy tube to percutaneous jejunostomy tube

(For fiberoptic jejunostomy through stoma, use 43235)

⊙ **44376** Small intestinal endoscopy, enteroscopy beyond second portion of duodenum, including ileum; diagnostic, with or without collection of specimen(s) by brushing or washing (separate procedure)

⊙ **44377**   with biopsy, single or multiple

⊙ **44378**   with control of bleeding (eg, injection, bipolar cautery, unipolar cautery, laser, heater probe, stapler, plasma coagulator)

⊙ **44379**   with transendoscopic stent placement (includes predilation)

⊙ **44380** Ileoscopy, through stoma; diagnostic, with or without collection of specimen(s) by brushing or washing (separate procedure)

⊙ **44382**   with biopsy, single or multiple

⊙ **44383**   with transendoscopic stent placement (includes predilation)

⊙ **44385** Endoscopic evaluation of small intestinal (abdominal or pelvic) pouch; diagnostic, with or without collection of specimen(s) by brushing or washing (separate procedure)

⊙ **44386**   with biopsy, single or multiple

⊙ **44388** Colonoscopy through stoma; diagnostic, with or without collection of specimen(s) by brushing or washing (separate procedure)

⊙ **44389**   with biopsy, single or multiple

⊙ **44390**   with removal of foreign body

⊙ **44391**   with control of bleeding (eg, injection, bipolar cautery, unipolar cautery, laser, heater probe, stapler, plasma coagulator)

⊙ **44392**   with removal of tumor(s), polyp(s), or other lesion(s) by hot biopsy forceps or bipolar cautery

⊙ **44393**   with ablation of tumor(s), polyp(s), or other lesion(s) not amenable to removal by hot biopsy forceps, bipolar cautery or snare technique

⊙ **44394**   with removal of tumor(s), polyp(s), or other lesion(s) by snare technique

(For colonoscopy per rectum, see 45330-45385)

⊙ **44397**   with transendoscopic stent placement (includes predilation)

Introduction

⊙⊘ **44500** Introduction of long gastrointestinal tube (eg, Miller-Abbott) (separate procedure)

(For radiological supervision and interpretation, use 74340)

(For naso- or oro-gastric tube placement, use 43752)

Repair

44602 Suture of small intestine (enterorrhaphy) for perforated ulcer, diverticulum, wound, injury or rupture; single perforation

44603   multiple perforations

44604 Suture of large intestine (colorrhaphy) for perforated ulcer, diverticulum, wound, injury or rupture (single or multiple perforations); without colostomy

44605   with colostomy

44615 Intestinal stricturoplasty (enterotomy and enterorrhaphy) with or without dilation, for intestinal obstruction

44620 Closure of enterostomy, large or small intestine;

44625   with resection and anastomosis other than colorectal

44626   with resection and colorectal anastomosis (eg, closure of Hartmann type procedure)

(For laparoscopic procedure, use 44227)

44640 Closure of intestinal cutaneous fistula

44650 Closure of enteroenteric or enterocolic fistula

44660 Closure of enterovesical fistula; without intestinal or bladder resection

44661   with intestine and/or bladder resection

(For closure of renocolic fistula, see 50525, 50526)

(For closure of gastrocolic fistula, use 43880)

(For closure of rectovesical fistula, see 45800, 45805)

44680 Intestinal plication (separate procedure)

Other Procedures

44700   Exclusion of small intestine from pelvis by mesh or other prosthesis, or native tissue (eg, bladder or omentum)

(For therapeutic radiation clinical treatment, see **Radiation Oncology** section)

+ 44701   Intraoperative colonic lavage (List separately in addition to code for primary procedure)

(Use 44701 in conjunction with 44140, 44145, 44150, or 44604 as appropriate)

(Do not report 44701 in conjunction with 44300, 44950-44960)

44715   Backbench standard preparation of cadaver or living donor intestine allograft prior to transplantation, including mobilization and fashioning of the superior mesenteric artery and vein

44720   Backbench reconstruction of cadaver or living donor intestine allograft prior to transplantation; venous anastomosis, each

44721   arterial anastomosis, each

44799   Unlisted procedure, intestine

(For unlisted laparoscopic procedure, intestine except rectum, use 44238)

Meckel's Diverticulum and the Mesentery

Excision

44800   Excision of Meckel's diverticulum (diverticulectomy) or omphalomesenteric duct

44820   Excision of lesion of mesentery (separate procedure)

(With intestine resection, see 44120 or 44140 et seq)

Suture

44850   Suture of mesentery (separate procedure)

(For reduction and repair of internal hernia, use 44050)

Other Procedures

44899   Unlisted procedure, Meckel's diverticulum and the mesentery

Appendix

Incision

44900   Incision and drainage of appendiceal abscess; open

⊙ **44901**   percutaneous

(For radiological supervision and interpretation, use 75989)

Excision

44950   Appendectomy;

(Incidental appendectomy during intra-abdominal surgery does not usually warrant a separate identification. If necessary to report, add modifier 52)

+ 44955   when done for indicated purpose at time of other major procedure (not as separate procedure) (List separately in addition to code for primary procedure)

44960   for ruptured appendix with abscess or generalized peritonitis

Laparoscopy

Surgical laparoscopy always includes diagnostic laparoscopy. To report a diagnostic laparoscopy (peritoneoscopy) (separate procedure), use 49320.

44970   Laparoscopy, surgical, appendectomy

44979   Unlisted laparoscopy procedure, appendix

Rectum

Incision

45000   Transrectal drainage of pelvic abscess

45005   Incision and drainage of submucosal abscess, rectum

45020   Incision and drainage of deep supralevator, pelvirectal, or retrorectal abscess

(See also 46050, 46060)

Excision

45100   Biopsy of anorectal wall, anal approach (eg, congenital megacolon)

(For endoscopic biopsy, use 45305)

45108   Anorectal myomectomy

45110   Proctectomy; complete, combined abdominoperineal, with colostomy

(For laparoscopic procedure, use 45395)

45111   partial resection of rectum, transabdominal approach

45112   Proctectomy, combined abdominoperineal, pull-through procedure (eg, colo-anal anastomosis)

(For colo-anal anastomosis with colonic reservoir or pouch, use 45119)

45113   Proctectomy, partial, with rectal mucosectomy, ileoanal anastomosis, creation of ileal reservoir (S or J), with or without loop ileostomy

45114   Proctectomy, partial, with anastomosis; abdominal and transsacral approach

45116   transsacral approach only (Kraske type)

Surgery: Digestive System

45119   Proctectomy, combined abdominoperineal pull-through procedure (eg, colo-anal anastomosis), with creation of colonic reservoir (eg, J-pouch), with diverting enterostomy when performed

(For laparoscopic procedure, use 45397)

45120   Proctectomy, complete (for congenital megacolon), abdominal and perineal approach; with pull-through procedure and anastomosis (eg, Swenson, Duhamel, or Soave type operation)

45121   with subtotal or total colectomy, with multiple biopsies

45123   Proctectomy, partial, without anastomosis, perineal approach

45126   Pelvic exenteration for colorectal malignancy, with proctectomy (with or without colostomy), with removal of bladder and ureteral transplantations, and/or hysterectomy, or cervicectomy, with or without removal of tube(s), with or without removal of ovary(s), or any combination thereof

45130   Excision of rectal procidentia, with anastomosis; perineal approach

45135   abdominal and perineal approach

45136   Excision of ileoanal reservoir with ileostomy

(Do not report 45136 in addition to 44005, 44120, 44310)

45150   Division of stricture of rectum

45160   Excision of rectal tumor by proctotomy, transsacral or transcoccygeal approach

►(45170 has been deleted. To report excision of rectal tumor, transanal approach, see 45171, 45172)◄

(For transanal endoscopic microsurgical [ie, TEMS] excision of rectal tumor, use 0184T)

● **45171**   Excision of rectal tumor, transanal approach; not including muscularis propria (ie, partial thickness)

● **45172**   including muscularis propria (ie, full thickness)

►(For destruction of rectal tumor, transanal approach, use 45190)◄

Destruction

45190   Destruction of rectal tumor (eg, electrodesiccation, electrosurgery, laser ablation, laser resection, cryosurgery) transanal approach

►(For excision of rectal tumor, transanal approach, see 45171, 45172)◄

Endoscopy

Definitions

Proctosigmoidoscopy is the examination of the rectum and sigmoid colon.

Sigmoidoscopy is the examination of the entire rectum, sigmoid colon and may include examination of a portion of the descending colon.

Colonoscopy is the examination of the entire colon, from the rectum to the cecum, and may include the examination of the terminal ileum.

For an incomplete colonoscopy, with full preparation for a colonoscopy, use a colonoscopy code with the modifier 52 and provide documentation.

Surgical endoscopy always includes diagnostic endoscopy.

►For computed tomographic colonography, see 74261-74263.◄

45300   Proctosigmoidoscopy, rigid; diagnostic, with or without collection of specimen(s) by brushing or washing (separate procedure)

⊙ **45303**   with dilation (eg, balloon, guide wire, bougie)

(For radiological supervision and interpretation, use 74360)

⊙ **45305**   with biopsy, single or multiple

⊙ **45307**   with removal of foreign body

⊙ **45308**   with removal of single tumor, polyp, or other lesion by hot biopsy forceps or bipolar cautery

⊙ **45309**   with removal of single tumor, polyp, or other lesion by snare technique

⊙ **45315**   with removal of multiple tumors, polyps, or other lesions by hot biopsy forceps, bipolar cautery or snare technique

⊙ **45317**   with control of bleeding (eg, injection, bipolar cautery, unipolar cautery, laser, heater probe, stapler, plasma coagulator)

⊙ **45320**   with ablation of tumor(s), polyp(s), or other lesion(s) not amenable to removal by hot biopsy forceps, bipolar cautery or snare technique (eg, laser)

⊙ **45321**   with decompression of volvulus

⊙ **45327**   with transendoscopic stent placement (includes predilation)

45330   Sigmoidoscopy, flexible; diagnostic, with or without collection of specimen(s) by brushing or washing (separate procedure)

45331   with biopsy, single or multiple

⊙ **45332**   with removal of foreign body

⊙ **45333**   with removal of tumor(s), polyp(s), or other lesion(s) by hot biopsy forceps or bipolar cautery

⊙ **45334**   with control of bleeding (eg, injection, bipolar cautery, unipolar cautery, laser, heater probe, stapler, plasma coagulator)

⊙ **45335**   with directed submucosal injection(s), any substance

⊙ **45337**   with decompression of volvulus, any method

⊙ **45338**   with removal of tumor(s), polyp(s), or other lesion(s) by snare technique

⊙ **45339**   with ablation of tumor(s), polyp(s), or other lesion(s) not amenable to removal by hot biopsy forceps, bipolar cautery or snare technique

⊙ **45340**   with dilation by balloon, 1 or more strictures

(Do not report 45340 in conjunction with 45345)

⊙ **45341**   with endoscopic ultrasound examination

⊙ **45342**   with transendoscopic ultrasound guided intramural or transmural fine needle aspiration/biopsy(s)

(Do not report 45341, 45342 in conjunction with 76942, 76975)

(For interpretation of specimen, see 88172-88173)

(For transrectal ultrasound utilizing rigid probe device, use 76872)

⊙ **45345**   with transendoscopic stent placement (includes predilation)

⊙ **45355**   Colonoscopy, rigid or flexible, transabdominal via colotomy, single or multiple

(For fiberoptic colonoscopy beyond 25cm to splenic flexure, see 45330-45345)

⊙ **45378**   Colonoscopy, flexible, proximal to splenic flexure; diagnostic, with or without collection of specimen(s) by brushing or washing, with or without colon decompression (separate procedure)

⊙ **45379**   with removal of foreign body

⊙ **45380**   with biopsy, single or multiple

⊙ **45381**   with directed submucosal injection(s), any substance

⊙ **45382**   with control of bleeding (eg, injection, bipolar cautery, unipolar cautery, laser, heater probe, stapler, plasma coagulator)

⊙ **45383**   with ablation of tumor(s), polyp(s), or other lesion(s) not amenable to removal by hot biopsy forceps, bipolar cautery or snare technique

⊙ **45384**   with removal of tumor(s), polyp(s), or other lesion(s) by hot biopsy forceps or bipolar cautery

⊙ **45385**   with removal of tumor(s), polyp(s), or other lesion(s) by snare technique

(For small intestine and stomal endoscopy, see 44360-44393)

⊙ **45386**   with dilation by balloon, 1 or more strictures

(Do not report 45386 in conjunction with 45387)

⊙ **45387**   with transendoscopic stent placement (includes predilation)

⊙ **45391**   with endoscopic ultrasound examination

(Do not report 45391 in conjunction with 45330, 45341, 45342, 45378, 76872)

⊙ **45392**   with transendoscopic ultrasound guided intramural or transmural fine needle aspiration/biopsy(s)

(Do not report 45392 in conjunction with 45330, 45341, 45342, 45378, 76872)

Laparoscopy

Surgical laparoscopy always includes diagnostic laparoscopy. To report a diagnostic laparoscopy (peritoneoscopy) (separate procedure), use 49320.

Excision

45395   Laparoscopy, surgical; proctectomy, complete, combined abdominoperineal, with colostomy

(For open procedure, use 45110)

45397   proctectomy, combined abdominoperineal pull-through procedure (eg, colo-anal anastomosis), with creation of colonic reservoir (eg, J-pouch), with diverting enterostomy, when performed

(For open procedure, use 45119)

Repair

45400   Laparoscopy, surgical; proctopexy (for prolapse)

(For open procedure, use 45540, 45541)

45402   proctopexy (for prolapse), with sigmoid resection

(For open procedure, use 45550)

45499   Unlisted laparoscopy procedure, rectum

Repair

45500   Proctoplasty; for stenosis

45505   for prolapse of mucous membrane

45520   Perirectal injection of sclerosing solution for prolapse

45540   Proctopexy (eg, for prolapse); abdominal approach

(For laparoscopic procedure, use 45400)

45541   perineal approach

45550   with sigmoid resection, abdominal approach

(For laparoscopic procedure, use 45402)

45560   Repair of rectocele (separate procedure)

(For repair of rectocele with posterior colporrhaphy, use 57250)

45562   Exploration, repair, and presacral drainage for rectal injury;

45563   with colostomy

45800   Closure of rectovesical fistula;

45805   with colostomy

Surgery: Digestive System

45820 Closure of rectourethral fistula;

45825 with colostomy

(For rectovaginal fistula closure, see 57300-57308)

Manipulation

45900 Reduction of procidentia (separate procedure) under anesthesia

45905 Dilation of anal sphincter (separate procedure) under anesthesia other than local

45910 Dilation of rectal stricture (separate procedure) under anesthesia other than local

45915 Removal of fecal impaction or foreign body (separate procedure) under anesthesia

Other Procedures

Surgical diagnostic anorectal exam (45990) includes the following elements: external perineal exam, digital rectal exam, pelvic exam (when performed), diagnostic anoscopy, and diagnostic rigid proctoscopy.

45990 Anorectal exam, surgical, requiring anesthesia (general, spinal, or epidural), diagnostic

(Do not report 45990 in conjunction with 45300-45327, 46600, 57410, 99170)

45999 Unlisted procedure, rectum

(For unlisted laparoscopic procedure, rectum, use 45499)

Anus

►For incision of thrombosed external hemorrhoid, use 46083. For ligation of internal hemorrhoid(s), see 46221, 46945, 46946. For excision of internal and/or external hemorrhoid(s), see 46250-46262, 46320. For injection of hemorrhoid(s), use 46500. For destruction of internal hemorrhoid(s) by thermal energy, use 46930. For destruction of hemorrhoid(s) by cryosurgery, use 46999. For hemorrhoidopexy, use 46947.◄

Incision

(For subcutaneous fistulotomy, use 46270)

46020 Placement of seton

(Do not report 46020 in addition to 46060, 46280, 46600)

46030 Removal of anal seton, other marker

46040 Incision and drainage of ischiorectal and/or perirectal abscess (separate procedure)

46045 Incision and drainage of intramural, intramuscular, or submucosal abscess, transanal, under anesthesia

46050 Incision and drainage, perianal abscess, superficial

(See also 45020, 46060)

46060 Incision and drainage of ischiorectal or intramural abscess, with fistulectomy or fistulotomy, submuscular, with or without placement of seton

(Do not report 46060 in addition to 46020)

(See also 45020)

46070 Incision, anal septum (infant)

(For anoplasty, see 46700-46705)

(Do not report modifier 63 in conjunction with 46070)

46080 Sphincterotomy, anal, division of sphincter (separate procedure)

46083 Incision of thrombosed hemorrhoid, external

Excision

▲ **46200** Fissurectomy, including sphincterotomy, when performed

►(46210, 46211 have been deleted. To report, use 46999)◄

46220 ►Code is out of numerical sequence. See 46200-46288◄

▲ **46221** Hemorrhoidectomy, internal, by rubber band ligation(s)

#▲ **46945** Hemorrhoidectomy, internal, by ligation other than rubber band; single hemorrhoid column/group

#▲ **46946** 2 or more hemorrhoid columns/groups

#▲ **46220** Excision of single external papilla or tag, anus

▲ **46230** Excision of multiple external papillae or tags, anus

#▲ **46320** Excision of thrombosed hemorrhoid, external

▲ **46250** Hemorrhoidectomy, external, 2 or more columns/groups

►(For hemorrhoidectomy, external, single column/group, use 46999)◄

▲ **46255** Hemorrhoidectomy, internal and external, single column/group;

46257 with fissurectomy

▲ **46258** with fistulectomy, including fissurectomy, when performed

▲ **46260** Hemorrhoidectomy, internal and external, 2 or more columns/groups;

46261 with fissurectomy

▲ **46262** with fistulectomy, including fissurectomy, when performed

46270 Surgical treatment of anal fistula (fistulectomy/fistulotomy); subcutaneous

▲ **46275** intersphincteric

▲ **46280** transsphincteric, suprasphincteric, extrasphincteric or multiple, including placement of seton, when performed

(Do not report 46280 in conjunction with 46020)

46285 second stage

46288   Closure of anal fistula with rectal advancement flap

46320   ►Code is out of numerical sequence. See 46200-46288◄

Introduction

46500   Injection of sclerosing solution, hemorrhoids

46505   Chemodenervation of internal anal sphincter

(For chemodenervation of other muscles, see 64612-64614, 64640)

(Report the specific service in conjunction with the specific substance(s) or drug(s) provided)

Endoscopy

Surgical endoscopy always includes diagnostic endoscopy.

46600   Anoscopy; diagnostic, with or without collection of specimen(s) by brushing or washing (separate procedure)

(Do not report 46600 in addition to 46020)

46604   with dilation (eg, balloon, guide wire, bougie)

46606   with biopsy, single or multiple

46608   with removal of foreign body

46610   with removal of single tumor, polyp, or other lesion by hot biopsy forceps or bipolar cautery

46611   with removal of single tumor, polyp, or other lesion by snare technique

46612   with removal of multiple tumors, polyps, or other lesions by hot biopsy forceps, bipolar cautery or snare technique

46614   with control of bleeding (eg, injection, bipolar cautery, unipolar cautery, laser, heater probe, stapler, plasma coagulator)

46615   with ablation of tumor(s), polyp(s), or other lesion(s) not amenable to removal by hot biopsy forceps, bipolar cautery or snare technique

Repair

46700   Anoplasty, plastic operation for stricture; adult

46705   infant

(For simple incision of anal septum, use 46070)

(Do not report modifier 63 in conjunction with 46705)

46706   Repair of anal fistula with fibrin glue

● **46707**   Repair of anorectal fistula with plug (eg, porcine small intestine submucosa [SIS])

46710   Repair of ileoanal pouch fistula/sinus (eg, perineal or vaginal), pouch advancement; transperineal approach

46712   combined transperineal and transabdominal approach

46715   Repair of low imperforate anus; with anoperineal fistula (cut-back procedure)

46716   with transposition of anoperineal or anovestibular fistula

(Do not report modifier 63 in conjunction with 46715, 46716)

46730   Repair of high imperforate anus without fistula; perineal or sacroperineal approach

46735   combined transabdominal and sacroperineal approaches

(Do not report modifier 63 in conjunction with 46730, 46735)

46740   Repair of high imperforate anus with rectourethral or rectovaginal fistula; perineal or sacroperineal approach

46742   combined transabdominal and sacroperineal approaches

(Do not report modifier 63 in conjunction with 46740, 46742)

46744   Repair of cloacal anomaly by anorectovaginoplasty and urethroplasty, sacroperineal approach

(Do not report modifier 63 in conjunction with 46744)

46746   Repair of cloacal anomaly by anorectovaginoplasty and urethroplasty, combined abdominal and sacroperineal approach;

46748   with vaginal lengthening by intestinal graft or pedicle flaps

46750   Sphincteroplasty, anal, for incontinence or prolapse; adult

46751   child

46753   Graft (Thiersch operation) for rectal incontinence and/or prolapse

46754   Removal of Thiersch wire or suture, anal canal

46760   Sphincteroplasty, anal, for incontinence, adult; muscle transplant

46761   levator muscle imbrication (Park posterior anal repair)

46762   implantation artificial sphincter

46947   Hemorrhoidopexy (eg, for prolapsing internal hemorrhoids) by stapling

Destruction

46900   Destruction of lesion(s), anus (eg, condyloma, papilloma, molluscum contagiosum, herpetic vesicle), simple; chemical

46910   electrodesiccation

46916   cryosurgery

46917   laser surgery

46922   surgical excision

46924   Destruction of lesion(s), anus (eg, condyloma, papilloma, molluscum contagiosum, herpetic vesicle), extensive (eg, laser surgery, electrosurgery, cryosurgery, chemosurgery)

Surgery: Digestive System

46930	Destruction of internal hemorrhoid(s) by thermal energy (eg, infrared coagulation, cautery, radiofrequency)

▶(46934-46936 have been deleted)◀

▶(46937, 46938 have been deleted. To report, use 45190)◀

46940	Curettage or cautery of anal fissure, including dilation of anal sphincter (separate procedure); initial
46942	subsequent
46945	▶Code is out of numerical sequence. See 46200-46288◀
46946	▶Code is out of numerical sequence. See 46200-46288◀
46947	▶Code is out of numerical sequence. See 46700-46947◀

Other Procedures

46999	Unlisted procedure, anus

Liver

Incision

47000	Biopsy of liver, needle; percutaneous

(If imaging guidance is performed, see 76942, 77002, 77012, 77021)

+ 47001	when done for indicated purpose at time of other major procedure (List separately in addition to code for primary procedure)

(If imaging guidance is performed, see 76942, 77002)

(For fine needle aspiration in conjunction with 47000, 47001, see 10021, 10022)

(For evaluation of fine needle aspirate in conjunction with 47000, 47001, see 88172, 88173)

47010	Hepatotomy; for open drainage of abscess or cyst, 1 or 2 stages
⊙ 47011	for percutaneous drainage of abscess or cyst, 1 or 2 stages

(For radiological supervision and interpretation, use 75989)

47015	Laparotomy, with aspiration and/or injection of hepatic parasitic (eg, amoebic or echinococcal) cyst(s) or abscess(es)

Excision

47100	Biopsy of liver, wedge
47120	Hepatectomy, resection of liver; partial lobectomy
47122	trisegmentectomy
47125	total left lobectomy

47130	total right lobectomy

Liver Transplantation

Liver allotransplantation involves three distinct components of physician work:

1. *Cadaver donor hepatectomy*, which includes harvesting the graft and cold preservation of the graft (perfusing with cold preservation solution and cold maintenance) (use 47133). *Living donor hepatectomy*, which includes harvesting the graft, cold preservation of the graft (perfusing with cold preservation solution and cold maintenance), and care of the donor (see 47140-47142).

2. *Backbench work*:

Standard preparation of the whole liver graft will include one of the following:

Preparation of whole liver graft (including cholecystectomy, if necessary, and dissection and removal of surrounding soft tissues to prepare vena cava, portal vein, hepatic artery, and common bile duct for implantation) (use 47143).

Preparation as described for whole liver graft, plus trisegment split into two partial grafts (use 47144).

Preparation as described for whole liver graft, plus lobe split into two partial grafts (use 47145).

Additional reconstruction of the liver graft may include venous and/or arterial anastomosis(es) (see 47146, 47147).

3. *Recipient liver allotransplantation*, which includes recipient hepatectomy (partial or whole), transplantation of the allograft (partial or whole), and care of the recipient (see 47135, 47136).

47133	Donor hepatectomy (including cold preservation), from cadaver donor
47135	Liver allotransplantation; orthotopic, partial or whole, from cadaver or living donor, any age
47136	heterotopic, partial or whole, from cadaver or living donor, any age
47140	Donor hepatectomy (including cold preservation), from living donor; left lateral segment only (segments II and III)
47141	total left lobectomy (segments II, III and IV)
47142	total right lobectomy (segments V, VI, VII and VIII)
47143	Backbench standard preparation of cadaver donor whole liver graft prior to allotransplantation, including cholecystectomy, if necessary, and dissection and removal of surrounding soft tissues to prepare the vena cava, portal vein, hepatic artery, and common bile duct for implantation; without trisegment or lobe split
47144	with trisegment split of whole liver graft into 2 partial liver grafts (ie, left lateral segment [segments II and III] and right trisegment [segments I and IV through VIII])

47145   with lobe split of whole liver graft into 2 partial liver grafts (ie, left lobe [segments II, III, and IV] and right lobe [segments I and V through VIII])

47146   Backbench reconstruction of cadaver or living donor liver graft prior to allotransplantation; venous anastomosis, each

47147   arterial anastomosis, each

(Do not report 47143-47147 in conjunction with 47120-47125, 47600, 47610)

Repair

47300   Marsupialization of cyst or abscess of liver

47350   Management of liver hemorrhage; simple suture of liver wound or injury

47360   complex suture of liver wound or injury, with or without hepatic artery ligation

47361   exploration of hepatic wound, extensive debridement, coagulation and/or suture, with or without packing of liver

47362   re-exploration of hepatic wound for removal of packing

Laparoscopy

Surgical laparoscopy always includes diagnostic laparoscopy. To report a diagnostic laparoscopy (peritoneoscopy) (separate procedure), use 49320.

47370   Laparoscopy, surgical, ablation of 1 or more liver tumor(s); radiofrequency

(For imaging guidance, use 76940)

47371   cryosurgical

(For imaging guidance, use 76940)

47379   Unlisted laparoscopic procedure, liver

Other Procedures

47380   Ablation, open, of 1 or more liver tumor(s); radiofrequency

(For imaging guidance, use 76940)

47381   cryosurgical

(For imaging guidance, use 76940)

⊙▲ **47382**   Ablation, 1 or more liver tumor(s), percutaneous, radiofrequency

(For imaging guidance and monitoring, see 76940, 77013, 77022)

47399   Unlisted procedure, liver

Biliary Tract

Incision

47400   Hepaticotomy or hepaticostomy with exploration, drainage, or removal of calculus

47420   Choledochotomy or choledochostomy with exploration, drainage, or removal of calculus, with or without cholecystotomy; without transduodenal sphincterotomy or sphincteroplasty

47425   with transduodenal sphincterotomy or sphincteroplasty

47460   Transduodenal sphincterotomy or sphincteroplasty, with or without transduodenal extraction of calculus (separate procedure)

47480   Cholecystotomy or cholecystostomy with exploration, drainage, or removal of calculus (separate procedure)

47490   Percutaneous cholecystostomy

(For radiological supervision and interpretation, use 75989)

Introduction

47500   Injection procedure for percutaneous transhepatic cholangiography

(For radiological supervision and interpretation, use 74320)

47505   Injection procedure for cholangiography through an existing catheter (eg, percutaneous transhepatic or T-tube)

(For radiological supervision and interpretation, use 74305)

47510   Introduction of percutaneous transhepatic catheter for biliary drainage

(For radiological supervision and interpretation, use 75980)

47511   Introduction of percutaneous transhepatic stent for internal and external biliary drainage

(For radiological supervision and interpretation, use 75982)

⊙▲ **47525**   Change of percutaneous biliary drainage catheter

(For radiological supervision and interpretation, use 75984)

47530   Revision and/or reinsertion of transhepatic tube

(For radiological supervision and interpretation, use 75984)

Surgery: Digestive System

Endoscopy

Surgical endoscopy always includes diagnostic endoscopy.

+ 47550   Biliary endoscopy, intraoperative (choledochoscopy) (List separately in addition to code for primary procedure)

47552   Biliary endoscopy, percutaneous via T-tube or other tract; diagnostic, with or without collection of specimen(s) by brushing and/or washing (separate procedure)

47553   with biopsy, single or multiple

47554   with removal of calculus/calculi

47555   with dilation of biliary duct stricture(s) without stent

47556   with dilation of biliary duct stricture(s) with stent

        (For ERCP, see 43260-43272, 74363)

        (If imaging guidance is performed, see 74363, 75982)

Laparoscopy

Surgical laparoscopy always includes diagnostic laparoscopy. To report a diagnostic laparoscopy (peritoneoscopy) (separate procedure), use 49320.

47560   Laparoscopy, surgical; with guided transhepatic cholangiography, without biopsy

47561   with guided transhepatic cholangiography with biopsy

47562   cholecystectomy

47563   cholecystectomy with cholangiography

47564   cholecystectomy with exploration of common duct

47570   cholecystoenterostomy

47579   Unlisted laparoscopy procedure, biliary tract

Excision

47600   Cholecystectomy;

47605   with cholangiography

        (For laparoscopic approach, see 47562-47564)

47610   Cholecystectomy with exploration of common duct;

        (For cholecystectomy with exploration of common duct with biliary endoscopy, use 47610 with 47550)

47612   with choledochoenterostomy

47620   with transduodenal sphincterotomy or sphincteroplasty, with or without cholangiography

47630   Biliary duct stone extraction, percutaneous via T-tube tract, basket, or snare (eg, Burhenne technique)

        (For radiological supervision and interpretation, use 74327)

47700   Exploration for congenital atresia of bile ducts, without repair, with or without liver biopsy, with or without cholangiography

        (Do not report modifier 63 in conjunction with 47700)

47701   Portoenterostomy (eg, Kasai procedure)

        (Do not report modifier 63 in conjunction with 47701)

47711   Excision of bile duct tumor, with or without primary repair of bile duct; extrahepatic

47712   intrahepatic

        (For anastomosis, see 47760-47800)

47715   Excision of choledochal cyst

Repair

        (47719 has been deleted)

47720   Cholecystoenterostomy; direct

        (For laparoscopic approach, use 47570)

47721   with gastroenterostomy

47740   Roux-en-Y

47741   Roux-en-Y with gastroenterostomy

47760   Anastomosis, of extrahepatic biliary ducts and gastrointestinal tract

47765   Anastomosis, of intrahepatic ducts and gastrointestinal tract

47780   Anastomosis, Roux-en-Y, of extrahepatic biliary ducts and gastrointestinal tract

47785   Anastomosis, Roux-en-Y, of intrahepatic biliary ducts and gastrointestinal tract

47800   Reconstruction, plastic, of extrahepatic biliary ducts with end-to-end anastomosis

47801   Placement of choledochal stent

47802   U-tube hepaticoenterostomy

47900   Suture of extrahepatic biliary duct for pre-existing injury (separate procedure)

Other Procedures

47999   Unlisted procedure, biliary tract

Pancreas

        (For peroral pancreatic endoscopic procedures, see 43260-43272)

Incision

48000   Placement of drains, peripancreatic, for acute pancreatitis;

48001   with cholecystostomy, gastrostomy, and jejunostomy

48020   Removal of pancreatic calculus

Surgery: Digestive System

Excision

48100   Biopsy of pancreas, open (eg, fine needle aspiration, needle core biopsy, wedge biopsy)

48102   Biopsy of pancreas, percutaneous needle

(For radiological supervision and interpretation, see 76942, 77002, 77012, 77021)

(For fine needle aspiration, use 10022)

(For evaluation of fine needle aspirate, see 88172, 88173)

48105   Resection or debridement of pancreas and peripancreatic tissue for acute necrotizing pancreatitis

48120   Excision of lesion of pancreas (eg, cyst, adenoma)

48140   Pancreatectomy, distal subtotal, with or without splenectomy; without pancreaticojejunostomy

48145   with pancreaticojejunostomy

48146   Pancreatectomy, distal, near-total with preservation of duodenum (Child-type procedure)

48148   Excision of ampulla of Vater

48150   Pancreatectomy, proximal subtotal with total duodenectomy, partial gastrectomy, choledochoenterostomy and gastrojejunostomy (Whipple-type procedure); with pancreatojejunostomy

48152   without pancreatojejunostomy

48153   Pancreatectomy, proximal subtotal with near-total duodenectomy, choledochoenterostomy and duodenojejunostomy (pylorus-sparing, Whipple-type procedure); with pancreatojejunostomy

48154   without pancreatojejunostomy

48155   Pancreatectomy, total

48160   Pancreatectomy, total or subtotal, with autologous transplantation of pancreas or pancreatic islet cells

Introduction

+ 48400   Injection procedure for intraoperative pancreatography (List separately in addition to code for primary procedure)

(For radiological supervision and interpretation, see 74300-74305)

Repair

48500   Marsupialization of pancreatic cyst

48510   External drainage, pseudocyst of pancreas; open

⊙ **48511**   percutaneous

(For radiological supervision and interpretation, use 75989)

48520   Internal anastomosis of pancreatic cyst to gastrointestinal tract; direct

48540   Roux-en-Y

48545   Pancreatorrhaphy for injury

48547   Duodenal exclusion with gastrojejunostomy for pancreatic injury

48548   Pancreaticojejunostomy, side-to-side anastomosis (Puestow-type operation)

Pancreas Transplantation

Pancreas allotransplantation involves three distinct components of physician work:

1. *Cadaver donor pancreatectomy*, which includes harvesting the pancreas graft, with or without duodenal segment, and cold preservation of the graft (perfusing with cold preservation solution and cold maintenance) (use 48550).

2. *Backbench work*:

Standard preparation of a cadaver donor pancreas allograft prior to transplantation includes dissection of the allograft from surrounding soft tissues, splenectomy, duodenotomy, ligation of bile duct, ligation of mesenteric vessels, and Y-graft arterial anastomoses from the iliac artery to the superior mesenteric artery and to the splenic artery (use 48551).

Additional reconstruction of a cadaver donor pancreas allograft prior to transplantation may include venous anastomosis(es) (use 48552).

3. *Recipient pancreas allotransplantation*, which includes transplantation of allograft, and care of the recipient (use 48554).

48550   Donor pancreatectomy (including cold preservation), with or without duodenal segment for transplantation

48551   Backbench standard preparation of cadaver donor pancreas allograft prior to transplantation, including dissection of allograft from surrounding soft tissues, splenectomy, duodenotomy, ligation of bile duct, ligation of mesenteric vessels, and Y-graft arterial anastomoses from iliac artery to superior mesenteric artery and to splenic artery

48552   Backbench reconstruction of cadaver donor pancreas allograft prior to transplantation, venous anastomosis, each

(Do not report 48551 and 48552 in conjunction with 35531, 35563, 35685, 38100-38102, 44010, 44820, 44850, 47460, 47505-47525, 47550-47556, 48100-48120, 48545)

48554   Transplantation of pancreatic allograft

48556   Removal of transplanted pancreatic allograft

Other Procedures

48999   Unlisted procedure, pancreas

Abdomen, Peritoneum, and Omentum

Incision

49000 Exploratory laparotomy, exploratory celiotomy with or without biopsy(s) (separate procedure)

(To report wound exploration due to penetrating trauma without laparotomy, use 20102)

49002 Reopening of recent laparotomy

(To report re-exploration of hepatic wound for removal of packing, use 47362)

49010 Exploration, retroperitoneal area with or without biopsy(s) (separate procedure)

(To report wound exploration due to penetrating trauma without laparotomy, use 20102)

49020 Drainage of peritoneal abscess or localized peritonitis, exclusive of appendiceal abscess; open

(For appendiceal abscess, use 44900)

⊙ **49021** percutaneous

(For radiological supervision and interpretation, use 75989)

49040 Drainage of subdiaphragmatic or subphrenic abscess; open

⊙ **49041** percutaneous

(For radiological supervision and interpretation, use 75989)

49060 Drainage of retroperitoneal abscess; open

⊙ **49061** percutaneous

(For laparoscopic drainage, use 49323)

(For radiological supervision and interpretation, use 75989)

49062 Drainage of extraperitoneal lymphocele to peritoneal cavity; open

49080 Peritoneocentesis, abdominal paracentesis, or peritoneal lavage (diagnostic or therapeutic); initial

49081 subsequent

(If imaging guidance is performed, see 76942, 77012)

Excision, Destruction

(For lysis of intestinal adhesions, use 44005)

49180 Biopsy, abdominal or retroperitoneal mass, percutaneous needle

(If imaging guidance is performed, see 76942, 77002, 77012, 77021)

(For fine needle aspiration, use 10021 or 10022)

(For evaluation of fine needle aspirate, see 88172, 88173)

(49200, 49201 have been deleted. To report, see 49203-49205, 58957, 58958)

49203 Excision or destruction, open, intra-abdominal tumors, cysts or endometriomas, 1 or more peritoneal, mesenteric, or retroperitoneal primary or secondary tumors; largest tumor 5 cm diameter or less

49204 largest tumor 5.1-10.0 cm diameter

49205 largest tumor greater than 10.0 cm diameter

(Do not report 49203-49205 in conjunction with 38770, 38780, 49000, 49010, 49215, 50010, 50205, 50225, 50236, 50250, 50290, 58900-58960)

(For partial or total nephrectomy, use 50220 or 50240 in conjunction with 49203-49205)

(For colectomy, use 44140 in conjunction with 49203-49205)

(For small bowel resection, use 44120 in conjunction with 49203-49205)

(For vena caval resection with reconstruction, use 49203-49205 in conjunction with 37799)

(For resection of recurrent ovarian, tubal, primary peritoneal, or uterine malignancy, see 58957, 58958)

(For cryoablation of renal tumors, see 50250, 50593)

49215 Excision of presacral or sacrococcygeal tumor

(Do not report modifier 63 in conjunction with 49215)

49220 Staging laparotomy for Hodgkins disease or lymphoma (includes splenectomy, needle or open biopsies of both liver lobes, possibly also removal of abdominal nodes, abdominal node and/or bone marrow biopsies, ovarian repositioning)

49250 Umbilectomy, omphalectomy, excision of umbilicus (separate procedure)

49255 Omentectomy, epiploectomy, resection of omentum (separate procedure)

Laparoscopy

Surgical laparoscopy always includes diagnostic laparoscopy. To report a diagnostic laparoscopy (peritoneoscopy), (separate procedure), use 49320.

For laparoscopic fulguration or excision of lesions of the ovary, pelvic viscera, or peritoneal surface use 58662.

49320 Laparoscopy, abdomen, peritoneum, and omentum, diagnostic, with or without collection of specimen(s) by brushing or washing (separate procedure)

49321 Laparoscopy, surgical; with biopsy (single or multiple)

49322 with aspiration of cavity or cyst (eg, ovarian cyst) (single or multiple)

49323 with drainage of lymphocele to peritoneal cavity

(For percutaneous or open drainage, see 49060, 49061)

49324   with insertion of intraperitoneal cannula or catheter, permanent

(For subcutaneous extension of intraperitoneal catheter with remote chest exit site, use 49435 in conjunction with 49324)

(For open insertion of permanent intraperitoneal cannula or catheter, use 49421)

49325   with revision of previously placed intraperitoneal cannula or catheter, with removal of intraluminal obstructive material if performed

+ **49326**   with omentopexy (omental tacking procedure) (List separately in addition to code for primary procedure)

(Use 49326 in conjunction with 49324, 49325)

49329   Unlisted laparoscopy procedure, abdomen, peritoneum and omentum

Introduction, Revision, Removal

49400   Injection of air or contrast into peritoneal cavity (separate procedure)

(For radiological supervision and interpretation, use 74190)

49402   Removal of peritoneal foreign body from peritoneal cavity

(For lysis of intestinal adhesions, use 44005)

⊙● **49411**   Placement of interstitial device(s) for radiation therapy guidance (eg, fiducial markers, dosimeter), percutaneous, intra-abdominal, intra-pelvic (except prostate), and/or retroperitoneum, single or multiple

▶(Report supply of device separately)◀

▶(For imaging guidance, see 76942, 77002, 77012, 77021)◀

▶(For percutaneous placement of interstitial device[s] for intra-thoracic radiation therapy guidance, use 32553)◀

49419   Insertion of intraperitoneal cannula or catheter, with subcutaneous reservoir, permanent (ie, totally implantable)

(For removal, use 49422)

49420   Insertion of intraperitoneal cannula or catheter for drainage or dialysis; temporary

49421   permanent

(For laparoscopic insertion of permanent intraperitoneal cannula or catheter, use 49324)

(For subcutaneous extension of intraperitoneal catheter with remote chest exit site, use 49435 in conjunction with 49421)

49422   Removal of permanent intraperitoneal cannula or catheter

(For removal of a temporary catheter/cannula, use appropriate E/M code)

49423   Exchange of previously placed abscess or cyst drainage catheter under radiological guidance (separate procedure)

(For radiological supervision and interpretation, use 75984)

49424   Contrast injection for assessment of abscess or cyst via previously placed drainage catheter or tube (separate procedure)

(For radiological supervision and interpretation, use 76080)

49425   Insertion of peritoneal-venous shunt

49426   Revision of peritoneal-venous shunt

(For shunt patency test, use 78291)

49427   Injection procedure (eg, contrast media) for evaluation of previously placed peritoneal-venous shunt

(For radiological supervision and interpretation, see 75809, 78291)

49428   Ligation of peritoneal-venous shunt

49429   Removal of peritoneal-venous shunt

+ **49435**   Insertion of subcutaneous extension to intraperitoneal cannula or catheter with remote chest exit site (List separately in addition to code for primary procedure)

(Use 49435 in conjunction with 49324, 49421)

49436   Delayed creation of exit site from embedded subcutaneous segment of intraperitoneal cannula or catheter

Initial Placement

Do not additionally report 43752 for placement of a nasogastric (NG) or orogastric (OG) tube to insufflate the stomach prior to percutaneous gastrointestinal tube placement. NG or OG tube placement is considered part of the procedure in this family of codes.

⊙ **49440**   Insertion of gastrostomy tube, percutaneous, under fluoroscopic guidance including contrast injection(s), image documentation and report

(For conversion to a gastro-jejunostomy tube at the time of initial gastrostomy tube placement, use 49440 in conjunction with 49446)

⊙ **49441**   Insertion of duodenostomy or jejunostomy tube, percutaneous, under fluoroscopic guidance including contrast injection(s), image documentation and report

(For conversion of gastrostomy tube to gastro-jejunostomy tube, use 49446)

⊙ **49442**   Insertion of cecostomy or other colonic tube, percutaneous, under fluoroscopic guidance including contrast injection(s), image documentation and report

Surgery: Digestive System

Conversion

⊙ **49446** Conversion of gastrostomy tube to gastro-jejunostomy tube, percutaneous, under fluoroscopic guidance including contrast injection(s), image documentation and report

(For conversion to a gastro-jejunostomy tube at the time of initial gastrostomy tube placement, use 49446 in conjunction with 49440)

Replacement

If an existing gastrostomy, duodenostomy, jejunostomy, gastro-jejunostomy, or cecostomy (or other colonic) tube is removed and a new tube is placed via a separate percutaneous access site, the placement of the new tube is not considered a replacement and would be reported using the appropriate initial placement codes 49440-49442.

49450 Replacement of gastrostomy or cecostomy (or other colonic) tube, percutaneous, under fluoroscopic guidance including contrast injection(s), image documentation and report

▶(To report a percutaneous change of a gastrostomy tube without imaging or endoscopic guidance, use 43760)◀

49451 Replacement of duodenostomy or jejunostomy tube, percutaneous, under fluoroscopic guidance including contrast injection(s), image documentation and report

49452 Replacement of gastro-jejunostomy tube, percutaneous, under fluoroscopic guidance including contrast injection(s), image documentation and report

Mechanical Removal of Obstructive Material

49460 Mechanical removal of obstructive material from gastrostomy, duodenostomy, jejunostomy, gastro-jejunostomy, or cecostomy (or other colonic) tube, any method, under fluoroscopic guidance including contrast injection(s), if performed, image documentation and report

(Do not report 49460 in conjunction with 49450-49452, 49465)

Other

49465 Contrast injection(s) for radiological evaluation of existing gastrostomy, duodenostomy, jejunostomy, gastro-jejunostomy, or cecostomy (or other colonic) tube, from a percutaneous approach including image documentation and report

(Do not report 49465 in conjunction with 49450-49460)

Repair

Hernioplasty, Herniorrhaphy, Herniotomy

The hernia repair codes in this section are categorized primarily by the type of hernia (inguinal, femoral, incisional, etc.).

Some types of hernias are further categorized as "initial" or "recurrent" based on whether or not the hernia has required previous repair(s).

Additional variables accounted for by some of the codes include patient age and clinical presentation (reducible vs. incarcerated or strangulated).

With the exception of the incisional hernia repairs (see 49560-49566) the use of mesh or other prostheses is not separately reported.

The excision/repair of strangulated organs or structures such as testicle(s), intestine, ovaries are reported by using the appropriate code for the excision/repair (eg, 44120, 54520, and 58940) in addition to the appropriate code for the repair of the strangulated hernia.

(For reduction and repair of intra-abdominal hernia, use 44050)

(For debridement of abdominal wall, see 11042, 11043)

(Codes 49491-49651 are unilateral procedures. To report bilateral procedure, report modifier 50 with the appropriate procedure code)

49491 Repair, initial inguinal hernia, preterm infant (younger than 37 weeks gestation at birth), performed from birth up to 50 weeks postconception age, with or without hydrocelectomy; reducible

49492   incarcerated or strangulated

(Do not report modifier 63 in conjunction with 49491, 49492)

(Postconception age equals gestational age at birth plus age of infant in weeks at the time of the hernia repair. Initial inguinal hernia repairs that are performed on preterm infants who are older than 50 weeks postconception age and younger than age 6 months at the time of surgery, should be reported using codes 49495, 49496)

49495 Repair, initial inguinal hernia, full term infant younger than age 6 months, or preterm infant older than 50 weeks postconception age and younger than age 6 months at the time of surgery, with or without hydrocelectomy; reducible

49496   incarcerated or strangulated

(Do not report modifier 63 in conjunction with 49495, 49496)

(Postconception age equals gestational age at birth plus age in weeks at the time of the hernia repair. Initial inguinal hernia repairs that are performed on preterm infants who are younger than or up to 50 weeks postconception age but younger than 6 months of age since birth, should be reported using codes 49491, 49492. Inguinal hernia repairs on infants age 6 months to younger than 5 years should be reported using codes 49500-49501)

49500   Repair initial inguinal hernia, age 6 months to younger than 5 years, with or without hydrocelectomy; reducible

49501   incarcerated or strangulated

49505   Repair initial inguinal hernia, age 5 years or older; reducible

49507   incarcerated or strangulated

(For inguinal hernia repair, with simple orchiectomy, see 49505 or 49507 and 54520)

(For inguinal hernia repair, with excision of hydrocele or spermatocele, see 49505 or 49507 and 54840 or 55040)

49520   Repair recurrent inguinal hernia, any age; reducible

49521   incarcerated or strangulated

49525   Repair inguinal hernia, sliding, any age

(For incarcerated or strangulated inguinal hernia repair, see 49496, 49501, 49507, 49521)

49540   Repair lumbar hernia

49550   Repair initial femoral hernia, any age; reducible

49553   incarcerated or strangulated

49555   Repair recurrent femoral hernia; reducible

49557   incarcerated or strangulated

49560   Repair initial incisional or ventral hernia; reducible

49561   incarcerated or strangulated

49565   Repair recurrent incisional or ventral hernia; reducible

49566   incarcerated or strangulated

+ 49568   Implantation of mesh or other prosthesis for open incisional or ventral hernia repair or mesh for closure of debridement for necrotizing soft tissue infection (List separately in addition to code for the incisional or ventral hernia repair)

(Use 49568 in conjunction with 11004-11006, 49560-49566)

49570   Repair epigastric hernia (eg, preperitoneal fat); reducible (separate procedure)

49572   incarcerated or strangulated

49580   Repair umbilical hernia, younger than age 5 years; reducible

49582   incarcerated or strangulated

49585   Repair umbilical hernia, age 5 years or older; reducible

49587   incarcerated or strangulated

49590   Repair spigelian hernia

49600   Repair of small omphalocele, with primary closure

(Do not report modifier 63 in conjunction with 49600)

49605   Repair of large omphalocele or gastroschisis; with or without prosthesis

49606   with removal of prosthesis, final reduction and closure, in operating room

(Do not report modifier 63 in conjunction with 49605, 49606)

49610   Repair of omphalocele (Gross type operation); first stage

49611   second stage

(Do not report modifier 63 in conjunction with 49610, 49611)

(For diaphragmatic or hiatal hernia repair, see 39502-39541)

(For surgical repair of omentum, use 49999)

Laparoscopy

Surgical laparoscopy always includes diagnostic laparoscopy. To report a diagnostic laparoscopy (peritoneoscopy) (separate procedure), use 49320.

49650   Laparoscopy, surgical; repair initial inguinal hernia

49651   repair recurrent inguinal hernia

49652   Laparoscopy, surgical, repair, ventral, umbilical, spigelian or epigastric hernia (includes mesh insertion, when performed); reducible

(Do not report 49652 in conjunction with 44180, 49568)

49653   incarcerated or strangulated

(Do not report 49653 in conjunction with 44180, 49568)

49654   Laparoscopy, surgical, repair, incisional hernia (includes mesh insertion, when performed); reducible

(Do not report 49654 in conjunction with 44180, 49568)

49655   incarcerated or strangulated

(Do not report 49655 in conjunction with 44180, 49568)

49656   Laparoscopy, surgical, repair, recurrent incisional hernia (includes mesh insertion, when performed); reducible

(Do not report 49656 in conjunction with 44180, 49568)

49657   incarcerated or strangulated

(Do not report 49657 in conjunction with 44180, 49568)

49659   Unlisted laparoscopy procedure, hernioplasty, herniorrhaphy, herniotomy

Surgery: Digestive System

Suture

49900   Suture, secondary, of abdominal wall for evisceration or dehiscence

(For suture of ruptured diaphragm, see 39540, 39541)

(For debridement of abdominal wall, see 11042, 11043)

Other Procedures

49904   Omental flap, extra-abdominal (eg, for reconstruction of sternal and chest wall defects)

(Code 49904 includes harvest and transfer. If a second surgeon harvests the omental flap, then the 2 surgeons should code 49904 as co-surgeons, using modifier 62)

+ 49905   Omental flap, intra-abdominal (List separately in addition to code for primary procedure)

(Do not report 49905 in conjunction with 44700)

49906   Free omental flap with microvascular anastomosis

(Do not report code 69990 in addition to 49906)

49999   Unlisted procedure, abdomen, peritoneum and omentum

Surgery: Digestive System

Urinary System

(For provision of chemotherapeutic agents, report both the specific service in addition to code(s) for the specific substance(s) or drug(s) provided)

Kidney

Incision

(For retroperitoneal exploration, abscess, tumor, or cyst, see 49010, 49060, 49203-49205)

50010   Renal exploration, not necessitating other specific procedures

(For laparoscopic ablation of renal mass lesion(s), use 50542)

50020   Drainage of perirenal or renal abscess; open

⊙ **50021**   percutaneous

(For radiological supervision and interpretation, use 75989)

50040   Nephrostomy, nephrotomy with drainage

50045   Nephrotomy, with exploration

(For renal endoscopy performed in conjunction with this procedure, see 50570-50580)

50060   Nephrolithotomy; removal of calculus

50065   secondary surgical operation for calculus

50070   complicated by congenital kidney abnormality

50075   removal of large staghorn calculus filling renal pelvis and calyces (including anatrophic pyelolithotomy)

50080   Percutaneous nephrostolithotomy or pyelostolithotomy, with or without dilation, endoscopy, lithotripsy, stenting, or basket extraction; up to 2 cm

50081   over 2 cm

(For establishment of nephrostomy without nephrostolithotomy, see 50040, 50395, 52334)

(For fluoroscopic guidance, see 76000, 76001)

50100   Transection or repositioning of aberrant renal vessels (separate procedure)

50120   Pyelotomy; with exploration

(For renal endoscopy performed in conjunction with this procedure, see 50570-50580)

50125   with drainage, pyelostomy

50130   with removal of calculus (pyelolithotomy, pelviolithotomy, including coagulum pyelolithotomy)

50135   complicated (eg, secondary operation, congenital kidney abnormality)

(For supply of anticarcinogenic agents, use 99070 in addition to code for primary procedure)

Excision

(For excision of retroperitoneal tumor or cyst, see 49203-49205)

(For laparoscopic ablation of renal mass lesion(s), use 50542)

⊙▲ **50200**   Renal biopsy; percutaneous, by trocar or needle

(For radiological supervision and interpretation, see 76942, 77002, 77012, 77021)

(For fine needle aspiration, use 10022)

(For evaluation of fine needle aspirate, see 88172, 88173)

50205   by surgical exposure of kidney

50220   Nephrectomy, including partial ureterectomy, any open approach including rib resection;

50225   complicated because of previous surgery on same kidney

50230   radical, with regional lymphadenectomy and/or vena caval thrombectomy

(When vena caval resection with reconstruction is necessary, use 37799)

50234   Nephrectomy with total ureterectomy and bladder cuff; through same incision

50236   through separate incision

50240   Nephrectomy, partial

(For laparoscopic partial nephrectomy, use 50543)

50250   Ablation, open, 1 or more renal mass lesion(s), cryosurgical, including intraoperative ultrasound, if performed

(For laparoscopic ablation of renal mass lesions, use 50542)

(For cryoablation of renal tumors, use 50593)

50280   Excision or unroofing of cyst(s) of kidney

(For laparoscopic ablation of renal cysts, use 50541)

50290   Excision of perinephric cyst

Renal Transplantation

Renal *auto*transplantation includes reimplantation of the autograft as the primary procedure, along with secondary extra-corporeal procedure(s) (eg, partial nephrectomy, nephrolithotomy) reported with modifier 51 (see 50380 and applicable secondary procedure(s)).

Renal *allo*transplantation involves three distinct components of physician work:

1. ***Cadaver donor nephrectomy, unilateral or bilateral***, which includes harvesting the graft(s) and cold preservation of the graft(s) (perfusing with cold preservation solution and cold maintenance) (use 50300). ***Living donor nephrectomy***, which includes harvesting the graft, cold preservation of the graft

Surgery: Urinary System

(perfusing with cold preservation solution and cold maintenance), and care of the donor (see 50320, 50547).

2. *Backbench work*:

Standard preparation of a cadaver donor renal allograft prior to transplantation including dissection and removal of perinephric fat, diaphragmatic and retroperitoneal attachments; excision of adrenal gland; and preparation of ureter(s), renal vein(s), and renal artery(s), ligating branches, as necessary (use 50323).

Standard preparation of a living donor renal allograft (open or laparoscopic) prior to transplantation including dissection and removal of perinephric fat and preparation of ureter(s), renal vein(s), and renal artery(s), ligating branches, as necessary (use 50325).

Additional reconstruction of a cadaver or living donor renal allograft prior to transplantation may include venous, arterial, and/or ureteral anastomosis(es) necessary for implantation (see 50327-50329).

3. *Recipient renal allotransplantation*, which includes transplantation of the allograft (with or without recipient nephrectomy) and care of the recipient (see 50360, 50365).

(For dialysis, see 90935-90999)

(For laparoscopic donor nephrectomy, use 50547)

(For laparoscopic drainage of lymphocele to peritoneal cavity, use 49323)

50300   Donor nephrectomy (including cold preservation); from cadaver donor, unilateral or bilateral

50320   open, from living donor

50323   Backbench standard preparation of cadaver donor renal allograft prior to transplantation, including dissection and removal of perinephric fat, diaphragmatic and retroperitoneal attachments, excision of adrenal gland, and preparation of ureter(s), renal vein(s), and renal artery(s), ligating branches, as necessary

(Do not report 50323 in conjunction with 60540, 60545)

50325   Backbench standard preparation of living donor renal allograft (open or laparoscopic) prior to transplantation, including dissection and removal of perinephric fat and preparation of ureter(s), renal vein(s), and renal artery(s), ligating branches, as necessary

50327   Backbench reconstruction of cadaver or living donor renal allograft prior to transplantation; venous anastomosis, each

50328   arterial anastomosis, each

50329   ureteral anastomosis, each

50340   Recipient nephrectomy (separate procedure)

(For bilateral procedure, report 50340 with modifier 50)

50360   Renal allotransplantation, implantation of graft; without recipient nephrectomy

50365   with recipient nephrectomy

(For bilateral procedure, report 50365 with modifier 50)

50370   Removal of transplanted renal allograft

50380   Renal autotransplantation, reimplantation of kidney

(For renal autotransplantation extra-corporeal [bench] surgery, use autotransplantation as the primary procedure and report secondary procedure[s] [eg, partial nephrectomy, nephrolithotomy] with modifier 51)

Introduction

Renal Pelvis Catheter Procedures

Internally Dwelling

⊙ 50382   Removal (via snare/capture) and replacement of internally dwelling ureteral stent via percutaneous approach, including radiological supervision and interpretation

(For bilateral procedure, use modifier 50)

(For removal and replacement of an internally dwelling ureteral stent via a transurethral approach, use 50385)

⊙ 50384   Removal (via snare/capture) of internally dwelling ureteral stent via percutaneous approach, including radiological supervision and interpretation

(For bilateral procedure, use modifier 50)

(Do not report 50382, 50384 in conjunction with 50395)

(For removal of an internally dwelling ureteral stent via a transurethral approach, use 50386)

⊙ 50385   Removal (via snare/capture) and replacement of internally dwelling ureteral stent via transurethral approach, without use of cystoscopy, including radiological supervision and interpretation

⊙ 50386   Removal (via snare/capture) of internally dwelling ureteral stent via transurethral approach, without use of cystoscopy, including radiological supervision and interpretation

Externally Accessible

⊙ 50387   Removal and replacement of externally accessible transnephric ureteral stent (eg, external/internal stent) requiring fluoroscopic guidance, including radiological supervision and interpretation

(For bilateral procedure, use modifier 50)

(For removal and replacement of externally accessible ureteral stent via ureterostomy or ilieal conduit, use 50688)

(For removal without replacement of an externally accessible ureteral stent not requiring fluoroscopic guidance, see **Evaluation and Management** services codes)

50389 Removal of nephrostomy tube, requiring fluoroscopic guidance (eg, with concurrent indwelling ureteral stent)

(Removal of nephrostomy tube not requiring fluoroscopic guidance is considered inherent to E/M services. Report the appropriate level of E/M service provided)

Other Introduction Procedures

50390 Aspiration and/or injection of renal cyst or pelvis by needle, percutaneous

(For radiological supervision and interpretation, see 74425, 74470, 76942, 77002, 77012, 77021)

(For evaluation of fine needle aspirate, see 88172, 88173)

50391 Instillation(s) of therapeutic agent into renal pelvis and/or ureter through established nephrostomy, pyelostomy or ureterostomy tube (eg, anticarcinogenic or antifungal agent)

50392 Introduction of intracatheter or catheter into renal pelvis for drainage and/or injection, percutaneous

(For radiological supervision and interpretation, see 74475, 76942, 77012)

50393 Introduction of ureteral catheter or stent into ureter through renal pelvis for drainage and/or injection, percutaneous

(For radiological supervision and interpretation, see 74480, 76942, 77002, 77012)

50394 Injection procedure for pyelography (as nephrostogram, pyelostogram, antegrade pyeloureterograms) through nephrostomy or pyelostomy tube, or indwelling ureteral catheter

(For radiological supervision and interpretation, use 74425)

50395 Introduction of guide into renal pelvis and/or ureter with dilation to establish nephrostomy tract, percutaneous

(For radiological supervision and interpretation, see 74475, 74480, 74485)

(For nephrostolithotomy, see 50080, 50081)

(For retrograde percutaneous nephrostomy, use 52334)

(For endoscopic surgery, see 50551-50561)

50396 Manometric studies through nephrostomy or pyelostomy tube, or indwelling ureteral catheter

(For radiological supervision and interpretation, see 74425, 74475, 74480)

50398 Change of nephrostomy or pyelostomy tube

(For radiological supervision and interpretation, use 75984)

Repair

50400 Pyeloplasty (Foley Y-pyeloplasty), plastic operation on renal pelvis, with or without plastic operation on ureter, nephropexy, nephrostomy, pyelostomy, or ureteral splinting; simple

50405 complicated (congenital kidney abnormality, secondary pyeloplasty, solitary kidney, calycoplasty)

(For laparoscopic approach, use 50544)

50500 Nephrorrhaphy, suture of kidney wound or injury

50520 Closure of nephrocutaneous or pyelocutaneous fistula

50525 Closure of nephrovisceral fistula (eg, renocolic), including visceral repair; abdominal approach

50526 thoracic approach

50540 Symphysiotomy for horseshoe kidney with or without pyeloplasty and/or other plastic procedure, unilateral or bilateral (1 operation)

Laparoscopy

Surgical laparoscopy always includes diagnostic laparoscopy. To report a diagnostic laparoscopy (peritoneoscopy) (separate procedure), use 49320.

50541 Laparoscopy, surgical; ablation of renal cysts

50542 ablation of renal mass lesion(s)

(For open procedure, see 50220-50240)

(For cryosurgical ablation, see 50250, 50593)

50543 partial nephrectomy

(For open procedure, use 50240)

50544 pyeloplasty

50545 radical nephrectomy (includes removal of Gerota's fascia and surrounding fatty tissue, removal of regional lymph nodes, and adrenalectomy)

(For open procedure, use 50230)

50546 nephrectomy, including partial ureterectomy

50547 donor nephrectomy (including cold preservation), from living donor

(For open procedure, use 50320)

(For backbench renal allograft standard preparation prior to transplantation, use 50325)

(For backbench renal allograft reconstruction prior to transplantation, see 50327-50329)

50548 nephrectomy with total ureterectomy

(For open procedure, see 50234, 50236)

50549 Unlisted laparoscopy procedure, renal

(For laparoscopic drainage of lymphocele to peritoneal cavity, use 49323)

Endoscopy

(For supplies and materials, use 99070)

50551 Renal endoscopy through established nephrostomy or pyelostomy, with or without irrigation, instillation, or ureteropyelography, exclusive of radiologic service;

50553 with ureteral catheterization, with or without dilation of ureter

50555 with biopsy

50557 with fulguration and/or incision, with or without biopsy

50561 with removal of foreign body or calculus

50562 with resection of tumor

(When procedures 50570-50580 provide a significant identifiable service, they may be added to 50045 and 50120)

50570 Renal endoscopy through nephrotomy or pyelotomy, with or without irrigation, instillation, or ureteropyelography, exclusive of radiologic service;

(For nephrotomy, use 50045)

(For pyelotomy, use 50120)

50572 with ureteral catheterization, with or without dilation of ureter

50574 with biopsy

50575 with endopyelotomy (includes cystoscopy, ureteroscopy, dilation of ureter and ureteral pelvic junction, incision of ureteral pelvic junction and insertion of endopyelotomy stent)

50576 with fulguration and/or incision, with or without biopsy

50580 with removal of foreign body or calculus

Other Procedures

50590 Lithotripsy, extracorporeal shock wave

⊙ **50592** Ablation, 1 or more renal tumor(s), percutaneous, unilateral, radiofrequency

(50592 is a unilateral procedure. For bilateral procedure, report 50592 with modifier 50)

(For imaging guidance and monitoring, see 76940, 77013, 77022)

⊙ **50593** Ablation, renal tumor(s), unilateral, percutaneous, cryotherapy

(50593 is a unilateral procedure. For bilateral procedure, report 50593 with modifier 50)

(For imaging guidance and monitoring, see codes 76940, 77013, 77022)

Ureter

Incision

50600 Ureterotomy with exploration or drainage (separate procedure)

(For ureteral endoscopy performed in conjunction with this procedure, see 50970-50980)

50605 Ureterotomy for insertion of indwelling stent, all types

50610 Ureterolithotomy; upper one-third of ureter

50620 middle one-third of ureter

50630 lower one-third of ureter

(For laparoscopic approach, use 50945)

(For transvesical ureterolithotomy, use 51060)

(For cystotomy with stone basket extraction of ureteral calculus, use 51065)

(For endoscopic extraction or manipulation of ureteral calculus, see 50080, 50081, 50561, 50961, 50980, 52320-52330, 52352, 52353)

Excision

(For ureterocele, see 51535, 52300)

50650 Ureterectomy, with bladder cuff (separate procedure)

50660 Ureterectomy, total, ectopic ureter, combination abdominal, vaginal and/or perineal approach

Introduction

50684 Injection procedure for ureterography or ureteropyelography through ureterostomy or indwelling ureteral catheter

(For radiological supervision and interpretation, use 74425)

50686 Manometric studies through ureterostomy or indwelling ureteral catheter

50688 Change of ureterostomy tube or externally accessible ureteral stent via ileal conduit

(If imaging guidance is performed, use 75984)

50690 Injection procedure for visualization of ileal conduit and/or ureteropyelography, exclusive of radiologic service

(For radiological supervision and interpretation, use 74425)

Repair

50700 Ureteroplasty, plastic operation on ureter (eg, stricture)

50715 Ureterolysis, with or without repositioning of ureter for retroperitoneal fibrosis

(For bilateral procedure, report 50715 with modifier 50)

50722 Ureterolysis for ovarian vein syndrome

50725 Ureterolysis for retrocaval ureter, with reanastomosis of upper urinary tract or vena cava

50727 Revision of urinary-cutaneous anastomosis (any type urostomy);

50728   with repair of fascial defect and hernia

50740 Ureteropyelostomy, anastomosis of ureter and renal pelvis

50750 Ureterocalycostomy, anastomosis of ureter to renal calyx

50760 Ureteroureterostomy

50770 Transureteroureterostomy, anastomosis of ureter to contralateral ureter

(Codes 50780-50785 include minor procedures to prevent vesicoureteral reflux)

50780 Ureteroneocystostomy; anastomosis of single ureter to bladder

(For bilateral procedure, report 50780 with modifier 50)

(When combined with cystourethroplasty or vesical neck revision, use 51820)

50782   anastomosis of duplicated ureter to bladder

50783   with extensive ureteral tailoring

50785   with vesico-psoas hitch or bladder flap

(For bilateral procedure, report 50785 with modifier 50)

50800 Ureteroenterostomy, direct anastomosis of ureter to intestine

(For bilateral procedure, report 50800 with modifier 50)

50810 Ureterosigmoidostomy, with creation of sigmoid bladder and establishment of abdominal or perineal colostomy, including intestine anastomosis

50815 Ureterocolon conduit, including intestine anastomosis

(For bilateral procedure, report 50815 with modifier 50)

50820 Ureteroileal conduit (ileal bladder), including intestine anastomosis (Bricker operation)

(For bilateral procedure, report 50820 with modifier 50)

(For combination of 50800-50820 with cystectomy, see 51580-51595)

50825 Continent diversion, including intestine anastomosis using any segment of small and/or large intestine (Kock pouch or Camey enterocystoplasty)

50830 Urinary undiversion (eg, taking down of ureteroileal conduit, ureterosigmoidostomy or ureteroenterostomy with ureteroureterostomy or ureteroneocystostomy)

50840 Replacement of all or part of ureter by intestine segment, including intestine anastomosis

(For bilateral procedure, report 50840 with modifier 50)

50845 Cutaneous appendico-vesicostomy

50860 Ureterostomy, transplantation of ureter to skin

(For bilateral procedure, report 50860 with modifier 50)

50900 Ureterorrhaphy, suture of ureter (separate procedure)

50920 Closure of ureterocutaneous fistula

50930 Closure of ureterovisceral fistula (including visceral repair)

50940 Deligation of ureter

(For ureteroplasty, ureterolysis, see 50700-50860)

Laparoscopy

Surgical laparoscopy always includes diagnostic laparoscopy. To report a diagnostic laparoscopy (peritoneoscopy) (separate procedure), use 49320.

50945 Laparoscopy, surgical; ureterolithotomy

50947   ureteroneocystostomy with cystoscopy and ureteral stent placement

50948   ureteroneocystostomy without cystoscopy and ureteral stent placement

(For open ureteroneocystostomy, see 50780-50785)

50949 Unlisted laparoscopy procedure, ureter

Endoscopy

50951 Ureteral endoscopy through established ureterostomy, with or without irrigation, instillation, or ureteropyelography, exclusive of radiologic service;

50953   with ureteral catheterization, with or without dilation of ureter

50955   with biopsy

50957   with fulguration and/or incision, with or without biopsy

50961   with removal of foreign body or calculus

(When procedures 50970-50980 provide a significant identifiable service, they may be added to 50600)

50970 Ureteral endoscopy through ureterotomy, with or without irrigation, instillation, or ureteropyelography, exclusive of radiologic service;

(For ureterotomy, use 50600)

50972   with ureteral catheterization, with or without dilation of ureter

50974   with biopsy

50976   with fulguration and/or incision, with or without biopsy

50980   with removal of foreign body or calculus

Surgery: Urinary System

Bladder

Incision

(51000 has been deleted. To report, use 51100)

(51005 has been deleted. To report, use 51101)

(51010 has been deleted. To report, use 51102)

51020 Cystotomy or cystostomy; with fulguration and/or insertion of radioactive material

51030 with cryosurgical destruction of intravesical lesion

51040 Cystostomy, cystotomy with drainage

51045 Cystotomy, with insertion of ureteral catheter or stent (separate procedure)

51050 Cystolithotomy, cystotomy with removal of calculus, without vesical neck resection

51060 Transvesical ureterolithotomy

51065 Cystotomy, with calculus basket extraction and/or ultrasonic or electrohydraulic fragmentation of ureteral calculus

51080 Drainage of perivesical or prevesical space abscess

Removal

51100 Aspiration of bladder; by needle

51101 by trocar or intracatheter

51102 with insertion of suprapubic catheter

(For imaging guidance, see 76942, 77002, 77012)

Excision

51500 Excision of urachal cyst or sinus, with or without umbilical hernia repair

51520 Cystotomy; for simple excision of vesical neck (separate procedure)

51525 for excision of bladder diverticulum, single or multiple (separate procedure)

51530 for excision of bladder tumor

(For transurethral resection, see 52234-52240, 52305)

51535 Cystotomy for excision, incision, or repair of ureterocele

(For bilateral procedure, report 51535 with modifier 50)

(For transurethral excision, use 52300)

51550 Cystectomy, partial; simple

51555 complicated (eg, postradiation, previous surgery, difficult location)

51565 Cystectomy, partial, with reimplantation of ureter(s) into bladder (ureteroneocystostomy)

51570 Cystectomy, complete; (separate procedure)

51575 with bilateral pelvic lymphadenectomy, including external iliac, hypogastric, and obturator nodes

51580 Cystectomy, complete, with ureterosigmoidostomy or ureterocutaneous transplantations;

51585 with bilateral pelvic lymphadenectomy, including external iliac, hypogastric, and obturator nodes

51590 Cystectomy, complete, with ureteroileal conduit or sigmoid bladder, including intestine anastomosis;

51595 with bilateral pelvic lymphadenectomy, including external iliac, hypogastric, and obturator nodes

51596 Cystectomy, complete, with continent diversion, any open technique, using any segment of small and/or large intestine to construct neobladder

51597 Pelvic exenteration, complete, for vesical, prostatic or urethral malignancy, with removal of bladder and ureteral transplantations, with or without hysterectomy and/or abdominoperineal resection of rectum and colon and colostomy, or any combination thereof

(For pelvic exenteration for gynecologic malignancy, use 58240)

Introduction

51600 Injection procedure for cystography or voiding urethrocystography

(For radiological supervision and interpretation, see 74430, 74455)

51605 Injection procedure and placement of chain for contrast and/or chain urethrocystography

(For radiological supervision and interpretation, use 74430)

51610 Injection procedure for retrograde urethrocystography

(For radiological supervision and interpretation, use 74450)

51700 Bladder irrigation, simple, lavage and/or instillation

(Codes 51701-51702 are reported only when performed independently. Do not report 51701-51702 when catheter insertion is an inclusive component of another procedure.)

51701 Insertion of non-indwelling bladder catheter (eg, straight catheterization for residual urine)

51702 Insertion of temporary indwelling bladder catheter; simple (eg, Foley)

51703 complicated (eg, altered anatomy, fractured catheter/balloon)

51705 Change of cystostomy tube; simple

51710 complicated

(If imaging guidance is performed, use 75984)

51715 Endoscopic injection of implant material into the submucosal tissues of the urethra and/or bladder neck

51720   Bladder instillation of anticarcinogenic agent (including retention time)

Urodynamics

►The following section (51725-51792) lists procedures that may be used separately or in many and varied combinations.◄

When multiple procedures are performed in the same investigative session, modifier 51 should be employed.

All procedures in this section imply that these services are performed by, or are under the direct supervision of, a physician and that all instruments, equipment, fluids, gases, probes, catheters, technician's fees, medications, gloves, trays, tubing and other sterile supplies be provided by the physician. When the physician only interprets the results and/or operates the equipment, a professional component, modifier 26, should be used to identify physicians' services.

51725   Simple cystometrogram (CMG) (eg, spinal manometer)

▲ **51726**   Complex cystometrogram (ie, calibrated electronic equipment);

● **51727**   with urethral pressure profile studies (ie, urethral closure pressure profile), any technique

● **51728**   with voiding pressure studies (ie, bladder voiding pressure), any technique

● **51729**   with voiding pressure studies (ie, bladder voiding pressure) and urethral pressure profile studies (ie, urethral closure pressure profile), any technique

+▲ **51797**   Voiding pressure studies, intra-abdominal (ie, rectal, gastric, intraperitoneal) (List separately in addition to code for primary procedure)

►(Use 51797 in conjunction with 51728, 51729)◄

51736   Simple uroflowmetry (UFR) (eg, stop-watch flow rate, mechanical uroflowmeter)

51741   Complex uroflowmetry (eg, calibrated electronic equipment)

►(51772 has been deleted. To report urethral pressure profile studies, see 51727, 51729)◄

51784   Electromyography studies (EMG) of anal or urethral sphincter, other than needle, any technique

51785   Needle electromyography studies (EMG) of anal or urethral sphincter, any technique

51792   Stimulus evoked response (eg, measurement of bulbocavernosus reflex latency time)

►(51795 has been deleted. To report bladder voiding pressure studies, see 51728, 51729)◄

51797   ►Code is out of numerical sequence. See 51725-51798◄

51798   Measurement of post-voiding residual urine and/or bladder capacity by ultrasound, non-imaging

Repair

51800   Cystoplasty or cystourethroplasty, plastic operation on bladder and/or vesical neck (anterior Y-plasty, vesical fundus resection), any procedure, with or without wedge resection of posterior vesical neck

51820   Cystourethroplasty with unilateral or bilateral ureteroneocystostomy

51840   Anterior vesicourethropexy, or urethropexy (eg, Marshall-Marchetti-Krantz, Burch); simple

51841   complicated (eg, secondary repair)

(For urethropexy (Pereyra type), use 57289)

51845   Abdomino-vaginal vesical neck suspension, with or without endoscopic control (eg, Stamey, Raz, modified Pereyra)

51860   Cystorrhaphy, suture of bladder wound, injury or rupture; simple

51865   complicated

51880   Closure of cystostomy (separate procedure)

51900   Closure of vesicovaginal fistula, abdominal approach

(For vaginal approach, see 57320-57330)

51920   Closure of vesicouterine fistula;

51925   with hysterectomy

(For closure of vesicoenteric fistula, see 44660, 44661)

(For closure of rectovesical fistula, see 45800-45805)

51940   Closure, exstrophy of bladder

(See also 54390)

51960   Enterocystoplasty, including intestinal anastomosis

51980   Cutaneous vesicostomy

Laparoscopy

Surgical laparoscopy always includes diagnostic laparoscopy. To report a diagnostic laparoscopy (peritoneoscopy) (separate procedure), use 49320.

51990   Laparoscopy, surgical; urethral suspension for stress incontinence

51992   sling operation for stress incontinence (eg, fascia or synthetic)

(For open sling operation for stress incontinence, use 57288)

(For reversal or removal of sling operation for stress incontinence, use 57287)

51999   Unlisted laparoscopy procedure, bladder

Endoscopy—Cystoscopy, Urethroscopy, Cystourethroscopy

Endoscopic descriptions are listed so that the main procedure can be identified without having to list all the minor related functions performed at the same time. For example: meatotomy, urethral calibration and/or dilation, urethroscopy, and cystoscopy prior to a transurethral resection of prostate; ureteral catheterization following extraction of ureteral calculus; internal urethrotomy and bladder neck fulguration when performing a cystourethroscopy for the female urethral syndrome. When the secondary procedure requires significant additional time and effort, it may be identified by the addition of modifier 22.

For example: urethrotomy performed for a documented pre-existing stricture or bladder neck contracture.

52000 Cystourethroscopy (separate procedure)

52001 Cystourethroscopy with irrigation and evacuation of multiple obstructing clots

(Do not report 52001 in conjunction with 52000)

52005 Cystourethroscopy, with ureteral catheterization, with or without irrigation, instillation, or ureteropyelography, exclusive of radiologic service;

52007   with brush biopsy of ureter and/or renal pelvis

52010 Cystourethroscopy, with ejaculatory duct catheterization, with or without irrigation, instillation, or duct radiography, exclusive of radiologic service

(For radiological supervision and interpretation, use 74440)

Transurethral Surgery

Urethra and Bladder

52204 Cystourethroscopy, with biopsy(s)

52214 Cystourethroscopy, with fulguration (including cryosurgery or laser surgery) of trigone, bladder neck, prostatic fossa, urethra, or periurethral glands

(For transurethral fulguration of prostate tissue performed within the postoperative period of 52601 or 52630 performed by the same physician, append modifier 78)

(For transurethral fulguration of prostate tissue performed within the postoperative period of a related procedure performed by the same physician, append modifier 78)

(For transurethral fulguration of prostate for postoperative bleeding performed by the same physician, append modifier 78)

52224 Cystourethroscopy, with fulguration (including cryosurgery or laser surgery) or treatment of MINOR (less than 0.5 cm) lesion(s) with or without biopsy

52234 Cystourethroscopy, with fulguration (including cryosurgery or laser surgery) and/or resection of; SMALL bladder tumor(s) (0.5 up to 2.0 cm)

52235   MEDIUM bladder tumor(s) (2.0 to 5.0 cm)

52240   LARGE bladder tumor(s)

52250 Cystourethroscopy with insertion of radioactive substance, with or without biopsy or fulguration

52260 Cystourethroscopy, with dilation of bladder for interstitial cystitis; general or conduction (spinal) anesthesia

52265   local anesthesia

52270 Cystourethroscopy, with internal urethrotomy; female

52275   male

52276 Cystourethroscopy with direct vision internal urethrotomy

52277 Cystourethroscopy, with resection of external sphincter (sphincterotomy)

52281 Cystourethroscopy, with calibration and/or dilation of urethral stricture or stenosis, with or without meatotomy, with or without injection procedure for cystography, male or female

▲ **52282** Cystourethroscopy, with insertion of permanent urethral stent

►(For placement of temporary prostatic urethral stent, use 53855)◄

52283 Cystourethroscopy, with steroid injection into stricture

52285 Cystourethroscopy for treatment of the female urethral syndrome with any or all of the following: urethral meatotomy, urethral dilation, internal urethrotomy, lysis of urethrovaginal septal fibrosis, lateral incisions of the bladder neck, and fulguration of polyp(s) of urethra, bladder neck, and/or trigone

52290 Cystourethroscopy; with ureteral meatotomy, unilateral or bilateral

52300   with resection or fulguration of orthotopic ureterocele(s), unilateral or bilateral

52301   with resection or fulguration of ectopic ureterocele(s), unilateral or bilateral

52305   with incision or resection of orifice of bladder diverticulum, single or multiple

52310 Cystourethroscopy, with removal of foreign body, calculus, or ureteral stent from urethra or bladder (separate procedure); simple

52315   complicated

52317 Litholapaxy: crushing or fragmentation of calculus by any means in bladder and removal of fragments; simple or small (less than 2.5 cm)

52318   complicated or large (over 2.5 cm)

Ureter and Pelvis

Therapeutic cystourethroscopy always includes diagnostic cystourethroscopy. To report a diagnostic cystourethroscopy, use 52000. Therapeutic cystourethroscopy with ureteroscopy and/or pyeloscopy always includes diagnostic cystourethroscopy with ureteroscopy and/or pyeloscopy. To report a diagnostic cystourethroscopy with ureteroscopy and/or pyeloscopy, use 52351.

Do not report 52000 in conjunction with 52320-52343.

Do not report 52351 in conjunction with 52344-52346, 52352-52355.

The insertion and removal of a temporary ureteral catheter (52005) during diagnostic or therapeutic cystourethroscopic with ureteroscopy and/or pyeloscopy is included in 52320-52355 and should not be reported separately.

To report insertion of a self-retaining, indwelling stent performed during diagnostic or therapeutic cystourethroscopy with ureteroscopy and/or pyeloscopy, report 52332, in addition to primary procedure(s) performed (52320-52355), and append modifier 51. 52332 is used to report a unilateral procedure unless otherwise specified.

For bilateral insertion of self-retaining, indwelling ureteral stents, use code 52332, and append modifier 50.

To report cystourethroscopic removal of a self-retaining, indwelling ureteral stent, see 52310, 52315, and append modifier 58, if appropriate.

52320 Cystourethroscopy (including ureteral catheterization); with removal of ureteral calculus

52325   with fragmentation of ureteral calculus (eg, ultrasonic or electro-hydraulic technique)

52327   with subureteric injection of implant material

52330   with manipulation, without removal of ureteral calculus

52332 Cystourethroscopy, with insertion of indwelling ureteral stent (eg, Gibbons or double-J type)

52334 Cystourethroscopy with insertion of ureteral guide wire through kidney to establish a percutaneous nephrostomy, retrograde

(For percutaneous nephrostolithotomy, see 50080, 50081; for establishment of nephrostomy tract only, use 50395)

(For cystourethroscopy, with ureteroscopy and/or pyeloscopy, see 52351-52355)

(For cystourethroscopy with incision, fulguration, or resection of congenital posterior urethral valves or obstructive hypertrophic mucosal folds, use 52400)

52341 Cystourethroscopy; with treatment of ureteral stricture (eg, balloon dilation, laser, electrocautery, and incision)

52342   with treatment of ureteropelvic junction stricture (eg, balloon dilation, laser, electrocautery, and incision)

52343   with treatment of intra-renal stricture (eg, balloon dilation, laser, electrocautery, and incision)

52344 Cystourethroscopy with ureteroscopy; with treatment of ureteral stricture (eg, balloon dilation, laser, electrocautery, and incision)

52345   with treatment of ureteropelvic junction stricture (eg, balloon dilation, laser, electrocautery, and incision)

52346   with treatment of intra-renal stricture (eg, balloon dilation, laser, electrocautery, and incision)

(For transurethral resection or incision of ejaculatory ducts, use 52402)

52351 Cystourethroscopy, with ureteroscopy and/or pyeloscopy; diagnostic

(For radiological supervision and interpretation, use 74485)

(Do not report 52351 in conjunction with 52341-52346, 52352-52355)

52352   with removal or manipulation of calculus (ureteral catheterization is included)

52353   with lithotripsy (ureteral catheterization is included)

52354   with biopsy and/or fulguration of ureteral or renal pelvic lesion

52355   with resection of ureteral or renal pelvic tumor

Vesical Neck and Prostate

52400 Cystourethroscopy with incision, fulguration, or resection of congenital posterior urethral valves, or congenital obstructive hypertrophic mucosal folds

52402 Cystourethroscopy with transurethral resection or incision of ejaculatory ducts

52450 Transurethral incision of prostate

52500 Transurethral resection of bladder neck (separate procedure)

(52510 has been deleted)

52601 Transurethral electrosurgical resection of prostate, including control of postoperative bleeding, complete (vasectomy, meatotomy, cystourethroscopy, urethral calibration and/or dilation, and internal urethrotomy are included)

(For other approaches, see 55801-55845)

(52606 has been deleted. For transurethral fulguration of prostate, use 52214)

(52612, 52614, 52620 have been deleted. For first stage transurethral partial resection of prostate, use 52601. For second stage partial resection of prostate, use 52601 with modifier 58. For transurethral resection of residual or regrowth of obstructive prostate tissue, use 52630)

Surgery: Urinary System

52630 Transurethral resection; residual or regrowth of obstructive prostate tissue including control of postoperative bleeding, complete (vasectomy, meatotomy, cystourethroscopy, urethral calibration and/or dilation, and internal urethrotomy are included)

(For resection of residual prostate tissue performed within the postoperative period of a related procedure performed by the same physician, append modifier 78)

52640 of postoperative bladder neck contracture

52647 Laser coagulation of prostate, including control of postoperative bleeding, complete (vasectomy, meatotomy, cystourethroscopy, urethral calibration and/or dilation, and internal urethrotomy are included if performed)

52648 Laser vaporization of prostate, including control of postoperative bleeding, complete (vasectomy, meatotomy, cystourethroscopy, urethral calibration and/or dilation, internal urethrotomy and transurethral resection of prostate are included if performed)

52649 Laser enucleation of the prostate with morcellation, including control of postoperative bleeding, complete (vasectomy, meatotomy, cystourethroscopy, urethral calibration and/or dilation, internal urethrotomy and transurethral resection of prostate are included if performed)

(Do not report 52649 in conjunction with 52000, 52276, 52281, 52601, 52647, 52648, 53020, 55250)

52700 Transurethral drainage of prostatic abscess

(For litholapaxy, use 52317, 52318)

Urethra

(For endoscopy, see cystoscopy, urethroscopy, cystourethroscopy, 52000-52700)

(For injection procedure for urethrocystography, see 51600-51610)

Incision

53000 Urethrotomy or urethrostomy, external (separate procedure); pendulous urethra

53010 perineal urethra, external

53020 Meatotomy, cutting of meatus (separate procedure); except infant

53025 infant

(Do not report modifier 63 in conjunction with 53025)

53040 Drainage of deep periurethral abscess

(For subcutaneous abscess, see 10060, 10061)

53060 Drainage of Skene's gland abscess or cyst

53080 Drainage of perineal urinary extravasation; uncomplicated (separate procedure)

53085 complicated

Excision

53200 Biopsy of urethra

53210 Urethrectomy, total, including cystostomy; female

53215 male

53220 Excision or fulguration of carcinoma of urethra

53230 Excision of urethral diverticulum (separate procedure); female

53235 male

53240 Marsupialization of urethral diverticulum, male or female

53250 Excision of bulbourethral gland (Cowper's gland)

53260 Excision or fulguration; urethral polyp(s), distal urethra

(For endoscopic approach, see 52214, 52224)

53265 urethral caruncle

53270 Skene's glands

53275 urethral prolapse

Repair

(For hypospadias, see 54300-54352)

53400 Urethroplasty; first stage, for fistula, diverticulum, or stricture (eg, Johannsen type)

53405 second stage (formation of urethra), including urinary diversion

53410 Urethroplasty, 1-stage reconstruction of male anterior urethra

53415 Urethroplasty, transpubic or perineal, 1-stage, for reconstruction or repair of prostatic or membranous urethra

53420 Urethroplasty, 2-stage reconstruction or repair of prostatic or membranous urethra; first stage

53425 second stage

53430 Urethroplasty, reconstruction of female urethra

53431 Urethroplasty with tubularization of posterior urethra and/or lower bladder for incontinence (eg, Tenago, Leadbetter procedure)

53440 Sling operation for correction of male urinary incontinence (eg, fascia or synthetic)

53442 Removal or revision of sling for male urinary incontinence (eg, fascia or synthetic)

53444 Insertion of tandem cuff (dual cuff)

53445 Insertion of inflatable urethral/bladder neck sphincter, including placement of pump, reservoir, and cuff

53446 Removal of inflatable urethral/bladder neck sphincter, including pump, reservoir, and cuff

53447 Removal and replacement of inflatable urethral/bladder neck sphincter including pump, reservoir, and cuff at the same operative session

53448 Removal and replacement of inflatable urethral/bladder neck sphincter including pump, reservoir, and cuff through an infected field at the same operative session including irrigation and debridement of infected tissue

(Do not report 11040-11043 in addition to 53448)

53449 Repair of inflatable urethral/bladder neck sphincter, including pump, reservoir, and cuff

53450 Urethromeatoplasty, with mucosal advancement

(For meatotomy, see 53020, 53025)

53460 Urethromeatoplasty, with partial excision of distal urethral segment (Richardson type procedure)

53500 Urethrolysis, transvaginal, secondary, open, including cystourethroscopy (eg, postsurgical obstruction, scarring)

(For urethrolysis by retropubic approach, use 53899)

(Do not report 53500 in conjunction with 52000)

53502 Urethrorrhaphy, suture of urethral wound or injury, female

53505 Urethrorrhaphy, suture of urethral wound or injury; penile

53510   perineal

53515   prostatomembranous

53520 Closure of urethrostomy or urethrocutaneous fistula, male (separate procedure)

(For closure of urethrovaginal fistula, use 57310)

(For closure of urethrorectal fistula, see 45820, 45825)

Manipulation

(For radiological supervision and interpretation, use 74485)

53600 Dilation of urethral stricture by passage of sound or urethral dilator, male; initial

53601   subsequent

53605 Dilation of urethral stricture or vesical neck by passage of sound or urethral dilator, male, general or conduction (spinal) anesthesia

(For dilation of urethral stricture, male, performed under local anesthesia, see 53600, 53601, 53620, 53621)

53620 Dilation of urethral stricture by passage of filiform and follower, male; initial

53621   subsequent

53660 Dilation of female urethra including suppository and/or instillation; initial

53661   subsequent

53665 Dilation of female urethra, general or conduction (spinal) anesthesia

(For urethral catheterization, see 51701-51703)

(For dilation of urethra performed under local anesthesia, female, see 53660, 53661)

Other Procedures

(For 2 or 3 glass urinalysis, use 81020)

53850 Transurethral destruction of prostate tissue; by microwave thermotherapy

53852   by radiofrequency thermotherapy

(53853 has been deleted. To report, use 55899)

● **53855** Insertion of a temporary prostatic urethral stent, including urethral measurement

►(For insertion of permanent urethral stent, use 52282)◄

53899 Unlisted procedure, urinary system

Surgery: Urinary System

Notes

⊙=Moderate sedation   +=Add-on code   ✔=FDA approval pending   #=Resequenced code

Male Genital System

Penis

Incision

(For abdominal perineal gangrene debridement, see 11004-11006)

54000   Slitting of prepuce, dorsal or lateral (separate procedure); newborn

(Do not report modifier 63 in conjunction with 54000)

54001   except newborn

54015   Incision and drainage of penis, deep

(For skin and subcutaneous abscess, see 10060-10160)

Destruction

54050   Destruction of lesion(s), penis (eg, condyloma, papilloma, molluscum contagiosum, herpetic vesicle), simple; chemical

54055   electrodesiccation

54056   cryosurgery

54057   laser surgery

54060   surgical excision

54065   Destruction of lesion(s), penis (eg, condyloma, papilloma, molluscum contagiosum, herpetic vesicle), extensive (eg, laser surgery, electrosurgery, cryosurgery, chemosurgery)

(For destruction or excision of other lesions, see **Integumentary System**)

Excision

54100   Biopsy of penis; (separate procedure)

54105   deep structures

54110   Excision of penile plaque (Peyronie disease);

54111   with graft to 5 cm in length

54112   with graft greater than 5 cm in length

54115   Removal foreign body from deep penile tissue (eg, plastic implant)

54120   Amputation of penis; partial

54125   complete

54130   Amputation of penis, radical; with bilateral inguinofemoral lymphadenectomy

54135   in continuity with bilateral pelvic lymphadenectomy, including external iliac, hypogastric and obturator nodes

(For lymphadenectomy (separate procedure), see 38760-38770)

54150   Circumcision, using clamp or other device with regional dorsal penile or ring block

(Do not report modifier 63 in conjunction with 54150)

(Report 54150 with modifier 52 when performed without dorsal penile or ring block)

54160   Circumcision, surgical excision other than clamp, device, or dorsal slit; neonate (28 days of age or less)

(Do not report modifier 63 in conjunction with 54160)

54161   older than 28 days of age

54162   Lysis or excision of penile post-circumcision adhesions

54163   Repair incomplete circumcision

54164   Frenulotomy of penis

(Do not report 54164 with circumcision codes 54150-54161, 54162, 54163)

Introduction

54200   Injection procedure for Peyronie disease;

54205   with surgical exposure of plaque

54220   Irrigation of corpora cavernosa for priapism

54230   Injection procedure for corpora cavernosography

(For radiological supervision and interpretation, use 74445)

54231   Dynamic cavernosometry, including intracavernosal injection of vasoactive drugs (eg, papaverine, phentolamine)

54235   Injection of corpora cavernosa with pharmacologic agent(s) (eg, papaverine, phentolamine)

54240   Penile plethysmography

54250   Nocturnal penile tumescence and/or rigidity test

Repair

(For other urethroplasties, see 53400-53430)

(For penile revascularization, use 37788)

54300   Plastic operation of penis for straightening of chordee (eg, hypospadias), with or without mobilization of urethra

54304   Plastic operation on penis for correction of chordee or for first stage hypospadias repair with or without transplantation of prepuce and/or skin flaps

54308   Urethroplasty for second stage hypospadias repair (including urinary diversion); less than 3 cm

54312   greater than 3 cm

54316   Urethroplasty for second stage hypospadias repair (including urinary diversion) with free skin graft obtained from site other than genitalia

54318   Urethroplasty for third stage hypospadias repair to release penis from scrotum (eg, third stage Cecil repair)

Surgery: Male Genital System

54322 1-stage distal hypospadias repair (with or without chordee or circumcision); with simple meatal advancement (eg, Magpi, V-flap)

54324 with urethroplasty by local skin flaps (eg, flip-flap, prepucial flap)

54326 with urethroplasty by local skin flaps and mobilization of urethra

54328 with extensive dissection to correct chordee and urethroplasty with local skin flaps, skin graft patch, and/or island flap

(For urethroplasty and straightening of chordee, use 54308)

54332 1-stage proximal penile or penoscrotal hypospadias repair requiring extensive dissection to correct chordee and urethroplasty by use of skin graft tube and/or island flap

54336 1-stage perineal hypospadias repair requiring extensive dissection to correct chordee and urethroplasty by use of skin graft tube and/or island flap

54340 Repair of hypospadias complications (ie, fistula, stricture, diverticula); by closure, incision, or excision, simple

54344 requiring mobilization of skin flaps and urethroplasty with flap or patch graft

54348 requiring extensive dissection and urethroplasty with flap, patch or tubed graft (includes urinary diversion)

54352 Repair of hypospadias cripple requiring extensive dissection and excision of previously constructed structures including re-release of chordee and reconstruction of urethra and penis by use of local skin as grafts and island flaps and skin brought in as flaps or grafts

54360 Plastic operation on penis to correct angulation

54380 Plastic operation on penis for epispadias distal to external sphincter;

54385 with incontinence

54390 with exstrophy of bladder

54400 Insertion of penile prosthesis; non-inflatable (semi-rigid)

54401 inflatable (self-contained)

(For removal or replacement of penile prosthesis, see 54415, 54416)

54405 Insertion of multi-component, inflatable penile prosthesis, including placement of pump, cylinders, and reservoir

(For reduced services, report 54405 with modifier 52)

54406 Removal of all components of a multi-component, inflatable penile prosthesis without replacement of prosthesis

(For reduced services, report 54406 with modifier 52)

54408 Repair of component(s) of a multi-component, inflatable penile prosthesis

54410 Removal and replacement of all component(s) of a multi-component, inflatable penile prosthesis at the same operative session

54411 Removal and replacement of all components of a multi-component inflatable penile prosthesis through an infected field at the same operative session, including irrigation and debridement of infected tissue

(For reduced services, report 54411 with modifier 52)

(Do not report 11040-11043 in addition to 54411)

54415 Removal of non-inflatable (semi-rigid) or inflatable (self-contained) penile prosthesis, without replacement of prosthesis

54416 Removal and replacement of non-inflatable (semi-rigid) or inflatable (self-contained) penile prosthesis at the same operative session

54417 Removal and replacement of non-inflatable (semi-rigid) or inflatable (self-contained) penile prosthesis through an infected field at the same operative session, including irrigation and debridement of infected tissue

(Do not report 11040-11043 in addition to 54417)

54420 Corpora cavernosa-saphenous vein shunt (priapism operation), unilateral or bilateral

54430 Corpora cavernosa-corpus spongiosum shunt (priapism operation), unilateral or bilateral

54435 Corpora cavernosa-glans penis fistulization (eg, biopsy needle, Winter procedure, rongeur, or punch) for priapism

54440 Plastic operation of penis for injury

Manipulation

54450 Foreskin manipulation including lysis of preputial adhesions and stretching

Testis

Excision

(For abdominal perineal gangrene debridement, see 11004-11006)

54500 Biopsy of testis, needle (separate procedure)

(For fine needle aspiration, see 10021, 10022)

(For evaluation of fine needle aspirate, see 88172, 88173)

54505 Biopsy of testis, incisional (separate procedure)

(For bilateral procedure, report 54505 with modifier 50)

(When combined with vasogram, seminal vesiculogram, or epididymogram, use 55300)

54512 Excision of extraparenchymal lesion of testis

Surgery: Male Genital System

54520   Orchiectomy, simple (including subcapsular), with or without testicular prosthesis, scrotal or inguinal approach

(For bilateral procedure, report 54520 with modifier 50)

54522   Orchiectomy, partial

54530   Orchiectomy, radical, for tumor; inguinal approach

54535   with abdominal exploration

(For orchiectomy with repair of hernia, see 49505 or 49507 and 54520)

(For radical retroperitoneal lymphadenectomy, use 38780)

Exploration

54550   Exploration for undescended testis (inguinal or scrotal area)

(For bilateral procedure, report 54550 with modifier 50)

54560   Exploration for undescended testis with abdominal exploration

(For bilateral procedure, report 54560 with modifier 50)

Repair

54600   Reduction of torsion of testis, surgical, with or without fixation of contralateral testis

54620   Fixation of contralateral testis (separate procedure)

54640   Orchiopexy, inguinal approach, with or without hernia repair

(For bilateral procedure, report 54640 with modifier 50)

(For inguinal hernia repair performed in conjunction with inguinal orchiopexy, see 49495-49525)

54650   Orchiopexy, abdominal approach, for intra-abdominal testis (eg, Fowler-Stephens)

(For laparoscopic approach, use 54692)

54660   Insertion of testicular prosthesis (separate procedure)

(For bilateral procedure, report 54660 with modifier 50)

54670   Suture or repair of testicular injury

54680   Transplantation of testis(es) to thigh (because of scrotal destruction)

Laparoscopy

Surgical laparoscopy always includes diagnostic laparoscopy. To report a diagnostic laparoscopy (peritoneoscopy) (separate procedure), use 49320.

54690   Laparoscopy, surgical; orchiectomy

54692   orchiopexy for intra-abdominal testis

54699   Unlisted laparoscopy procedure, testis

Epididymis

Incision

54700   Incision and drainage of epididymis, testis and/or scrotal space (eg, abscess or hematoma)

(For debridement of necrotizing soft tissue infection of external genitalia, see 11004-11006)

Excision

54800   Biopsy of epididymis, needle

(For fine needle aspiration, see 10021, 10022)

(For evaluation of fine needle aspirate, see 88172, 88173)

54830   Excision of local lesion of epididymis

54840   Excision of spermatocele, with or without epididymectomy

54860   Epididymectomy; unilateral

54861   bilateral

Exploration

54865   Exploration of epididymis, with or without biopsy

Repair

54900   Epididymovasostomy, anastomosis of epididymis to vas deferens; unilateral

54901   bilateral

(For operating microscope, use 69990)

Tunica Vaginalis

Incision

55000   Puncture aspiration of hydrocele, tunica vaginalis, with or without injection of medication

Excision

55040   Excision of hydrocele; unilateral

55041   bilateral

(With hernia repair, see 49495-49501)

Repair

55060   Repair of tunica vaginalis hydrocele (Bottle type)

Surgery: Male Genital System

Scrotum

Incision

55100 Drainage of scrotal wall abscess

(See also 54700)

(For debridement of necrotizing soft tissue infection of external genitalia, see 11004-11006)

55110 Scrotal exploration

55120 Removal of foreign body in scrotum

Excision

(For excision of local lesion of skin of scrotum, see **Integumentary System**)

55150 Resection of scrotum

Repair

55175 Scrotoplasty; simple

55180   complicated

Vas Deferens

Incision

55200 Vasotomy, cannulization with or without incision of vas, unilateral or bilateral (separate procedure)

Excision

55250 Vasectomy, unilateral or bilateral (separate procedure), including postoperative semen examination(s)

Introduction

55300 Vasotomy for vasograms, seminal vesiculograms, or epididymograms, unilateral or bilateral

(For radiological supervision and interpretation, use 74440)

(When combined with biopsy of testis, see 54505 and use modifier 51)

Repair

55400 Vasovasostomy, vasovasorrhaphy

(For bilateral procedure, report 55400 with modifier 50)

(For operating microscope, use 69990)

Suture

55450 Ligation (percutaneous) of vas deferens, unilateral or bilateral (separate procedure)

Spermatic Cord

Excision

55500 Excision of hydrocele of spermatic cord, unilateral (separate procedure)

55520 Excision of lesion of spermatic cord (separate procedure)

55530 Excision of varicocele or ligation of spermatic veins for varicocele; (separate procedure)

55535   abdominal approach

55540   with hernia repair

Laparoscopy

Surgical laparoscopy always includes diagnostic laparoscopy. To report a diagnostic laparoscopy (peritoneoscopy) (separate procedure), use 49320.

55550 Laparoscopy, surgical, with ligation of spermatic veins for varicocele

55559 Unlisted laparoscopy procedure, spermatic cord

Seminal Vesicles

Incision

55600 Vesiculotomy;

(For bilateral procedure, report 55600 with modifier 50)

55605   complicated

Excision

55650 Vesiculectomy, any approach

(For bilateral procedure, report 55650 with modifier 50)

55680 Excision of Mullerian duct cyst

(For injection procedure, see 52010, 55300)

Prostate

Incision

55700 Biopsy, prostate; needle or punch, single or multiple, any approach

(If imaging guidance is performed, use 76942)

(For fine needle aspiration, see 10021, 10022)

(For evaluation of fine needle aspirate, see 88172, 88173)

(For transperineal stereotactic template guided saturation prostate biopsies, use 55706)

55705   incisional, any approach

Surgery: Male Genital System

55706   Biopsies, prostate, needle, transperineal, stereotactic template guided saturation sampling, including imaging guidance

       (Do not report 55706 in conjunction with 55700)

55720   Prostatotomy, external drainage of prostatic abscess, any approach; simple

55725   complicated

       (For transurethral drainage, use 52700)

Excision

       (For transurethral removal of prostate, see 52601-52640)

       (For transurethral destruction of prostate, see 53850-53852)

       (For limited pelvic lymphadenectomy for staging (separate procedure), use 38562)

       (For independent node dissection, see 38770-38780)

55801   Prostatectomy, perineal, subtotal (including control of postoperative bleeding, vasectomy, meatotomy, urethral calibration and/or dilation, and internal urethrotomy)

55810   Prostatectomy, perineal radical;

55812   with lymph node biopsy(s) (limited pelvic lymphadenectomy)

55815   with bilateral pelvic lymphadenectomy, including external iliac, hypogastric and obturator nodes

       (If 55815 is carried out on separate days, use 38770 with modifier 50 and 55810)

55821   Prostatectomy (including control of postoperative bleeding, vasectomy, meatotomy, urethral calibration and/or dilation, and internal urethrotomy); suprapubic, subtotal, 1 or 2 stages

55831   retropubic, subtotal

55840   Prostatectomy, retropubic radical, with or without nerve sparing;

55842   with lymph node biopsy(s) (limited pelvic lymphadenectomy)

55845   with bilateral pelvic lymphadenectomy, including external iliac, hypogastric, and obturator nodes

       (If 55845 is carried out on separate days, use 38770 with modifier 50 and 55840)

       (For laparoscopic retropubic radical prostatectomy, use 55866)

55860   Exposure of prostate, any approach, for insertion of radioactive substance;

       (For application of interstitial radioelement, see 77776-77778)

55862   with lymph node biopsy(s) (limited pelvic lymphadenectomy)

55865   with bilateral pelvic lymphadenectomy, including external iliac, hypogastric and obturator nodes

Laparoscopy

Surgical laparoscopy always includes diagnostic laparoscopy. To report a diagnostic laparoscopy (peritoneoscopy) (separate procedure), use 49320.

55866   Laparoscopy, surgical prostatectomy, retropubic radical, including nerve sparing

       (For open procedure, use 55840)

Other Procedures

       (For artificial insemination, see 58321, 58322)

55870   Electroejaculation

▲ **55873**   Cryosurgical ablation of the prostate (includes ultrasonic guidance and monitoring)

55875   Transperineal placement of needles or catheters into prostate for interstitial radioelement application, with or without cystoscopy

       (For placement of needles or catheters into pelvic organs and/or genitalia [except prostate] for interstitial radioelement application, use 55920)

       (For interstitial radioelement application, see 77776-77787)

       (For ultrasonic guidance for interstitial radioelement application, use 76965)

▲ **55876**   Placement of interstitial device(s) for radiation therapy guidance (eg, fiducial markers, dosimeter), percutaneous, prostate, single or multiple

       (Report supply of device separately)

       (For imaging guidance, see 76942, 77002, 77012, 77021)

55899   Unlisted procedure, male genital system

Reproductive System Procedures

55920   Placement of needles or catheters into pelvic organs and/or genitalia (except prostate) for subsequent interstitial radioelement application

       (For placement of needles or catheters into prostate, use 55875)

       (For insertion of uterine tandems and/or vaginal ovoids for clinical brachytherapy, use 57155)

       (For insertion of Heyman capsules for clinical brachytherapy, use 58346)

Intersex Surgery

55970   Intersex surgery; male to female

55980   female to male

Surgery: Male Genital System

Notes

⊙=Moderate sedation   ✚=Add-on code   ✗=FDA approval pending   #=Resequenced code

Female Genital System

(For pelvic laparotomy, use 49000)

(For excision or destruction of endometriomas, open method, see 49203-49205, 58957, 58958)

(For paracentesis, see 49080, 49081)

(For secondary closure of abdominal wall evisceration or disruption, use 49900)

(For fulguration or excision of lesions, laparoscopic approach, use 58662)

(For chemotherapy, see 96401-96549)

Vulva, Perineum, and Introitus

Definitions

The following definitions apply to the vulvectomy codes (56620-56640):

A *simple* procedure is the removal of skin and superficial subcutaneous tissues.

A *radical* procedure is the removal of skin and deep subcutaneous tissue.

A *partial* procedure is the removal of less than 80% of the vulvar area.

A *complete* procedure is the removal of greater than 80% of the vulvar area.

Incision

(For incision and drainage of sebaceous cyst, furuncle, or abscess, see 10040, 10060, 10061)

56405   Incision and drainage of vulva or perineal abscess

56420   Incision and drainage of Bartholin's gland abscess

(For incision and drainage of Skene's gland abscess or cyst, use 53060)

56440   Marsupialization of Bartholin's gland cyst

56441   Lysis of labial adhesions

56442   Hymenotomy, simple incision

Destruction

56501   Destruction of lesion(s), vulva; simple (eg, laser surgery, electrosurgery, cryosurgery, chemosurgery)

56515   extensive (eg, laser surgery, electrosurgery, cryosurgery, chemosurgery)

(For destruction of Skene's gland cyst or abscess, use 53270)

(For cautery destruction of urethral caruncle, use 53265)

Excision

56605   Biopsy of vulva or perineum (separate procedure); 1 lesion

+ 56606   each separate additional lesion (List separately in addition to code for primary procedure)

(Use 56606 in conjunction with 56605)

(For excision of local lesion, see 11420-11426, 11620-11626)

56620   Vulvectomy simple; partial

56625   complete

(For skin graft, see 15002 et seq)

56630   Vulvectomy, radical, partial;

(For skin graft, if used, see 15004-15005, 15120, 15121, 15240, 15241)

56631   with unilateral inguinofemoral lymphadenectomy

56632   with bilateral inguinofemoral lymphadenectomy

56633   Vulvectomy, radical, complete;

56634   with unilateral inguinofemoral lymphadenectomy

56637   with bilateral inguinofemoral lymphadenectomy

56640   Vulvectomy, radical, complete, with inguinofemoral, iliac, and pelvic lymphadenectomy

(For bilateral procedure, report 56640 with modifier 50)

(For lymphadenectomy, see 38760-38780)

56700   Partial hymenectomy or revision of hymenal ring

56740   Excision of Bartholin's gland or cyst

(For excision of Skene's gland, use 53270)

(For excision of urethral caruncle, use 53265)

(For excision or fulguration of urethral carcinoma, use 53220)

(For excision or marsupialization of urethral diverticulum, see 53230, 53240)

Repair

(For repair of urethra for mucosal prolapse, use 53275)

56800   Plastic repair of introitus

56805   Clitoroplasty for intersex state

56810   Perineoplasty, repair of perineum, nonobstetrical (separate procedure)

(See also 56800)

(For repair of wounds to genitalia, see 12001-12007, 12041-12047, 13131-13133)

(For repair of recent injury of vagina and perineum, nonobstetrical, use 57210)

Surgery: Female Genital System

(For anal sphincteroplasty, see 46750, 46751)

(For episiorrhaphy, episioperineorrhaphy for recent injury of vulva and/or perineum, nonobstetrical, use 57210)

Endoscopy

56820 Colposcopy of the vulva;

56821 with biopsy(s)

(For colposcopic examinations/procedures involving the vagina, see 57420, 57421; cervix, see 57452-57461)

Vagina

Incision

57000 Colpotomy; with exploration

57010 with drainage of pelvic abscess

57020 Colpocentesis (separate procedure)

57022 Incision and drainage of vaginal hematoma; obstetrical/postpartum

57023 non-obstetrical (eg, post-trauma, spontaneous bleeding)

Destruction

57061 Destruction of vaginal lesion(s); simple (eg, laser surgery, electrosurgery, cryosurgery, chemosurgery)

57065 extensive (eg, laser surgery, electrosurgery, cryosurgery, chemosurgery)

Excision

57100 Biopsy of vaginal mucosa; simple (separate procedure)

57105 extensive, requiring suture (including cysts)

57106 Vaginectomy, partial removal of vaginal wall;

57107 with removal of paravaginal tissue (radical vaginectomy)

57109 with removal of paravaginal tissue (radical vaginectomy) with bilateral total pelvic lymphadenectomy and para-aortic lymph node sampling (biopsy)

57110 Vaginectomy, complete removal of vaginal wall;

57111 with removal of paravaginal tissue (radical vaginectomy)

57112 with removal of paravaginal tissue (radical vaginectomy) with bilateral total pelvic lymphadenectomy and para-aortic lymph node sampling (biopsy)

57120 Colpocleisis (Le Fort type)

57130 Excision of vaginal septum

57135 Excision of vaginal cyst or tumor

Introduction

57150 Irrigation of vagina and/or application of medicament for treatment of bacterial, parasitic, or fungoid disease

57155 Insertion of uterine tandems and/or vaginal ovoids for clinical brachytherapy

(For placement of needles or catheters into pelvic organs and/or genitalia [except prostate] for interstitial radioelement application, use 55920)

(For insertion of radioelement sources or ribbons, see 77761-77763, 77785-77787)

57160 Fitting and insertion of pessary or other intravaginal support device

57170 Diaphragm or cervical cap fitting with instructions

57180 Introduction of any hemostatic agent or pack for spontaneous or traumatic nonobstetrical vaginal hemorrhage (separate procedure)

Repair

(For urethral suspension, Marshall-Marchetti-Krantz type, abdominal approach, see 51840, 51841)

(For laparoscopic suspension, use 51990)

57200 Colporrhaphy, suture of injury of vagina (nonobstetrical)

57210 Colpoperineorrhaphy, suture of injury of vagina and/or perineum (nonobstetrical)

57220 Plastic operation on urethral sphincter, vaginal approach (eg, Kelly urethral plication)

57230 Plastic repair of urethrocele

57240 Anterior colporrhaphy, repair of cystocele with or without repair of urethrocele

57250 Posterior colporrhaphy, repair of rectocele with or without perineorrhaphy

(For repair of rectocele (separate procedure) without posterior colporrhaphy, use 45560)

57260 Combined anteroposterior colporrhaphy;

57265 with enterocele repair

+ 57267 Insertion of mesh or other prosthesis for repair of pelvic floor defect, each site (anterior, posterior compartment), vaginal approach (List separately in addition to code for primary procedure)

(Use 57267 in conjunction with 45560, 57240-57265, 57285)

57268 Repair of enterocele, vaginal approach (separate procedure)

57270 Repair of enterocele, abdominal approach (separate procedure)

57280 Colpopexy, abdominal approach

57282 Colpopexy, vaginal; extra-peritoneal approach (sacrospinous, iliococcygeus)

57283   intra-peritoneal approach (uterosacral, levator myorrhaphy)

57284   Paravaginal defect repair (including repair of cystocele, if performed); open abdominal approach

(Do not report 57284 in conjunction with 51840, 51841, 51990, 57240, 57260, 57265, 58152, 58267)

57285   vaginal approach

(Do not report 57285 in conjunction with 51990, 57240, 57260, 57265, 58267)

57287   Removal or revision of sling for stress incontinence (eg, fascia or synthetic)

57288   Sling operation for stress incontinence (eg, fascia or synthetic)

(For laparoscopic approach, use 51992)

57289   Pereyra procedure, including anterior colporrhaphy

57291   Construction of artificial vagina; without graft

57292   with graft

57295   Revision (including removal) of prosthetic vaginal graft; vaginal approach

57296   open abdominal approach

▶(For laparoscopic approach, use 57426)◀

57300   Closure of rectovaginal fistula; vaginal or transanal approach

57305   abdominal approach

57307   abdominal approach, with concomitant colostomy

57308   transperineal approach, with perineal body reconstruction, with or without levator plication

57310   Closure of urethrovaginal fistula;

57311   with bulbocavernosus transplant

57320   Closure of vesicovaginal fistula; vaginal approach

(For concomitant cystostomy, see 51020-51040, 51101, 51102)

57330   transvesical and vaginal approach

(For abdominal approach, use 51900)

57335   Vaginoplasty for intersex state

Manipulation

57400   Dilation of vagina under anesthesia (other than local)

57410   Pelvic examination under anesthesia (other than local)

57415   Removal of impacted vaginal foreign body (separate procedure) under anesthesia (other than local)

(For removal without anesthesia of an impacted vaginal foreign body, use the appropriate E/M code)

▶Endoscopy/Laparoscopy◀

57420   Colposcopy of the entire vagina, with cervix if present;

57421   with biopsy(s) of vagina/cervix

(For colposcopic visualization of cervix and adjacent upper vagina, use 57452)

(When reporting colposcopies of multiple sites, use modifier 51 as appropriate. For colposcopic examinations/procedures involving the vulva, see 56820, 56821; cervix, see 57452-57461)

(For endometrial sampling (biopsy) performed in conjunction with colposcopy, use 58110)

57423   Paravaginal defect repair (including repair of cystocele, if performed), laparoscopic approach

(Do not report 57423 in conjunction with 49320, 51840, 51841, 51990, 57240, 57260, 58152, 58267)

57425   Laparoscopy, surgical, colpopexy (suspension of vaginal apex)

● **57426**   Revision (including removal) of prosthetic vaginal graft, laparoscopic approach

▶(For vaginal approach, see 57295. For open abdominal approach, see 57296)◀

Cervix Uteri

(For cervicography, see Category III code 0003T)

Endoscopy

(For colposcopic examinations/procedures involving the vulva, see 56820, 56821; vagina, see 57420, 57421)

57452   Colposcopy of the cervix including upper/adjacent vagina;

(Do not report 57452 in addition to 57454-57461)

57454   with biopsy(s) of the cervix and endocervical curettage

57455   with biopsy(s) of the cervix

57456   with endocervical curettage

57460   with loop electrode biopsy(s) of the cervix

57461   with loop electrode conization of the cervix

(Do not report 57456 in addition to 57461)

(For endometrial sampling [biopsy] performed in conjunction with colposcopy, use 58110)

Excision

(For radical surgical procedures, see 58200-58240)

57500   Biopsy of cervix, single or multiple, or local excision of lesion, with or without fulguration (separate procedure)

57505   Endocervical curettage (not done as part of a dilation and curettage)

57510 Cautery of cervix; electro or thermal

57511   cryocautery, initial or repeat

57513   laser ablation

57520 Conization of cervix, with or without fulguration, with or without dilation and curettage, with or without repair; cold knife or laser

(See also 58120)

57522   loop electrode excision

57530 Trachelectomy (cervicectomy), amputation of cervix (separate procedure)

57531 Radical trachelectomy, with bilateral total pelvic lymphadenectomy and para-aortic lymph node sampling biopsy, with or without removal of tube(s), with or without removal of ovary(s)

(For radical abdominal hysterectomy, use 58210)

57540 Excision of cervical stump, abdominal approach;

57545   with pelvic floor repair

57550 Excision of cervical stump, vaginal approach;

57555   with anterior and/or posterior repair

57556   with repair of enterocele

(For insertion of intrauterine device, use 58300)

(For insertion of any hemostatic agent or pack for control of spontaneous non-obstetrical hemorrhage, see 57180)

57558 Dilation and curettage of cervical stump

Repair

57700 Cerclage of uterine cervix, nonobstetrical

57720 Trachelorrhaphy, plastic repair of uterine cervix, vaginal approach

Manipulation

57800 Dilation of cervical canal, instrumental (separate procedure)

Corpus Uteri

Excision

58100 Endometrial sampling (biopsy) with or without endocervical sampling (biopsy), without cervical dilation, any method (separate procedure)

(For endocervical curettage only, use 57505)

(For endometrial sampling (biopsy) performed in conjunction with colposcopy (57420, 57421, 57452-57461), use 58110)

+ 58110 Endometrial sampling (biopsy) performed in conjunction with colposcopy (List separately in addition to code for primary procedure)

(Use 58110 in conjunction with 57420, 57421, 57452-57461)

58120 Dilation and curettage, diagnostic and/or therapeutic (nonobstetrical)

(For postpartum hemorrhage, use 59160)

58140 Myomectomy, excision of fibroid tumor(s) of uterus, 1 to 4 intramural myoma(s) with total weight of 250 g or less and/or removal of surface myomas; abdominal approach

58145   vaginal approach

58146 Myomectomy, excision of fibroid tumor(s) of uterus, 5 or more intramural myomas and/or intramural myomas with total weight greater than 250 g, abdominal approach

(Do not report 58146 in addition to 58140-58145, 58150-58240)

Hysterectomy Procedures

58150 Total abdominal hysterectomy (corpus and cervix), with or without removal of tube(s), with or without removal of ovary(s);

58152   with colpo-urethrocystopexy (eg, Marshall-Marchetti-Krantz, Burch)

(For urethrocystopexy without hysterectomy, see 51840, 51841)

58180 Supracervical abdominal hysterectomy (subtotal hysterectomy), with or without removal of tube(s), with or without removal of ovary(s)

58200 Total abdominal hysterectomy, including partial vaginectomy, with para-aortic and pelvic lymph node sampling, with or without removal of tube(s), with or without removal of ovary(s)

58210 Radical abdominal hysterectomy, with bilateral total pelvic lymphadenectomy and para-aortic lymph node sampling (biopsy), with or without removal of tube(s), with or without removal of ovary(s)

(For radical hysterectomy with ovarian transposition, use also 58825)

58240 Pelvic exenteration for gynecologic malignancy, with total abdominal hysterectomy or cervicectomy, with or without removal of tube(s), with or without removal of ovary(s), with removal of bladder and ureteral transplantations, and/or abdominoperineal resection of rectum and colon and colostomy, or any combination thereof

(For pelvic exenteration for lower urinary tract or male genital malignancy, use 51597)

58260 Vaginal hysterectomy, for uterus 250 g or less;

58262   with removal of tube(s), and/or ovary(s)

58263	with removal of tube(s), and/or ovary(s), with repair of enterocele

(Do not report 58263 in addition to 57283)

58267   with colpo-urethrocystopexy (Marshall-Marchetti-Krantz type, Pereyra type) with or without endoscopic control

58270   with repair of enterocele

(For repair of enterocele with removal of tubes and/or ovaries, use 58263)

58275   Vaginal hysterectomy, with total or partial vaginectomy;

58280   with repair of enterocele

58285   Vaginal hysterectomy, radical (Schauta type operation)

58290   Vaginal hysterectomy, for uterus greater than 250 g;

58291   with removal of tube(s) and/or ovary(s)

58292   with removal of tube(s) and/or ovary(s), with repair of enterocele

58293   with colpo-urethrocystopexy (Marshall-Marchetti-Krantz type, Pereyra type) with or without endoscopic control

58294   with repair of enterocele

Introduction

(For insertion/removal of implantable contraceptive capsules, see 11975, 11976, 11977)

58300   Insertion of intrauterine device (IUD)

58301   Removal of intrauterine device (IUD)

58321   Artificial insemination; intra-cervical

58322   intra-uterine

58323   Sperm washing for artificial insemination

58340   Catheterization and introduction of saline or contrast material for saline infusion sonohysterography (SIS) or hysterosalpingography

(For radiological supervision and interpretation of saline infusion sonohysterography, use 76831)

(For radiological supervision and interpretation of hysterosalpingography, use 74740)

58345   Transcervical introduction of fallopian tube catheter for diagnosis and/or re-establishing patency (any method), with or without hysterosalpingography

(For radiological supervision and interpretation, use 74742)

58346   Insertion of Heyman capsules for clinical brachytherapy

(For placement of needles or catheters into pelvic organs and/or genitalia [except prostate] for interstitial radioelement application, use 55920)

(For insertion of radioelement sources or ribbons, see 77761-77763, 77785-77787)

58350   Chromotubation of oviduct, including materials

(For materials supplied by physician, use 99070)

58353   Endometrial ablation, thermal, without hysteroscopic guidance

(For hysteroscopic procedure, use 58563)

58356   Endometrial cryoablation with ultrasonic guidance, including endometrial curettage, when performed

(Do not report 58356 in conjunction with 58100, 58120, 58340, 76700, 76856)

Repair

58400   Uterine suspension, with or without shortening of round ligaments, with or without shortening of sacrouterine ligaments; (separate procedure)

58410   with presacral sympathectomy

(For anastomosis of tubes to uterus, use 58752)

58520   Hysterorrhaphy, repair of ruptured uterus (nonobstetrical)

58540   Hysteroplasty, repair of uterine anomaly (Strassman type)

(For closure of vesicouterine fistula, use 51920)

Laparoscopy/Hysteroscopy

Surgical laparoscopy always includes diagnostic laparoscopy. To report a diagnostic laparoscopy (peritoneoscopy) (separate procedure), use 49320. To report a diagnostic hysteroscopy (separate procedure), use 58555.

58541   Laparoscopy, surgical, supracervical hysterectomy, for uterus 250 g or less;

58542   with removal of tube(s) and/or ovary(s)

(Do not report 58541, 58542 in conjunction with 49320, 57000, 57180, 57410, 58140-58146, 58545, 58546, 58561, 58661, 58670, 58671)

58543   Laparoscopy, surgical, supracervical hysterectomy, for uterus greater than 250 g;

58544   with removal of tube(s) and/or ovary(s)

(Do not report 58543-58544 in conjunction with 49320, 57000, 57180, 57410, 58140-58146, 58545, 58546, 58561, 58661, 58670, 58671)

58545   Laparoscopy, surgical, myomectomy, excision; 1 to 4 intramural myomas with total weight of 250 g or less and/or removal of surface myomas

58546   5 or more intramural myomas and/or intramural myomas with total weight greater than 250 g

58548   Laparoscopy, surgical, with radical hysterectomy, with bilateral total pelvic lymphadenectomy and para-aortic lymph node sampling (biopsy), with removal of tube(s) and ovary(s), if performed

(Do not report 58548 in conjunction with 38570-38572, 58210, 58285, 58550-58554)

Surgery: Female Genital System

58550   Laparoscopy, surgical, with vaginal hysterectomy, for uterus 250 g or less;

58552   with removal of tube(s) and/or ovary(s)

(Do not report 58550-58552 in conjunction with 49320, 57000, 57180, 57410, 58140-58146, 58545, 58546, 58561, 58661, 58670, 58671)

58553   Laparoscopy, surgical, with vaginal hysterectomy, for uterus greater than 250 g;

58554   with removal of tube(s) and/or ovary(s)

(Do not report 58553-58554 in conjunction with 49320, 57000, 57180, 57410, 58140-58146, 58545, 58546, 58561, 58661, 58670, 58671)

58555   Hysteroscopy, diagnostic (separate procedure)

58558   Hysteroscopy, surgical; with sampling (biopsy) of endometrium and/or polypectomy, with or without D & C

58559   with lysis of intrauterine adhesions (any method)

58560   with division or resection of intrauterine septum (any method)

58561   with removal of leiomyomata

58562   with removal of impacted foreign body

58563   with endometrial ablation (eg, endometrial resection, electrosurgical ablation, thermoablation)

58565   with bilateral fallopian tube cannulation to induce occlusion by placement of permanent implants

(Do not report 58565 in conjunction with 58555 or 57800)

(For unilateral procedure, use modifier 52)

58570   Laparoscopy, surgical, with total hysterectomy, for uterus 250 g or less;

58571   with removal of tube(s) and/or ovary(s)

58572   Laparoscopy, surgical, with total hysterectomy, for uterus greater than 250 g;

58573   with removal of tube(s) and/or ovary(s)

(Do not report 58570-58573 in conjunction with 49320, 57000, 57180, 57410, 58140-58146, 58150, 58545, 58546, 58561, 58661, 58670, 58671)

58578   Unlisted laparoscopy procedure, uterus

58579   Unlisted hysteroscopy procedure, uterus

Oviduct/Ovary

Incision

58600   Ligation or transection of fallopian tube(s), abdominal or vaginal approach, unilateral or bilateral

58605   Ligation or transection of fallopian tube(s), abdominal or vaginal approach, postpartum, unilateral or bilateral, during same hospitalization (separate procedure)

(For laparoscopic procedures, use 58670, 58671)

+ 58611   Ligation or transection of fallopian tube(s) when done at the time of cesarean delivery or intra-abdominal surgery (not a separate procedure) (List separately in addition to code for primary procedure)

58615   Occlusion of fallopian tube(s) by device (eg, band, clip, Falope ring) vaginal or suprapubic approach

(For laparoscopic approach, use 58671)

(For lysis of adnexal adhesions, use 58740)

Laparoscopy

Surgical laparoscopy always includes diagnostic laparoscopy. To report a diagnostic laparoscopy (peritoneoscopy) (separate procedure), use 49320.

58660   Laparoscopy, surgical; with lysis of adhesions (salpingolysis, ovariolysis) (separate procedure)

58661   with removal of adnexal structures (partial or total oophorectomy and/or salpingectomy)

58662   with fulguration or excision of lesions of the ovary, pelvic viscera, or peritoneal surface by any method

58670   with fulguration of oviducts (with or without transection)

58671   with occlusion of oviducts by device (eg, band, clip, or Falope ring)

58672   with fimbrioplasty

58673   with salpingostomy (salpingoneostomy)

(Codes 58672 and 58673 are used to report unilateral procedures. For bilateral procedure, use modifier 50)

58679   Unlisted laparoscopy procedure, oviduct, ovary

(For laparoscopic aspiration of ovarian cyst, use 49322)

(For laparoscopic biopsy of the ovary or fallopian tube, use 49321)

Excision

58700   Salpingectomy, complete or partial, unilateral or bilateral (separate procedure)

58720   Salpingo-oophorectomy, complete or partial, unilateral or bilateral (separate procedure)

Repair

58740   Lysis of adhesions (salpingolysis, ovariolysis)

(For laparoscopic approach, use 58660)

(For excision or destruction of endometriomas, open method, see 49203-49205, 58957, 58958)

(For fulguration or excision of lesions, laparoscopic approach, use 58662)

58750   Tubotubal anastomosis

58752   Tubouterine implantation

Surgery: Female Genital System

58760   Fimbrioplasty

(For laparoscopic approach, use 58672)

58770   Salpingostomy (salpingoneostomy)

(For laparoscopic approach, use 58673)

Ovary

Incision

58800   Drainage of ovarian cyst(s), unilateral or bilateral (separate procedure); vaginal approach

58805   abdominal approach

58820   Drainage of ovarian abscess; vaginal approach, open

58822   abdominal approach

⊙ **58823**   Drainage of pelvic abscess, transvaginal or transrectal approach, percutaneous (eg, ovarian, pericolic)

(For radiological supervision and interpretation, use 75989)

58825   Transposition, ovary(s)

Excision

58900   Biopsy of ovary, unilateral or bilateral (separate procedure)

(For laparoscopic biopsy of the ovary or fallopian tube, use 49321)

58920   Wedge resection or bisection of ovary, unilateral or bilateral

58925   Ovarian cystectomy, unilateral or bilateral

58940   Oophorectomy, partial or total, unilateral or bilateral;

(For oophorectomy with concomitant debulking for ovarian malignancy, use 58952)

58943   for ovarian, tubal or primary peritoneal malignancy, with para-aortic and pelvic lymph node biopsies, peritoneal washings, peritoneal biopsies, diaphragmatic assessments, with or without salpingectomy(s), with or without omentectomy

58950   Resection (initial) of ovarian, tubal or primary peritoneal malignancy with bilateral salpingo-oophorectomy and omentectomy;

58951   with total abdominal hysterectomy, pelvic and limited para-aortic lymphadenectomy

58952   with radical dissection for debulking (ie, radical excision or destruction, intra-abdominal or retroperitoneal tumors)

(For resection of recurrent ovarian, tubal, primary peritoneal, or uterine malignancy, see 58957, 58958)

58953   Bilateral salpingo-oophorectomy with omentectomy, total abdominal hysterectomy and radical dissection for debulking;

58954   with pelvic lymphadenectomy and limited para-aortic lymphadenectomy

58956   Bilateral salpingo-oophorectomy with total omentectomy, total abdominal hysterectomy for malignancy

(Do not report 58956 in conjunction with 49255, 58150, 58180, 58262, 58263, 58550, 58661, 58700, 58720, 58900, 58925, 58940, 58957, 58958)

58957   Resection (tumor debulking) of recurrent ovarian, tubal, primary peritoneal, uterine malignancy (intra-abdominal, retroperitoneal tumors), with omentectomy, if performed;

58958   with pelvic lymphadenectomy and limited para-aortic lymphadenectomy

(Do not report 58957, 58958 in conjunction with 38770, 38780, 44005, 49000, 49203-49215, 49255, 58900-58960)

58960   Laparotomy, for staging or restaging of ovarian, tubal, or primary peritoneal malignancy (second look), with or without omentectomy, peritoneal washing, biopsy of abdominal and pelvic peritoneum, diaphragmatic assessment with pelvic and limited para-aortic lymphadenectomy

(Do not report 58960 in conjunction with 58957, 58958)

In Vitro Fertilization

58970   Follicle puncture for oocyte retrieval, any method

(For radiological supervision and interpretation, use 76948)

58974   Embryo transfer, intrauterine

58976   Gamete, zygote, or embryo intrafallopian transfer, any method

(For laparoscopic adnexal procedures, see 58660-58673)

Other Procedures

58999   Unlisted procedure, female genital system (nonobstetrical)

Maternity Care and Delivery

The services normally provided in uncomplicated maternity cases include antepartum care, delivery, and postpartum care.

Antepartum care includes the initial and subsequent history, physical examinations, recording of weight, blood pressures, fetal heart tones, routine chemical urinalysis, and monthly visits up to 28 weeks gestation, biweekly visits to 36 weeks gestation, and weekly visits until delivery. Any other visits or services within this time period should be coded separately.

Surgery: Female Genital System

Delivery services include admission to the hospital, the admission history and physical examination, management of uncomplicated labor, vaginal delivery (with or without episiotomy, with or without forceps), or cesarean delivery. Medical problems complicating labor and delivery management may require additional resources and should be identified by utilizing the codes in the **Medicine** and **Evaluation and Management Services** section in addition to codes for maternity care.

Postpartum care includes hospital and office visits following vaginal or cesarean section delivery.

For medical complications of pregnancy (eg, cardiac problems, neurological problems, diabetes, hypertension, toxemia, hyperemesis, pre-term labor, premature rupture of membranes), see services in the **Medicine** and **Evaluation and Management Services** section.

For surgical complications of pregnancy (eg, appendectomy, hernia, ovarian cyst, Bartholin cyst), see services in the **Surgery** section.

If a physician provides all or part of the antepartum and/or postpartum patient care but does not perform delivery due to termination of pregnancy by abortion or referral to another physician for delivery, see the antepartum and postpartum care codes 59425-59426 and 59430.

(For circumcision of newborn, see 54150, 54160)

►Antepartum and Fetal Invasive Services◄

►(For fetal intrauterine transfusion, use 36460)◄

►(For unlisted fetal invasive procedure, use 59897)◄

59000 Amniocentesis; diagnostic

(For radiological supervision and interpretation, use 76946)

59001 therapeutic amniotic fluid reduction (includes ultrasound guidance)

59012 Cordocentesis (intrauterine), any method

(For radiological supervision and interpretation, use 76941)

59015 Chorionic villus sampling, any method

(For radiological supervision and interpretation, use 76945)

59020 Fetal contraction stress test

59025 Fetal non-stress test

59030 Fetal scalp blood sampling

(For repeat fetal scalp blood sampling, use 59030 and see modifiers 76 and 77)

59050 Fetal monitoring during labor by consulting physician (ie, non-attending physician) with written report; supervision and interpretation

59051 interpretation only

59070 Transabdominal amnioinfusion, including ultrasound guidance

59072 Fetal umbilical cord occlusion, including ultrasound guidance

59074 Fetal fluid drainage (eg, vesicocentesis, thoracocentesis, paracentesis), including ultrasound guidance

59076 Fetal shunt placement, including ultrasound guidance

Excision

59100 Hysterotomy, abdominal (eg, for hydatidiform mole, abortion)

(When tubal ligation is performed at the same time as hysterotomy, use 58611 in addition to 59100)

59120 Surgical treatment of ectopic pregnancy; tubal or ovarian, requiring salpingectomy and/or oophorectomy, abdominal or vaginal approach

59121 tubal or ovarian, without salpingectomy and/or oophorectomy

59130 abdominal pregnancy

59135 interstitial, uterine pregnancy requiring total hysterectomy

59136 interstitial, uterine pregnancy with partial resection of uterus

59140 cervical, with evacuation

59150 Laparoscopic treatment of ectopic pregnancy; without salpingectomy and/or oophorectomy

59151 with salpingectomy and/or oophorectomy

59160 Curettage, postpartum

Introduction

(For intrauterine fetal transfusion, use 36460)

(For introduction of hypertonic solution and/or prostaglandins to initiate labor, see 59850-59857)

59200 Insertion of cervical dilator (eg, laminaria, prostaglandin) (separate procedure)

Repair

(For tracheloplasty, use 57700)

59300 Episiotomy or vaginal repair, by other than attending physician

59320 Cerclage of cervix, during pregnancy; vaginal

59325 abdominal

59350 Hysterorrhaphy of ruptured uterus

Surgery: Female Genital System

Vaginal Delivery, Antepartum and Postpartum Care

59400   Routine obstetric care including antepartum care, vaginal delivery (with or without episiotomy, and/or forceps) and postpartum care

59409   Vaginal delivery only (with or without episiotomy and/or forceps);

59410   including postpartum care

59412   External cephalic version, with or without tocolysis

(Use 59412 in addition to code[s] for delivery)

59414   Delivery of placenta (separate procedure)

(For antepartum care only, see 59425, 59426 or appropriate E/M code(s))

(For 1-3 antepartum care visits, see appropriate E/M code(s))

59425   Antepartum care only; 4-6 visits

59426   7 or more visits

59430   Postpartum care only (separate procedure)

Cesarean Delivery

(For standby attendance for infant, use 99360)

(For low cervical cesarean section, see 59510, 59515, 59525)

59510   Routine obstetric care including antepartum care, cesarean delivery, and postpartum care

59514   Cesarean delivery only;

59515   including postpartum care

(For classic cesarean section, see 59510, 59515, 59525)

+ 59525   Subtotal or total hysterectomy after cesarean delivery (List separately in addition to code for primary procedure)

(Use 59525 in conjunction with 59510, 59514, 59515, 59618, 59620, 59622)

(For extraperitoneal cesarean section, or cesarean section with subtotal or total hysterectomy, see 59510, 59515, 59525)

Delivery After Previous Cesarean Delivery

Patients who have had a previous cesarean delivery and now present with the expectation of a vaginal delivery are coded using codes 59610-59622. If the patient has a successful vaginal delivery after a previous cesarean delivery (VBAC), use codes 59610-59614. If the attempt is unsuccessful and another cesarean delivery is carried out, use codes 59618-59622. To report elective cesarean deliveries use code 59510, 59514 or 59515.

59610   Routine obstetric care including antepartum care, vaginal delivery (with or without episiotomy, and/or forceps) and postpartum care, after previous cesarean delivery

59612   Vaginal delivery only, after previous cesarean delivery (with or without episiotomy and/or forceps);

59614   including postpartum care

59618   Routine obstetric care including antepartum care, cesarean delivery, and postpartum care, following attempted vaginal delivery after previous cesarean delivery

59620   Cesarean delivery only, following attempted vaginal delivery after previous cesarean delivery;

59622   including postpartum care

Abortion

(For medical treatment of spontaneous complete abortion, any trimester, use E/M codes 99201-99233)

(For surgical treatment of spontaneous abortion, use 59812)

59812   Treatment of incomplete abortion, any trimester, completed surgically

59820   Treatment of missed abortion, completed surgically; first trimester

59821   second trimester

59830   Treatment of septic abortion, completed surgically

59840   Induced abortion, by dilation and curettage

59841   Induced abortion, by dilation and evacuation

59850   Induced abortion, by 1 or more intra-amniotic injections (amniocentesis-injections), including hospital admission and visits, delivery of fetus and secundines;

59851   with dilation and curettage and/or evacuation

59852   with hysterotomy (failed intra-amniotic injection)

(For insertion of cervical dilator, use 59200)

59855   Induced abortion, by 1 or more vaginal suppositories (eg, prostaglandin) with or without cervical dilation (eg, laminaria), including hospital admission and visits, delivery of fetus and secundines;

59856   with dilation and curettage and/or evacuation

59857   with hysterotomy (failed medical evacuation)

Other Procedures

59866   Multifetal pregnancy reduction(s) (MPR)

59870   Uterine evacuation and curettage for hydatidiform mole

59871   Removal of cerclage suture under anesthesia (other than local)

▲ **59897**   Unlisted fetal invasive procedure, including ultrasound guidance, when performed

59898   Unlisted laparoscopy procedure, maternity care and delivery

59899   Unlisted procedure, maternity care and delivery

Surgery: Female Genital System

Endocrine System

(For pituitary and pineal surgery, see **Nervous System**)

Thyroid Gland

Incision

60000 Incision and drainage of thyroglossal duct cyst, infected

Excision

(60001 has been deleted. To report, use 60300)

60100 Biopsy thyroid, percutaneous core needle

(If imaging guidance is performed, see 76942, 77002, 77012, 77021)

(For fine needle aspiration, use 10021 or 10022)

(For evaluation of fine needle aspirate, see 88172, 88173)

60200 Excision of cyst or adenoma of thyroid, or transection of isthmus

60210 Partial thyroid lobectomy, unilateral; with or without isthmusectomy

60212   with contralateral subtotal lobectomy, including isthmusectomy

60220 Total thyroid lobectomy, unilateral; with or without isthmusectomy

60225   with contralateral subtotal lobectomy, including isthmusectomy

60240 Thyroidectomy, total or complete

(For thyroidectomy, subtotal or partial, use 60271)

60252 Thyroidectomy, total or subtotal for malignancy; with limited neck dissection

60254   with radical neck dissection

60260 Thyroidectomy, removal of all remaining thyroid tissue following previous removal of a portion of thyroid

(For bilateral procedure, report 60260 with modifier 50)

60270 Thyroidectomy, including substernal thyroid; sternal split or transthoracic approach

60271   cervical approach

60280 Excision of thyroglossal duct cyst or sinus;

60281   recurrent

(For thyroid ultrasonography, use 76536)

Removal

60300 Aspiration and/or injection, thyroid cyst

(For fine needle aspiration, see 10021, 10022)

(If imaging guidance is performed, see 76942, 77012)

Parathyroid, Thymus, Adrenal Glands, Pancreas, and Carotid Body

Excision

(For pituitary and pineal surgery, see **Nervous System**)

60500 Parathyroidectomy or exploration of parathyroid(s);

60502   re-exploration

60505   with mediastinal exploration, sternal split or transthoracic approach

+ 60512 Parathyroid autotransplantation (List separately in addition to code for primary procedure)

(Use 60512 in conjunction with 60500, 60502, 60505, 60212, 60225, 60240, 60252, 60254, 60260, 60270, 60271)

60520 Thymectomy, partial or total; transcervical approach (separate procedure)

60521   sternal split or transthoracic approach, without radical mediastinal dissection (separate procedure)

60522   sternal split or transthoracic approach, with radical mediastinal dissection (separate procedure)

60540 Adrenalectomy, partial or complete, or exploration of adrenal gland with or without biopsy, transabdominal, lumbar or dorsal (separate procedure);

60545   with excision of adjacent retroperitoneal tumor

(Do not report 60540, 60545 in conjunction with 50323)

(For bilateral procedure, report 60540 with modifier 50)

(For excision of remote or disseminated pheochromocytoma, see 49203-49205)

(For laparoscopic approach, use 60650)

60600 Excision of carotid body tumor; without excision of carotid artery

60605   with excision of carotid artery

Laparoscopy

Surgical laparoscopy always includes diagnostic laparoscopy. To report a diagnostic laparoscopy (peritoneoscopy) (separate procedure), use 49320.

60650 Laparoscopy, surgical, with adrenalectomy, partial or complete, or exploration of adrenal gland with or without biopsy, transabdominal, lumbar or dorsal

60659 Unlisted laparoscopy procedure, endocrine system

Other Procedures

60699 Unlisted procedure, endocrine system

Surgery: Endocrine System

Nervous System

Skull, Meninges, and Brain

(For injection procedure for cerebral angiography, see 36100-36218)

(For injection procedure for ventriculography, see 61026, 61120)

(For injection procedure for pneumoencephalography, use 61055)

Injection, Drainage, or Aspiration

61000 Subdural tap through fontanelle, or suture, infant, unilateral or bilateral; initial

61001   subsequent taps

61020 Ventricular puncture through previous burr hole, fontanelle, suture, or implanted ventricular catheter/reservoir; without injection

61026   with injection of medication or other substance for diagnosis or treatment

61050 Cisternal or lateral cervical (C1-C2) puncture; without injection (separate procedure)

61055   with injection of medication or other substance for diagnosis or treatment (eg, C1-C2)

(For radiological supervision and interpretation, see **Radiology**)

61070 Puncture of shunt tubing or reservoir for aspiration or injection procedure

(For radiological supervision and interpretation, use 75809)

Twist Drill, Burr Hole(s), or Trephine

61105 Twist drill hole for subdural or ventricular puncture

⊘ **61107** Twist drill hole(s) for subdural, intracerebral, or ventricular puncture; for implanting ventricular catheter, pressure recording device, or other intracerebral monitoring device

(For intracranial neuroendoscopic ventricular catheter placement, use 62160)

(For twist drill or burr hole performed to place thermal perfusion probe, use Category III code 0077T)

61108   for evacuation and/or drainage of subdural hematoma

61120 Burr hole(s) for ventricular puncture (including injection of gas, contrast media, dye, or radioactive material)

61140 Burr hole(s) or trephine; with biopsy of brain or intracranial lesion

61150   with drainage of brain abscess or cyst

61151   with subsequent tapping (aspiration) of intracranial abscess or cyst

61154 Burr hole(s) with evacuation and/or drainage of hematoma, extradural or subdural

(For bilateral procedure, report 61154 with modifier 50)

61156 Burr hole(s); with aspiration of hematoma or cyst, intracerebral

61210   for implanting ventricular catheter, reservoir, EEG electrode(s), pressure recording device, or other cerebral monitoring device (separate procedure)

(For intracranial neuroendoscopic ventricular catheter placement, use 62160)

61215 Insertion of subcutaneous reservoir, pump or continuous infusion system for connection to ventricular catheter

(For refilling and maintenance of an implantable infusion pump for spinal or brain drug therapy, use 95990)

(For chemotherapy, use 96450)

61250 Burr hole(s) or trephine, supratentorial, exploratory, not followed by other surgery

(For bilateral procedure, report 61250 with modifier 50)

61253 Burr hole(s) or trephine, infratentorial, unilateral or bilateral

(If burr hole[s] or trephine are followed by craniotomy at same operative session, use 61304-61321; do not use 61250 or 61253)

Craniectomy or Craniotomy

61304 Craniectomy or craniotomy, exploratory; supratentorial

61305   infratentorial (posterior fossa)

61312 Craniectomy or craniotomy for evacuation of hematoma, supratentorial; extradural or subdural

61313   intracerebral

61314 Craniectomy or craniotomy for evacuation of hematoma, infratentorial; extradural or subdural

61315   intracerebellar

+ **61316** Incision and subcutaneous placement of cranial bone graft (List separately in addition to code for primary procedure)

(Use 61316 in conjunction with 61304, 61312, 61313, 61322, 61323, 61340, 61570, 61571, 61680-61705)

61320 Craniectomy or craniotomy, drainage of intracranial abscess; supratentorial

61321   infratentorial

61322 Craniectomy or craniotomy, decompressive, with or without duraplasty, for treatment of intracranial hypertension, without evacuation of associated intraparenchymal hematoma; without lobectomy

(Do not report 61313 in addition to 61322)

(For subtemporal decompression, use 61340)

Surgery: Nervous System

61323   with lobectomy

(Do not report 61313 in addition to 61323)

(For subtemporal decompression, use 61340)

61330   Decompression of orbit only, transcranial approach

(For bilateral procedure, report 61330 with modifier 50)

61332   Exploration of orbit (transcranial approach); with biopsy

61333   with removal of lesion

61334   with removal of foreign body

61340   Subtemporal cranial decompression (pseudotumor cerebri, slit ventricle syndrome)

(For bilateral procedure, report 61340 with modifier 50)

(For decompressive craniotomy or craniectomy for intracranial hypertension, without hematoma evacuation, see 61322, 61323)

61343   Craniectomy, suboccipital with cervical laminectomy for decompression of medulla and spinal cord, with or without dural graft (eg, Arnold-Chiari malformation)

61345   Other cranial decompression, posterior fossa

(For orbital decompression by lateral wall approach, Kroenlein type, use 67445)

61440   Craniotomy for section of tentorium cerebelli (separate procedure)

61450   Craniectomy, subtemporal, for section, compression, or decompression of sensory root of gasserian ganglion

61458   Craniectomy, suboccipital; for exploration or decompression of cranial nerves

61460   for section of 1 or more cranial nerves

61470   for medullary tractotomy

61480   for mesencephalic tractotomy or pedunculotomy

61490   Craniotomy for lobotomy, including cingulotomy

(For bilateral procedure, report 61490 with modifier 50)

61500   Craniectomy; with excision of tumor or other bone lesion of skull

61501   for osteomyelitis

61510   Craniectomy, trephination, bone flap craniotomy; for excision of brain tumor, supratentorial, except meningioma

61512   for excision of meningioma, supratentorial

61514   for excision of brain abscess, supratentorial

61516   for excision or fenestration of cyst, supratentorial

(For excision of pituitary tumor or craniopharyngioma, see 61545, 61546, 61548)

+ 61517 Implantation of brain intracavitary chemotherapy agent (List separately in addition to code for primary procedure)

(Use 61517 only in conjunction with 61510 or 61518)

(Do not report 61517 for brachytherapy insertion. For intracavitary insertion of radioelement sources or ribbons, see 77785-77787)

61518   Craniectomy for excision of brain tumor, infratentorial or posterior fossa; except meningioma, cerebellopontine angle tumor, or midline tumor at base of skull

61519   meningioma

61520   cerebellopontine angle tumor

61521   midline tumor at base of skull

61522   Craniectomy, infratentorial or posterior fossa; for excision of brain abscess

61524   for excision or fenestration of cyst

61526   Craniectomy, bone flap craniotomy, transtemporal (mastoid) for excision of cerebellopontine angle tumor;

61530   combined with middle/posterior fossa craniotomy/craniectomy

61531   Subdural implantation of strip electrodes through 1 or more burr or trephine hole(s) for long-term seizure monitoring

(For stereotactic implantation of electrodes, use 61760)

(For craniotomy for excision of intracranial arteriovenous malformation, see 61680-61692)

61533   Craniotomy with elevation of bone flap; for subdural implantation of an electrode array, for long-term seizure monitoring

(For continuous EEG monitoring, see 95950-95954)

61534   for excision of epileptogenic focus without electrocorticography during surgery

61535   for removal of epidural or subdural electrode array, without excision of cerebral tissue (separate procedure)

61536   for excision of cerebral epileptogenic focus, with electrocorticography during surgery (includes removal of electrode array)

61537   for lobectomy, temporal lobe, without electrocorticography during surgery

61538   for lobectomy, temporal lobe, with electrocorticography during surgery

61539   for lobectomy, other than temporal lobe, partial or total, with electrocorticography during surgery

61540   for lobectomy, other than temporal lobe, partial or total, without electrocorticography during surgery

61541   for transection of corpus callosum

61542   for total hemispherectomy

61543   for partial or subtotal (functional) hemispherectomy

61544   for excision or coagulation of choroid plexus

61545   for excision of craniopharyngioma

(For craniotomy for selective amygdalohippocampectomy, use 61566)

(For craniotomy for multiple subpial transections during surgery, use 61567)

61546   Craniotomy for hypophysectomy or excision of pituitary tumor, intracranial approach

61548   Hypophysectomy or excision of pituitary tumor, transnasal or transseptal approach, nonstereotactic

(Do not report code 69990 in addition to code 61548)

61550   Craniectomy for craniosynostosis; single cranial suture

61552   multiple cranial sutures

(For cranial reconstruction for orbital hypertelorism, see 21260-21263)

(For reconstruction, see 21172-21180)

61556   Craniotomy for craniosynostosis; frontal or parietal bone flap

61557   bifrontal bone flap

61558   Extensive craniectomy for multiple cranial suture craniosynostosis (eg, cloverleaf skull); not requiring bone grafts

61559   recontouring with multiple osteotomies and bone autografts (eg, barrel-stave procedure) (includes obtaining grafts)

(For reconstruction, see 21172-21180)

61563   Excision, intra and extracranial, benign tumor of cranial bone (eg, fibrous dysplasia); without optic nerve decompression

61564   with optic nerve decompression

(For reconstruction, see 21181-21183)

61566   Craniotomy with elevation of bone flap; for selective amygdalohippocampectomy

61567   for multiple subpial transections, with electrocorticography during surgery

61570   Craniectomy or craniotomy; with excision of foreign body from brain

61571   with treatment of penetrating wound of brain

(For sequestrectomy for osteomyelitis, use 61501)

61575   Transoral approach to skull base, brain stem or upper spinal cord for biopsy, decompression or excision of lesion;

61576   requiring splitting of tongue and/or mandible (including tracheostomy)

(For arthrodesis, use 22548)

Surgery of Skull Base

The surgical management of lesions involving the skull base (base of anterior, middle, and posterior cranial fossae) often requires the skills of several surgeons of different surgical specialties working together or in tandem during the operative session. These operations are usually not staged because of the need for definitive closure of dura, subcutaneous tissues, and skin to avoid serious infections such as osteomyelitis and/or meningitis.

The procedures are categorized according to (1) *approach procedure* necessary to obtain adequate exposure to the lesion (pathologic entity), (2) *definitive procedure(s)* necessary to biopsy, excise or otherwise treat the lesion, and (3) *repair/reconstruction* of the defect present following the definitive procedure(s).

The *approach procedure* is described according to anatomical area involved, ie, anterior cranial fossa, middle cranial fossa, posterior cranial fossa, and brain stem or upper spinal cord.

The *definitive procedure(s)* describes the repair, biopsy, resection, or excision of various lesions of the skull base and, when appropriate, primary closure of the dura, mucous membranes, and skin.

The *repair/reconstruction procedure(s)* is reported separately if extensive dural grafting, cranioplasty, local or regional myocutaneous pedicle flaps, or extensive skin grafts are required.

For primary closure, see the appropriate codes (ie, 15732, 15756-15758).

When one surgeon performs the approach procedure, another surgeon performs the definitive procedure, and another surgeon performs the repair/reconstruction procedure, each surgeon reports only the code for the specific procedure performed.

If one surgeon performs more than one procedure (ie, approach procedure and definitive procedure), then both codes are reported, adding modifier 51 to the secondary, additional procedure(s).

Approach Procedures

Anterior Cranial Fossa

61580   Craniofacial approach to anterior cranial fossa; extradural, including lateral rhinotomy, ethmoidectomy, sphenoidectomy, without maxillectomy or orbital exenteration

61581   extradural, including lateral rhinotomy, orbital exenteration, ethmoidectomy, sphenoidectomy and/or maxillectomy

61582   extradural, including unilateral or bifrontal craniotomy, elevation of frontal lobe(s), osteotomy of base of anterior cranial fossa

61583   intradural, including unilateral or bifrontal craniotomy, elevation or resection of frontal lobe, osteotomy of base of anterior cranial fossa

61584   Orbitocranial approach to anterior cranial fossa, extradural, including supraorbital ridge osteotomy and elevation of frontal and/or temporal lobe(s); without orbital exenteration

61585   with orbital exenteration

61586   Bicoronal, transzygomatic and/or LeFort I osteotomy approach to anterior cranial fossa with or without internal fixation, without bone graft

Middle Cranial Fossa

61590   Infratemporal pre-auricular approach to middle cranial fossa (parapharyngeal space, infratemporal and midline skull base, nasopharynx), with or without disarticulation of the mandible, including parotidectomy, craniotomy, decompression and/or mobilization of the facial nerve and/or petrous carotid artery

61591   Infratemporal post-auricular approach to middle cranial fossa (internal auditory meatus, petrous apex, tentorium, cavernous sinus, parasellar area, infratemporal fossa) including mastoidectomy, resection of sigmoid sinus, with or without decompression and/or mobilization of contents of auditory canal or petrous carotid artery

61592   Orbitocranial zygomatic approach to middle cranial fossa (cavernous sinus and carotid artery, clivus, basilar artery or petrous apex) including osteotomy of zygoma, craniotomy, extra- or intradural elevation of temporal lobe

Posterior Cranial Fossa

61595   Transtemporal approach to posterior cranial fossa, jugular foramen or midline skull base, including mastoidectomy, decompression of sigmoid sinus and/or facial nerve, with or without mobilization

61596   Transcochlear approach to posterior cranial fossa, jugular foramen or midline skull base, including labyrinthectomy, decompression, with or without mobilization of facial nerve and/or petrous carotid artery

61597   Transcondylar (far lateral) approach to posterior cranial fossa, jugular foramen or midline skull base, including occipital condylectomy, mastoidectomy, resection of C1-C3 vertebral body(s), decompression of vertebral artery, with or without mobilization

61598   Transpetrosal approach to posterior cranial fossa, clivus or foramen magnum, including ligation of superior petrosal sinus and/or sigmoid sinus

Definitive Procedures

Base of Anterior Cranial Fossa

61600   Resection or excision of neoplastic, vascular or infectious lesion of base of anterior cranial fossa; extradural

61601   intradural, including dural repair, with or without graft

Base of Middle Cranial Fossa

61605   Resection or excision of neoplastic, vascular or infectious lesion of infratemporal fossa, parapharyngeal space, petrous apex; extradural

61606   intradural, including dural repair, with or without graft

61607   Resection or excision of neoplastic, vascular or infectious lesion of parasellar area, cavernous sinus, clivus or midline skull base; extradural

61608   intradural, including dural repair, with or without graft

Codes 61609-61612 are reported in addition to code(s) for primary procedure(s) 61605-61608. Report only one transection or ligation of carotid artery code per operative session.

+ 61609   Transection or ligation, carotid artery in cavernous sinus; without repair (List separately in addition to code for primary procedure)

+ 61610   with repair by anastomosis or graft (List separately in addition to code for primary procedure)

+ 61611   Transection or ligation, carotid artery in petrous canal; without repair (List separately in addition to code for primary procedure)

+ 61612   with repair by anastomosis or graft (List separately in addition to code for primary procedure)

61613   Obliteration of carotid aneurysm, arteriovenous malformation, or carotid-cavernous fistula by dissection within cavernous sinus

Base of Posterior Cranial Fossa

61615   Resection or excision of neoplastic, vascular or infectious lesion of base of posterior cranial fossa, jugular foramen, foramen magnum, or C1-C3 vertebral bodies; extradural

61616   intradural, including dural repair, with or without graft

Repair and/or Reconstruction of Surgical Defects of Skull Base

61618   Secondary repair of dura for cerebrospinal fluid leak, anterior, middle or posterior cranial fossa following surgery of the skull base; by free tissue graft (eg, pericranium, fascia, tensor fascia lata, adipose tissue, homologous or synthetic grafts)

61619   by local or regionalized vascularized pedicle flap or myocutaneous flap (including galea, temporalis, frontalis or occipitalis muscle)

Surgery: Nervous System

Endovascular Therapy

61623   Endovascular temporary balloon arterial occlusion, head or neck (extracranial/intracranial) including selective catheterization of vessel to be occluded, positioning and inflation of occlusion balloon, concomitant neurological monitoring, and radiologic supervision and interpretation of all angiography required for balloon occlusion and to exclude vascular injury post occlusion

(If selective catheterization and angiography of arteries other than artery to be occluded is performed, use appropriate catheterization and radiologic supervision and interpretation codes)

(If complete diagnostic angiography of the artery to be occluded is performed immediately prior to temporary occlusion, use appropriate radiologic supervision and interpretation codes only)

61624   Transcatheter permanent occlusion or embolization (eg, for tumor destruction, to achieve hemostasis, to occlude a vascular malformation), percutaneous, any method; central nervous system (intracranial, spinal cord)

(See also 37204)

(For radiological supervision and interpretation, use 75894)

61626   non-central nervous system, head or neck (extracranial, brachiocephalic branch)

(See also 37204)

(For radiological supervision and interpretation, use 75894)

61630   Balloon angioplasty, intracranial (eg, atherosclerotic stenosis), percutaneous

61635   Transcatheter placement of intravascular stent(s), intracranial (eg, atherosclerotic stenosis), including balloon angioplasty, if performed

(61630 and 61635 include all selective vascular catheterization of the target vascular family, all diagnostic imaging for arteriography of the target vascular family, and all related radiological supervision and interpretation. When diagnostic arteriogram (including imaging and selective catheterization) confirms the need for angioplasty or stent placement, 61630 and 61635 are inclusive of these services. If angioplasty or stenting are not indicated, then the appropriate codes for selective catheterization and imaging should be reported in lieu of 61630 and 61635)

61640   Balloon dilatation of intracranial vasospasm, percutaneous; initial vessel

+ 61641   each additional vessel in same vascular family (List separately in addition to code for primary procedure)

+ 61642   each additional vessel in different vascular family (List separately in addition to code for primary procedure)

(Use 61641 and 61642 in conjunction with 61640)

(61640, 61641, 61642 include all selective vascular catheterization of the target vessel, contrast injection(s), vessel measurement, roadmapping, postdilatation angiography, and fluoroscopic guidance for the balloon dilatation)

Surgery for Aneurysm, Arteriovenous Malformation, or Vascular Disease

Includes craniotomy when appropriate for procedure.

61680   Surgery of intracranial arteriovenous malformation; supratentorial, simple

61682   supratentorial, complex

61684   infratentorial, simple

61686   infratentorial, complex

61690   dural, simple

61692   dural, complex

61697   Surgery of complex intracranial aneurysm, intracranial approach; carotid circulation

61698   vertebrobasilar circulation

(61697, 61698 involve aneurysms that are larger than 15 mm or with calcification of the aneurysm neck, or with incorporation of normal vessels into the aneurysm neck, or a procedure requiring temporary vessel occlusion, trapping or cardiopulmonary bypass to successfully treat the aneurysm)

61700   Surgery of simple intracranial aneurysm, intracranial approach; carotid circulation

61702   vertebrobasilar circulation

61703   Surgery of intracranial aneurysm, cervical approach by application of occluding clamp to cervical carotid artery (Selverstone-Crutchfield type)

(For cervical approach for direct ligation of carotid artery, see 37600-37606)

61705   Surgery of aneurysm, vascular malformation or carotid-cavernous fistula; by intracranial and cervical occlusion of carotid artery

61708   by intracranial electrothrombosis

(For ligation or gradual occlusion of internal/common carotid artery, see 37605, 37606)

61710   by intra-arterial embolization, injection procedure, or balloon catheter

61711   Anastomosis, arterial, extracranial-intracranial (eg, middle cerebral/cortical) arteries

(For carotid or vertebral thromboendarterectomy, use 35301)

(Use 69990 when the surgical microscope is employed for the microsurgical procedure. Do not use 69990 for visualization with magnifying loupes or corrected vision)

Surgery: Nervous System

Stereotaxis

61720 Creation of lesion by stereotactic method, including burr hole(s) and localizing and recording techniques, single or multiple stages; globus pallidus or thalamus

61735 subcortical structure(s) other than globus pallidus or thalamus

61750 Stereotactic biopsy, aspiration, or excision, including burr hole(s), for intracranial lesion;

61751 with computed tomography and/or magnetic resonance guidance

(For radiological supervision and interpretation of computerized tomography, see 70450, 70460, or 70470 as appropriate)

(For radiological supervision and interpretation of magnetic resonance imaging, see 70551, 70552, or 70553 as appropriate)

61760 Stereotactic implantation of depth electrodes into the cerebrum for long-term seizure monitoring

61770 Stereotactic localization, including burr hole(s), with insertion of catheter(s) or probe(s) for placement of radiation source

61790 Creation of lesion by stereotactic method, percutaneous, by neurolytic agent (eg, alcohol, thermal, electrical, radiofrequency); gasserian ganglion

61791 trigeminal medullary tract

(61793 has been deleted. To report, see 61796-61800, 63620-63621)

Stereotactic Radiosurgery (Cranial)

Cranial stereotactic radiosurgery is a distinct procedure that utilizes externally generated ionizing radiation to inactivate or eradicate defined target(s) in the head without the need to make an incision. The target is defined by and the treatment is delivered using high-resolution stereotactic imaging. Stereotactic radiosurgery codes and headframe application procedures are reported by the neurosurgeon. The radiation oncologist reports the appropriate code(s) for clinical treatment planning, physics and dosimetry, treatment delivery, and management from the **Radiation Oncology** section (77261-77790). Any necessary planning, dosimetry, targeting, positioning, or blocking by the neurosurgeon is included in the stereotactic radiation surgery services. The same physician should not report stereotactic radiosurgery services with radiation treatment management codes (77427-77435).

Cranial stereotactic radiosurgery is typically performed in a single planning and treatment session, using a rigidly attached stereotactic guiding device, other immobilization technology and/or a stereotactic image-guidance system, but can be performed with more than one planning session and in a limited number of treatment sessions, up to a maximum of five sessions. Do not report stereotactic radiosurgery more than once per lesion per course of treatment when the treatment requires more than one session.

Codes 61796 and 61797 involve stereotactic radiosurgery for simple cranial lesions. Simple cranial lesions are lesions less than 3.5 cm in maximum dimension that do not meet the definition of a complex lesion provided below. Report code 61796 when all lesions are simple.

Codes 61798 and 61799 involve stereotactic radiosurgery for complex cranial lesions and procedures that create therapeutic lesions (eg, thalamotomy or pallidotomy). All lesions 3.5 cm in maximum dimension or greater are complex. When performing therapeutic lesion creation procedures, report code 61798 only once regardless of the number of lesions created. Schwannomas, arterio-venous malformations, pituitary tumors, glomus tumors, pineal region tumors and cavernous sinus/parasellar/petroclival tumors are complex. Any lesion that is adjacent (5mm or less) to the optic nerve/optic chasm/optic tract or within the brainstem is complex. If treating multiple lesions, and any single lesion treated is complex, use 61798.

Do not report codes 61796-61800 in conjunction with code 20660.

Codes 61796-61799 include computer-assisted planning. Do not report codes 61796-61799 in conjunction with 61795.

▶(For intensity modulated beam delivery plan and treatment, see 77301, 77418. For stereotactic body radiation therapy, see 77373, 77435)◀

+ 61795 Stereotactic computer-assisted volumetric (navigational) procedure, intracranial, extracranial, or spinal (List separately in addition to code for primary procedure)

61796 Stereotactic radiosurgery (particle beam, gamma ray, or linear accelerator); 1 simple cranial lesion

(Do not report 61796 more than once per course of treatment)

(Do not report 61796 in conjunction with 61798)

+ 61797 each additional cranial lesion, simple (List separately in addition to code for primary procedure)

(Use 61797 in conjunction with 61796, 61798)

(For each course of treatment, 61797 and 61799 may be reported no more than once per lesion. Do not report any combination of 61797 and 61799 more than 4 times for entire course of treatment regardless of number of lesions treated)

61798 1 complex cranial lesion

(Do not report 61798 more than once per course of treatment)

(Do not report 61798 in conjunction with 61796)

+ 61799   each additional cranial lesion, complex (List separately in addition to code for primary procedure)

(Use 61799 in conjunction with 61798)

(For each course of treatment, 61797 and 61799 may be reported no more than once per lesion. Do not report any combination of 61797 and 61799 more than 4 times for entire course of treatment regardless of number of lesions treated)

+ 61800   Application of stereotactic headframe for stereotactic radiosurgery (List separately in addition to code for primary procedure)

(Use 61800 in conjunction with 61796, 61798)

Neurostimulators (Intracranial)

Codes 61850-61888 apply to both simple and complex neurostimulators. For initial or subsequent electronic analysis and programming of neurostimulator pulse generators, see codes 95970-95975.

Microelectrode recording, when performed by the operating surgeon in association with implantation of neurostimulator electrode arrays, is an inclusive service and should not be reported separately. If another physician participates in neurophysiological mapping during a deep brain stimulator implantation procedure, this service may be reported by the other physician with codes 95961-95962.

61850   Twist drill or burr hole(s) for implantation of neurostimulator electrodes, cortical

61860   Craniectomy or craniotomy for implantation of neurostimulator electrodes, cerebral, cortical

61863   Twist drill, burr hole, craniotomy, or craniectomy with stereotactic implantation of neurostimulator electrode array in subcortical site (eg, thalamus, globus pallidus, subthalamic nucleus, periventricular, periaqueductal gray), without use of intraoperative microelectrode recording; first array

+ 61864   each additional array (List separately in addition to primary procedure)

(Use 61864 in conjunction with 61863)

61867   Twist drill, burr hole, craniotomy, or craniectomy with stereotactic implantation of neurostimulator electrode array in subcortical site (eg, thalamus, globus pallidus, subthalamic nucleus, periventricular, periaqueductal gray), with use of intraoperative microelectrode recording; first array

+ 61868   each additional array (List separately in addition to primary procedure)

(Use 61868 in conjunction with 61867)

61870   Craniectomy for implantation of neurostimulator electrodes, cerebellar; cortical

61875   subcortical

61880   Revision or removal of intracranial neurostimulator electrodes

61885   Insertion or replacement of cranial neurostimulator pulse generator or receiver, direct or inductive coupling; with connection to a single electrode array

61886   with connection to 2 or more electrode arrays

(For open placement of cranial nerve (eg, vagal, trigeminal) neurostimulator electrode(s), use 64573)

(For percutaneous placement of cranial nerve (eg, vagal, trigeminal) neurostimulator electrode(s), use 64553)

(For revision or removal of cranial nerve (eg, vagal, trigeminal) neurostimulator electrode(s), use 64585)

61888   Revision or removal of cranial neurostimulator pulse generator or receiver

(Do not report 61888 in conjunction with 61885 or 61886 for the same pulse generator)

Repair

62000   Elevation of depressed skull fracture; simple, extradural

62005   compound or comminuted, extradural

62010   with repair of dura and/or debridement of brain

62100   Craniotomy for repair of dural/cerebrospinal fluid leak, including surgery for rhinorrhea/otorrhea

(For repair of spinal dural/CSF leak, see 63707, 63709)

62115   Reduction of craniomegalic skull (eg, treated hydrocephalus); not requiring bone grafts or cranioplasty

62116   with simple cranioplasty

62117   requiring craniotomy and reconstruction with or without bone graft (includes obtaining grafts)

62120   Repair of encephalocele, skull vault, including cranioplasty

62121   Craniotomy for repair of encephalocele, skull base

62140   Cranioplasty for skull defect; up to 5 cm diameter

62141   larger than 5 cm diameter

62142   Removal of bone flap or prosthetic plate of skull

62143   Replacement of bone flap or prosthetic plate of skull

62145   Cranioplasty for skull defect with reparative brain surgery

62146   Cranioplasty with autograft (includes obtaining bone grafts); up to 5 cm diameter

62147   larger than 5 cm diameter

+ 62148   Incision and retrieval of subcutaneous cranial bone graft for cranioplasty (List separately in addition to code for primary procedure)

(Use 62148 in conjunction with 62140-62147)

Surgery: Nervous System

Neuroendoscopy

Surgical endoscopy always includes diagnostic endoscopy.

+ 62160   Neuroendoscopy, intracranial, for placement or replacement of ventricular catheter and attachment to shunt system or external drainage (List separately in addition to code for primary procedure)

(Use 62160 only in conjunction with 61107, 61210, 62220-62230, 62258)

62161   Neuroendoscopy, intracranial; with dissection of adhesions, fenestration of septum pellucidum or intraventricular cysts (including placement, replacement, or removal of ventricular catheter)

62162   with fenestration or excision of colloid cyst, including placement of external ventricular catheter for drainage

62163   with retrieval of foreign body

62164   with excision of brain tumor, including placement of external ventricular catheter for drainage

62165   with excision of pituitary tumor, transnasal or trans-sphenoidal approach

Cerebrospinal Fluid (CSF) Shunt

62180   Ventriculocisternostomy (Torkildsen type operation)

62190   Creation of shunt; subarachnoid/subdural-atrial, -jugular, -auricular

62192   subarachnoid/subdural-peritoneal, -pleural, other terminus

62194   Replacement or irrigation, subarachnoid/subdural catheter

62200   Ventriculocisternostomy, third ventricle;

62201   stereotactic, neuroendoscopic method

(For intracranial neuroendoscopic procedures, see 62161-62165)

62220   Creation of shunt; ventriculo-atrial, -jugular, -auricular

(For intracranial neuroendoscopic ventricular catheter placement, use 62160)

62223   ventriculo-peritoneal, -pleural, other terminus

(For intracranial neuroendoscopic ventricular catheter placement, use 62160)

62225   Replacement or irrigation, ventricular catheter

(For intracranial neuroendoscopic ventricular catheter placement, use 62160)

62230   Replacement or revision of cerebrospinal fluid shunt, obstructed valve, or distal catheter in shunt system

(For intracranial neuroendoscopic ventricular catheter placement, use 62160)

62252   Reprogramming of programmable cerebrospinal shunt

62256   Removal of complete cerebrospinal fluid shunt system; without replacement

62258   with replacement by similar or other shunt at same operation

(For percutaneous irrigation or aspiration of shunt reservoir, use 61070)

(For reprogramming of programmable CSF shunt, use 62252)

(For intracranial neuroendoscopic ventricular catheter placement, use 62160)

Spine and Spinal Cord

(For application of caliper or tongs, use 20660)

(For treatment of fracture or dislocation of spine, see 22305-22327)

Injection, Drainage, or Aspiration

Injection of contrast during fluoroscopic guidance and localization is an inclusive component of 62263, 62264, 62267, 62270-62273, 62280-62282, 62310-62319. Fluoroscopic guidance and localization is reported with 77003, unless a formal contrast study (myelography, epidurography, or arthrography) is performed, in which case the use of fluoroscopy is included in the supervision and interpretation codes.

For radiologic supervision and interpretation of epidurography, use 72275. Code 72275 is only to be used when an epidurogram is performed, images documented, and a formal radiologic report is issued.

Code 62263 describes a catheter-based treatment involving targeted injection of various substances (eg, hypertonic saline, steroid, anesthetic) via an indwelling epidural catheter. Code 62263 includes percutaneous insertion and removal of an epidural catheter (remaining in place over a several-day period), for the administration of multiple injections of a neurolytic agent(s) performed during serial treatment sessions (ie, spanning two or more treatment days). If required, adhesions or scarring may also be lysed by mechanical means. Code 62263 is **not** reported for each adhesiolysis treatment, but should be reported **once** to describe the entire series of injections/infusions spanning two or more treatment days.

Code 62264 describes multiple adhesiolysis treatment sessions performed on the same day. Adhesions or scarring may be lysed by injections of neurolytic agent(s). If required, adhesions or scarring may also be lysed mechanically using a percutaneously-deployed catheter.

Codes 62263 and 62264 include the procedure of injections of contrast for epidurography (72275) and fluoroscopic guidance and localization (77003) during initial or subsequent sessions.

Surgery: Nervous System

(Report 01996 for daily hospital management of continuous epidural or subarachnoid drug administration performed in conjunction with 62318-62319)

62263   Percutaneous lysis of epidural adhesions using solution injection (eg, hypertonic saline, enzyme) or mechanical means (eg, catheter) including radiologic localization (includes contrast when administered), multiple adhesiolysis sessions; 2 or more days

(62263 includes codes 72275 and 77003)

62264   1 day

(Do not report 62264 with 62263)

(62264 includes codes 72275 and 77003)

62267   Percutaneous aspiration within the nucleus pulposus, intervertebral disc, or paravertebral tissue for diagnostic purposes

▶(For imaging, use 77003)◀

(Do not report 62267 in conjunction with 10022, 20225, 62287, 62290, 62291)

62268   Percutaneous aspiration, spinal cord cyst or syrinx

(For radiological supervision and interpretation, see 76942, 77002, 77012)

62269   Biopsy of spinal cord, percutaneous needle

(For radiological supervision and interpretation, see 76942, 77002, 77012)

(For fine needle aspiration, see 10021, 10022)

(For evaluation of fine needle aspirate, see 88172, 88173)

62270   Spinal puncture, lumbar, diagnostic

62272   Spinal puncture, therapeutic, for drainage of cerebrospinal fluid (by needle or catheter)

62273   Injection, epidural, of blood or clot patch

(For injection of diagnostic or therapeutic substance(s), see 62310, 62311, 62318, 62319)

62280   Injection/infusion of neurolytic substance (eg, alcohol, phenol, iced saline solutions), with or without other therapeutic substance; subarachnoid

62281   epidural, cervical or thoracic

62282   epidural, lumbar, sacral (caudal)

62284   Injection procedure for myelography and/or computed tomography, spinal (other than C1-C2 and posterior fossa)

(For injection procedure at C1-C2, use 61055)

(For radiological supervision and interpretation, see **Radiology**)

62287   Decompression procedure, percutaneous, of nucleus pulposus of intervertebral disc, any method, single or multiple levels, lumbar (eg, manual or automated percutaneous discectomy, percutaneous laser discectomy)

(For fluoroscopic guidance, use 77003)

(Do not report 62287 in conjunction with 62267)

(For injection of non-neurolytic diagnostic or therapeutic substance(s), see 62310, 62311)

62290   Injection procedure for discography, each level; lumbar

62291   cervical or thoracic

(For radiological supervision and interpretation, see 72285, 72295)

62292   Injection procedure for chemonucleolysis, including discography, intervertebral disc, single or multiple levels, lumbar

62294   Injection procedure, arterial, for occlusion of arteriovenous malformation, spinal

62310   Injection, single (not via indwelling catheter), not including neurolytic substances, with or without contrast (for either localization or epidurography), of diagnostic or therapeutic substance(s) (including anesthetic, antispasmodic, opioid, steroid, other solution), epidural or subarachnoid; cervical or thoracic

62311   lumbar, sacral (caudal)

62318   Injection, including catheter placement, continuous infusion or intermittent bolus, not including neurolytic substances, with or without contrast (for either localization or epidurography), of diagnostic or therapeutic substance(s) (including anesthetic, antispasmodic, opioid, steroid, other solution), epidural or subarachnoid; cervical or thoracic

62319   lumbar, sacral (caudal)

(For transforaminal epidural injection, see 64479-64484)

(Report 01996 for daily hospital management of continuous epidural or subarachnoid drug administration performed in conjunction with 62318-62319)

Catheter Implantation

(For percutaneous placement of intrathecal or epidural catheter, see codes 62270-62273, 62280-62284, 62310-62319)

62350   Implantation, revision or repositioning of tunneled intrathecal or epidural catheter, for long-term medication administration via an external pump or implantable reservoir/infusion pump; without laminectomy

62351   with laminectomy

(For refilling and maintenance of an implantable infusion pump for spinal or brain drug therapy, see 95990, 95991)

62355   Removal of previously implanted intrathecal or epidural catheter

Reservoir/Pump Implantation

62360   Implantation or replacement of device for intrathecal or epidural drug infusion; subcutaneous reservoir

62361   nonprogrammable pump

Surgery: Nervous System

62362   programmable pump, including preparation of pump, with or without programming

62365   Removal of subcutaneous reservoir or pump, previously implanted for intrathecal or epidural infusion

62367   Electronic analysis of programmable, implanted pump for intrathecal or epidural drug infusion (includes evaluation of reservoir status, alarm status, drug prescription status); without reprogramming

62368   with reprogramming

(For refilling and maintenance of an implantable infusion pump for spinal or brain drug therapy, use 95990-95991)

Posterior Extradural Laminotomy or Laminectomy for Exploration/Decompression of Neural Elements or Excision of Herniated Intervertebral Discs

(When 63001-63048 are followed by arthrodesis, see 22590-22614)

63001   Laminectomy with exploration and/or decompression of spinal cord and/or cauda equina, without facetectomy, foraminotomy or discectomy (eg, spinal stenosis), 1 or 2 vertebral segments; cervical

63003   thoracic

63005   lumbar, except for spondylolisthesis

63011   sacral

63012   Laminectomy with removal of abnormal facets and/or pars inter-articularis with decompression of cauda equina and nerve roots for spondylolisthesis, lumbar (Gill type procedure)

63015   Laminectomy with exploration and/or decompression of spinal cord and/or cauda equina, without facetectomy, foraminotomy or discectomy (eg, spinal stenosis), more than 2 vertebral segments; cervical

63016   thoracic

63017   lumbar

63020   Laminotomy (hemilaminectomy), with decompression of nerve root(s), including partial facetectomy, foraminotomy and/or excision of herniated intervertebral disc, including open and endoscopically-assisted approaches; 1 interspace, cervical

(For bilateral procedure, report 63020 with modifier 50)

63030   1 interspace, lumbar

(For bilateral procedure, report 63030 with modifier 50)

+ 63035   each additional interspace, cervical or lumbar (List separately in addition to code for primary procedure)

(Use 63035 in conjunction with 63020-63030)

(For bilateral procedure, report 63035 with modifier 50)

63040   Laminotomy (hemilaminectomy), with decompression of nerve root(s), including partial facetectomy, foraminotomy and/or excision of herniated intervertebral disc, reexploration, single interspace; cervical

(For bilateral procedure, report 63040 with modifier 50)

63042   lumbar

(For bilateral procedure, report 63042 with modifier 50)

+ 63043   each additional cervical interspace (List separately in addition to code for primary procedure)

(Use 63043 in conjunction with 63040)

(For bilateral procedure, report 63043 with modifier 50)

+ 63044   each additional lumbar interspace (List separately in addition to code for primary procedure)

(Use 63044 in conjunction with 63042)

(For bilateral procedure, report 63044 with modifier 50)

63045   Laminectomy, facetectomy and foraminotomy (unilateral or bilateral with decompression of spinal cord, cauda equina and/or nerve root[s], [eg, spinal or lateral recess stenosis]), single vertebral segment; cervical

63046   thoracic

63047   lumbar

+ 63048   each additional segment, cervical, thoracic, or lumbar (List separately in addition to code for primary procedure)

(Use 63048 in conjunction with 63045-63047)

63050   Laminoplasty, cervical, with decompression of the spinal cord, 2 or more vertebral segments;

63051   with reconstruction of the posterior bony elements (including the application of bridging bone graft and non-segmental fixation devices (eg, wire, suture, mini-plates), when performed)

(Do not report 63050 or 63051 in conjunction with 22600, 22614, 22840-22842, 63001, 63015, 63045, 63048, 63295 for the same vertebral segment(s))

Transpedicular or Costovertebral Approach for Posterolateral Extradural Exploration/Decompression

63055   Transpedicular approach with decompression of spinal cord, equina and/or nerve root(s) (eg, herniated intervertebral disc), single segment; thoracic

63056   lumbar (including transfacet, or lateral extraforaminal approach) (eg, far lateral herniated intervertebral disc)

+ 63057   each additional segment, thoracic or lumbar (List separately in addition to code for primary procedure)

(Use 63057 in conjunction with 63055, 63056)

63064   Costovertebral approach with decompression of spinal cord or nerve root(s) (eg, herniated intervertebral disc), thoracic; single segment

+ 63066   each additional segment (List separately in addition to code for primary procedure)

(Use 63066 in conjunction with 63064)

(For excision of thoracic intraspinal lesions by laminectomy, see 63266, 63271, 63276, 63281, 63286)

Anterior or Anterolateral Approach for Extradural Exploration/Decompression

For the following codes, when two surgeons work together as primary surgeons performing distinct part(s) of spinal cord exploration/decompression operation, each surgeon should report his/her distinct operative work by appending modifier 62 to the procedure code (and any associated add-on codes for that procedure code as long as both surgeons continue to work together as primary surgeons). In this situation, modifier 62 may be appended to the definitive procedure code(s) 63075, 63077, 63081, 63085, 63087, 63090 and, as appropriate, to associated additional interspace add-on code(s) 63076, 63078 or additional segment add-on code(s) 63082, 63086, 63088, 63091 as long as both surgeons continue to work together as primary surgeons.

63075   Discectomy, anterior, with decompression of spinal cord and/or nerve root(s), including osteophytectomy; cervical, single interspace

+ 63076   cervical, each additional interspace (List separately in addition to code for primary procedure)

(Use 63076 in conjunction with 63075)

63077   thoracic, single interspace

+ 63078   thoracic, each additional interspace (List separately in addition to code for primary procedure)

(Use 63078 in conjunction with 63077)

(Do not report code 69990 in addition to codes 63075-63078)

63081   Vertebral corpectomy (vertebral body resection), partial or complete, anterior approach with decompression of spinal cord and/or nerve root(s); cervical, single segment

+ 63082   cervical, each additional segment (List separately in addition to code for primary procedure)

(Use 63082 in conjunction with 63081)

(For transoral approach, see 61575, 61576)

63085   Vertebral corpectomy (vertebral body resection), partial or complete, transthoracic approach with decompression of spinal cord and/or nerve root(s); thoracic, single segment

+ 63086   thoracic, each additional segment (List separately in addition to code for primary procedure)

(Use 63086 in conjunction with 63085)

63087   Vertebral corpectomy (vertebral body resection), partial or complete, combined thoracolumbar approach with decompression of spinal cord, cauda equina or nerve root(s), lower thoracic or lumbar; single segment

+ 63088   each additional segment (List separately in addition to code for primary procedure)

(Use 63088 in conjunction with 63087)

63090   Vertebral corpectomy (vertebral body resection), partial or complete, transperitoneal or retroperitoneal approach with decompression of spinal cord, cauda equina or nerve root(s), lower thoracic, lumbar, or sacral; single segment

+ 63091   each additional segment (List separately in addition to code for primary procedure)

(Use 63091 in conjunction with 63090)

(Procedures 63081-63091 include discectomy above and/or below vertebral segment)

(If followed by arthrodesis, see 22548-22812)

(For reconstruction of spine, use appropriate vertebral corpectomy codes 63081-63091, bone graft codes 20930-20938, arthrodesis codes 22548-22812, and spinal instrumentation codes 22840-22855)

Lateral Extracavitary Approach for Extradural Exploration/Decompression

63101   Vertebral corpectomy (vertebral body resection), partial or complete, lateral extracavitary approach with decompression of spinal cord and/or nerve root(s) (eg, for tumor or retropulsed bone fragments); thoracic, single segment

63102   lumbar, single segment

+ 63103   thoracic or lumbar, each additional segment (List separately in addition to code for primary procedure)

(Use 63103 in conjunction with 63101 and 63102)

Incision

63170   Laminectomy with myelotomy (eg, Bischof or DREZ type), cervical, thoracic, or thoracolumbar

63172   Laminectomy with drainage of intramedullary cyst/syrinx; to subarachnoid space

63173   to peritoneal or pleural space

63180   Laminectomy and section of dentate ligaments, with or without dural graft, cervical; 1 or 2 segments

63182   more than 2 segments

63185   Laminectomy with rhizotomy; 1 or 2 segments

63190   more than 2 segments

63191   Laminectomy with section of spinal accessory nerve

(For bilateral procedure, report 63191 with modifier 50)

(For resection of sternocleidomastoid muscle, use 21720)

▲=Revised code   ●=New code   ▶ ◀=Contains new or revised text   ⊘=Modifier 51 exempt

63194 Laminectomy with cordotomy, with section of 1 spinothalamic tract, 1 stage; cervical

63195   thoracic

63196 Laminectomy with cordotomy, with section of both spinothalamic tracts, 1 stage; cervical

63197   thoracic

63198 Laminectomy with cordotomy with section of both spinothalamic tracts, 2 stages within 14 days; cervical

63199   thoracic

63200 Laminectomy, with release of tethered spinal cord, lumbar

Excision by Laminectomy of Lesion Other Than Herniated Disc

63250 Laminectomy for excision or occlusion of arteriovenous malformation of spinal cord; cervical

63251   thoracic

63252   thoracolumbar

63265 Laminectomy for excision or evacuation of intraspinal lesion other than neoplasm, extradural; cervical

63266   thoracic

63267   lumbar

63268   sacral

63270 Laminectomy for excision of intraspinal lesion other than neoplasm, intradural; cervical

63271   thoracic

63272   lumbar

63273   sacral

63275 Laminectomy for biopsy/excision of intraspinal neoplasm; extradural, cervical

63276   extradural, thoracic

63277   extradural, lumbar

63278   extradural, sacral

63280   intradural, extramedullary, cervical

63281   intradural, extramedullary, thoracic

63282   intradural, extramedullary, lumbar

63283   intradural, sacral

63285   intradural, intramedullary, cervical

63286   intradural, intramedullary, thoracic

63287   intradural, intramedullary, thoracolumbar

63290   combined extradural-intradural lesion, any level

(For drainage of intramedullary cyst/syrinx, use 63172, 63173)

+ 63295 Osteoplastic reconstruction of dorsal spinal elements, following primary intraspinal procedure (List separately in addition to code for primary procedure)

(Use 63295 in conjunction with 63172, 63173, 63185, 63190, 63200-63290)

(Do not report 63295 in conjunction with 22590-22614, 22840-22844, 63050, 63051 for the same vertebral segment(s))

Excision, Anterior or Anterolateral Approach, Intraspinal Lesion

For the following codes, when two surgeons work together as primary surgeons performing distinct part(s) of an anterior approach for an intraspinal excision, each surgeon should report his/her distinct operative work by appending modifier 62 to the single definitive procedure code. In this situation, modifier 62 may be appended to the definitive procedure code(s) 63300-63307 and, as appropriate, to the associated additional segment add-on code 63308 as long as both surgeons continue to work together as primary surgeons.

(For arthrodesis, see 22548-22585)

(For reconstruction of spine, see 20930-20938)

63300 Vertebral corpectomy (vertebral body resection), partial or complete, for excision of intraspinal lesion, single segment; extradural, cervical

63301   extradural, thoracic by transthoracic approach

63302   extradural, thoracic by thoracolumbar approach

63303   extradural, lumbar or sacral by transperitoneal or retroperitoneal approach

63304   intradural, cervical

63305   intradural, thoracic by transthoracic approach

63306   intradural, thoracic by thoracolumbar approach

63307   intradural, lumbar or sacral by transperitoneal or retroperitoneal approach

+ 63308   each additional segment (List separately in addition to codes for single segment)

(Use 63308 in conjunction with 63300-63307)

Stereotaxis

63600 Creation of lesion of spinal cord by stereotactic method, percutaneous, any modality (including stimulation and/or recording)

63610 Stereotactic stimulation of spinal cord, percutaneous, separate procedure not followed by other surgery

63615 Stereotactic biopsy, aspiration, or excision of lesion, spinal cord

Stereotactic Radiosurgery (Spinal)

Spinal stereotactic radiosurgery is a distinct procedure that utilizes externally generated ionizing radiation to inactivate or eradicate defined target(s) in the spine without the need to make an incision. The target is defined by and the treatment is delivered using high-resolution stereotactic imaging. These codes are reported by the surgeon. The radiation oncologist reports the appropriate code(s) for clinical treatment planning, physics and dosimetry, treatment delivery and management from the **Radiation Oncology** section (77261-77790). Any necessary planning, dosimetry, targeting, positioning, or blocking by the neurosurgeon is included in the stereotactic radiation surgery services. The same physician should not report stereotactic radiosurgery services with radiation treatment management codes (77427-77432).

Spinal stereotactic radiosurgery is typically performed in a single planning and treatment session using a stereotactic image-guidance system, but can be performed with a planning session and in a limited number of treatment sessions, up to a maximum of five sessions. Do not report stereotactic radiosurgery more than once per lesion per course of treatment when the treatment requires greater than one session.

Stereotactic spinal surgery is only used when the tumor being treated affects spinal neural tissue or abuts the dura mater. Arteriovenous malformations must be subdural. For other radiation services of the spine, see **Radiation Oncology** services.

Codes 63620, 63621 include computer-assisted planning. Do not report 63620, 63621 in conjunction with 61795.

> ►(For intensity modulated beam delivery plan and treatment, see 77301, 77418. For stereotactic body radiation therapy, see 77373, 77435)◄

63620   Stereotactic radiosurgery (particle beam, gamma ray, or linear accelerator); 1 spinal lesion

(Do not report 63620 more than once per course of treatment)

+ 63621   each additional spinal lesion (List separately in addition to code for primary procedure)

(Report 63621 in conjunction with 63620)

(For each course of treatment, 63621 may be reported no more than once per lesion. Do not report 63621 more than 2 times for entire course of treatment regardless of number of lesions treated)

Neurostimulators (Spinal)

Codes 63650-63688 apply to both simple and complex neurostimulators. For initial or subsequent electronic analysis and programming of neurostimulator pulse generators, see codes 95970-95975.

►Codes 63650, 63655, and 63661-63664 describe the operative placement, revision, replacement, or removal of the spinal neurostimulator system components to provide spinal electrical stimulation. A neurostimulator system includes an implanted neurostimulator, external controller, extension, and collection of contacts. Multiple contacts or electrodes (4 or more) provide the actual electrical stimulation in the epidural space.

For percutaneously placed neurostimulator systems (63650, 63661, 63663), the contacts are on a catheter-like lead. An array defines the collection of contacts that are on one catheter.

For systems placed via an open surgical exposure (63655, 63662, 63664), the contacts are on a plate or paddle-shaped surface.

Do not report 63661 or 63663 when removing or replacing a temporary percutaneously placed array for an external generator.◄

63650   Percutaneous implantation of neurostimulator electrode array, epidural

63655   Laminectomy for implantation of neurostimulator electrodes, plate/paddle, epidural

> ►(63660 has been deleted. To report, see 63661-63664)◄

● 63661   Removal of spinal neurostimulator electrode percutaneous array(s), including fluoroscopy, when performed

● 63662   Removal of spinal neurostimulator electrode plate/paddle(s) placed via laminotomy or laminectomy, including fluoroscopy, when performed

● 63663   Revision including replacement, when performed, of spinal neurostimulator electrode percutaneous array(s), including fluoroscopy, when performed

> ►(Do not report 63663 in conjunction with 63661, 63662 for the same spinal level)◄

● 63664   Revision including replacement, when performed, of spinal neurostimulator electrode plate/paddle(s) placed via laminotomy or laminectomy, including fluoroscopy, when performed

> ►(Do not report 63664 in conjunction with 63661, 63662 for the same spinal level)◄

63685   Insertion or replacement of spinal neurostimulator pulse generator or receiver, direct or inductive coupling

(Do not report 63685 in conjunction with 63688 for the same pulse generator or receiver)

63688   Revision or removal of implanted spinal neurostimulator pulse generator or receiver

(For electronic analysis of implanted neurostimulator pulse generator system, see 95970-95975)

Surgery: Nervous System

Repair

63700   Repair of meningocele; less than 5 cm diameter

63702   larger than 5 cm diameter

(Do not use modifier 63 in conjunction with 63700, 63702)

63704   Repair of myelomeningocele; less than 5 cm diameter

63706   larger than 5 cm diameter

(Do not use modifier 63 in conjunction with 63704, 63706)

(For complex skin closure, see **Integumentary System**)

63707   Repair of dural/cerebrospinal fluid leak, not requiring laminectomy

63709   Repair of dural/cerebrospinal fluid leak or pseudomeningocele, with laminectomy

63710   Dural graft, spinal

(For laminectomy and section of dentate ligaments, with or without dural graft, cervical, see 63180, 63182)

Shunt, Spinal CSF

63740   Creation of shunt, lumbar, subarachnoid-peritoneal, -pleural, or other; including laminectomy

63741   percutaneous, not requiring laminectomy

63744   Replacement, irrigation or revision of lumbosubarachnoid shunt

63746   Removal of entire lumbosubarachnoid shunt system without replacement

(For insertion of subarachnoid catheter with reservoir and/or pump for intermittent or continuous infusion of drug including laminectomy, see 62351 and 62360, 62361 or 62362)

(For insertion or replacement of subarachnoid or epidural catheter, with reservoir and/or pump for drug infusion without laminectomy, see 62350 and 62360, 62361 or 62362)

Extracranial Nerves, Peripheral Nerves, and Autonomic Nervous System

(For intracranial surgery on cranial nerves, see 61450, 61460, 61790)

Introduction/Injection of Anesthetic Agent (Nerve Block), Diagnostic or Therapeutic

►(For destruction by neurolytic agent or chemodenervation, see 62280-62282, 64600-64681)◄

►(For epidural or subarachnoid injection, see 62310-62319)◄

►(Codes 64479-64495 are unilateral procedures. For bilateral procedures, use modifier 50)◄

►(For fluoroscopic guidance and localization for needle placement and injection in conjunction with 64479-64484, use 77003)◄

Somatic Nerves

64400   Injection, anesthetic agent; trigeminal nerve, any division or branch

64402   facial nerve

64405   greater occipital nerve

64408   vagus nerve

64410   phrenic nerve

64412   spinal accessory nerve

64413   cervical plexus

64415   brachial plexus, single

64416   brachial plexus, continuous infusion by catheter (including catheter placement)

(Do not report 64416 in conjunction with 01996)

64417   axillary nerve

64418   suprascapular nerve

64420   intercostal nerve, single

64421   intercostal nerves, multiple, regional block

64425   ilioinguinal, iliohypogastric nerves

64430   pudendal nerve

64435   paracervical (uterine) nerve

64445   sciatic nerve, single

64446   sciatic nerve, continuous infusion by catheter (including catheter placement)

(Do not report 64446 in conjunction with 01996)

64447   femoral nerve, single

(Do not report 64447 in conjunction with 01996)

64448   femoral nerve, continuous infusion by catheter (including catheter placement)

(Do not report 64448 in conjunction with 01996)

64449   lumbar plexus, posterior approach, continuous infusion by catheter (including catheter placement)

(Do not report 64449 in conjunction with 01996)

64450   other peripheral nerve or branch

64455   Injection(s), anesthetic agent and/or steroid, plantar common digital nerve(s) (eg, Morton's neuroma)

(Do not report 64455 in conjunction with 64632)

►(Codes 64470-64476 have been deleted. To report, see 64490-64495)◄

64479   Injection, anesthetic agent and/or steroid, transforaminal epidural; cervical or thoracic, single level

+ 64480   cervical or thoracic, each additional level (List separately in addition to code for primary procedure)

          (Use 64480 in conjunction with 64479)

64483   lumbar or sacral, single level

+ 64484   lumbar or sacral, each additional level (List separately in addition to code for primary procedure)

          (Use 64484 in conjunction with 64483)

▶Paravertebral Spinal Nerves and Branches◀

▶(Image guidance [fluoroscopy or CT] and any injection of contrast are inclusive components of 64490-64495. Imaging guidance and localization are required for the performance of paravertebral facet joint injections described by codes 64490-64495. If imaging is not used, report 20550-20553. If ultrasound guidance is used, report 64999)◀

▶(For bilateral procedures, use modifier 50)◀

▶(For injection of the T12-L1 joint, or nerves innervating that joint, use 64493)◀

● **64490**   Injection(s), diagnostic or therapeutic agent, paravertebral facet (zygapophyseal) joint (or nerves innervating that joint) with image guidance (fluoroscopy or CT), cervical or thoracic; single level

+● **64491**   second level (List separately in addition to code for primary procedure)

+● **64492**   third and any additional level(s) (List separately in addition to code for primary procedure)

          ▶(Do not report 64492 more than once per day)◀

          ▶(Use 64491, 64492 in conjunction with 64490)◀

● **64493**   Injection(s), diagnostic or therapeutic agent, paravertebral facet (zygapophyseal) joint (or nerves innervating that joint) with image guidance (fluoroscopy or CT), lumbar or sacral; single level

+● **64494**   second level (List separately in addition to code for primary procedure)

+● **64495**   third and any additional level(s) (List separately in addition to code for primary procedure)

          ▶(Do not report 64495 more than once per day)◀

          ▶(Use 64494, 64495 in conjunction with 64493)◀

▶Autonomic Nerves◀

64505   Injection, anesthetic agent; sphenopalatine ganglion

64508   carotid sinus (separate procedure)

64510   stellate ganglion (cervical sympathetic)

64517   superior hypogastric plexus

64520   lumbar or thoracic (paravertebral sympathetic)

64530   celiac plexus, with or without radiologic monitoring

Neurostimulators (Peripheral Nerve)

Codes 64553-64595 apply to both simple and complex neurostimulators. For initial or subsequent electronic analysis and programming of neurostimulator pulse generators, see codes 95970-95975.

64550   Application of surface (transcutaneous) neurostimulator

64553   Percutaneous implantation of neurostimulator electrodes; cranial nerve

          (For open placement of cranial nerve (eg, vagal, trigeminal) neurostimulator pulse generator or receiver, see 61885, 61886, as appropriate)

64555   peripheral nerve (excludes sacral nerve)

64560   autonomic nerve

64561   sacral nerve (transforaminal placement)

64565   neuromuscular

64573   Incision for implantation of neurostimulator electrodes; cranial nerve

          (For open placement of cranial nerve (eg, vagal, trigeminal) neurostimulator pulse generator or receiver, see 61885, 61886, as appropriate)

          (For revision or removal of cranial nerve (eg, vagal, trigeminal) neurostimulator pulse generator or receiver, use 61888)

64575   peripheral nerve (excludes sacral nerve)

64577   autonomic nerve

64580   neuromuscular

64581   sacral nerve (transforaminal placement)

64585   Revision or removal of peripheral neurostimulator electrodes

64590   Insertion or replacement of peripheral or gastric neurostimulator pulse generator or receiver, direct or inductive coupling

          (Do not report 64590 in conjunction with 64595)

64595   Revision or removal of peripheral or gastric neurostimulator pulse generator or receiver

Surgery: Nervous System

Destruction by Neurolytic Agent (eg, Chemical, Thermal, Electrical or Radiofrequency)

Codes 64600-64681 include the injection of other therapeutic agents (eg, corticosteroids). (For therapies that are not destructive of the target nerve [eg, pulsed radiofrequency]), use 64999)

Somatic Nerves

64600 Destruction by neurolytic agent, trigeminal nerve; supraorbital, infraorbital, mental, or inferior alveolar branch

64605 second and third division branches at foramen ovale

64610 second and third division branches at foramen ovale under radiologic monitoring

64612 Chemodenervation of muscle(s); muscle(s) innervated by facial nerve (eg, for blepharospasm, hemifacial spasm)

64613 neck muscle(s) (eg, for spasmodic torticollis, spasmodic dysphonia)

64614 extremity(s) and/or trunk muscle(s) (eg, for dystonia, cerebral palsy, multiple sclerosis)

(For chemodenervation guided by needle electromyography or muscle electrical stimulation, see 95873, 95874)

(For chemodenervation for strabismus involving the extraocular muscles, use 67345)

(For chemodenervation of internal anal sphincter, use 46505)

64620 Destruction by neurolytic agent, intercostal nerve

(For fluoroscopic guidance and localization for needle placement and neurolysis in conjunction with 64622-64627, use 77003)

64622 Destruction by neurolytic agent, paravertebral facet joint nerve; lumbar or sacral, single level

(For bilateral procedure, report 64622 with modifier 50)

+ 64623 lumbar or sacral, each additional level (List separately in addition to code for primary procedure)

(Use 64623 in conjunction with 64622)

(For bilateral procedure, report 64623 with modifier 50)

64626 cervical or thoracic, single level

(For bilateral procedure, report 64626 with modifier 50)

+ 64627 cervical or thoracic, each additional level (List separately in addition to code for primary procedure)

(Use 64627 in conjunction with 64626)

(For bilateral procedure, report 64627 with modifier 50)

64630 Destruction by neurolytic agent; pudendal nerve

64632 plantar common digital nerve

(Do not report 64632 in conjunction with 64455)

64640 other peripheral nerve or branch

Sympathetic Nerves

64650 Chemodenervation of eccrine glands; both axillae

64653 other area(s) (eg, scalp, face, neck), per day

(Report the specific service in conjunction with code(s) for the specific substance(s) or drug(s) provided)

(For chemodenervation of extremities (eg, hands or feet), use 64999)

64680 Destruction by neurolytic agent, with or without radiologic monitoring; celiac plexus

64681 superior hypogastric plexus

Neuroplasty (Exploration, Neurolysis or Nerve Decompression)

Neuroplasty is the decompression or freeing of intact nerve from scar tissue, including external neurolysis and/or transposition.

(For internal neurolysis requiring use of operating microscope, use 64727)

(For facial nerve decompression, use 69720)

(For neuroplasty with nerve wrapping, see 64702-64727, 64999)

64702 Neuroplasty; digital, 1 or both, same digit

64704 nerve of hand or foot

64708 Neuroplasty, major peripheral nerve, arm or leg; other than specified

64712 sciatic nerve

64713 brachial plexus

64714 lumbar plexus

64716 Neuroplasty and/or transposition; cranial nerve (specify)

64718 ulnar nerve at elbow

64719 ulnar nerve at wrist

64721 median nerve at carpal tunnel

(For arthroscopic procedure, use 29848)

64722 Decompression; unspecified nerve(s) (specify)

64726 plantar digital nerve

+ 64727 Internal neurolysis, requiring use of operating microscope (List separately in addition to code for neuroplasty) (Neuroplasty includes external neurolysis)

(Do not report code 69990 in addition to code 64727)

Transection or Avulsion

(For stereotactic lesion of gasserian ganglion, use 61790)

64732 Transection or avulsion of; supraorbital nerve

64734 infraorbital nerve

64736 mental nerve

64738 inferior alveolar nerve by osteotomy

64740 lingual nerve

64742 facial nerve, differential or complete

64744 greater occipital nerve

64746 phrenic nerve

(For section of recurrent laryngeal nerve, use 31595)

64752 vagus nerve (vagotomy), transthoracic

64755 vagus nerves limited to proximal stomach (selective proximal vagotomy, proximal gastric vagotomy, parietal cell vagotomy, supra- or highly selective vagotomy)

(For laparoscopic approach, use 43652)

64760 vagus nerve (vagotomy), abdominal

(For laparoscopic approach, use 43651)

64761 pudendal nerve

(For bilateral procedure, report 64761 with modifier 50)

64763 Transection or avulsion of obturator nerve, extrapelvic, with or without adductor tenotomy

(For bilateral procedure, report 64763 with modifier 50)

64766 Transection or avulsion of obturator nerve, intrapelvic, with or without adductor tenotomy

(For bilateral procedure, report 64766 with modifier 50)

64771 Transection or avulsion of other cranial nerve, extradural

64772 Transection or avulsion of other spinal nerve, extradural

(For excision of tender scar, skin and subcutaneous tissue, with or without tiny neuroma, see 11400-11446, 13100-13153)

Excision

Somatic Nerves

(For Morton neurectomy, use 28080)

64774 Excision of neuroma; cutaneous nerve, surgically identifiable

64776 digital nerve, 1 or both, same digit

+ 64778 digital nerve, each additional digit (List separately in addition to code for primary procedure)

(Use 64778 in conjunction with 64776)

64782 hand or foot, except digital nerve

+ 64783 hand or foot, each additional nerve, except same digit (List separately in addition to code for primary procedure)

(Use 64783 in conjunction with 64782)

64784 major peripheral nerve, except sciatic

64786 sciatic nerve

+ 64787 Implantation of nerve end into bone or muscle (List separately in addition to neuroma excision)

(Use 64787 in conjunction with 64774-64786)

64788 Excision of neurofibroma or neurolemmoma; cutaneous nerve

64790 major peripheral nerve

64792 extensive (including malignant type)

64795 Biopsy of nerve

Sympathetic Nerves

64802 Sympathectomy, cervical

(For bilateral procedure, report 64802 with modifier 50)

64804 Sympathectomy, cervicothoracic

(For bilateral procedure, report 64804 with modifier 50)

64809 Sympathectomy, thoracolumbar

(For bilateral procedure, report 64809 with modifier 50)

64818 Sympathectomy, lumbar

(For bilateral procedure, report 64818 with modifier 50)

64820 Sympathectomy; digital arteries, each digit

(Do not report 69990 in addition to code 64820)

64821 radial artery

(Do not report 69990 in addition to code 64821)

64822 ulnar artery

(Do not report 69990 in addition to code 64822)

64823 superficial palmar arch

(Do not report 69990 in addition to code 64823)

Neurorrhaphy

64831 Suture of digital nerve, hand or foot; 1 nerve

+ 64832 each additional digital nerve (List separately in addition to code for primary procedure)

(Use 64832 in conjunction with 64831)

64834 Suture of 1 nerve; hand or foot, common sensory nerve

64835 median motor thenar

64836 ulnar motor

Surgery: Nervous System

+ **64837**   Suture of each additional nerve, hand or foot (List separately in addition to code for primary procedure)

(Use 64837 in conjunction with 64834-64836)

64840   Suture of posterior tibial nerve

64856   Suture of major peripheral nerve, arm or leg, except sciatic; including transposition

64857   without transposition

64858   Suture of sciatic nerve

+ **64859**   Suture of each additional major peripheral nerve (List separately in addition to code for primary procedure)

(Use 64859 in conjunction with 64856, 64857)

64861   Suture of; brachial plexus

64862   lumbar plexus

64864   Suture of facial nerve; extracranial

64865   infratemporal, with or without grafting

64866   Anastomosis; facial-spinal accessory

64868   facial-hypoglossal

64870   facial-phrenic

+ **64872**   Suture of nerve; requiring secondary or delayed suture (List separately in addition to code for primary neurorrhaphy)

(Use 64872 in conjunction with 64831-64865)

+ **64874**   requiring extensive mobilization, or transposition of nerve (List separately in addition to code for nerve suture)

(Use 64874 in conjunction with 64831-64865)

+ **64876**   requiring shortening of bone of extremity (List separately in addition to code for nerve suture)

(Use 64876 in conjunction with 64831-64865)

Neurorrhaphy With Nerve Graft, Vein Graft, or Conduit

64885   Nerve graft (includes obtaining graft), head or neck; up to 4 cm in length

64886   more than 4 cm length

64890   Nerve graft (includes obtaining graft), single strand, hand or foot; up to 4 cm length

64891   more than 4 cm length

64892   Nerve graft (includes obtaining graft), single strand, arm or leg; up to 4 cm length

64893   more than 4 cm length

64895   Nerve graft (includes obtaining graft), multiple strands (cable), hand or foot; up to 4 cm length

64896   more than 4 cm length

64897   Nerve graft (includes obtaining graft), multiple strands (cable), arm or leg; up to 4 cm length

64898   more than 4 cm length

+ **64901**   Nerve graft, each additional nerve; single strand (List separately in addition to code for primary procedure)

(Use 64901 in conjunction with 64885-64893)

+ **64902**   multiple strands (cable) (List separately in addition to code for primary procedure)

(Use 64902 in conjunction with 64885, 64886, 64895-64898)

64905   Nerve pedicle transfer; first stage

64907   second stage

64910   Nerve repair; with synthetic conduit or vein allograft (eg, nerve tube), each nerve

64911   with autogenous vein graft (includes harvest of vein graft), each nerve

(Do not report 69990 in addition to 64910, 64911)

Other Procedures

64999   Unlisted procedure, nervous system

Eye and Ocular Adnexa

(For diagnostic and treatment ophthalmological services, see **Medicine, Ophthalmology,** and 92002 et seq)

(Do not report code 69990 in addition to codes 65091-68850)

Eyeball

Removal of Eye

65091   Evisceration of ocular contents; without implant

65093   with implant

65101   Enucleation of eye; without implant

65103   with implant, muscles not attached to implant

65105   with implant, muscles attached to implant

(For conjunctivoplasty after enucleation, see 68320 et seq)

65110   Exenteration of orbit (does not include skin graft), removal of orbital contents; only

65112   with therapeutic removal of bone

65114   with muscle or myocutaneous flap

(For skin graft to orbit (split skin), see 15120, 15121; free, full thickness, see 15260, 15261)

(For eyelid repair involving more than skin, see 67930 et seq)

Secondary Implant(s) Procedures

An ocular implant is an implant inside muscular cone; an orbital implant is an implant outside muscular cone.

65125   Modification of ocular implant with placement or replacement of pegs (eg, drilling receptacle for prosthesis appendage) (separate procedure)

65130   Insertion of ocular implant secondary; after evisceration, in scleral shell

65135   after enucleation, muscles not attached to implant

65140   after enucleation, muscles attached to implant

65150   Reinsertion of ocular implant; with or without conjunctival graft

65155   with use of foreign material for reinforcement and/or attachment of muscles to implant

65175   Removal of ocular implant

(For orbital implant (implant outside muscle cone) insertion, use 67550; removal, use 67560)

Removal of Foreign Body

(For removal of implanted material: ocular implant, use 65175; anterior segment implant, use 65920; posterior segment implant, use 67120; orbital implant, use 67560)

(For diagnostic x-ray for foreign body, use 70030)

(For diagnostic echography for foreign body, use 76529)

(For removal of foreign body from orbit: frontal approach, use 67413; lateral approach, use 67430; transcranial approach, use 61334)

(For removal of foreign body from eyelid, embedded, use 67938)

(For removal of foreign body from lacrimal system, use 68530)

65205   Removal of foreign body, external eye; conjunctival superficial

65210   conjunctival embedded (includes concretions), subconjunctival, or scleral nonperforating

65220   corneal, without slit lamp

65222   corneal, with slit lamp

(For repair of corneal laceration with foreign body, use 65275)

65235   Removal of foreign body, intraocular; from anterior chamber of eye or lens

(For removal of implanted material from anterior segment, use 65920)

65260   from posterior segment, magnetic extraction, anterior or posterior route

65265   from posterior segment, nonmagnetic extraction

(For removal of implanted material from posterior segment, use 67120)

Repair of Laceration

(For fracture of orbit, see 21385 et seq)

(For repair of wound of eyelid, skin, linear, simple, see 12011-12018; intermediate, layered closure, see 12051-12057; linear, complex, see 13150-13160; other, see 67930, 67935)

(For repair of wound of lacrimal system, use 68700)

(For repair of operative wound, use 66250)

65270   Repair of laceration; conjunctiva, with or without nonperforating laceration sclera, direct closure

65272   conjunctiva, by mobilization and rearrangement, without hospitalization

65273   conjunctiva, by mobilization and rearrangement, with hospitalization

65275   cornea, nonperforating, with or without removal foreign body

Surgery: Ocular System

| 65280 | cornea and/or sclera, perforating, not involving uveal tissue |

65285   cornea and/or sclera, perforating, with reposition or resection of uveal tissue

65286   application of tissue glue, wounds of cornea and/or sclera

(Repair of laceration includes use of conjunctival flap and restoration of anterior chamber, by air or saline injection when indicated)

(For repair of iris or ciliary body, use 66680)

65290   Repair of wound, extraocular muscle, tendon and/or Tenon's capsule

Anterior Segment

Cornea

Excision

65400   Excision of lesion, cornea (keratectomy, lamellar, partial), except pterygium

65410   Biopsy of cornea

65420   Excision or transposition of pterygium; without graft

65426   with graft

Removal or Destruction

65430   Scraping of cornea, diagnostic, for smear and/or culture

65435   Removal of corneal epithelium; with or without chemocauterization (abrasion, curettage)

65436   with application of chelating agent (eg, EDTA)

65450   Destruction of lesion of cornea by cryotherapy, photocoagulation or thermocauterization

65600   Multiple punctures of anterior cornea (eg, for corneal erosion, tattoo)

Keratoplasty

Corneal transplant includes use of fresh or preserved grafts. The preparation of donor material is included for penetrating or anterior lamellar keratoplasty, but reported separately for endothelial keratoplasty. Do not report 65710-65757 in conjunction with 92025.

(Keratoplasty excludes refractive keratoplasty procedures, 65760, 65765, and 65767)

65710   Keratoplasty (corneal transplant); anterior lamellar

65730   penetrating (except in aphakia or pseudophakia)

65750   penetrating (in aphakia)

65755   penetrating (in pseudophakia)

65756   endothelial

+ 65757   Backbench preparation of corneal endothelial allograft prior to transplantation (List separately in addition to code for primary procedure)

(Use 65757 in conjunction with 65756)

Other Procedures

Do not report 65760-65771 in conjunction with 92025.

65760   Keratomileusis

65765   Keratophakia

65767   Epikeratoplasty

65770   Keratoprosthesis

65771   Radial keratotomy

65772   Corneal relaxing incision for correction of surgically induced astigmatism

65775   Corneal wedge resection for correction of surgically induced astigmatism

(For fitting of contact lens for treatment of disease, use 92070)

(For unlisted procedures on cornea, use 66999)

65780   Ocular surface reconstruction; amniotic membrane transplantation

65781   limbal stem cell allograft (eg, cadaveric or living donor)

65782   limbal conjunctival autograft (includes obtaining graft)

(For harvesting conjunctival allograft, living donor, use 68371)

Anterior Chamber

Incision

65800   Paracentesis of anterior chamber of eye (separate procedure); with diagnostic aspiration of aqueous

65805   with therapeutic release of aqueous

65810   with removal of vitreous and/or discission of anterior hyaloid membrane, with or without air injection

65815   with removal of blood, with or without irrigation and/or air injection

(For injection, see 66020-66030)

(For removal of blood clot, use 65930)

65820   Goniotomy

(Do not report modifier 63 in conjunction with 65820)

(For use of ophthalmic endoscope with 65820, use 66990)

65850   Trabeculotomy ab externo

⊙=Moderate sedation   +=Add-on code   ✗=FDA approval pending   #=Resequenced code

Surgery: Ocular System

65855   Trabeculoplasty by laser surgery, 1 or more sessions (defined treatment series)

(If re-treatment is necessary after several months because of disease progression, a new treatment or treatment series should be reported with a modifier, if necessary, to indicate lesser or greater complexity)

(For trabeculectomy, use 66170)

65860   Severing adhesions of anterior segment, laser technique (separate procedure)

65865   Severing adhesions of anterior segment of eye, incisional technique (with or without injection of air or liquid) (separate procedure); goniosynechiae

(For trabeculoplasty by laser surgery, use 65855)

65870   anterior synechiae, except goniosynechiae

65875   posterior synechiae

(For use of ophthalmic endoscope with 65875, use 66990)

65880   corneovitreal adhesions

(For laser surgery, use 66821)

Removal

65900   Removal of epithelial downgrowth, anterior chamber of eye

65920   Removal of implanted material, anterior segment of eye

(For use of ophthalmic endoscope with 65920, use 66990)

65930   Removal of blood clot, anterior segment of eye

Introduction

66020   Injection, anterior chamber of eye (separate procedure); air or liquid

66030   medication

(For unlisted procedures on anterior segment, use 66999)

Anterior Sclera

Excision

(For removal of intraocular foreign body, use 65235)

(For operations on posterior sclera, use 67250, 67255)

66130   Excision of lesion, sclera

66150   Fistulization of sclera for glaucoma; trephination with iridectomy

66155   thermocauterization with iridectomy

66160   sclerectomy with punch or scissors, with iridectomy

66165   iridencleisis or iridotasis

66170   trabeculectomy ab externo in absence of previous surgery

(For trabeculotomy ab externo, use 65850)

(For repair of operative wound, use 66250)

(For dilation of Schlemm's Canal with or without retention of device, see 0176T, 0177T)

66172   trabeculectomy ab externo with scarring from previous ocular surgery or trauma (includes injection of antifibrotic agents)

(For transciliary body sclera fistulization, use Category III code 0123T)

Aqueous Shunt

66180   Aqueous shunt to extraocular reservoir (eg, Molteno, Schocket, Denver-Krupin)

66185   Revision of aqueous shunt to extraocular reservoir

(For removal of implanted shunt, use 67120)

Repair or Revision

(For scleral procedures in retinal surgery, see 67101 et seq)

66220   Repair of scleral staphyloma; without graft

66225   with graft

(For scleral reinforcement, see 67250, 67255)

66250   Revision or repair of operative wound of anterior segment, any type, early or late, major or minor procedure

(For unlisted procedures on anterior sclera, use 66999)

Iris, Ciliary Body

Incision

66500   Iridotomy by stab incision (separate procedure); except transfixion

66505   with transfixion as for iris bombe

(For iridotomy by photocoagulation, use 66761)

Excision

66600   Iridectomy, with corneoscleral or corneal section; for removal of lesion

66605   with cyclectomy

66625   peripheral for glaucoma (separate procedure)

66630   sector for glaucoma (separate procedure)

66635   optical (separate procedure)

(For coreoplasty by photocoagulation, use 66762)

Surgery: Ocular System

Repair

66680 Repair of iris, ciliary body (as for iridodialysis)

(For reposition or resection of uveal tissue with perforating wound of cornea or sclera, use 65285)

66682 Suture of iris, ciliary body (separate procedure) with retrieval of suture through small incision (eg, McCannel suture)

Destruction

66700 Ciliary body destruction; diathermy

66710 cyclophotocoagulation, transscleral

66711 cyclophotocoagulation, endoscopic

(Do not report 66711 in conjunction with 66990)

⊙ **66720** cryotherapy

66740 cyclodialysis

66761 Iridotomy/iridectomy by laser surgery (eg, for glaucoma) (1 or more sessions)

66762 Iridoplasty by photocoagulation (1 or more sessions) (eg, for improvement of vision, for widening of anterior chamber angle)

66770 Destruction of cyst or lesion iris or ciliary body (nonexcisional procedure)

(For excision lesion iris, ciliary body, see 66600, 66605; for removal of epithelial downgrowth, use 65900)

(For unlisted procedures on iris, ciliary body, use 66999)

Lens

Incision

66820 Discission of secondary membranous cataract (opacified posterior lens capsule and/or anterior hyaloid); stab incision technique (Ziegler or Wheeler knife)

66821 laser surgery (eg, YAG laser) (1 or more stages)

66825 Repositioning of intraocular lens prosthesis, requiring an incision (separate procedure)

Removal

Lateral canthotomy, iridectomy, iridotomy, anterior capsulotomy, posterior capsulotomy, the use of viscoelastic agents, enzymatic zonulysis, use of other pharmacologic agents, and subconjunctival or sub-tenon injections are included as part of the code for the extraction of lens.

66830 Removal of secondary membranous cataract (opacified posterior lens capsule and/or anterior hyaloid) with corneo-scleral section, with or without iridectomy (iridocapsulotomy, iridocapsulectomy)

66840 Removal of lens material; aspiration technique, 1 or more stages

66850 phacofragmentation technique (mechanical or ultrasonic) (eg, phacoemulsification), with aspiration

66852 pars plana approach, with or without vitrectomy

66920 intracapsular

66930 intracapsular, for dislocated lens

66940 extracapsular (other than 66840, 66850, 66852)

(For removal of intralenticular foreign body without lens extraction, use 65235)

(For repair of operative wound, use 66250)

Intraocular Lens Procedures

66982 Extracapsular cataract removal with insertion of intraocular lens prosthesis (1-stage procedure), manual or mechanical technique (eg, irrigation and aspiration or phacoemulsification), complex, requiring devices or techniques not generally used in routine cataract surgery (eg, iris expansion device, suture support for intraocular lens, or primary posterior capsulorrhexis) or performed on patients in the amblyogenic developmental stage

66983 Intracapsular cataract extraction with insertion of intraocular lens prosthesis (1 stage procedure)

66984 Extracapsular cataract removal with insertion of intraocular lens prosthesis (1 stage procedure), manual or mechanical technique (eg, irrigation and aspiration or phacoemulsification)

(For complex extracapsular cataract removal, use 66982)

66985 Insertion of intraocular lens prosthesis (secondary implant), not associated with concurrent cataract removal

(To code implant at time of concurrent cataract surgery, see 66982, 66983, 66984)

(For intraocular lens prosthesis supplied by physician, use 99070)

(For ultrasonic determination of intraocular lens power, use 76519)

(For removal of implanted material from anterior segment, use 65920)

(For secondary fixation (separate procedure), use 66682)

(For use of ophthalmic endoscope with 66985, use 66990)

66986 Exchange of intraocular lens

(For use of ophthalmic endoscope with 66986, use 66990)

Other Procedures

+ 66990   Use of ophthalmic endoscope (List separately in addition
to code for primary procedure)

►(66990 may be used only with codes 65820, 65875,
65920, 66985, 66986, 67036, 67039, 67040, 67041,
67042, 67043, 67112, 67113)◄

66999   Unlisted procedure, anterior segment of eye

Posterior Segment

Vitreous

67005   Removal of vitreous, anterior approach (open sky
technique or limbal incision); partial removal

67010   subtotal removal with mechanical vitrectomy

(For removal of vitreous by paracentesis of anterior
chamber, use 65810)

(For removal of corneovitreal adhesions, use 65880)

67015   Aspiration or release of vitreous, subretinal or choroidal
fluid, pars plana approach (posterior sclerotomy)

67025   Injection of vitreous substitute, pars plana or limbal
approach (fluid-gas exchange), with or without aspiration
(separate procedure)

67027   Implantation of intravitreal drug delivery system (eg,
ganciclovir implant), includes concomitant removal of
vitreous

(For removal, use 67121)

67028   Intravitreal injection of a pharmacologic agent (separate
procedure)

67030   Discission of vitreous strands (without removal), pars
plana approach

67031   Severing of vitreous strands, vitreous face adhesions,
sheets, membranes or opacities, laser surgery (1 or more
stages)

67036   Vitrectomy, mechanical, pars plana approach;

(For application of intraocular epiretinal radiation with
67036, use 0190T)

(67038 has been deleted. To report, see 67041, 67042,
67043)

67039   with focal endolaser photocoagulation

67040   with endolaser panretinal photocoagulation

67041   with removal of preretinal cellular membrane (eg,
macular pucker)

67042   with removal of internal limiting membrane of retina
(eg, for repair of macular hole, diabetic macular
edema), includes, if performed, intraocular
tamponade (ie, air, gas or silicone oil)

67043   with removal of subretinal membrane (eg, choroidal
neovascularization), includes, if performed,
intraocular tamponade (ie, air, gas or silicone oil) and
laser photocoagulation

(For use of ophthalmic endoscope with 67036, 67039,
67040-67043, use 66990)

(For associated lensectomy, use 66850)

(For use of vitrectomy in retinal detachment surgery, see
67108, 67113)

(For associated removal of foreign body, see 65260,
65265)

(For unlisted procedures on vitreous, use 67299)

Retina or Choroid

Repair

(If diathermy, cryotherapy and/or photocoagulation are
combined, report under principal modality used)

67101   Repair of retinal detachment, 1 or more sessions;
cryotherapy or diathermy, with or without drainage of
subretinal fluid

67105   photocoagulation, with or without drainage of
subretinal fluid

67107   Repair of retinal detachment; scleral buckling (such as
lamellar scleral dissection, imbrication or encircling
procedure), with or without implant, with or without
cryotherapy, photocoagulation, and drainage of subretinal
fluid

67108   with vitrectomy, any method, with or without air or
gas tamponade, focal endolaser photocoagulation,
cryotherapy, drainage of subretinal fluid, scleral
buckling, and/or removal of lens by same technique

67110   by injection of air or other gas (eg, pneumatic
retinopexy)

67112   by scleral buckling or vitrectomy, on patient having
previous ipsilateral retinal detachment repair(s) using
scleral buckling or vitrectomy techniques

(For aspiration or drainage of subretinal or subchoroidal
fluid, use 67015)

(For use of ophthalmic endoscope with 67112, use 66990)

67113   Repair of complex retinal detachment (eg, proliferative
vitreoretinopathy, stage C-1 or greater, diabetic traction
retinal detachment, retinopathy of prematurity, retinal
tear of greater than 90 degrees), with vitrectomy and
membrane peeling, may include air, gas, or silicone oil
tamponade, cryotherapy, endolaser photocoagulation,
drainage of subretinal fluid, scleral buckling, and/or
removal of lens

(To report vitrectomy, pars plana approach, other than in
retinal detachment surgery, see 67036-67043)

►(For use of ophthalmic endoscope with 67113, use
66990)◄

Surgery: Ocular System

67115 Release of encircling material (posterior segment)

67120 Removal of implanted material, posterior segment; extraocular

67121 intraocular

(For removal from anterior segment, use 65920)

(For removal of foreign body, see 65260, 65265)

Prophylaxis

▶Codes 67141, 67145 include treatment at one or more sessions that may occur at different encounters. These codes should be reported once during a defined treatment period.◀

Repetitive services. The services listed below are often performed in multiple sessions or groups of sessions. The methods of reporting vary.

The following descriptors are intended to include all sessions in a defined treatment period.

67141 Prophylaxis of retinal detachment (eg, retinal break, lattice degeneration) without drainage, 1 or more sessions; cryotherapy, diathermy

67145 photocoagulation (laser or xenon arc)

Destruction

▶Codes 67208, 67210, 67218, 67220, 67227, 67228, 67229 include treatment at one or more sessions that may occur at different encounters. These codes should be reported once during a defined treatment period.◀

67208 Destruction of localized lesion of retina (eg, macular edema, tumors), 1 or more sessions; cryotherapy, diathermy

67210 photocoagulation

67218 radiation by implantation of source (includes removal of source)

67220 Destruction of localized lesion of choroid (eg, choroidal neovascularization); photocoagulation (eg, laser), 1 or more sessions

(For destruction of macular drusen, photocoagulation, use Category III code 0017T)

(For destruction of localized lesion of choroid by transpupillary thermotherapy, use Category III code 0016T)

67221 photodynamic therapy (includes intravenous infusion)

+ 67225 photodynamic therapy, second eye, at single session (List separately in addition to code for primary eye treatment)

(Use 67225 in conjunction with 67221)

67227 Destruction of extensive or progressive retinopathy (eg, diabetic retinopathy), 1 or more sessions, cryotherapy, diathermy

67228 Treatment of extensive or progressive retinopathy, 1 or more sessions; (eg, diabetic retinopathy), photocoagulation

67229 preterm infant (less than 37 weeks gestation at birth), performed from birth up to 1 year of age (eg, retinopathy of prematurity), photocoagulation or cryotherapy

(For bilateral procedure, use modifier 50)

(For unlisted procedures on retina, use 67299)

Posterior Sclera

Repair

(For excision lesion sclera, use 66130)

67250 Scleral reinforcement (separate procedure); without graft

67255 with graft

(For repair scleral staphyloma, see 66220, 66225)

Other Procedures

67299 Unlisted procedure, posterior segment

Ocular Adnexa

Extraocular Muscles

67311 Strabismus surgery, recession or resection procedure; 1 horizontal muscle

67312 2 horizontal muscles

67314 1 vertical muscle (excluding superior oblique)

67316 2 or more vertical muscles (excluding superior oblique)

(For adjustable sutures, use 67335 in addition to codes 67311-67334 for primary procedure reflecting number of muscles operated on)

67318 Strabismus surgery, any procedure, superior oblique muscle

+ 67320 Transposition procedure (eg, for paretic extraocular muscle), any extraocular muscle (specify) (List separately in addition to code for primary procedure)

(Use 67320 in conjunction with 67311-67318)

+ 67331 Strabismus surgery on patient with previous eye surgery or injury that did not involve the extraocular muscles (List separately in addition to code for primary procedure)

(Use 67331 in conjunction with 67311-67318)

Surgery: Ocular System

+ 67332 Strabismus surgery on patient with scarring of extraocular muscles (eg, prior ocular injury, strabismus or retinal detachment surgery) or restrictive myopathy (eg, dysthyroid ophthalmopathy) (List separately in addition to code for primary procedure)

(Use 67332 in conjunction with 67311-67318)

+ 67334 Strabismus surgery by posterior fixation suture technique, with or without muscle recession (List separately in addition to code for primary procedure)

(Use 67334 in conjunction with 67311-67318)

+ 67335 Placement of adjustable suture(s) during strabismus surgery, including postoperative adjustment(s) of suture(s) (List separately in addition to code for specific strabismus surgery)

(Use 67335 in conjunction with 67311-67334)

+ 67340 Strabismus surgery involving exploration and/or repair of detached extraocular muscle(s) (List separately in addition to code for primary procedure)

(Use 67340 in conjunction with 67311-67334)

67343 Release of extensive scar tissue without detaching extraocular muscle (separate procedure)

(Use 67343 in conjunction with 67311-67340, when such procedures are performed other than on the affected muscle)

67345 Chemodenervation of extraocular muscle

(For chemodenervation for blepharospasm and other neurological disorders, see 64612 and 64613)

67346 Biopsy of extraocular muscle

(For repair of wound, extraocular muscle, tendon or Tenon's capsule, use 65290)

Other Procedures

67399 Unlisted procedure, ocular muscle

Orbit

Exploration, Excision, Decompression

67400 Orbitotomy without bone flap (frontal or transconjunctival approach); for exploration, with or without biopsy

67405   with drainage only

67412   with removal of lesion

67413   with removal of foreign body

67414   with removal of bone for decompression

67415 Fine needle aspiration of orbital contents

(For exenteration, enucleation, and repair, see 65101 et seq; for optic nerve decompression, use 67570)

67420 Orbitotomy with bone flap or window, lateral approach (eg, Kroenlein); with removal of lesion

67430   with removal of foreign body

67440   with drainage

67445   with removal of bone for decompression

(For optic nerve sheath decompression, use 67570)

67450   for exploration, with or without biopsy

(For orbitotomy, transcranial approach, see 61330-61334)

(For orbital implant, see 67550, 67560)

(For removal of eyeball or for repair after removal, see 65091-65175)

Other Procedures

67500 Retrobulbar injection; medication (separate procedure, does not include supply of medication)

67505   alcohol

67515 Injection of medication or other substance into Tenon's capsule

(For subconjunctival injection, use 68200)

67550 Orbital implant (implant outside muscle cone); insertion

67560   removal or revision

(For ocular implant (implant inside muscle cone), see 65093-65105, 65130-65175)

(For treatment of fractures of malar area, orbit, see 21355 et seq)

67570 Optic nerve decompression (eg, incision or fenestration of optic nerve sheath)

67599 Unlisted procedure, orbit

Eyelids

Incision

67700 Blepharotomy, drainage of abscess, eyelid

67710 Severing of tarsorrhaphy

67715 Canthotomy (separate procedure)

(For canthoplasty, use 67950)

(For division of symblepharon, use 68340)

Excision, Destruction

Codes for removal of lesion include more than skin (ie, involving lid margin, tarsus, and/or palpebral conjunctiva).

(For removal of lesion, involving mainly skin of eyelid, see 11310-11313; 11440-11446, 11640-11646; 17000-17004)

(For repair of wounds, blepharoplasty, grafts, reconstructive surgery, see 67930-67975)

67800 Excision of chalazion; single

Surgery: Ocular System

67801	multiple, same lid
67805	multiple, different lids
67808	under general anesthesia and/or requiring hospitalization, single or multiple
67810	Biopsy of eyelid
67820	Correction of trichiasis; epilation, by forceps only
67825	epilation by other than forceps (eg, by electrosurgery, cryotherapy, laser surgery)
67830	incision of lid margin
67835	incision of lid margin, with free mucous membrane graft
67840	Excision of lesion of eyelid (except chalazion) without closure or with simple direct closure

(For excision and repair of eyelid by reconstructive surgery, see 67961, 67966)

67850	Destruction of lesion of lid margin (up to 1 cm)

(For Mohs micrographic surgery, see 17311-17315)

(For initiation or follow-up care of topical chemotherapy (eg, 5-FU or similar agents), see appropriate office visits)

Tarsorrhaphy

67875	Temporary closure of eyelids by suture (eg, Frost suture)
67880	Construction of intermarginal adhesions, median tarsorrhaphy, or canthorrhaphy;
67882	with transposition of tarsal plate

(For severing of tarsorrhaphy, use 67710)

(For canthoplasty, reconstruction canthus, use 67950)

(For canthotomy, use 67715)

Repair (Brow Ptosis, Blepharoptosis, Lid Retraction, Ectropion, Entropion)

67900	Repair of brow ptosis (supraciliary, mid-forehead or coronal approach)

(For forehead rhytidectomy, use 15824)

67901	Repair of blepharoptosis; frontalis muscle technique with suture or other material (eg, banked fascia)
67902	frontalis muscle technique with autologous fascial sling (includes obtaining fascia)
67903	(tarso) levator resection or advancement, internal approach
67904	(tarso) levator resection or advancement, external approach
67906	superior rectus technique with fascial sling (includes obtaining fascia)
67908	conjunctivo-tarso-Muller's muscle-levator resection (eg, Fasanella-Servat type)

67909	Reduction of overcorrection of ptosis
67911	Correction of lid retraction

(For obtaining autogenous graft materials, see 20920, 20922 or 20926)

(For correction of trichiasis by mucous membrane graft, use 67835)

67912	Correction of lagophthalmos, with implantation of upper eyelid lid load (eg, gold weight)
67914	Repair of ectropion; suture
67915	thermocauterization
67916	excision tarsal wedge
67917	extensive (eg, tarsal strip operations)

(For correction of everted punctum, use 68705)

67921	Repair of entropion; suture
67922	thermocauterization
67923	excision tarsal wedge
67924	extensive (eg, tarsal strip or capsulopalpebral fascia repairs operation)

(For repair of cicatricial ectropion or entropion requiring scar excision or skin graft, see also 67961 et seq)

Reconstruction

Codes for blepharoplasty involve more than skin (ie, involving lid margin, tarsus, and/or palpebral conjunctiva).

67930	Suture of recent wound, eyelid, involving lid margin, tarsus, and/or palpebral conjunctiva direct closure; partial thickness
67935	full thickness
67938	Removal of embedded foreign body, eyelid

(For repair of skin of eyelid, see 12011-12018; 12051-12057; 13150-13153)

(For tarsorrhaphy, canthorrhaphy, see 67880, 67882)

(For repair of blepharoptosis and lid retraction, see 67901-67911)

(For blepharoplasty for entropion, ectropion, see 67916, 67917, 67923, 67924)

(For correction of blepharochalasis (blepharorhytidectomy), see 15820-15823)

(For repair of skin of eyelid, adjacent tissue transfer, see 14060, 14061; preparation for graft, use 15004; free graft, see 15120, 15121, 15260, 15261)

(For excision of lesion of eyelid, use 67800 et seq)

(For repair of lacrimal canaliculi, use 68700)

67950	Canthoplasty (reconstruction of canthus)

Surgery: Ocular System

67961   Excision and repair of eyelid, involving lid margin, tarsus, conjunctiva, canthus, or full thickness, may include preparation for skin graft or pedicle flap with adjacent tissue transfer or rearrangement; up to one-fourth of lid margin

67966   over one-fourth of lid margin

(For canthoplasty, use 67950)

(For free skin grafts, see 15120, 15121, 15260, 15261)

(For tubed pedicle flap preparation, use 15576; for delay, use 15630; for attachment, use 15650)

67971   Reconstruction of eyelid, full thickness by transfer of tarsoconjunctival flap from opposing eyelid; up to two-thirds of eyelid, 1 stage or first stage

67973   total eyelid, lower, 1 stage or first stage

67974   total eyelid, upper, 1 stage or first stage

67975   second stage

Other Procedures

67999   Unlisted procedure, eyelids

Conjunctiva

(For removal of foreign body, see 65205 et seq)

Incision and Drainage

68020   Incision of conjunctiva, drainage of cyst

68040   Expression of conjunctival follicles (eg, for trachoma)

Excision and/or Destruction

68100   Biopsy of conjunctiva

68110   Excision of lesion, conjunctiva; up to 1 cm

68115   over 1 cm

68130   with adjacent sclera

68135   Destruction of lesion, conjunctiva

Injection

(For injection into Tenon's capsule or retrobulbar injection, see 67500-67515)

68200   Subconjunctival injection

Conjunctivoplasty

(For wound repair, see 65270-65273)

68320   Conjunctivoplasty; with conjunctival graft or extensive rearrangement

68325   with buccal mucous membrane graft (includes obtaining graft)

68326   Conjunctivoplasty, reconstruction cul-de-sac; with conjunctival graft or extensive rearrangement

68328   with buccal mucous membrane graft (includes obtaining graft)

68330   Repair of symblepharon; conjunctivoplasty, without graft

68335   with free graft conjunctiva or buccal mucous membrane (includes obtaining graft)

68340   division of symblepharon, with or without insertion of conformer or contact lens

Other Procedures

68360   Conjunctival flap; bridge or partial (separate procedure)

68362   total (such as Gunderson thin flap or purse string flap)

(For conjunctival flap for perforating injury, see 65280, 65285)

(For repair of operative wound, use 66250)

(For removal of conjunctival foreign body, see 65205, 65210)

68371   Harvesting conjunctival allograft, living donor

68399   Unlisted procedure, conjunctiva

Lacrimal System

Incision

68400   Incision, drainage of lacrimal gland

68420   Incision, drainage of lacrimal sac (dacryocystotomy or dacryocystostomy)

68440   Snip incision of lacrimal punctum

Excision

68500   Excision of lacrimal gland (dacryoadenectomy), except for tumor; total

68505   partial

68510   Biopsy of lacrimal gland

68520   Excision of lacrimal sac (dacryocystectomy)

68525   Biopsy of lacrimal sac

68530   Removal of foreign body or dacryolith, lacrimal passages

68540   Excision of lacrimal gland tumor; frontal approach

68550   involving osteotomy

Repair

68700   Plastic repair of canaliculi

68705   Correction of everted punctum, cautery

68720   Dacryocystorhinostomy (fistulization of lacrimal sac to nasal cavity)

Surgery: Ocular System

68745 Conjunctivorhinostomy (fistulization of conjunctiva to nasal cavity); without tube

68750 with insertion of tube or stent

68760 Closure of the lacrimal punctum; by thermocauterization, ligation, or laser surgery

68761 by plug, each

68770 Closure of lacrimal fistula (separate procedure)

Probing and/or Related Procedures

68801 Dilation of lacrimal punctum, with or without irrigation

(To report a bilateral procedure, use 68801 with modifier 50)

68810 Probing of nasolacrimal duct, with or without irrigation;

(For bilateral procedure, report 68810 with modifier 50)

68811 requiring general anesthesia

(For bilateral procedure, report 68811 with modifier 50)

68815 with insertion of tube or stent

(See also 92018)

(For bilateral procedure, report 68815 with modifier 50)

68816 with transluminal balloon catheter dilation

(Do not report 68816 in conjunction with 68810, 68811, 68815)

(For bilateral procedure, report 68816 with modifier 50)

68840 Probing of lacrimal canaliculi, with or without irrigation

68850 Injection of contrast medium for dacryocystography

(For radiological supervision and interpretation, see 70170, 78660)

Other Procedures

68899 Unlisted procedure, lacrimal system

Surgery: Ocular System

Auditory System

(For diagnostic services (eg, audiometry, vestibular tests), see 92502 et seq)

External Ear

Incision

69000   Drainage external ear, abscess or hematoma; simple

69005   complicated

69020   Drainage external auditory canal, abscess

69090   Ear piercing

Excision

69100   Biopsy external ear

69105   Biopsy external auditory canal

69110   Excision external ear; partial, simple repair

69120   complete amputation

(For reconstruction of ear, see 15120 et seq)

69140   Excision exostosis(es), external auditory canal

69145   Excision soft tissue lesion, external auditory canal

69150   Radical excision external auditory canal lesion; without neck dissection

69155   with neck dissection

(For resection of temporal bone, use 69535)

(For skin grafting, see 15004-15261)

Removal

69200   Removal foreign body from external auditory canal; without general anesthesia

69205   with general anesthesia

69210   Removal impacted cerumen (separate procedure), 1 or both ears

69220   Debridement, mastoidectomy cavity, simple (eg, routine cleaning)

(For bilateral procedure, report 69220 with modifier 50)

69222   Debridement, mastoidectomy cavity, complex (eg, with anesthesia or more than routine cleaning)

(For bilateral procedure, report 69222 with modifier 50)

Repair

▶(For suture of wound or injury of external ear, see 12011-14302)◀

⊙ **69300**   Otoplasty, protruding ear, with or without size reduction

(For bilateral procedure, report 69300 with modifier 50)

69310   Reconstruction of external auditory canal (meatoplasty) (eg, for stenosis due to injury, infection) (separate procedure)

69320   Reconstruction external auditory canal for congenital atresia, single stage

(For combination with middle ear reconstruction, see 69631, 69641)

(For other reconstructive procedures with grafts (eg, skin, cartilage, bone), see 13150-15760, 21230-21235)

Other Procedures

(For otoscopy under general anesthesia, use 92502)

69399   Unlisted procedure, external ear

Middle Ear

Introduction

69400   Eustachian tube inflation, transnasal; with catheterization

69401   without catheterization

69405   Eustachian tube catheterization, transtympanic

Incision

69420   Myringotomy including aspiration and/or eustachian tube inflation

69421   Myringotomy including aspiration and/or eustachian tube inflation requiring general anesthesia

69424   Ventilating tube removal requiring general anesthesia

(For bilateral procedure, report 69424 with modifier 50)

(Do not report code 69424 in conjunction with 69205, 69210, 69420, 69421, 69433-69676, 69710-69745, 69801-69930)

69433   Tympanostomy (requiring insertion of ventilating tube), local or topical anesthesia

(For bilateral procedure, report 69433 with modifier 50)

69436   Tympanostomy (requiring insertion of ventilating tube), general anesthesia

(For bilateral procedure, report 69436 with modifier 50)

69440   Middle ear exploration through postauricular or ear canal incision

(For atticotomy, see 69601 et seq)

69450   Tympanolysis, transcanal

Excision

69501   Transmastoid antrotomy (simple mastoidectomy)

69502   Mastoidectomy; complete

69505   modified radical

69511   radical

(For skin graft, see 15004 et seq)

(For mastoidectomy cavity debridement, see 69220, 69222)

69530   Petrous apicectomy including radical mastoidectomy

69535   Resection temporal bone, external approach

(For middle fossa approach, see 69950-69970)

69540   Excision aural polyp

69550   Excision aural glomus tumor; transcanal

69552   transmastoid

69554   extended (extratemporal)

Repair

69601   Revision mastoidectomy; resulting in complete mastoidectomy

69602   resulting in modified radical mastoidectomy

69603   resulting in radical mastoidectomy

69604   resulting in tympanoplasty

(For planned secondary tympanoplasty after mastoidectomy, see 69631, 69632)

69605   with apicectomy

(For skin graft, see 15120, 15121, 15260, 15261)

69610   Tympanic membrane repair, with or without site preparation of perforation for closure, with or without patch

69620   Myringoplasty (surgery confined to drumhead and donor area)

69631   Tympanoplasty without mastoidectomy (including canalplasty, atticotomy and/or middle ear surgery), initial or revision; without ossicular chain reconstruction

69632   with ossicular chain reconstruction (eg, postfenestration)

69633   with ossicular chain reconstruction and synthetic prosthesis (eg, partial ossicular replacement prosthesis [PORP], total ossicular replacement prosthesis [TORP])

69635   Tympanoplasty with antrotomy or mastoidotomy (including canalplasty, atticotomy, middle ear surgery, and/or tympanic membrane repair); without ossicular chain reconstruction

69636   with ossicular chain reconstruction

69637   with ossicular chain reconstruction and synthetic prosthesis (eg, partial ossicular replacement prosthesis [PORP], total ossicular replacement prosthesis [TORP])

69641   Tympanoplasty with mastoidectomy (including canalplasty, middle ear surgery, tympanic membrane repair); without ossicular chain reconstruction

69642   with ossicular chain reconstruction

69643   with intact or reconstructed wall, without ossicular chain reconstruction

69644   with intact or reconstructed canal wall, with ossicular chain reconstruction

69645   radical or complete, without ossicular chain reconstruction

69646   radical or complete, with ossicular chain reconstruction

69650   Stapes mobilization

69660   Stapedectomy or stapedotomy with reestablishment of ossicular continuity, with or without use of foreign material;

69661   with footplate drill out

69662   Revision of stapedectomy or stapedotomy

69666   Repair oval window fistula

69667   Repair round window fistula

69670   Mastoid obliteration (separate procedure)

69676   Tympanic neurectomy

(For bilateral procedure, report 69676 with modifier 50)

Other Procedures

69700   Closure postauricular fistula, mastoid (separate procedure)

69710   Implantation or replacement of electromagnetic bone conduction hearing device in temporal bone

(Replacement procedure includes removal of old device)

69711   Removal or repair of electromagnetic bone conduction hearing device in temporal bone

69714   Implantation, osseointegrated implant, temporal bone, with percutaneous attachment to external speech processor/cochlear stimulator; without mastoidectomy

69715   with mastoidectomy

69717   Replacement (including removal of existing device), osseointegrated implant, temporal bone, with percutaneous attachment to external speech processor/cochlear stimulator; without mastoidectomy

69718   with mastoidectomy

69720   Decompression facial nerve, intratemporal; lateral to geniculate ganglion

69725   including medial to geniculate ganglion

69740   Suture facial nerve, intratemporal, with or without graft or decompression; lateral to geniculate ganglion

69745   including medial to geniculate ganglion

(For extracranial suture of facial nerve, use 64864)

69799   Unlisted procedure, middle ear

Surgery: Auditory System

Inner Ear

Incision and/or Destruction

69801   Labyrinthotomy, with or without cryosurgery including other nonexcisional destructive procedures or perfusion of vestibuloactive drugs (single or multiple perfusions); transcanal

(69801 includes all required infusions performed on initial and subsequent days of treatment)

69802   with mastoidectomy

69805   Endolymphatic sac operation; without shunt

69806   with shunt

69820   Fenestration semicircular canal

69840   Revision fenestration operation

Excision

69905   Labyrinthectomy; transcanal

69910   with mastoidectomy

69915   Vestibular nerve section, translabyrinthine approach

(For transcranial approach, use 69950)

Introduction

69930   Cochlear device implantation, with or without mastoidectomy

Other Procedures

69949   Unlisted procedure, inner ear

Temporal Bone, Middle Fossa Approach

(For external approach, use 69535)

69950   Vestibular nerve section, transcranial approach

69955   Total facial nerve decompression and/or repair (may include graft)

69960   Decompression internal auditory canal

69970   Removal of tumor, temporal bone

Other Procedures

69979   Unlisted procedure, temporal bone, middle fossa approach

Operating Microscope

The surgical microscope is employed when the surgical services are performed using the techniques of microsurgery. Code 69990 should be reported (without modifier 51 appended) in addition to the code for the primary procedure performed. Do not use 69990 for visualization with magnifying loupes or corrected vision. Do not report 69990 in addition to procedures where use of the operating microscope is an inclusive component (15756-15758, 15842, 19364, 19368, 20955-20962, 20969-20973, 22856-22861, 26551-26554, 26556, 31526, 31531, 31536, 31541, 31545, 31546, 31561, 31571, 43116, 43496, 49906, 61548, 63075-63078, 64727, 64820-64823, 65091-68850, 0184T).

+ 69990   Microsurgical techniques, requiring use of operating microscope (List separately in addition to code for primary procedure)

Notes

⊙=Moderate sedation   ✚=Add-on code   ✗=FDA approval pending   #=Resequenced code

Radiology Guidelines (Including Nuclear Medicine and Diagnostic Ultrasound)

Items used by all physicians in reporting their services are presented in the **Introduction.** Some of the commonalities are repeated here for the convenience of those physicians referring to this section on **Radiology (Including Nuclear Medicine and Diagnostic Ultrasound).** Other definitions and items unique to Radiology are also listed.

Subject Listings

Subject listings apply when radiological services are performed by or under the responsible supervision of a physician.

Separate Procedures

Some of the procedures or services listed in the CPT codebook that are commonly carried out as an integral component of a total service or procedure have been identified by the inclusion of the term "separate procedure." The codes designated as "separate procedure" should not be reported in addition to the code for the total procedure or service of which it is considered an integral component.

However, when a procedure or service that is designated as a "separate procedure" is carried out independently or considered to be unrelated or distinct from other procedures/services provided at that time, it may be reported by itself, or in addition to other procedures/services by appending modifier 59 to the specific "separate procedure" code to indicate that the procedure is not considered to be a component of another procedure, but is a distinct, independent procedure. This may represent a different session or patient encounter, different procedure or surgery, different site or organ system, separate incision/excision, separate lesion, separate injury, or area of injury in extensive injuries.

Unlisted Service or Procedure

A service or procedure may be provided that is not listed in this edition of the CPT codebook. When reporting such a service, the appropriate "Unlisted Procedure" code may be used to indicate the service, identifying it by "Special Report" as discussed below. The "Unlisted Procedures" and accompanying codes for **Radiology (Including Nuclear Medicine and Diagnostic Ultrasound)** are as follows:

76496   Unlisted fluoroscopic procedure (eg, diagnostic, interventional)

76497   Unlisted computed tomography procedure (eg, diagnostic, interventional)

76498   Unlisted magnetic resonance procedure (eg, diagnostic, interventional)

76499   Unlisted diagnostic radiographic procedure

76999   Unlisted ultrasound procedure (eg, diagnostic, interventional)

77299   Unlisted procedure, therapeutic radiology clinical treatment planning

77399   Unlisted procedure, medical radiation physics, dosimetry and treatment devices, and special services

77499   Unlisted procedure, therapeutic radiology treatment management

77799   Unlisted procedure, clinical brachytherapy

78099   Unlisted endocrine procedure, diagnostic nuclear medicine

78199   Unlisted hematopoietic, reticuloendothelial and lymphatic procedure, diagnostic nuclear medicine

78299   Unlisted gastrointestinal procedure, diagnostic nuclear medicine

78399   Unlisted musculoskeletal procedure, diagnostic nuclear medicine

78499   Unlisted cardiovascular procedure, diagnostic nuclear medicine

Radiology Guidelines

78599   Unlisted respiratory procedure, diagnostic nuclear medicine

78699   Unlisted nervous system procedure, diagnostic nuclear medicine

78799   Unlisted genitourinary procedure, diagnostic nuclear medicine

78999   Unlisted miscellaneous procedure, diagnostic nuclear medicine

79999   Radiopharmaceutical therapy, unlisted procedure

Special Report

▶A service that is rarely provided, unusual, variable, or new may require a special report. Pertinent information should include an adequate definition or description of the nature, extent, and need for the procedure; and the time, effort, and equipment necessary to provide the service.◄

Supervision and Interpretation

When a procedure is performed by two physicians, the radiologic portion of the procedure is designated as "radiological supervision and interpretation." When a physician performs both the procedure and provides imaging supervision and interpretation, a combination of procedure codes outside the 70000 series and imaging supervision and interpretation codes are to be used.

(The Radiological Supervision and Interpretation codes arc not applicable to the Radiation Oncology subsection.)

Administration of Contrast Material(s)

The phrase "with contrast" used in the codes for procedures performed using contrast for imaging enhancement represents contrast material administered intravascularly, intra-articularly or intrathecally.

For intra-articular injection, use the appropriate joint injection code. If radiographic arthrography is performed, also use the arthrography supervision and interpretation code for the appropriate joint (which includes fluoroscopy). If computed tomography (CT) or magnetic resonance (MR) arthrography are performed without radiographic arthrography, use the appropriate joint injection code, the appropriate CT or MR code ("with contrast" or "without followed by contrast"), and the appropriate imaging guidance code for needle placement for contrast injection.

For spine examinations using computed tomography, magnetic resonance imaging, magnetic resonance angiography, "with contrast" includes intrathecal or intravascular injection. For intrathecal injection, use also 61055 or 62284.

Injection of intravascular contrast material is part of the "with contrast" CT, computed tomographic angiography (CTA), magnetic resonance imaging (MRI), and magnetic resonance angiography (MRA) procedures.

Oral and/or rectal contrast administration alone does not qualify as a study "with contrast."

Written Report(s)

A written report signed by the interpreting physician should be considered an integral part of a radiologic procedure or interpretation.

Radiology

Diagnostic Radiology (Diagnostic Imaging)

Head and Neck

70010 Myelography, posterior fossa, radiological supervision and interpretation

70015 Cisternography, positive contrast, radiological supervision and interpretation

70030 Radiologic examination, eye, for detection of foreign body

70100 Radiologic examination, mandible; partial, less than 4 views

70110 complete, minimum of 4 views

70120 Radiologic examination, mastoids; less than 3 views per side

70130 complete, minimum of 3 views per side

70134 Radiologic examination, internal auditory meati, complete

70140 Radiologic examination, facial bones; less than 3 views

70150 complete, minimum of 3 views

70160 Radiologic examination, nasal bones, complete, minimum of 3 views

70170 Dacryocystography, nasolacrimal duct, radiological supervision and interpretation

70190 Radiologic examination; optic foramina

70200 orbits, complete, minimum of 4 views

70210 Radiologic examination, sinuses, paranasal, less than 3 views

70220 Radiologic examination, sinuses, paranasal, complete, minimum of 3 views

70240 Radiologic examination, sella turcica

70250 Radiologic examination, skull; less than 4 views

70260 complete, minimum of 4 views

70300 Radiologic examination, teeth; single view

70310 partial examination, less than full mouth

70320 complete, full mouth

70328 Radiologic examination, temporomandibular joint, open and closed mouth; unilateral

70330 bilateral

70332 Temporomandibular joint arthrography, radiological supervision and interpretation

(Do not report 70332 in conjunction with 77002)

70336 Magnetic resonance (eg, proton) imaging, temporomandibular joint(s)

70350 Cephalogram, orthodontic

70355 Orthopantogram

70360 Radiologic examination; neck, soft tissue

70370 pharynx or larynx, including fluoroscopy and/or magnification technique

70371 Complex dynamic pharyngeal and speech evaluation by cine or video recording

70373 Laryngography, contrast, radiological supervision and interpretation

70380 Radiologic examination, salivary gland for calculus

70390 Sialography, radiological supervision and interpretation

70450 Computed tomography, head or brain; without contrast material

70460 with contrast material(s)

70470 without contrast material, followed by contrast material(s) and further sections

(To report 3D rendering, see 76376, 76377)

70480 Computed tomography, orbit, sella, or posterior fossa or outer, middle, or inner ear; without contrast material

70481 with contrast material(s)

70482 without contrast material, followed by contrast material(s) and further sections

(To report 3D rendering, see 76376, 76377)

70486 Computed tomography, maxillofacial area; without contrast material

70487 with contrast material(s)

70488 without contrast material, followed by contrast material(s) and further sections

(To report 3D rendering, see 76376, 76377)

70490 Computed tomography, soft tissue neck; without contrast material

70491 with contrast material(s)

70492 without contrast material followed by contrast material(s) and further sections

(To report 3D rendering, see 76376, 76377)

(For cervical spine, see 72125, 72126)

70496 Computed tomographic angiography, head, with contrast material(s), including noncontrast images, if performed, and image postprocessing

Radiology

70498   Computed tomographic angiography, neck, with contrast material(s), including noncontrast images, if performed, and image postprocessing

70540   Magnetic resonance (eg, proton) imaging, orbit, face, and/or neck; without contrast material(s)

(For head or neck magnetic resonance angiography studies, see 70544-70546, 70547-70549)

70542   with contrast material(s)

70543   without contrast material(s), followed by contrast material(s) and further sequences

(Report 70540-70543 once per imaging session)

70544   Magnetic resonance angiography, head; without contrast material(s)

70545   with contrast material(s)

70546   without contrast material(s), followed by contrast material(s) and further sequences

70547   Magnetic resonance angiography, neck; without contrast material(s)

70548   with contrast material(s)

70549   without contrast material(s), followed by contrast material(s) and further sequences

70551   Magnetic resonance (eg, proton) imaging, brain (including brain stem); without contrast material

70552   with contrast material(s)

70553   without contrast material, followed by contrast material(s) and further sequences

(For magnetic spectroscopy, use 76390)

Functional MRI involves identification and mapping of stimulation of brain function. When neurofunctional tests are administered by a technologist or other non-physician or non-psychologist, use 70554. When neurofunctional tests are entirely administered by a physician or psychologist, use 70555.

70554   Magnetic resonance imaging, brain, functional MRI; including test selection and administration of repetitive body part movement and/or visual stimulation, not requiring physician or psychologist administration

(Do not report 70554 in conjunction with 96020)

70555   requiring physician or psychologist administration of entire neurofunctional testing

(Do not report 70555 unless 96020 is performed)

(Do not report 70554, 70555 in conjunction with 70551-70553 unless a separate diagnostic MRI is performed)

70557   Magnetic resonance (eg, proton) imaging, brain (including brain stem and skull base), during open intracranial procedure (eg, to assess for residual tumor or residual vascular malformation); without contrast material

70558   with contrast material(s)

70559   without contrast material(s), followed by contrast material(s) and further sequences

(For stereotactic biopsy of intracranial lesion with magnetic resonance guidance, use 61751. 70557, 70558 or 70559 may be reported only if a separate report is generated. Report only 1 of the above codes once per operative session. Do not use these codes in conjunction with 61751, 77021, 77022)

Chest

(For fluoroscopic or ultrasonic guidance for needle placement procedures (eg, biopsy, aspiration, injection, localization device) of the thorax, see 76942, 77002)

71010   Radiologic examination, chest; single view, frontal

71015   stereo, frontal

71020   Radiologic examination, chest, 2 views, frontal and lateral;

71021   with apical lordotic procedure

71022   with oblique projections

71023   with fluoroscopy

71030   Radiologic examination, chest, complete, minimum of 4 views;

(For concurrent computer-aided detection [CAD] performed in addition to codes 71010, 71020, 71021, 71022, and 71030, use 0174T. Do not report 71010, 71020, 71021, 71022, and 71030 in conjunction with 0175T for CAD performed remotely from the primary interpretation)

71034   with fluoroscopy

(For separate chest fluoroscopy, use 76000)

71035   Radiologic examination, chest, special views (eg, lateral decubitus, Bucky studies)

71040   Bronchography, unilateral, radiological supervision and interpretation

71060   Bronchography, bilateral, radiological supervision and interpretation

71090   Insertion pacemaker, fluoroscopy and radiography, radiological supervision and interpretation

(For procedure, see appropriate organ or site)

71100   Radiologic examination, ribs, unilateral; 2 views

71101   including posteroanterior chest, minimum of 3 views

71110   Radiologic examination, ribs, bilateral; 3 views

71111   including posteroanterior chest, minimum of 4 views

71120   Radiologic examination; sternum, minimum of 2 views

71130   sternoclavicular joint or joints, minimum of 3 views

71250   Computed tomography, thorax; without contrast material

71260   with contrast material(s)

Radiology

71270   without contrast material, followed by contrast material(s) and further sections

►(For cardiac computed tomography of the heart, see 75571-75574)◄

(To report 3D rendering, see 76376, 76377)

71275   Computed tomographic angiography, chest (noncoronary), with contrast material(s), including noncontrast images, if performed, and image postprocessing

►(For coronary artery computed tomographic angiography including calcification score and/or cardiac morphology, use 75574)◄

71550   Magnetic resonance (eg, proton) imaging, chest (eg, for evaluation of hilar and mediastinal lymphadenopathy); without contrast material(s)

71551   with contrast material(s)

71552   without contrast material(s), followed by contrast material(s) and further sequences

(For breast MRI, see 77058, 77059)

71555   Magnetic resonance angiography, chest (excluding myocardium), with or without contrast material(s)

Spine and Pelvis

72010   Radiologic examination, spine, entire, survey study, anteroposterior and lateral

72020   Radiologic examination, spine, single view, specify level

72040   Radiologic examination, spine, cervical; 2 or 3 views

72050   minimum of 4 views

72052   complete, including oblique and flexion and/or extension studies

72069   Radiologic examination, spine, thoracolumbar, standing (scoliosis)

72070   Radiologic examination, spine; thoracic, 2 views

72072   thoracic, 3 views

72074   thoracic, minimum of 4 views

72080   thoracolumbar, 2 views

72090   scoliosis study, including supine and erect studies

72100   Radiologic examination, spine, lumbosacral; 2 or 3 views

72110   minimum of 4 views

72114   complete, including bending views

72120   Radiologic examination, spine, lumbosacral, bending views only, minimum of 4 views

(Contrast material in CT of spine is either by intrathecal or intravenous injection. For intrathecal injection, use also 61055 or 62284. IV injection of contrast material is part of the CT procedure)

72125   Computed tomography, cervical spine; without contrast material

72126   with contrast material

72127   without contrast material, followed by contrast material(s) and further sections

(For intrathecal injection procedure, see 61055, 62284)

72128   Computed tomography, thoracic spine; without contrast material

72129   with contrast material

(For intrathecal injection procedure, see 61055, 62284)

72130   without contrast material, followed by contrast material(s) and further sections

(For intrathecal injection procedure, see 61055, 62284)

72131   Computed tomography, lumbar spine; without contrast material

72132   with contrast material

72133   without contrast material, followed by contrast material(s) and further sections

(For intrathecal injection procedure, see 61055, 62284)

(To report 3D rendering, see 76376, 76377)

72141   Magnetic resonance (eg, proton) imaging, spinal canal and contents, cervical; without contrast material

72142   with contrast material(s)

(For cervical spinal canal imaging without contrast material followed by contrast material, use 72156)

72146   Magnetic resonance (eg, proton) imaging, spinal canal and contents, thoracic; without contrast material

72147   with contrast material(s)

(For thoracic spinal canal imaging without contrast material followed by contrast material, use 72157)

72148   Magnetic resonance (eg, proton) imaging, spinal canal and contents, lumbar; without contrast material

72149   with contrast material(s)

(For lumbar spinal canal imaging without contrast material followed by contrast material, use 72158)

72156   Magnetic resonance (eg, proton) imaging, spinal canal and contents, without contrast material, followed by contrast material(s) and further sequences; cervical

72157   thoracic

72158   lumbar

72159   Magnetic resonance angiography, spinal canal and contents, with or without contrast material(s)

72170   Radiologic examination, pelvis; 1 or 2 views

72190   complete, minimum of 3 views

(For pelvimetry, use 74710)

Radiology

72191 Computed tomographic angiography, pelvis, with contrast material(s), including noncontrast images, if performed, and image postprocessing

(For CTA aorto-iliofemoral runoff, use 75635)

72192 Computed tomography, pelvis; without contrast material

72193 with contrast material(s)

72194 without contrast material, followed by contrast material(s) and further sections

(To report 3D rendering, see 76376, 76377)

▶(For computed tomographic colonography, diagnostic, see 74261-74262. For computed tomographic colonography, screening, use 74263)◀

▶(Do not report 72192-72194 in conjunction with 74261-74263)◀

72195 Magnetic resonance (eg, proton) imaging, pelvis; without contrast material(s)

72196 with contrast material(s)

72197 without contrast material(s), followed by contrast material(s) and further sequences

72198 Magnetic resonance angiography, pelvis, with or without contrast material(s)

72200 Radiologic examination, sacroiliac joints; less than 3 views

72202 3 or more views

72220 Radiologic examination, sacrum and coccyx, minimum of 2 views

72240 Myelography, cervical, radiological supervision and interpretation

(For complete cervical myelography, see 61055, 62284, 72240)

72255 Myelography, thoracic, radiological supervision and interpretation

(For complete thoracic myelography, see 61055, 62284, 72255)

72265 Myelography, lumbosacral, radiological supervision and interpretation

(For complete lumbosacral myelography, see 61055, 62284, 72265)

72270 Myelography, 2 or more regions (eg, lumbar/thoracic, cervical/thoracic, lumbar/cervical, lumbar/thoracic/cervical), radiological supervision and interpretation

(For complete myelography of entire spinal canal, see 61055, 62284, 72270)

72275 Epidurography, radiological supervision and interpretation

(72275 includes 77003)

(For injection procedure, see 62280-62282, 62310-62319, 64479-64484)

(Use 72275 only when an epidurogram is performed, images documented, and a formal radiologic report is issued)

72285 Discography, cervical or thoracic, radiological supervision and interpretation

▲ **72291** Radiological supervision and interpretation, percutaneous vertebroplasty, vertebral augmentation, or sacral augmentation (sacroplasty), including cavity creation, per vertebral body or sacrum; under fluoroscopic guidance

▲ **72292** under CT guidance

▶(For procedure, see 22520-22525, 0200T, 0201T)◀

72295 Discography, lumbar, radiological supervision and interpretation

Upper Extremities

(For stress views, any joint, use 77071)

73000 Radiologic examination; clavicle, complete

73010 scapula, complete

73020 Radiologic examination, shoulder; 1 view

73030 complete, minimum of 2 views

73040 Radiologic examination, shoulder, arthrography, radiological supervision and interpretation

(Do not report 77002 in conjunction with 73040)

73050 Radiologic examination; acromioclavicular joints, bilateral, with or without weighted distraction

73060 humerus, minimum of 2 views

73070 Radiologic examination, elbow; 2 views

73080 complete, minimum of 3 views

73085 Radiologic examination, elbow, arthrography, radiological supervision and interpretation

(Do not report 77002 in conjunction with 73085)

73090 Radiologic examination; forearm, 2 views

73092 upper extremity, infant, minimum of 2 views

73100 Radiologic examination, wrist; 2 views

73110 complete, minimum of 3 views

73115 Radiologic examination, wrist, arthrography, radiological supervision and interpretation

(Do not report 77002 in conjunction with 73115)

73120 Radiologic examination, hand; 2 views

73130 minimum of 3 views

73140 Radiologic examination, finger(s), minimum of 2 views

73200 Computed tomography, upper extremity; without contrast material

73201 with contrast material(s)

Radiology

73202   without contrast material, followed by contrast material(s) and further sections

(To report 3D rendering, see 76376, 76377)

73206   Computed tomographic angiography, upper extremity, with contrast material(s), including noncontrast images, if performed, and image postprocessing

73218   Magnetic resonance (eg, proton) imaging, upper extremity, other than joint; without contrast material(s)

73219   with contrast material(s)

73220   without contrast material(s), followed by contrast material(s) and further sequences

73221   Magnetic resonance (eg, proton) imaging, any joint of upper extremity; without contrast material(s)

73222   with contrast material(s)

73223   without contrast material(s), followed by contrast material(s) and further sequences

73225   Magnetic resonance angiography, upper extremity, with or without contrast material(s)

Lower Extremities

(For stress views, any joint, use 77071)

73500   Radiologic examination, hip, unilateral; 1 view

73510   complete, minimum of 2 views

73520   Radiologic examination, hips, bilateral, minimum of 2 views of each hip, including anteroposterior view of pelvis

73525   Radiologic examination, hip, arthrography, radiological supervision and interpretation

(Do not report 73525 in conjunction with 77002)

73530   Radiologic examination, hip, during operative procedure

73540   Radiologic examination, pelvis and hips, infant or child, minimum of 2 views

73542   Radiological examination, sacroiliac joint arthrography, radiological supervision and interpretation

(Do not report 73542 in conjunction with 77002)

(For procedure, use 27096. If formal arthrography is not performed, recorded, and a formal radiologic report is not issued, use 77003 for fluoroscopic guidance for sacroiliac joint injections)

73550   Radiologic examination, femur, 2 views

73560   Radiologic examination, knee; 1 or 2 views

73562   3 views

73564   complete, 4 or more views

73565   both knees, standing, anteroposterior

73580   Radiologic examination, knee, arthrography, radiological supervision and interpretation

(Do not report 73580 in conjunction with 77002)

73590   Radiologic examination; tibia and fibula, 2 views

73592   lower extremity, infant, minimum of 2 views

73600   Radiologic examination, ankle; 2 views

73610   complete, minimum of 3 views

73615   Radiologic examination, ankle, arthrography, radiological supervision and interpretation

(Do not report 73615 in conjunction with 77002)

73620   Radiologic examination, foot; 2 views

73630   complete, minimum of 3 views

73650   Radiologic examination; calcaneus, minimum of 2 views

73660   toe(s), minimum of 2 views

73700   Computed tomography, lower extremity; without contrast material

73701   with contrast material(s)

73702   without contrast material, followed by contrast material(s) and further sections

(To report 3D rendering, see 76376, 76377)

73706   Computed tomographic angiography, lower extremity, with contrast material(s), including noncontrast images, if performed, and image postprocessing

(For CTA aorto-iliofemoral runoff, use 75635)

73718   Magnetic resonance (eg, proton) imaging, lower extremity other than joint; without contrast material(s)

73719   with contrast material(s)

73720   without contrast material(s), followed by contrast material(s) and further sequences

73721   Magnetic resonance (eg, proton) imaging, any joint of lower extremity; without contrast material

73722   with contrast material(s)

73723   without contrast material(s), followed by contrast material(s) and further sequences

73725   Magnetic resonance angiography, lower extremity, with or without contrast material(s)

Abdomen

74000   Radiologic examination, abdomen; single anteroposterior view

74010   anteroposterior and additional oblique and cone views

74020   complete, including decubitus and/or erect views

74022   complete acute abdomen series, including supine, erect, and/or decubitus views, single view chest

74150   Computed tomography, abdomen; without contrast material

74160   with contrast material(s)

Radiology

74170 without contrast material, followed by contrast material(s) and further sections

(To report 3D rendering, see 76376, 76377)

▶(For computed tomographic colonography, diagnostic, see 74261-74262. For computed tomographic colonography, screening, use 74263)◀

▶(Do not report 74150-74170 in conjunction with 74261-74263)◀

74175 Computed tomographic angiography, abdomen, with contrast material(s), including noncontrast images, if performed, and image postprocessing

(For CTA aorto-iliofemoral runoff, use 75635)

74181 Magnetic resonance (eg, proton) imaging, abdomen; without contrast material(s)

74182 with contrast material(s)

74183 without contrast material(s), followed by with contrast material(s) and further sequences

74185 Magnetic resonance angiography, abdomen, with or without contrast material(s)

74190 Peritoneogram (eg, after injection of air or contrast), radiological supervision and interpretation

(For procedure, use 49400)

(For computed tomography, see 72192 or 74150)

Gastrointestinal Tract

(For percutaneous placement of gastrostomy tube, use 43246)

74210 Radiologic examination; pharynx and/or cervical esophagus

74220 esophagus

74230 Swallowing function, with cineradiography/videoradiography

74235 Removal of foreign body(s), esophageal, with use of balloon catheter, radiological supervision and interpretation

(For procedure, see 43215, 43247)

74240 Radiologic examination, gastrointestinal tract, upper; with or without delayed films, without KUB

74241 with or without delayed films, with KUB

74245 with small intestine, includes multiple serial films

74246 Radiological examination, gastrointestinal tract, upper, air contrast, with specific high density barium, effervescent agent, with or without glucagon; with or without delayed films, without KUB

74247 with or without delayed films, with KUB

74249 with small intestine follow-through

74250 Radiologic examination, small intestine, includes multiple serial films;

74251 via enteroclysis tube

74260 Duodenography, hypotonic

● **74261** Computed tomographic (CT) colonography, diagnostic, including image postprocessing; without contrast material

● **74262** with contrast material(s) including non-contrast images, if performed

▶(Do not report 74261, 74262 in conjunction with 72192-72194, 74150-74170, 74263, 76376, 76377)◀

● **74263** Computed tomographic (CT) colonography, screening, including image postprocessing

▶(Do not report 74263 in conjunction with 72192-72194, 74150-74170, 74261, 74262, 76376, 76377)◀

74270 Radiologic examination, colon; contrast (eg, barium) enema, with or without KUB

74280 air contrast with specific high density barium, with or without glucagon

74283 Therapeutic enema, contrast or air, for reduction of intussusception or other intraluminal obstruction (eg, meconium ileus)

74290 Cholecystography, oral contrast;

74291 additional or repeat examination or multiple day examination

74300 Cholangiography and/or pancreatography; intraoperative, radiological supervision and interpretation

+ **74301** additional set intraoperative, radiological supervision and interpretation (List separately in addition to code for primary procedure)

(Use 74301 in conjunction with 74300)

74305 through existing catheter, radiological supervision and interpretation

(For procedure, see 47505, 48400, 47560-47561, 47563)

(For biliary duct stone extraction, percutaneous, see 47630, 74327)

74320 Cholangiography, percutaneous, transhepatic, radiological supervision and interpretation

74327 Postoperative biliary duct calculus removal, percutaneous via T-tube tract, basket, or snare (eg, Burhenne technique), radiological supervision and interpretation

(For procedure, use 47630)

74328 Endoscopic catheterization of the biliary ductal system, radiological supervision and interpretation

(For procedure, see 43260-43272 as appropriate)

74329 Endoscopic catheterization of the pancreatic ductal system, radiological supervision and interpretation

(For procedure, see 43260-43272 as appropriate)

74330 Combined endoscopic catheterization of the biliary and pancreatic ductal systems, radiological supervision and interpretation

(For procedure, see 43260-43272 as appropriate)

74340 Introduction of long gastrointestinal tube (eg, Miller-Abbott), including multiple fluoroscopies and films, radiological supervision and interpretation

(For tube placement, use 44500)

(74350 has been deleted. To report gastrostomy tube placement, use 49440)

74355 Percutaneous placement of enteroclysis tube, radiological supervision and interpretation

74360 Intraluminal dilation of strictures and/or obstructions (eg, esophagus), radiological supervision and interpretation

74363 Percutaneous transhepatic dilation of biliary duct stricture with or without placement of stent, radiological supervision and interpretation

(For procedure, see 47510, 47511, 47555, 47556)

Urinary Tract

74400 Urography (pyelography), intravenous, with or without KUB, with or without tomography

74410 Urography, infusion, drip technique and/or bolus technique;

74415   with nephrotomography

74420 Urography, retrograde, with or without KUB

74425 Urography, antegrade (pyelostogram, nephrostogram, loopogram), radiological supervision and interpretation

74430 Cystography, minimum of 3 views, radiological supervision and interpretation

74440 Vasography, vesiculography, or epididymography, radiological supervision and interpretation

74445 Corpora cavernosography, radiological supervision and interpretation

74450 Urethrocystography, retrograde, radiological supervision and interpretation

74455 Urethrocystography, voiding, radiological supervision and interpretation

74470 Radiologic examination, renal cyst study, translumbar, contrast visualization, radiological supervision and interpretation

74475 Introduction of intracatheter or catheter into renal pelvis for drainage and/or injection, percutaneous, radiological supervision and interpretation

74480 Introduction of ureteral catheter or stent into ureter through renal pelvis for drainage and/or injection, percutaneous, radiological supervision and interpretation

(For transurethral surgery [ureter and pelvis], see 52320-52355)

74485 Dilation of nephrostomy, ureters, or urethra, radiological supervision and interpretation

(For dilation of ureter without radiologic guidance, use 52341, 52344)

(For change of nephrostomy or pyelostomy tube, use 50398)

Gynecological and Obstetrical

(For abdomen and pelvis, see 72170-72190, 74000-74170)

74710 Pelvimetry, with or without placental localization

74740 Hysterosalpingography, radiological supervision and interpretation

(For introduction of saline or contrast for hysterosalpingography, see 58340)

74742 Transcervical catheterization of fallopian tube, radiological supervision and interpretation

(For procedure, use 58345)

74775 Perineogram (eg, vaginogram, for sex determination or extent of anomalies)

Heart

▶Cardiac magnetic imaging differs from traditional magnetic resonance imaging (MRI) in its ability to provide a physiologic evaluation of cardiac function. Traditional MRI relies on static images to obtain clinical diagnoses based upon anatomic information. Improvement in spatial and temporal resolution has expanded the application from an anatomic test and includes physiologic evaluation of cardiac function. Flow and velocity assessment for valves and intracardiac shunts is performed in addition to a function and morphologic evaluation. Use 75559 with 75565 to report flow with pharmacologic wall motion stress evaluation without contrast. Use 75563 with 75565 to report flow with pharmacologic perfusion stress with contrast.

Cardiac MRI for velocity flow mapping can be reported in conjunction with 75557, 75559, 75561, or 75563.

Listed procedures may be performed independently or in the course of overall medical care. If the physician providing these services is also responsible for diagnostic workup and/or follow-up care of the patient, see appropriate sections also. Only one procedure in the series 75557-75563 is appropriately reported per session. Only one add-on code for flow velocity can be reported per session.

Cardiac MRI studies may be performed at rest and/or during pharmacologic stress. Therefore, the appropriate stress testing code from the 93015-93018 series should be reported in addition to 75559 or 75563.

Radiology

Cardiac computed tomography (CT) and coronary computed tomographic angiography (CTA) include the axial source images of the pre-contrast, arterial phase sequence, and venous phase sequence (if performed), as well as the two-dimensional and three-dimensional reformatted images resulting from the study, including cine review. Contrast enhanced cardiac CT and coronary CTA codes 75571-75574 include any quantitative assessment when performed as part of the same encounter. Report only one computed tomography heart service per encounter.◄

> (For separate injection procedures for vascular radiology, see **Surgery** section, 36000-36299)

> (For cardiac catheterization procedures, see 93501-93556)

> ►(75552-75556 have been deleted. To report, see 75557, 75559, 75561, 75563, 75565)◄

75557   Cardiac magnetic resonance imaging for morphology and function without contrast material;

75559   with stress imaging

75561   Cardiac magnetic resonance imaging for morphology and function without contrast material(s), followed by contrast material(s) and further sequences;

75563   with stress imaging

> ►(75558, 75560, 75562, 75564 have been deleted. To report flow velocity, use 75565)◄

+● **75565**   Cardiac magnetic resonance imaging for velocity flow mapping (List separately in addition to code for primary procedure)

> ►(Use 75565 in conjunction with 75557, 75559, 75561, 75563)◄

> ►(Do not report 75557, 75559, 75561, 75563, 75565 in conjunction with 76376, 76377)◄

● **75571**   Computed tomography, heart, without contrast material, with quantitative evaluation of coronary calcium

● **75572**   Computed tomography, heart, with contrast material, for evaluation of cardiac structure and morphology (including 3D image postprocessing, assessment of cardiac function, and evaluation of venous structures, if performed)

● **75573**   Computed tomography, heart, with contrast material, for evaluation of cardiac structure and morphology in the setting of congenital heart disease (including 3D image postprocessing, assessment of LV cardiac function, RV structure and function and evaluation of venous structures, if performed)

● **75574**   Computed tomographic angiography, heart, coronary arteries and bypass grafts (when present), with contrast material, including 3D image postprocessing (including evaluation of cardiac structure and morphology, assessment of cardiac function, and evaluation of venous structures, if performed)

Vascular Procedures

Aorta and Arteries

Selective vascular catheterizations should be coded to include introduction and all lesser order selective catheterizations used in the approach (eg, the description for a selective right middle cerebral artery catheterization includes the introduction and placement catheterization of the right common and internal carotid arteries).

Additional second and/or third order arterial catheterizations within the same family of arteries supplied by a single first order artery should be expressed by 36218 or 36248. Additional first order or higher catheterizations in vascular families supplied by a first order vessel different from a previously selected and coded family should be separately coded using the conventions described above.

For angiography performed in conjunction with therapeutic transcatheter radiological supervision and interpretation services, see the **Radiology Transcatheter Procedures** guidelines.

Diagnostic angiography (radiological supervision and interpretation) codes should NOT be used with interventional procedures for:

1. Contrast injections, angiography, roadmapping, and/or fluoroscopic guidance for the intervention,

2. Vessel measurement, and

3. Post-angioplasty/stent angiography,

as this work is captured in the radiological supervision and interpretation code(s).

Diagnostic angiography performed at the time of an interventional procedure is separately reportable if:

1. No prior catheter-based angiographic study is available and a full diagnostic study is performed, and the decision to intervene is based on the diagnostic study, OR

2. A prior study is available, but as documented in the medical record:

   a. The patient's condition with respect to the clinical indication has changed since the prior study, OR

   b. There is inadequate visualization of the anatomy and/or pathology, OR

   c. There is a clinical change during the procedure that requires new evaluation outside the target area of intervention.

Diagnostic angiography performed at a separate setting from an interventional procedure is separately reported.

Diagnostic angiography performed at the time of an interventional procedure is NOT separately reportable if it is specifically included in the interventional code descriptor.

(For intravenous procedure, see 36000-36013, 36400-36425 and 36100-36248 for intra-arterial procedure)

(For radiological supervision and interpretation, see 75600-75978)

75600 Aortography, thoracic, without serialography, radiological supervision and interpretation

(For injection procedure, use 93544)

75605 Aortography, thoracic, by serialography, radiological supervision and interpretation

(For injection procedure, use 93544)

75625 Aortography, abdominal, by serialography, radiological supervision and interpretation

(For injection procedure, use 93544)

75630 Aortography, abdominal plus bilateral iliofemoral lower extremity, catheter, by serialography, radiological supervision and interpretation

75635 Computed tomographic angiography, abdominal aorta and bilateral iliofemoral lower extremity runoff, with contrast material(s), including noncontrast images, if performed, and image postprocessing

75650 Angiography, cervicocerebral, catheter, including vessel origin, radiological supervision and interpretation

75658 Angiography, brachial, retrograde, radiological supervision and interpretation

75660 Angiography, external carotid, unilateral, selective, radiological supervision and interpretation

75662 Angiography, external carotid, bilateral, selective, radiological supervision and interpretation

75665 Angiography, carotid, cerebral, unilateral, radiological supervision and interpretation

75671 Angiography, carotid, cerebral, bilateral, radiological supervision and interpretation

75676 Angiography, carotid, cervical, unilateral, radiological supervision and interpretation

75680 Angiography, carotid, cervical, bilateral, radiological supervision and interpretation

75685 Angiography, vertebral, cervical, and/or intracranial, radiological supervision and interpretation

75705 Angiography, spinal, selective, radiological supervision and interpretation

75710 Angiography, extremity, unilateral, radiological supervision and interpretation

75716 Angiography, extremity, bilateral, radiological supervision and interpretation

75722 Angiography, renal, unilateral, selective (including flush aortogram), radiological supervision and interpretation

75724 Angiography, renal, bilateral, selective (including flush aortogram), radiological supervision and interpretation

75726 Angiography, visceral, selective or supraselective (with or without flush aortogram), radiological supervision and interpretation

(For selective angiography, each additional visceral vessel studied after basic examination, use 75774)

75731 Angiography, adrenal, unilateral, selective, radiological supervision and interpretation

75733 Angiography, adrenal, bilateral, selective, radiological supervision and interpretation

75736 Angiography, pelvic, selective or supraselective, radiological supervision and interpretation

75741 Angiography, pulmonary, unilateral, selective, radiological supervision and interpretation

(For injection procedure, use 93541)

75743 Angiography, pulmonary, bilateral, selective, radiological supervision and interpretation

(For injection procedure, use 93541)

75746 Angiography, pulmonary, by nonselective catheter or venous injection, radiological supervision and interpretation

(For injection procedure, use 93541)

(For introduction of catheter, injection procedure, see 93501-93533, 93539, 93540, 93545, 93556)

75756 Angiography, internal mammary, radiological supervision and interpretation

(For introduction of catheter, injection procedure, see 93501-93533, 93545, 93556)

+ 75774 Angiography, selective, each additional vessel studied after basic examination, radiological supervision and interpretation (List separately in addition to code for primary procedure)

(Use 75774 in addition to code for specific initial vessel studied)

►(For angiography, see 36147, 75600-75774, 75791)◄

(For catheterizations, see codes 36215-36248)

(For introduction of catheter, injection procedure, see 93501-93533, 93545, 93555, 93556)

►(75790 has been deleted. To report, see 36147, 75791)◄

● 75791 Angiography, arteriovenous shunt (eg, dialysis patient fistula/graft), complete evaluation of dialysis access, including fluoroscopy, image documentation and report (includes injections of contrast and all necessary imaging from the arterial anastomosis and adjacent artery through entire venous outflow including the inferior or superior vena cava), radiological supervision and interpretation

►(Do not report 75791 in conjunction with 36147, 36148)◄

►(For introduction of catheter, if necessary, see 36140, 36215-36217, 36245-36247)◄

Radiology

▶(Use 75791 only if radiological evaluation is performed through an already existing access into the shunt or from an access that is not a direct puncture of the shunt)◄

▶(For radiological evaluation with needle/catheter introduction, AV dialysis shunt, complete procedure, use 36147)◄

Veins and Lymphatics

For venography performed in conjunction with therapeutic transcatheter radiological supervision and interpretation services, see the **Radiology Transcatheter Procedures** guidelines.

Diagnostic venography (radiological supervision and interpretation) codes should NOT be used with interventional procedures for:

1. Contrast injections, venography, roadmapping, and/or fluoroscopic guidance for the intervention,

2. Vessel measurement, and

3. Post-angioplasty/stent venography,

as this work is captured in the radiological supervision and interpretation code(s).

Diagnostic venography performed at the time of an interventional procedure is separately reportable if:

1. No prior catheter-based venographic study is available and a full diagnostic study is performed, and decision to intervene is based on the diagnostic study, OR

2. A prior study is available, but as documented in the medical record:

   a. The patient's condition with respect to the clinical indication has changed since the prior study, OR

   b. There is inadequate visualization of the anatomy and/or pathology, OR

   c. There is a clinical change during the procedure that requires new evaluation outside the target area of intervention.

Diagnostic venography performed at a separate setting from an interventional procedure is separately reported.

Diagnostic venography performed at the time of an interventional procedure is NOT separately reportable if it is specifically included in the interventional code descriptor.

(For injection procedure for venous system, see 36000-36015, 36400-36510)

(For injection procedure for lymphatic system, use 38790)

75801 Lymphangiography, extremity only, unilateral, radiological supervision and interpretation

75803 Lymphangiography, extremity only, bilateral, radiological supervision and interpretation

75805 Lymphangiography, pelvic/abdominal, unilateral, radiological supervision and interpretation

75807 Lymphangiography, pelvic/abdominal, bilateral, radiological supervision and interpretation

75809 Shuntogram for investigation of previously placed indwelling nonvascular shunt (eg, LeVeen shunt, ventriculoperitoneal shunt, indwelling infusion pump), radiological supervision and interpretation

(For procedure, see 49427 or 61070)

75810 Splenoportography, radiological supervision and interpretation

75820 Venography, extremity, unilateral, radiological supervision and interpretation

75822 Venography, extremity, bilateral, radiological supervision and interpretation

75825 Venography, caval, inferior, with serialography, radiological supervision and interpretation

75827 Venography, caval, superior, with serialography, radiological supervision and interpretation

75831 Venography, renal, unilateral, selective, radiological supervision and interpretation

75833 Venography, renal, bilateral, selective, radiological supervision and interpretation

75840 Venography, adrenal, unilateral, selective, radiological supervision and interpretation

75842 Venography, adrenal, bilateral, selective, radiological supervision and interpretation

75860 Venography, venous sinus (eg, petrosal and inferior sagittal) or jugular, catheter, radiological supervision and interpretation

75870 Venography, superior sagittal sinus, radiological supervision and interpretation

75872 Venography, epidural, radiological supervision and interpretation

75880 Venography, orbital, radiological supervision and interpretation

75885 Percutaneous transhepatic portography with hemodynamic evaluation, radiological supervision and interpretation

75887 Percutaneous transhepatic portography without hemodynamic evaluation, radiological supervision and interpretation

75889 Hepatic venography, wedged or free, with hemodynamic evaluation, radiological supervision and interpretation

75891 Hepatic venography, wedged or free, without hemodynamic evaluation, radiological supervision and interpretation

75893 Venous sampling through catheter, with or without angiography (eg, for parathyroid hormone, renin), radiological supervision and interpretation

(For procedure, use 36500)

Radiology

Transcatheter Procedures

Therapeutic transcatheter radiological supervision and interpretation code(s) include the following services associated with that intervention:

1. Contrast injections, angiography/venography, roadmapping, and fluoroscopic guidance for the intervention,

2. Vessel measurement, and

3. Completion angiography/venography (except for those uses permitted by 75898).

Unless specifically included in the code descriptor, diagnostic angiography/venography performed at the time of transcatheter therapeutic radiological and interpretation service(s) is separately reportable (eg, no prior catheter-based diagnostic angiography/venography study of the target vessel is available, prior diagnostic study is inadequate, patient's condition with respect to the clinical indication has changed since the prior study or during the intervention). See 75600-75893.

Codes 75956 and 75957 include all angiography of the thoracic aorta and its branches for diagnostic imaging prior to deployment of the primary endovascular devices (including all routine components of modular devices), fluoroscopic guidance in the delivery of the endovascular components, and intraprocedural arterial angiography (eg, confirm position, detect endoleak, evaluate runoff).

Code 75958 includes the analogous services for placement of each proximal thoracic endovascular extension. Code 75959 includes the analogous services for placement of a distal thoracic endovascular extension(s) placed during a procedure after the primary repair.

75894   Transcatheter therapy, embolization, any method, radiological supervision and interpretation

(For uterine fibroid embolization [uterine artery embolization performed to treat uterine fibroids], use 37210)

(For obstetrical and gynecologic embolization procedures other than uterine fibroid embolization [eg, embolization to treat obstetrical or postpartum hemorrhage], use 37204)

75896   Transcatheter therapy, infusion, any method (eg, thrombolysis other than coronary), radiological supervision and interpretation

(For infusion for coronary disease, see 92975, 92977)

75898   Angiography through existing catheter for follow-up study for transcatheter therapy, embolization or infusion

75900   Exchange of a previously placed intravascular catheter during thrombolytic therapy with contrast monitoring, radiological supervision and interpretation

(For procedure, use 37209)

75901   Mechanical removal of pericatheter obstructive material (eg, fibrin sheath) from central venous device via separate venous access, radiologic supervision and interpretation

(For procedure, use 36595)

(For venous catheterization, see 36010-36012)

75902   Mechanical removal of intraluminal (intracatheter) obstructive material from central venous device through device lumen, radiologic supervision and interpretation

(For procedure, use 36596)

(For venous catheterization, see 36010-36012)

75940   Percutaneous placement of IVC filter, radiological supervision and interpretation

75945   Intravascular ultrasound (non-coronary vessel), radiological supervision and interpretation; initial vessel

+ 75946   each additional non-coronary vessel (List separately in addition to code for primary procedure)

(Use 75946 in conjunction with 75945)

(For catheterizations, see codes 36215-36248)

(For transcatheter therapies, see codes 37200-37208, 61624, 61626)

(For procedure, see 37250, 37251)

75952   Endovascular repair of infrarenal abdominal aortic aneurysm or dissection, radiological supervision and interpretation

(For implantation of endovascular grafts, see 34800-34808)

(For radiologic supervision and interpretation of endovascular repair of abdominal aortic aneurysm involving visceral vessels, see Category III codes 0078T-0081T)

75953   Placement of proximal or distal extension prosthesis for endovascular repair of infrarenal aortic or iliac artery aneurysm, pseudoaneurysm, or dissection, radiological supervision and interpretation

(For implantation of endovascular extension prostheses, see 34825, 34826)

75954   Endovascular repair of iliac artery aneurysm, pseudoaneurysm, arteriovenous malformation, or trauma, radiological supervision and interpretation

(For implantation of endovascular graft, see 34900)

75956   Endovascular repair of descending thoracic aorta (eg, aneurysm, pseudoaneurysm, dissection, penetrating ulcer, intramural hematoma, or traumatic disruption); involving coverage of left subclavian artery origin, initial endoprosthesis plus descending thoracic aortic extension(s), if required, to level of celiac artery origin, radiological supervision and interpretation

(For implantation of endovascular graft, use 33880)

Radiology

75957   not involving coverage of left subclavian artery origin, initial endoprosthesis plus descending thoracic aortic extension(s), if required, to level of celiac artery origin, radiological supervision and interpretation

(For implantation of endovascular graft, use 33881)

75958   Placement of proximal extension prosthesis for endovascular repair of descending thoracic aorta (eg, aneurysm, pseudoaneurysm, dissection, penetrating ulcer, intramural hematoma, or traumatic disruption), radiological supervision and interpretation

(Report 75958 for each proximal extension)

(For implantation of proximal endovascular extension, see 33883, 33884)

75959   Placement of distal extension prosthesis(s) (delayed) after endovascular repair of descending thoracic aorta, as needed, to level of celiac origin, radiological supervision and interpretation

(Do not report 75959 in conjunction with 75956, 75957)

(Report 75959 once, regardless of number of modules deployed)

(For implantation of distal endovascular extension, use 33886)

75960   Transcatheter introduction of intravascular stent(s) (except coronary, carotid, and vertebral vessel), percutaneous and/or open, radiological supervision and interpretation, each vessel

(For procedure, see 37205-37208)

(For radiologic supervision and interpretation for transcatheter placement of extracranial vertebral or intrathoracic carotid artery stent(s), see Category III codes 0075T, 0076T)

75961   Transcatheter retrieval, percutaneous, of intravascular foreign body (eg, fractured venous or arterial catheter), radiological supervision and interpretation

(For procedure, use 37203)

75962   Transluminal balloon angioplasty, peripheral artery, radiological supervision and interpretation

+ 75964   Transluminal balloon angioplasty, each additional peripheral artery, radiological supervision and interpretation (List separately in addition to code for primary procedure)

(Use 75964 in conjunction with 75962)

75966   Transluminal balloon angioplasty, renal or other visceral artery, radiological supervision and interpretation

+ 75968   Transluminal balloon angioplasty, each additional visceral artery, radiological supervision and interpretation (List separately in addition to code for primary procedure)

(Use 75968 in conjunction with 75966)

(For percutaneous transluminal coronary angioplasty, see 92982-92984)

75970   Transcatheter biopsy, radiological supervision and interpretation

(For injection procedure only for transcatheter therapy or biopsy, see 36100-36299)

(For transcatheter renal and ureteral biopsy, use 52007)

(For percutaneous needle biopsy of pancreas, use 48102; of retroperitoneal lymph node or mass, use 49180)

75978   Transluminal balloon angioplasty, venous (eg, subclavian stenosis), radiological supervision and interpretation

75980   Percutaneous transhepatic biliary drainage with contrast monitoring, radiological supervision and interpretation

75982   Percutaneous placement of drainage catheter for combined internal and external biliary drainage or of a drainage stent for internal biliary drainage in patients with an inoperable mechanical biliary obstruction, radiological supervision and interpretation

75984   Change of percutaneous tube or drainage catheter with contrast monitoring (eg, genitourinary system, abscess), radiological supervision and interpretation

(For percutaneous replacement of gastrostomy, duodenostomy, jejunostomy, gastro-jejunostomy, or cecostomy [or other colonic] tube including fluoroscopic imaging guidance, see 49450-49452)

(For change of nephrostomy or pyelostomy tube only, use 50398)

(For introduction procedure only for percutaneous biliary drainage, see 47510, 47511)

(For percutaneous cholecystostomy, use 47490)

(For change of percutaneous biliary drainage catheter only, use 47525)

(For percutaneous nephrostolithotomy or pyelostolithotomy, see 50080, 50081)

(For removal and/or replacement of an internally dwelling ureteral stent via a transurethral approach, see 50385-50386)

75989   Radiological guidance (ie, fluoroscopy, ultrasound, or computed tomography), for percutaneous drainage (eg, abscess, specimen collection), with placement of catheter, radiological supervision and interpretation

Transluminal Atherectomy

75992   Transluminal atherectomy, peripheral artery, radiological supervision and interpretation

(For procedure, see 35481-35485, 35491-35495)

+ 75993   Transluminal atherectomy, each additional peripheral artery, radiological supervision and interpretation (List separately in addition to code for primary procedure)

(Use 75993 in conjunction with 75992)

(For procedure, see 35481-35485, 35491-35495)

Radiology

75994   Transluminal atherectomy, renal, radiological supervision and interpretation

(For procedure, see 35480, 35490)

75995   Transluminal atherectomy, visceral, radiological supervision and interpretation

(For procedure, see 35480, 35490)

+ **75996**   Transluminal atherectomy, each additional visceral artery, radiological supervision and interpretation (List separately in addition to code for primary procedure)

(Use 75996 in conjunction with 75995)

(For procedure, see 35480, 35490)

Other Procedures

(For computed tomography cerebral perfusion analysis, see Category III code 0042T)

(For arthrography of shoulder, use 73040; elbow, use 73085; wrist, use 73115; hip, use 73525; knee, use 73580; ankle, use 73615)

76000   Fluoroscopy (separate procedure), up to 1 hour physician time, other than 71023 or 71034 (eg, cardiac fluoroscopy)

76001   Fluoroscopy, physician time more than 1 hour, assisting a nonradiologic physician (eg, nephrostolithotomy, ERCP, bronchoscopy, transbronchial biopsy)

76010   Radiologic examination from nose to rectum for foreign body, single view, child

76080   Radiologic examination, abscess, fistula or sinus tract study, radiological supervision and interpretation

(For contrast injection[s] and radiological assessment of gastrostomy, duodenostomy, jejunostomy, gastro-jejunostomy, or cecostomy [or other colonic] tube including fluoroscopic imaging guidance, use 49465)

76098   Radiological examination, surgical specimen

76100   Radiologic examination, single plane body section (eg, tomography), other than with urography

76101   Radiologic examination, complex motion (ie, hypercycloidal) body section (eg, mastoid polytomography), other than with urography; unilateral

76102   bilateral

(For nephrotomography, use 74415)

76120   Cineradiography/videoradiography, except where specifically included

+ **76125**   Cineradiography/videoradiography to complement routine examination (List separately in addition to code for primary procedure)

76140   Consultation on X-ray examination made elsewhere, written report

76150   Xeroradiography

(76150 is to be used for non-mammographic studies only)

76350   Subtraction in conjunction with contrast studies

(2D reformatting is no longer separately reported. To report 3D rendering, see 76376, 76377)

(76376, 76377 require concurrent physician supervision of image postprocessing 3D manipulation of volumetric data set and image rendering)

76376   3D rendering with interpretation and reporting of computed tomography, magnetic resonance imaging, ultrasound, or other tomographic modality; not requiring image postprocessing on an independent workstation

(Use 76376 in conjunction with code[s] for base imaging procedure[s])

►(Do not report 76376 in conjunction with 31627, 70496, 70498, 70544-70549, 71275, 71555, 72159, 72191, 72198, 73206, 73225, 73706, 73725, 74175, 74185, 74261-74263, 75557, 75559, 75561, 75563, 75565, 75571-75574, 75635, 76377, 78000-78999, 0159T)◄

76377   requiring image postprocessing on an independent workstation

(Use 76377 in conjunction with code[s] for base imaging procedure[s])

►(Do not report 76377 in conjunction with 70496, 70498, 70544-70549, 71275, 71555, 72159, 72191, 72198, 73206, 73225, 73706, 73725, 74175, 74185, 74261-74263, 75557, 75559, 75561, 75563, 75565, 75571-75574, 75635, 76376, 78000-78999, 0159T)◄

(To report computer-aided detection, including computer algorithm analysis of MRI data for lesion detection/characterization, pharmacokinetic analysis, breast MRI, use Category III code 0159T)

76380   Computed tomography, limited or localized follow-up study

76390   Magnetic resonance spectroscopy

(For magnetic resonance imaging, use appropriate MRI body site code)

76496   Unlisted fluoroscopic procedure (eg, diagnostic, interventional)

76497   Unlisted computed tomography procedure (eg, diagnostic, interventional)

76498   Unlisted magnetic resonance procedure (eg, diagnostic, interventional)

76499   Unlisted diagnostic radiographic procedure

Radiology

Diagnostic Ultrasound

All diagnostic ultrasound examinations require permanently recorded images with measurements, when such measurements are clinically indicated. For those codes whose sole diagnostic goal is a biometric measure (ie, 76514, 76516, and 76519), permanently recorded images are not required. A final, written report should be issued for inclusion in the patient's medical record. The prescription form for the intraocular lens satisfies the written report requirement for 76519. For those anatomic regions that have "complete" and "limited" ultrasound codes, note the elements that comprise a "complete" exam. The report should contain a description of these elements or the reason that an element could not be visualized (eg, obscured by bowel gas, surgically absent).

If less than the required elements for a "complete" exam are reported (eg, limited number of organs or limited portion of region evaluated), the "limited" code for that anatomic region should be used once per patient exam session. A "limited" exam of an anatomic region should not be reported for the same exam session as a "complete" exam of that same region.

Evaluation of vascular structures using both color and spectral Doppler is separately reportable. To report, see **Noninvasive Vascular Diagnostic Studies** (93875-93990). However, color Doppler alone, when performed for anatomic structure identification in conjunction with a real-time ultrasound examination, is not reported separately.

Ultrasound guidance procedures also require permanently recorded images of the site to be localized, as well as a documented description of the localization process, either separately or within the report of the procedure for which the guidance is utilized.

Use of ultrasound, without thorough evaluation of organ(s) or anatomic region, image documentation, and final, written report, is not separately reportable.

Definitions

A-mode implies a one-dimensional ultrasonic measurement procedure.

M-mode implies a one-dimensional ultrasonic measurement procedure with movement of the trace to record amplitude and velocity of moving echo-producing structures.

B-scan implies a two-dimensional ultrasonic scanning procedure with a two-dimensional display.

Real-time scan implies a two-dimensional ultrasonic scanning procedure with display of both two-dimensional structure and motion with time.

> (To report diagnostic vascular ultrasound studies, see 93875-93990)

> (For focused ultrasound ablation treatment of uterine leiomyomata, see Category III codes 0071T, 0072T)

Head and Neck

76506 Echoencephalography, real time with image documentation (gray scale) (for determination of ventricular size, delineation of cerebral contents, and detection of fluid masses or other intracranial abnormalities), including A-mode encephalography as secondary component where indicated

76510 Ophthalmic ultrasound, diagnostic; B-scan and quantitative A-scan performed during the same patient encounter

76511 quantitative A-scan only

76512 B-scan (with or without superimposed non-quantitative A-scan)

76513 anterior segment ultrasound, immersion (water bath) B-scan or high resolution biomicroscopy

> (For scanning computerized ophthalmic diagnostic imaging of the anterior and posterior segments using technology other than ultrasound, see 92135, 0187T)

76514 corneal pachymetry, unilateral or bilateral (determination of corneal thickness)

76516 Ophthalmic biometry by ultrasound echography, A-scan;

76519 with intraocular lens power calculation

> (For partial coherence interferometry, use 92136)

76529 Ophthalmic ultrasonic foreign body localization

76536 Ultrasound, soft tissues of head and neck (eg, thyroid, parathyroid, parotid), real time with image documentation

Chest

76604 Ultrasound, chest (includes mediastinum), real time with image documentation

76645 Ultrasound, breast(s) (unilateral or bilateral), real time with image documentation

Abdomen and Retroperitoneum

A complete ultrasound examination of the abdomen (76700) consists of real time scans of the liver, gall bladder, common bile duct, pancreas, spleen, kidneys, and the upper abdominal aorta and inferior vena cava including any demonstrated abdominal abnormality.

A complete ultrasound examination of the retroperitoneum (76770) consists of real time scans of the kidneys, abdominal aorta, common iliac artery origins, and inferior vena cava, including any demonstrated retroperitoneal abnormality. Alternatively, if clinical history suggests urinary tract pathology, complete evaluation of the kidneys and urinary bladder also comprises a complete retroperitoneal ultrasound.

Use of ultrasound, without thorough evaluation of organ(s) or anatomic region, image documentation and final, written report, is not separately reportable.

76700 Ultrasound, abdominal, real time with image documentation; complete

76705 limited (eg, single organ, quadrant, follow-up)

76770 Ultrasound, retroperitoneal (eg, renal, aorta, nodes), real time with image documentation; complete

76775 limited

76776 Ultrasound, transplanted kidney, real time and duplex Doppler with image documentation

(For ultrasound of transplanted kidney without duplex Doppler, use 76775)

(Do not report 76776 in conjunction with 93975, 93976)

Spinal Canal

76800 Ultrasound, spinal canal and contents

Pelvis

Obstetrical

Codes 76801 and 76802 include determination of the number of gestational sacs and fetuses, gestational sac/fetal measurements appropriate for gestation (younger than 14 weeks 0 days), survey of visible fetal and placental anatomic structure, qualitative assessment of amniotic fluid volume/gestational sac shape and examination of the maternal uterus and adnexa.

Codes 76805 and 76810 include determination of number of fetuses and amniotic/chorionic sacs, measurements appropriate for gestational age (older than or equal to 14 weeks 0 days), survey of intracranial/spinal/abdominal anatomy, 4 chambered heart, umbilical cord insertion site, placenta location and amniotic fluid assessment and, when visible, examination of maternal adnexa.

Codes 76811 and 76812 include all elements of codes 76805 and 76810 plus detailed anatomic evaluation of the fetal brain/ventricles, face, heart/outflow tracts and chest anatomy, abdominal organ specific anatomy, number/length/architecture of limbs and detailed evaluation of the umbilical cord and placenta and other fetal anatomy as clinically indicated.

Report should document the results of the evaluation of each element described above or the reason for non-visualization.

Code 76815 represents a focused "quick look" exam limited to the assessment of one or more of the elements listed in code 76815.

Code 76816 describes an examination designed to reassess fetal size and interval growth or reevaluate one or more anatomic abnormalities of a fetus previously demonstrated on ultrasound, and should be coded once for each fetus requiring reevaluation using modifier 59 for each fetus after the first.

Code 76817 describes a transvaginal obstetric ultrasound performed separately or in addition to one of the transabdominal examinations described above. For transvaginal examinations performed for non-obstetrical purposes, use code 76830.

76801 Ultrasound, pregnant uterus, real time with image documentation, fetal and maternal evaluation, first trimester (< 14 weeks 0 days), transabdominal approach; single or first gestation

(To report first trimester fetal nuchal translucency measurement, use 76813)

+ 76802 each additional gestation (List separately in addition to code for primary procedure)

(Use 76802 in conjunction with 76801)

(To report first trimester fetal nuchal translucency measurement, use 76814)

76805 Ultrasound, pregnant uterus, real time with image documentation, fetal and maternal evaluation, after first trimester (> or = 14 weeks 0 days), transabdominal approach; single or first gestation

+ 76810 each additional gestation (List separately in addition to code for primary procedure)

(Use 76810 in conjunction with 76805)

76811 Ultrasound, pregnant uterus, real time with image documentation, fetal and maternal evaluation plus detailed fetal anatomic examination, transabdominal approach; single or first gestation

+ 76812 each additional gestation (List separately in addition to code for primary procedure)

(Use 76812 in conjunction with 76811)

76813 Ultrasound, pregnant uterus, real time with image documentation, first trimester fetal nuchal translucency measurement, transabdominal or transvaginal approach; single or first gestation

+ 76814 each additional gestation (List separately in addition to code for primary procedure)

(Use 76814 in conjunction with 76813)

76815 Ultrasound, pregnant uterus, real time with image documentation, limited (eg, fetal heart beat, placental location, fetal position and/or qualitative amniotic fluid volume), 1 or more fetuses

(Use 76815 only once per exam and not per element)

(To report first trimester fetal nuchal translucency measurement, see 76813, 76814)

76816 Ultrasound, pregnant uterus, real time with image documentation, follow-up (eg, re-evaluation of fetal size by measuring standard growth parameters and amniotic fluid volume, re-evaluation of organ system(s) suspected or confirmed to be abnormal on a previous scan), transabdominal approach, per fetus

(Report 76816 with modifier 59 for each additional fetus examined in a multiple pregnancy)

76817 Ultrasound, pregnant uterus, real time with image documentation, transvaginal

(For non-obstetrical transvaginal ultrasound, use 76830)

(If transvaginal examination is done in addition to transabdominal obstetrical ultrasound exam, use 76817 in addition to appropriate transabdominal exam code)

76818 Fetal biophysical profile; with non-stress testing

76819 without non-stress testing

(Fetal biophysical profile assessments for the second and any additional fetuses, should be reported separately by code 76818 or 76819 with the modifier 59 appended)

(For amniotic fluid index without non-stress test, use 76815)

76820 Doppler velocimetry, fetal; umbilical artery

76821 middle cerebral artery

76825 Echocardiography, fetal, cardiovascular system, real time with image documentation (2D), with or without M-mode recording;

76826 follow-up or repeat study

76827 Doppler echocardiography, fetal, pulsed wave and/or continuous wave with spectral display; complete

76828 follow-up or repeat study

(To report the use of color mapping, use 93325)

Nonobstetrical

Code 76856 includes the complete evaluation of the female pelvic anatomy. Elements of this examination include a description and measurements of the uterus and adnexal structures, measurement of the endometrium, measurement of the bladder (when applicable), and a description of any pelvic pathology (eg, ovarian cysts, uterine leiomyomata, free pelvic fluid).

Code 76856 is also applicable to a complete evaluation of the male pelvis. Elements of the examination include evaluation and measurement (when applicable) of the urinary bladder, evaluation of the prostate and seminal vesicles to the extent that they are visualized transabdominally, and any pelvic pathology (eg, bladder tumor, enlarged prostate, free pelvic fluid, pelvic abscess).

Code 76857 represents a focused examination limited to the assessment of one or more elements listed in code 76856 and/or the reevaluation of one or more pelvic abnormalities previously demonstrated on ultrasound. Code 76857, rather than 76770, should be utilized if the urinary bladder alone (ie, not including the kidneys) is imaged, whereas code 51798 should be utilized if a bladder volume or post-void residual measurement is obtained without imaging the bladder.

Use of ultrasound, without thorough evaluation of organ(s) or anatomic region, image documentation, and final, written report, is not separately reportable.

76830 Ultrasound, transvaginal

(For obstetrical transvaginal ultrasound, use 76817)

(If transvaginal examination is done in addition to transabdominal non-obstetrical ultrasound exam, use 76830 in addition to appropriate transabdominal exam code)

76831 Saline infusion sonohysterography (SIS), including color flow Doppler, when performed

(For introduction of saline for saline infusion sonohysterography, use 58340)

76856 Ultrasound, pelvic (nonobstetric), real time with image documentation; complete

76857 limited or follow-up (eg, for follicles)

Genitalia

76870 Ultrasound, scrotum and contents

76872 Ultrasound, transrectal;

76873 prostate volume study for brachytherapy treatment planning (separate procedure)

Extremities

76880 Ultrasound, extremity, nonvascular, real time with image documentation

76885 Ultrasound, infant hips, real time with imaging documentation; dynamic (requiring physician manipulation)

76886 limited, static (not requiring physician manipulation)

Radiology

Ultrasonic Guidance Procedures

76930   Ultrasonic guidance for pericardiocentesis, imaging supervision and interpretation

76932   Ultrasonic guidance for endomyocardial biopsy, imaging supervision and interpretation

76936   Ultrasound guided compression repair of arterial pseudoaneurysm or arteriovenous fistulae (includes diagnostic ultrasound evaluation, compression of lesion and imaging)

+ 76937   Ultrasound guidance for vascular access requiring ultrasound evaluation of potential access sites, documentation of selected vessel patency, concurrent realtime ultrasound visualization of vascular needle entry, with permanent recording and reporting (List separately in addition to code for primary procedure)

▶(Do not use 76937 in conjunction with 37760, 37761, or 76942)◀

(If extremity venous non-invasive vascular diagnostic study is performed separate from venous access guidance, use 93965, 93970 or 93971)

76940   Ultrasound guidance for, and monitoring of, parenchymal tissue ablation

(Do not report 76940 in conjunction with 76998)

(For ablation, see 32998, 47370-47382, 50592, 50593)

76941   Ultrasonic guidance for intrauterine fetal transfusion or cordocentesis, imaging supervision and interpretation

(For procedure, see 36460, 59012)

76942   Ultrasonic guidance for needle placement (eg, biopsy, aspiration, injection, localization device), imaging supervision and interpretation

▶(Do not report 76942 in conjunction with 37760, 37761, 43232, 43237, 43242, 45341, 45342, or 76975)◀

76945   Ultrasonic guidance for chorionic villus sampling, imaging supervision and interpretation

(For procedure, use 59015)

76946   Ultrasonic guidance for amniocentesis, imaging supervision and interpretation

76948   Ultrasonic guidance for aspiration of ova, imaging supervision and interpretation

76950   Ultrasonic guidance for placement of radiation therapy fields

▶(For placement of interstitial device[s] for radiation therapy guidance, see 31627, 32553, 49411, 55876)◀

76965   Ultrasonic guidance for interstitial radioelement application

Other Procedures

76970   Ultrasound study follow-up (specify)

76975   Gastrointestinal endoscopic ultrasound, supervision and interpretation

(Do not report 76975 in conjunction with 43231, 43232, 43237, 43238, 43242, 43259, 45341, 45342, or 76942)

76977   Ultrasound bone density measurement and interpretation, peripheral site(s), any method

76998   Ultrasonic guidance, intraoperative

▶(Do not report 76998 in conjunction with 36475-36479, 37760, 37761, 47370-47382)◀

(For ultrasound guidance for open and laparoscopic radiofrequency tissue ablation, use 76940)

76999   Unlisted ultrasound procedure (eg, diagnostic, interventional)

Radiologic Guidance

Fluoroscopic Guidance

+ 77001   Fluoroscopic guidance for central venous access device placement, replacement (catheter only or complete), or removal (includes fluoroscopic guidance for vascular access and catheter manipulation, any necessary contrast injections through access site or catheter with related venography radiologic supervision and interpretation, and radiographic documentation of final catheter position) (List separately in addition to code for primary procedure)

(Do not use 77001 in conjunction with 77002)

(If formal extremity venography is performed from separate venous access and separately interpreted, use 36005 and 75820, 75822, 75825, or 75827)

77002   Fluoroscopic guidance for needle placement (eg, biopsy, aspiration, injection, localization device)

(See appropriate surgical code for procedure and anatomic location)

(77002 includes all radiographic arthrography with the exception of supervision and interpretation for CT and MR arthrography)

(Do not report 77002 in addition to 70332, 73040, 73085, 73115, 73525, 73580, 73615)

(77002 is included in the organ/anatomic specific radiological supervision and interpretation procedures 49440, 74320, 74355, 74445, 74470, 74475, 75809, 75810, 75885, 75887, 75980, 75982, 75989)

Radiology

▲ **77003** Fluoroscopic guidance and localization of needle or catheter tip for spine or paraspinous diagnostic or therapeutic injection procedures (epidural, transforaminal epidural, subarachnoid, or sacroiliac joint), including neurolytic agent destruction

(Injection of contrast during fluoroscopic guidance and localization [77003] is included in 22526, 22527, 62263, 62264, 62267, 62270-62282, 62310-62319)

(Fluoroscopic guidance for subarachnoid puncture for diagnostic radiographic myelography is included in supervision and interpretation codes 72240-72270)

(For epidural or subarachnoid needle or catheter placement and injection, see 62270-62282, 62310-62319)

(For sacroiliac joint arthrography, see 27096, 73542. If formal arthrography is not performed and recorded, and a formal radiographic report is not issued, use 77003 for fluoroscopic guidance for sacroiliac joint injections)

►(For paravertebral facet joint injection, see 64490-64495. For transforaminal epidural needle placement and injection, see 64479-64484)◄

(For destruction by neurolytic agent, see 64600-64680)

(For percutaneous or endoscopic lysis of epidural adhesions, 62263, 62264 include fluoroscopic guidance and localization)

Computed Tomography Guidance

77011 Computed tomography guidance for stereotactic localization

77012 Computed tomography guidance for needle placement (eg, biopsy, aspiration, injection, localization device), radiological supervision and interpretation

77013 Computed tomography guidance for, and monitoring of, parenchymal tissue ablation

(Do not report 77013 in conjunction with 20982)

(For percutaneous radiofrequency ablation, see 32998, 47382, 50592, 50593)

77014 Computed tomography guidance for placement of radiation therapy fields

►(For placement of interstitial device[s] for radiation therapy guidance, see 31627, 32553, 49411, 55876)◄

Magnetic Resonance Guidance

77021 Magnetic resonance guidance for needle placement (eg, for biopsy, needle aspiration, injection, or placement of localization device) radiological supervision and interpretation

(For procedure, see appropriate organ or site)

77022 Magnetic resonance guidance for, and monitoring of, parenchymal tissue ablation

(For percutaneous radiofrequency ablation, see 32998, 47382, 50592, 50593)

(For focused ultrasound ablation treatment of uterine leiomyomata, see Category III codes 0071T, 0072T)

Other Radiologic Guidance

77031 Stereotactic localization guidance for breast biopsy or needle placement (eg, for wire localization or for injection), each lesion, radiological supervision and interpretation

(For procedure, see 10022, 19000-19103, 19290, 19291)

(For injection for sentinel node localization without lymphoscintigraphy, use 38792)

77032 Mammographic guidance for needle placement, breast (eg, for wire localization or for injection), each lesion, radiological supervision and interpretation

(For procedure, see 10022, 19000, 19102, 19103, 19290, 19291)

(For injection for sentinel node localization without lymphoscintigraphy, use 38792)

Breast, Mammography

(For mammographic guidance for needle placement of breast lesion, use 77032)

✚ **77051** Computer-aided detection (computer algorithm analysis of digital image data for lesion detection) with further physician review for interpretation, with or without digitization of film radiographic images; diagnostic mammography (List separately in addition to code for primary procedure)

(Use 77051 in conjunction with 77055, 77056)

✚ **77052** screening mammography (List separately in addition to code for primary procedure)

(Use 77052 in conjunction with 77057)

77053 Mammary ductogram or galactogram, single duct, radiological supervision and interpretation

(For mammary ductogram or galactogram injection, use 19030)

77054 Mammary ductogram or galactogram, multiple ducts, radiological supervision and interpretation

77055 Mammography; unilateral

77056 bilateral

(Use 77055, 77056 in conjunction with 77051 for computer-aided detection applied to a diagnostic mammogram)

Radiology

77057 Screening mammography, bilateral (2-view film study of each breast)

(Use 77057 in conjunction with 77052 for computer-aided detection applied to a screening mammogram)

(For electrical impedance breast scan, use 76499)

77058 Magnetic resonance imaging, breast, without and/or with contrast material(s); unilateral

77059   bilateral

Bone/Joint Studies

77071 Manual application of stress performed by physician for joint radiography, including contralateral joint if indicated

(For radiographic interpretation of stressed images, see appropriate anatomic site and number of views)

77072 Bone age studies

77073 Bone length studies (orthoroentgenogram, scanogram)

77074 Radiologic examination, osseous survey; limited (eg, for metastases)

77075   complete (axial and appendicular skeleton)

77076 Radiologic examination, osseous survey, infant

77077 Joint survey, single view, 2 or more joints (specify)

77078 Computed tomography, bone mineral density study, 1 or more sites; axial skeleton (eg, hips, pelvis, spine)

77079   appendicular skeleton (peripheral) (eg, radius, wrist, heel)

77080 Dual-energy X-ray absorptiometry (DXA), bone density study, 1 or more sites; axial skeleton (eg, hips, pelvis, spine)

77081   appendicular skeleton (peripheral) (eg, radius, wrist, heel)

77082   vertebral fracture assessment

(For dual energy x-ray absorptiometry [DXA] body composition study, use 76499)

77083 Radiographic absorptiometry (eg, photodensitometry, radiogrammetry), 1 or more sites

77084 Magnetic resonance (eg, proton) imaging, bone marrow blood supply

Radiation Oncology

Listings for Radiation Oncology provide for teletherapy and brachytherapy to include initial consultation, clinical treatment planning, simulation, medical radiation physics, dosimetry, treatment devices, special services, and clinical treatment management procedures. They include normal follow-up care during course of treatment and for three months following its completion.

When a service or procedure is provided that is not listed in this edition of the CPT codebook it should be identified by a Special Report (see page 304) and one of the following unlisted procedure codes:

77299 Unlisted procedure, therapeutic radiology clinical treatment planning

77399 Unlisted procedure, medical radiation physics, dosimetry and treatment devices, and special services

77499 Unlisted procedure, therapeutic radiology treatment management

77799 Unlisted procedure, clinical brachytherapy

For treatment by injectable or ingestible isotopes, see subsection **Nuclear Medicine.**

Consultation: Clinical Management

Preliminary consultation, evaluation of patient prior to decision to treat, or full medical care (in addition to treatment management) when provided by the therapeutic radiologist may be identified by the appropriate procedure codes from **Evaluation and Management, Medicine,** or **Surgery** sections.

Clinical Treatment Planning (External and Internal Sources)

The clinical treatment planning process is a complex service including interpretation of special testing, tumor localization, treatment volume determination, treatment time/dosage determination, choice of treatment modality, determination of number and size of treatment ports, selection of appropriate treatment devices, and other procedures.

Definitions

Simple planning requires a single treatment area of interest encompassed in a single port or simple parallel opposed ports with simple or no blocking.

Intermediate planning requires 3 or more converging ports, 2 separate treatment areas, multiple blocks, or special time dose constraints.

Complex planning requires highly complex blocking, custom shielding blocks, tangential ports, special wedges or compensators, three or more separate treatment areas, rotational or special beam considerations, combination of therapeutic modalities.

77261 Therapeutic radiology treatment planning; simple

77262   intermediate

77263   complex

Definitions

Simple simulation of a single treatment area with either a single port or parallel opposed ports. Simple or no blocking.

Radiology

Intermediate simulation of three or more converging ports, two separate treatment areas, multiple blocks.

Complex simulation of tangential portals, three or more treatment areas, rotation or arc therapy, complex blocking, custom shielding blocks, brachytherapy source verification, hyperthermia probe verification, any use of contrast materials.

Three-dimensional (3D) computer-generated 3D reconstruction of tumor volume and surrounding critical normal tissue structures from direct CT scans and/or MRI data in preparation for non-coplanar or coplanar therapy. The simulation uses documented 3D beam's eye view volume-dose displays of multiple or moving beams. Documentation with 3D volume reconstruction and dose distribution is required.

Simulation may be carried out on a dedicated simulator, a radiation therapy treatment unit, or diagnostic X-ray machine.

77280 Therapeutic radiology simulation-aided field setting; simple

77285 intermediate

77290 complex

77295 3-dimensional

77299 Unlisted procedure, therapeutic radiology clinical treatment planning

Medical Radiation Physics, Dosimetry, Treatment Devices, and Special Services

77300 Basic radiation dosimetry calculation, central axis depth dose calculation, TDF, NSD, gap calculation, off axis factor, tissue inhomogeneity factors, calculation of non-ionizing radiation surface and depth dose, as required during course of treatment, only when prescribed by the treating physician

77301 Intensity modulated radiotherapy plan, including dose-volume histograms for target and critical structure partial tolerance specifications

(Dose plan is optimized using inverse or forward planning technique for modulated beam delivery [eg, binary, dynamic MLC] to create highly conformal dose distribution. Computer plan distribution must be verified for positional accuracy based on dosimetric verification of the intensity map with verification of treatment set-up and interpretation of verification methodology)

77305 Teletherapy, isodose plan (whether hand or computer calculated); simple (1 or 2 parallel opposed unmodified ports directed to a single area of interest)

77310 intermediate (3 or more treatment ports directed to a single area of interest)

77315 complex (mantle or inverted Y, tangential ports, the use of wedges, compensators, complex blocking, rotational beam, or special beam considerations)

(Only 1 teletherapy isodose plan may be reported for a given course of therapy to a specific treatment area)

77321 Special teletherapy port plan, particles, hemibody, total body

77326 Brachytherapy isodose plan; simple (calculation made from single plane, 1 to 4 sources/ribbon application, remote afterloading brachytherapy, 1 to 8 sources)

(For definition of source/ribbon, see page 332)

77327 intermediate (multiplane dosage calculations, application involving 5 to 10 sources/ribbons, remote afterloading brachytherapy, 9 to 12 sources)

77328 complex (multiplane isodose plan, volume implant calculations, over 10 sources/ribbons used, special spatial reconstruction, remote afterloading brachytherapy, over 12 sources)

77331 Special dosimetry (eg, TLD, microdosimetry) (specify), only when prescribed by the treating physician

77332 Treatment devices, design and construction; simple (simple block, simple bolus)

77333 intermediate (multiple blocks, stents, bite blocks, special bolus)

77334 complex (irregular blocks, special shields, compensators, wedges, molds or casts)

77336 Continuing medical physics consultation, including assessment of treatment parameters, quality assurance of dose delivery, and review of patient treatment documentation in support of the radiation oncologist, reported per week of therapy

● **77338** Multi-leaf collimator (MLC) device(s) for intensity modulated radiation therapy (IMRT), design and construction per IMRT plan

▶(Do not report 77338 more than once per IMRT plan)◀

▶(For immobilization in IMRT treatment, see 77332-77334)◀

▶(Do not report 77338 in conjunction with 0073T, compensator based IMRT)◀

77370 Special medical radiation physics consultation

Stereotactic Radiation Treatment Delivery

⊙▲ **77371** Radiation treatment delivery, stereotactic radiosurgery (SRS), complete course of treatment of cranial lesion(s) consisting of 1 session; multi-source Cobalt 60 based

77372 linear accelerator based

(For radiation treatment management, use 77432)

77373   Stereotactic body radiation therapy, treatment delivery, per fraction to 1 or more lesions, including image guidance, entire course not to exceed 5 fractions

(Do not report 77373 in conjunction with 77401-77416, 77418)

(For single fraction cranial lesion[s], see 77371, 77372)

Other Procedures

77399   Unlisted procedure, medical radiation physics, dosimetry and treatment devices, and special services

Radiation Treatment Delivery

(Radiation treatment delivery [77401-77416] recognizes the technical component and the various energy levels)

▶(For intra-fraction localization and tracking of target, use 0197T)◀

77401   Radiation treatment delivery, superficial and/or ortho voltage

77402   Radiation treatment delivery, single treatment area, single port or parallel opposed ports, simple blocks or no blocks; up to 5 MeV

77403   6-10 MeV

77404   11-19 MeV

77406   20 MeV or greater

77407   Radiation treatment delivery, 2 separate treatment areas, 3 or more ports on a single treatment area, use of multiple blocks; up to 5 MeV

77408   6-10 MeV

77409   11-19 MeV

77411   20 MeV or greater

77412   Radiation treatment delivery, 3 or more separate treatment areas, custom blocking, tangential ports, wedges, rotational beam, compensators, electron beam; up to 5 MeV

77413   6-10 MeV

77414   11-19 MeV

77416   20 MeV or greater

77417   Therapeutic radiology port film(s)

77418   Intensity modulated treatment delivery, single or multiple fields/arcs, via narrow spatially and temporally modulated beams, binary, dynamic MLC, per treatment session

(For intensity modulated treatment planning, use 77301)

(For compensator-based beam modulation treatment delivery, use Category III code 0073T)

77421   Stereoscopic X-ray guidance for localization of target volume for the delivery of radiation therapy

(Do not report 77421 in conjunction with 77432, 77435)

▶(For placement of interstitial device[s] for radiation therapy guidance, see 31627, 32553, 49411, 55876)◀

Neutron Beam Treatment Delivery

77422   High energy neutron radiation treatment delivery; single treatment area using a single port or parallel-opposed ports with no blocks or simple blocking

77423   1 or more isocenter(s) with coplanar or non-coplanar geometry with blocking and/or wedge, and/or compensator(s)

Radiation Treatment Management

Radiation treatment management is reported in units of five fractions or treatment sessions, regardless of the actual time period in which the services are furnished. The services need not be furnished on consecutive days. Multiple fractions representing two or more treatment sessions furnished on the same day may be counted separately as long as there has been a distinct break in therapy sessions, and the fractions are of the character usually furnished on different days. Code 77427 is also reported if there are three or four fractions beyond a multiple of five at the end of a course of treatment; one or two fractions beyond a multiple of five at the end of a course of treatment are not reported separately. The professional services furnished during treatment management typically consist of:

- Review of port films;

- Review of dosimetry, dose delivery, and treatment parameters;

- Review of patient treatment set-up;

- Examination of patient for medical evaluation and management (eg, assessment of the patient's response to treatment, coordination of care and treatment, review of imaging and/or lab test results).

77427   Radiation treatment management, 5 treatments

77431   Radiation therapy management with complete course of therapy consisting of 1 or 2 fractions only

(77431 is not to be used to fill in the last week of a long course of therapy)

77432   Stereotactic radiation treatment management of cranial lesion(s) (complete course of treatment consisting of 1 session)

(The same physician should not report both stereotactic radiosurgery services [61796-61800] and radiation treatment management [77432 or 77435] for cranial lesions)

(For stereotactic body radiation therapy treatment, use 77435)

Radiology

77435 Stereotactic body radiation therapy, treatment management, per treatment course, to 1 or more lesions, including image guidance, entire course not to exceed 5 fractions

(Do not report 77435 in conjunction with 77427-77432)

(The same physician should not report both stereotactic radiosurgery services [63620, 63621] and radiation treatment management [77435] for extracranial lesions)

77470 Special treatment procedure (eg, total body irradiation, hemibody radiation, per oral, endocavitary or intraoperative cone irradiation)

(77470 assumes that the procedure is performed 1 or more times during the course of therapy, in addition to daily or weekly patient management)

77499 Unlisted procedure, therapeutic radiology treatment management

Proton Beam Treatment Delivery

Definitions

Simple proton treatment delivery to a single treatment area utilizing a single non-tangential/oblique port, custom block with compensation (77522) and without compensation (77520).

Intermediate proton treatment delivery to one or more treatment areas utilizing two or more ports or one or more tangential/oblique ports, with custom blocks and compensators.

Complex proton treatment delivery to one or more treatment areas utilizing two or more ports per treatment area with matching or patching fields and/or multiple isocenters, with custom blocks and compensators.

77520 Proton treatment delivery; simple, without compensation

77522 simple, with compensation

77523 intermediate

77525 complex

Hyperthermia

Hyperthermia treatments as listed in this section include external (superficial and deep), interstitial, and intracavitary.

Radiation therapy when given concurrently is listed separately.

Hyperthermia is used only as an adjunct to radiation therapy or chemotherapy. It may be induced by a variety of sources (eg, microwave, ultrasound, low energy radio-frequency conduction, or by probes).

The listed treatments include management during the course of therapy and follow-up care for three months after completion.

Preliminary consultation is not included (see **Evaluation and Management** 99241-99255).

Physics planning and interstitial insertion of temperature sensors, and use of external or interstitial heat generating sources are included.

The following descriptors are included in the treatment schedule:

⊙ **77600** Hyperthermia, externally generated; superficial (ie, heating to a depth of 4 cm or less)

⊙ **77605** deep (ie, heating to depths greater than 4 cm)

⊙ **77610** Hyperthermia generated by interstitial probe(s); 5 or fewer interstitial applicators

⊙ **77615** more than 5 interstitial applicators

Clinical Intracavitary Hyperthermia

77620 Hyperthermia generated by intracavitary probe(s)

Clinical Brachytherapy

Clinical brachytherapy requires the use of either natural or man-made radioelements applied into or around a treatment field of interest. The supervision of radioelements and dose interpretation are performed solely by the therapeutic radiologist.

Services 77750-77799 include admission to the hospital and daily visits.

For insertion of ovoids and tandems, use 57155.

For insertion of Heyman capsules, use 58346.

Definitions

(Sources refer to intracavitary placement or permanent interstitial placement; ribbons refer to temporary interstitial placement)

A simple application has one to four sources/ribbons.

An intermediate application has five to 10 sources/ribbons.

A complex application has greater than 10 sources/ribbons.

(For high dose rate electronic brachytherapy, per fraction, use Category III code 0182T)

77750 Infusion or instillation of radioelement solution (includes 3-month follow-up care)

(For administration of radiolabeled monoclonal antibodies, use 79403)

(For non-antibody radiopharmaceutical therapy by intravenous administration only, not including 3-month follow-up care, use 79101)

77761 Intracavitary radiation source application; simple

77762 intermediate

77763 complex

(Do not report 77761-77763 in conjunction with Category III code 0182T)

77776 Interstitial radiation source application; simple

77777   intermediate

77778   complex

(Do not report 77776-77778 in conjunction with Category III code 0182T)

(77781 has been deleted. To report, see 77785, 77786)

(77782-77784 have been deleted. To report, see 77785-77787)

77785   Remote afterloading high dose rate radionuclide brachytherapy; 1 channel

77786   2-12 channels

77787   over 12 channels

▶(Do not report 77785-77787 in conjunction with Category III code 0182T)◀

77789   Surface application of radiation source

(Do not report 77789 in conjunction with Category III code 0182T)

77790   Supervision, handling, loading of radiation source

77799   Unlisted procedure, clinical brachytherapy

Nuclear Medicine

Listed procedures may be performed independently or in the course of overall medical care. If the physician providing these services is also responsible for diagnostic work-up and/or follow-up care of patient, see appropriate sections also.

Radioimmunoassay tests are found in the **Clinical Pathology** section (codes 82000-84999). These codes can be appropriately used by any specialist performing such tests in a laboratory licensed and/or certified for radioimmunoassays. The reporting of these tests is not confined to clinical pathology laboratories alone.

The services listed do not include the radiopharmaceutical or drug. Diagnostic and therapeutic radiopharmaceuticals and drugs supplied by the physician should be reported separately using the appropriate supply code(s), in addition to the procedure code.

Diagnostic

Endocrine System

78000   Thyroid uptake; single determination

78001   multiple determinations

78003   stimulation, suppression or discharge (not including initial uptake studies)

78006   Thyroid imaging, with uptake; single determination

78007   multiple determinations

78010   Thyroid imaging; only

78011   with vascular flow

78015   Thyroid carcinoma metastases imaging; limited area (eg, neck and chest only)

78016   with additional studies (eg, urinary recovery)

78018   whole body

+ 78020   Thyroid carcinoma metastases uptake (List separately in addition to code for primary procedure)

(Use 78020 in conjunction with 78018 only)

78070   Parathyroid imaging

78075   Adrenal imaging, cortex and/or medulla

78099   Unlisted endocrine procedure, diagnostic nuclear medicine

(For chemical analysis, see **Chemistry** section)

Hematopoietic, Reticuloendothelial and Lymphatic System

78102   Bone marrow imaging; limited area

78103   multiple areas

78104   whole body

78110   Plasma volume, radiopharmaceutical volume-dilution technique (separate procedure); single sampling

78111   multiple samplings

78120   Red cell volume determination (separate procedure); single sampling

78121   multiple samplings

78122   Whole blood volume determination, including separate measurement of plasma volume and red cell volume (radiopharmaceutical volume-dilution technique)

78130   Red cell survival study;

78135   differential organ/tissue kinetics (eg, splenic and/or hepatic sequestration)

78140   Labeled red cell sequestration, differential organ/tissue (eg, splenic and/or hepatic)

78185   Spleen imaging only, with or without vascular flow

(If combined with liver study, use procedures 78215 and 78216)

78190   Kinetics, study of platelet survival, with or without differential organ/tissue localization

78191   Platelet survival study

78195   Lymphatics and lymph nodes imaging

(For sentinel node identification without scintigraphy imaging, use 38792)

(For sentinel node excision, see 38500-38542)

78199   Unlisted hematopoietic, reticuloendothelial and lymphatic procedure, diagnostic nuclear medicine

(For chemical analysis, see **Chemistry** section)

Radiology

Gastrointestinal System

78201   Liver imaging; static only

78202   with vascular flow

(For spleen imaging only, use 78185)

78205   Liver imaging (SPECT);

78206   with vascular flow

78215   Liver and spleen imaging; static only

78216   with vascular flow

78220   Liver function study with hepatobiliary agents, with serial images

78223   Hepatobiliary ductal system imaging, including gallbladder, with or without pharmacologic intervention, with or without quantitative measurement of gallbladder function

78230   Salivary gland imaging;

78231   with serial images

78232   Salivary gland function study

78258   Esophageal motility

78261   Gastric mucosa imaging

78262   Gastroesophageal reflux study

78264   Gastric emptying study

78267   Urea breath test, C-14 (isotopic); acquisition for analysis

78268   analysis

78270   Vitamin B-12 absorption study (eg, Schilling test); without intrinsic factor

78271   with intrinsic factor

78272   Vitamin B-12 absorption studies combined, with and without intrinsic factor

78278   Acute gastrointestinal blood loss imaging

78282   Gastrointestinal protein loss

78290   Intestine imaging (eg, ectopic gastric mucosa, Meckel's localization, volvulus)

78291   Peritoneal-venous shunt patency test (eg, for LeVeen, Denver shunt)

(For injection procedure, use 49427)

78299   Unlisted gastrointestinal procedure, diagnostic nuclear medicine

Musculoskeletal System

Bone and joint imaging can be used in the diagnosis of a variety of inflammatory processes (eg, osteomyelitis), as well as for localization of primary and/or metastatic neoplasms.

78300   Bone and/or joint imaging; limited area

78305   multiple areas

78306   whole body

78315   3 phase study

78320   tomographic (SPECT)

78350   Bone density (bone mineral content) study, 1 or more sites; single photon absorptiometry

78351   dual photon absorptiometry, 1 or more sites

(For radiographic bone density [photodensitometry], use 77083)

78399   Unlisted musculoskeletal procedure, diagnostic nuclear medicine

Cardiovascular System

►Myocardial perfusion and cardiac blood pool imaging studies may be performed at rest and/or during stress. When performed during exercise and/or pharmacologic stress, the appropriate stress testing code from the 93015-93018 series should be reported in addition to 78451-78454, 78472-78492.◄

78414   Determination of central c-v hemodynamics (non-imaging) (eg, ejection fraction with probe technique) with or without pharmacologic intervention or exercise, single or multiple determinations

78428   Cardiac shunt detection

78445   Non-cardiac vascular flow imaging (ie, angiography, venography)

● **78451**   Myocardial perfusion imaging, tomographic (SPECT) (including attenuation correction, qualitative or quantitative wall motion, ejection fraction by first pass or gated technique, additional quantification, when performed); single study, at rest or stress (exercise or pharmacologic)

● **78452**   multiple studies, at rest and/or stress (exercise or pharmacologic) and/or redistribution and/or rest reinjection

● **78453**   Myocardial perfusion imaging, planar (including qualitative or quantitative wall motion, ejection fraction by first pass or gated technique, additional quantification, when performed); single study, at rest or stress (exercise or pharmacologic)

● **78454**   multiple studies, at rest and/or stress (exercise or pharmacologic) and/or redistribution and/or rest reinjection

78456   Acute venous thrombosis imaging, peptide

78457   Venous thrombosis imaging, venogram; unilateral

78458   bilateral

78459   Myocardial imaging, positron emission tomography (PET), metabolic evaluation

(For myocardial perfusion study, see 78491-78492)

►(78460–78465 have been deleted. To report, see 78451–78454)◄

Radiology

78466   Myocardial imaging, infarct avid, planar; qualitative or quantitative

78468   with ejection fraction by first pass technique

78469   tomographic SPECT with or without quantification

78472   Cardiac blood pool imaging, gated equilibrium; planar, single study at rest or stress (exercise and/or pharmacologic), wall motion study plus ejection fraction, with or without additional quantitative processing

       (For assessment of right ventricular ejection fraction by first pass technique, use 78496)

78473   multiple studies, wall motion study plus ejection fraction, at rest and stress (exercise and/or pharmacologic), with or without additional quantification

       ►(Do not report 78472, 78473 in conjunction with 78451-78454, 78481, 78483, 78494)◄

       ►(78478, 78480 have been deleted. To report, see 78451–78454)◄

78481   Cardiac blood pool imaging (planar), first pass technique; single study, at rest or with stress (exercise and/or pharmacologic), wall motion study plus ejection fraction, with or without quantification

78483   multiple studies, at rest and with stress (exercise and/or pharmacologic), wall motion study plus ejection fraction, with or without quantification

       (For cerebral blood flow study, use 78610)

       ►(Do not report 78481-78483 in conjunction with 78451–78454)◄

78491   Myocardial imaging, positron emission tomography (PET), perfusion; single study at rest or stress

78492   multiple studies at rest and/or stress

78494   Cardiac blood pool imaging, gated equilibrium, SPECT, at rest, wall motion study plus ejection fraction, with or without quantitative processing

+ 78496   Cardiac blood pool imaging, gated equilibrium, single study, at rest, with right ventricular ejection fraction by first pass technique (List separately in addition to code for primary procedure)

       (Use 78496 in conjunction with 78472)

78499   Unlisted cardiovascular procedure, diagnostic nuclear medicine

Respiratory System

78580   Pulmonary perfusion imaging, particulate

       ►(Do not report 78580 in conjunction with 78451-78454)◄

78584   Pulmonary perfusion imaging, particulate, with ventilation; single breath

78585   rebreathing and washout, with or without single breath

78586   Pulmonary ventilation imaging, aerosol; single projection

78587   multiple projections (eg, anterior, posterior, lateral views)

78588   Pulmonary perfusion imaging, particulate, with ventilation imaging, aerosol, 1 or multiple projections

78591   Pulmonary ventilation imaging, gaseous, single breath, single projection

78593   Pulmonary ventilation imaging, gaseous, with rebreathing and washout with or without single breath; single projection

78594   multiple projections (eg, anterior, posterior, lateral views)

78596   Pulmonary quantitative differential function (ventilation/perfusion) study

78599   Unlisted respiratory procedure, diagnostic nuclear medicine

Nervous System

78600   Brain imaging, less than 4 static views;

78601   with vascular flow

78605   Brain imaging, minimum 4 static views;

78606   with vascular flow

78607   Brain imaging, tomographic (SPECT)

78608   Brain imaging, positron emission tomography (PET); metabolic evaluation

78609   perfusion evaluation

78610   Brain imaging, vascular flow only

       (78615 has been deleted. To report, use 78610)

78630   Cerebrospinal fluid flow, imaging (not including introduction of material); cisternography

       (For injection procedure, see 61000-61070, 62270-62319)

78635   ventriculography

       (For injection procedure, see 61000-61070, 62270-62294)

78645   shunt evaluation

       (For injection procedure, see 61000-61070, 62270-62294)

78647   tomographic (SPECT)

78650   Cerebrospinal fluid leakage detection and localization

       (For injection procedure, see 61000-61070, 62270-62294)

78660   Radiopharmaceutical dacryocystography

78699   Unlisted nervous system procedure, diagnostic nuclear medicine

Radiology

Genitourinary System

78700 Kidney imaging morphology;

78701   with vascular flow

78707   with vascular flow and function, single study without pharmacological intervention

78708   with vascular flow and function, single study, with pharmacological intervention (eg, angiotensin converting enzyme inhibitor and/or diuretic)

78709   with vascular flow and function, multiple studies, with and without pharmacological intervention (eg, angiotensin converting enzyme inhibitor and/or diuretic)

(For introduction of radioactive substance in association with renal endoscopy, see 77776-77778)

78710   tomographic (SPECT)

78725 Kidney function study, non-imaging radioisotopic study

+ 78730 Urinary bladder residual study (List separately in addition to code for primary procedure)

(Use 78730 in conjunction with 78740)

(For measurement of postvoid residual urine and/or bladder capacity by ultrasound, nonimaging, use 51798)

(For ultrasound imaging of the bladder only, with measurement of postvoid residual urine when performed, use 76857)

78740 Ureteral reflux study (radiopharmaceutical voiding cystogram)

(Use 78740 in conjunction with 78730 for urinary bladder residual study)

(For catheterization, see 51701, 51702, 51703)

78761 Testicular imaging with vascular flow

78799 Unlisted genitourinary procedure, diagnostic nuclear medicine

(For chemical analysis, see **Chemistry** section)

Other Procedures

(For specific organ, see appropriate heading)

(For radiophosphorus tumor identification, ocular, see 78800)

78800 Radiopharmaceutical localization of tumor or distribution of radiopharmaceutical agent(s); limited area

(For specific organ, see appropriate heading)

78801   multiple areas

78802   whole body, single day imaging

78803   tomographic (SPECT)

78804   whole body, requiring 2 or more days imaging

78805 Radiopharmaceutical localization of inflammatory process; limited area

78806   whole body

78807   tomographic (SPECT)

(For imaging bone infectious or inflammatory disease with a bone imaging radiopharmaceutical, see 78300, 78305, 78306)

78808 Injection procedure for radiopharmaceutical localization by non-imaging probe study, intravenous (eg, parathyroid adenoma)

(For sentinel lymph node identification, use 38792)

(For PET of brain, see 78608, 78609)

(For PET myocardial imaging, see 78459, 78491, 78492)

78811 Positron emission tomography (PET) imaging; limited area (eg, chest, head/neck)

78812   skull base to mid-thigh

78813   whole body

78814 Positron emission tomography (PET) with concurrently acquired computed tomography (CT) for attenuation correction and anatomical localization imaging; limited area (eg, chest, head/neck)

78815   skull base to mid-thigh

78816   whole body

(Report 78811-78816 only once per imaging session)

(Computed tomography [CT] performed for other than attenuation correction and anatomical localization is reported using the appropriate site specific CT code with modifier 59)

(78890, 78891 have been deleted)

78999 Unlisted miscellaneous procedure, diagnostic nuclear medicine

Therapeutic

The oral and intravenous administration codes in this section are inclusive of the mode of administration. For intra-arterial, intra-cavitary, and intra-articular administration, also use the appropriate injection and/or procedure codes, as well as imaging guidance and radiological supervision and interpretation codes, when appropriate.

79005 Radiopharmaceutical therapy, by oral administration

(For monoclonal antibody therapy, use 79403)

79101 Radiopharmaceutical therapy, by intravenous administration

▶(Do not report 79101 in conjunction with 36400, 36410, 79403, 96360, 96374 or 96375, 96409)◀

(For radiolabeled monoclonal antibody by intravenous infusion, use 79403)

(For infusion or instillation of non-antibody radioelement solution that includes 3 months follow-up care, use 77750)

Radiology

79200   Radiopharmaceutical therapy, by intracavitary administration

79300   Radiopharmaceutical therapy, by interstitial radioactive colloid administration

79403   Radiopharmaceutical therapy, radiolabeled monoclonal antibody by intravenous infusion

(For pre-treatment imaging, see 78802, 78804)

(Do not report 79403 in conjunction with 79101)

79440   Radiopharmaceutical therapy, by intra-articular administration

79445   Radiopharmaceutical therapy, by intra-arterial particulate administration

►(Do not report 79445 in conjunction with 96373, 96420)◄

(Use appropriate procedural and radiological supervision and interpretation codes for the angiographic and interventional procedures provided prerequisite to intra-arterial radiopharmaceutical therapy)

79999   Radiopharmaceutical therapy, unlisted procedure

Radiology

Notes

⊙=Moderate sedation   ✚=Add-on code   ✎=FDA approval pending   #=Resequenced code

Pathology and Laboratory Guidelines

Items used by all physicians in reporting their services are presented in the **Introduction.** Some of the commonalities are repeated here for the convenience of those physicians referring to this section on **Pathology and Laboratory.** Other definitions and items unique to Pathology and Laboratory are also listed.

Services in Pathology and Laboratory

Services in Pathology and Laboratory are provided by a physician or by technologists under responsible supervision of a physician.

Separate or Multiple Procedures

It is appropriate to designate multiple procedures that are rendered on the same date by separate entries.

Unlisted Service or Procedure

A service or procedure may be provided that is not listed in this edition of the CPT codebook. When reporting such a service, the appropriate "Unlisted Procedure" code may be used to indicate the service, identifying it by "Special Report" as discussed below. The "Unlisted Procedures" and accompanying codes for **Pathology and Laboratory** are as follows:

81099	Unlisted urinalysis procedure
84999	Unlisted chemistry procedure
85999	Unlisted hematology and coagulation procedure
86486	unlisted antigen, each
86849	Unlisted immunology procedure
86999	Unlisted transfusion medicine procedure
87999	Unlisted microbiology procedure
88099	Unlisted necropsy (autopsy) procedure
88199	Unlisted cytopathology procedure
88299	Unlisted cytogenetic study
88399	Unlisted surgical pathology procedure
89240	Unlisted miscellaneous pathology test
● **89398**	Unlisted reproductive medicine laboratory procedure

Special Report

▶A service that is rarely provided, unusual, variable, or new may require a special report. Pertinent information should include an adequate definition or description of the nature, extent, and need for the procedure; and the time, effort, and equipment necessary to provide the service.◀

Notes

⊙=Moderate sedation   ✛=Add-on code   ⟋=FDA approval pending   #=Resequenced code

Pathology and Laboratory Guidelines

Pathology and Laboratory

Organ or Disease-Oriented Panels

These panels were developed for coding purposes only and should not be interpreted as clinical parameters. The tests listed with each panel identify the defined components of that panel.

These panel components are not intended to limit the performance of other tests. If one performs tests in addition to those specifically indicated for a particular panel, those tests should be reported separately in addition to the panel code.

▶Do not report two or more panel codes that include any of the same constituent tests performed from the same patient collection. If a group of tests overlaps two or more panels, report the panel that incorporates the greater number of tests to fulfill the code definition and report the remaining tests using individual test codes (eg, do not report 80047 in conjunction with 80053)◀

80047   Basic metabolic panel (Calcium, ionized)

This panel must include the following:

Calcium, ionized (82330)

Carbon dioxide (82374)

Chloride (82435)

Creatinine (82565)

Glucose (82947)

Potassium (84132)

Sodium (84295)

Urea Nitrogen (BUN) (84520)

80048   Basic metabolic panel (Calcium, total)

This panel must include the following:

Calcium, total (82310)

Carbon dioxide (82374)

Chloride (82435)

Creatinine (82565)

Glucose (82947)

Potassium (84132)

Sodium (84295)

Urea nitrogen (BUN) (84520)

80050   General health panel

This panel must include the following:

Comprehensive metabolic panel (80053)

Blood count, complete (CBC), automated and automated differential WBC count (85025 or 85027 and 85004)

OR

Blood count, complete (CBC), automated (85027) and appropriate manual differential WBC count (85007 or 85009)

Thyroid stimulating hormone (TSH) (84443)

80051   Electrolyte panel

This panel must include the following:

Carbon dioxide (82374)

Chloride (82435)

Potassium (84132)

Sodium (84295)

80053   Comprehensive metabolic panel

This panel must include the following:

Albumin (82040)

Bilirubin, total (82247)

Calcium, total (82310)

Carbon dioxide (bicarbonate) (82374)

Chloride (82435)

Creatinine (82565)

Glucose (82947)

Phosphatase, alkaline (84075)

Potassium (84132)

Protein, total (84155)

Sodium (84295)

Transferase, alanine amino (ALT) (SGPT) (84460)

Transferase, aspartate amino (AST) (SGOT) (84450)

Urea nitrogen (BUN) (84520)

▲ **80055**   Obstetric panel

This panel must include the following:

Blood count, complete (CBC), automated and automated differential WBC count (85025 or 85027 and 85004)

OR

Blood count, complete (CBC), automated (85027) and appropriate manual differential WBC count (85007 or 85009)

Hepatitis B surface antigen (HBsAg) (87340)

Antibody, rubella (86762)

Syphilis test, non-treponemal antibody; qualitative (eg, VDRL, RPR, ART) (86592)

Antibody screen, RBC, each serum technique (86850)

Blood typing, ABO (86900) AND

Blood typing, Rh (D) (86901)

►(When syphilis screening is performed using a treponemal antibody approach [86780], do not use 80055. Use the individual codes for the tests performed in the obstetric panel)◄

80061   Lipid panel

This panel must include the following:

Cholesterol, serum, total (82465)

Lipoprotein, direct measurement, high density cholesterol (HDL cholesterol) (83718)

Triglycerides (84478)

80069   Renal function panel

This panel must include the following:

Albumin (82040)

Calcium, total (82310)

Carbon dioxide (bicarbonate) (82374)

Chloride (82435)

Creatinine (82565)

Glucose (82947)

Phosphorus inorganic (phosphate) (84100)

Potassium (84132)

Sodium (84295)

Urea nitrogen (BUN) (84520)

80074   Acute hepatitis panel

This panel must include the following:

Hepatitis A antibody (HAAb), IgM antibody (86709)

Hepatitis B core antibody (HBcAb), IgM antibody (86705)

Hepatitis B surface antigen (HBsAg) (87340)

Hepatitis C antibody (86803)

80076   Hepatic function panel

This panel must include the following:

Albumin (82040)

Bilirubin, total (82247)

Bilirubin, direct (82248)

Phosphatase, alkaline (84075)

Protein, total (84155)

Transferase, alanine amino (ALT) (SGPT) (84460)

Transferase, aspartate amino (AST) (SGOT) (84450)

Drug Testing

The following list contains examples of drugs or classes of drugs that are commonly assayed by qualitative screen, followed by confirmation with a second method:

- Alcohols
- Amphetamines
- Barbiturates
- Benzodiazepines
- Cocaine and metabolites
- Methadones
- Methaqualones
- Opiates
- Phencyclidines
- Phenothiazines
- Propoxyphenes
- Tetrahydrocannabinoids
- Tricyclic antidepressants

Confirmed drugs may also be quantitated.

Use 80100 for each multiple drug class chromatographic procedure. Use 80102 for each procedure necessary for confirmation. For chromatography, each combination of stationary and mobile phase is to be counted as one procedure. For example, if detection of three drugs by chromatography requires one stationary phase with three mobile phases, use 80100 three times. However, if multiple drugs can be detected using a single analysis (eg, one stationary phase with one mobile phase), use 80100 only once.

For quantitation of drugs screened, use appropriate code in **Chemistry** section (82000-84999) or **Therapeutic Drug Assay** section (80150-80299).

80100   Drug screen, qualitative; multiple drug classes chromatographic method, each procedure

80101   single drug class method (eg, immunoassay, enzyme assay), each drug class

80102   Drug confirmation, each procedure

80103   Tissue preparation for drug analysis

Therapeutic Drug Assays

The material for examination may be from any source. Examination is quantitative. For nonquantitative testing, see Drug Testing (80100-80103).

80150   Amikacin

80152   Amitriptyline

80154   Benzodiazepines

80156	Carbamazepine; total
80157	free
80158	Cyclosporine
80160	Desipramine
80162	Digoxin
80164	Dipropylacetic acid (valproic acid)
80166	Doxepin
80168	Ethosuximide
80170	Gentamicin
80172	Gold
80173	Haloperidol
80174	Imipramine
80176	Lidocaine
80178	Lithium
80182	Nortriptyline
80184	Phenobarbital
80185	Phenytoin; total
80186	free
80188	Primidone
80190	Procainamide;
80192	with metabolites (eg, n-acetyl procainamide)
80194	Quinidine
80195	Sirolimus
80196	Salicylate
80197	Tacrolimus
80198	Theophylline
80200	Tobramycin
80201	Topiramate
80202	Vancomycin
80299	Quantitation of drug, not elsewhere specified

Evocative/Suppression Testing

The following test panels involve the administration of evocative or suppressive agents, and the baseline and subsequent measurement of their effects on chemical constituents. These codes are to be used for the reporting of the laboratory component of the overall testing protocol. For the physician's administration of the evocative or suppressive agents, see 96360, 96361, 96372-96374, 96375; for the supplies and drugs, see 99070. To report physician attendance and monitoring during the testing, use the appropriate evaluation and management code, including the prolonged physician care codes if required. Prolonged physician care codes are not separately reported when evocative/suppression testing involves prolonged infusions reported with 96360, 96361. In the code descriptors where reference is made to a particular analyte (eg, Cortisol: 82533 x 2) the "x 2" refers to the number of times the test for that particular analyte is performed.

80400	ACTH stimulation panel; for adrenal insufficiency
	This panel must include the following:
	Cortisol (82533 x 2)
80402	for 21 hydroxylase deficiency
	This panel must include the following:
	Cortisol (82533 x 2)
	17 hydroxyprogesterone (83498 x 2)
80406	for 3 beta-hydroxydehydrogenase deficiency
	This panel must include the following:
	Cortisol (82533 x 2)
	17 hydroxypregnenolone (84143 x 2)
80408	Aldosterone suppression evaluation panel (eg, saline infusion)
	This panel must include the following:
	Aldosterone (82088 x 2)
	Renin (84244 x 2)
80410	Calcitonin stimulation panel (eg, calcium, pentagastrin)
	This panel must include the following:
	Calcitonin (82308 x 3)
80412	Corticotropic releasing hormone (CRH) stimulation panel
	This panel must include the following:
	Cortisol (82533 x 6)
	Adrenocorticotropic hormone (ACTH) (82024 x 6)
80414	Chorionic gonadotropin stimulation panel; testosterone response
	This panel must include the following:
	Testosterone (84403 x 2 on 3 pooled blood samples)
80415	estradiol response
	This panel must include the following:
	Estradiol (82670 x 2 on 3 pooled blood samples)
80416	Renal vein renin stimulation panel (eg, captopril)
	This panel must include the following:
	Renin (84244 x 6)
80417	Peripheral vein renin stimulation panel (eg, captopril)
	This panel must include the following:
	Renin (84244 x 2)

80418 Combined rapid anterior pituitary evaluation panel

This panel must include the following:

Adrenocorticotropic hormone (ACTH) (82024 x 4)

Luteinizing hormone (LH) (83002 x 4)

Follicle stimulating hormone (FSH) (83001 x 4)

Prolactin (84146 x 4)

Human growth hormone (HGH) (83003 x 4)

Cortisol (82533 x 4)

Thyroid stimulating hormone (TSH) (84443 x 4)

80420 Dexamethasone suppression panel, 48 hour

This panel must include the following:

Free cortisol, urine (82530 x 2)

Cortisol (82533 x 2)

Volume measurement for timed collection (81050 x 2)

(For single dose dexamethasone, use 82533)

80422 Glucagon tolerance panel; for insulinoma

This panel must include the following:

Glucose (82947 x 3)

Insulin (83525 x 3)

80424 for pheochromocytoma

This panel must include the following:

Catecholamines, fractionated (82384 x 2)

80426 Gonadotropin releasing hormone stimulation panel

This panel must include the following:

Follicle stimulating hormone (FSH) (83001 x 4)

Luteinizing hormone (LH) (83002 x 4)

80428 Growth hormone stimulation panel (eg, arginine infusion, l-dopa administration)

This panel must include the following:

Human growth hormone (HGH) (83003 x 4)

80430 Growth hormone suppression panel (glucose administration)

This panel must include the following:

Glucose (82947 x 3)

Human growth hormone (HGH) (83003 x 4)

80432 Insulin-induced C-peptide suppression panel

This panel must include the following:

Insulin (83525)

C-peptide (84681 x 5)

Glucose (82947 x 5)

80434 Insulin tolerance panel; for ACTH insufficiency

This panel must include the following:

Cortisol (82533 x 5)

Glucose (82947 x 5)

80435 for growth hormone deficiency

This panel must include the following:

Glucose (82947 x 5)

Human growth hormone (HGH) (83003 x 5)

80436 Metyrapone panel

This panel must include the following:

Cortisol (82533 x 2)

11 deoxycortisol (82634 x 2)

80438 Thyrotropin releasing hormone (TRH) stimulation panel; 1 hour

This panel must include the following:

Thyroid stimulating hormone (TSH) (84443 x 3)

80439 2 hour

This panel must include the following:

Thyroid stimulating hormone (TSH) (84443 x 4)

80440 for hyperprolactinemia

This panel must include the following:

Prolactin (84146 x 3)

Consultations (Clinical Pathology)

A clinical pathology consultation is a service, including a written report, rendered by the pathologist in response to a request from an attending physician in relation to a test result(s) requiring additional medical interpretive judgment.

Reporting of a test result(s) without medical interpretive judgment is not considered a clinical pathology consultation.

80500 Clinical pathology consultation; limited, without review of patient's history and medical records

80502 comprehensive, for a complex diagnostic problem, with review of patient's history and medical records

(These codes may also be used for pharmacokinetic consultations)

(For consultations involving the examination and evaluation of the patient, see 99241-99255)

Pathology and Laboratory

Urinalysis

For specific analyses, see appropriate section.

81000   Urinalysis, by dip stick or tablet reagent for bilirubin, glucose, hemoglobin, ketones, leukocytes, nitrite, pH, protein, specific gravity, urobilinogen, any number of these constituents; non-automated, with microscopy

81001   automated, with microscopy

81002   non-automated, without microscopy

81003   automated, without microscopy

81005   Urinalysis; qualitative or semiquantitative, except immunoassays

(For non-immunoassay reagent strip urinalysis, see 81000, 81002)

(For immunoassay, qualitative or semiquantitative, use 83518)

(For microalbumin, see 82043, 82044)

81007   bacteriuria screen, except by culture or dipstick

(For culture, see 87086-87088)

(For dipstick, use 81000 or 81002)

81015   microscopic only

(For sperm evaluation for retrograde ejaculation, use 89331)

81020   2 or 3 glass test

81025   Urine pregnancy test, by visual color comparison methods

81050   Volume measurement for timed collection, each

81099   Unlisted urinalysis procedure

Chemistry

The material for examination may be from any source unless otherwise specified in the code descriptor. When an analyte is measured in multiple specimens from different sources, or in specimens that are obtained at different times, the analyte is reported separately for each source and for each specimen. The examination is quantitative unless specified. To report an organ or disease oriented panel, see codes 80048-80076.

When a code describes a method where measurement of multiple analytes may require one or several procedures, each procedure is coded separately (eg, 82491-82492, 82541-82544). For example, if two analytes are measured using column chromatography using a single stationary or mobile phase, use 82492. If the same two analytes are measured using different stationary or mobile phase conditions, 82491 would be used twice. If a total of four analytes are measured where two analytes are measured with a single stationary and mobile phase, and the other two analytes are measured using a different stationary and

mobile phase, use 82492 twice. If a total of three analytes are measured where two analytes are measured using a single stationary or mobile phase condition, and the third analyte is measured separately using a different stationary or mobile phase procedure, use 82492 once for the two analytes measured under the same condition, and use 82491 once for the third analyte measured separately.

Clinical information derived from the results of laboratory data that is mathematically calculated (eg, free thyroxine index [T7]) is considered part of the test procedure and therefore is not a separately reportable service.

82000   Acetaldehyde, blood

82003   Acetaminophen

82009   Acetone or other ketone bodies, serum; qualitative

82010   quantitative

82013   Acetylcholinesterase

(Acid, gastric, see gastric acid, 82926, 82928)

(Acid phosphatase, see 84060-84066)

82016   Acylcarnitines; qualitative, each specimen

82017   quantitative, each specimen

(For carnitine, use 82379)

82024   Adrenocorticotropic hormone (ACTH)

82030   Adenosine, 5-monophosphate, cyclic (cyclic AMP)

82040   Albumin; serum, plasma or whole blood

82042   urine or other source, quantitative, each specimen

82043   urine, microalbumin, quantitative

82044   urine, microalbumin, semiquantitative (eg, reagent strip assay)

(For prealbumin, use 84134)

82045   ischemia modified

82055   Alcohol (ethanol); any specimen except breath

(For other volatiles, alcohol, use 84600)

82075   breath

82085   Aldolase

82088   Aldosterone

(Alkaline phosphatase, see 84075, 84080)

82101   Alkaloids, urine, quantitative

(Alphaketoglutarate, see 82009, 82010)

(Alpha tocopherol [Vitamin E], use 84446)

82103   Alpha-1-antitrypsin; total

82104   phenotype

82105   Alpha-fetoprotein (AFP); serum

82106   amniotic fluid

Pathology and Laboratory

82107	AFP-L3 fraction isoform and total AFP (including ratio)
82108	Aluminum
82120	Amines, vaginal fluid, qualitative
	(For combined pH and amines test for vaginitis, use 82120 and 83986)
82127	Amino acids; single, qualitative, each specimen
82128	multiple, qualitative, each specimen
82131	single, quantitative, each specimen
82135	Aminolevulinic acid, delta (ALA)
82136	Amino acids, 2 to 5 amino acids, quantitative, each specimen
82139	Amino acids, 6 or more amino acids, quantitative, each specimen
82140	Ammonia
82143	Amniotic fluid scan (spectrophotometric)
	(For L/S ratio, use 83661)
	(Amobarbital, see 80100-80103 for qualitative analysis, 82205 for quantitative analysis)
82145	Amphetamine or methamphetamine
	(For qualitative analysis, see 80100-80103)
82150	Amylase
82154	Androstanediol glucuronide
82157	Androstenedione
82160	Androsterone
82163	Angiotensin II
82164	Angiotensin I - converting enzyme (ACE)
	(Antidiuretic hormone (ADH), use 84588)
	(Antimony, use 83015)
	(Antitrypsin, alpha-1-, see 82103, 82104)
82172	Apolipoprotein, each
82175	Arsenic
	(For heavy metal screening, use 83015)
82180	Ascorbic acid (Vitamin C), blood
	(Aspirin, see acetylsalicylic acid, 80196)
	(Atherogenic index, blood, ultracentrifugation, quantitative, use 83701)
82190	Atomic absorption spectroscopy, each analyte
82205	Barbiturates, not elsewhere specified
	(For qualitative analysis, see 80100-80103)
	(For B-Natriuretic peptide, use 83880)
82232	Beta-2 microglobulin
	(Bicarbonate, use 82374)
82239	Bile acids; total

82240	cholylglycine
	(For bile pigments, urine, see 81000-81005)
82247	Bilirubin; total
82248	direct
82252	feces, qualitative
82261	Biotinidase, each specimen
82270	Blood, occult, by peroxidase activity (eg, guaiac), qualitative; feces, consecutive collected specimens with single determination, for colorectal neoplasm screening (ie, patient was provided 3 cards or single triple card for consecutive collection)
82271	other sources
82272	Blood, occult, by peroxidase activity (eg, guaiac), qualitative, feces, 1-3 simultaneous determinations, performed for other than colorectal neoplasm screening
	(Blood urea nitrogen [BUN], see 84520, 84525)
82274	Blood, occult, by fecal hemoglobin determination by immunoassay, qualitative, feces, 1-3 simultaneous determinations
82286	Bradykinin
82300	Cadmium
▲ 82306	Vitamin D; 25 hydroxy, includes fraction(s), if performed
#▲ 82652	1, 25 dihydroxy, includes fraction(s), if performed
	►(82307 has been deleted. For 25 hydroxy vitamin D, use 82306)◄
82308	Calcitonin
82310	Calcium; total
82330	ionized
82331	after calcium infusion test
82340	urine quantitative, timed specimen
82355	Calculus; qualitative analysis
82360	quantitative analysis, chemical
82365	infrared spectroscopy
82370	X-ray diffraction
	(Carbamates, see individual listings)
82373	Carbohydrate deficient transferrin
82374	Carbon dioxide (bicarbonate)
	(See also 82803)
82375	Carboxyhemoglobin; quantitative
82376	qualitative
	(For transcutaneous measurement of carboxyhemoglobin, use 88740)
82378	Carcinoembryonic antigen (CEA)
82379	Carnitine (total and free), quantitative, each specimen
	(For acylcarnitine, see 82016, 82017)

Pathology and Laboratory

82380	Carotene
82382	Catecholamines; total urine
82383	blood
82384	fractionated
	(For urine metabolites, see 83835, 84585)
82387	Cathepsin-D
82390	Ceruloplasmin
82397	Chemiluminescent assay
82415	Chloramphenicol
82435	Chloride; blood
82436	urine
82438	other source
	(For sweat collection by iontophoresis, use 89230)
82441	Chlorinated hydrocarbons, screen
	(Chlorpromazine, use 84022)
	▶(Cholecalciferol [Vitamin D], use 82306)◀
82465	Cholesterol, serum or whole blood, total
	(For high density lipoprotein [HDL], use 83718)
82480	Cholinesterase; serum
82482	RBC
82485	Chondroitin B sulfate, quantitative
	(Chorionic gonadotropin, see gonadotropin, 84702, 84703)
82486	Chromatography, qualitative; column (eg, gas liquid or HPLC), analyte not elsewhere specified
82487	paper, 1-dimensional, analyte not elsewhere specified
82488	paper, 2-dimensional, analyte not elsewhere specified
82489	thin layer, analyte not elsewhere specified
82491	Chromatography, quantitative, column (eg, gas liquid or HPLC); single analyte not elsewhere specified, single stationary and mobile phase
82492	multiple analytes, single stationary and mobile phase
82495	Chromium
82507	Citrate
82520	Cocaine or metabolite
	(Cocaine, qualitative analysis, see 80100-80103)
	(Codeine, qualitative analysis, see 80100-80103)
	(Codeine, quantitative analysis, see 82101)
	(Complement, see 86160-86162)
82523	Collagen cross links, any method

82525	Copper
	(Coproporphyrin, see 84119, 84120)
	(Corticosteroids, use 83491)
82528	Corticosterone
82530	Cortisol; free
82533	total
	(C-peptide, use 84681)
82540	Creatine
82541	Column chromatography/mass spectrometry (eg, GC/MS, or HPLC/MS), analyte not elsewhere specified; qualitative, single stationary and mobile phase
82542	quantitative, single stationary and mobile phase
82543	stable isotope dilution, single analyte, quantitative, single stationary and mobile phase
82544	stable isotope dilution, multiple analytes, quantitative, single stationary and mobile phase
82550	Creatine kinase (CK), (CPK); total
82552	isoenzymes
82553	MB fraction only
82554	isoforms
82565	Creatinine; blood
82570	other source
82575	clearance
82585	Cryofibrinogen
82595	Cryoglobulin, qualitative or semi-quantitative (eg, cryocrit)
	(For quantitative, cryoglobulin, see 82784, 82785)
	(Crystals, pyrophosphate vs urate, use 89060)
82600	Cyanide
82607	Cyanocobalamin (Vitamin B-12);
82608	unsaturated binding capacity
	(Cyclic AMP, use 82030)
	(Cyclic GMP, use 83008)
	(Cyclosporine, use 80158)
82610	Cystatin C
82615	Cystine and homocystine, urine, qualitative
82626	Dehydroepiandrosterone (DHEA)
82627	Dehydroepiandrosterone-sulfate (DHEA-S)
	(Delta-aminolevulinic acid (ALA), use 82135)
82633	Desoxycorticosterone, 11-
82634	Deoxycortisol, 11-
	(Dexamethasone suppression test, use 80420)
	(Diastase, urine, use 82150)

Pathology and Laboratory

82638   Dibucaine number

(Dichloroethane, use 84600)

(Dichloromethane, use 84600)

(Diethylether, use 84600)

82646   Dihydrocodeinone

(For qualitative analysis, see 80100-80103)

82649   Dihydromorphinone

(For qualitative analysis, see 80100-80103)

82651   Dihydrotestosterone (DHT)

82652   ▶Code is out of numerical sequence. See 82000-84999◀

82654   Dimethadione

(For qualitative analysis, see 80100-80103)

(Diphenylhydantoin, use 80185)

(Dipropylacetic acid, use 80164)

(Dopamine, see 82382-82384)

(Duodenal contents, see individual enzymes; for intubation and collection, use 89100)

82656   Elastase, pancreatic (EL-1), fecal, qualitative or semi-quantitative

82657   Enzyme activity in blood cells, cultured cells, or tissue, not elsewhere specified; nonradioactive substrate, each specimen

82658   radioactive substrate, each specimen

82664   Electrophoretic technique, not elsewhere specified

(Endocrine receptor assays, see 84233-84235)

82666   Epiandrosterone

(Epinephrine, see 82382-82384)

82668   Erythropoietin

82670   Estradiol

82671   Estrogens; fractionated

82672   total

(Estrogen receptor assay, use 84233)

82677   Estriol

82679   Estrone

(Ethanol, see 82055 and 82075)

82690   Ethchlorvynol

(Ethyl alcohol, see 82055 and 82075)

82693   Ethylene glycol

82696   Etiocholanolone

(For fractionation of ketosteroids, use 83593)

82705   Fat or lipids, feces; qualitative

82710   quantitative

82715   Fat differential, feces, quantitative

82725   Fatty acids, nonesterified

82726   Very long chain fatty acids

(For long-chain [C20-22] omega-3 fatty acids in red blood cell [RBC] membranes, use Category III code 0111T)

82728   Ferritin

(Fetal hemoglobin, see hemoglobin 83030, 83033, and 85460)

(Fetoprotein, alpha-1, see 82105, 82106)

82731   Fetal fibronectin, cervicovaginal secretions, semi-quantitative

82735   Fluoride

82742   Flurazepam

(For qualitative analysis, see 80100-80103)

(Foam stability test, use 83662)

82746   Folic acid; serum

82747   RBC

(Follicle stimulating hormone [FSH], use 83001)

82757   Fructose, semen

(Fructosamine, use 82985)

(Fructose, TLC screen, use 84375)

82759   Galactokinase, RBC

82760   Galactose

82775   Galactose-1-phosphate uridyl transferase; quantitative

82776   screen

▲ 82784   Gammaglobulin (immunoglobulin); IgA, IgD, IgG, IgM, each

▲ 82785   IgE

(For allergen specific IgE, see 86003, 86005)

▲ 82787   immunoglobulin subclasses (eg, IgG1, 2, 3, or 4), each

(Gamma-glutamyltransferase [GGT], use 82977)

82800   Gases, blood, pH only

82803   Gases, blood, any combination of pH, pCO_2, pO_2, CO_2, HCO_3 (including calculated O_2 saturation);

(Use 82803 for 2 or more of the above listed analytes)

82805   with O_2 saturation, by direct measurement, except pulse oximetry

82810   Gases, blood, O_2 saturation only, by direct measurement, except pulse oximetry

(For pulse oximetry, use 94760)

82820   Hemoglobin-oxygen affinity (pO_2 for 50% hemoglobin saturation with oxygen)

82926   Gastric acid, free and total, each specimen

82928   Gastric acid, free or total, each specimen

Pathology and Laboratory

82938 Gastrin after secretin stimulation

82941 Gastrin

(Gentamicin, use 80170)

(GGT, use 82977)

(GLC, gas liquid chromatography, use 82486)

82943 Glucagon

82945 Glucose, body fluid, other than blood

82946 Glucagon tolerance test

82947 Glucose; quantitative, blood (except reagent strip)

82948   blood, reagent strip

82950   post glucose dose (includes glucose)

82951   tolerance test (GTT), 3 specimens (includes glucose)

82952   tolerance test, each additional beyond 3 specimens

82953   tolbutamide tolerance test

(For insulin tolerance test, see 80434, 80435)

(For leucine tolerance test, use 80428)

(For semiquantitative urine glucose, see 81000, 81002, 81005, 81099)

82955 Glucose-6-phosphate dehydrogenase (G6PD); quantitative

82960   screen

(For glucose tolerance test with medication, use 96374 in addition)

82962 Glucose, blood by glucose monitoring device(s) cleared by the FDA specifically for home use

82963 Glucosidase, beta

82965 Glutamate dehydrogenase

82975 Glutamine (glutamic acid amide)

82977 Glutamyltransferase, gamma (GGT)

82978 Glutathione

82979 Glutathione reductase, RBC

82980 Glutethimide

(Glycohemoglobin, use 83036)

82985 Glycated protein

(Gonadotropin, chorionic, see 84702, 84703)

83001 Gonadotropin; follicle stimulating hormone (FSH)

83002   luteinizing hormone (LH)

(For luteinizing releasing factor [LRH], use 83727)

83003 Growth hormone, human (HGH) (somatotropin)

(For antibody to human growth hormone, use 86277)

83008 Guanosine monophosphate (GMP), cyclic

83009 Helicobacter pylori, blood test analysis for urease activity, non-radioactive isotope (eg, C-13)

(For H. pylori, breath test analysis for urease activity, see 83013, 83014)

83010 Haptoglobin; quantitative

83012   phenotypes

83013 Helicobacter pylori; breath test analysis for urease activity, non-radioactive isotope (eg, C-13)

83014   drug administration

(For H. pylori, stool, use 87338. For H. pylori, liquid scintillation counter, see 78267, 78268. For H. pylori, enzyme immunoassay, use 87339)

(For H. pylori, blood test analysis for urease activity, use 83009)

83015 Heavy metal (eg, arsenic, barium, beryllium, bismuth, antimony, mercury); screen

83018   quantitative, each

83020 Hemoglobin fractionation and quantitation; electrophoresis (eg, A2, S, C, and/or F)

83021   chromatography (eg, A2, S, C, and/or F)

(For glycosylated [A1c] hemoglobin analysis, by chromatography, in the absence of an identified hemoglobin variant, use 83036)

83026 Hemoglobin; by copper sulfate method, non-automated

83030   F (fetal), chemical

83033   F (fetal), qualitative

83036   glycosylated (A1C)

(For glycosylated [A1c] hemoglobin analysis, by chromatography, in the setting of an identified hemoglobin variant, use 83021)

(For fecal hemoglobin detection by immunoassay, use 82274)

83037   glycosylated (A1C) by device cleared by FDA for home use

83045   methemoglobin, qualitative

83050   methemoglobin, quantitative

(For transcutaneous quantitative methemoglobin determination, use 88741)

83051   plasma

83055   sulfhemoglobin, qualitative

83060   sulfhemoglobin, quantitative

83065   thermolabile

83068   unstable, screen

83069   urine

83070 Hemosiderin; qualitative

| 83071 | quantitative |

(Heroin, see 80100-80103)

(HIAA, use 83497)

(High performance liquid chromatography [HPLC], use 82486)

| 83080 | b-Hexosaminidase, each assay |
| 83088 | Histamine |

(Hollander test, use 91052)

| 83090 | Homocysteine |
| 83150 | Homovanillic acid (HVA) |

(Hormones, see individual alphabetic listings in **Chemistry** section)

(Hydrogen breath test, use 91065)

| 83491 | Hydroxycorticosteroids, 17- (17-OHCS) |

(For cortisol, see 82530, 82533. For deoxycortisol, use 82634)

| 83497 | Hydroxyindolacetic acid, 5-(HIAA) |

(For urine qualitative test, use 81005)

(5-Hydroxytryptamine, use 84260)

83498	Hydroxyprogesterone, 17-d
83499	Hydroxyprogesterone, 20-
83500	Hydroxyproline; free
83505	total
▲ 83516	Immunoassay for analyte other than infectious agent antibody or infectious agent antigen; qualitative or semiquantitative, multiple step method
▲ 83518	qualitative or semiquantitative, single step method (eg, reagent strip)
▲ 83519	quantitative, by radioimmunoassay (eg, RIA)
▲ 83520	quantitative, not otherwise specified

(For immunoassays for antibodies to infectious agent antigens, see analyte and method specific codes in the **Immunology** section)

(For immunoassay of tumor antigen not elsewhere specified, use 86316)

(Immunoglobulins, see 82784, 82785)

| 83525 | Insulin; total |

(For proinsulin, use 84206)

| 83527 | free |
| 83528 | Intrinsic factor |

(For intrinsic factor antibodies, use 86340)

| 83540 | Iron |
| 83550 | Iron binding capacity |

| 83570 | Isocitric dehydrogenase (IDH) |

(Isonicotinic acid hydrazide, INH, see code for specific method)

(Isopropyl alcohol, use 84600)

| 83582 | Ketogenic steroids, fractionation |

(Ketone bodies, for serum, see 82009, 82010; for urine, see 81000-81003)

83586	Ketosteroids, 17- (17-KS); total
83593	fractionation
83605	Lactate (lactic acid)
83615	Lactate dehydrogenase (LD), (LDH);
83625	isoenzymes, separation and quantitation
83630	Lactoferrin, fecal; qualitative
83631	quantitative
83632	Lactogen, human placental (HPL) human chorionic somatomammotropin
83633	Lactose, urine; qualitative
83634	quantitative

(For tolerance, see 82951, 82952)

(For breath hydrogen test for lactase deficiency, use 91065)

83655	Lead
83661	Fetal lung maturity assessment; lecithin sphingomyelin (L/S) ratio
83662	foam stability test
83663	fluorescence polarization
83664	lamellar body density

(For phosphatidylglycerol, use 84081)

83670	Leucine aminopeptidase (LAP)
83690	Lipase
83695	Lipoprotein (a)
83698	Lipoprotein-associated phospholipase A_2 (Lp-PLA$_2$)
83700	Lipoprotein, blood; electrophoretic separation and quantitation
83701	high resolution fractionation and quantitation of lipoproteins including lipoprotein subclasses when performed (eg, electrophoresis, ultracentrifugation)
83704	quantitation of lipoprotein particle numbers and lipoprotein particle subclasses (eg, by nuclear magnetic resonance spectroscopy)
83718	Lipoprotein, direct measurement; high density cholesterol (HDL cholesterol)
83719	VLDL cholesterol

Pathology and Laboratory

83721   LDL cholesterol

(For fractionation by high resolution electrophoresis or ultracentrifugation, use 83701)

(For lipoprotein particle numbers and subclasses analysis by nuclear magnetic resonance spectroscopy, use 83704)

83727   Luteinizing releasing factor (LRH)

(Luteinizing hormone [LH], use 83002)

(For qualitative analysis, see 80100-80103)

(Macroglobulins, alpha-2, use 86329)

83735   Magnesium

83775   Malate dehydrogenase

(Maltose tolerance, see 82951, 82952)

(Mammotropin, use 84146)

83785   Manganese

(Marijuana, see 80100-80103)

83788   Mass spectrometry and tandem mass spectrometry (MS, MS/MS), analyte not elsewhere specified; qualitative, each specimen

83789   quantitative, each specimen

83805   Meprobamate

(For qualitative analysis, see 80100-80103)

83825   Mercury, quantitative

(Mercury screen, use 83015)

83835   Metanephrines

(For catecholamines, see 82382-82384)

83840   Methadone

(For methadone qualitative analysis, see 80100-80103)

(Methamphetamine, see 80100-80103, 82145)

(Methanol, use 84600)

83857   Methemalbumin

(Methemoglobin, see hemoglobin 83045, 83050)

83858   Methsuximide

(Methyl alcohol, use 84600)

(Microalbumin, see 82043 for quantitative, see 82044 for semiquantitative)

(Microglobulin, beta-2, use 82232)

83864   Mucopolysaccharides, acid; quantitative

83866   screen

83872   Mucin, synovial fluid (Ropes test)

83873   Myelin basic protein, cerebrospinal fluid

(For oligoclonal bands, use 83916)

83874   Myoglobin

(Nalorphine, use 83925)

83876   Myeloperoxidase (MPO)

83880   Natriuretic peptide

83883   Nephelometry, each analyte not elsewhere specified

83885   Nickel

83887   Nicotine

Codes 83890-83914 are intended for use with molecular diagnostic techniques for analysis of nucleic acids.

Codes 83890-83914 are coded by procedure rather than analyte.

Code separately for each procedure used in an analysis. For example, a procedure requiring isolation of DNA, restriction endonuclease digestion, electrophoresis, and nucleic acid probe amplification would be coded 83890, 83892, 83894, and 83898.

When molecular diagnostic procedures are performed to test for oncology, hematology, neurology or inherited disorder, use the appropriate modifier to specify probe type or condition tested. (See **Appendix I** for a listing of appropriate modifiers to report with molecular diagnostic and cytogenetic procedures.)

Each nucleic acid preparation may include a digestate, undigested nucleic acid, or other uniquely modified nucleic acid sample (eg, newly synthesized oligonucleotide).

►(For microbial identification, see 87149, 87150, 87152, 87153, 87470-87801)◄

(For array technology using more than 10 probes, see 88384-88386)

83890   Molecular diagnostics; molecular isolation or extraction, each nucleic acid type (ie, DNA or RNA)

83891   isolation or extraction of highly purified nucleic acid, each nucleic acid type (ie, DNA or RNA)

83892   enzymatic digestion, each enzyme treatment

83893   dot/slot blot production, each nucleic acid preparation

83894   separation by gel electrophoresis (eg, agarose, polyacrylamide), each nucleic acid preparation

83896   nucleic acid probe, each

83897   nucleic acid transfer (eg, Southern, Northern), each nucleic acid preparation

83898   amplification, target, each nucleic acid sequence

(For multiplex target amplification, see 83900, 83901)

(For signal amplification, use 83908)

83900   amplification, target, multiplex, first 2 nucleic acid sequences

+ 83901   amplification, target, multiplex, each additional nucleic acid sequence beyond 2 (List separately in addition to code for primary procedure)

(Use 83901 in conjunction with 83900)

Pathology and Laboratory

83902	reverse transcription
83903	mutation scanning, by physical properties (eg, single strand conformational polymorphisms [SSCP], heteroduplex, denaturing gradient gel electrophoresis [DGGE], RNA'ase A), single segment, each
83904	mutation identification by sequencing, single segment, each segment
83905	mutation identification by allele specific transcription, single segment, each segment
83906	mutation identification by allele specific translation, single segment, each segment
83907	lysis of cells prior to nucleic acid extraction (eg, stool specimens, paraffin embedded tissue), each specimen
83908	amplification, signal, each nucleic acid sequence

(For target amplification, see 83898, 83900, 83901)

83909	separation and identification by high resolution technique (eg, capillary electrophoresis), each nucleic acid preparation
83912	interpretation and report
83913	RNA stabilization
83914	Mutation identification by enzymatic ligation or primer extension, single segment, each segment (eg, oligonucleotide ligation assay [OLA], single base chain extension [SBCE], or allele-specific primer extension [ASPE])
83915	Nucleotidase 5'-
83916	Oligoclonal immune (oligoclonal bands)
83918	Organic acids; total, quantitative, each specimen
83919	qualitative, each specimen
83921	Organic acid, single, quantitative
83925	Opiate(s), drug and metabolites, each procedure
83930	Osmolality; blood
83935	urine
83937	Osteocalcin (bone g1a protein)
83945	Oxalate
83950	Oncoprotein; HER-2/neu

(For tissue, see 88342, 88365)

83951	des-gamma-carboxy-prothrombin (DCP)
83970	Parathormone (parathyroid hormone)

(Pesticide, quantitative, see code for specific method. For screen for chlorinated hydrocarbons, use 82441)

▲ 83986	pH; body fluid, not otherwise specified
● 83987	exhaled breath condensate

(For blood pH, see 82800, 82803)

83992	Phencyclidine (PCP)

(For qualitative analysis, see 80100-80103)

(Phenobarbital, use 80184)

83993	Calprotectin, fecal
84022	Phenothiazine

(For qualitative analysis, see 80100, 80101)

84030	Phenylalanine (PKU), blood

(Phenylalanine-tyrosine ratio, see 84030, 84510)

84035	Phenylketones, qualitative
84060	Phosphatase, acid; total
84061	forensic examination
84066	prostatic
84075	Phosphatase, alkaline;
84078	heat stable (total not included)
84080	isoenzymes
84081	Phosphatidylglycerol

(Phosphates inorganic, use 84100)

(Phosphates, organic, see code for specific method. For cholinesterase, see 82480, 82482)

84085	Phosphogluconate, 6-, dehydrogenase, RBC
84087	Phosphohexose isomerase
84100	Phosphorus inorganic (phosphate);
84105	urine

(Pituitary gonadotropins, see 83001-83002)

(PKU, see 84030, 84035)

84106	Porphobilinogen, urine; qualitative
84110	quantitative
84119	Porphyrins, urine; qualitative
84120	quantitation and fractionation
84126	Porphyrins, feces; quantitative
84127	qualitative

(Porphyrin precursors, see 82135, 84106, 84110)

(For protoporphyrin, RBC, see 84202, 84203)

84132	Potassium; serum, plasma or whole blood
84133	urine
84134	Prealbumin

(For microalbumin, see 82043, 82044)

84135	Pregnanediol
84138	Pregnanetriol
84140	Pregnenolone
84143	17-hydroxypregnenolone

Pathology and Laboratory

84144	Progesterone
	(Progesterone receptor assay, use 84234)
	(For proinsulin, use 84206)
● **84145**	Procalcitonin (PCT)
84146	Prolactin
84150	Prostaglandin, each
84152	Prostate specific antigen (PSA); complexed (direct measurement)
84153	total
84154	free
84155	Protein, total, except by refractometry; serum, plasma or whole blood
84156	urine
84157	other source (eg, synovial fluid, cerebrospinal fluid)
84160	Protein, total, by refractometry, any source
	(For urine total protein by dipstick method, use 81000-81003)
84163	Pregnancy-associated plasma protein-A (PAPP-A)
84165	Protein; electrophoretic fractionation and quantitation, serum
84166	electrophoretic fractionation and quantitation, other fluids with concentration (eg, urine, CSF)
84181	Western Blot, with interpretation and report, blood or other body fluid
84182	Western Blot, with interpretation and report, blood or other body fluid, immunological probe for band identification, each
	(For Western Blot tissue analysis, use 88371)
84202	Protoporphyrin, RBC; quantitative
84203	screen
84206	Proinsulin
	(Pseudocholinesterase, use 82480)
84207	Pyridoxal phosphate (Vitamin B-6)
84210	Pyruvate
84220	Pyruvate kinase
84228	Quinine
84233	Receptor assay; estrogen
84234	progesterone
84235	endocrine, other than estrogen or progesterone (specify hormone)
84238	non-endocrine (specify receptor)
84244	Renin

84252	Riboflavin (Vitamin B-2)
	(Salicylates, use 80196)
	(Secretin test, see 99070, 89100 and appropriate analyses)
84255	Selenium
84260	Serotonin
	(For urine metabolites (HIAA), use 83497)
84270	Sex hormone binding globulin (SHBG)
84275	Sialic acid
	(Sickle hemoglobin, use 85660)
84285	Silica
84295	Sodium; serum, plasma or whole blood
84300	urine
84302	other source
	(Somatomammotropin, use 83632)
	(Somatotropin, use 83003)
84305	Somatomedin
84307	Somatostatin
84311	Spectrophotometry, analyte not elsewhere specified
84315	Specific gravity (except urine)
	(For specific gravity, urine, see 81000-81003)
	(Stone analysis, see 82355-82370)
84375	Sugars, chromatographic, TLC or paper chromatography
84376	Sugars (mono-, di-, and oligosaccharides); single qualitative, each specimen
84377	multiple qualitative, each specimen
84378	single quantitative, each specimen
84379	multiple quantitative, each specimen
84392	Sulfate, urine
	(Sulfhemoglobin, see hemoglobin, 83055, 83060)
	(T-3, see 84479-84481)
	(T-4, see 84436-84439)
84402	Testosterone; free
84403	total
84425	Thiamine (Vitamin B-1)
84430	Thiocyanate
● **84431**	Thromboxane metabolite(s), including thromboxane if performed, urine
	▶(For concurrent urine creatinine determination, use 84431 in conjunction with 82570)◀

84432   Thyroglobulin

(Thyroglobulin, antibody, use 86800)

(Thyrotropin releasing hormone [TRH] test, see 80438, 80439)

84436   Thyroxine; total

84437   requiring elution (eg, neonatal)

84439   free

84442   Thyroxine binding globulin (TBG)

84443   Thyroid stimulating hormone (TSH)

84445   Thyroid stimulating immune globulins (TSI)

(Tobramycin, use 80200)

84446   Tocopherol alpha (Vitamin E)

(Tolbutamide tolerance, use 82953)

84449   Transcortin (cortisol binding globulin)

84450   Transferase; aspartate amino (AST) (SGOT)

84460   alanine amino (ALT) (SGPT)

84466   Transferrin

(Iron binding capacity, use 83550)

84478   Triglycerides

84479   Thyroid hormone (T3 or T4) uptake or thyroid hormone binding ratio (THBR)

84480   Triiodothyronine T3; total (TT-3)

84481   free

84482   reverse

84484   Troponin, quantitative

(For troponin, qualitative assay, use 84512)

84485   Trypsin; duodenal fluid

84488   feces, qualitative

84490   feces, quantitative, 24-hour collection

84510   Tyrosine

(Urate crystal identification, use 89060)

84512   Troponin, qualitative

(For troponin, quantitative assay, use 84484)

84520   Urea nitrogen; quantitative

84525   semiquantitative (eg, reagent strip test)

84540   Urea nitrogen, urine

84545   Urea nitrogen, clearance

84550   Uric acid; blood

84560   other source

84577   Urobilinogen, feces, quantitative

84578   Urobilinogen, urine; qualitative

84580   quantitative, timed specimen

84583   semiquantitative

(Uroporphyrins, use 84120)

(Valproic acid [dipropylacetic acid], use 80164)

84585   Vanillylmandelic acid (VMA), urine

84586   Vasoactive intestinal peptide (VIP)

84588   Vasopressin (antidiuretic hormone, ADH)

84590   Vitamin A

(Vitamin B-1, use 84425)

(Vitamin B-2, use 84252)

(Vitamin B-6, use 84207)

(Vitamin B-12, use 82607)

(Vitamin B-12, absorption (Schilling), see 78270, 78271)

(Vitamin C, use 82180)

▶(Vitamin D, see 82306, 82652)◀

(Vitamin E, use 84446)

84591   Vitamin, not otherwise specified

84597   Vitamin K

(VMA, use 84585)

84600   Volatiles (eg, acetic anhydride, carbon tetrachloride, dichloroethane, dichloromethane, diethylether, isopropyl alcohol, methanol)

(For acetaldehyde, use 82000)

(Volume, blood, RISA or Cr-51, see 78110, 78111)

84620   Xylose absorption test, blood and/or urine

(For administration, use 99070)

84630   Zinc

84681   C-peptide

84702   Gonadotropin, chorionic (hCG); quantitative

84703   qualitative

(For urine pregnancy test by visual color comparison, use 81025)

84704   free beta chain

84830   Ovulation tests, by visual color comparison methods for human luteinizing hormone

84999   Unlisted chemistry procedure

Hematology and Coagulation

(For blood banking procedures, see **Transfusion Medicine**)

(Agglutinins, see **Immunology**)

(Antiplasmin, use 85410)

(Antithrombin III, see 85300, 85301)

85002	Bleeding time
85004	Blood count; automated differential WBC count
85007	blood smear, microscopic examination with manual differential WBC count
85008	blood smear, microscopic examination without manual differential WBC count
	(For other fluids [eg, CSF], see 89050, 89051)
85009	manual differential WBC count, buffy coat
	(Eosinophils, nasal smear, use 89190)
85013	spun microhematocrit
85014	hematocrit (Hct)
85018	hemoglobin (Hgb)
	(For other hemoglobin determination, see 83020-83069)
	(For immunoassay, hemoglobin, fecal, use 82274)
	▶(For transcutaneous hemoglobin measurement, use 88738)◀
85025	complete (CBC), automated (Hgb, Hct, RBC, WBC and platelet count) and automated differential WBC count
85027	complete (CBC), automated (Hgb, Hct, RBC, WBC and platelet count)
85032	manual cell count (erythrocyte, leukocyte, or platelet) each
85041	red blood cell (RBC), automated
	(Do not report code 85041 in conjunction with 85025 or 85027)
85044	reticulocyte, manual
85045	reticulocyte, automated
85046	reticulocytes, automated, including 1 or more cellular parameters (eg, reticulocyte hemoglobin content [CHr], immature reticulocyte fraction [IRF], reticulocyte volume [MRV], RNA content), direct measurement
85048	leukocyte (WBC), automated
85049	platelet, automated
85055	Reticulated platelet assay
85060	Blood smear, peripheral, interpretation by physician with written report
85097	Bone marrow, smear interpretation
	(For special stains, see 88312, 88313)
	(For bone biopsy, see 20220, 20225, 20240, 20245, 20250, 20251)
85130	Chromogenic substrate assay
	(Circulating anti-coagulant screen [mixing studies], see 85611, 85732)
85170	Clot retraction
85175	Clot lysis time, whole blood dilution
	(Clotting factor I [fibrinogen], see 85384, 85385)
85210	Clotting; factor II, prothrombin, specific
	(See also 85610-85613)
85220	factor V (AcG or proaccelerin), labile factor
85230	factor VII (proconvertin, stable factor)
85240	factor VIII (AHG), 1-stage
85244	factor VIII related antigen
85245	factor VIII, VW factor, ristocetin cofactor
85246	factor VIII, VW factor antigen
85247	factor VIII, von Willebrand factor, multimetric analysis
85250	factor IX (PTC or Christmas)
85260	factor X (Stuart-Prower)
85270	factor XI (PTA)
85280	factor XII (Hageman)
85290	factor XIII (fibrin stabilizing)
85291	factor XIII (fibrin stabilizing), screen solubility
85292	prekallikrein assay (Fletcher factor assay)
85293	high molecular weight kininogen assay (Fitzgerald factor assay)
85300	Clotting inhibitors or anticoagulants; antithrombin III, activity
85301	antithrombin III, antigen assay
85302	protein C, antigen
85303	protein C, activity
85305	protein S, total
85306	protein S, free
85307	Activated Protein C (APC) resistance assay
85335	Factor inhibitor test
85337	Thrombomodulin
	(For mixing studies for inhibitors, use 85732)
85345	Coagulation time; Lee and White
85347	activated
85348	other methods
	(Differential count, see 85007 et seq)
	(Duke bleeding time, use 85002)
	(Eosinophils, nasal smear, use 89190)
85360	Euglobulin lysis
	(Fetal hemoglobin, see 83030, 83033, 85460)
85362	Fibrin(ogen) degradation (split) products (FDP) (FSP); agglutination slide, semiquantitative
	(Immunoelectrophoresis, use 86320)

Pathology and Laboratory

85366	paracoagulation
85370	quantitative
85378	Fibrin degradation products, D-dimer; qualitative or semiquantitative
85379	quantitative

(For ultrasensitive and standard sensitivity quantitative D-dimer, use 85379)

85380	ultrasensitive (eg, for evaluation for venous thromboembolism), qualitative or semiquantitative
85384	Fibrinogen; activity
85385	antigen
85390	Fibrinolysins or coagulopathy screen, interpretation and report
85396	Coagulation/fibrinolysis assay, whole blood (eg, viscoelastic clot assessment), including use of any pharmacologic additive(s), as indicated, including interpretation and written report, per day
85397	Coagulation and fibrinolysis, functional activity, not otherwise specified (eg, ADAMTS-13), each analyte
85400	Fibrinolytic factors and inhibitors; plasmin
85410	alpha-2 antiplasmin
85415	plasminogen activator
85420	plasminogen, except antigenic assay
85421	plasminogen, antigenic assay

(Fragility, red blood cell, see 85547, 85555-85557)

85441	Heinz bodies; direct
85445	induced, acetyl phenylhydrazine

(Hematocrit [PCV], see 85014, 85025, 85027)

(Hemoglobin, see 83020-83068, 85018, 85025, 85027)

85460	Hemoglobin or RBCs, fetal, for fetomaternal hemorrhage; differential lysis (Kleihauer-Betke)

(See also 83030, 83033)

(Hemolysins, see 86940, 86941)

85461	rosette
85475	Hemolysin, acid

(See also 86940, 86941)

85520	Heparin assay
85525	Heparin neutralization
85530	Heparin-protamine tolerance test
85536	Iron stain, peripheral blood

(For iron stains on bone marrow or other tissues with physician evaluation, use 88313)

85540	Leukocyte alkaline phosphatase with count
85547	Mechanical fragility, RBC
85549	Muramidase

(Nitroblue tetrazolium dye test, use 86384)

85555	Osmotic fragility, RBC; unincubated
85557	incubated

(Packed cell volume, use 85013)

(Partial thromboplastin time, see 85730, 85732)

(Parasites, blood [eg, malaria smears], use 87207)

(Plasmin, use 85400)

(Plasminogen, use 85420)

(Plasminogen activator, use 85415)

85576	Platelet, aggregation (in vitro), each agent

▶(For thromboxane metabolite[s], including thromboxane, if performed, measurement[s] in urine, use 84431)◀

85597	Platelet neutralization
85610	Prothrombin time;
85611	substitution, plasma fractions, each
85612	Russell viper venom time (includes venom); undiluted
85613	diluted

(Red blood cell count, see 85025, 85027, 85041)

85635	Reptilase test

(Reticulocyte count, see 85044, 85045)

85651	Sedimentation rate, erythrocyte; non-automated
85652	automated
85660	Sickling of RBC, reduction

(Hemoglobin electrophoresis, use 83020)

(Smears [eg, for parasites, malaria], use 87207)

85670	Thrombin time; plasma
85675	titer
85705	Thromboplastin inhibition, tissue

(For individual clotting factors, see 85245-85247)

85730	Thromboplastin time, partial (PTT); plasma or whole blood
85732	substitution, plasma fractions, each
85810	Viscosity

(von Willebrand factor assay, see 85245-85247)

(WBC count, see 85025, 85027, 85048, 89050)

85999	Unlisted hematology and coagulation procedure

Immunology

(Acetylcholine receptor antibody, see 83519, 86255, 86256)

(Actinomyces, antibodies to, use 86602)

(Adrenal cortex antibodies, see 86255, 86256)

86000   Agglutinins, febrile (eg, Brucella, Francisella, Murine typhus, Q fever, Rocky Mountain spotted fever, scrub typhus), each antigen

(For antibodies to infectious agents, see 86602-86804)

86001   Allergen specific IgG quantitative or semiquantitative, each allergen

(Agglutinins and autohemolysins, see 86940, 86941)

86003   Allergen specific IgE; quantitative or semiquantitative, each allergen

(For total quantitative IgE, use 82785)

86005   qualitative, multiallergen screen (dipstick, paddle, or disk)

(For total qualitative IgE, use 83518)

(Alpha-1 antitrypsin, see 82103, 82104)

(Alpha-1 feto-protein, see 82105, 82106)

(Anti-AChR [acetylcholine receptor] antibody titer, see 86255, 86256)

(Anticardiolipin antibody, use 86147)

(Anti-DNA, use 86225)

(Anti-deoxyribonuclease titer, use 86215)

86021   Antibody identification; leukocyte antibodies

86022   platelet antibodies

86023   platelet associated immunoglobulin assay

86038   Antinuclear antibodies (ANA);

86039   titer

(Antistreptococcal antibody, ie, anti-DNAse, use 86215)

(Antistreptokinase titer, use 86590)

86060   Antistreptolysin O; titer

(For antibodies to infectious agents, see 86602-86804)

86063   screen

(For antibodies to infectious agents, see 86602-86804)

(Blastomyces, antibodies to, use 86612)

86077   Blood bank physician services; difficult cross match and/or evaluation of irregular antibody(s), interpretation and written report

86078   investigation of transfusion reaction including suspicion of transmissible disease, interpretation and written report

86079   authorization for deviation from standard blood banking procedures (eg, use of outdated blood, transfusion of Rh incompatible units), with written report

(Brucella, antibodies to, use 86622)

(Candida, antibodies to, use 86628. For skin testing, use 86485)

86140   C-reactive protein;

(Candidiasis, use 86628)

86141   high sensitivity (hsCRP)

86146   Beta 2 Glycoprotein I antibody, each

86147   Cardiolipin (phospholipid) antibody, each Ig class

86148   Anti-phosphatidylserine (phospholipid) antibody

(To report antiprothrombin [phospholipid cofactor] antibody, use Category III code 0030T)

86155   Chemotaxis assay, specify method

(Clostridium difficile toxin, use 87230)

(Coccidioides, antibodies to, see 86635. For skin testing, use 86490)

86156   Cold agglutinin; screen

86157   titer

86160   Complement; antigen, each component

86161   functional activity, each component

86162   total hemolytic (CH50)

86171   Complement fixation tests, each antigen

(Coombs test, see 86880-86886)

86185   Counterimmunoelectrophoresis, each antigen

(Cryptococcus, antibodies to, use 86641)

86200   Cyclic citrullinated peptide (CCP), antibody

86215   Deoxyribonuclease, antibody

86225   Deoxyribonucleic acid (DNA) antibody; native or double stranded

(Echinococcus, antibodies to, see code for specific method)

(For HIV antibody tests, see 86701-86703)

86226   single stranded

(Anti D.S., DNA, IFA, eg, using C.Lucilae, see 86255 and 86256)

86235   Extractable nuclear antigen, antibody to, any method (eg, nRNP, SS-A, SS-B, Sm, RNP, Sc170, J01), each antibody

86243   Fc receptor

(Filaria, antibodies to, see code for specific method)

86255   Fluorescent noninfectious agent antibody; screen, each antibody

Pathology and Laboratory

86256   titer, each antibody

(Fluorescent technique for antigen identification in tissue, use 88346; for indirect fluorescence, use 88347)

(FTA, see 86781)

(Gel [agar] diffusion tests, use 86331)

86277   Growth hormone, human (HGH), antibody

86280   Hemagglutination inhibition test (HAI)

(For rubella, use 86762)

(For antibodies to infectious agents, see 86602-86804)

86294   Immunoassay for tumor antigen, qualitative or semiquantitative (eg, bladder tumor antigen)

86300   Immunoassay for tumor antigen, quantitative; CA 15-3 (27.29)

86301   CA 19-9

86304   CA 125

(For measurement of serum HER-2/neu oncoprotein, see 83950)

(For hepatitis delta agent, antibody, use 86692)

● 86305   Human epididymis protein 4 (HE4)

86308   Heterophile antibodies; screening

(For antibodies to infectious agents, see 86602-86804)

86309   titer

(For antibodies to infectious agents, see 86602-86804)

86310   titers after absorption with beef cells and guinea pig kidney

(Histoplasma, antibodies to, use 86698. For skin testing, use 86510)

(For antibodies to infectious agents, see 86602-86804)

(Human growth hormone antibody, use 86277)

86316   Immunoassay for tumor antigen, other antigen, quantitative (eg, CA 50, 72-4, 549), each

86317   Immunoassay for infectious agent antibody, quantitative, not otherwise specified

(For immunoassay techniques for antigens, see 83516, 83518, 83519, 83520, 87301-87450, 87810-87899)

(For particle agglutination procedures, use 86403)

86318   Immunoassay for infectious agent antibody, qualitative or semiquantitative, single step method (eg, reagent strip)

86320   Immunoelectrophoresis; serum

86325   other fluids (eg, urine, cerebrospinal fluid) with concentration

86327   crossed (2-dimensional assay)

86329   Immunodiffusion; not elsewhere specified

86331   gel diffusion, qualitative (Ouchterlony), each antigen or antibody

86332   Immune complex assay

86334   Immunofixation electrophoresis; serum

86335   other fluids with concentration (eg, urine, CSF)

86336   Inhibin A

86337   Insulin antibodies

86340   Intrinsic factor antibodies

(Leptospira, antibodies to, use 86720)

(Leukoagglutinins, use 86021)

86341   Islet cell antibody

86343   Leukocyte histamine release test (LHR)

86344   Leukocyte phagocytosis

● 86352   Cellular function assay involving stimulation (eg, mitogen or antigen) and detection of biomarker (eg, ATP)

86353   Lymphocyte transformation, mitogen (phytomitogen) or antigen induced blastogenesis

(Malaria antibodies, use 86750)

▶(For cellular function assay involving stimulation and detection of biomarker, use 86352)◀

86355   B cells, total count

86356   Mononuclear cell antigen, quantitative (eg, flow cytometry), not otherwise specified, each antigen

(Do not report 88187-88189 for interpretation of 86355, 86356, 86357, 86359, 86360, 86361, 86367)

86357   Natural killer (NK) cells, total count

86359   T cells; total count

86360   absolute CD4 and CD8 count, including ratio

86361   absolute CD4 count

86367   Stem cells (ie, CD34), total count

(For flow cytometric immunophenotyping for the assessment of potential hematolymphoid neoplasia, see 88184-88189)

86376   Microsomal antibodies (eg, thyroid or liver-kidney), each

86378   Migration inhibitory factor test (MIF)

(Mitochondrial antibody, liver, see 86255, 86256)

(Mononucleosis, see 86308-86310)

86382   Neutralization test, viral

86384   Nitroblue tetrazolium dye test (NTD)

(Ouchterlony diffusion, use 86331)

(Platelet antibodies, see 86022, 86023)

86403   Particle agglutination; screen, each antibody

86406   titer, each antibody

(Pregnancy test, see 84702, 84703)

(Rapid plasma reagin test (RPR), see 86592, 86593)

Pathology and Laboratory

86430 Rheumatoid factor; qualitative

86431   quantitative

(Serologic test for syphilis, see 86592, 86593)

86480 Tuberculosis test, cell mediated immunity measurement of gamma interferon antigen response

86485 Skin test; candida

(For antibody, candida, use 86628)

86486   unlisted antigen, each

86490   coccidioidomycosis

86510   histoplasmosis

(For histoplasma, antibody, use 86698)

86580   tuberculosis, intradermal

(For tuberculosis test, cell mediated immunity measurement of gamma interferon antigen response, use 86480)

(For skin tests for allergy, see 95010-95199)

(Smooth muscle antibody, see 86255, 86256)

(Sporothrix, antibodies to, see code for specific method)

(86586 has been deleted. For skin testing, unlisted antigen, use 86486. For flow cytometry, quantitative, not otherwise specified, use 86356)

86590 Streptokinase, antibody

(For antibodies to infectious agents, see 86602-86804)

(Streptolysin O antibody, see antistreptolysin O, 86060, 86063)

▲ **86592** Syphilis test, non-treponemal antibody; qualitative (eg, VDRL, RPR, ART)

(For antibodies to infectious agents, see 86602-86804)

▲ **86593**   quantitative

(For antibodies to infectious agents, see 86602-86804)

(Tetanus antibody, use 86774)

(Thyroglobulin antibody, use 86800)

(Thyroglobulin, use 84432)

(Thyroid microsomal antibody, use 86376)

(For toxoplasma antibody, see 86777-86778)

The following codes (86602-86804) are qualitative or semiquantitative immunoassays performed by multiple-step methods for the detection of antibodies to infectious agents. For immunoassays by single-step method (eg, reagent strips), use code 86318. Procedures for the identification of antibodies should be coded as precisely as possible. For example, an antibody to a virus could be coded with increasing specificity for virus, family, genus, species, or type. In some cases, further precision may be added to codes by specifying the class of immunoglobulin being detected. When multiple tests are done to detect antibodies to organisms classified more precisely than the specificity allowed by available codes, it is appropriate to code each as a separate service. For example, a test for antibody to an enterovirus is coded as 86658. Coxsackie viruses are enteroviruses, but there are no codes for the individual species of enterovirus. If assays are performed for antibodies to coxsackie A and B species, each assay should be separately coded. Similarly, if multiple assays are performed for antibodies of different immunoglobulin classes, each assay should be coded separately. When a coding option exists for reporting IgM specific antibodies (eg, 86632), the corresponding nonspecific code (eg, 86631) may be reported for performance of either an antibody analysis not specific for a particular immunoglobulin class or for an IgG analysis.

(For the detection of antibodies other than those to infectious agents, see specific antibody [eg, 86021-86023, 86376, 86800, 86850-86870] or specific method [eg, 83516, 86255, 86256]).

(For infectious agent/antigen detection, see 87260-87899)

86602 Antibody; actinomyces

86603   adenovirus

86606   Aspergillus

86609   bacterium, not elsewhere specified

86611   Bartonella

86612   Blastomyces

86615   Bordetella

86617   Borrelia burgdorferi (Lyme disease) confirmatory test (eg, Western Blot or immunoblot)

86618   Borrelia burgdorferi (Lyme disease)

86619   Borrelia (relapsing fever)

86622   Brucella

86625   Campylobacter

86628   Candida

(For skin test, candida, use 86485)

86631   Chlamydia

86632   Chlamydia, IgM

(For chlamydia antigen, see 87270, 87320. For fluorescent antibody technique, see 86255, 86256)

86635   Coccidioides

86638   Coxiella burnetii (Q fever)

86641   Cryptococcus

86644   cytomegalovirus (CMV)

86645   cytomegalovirus (CMV), IgM

86648   Diphtheria

86651   encephalitis, California (La Crosse)

86652   encephalitis, Eastern equine

Pathology and Laboratory

86653	encephalitis, St. Louis
86654	encephalitis, Western equine
86658	enterovirus (eg, coxsackie, echo, polio)

(Trichinella, antibodies to, use 86784)

(Trypanosoma, antibodies to, see code for specific method)

(Tuberculosis, use 86580 for skin testing)

(Viral antibodies, see code for specific method)

86663	Epstein-Barr (EB) virus, early antigen (EA)
86664	Epstein-Barr (EB) virus, nuclear antigen (EBNA)
86665	Epstein-Barr (EB) virus, viral capsid (VCA)
86666	Ehrlichia
86668	Francisella tularensis
86671	fungus, not elsewhere specified
86674	Giardia lamblia
86677	Helicobacter pylori
86682	helminth, not elsewhere specified
86684	Haemophilus influenza
86687	HTLV-I
86688	HTLV-II
86689	HTLV or HIV antibody, confirmatory test (eg, Western Blot)
86692	hepatitis, delta agent

(For hepatitis delta agent, antigen, use 87380)

86694	herpes simplex, non-specific type test
86695	herpes simplex, type 1
86696	herpes simplex, type 2
86698	histoplasma
86701	HIV-1
86702	HIV-2
86703	HIV-1 and HIV-2, single assay

(When HIV antibody immunoassay [HIV testing 86701-86703] is performed using a kit or transportable instrument that wholly or in part consists of a single use, disposable analytical chamber, the service may be identified by adding modifier 92 to the usual code)

(For HIV-1 antigen, use 87390)

(For HIV-2 antigen, use 87391)

(For confirmatory test for HIV antibody (eg, Western Blot), use 86689)

86704	Hepatitis B core antibody (HBcAb); total
86705	IgM antibody
86706	Hepatitis B surface antibody (HBsAb)
86707	Hepatitis Be antibody (HBeAb)

86708	Hepatitis A antibody (HAAb); total
86709	IgM antibody
86710	Antibody; influenza virus
86713	Legionella
86717	Leishmania
86720	Leptospira
86723	Listeria monocytogenes
86727	lymphocytic choriomeningitis
86729	lymphogranuloma venereum
86732	mucormycosis
86735	mumps
86738	mycoplasma
86741	Neisseria meningitidis
86744	Nocardia
86747	parvovirus
86750	Plasmodium (malaria)
86753	protozoa, not elsewhere specified
86756	respiratory syncytial virus
86757	Rickettsia
86759	rotavirus
86762	rubella
86765	rubeola
86768	Salmonella
86771	Shigella
86774	tetanus
86777	Toxoplasma
86778	Toxoplasma, IgM
● 86780	Treponema pallidum

►(86781 has been deleted)◄

►(For syphilis testing by non-treponemal antibody analysis, see 86592-86593)◄

86784	Trichinella
86787	varicella-zoster
86788	West Nile virus, IgM
86789	West Nile virus
86790	virus, not elsewhere specified
86793	Yersinia
86800	Thyroglobulin antibody

(For thyroglobulin, use 84432)

86803	Hepatitis C antibody;
86804	confirmatory test (eg, immunoblot)

Tissue Typing

86805   Lymphocytotoxicity assay, visual crossmatch; with titration

86806   without titration

86807   Serum screening for cytotoxic percent reactive antibody (PRA); standard method

86808   quick method

86812   HLA typing; A, B, or C (eg, A10, B7, B27), single antigen

86813   A, B, or C, multiple antigens

86816   DR/DQ, single antigen

86817   DR/DQ, multiple antigens

86821   lymphocyte culture, mixed (MLC)

86822   lymphocyte culture, primed (PLC)

(For HLA typing by molecular pathology techniques, see 83890-83914 with appropriate genetic testing modifiers 4A-4G)

● **86825**   Human leukocyte antigen (HLA) crossmatch, non-cytotoxic (eg, using flow cytometry); first serum sample or dilution

+● **86826**   each additional serum sample or sample dilution (List separately in addition to primary procedure)

▶(Do not report 86825, 86826 in conjunction with 86355, 86359, 88184-88189 for antibody surface markers integral to crossmatch testing)◀

▶(For autologous HLA crossmatch, see 86825, 86826)◀

▶(For lymphocytotoxicity visual crossmatch, see 86805, 86806)◀

86849   Unlisted immunology procedure

Transfusion Medicine

(For apheresis, use 36511, 36512)

(For therapeutic phlebotomy, use 99195)

86850   Antibody screen, RBC, each serum technique

86860   Antibody elution (RBC), each elution

86870   Antibody identification, RBC antibodies, each panel for each serum technique

86880   Antihuman globulin test (Coombs test); direct, each antiserum

86885   indirect, qualitative, each reagent red cell

86886   indirect, each antibody titer

(For indirect antihuman globulin [Coombs] test for RBC antibody screening, use 86850)

(For indirect antihuman globulin [Coombs] test for RBC antibody identification using reagent red cell panels, use 86870)

86890   Autologous blood or component, collection processing and storage; predeposited

86891   intra- or postoperative salvage

(For physician services to autologous donors, see 99201-99204)

86900   Blood typing; ABO

86901   Rh (D)

86903   antigen screening for compatible blood unit using reagent serum, per unit screened

86904   antigen screening for compatible unit using patient serum, per unit screened

86905   RBC antigens, other than ABO or Rh (D), each

86906   Rh phenotyping, complete

86910   Blood typing, for paternity testing, per individual; ABO, Rh and MN

86911   each additional antigen system

86920   Compatibility test each unit; immediate spin technique

86921   incubation technique

86922   antiglobulin technique

86923   electronic

(Do not use 86923 in conjunction with 86920-86922 for same unit crossmatch)

86927   Fresh frozen plasma, thawing, each unit

86930   Frozen blood, each unit; freezing (includes preparation)

86931   thawing

86932   freezing (includes preparation) and thawing

86940   Hemolysins and agglutinins; auto, screen, each

86941   incubated

86945   Irradiation of blood product, each unit

86950   Leukocyte transfusion

(For leukapheresis, use 36511)

86960   Volume reduction of blood or blood product (eg, red blood cells or platelets), each unit

86965   Pooling of platelets or other blood products

86970   Pretreatment of RBCs for use in RBC antibody detection, identification, and/or compatibility testing; incubation with chemical agents or drugs, each

86971   incubation with enzymes, each

86972   by density gradient separation

86975   Pretreatment of serum for use in RBC antibody identification; incubation with drugs, each

86976   by dilution

86977   incubation with inhibitors, each

86978   by differential red cell absorption using patient RBCs or RBCs of known phenotype, each absorption

Pathology and Laboratory

86985   Splitting of blood or blood products, each unit

86999   Unlisted transfusion medicine procedure

Microbiology

Includes bacteriology, mycology, parasitology, and virology.

▶Presumptive identification of microorganisms is defined as identification by colony morphology, growth on selective media, Gram stains, or up to three tests (eg, catalase, oxidase, indole, urease). Definitive identification of microorganisms is defined as an identification to the genus or species level that requires additional tests (eg, biochemical panels, slide cultures). If additional studies involve molecular probes, nucleic acid sequencing, chromatography, or immunologic techniques, these should be separately coded using 87140-87158, in addition to definitive identification codes. The molecular diagnostic codes (eg, 83890-83914) are not to be used in combination with or instead of the procedures represented by 87140-87158. For multiple specimens/sites use modifier 59. For repeat laboratory tests performed on the same day, use modifier 91.◀

87001   Animal inoculation, small animal; with observation

87003   with observation and dissection

87015   Concentration (any type), for infectious agents

(Do not report 87015 in conjunction with 87177)

87040   Culture, bacterial; blood, aerobic, with isolation and presumptive identification of isolates (includes anaerobic culture, if appropriate)

87045   stool, aerobic, with isolation and preliminary examination (eg, KIA, LIA), Salmonella and Shigella species

87046   stool, aerobic, additional pathogens, isolation and presumptive identification of isolates, each plate

87070   any other source except urine, blood or stool, aerobic, with isolation and presumptive identification of isolates

(For urine, use 87088)

87071   quantitative, aerobic with isolation and presumptive identification of isolates, any source except urine, blood or stool

(For urine, use 87088)

87073   quantitative, anaerobic with isolation and presumptive identification of isolates, any source except urine, blood or stool

(For definitive identification of isolates, use 87076 or 87077. For typing of isolates see 87140-87158)

87075   any source, except blood, anaerobic with isolation and presumptive identification of isolates

87076   anaerobic isolate, additional methods required for definitive identification, each isolate

87077   aerobic isolate, additional methods required for definitive identification, each isolate

87081   Culture, presumptive, pathogenic organisms, screening only;

87084   with colony estimation from density chart

87086   Culture, bacterial; quantitative colony count, urine

87088   with isolation and presumptive identification of each isolate, urine

87101   Culture, fungi (mold or yeast) isolation, with presumptive identification of isolates; skin, hair, or nail

87102   other source (except blood)

87103   blood

87106   Culture, fungi, definitive identification, each organism; yeast

87107   mold

87109   Culture, mycoplasma, any source

87110   Culture, chlamydia, any source

(For immunofluorescence staining of shell vials, use 87140)

87116   Culture, tubercle or other acid-fast bacilli (eg, TB, AFB, mycobacteria) any source, with isolation and presumptive identification of isolates

(For concentration, use 87015)

87118   Culture, mycobacterial, definitive identification, each isolate

87140   Culture, typing; immunofluorescent method, each antiserum

87143   gas liquid chromatography (GLC) or high pressure liquid chromatography (HPLC) method

87147   immunologic method, other than immunofluoresence (eg, agglutination grouping), per antiserum

▲ **87149**   identification by nucleic acid (DNA or RNA) probe, direct probe technique, per culture or isolate, each organism probed

▶(Do not report 87149 in conjunction with 83890-83914)◀

● **87150**   identification by nucleic acid (DNA or RNA) probe, amplified probe technique, per culture or isolate, each organism probed

▶(Do not report 87150 in conjunction with 83890-83914)◀

87152   identification by pulse field gel typing

▶(Do not report 87152 in conjunction with 83890-83914)◀

● **87153**   identification by nucleic acid sequencing method, each isolate (eg, sequencing of the 16S rRNA gene)

Pathology and Laboratory

87158   other methods

87164   Dark field examination, any source (eg, penile, vaginal, oral, skin); includes specimen collection

87166   without collection

87168   Macroscopic examination; arthropod

87169   parasite

87172   Pinworm exam (eg, cellophane tape prep)

87176   Homogenization, tissue, for culture

87177   Ova and parasites, direct smears, concentration and identification

(Do not report 87177 in conjunction with 87015)

(For direct smears from a primary source, use 87207)

(For coccidia or microsporidia exam, use 87207)

(For complex special stain (trichrome, iron hematoxylin), use 87209)

(For nucleic acid probes in cytologic material, use 88365)

87181   Susceptibility studies, antimicrobial agent; agar dilution method, per agent (eg, antibiotic gradient strip)

87184   disk method, per plate (12 or fewer agents)

87185   enzyme detection (eg, beta lactamase), per enzyme

87186   microdilution or agar dilution (minimum inhibitory concentration [MIC] or breakpoint), each multi-antimicrobial, per plate

+ 87187   microdilution or agar dilution, minimum lethal concentration (MLC), each plate (List separately in addition to code for primary procedure)

(Use 87187 in conjunction with 87186 or 87188)

87188   macrobroth dilution method, each agent

87190   mycobacteria, proportion method, each agent

(For other mycobacterial susceptibility studies, see 87181, 87184, 87186, or 87188)

87197   Serum bactericidal titer (Schlicter test)

87205   Smear, primary source with interpretation; Gram or Giemsa stain for bacteria, fungi, or cell types

87206   fluorescent and/or acid fast stain for bacteria, fungi, parasites, viruses or cell types

87207   special stain for inclusion bodies or parasites (eg, malaria, coccidia, microsporidia, trypanosomes, herpes viruses)

(For direct smears with concentration and identification, use 87177)

(For thick smear preparation, use 87015)

(For fat, meat, fibers, nasal eosinophils, and starch, see miscellaneous section)

87209   complex special stain (eg, trichrome, iron hemotoxylin) for ova and parasites

87210   wet mount for infectious agents (eg, saline, India ink, KOH preps)

(For KOH examination of skin, hair or nails, see 87220)

87220   Tissue examination by KOH slide of samples from skin, hair, or nails for fungi or ectoparasite ova or mites (eg, scabies)

87230   Toxin or antitoxin assay, tissue culture (eg, Clostridium difficile toxin)

87250   Virus isolation; inoculation of embryonated eggs, or small animal, includes observation and dissection

87252   tissue culture inoculation, observation, and presumptive identification by cytopathic effect

87253   tissue culture, additional studies or definitive identification (eg, hemabsorption, neutralization, immunofluoresence stain), each isolate

(Electron microscopy, use 88348)

(Inclusion bodies in tissue sections, see 88304-88309; in smears, see 87207-87210; in fluids, use 88106)

87254   centrifuge enhanced (shell vial) technique, includes identification with immunofluorescence stain, each virus

(Report 87254 in addition to 87252 as appropriate)

87255   including identification by non-immunologic method, other than by cytopathic effect (eg, virus specific enzymatic activity)

▶These codes are intended for primary source only. For similar studies on culture material, refer to codes 87140-87158. Infectious agents by antigen detection, immunofluorescence microscopy, or nucleic acid probe techniques should be reported as precisely as possible. The molecular diagnostic codes (eg, 83890-83914) are not to be used in combination with or instead of the procedures represented by 87470-87801. The most specific code possible should be reported. If there is no specific agent code, the general methodology code (eg, 87299, 87449, 87450, 87797, 87798, 87799, 87899) should be used. For identification of antibodies to many of the listed infectious agents, see 86602-86804. When separate results are reported for different species or strain of organisms, each result should be coded separately. Use modifier 59 when separate results are reported for different species or strains that are described by the same code.◀

87260   Infectious agent antigen detection by immunofluorescent technique; adenovirus

87265   Bordetella pertussis/parapertussis

87267   Enterovirus, direct fluorescent antibody (DFA)

87269   giardia

87270   Chlamydia trachomatis

87271   Cytomegalovirus, direct fluorescent antibody (DFA)

87272   cryptosporidium

Pathology and Laboratory

87273	Herpes simplex virus type 2
87274	Herpes simplex virus type 1
87275	influenza B virus
87276	influenza A virus
87277	Legionella micdadei
87278	Legionella pneumophila
87279	Parainfluenza virus, each type
87280	respiratory syncytial virus
87281	Pneumocystis carinii
87283	Rubeola
87285	Treponema pallidum
87290	Varicella zoster virus
87299	not otherwise specified, each organism

87300 Infectious agent antigen detection by immunofluorescent technique, polyvalent for multiple organisms, each polyvalent antiserum

(For physician evaluation of infectious disease agents by immunofluorescence, use 88346)

87301 Infectious agent antigen detection by enzyme immunoassay technique, qualitative or semiquantitative, multiple-step method; adenovirus enteric types 40/41

87305	Aspergillus
87320	Chlamydia trachomatis
87324	Clostridium difficile toxin(s)
87327	Cryptococcus neoformans

(For Cryptococcus latex agglutination, use 86403)

87328	cryptosporidium
87329	giardia
87332	cytomegalovirus
87335	Escherichia coli 0157

(For giardia antigen, use 87329)

87336	Entamoeba histolytica dispar group
87337	Entamoeba histolytica group
87338	Helicobacter pylori, stool
87339	Helicobacter pylori

(For H. pylori, stool, use 87338. For H. pylori, breath and blood by mass spectrometry, see 83013, 83014. For H. pylori, liquid scintillation counter, see 78267, 78268)

87340	hepatitis B surface antigen (HBsAg)
87341	hepatitis B surface antigen (HBsAg) neutralization
87350	hepatitis Be antigen (HBeAg)
87380	hepatitis, delta agent
87385	Histoplasma capsulatum
87390	HIV-1
87391	HIV-2
87400	Influenza, A or B, each
87420	respiratory syncytial virus
87425	rotavirus
87427	Shiga-like toxin
87430	Streptococcus, group A

87449 Infectious agent antigen detection by enzyme immunoassay technique qualitative or semiquantitative; multiple step method, not otherwise specified, each organism

87450 single step method, not otherwise specified, each organism

87451 multiple step method, polyvalent for multiple organisms, each polyvalent antiserum

87470 Infectious agent detection by nucleic acid (DNA or RNA); Bartonella henselae and Bartonella quintana, direct probe technique

87471	Bartonella henselae and Bartonella quintana, amplified probe technique
87472	Bartonella henselae and Bartonella quintana, quantification
87475	Borrelia burgdorferi, direct probe technique
87476	Borrelia burgdorferi, amplified probe technique
87477	Borrelia burgdorferi, quantification
87480	Candida species, direct probe technique
87481	Candida species, amplified probe technique
87482	Candida species, quantification
87485	Chlamydia pneumoniae, direct probe technique
87486	Chlamydia pneumoniae, amplified probe technique
87487	Chlamydia pneumoniae, quantification
87490	Chlamydia trachomatis, direct probe technique
87491	Chlamydia trachomatis, amplified probe technique
87492	Chlamydia trachomatis, quantification
● 87493	Clostridium difficile, toxin gene(s), amplified probe technique
87495	cytomegalovirus, direct probe technique
87496	cytomegalovirus, amplified probe technique
87497	cytomegalovirus, quantification
87498	enterovirus, amplified probe technique
87500	vancomycin resistance (eg, enterococcus species van A, van B), amplified probe technique
87510	Gardnerella vaginalis, direct probe technique
87511	Gardnerella vaginalis, amplified probe technique
87512	Gardnerella vaginalis, quantification

Pathology and Laboratory

87515	hepatitis B virus, direct probe technique
87516	hepatitis B virus, amplified probe technique
87517	hepatitis B virus, quantification
87520	hepatitis C, direct probe technique
87521	hepatitis C, amplified probe technique
87522	hepatitis C, quantification
87525	hepatitis G, direct probe technique
87526	hepatitis G, amplified probe technique
87527	hepatitis G, quantification
87528	Herpes simplex virus, direct probe technique
87529	Herpes simplex virus, amplified probe technique
87530	Herpes simplex virus, quantification
87531	Herpes virus-6, direct probe technique
87532	Herpes virus-6, amplified probe technique
87533	Herpes virus-6, quantification
87534	HIV-1, direct probe technique
87535	HIV-1, amplified probe technique
87536	HIV-1, quantification
87537	HIV-2, direct probe technique
87538	HIV-2, amplified probe technique
87539	HIV-2, quantification
87540	Legionella pneumophila, direct probe technique
87541	Legionella pneumophila, amplified probe technique
87542	Legionella pneumophila, quantification
87550	Mycobacteria species, direct probe technique
87551	Mycobacteria species, amplified probe technique
87552	Mycobacteria species, quantification
87555	Mycobacteria tuberculosis, direct probe technique
87556	Mycobacteria tuberculosis, amplified probe technique
87557	Mycobacteria tuberculosis, quantification
87560	Mycobacteria avium-intracellulare, direct probe technique
87561	Mycobacteria avium-intracellulare, amplified probe technique
87562	Mycobacteria avium-intracellulare, quantification
87580	Mycoplasma pneumoniae, direct probe technique
87581	Mycoplasma pneumoniae, amplified probe technique
87582	Mycoplasma pneumoniae, quantification
87590	Neisseria gonorrhoeae, direct probe technique
87591	Neisseria gonorrhoeae, amplified probe technique
87592	Neisseria gonorrhoeae, quantification
87620	papillomavirus, human, direct probe technique

87621	papillomavirus, human, amplified probe technique
87622	papillomavirus, human, quantification
87640	Staphylococcus aureus, amplified probe technique
87641	Staphylococcus aureus, methicillin resistant, amplified probe technique

(For assays that detect methicillin resistance and identify Staphylococcus aureus using a single nucleic acid sequence, use 87641)

87650	Streptococcus, group A, direct probe technique
87651	Streptococcus, group A, amplified probe technique
87652	Streptococcus, group A, quantification
87653	Streptococcus, group B, amplified probe technique
87660	Trichomonas vaginalis, direct probe technique
87797	Infectious agent detection by nucleic acid (DNA or RNA), not otherwise specified; direct probe technique, each organism
87798	amplified probe technique, each organism
87799	quantification, each organism
87800	Infectious agent detection by nucleic acid (DNA or RNA), multiple organisms; direct probe(s) technique
87801	amplified probe(s) technique

(For each specific organism nucleic acid detection from a primary source, see 87470-87660. For detection of specific infectious agents not otherwise specified, see 87797, 87798, or 87799 1 time for each agent)

87802	Infectious agent antigen detection by immunoassay with direct optical observation; Streptococcus, group B
87803	Clostridium difficile toxin A
87804	Influenza
87807	respiratory syncytial virus
87808	Trichomonas vaginalis
87809	adenovirus
87810	Chlamydia trachomatis
87850	Neisseria gonorrhoeae
87880	Streptococcus, group A
87899	not otherwise specified
87900	Infectious agent drug susceptibility phenotype prediction using regularly updated genotypic bioinformatics
87901	Infectious agent genotype analysis by nucleic acid (DNA or RNA); HIV-1, reverse transcriptase and protease

(For infectious agent drug susceptibility phenotype prediction for HIV-1, use 87900)

87902	Hepatitis C virus
87903	Infectious agent phenotype analysis by nucleic acid (DNA or RNA) with drug resistance tissue culture analysis, HIV 1; first through 10 drugs tested

Pathology and Laboratory

+ 87904   each additional drug tested (List separately in addition to code for primary procedure)

    (Use 87904 in conjunction with 87903)

87905   Infectious agent enzymatic activity other than virus (eg, sialidase activity in vaginal fluid)

    (For virus isolation including identification by non-immunologic method, other than by cytopathic effect, use 87255)

87999   Unlisted microbiology procedure

Anatomic Pathology

Postmortem Examination

Procedures 88000 through 88099 represent physician services only. Use modifier 90 for outside laboratory services.

88000   Necropsy (autopsy), gross examination only; without CNS

88005   with brain

88007   with brain and spinal cord

88012   infant with brain

88014   stillborn or newborn with brain

88016   macerated stillborn

88020   Necropsy (autopsy), gross and microscopic; without CNS

88025   with brain

88027   with brain and spinal cord

88028   infant with brain

88029   stillborn or newborn with brain

88036   Necropsy (autopsy), limited, gross and/or microscopic; regional

88037   single organ

88040   Necropsy (autopsy); forensic examination

88045   coroner's call

88099   Unlisted necropsy (autopsy) procedure

Cytopathology

88104   Cytopathology, fluids, washings or brushings, except cervical or vaginal; smears with interpretation

88106   simple filter method with interpretation

88107   smears and simple filter preparation with interpretation

    (For nongynecological selective cellular enhancement including filter transfer techniques, use 88112)

88108   Cytopathology, concentration technique, smears and interpretation (eg, Saccomanno technique)

    (For cervical or vaginal smears, see 88150-88155)

    (For gastric intubation with lavage, see 89130-89141, 91055)

    (For x-ray localization, use 74340)

88112   Cytopathology, selective cellular enhancement technique with interpretation (eg, liquid based slide preparation method), except cervical or vaginal

    (Do not report 88112 with 88108)

88125   Cytopathology, forensic (eg, sperm)

88130   Sex chromatin identification; Barr bodies

88140   peripheral blood smear, polymorphonuclear drumsticks

    (For Guard stain, use 88313)

Codes 88141-88155, 88164-88167, 88174-88175 are used to report cervical or vaginal screening by various methods and to report physician interpretation services. Use codes 88150-88154 to report conventional Pap smears that are examined using non-Bethesda reporting. Use codes 88164-88167 to report conventional Pap smears that are examined using the Bethesda System of reporting. Use codes 88142-88143 to report liquid-based specimens processed as thin-layer preparations that are examined using any system of reporting (Bethesda or non-Bethesda). Use codes 88174-88175 to report automated screening of liquid-based specimens that are examined using any system of reporting (Bethesda or non-Bethesda). Within each of these three code families choose the one code that describes the screening method(s) used. Codes 88141 and 88155 should be reported in addition to the screening code chosen when the additional services are provided. Manual rescreening requires a complete visual reassessment of the entire slide initially screened by either an automated or manual process. Manual review represents an assessment of selected cells or regions of a slide identified by initial automated review.

88141   Cytopathology, cervical or vaginal (any reporting system), requiring interpretation by physician

    (Use 88141 in conjunction with 88142-88154, 88164-88167, 88174-88175)

88142   Cytopathology, cervical or vaginal (any reporting system), collected in preservative fluid, automated thin layer preparation; manual screening under physician supervision

88143   with manual screening and rescreening under physician supervision

    (For automated screening of automated thin layer preparation, see 88174, 88175)

88147   Cytopathology smears, cervical or vaginal; screening by automated system under physician supervision

88148	screening by automated system with manual rescreening under physician supervision
88150	Cytopathology, slides, cervical or vaginal; manual screening under physician supervision
88152	with manual screening and computer-assisted rescreening under physician supervision
88153	with manual screening and rescreening under physician supervision
88154	with manual screening and computer-assisted rescreening using cell selection and review under physician supervision

+ 88155 Cytopathology, slides, cervical or vaginal, definitive hormonal evaluation (eg, maturation index, karyopyknotic index, estrogenic index) (List separately in addition to code[s] for other technical and interpretation services)

(Use 88155 in conjunction with 88142-88154, 88164-88167, 88174-88175)

88160 Cytopathology, smears, any other source; screening and interpretation

88161 preparation, screening and interpretation

88162 extended study involving over 5 slides and/or multiple stains

(For aerosol collection of sputum, use 89220)

(For special stains, see 88312-88314)

88164 Cytopathology, slides, cervical or vaginal (the Bethesda System); manual screening under physician supervision

88165 with manual screening and rescreening under physician supervision

88166 with manual screening and computer-assisted rescreening under physician supervision

88167 with manual screening and computer-assisted rescreening using cell selection and review under physician supervision

(To report collection of specimen via fine needle aspiration, see 10021, 10022)

88172 Cytopathology, evaluation of fine needle aspirate; immediate cytohistologic study to determine adequacy of specimen(s)

88173 interpretation and report

(For fine needle aspirate, see 10021, 10022)

(Do not report 88172, 88173 in conjunction with 88333 and 88334 for the same specimen)

88174 Cytopathology, cervical or vaginal (any reporting system), collected in preservative fluid, automated thin layer preparation; screening by automated system, under physician supervision

88175 with screening by automated system and manual rescreening or review, under physician supervision

(For manual screening, see 88142, 88143)

88182 Flow cytometry, cell cycle or DNA analysis

(For DNA ploidy analysis by morphometric technique, use 88358)

88184 Flow cytometry, cell surface, cytoplasmic, or nuclear marker, technical component only; first marker

+ 88185 each additional marker (List separately in addition to code for first marker)

(Report 88185 in conjunction with 88184)

88187 Flow cytometry, interpretation; 2 to 8 markers

88188 9 to 15 markers

88189 16 or more markers

(Do not report 88187-88189 for interpretation of 86355, 86356, 86357, 86359, 86360, 86361, 86367)

88199 Unlisted cytopathology procedure

(For electron microscopy, see 88348, 88349)

Cytogenetic Studies

When molecular diagnostic procedures are performed to test for oncologic or inherited disorder, use the appropriate modifier to specify probe type or condition tested. (See **Appendix I** for a listing of appropriate modifiers to report with molecular diagnostic and cytogenetic procedures.)

(For acetylcholinesterase, use 82013)

(For alpha-fetoprotein, serum or amniotic fluid, see 82105, 82106)

(For laser microdissection of cells from tissue sample, see 88380)

88230 Tissue culture for non-neoplastic disorders; lymphocyte

88233 skin or other solid tissue biopsy

88235 amniotic fluid or chorionic villus cells

88237 Tissue culture for neoplastic disorders; bone marrow, blood cells

88239 solid tumor

88240 Cryopreservation, freezing and storage of cells, each cell line

(For therapeutic cryopreservation and storage, use 38207)

88241 Thawing and expansion of frozen cells, each aliquot

(For therapeutic thawing of previous harvest, use 38208)

88245 Chromosome analysis for breakage syndromes; baseline Sister Chromatid Exchange (SCE), 20-25 cells

88248 baseline breakage, score 50-100 cells, count 20 cells, 2 karyotypes (eg, for ataxia telangiectasia, Fanconi anemia, fragile X)

88249 score 100 cells, clastogen stress (eg, diepoxybutane, mitomycin C, ionizing radiation, UV radiation)

Pathology and Laboratory

88261   Chromosome analysis; count 5 cells, 1 karyotype, with banding

88262   count 15-20 cells, 2 karyotypes, with banding

88263   count 45 cells for mosaicism, 2 karyotypes, with banding

88264   analyze 20-25 cells

88267   Chromosome analysis, amniotic fluid or chorionic villus, count 15 cells, 1 karyotype, with banding

88269   Chromosome analysis, in situ for amniotic fluid cells, count cells from 6-12 colonies, 1 karyotype, with banding

88271   Molecular cytogenetics; DNA probe, each (eg, FISH)

88272   chromosomal in situ hybridization, analyze 3-5 cells (eg, for derivatives and markers)

88273   chromosomal in situ hybridization, analyze 10-30 cells (eg, for microdeletions)

88274   interphase in situ hybridization, analyze 25-99 cells

88275   interphase in situ hybridization, analyze 100-300 cells

88280   Chromosome analysis; additional karyotypes, each study

88283   additional specialized banding technique (eg, NOR, C-banding)

88285   additional cells counted, each study

88289   additional high resolution study

88291   Cytogenetics and molecular cytogenetics, interpretation and report

88299   Unlisted cytogenetic study

Surgical Pathology

Services 88300 through 88309 include accession, examination, and reporting. They do not include the services designated in codes 88311 through 88365 and 88399, which are coded in addition when provided.

The unit of service for codes 88300 through 88309 is the specimen.

A specimen is defined as tissue or tissues that is (are) submitted for individual and separate attention, requiring individual examination and pathologic diagnosis. Two or more such specimens from the same patient (eg, separately identified endoscopic biopsies, skin lesions) are each appropriately assigned an individual code reflective of its proper level of service.

Service code 88300 is used for any specimen that in the opinion of the examining pathologist can be accurately diagnosed without microscopic examination. Service code 88302 is used when gross and microscopic examination is performed on a specimen to confirm identification and the absence of disease. Service codes 88304 through 88309 describe all other specimens requiring gross and microscopic examination, and represent additional

ascending levels of physician work. Levels 88302 through 88309 are specifically defined by the assigned specimens.

Any unlisted specimen should be assigned to the code which most closely reflects the physician work involved when compared to other specimens assigned to that code.

(Do not report 88302-88309 on the same specimen as part of Mohs surgery)

88300   **Level I** - Surgical pathology, gross examination only

88302   **Level II** - Surgical pathology, gross and microscopic examination

Appendix, incidental

Fallopian tube, sterilization

Fingers/toes, amputation, traumatic

Foreskin, newborn

Hernia sac, any location

Hydrocele sac

Nerve

Skin, plastic repair

Sympathetic ganglion

Testis, castration

Vaginal mucosa, incidental

Vas deferens, sterilization

88304   **Level III** - Surgical pathology, gross and microscopic examination

Abortion, induced

Abscess

Aneurysm - arterial/ventricular

Anus, tag

Appendix, other than incidental

Artery, atheromatous plaque

Bartholin's gland cyst

Bone fragment(s), other than pathologic fracture

Bursa/synovial cyst

Carpal tunnel tissue

Cartilage, shavings

Cholesteatoma

Colon, colostomy stoma

Conjunctiva - biopsy/pterygium

Cornea

Diverticulum - esophagus/small intestine

Dupuytren's contracture tissue

Femoral head, other than fracture

Fissure/fistula

Pathology and Laboratory

Foreskin, other than newborn

Gallbladder

Ganglion cyst

Hematoma

Hemorrhoids

Hydatid of Morgagni

Intervertebral disc

Joint, loose body

Meniscus

Mucocele, salivary

Neuroma - Morton's/traumatic

Pilonidal cyst/sinus

Polyps, inflammatory - nasal/sinusoidal

Skin - cyst/tag/debridement

Soft tissue, debridement

Soft tissue, lipoma

Spermatocele

Tendon/tendon sheath

Testicular appendage

Thrombus or embolus

Tonsil and/or adenoids

Varicocele

Vas deferens, other than sterilization

Vein, varicosity

88305 **Level IV** - Surgical pathology, gross and microscopic examination

Abortion - spontaneous/missed

Artery, biopsy

Bone marrow, biopsy

Bone exostosis

Brain/meninges, other than for tumor resection

Breast, biopsy, not requiring microscopic evaluation of surgical margins

Breast, reduction mammoplasty

Bronchus, biopsy

Cell block, any source

Cervix, biopsy

Colon, biopsy

Duodenum, biopsy

Endocervix, curettings/biopsy

Endometrium, curettings/biopsy

Esophagus, biopsy

Extremity, amputation, traumatic

Fallopian tube, biopsy

Fallopian tube, ectopic pregnancy

Femoral head, fracture

Fingers/toes, amputation, non-traumatic

Gingiva/oral mucosa, biopsy

Heart valve

Joint, resection

Kidney, biopsy

Larynx, biopsy

Leiomyoma(s), uterine myomectomy - without uterus

Lip, biopsy/wedge resection

Lung, transbronchial biopsy

Lymph node, biopsy

Muscle, biopsy

Nasal mucosa, biopsy

Nasopharynx/oropharynx, biopsy

Nerve, biopsy

Odontogenic/dental cyst

Omentum, biopsy

Ovary with or without tube, non-neoplastic

Ovary, biopsy/wedge resection

Parathyroid gland

Peritoneum, biopsy

Pituitary tumor

Placenta, other than third trimester

Pleura/pericardium - biopsy/tissue

Polyp, cervical/endometrial

Polyp, colorectal

Polyp, stomach/small intestine

Prostate, needle biopsy

Prostate, TUR

Salivary gland, biopsy

Sinus, paranasal biopsy

Skin, other than cyst/tag/debridement/plastic repair

Small intestine, biopsy

Soft tissue, other than tumor/mass/lipoma/debridement

Spleen

Stomach, biopsy

Synovium

Testis, other than tumor/biopsy/castration

Pathology and Laboratory

Thyroglossal duct/brachial cleft cyst

Tongue, biopsy

Tonsil, biopsy

Trachea, biopsy

Ureter, biopsy

Urethra, biopsy

Urinary bladder, biopsy

Uterus, with or without tubes and ovaries, for prolapse

Vagina, biopsy

Vulva/labia, biopsy

88307 **Level V** - Surgical pathology, gross and microscopic examination

Adrenal, resection

Bone - biopsy/curettings

Bone fragment(s), pathologic fracture

Brain, biopsy

Brain/meninges, tumor resection

Breast, excision of lesion, requiring microscopic evaluation of surgical margins

Breast, mastectomy - partial/simple

Cervix, conization

Colon, segmental resection, other than for tumor

Extremity, amputation, non-traumatic

Eye, enucleation

Kidney, partial/total nephrectomy

Larynx, partial/total resection

Liver, biopsy - needle/wedge

Liver, partial resection

Lung, wedge biopsy

Lymph nodes, regional resection

Mediastinum, mass

Myocardium, biopsy

Odontogenic tumor

Ovary with or without tube, neoplastic

Pancreas, biopsy

Placenta, third trimester

Prostate, except radical resection

Salivary gland

Sentinel lymph node

Small intestine, resection, other than for tumor

Soft tissue mass (except lipoma) - biopsy/simple excision

Stomach - subtotal/total resection, other than for tumor

Testis, biopsy

Thymus, tumor

Thyroid, total/lobe

Ureter, resection

Urinary bladder, TUR

Uterus, with or without tubes and ovaries, other than neoplastic/prolapse

88309 **Level VI** - Surgical pathology, gross and microscopic examination

Bone resection

Breast, mastectomy - with regional lymph nodes

Colon, segmental resection for tumor

Colon, total resection

Esophagus, partial/total resection

Extremity, disarticulation

Fetus, with dissection

Larynx, partial/total resection - with regional lymph nodes

Lung - total/lobe/segment resection

Pancreas, total/subtotal resection

Prostate, radical resection

Small intestine, resection for tumor

Soft tissue tumor, extensive resection

Stomach - subtotal/total resection for tumor

Testis, tumor

Tongue/tonsil -resection for tumor

Urinary bladder, partial/total resection

Uterus, with or without tubes and ovaries, neoplastic

Vulva, total/subtotal resection

(For fine needle aspiration, see 10021, 10022)

(For evaluation of fine needle aspirate, see 88172-88173)

(Do not report 88302-88309 on the same specimen as part of Mohs surgery)

+ **88311** Decalcification procedure (List separately in addition to code for surgical pathology examination)

▲ **88312** Special stains; Group I for microorganisms (eg, Gridley, acid fast, methenamine silver), including interpretation and report, each

▲ **88313** Group II, all other (eg, iron, trichrome), except immunocytochemistry and immunoperoxidase stains, including interpretation and report, each

(For immunocytochemistry and immunoperoxidase tissue studies, use 88342)

+▲ **88314**   histochemical staining with frozen section(s), including interpretation and report (List separately in addition to code for primary procedure)

▶(Use 88314 in conjunction with 88302-88309)◀

(Do not report 88314 with 17311-17315 for routine frozen section stain [eg, hematoxylin and eosin, toluidine blue], performed during Mohs surgery. When a nonroutine histochemical stain on frozen tissue is utilized, report 88314 with modifier 59)

88318   Determinative histochemistry to identify chemical components (eg, copper, zinc)

88319   Determinative histochemistry or cytochemistry to identify enzyme constituents, each

88321   Consultation and report on referred slides prepared elsewhere

88323   Consultation and report on referred material requiring preparation of slides

88325   Consultation, comprehensive, with review of records and specimens, with report on referred material

88329   Pathology consultation during surgery;

88331   first tissue block, with frozen section(s), single specimen

88332   each additional tissue block with frozen section(s)

88333   cytologic examination (eg, touch prep, squash prep), initial site

88334   cytologic examination (eg, touch prep, squash prep), each additional site

(For intraoperative consultation on a specimen requiring both frozen section and cytologic evaluation, use 88331 and 88334)

(For percutaneous needle biopsy requiring intraprocedural cytologic examination, use 88333)

(Do not report 88333 and 88334 for non-intraoperative cytologic examination, see 88160-88162)

(Do not report 88333 and 88334 for intraprocedural cytologic evaluation of fine needle aspirate, see 88172)

88342   Immunohistochemistry (including tissue immunoperoxidase), each antibody

(Do not report 88342 in conjunction with 88360 or 88361 for the same antibody)

(For quantitative or semiquantitative immunohistochemistry, see 88360, 88361)

88346   Immunofluorescent study, each antibody; direct method

88347   indirect method

88348   Electron microscopy; diagnostic

88349   scanning

88355   Morphometric analysis; skeletal muscle

88356   nerve

88358   tumor (eg, DNA ploidy)

(Do not report 88358 with 88313 unless each procedure is for a different special stain)

88360   Morphometric analysis, tumor immunohistochemistry (eg, Her-2/neu, estrogen receptor/progesterone receptor), quantitative or semiquantitative, each antibody; manual

88361   using computer-assisted technology

(Do not report 88360, 88361 with 88342 unless each procedure is for a different antibody)

(For morphometric analysis using in situ hybridization techniques, see 88367, 88368)

(When semi-thin plastic-embedded sections are performed in conjunction with morphometric analysis, only the morphometric analysis should be reported; if performed as an independent procedure, see codes 88300-88309 for surgical pathology.)

88362   Nerve teasing preparations

88365   In situ hybridization (eg, FISH), each probe

(Do not report 88365 in conjunction with 88367, 88368 for the same probe)

88367   Morphometric analysis, in situ hybridization (quantitative or semi-quantitative) each probe; using computer-assisted technology

88368   manual

88371   Protein analysis of tissue by Western Blot, with interpretation and report;

88372   immunological probe for band identification, each

88380   Microdissection (ie, sample preparation of microscopically identified target); laser capture

88381   manual

(Do not report 88380 in conjunction with 88381)

88384   Array-based evaluation of multiple molecular probes; 11 through 50 probes

88385   51 through 250 probes

88386   251 through 500 probes

(For preparation of array-based evaluation, see 83890-83892, 83898-83901)

(For preparation and analyses of less than 11 probes, see 83890-83914)

● **88387**   Macroscopic examination, dissection, and preparation of tissue for non-microscopic analytical studies (eg, nucleic acid-based molecular studies); each tissue preparation (eg, a single lymph node)

▶(Do not report 88387 for tissue preparation for microbiologic cultures or flow cytometric studies)◀

▶(Do not report 88387 in conjunction with 88388, 88329-88334)◀

Pathology and Laboratory

+● 88388   in conjunction with a touch imprint, intraoperative consultation, or frozen section, each tissue preparation (eg, a single lymph node) (List separately in addition to code for primary procedure)

▶(Use 88388 in conjunction with 88329-88334)◀

▶(Do not report 88387 or 88388 for tissue preparation for microbiologic cultures or flow cytometric studies)◀

88399   Unlisted surgical pathology procedure

(88400 has been deleted. To report, use 88720)

In Vivo (eg, Transcutaneous) Laboratory Procedures

88720   Bilirubin, total, transcutaneous

(For transdermal oxygen saturation, see 94760-94762)

● 88738   Hemoglobin (Hgb), quantitative, transcutaneous

▶(For in vitro hemoglobin measurement, use 85018)◀

88740   Hemoglobin, quantitative, transcutaneous, per day; carboxyhemoglobin

(For in vitro carboxyhemoglobin measurement, use 82375)

88741   methemoglobin

(For in vitro quantitative methemoglobin determination, use 83050)

Other Procedures

89049   Caffeine halothane contracture test (CHCT) for malignant hyperthermia susceptibility, including interpretation and report

89050   Cell count, miscellaneous body fluids (eg, cerebrospinal fluid, joint fluid), except blood;

89051   with differential count

89055   Leukocyte assessment, fecal, qualitative or semiquantitative

89060   Crystal identification by light microscopy with or without polarizing lens analysis, tissue or any body fluid (except urine)

(Do not report 89060 for crystal identification on paraffin-embedded tissue)

89100   Duodenal intubation and aspiration; single specimen (eg, simple bile study or afferent loop culture) plus appropriate test procedure

89105   collection of multiple fractional specimens with pancreatic or gallbladder stimulation, single or double lumen tube

(For radiological localization, use 74340)

(For chemical analyses, see **Chemistry,** this section)

(Electrocardiogram, see 93000-93268)

(Esophagus acid perfusion test [Bernstein], see 91030)

89125   Fat stain, feces, urine, or respiratory secretions

89130   Gastric intubation and aspiration, diagnostic, each specimen, for chemical analyses or cytopathology;

89132   after stimulation

89135   Gastric intubation, aspiration, and fractional collections (eg, gastric secretory study); 1 hour

89136   2 hours

89140   2 hours including gastric stimulation (eg, histalog, pentagastrin)

89141   3 hours, including gastric stimulation

(For gastric lavage, therapeutic, use 91105)

(For radiologic localization of gastric tube, use 74340)

(For chemical analyses, see 82926, 82928)

(Joint fluid chemistry, see **Chemistry,** this section)

89160   Meat fibers, feces

89190   Nasal smear for eosinophils

(Occult blood, feces, use 82270)

(Paternity tests, use 86910)

89220   Sputum, obtaining specimen, aerosol induced technique (separate procedure)

89225   Starch granules, feces

89230   Sweat collection by iontophoresis

89235   Water load test

89240   Unlisted miscellaneous pathology test

Reproductive Medicine Procedures

89250   Culture of oocyte(s)/embryo(s), less than 4 days;

89251   with co-culture of oocyte(s)/embryos

(For extended culture of oocyte[s]/embryo[s], see 89272)

89253   Assisted embryo hatching, microtechniques (any method)

89254   Oocyte identification from follicular fluid

89255   Preparation of embryo for transfer (any method)

89257   Sperm identification from aspiration (other than seminal fluid)

(For semen analysis, see 89300-89320)

(For sperm identification from testis tissue, use 89264)

89258   Cryopreservation; embryo(s)

Pathology and Laboratory

89259   sperm

(For cryopreservation of reproductive tissue, testicular, use 89335)

89260   Sperm isolation; simple prep (eg, sperm wash and swim-up) for insemination or diagnosis with semen analysis

89261   complex prep (eg, Percoll gradient, albumin gradient) for insemination or diagnosis with semen analysis

(For semen analysis without sperm wash or swim-up, use 89320)

89264   Sperm identification from testis tissue, fresh or cryopreserved

(For biopsy of testis, see 54500, 54505)

(For sperm identification from aspiration, use 89257)

(For semen analysis, see 89300-89320)

89268   Insemination of oocytes

89272   Extended culture of oocyte(s)/embryo(s), 4-7 days

89280   Assisted oocyte fertilization, microtechnique; less than or equal to 10 oocytes

89281   greater than 10 oocytes

89290   Biopsy, oocyte polar body or embryo blastomere, microtechnique (for pre-implantation genetic diagnosis); less than or equal to 5 embryos

89291   greater than 5 embryos

89300   Semen analysis; presence and/or motility of sperm including Huhner test (post coital)

89310   motility and count (not including Huhner test)

89320   volume, count, motility, and differential

(Skin tests, see 86485-86580 and 95010-95199)

89321   sperm presence and motility of sperm, if performed

►(To report Hyaluronan binding assay [HBA], use 89398)◄

89322   volume, count, motility, and differential using strict morphologic criteria (eg, Kruger)

89325   Sperm antibodies

(For medicolegal identification of sperm, use 88125)

89329   Sperm evaluation; hamster penetration test

89330   cervical mucus penetration test, with or without spinnbarkeit test

89331   Sperm evaluation, for retrograde ejaculation, urine (sperm concentration, motility, and morphology, as indicated)

(For semen analysis on concurrent semen specimen, see 89300-89322 in conjunction with 89331)

(For detection of sperm in urine, use 81015)

89335   Cryopreservation, reproductive tissue, testicular

(For cryopreservation of embryo[s], use 89258. For cryopreservation of sperm, use 89259)

►(For cryopreservation, ovarian reproductive tissue, oocytes, use 89240)◄

89342   Storage (per year); embryo(s)

89343   sperm/semen

89344   reproductive tissue, testicular/ovarian

89346   oocyte(s)

89352   Thawing of cryopreserved; embryo(s)

89353   sperm/semen, each aliquot

89354   reproductive tissue, testicular/ovarian

89356   oocytes, each aliquot

● **89398**   Unlisted reproductive medicine laboratory procedure

Pathology and Laboratory

Notes

Medicine Guidelines

In addition to the definitions and commonly used terms presented in the **Introduction**, several other items unique to this section on **Medicine** are defined or identified here.

Multiple Procedures

It is appropriate to designate multiple procedures that are rendered on the same date by separate entries. For example: If individual medical psychotherapy (90829) is rendered in addition to subsequent hospital care (eg, 99231), the psychotherapy would be reported separately from the hospital visit. In this instance, both 99231 and 90829 would be reported.

Add-on Codes

Some of the listed procedures are commonly carried out in addition to the primary procedure performed. All add-on codes found in the CPT codebook are exempt from the multiple procedure concept. They are exempt from the use of modifier 51, as these procedures are not reported as stand-alone codes. These additional or supplemental procedures are designated as "add-on" codes. Add-on codes in the CPT codebook can be readily identified by specific descriptor nomenclature which includes phrases such as "each additional" or "(List separately in addition to primary procedure)."

Separate Procedures

Some of the procedures or services listed in the CPT codebook that are commonly carried out as an integral component of a total service or procedure have been identified by the inclusion of the term "separate procedure." The codes designated as "separate procedure" should not be reported in addition to the code for the total procedure or service of which it is considered an integral component.

However, when a procedure or service that is designated as a "separate procedure" is carried out independently or considered to be unrelated or distinct from other procedures/services provided at that time, it may be reported by itself, or in addition to other procedures/services by appending modifier 59 to the specific "separate procedure" code to indicate that the procedure is not considered to be a component of

another procedure, but is a distinct, independent procedure. This may represent a different session or patient encounter, different procedure or surgery, different site or organ system, separate incision/excision, separate lesion, or separate injury (or area of injury in extensive injuries).

Unlisted Service or Procedure

A service or procedure may be provided that is not listed in this edition of the CPT codebook. When reporting such a service, the appropriate "Unlisted Procedure" code may be used to indicate the service, identifying it by "Special Report" as discussed on this page. The "Unlisted Procedures" and accompanying codes for **Medicine** are as follows:

90399	Unlisted immune globulin
90749	Unlisted vaccine/toxoid
90899	Unlisted psychiatric service or procedure
90999	Unlisted dialysis procedure, inpatient or outpatient
91299	Unlisted diagnostic gastroenterology procedure
92499	Unlisted ophthalmological service or procedure
92700	Unlisted otorhinolaryngological service or procedure
93799	Unlisted cardiovascular service or procedure
94799	Unlisted pulmonary service or procedure
95199	Unlisted allergy/clinical immunologic service or procedure
95999	Unlisted neurological or neuromuscular diagnostic procedure
96379	Unlisted therapeutic, prophylactic, or diagnostic intravenous or intra-arterial injection or infusion
96549	Unlisted chemotherapy procedure
96999	Unlisted special dermatological service or procedure
97039	Unlisted modality (specify type and time if constant attendance)
97139	Unlisted therapeutic procedure (specify)
97799	Unlisted physical medicine/rehabilitation service or procedure
99199	Unlisted special service, procedure or report
99600	Unlisted home visit service or procedure

Special Report

▶A service that is rarely provided, unusual, variable, or new may require a special report. Pertinent information should include an adequate definition or description of the nature, extent, and need for the procedure; and the time, effort, and equipment necessary to provide the service.◀

Materials Supplied by Physician

Supplies and materials provided by the physician (eg, sterile trays/drugs), over and above those usually included with the procedure(s) rendered are reported separately. List drugs, trays, supplies, and materials provided. Identify as 99070 or specific supply code.

Medicine

►Immune Globulins, Serum or Recombinant Products◄

►Codes 90281-90399 identify the serum globulins, extracted from human blood; or recombinant immune globulin products created in a laboratory through genetic modification of human and/or animal proteins. Both are reported in addition to the administration codes 96365-96368, 96372, 96374, 96375 as appropriate. Modifier 51 should not be reported with this section of products codes when performed with another procedure. The serum or recombinant globulin products listed here include broad-spectrum anti-infective immune globulins, antitoxins, various isoantibodies, and monoclonal antibodies.◄

90281 Immune globulin (Ig), human, for intramuscular use

90283 Immune globulin (IgIV), human, for intravenous use

90284 Immune globulin (SCIg), human, for use in subcutaneous infusions, 100 mg, each

90287 Botulinum antitoxin, equine, any route

90288 Botulism immune globulin, human, for intravenous use

90291 Cytomegalovirus immune globulin (CMV-IgIV), human, for intravenous use

90296 Diphtheria antitoxin, equine, any route

90371 Hepatitis B immune globulin (HBIg), human, for intramuscular use

90375 Rabies immune globulin (RIg), human, for intramuscular and/or subcutaneous use

90376 Rabies immune globulin, heat-treated (RIg-HT), human, for intramuscular and/or subcutaneous use

▲ **90378** Respiratory syncytial virus, monoclonal antibody, recombinant, for intramuscular use, 50 mg, each

►(90379 has been deleted)◄

90384 Rho(D) immune globulin (RhIg), human, full-dose, for intramuscular use

90385 Rho(D) immune globulin (RhIg), human, mini-dose, for intramuscular use

90386 Rho(D) immune globulin (RhIgIV), human, for intravenous use

90389 Tetanus immune globulin (TIg), human, for intramuscular use

90393 Vaccinia immune globulin, human, for intramuscular use

90396 Varicella-zoster immune globulin, human, for intramuscular use

90399 Unlisted immune globulin

Immunization Administration for Vaccines/Toxoids

Codes 90465-90474 must be reported in addition to the vaccine and toxoid code(s) 90476-90749.

Report codes 90465-90468 only when the physician provides face-to-face counseling of the patient and family during the administration of a vaccine. For immunization administration of any vaccine that is not accompanied by face-to-face physician counseling to the patient/family, report codes 90471-90474.

If a significant separately identifiable Evaluation and Management service (eg, office or other outpatient services, preventive medicine services) is performed, the appropriate E/M service code should be reported in addition to the vaccine and toxoid administration codes.

(For allergy testing, see 95004 et seq)

(For skin testing of bacterial, viral, fungal extracts, see 86485-86580)

(For therapeutic or diagnostic injections, see 96372-96379)

90465 Immunization administration younger than 8 years of age (includes percutaneous, intradermal, subcutaneous, or intramuscular injections) when the physician counsels the patient/family; first injection (single or combination vaccine/toxoid), per day

(Do not report 90465 in conjunction with 90467)

+ **90466** each additional injection (single or combination vaccine/toxoid), per day (List separately in addition to code for primary procedure)

(Use 90466 in conjunction with 90465 or 90467)

90467 Immunization administration younger than age 8 years (includes intranasal or oral routes of administration) when the physician counsels the patient/family; first administration (single or combination vaccine/toxoid), per day

(Do not report 90467 in conjunction with 90465)

+ **90468** each additional administration (single or combination vaccine/toxoid), per day (List separately in addition to code for primary procedure)

(Use 90468 in conjunction with 90465 or 90467)

90471 Immunization administration (includes percutaneous, intradermal, subcutaneous, or intramuscular injections); 1 vaccine (single or combination vaccine/toxoid)

(Do not report 90471 in conjunction with 90473)

Medicine

+ 90472   each additional vaccine (single or combination vaccine/toxoid) (List separately in addition to code for primary procedure)

(Use 90472 in conjunction with 90471 or 90473)

(For administration of immune globulins, see 90281-90399, 96360, 96361, 96365-96368, 96374)

(For intravesical administration of BCG vaccine, see 51720, 90586)

90473   Immunization administration by intranasal or oral route; 1 vaccine (single or combination vaccine/toxoid)

(Do not report 90473 in conjunction with 90471)

+ 90474   each additional vaccine (single or combination vaccine/toxoid) (List separately in addition to code for primary procedure)

(Use 90474 in conjunction with 90471 or 90473)

Vaccines, Toxoids

To assist users to report the most recent new or revised vaccine product codes, the American Medical Association (AMA) currently uses the CPT Website, which features updates of CPT Editorial Panel actions regarding these products. Once approved by the CPT Editorial Panel, these codes will be made available for release on a semi-annual (twice a year: July 1 and January 1) basis. As part of the electronic distribution, there is a six-month implementation period from the initial release date (ie, codes released on January 1 are eligible for use on July 1 and codes released on July 1 are eligible for use January 1).

The CPT Editorial Panel, in recognition of the public health interest in vaccine products, has chosen to publish new vaccine product codes prior to approval by the U. S. Food and Drug Administration (FDA). These codes are indicated with the ✗ symbol and will be tracked by the AMA to monitor FDA approval status. Once the FDA status changes to approval, the ✗ symbol will be removed. CPT users should refer to the AMA Internet site (www.ama-assn.org/ama/pub/category/10902.html) for the most up-to-date information on codes with the ✗ symbol.

Codes 90476-90748 identify the vaccine product **only.** To report the administration of a vaccine/toxoid, the vaccine/toxoid product codes 90476-90749 must be used in addition to an immunization administration code(s) 90465-90474. Modifier 51 should not be reported for the vaccines, toxoids when performed with these administration procedures.

If a significantly separately identifiable Evaluation and Management (E/M) service (eg, office or other outpatient services, preventive medicine services) is performed, the appropriate E/M service code should be reported in addition to the vaccine and toxoid administration codes.

To meet the reporting requirements of immunization registries, vaccine distribution programs, and reporting systems (eg, Vaccine Adverse Event Reporting System) the exact vaccine product administered needs to be reported. Multiple codes for a particular vaccine are provided in the CPT codebook when the schedule (number of doses or timing) differs for two or more products of the same vaccine type (eg, hepatitis A, Hib) or the vaccine product is available in more than one chemical formulation, dosage, or route of administration.

▶The "when administered to" age descriptions included in CPT vaccine codes are not intended to identify a product's licensed age indication. The term "preservative free" includes use for vaccines that contain no preservative and vaccines that contain trace amounts of preservative agents that are not present in a sufficient concentration for the purpose of preserving the final vaccine formulation. The absence of a designation regarding a preservative does not necessarily indicate the presence or absence of preservative in the vaccine. Refer to the product's prescribing information (PI) for the licensed age indication before administering vaccine to a patient.◀

Separate codes are available for combination vaccines (eg, DTP-Hib, DtaP-Hib, HepB-Hib). It is inappropriate to code each component of a combination vaccine separately. If a specific vaccine code is not available, the unlisted procedure code should be reported, until a new code becomes available.

(For immune globulins, see codes 90281-90399, 96365-96368, 96372-96375 for administration of immune globulins)

90476   Adenovirus vaccine, type 4, live, for oral use

90477   Adenovirus vaccine, type 7, live, for oral use

90581   Anthrax vaccine, for subcutaneous use

90585   Bacillus Calmette-Guerin vaccine (BCG) for tuberculosis, live, for percutaneous use

90586   Bacillus Calmette-Guerin vaccine (BCG) for bladder cancer, live, for intravesical use

90632   Hepatitis A vaccine, adult dosage, for intramuscular use

90633   Hepatitis A vaccine, pediatric/adolescent dosage-2 dose schedule, for intramuscular use

90634   Hepatitis A vaccine, pediatric/adolescent dosage-3 dose schedule, for intramuscular use

90636   Hepatitis A and hepatitis B vaccine (HepA-HepB), adult dosage, for intramuscular use

90645   Hemophilus influenza b vaccine (Hib), HbOC conjugate (4 dose schedule), for intramuscular use

90646   Hemophilus influenza b vaccine (Hib), PRP-D conjugate, for booster use only, intramuscular use

90647   Hemophilus influenza b vaccine (Hib), PRP-OMP conjugate (3 dose schedule), for intramuscular use

90648   Hemophilus influenza b vaccine (Hib), PRP-T conjugate (4 dose schedule), for intramuscular use

90649   Human Papilloma virus (HPV) vaccine, types 6, 11, 16, 18 (quadrivalent), 3 dose schedule, for intramuscular use

✗ **90650**   Human Papilloma virus (HPV) vaccine, types 16, 18, bivalent, 3 dose schedule, for intramuscular use

90655   Influenza virus vaccine, split virus, preservative free, when administered to children 6-35 months of age, for intramuscular use

90656   Influenza virus vaccine, split virus, preservative free, when administered to individuals 3 years and older, for intramuscular use

90657   Influenza virus vaccine, split virus, when administered to children 6-35 months of age, for intramuscular use

90658   Influenza virus vaccine, split virus, when administered to individuals 3 years of age and older, for intramuscular use

90660   Influenza virus vaccine, live, for intranasal use

✗ **90661**   Influenza virus vaccine, derived from cell cultures, subunit, preservative and antibiotic free, for intramuscular use

✗ **90662**   Influenza virus vaccine, split virus, preservative free, enhanced immunogenicity via increased antigen content, for intramuscular use

✗ **90663**   Influenza virus vaccine, pandemic formulation

90665   Lyme disease vaccine, adult dosage, for intramuscular use

▲ **90669**   Pneumococcal conjugate vaccine, 7 valent, for intramuscular use

✗● **90670** Pneumococcal conjugate vaccine, 13 valent, for intramuscular use

90675   Rabies vaccine, for intramuscular use

90676   Rabies vaccine, for intradermal use

90680   Rotavirus vaccine, pentavalent, 3 dose schedule, live, for oral use

90681   Rotavirus vaccine, human, attenuated, 2 dose schedule, live, for oral use

90690   Typhoid vaccine, live, oral

90691   Typhoid vaccine, Vi capsular polysaccharide (ViCPs), for intramuscular use

90692   Typhoid vaccine, heat- and phenol-inactivated (H-P), for subcutaneous or intradermal use

90693   Typhoid vaccine, acetone-killed, dried (AKD), for subcutaneous use (U.S. military)

90696   Diphtheria, tetanus toxoids, acellular pertussis vaccine and poliovirus vaccine, inactivated (DTaP-IPV), when administered to children 4 through 6 years of age, for intramuscular use

90698   Diphtheria, tetanus toxoids, acellular pertussis vaccine, haemophilus influenza Type B, and poliovirus vaccine, inactivated (DTaP - Hib - IPV), for intramuscular use

90700   Diphtheria, tetanus toxoids, and acellular pertussis vaccine (DTaP), when administered to individuals younger than 7 years, for intramuscular use

90701   Diphtheria, tetanus toxoids, and whole cell pertussis vaccine (DTP), for intramuscular use

90702   Diphtheria and tetanus toxoids (DT) adsorbed when administered to individuals younger than 7 years, for intramuscular use

90703   Tetanus toxoid adsorbed, for intramuscular use

90704   Mumps virus vaccine, live, for subcutaneous use

90705   Measles virus vaccine, live, for subcutaneous use

90706   Rubella virus vaccine, live, for subcutaneous use

90707   Measles, mumps and rubella virus vaccine (MMR), live, for subcutaneous use

90708   Measles and rubella virus vaccine, live, for subcutaneous use

90710   Measles, mumps, rubella, and varicella vaccine (MMRV), live, for subcutaneous use

90712   Poliovirus vaccine, (any type[s]) (OPV), live, for oral use

90713   Poliovirus vaccine, inactivated (IPV), for subcutaneous or intramuscular use

90714   Tetanus and diphtheria toxoids (Td) adsorbed, preservative free, when administered to individuals 7 years or older, for intramuscular use

90715   Tetanus, diphtheria toxoids and acellular pertussis vaccine (Tdap), when administered to individuals 7 years or older, for intramuscular use

90716   Varicella virus vaccine, live, for subcutaneous use

90717   Yellow fever vaccine, live, for subcutaneous use

90718   Tetanus and diphtheria toxoids (Td) adsorbed when administered to individuals 7 years or older, for intramuscular use

90719   Diphtheria toxoid, for intramuscular use

90720   Diphtheria, tetanus toxoids, and whole cell pertussis vaccine and Hemophilus influenza B vaccine (DTP-Hib), for intramuscular use

90721   Diphtheria, tetanus toxoids, and acellular pertussis vaccine and Hemophilus influenza B vaccine (DtaP-Hib), for intramuscular use

90723   Diphtheria, tetanus toxoids, acellular pertussis vaccine, Hepatitis B, and poliovirus vaccine, inactivated (DtaP-HepB-IPV), for intramuscular use

90725   Cholera vaccine for injectable use

90727   Plague vaccine, for intramuscular use

Medicine

90732   Pneumococcal polysaccharide vaccine, 23-valent, adult or immunosuppressed patient dosage, when administered to individuals 2 years or older, for subcutaneous or intramuscular use

90733   Meningococcal polysaccharide vaccine (any group(s)), for subcutaneous use

90734   Meningococcal conjugate vaccine, serogroups A, C, Y and W-135 (tetravalent), for intramuscular use

90735   Japanese encephalitis virus vaccine, for subcutaneous use

90736   Zoster (shingles) vaccine, live, for subcutaneous injection

▲ **90738**   Japanese encephalitis virus vaccine, inactivated, for intramuscular use

90740   Hepatitis B vaccine, dialysis or immunosuppressed patient dosage (3 dose schedule), for intramuscular use

90743   Hepatitis B vaccine, adolescent (2 dose schedule), for intramuscular use

90744   Hepatitis B vaccine, pediatric/adolescent dosage (3 dose schedule), for intramuscular use

90746   Hepatitis B vaccine, adult dosage, for intramuscular use

90747   Hepatitis B vaccine, dialysis or immunosuppressed patient dosage (4 dose schedule), for intramuscular use

90748   Hepatitis B and Hemophilus influenza b vaccine (HepB-Hib), for intramuscular use

90749   Unlisted vaccine/toxoid

(90760 has been deleted. To report, use 96360)

(90761 has been deleted. To report, use 96361)

(90765 has been deleted. To report, use 96365)

(90766 has been deleted. To report, use 96366)

(90767 has been deleted. To report, use 96367)

(90768 has been deleted. To report, use 96368)

(90769 has been deleted. To report, use 96369)

(90770 has been deleted. To report, use 96370)

(90771 has been deleted. To report, use 96371)

(90772 has been deleted. To report, use 96372)

(90773 has been deleted. To report, use 96373)

(90774 has been deleted. To report, use 96374)

(90775 has been deleted. To report, use 96375)

(90776 has been deleted. To report, use 96376)

(90779 has been deleted. To report, use 96379)

Psychiatry

Hospital care by the attending physician in treating a psychiatric inpatient or partial hospitalization may be initial or subsequent in nature (see 99221-99233) and may include exchanges with nursing and ancillary personnel. Hospital care services involve a variety of responsibilities unique to the medical management of inpatients, such as physician hospital orders, interpretation of laboratory or other medical diagnostic studies and observations.

Some patients receive hospital evaluation and management services only and others receive evaluation and management services and other procedures. If other procedures such as electroconvulsive therapy or psychotherapy are rendered in addition to hospital evaluation and management services, these should be listed separately (ie, hospital care service plus electroconvulsive therapy or when psychotherapy is done, an appropriate code defining psychotherapy with medical evaluation and management services). Modifier 22 may be used to indicate a more extensive service. Modifier 52 may be used to signify a service that is reduced or less extensive than the usual procedure.

Other evaluation and management services, such as office medical service or other patient encounters, may be described as listed in the section on **Evaluation and Management,** if appropriate.

The evaluation and management services should not be reported separately, when reporting codes 90805, 90807, 90809, 90811, 90813, 90815, 90817, 90819, 90822, 90824, 90827, 90829.

Consultation for psychiatric evaluation of a patient includes examination of a patient and exchange of information with the primary physician and other informants such as nurses or family members, and preparation of a report. These consultation services (99241-99255) are limited to initial or follow-up evaluation and do not involve psychiatric treatment.

Psychiatric Diagnostic or Evaluative Interview Procedures

Psychiatric diagnostic interview examination includes a history, mental status, and a disposition, and may include communication with family or other sources, ordering and medical interpretation of laboratory or other medical diagnostic studies. In certain circumstances other informants will be seen in lieu of the patient.

Interactive psychiatric diagnostic interview examination is typically furnished to children. It involves the use of physical aids and non-verbal communication to overcome barriers to therapeutic interaction between the clinician and a patient who has not yet developed, or has lost, either the expressive language communication skills to explain his/her symptoms and response to treatment, or the receptive communication skills to understand the clinician if he/she were to use ordinary adult language for communication.

90801   Psychiatric diagnostic interview examination

90802   Interactive psychiatric diagnostic interview examination using play equipment, physical devices, language interpreter, or other mechanisms of communication

Psychiatric Therapeutic Procedures

Psychotherapy is the treatment for mental illness and behavioral disturbances in which the clinician establishes a professional contract with the patient and, through definitive therapeutic communication, attempts to alleviate the emotional disturbances, reverse or change maladaptive patterns of behavior, and encourage personality growth and development. The codes for reporting psychotherapy are divided into two broad categories: Interactive Psychotherapy; and Insight Oriented, Behavior Modifying and/or Supportive Psychotherapy.

Interactive psychotherapy is typically furnished to children. It involves the use of physical aids and non-verbal communication to overcome barriers to therapeutic interaction between the clinician and a patient who has not yet developed, or has lost, either the expressive language communication skills to explain his/her symptoms and response to treatment, or the receptive communication skills to understand the clinician if he/she were to use ordinary adult language for communication.

Insight oriented, behavior modifying and/or supportive psychotherapy refers to the development of insight or affective understanding, the use of behavior modification techniques, the use of supportive interactions, the use of cognitive discussion of reality, or any combination of the above to provide therapeutic change.

Some patients receive psychotherapy only and others receive psychotherapy and medical evaluation and management services. These evaluation and management services involve a variety of responsibilities unique to the medical management of psychiatric patients, such as medical diagnostic evaluation (eg, evaluation of comorbid medical conditions, drug interactions, and physical examinations), drug management when indicated, physician orders, interpretation of laboratory or other medical diagnostic studies and observations.

In reporting psychotherapy, the appropriate code is chosen on the basis of the type of psychotherapy (interactive using non-verbal techniques versus insight oriented, behavior modifying and/or supportive using verbal techniques), the place of service (office versus inpatient), the face-to-face time spent with the patient during psychotherapy, and whether evaluation and management services are furnished on the same date of service as psychotherapy.

To report medical evaluation and management services furnished on a day when psychotherapy is not provided, select the appropriate code from the **Evaluation and Management Services Guidelines.**

Office or Other Outpatient Facility

Insight Oriented, Behavior Modifying and/or Supportive Psychotherapy

90804   Individual psychotherapy, insight oriented, behavior modifying and/or supportive, in an office or outpatient facility, approximately 20 to 30 minutes face-to-face with the patient;

90805   with medical evaluation and management services

90806   Individual psychotherapy, insight oriented, behavior modifying and/or supportive, in an office or outpatient facility, approximately 45 to 50 minutes face-to-face with the patient;

90807   with medical evaluation and management services

90808   Individual psychotherapy, insight oriented, behavior modifying and/or supportive, in an office or outpatient facility, approximately 75 to 80 minutes face-to-face with the patient;

90809   with medical evaluation and management services

Interactive Psychotherapy

90810   Individual psychotherapy, interactive, using play equipment, physical devices, language interpreter, or other mechanisms of non-verbal communication, in an office or outpatient facility, approximately 20 to 30 minutes face-to-face with the patient;

90811   with medical evaluation and management services

90812   Individual psychotherapy, interactive, using play equipment, physical devices, language interpreter, or other mechanisms of non-verbal communication, in an office or outpatient facility, approximately 45 to 50 minutes face-to-face with the patient;

90813   with medical evaluation and management services

90814   Individual psychotherapy, interactive, using play equipment, physical devices, language interpreter, or other mechanisms of non-verbal communication, in an office or outpatient facility, approximately 75 to 80 minutes face-to-face with the patient;

90815   with medical evaluation and management services

Medicine

Inpatient Hospital, Partial Hospital or Residential Care Facility

Insight Oriented, Behavior Modifying and/or Supportive Psychotherapy

90816   Individual psychotherapy, insight oriented, behavior modifying and/or supportive, in an inpatient hospital, partial hospital or residential care setting, approximately 20 to 30 minutes face-to-face with the patient;

90817   with medical evaluation and management services

90818   Individual psychotherapy, insight oriented, behavior modifying and/or supportive, in an inpatient hospital, partial hospital or residential care setting, approximately 45 to 50 minutes face-to-face with the patient;

90819   with medical evaluation and management services

90821   Individual psychotherapy, insight oriented, behavior modifying and/or supportive, in an inpatient hospital, partial hospital or residential care setting, approximately 75 to 80 minutes face-to-face with the patient;

90822   with medical evaluation and management services

Interactive Psychotherapy

90823   Individual psychotherapy, interactive, using play equipment, physical devices, language interpreter, or other mechanisms of non-verbal communication, in an inpatient hospital, partial hospital or residential care setting, approximately 20 to 30 minutes face-to-face with the patient;

90824   with medical evaluation and management services

90826   Individual psychotherapy, interactive, using play equipment, physical devices, language interpreter, or other mechanisms of non-verbal communication, in an inpatient hospital, partial hospital or residential care setting, approximately 45 to 50 minutes face-to-face with the patient;

90827   with medical evaluation and management services

90828   Individual psychotherapy, interactive, using play equipment, physical devices, language interpreter, or other mechanisms of non-verbal communication, in an inpatient hospital, partial hospital or residential care setting, approximately 75 to 80 minutes face-to-face with the patient;

90829   with medical evaluation and management services

Other Psychotherapy

90845   Psychoanalysis

90846   Family psychotherapy (without the patient present)

90847   Family psychotherapy (conjoint psychotherapy) (with patient present)

90849   Multiple-family group psychotherapy

90853   Group psychotherapy (other than of a multiple-family group)

90857   Interactive group psychotherapy

Other Psychiatric Services or Procedures

(For repetitive transcranial magnetic stimulation for treatment of clinical depression, see Category III codes 0160T, 0161T)

(For analysis/programming of neurostimulators used for vagus nerve stimulation therapy, see 95970, 95974, 95975)

90862   Pharmacologic management, including prescription, use, and review of medication with no more than minimal medical psychotherapy

90865   Narcosynthesis for psychiatric diagnostic and therapeutic purposes (eg, sodium amobarbital (Amytal) interview)

90870   Electroconvulsive therapy (includes necessary monitoring)

90875   Individual psychophysiological therapy incorporating biofeedback training by any modality (face-to-face with the patient), with psychotherapy (eg, insight oriented, behavior modifying or supportive psychotherapy); approximately 20-30 minutes

90876   approximately 45-50 minutes

90880   Hypnotherapy

90882   Environmental intervention for medical management purposes on a psychiatric patient's behalf with agencies, employers, or institutions

90885   Psychiatric evaluation of hospital records, other psychiatric reports, psychometric and/or projective tests, and other accumulated data for medical diagnostic purposes

90887   Interpretation or explanation of results of psychiatric, other medical examinations and procedures, or other accumulated data to family or other responsible persons, or advising them how to assist patient

90889   Preparation of report of patient's psychiatric status, history, treatment, or progress (other than for legal or consultative purposes) for other physicians, agencies, or insurance carriers

90899   Unlisted psychiatric service or procedure

Biofeedback

(For psychophysiological therapy incorporating biofeedback training, see 90875, 90876)

90901   Biofeedback training by any modality

90911   Biofeedback training, perineal muscles, anorectal or urethral sphincter, including EMG and/or manometry

(For testing of rectal sensation, tone and compliance, use 91120)

(For incontinence treatment by pulsed magnetic neuromodulation, use 53899)

Dialysis

(90918, 90922 have been deleted. To report ESRD-related services for patients younger than 2 years of age, see 90951-90953, 90963, 90967)

(90919, 90923 have been deleted. To report ESRD-related services for patients between 2 and 11 years of age, see 90954-90956, 90964, 90968)

(90920, 90924 have been deleted. To report ESRD-related services for patients between 12 and 19 years of age, see 90957-90959, 90965, 90969)

(90921, 90925 have been deleted. To report ESRD-related services for patients 20 years of age and older, see 90960-90962, 90966, 90970)

Hemodialysis

Codes 90935, 90937 are reported to describe the hemodialysis procedure with all evaluation and management services related to the patient's renal disease on the day of the hemodialysis procedure. These codes are used for inpatient ESRD and non-ESRD procedures or for outpatient non-ESRD dialysis services. Code 90935 is reported if only one evaluation of the patient is required related to that hemodialysis procedure. Code 90937 is reported when patient re-evaluation(s) is required during a hemodialysis procedure. Use modifier 25 with Evaluation and Management codes for separately identifiable services unrelated to the dialysis procedure or renal failure which cannot be rendered during the dialysis session.

(For home visit hemodialysis services performed by a non-physician health care professional, use 99512)

(For cannula declotting, see 36831, 36833, 36860, 36861)

(For declotting of implanted vascular access device or catheter by thrombolytic agent, use 36593)

(For collection of blood specimen from a partially or completely implantable venous access device, use 36591)

(For prolonged physician attendance, see 99354-99360)

90935   Hemodialysis procedure with single physician evaluation

90937   Hemodialysis procedure requiring repeated evaluation(s) with or without substantial revision of dialysis prescription

90940   Hemodialysis access flow study to determine blood flow in grafts and arteriovenous fistulae by an indicator method

(For duplex scan of hemodialysis access, use 93990)

Miscellaneous Dialysis Procedures

Codes 90945, 90947 describe dialysis procedures other than hemodialysis (eg, peritoneal dialysis, hemofiltration or continuous renal replacement therapies), and all evaluation and management services related to the patient's renal disease on the day of the procedure. Code 90945 is reported if only one evaluation of the patient is required related to that procedure. Code 90947 is reported when patient re-evaluation(s) is required during a procedure. Utilize modifier 25 with Evaluation and Management codes for separately identifiable services unrelated to the procedure or the renal failure which cannot be rendered during the dialysis session.

(For insertion of intraperitoneal cannula or catheter, see 49420, 49421)

(For prolonged physician attendance, see 99354-99360)

90945   Dialysis procedure other than hemodialysis (eg, peritoneal dialysis, hemofiltration, or other continuous renal replacement therapies), with single physician evaluation

(For home infusion of peritoneal dialysis, use 99601, 99602)

90947   Dialysis procedure other than hemodialysis (eg, peritoneal dialysis, hemofiltration, or other continuous renal replacement therapies) requiring repeated physician evaluations, with or without substantial revision of dialysis prescription

End-Stage Renal Disease Services

Codes 90951-90962 are reported **once** per month to distinguish age-specific services related to the patient's end-stage renal disease (ESRD) performed in an outpatient setting with three levels of service based on the number of face-to-face visits. ESRD-related physician services include establishment of a dialyzing cycle, outpatient evaluation and management of the dialysis visits, telephone calls, and patient management during the dialysis provided during a full month. In the circumstances where the patient has had a complete assessment visit during the month and services are provided over a period of less than a month, 90951-90962 may be used according to the number of visits performed.

Codes 90963-90966 are reported once per month for a full month of service to distinguish age-specific services for end-stage renal disease (ESRD) services for home dialysis patients.

For ESRD and non-ESRD dialysis services performed in an inpatient setting, and for non-ESRD dialysis services performed in an outpatient setting, see 90935-90937 and 90945-90947.

Evaluation and Management services unrelated to ESRD services that cannot be performed during the dialysis session may be reported separately.

Codes 90967-90970 are reported to distinguish age-specific services for end-stage renal disease (ESRD) services for less than a full month of service, per day, for services provided under the following circumstances: home dialysis patients less than a full month, transient patients, partial month where there was one or more face-to-face visits without the complete assessment, the patient was hospitalized before a complete assessment was furnished, dialysis was stopped due to recovery or death, or the patient received a kidney transplant. For reporting purposes, each month is considered 30 days.

Examples:

ESRD-related services:

ESRD-related services are initiated on July 1 for a 57-year-old male. On July 11, he is admitted to the hospital as an inpatient and is discharged on July 27. He has had a complete assessment and the physician has performed two face-to-face visits prior to admission. Another face-to-face visit occurs after discharge during the month.

In this example, 90961 is reported for the three face-to-face outpatient visits. Report inpatient E/M services as appropriate. Dialysis procedures rendered during the hospitalization (July 11-27) should be reported as appropriate (90935-90937, 90945-90947).

If the patient did not have a complete assessment during the month or was a transient or dialysis was stopped due to recovery or death, 90970 would be used to report each day outside the inpatient hospitalization as described in the home dialysis example below.

ESRD-related services for the home dialysis patient:

Home ESRD-related services are initiated on July 1 for a 57-year-old male. On July 11, he is admitted to the hospital as an inpatient and is discharged on July 27.

In this example, 90970 should be reported for each day outside of the inpatient hospitalization (30 days/month less 17 days/hospitalization = 13 days). Report inpatient E/M services as appropriate. Dialysis procedures rendered during the hospitalization (July 11-27) should be reported as appropriate (90935-90937, 90945-90947).

90951 End-stage renal disease (ESRD) related services monthly, for patients younger than 2 years of age to include monitoring for the adequacy of nutrition, assessment of growth and development, and counseling of parents; with 4 or more face-to-face physician visits per month

90952 with 2-3 face-to-face physician visits per month

90953 with 1 face-to-face physician visit per month

90954 End-stage renal disease (ESRD) related services monthly, for patients 2-11 years of age to include monitoring for the adequacy of nutrition, assessment of growth and development, and counseling of parents; with 4 or more face-to-face physician visits per month

90955 with 2-3 face-to-face physician visits per month

90956 with 1 face-to-face physician visit per month

90957 End-stage renal disease (ESRD) related services monthly, for patients 12-19 years of age to include monitoring for the adequacy of nutrition, assessment of growth and development, and counseling of parents; with 4 or more face-to-face physician visits per month

90958 with 2-3 face-to-face physician visits per month

90959 with 1 face-to-face physician visit per month

90960 End-stage renal disease (ESRD) related services monthly, for patients 20 years of age and older; with 4 or more face-to-face physician visits per month

90961 with 2-3 face-to-face physician visits per month

90962 with 1 face-to-face physician visit per month

90963 End-stage renal disease (ESRD) related services for home dialysis per full month, for patients younger than 2 years of age to include monitoring for the adequacy of nutrition, assessment of growth and development, and counseling of parents

90964 End-stage renal disease (ESRD) related services for home dialysis per full month, for patients 2-11 years of age to include monitoring for the adequacy of nutrition, assessment of growth and development, and counseling of parents

90965 End-stage renal disease (ESRD) related services for home dialysis per full month, for patients 12-19 years of age to include monitoring for the adequacy of nutrition, assessment of growth and development, and counseling of parents

90966 End-stage renal disease (ESRD) related services for home dialysis per full month, for patients 20 years of age and older

90967 End-stage renal disease (ESRD) related services for dialysis less than a full month of service, per day; for patients younger than 2 years of age

90968 for patients 2-11 years of age

90969 for patients 12-19 years of age

90970 for patients 20 years of age and older

Other Dialysis Procedures

90989 Dialysis training, patient, including helper where applicable, any mode, completed course

90993 Dialysis training, patient, including helper where applicable, any mode, course not completed, per training session

90997 Hemoperfusion (eg, with activated charcoal or resin)

90999 Unlisted dialysis procedure, inpatient or outpatient

Gastroenterology

(For duodenal intubation and aspiration, see 89100-89105)

(For gastrointestinal radiologic procedures, see 74210-74363)

(For esophagoscopy procedures, see 43200-43228; upper GI endoscopy 43234-43259; endoscopy, small intestine and stomal 44360-44393; proctosigmoidoscopy 45300-45321; sigmoidoscopy 45330-45339; colonoscopy 45355-45385; anoscopy 46600-46615)

91000 Esophageal intubation and collection of washings for cytology, including preparation of specimens (separate procedure)

91010 Esophageal motility (manometric study of the esophagus and/or gastroesophageal junction) study;

91011   with mecholyl or similar stimulant

91012   with acid perfusion studies

91020 Gastric motility (manometric) studies

91022 Duodenal motility (manometric) study

(If gastrointestinal endoscopy is performed, use 43235)

(If fluoroscopy is performed, use 76000)

(If gastric motility study is performed, use 91020)

91030 Esophagus, acid perfusion (Bernstein) test for esophagitis

91034 Esophagus, gastroesophageal reflux test; with nasal catheter pH electrode(s) placement, recording, analysis and interpretation

91035   with mucosal attached telemetry pH electrode placement, recording, analysis and interpretation

91037 Esophageal function test, gastroesophageal reflux test with nasal catheter intraluminal impedance electrode(s) placement, recording, analysis and interpretation;

91038   prolonged (greater than 1 hour, up to 24 hours)

91040 Esophageal balloon distension provocation study

(For balloon dilatation with endoscopy, see 43220, 43249, 43456, or 43458)

91052 Gastric analysis test with injection of stimulant of gastric secretion (eg, histamine, insulin, pentagastrin, calcium and secretin)

(For gastric biopsy by capsule, peroral, via tube, 1 or more specimens, use 43600)

(For gastric laboratory procedures, see also 89130-89141)

91055 Gastric intubation, washings, and preparing slides for cytology (separate procedure)

(For gastric lavage, therapeutic, use 91105)

(For biopsy by capsule, small intestine, per oral, via tube [1 or more specimens], use 44100)

91065 Breath hydrogen test (eg, for detection of lactase deficiency, fructose intolerance, bacterial overgrowth, or oro-cecal gastrointestinal transit)

(For H. pylori breath test analysis, use 83013 for non-radioactive (C-13) isotope or 78268 for radioactive (C-14) isotope)

(91100 has been deleted)

(To report placement of an esophageal tamponade tube for management of variceal bleeding, use 43460. To report placement of a long intestinal Miller-Abbott tube, use 44500)

91105 Gastric intubation, and aspiration or lavage for treatment (eg, for ingested poisons)

(For cholangiography, see 47500, 74320)

(For abdominal paracentesis, see 49080, 49081; with instillation of medication, see 96440, 96445)

(For peritoneoscopy, use 49320; with biopsy, use 49321)

(For peritoneoscopy and guided transhepatic cholangiography, use 47560; with biopsy, use 47561)

(For splenoportography, see 38200, 75810)

91110 Gastrointestinal tract imaging, intraluminal (eg, capsule endoscopy), esophagus through ileum, with physician interpretation and report

(Visualization of the colon is not reported separately)

(Append modifier 52 if the ileum is not visualized)

91111 Gastrointestinal tract imaging, intraluminal (eg, capsule endoscopy), esophagus with physician interpretation and report

(Do not report 91111 in conjunction with 91110)

91120 Rectal sensation, tone, and compliance test (ie, response to graded balloon distention)

(For biofeedback training, use 90911)

(For anorectal manometry, use 91122)

91122 Anorectal manometry

91123 Pulsed irrigation of fecal impaction

Gastric Physiology

91132 Electrogastrography, diagnostic, transcutaneous;

91133   with provocative testing

Other Procedures

91299 Unlisted diagnostic gastroenterology procedure

Medicine

Ophthalmology

(For surgical procedures, see **Surgery,** Eye and Ocular Adnexa, 65091 et seq)

Definitions

Intermediate ophthalmological services describes an evaluation of a new or existing condition complicated with a new diagnostic or management problem not necessarily relating to the primary diagnosis, including history, general medical observation, external ocular and adnexal examination and other diagnostic procedures as indicated; may include the use of mydriasis for ophthalmoscopy.

For example:

a. Review of history, external examination, ophthalmoscopy, biomicroscopy for an acute complicated condition (eg, iritis) not requiring comprehensive ophthalmological services.

b. Review of interval history, external examination, ophthalmoscopy, biomicroscopy and tonometry in established patient with known cataract not requiring comprehensive ophthalmological services.

Comprehensive ophthalmological services describes a general evaluation of the complete visual system. The comprehensive services constitute a single service entity but need not be performed at one session. The service includes history, general medical observation, external and ophthalmoscopic examinations, gross visual fields and basic sensorimotor examination. It often includes, as indicated: biomicroscopy, examination with cycloplegia or mydriasis and tonometry. It always includes initiation of diagnostic and treatment programs.

Intermediate and comprehensive ophthalmological services constitute integrated services in which medical decision making cannot be separated from the examining techniques used. Itemization of service components, such as slit lamp examination, keratometry, routine ophthalmoscopy, retinoscopy, tonometry, or motor evaluation is not applicable.

For example:

The comprehensive services required for diagnosis and treatment of a patient with symptoms indicating possible disease of the visual system, such as glaucoma, cataract or retinal disease, or to rule out disease of the visual system, new or established patient.

Initiation of diagnostic and treatment program includes the prescription of medication, and arranging for special ophthalmological diagnostic or treatment services, consultations, laboratory procedures and radiological services.

Special ophthalmological services describes services in which a special evaluation of part of the visual system is made, which goes beyond the services included under general ophthalmological services, or in which special treatment is given. Special ophthalmological services may be reported in addition to the general ophthalmological services or evaluation and management services.

For example:

Fluorescein angioscopy, quantitative visual field examination, refraction or extended color vision examination (such as Nagel's anomaloscope) should be separately reported.

Prescription of lenses, when required, is included in 92015. It includes specification of lens type (monofocal, bifocal, other), lens power, axis, prism, absorptive factor, impact resistance, and other factors.

Interpretation and report by the physician is an integral part of special ophthalmological services where indicated. Technical procedures (which may or may not be performed by the physician personally) are often part of the service, but should not be mistaken to constitute the service itself.

General Ophthalmological Services

New Patient

Solely for the purposes of distinguishing between new and established patients, **professional services** are those face-to-face services rendered by a physician and reported by a specific code(s). A new patient is one who has not received any professional services from the physician or another physician of the same specialty who belongs to the same group practice within the past three years.

92002   Ophthalmological services: medical examination and evaluation with initiation of diagnostic and treatment program; intermediate, new patient

92004   comprehensive, new patient, 1 or more visits

Established Patient

Solely for the purposes of distinguishing between new and established patients, **professional services** are those face-to-face services rendered by a physician and reported by a specific code(s). An established patient is one who has received professional services from the physician or another physician of the same specialty who belongs to the same group practice within the past three years.

92012   Ophthalmological services: medical examination and evaluation, with initiation or continuation of diagnostic and treatment program; intermediate, established patient

92014   comprehensive, established patient, 1 or more visits

(For surgical procedures, see **Surgery,** Eye and Ocular Adnexa, 65091 et seq)

Medicine

Special Ophthalmological Services

92015   Determination of refractive state

92018   Ophthalmological examination and evaluation, under general anesthesia, with or without manipulation of globe for passive range of motion or other manipulation to facilitate diagnostic examination; complete

92019   limited

92020   Gonioscopy (separate procedure)

(For gonioscopy under general anesthesia, use 92018)

92025   Computerized corneal topography, unilateral or bilateral, with interpretation and report

(Do not report 92025 in conjunction with 65710-65771)

(92025 is not used for manual keratoscopy, which is part of a single system Evaluation and Management or ophthalmological service)

92060   Sensorimotor examination with multiple measurements of ocular deviation (eg, restrictive or paretic muscle with diplopia) with interpretation and report (separate procedure)

92065   Orthoptic and/or pleoptic training, with continuing medical direction and evaluation

92070   Fitting of contact lens for treatment of disease, including supply of lens

92081   Visual field examination, unilateral or bilateral, with interpretation and report; limited examination (eg, tangent screen, Autoplot, arc perimeter, or single stimulus level automated test, such as Octopus 3 or 7 equivalent)

92082   intermediate examination (eg, at least 2 isopters on Goldmann perimeter, or semiquantitative, automated suprathreshold screening program, Humphrey suprathreshold automatic diagnostic test, Octopus program 33)

92083   extended examination (eg, Goldmann visual fields with at least 3 isopters plotted and static determination within the central 30°, or quantitative, automated threshold perimetry, Octopus program G-1, 32 or 42, Humphrey visual field analyzer full threshold programs 30-2, 24-2, or 30/60-2)

(Gross visual field testing (eg, confrontation testing) is a part of general ophthalmological services and is not reported separately)

92100   Serial tonometry (separate procedure) with multiple measurements of intraocular pressure over an extended time period with interpretation and report, same day (eg, diurnal curve or medical treatment of acute elevation of intraocular pressure)

92120   Tonography with interpretation and report, recording indentation tonometer method or perilimbal suction method

▶(For measurement of ocular blood flow, use Category III code 0198T)◀

92130   Tonography with water provocation

92135   Scanning computerized ophthalmic diagnostic imaging, posterior segment, (eg, scanning laser) with interpretation and report, unilateral

92136   Ophthalmic biometry by partial coherence interferometry with intraocular lens power calculation

92140   Provocative tests for glaucoma, with interpretation and report, without tonography

Ophthalmoscopy

Routine ophthalmoscopy is part of general and special ophthalmologic services whenever indicated. It is a non-itemized service and is not reported separately.

92225   Ophthalmoscopy, extended, with retinal drawing (eg, for retinal detachment, melanoma), with interpretation and report; initial

92226   subsequent

92230   Fluorescein angioscopy with interpretation and report

92235   Fluorescein angiography (includes multiframe imaging) with interpretation and report

92240   Indocyanine-green angiography (includes multiframe imaging) with interpretation and report

92250   Fundus photography with interpretation and report

92260   Ophthalmodynamometry

(For ophthalmoscopy under general anesthesia, use 92018)

Other Specialized Services

92265   Needle oculoelectromyography, 1 or more extraocular muscles, 1 or both eyes, with interpretation and report

92270   Electro-oculography with interpretation and report

92275   Electroretinography with interpretation and report

(For electronystagmography for vestibular function studies, see 92541 et seq)

(For ophthalmic echography (diagnostic ultrasound), see 76511-76529)

92283   Color vision examination, extended, eg, anomaloscope or equivalent

(Color vision testing with pseudoisochromatic plates [such as HRR or Ishihara] is not reported separately. It is included in the appropriate general or ophthalmological service, or 99172)

92284   Dark adaptation examination with interpretation and report

92285   External ocular photography with interpretation and report for documentation of medical progress (eg, close-up photography, slit lamp photography, goniophotography, stereo-photography)

Medicine

92286   Special anterior segment photography with interpretation and report; with specular endothelial microscopy and cell count

92287   with fluorescein angiography

Contact Lens Services

The prescription of contact lens includes specification of optical and physical characteristics (such as power, size, curvature, flexibility, gas-permeability). It is NOT a part of the general ophthalmological services.

The fitting of contact lens includes instruction and training of the wearer and incidental revision of the lens during the training period.

Follow-up of successfully fitted extended wear lenses is reported as part of a general ophthalmological service (92012 et seq).

The supply of contact lenses may be reported as part of the service of fitting. It may also be reported separately by using the appropriate supply codes.

(For therapeutic or surgical use of contact lens, see 68340, 92070)

92310   Prescription of optical and physical characteristics of and fitting of contact lens, with medical supervision of adaptation; corneal lens, both eyes, except for aphakia

(For prescription and fitting of 1 eye, add modifier 52)

92311   corneal lens for aphakia, 1 eye

92312   corneal lens for aphakia, both eyes

92313   corneoscleral lens

92314   Prescription of optical and physical characteristics of contact lens, with medical supervision of adaptation and direction of fitting by independent technician; corneal lens, both eyes except for aphakia

(For prescription and fitting of 1 eye, add modifier 52)

92315   corneal lens for aphakia, 1 eye

92316   corneal lens for aphakia, both eyes

92317   corneoscleral lens

92325   Modification of contact lens (separate procedure), with medical supervision of adaptation

92326   Replacement of contact lens

(For prescription, fitting, and/or medical supervision of ocular prosthetic adaptation by a physician, see Evaluation and Management services or General Ophthalmological service codes 92002-92014)

Spectacle Services (Including Prosthesis for Aphakia)

Prescription of lenses, when required, is included in 92015 Determination of refractive state. It includes specification of lens type (monofocal, bifocal, other), lens power, axis, prism, absorptive factor, impact resistance, and other factors.

Fitting of spectacles is a separate service; when provided by the physician, it is reported as indicated by 92340-92371.

Fitting includes measurement of anatomical facial characteristics, the writing of laboratory specifications, and the final adjustment of the spectacles to the visual axes and anatomical topography. Presence of physician is not required.

Supply of materials is a separate service component; it is not part of the service of fitting spectacles.

92340   Fitting of spectacles, except for aphakia; monofocal

92341   bifocal

92342   multifocal, other than bifocal

92352   Fitting of spectacle prosthesis for aphakia; monofocal

92353   multifocal

92354   Fitting of spectacle mounted low vision aid; single element system

92355   telescopic or other compound lens system

92358   Prosthesis service for aphakia, temporary (disposable or loan, including materials)

92370   Repair and refitting spectacles; except for aphakia

92371   spectacle prosthesis for aphakia

Other Procedures

92499   Unlisted ophthalmological service or procedure

Special Otorhinolaryngologic Services

Diagnostic or treatment procedures that are reported as evaluation and management services (eg, otoscopy, anterior rhinoscopy, tuning fork test, removal of non-impacted cerumen) are not reported separately.

Special otorhinolaryngologic services are those diagnostic and treatment services not included in an Evaluation and Management service. These services are reported separately, using codes 92502-92700.

Code 92506 is used to report evaluation of speech production, receptive language, and expressive language abilities. Tests may examine speech sound production, articulatory movements of oral musculature, the patient's ability to understand the meaning and intent of written and verbal expressions, and the appropriate formulation and utterance of expressive thought. In contrast, 92626 and 92627 are reported for an evaluation of auditory rehabilitation status determining the patient's ability to use residual hearing in order to identify the acoustic characteristics of sounds associated with speech communication.

(For laryngoscopy with stroboscopy, use 31579)

92502   Otolaryngologic examination under general anesthesia

92504   Binocular microscopy (separate diagnostic procedure)

92506   Evaluation of speech, language, voice, communication, and/or auditory processing

92507   Treatment of speech, language, voice, communication, and/or auditory processing disorder; individual

92508   group, 2 or more individuals

(For auditory rehabilitation, prelingual hearing loss, use 92630)

(For auditory rehabilitation, postlingual hearing loss, use 92633)

(For cochlear implant programming, see 92601-92604)

92511   Nasopharyngoscopy with endoscope (separate procedure)

92512   Nasal function studies (eg, rhinomanometry)

92516   Facial nerve function studies (eg, electroneuronography)

92520   Laryngeal function studies (ie, aerodynamic testing and acoustic testing)

(For performance of a single test, use modifier 52)

(To report flexible fiberoptic laryngeal evaluation of swallowing and laryngeal sensory testing, see 92611-92617)

(To report other testing of laryngeal function (eg, electroglottography), use 92700)

92526   Treatment of swallowing dysfunction and/or oral function for feeding

Vestibular Function Tests, Without Electrical Recording

92531   Spontaneous nystagmus, including gaze

92532   Positional nystagmus test

(Do not report 92531, 92532 with evaluation and management services)

92533   Caloric vestibular test, each irrigation (binaural, bithermal stimulation constitutes 4 tests)

92534   Optokinetic nystagmus test

Vestibular Function Tests, With Recording (eg, ENG)

● **92540**   Basic vestibular evaluation, includes spontaneous nystagmus test with eccentric gaze fixation nystagmus, with recording, positional nystagmus test, minimum of 4 positions, with recording, optokinetic nystagmus test, bidirectional foveal and peripheral stimulation, with recording, and oscillating tracking test, with recording

►(Do not report 92540 in conjunction with 92541, 92542, 92544, or 92545)◄

92541   Spontaneous nystagmus test, including gaze and fixation nystagmus, with recording

►(Do not report 92541 in conjunction with 92542, 92544, 92545)◄

92542   Positional nystagmus test, minimum of 4 positions, with recording

►(Do not report 92542 in conjunction with 92541, 92544, 92545)◄

92543   Caloric vestibular test, each irrigation (binaural, bithermal stimulation constitutes 4 tests), with recording

92544   Optokinetic nystagmus test, bidirectional, foveal or peripheral stimulation, with recording

►(Do not report 92544 in conjunction with 92541, 92542, 92545)◄

92545   Oscillating tracking test, with recording

92546   Sinusoidal vertical axis rotational testing

+ **92547**   Use of vertical electrodes (List separately in addition to code for primary procedure)

(Use 92547 in conjunction with 92541-92546)

(For unlisted vestibular tests, use 92700)

92548   Computerized dynamic posturography

Audiologic Function Tests

The audiometric tests listed below require the use of calibrated electronic equipment, recording of results and a report with interpretation. Hearing tests (such as whispered voice, tuning fork) that are otorhinolaryngologic Evaluation and Management services are not reported separately. All services include testing of both ears. Use modifier 52 if a test is applied to one ear instead of two ears. All codes (except 92559) apply to testing of individuals. For testing of groups, use 92559 and specify test(s) used.

(For evaluation of speech, language and/or hearing problems through observation and assessment of performance, use 92506)

● **92550**   Tympanometry and reflex threshold measurements

►(Do not report 92550 in conjunction with 92567, 92568)◄

92551   Screening test, pure tone, air only

Medicine

92552   Pure tone audiometry (threshold); air only

92553   air and bone

92555   Speech audiometry threshold;

92556   with speech recognition

92557   Comprehensive audiometry threshold evaluation and speech recognition (92553 and 92556 combined)

(For hearing aid evaluation and selection, see 92590-92595)

92559   Audiometric testing of groups

92560   Bekesy audiometry; screening

92561   diagnostic

92562   Loudness balance test, alternate binaural or monaural

92563   Tone decay test

92564   Short increment sensitivity index (SISI)

92565   Stenger test, pure tone

92567   Tympanometry (impedance testing)

92568   Acoustic reflex testing, threshold

▶(92569 has been deleted. For acoustic reflex decay testing performed in conjunction with tympanometry, use 92570)◀

● 92570   Acoustic immittance testing, includes tympanometry (impedance testing), acoustic reflex threshold testing, and acoustic reflex decay testing

▶(Do not report 92570 in conjunction with 92567, 92568)◀

92571   Filtered speech test

92572   Staggered spondaic word test

92575   Sensorineural acuity level test

92576   Synthetic sentence identification test

92577   Stenger test, speech

92579   Visual reinforcement audiometry (VRA)

92582   Conditioning play audiometry

92583   Select picture audiometry

92584   Electrocochleography

92585   Auditory evoked potentials for evoked response audiometry and/or testing of the central nervous system; comprehensive

92586   limited

92587   Evoked otoacoustic emissions; limited (single stimulus level, either transient or distortion products)

92588   comprehensive or diagnostic evaluation (comparison of transient and/or distortion product otoacoustic emissions at multiple levels and frequencies)

(For central auditory function evaluation, see 92620, 92621)

92590   Hearing aid examination and selection; monaural

92591   binaural

92592   Hearing aid check; monaural

92593   binaural

92594   Electroacoustic evaluation for hearing aid; monaural

92595   binaural

92596   Ear protector attenuation measurements

92597   Evaluation for use and/or fitting of voice prosthetic device to supplement oral speech

(To report augmentative and alternative communication device services, see 92605, 92607, 92608)

Evaluative and Therapeutic Services

Codes 92601 and 92603 describe post-operative analysis and fitting of previously placed external devices, connection to the cochlear implant, and programming of the stimulator. Codes 92602 and 92604 describe subsequent sessions for measurements and adjustment of the external transmitter and re-programming of the internal stimulator.

(For placement of cochlear implant, use 69930)

92601   Diagnostic analysis of cochlear implant, patient younger than 7 years of age; with programming

92602   subsequent reprogramming

(Do not report 92602 in addition to 92601)

(For aural rehabilitation services following cochlear implant, including evaluation of rehabilitation status, see 92626-92627, 92630-92633)

92603   Diagnostic analysis of cochlear implant, age 7 years or older; with programming

92604   subsequent reprogramming

(Do not report 92604 in addition to 92603)

92605   Evaluation for prescription of non-speech-generating augmentative and alternative communication device

92606   Therapeutic service(s) for the use of non-speech-generating device, including programming and modification

92607   Evaluation for prescription for speech-generating augmentative and alternative communication device, face-to-face with the patient; first hour

(For evaluation for prescription of a non-speech-generating device, use 92605)

✚ 92608   each additional 30 minutes (List separately in addition to code for primary procedure)

(Use 92608 in conjunction with 92607)

92609   Therapeutic services for the use of speech-generating device, including programming and modification

(For therapeutic service(s) for the use of a non-speech-generating device, use 92606)

92610   Evaluation of oral and pharyngeal swallowing function

(For motion fluoroscopic evaluation of swallowing function, use 92611)

(For flexible endoscopic examination, use 92612-92617)

92611   Motion fluoroscopic evaluation of swallowing function by cine or video recording

(For radiological supervision and interpretation, use 74230)

(For evaluation of oral and pharyngeal swallowing function, use 92610)

(For flexible fiberoptic diagnostic laryngoscopy, use 31575. Do not report 31575 in conjunction with 92612-92617)

92612   Flexible fiberoptic endoscopic evaluation of swallowing by cine or video recording;

(If flexible fiberoptic or endoscopic evaluation of swallowing is performed without cine or video recording, use 92700)

92613   physician interpretation and report only

(To report an evaluation of oral and pharyngeal swallowing function, use 92610)

(To report motion fluoroscopic evaluation of swallowing function, use 92611)

92614   Flexible fiberoptic endoscopic evaluation, laryngeal sensory testing by cine or video recording;

(If flexible fiberoptic or endoscopic evaluation of swallowing is performed without cine or video recording, use 92700)

92615   physician interpretation and report only

92616   Flexible fiberoptic endoscopic evaluation of swallowing and laryngeal sensory testing by cine or video recording;

(If flexible fiberoptic or endoscopic evaluation of swallowing is performed without cine or video recording, use 92700)

92617   physician interpretation and report only

92620   Evaluation of central auditory function, with report; initial 60 minutes

92621   each additional 15 minutes

(Do not report 92620, 92621 in conjunction with 92506)

92625   Assessment of tinnitus (includes pitch, loudness matching, and masking)

(Do not report 92625 in conjunction with 92562)

(For unilateral assessment, use modifier 52)

92626   Evaluation of auditory rehabilitation status; first hour

+ 92627   each additional 15 minutes (List separately in addition to code for primary procedure)

(Use 92627 in conjunction with 92626)

(When reporting 92626, 92627, use the face-to-face time with the patient or family)

92630   Auditory rehabilitation; prelingual hearing loss

92633   postlingual hearing loss

Special Diagnostic Procedures

92640   Diagnostic analysis with programming of auditory brainstem implant, per hour

(Report nonprogramming services separately [eg, cardiac monitoring])

Other Procedures

92700   Unlisted otorhinolaryngological service or procedure

Cardiovascular

Therapeutic Services and Procedures

(For nonsurgical septal reduction therapy [eg, alcohol ablation], use 93799)

92950   Cardiopulmonary resuscitation (eg, in cardiac arrest)

(See also critical care services, 99291, 99292)

⊙ **92953**   Temporary transcutaneous pacing

(For physician direction of ambulance or rescue personnel outside the hospital, use 99288)

⊙ **92960**   Cardioversion, elective, electrical conversion of arrhythmia; external

⊙ **92961**   internal (separate procedure)

►(Do not report 92961 in conjunction with 93282-93284, 93287, 93289, 93295, 93296, 93618-93624, 93631, 93640-93642, 93650-93652, 93662)◄

92970   Cardioassist-method of circulatory assist; internal

92971   external

(For balloon atrial-septostomy, use 92992)

(For placement of catheters for use in circulatory assist devices such as intra-aortic balloon pump, use 33970)

⊙**+ 92973**   Percutaneous transluminal coronary thrombectomy (List separately in addition to code for primary procedure)

(Use 92973 in conjunction with 92980, 92982)

Medicine

⊙+ **92974**   Transcatheter placement of radiation delivery device for subsequent coronary intravascular brachytherapy (List separately in addition to code for primary procedure)

(Use 92974 in conjunction with 92980, 92982, 92995, 93508)

▶(For intravascular radioelement application, see 77785-77787)◀

⊙ **92975**   Thrombolysis, coronary; by intracoronary infusion, including selective coronary angiography

92977   by intravenous infusion

(For thrombolysis of vessels other than coronary, see 37201, 75896)

(For cerebral thrombolysis, use 37195)

⊙+ **92978**   Intravascular ultrasound (coronary vessel or graft) during diagnostic evaluation and/or therapeutic intervention including imaging supervision, interpretation and report; initial vessel (List separately in addition to code for primary procedure)

⊙+ **92979**   each additional vessel (List separately in addition to code for primary procedure)

(Use 92979 in conjunction with 92978)

(Intravascular ultrasound services include all transducer manipulations and repositioning within the specific vessel being examined, both before and after therapeutic intervention [eg, stent placement])

▶(For intravascular spectroscopy, use 0205T)◀

⊙ **92980**   Transcatheter placement of an intracoronary stent(s), percutaneous, with or without other therapeutic intervention, any method; single vessel

⊙+ **92981**   each additional vessel (List separately in addition to code for primary procedure)

(Use 92981 in conjunction with 92980)

(Codes 92980, 92981 are used to report coronary artery stenting. Coronary angioplasty [92982, 92984] or atherectomy [92995, 92996], in the same artery, is considered part of the stenting procedure and is not reported separately. Codes 92973 [percutaneous transluminal coronary thombectomy], 92974 [coronary brachytherapy] and 92978, 92979 [intravascular ultrasound] are add-on codes for reporting procedures performed in addition to coronary stenting, atherectomy, and angioplasty and are not included in the "therapeutic interventions" in 92980)

(To report additional vessels treated by angioplasty or atherectomy only during the same session, see 92984, 92996)

(To report transcatheter placement of radiation delivery device for coronary intravascular brachytherapy, use 92974)

▶(For intravascular radioelement application, see 77785-77787)◀

⊙ **92982**   Percutaneous transluminal coronary balloon angioplasty; single vessel

⊙+ **92984**   each additional vessel (List separately in addition to code for primary procedure)

(Use 92984 in conjunction with 92980, 92982, 92995)

(For stent placement following completion of angioplasty or atherectomy, see 92980, 92981)

(To report transcatheter placement of radiation delivery device for coronary intravascular brachytherapy, use 92974)

▶(For intravascular radioelement application, see 77785-77787)◀

⊙ **92986**   Percutaneous balloon valvuloplasty; aortic valve

⊙ **92987**   mitral valve

92990   pulmonary valve

92992   Atrial septectomy or septostomy; transvenous method, balloon (eg, Rashkind type) (includes cardiac catheterization)

92993   blade method (Park septostomy) (includes cardiac catheterization)

⊙ **92995**   Percutaneous transluminal coronary atherectomy, by mechanical or other method, with or without balloon angioplasty; single vessel

⊙+ **92996**   each additional vessel (List separately in addition to code for primary procedure)

(Use 92996 in conjunction with 92980, 92982, 92995)

(For stent placement following completion of angioplasty or atherectomy, see 92980, 92981)

(To report additional vessels treated by angioplasty only during the same session, use 92984)

92997   Percutaneous transluminal pulmonary artery balloon angioplasty; single vessel

+ **92998**   each additional vessel (List separately in addition to code for primary procedure)

(Use 92998 in conjunction with 92997)

Cardiography

Codes 93040-93042 are appropriate when an order for the test is triggered by an event, the rhythm strip is used to help diagnose the presence or absence of an arrhythmia, and a report is generated. There must be a specific order for an electrocardiogram or rhythm strip followed by a separate, signed, written, and retrievable report. It is not appropriate to use these codes for reviewing the telemetry monitor strips taken from a monitoring system. The need for an electrocardiogram or rhythm strip should be supported by documentation in the patient medical record.

Cardiovascular monitoring services are diagnostic medical procedures using in-person and remote technology to assess cardiovascular rhythm (ECG) data.

Medicine

Attended surveillance: is the immediate availability of a remote technician to respond to rhythm or device alert transmissions from a patient, either from an implanted or wearable monitoring or therapy device, as they are generated and transmitted to the remote surveillance location or center.

▶***Electrocardiographic rhythm derived elements:*** elements derived from recordings of the electrical activation of the heart including, but not limited to heart rhythm, rate, ST analysis, heart rate variability, T-wave alternans.◀

Mobile cardiovascular telemetry (MCT): continuously records the electrocardiographic rhythm from external electrodes placed on the patient's body. Segments of the ECG data are automatically (without patient intervention) transmitted to a remote surveillance location by cellular or landline telephone signal. The segments of the rhythm, selected for transmission, are triggered automatically (MCT device algorithm) by rapid and slow heart rates or by the patient during a symptomatic episode. There is continuous real time data analysis by preprogrammed algorithms in the device and attended surveillance of the transmitted rhythm segments by a surveillance center technician to evaluate any arrhythmias and to determine signal quality. The surveillance center technician reviews the data and notifies the physician depending on the prescribed criteria.

ECG rhythm derived elements are distinct from physiologic data, even when the same device is capable of producing both. Implantable cardiovascular monitor (ICM) device services are always separately reported from Implantable cardioverter-defibrillator (ICD) service.

For other services related to a wearable defibrillator, see 93745.

(For echocardiography, see 93303-93350)

(For electrocardiogram, 64 leads or greater, with graphic presentation and analysis, see 0178T-0180T)

93000   Electrocardiogram, routine ECG with at least 12 leads; with interpretation and report

93005   tracing only, without interpretation and report

93010   interpretation and report only

(For ECG monitoring, see 99354-99360)

93012   Telephonic transmission of post-symptom electrocardiogram rhythm strip(s), 24-hour attended monitoring, per 30 day period of time; tracing only

93014   physician review with interpretation and report only

(Do not report 93014 in conjunction with 93228, 93229)

93015   Cardiovascular stress test using maximal or submaximal treadmill or bicycle exercise, continuous electrocardiographic monitoring, and/or pharmacological stress; with physician supervision, with interpretation and report

93016   physician supervision only, without interpretation and report

93017   tracing only, without interpretation and report

93018   interpretation and report only

(For inert gas rebreathing measurement, see Category III codes 0104T, 0105T)

93024   Ergonovine provocation test

93025   Microvolt T-wave alternans for assessment of ventricular arrhythmias

93040   Rhythm ECG, 1-3 leads; with interpretation and report

93041   tracing only without interpretation and report

93042   interpretation and report only

93224   Wearable electrocardiographic rhythm derived monitoring for 24 hours by continuous original waveform recording and storage, with visual superimposition scanning; includes recording, scanning analysis with report, physician review and interpretation

93225   recording (includes connection, recording, and disconnection)

93226   scanning analysis with report

93227   physician review and interpretation

93228   Wearable mobile cardiovascular telemetry with electrocardiographic recording, concurrent computerized real time data analysis and greater than 24 hours of accessible ECG data storage (retrievable with query) with ECG triggered and patient selected events transmitted to a remote attended surveillance center for up to 30 days; physician review and interpretation with report

(Report 93228 only once per 30 days)

(Do not report 93228 in conjunction with 93014)

93229   technical support for connection and patient instructions for use, attended surveillance, analysis and physician prescribed transmission of daily and emergent data reports

(Report 93229 only once per 30 days)

(Do not report 93229 in conjunction with 93014)

(For wearable cardiovascular monitors that do not perform automatic ECG triggered transmissions to an attended surveillance center, see 93224-93227, 93230-93272)

93230   Wearable electrocardiographic rhythm derived monitoring for 24 hours by continuous original waveform recording and storage without superimposition scanning utilizing a device capable of producing a full miniaturized printout; includes recording, microprocessor-based analysis with report, physician review and interpretation

93231   recording (includes connection, recording, and disconnection)

93232   microprocessor-based analysis with report

93233   physician review and interpretation

Medicine

93235   Wearable electrocardiographic rhythm derived monitoring for 24 hours by continuous computerized monitoring and non-continuous recording, and real-time data analysis utilizing a device capable of producing intermittent full-sized waveform tracings, possibly patient activated; includes monitoring and real-time data analysis with report, physician review and interpretation

93236   monitoring and real-time data analysis with report

93237   physician review and interpretation

(For wearable mobile telemetry with ECG triggered transmissions to an attended surveillance center, see 93228, 93229)

93268   Wearable patient activated electrocardiographic rhythm derived event recording with presymptom memory loop, 24-hour attended monitoring, per 30 day period of time; includes transmission, physician review and interpretation

93270   recording (includes connection, recording, and disconnection)

93271   monitoring, receipt of transmissions, and analysis

93272   physician review and interpretation

(For postsymptom recording, see 93012, 93014)

(For implanted patient activated cardiac event recording, see 33282, 93285, 93291, 93298)

93278   Signal-averaged electrocardiography (SAECG), with or without ECG

(For interpretation and report only, use 93278 with modifier 26)

(For unlisted cardiographic procedure, use 93799)

▶Implantable and Wearable Cardiac Device Evaluations◀

▶Cardiac device evaluation services are diagnostic medical procedures using in-person and remote technology to assess device therapy and cardiovascular physiologic data. Codes 93279-93299 describe this technology and technical/professional physician and service center practice. Codes 93279-93292 are reported per procedure. Codes 93293-93296 are reported no more than **once** every 90 days. Do not report 93293-93296 if the monitoring period is less than 30 days. Codes 93297, 93298 are reported no more than **once** up to every 30 days. Do not report 93297-93299 if the monitoring period is less than 10 days.

A service center may report 93296 or 93299 during a period in which a physician performs an in-person interrogation device evaluation. A physician may not report an in-person and remote interrogation of the same device during the same period. Report only remote services when an in-person interrogation device evaluation is performed during a period of remote interrogation device evaluation. A period is established by

the initiation of the remote monitoring or the 91st day of a pacemaker or implantable cardioverter-defibrillator (ICD) monitoring or the 31st day of an implantable loop recorder (ILR) or implantable cardiovascular monitor (ICM) monitoring and extends for the subsequent 90 or 30 days, respectively, for which remote monitoring is occurring. Programming device evaluations and in-person interrogation device evaluations may not be reported on the same date by the same physician. Programming device evaluations and remote interrogation device evaluations may both be reported during the remote interrogation device evaluation period.

For monitoring by wearable devices, see 93224-93272.◀

ECG rhythm derived elements are distinct from physiologic data, even when the same device is capable of producing both. ICM device services are always separately reported from ICD services. When ILR data is derived from an ICD or pacemaker, do not report ILR services with pacemaker or ICD services.

For other services related to a wearable defibrillator, use 93745.

Do not report 93012, 93014 when performing 93279-93289, 93291-93296 or 93298-93299. Do not report 93040-93042 when performing 93279-93289, 93291-93296, or 93298-93299.

The pacemaker and ICD interrogation device evaluations, peri-procedural device evaluations and programming, and programming device evaluations may not be reported in conjunction with pacemaker or ICD device and/or lead insertion or revision services by the same physician.

The following definitions and instructions apply to codes 93279-93299:

Attended surveillance: the immediate availability of a remote technician to respond to rhythm or device alert transmissions from a patient, either from an implanted or wearable monitoring or therapy device, as they are generated and transmitted to the remote surveillance location or center.

Device, single lead: a pacemaker or implantable cardioverter-defibrillator with pacing and sensing function in only one chamber of the heart.

Device, dual lead: a pacemaker or implantable cardioverter-defibrillator with pacing and sensing function in only two chambers of the heart.

Device, multiple lead: a pacemaker or implantable cardioverter-defibrillator with pacing and sensing function in three or more chambers of the heart.

▶***Electrocardiographic rhythm derived elements:*** elements derived from recordings of the electrical activation of the heart including, but not limited to heart rhythm, rate, ST analysis, heart rate variability, T-wave alternans.◀

Implantable cardiovascular monitor (ICM): an implantable cardiovascular device used to assist the physician in the management of non-rhythm related cardiac conditions such as heart failure. The device collects longitudinal physiologic cardiovascular data elements from one or more internal sensors (such as right ventricular pressure, left atrial pressure or an index of lung water) and/or external sensors (such as blood pressure or body weight) for patient assessment and management. The data are stored and transmitted to the physician by either local telemetry or remotely to an Internet based file server or surveillance technician. The function of the ICM may be an additional function of an implantable cardiac device (eg, implantable cardioverter-defibrillator) or a function of a stand-alone device. When ICM functionality is included in an ICD device, the ICM data and the ICD heart rhythm data such as sensing, pacing and tachycardia detection therapy are distinct and therefore, the monitoring processes are distinct.

Implantable cardioverter-defibrillator (ICD): an implantable device that provides high-energy and low-energy stimulation to one or more chambers of the heart to terminate rapid heart rhythms called tachycardia or fibrillation. ICDs also have pacemaker functions to treat slow heart rhythms called bradycardia. In addition to the tachycardia and bradycardia functions, the ICD may or may not include the functionality of an implantable cardiovascular monitor or an implantable loop recorder.

Implantable loop recorder (ILR): an implantable device that continuously records the electrocardiographic rhythm triggered automatically by rapid and slow heart rates or by the patient during a symptomatic episode. The ILR function may be the only function of the device or it may be part of a pacemaker or implantable cardioverter-defibrillator device. The data are stored and transmitted to the physician by either local telemetry or remotely to an Internet based file server or surveillance technician.

►*Interrogation device evaluation:* an evaluation of an implantable device such as a cardiac pacemaker, implantable cardioverter-defibrillator, implantable cardiovascular monitor, or implantable loop recorder. Using an office, hospital, or emergency room instrument or via a remote interrogation system, stored and measured information about the lead(s) when present, sensor(s) when present, battery and the implanted device function, as well as data collected about the patient's heart rhythm and heart rate is retrieved. The retrieved information is evaluated to determine the current programming of the device and to evaluate certain aspects of the device function such as battery voltage, lead impedance, tachycardia detection settings, and rhythm treatment settings.◄

The components that must be evaluated for the various types of implantable cardiac devices are listed below. (The required components for both remote and in-person interrogations are the same.)

Pacemaker: Programmed parameters, lead(s), battery, capture and sensing function and heart rhythm.

Implantable cardioverter-defibrillator: Programmed parameters, lead(s), battery, capture and sensing function, presence or absence of therapy for ventricular tachyarrhythmias and underlying heart rhythm.

Implantable cardiovascular monitor: Programmed parameters and analysis of at least one recorded physiologic cardiovascular data element from either internal or external sensors.

Implantable loop recorder: Programmed parameters and the heart rate and rhythm during recorded episodes from both patient initiated and device algorithm detected events, when present.

Interrogation device evaluation (remote): a procedure performed for patients with pacemakers, implantable cardioverter-defibrillators or implantable loop recorders using data obtained remotely. All device functions, including the programmed parameters, lead(s), battery, capture and sensing function, presence or absence of therapy for ventricular tachyarrhythmias (for ICDs) and underlying heart rhythm are evaluated.

The components that must be evaluated for the various types of implantable cardiac devices are listed below. (The required components for both remote and in person interrogations are the same.)

Pacemaker: Programmed parameters, lead(s), battery, capture and sensing function, and heart rhythm.

Implantable cardioverter-defibrillator: Programmed parameters, lead(s), battery, capture and sensing function, presence or absence of therapy for ventricular tachyarrhythmias, and underlying heart rhythm.

Implantable cardiovascular monitor: Programmed parameters and analysis of at least one recorded physiologic cardiovascular data element from either internal or external sensors.

Implantable loop recorder: Programmed parameters and the heart rate and rhythm during recorded episodes from both patient-initiated and device algorithm detected events, when present.

Pacemaker: an implantable device that provides low energy localized stimulation to one or more chambers of the heart to initiate contraction in that chamber.

Peri-procedural device evaluation and programming: an evaluation of an implantable device system (either a pacemaker or implantable cardioverter defibrillator) to adjust the device to settings appropriate for the patient prior to a surgery, procedure, or test. The device system data are interrogated to evaluate the lead(s), sensor(s), and battery in addition to review of stored information, including patient and system measurements. The device is programmed to settings appropriate for the surgery, procedure, or test, as required. A second evaluation and programming are performed after the surgery, procedure,

Medicine

or test to provide settings appropriate to the post procedural situation, as required. If one provider performs both the pre- and post-evaluation and programming service, the appropriate code, either 93286 or 93287, would be reported two times. If one provider performs the pre-surgical service and a separate provider performs the post-surgical service, each reports either 93286 or 93287 only one time.

Physiologic cardiovascular data elements: data elements from one or more internal sensors (such as right ventricular pressure, left atrial pressure or an index of lung water) and/or external sensors (such as blood pressure or body weight) for patient assessement and management. It does not include ECG rhythm derived data elements.

▶*Programming device evaluation (in person):* a procedure performed for patients with a pacemaker, implantable cardioverter-defibrillator, or implantable loop recorder. All device functions, including the battery, programmable settings and lead(s), when present, are evaluated. To assess capture thresholds, iterative adjustments (eg, progressive changes in pacing output of a pacing lead) of the programmable parameters are conducted. The iterative adjustments provide information that permits the operator to assess and select the most appropriate final program parameters to provide for consistent delivery of the appropriate therapy and to verify the function of the device. The final program parameters may or may not change after evaluation.◀

The programming device evaluation includes all of the components of the interrogation device evaluation (remote) or the interrogation device evaluation (in person), and it includes the selection of patient specific programmed parameters depending on the type of device.

The components that must be evaluated for the various types of programming device evaluations are listed below. (See also required interrogation device evaluation [remote and in person] components above.)

Pacemaker: Programmed parameters, lead(s), battery, capture and sensing function, and heart rhythm. Often, but not always, the sensor rate response, lower and upper heart rates, AV intervals, pacing voltage and pulse duration, sensing value, and diagnostics will be adjusted during a programming evaluation.

Implantable cardioverter-defibrillator: Programmed parameters, lead(s), battery, capture and sensing function, presence or absence of therapy for ventricular tachyarrhythmias and underlying heart rhythm. Often, but not always, the sensor rate response, lower and upper heart rates, AV intervals, pacing voltage and pulse duration, sensing value, and diagnostics will be adjusted during a programming evaluation. In addition, ventricular tachycardia detection and therapies are sometimes altered depending on the interrogated data, patient's rhythm, symptoms, and condition.

Implantable loop recorder: Programmed parameters and the heart rhythm during recorded episodes from both patient initiated and device algorithm detected events. Often, but not always, the tachycardia and bradycardia detection criteria will be adjusted during a programming evaluation.

Transtelephonic rhythm strip pacemaker evaluation: service of transmission of an electrocardiographic rhythm strip over the telephone by the patient using a transmitter and recorded by a receiving location using a receiver/recorder (also commonly known as transtelephonic pacemaker monitoring). The electrocardiographic rhythm strip is recorded both with and without a magnet applied over the pacemaker. The rhythm strip is evaluated for heart rate and rhythm, atrial and ventricular capture (if observed) and atrial and ventricular sensing (if observed). In addition, the battery status of the pacemaker is determined by measurement of the paced rate on the electrocardiographic rhythm strip recorded with the magnet applied.

▲ **93279** Programming device evaluation (in person) with iterative adjustment of the implantable device to test the function of the device and select optimal permanent programmed values with physician analysis, review and report; single lead pacemaker system

(Do not report 93279 in conjunction with 93286, 93288)

▲ **93280** dual lead pacemaker system

(Do not report 93280 in conjunction with 93286, 93288)

▲ **93281** multiple lead pacemaker system

(Do not report 93281 in conjunction with 93286, 93288)

▲ **93282** single lead implantable cardioverter-defibrillator system

(Do not report 93282 in conjunction with 93287, 93289, 93745)

▲ **93283** dual lead implantable cardioverter-defibrillator system

(Do not report 93283 in conjunction with 93287, 93289)

▲ **93284** multiple lead implantable cardioverter-defibrillator system

(Do not report 93284 in conjunction with 93287, 93289)

▲ **93285** implantable loop recorder system

▶(Do not report 93285 in conjunction with 33282, 93279-93284, 93291)◀

▲ **93286** Peri-procedural device evaluation (in person) and programming of device system parameters before or after a surgery, procedure, or test with physician analysis, review and report; single, dual, or multiple lead pacemaker system

(Report 93286 once before and once after surgery, procedure, or test, when device evaluation and programming is performed before and after surgery, procedure, or test)

⊙=Moderate sedation ✚=Add-on code ✔=FDA approval pending #=Resequenced code

(Do not report 93286 in conjunction with 93279-93281, 93288)

▲ **93287**   single, dual, or multiple lead implantable cardioverter-defibrillator system

(Report 93287 once before and once after surgery, procedure, or test, when device evaluation and programming is performed before and after surgery, procedure, or test)

(Do not report 93287 in conjunction with 93282-93284, 93289)

93288   Interrogation device evaluation (in person) with physician analysis, review and report, includes connection, recording and disconnection per patient encounter; single, dual, or multiple lead pacemaker system

(Do not report 93288 in conjunction with 93279-93281, 93286, 93294, 93296)

93289   single, dual, or multiple lead implantable cardioverter-defibrillator system, including analysis of heart rhythm derived data elements

(For monitoring physiologic cardiovascular data elements derived from an ICD, use 93290)

(Do not report 93289 in conjunction with 93282-93284, 93287, 93295, 93296)

93290   implantable cardiovascular monitor system, including analysis of 1 or more recorded physiologic cardiovascular data elements from all internal and external sensors

(For heart rhythm derived data elements, use 93289)

(Do not report 93290 in conjunction with 93297, 93299)

93291   implantable loop recorder system, including heart rhythm derived data analysis

(Do not report 93291 in conjunction with 33282, 93288-93290, 93298, 93299)

93292   wearable defibrillator system

(Do not report 93292 in conjunction with 93745)

93293   Transtelephonic rhythm strip pacemaker evaluation(s) single, dual, or multiple lead pacemaker system, includes recording with and without magnet application with physician analysis, review and report(s), up to 90 days

(Do not report 93293 in conjunction with 93294)

(For in person evaluation, see 93040, 93041, 93042)

(Report 93293 only once per 90 days)

93294   Interrogation device evaluation(s) (remote), up to 90 days; single, dual, or multiple lead pacemaker system with interim physician analysis, review(s) and report(s)

(Do not report 93294 in conjunction with 93288, 93293)

(Report 93294 only once per 90 days)

93295   single, dual, or multiple lead implantable cardioverter-defibrillator system with interim physician analysis, review(s) and report(s)

(For remote monitoring of physiologic cardiovascular data elements derived from an ICD, use 93297)

(Do not report 93295 in conjunction with 93289)

(Report 93295 only once per 90 days)

93296   single, dual, or multiple lead pacemaker system or implantable cardioverter-defibrillator system, remote data acquisition(s), receipt of transmissions and technician review, technical support and distribution of results

(Do not report 93296 in conjunction with 93288, 93289, 93299)

(Report 93296 only once per 90 days)

93297   Interrogation device evaluation(s), (remote) up to 30 days; implantable cardiovascular monitor system, including analysis of 1 or more recorded physiologic cardiovascular data elements from all internal and external sensors, physician analysis, review(s) and report(s)

(For heart rhythm derived data elements, use 93295)

(Do not report 93297 in conjunction with 93290, 93298)

(Report 93297 only once per 30 days)

93298   implantable loop recorder system, including analysis of recorded heart rhythm data, physician analysis, review(s) and report(s)

▶(Do not report 93298 in conjunction with 33282, 93291, 93297)◀

(Report 93298 only once per 30 days)

93299   implantable cardiovascular monitor system or implantable loop recorder system, remote data acquisition(s), receipt of transmissions and technician review, technical support and distribution of results

(Do not report 93299 in conjunction with 93290, 93291, 93296)

(Report 93299 only once per 30 days)

Echocardiography

Echocardiography includes obtaining ultrasonic signals from the heart and great vessels, with real time image and/or Doppler ultrasonic signal documentation, with interpretation and report. When interpretation is performed separately, use modifier 26.

▶A complete transthoracic echocardiogram without spectral or color flow Doppler (93307) is a comprehensive procedure that includes 2-dimensional and, when performed, selected M-mode examination of the left and right atria, left and right ventricles, the aortic, mitral, and tricuspid valves, the pericardium, and

Medicine

adjacent portions of the aorta. Multiple views are required to obtain a complete functional and anatomic evaluation, and appropriate measurements are obtained and recorded. Despite significant effort, identification and measurement of some structures may not always be possible. In such instances, the reason that an element could not be visualized must be documented. Additional structures that may be visualized (eg, pulmonary veins, pulmonary artery, pulmonic valve, inferior vena cava) would be included as part of the service.

A complete transthoracic echocardiogram with spectral and color flow Doppler (93306) is a comprehensive procedure that includes spectral Doppler and color flow Doppler in addition to the 2-dimensional and selected M-mode examinations, when performed. Spectral Doppler (93320, 93321) and color flow Doppler (93325) provide information regarding intracardiac blood flow and hemodynamics.◄

A follow-up or limited echocardiographic study (93308) is an examination that does not evaluate or document the attempt to evaluate all the structures that comprise the complete echocardiographic exam. This is typically limited to, or performed in follow-up of a focused clinical concern.

In stress echocardiography, echocardiographic images are recorded from multiple cardiac windows before, after, and in some protocols, during stress. The stress is achieved by (1) walking on a treadmill; (2) using a bicycle (supine or upright); or (3) the administration of pharmacological agents that either simulate exercise (by increasing heart rate, blood pressure, or myocardial contractility) or alter coronary flow (vasodilation). The patient's ECG, heart rate, and blood pressure are monitored at baseline, throughout the procedure and during recovery. Reports are prepared to evaluate (1) the duration of stress, the reason for stopping, and the hemodynamic response to stress; (2) the electrocardiographic response to stress; and (3) the echocardiographic response to stress.

►When a stress echocardiogram is performed with a complete cardiovascular stress test (93015) (continuous electrocardiographic monitoring, physician supervision, interpretation and report), use 93351. Code 93350 is used to report the performance and interpretation of a stress echocardiogram only, with the components of the cardiovascular stress test reported separately using the appropriate codes (93016–93018).◄

When left ventricular endocardial borders cannot be adequately identified by standard echocardiographic imaging, echocardiographic contrast may be infused intravenously both at rest and with stress to achieve that purpose. Code 93352 is used to report the administration of echocardiographic contrast agent in conjunction with the stress echocardiography codes (93350 or 93351). Supply of contrast agent and/or drugs used for pharmacological stress is reported separately in addition to the procedure code.

Report of an echocardiographic study, whether complete or limited, includes an interpretation of all obtained information, documentation of all clinically relevant findings including quantitative measurements obtained, plus a description of any recognized abnormalities. Pertinent images, videotape, and/or digital data are archived for permanent storage and are available for subsequent review. Use of echocardiography not meeting these criteria is not separately reportable.

Use of ultrasound, without thorough evaluation of organ(s) or anatomic region, image documentation and final, written report, is not separately reportable.

(For fetal echocardiography, see 76825-76828)

93303   Transthoracic echocardiography for congenital cardiac anomalies; complete

93304   follow-up or limited study

93306   Echocardiography, transthoracic, real-time with image documentation (2D), includes M-mode recording, when performed, complete, with spectral Doppler echocardiography, and with color flow Doppler echocardiography

(For transthoracic echocardiography without spectral and color Doppler, use 93307)

93307   Echocardiography, transthoracic, real-time with image documentation (2D), includes M-mode recording, when performed, complete, without spectral or color Doppler echocardiography

(Do not report 93307 in conjunction with 93320, 93321, 93325)

93308   Echocardiography, transthoracic, real-time with image documentation (2D), includes M-mode recording, when performed, follow-up or limited study

⊙ 93312   Echocardiography, transesophageal, real-time with image documentation (2D) (with or without M-mode recording); including probe placement, image acquisition, interpretation and report

⊙ 93313   placement of transesophageal probe only

⊙ 93314   image acquisition, interpretation and report only

⊙ 93315   Transesophageal echocardiography for congenital cardiac anomalies; including probe placement, image acquisition, interpretation and report

⊙ 93316   placement of transesophageal probe only

⊙ 93317   image acquisition, interpretation and report only

⊙ 93318   Echocardiography, transesophageal (TEE) for monitoring purposes, including probe placement, real time 2-dimensional image acquisition and interpretation leading to ongoing (continuous) assessment of (dynamically changing) cardiac pumping function and to therapeutic measures on an immediate time basis

+ 93320   Doppler echocardiography, pulsed wave and/or continuous wave with spectral display (List separately in addition to codes for echocardiographic imaging); complete

(Use 93320 in conjunction with 93303, 93304, 93312, 93314, 93315, 93317, 93350, 93351)

+ 93321   follow-up or limited study (List separately in addition to codes for echocardiographic imaging)

(Use 93321 in conjunction with 93303, 93304, 93308, 93312, 93314, 93315, 93317, 93350, 93351)

+ 93325   Doppler echocardiography color flow velocity mapping (List separately in addition to codes for echocardiography)

(Use 93325 in conjunction with 76825, 76826, 76827, 76828, 93303, 93304, 93308, 93312, 93314, 93315, 93317, 93350, 93351)

93350   Echocardiography, transthoracic, real-time with image documentation (2D), includes M-mode recording, when performed, during rest and cardiovascular stress test using treadmill, bicycle exercise and/or pharmacologically induced stress, with interpretation and report;

▶(Stress testing codes 93016-93018 should be reported, when appropriate, in conjunction with 93350 to capture the cardiovascular stress portion of the study)◀

▶(Do not report 93350 in conjunction with 93015)◀

93351   including performance of continuous electrocardiographic monitoring, with physician supervision

(Do not report 93351 in conjunction with 93015-93018, 93350)

+ 93352   Use of echocardiographic contrast agent during stress echocardiography (List separately in addition to code for primary procedure)

(Do not report 93352 more than once per stress echocardiogram)

(Use 93352 in conjunction with 93350, 93351)

Cardiac Catheterization

Cardiac catheterization is a diagnostic medical procedure which includes introduction, positioning and repositioning of catheter(s), when necessary, recording of intracardiac and intravascular pressure, obtaining blood samples for measurement of blood gases or dilution curves and cardiac output measurements (Fick or other method, with or without rest and exercise and/or studies) with or without electrode catheter placement, final evaluation and report of procedure. When selective injection procedures are performed without a preceding cardiac catheterization, these services should be reported using codes in the Vascular Injection Procedures section, 36011-36015 and 36215-36218.

When coronary artery, arterial coronary conduit or venous bypass graft angiography is performed without concomitant left heart cardiac catheterization, use 93508. Injection procedures 93539, 93540, 93544, and 93545 represent separate identifiable services and may be reported in conjunction with one another in addition to 93508, as appropriate. To report imaging supervision, interpretation and report in conjunction with 93508, use 93556.

Modifier 51 should not be appended to 93503, 93539, 93540, 93544-93556.

⊙ **93501**   Right heart catheterization

(For bundle of His recording, use 93600)

⊘ **93503**   Insertion and placement of flow directed catheter (eg, Swan-Ganz) for monitoring purposes

(For subsequent monitoring, see 99356-99357)

⊙ **93505**   Endomyocardial biopsy

⊙ **93508**   Catheter placement in coronary artery(s), arterial coronary conduit(s), and/or venous coronary bypass graft(s) for coronary angiography without concomitant left heart catheterization

(93508 is to be used only when left heart catheterization 93510, 93511, 93524, 93526 is not performed)

(93508 is to be used only once per procedure)

(To report transcatheter placement of radiation delivery device for coronary intravascular brachytherapy, use 92974)

▶(For intravascular radioelement application, see 77785-77787)◀

⊙ **93510**   Left heart catheterization, retrograde, from the brachial artery, axillary artery or femoral artery; percutaneous

⊙ **93511**   by cutdown

⊙ **93514**   Left heart catheterization by left ventricular puncture

⊙ **93524**   Combined transseptal and retrograde left heart catheterization

⊙ **93526**   Combined right heart catheterization and retrograde left heart catheterization

⊙ **93527**   Combined right heart catheterization and transseptal left heart catheterization through intact septum (with or without retrograde left heart catheterization)

⊙ **93528**   Combined right heart catheterization with left ventricular puncture (with or without retrograde left heart catheterization)

⊙ **93529**   Combined right heart catheterization and left heart catheterization through existing septal opening (with or without retrograde left heart catheterization)

⊙ **93530**   Right heart catheterization, for congenital cardiac anomalies

93531   Combined right heart catheterization and retrograde left heart catheterization, for congenital cardiac anomalies

Medicine

93532   Combined right heart catheterization and transseptal left heart catheterization through intact septum with or without retrograde left heart catheterization, for congenital cardiac anomalies

93533   Combined right heart catheterization and transseptal left heart catheterization through existing septal opening, with or without retrograde left heart catheterization, for congenital cardiac anomalies

Injection Procedures

When injection procedures are performed in conjunction with cardiac catheterization, these services do not include introduction of catheters but do include repositioning of catheters when necessary and use of automatic power injectors. Injection procedures 93539-93545 represent separate identifiable services and may be coded in conjunction with one another when appropriate. The technical details of angiography, supervision of filming and processing, interpretation, and report are not included. To report radiological supervision, interpretation, and report for 93542 or 93543, use 93555. To report radiological supervision, interpretation, and report for 93539, 93540, 93541, 93544, or 93545, use 93556. Modifier 51 should not be appended to 93539, 93540, 93544-93556.

⊙⊘ **93539**   Injection procedure during cardiac catheterization; for selective opacification of arterial conduits (eg, internal mammary), whether native or used for bypass

⊙⊘ **93540**   for selective opacification of aortocoronary venous bypass grafts, 1 or more coronary arteries

⊙ **93541**   for pulmonary angiography

⊙ **93542**   for selective right ventricular or right atrial angiography

⊙ **93543**   for selective left ventricular or left atrial angiography

⊙⊘ **93544**   for aortography

⊙⊘ **93545**   for selective coronary angiography (injection of radiopaque material may be by hand)

⊙⊘ **93555**   Imaging supervision, interpretation and report for injection procedure(s) during cardiac catheterization; ventricular and/or atrial angiography

⊙⊘ **93556**   pulmonary angiography, aortography, and/or selective coronary angiography including venous bypass grafts and arterial conduits (whether native or used in bypass)

⊙ **93561**   Indicator dilution studies such as dye or thermal dilution, including arterial and/or venous catheterization; with cardiac output measurement (separate procedure)

⊙ **93562**   subsequent measurement of cardiac output

(93561, 93562 are not to be used with cardiac catheterization codes)

(For radioisotope method of cardiac output, see 78472, 78473, or 78481)

⊙+ **93571**   Intravascular Doppler velocity and/or pressure derived coronary flow reserve measurement (coronary vessel or graft) during coronary angiography including pharmacologically induced stress; initial vessel (List separately in addition to code for primary procedure)

⊙+ **93572**   each additional vessel (List separately in addition to code for primary procedure)

(Intravascular distal coronary blood flow velocity measurements include all Doppler transducer manipulations and repositioning within the specific vessel being examined, during coronary angiography or therapeutic intervention [eg, angioplasty])

(For unlisted cardiac catheterization procedure, use 93799)

Repair of Septal Defect

93580   Percutaneous transcatheter closure of congenital interatrial communication (ie, Fontan fenestration, atrial septal defect) with implant

(Percutaneous transcatheter closure of atrial septal defect includes a right heart catheterization procedure. Code 93580 includes injection of contrast for atrial and ventricular angiograms. Codes 93501, 93529-93533, 93539, 93543, 93555 should not be reported separately in addition to code 93580)

93581   Percutaneous transcatheter closure of a congenital ventricular septal defect with implant

(Percutaneous transcatheter closure of ventricular septal defect includes a right heart catheterization procedure. Code 93581 includes injection of contrast for atrial and ventricular angiograms. Codes 93501, 93529-93533, 93539, 93543, 93555 should not be reported separately in addition to code 93581)

(For ventricular septal defect closure via transmyocardial implant delivery, see 0166T, 0167T)

(For echocardiographic services performed in addition to 93580, 93581, see 93303-93317, 93662 as appropriate)

Intracardiac Electrophysiological Procedures/Studies

Intracardiac electrophysiologic studies (EPS) are an invasive diagnostic medical procedure which include the insertion and repositioning of electrode catheters, recording of electrograms before and during pacing or programmed stimulation of multiple locations in the heart, analysis of recorded information, and report of the procedure. Electrophysiologic studies are most often performed with two or more electrode catheters. In many circumstances, patients with arrhythmias are evaluated and treated at the same encounter. In this situation, a diagnostic *electrophysiologic study* is performed, induced tachycardia(s) are *mapped*, and on the basis of the diagnostic and mapping information, the tissue is *ablated*. Electrophysiologic study(ies), mapping, and ablation

Medicine

represent distinctly different procedures, requiring individual reporting whether performed on the same or subsequent dates.

Definitions

Arrhythmia Induction: In most electrophysiologic studies, an attempt is made to induce arrhythmia(s) from single or multiple sites within the heart. Arrhythmia induction is achieved by performing pacing at different rates, programmed stimulation (introduction of critically timed electrical impulses), and other techniques. Because arrhythmia induction occurs via the same catheter(s) inserted for the electrophysiologic study(ies), catheter insertion and temporary pacemaker codes are not additionally reported. Codes 93600-93603, 93610-93612 and 93618 are used to describe unusual situations where there may be recording, pacing or an attempt at arrhythmia induction from only one site in the heart. Code 93619 describes only evaluation of the sinus node, atrioventricular node and His-Purkinje conduction system, without arrhythmia induction. Codes 93620-93624 and 93640-93642 all include recording, pacing and attempted arrhythmia induction from one or more site(s) in the heart.

Mapping: Mapping is a distinct procedure performed in addition to a diagnostic electrophysiologic procedure and should be separately reported using 93609 or 93613. Do not report standard mapping (93609) in addition to 3D mapping (93613). When a tachycardia is induced, the site of tachycardia origination or its electrical path through the heart is often defined by mapping. Mapping creates a multidimensional depiction of a tachycardia by recording multiple electrograms obtained sequentially or simultaneously from multiple catheter sites in the heart. Depending upon the technique, certain types of mapping catheters may be repositioned from point-to-point within the heart, allowing sequential recording from the various sites to construct maps. Other types of mapping catheters allow mapping without a point-to-point technique by allowing simultaneous recording from many electrodes on the same catheter and computer-assisted three dimensional reconstruction of the tachycardia activation sequence.

Ablation: Once the part of the heart involved in the tachycardia is localized, the tachycardia may be treated by ablation (the delivery of a radiofrequency energy to the area to selectively destroy cardiac tissue). Ablation procedures (93651-93652) may be performed: independently on a date subsequent to a diagnostic electrophysiologic study and mapping; or, at the time a diagnostic electrophysiologic study, tachycardia(s) induction and mapping is performed. When an electrophysiologic study, mapping, and ablation are performed on the same date, each procedure should be separately reported. In reporting catheter ablation, 93651 and/or 93652 should be reported once to describe ablation of cardiac arrhythmias, regardless of the number of arrhythmias ablated.

Modifier 51 should not be appended to 93600-93603, 93610, 93612, 93615-93618, 93631.

⊘ **93600** Bundle of His recording

⊘ **93602** Intra-atrial recording

⊘ **93603** Right ventricular recording

⊙+ **93609** Intraventricular and/or intra-atrial mapping of tachycardia site(s) with catheter manipulation to record from multiple sites to identify origin of tachycardia (List separately in addition to code for primary procedure)

(Use 93609 in conjunction with 93620, 93651, 93652)

(Do not report 93609 in addition to 93613)

⊘ **93610** Intra-atrial pacing

⊘ **93612** Intraventricular pacing

(Do not report 93612 in conjunction with 93620-93622)

⊙+ **93613** Intracardiac electrophysiologic 3-dimensional mapping (List separately in addition to code for primary procedure)

(Use 93613 in conjunction with 93620, 93651, 93652)

(Do not report 93613 in addition to 93609)

⊙⊘ **93615** Esophageal recording of atrial electrogram with or without ventricular electrogram(s);

⊙⊘ **93616**   with pacing

⊙⊘ **93618** Induction of arrhythmia by electrical pacing

(For intracardiac phonocardiogram, use 93799)

⊙ **93619** Comprehensive electrophysiologic evaluation with right atrial pacing and recording, right ventricular pacing and recording, His bundle recording, including insertion and repositioning of multiple electrode catheters, without induction or attempted induction of arrhythmia

(Do not report 93619 in conjunction with 93600, 93602, 93610, 93612, 93618, or 93620-93622)

⊙ **93620** Comprehensive electrophysiologic evaluation including insertion and repositioning of multiple electrode catheters with induction or attempted induction of arrhythmia; with right atrial pacing and recording, right ventricular pacing and recording, His bundle recording

(Do not report 93620 in conjunction with 93600, 93602, 93610, 93612, 93618 or 93619)

⊙+ **93621**   with left atrial pacing and recording from coronary sinus or left atrium (List separately in addition to code for primary procedure)

(Use 93621 in conjunction with 93620)

⊙+ **93622**   with left ventricular pacing and recording (List separately in addition to code for primary procedure)

(Use 93622 in conjunction with 93620)

+ **93623** Programmed stimulation and pacing after intravenous drug infusion (List separately in addition to code for primary procedure)

(Use 93623 in conjunction with 93619, 93620)

Medicine

⊙ **93624**   Electrophysiologic follow-up study with pacing and recording to test effectiveness of therapy, including induction or attempted induction of arrhythmia

⊘ **93631**   Intra-operative epicardial and endocardial pacing and mapping to localize the site of tachycardia or zone of slow conduction for surgical correction

(For operative ablation of an arrhythmogenic focus or pathway by a separate provider, see 33250-33261)

⊙ **93640**   Electrophysiologic evaluation of single or dual chamber pacing cardioverter-defibrillator leads including defibrillation threshold evaluation (induction of arrhythmia, evaluation of sensing and pacing for arrhythmia termination) at time of initial implantation or replacement;

⊙ **93641**   with testing of single or dual chamber pacing cardioverter-defibrillator pulse generator

▶(For subsequent or periodic electronic analysis and/or reprogramming of single or dual chamber pacing cardioverter-defibrillators, see 93282, 93283, 93289, 93292, 93295, 93642)◀

⊙ **93642**   Electrophysiologic evaluation of single or dual chamber pacing cardioverter-defibrillator (includes defibrillation threshold evaluation, induction of arrhythmia, evaluation of sensing and pacing for arrhythmia termination, and programming or reprogramming of sensing or therapeutic parameters)

⊙ **93650**   Intracardiac catheter ablation of atrioventricular node function, atrioventricular conduction for creation of complete heart block, with or without temporary pacemaker placement

⊙ **93651**   Intracardiac catheter ablation of arrhythmogenic focus; for treatment of supraventricular tachycardia by ablation of fast or slow atrioventricular pathways, accessory atrioventricular connections or other atrial foci, singly or in combination

⊙ **93652**   for treatment of ventricular tachycardia

93660   Evaluation of cardiovascular function with tilt table evaluation, with continuous ECG monitoring and intermittent blood pressure monitoring, with or without pharmacological intervention

(For testing of autonomic nervous system function, see 95921-95923)

✛ **93662**   Intracardiac echocardiography during therapeutic/diagnostic intervention, including imaging supervision and interpretation (List separately in addition to code for primary procedure)

(Use 93662 in conjunction with 92987, 93527, 93532, 93580, 93581, 93621, 93622, 93651, or 93652, as appropriate)

(Do not report 92961 in addition to 93662)

Peripheral Arterial Disease Rehabilitation

Peripheral arterial disease (PAD) rehabilitative physical exercise consists of a series of sessions, lasting 45-60 minutes per session, involving use of either a motorized treadmill or a track to permit each patient to achieve symptom-limited claudication. Each session is supervised by an exercise physiologist or nurse. The supervising provider monitors the individual patient's claudication threshold and other cardiovascular limitations for adjustment of workload. During this supervised rehabilitation program, the development of new arrhythmias, symptoms that might suggest angina or the continued inability of the patient to progress to an adequate level of exercise may require physician review and examination of the patient. These physician services would be separately reported with an appropriate level E/M service code.

93668   Peripheral arterial disease (PAD) rehabilitation, per session

Noninvasive Physiologic Studies and Procedures

(For arterial cannulization and recording of direct arterial pressure, use 36620)

(For radiographic injection procedures, see 36000-36299)

(For vascular cannulization for hemodialysis, see 36800-36821)

(For chemotherapy for malignant disease, see 96409-96549)

(For penile plethysmography, use 54240)

▲ **93701**   Bioimpedance-derived physiologic cardiovascular analysis

▶(For left ventricular filling pressure indirect measurement by computerized calibration of the arterial waveform response to Valsalva, use 93799)◀

93720   Plethysmography, total body; with interpretation and report

93721   tracing only, without interpretation and report

93722   interpretation and report only

(For regional plethysmography, see 93875-93931)

93724   Electronic analysis of antitachycardia pacemaker system (includes electrocardiographic recording, programming of device, induction and termination of tachycardia via implanted pacemaker, and interpretation of recordings)

(93727 has been deleted. For programming of implantable loop recorder, use 93285. For interrogation of implantable loop recorder, see 93291, 93298)

(93731, 93732 have been deleted. For interrogation of dual lead pacemaker, see 93288, 93294. For programming of dual chamber pacemaker, use 93280)

Medicine

(93733 has been deleted. For transtelephonic rhythm strip pacemaker, single and dual, or multiple lead pacemaker evaluation, use 93293)

(93734, 93735 have been deleted. For interrogation of single lead pacemaker, see 93288, 93294. For programming of single lead pacemaker, use 93279)

(93736 has been deleted. For transtelephonic rhythm strip pacemaker, single and dual, or multiple lead pacemaker evaluation, use 93293)

93740   Temperature gradient studies

(93741, 93742 have been deleted. For interrogation of single implantable cardioverter-defibrillator [ICD], see 93289, 93295. For programming of single ICD, use 93282. For interrogation of wearable cardioverter-defibrillator, use 93292)

(93743, 93744 have been deleted. For interrogation of dual implantable cardioverter-defibrillator [ICD], see 93289, 93295. For programming of dual ICD, use 93283)

93745   Initial set-up and programming by a physician of wearable cardioverter-defibrillator includes initial programming of system, establishing baseline electronic ECG, transmission of data to data repository, patient instruction in wearing system and patient reporting of problems or events

(Do not report 93745 in conjunction with 93282, 93292)

● **93750**   Interrogation of ventricular assist device (VAD), in person, with physician analysis of device parameters (eg, drivelines, alarms, power surges), review of device function (eg, flow and volume status, septum status, recovery), with programming, if performed, and report

▶(Do not report 93750 in conjunction with 33975, 33976, 33979, 33981-33983)◀

(93760, 93762 have been deleted)

93770   Determination of venous pressure

(For central venous cannulization see 36555-36556, 36500)

93784   Ambulatory blood pressure monitoring, utilizing a system such as magnetic tape and/or computer disk, for 24 hours or longer; including recording, scanning analysis, interpretation and report

93786   recording only

93788   scanning analysis with report

93790   physician review with interpretation and report

Other Procedures

93797   Physician services for outpatient cardiac rehabilitation; without continuous ECG monitoring (per session)

93798   with continuous ECG monitoring (per session)

93799   Unlisted cardiovascular service or procedure

Noninvasive Vascular Diagnostic Studies

Vascular studies include patient care required to perform the studies, supervision of the studies and interpretation of study results with copies for patient records of hard copy output with analysis of all data, including bidirectional vascular flow or imaging when provided.

The use of a simple hand-held or other Doppler device that does not produce hard copy output, or that produces a record that does not permit analysis of bidirectional vascular flow, is considered to be part of the physical examination of the vascular system and is not separately reported.

Duplex scan (eg, 93880, 93882) describes an ultrasonic scanning procedure for characterizing the pattern and direction of blood flow in arteries or veins with the production of real-time images integrating B-mode two-dimensional vascular structure, Doppler spectral analysis, and color flow Doppler imaging.

Noninvasive physiologic studies are performed using equipment separate and distinct from the duplex scanner. Codes 93875, 93965, 93922, 93923, and 93924 describe the evaluation of non-imaging physiologic recordings of pressures, Doppler analysis of bi-directional blood flow, plethysmography, and/or oxygen tension measurements appropriate for the anatomic area studied.

Cerebrovascular Arterial Studies

A complete transcranial Doppler (TCD) study (93886) includes ultrasound evaluation of the right and left anterior circulation territories and the posterior circulation territory (to include vertebral arteries and basilar artery). In a limited TCD study (93888) there is ultrasound evaluation of two or fewer of these territories. For TCD, ultrasound evaluation is a reasonable and concerted attempt to identify arterial signals through an acoustic window.

93875   Noninvasive physiologic studies of extracranial arteries, complete bilateral study (eg, periorbital flow direction with arterial compression, ocular pneumoplethysmography, Doppler ultrasound spectral analysis)

93880   Duplex scan of extracranial arteries; complete bilateral study

93882   unilateral or limited study

(To report common carotid intima-media thickness (IMT) study for evaluation of atherosclerotic burden or coronary heart disease risk factor assessment, use Category III code 0126T)

93886   Transcranial Doppler study of the intracranial arteries; complete study

93888   limited study

Medicine

93890   vasoreactivity study

93892   emboli detection without intravenous microbubble injection

93893   emboli detection with intravenous microbubble injection

(Do not report 93890-93893 in conjunction with 93888)

Extremity Arterial Studies (Including Digits)

93922   Noninvasive physiologic studies of upper or lower extremity arteries, single level, bilateral (eg, ankle/brachial indices, Doppler waveform analysis, volume plethysmography, transcutaneous oxygen tension measurement)

93923   Noninvasive physiologic studies of upper or lower extremity arteries, multiple levels or with provocative functional maneuvers, complete bilateral study (eg, segmental blood pressure measurements, segmental Doppler waveform analysis, segmental volume plethysmography, segmental transcutaneous oxygen tension measurements, measurements with postural provocative tests, measurements with reactive hyperemia)

93924   Noninvasive physiologic studies of lower extremity arteries, at rest and following treadmill stress testing, complete bilateral study

93925   Duplex scan of lower extremity arteries or arterial bypass grafts; complete bilateral study

93926   unilateral or limited study

93930   Duplex scan of upper extremity arteries or arterial bypass grafts; complete bilateral study

93931   unilateral or limited study

Extremity Venous Studies (Including Digits)

93965   Noninvasive physiologic studies of extremity veins, complete bilateral study (eg, Doppler waveform analysis with responses to compression and other maneuvers, phleborheography, impedance plethysmography)

93970   Duplex scan of extremity veins including responses to compression and other maneuvers; complete bilateral study

93971   unilateral or limited study

Visceral and Penile Vascular Studies

93975   Duplex scan of arterial inflow and venous outflow of abdominal, pelvic, scrotal contents and/or retroperitoneal organs; complete study

93976   limited study

93978   Duplex scan of aorta, inferior vena cava, iliac vasculature, or bypass grafts; complete study

93979   unilateral or limited study

93980   Duplex scan of arterial inflow and venous outflow of penile vessels; complete study

93981   follow-up or limited study

93982   Noninvasive physiologic study of implanted wireless pressure sensor in aneurysmal sac following endovascular repair, complete study including recording, analysis of pressure and waveform tracings, interpretation and report

(Do not report 93982 in conjunction with 34806)

Extremity Arterial-Venous Studies

93990   Duplex scan of hemodialysis access (including arterial inflow, body of access and venous outflow)

(For measurement of hemodialysis access flow using indicator dilution methods, use 90940)

Pulmonary

Ventilator Management

94002   Ventilation assist and management, initiation of pressure or volume preset ventilators for assisted or controlled breathing; hospital inpatient/observation, initial day

94003   hospital inpatient/observation, each subsequent day

94004   nursing facility, per day

(Do not report 94002-94004 in conjunction with Evaluation and Management services 99201-99499)

94005   Home ventilator management care plan oversight of a patient (patient not present) in home, domiciliary or rest home (eg, assisted living) requiring review of status, review of laboratories and other studies and revision of orders and respiratory care plan (as appropriate), within a calendar month, 30 minutes or more

(Do not report 94005 in conjunction with 99339, 99340, 99374-99378)

(Ventilator management care plan oversight is reported separately from home or domiciliary, rest home [eg, assisted living] services. A physician may report 94005, when performed, including when a different physician reports 99339, 99340, 99374-99378 for the same 30 days)

Other Procedures

Codes 94010-94799 include laboratory procedure(s) and interpretation of test results. If a separate identifiable Evaluation and Management service is performed, the appropriate E/M service code should be reported in addition to 94010-94799.

Medicine

94010 Spirometry, including graphic record, total and timed vital capacity, expiratory flow rate measurement(s), with or without maximal voluntary ventilation

⊙● **94011** Measurement of spirometric forced expiratory flows in an infant or child through 2 years of age

⊙● **94012** Measurement of spirometric forced expiratory flows, before and after bronchodilator, in an infant or child through 2 years of age

⊙● **94013** Measurement of lung volumes (ie, functional residual capacity [FRC], forced vital capacity [FVC], and expiratory reserve volume [ERV]) in an infant or child through 2 years of age

94014 Patient-initiated spirometric recording per 30-day period of time; includes reinforced education, transmission of spirometric tracing, data capture, analysis of transmitted data, periodic recalibration and physician review and interpretation

94015 recording (includes hook-up, reinforced education, data transmission, data capture, trend analysis, and periodic recalibration)

94016 physician review and interpretation only

94060 Bronchodilation responsiveness, spirometry as in 94010, pre- and post-bronchodilator administration

(Report bronchodilator supply separately with 99070 or appropriate supply code)

(For prolonged exercise test for bronchospasm with pre- and post-spirometry, use 94620)

94070 Bronchospasm provocation evaluation, multiple spirometric determinations as in 94010, with administered agents (eg, antigen[s], cold air, methacholine)

(Report antigen[s] administration separately with 99070 or appropriate supply code)

94150 Vital capacity, total (separate procedure)

94200 Maximum breathing capacity, maximal voluntary ventilation

94240 Functional residual capacity or residual volume: helium method, nitrogen open circuit method, or other method

94250 Expired gas collection, quantitative, single procedure (separate procedure)

94260 Thoracic gas volume

(For plethysmography, see 93720-93722)

94350 Determination of maldistribution of inspired gas: multiple breath nitrogen washout curve including alveolar nitrogen or helium equilibration time

94360 Determination of resistance to airflow, oscillatory or plethysmographic methods

94370 Determination of airway closing volume, single breath tests

94375 Respiratory flow volume loop

94400 Breathing response to CO_2 (CO_2 response curve)

94450 Breathing response to hypoxia (hypoxia response curve)

(For high altitude simulation test [HAST], see 94452, 94453)

94452 High altitude simulation test (HAST), with physician interpretation and report;

(For obtaining arterial blood gases, use 36600)

(Do not report 94452 in conjunction with 94453, 94760, 94761)

94453 with supplemental oxygen titration

(For obtaining arterial blood gases, use 36600)

(Do not report 94453 in conjunction with 94452, 94760, 94761)

⊘ **94610** Intrapulmonary surfactant administration by a physician through endotracheal tube

▶(Do not report 94610 in conjunction with 99468-99472)◀

(For endotracheal intubation, use 31500)

(Report 94610 once per dosing episode)

94620 Pulmonary stress testing; simple (eg, 6-minute walk test, prolonged exercise test for bronchospasm with pre- and post-spirometry and oximetry)

94621 complex (including measurements of CO_2 production, O_2 uptake, and electrocardiographic recordings)

94640 Pressurized or nonpressurized inhalation treatment for acute airway obstruction or for sputum induction for diagnostic purposes (eg, with an aerosol generator, nebulizer, metered dose inhaler or intermittent positive pressure breathing [IPPB] device)

(For more than 1 inhalation treatment performed on the same date, append modifier 76)

(For continuous inhalation treatment of 1 hour or more, see 94644, 94645)

94642 Aerosol inhalation of pentamidine for pneumocystis carinii pneumonia treatment or prophylaxis

94644 Continuous inhalation treatment with aerosol medication for acute airway obstruction; first hour

(For services of less than 1 hour, use 94640)

+ **94645** each additional hour (List separately in addition to code for primary procedure)

(Use 94645 in conjunction with 94644)

94660 Continuous positive airway pressure ventilation (CPAP), initiation and management

94662 Continuous negative pressure ventilation (CNP), initiation and management

Medicine

94664   Demonstration and/or evaluation of patient utilization of an aerosol generator, nebulizer, metered dose inhaler or IPPB device

(94664 can be reported 1 time only per day of service)

94667   Manipulation chest wall, such as cupping, percussing, and vibration to facilitate lung function; initial demonstration and/or evaluation

94668   subsequent

94680   Oxygen uptake, expired gas analysis; rest and exercise, direct, simple

94681   including CO_2 output, percentage oxygen extracted

94690   rest, indirect (separate procedure)

(For single arterial puncture, use 36600)

94720   Carbon monoxide diffusing capacity (eg, single breath, steady state)

94725   Membrane diffusion capacity

94750   Pulmonary compliance study (eg, plethysmography, volume and pressure measurements)

94760   Noninvasive ear or pulse oximetry for oxygen saturation; single determination

(For blood gases, see 82803-82810)

94761   multiple determinations (eg, during exercise)

94762   by continuous overnight monitoring (separate procedure)

(For other in vivo laboratory procedures, see 88720-88741)

94770   Carbon dioxide, expired gas determination by infrared analyzer

(For bronchoscopy, see 31622-31656)

(For placement of flow directed catheter, use 93503)

(For venipuncture, use 36410)

(For central venous catheter placement, see 36555-36556)

(For arterial puncture, use 36600)

(For arterial catheterization, use 36620)

(For thoracentesis, use 32421)

(For phlebotomy, therapeutic, use 99195)

(For lung biopsy, needle, use 32405)

(For intubation, orotracheal or nasotracheal, use 31500)

94772   Circadian respiratory pattern recording (pediatric pneumogram), 12-24 hour continuous recording, infant

(Separate procedure codes for electromyograms, EEG, ECG, and recordings of respiration are excluded when 94772 is reported)

94774   Pediatric home apnea monitoring event recording including respiratory rate, pattern and heart rate per 30-day period of time; includes monitor attachment, download of data, physician review, interpretation, and preparation of a report

(Do not report 94774 in conjunction with 94775-94777 during the same reporting period)

94775   monitor attachment only (includes hook-up, initiation of recording and disconnection)

94776   monitoring, download of information, receipt of transmission(s) and analyses by computer only

94777   physician review, interpretation and preparation of report only

(When oxygen saturation monitoring is used in addition to heart rate and respiratory monitoring, it is not reported separately)

(Do not report 94774-94777 in conjunction with 93224-93272)

(Do not report apnea recording device separately)

(For sleep study, see 95805-95811)

94799   Unlisted pulmonary service or procedure

Allergy and Clinical Immunology

Definitions

Immunotherapy (desensitization, hyposensitization) is the parenteral administration of allergenic extracts as antigens at periodic intervals, usually on an increasing dosage scale to a dosage which is maintained as maintenance therapy. Indications for immunotherapy are determined by appropriate diagnostic procedures coordinated with clinical judgment and knowledge of the natural history of allergic diseases.

Other therapy: for medical conferences on the use of mechanical and electronic devices (precipitators, air conditioners, air filters, humidifiers, dehumidifiers), climatotherapy, physical therapy, occupational and recreational therapy, see **Evaluation and Management** section.

Do not report Evaluation and Management (E/M) services for test interpretation and report. If a significant separately identifiable E/M service is performed, the appropriate E/M service code should be reported using modifier 25.

Allergy Testing

(For allergy laboratory tests, see 86000-86999)

(For therapy for severe or intractable allergic disease, see 96365-96368, 96372, 96374, 96375)

95004 Percutaneous tests (scratch, puncture, prick) with allergenic extracts, immediate type reaction, including test interpretation and report by a physician, specify number of tests

95010 Percutaneous tests (scratch, puncture, prick) sequential and incremental, with drugs, biologicals or venoms, immediate type reaction, including test interpretation and report by a physician, specify number of tests

95012 Nitric oxide expired gas determination

(For nitric oxide determination by spectroscopy, use Category III code 0064T)

95015 Intracutaneous (intradermal) tests, sequential and incremental, with drugs, biologicals, or venoms, immediate type reaction, including test interpretation and report by a physician, specify number of tests

95024 Intracutaneous (intradermal) tests with allergenic extracts, immediate type reaction, including test interpretation and report by a physician, specify number of tests

95027 Intracutaneous (intradermal) tests, sequential and incremental, with allergenic extracts for airborne allergens, immediate type reaction, including test interpretation and report by a physician, specify number of tests

95028 Intracutaneous (intradermal) tests with allergenic extracts, delayed type reaction, including reading, specify number of tests

95044 Patch or application test(s) (specify number of tests)

95052 Photo patch test(s) (specify number of tests)

95056 Photo tests

95060 Ophthalmic mucous membrane tests

95065 Direct nasal mucous membrane test

95070 Inhalation bronchial challenge testing (not including necessary pulmonary function tests); with histamine, methacholine, or similar compounds

95071   with antigens or gases, specify

(For pulmonary function tests, see 94060, 94070)

95075 Ingestion challenge test (sequential and incremental ingestion of test items, eg, food, drug or other substance such as metabisulfite)

Allergen Immunotherapy

Codes 95115-95199 include the professional services necessary for allergen immunotherapy. Office visit codes may be used in addition to allergen immunotherapy if other identifiable services are provided at that time.

95115 Professional services for allergen immunotherapy not including provision of allergenic extracts; single injection

95117   2 or more injections

95120 Professional services for allergen immunotherapy in prescribing physicians office or institution, including provision of allergenic extract; single injection

95125   2 or more injections

95130   single stinging insect venom

95131   2 stinging insect venoms

95132   3 stinging insect venoms

95133   4 stinging insect venoms

95134   5 stinging insect venoms

95144 Professional services for the supervision of preparation and provision of antigens for allergen immunotherapy, single dose vial(s) (specify number of vials)

(A single dose vial contains a single dose of antigen administered in 1 injection)

95145 Professional services for the supervision of preparation and provision of antigens for allergen immunotherapy (specify number of doses); single stinging insect venom

95146   2 single stinging insect venoms

95147   3 single stinging insect venoms

95148   4 single stinging insect venoms

95149   5 single stinging insect venoms

95165 Professional services for the supervision of preparation and provision of antigens for allergen immunotherapy; single or multiple antigens (specify number of doses)

95170   whole body extract of biting insect or other arthropod (specify number of doses)

(For allergy immunotherapy reporting, a dose is the amount of antigen[s] administered in a single injection from a multiple dose vial)

95180 Rapid desensitization procedure, each hour (eg, insulin, penicillin, equine serum)

95199 Unlisted allergy/clinical immunologic service or procedure

(For skin testing of bacterial, viral, fungal extracts, see 86485-86580, 95028)

(For special reports on allergy patients, use 99080)

(For testing procedures such as radioallergosorbent testing [RAST], rat mast cell technique [RMCT], mast cell degranulation test [MCDT], lymphocytic transformation test [LTT], leukocyte histamine release [LHR], migration inhibitory factor test [MIF], transfer factor test [TFT], nitroblue tetrazolium dye test [NTD], see Immunology section in **Pathology** or use 95199)

Endocrinology

95250   Ambulatory continuous glucose monitoring of interstitial tissue fluid via a subcutaneous sensor for a minimum of 72 hours; sensor placement, hook-up, calibration of monitor, patient training, removal of sensor, and printout of recording

(Do not report 95250 more than once per month)

(Do not report 95250 in conjunction with 99091)

95251   interpretation and report

(Do not report 95251 more than once per month)

(Do not report 95251 in conjunction with 99091)

Neurology and Neuromuscular Procedures

Neurologic services are typically consultative, and any of the levels of consultation (99241-99255) may be appropriate.

In addition, services and skills outlined under **Evaluation and Management** levels of service appropriate to neurologic illnesses should be reported similarly.

The EEG, autonomic function, evoked potential, reflex tests, EMG, NCV, and MEG services (95812-95829 and 95860-95967) include recording, interpretation by a physician, and report. For interpretation only, use modifier 26. For EMG guidance, see 95873, 95874.

(For repetitive transcranial magnetic stimulation for treatment of clinical depression, see Category III codes 0160T, 0161T)

(Do not report codes 95860-95875 in addition to 96000-96004)

Sleep Testing

Sleep studies and polysomnography refer to the continuous and simultaneous monitoring and recording of various physiological and pathophysiological parameters of sleep for 6 or more hours with physician review, interpretation and report. The studies are performed to diagnose a variety of sleep disorders and to evaluate a patient's response to therapies such as nasal continuous positive airway pressure (NCPAP).

Polysomnography is distinguished from sleep studies by the inclusion of sleep staging which is defined to include a 1-4 lead electroencephalogram (EEG), an electro-oculogram (EOG), and a submental electromyogram (EMG). Additional parameters of sleep include (1) ECG; (2) airflow; (3) ventilation and respiratory effort; (4) gas exchange by oximetry, transcutaneous monitoring, or end tidal gas analysis; (5) extremity muscle activity, motor activity-movement; (6) extended EEG monitoring; (7) penile tumescence; (8) gastroesophageal reflux; (9) continuous blood pressure monitoring; (10) snoring; (11) body positions; etc.

The sleep services (95805-95811) include recording, interpretation and report. For interpretation only, use modifier 26.

For a study to be reported as polysomnography, sleep must be recorded and staged.

(Report with modifier 52 if less than 6 hours of recording or in other cases of reduced services as appropriate)

(For unattended sleep study, use 95806)

95803   Actigraphy testing, recording, analysis, interpretation, and report (minimum of 72 hours to 14 consecutive days of recording)

(Do not report 95803 more than once in any 14 day period)

(Do not report 95803 in conjunction with 95806-95811)

95805   Multiple sleep latency or maintenance of wakefulness testing, recording, analysis and interpretation of physiological measurements of sleep during multiple trials to assess sleepiness

▲ **95806**   Sleep study, unattended, simultaneous recording of, heart rate, oxygen saturation, respiratory airflow, and respiratory effort (eg, thoracoabdominal movement)

(Do not report 95806 in conjunction with 93012, 93014, 93041-93227, 93228, 93229, 93230-93272, 0203T, 0204T)

(For unattended sleep study that measures heart rate, oxygen saturation, respiratory analysis, and sleep time, use 0203T)

(For unattended sleep study that measures heart rate, oxygen saturation, and respiratory analysis, use 0204T)

95807   Sleep study, simultaneous recording of ventilation, respiratory effort, ECG or heart rate, and oxygen saturation, attended by a technologist

95808   Polysomnography; sleep staging with 1-3 additional parameters of sleep, attended by a technologist

95810   sleep staging with 4 or more additional parameters of sleep, attended by a technologist

95811   sleep staging with 4 or more additional parameters of sleep, with initiation of continuous positive airway pressure therapy or bilevel ventilation, attended by a technologist

Routine Electroencephalography (EEG)

EEG codes 95812-95822 include hyperventilation and/or photic stimulation when appropriate. Routine EEG codes 95816-95822 include 20 to 40 minutes of recording. Extended EEG codes 95812-95813 include reporting times longer than 40 minutes.

95812   Electroencephalogram (EEG) extended monitoring; 41-60 minutes

95813   greater than 1 hour

95816   Electroencephalogram (EEG); including recording awake and drowsy

95819   including recording awake and asleep

95822   recording in coma or sleep only

95824   cerebral death evaluation only

95827   all night recording

(For 24-hour EEG monitoring, see 95950-95953 or 95956)

(For EEG during nonintracranial surgery, use 95955)

(For Wada test, use 95958)

(For digital analysis of EEG, use 95957)

95829   Electrocorticogram at surgery (separate procedure)

95830   Insertion by physician of sphenoidal electrodes for electroencephalographic (EEG) recording

Muscle and Range of Motion Testing

95831   Muscle testing, manual (separate procedure) with report; extremity (excluding hand) or trunk

95832   hand, with or without comparison with normal side

95833   total evaluation of body, excluding hands

95834   total evaluation of body, including hands

95851   Range of motion measurements and report (separate procedure); each extremity (excluding hand) or each trunk section (spine)

95852   hand, with or without comparison with normal side

95857   Tensilon test for myasthenia gravis

Electromyography

Needle electromyographic procedures include the interpretation of electrical waveforms measured by equipment that produces both visible and audible components of electrical signals recorded from the muscle(s) studied by the needle electrode.

95860   Needle electromyography; 1 extremity with or without related paraspinal areas

95861   2 extremities with or without related paraspinal areas

(For dynamic electromyography performed during motion analysis studies, see 96002-96003)

95863   3 extremities with or without related paraspinal areas

95864   4 extremities with or without related paraspinal areas

95865   larynx

(Do not report modifier 50 in conjunction with 95865)

(For unilateral procedure, report modifier 52 in conjunction with 95865)

95866   hemidiaphragm

95867   cranial nerve supplied muscle(s), unilateral

95868   cranial nerve supplied muscles, bilateral

95869   thoracic paraspinal muscles (excluding T1 or T12)

95870   limited study of muscles in 1 extremity or non-limb (axial) muscles (unilateral or bilateral), other than thoracic paraspinal, cranial nerve supplied muscles, or sphincters

(To report a complete study of the extremities, see 95860-95864)

(For anal or urethral sphincter, detrusor, urethra, perineum musculature, see 51785-51792)

(For eye muscles, use 92265)

95872   Needle electromyography using single fiber electrode, with quantitative measurement of jitter, blocking and/or fiber density, any/all sites of each muscle studied

Guidance for Chemodenervation and Ischemic Muscle Testing

+ 95873   Electrical stimulation for guidance in conjunction with chemodenervation (List separately in addition to code for primary procedure)

+ 95874   Needle electromyography for guidance in conjunction with chemodenervation (List separately in addition to code for primary procedure)

(Use 95873, 95874 in conjunction with 64612-64614)

(Do not report 95874 in conjunction with 95873)

(Do not report 95873, 95874 in conjunction with 95860-95870)

95875   Ischemic limb exercise test with serial specimen(s) acquisition for muscle(s) metabolite(s)

(For listing of nerves considered for separate study, see **Appendix J**)

Nerve Conduction Tests

▶The following applies to nerve conduction tests (95900-95904): Codes 95900-95904 describe nerve conduction tests when performed with individually placed stimulating, recording, and ground electrodes. The stimulating, recording, and ground electrode placement and the test design must be individualized to the patient's unique anatomy. Nerves tested must be limited to the specific nerves and conduction studies needed for the particular clinical question being investigated. The

Medicine

stimulating electrode must be placed directly over the nerve to be tested, and stimulation parameters properly adjusted to avoid stimulating other nerves or nerve branches. In most motor nerve conduction studies, and in some sensory and mixed nerve conduction studies, both proximal and distal stimulation will be used. Motor nerve conduction study recordings must be made from electrodes placed directly over the motor point of the specific muscle to be tested. Sensory nerve conduction study recordings must be made from electrodes placed directly over the specific nerve to be tested. Waveforms must be reviewed on site in real time, and the technique (stimulus site, recording site, ground site, filter settings) must be adjusted, as appropriate, as the test proceeds in order to minimize artifact, and to minimize the chances of unintended stimulation of adjacent nerves and the unintended recording from adjacent muscles or nerves. Reports must be prepared on site by the examiner, and consist of the work product of the interpretation of numerous test results, using well-established techniques to assess the amplitude, latency, and configuration of waveforms elicited by stimulation at each site of each nerve tested. This includes the calculation of nerve conduction velocities, sometimes including specialized F-wave indices, along with comparison to normal values, summarization of clinical and electrodiagnostic data, and physician or other qualified health care professional interpretation.

Code 95905 describes nerve conduction tests when performed with preconfigured electrodes customized to a specific anatomic site.◄

⊘ **95900**   Nerve conduction, amplitude and latency/velocity study, each nerve; motor, without F-wave study

⊘ **95903**   motor, with F-wave study

⊘ **95904**   sensory

(Report 95900, 95903, and/or 95904 only once when multiple sites on the same nerve are stimulated or recorded)

⊘● **95905**   Motor and/or sensory nerve conduction, using preconfigured electrode array(s), amplitude and latency/velocity study, each limb, includes F-wave study when performed, with interpretation and report

►(Report 95905 only once per limb studied)◄

►(Do not report 95905 in conjunction with 95900-95904, 95934-95936)◄

Intraoperative Neurophysiology

+ **95920**   Intraoperative neurophysiology testing, per hour (List separately in addition to code for primary procedure)

(Use 95920 in conjunction with the study performed, 92585, 95822, 95860, 95861, 95867, 95868, 95870, 95900, 95904, 95925-95937)

(Code 95920 describes ongoing electrophysiologic testing and monitoring performed during surgical procedures. Code 95920 is reported per hour of service, and includes only the ongoing electrophysiologic monitoring time distinct from performance of specific type(s) of baseline electrophysiologic study(s) (95860, 95861, 95867, 95868, 95870, 95900, 95904, 95928, 95929, 95933-95937) or interpretation of specific type(s) of baseline electrophysiologic study(s) (92585, 95822, 95870, 95925-95928, 95929, 95930). The time spent performing or interpreting the baseline electrophysiologic study(s) should not be counted as intraoperative monitoring, but represents separately reportable procedures. Code 95920 should be used once per hour even if multiple electrophysiologic studies are performed. The baseline electrophysiologic study(s) should be used once per operative session.)

(For electrocorticography, use 95829)

(For intraoperative EEG during nonintracranial surgery, use 95955)

(For intraoperative functional cortical or subcortical mapping, see 95961-95962)

(For intraoperative neurostimulator programming and analysis, see 95970-95975)

Autonomic Function Tests

95921   Testing of autonomic nervous system function; cardiovagal innervation (parasympathetic function), including 2 or more of the following: heart rate response to deep breathing with recorded R-R interval, Valsalva ratio, and 30:15 ratio

95922   vasomotor adrenergic innervation (sympathetic adrenergic function), including beat-to-beat blood pressure and R-R interval changes during Valsalva maneuver and at least 5 minutes of passive tilt

95923   sudomotor, including 1 or more of the following: quantitative sudomotor axon reflex test (QSART), silastic sweat imprint, thermoregulatory sweat test, and changes in sympathetic skin potential

Evoked Potentials and Reflex Tests

95925   Short-latency somatosensory evoked potential study, stimulation of any/all peripheral nerves or skin sites, recording from the central nervous system; in upper limbs

95926   in lower limbs

95927   in the trunk or head

(To report a unilateral study, use modifier 52)

(For auditory evoked potentials, use 92585)

95928   Central motor evoked potential study (transcranial motor stimulation); upper limbs

95929   lower limbs

95930   Visual evoked potential (VEP) testing central nervous system, checkerboard or flash

95933 Orbicularis oculi (blink) reflex, by electrodiagnostic testing

95934 H-reflex, amplitude and latency study; record gastrocnemius/soleus muscle

95936 record muscle other than gastrocnemius/soleus muscle

(To report a bilateral study, use modifier 50)

95937 Neuromuscular junction testing (repetitive stimulation, paired stimuli), each nerve, any 1 method

Special EEG Tests

95950 Monitoring for identification and lateralization of cerebral seizure focus, electroencephalographic (eg, 8 channel EEG) recording and interpretation, each 24 hours

95951 Monitoring for localization of cerebral seizure focus by cable or radio, 16 or more channel telemetry, combined electroencephalographic (EEG) and video recording and interpretation (eg, for presurgical localization), each 24 hours

95953 Monitoring for localization of cerebral seizure focus by computerized portable 16 or more channel EEG, electroencephalographic (EEG) recording and interpretation, each 24 hours

95954 Pharmacological or physical activation requiring physician attendance during EEG recording of activation phase (eg, thiopental activation test)

95955 Electroencephalogram (EEG) during nonintracranial surgery (eg, carotid surgery)

95956 Monitoring for localization of cerebral seizure focus by cable or radio, 16 or more channel telemetry, electroencephalographic (EEG) recording and interpretation, each 24 hours

95957 Digital analysis of electroencephalogram (EEG) (eg, for epileptic spike analysis)

95958 Wada activation test for hemispheric function, including electroencephalographic (EEG) monitoring

95961 Functional cortical and subcortical mapping by stimulation and/or recording of electrodes on brain surface, or of depth electrodes, to provoke seizures or identify vital brain structures; initial hour of physician attendance

+ 95962 each additional hour of physician attendance (List separately in addition to code for primary procedure)

(Use 95962 in conjunction with 95961)

95965 Magnetoencephalography (MEG), recording and analysis; for spontaneous brain magnetic activity (eg, epileptic cerebral cortex localization)

95966 for evoked magnetic fields, single modality (eg, sensory, motor, language, or visual cortex localization)

+ 95967 for evoked magnetic fields, each additional modality (eg, sensory, motor, language, or visual cortex localization) (List separately in addition to code for primary procedure)

(Use 95967 in conjunction with 95966)

(For electroencephalography performed in addition to magnetoencephalography, see 95812-95827)

(For somatosensory evoked potentials, auditory evoked potentials, and visual evoked potentials performed in addition to magnetic evoked field responses, see 92585, 95925, 95926, and/or 95930)

(For computerized tomography performed in addition to magnetoencephalography, see 70450-70470, 70496)

(For magnetic resonance imaging performed in addition to magnetoencephalography, see 70551-70553)

Neurostimulators, Analysis-Programming

A simple neurostimulator pulse generator/transmitter (95970, 95971) is one capable of affecting three or fewer of the following: pulse amplitude, pulse duration, pulse frequency, eight or more electrode contacts, cycling, stimulation train duration, train spacing, number of programs, number of channels, alternating electrode polarities, dose time (stimulation parameters changing in time periods of minutes including dose lockout times), more than one clinical feature (eg, rigidity, dyskinesia, tremor). A complex neurostimulator pulse generator/ transmitter (95970, 95972- 95975) is one capable of affecting more than three of the above.

Code 95970 describes subsequent electronic analysis of a previously-implanted simple or complex brain, spinal cord, or peripheral neurostimulator pulse generator system, without reprogramming. Code 95971 describes intraoperative or subsequent electronic analysis of an implanted simple spinal cord, or peripheral (ie, peripheral nerve, autonomic nerve, neuromuscular) neurostimulator pulse generator system, with programming. Codes 95972 and 95973 describe intraoperative (at initial insertion/revision) or subsequent electronic analysis of an implanted complex spinal cord or peripheral (except cranial nerve) neurostimulator pulse generator system, with programming. Codes 95974 and 95975 describe intraoperative (at initial insertion/revision) or subsequent electronic analysis of an implanted complex cranial nerve neurostimulator pulse generator system, with programming. Codes 95978 and 95979 describe initial or subsequent electronic analysis of an implanted brain neurostimulator pulse generator system, with programming.

Medicine

Code 95980 describes intraoperative electronic analysis of an implanted gastric neurostimulator pulse generator system, with programming; code 95981 describes subsequent analysis of the device; code 95982 describes subsequent analysis and reprogramming. For electronic analysis and reprogramming of gastric neurostimulator, lesser curvature, see 95980-95982.

(For insertion of neurostimulator pulse generator, see 61885, 63685, 64590)

(For revision or removal of neurostimulator pulse generator or receiver, see 61888, 63688, 64595)

▶(For implantation of neurostimulator electrodes, see 43647, 43881, 61850-61875, 63650-63655, 64553-64580, 0155T, 0157T. For revision or removal of neurostimulator electrodes, see 43648, 43882, 61880, 63661-63664, 64585, 0156T, 0158T)◀

95970 Electronic analysis of implanted neurostimulator pulse generator system (eg, rate, pulse amplitude and duration, configuration of wave form, battery status, electrode selectability, output modulation, cycling, impedance and patient compliance measurements); simple or complex brain, spinal cord, or peripheral (ie, cranial nerve, peripheral nerve, autonomic nerve, neuromuscular) neurostimulator pulse generator/transmitter, without reprogramming

95971 simple spinal cord, or peripheral (ie, peripheral nerve, autonomic nerve, neuromuscular) neurostimulator pulse generator/transmitter, with intraoperative or subsequent programming

95972 complex spinal cord, or peripheral (except cranial nerve) neurostimulator pulse generator/transmitter, with intraoperative or subsequent programming, first hour

+ 95973 complex spinal cord, or peripheral (except cranial nerve) neurostimulator pulse generator/transmitter, with intraoperative or subsequent programming, each additional 30 minutes after first hour (List separately in addition to code for primary procedure)

(Use 95973 in conjunction with 95972)

95974 complex cranial nerve neurostimulator pulse generator/transmitter, with intraoperative or subsequent programming, with or without nerve interface testing, first hour

+ 95975 complex cranial nerve neurostimulator pulse generator/transmitter, with intraoperative or subsequent programming, each additional 30 minutes after first hour (List separately in addition to code for primary procedure)

(Use 95975 in conjunction with 95974)

(For electronic analysis programming of gastric neurostimulator, lesser curvature, use Category III code 0162T)

95978 Electronic analysis of implanted neurostimulator pulse generator system (eg, rate, pulse amplitude and duration, battery status, electrode selectability and polarity, impedance and patient compliance measurements), complex deep brain neurostimulator pulse generator/transmitter, with initial or subsequent programming; first hour

+ 95979 each additional 30 minutes after first hour (List separately in addition to code for primary procedure)

(Use 95979 in conjunction with 95978)

95980 Electronic analysis of implanted neurostimulator pulse generator system (eg, rate, pulse amplitude and duration, configuration of wave form, battery status, electrode selectability, output modulation, cycling, impedance and patient measurements) gastric neurostimulator pulse generator/transmitter; intraoperative, with programming

95981 subsequent, without reprogramming

95982 subsequent, with reprogramming

Other Procedures

95990 Refilling and maintenance of implantable pump or reservoir for drug delivery, spinal (intrathecal, epidural) or brain (intraventricular);

(For analysis and/or reprogramming of implantable infusion pump, see 62367-62368)

(For refill and maintenance of implanted infusion pump or reservoir for systemic drug therapy [eg, chemotherapy or insulin], use 96522)

95991 administered by physician

⊘ **95992** Canalith repositioning procedure(s) (eg, Epley maneuver, Semont maneuver), per day

(Do not report 95992 in conjunction with 92531, 92532)

95999 Unlisted neurological or neuromuscular diagnostic procedure

Motion Analysis

Codes 96000-96004 describe services performed as part of a major therapeutic or diagnostic decision making process. Motion analysis is performed in a dedicated motion analysis laboratory (ie, a facility capable of performing videotaping from the front, back and both sides, computerized 3D kinematics, 3D kinetics, and dynamic electromyography). Code 96000 may include 3D kinetics and stride characteristics. Codes 96002-96003 describe dynamic electromyography.

Code 96004 should only be reported once regardless of the number of study(ies) reviewed/interpreted.

(For performance of needle electromyography procedures, see 95860-95875)

(For gait training, use 97116)

96000 Comprehensive computer-based motion analysis by video-taping and 3D kinematics;

96001   with dynamic plantar pressure measurements during walking

96002   Dynamic surface electromyography, during walking or other functional activities, 1-12 muscles

96003   Dynamic fine wire electromyography, during walking or other functional activities, 1 muscle

(Do not report 96002, 96003 in conjunction with 95860-95864, 95869-95872)

96004   Physician review and interpretation of comprehensive computer-based motion analysis, dynamic plantar pressure measurements, dynamic surface electromyography during walking or other functional activities, and dynamic fine wire electromyography, with written report

Functional Brain Mapping

Code 96020 includes selection and administration of testing of language, memory, cognition, movement, sensation, and other neurological functions when conducted in association with functional neuroimaging, monitoring of performance of this testing, and determination of validity of neurofunctional testing relative to separately interpreted functional magnetic resonance images.

96020   Neurofunctional testing selection and administration during noninvasive imaging functional brain mapping, with test administered entirely by a physician or psychologist, with review of test results and report

(For functional magnetic resonance imaging [fMRI], brain, use 70555)

(Do not report 96020 in conjunction with 96101-96103, 96116-96120)

(Do not report 96020 in conjunction with 70554)

(Evaluation and Management services codes should not be reported on the same day as 96020)

Medical Genetics and Genetic Counseling Services

These services are provided by trained genetic counselors and may include obtaining a structured family genetic history, pedigree construction, analysis for genetic risk assessment, and counseling of the patient and family. These activities may be provided during one or more sessions and may include review of medical data and family information, face-to-face interviews, and counseling services.

96040   Medical genetics and genetic counseling services, each 30 minutes face-to-face with patient/family

(For genetic counseling and education provided by a physician to an individual, see the appropriate Evaluation and Management codes)

(For genetic counseling and education provided by a physician to a group, use 99078)

(For education regarding genetic risks by a nonphysician to a group, see 98961, 98962)

(For genetic counseling and/or risk factor reduction intervention provided by a physician to patient(s) without symptoms or established disease, see 99401-99412)

Central Nervous System Assessments/Tests (eg, Neuro-Cognitive, Mental Status, Speech Testing)

The following codes are used to report the services provided during testing of the cognitive function of the central nervous system. The testing of cognitive processes, visual motor responses, and abstractive abilities is accomplished by the combination of several types of testing procedures. It is expected that the administration of these tests will generate material that will be formulated into a report.

(For development of cognitive skills, see 97532, 97533)

(For mini-mental status examination performed by a physician, see **Evaluation and Management** services codes)

96101   Psychological testing (includes psychodiagnostic assessment of emotionality, intellectual abilities, personality and psychopathology, eg, MMPI, Rorschach, WAIS), per hour of the psychologist's or physician's time, both face-to-face time administering tests to the patient and time interpreting these test results and preparing the report

(96101 is also used in those circumstances when additional time is necessary to integrate other sources of clinical data, including previously completed and reported technician- and computer-administered tests)

(Do not report 96101 for the interpretation and report of 96102, 96103)

96102   Psychological testing (includes psychodiagnostic assessment of emotionality, intellectual abilities, personality and psychopathology, eg, MMPI and WAIS), with qualified health care professional interpretation and report, administered by technician, per hour of technician time, face-to-face

96103   Psychological testing (includes psychodiagnostic assessment of emotionality, intellectual abilities, personality and psychopathology, eg, MMPI), administered by a computer, with qualified health care professional interpretation and report

Medicine

96105 Assessment of aphasia (includes assessment of expressive and receptive speech and language function, language comprehension, speech production ability, reading, spelling, writing, eg, by Boston Diagnostic Aphasia Examination) with interpretation and report, per hour

96110 Developmental testing; limited (eg, Developmental Screening Test II, Early Language Milestone Screen), with interpretation and report

96111 extended (includes assessment of motor, language, social, adaptive and/or cognitive functioning by standardized developmental instruments) with interpretation and report

96116 Neurobehavioral status exam (clinical assessment of thinking, reasoning and judgment, eg, acquired knowledge, attention, language, memory, planning and problem solving, and visual spatial abilities), per hour of the psychologist's or physician's time, both face-to-face time with the patient and time interpreting test results and preparing the report

96118 Neuropsychological testing (eg, Halstead-Reitan Neuropsychological Battery, Wechsler Memory Scales and Wisconsin Card Sorting Test), per hour of the psychologist's or physician's time, both face-to-face time administering tests to the patient and time interpreting these test results and preparing the report

(96118 is also used in those circumstances when additional time is necessary to integrate other sources of clinical data, including previously completed and reported technician- and computer-administered tests)

(Do not report 96118 for the interpretation and report of 96119 or 96120)

96119 Neuropsychological testing (eg, Halstead-Reitan Neuropsychological Battery, Wechsler Memory Scales and Wisconsin Card Sorting Test), with qualified health care professional interpretation and report, administered by technician, per hour of technician time, face-to-face

96120 Neuropsychological testing (eg, Wisconsin Card Sorting Test), administered by a computer, with qualified health care professional interpretation and report

96125 Standardized cognitive performance testing (eg, Ross Information Processing Assessment) per hour of a qualified health care professional's time, both face-to-face time administering tests to the patient and time interpreting these test results and preparing the report

(For psychological and neuropsychological testing by a physician or psychologist, see 96101-96103, 96118-96120)

Health and Behavior Assessment/Intervention

Health and behavior assessment procedures are used to identify the psychological, behavioral, emotional, cognitive, and social factors important to the prevention, treatment, or management of physical health problems.

The focus of the assessment is not on mental health but on the biopsychosocial factors important to physical health problems and treatments. The focus of the intervention is to improve the patient's health and well-being utilizing cognitive, behavioral, social, and/or psychophysiological procedures designed to ameliorate specific disease-related problems.

Codes 96150-96155 describe services offered to patients who present with primary physical illnesses, diagnoses, or symptoms and may benefit from assessments and interventions that focus on the biopsychosocial factors related to the patient's health status. These services do not represent preventive medicine counseling and risk factor reduction interventions.

For patients that require psychiatric services (90801-90899) as well as health and behavior assessment/intervention (96150-96155), report the predominant service performed. Do not report 96150-96155 in conjunction with 90801-90899 on the same date.

Evaluation and Management services codes (including Counseling Risk Factor Reduction and Behavior Change Intervention [99401-99412]), should not be reported on the same day.

(For health and behavior assessment and/or intervention performed by a physician, see **Evaluation and Management** or **Preventive Medicine** services codes)

96150 Health and behavior assessment (eg, health-focused clinical interview, behavioral observations, psychophysiological monitoring, health-oriented questionnaires), each 15 minutes face-to-face with the patient; initial assessment

96151 re-assessment

96152 Health and behavior intervention, each 15 minutes, face-to-face; individual

96153 group (2 or more patients)

96154 family (with the patient present)

96155 family (without the patient present)

Medicine

Hydration, Therapeutic, Prophylactic, Diagnostic Injections and Infusions, and Chemotherapy and Other Highly Complex Drug or Highly Complex Biologic Agent Administration

Physician work related to hydration, injection, and infusion services predominantly involves affirmation of treatment plan and direct supervision of staff.

If a significant, separately identifiable Evaluation and Management service is performed, the appropriate E/M service code should be reported using modifier 25 in addition to 96360-96549. For same day E/M service, a different diagnosis is not required.

If performed to facilitate the infusion or injection, the following services are included and are not reported separately:

a. Use of local anesthesia

b. IV start

c. Access to indwelling IV, subcutaneous catheter or port

d. Flush at conclusion of infusion

e. Standard tubing, syringes, and supplies

(For declotting a catheter or port, use 36593)

When multiple drugs are administered, report the service(s) and the specific materials or drugs for each.

When administering multiple infusions, injections or combinations, only one "initial" service code should be reported, unless protocol requires that two separate IV sites must be used. If an injection or infusion is of a subsequent or concurrent nature, even if it is the first such service within that group of services, then a subsequent or concurrent code from the appropriate section should be reported (eg, the first IV push given subsequent to an initial one-hour infusion is reported using a subsequent IV push code).

▶In order to determine which service should be reported as the initial service when there is more than one type of service, hierarchies have been created. These vary by whether the physician or a facility is reporting. The order of selection for physicians is based upon the physician knowledge of the clinical condition(s) and treatment(s). The hierarchy that facilities are to use is based upon a structural algorithm. When these codes are reported by the physician, the "initial" code that best describes the key or primary reason for the encounter should always be reported irrespective of the order in which the infusions or injections occur.◀

▶When these codes are reported *by the facility*, the following instructions apply. The initial code should be selected using a hierarchy whereby chemotherapy services are primary to therapeutic, prophylactic, and diagnostic services which are primary to hydration services. Infusions are primary to pushes, which are primary to injections. This hierarchy is to be followed by facilities and supersedes parenthetical instructions for add-on codes that suggest an add-on of a higher hierarchical position may be reported in conjunction with a base code of a lower position. (For example, the hierarchy would not permit reporting 96376 with 96360, as 96376 is a higher order code. IV push is primary to hydration.)◀

When reporting codes for which infusion time is a factor, use the actual time over which the infusion is administered. Intravenous or intra-arterial push is defined as: (a) an injection in which the health care professional who administers the substance/drug is continuously present to administer the injection and observe the patient, or (b) an infusion of 15 minutes or less.

Hydration

Codes 96360-96361 are intended to report a hydration IV infusion to consist of a pre-packaged fluid and electrolytes (eg, normal saline, D5-1/2 normal saline+30mEq KCl/liter), but are not used to report infusion of drugs or other substances. Hydration IV infusions typically require direct physician supervision for purposes of consent, safety oversight, or intraservice supervision of staff. Typically such infusions require little special handling to prepare or dispose of, and staff that administer these do not typically require advanced practice training. After initial set-up, infusion typically entails little patient risk and thus little monitoring. These codes are not intended to be reported by the physician in the facility setting.

96360 Intravenous infusion, hydration; initial, 31 minutes to 1 hour

(Do not report 96360 if performed as a concurrent infusion service)

(Do not report intravenous infusion for hydration of 30 minutes or less)

+ 96361 each additional hour (List separately in addition to code for primary procedure)

(Use 96361 in conjunction with 96360)

(Report 96361 for hydration infusion intervals of greater than 30 minutes beyond 1 hour increments)

(Report 96361 to identify hydration if provided as a secondary or subsequent service after a different initial service [96360, 96365, 96374, 96409, 96413] is administered through the same IV access)

Medicine

Therapeutic, Prophylactic, and Diagnostic Injections and Infusions (Excludes Chemotherapy and Other Highly Complex Drug or Highly Complex Biologic Agent Administration)

A therapeutic, prophylactic, or diagnostic IV infusion or injection (other than hydration) is for the administration of substances/drugs. When fluids are used to administer the drug(s), the administration of the fluid is considered incidental hydration and is not separately reportable. These services typically require direct physician supervision for any or all purposes of patient assessment, provision of consent, safety oversight, and intra-service supervision of staff. Typically, such infusions require special consideration to prepare, dose or dispose of, require practice training and competency for staff who administer the infusions, and require periodic patient assessment with vital sign monitoring during the infusion. These codes are not intended to be reported by the physician in the facility setting.

See codes 96401-96549 for the administration of chemotherapy or other highly complex drug or highly complex biologic agent services. These highly complex services require advanced practice training and competency for staff who provide these services; special considerations for preparation, dosage or disposal; and commonly, these services entail significant patient risk and frequent monitoring. Examples are frequent changes in the infusion rate, prolonged presence of nurse administering the solution for patient monitoring and infusion adjustments, and frequent conferring with the physician about these issues.

(Do not report 96365-96379 with codes for which IV push or infusion is an inherent part of the procedure [eg, administration of contrast material for a diagnostic imaging study])

96365 Intravenous infusion, for therapy, prophylaxis, or diagnosis (specify substance or drug); initial, up to 1 hour

+ 96366 each additional hour (List separately in addition to code for primary procedure)

(Report 96366 in conjunction with 96365, 96367)

(Report 96366 for additional hour[s] of sequential infusion)

(Report 96366 for infusion intervals of greater than 30 minutes beyond 1 hour increments)

+ 96367 additional sequential infusion, up to 1 hour (List separately in addition to code for primary procedure)

(Report 96367 in conjunction with 96365, 96374, 96409, 96413 if provided as a secondary or subsequent service after a different initial service is administered through the same IV access. Report 96367 only once per sequential infusion of same infusate mix)

+ 96368 concurrent infusion (List separately in addition to code for primary procedure)

(Report 96368 only once per encounter)

(Report 96368 in conjunction with 96365, 96366, 96413, 96415, 96416)

96369 Subcutaneous infusion for therapy or prophylaxis (specify substance or drug); initial, up to 1 hour, including pump set-up and establishment of subcutaneous infusion site(s)

(For infusions of 15 minutes or less, use 96372)

+ 96370 each additional hour (List separately in addition to code for primary procedure)

(Use 96370 in conjunction with 96369)

(Use 96370 for infusion intervals of greater than 30 minutes beyond 1 hour increments)

+ 96371 additional pump set-up with establishment of new subcutaneous infusion site(s) (List separately in addition to code for primary procedure)

(Use 96371 in conjunction with 96369)

(Use 96369, 96371 only once per encounter)

96372 Therapeutic, prophylactic, or diagnostic injection (specify substance or drug); subcutaneous or intramuscular

(For administration of vaccines/toxoids, see 96365, 96366, 90471, 90472)

(Report 96372 for non-antineoplastic hormonal therapy injections)

(Report 96401 for anti-neoplastic nonhormonal injection therapy)

(Report 96402 for anti-neoplastic hormonal injection therapy)

(Physicians do not report 96372 for injections given without direct physician supervision. To report, use 99211. Hospitals may report 96372 when the physician is not present)

(96372 does not include injections for allergen immunotherapy. For allergen immunotherapy injections, see 95115-95117)

96373 intra-arterial

96374 intravenous push, single or initial substance/drug

+ 96375 each additional sequential intravenous push of a new substance/drug (List separately in addition to code for primary procedure)

(Use 96375 in conjunction with 96365, 96374, 96409, 96413)

(Report 96375 to identify intravenous push of a new substance/drug if provided as a secondary or subsequent service after a different initial service is administered through the same IV access)

+ 96376   each additional sequential intravenous push of the same substance/drug provided in a facility (List separately in addition to code for primary procedure)

(Do not report 96376 for a push performed within 30 minutes of a reported push of the same substance or drug)

(96376 may be reported by facilities only)

96379   Unlisted therapeutic, prophylactic, or diagnostic intravenous or intra-arterial injection or infusion

(For allergy immunology, see 95004 et seq)

Chemotherapy and Other Highly Complex Drug or Highly Complex Biologic Agent Administration

Chemotherapy administration codes 96401-96549 apply to parenteral administration of non-radionuclide anti-neoplastic drugs; and also to anti-neoplastic agents provided for treatment of noncancer diagnoses (eg, cyclophosphamide for auto-immune conditions) or to substances such as certain monoclonal antibody agents, and other biologic response modifiers. The highly complex infusion of chemotherapy or other drug or biologic agents requires physician work and/or clinical staff monitoring well beyond that of therapeutic drug agents (96360-96379) because the incidence of severe adverse patient reactions are typically greater. These services can be provided by any physician. Chemotherapy services are typically highly complex and require direct physician supervision for any or all purposes of patient assessment, provision of consent, safety oversight, and intraservice supervision of staff. Typically, such chemotherapy services require advanced practice training and competency for staff who provide these services; special considerations for preparation, dosage, or disposal; and commonly, these services entail significant patient risk and frequent monitoring. Examples are frequent changes in the infusion rate, prolonged presence of the nurse administering the solution for patient monitoring and infusion adjustments, and frequent conferring with the physician about these issues. When performed to facilitate the infusion of injection, preparation of chemotherapy agent(s), highly complex agent(s), or other highly complex drugs is included and is not reported separately. To report infusions that do not require this level of complexity, see 96360-96379. Codes 96401-96402, 96409-96425, 96521-96523 are not intended to be reported by the physician in the facility setting.

The term "chemotherapy" in 96401-96549 includes other highly complex drugs or highly complex biologic agents.

Report separate codes for each parenteral method of administration employed when chemotherapy is administered by different techniques. The administration of medications (eg, antibiotics, steroidal agents, antiemetics, narcotics, analgesics) administered

independently or sequentially as supportive management of chemotherapy administration, should be separately reported using 96360, 96361, 96365, 96379 as appropriate.

Report both the specific service as well as code(s) for the specific substance(s) or drug(s) provided. The fluid used to administer the drug(s) is considered incidental hydration and is not separately reportable.

Regional (isolation) chemotherapy perfusion should be reported using the codes for arterial infusion (96420-96425). Placement of the intra-arterial catheter should be reported using the appropriate code from the **Cardiovascular Surgery** section. Placement of arterial and venous cannula(s) for extracorporeal circulation via a membrane oxygenator perfusion pump should be reported using 36823. Code 36823 includes dose calculation and administration of the chemotherapy agent by injection into the perfusate. Do not report 96409-96425 in conjunction with 36823.

(For home infusion services, see 99601-99602)

Injection and Intravenous Infusion Chemotherapy and Other Highly Complex Drug or Highly Complex Biologic Agent Administration

Intravenous or intra-arterial push is defined as: (a) an injection in which the healthcare professional who administers the substance/drug is continuously present to administer the injection and observe the patient, or (b) an infusion of 15 minutes or less.

96401   Chemotherapy administration, subcutaneous or intramuscular; non-hormonal anti-neoplastic

96402   hormonal anti-neoplastic

96405   Chemotherapy administration; intralesional, up to and including 7 lesions

96406   intralesional, more than 7 lesions

96409   intravenous, push technique, single or initial substance/drug

+ 96411   intravenous, push technique, each additional substance/drug (List separately in addition to code for primary procedure)

(Use 96411 in conjunction with 96409, 96413)

96413   Chemotherapy administration, intravenous infusion technique; up to 1 hour, single or initial substance/drug

(Report 96361 to identify hydration if administered as a secondary or subsequent service in association with 96413 through the same IV access)

(Report 96366, 96367, 96375 to identify therapeutic, prophylactic, or diagnostic drug infusion or injection, if administered as a secondary or subsequent service in association with 96413 through the same IV access)

Medicine

+ 96415   each additional hour (List separately in addition to code for primary procedure)

(Use 96415 in conjunction with 96413)

(Report 96415 for infusion intervals of greater than 30 minutes beyond 1-hour increments)

96416   initiation of prolonged chemotherapy infusion (more than 8 hours), requiring use of a portable or implantable pump

(For refilling and maintenance of a portable pump or an implantable infusion pump or reservoir for drug delivery, see 96521-96523)

+ 96417   each additional sequential infusion (different substance/drug), up to 1 hour (List separately in addition to code for primary procedure)

(Use 96417 in conjunction with 96413)

(Report only once per sequential infusion. Report 96415 for additional hour(s) of sequential infusion)

Intra-Arterial Chemotherapy and Other Highly Complex Drug or Highly Complex Biologic Agent Administration

96420   Chemotherapy administration, intra-arterial; push technique

96422   infusion technique, up to 1 hour

+ 96423   infusion technique, each additional hour (List separately in addition to code for primary procedure)

(Use 96423 in conjunction with 96422)

(Report 96423 for infusion intervals of greater than 30 minutes beyond 1-hour increments)

(For regional chemotherapy perfusion via membrane oxygenator perfusion pump to an extremity, use 36823)

96425   infusion technique, initiation of prolonged infusion (more than 8 hours), requiring the use of a portable or implantable pump

(For refilling and maintenance of a portable pump or an implantable infusion pump or reservoir for drug delivery, see 96521-96523)

Other Injection and Infusion Services

Code 96523 does not require direct physician supervision. Codes 96521-96523 may be reported when these devices are used for therapeutic drugs other than chemotherapy.

(For collection of blood specimen from a completely implantable venous access device, use 36591)

96440   Chemotherapy administration into pleural cavity, requiring and including thoracentesis

96445   Chemotherapy administration into peritoneal cavity, requiring and including peritoneocentesis

96450   Chemotherapy administration, into CNS (eg, intrathecal), requiring and including spinal puncture

(For intravesical (bladder) chemotherapy administration, use 51720)

(For insertion of subarachnoid catheter and reservoir for infusion of drug, see 62350, 62351, 62360-62362; for insertion of intraventricular catheter and reservoir, see 61210, 61215)

96521   Refilling and maintenance of portable pump

96522   Refilling and maintenance of implantable pump or reservoir for drug delivery, systemic (eg, intravenous, intra-arterial)

(For refilling and maintenance of an implantable infusion pump for spinal or brain drug infusion, use 95990-95991)

96523   Irrigation of implanted venous access device for drug delivery systems

(Do not report 96523 if any other services are provided on the same day)

96542   Chemotherapy injection, subarachnoid or intraventricular via subcutaneous reservoir, single or multiple agents

(For radioactive isotope therapy, use 79005)

96549   Unlisted chemotherapy procedure

Photodynamic Therapy

(To report ocular photodynamic therapy, use 67221)

96567   Photodynamic therapy by external application of light to destroy premalignant and/or malignant lesions of the skin and adjacent mucosa (eg, lip) by activation of photosensitive drug(s), each phototherapy exposure session

+▲ 96570   Photodynamic therapy by endoscopic application of light to ablate abnormal tissue via activation of photosensitive drug(s); first 30 minutes (List separately in addition to code for endoscopy or bronchoscopy procedures of lung and gastrointestinal tract)

+▲ 96571   each additional 15 minutes (List separately in addition to code for endoscopy or bronchoscopy procedures of lung and gastrointestinal tract)

(96570, 96571 are to be used in addition to bronchoscopy, endoscopy codes)

(Use 96570, 96571 in conjunction with 31641, 43228 as appropriate)

Special Dermatological Procedures

Dermatologic services are typically consultative, and any of the five levels of consultation (99241-99255) may be appropriate.

In addition, services and skills outlined under **Evaluation and Management** levels of service appropriate to dermatologic illnesses should be coded similarly.

> (For intralesional injections, see 11900, 11901)

> (For Tzanck smear, see 88160-88161)

96900   Actinotherapy (ultraviolet light)

96902   Microscopic examination of hairs plucked or clipped by the examiner (excluding hair collected by the patient) to determine telogen and anagen counts, or structural hair shaft abnormality

96904   Whole body integumentary photography, for monitoring of high risk patients with dysplastic nevus syndrome or a history of dysplastic nevi, or patients with a personal or familial history of melanoma

96910   Photochemotherapy; tar and ultraviolet B (Goeckerman treatment) or petrolatum and ultraviolet B

96912   psoralens and ultraviolet A (PUVA)

96913   Photochemotherapy (Goeckerman and/or PUVA) for severe photoresponsive dermatoses requiring at least 4-8 hours of care under direct supervision of the physician (includes application of medication and dressings)

96920   Laser treatment for inflammatory skin disease (psoriasis); total area less than 250 sq cm

96921   250 sq cm to 500 sq cm

96922   over 500 sq cm

> ►(For laser destruction of premalignant lesions, see 17000-17004)◄

> ►(For laser destruction of cutaneous vascular proliferative lesions, see 17106-17108)◄

> ►(For laser destruction of benign lesions, see 17110-17111)◄

> ►(For laser destruction of malignant lesions, see 17260-17286)◄

96999   Unlisted special dermatological service or procedure

Physical Medicine and Rehabilitation

Codes 97001-97755 should be used to report each distinct procedure performed. Do not append modifier 51 to 97001-97755.

> (For muscle testing, range of joint motion, electromyography, see 95831 et seq)

> (For biofeedback training by EMG, use 90901)

> (For transcutaneous nerve stimulation (TNS), use 64550)

97001   Physical therapy evaluation

97002   Physical therapy re-evaluation

97003   Occupational therapy evaluation

97004   Occupational therapy re-evaluation

97005   Athletic training evaluation

97006   Athletic training re-evaluation

Modalities

Any physical agent applied to produce therapeutic changes to biologic tissue; includes but not limited to thermal, acoustic, light, mechanical, or electric energy.

Supervised

The application of a modality that does not require direct (one-on-one) patient contact by the provider.

97010   Application of a modality to 1 or more areas; hot or cold packs

97012   traction, mechanical

97014   electrical stimulation (unattended)

> (For acupuncture with electrical stimulation, see 97813, 97814)

97016   vasopneumatic devices

97018   paraffin bath

97022   whirlpool

97024   diathermy (eg, microwave)

97026   infrared

97028   ultraviolet

Constant Attendance

The application of a modality that requires direct (one-on-one) patient contact by the provider.

97032   Application of a modality to 1 or more areas; electrical stimulation (manual), each 15 minutes

97033   iontophoresis, each 15 minutes

97034   contrast baths, each 15 minutes

97035   ultrasound, each 15 minutes

97036   Hubbard tank, each 15 minutes

97039   Unlisted modality (specify type and time if constant attendance)

Therapeutic Procedures

A manner of effecting change through the application of clinical skills and/or services that attempt to improve function.

Physician or therapist required to have direct (one-on-one) patient contact.

97110   Therapeutic procedure, 1 or more areas, each 15 minutes; therapeutic exercises to develop strength and endurance, range of motion and flexibility

Medicine

97112   neuromuscular reeducation of movement, balance, coordination, kinesthetic sense, posture, and/or proprioception for sitting and/or standing activities

97113   aquatic therapy with therapeutic exercises

97116   gait training (includes stair climbing)

(Use 96000-96003 to report comprehensive gait and motion analysis procedures)

97124   massage, including effleurage, petrissage and/or tapotement (stroking, compression, percussion)

(For myofascial release, use 97140)

97139   Unlisted therapeutic procedure (specify)

97140   Manual therapy techniques (eg, mobilization/manipulation, manual lymphatic drainage, manual traction), 1 or more regions, each 15 minutes

97150   Therapeutic procedure(s), group (2 or more individuals)

(Report 97150 for each member of group)

(Group therapy procedures involve constant attendance of the physician or therapist, but by definition do not require one-on-one patient contact by the physician or therapist)

(For manipulation under general anesthesia, see appropriate anatomic section in **Musculoskeletal System**)

(For osteopathic manipulative treatment [OMT], see 98925-98929)

97530   Therapeutic activities, direct (one-on-one) patient contact by the provider (use of dynamic activities to improve functional performance), each 15 minutes

97532   Development of cognitive skills to improve attention, memory, problem solving (includes compensatory training), direct (one-on-one) patient contact by the provider, each 15 minutes

97533   Sensory integrative techniques to enhance sensory processing and promote adaptive responses to environmental demands, direct (one-on-one) patient contact by the provider, each 15 minutes

97535   Self-care/home management training (eg, activities of daily living (ADL) and compensatory training, meal preparation, safety procedures, and instructions in use of assistive technology devices/adaptive equipment) direct one-on-one contact by provider, each 15 minutes

97537   Community/work reintegration training (eg, shopping, transportation, money management, avocational activities and/or work environment/modification analysis, work task analysis, use of assistive technology device/adaptive equipment), direct one-on-one contact by provider, each 15 minutes

(For wheelchair management/propulsion training, use 97542)

97542   Wheelchair management (eg, assessment, fitting, training), each 15 minutes

97545   Work hardening/conditioning; initial 2 hours

+ 97546   each additional hour (List separately in addition to code for primary procedure)

(Use 97546 in conjunction with 97545)

Active Wound Care Management

Active wound care procedures are performed to remove devitalized and/or necrotic tissue and promote healing. Provider is required to have direct (one-on-one) patient contact.

(Do not report 97597-97602 in conjunction with 11040-11044)

97597   Removal of devitalized tissue from wound(s), selective debridement, without anesthesia (eg, high pressure waterjet with/without suction, sharp selective debridement with scissors, scalpel and forceps), with or without topical application(s), wound assessment, and instruction(s) for ongoing care, may include use of a whirlpool, per session; total wound(s) surface area less than or equal to 20 square centimeters

97598   total wound(s) surface area greater than 20 square centimeters

97602   Removal of devitalized tissue from wound(s), non-selective debridement, without anesthesia (eg, wet-to-moist dressings, enzymatic, abrasion), including topical application(s), wound assessment, and instruction(s) for ongoing care, per session

97605   Negative pressure wound therapy (eg, vacuum assisted drainage collection), including topical application(s), wound assessment, and instruction(s) for ongoing care, per session; total wound(s) surface area less than or equal to 50 square centimeters

97606   total wound(s) surface area greater than 50 square centimeters

Tests and Measurements

Requires direct one-on-one patient contact.

(For muscle testing, manual or electrical, joint range of motion, electromyography or nerve velocity determination, see 95831-95904)

97750   Physical performance test or measurement (eg, musculoskeletal, functional capacity), with written report, each 15 minutes

97755   Assistive technology assessment (eg, to restore, augment or compensate for existing function, optimize functional tasks and/or maximize environmental accessibility), direct one-on-one contact by provider, with written report, each 15 minutes

(To report augmentative and alternative communication devices, see 92605, 92607)

Orthotic Management and Prosthetic Management

97760 Orthotic(s) management and training (including assessment and fitting when not otherwise reported), upper extremity(s), lower extremity(s) and/or trunk, each 15 minutes

(Code 97760 should not be reported with 97116 for the same extremity)

97761 Prosthetic training, upper and/or lower extremity(s), each 15 minutes

97762 Checkout for orthotic/prosthetic use, established patient, each 15 minutes

Other Procedures

(For extracorporeal shock wave musculoskeletal therapy, see Category III codes 0019T, 0101T, 0102T)

97799 Unlisted physical medicine/rehabilitation service or procedure

Medical Nutrition Therapy

97802 Medical nutrition therapy; initial assessment and intervention, individual, face-to-face with the patient, each 15 minutes

97803 re-assessment and intervention, individual, face-to-face with the patient, each 15 minutes

97804 group (2 or more individual(s)), each 30 minutes

(For medical nutrition therapy assessment and/or intervention performed by a physician, see **Evaluation and Management** or **Preventive Medicine** service codes)

Acupuncture

Acupuncture is reported based on 15-minute increments of personal (face-to-face) contact with the patient, not the duration of acupuncture needle(s) placement.

If no electrical stimulation is used during a 15-minute increment, use 97810, 97811. If electrical stimulation of any needle is used during a 15-minute increment, use 97813, 97814.

Only one code may be reported for each 15-minute increment. Use either 97810 or 97813 for the initial 15-minute increment. Only one initial code is reported per day.

Evaluation and Management services may be reported separately, using modifier 25, if the patient's condition requires a significant separately identifiable E/M service, above and beyond the usual preservice and postservice

work associated with the acupuncture services. The time of the E/M service is not included in the time of the acupuncture service.

97810 Acupuncture, 1 or more needles; without electrical stimulation, initial 15 minutes of personal one-on-one contact with the patient

(Do not report 97810 in conjunction with 97813)

+ 97811 without electrical stimulation, each additional 15 minutes of personal one-on-one contact with the patient, with re-insertion of needle(s) (List separately in addition to code for primary procedure)

(Use 97811 in conjunction with 97810, 97813)

97813 with electrical stimulation, initial 15 minutes of personal one-on-one contact with the patient

(Do not report 97813 in conjunction with 97810)

+ 97814 with electrical stimulation, each additional 15 minutes of personal one-on-one contact with the patient, with re-insertion of needle(s) (List separately in addition to code for primary procedure)

(Use 97814 in conjunction with 97810, 97813)

Osteopathic Manipulative Treatment

Osteopathic manipulative treatment (OMT) is a form of manual treatment applied by a physician to eliminate or alleviate somatic dysfunction and related disorders. This treatment may be accomplished by a variety of techniques.

Evaluation and Management services may be reported separately if, using modifier 25, the patient's condition requires a significant separately identifiable E/M service, above and beyond the usual preservice and postservice work associated with the procedure. The E/M service may be caused or prompted by the same symptoms or condition for which the OMT service was provided. As such, different diagnoses are not required for the reporting of the OMT and E/M service on the same date.

Body regions referred to are: head region; cervical region; thoracic region; lumbar region; sacral region; pelvic region; lower extremities; upper extremities; rib cage region; abdomen and viscera region.

98925 Osteopathic manipulative treatment (OMT); 1-2 body regions involved

98926 3-4 body regions involved

98927 5-6 body regions involved

98928 7-8 body regions involved

98929 9-10 body regions involved

Chiropractic Manipulative Treatment

Chiropractic manipulative treatment (CMT) is a form of manual treatment to influence joint and neurophysiological function. This treatment may be accomplished using a variety of techniques.

The chiropractic manipulative treatment codes include a pre-manipulation patient assessment. Additional Evaluation and Management services may be reported separately using modifier 25, if the patient's condition requires a significant separately identifiable E/M service, above and beyond the usual preservice and postservice work associated with the procedure. The E/M service may be caused or prompted by the same symptoms or condition for which the CMT service was provided. As such, different diagnoses are not required for the reporting of the CMT and E/M service on the same date.

For purposes of CMT, the five spinal regions referred to are: cervical region (includes atlanto-occipital joint); thoracic region (includes costovertebral and costotransverse joints); lumbar region; sacral region; and pelvic (sacro-iliac joint) region. The five extraspinal regions referred to are: head (including temporomandibular joint, excluding atlanto-occipital) region; lower extremities; upper extremities; rib cage (excluding costotransverse and costovertebral joints) and abdomen.

98940 Chiropractic manipulative treatment (CMT); spinal, 1-2 regions

98941 spinal, 3-4 regions

98942 spinal, 5 regions

98943 extraspinal, 1 or more regions

Education and Training for Patient Self-Management

The following codes are used to report educational and training services prescribed by a physician and provided by a qualified, nonphysician healthcare professional using a standardized curriculum to an individual or a group of patients for the treatment of established illness(s)/disease(s) or to delay comorbidity(s). Education and training for patient self-management may be reported with these codes only when using a standardized curriculum as described below. This curriculum may be modified as necessary for the clinical needs, cultural norms and health literacy of the individual patient(s).

The purpose of the educational and training services is to teach the patient (may include caregiver[s]) how to effectively self-manage the patient's illness(s)/disease(s) or delay disease comorbidity(s) in conjunction with the patient's professional healthcare team. Education and

training related to subsequent reinforcement or due to changes in the patient's condition or treatment plan are reported in the same manner as the original education and training. The type of education and training provided for the patient's clinical condition will be identified by the appropriate diagnosis code(s) reported.

The qualifications of the nonphysician healthcare professionals and the content of the educational and training program must be consistent with guidelines or standards established or recognized by a physician society, nonphysician healthcare professional society/association, or other appropriate source.

(For counseling and education provided by a physician to an individual, see the appropriate Evaluation and Management codes)

(For counseling and education provided by a physician to a group, use 99078)

(For counseling and/or risk factor reduction intervention provided by a physician to patient(s) without symptoms or established disease, see 99401-99412)

(For medical nutrition therapy, see 97802-97804)

(For health and behavior assessment/intervention that is not part of a standardized curriculum, see 96150-96155)

(For education provided as genetic counseling services, use 96040. For education to a group regarding genetic risks, see 98961, 98962)

98960 Education and training for patient self-management by a qualified, nonphysician health care professional using a standardized curriculum, face-to-face with the patient (could include caregiver/family) each 30 minutes; individual patient

98961 2-4 patients

98962 5-8 patients

Non-Face-to-Face Nonphysician Services

Telephone Services

Telephone services are non-face-to-face assessment and management services provided by a qualified health care professional to a patient using the telephone. These codes are used to report episodes of care by the qualified health care professional initiated by an established patient or guardian of an established patient. If the telephone service ends with a decision to see the patient within 24 hours or the next available urgent visit appointment, the code is not reported; rather the encounter is considered part of the preservice work of the subsequent assessment and management service, procedure and visit. Likewise, if the telephone call refers to a service performed and reported by the qualified health care professional within the previous seven days (either qualified health care professional requested or unsolicited patient follow-up) or within the postoperative period of the previously completed procedure, then the service(s) are considered part of that previous service or procedure. (Do not report 98966-98969 if reporting 98966-98969 performed in the previous seven days.)

(For telephone services provided by a physician, see 99441-99443)

98966 Telephone assessment and management service provided by a qualified nonphysician health care professional to an established patient, parent, or guardian not originating from a related assessment and management service provided within the previous 7 days nor leading to an assessment and management service or procedure within the next 24 hours or soonest available appointment; 5-10 minutes of medical discussion

98967 11-20 minutes of medical discussion

98968 21-30 minutes of medical discussion

On-line Medical Evaluation

An on-line electronic medical evaluation is a non-face-to-face assessment and management service by a qualified health care professional to a patient using Internet resources in response to a patient's on-line inquiry. Reportable services involve the qualified health care professional's personal timely response to the patient's inquiry and must involve permanent storage (electronic or hard copy) of the encounter. This service is reported only once for the same episode of care during a seven-day period, although multiple qualified healthcare professionals could report their exchange with the same patient. If the on-line medical evaluation refers to an assessment and management service previously performed and reported by the qualified health care professional within the previous seven days (either qualified health care professional requested or unsolicited patient follow-up) or within the postoperative period of the previously completed procedure, then the service(s) are considered covered by the previous assessment and management office service or procedure. A reportable service encompasses the sum of communication (eg, related telephone calls, prescription provision, laboratory orders) pertaining to the on-line patient encounter.

(For an on-line medical evaluation provided by a physician, use 99444)

98969 Online assessment and management service provided by a qualified nonphysician health care professional to an established patient, guardian, or health care provider not originating from a related assessment and management service provided within the previous 7 days, using the Internet or similar electronic communications network

(Do not report 98969 when using 99339-99340, 99374-99380 for the same communication[s])

(Do not report 98969 for anticoagulation management when reporting 99363, 99364)

Special Services, Procedures and Reports

The procedures with code numbers 99000 through 99091 provide the reporting physician or other qualified healthcare professional with the means of identifying the completion of special reports and services that are an adjunct to the basic services rendered. The specific number assigned indicates the special circumstances under which a basic procedure is performed.

Code 99091 should be reported no more than once in a 30-day period to include the physician or health care provider time involved with data accession, review and interpretation, modification of care plan as necessary (including communication to patient and/or caregiver), and associated documentation.

If the services described by 99091 are provided on the same day the patient presents for an E/M service, these services should be considered part of the E/M service and not separately reported.

Do not report 99091 if it occurs within 30 days of care plan oversight services 99374-99380. Do not report 99091 if other more specific CPT codes exist (eg, 93014, 93227, 93233, 93272 for cardiographic services; 95250 for continuous glucose monitoring). Do not report 99091 for transfer and interpretation of data from hospital or clinical laboratory computers.

Codes 99050-99060 are reported in addition to an associated basic service. Typically only a single adjunct code from among 99050-99060 would be reported per patient encounter. However, there may be circumstances in which reporting multiple adjunct codes per patient encounter may be appropriate.

Miscellaneous Services

99000 Handling and/or conveyance of specimen for transfer from the physician's office to a laboratory

99001 Handling and/or conveyance of specimen for transfer from the patient in other than a physician's office to a laboratory (distance may be indicated)

99002 Handling, conveyance, and/or any other service in connection with the implementation of an order involving devices (eg, designing, fitting, packaging, handling, delivery or mailing) when devices such as orthotics, protectives, prosthetics are fabricated by an outside laboratory or shop but which items have been designed, and are to be fitted and adjusted by the attending physician

(For routine collection of venous blood, use 36415)

Medicine

99024   Postoperative follow-up visit, normally included in the surgical package, to indicate that an evaluation and management service was performed during a postoperative period for a reason(s) related to the original procedure

(As a component of a surgical "package," see **Surgery Guidelines**)

99026   Hospital mandated on call service; in-hospital, each hour

99027   out-of-hospital, each hour

(For physician standby services requiring prolonged physician attendance, use 99360, as appropriate. Time spent performing separately reportable procedure(s) or service(s) should not be included in the time reported as mandated on call service)

99050   Services provided in the office at times other than regularly scheduled office hours, or days when the office is normally closed (eg, holidays, Saturday or Sunday), in addition to basic service

99051   Service(s) provided in the office during regularly scheduled evening, weekend, or holiday office hours, in addition to basic service

99053   Service(s) provided between 10:00 PM and 8:00 AM at 24-hour facility, in addition to basic service

99056   Service(s) typically provided in the office, provided out of the office at request of patient, in addition to basic service

99058   Service(s) provided on an emergency basis in the office, which disrupts other scheduled office services, in addition to basic service

99060   Service(s) provided on an emergency basis, out of the office, which disrupts other scheduled office services, in addition to basic service

99070   Supplies and materials (except spectacles), provided by the physician over and above those usually included with the office visit or other services rendered (list drugs, trays, supplies, or materials provided)

(For supply of spectacles, use the appropriate supply codes)

99071   Educational supplies, such as books, tapes, and pamphlets, provided by the physician for the patient's education at cost to physician

99075   Medical testimony

99078   Physician educational services rendered to patients in a group setting (eg, prenatal, obesity, or diabetic instructions)

99080   Special reports such as insurance forms, more than the information conveyed in the usual medical communications or standard reporting form

(Do not report 99080 in conjunction with 99455, 99456 for the completion of Workmen's Compensation forms)

99082   Unusual travel (eg, transportation and escort of patient)

99090   Analysis of clinical data stored in computers (eg, ECGs, blood pressures, hematologic data)

(For physician/health care professional collection and interpretation of physiologic data stored/transmitted by patient/caregiver, see 99091)

(Do not report 99090 if other more specific CPT codes exist, eg, 93227, 93233, 93272 for cardiographic services; 95250 for continuous glucose monitoring, 97750 for musculoskeletal function testing)

99091   Collection and interpretation of physiologic data (eg, ECG, blood pressure, glucose monitoring) digitally stored and/or transmitted by the patient and/or caregiver to the physician or other qualified health care professional, requiring a minimum of 30 minutes of time

Qualifying Circumstances for Anesthesia

(For explanation of these services, see **Anesthesia Guidelines**)

+ 99100   Anesthesia for patient of extreme age, younger than 1 year and older than 70 (List separately in addition to code for primary anesthesia procedure)

(For procedure performed on infants younger than 1 year of age at time of surgery, see 00326, 00561, 00834, 00836)

+ 99116   Anesthesia complicated by utilization of total body hypothermia (List separately in addition to code for primary anesthesia procedure)

+ 99135   Anesthesia complicated by utilization of controlled hypotension (List separately in addition to code for primary anesthesia procedure)

+ 99140   Anesthesia complicated by emergency conditions (specify) (List separately in addition to code for primary anesthesia procedure)

(An emergency is defined as existing when delay in treatment of the patient would lead to a significant increase in the threat to life or body part.)

Moderate (Conscious) Sedation

Moderate (conscious) sedation is a drug induced depression of consciousness during which patients respond purposefully to verbal commands, either alone or accompanied by light tactile stimulation. No interventions are required to maintain a patent airway, and spontaneous ventilation is adequate. Cardiovascular function is usually maintained.

Moderate sedation does not include minimal sedation (anxiolysis), deep sedation or monitored anesthesia care (00100-01999).

When providing moderate sedation, the following services are included and NOT reported separately:

- Assessment of the patient (not included in intraservice time);

- Establishment of IV access and fluids to maintain patency, when performed;

- Administration of agent(s);

- Maintenance of sedation;

- Monitoring of oxygen saturation, heart rate and blood pressure; and

- Recovery (not included in intraservice time).

Intraservice time starts with the administration of the sedation agent(s), requires continuous face-to-face attendance, and ends at the conclusion of personal contact by the physician providing the sedation.

Do not report 99143-99150 in conjunction with 94760-94762.

Do not report 99143-99145 in conjunction with codes listed in Appendix G. Do not report 99148-99150 in conjunction with codes listed in Appendix G when performed in the nonfacility setting.

When a second physician other than the healthcare professional performing the diagnostic or therapeutic services provides moderate sedation in the facility setting (eg, hospital, outpatient hospital/ambulatory surgery center, skilled nursing facility) for the procedures listed in Appendix G, the second physician reports 99148-99150. However, for the circumstance in which these services are performed by the second physician in the nonfacility setting (eg, physician office, freestanding imaging center), codes 99148-99150 are not reported.

⊘ **99143**   Moderate sedation services (other than those services described by codes 00100-01999) provided by the same physician performing the diagnostic or therapeutic service that the sedation supports, requiring the presence of an independent trained observer to assist in the monitoring of the patient's level of consciousness and physiological status; younger than 5 years of age, first 30 minutes intra-service time

⊘ **99144**   age 5 years or older, first 30 minutes intra-service time

+ **99145**   each additional 15 minutes intra-service time (List separately in addition to code for primary service)

(Use 99145 in conjunction with 99143, 99144)

99148   Moderate sedation services (other than those services described by codes 00100-01999), provided by a physician other than the health care professional performing the diagnostic or therapeutic service that the sedation supports; younger than 5 years of age, first 30 minutes intra-service time

99149   age 5 years or older, first 30 minutes intra-service time

+ **99150**   each additional 15 minutes intra-service time (List separately in addition to code for primary service)

(Use 99150 in conjunction with 99148, 99149)

Other Services and Procedures

99170   Anogenital examination with colposcopic magnification in childhood for suspected trauma

(For conscious sedation, use 99143-99150)

99172   Visual function screening, automated or semi-automated bilateral quantitative determination of visual acuity, ocular alignment, color vision by pseudoisochromatic plates, and field of vision (may include all or some screening of the determination[s] for contrast sensitivity, vision under glare)

(This service must employ graduated visual acuity stimuli that allow a quantitative determination of visual acuity [eg, Snellen chart]. This service may not be used in addition to a general ophthalmological service or an E/M service)

(Do not report 99172 in conjunction with 99173)

99173   Screening test of visual acuity, quantitative, bilateral

(The screening test used must employ graduated visual acuity stimuli that allow a quantitative estimate of visual acuity [eg, Snellen chart]. Other identifiable services unrelated to this screening test provided at the same time may be reported separately [eg, preventive medicine services]. When acuity is measured as part of a general ophthalmological service or of an E/M service of the eye, it is a diagnostic examination and not a screening test.)

(Do not report 99173 in conjunction with 99172)

99174   Ocular photoscreening with interpretation and report, bilateral

(Do not report 99174 in conjunction with 92002-92014, 99172, 99173)

99175   Ipecac or similar administration for individual emesis and continued observation until stomach adequately emptied of poison

(For diagnostic intubation, see 82926-82928, 89130-89141)

(For gastric lavage for diagnostic purposes, see 91055)

99183   Physician attendance and supervision of hyperbaric oxygen therapy, per session

(Evaluation and Management services and/or procedures [eg, wound debridement] provided in a hyperbaric oxygen treatment facility in conjunction with a hyperbaric oxygen therapy session should be reported separately)

▶(99185, 99186 have been deleted)◀

Medicine

99190   Assembly and operation of pump with oxygenator or heat exchanger (with or without ECG and/or pressure monitoring); each hour

99191   45 minutes

99192   30 minutes

99195   Phlebotomy, therapeutic (separate procedure)

99199   Unlisted special service, procedure or report

Home Health Procedures/Services

These codes are used by non-physician health care professionals. Physicians should utilize the home visit codes 99341-99350 and utilize CPT codes other than 99500-99600 for any additional procedure/service provided to a patient living in a residence.

The following codes are used to report services provided in a patient's residence (including assisted living apartments, group homes, nontraditional private homes, custodial care facilities, or schools).

Health care professionals who are authorized to use Evaluation and Management (E/M) Home Visit codes (99341-99350) may report 99500-99600 in addition to 99341-99350 if both services are performed. E/M services may be reported separately, using modifier 25, if the patient's condition requires a significant separately identifiable E/M service, above and beyond the home health service(s)/procedure(s) codes 99500-99600.

99500   Home visit for prenatal monitoring and assessment to include fetal heart rate, non-stress test, uterine monitoring, and gestational diabetes monitoring

99501   Home visit for postnatal assessment and follow-up care

99502   Home visit for newborn care and assessment

99503   Home visit for respiratory therapy care (eg, bronchodilator, oxygen therapy, respiratory assessment, apnea evaluation)

99504   Home visit for mechanical ventilation care

99505   Home visit for stoma care and maintenance including colostomy and cystostomy

99506   Home visit for intramuscular injections

99507   Home visit for care and maintenance of catheter(s) (eg, urinary, drainage, and enteral)

99509   Home visit for assistance with activities of daily living and personal care

(To report self-care/home management training, see 97535)

(To report home medical nutrition assessment and intervention services, see 97802-97804)

(To report home speech therapy services, see 92507-92508)

99510   Home visit for individual, family, or marriage counseling

99511   Home visit for fecal impaction management and enema administration

99512   Home visit for hemodialysis

(For home infusion of peritoneal dialysis, use 99601, 99602)

99600   Unlisted home visit service or procedure

Home Infusion Procedures/Services

99601   Home infusion/specialty drug administration, per visit (up to 2 hours);

+ 99602   each additional hour (List separately in addition to code for primary procedure)

(Use 99602 in conjunction with 99601)

Medication Therapy Management Services

Medication therapy management service(s) (MTMS) describe face-to-face patient assessment and intervention as appropriate, by a pharmacist, upon request. MTMS is provided to optimize the response to medications or to manage treatment-related medication interactions or complications.

MTMS includes the following documented elements: review of the pertinent patient history, medication profile (prescription and nonprescription), and recommendations for improving health outcomes and treatment compliance. These codes are not to be used to describe the provision of product-specific information at the point of dispensing or any other routine dispensing-related activities.

99605   Medication therapy management service(s) provided by a pharmacist, individual, face-to-face with patient, with assessment and intervention if provided; initial 15 minutes, new patient

99606   initial 15 minutes, established patient

+ 99607   each additional 15 minutes (List separately in addition to code for primary service)

(Use 99607 in conjunction with 99605, 99606)

⊙=Moderate sedation   ✦=Add-on code   ✒=FDA approval pending   #=Resequenced code

Medicine

Category II Codes

The following section of *Current Procedural Terminology* (CPT) contains a set of supplemental tracking codes that can be used for performance measurement. It is anticipated that the use of Category II codes for performance measurement will decrease the need for record abstraction and chart review, and thereby minimize administrative burden on physicians, other health care professionals, hospitals, and entities seeking to measure the quality of patient care. These codes are intended to facilitate data collection about the quality of care rendered by coding certain services and test results that support nationally established performance measures and that have an evidence base as contributing to quality patient care.

The use of these codes is optional. The codes are not required for correct coding and may not be used as a substitute for Category I codes.

These codes describe clinical components that may be typically included in evaluation and management services or clinical services and, therefore, do not have a relative value associated with them. Category II codes may also describe results from clinical laboratory or radiology tests and other procedures, identified processes intended to address patient safety practices, or services reflecting compliance with state or federal law.

Category II codes described in this section make use of alphabetical characters as the 5th character in the string (ie, 4 digits followed by the letter **F**). These digits are not intended to reflect the placement of the code in the regular (Category I) part of the CPT codebook. To promote understanding of these codes and their associated measures, users are referred to Appendix H, which contains information about performance measurement exclusion modifiers, measures, and the measure's source.

Cross-references to the measures associated with each Category II code and their source are included for reference in Appendix H. In addition, acronyms for the related diseases or clinical condition(s) have been added at the end of each code descriptor to identify the topic or clinical category in which that code is included. A complete listing of the diseases/clinical conditions, and their acronyms are provided in alphabetical order in Appendix H. Users should review the complete measure(s) associated with each code prior to implementation.

Category II codes are reviewed by the Performance Measures Advisory Group (PMAG), an advisory body to the CPT Editorial Panel and the CPT/HCPAC Advisory Committee. The PMAG is comprised of performance measurement experts representing the Agency for Healthcare Research and Quality (AHRQ), the American Medical Association (AMA), the Centers for Medicare and Medicaid Services (CMS), The Joint Commission (TJC), the National Committee for Quality Assurance (NCQA), and the Physician Consortium for Performance Improvement® (PCPI). The PMAG may seek additional expertise and/or input from other national health care organizations, as necessary, for the development of tracking codes. These may include national medical specialty societies, other national health care professional associations, accrediting bodies, and federal regulatory agencies.

The most current listing of Category II codes, including guidelines, Code Change Proposal forms, and release and implementation dates for Category II codes may be accessed at http://www.ama-assn.org/go/cpt.

> (For blood pressure measured, use 2000F)
>
> (For tobacco use cessation intervention, pharmacologic therapy, use 4001F)

Modifiers

The following performance measurement modifiers may be used for Category II codes to indicate that a service specified in the associated measure(s) was considered but, due to either medical, patient, or system circumstance(s) documented in the medical record, the service was not provided. These modifiers serve as denominator exclusions from the performance measure. The user should note that not all listed measures provide for exclusions (see Appendix H for more discussion regarding exclusion criteria).

Category II modifiers should only be reported with Category II codes—they should not be reported with Category I or Category III codes. In addition, the modifiers in the Category II section should only be used where specified in the guidelines, reporting instructions, parenthetic notes, or code descriptor language listed in the Category II section (code listing and Appendix H).

1P Performance Measure Exclusion Modifier due to Medical Reasons

Reasons include:

- Not indicated (absence of organ/limb, already received/performed, other)

- Contraindicated (patient allergic history, potential adverse drug interaction, other)

Category II Codes

Other medical reasons

2P Performance Measure Exclusion Modifier due to Patient Reasons

Reasons include:

- Patient declined
- Economic, social, or religious reasons
- Other patient reasons

3P Performance Measure Exclusion Modifier due to System Reasons

Reasons include:

- Resources to perform the services not available
- Insurance coverage/payor-related limitations
- Other reasons attributable to health care delivery system

Modifier 8P is intended to be used as a "reporting modifier" to allow the reporting of circumstances when an action described in a measure's numerator is not performed and the reason is not otherwise specified.

8P Performance measure reporting modifier—action not performed, reason not otherwise specified

Composite Codes

Composite codes combine several measures grouped within a single code descriptor to facilitate reporting for a clinical condition when all components are met. If only some of the components are met or if services are provided in addition to those included in the composite code, they may be reported individually using the corresponding CPT Category II codes for those services.

0001F Heart failure assessed (includes assessment of all the following components) (CAD, HF)[1]:

Blood pressure measured (2000F)[1]

Level of activity assessed (1003F)[1]

Clinical symptoms of volume overload (excess) assessed (1004F)[1]

Weight, recorded (2001F)[1]

Clinical signs of volume overload (excess) assessed (2002F)[1]

(To report blood pressure measured, use 2000F)

0005F Osteoarthritis assessed (OA)[1]

Includes assessment of all the following components:

Osteoarthritis symptoms and functional status assessed (1006F)[1]

Use of anti-inflammatory or over-the-counter (OTC) analgesic medications assessed (1007F)[1]

Initial examination of the involved joint(s) (includes visual inspection, palpation, range of motion) (2004F)[1]

(To report tobacco use cessation intervention, use 4001F)

0012F Community-acquired bacterial pneumonia assessment (includes all of the following components) (CAP)[1]:

Co-morbid conditions assessed (1026F)[1]

Vital signs recorded (2010F)[1]

Mental status assessed (2014F)[1]

Hydration status assessed (2018F)[1]

0014F Comprehensive preoperative assessment performed for cataract surgery with intraocular lens (IOL) placement (includes assessment of all of the following components) (EC)[5]:

Dilated fundus evaluation performed within 12 months prior to cataract surgery (2020F)[5]

Pre-surgical (cataract) axial length, corneal power measurement and method of intraocular lens power calculation documented (must be performed within 12 months prior to surgery) (3073F)[5]

Preoperative assessment of functional or medical indication(s) for surgery prior to the cataract surgery with intraocular lens placement (must be performed within 12 months prior to cataract surgery) (3325F)[5]

0015F Melanoma follow up completed (includes assessment of all of the following components) (ML)[5]:

History obtained regarding new or changing moles (1050F)[5]

Complete physical skin exam performed (2029F)[5]

Patient counseled to perform a monthly self skin examination (5005F)[5]

Patient Management

Patient management codes describe utilization measures or measures of patient care provided for specific clinical purposes (eg, prenatal care, pre- and post-surgical care).

Footnotes
[1] Physician Consortium for Performance Improvement® (PCPI), www.physicianconsortium.org
[2] National Committee on Quality Assurance (NCQA), Health Employer Data Information Set (HEDIS®), www.ncqa.org
[3] The Joint Commission (TJC) ORYX Initiative Performance Measures, www.thejointcommission.org
[4] National Diabetes Quality Improvement Alliance (NDQIA), www.nationaldiabetesalliance.org
[5] Joint measure from the Physician Consortium for Performance Improvement, www.physicianconsortium.org and National Committee on Quality Assurance (NCQA), www.ncqa.org
[6] The Society of Thoracic Surgeons, www.sts.org, National Quality Forum, www.qualityforum.org

0500F   Initial prenatal care visit (report at first prenatal encounter with health care professional providing obstetrical care. Report also date of visit and, in a separate field, the date of the last menstrual period [LMP] (Prenatal)[2]

0501F   Prenatal flow sheet documented in medical record by first prenatal visit (documentation includes at minimum blood pressure, weight, urine protein, uterine size, fetal heart tones, and estimated date of delivery). Report also: date of visit and, in a separate field, the date of the last menstrual period [LMP] (Note: If reporting 0501F Prenatal flow sheet, it is not necessary to report 0500F Initial prenatal care visit) (Prenatal)[1]

0502F   Subsequent prenatal care visit (Prenatal)[2]

[Excludes: patients who are seen for a condition unrelated to pregnancy or prenatal care (eg, an upper respiratory infection; patients seen for consultation only, not for continuing care)]

0503F   Postpartum care visit (Prenatal)[2]

0505F   Hemodialysis plan of care documented (ESRD, P-ESRD)[1]

0507F   Peritoneal dialysis plan of care documented (ESRD)[1]

0509F   Urinary incontinence plan of care documented (GER)[5]

0513F   Elevated blood pressure plan of care documented (CKD)[1]

0514F   Plan of care for elevated hemoglobin level documented for patient receiving Erythropoiesis-Stimulating Agent therapy (ESA) (CKD)[1]

0516F   Anemia plan of care documented (ESRD)[1]

0517F   Glaucoma plan of care documented (EC)[5]

0518F   Falls plan of care documented (GER)[5]

▲ **0519F**   Planned chemotherapy regimen, including at a minimum: drug(s) prescribed, dose, and duration, documented prior to initiation of a new treatment regimen (ONC)[1]

▲ **0520F**   Radiation dose limits to normal tissues established prior to the initiation of a course of 3D conformal radiation for a minimum of 2 tissue/organ (ONC)[1]

▲ **0521F**   Plan of care to address pain documented (COA)[2] (ONC)[1]

0525F   Initial visit for episode (BkP)[2]

0526F   Subsequent visit for episode (BkP)[2]

● **0528F**   Recommended follow-up interval for repeat colonoscopy of at least 10 years documented in colonoscopy report (End/Polyp)[5]

● **0529F**   Interval of 3 or more years since patient's last colonoscopy, documented (End/Polyp)[5]

● **0535F**   Dyspnea management plan of care, documented (Pall Cr)[5]

● **0540F**   Glucorticoid Management Plan Documented (RA)[5]

● **0575F**   HIV RNA control plan of care, documented (HIV)[5]

Patient History

Patient history codes describe measures for select aspects of patient history or review of systems.

1000F   Tobacco use assessed (CAD, CAP, COPD, PV)[1] (DM)[4]

1002F   Anginal symptoms and level of activity assessed (CAD)[1]

1003F   Level of activity assessed (HF)[1]

1004F   Clinical symptoms of volume overload (excess) assessed (HF)[1]

1005F   Asthma symptoms evaluated (includes physician documentation of numeric frequency of symptoms or patient completion of an asthma assessment tool/survey/questionnaire) (Asthma)[1]

1006F   Osteoarthritis symptoms and functional status assessed (may include the use of a standardized scale or the completion of an assessment questionnaire, such as the SF-36, AAOS Hip & Knee Questionnaire) (OA)[1]

[Instructions: Report when osteoarthritis is addressed during the patient encounter]

1007F   Use of anti-inflammatory or analgesic over-the-counter (OTC) medications for symptom relief assessed (OA)[1]

1008F   Gastrointestinal and renal risk factors assessed for patients on prescribed or OTC non-steroidal anti-inflammatory drug (NSAID) (OA)[1]

1015F   Chronic obstructive pulmonary disease (COPD) symptoms assessed (Includes assessment of at least 1 of the following: dyspnea, cough/sputum, wheezing), or respiratory symptom assessment tool completed (COPD)[1]

1018F   Dyspnea assessed, not present (COPD)[1]

1019F   Dyspnea assessed, present (COPD)[1]

1022F   Pneumococcus immunization status assessed (CAP, COPD)[1]

1026F   Co-morbid conditions assessed (eg, includes assessment for presence or absence of: malignancy, liver disease, congestive heart failure, cerebrovascular disease, renal disease, chronic obstructive pulmonary disease, asthma, diabetes, other co-morbid conditions) (CAP)[1]

Footnotes

[1] Physician Consortium for Performance Improvement® (PCPI), www.physicianconsortium.org

[2] National Committee on Quality Assurance (NCQA), Health Employer Data Information Set (HEDIS®), www.ncqa.org

[3] The Joint Commission (TJC) ORYX Initiative Performance Measures, www.thejointcommission.org

[4] National Diabetes Quality Improvement Alliance (NDQIA), www.nationaldiabetesalliance.org

[5] Joint measure from the Physician Consortium for Performance Improvement, www.physicianconsortium.org and National Committee on Quality Assurance (NCQA), www.ncqa.org

[6] The Society of Thoracic Surgeons, www.sts.org, National Quality Forum, www.qualityforum.org

Category II Codes

Category II Codes

1030F   Influenza immunization status assessed (CAP)[1]

1034F   Current tobacco smoker (CAD, CAP, COPD, PV)[1] (DM)[4]

1035F   Current smokeless tobacco user (eg, chew, snuff) (PV)[1]

1036F   Current tobacco non-user (CAD, CAP, COPD, PV)[1] (DM)[4]

1038F   Persistent asthma (mild, moderate or severe) (Asthma)[1]

1039F   Intermittent asthma (Asthma)[1]

1040F   DSM-IV™ criteria for major depressive disorder documented at the initial evaluation (MDD)[1]

1050F   History obtained regarding new or changing moles (ML)[5]

1055F   Visual functional status assessed (EC)[5]

1060F   Documentation of permanent OR persistent OR paroxysmal atrial fibrillation (STR)[5]

1061F   Documentation of absence of permanent AND persistent AND paroxysmal atrial fibrillation (STR)[5]

1065F   Ischemic stroke symptom onset of less than 3 hours prior to arrival (STR)[5]

1066F   Ischemic stroke symptom onset greater than or equal to 3 hours prior to arrival (STR)[5]

1070F   Alarm symptoms (involuntary weight loss, dysphagia, or gastrointestinal bleeding) assessed; none present (GERD)[5]

1071F   1 or more present (GERD)[5]

(1080F has been deleted. To report Surrogate decision maker or advance care plan documented in the medical record, report code 1123F or 1124F.)

1090F   Presence or absence of urinary incontinence assessed (GER)[5]

1091F   Urinary incontinence characterized (eg, frequency, volume, timing, type of symptoms, how bothersome) (GER)[5]

1100F   Patient screened for future fall risk; documentation of 2 or more falls in the past year or any fall with injury in the past year (GER)[5]

1101F   documentation of no falls in the past year or only 1 fall without injury in the past year (GER)[5]

1110F   Patient discharged from an inpatient facility (eg, hospital, skilled nursing facility, or rehabilitation facility) within the last 60 days (GER)[5]

1111F   Discharge medications reconciled with the current medication list in outpatient medical record (COA)[2] (GER)[5]

1116F   Auricular or periauricular pain assessed (AOE)[1]

1118F   GERD symptoms assessed after 12 months of therapy (GERD)[5]

1119F   Initial evaluation for condition (HEP C)[1]

1121F   Subsequent evaluation for condition (HEP C)[1]

1123F   Advance Care Planning discussed and documented advance care plan or surrogate decision maker documented in the medical record (GER, Pall Cr)[5]

1124F   Advance Care Planning discussed and documented in the medical record – patient did not wish or was not able to name a surrogate decision maker or provide an advance care plan (GER, Pall Cr)[5]

1125F   Pain severity quantified; pain present (COA)[2] (ONC)[1]

1126F   no pain present (COA)[2] (ONC)[1]

1127F   New episode for condition (ML)[5]

1128F   Subsequent episode for condition (ML)[5]

1130F   Back pain and function assessed, including all of the following: Pain assessment AND functional status AND patient history, including notation of presence or absence of "red flags" (warning signs) AND assessment of prior treatment and response, AND employment status (BkP)[2]

1134F   Episode of back pain lasting 6 weeks or less (BkP)[2]

1135F   Episode of back pain lasting longer than 6 weeks (BkP)[2]

1136F   Episode of back pain lasting 12 weeks or less (BkP)[2]

1137F   Episode of back pain lasting longer than 12 weeks (BkP)[2]

● **1150F**   Documentation that a patient has a substantial risk of death within 1 year (Pall Cr)[5]

● **1151F**   Documentation that a patient does not have a substantial risk of death within one year (Pall Cr)[5]

● **1152F**   Documentation of advanced disease diagnosis, goals of care prioritize comfort (Pall Cr)[5]

● **1153F**   Documentation of advanced disease diagnosis, goals of care do not prioritize comfort (Pall Cr)[5]

● **1157F**   Advance care plan or similar legal document present in the medical record (COA)[2]

● **1158F**   Advance care planning discussion documented in the medical record (COA)[2]

● **1159F**   Medication list documented in medical record (COA)[2]

● **1160F**   Review of all medications by a prescribing practitioner or clinical pharmacist (such as, prescriptions, OTCs, herbal therapies and supplements) documented in the medical record (COA)[2]

● **1170F**   Functional status assessed (COA)[2] (RA)[5]

Footnotes

[1] Physician Consortium for Performance Improvement® (PCPI), www.physicianconsortium.org

[2] National Committee on Quality Assurance (NCQA), Health Employer Data Information Set (HEDIS®), www.ncqa.org

[3] The Joint Commission (TJC) ORYX Initiative Performance Measures, www.thejointcommission.org

[4] National Diabetes Quality Improvement Alliance (NDQIA), www.nationaldiabetesalliance.org

[5] Joint measure from the Physician Consortium for Performance Improvement, www.physicianconsortium.org and National Committee on Quality Assurance (NCQA), www.ncqa.org

[6] The Society of Thoracic Surgeons, www.sts.org, National Quality Forum, www.qualityforum.org

● **1180F** All specified thromboembolic risk factors assessed (AFIB)[1]

● **1220F** Patient screened for depression (SUD)[5]

Physical Examination

Physical examination codes describe aspects of physical examination or clinical assessment.

2000F Blood pressure measured (CAD, CKD, HF, HTN)[1](DM)[2,4]

2001F Weight recorded (HF, PAG)[1]

2002F Clinical signs of volume overload (excess) assessed (HF)[1]

2004F Initial examination of the involved joint(s) (includes visual inspection, palpation, range of motion) (OA)[1]

[Instructions: Report only for initial osteoarthritis visit or for visits for new joint involvement]

2010F Vital signs (temperature, pulse, respiratory rate, and blood pressure) documented and reviewed (CAP)[1] (EM)[5]

2014F Mental status assessed (CAP)[1] (EM)[5]

2018F Hydration status assessed (normal/mildly dehydrated/severely dehydrated) (CAP)[1]

2019F Dilated macular exam performed, including documentation of the presence or absence of macular thickening or hemorrhage AND the level of macular degeneration severity (EC)[5]

2020F Dilated fundus evaluation performed within 12 months prior to cataract surgery (EC)[5]

2021F Dilated macular or fundus exam performed, including documentation of the presence or absence of macular edema AND level of severity of retinopathy (EC)[5]

2022F Dilated retinal eye exam with interpretation by an ophthalmologist or optometrist documented and reviewed (DM)[2,4]

2024F 7 standard field stereoscopic photos with interpretation by an ophthalmologist or optometrist documented and reviewed (DM)[2,4]

2026F Eye imaging validated to match diagnosis from 7 standard field stereoscopic photos results documented and reviewed (DM)[2,4]

2027F Optic nerve head evaluation performed (EC)[5]

2028F Foot examination performed (includes examination through visual inspection, sensory exam with monofilament, and pulse exam – report when any of the 3 components are completed) (DM)[4]

2029F Complete physical skin exam performed (ML)[5]

2030F Hydration status documented, normally hydrated (PAG)[1]

2031F Hydration status documented, dehydrated (PAG)[1]

2035F Tympanic membrane mobility assessed with pneumatic otoscopy or tympanometry (OME)[1]

2040F Physical examination on the date of the initial visit for low back pain performed, in accordance with specifications (BkP)[2]

2044F Documentation of mental health assessment prior to intervention (back surgery or epidural steroid injection) or for back pain episode lasting longer than 6 weeks (BkP)[2]

● **2050F** Wound characteristics including size AND nature of wound base tissue AND amount of drainage prior to debridement documented (CWC)[5]

Diagnostic/Screening Processes or Results

Diagnostic/screening processes or results codes describe results of tests ordered (clinical laboratory tests, radiological or other procedural examinations, and conclusions of medical decision-making).

(Code 3000F has been deleted. To report blood pressure use the corresponding systolic codes (3074F, 3075F, 3077F) and diastolic codes (3078F, 3079F, 3080F)

(Code 3002F has been deleted. To report blood pressure use the corresponding systolic codes (3074F, 3075F, 3077F) and diastolic codes (3078F, 3079F, 3080F)

3006F Chest X-ray results documented and reviewed (CAP)[1]

3011F Lipid panel results documented and reviewed (must include total cholesterol, HDL-C, triglycerides and calculated LDL-C) (CAD)[1]

3014F Screening mammography results documented and reviewed (PV)[1,2]

● **3016F** Patient screened for unhealthy alcohol use using a systematic screening method (PV)[1]

3017F Colorectal cancer screening results documented and reviewed (PV)[1,2]

● **3018F** Pre-procedure risk assessment AND depth of insertion AND quality of the bowel prep AND complete description of polyp(s) found, including location of each polyp, size, number and gross morphology AND recommendations for follow-up in final colonoscopy report documented (End/Polyp)[5]

Footnotes
[1] Physician Consortium for Performance Improvement® (PCPI), www.physicianconsortium.org
[2] National Committee on Quality Assurance (NCQA), Health Employer Data Information Set (HEDIS®), www.ncqa.org
[3] The Joint Commission (TJC) ORYX Initiative Performance Measures, www.thejointcommission.org
[4] National Diabetes Quality Improvement Alliance (NDQIA), www.nationaldiabetesalliance.org
[5] Joint measure from the Physician Consortium for Performance Improvement, www.physicianconsortium.org and National Committee on Quality Assurance (NCQA), www.ncqa.org
[6] The Society of Thoracic Surgeons, www.sts.org, National Quality Forum, www.qualityforum.org

Category II Codes

3020F Left ventricular function (LVF) assessment (eg, echocardiography, nuclear test, or ventriculography) documented in the medical record (Includes quantitative or qualitative assessment results) (HF)[1]

3021F Left ventricular ejection fraction (LVEF) less than 40% or documentation of moderately or severely depressed left ventricular systolic function (CAD, HF)[1]

3022F Left ventricular ejection fraction (LVEF) greater than or equal to 40% or documentation as normal or mildly depressed left ventricular systolic function (CAD, HF)[1]

3023F Spirometry results documented and reviewed (COPD)[1]

3025F Spirometry test results demonstrate FEV_1/FVC less than 70% with COPD symptoms (eg, dyspnea, cough/sputum, wheezing) (CAP, COPD)[1]

3027F Spirometry test results demonstrate FEV_1/FVC greater than or equal to 70% or patient does not have COPD symptoms (COPD)[1]

3028F Oxygen saturation results documented and reviewed (includes assessment through pulse oximetry or arterial blood gas measurement) (CAP, COPD)[1] (EM)[5]

3035F Oxygen saturation less than or equal to 88 % or a PaO_2 less than or equal to 55 mm Hg (COPD)[1].

3037F Oxygen saturation greater than 88% or PaO_2 greater than 55 mmHg (COPD)[1]

3040F Functional expiratory volume (FEV_1) less than 40% of predicted value (COPD)[1]

3042F Functional expiratory volume (FEV_1) greater than or equal to 40% of predicted value (COPD)[1]

3044F Most recent hemoglobin A1c (HbA1c) level less than 7.0% (DM)[2,4]

3045F Most recent hemoglobin A1c (HbA1c) level 7.0 – 9.0 % (DM)[2,4]

3046F Most recent hemoglobin A1c level greater than 9.0% (DM)[4]

(Code 3047F has been deleted. To report most recent hemoglobin A1c level less than or equal to 9.0%, see codes 3044F-3045F)

3048F Most recent LDL-C less than 100 mg/dL (DM)[4]

3049F Most recent LDL-C 100-129 mg/dL (DM)[4]

3050F Most recent LDL-C greater than or equal to 130 mg/dL (DM)[4]

3060F Positive microalbuminuria test result documented and reviewed (DM)[2,4]

3061F Negative microalbuminuria test result documented and reviewed (DM)[2,4]

3062F Positive macroalbuminuria test result documented and reviewed (DM)[2,4]

3066F Documentation of treatment for nephropathy (eg, patient receiving dialysis, patient being treated for ESRD, CRF, ARF, or renal insufficiency, any visit to a nephrologist) (DM)[2,4]

3072F Low risk for retinopathy (no evidence of retinopathy in the prior year) (DM)[2,4]

3073F Pre-surgical (cataract) axial length, corneal power measurement and method of intraocular lens power calculation documented within 12 months prior to surgery (EC)[5]

3074F Most recent systolic blood pressure less than 130 mm Hg (DM)[2,4] (HTN, CKD)[1]

3075F Most recent systolic blood pressure 130 - 139 mm Hg (DM)[2,4] (HTN, CKD)[1]

(Code 3076F has been deleted. To report most recent systolic blood pressure less than 140 mm Hg, see codes 3074F-3075F)

3077F Most recent systolic blood pressure greater than or equal to 140 mm Hg (HTN, CKD)[1] (DM)[2,4]

3078F Most recent diastolic blood pressure less than 80 mm Hg (HTN, CKD)[1] (DM)[2,4]

3079F Most recent diastolic blood pressure 80-89 mm Hg (HTN, CKD)[1] (DM)[2,4]

3080F Most recent diastolic blood pressure grreater than or equal to 90 mm Hg (HTN, CKD)[1] (DM)[2,4]

3082F Kt/V less than 1.2 (Clearance of urea [Kt]/volume [V]) (ESRD, P-ESRD)[1]

3083F Kt/V equal to or greater than 1.2 and less than 1.7 (Clearance of urea [Kt]/volume [V]) (ESRD, P-ESRD)[1]

3084F Kt/V greater than or equal to 1.7 (Clearance of urea [Kt]/volume [V]) (ESRD, P-ESRD)[1]

3085F Suicide risk assessed (MDD)[1]

3088F Major depressive disorder, mild (MDD)[1]

3089F Major depressive disorder, moderate (MDD)[1]

3090F Major depressive disorder, severe without psychotic features (MDD)[1]

3091F Major depressive disorder, severe with psychotic features (MDD)[1]

3092F Major depressive disorder, in remission (MDD)[1]

3093F Documentation of new diagnosis of initial or recurrent episode of major depressive disorder (MDD)[1]

Footnotes

[1] Physician Consortium for Performance Improvement® (PCPI), www.physicianconsortium.org

[2] National Committee on Quality Assurance (NCQA), Health Employer Data Information Set (HEDIS®), www.ncqa.org

[3] The Joint Commission (TJC) ORYX Initiative Performance Measures, www.thejointcommission.org

[4] National Diabetes Quality Improvement Alliance (NDQIA), www.nationaldiabetesalliance.org

[5] Joint measure from the Physician Consortium for Performance Improvement, www.physicianconsortium.org and National Committee on Quality Assurance (NCQA), www.ncqa.org

[6] The Society of Thoracic Surgeons, www.sts.org, National Quality Forum, www.qualityforum.org

Category II Codes

3095F   Central dual-energy X-ray absorptiometry (DXA) results documented (OP)[5]

3096F   Central dual-energy X-ray absorptiometry (DXA) ordered (OP)[5]

3100F   Carotid imaging study report (includes direct or indirect reference to measurements of distal internal carotid diameter as the denominator for stenosis measurement) (STR, RAD)[5]

(Code 3101F has been deleted)

(Code 3102F has been deleted)

3110F   Presence or absence of hemorrhage and mass lesion and acute infarction documented in final CT or MRI report (STR)[5]

3111F   CT or MRI of the brain performed within 24 hours of arrival to the hospital (STR)[5]

3112F   CT or MRI of the brain performed greater than 24 hours after arrival to the hospital (STR)[5]

3120F   12-Lead ECG Performed (EM)[5]

3130F   Upper gastrointestinal endoscopy performed (GERD)[5]

3132F   Documentation of referral for upper gastrointestinal endoscopy (GERD)[5]

3140F   Upper gastrointestinal endoscopy report indicates suspicion of Barrett's esophagus (GERD)[5]

3141F   Upper gastrointestinal endoscopy report indicates no suspicion of Barrett's esophagus (GERD)[5]

3142F   Barium swallow test ordered (GERD)[1]

(Code 3143F has been deleted. To report documentation of barium swallow study, use code 3142F)

3150F   Forceps esophageal biopsy performed (GERD)[5]

3155F   Cytogenetic testing performed on bone marrow at time of diagnosis or prior to initiating treatment (HEM)[1]

3160F   Documentation of iron stores prior to initiating erythropoietin therapy (HEM)[1]

3170F   Flow cytometry studies performed at time of diagnosis or prior to initiating treatment (HEM)[1]

3200F   Barium swallow test not ordered (GERD)[5]

3210F   Group A Strep Test Performed (PHAR)[2]

3215F   Patient has documented immunity to Hepatitis A (HEP-C)[1]

3216F   Patient has documented immunity to Hepatitis B (HEP-C)[1]

(3217F has been deleted)

3218F   RNA testing for Hepatitis C documented as performed within 6 months prior to initiation of antiviral treatment for Hepatitis C (HEP-C)[1]

(3219F has been deleted)

3220F   Hepatitis C quantitative RNA testing documented as performed at 12 weeks from initiation of antiviral treatment (HEP-C)[1]

3230F   Documentation that hearing test was performed within 6 months prior to tympanostomy tube insertion (OME)[1]

● **3250F**   Specimen site other than anatomic location of primary tumor (PATH)[1]

3260F   pT category (primary tumor), pN category (regional lymph nodes), and histologic grade documented in pathology report (PATH)[1]

3265F   Ribonucleic acid (RNA) testing for Hepatitis C viremia ordered or results documented (HEP C)[1]

3266F   Hepatitis C genotype testing documented as performed prior to initiation of antiviral treatment for Hepatitis C (HEP C)[1]

3268F   Prostate-specific antigen (PSA), AND primary tumor (T) stage, AND Gleason score documented prior to initiation of treatment (PRCA)[1]

3269F   Bone scan performed prior to initiation of treatment or at any time since diagnosis of prostate cancer (PRCA)[1]

3270F   Bone scan not performed prior to initiation of treatment nor at any time since diagnosis of prostate cancer (PRCA)[1]

3271F   Low risk of recurrence, prostate cancer (PRCA)[1]

3272F   Intermediate risk of recurrence, prostate cancer (PRCA)[1]

3273F   High risk of recurrence, prostate cancer (PRCA)[1]

3274F   Prostate cancer risk of recurrence not determined or neither low, intermediate nor high (PRCA)[1]

3278F   Serum levels of calcium, phosphorus, intact Parathyroid Hormone (PTH) and lipid profile ordered (CKD)[1]

3279F   Hemoglobin level greater than or equal to 13 g/dL (CKD, ESRD)[1]

3280F   Hemoglobin level 11 g/dL to 12.9 g/dL (CKD, ESRD)[1]

3281F   Hemoglobin level less than 11 g/dL (CKD, ESRD)[1]

3284F   Intraocular pressure (IOP) reduced by a value of greater than or equal to 15% from the pre-intervention level (EC)[5]

3285F   Intraocular pressure (IOP) reduced by a value less than 15% from the pre-intervention level (EC)[5]

3288F   Falls risk assessment documented (GER)[5]

Footnotes

[1] Physician Consortium for Performance Improvement® (PCPI), www.physicianconsortium.org

[2] National Committee on Quality Assurance (NCQA), Health Employer Data Information Set (HEDIS®), www.ncqa.org

[3] The Joint Commission (TJC) ORYX Initiative Performance Measures, www.thejointcommission.org

[4] National Diabetes Quality Improvement Alliance (NDQIA), www.nationaldiabetesalliance.org

[5] Joint measure from the Physician Consortium for Performance Improvement, www.physicianconsortium.org and National Committee on Quality Assurance (NCQA), www.ncqa.org

[6] The Society of Thoracic Surgeons, www.sts.org, National Quality Forum, www.qualityforum.org

Category II Codes

3290F Patient is D (Rh) negative and unsensitized (Pre-Cr)[1]

3291F Patient is D (Rh) positive or sensitized (Pre-Cr)[1]

3292F HIV testing ordered or documented and reviewed during the first or second prenatal visit (Pre-Cr)[1]

3300F American Joint Committee on Cancer (AJCC) stage documented and reviewed (ONC)[1]

3301F Cancer stage documented in medical record as metastatic and reviewed (ONC)[1]

▶(Codes 3302F-3312F have been deleted.

To report measures for cancer staging, see 3321F-3390F.)◀

3315F Estrogen receptor (ER) or progesterone receptor (PR) positive breast cancer (ONC)[1]

3316F Estrogen receptor (ER) and progesterone receptor (PR) negative breast cancer (ONC)[1]

3317F Pathology report confirming malignancy documented in the medical record and reviewed prior to the initiation of chemotherapy (ONC)[1]

3318F Pathology report confirming malignancy documented in the medical record and reviewed prior to the initiation of radiation therapy (ONC)[1]

3319F 1 of the following diagnostic imaging studies ordered: chest x-ray, CT, Ultrasound, MRI, PET, or nuclear medicine scans (ML)[5]

3320F None of the following diagnostic imaging studies ordered: chest X-ray, CT, Ultrasound, MRI, PET, or nuclear medicine scans (ML)[5]

● **3321F** AJCC Cancer Stage 0 or IA Melanoma, documented (ML)[5]

● **3322F** Melanoma greater than AJCC Stage 0 or IA (ML)[5]

3325F Preoperative assessment of functional or medical indication(s) for surgery prior to the cataract surgery with intraocular lens placement (must be performed within 12 months prior to cataract surgery) (EC)[5]

3330F Imaging study ordered (BkP)[2]

3331F Imaging study not ordered (BkP)[2]

3340F Mammogram assessment category of "incomplete: need additional imaging evaluation", documented (RAD)[5]

3341F Mammogram assessment category of "negative" documented (RAD)[5]

3342F Mammogram assessment category of "benign", documented (RAD)[5]

3343F Mammogram assessment category of "probably benign", documented (RAD)[5]

3344F Mammogram assessment category of "suspicious", documented (RAD)[5]

3345F Mammogram assessment category of "highly suggestive of malignancy", documented (RAD)[5]

3350F Mammogram assessment category of "known biopsy proven malignancy", documented (RAD)[5]

3351F Negative screen for depressive symptoms as categorized by using a standardized depression screening/assessment tool (MDD)[2]

3352F No significant depressive symptoms as categorized by using a standardized depression assessment tool (MDD)[2]

3353F Mild to moderate depressive symptoms as categorized by using a standardized depression screening/assessment tool (MDD)[2]

3354F Clinically significant depressive symptoms as categorized by using a standardized depression screening/assessment tool (MDD)[2]

● **3370F** AJCC Breast Cancer Stage 0 documented (ONC)[1]

● **3372F** AJCC Breast Cancer Stage I: T1mic, T1a or T1b (tumor size ≤ 1 cm) documented (ONC)[1]

● **3374F** AJCC Breast Cancer Stage I: T1c (tumor size > 1 cm to 2 cm) documented (ONC)[1]

● **3376F** AJCC Breast Cancer Stage II documented (ONC)[1]

● **3378F** AJCC Breast Cancer Stage III documented (ONC)[1]

● **3380F** AJCC Breast Cancer Stage IV documented (ONC)[1]

● **3382F** AJCC colon cancer, Stage 0 documented (ONC)[1]

● **3384F** AJCC colon cancer, Stage I documented (ONC)[1]

● **3386F** AJCC colon cancer, Stage II documented (ONC)[1]

● **3388F** AJCC colon cancer, Stage III documented (ONC)[1]

● **3390F** AJCC colon cancer, Stage IV documented (ONC)[1]

● **3450F** Dyspnea screened, no dyspnea or mild dyspnea (Pall Cr)[5]

● **3451F** Dyspnea screened, moderate or severe dyspnea (Pall Cr)[5]

● **3452F** Dyspnea not screened (Pall Cr)[5]

● **3455F** TB screening performed and results interpreted within six months prior to initiation of first-time biologic disease modifying anti-rheumatic drug therapy for RA (RA)[5]

● **3470F** Rheumatoid arthritis (RA) disease activity, low (RA)[5]

● **3471F** Rheumatoid arthritis (RA) disease activity, moderate (RA)[5]

● **3472F** Rheumatoid arthritis (RA) disease activity, high (RA)[5]

Footnotes

[1] Physician Consortium for Performance Improvement® (PCPI), www.physicianconsortium.org

[2] National Committee on Quality Assurance (NCQA), Health Employer Data Information Set (HEDIS®), www.ncqa.org

[3] The Joint Commission (TJC) ORYX Initiative Performance Measures, www.thejointcommission.org

[4] National Diabetes Quality Improvement Alliance (NDQIA), www.nationaldiabetesalliance.org

[5] Joint measure from the Physician Consortium for Performance Improvement, www.physicianconsortium.org and National Committee on Quality Assurance (NCQA), www.ncqa.org

[6] The Society of Thoracic Surgeons, www.sts.org, National Quality Forum, www.qualityforum.org

Category II Codes

● **3475F** Disease prognosis for rheumatoid arthritis assessed, poor prognosis documented (RA)[5]

● **3476F** Disease prognosis for rheumatoid arthritis assessed, good prognosis documented (RA)[5]

● **3490F** History of AIDS-defining condition (HIV)[5]

● **3491F** HIV indeterminate (infants of undetermined HIV status born of HIV-infected mothers) (HIV)[5]

● **3492F** History of nadir CD4+ cell count <350 cells/mm^3 (HIV)[5]

● **3493F** No history of nadir CD4+ cell count <350 cells/mm^3 AND no history of AIDS-defining condition (HIV)[5]

● **3494F** CD4+ cell count <200 cells/mm^3 (HIV)[5]

● **3495F** CD4+ cell count 200 – 499 cells/mm^3 (HIV)[5]

● **3496F** CD4+ cell count ≥500 cells/mm^3 (HIV)[5]

● **3497F** CD4+ cell percentage <15% (HIV)[5]

● **3498F** CD4+ cell percentage ≥15% (HIV)[5]

● **3500F** CD4+ cell count or CD4+ cell percentage documented as performed (HIV)[5]

● **3502F** HIV RNA viral load below limits of quantification (HIV)[5]

● **3503F** HIV RNA viral load not below limits of quantification (HIV)[5]

● **3510F** Documentation that tuberculosis (TB) screening test performed and results interpreted (HIV)[5]

● **3511F** Chlamydia and gonorrhea screenings documented as performed (HIV)[5]

● **3512F** Syphilis screening documented as performed (HIV)[5]

● **3513F** Hepatitis B screening documented as performed (HIV)[5]

● **3514F** Hepatitis C screening documented as performed (HIV)[5]

● **3515F** Patient has documented immunity to Hepatitis C (HIV)[5]

● **3550F** Low risk for thromboembolism (AFIB)[1]

● **3551F** Intermediate risk for thromboembolism (AFIB)[1]

● **3552F** High risk for thromboembolism (AFIB)[1]

● **3555F** Patient had International Normalized Ratio (INR) measurement performed (AFIB)[1]

● **3570F** Final report for bone scintigraphy study includes correlation with existing relevant imaging studies (eg, x-ray, MRI, CT) corresponding to the same anatomical region in question (NUC_MED)[1]

● **3572F** Patient considered to be potentially at risk for fracture in a weight-bearing site (NUC_MED)[1]

● **3573F** Patient not considered to be potentially at risk for fracture in a weight-bearing site (NUC_MED)[1]

Therapeutic, Preventive, or Other Interventions

Therapeutic, preventive, or other interventions codes describe pharmacologic, procedural, or behavioral therapies, including preventive services such as patient education and counseling.

4000F Tobacco use cessation intervention, counseling (COPD, CAP, CAD)[1](DM)[4](PV)[2]

4001F Tobacco use cessation intervention, pharmacologic therapy (COPD, CAD, CAP, PV)[1] (DM)[4](PV)[2]

4002F Statin therapy, prescribed (CAD)[1]

4003F Patient education, written/oral, appropriate for patients with heart failure, performed (HF)[1]

4005F Pharmacologic therapy (other than minerals/vitamins) for osteoporosis prescribed (OP)[5]

4006F Beta-blocker therapy prescribed (CAD, HF)[1]

(4007F has been deleted. To report age related eye disease study (AREDS) formulation prescribed or recommended, use code 4177F)

4009F Angiotensin converting enzyme (ACE) inhibitor or angiotensin receptor blocker (ARB) therapy prescribed (HF, CAD, CKD)[1], (DM)[2]

▲ **4011F** Oral antiplatelet therapy prescribed (CAD)[1]

4012F Warfarin therapy prescribed (HF)[1]

4014F Written discharge instructions provided to heart failure patients discharged home (Instructions include all of the following components: activity level, diet, discharge medications, follow-up appointment, weight monitoring, what to do if symptoms worsen) (HF)[3]

(Excludes patients less than 18 years of age)

4015F Persistent asthma, preferred long term control medication or an acceptable alternative treatment, prescribed (Asthma)[1]

(Note: There are no medical exclusion criteria)

(Do not report modifier 1P with 4015F)

(To report patient reasons for not prescribing, use modifier 2P)

Footnotes

[1] Physician Consortium for Performance Improvement® (PCPI), www.physicianconsortium.org

[2] National Committee on Quality Assurance (NCQA), Health Employer Data Information Set (HEDIS®), www.ncqa.org

[3] The Joint Commission (TJC) ORYX Initiative Performance Measures, www.thejointcommission.org

[4] National Diabetes Quality Improvement Alliance (NDQIA), www.nationaldiabetesalliance.org

[5] Joint measure from the Physician Consortium for Performance Improvement, www.physicianconsortium.org and National Committee on Quality Assurance (NCQA), www.ncqa.org

[6] The Society of Thoracic Surgeons, www.sts.org, National Quality Forum, www.qualityforum.org

Category II Codes

4016F Anti-inflammatory/analgesic agent prescribed (OA)[1]

(Use for prescribed or continued medication[s], including over-the-counter medication[s])

4017F Gastrointestinal prophylaxis for NSAID use prescribed (OA)[1]

4018F Therapeutic exercise for the involved joint(s) instructed or physical or occupational therapy prescribed (OA)[1]

4019F Documentation of receipt of counseling on exercise AND either both calcium and vitamin D use or counseling regarding both calcium and vitamin D use (OP)[5]

4025F Inhaled bronchodilator prescribed (COPD)[1]

4030F Long-term oxygen therapy prescribed (more than 15 hours per day) (COPD)[1]

4033F Pulmonary rehabilitation exercise training recommended (COPD)[1]

(Report 4033F with 1019F)

4035F Influenza immunization recommended (COPD)[1]

4037F Influenza immunization ordered or administered (COPD, PV, CKD, ESRD)[1]

4040F Pneumococcal vaccine administered or previously received (COPD)[1], (PV)[2]

4041F Documentation of order for cefazolin OR cefuroxime for antimicrobial prophylaxis (PERI 2)[5]

4042F Documentation that prophylactic antibiotics were neither given within 4 hours prior to surgical incision nor given intraoperatively (PERI 2)[5]

4043F Documentation that an order was given to discontinue prophylactic antibiotics within 48 hours of surgical end time, cardiac procedures (PERI 2)[5]

4044F Documentation that an order was given for venous thromboembolism (VTE) prophylaxis to be given within 24 hours prior to incision time or 24 hours after surgery end time (PERI 2)[5]

4045F Appropriate empiric antibiotic prescribed (CAP)[1], (EM)[5]

4046F Documentation that prophylactic antibiotics were given within 4 hours prior to surgical incision or given intraoperatively (PERI 2)[5]

4047F Documentation of order for prophylactic antibiotics to be given within 1 hour (if fluoroquinolone or vancomycin, 2 hours) prior to surgical incision (or start of procedure when no incision is required) (PERI 2)[5]

4048F Documentation that prophylactic antibiotic was given within 1 hour (if fluoroquinolone or vancomycin, 2 hours) prior to surgical incision (or start of procedure when no incision is required) (PERI 2)[5]

4049F Documentation that order was given to discontinue prophylactic antibiotics within 24 hours of surgical end time, non-cardiac procedure (PERI 2)[5]

4050F Hypertension plan of care documented as appropriate (HTN)[1]

4051F Referred for an arteriovenous (AV) fistula (ESRD, CKD)[1]

4052F Hemodialysis via functioning arteriovenous (AV) fistula (ESRD)[1]

4053F Hemodialysis via functioning arteriovenous (AV) graft (ESRD)[1]

4054F Hemodialysis via catheter (ESRD)[1]

4055F Patient receiving peritoneal dialysis (ESRD)[1]

4056F Appropriate oral rehydration solution recommended (PAG)[1]

4058F Pediatric gastroenteritis education provided to caregiver (PAG)[1]

4060F Psychotherapy services provided (MDD)[1]

4062F Patient referral for psychotherapy documented (MDD)[1]

4064F Antidepressant pharmacotherapy prescribed (MDD)[1]

4065F Antipsychotic pharmacotherapy prescribed (MDD)[1]

4066F Electroconvulsive therapy (ECT) provided (MDD)[1]

4067F Patient referral for electroconvulsive therapy (ECT) documented (MDD)[1]

4070F Deep vein thrombosis (DVT) prophylaxis received by end of hospital day 2 (STR)[5]

4073F Oral antiplatelet therapy prescribed at discharge (STR)[5]

4075F Anticoagulant therapy prescribed at discharge (STR)[5]

4077F Documentation that tissue plasminogen activator (t-PA) administration was considered (STR)[5]

4079F Documentation that rehabilitation services were considered (STR)[5]

4084F Aspirin received within 24 hours before emergency department arrival or during emergency department stay (EM)[5]

4090F Patient receiving erythropoietin therapy (HEM)[1]

4095F Patient not receiving erythropoietin therapy (HEM)[1]

4100F Bisphosphonate therapy, intravenous, ordered or received (HEM)[1]

4110F Internal mammary artery graft performed for primary, isolated coronary artery bypass graft procedure (CABG)[6]

Footnotes

[1] Physician Consortium for Performance Improvement® (PCPI), www.physicianconsortium.org

[2] National Committee on Quality Assurance (NCQA), Health Employer Data Information Set (HEDIS®), www.ncqa.org

[3] The Joint Commission (TJC) ORYX Initiative Performance Measures, www.thejointcommission.org

[4] National Diabetes Quality Improvement Alliance (NDQIA), www.nationaldiabetesalliance.org

[5] Joint measure from the Physician Consortium for Performance Improvement, www.physicianconsortium.org and National Committee on Quality Assurance (NCQA), www.ncqa.org

[6] The Society of Thoracic Surgeons, www.sts.org, National Quality Forum, www.qualityforum.org

Category II Codes

4115F Beta blocker administered within 24 hours prior to surgical incision (CABG)[6]

4120F Antibiotic prescribed or dispensed (URI, PHAR)[2], (A-BRONCH)[2]

4124F Antibiotic neither prescribed nor dispensed (URI, PHAR)[2], (A-BRONCH)[2]

4130F Topical preparations (including OTC) prescribed for acute otitis externa (AOE)[1]

4131F Systemic antimicrobial therapy prescribed (AOE)[1]

4132F Systemic antimicrobial therapy not prescribed (AOE)[1]

4133F Antihistamines or decongestants prescribed or recommended (OME)[1]

4134F Antihistamines or decongestants neither prescribed nor recommended (OME)[1]

4135F Systemic corticosteroids prescribed (OME)[1]

4136F Systemic corticosteroids not prescribed (OME)[1]

● **4148F** Hepatitis A vaccine injection administered or previously received (HEP-C)[1]

● **4149F** Hepatitis B vaccine injection administered or previously received (HEP-C)[1]

4150F Patient receiving antiviral treatment for Hepatitis C (HEP-C)[1]

4151F Patient not receiving antiviral treatment for Hepatitis C (HEP-C)[1]

▶(Code 4152F has been deleted.)◀

4153F Combination peginterferon and ribavirin therapy prescribed (HEP-C)[1]

▶(Code 4154F has been deleted.)◀

4155F Hepatitis A vaccine series previously received (HEP-C)[1]

▶(Code 4156F has been deleted.)◀

4157F Hepatitis B vaccine series previously received (HEP-C)[1]

▲ **4158F** Patient counseled about risks of alcohol use (HEP-C)[1]

4159F Counseling regarding contraception received prior to initiation of antiviral treatment (HEP-C)[1]

4163F Patient counseling at a minimum on all of the following treatment options for clinically localized prostate cancer: active surveillance, AND interstitial prostate brachytherapy, AND external beam radiotherapy, AND radical prostatectomy, provided prior to initiation of treatment (PRCA)[1]

4164F Adjuvant (ie, in combination with external beam radiotherapy to the prostate for prostate cancer) hormonal therapy (gonadotropin-releasing hormone [GnRH] agonist or antagonist) prescribed/administered (PRCA)[1]

4165F 3-dimensional conformal radiotherapy (3D-CRT) or intensity modulated radiation therapy (IMRT) received (PRCA)[1]

4167F Head of bed elevation (30-45 degrees) on first ventilator day ordered (CRIT)[1]

4168F Patient receiving care in the intensive care unit (ICU) and receiving mechanical ventilation, 24 hours or less (CRIT)[1]

4169F Patient either not receiving care in the intensive care unit (ICU) OR not receiving mechanical ventilation OR receiving mechanical ventilation greater than 24 hours (CRIT)[1]

4171F Patient receiving erythropoiesis-stimulating agents (ESA) therapy (CKD)[1]

4172F Patient not receiving erythropoiesis-stimulating agents (ESA) therapy (CKD)[1]

4174F Counseling about the potential impact of glaucoma on visual functioning and quality of life, and importance of treatment adherence provided to patient and/or caregiver(s) (EC)[5]

4175F Best-corrected visual acuity of 20/40 or better (distance or near) achieved within the 90 days following cataract surgery (EC)[5]

4176F Counseling about value of protection from UV light and lack of proven efficacy of nutritional supplements in prevention or progression of cataract development provided to patient and/or caregiver(s) (NMA No Measure Associated)

4177F Counseling about the benefits and/or risks of the Age-Related Eye Disease Study (AREDS) formulation for preventing progression of age-related macular degeneration (AMD) provided to patient and/or caregiver(s) (EC)[5]

4178F Anti-D immune globulin received between 26 and 30 weeks gestation (Pre-Cr)[1]

4179F Tamoxifen or aromatase inhibitor (AI) prescribed (ONC)[1]

▲ **4180F** Adjuvant chemotherapy referred, prescribed, or previously received for Stage III colon cancer (ONC)[1]

4181F Conformal radiation therapy received (NMA-No Measure Assoc.)

4182F Conformal radiation therapy not received (NMA-No Measure Assoc.)

Footnotes

[1] Physician Consortium for Performance Improvement® (PCPI), www.physicianconsortium.org

[2] National Committee on Quality Assurance (NCQA), Health Employer Data Information Set (HEDIS®), www.ncqa.org

[3] The Joint Commission (TJC) ORYX Initiative Performance Measures, www.thejointcommission.org

[4] National Diabetes Quality Improvement Alliance (NDQIA), www.nationaldiabetesalliance.org

[5] Joint measure from the Physician Consortium for Performance Improvement, www.physicianconsortium.org and National Committee on Quality Assurance (NCQA), www.ncqa.org

[6] The Society of Thoracic Surgeons, www.sts.org, National Quality Forum, www.qualityforum.org

 ▲=Revised code   ●=New code   ▶ ◀=Contains new or revised text   ⊘=Modifier 51 exempt

Category II Codes

4185F   Continuous (12-months) therapy with proton pump inhibitor (PPI) or histamine H2 receptor antagonist (H2RA) received (GERD)[5]

4186F   No continuous (12-months) therapy with either proton pump inhibitor (PPI) or histamine H2 receptor antagonist (H2RA) received (GERD)[5]

4187F   Disease modifying anti-rheumatic drug therapy prescribed or dispensed (RA)[2]

4188F   Appropriate angiotensin converting enzyme (ACE)/angiotensin receptor blockers (ARB) therapeutic monitoring test ordered or performed (AM)[2]

4189F   Appropriate digoxin therapeutic monitoring test ordered or performed (AM)[2]

4190F   Appropriate diuretic therapeutic monitoring test ordered or performed (AM)[2]

4191F   Appropriate anticonvulsant therapeutic monitoring test ordered or performed (AM)[2]

● 4192F   Patient not receiving glucocorticoid therapy (RA)[5]

● 4193F   Patient receiving <10 mg daily prednisone (or equivalent), or RA activity is worsening, or glucocorticoid use is for less than 6 months (RA)[5]

● 4194F   Patient receiving ≥10 mg daily prednisone (or equivalent) for longer than 6 months, and improvement or no change in disease activity (RA)[5]

● 4195F   Patient receiving first-time biologic disease modifying anti-rheumatic drug therapy for rheumatoid arthritis (RA)[5]

● 4196F   Patient not receiving first-time biologic disease modifying anti-rheumatic drug therapy for rheumatoid arthritis (RA)[5]

▲ 4200F   External beam radiotherapy as primary therapy to prostate with or without nodal irradiation (PRCA)[1]

▲ 4201F   External beam radiotherapy with or without nodal irradiation as adjuvant or salvage therapy for prostate cancer patient (PRCA)[1]

4210F   Angiotensin converting enzyme (ACE) or angiotensin receptor blockers (ARB) medication therapy for 6 months or more (MM)[2]

4220F   Digoxin medication therapy for 6 months or more (MM)[2]

4221F   Diuretic medication therapy for 6 months or more (MM)[2]

4230F   Anticonvulsant medication therapy for 6 months or more (MM)[2]

4240F   Instruction in therapeutic exercise with follow-up by the physician provided to patients during episode of back pain lasting longer than 12 weeks (BkP)[2]

4242F   Counseling for supervised exercise program provided to patients during episode of back pain lasting longer than 12 weeks (BkP)[2]

4245F   Patient counseled during the initial visit to maintain or resume normal activities (BkP)[2]

4248F   Patient counseled during the initial visit for an episode of back pain against bed rest lasting 4 days or longer (BkP)[2]

▲ 4250F   Active warming used intraoperatively for the purpose of maintaining normothermia, OR at least 1 body temperature equal to or greater than 36 degrees Centigrade (or 96.8 degrees Fahrenheit) recorded within the 30 minutes immediately before or the 15 minutes immediately after anesthesia end time (CRIT)[1]

● 4260F   Wound surface culture technique used (CWC)[5]

● 4261F   Technique other than surface culture of the wound exudate used (eg, Levine/deep swab technique, semi-quantitative or quantitative swab technique) OR wound surface culture technique not used (CWC)[5]

● 4265F   Use of wet to dry dressings prescribed or recommended (CWC)[5]

● 4266F   Use of wet to dry dressings neither prescribed nor recommended (CWC)[5]

● 4267F   Compression therapy prescribed (CWC)[5]

● 4268F   Patient education regarding the need for long term compression therapy including interval replacement of compression stockings received (CWC)[5]

● 4269F   Appropriate method of offloading (pressure relief) prescribed (CWC)[5]

● 4270F   Patient receiving potent antiretroviral therapy for 6 months or longer (HIV)[5]

● 4271F   Patient receiving potent antiretroviral therapy for less than 6 months or not receiving potent antiretroviral therapy (HIV)[5]

● 4274F   Influenza immunization administered or previously received (HIV)[5] (P-ESRD)[1]

● 4275F   Hepatitis B vaccine injection administered or previously received (HIV)[5]

● 4276F   Potent antiretroviral therapy prescribed (HIV)[5]

● 4279F   Pneumocystis jiroveci pneumonia prophylaxis prescribed (HIV)[5]

● 4280F   Pneumocystis jiroveci pneumonia prophylaxis prescribed within 3 months of low CD4+ cell count or percentage (HIV)[5]

● 4290F   Patient screened for injection drug use (HIV)[5]

● 4293F   Patient screened for high-risk sexual behavior (HIV)[5]

Footnotes

[1] Physician Consortium for Performance Improvement® (PCPI), www.physicianconsortium.org

[2] National Committee on Quality Assurance (NCQA), Health Employer Data Information Set (HEDIS®), www.ncqa.org

[3] The Joint Commission (TJC) ORYX Initiative Performance Measures, www.thejointcommission.org

[4] National Diabetes Quality Improvement Alliance (NDQIA), www.nationaldiabetesalliance.org

[5] Joint measure from the Physician Consortium for Performance Improvement, www.physicianconsortium.org and National Committee on Quality Assurance (NCQA), www.ncqa.org

[6] The Society of Thoracic Surgeons, www.sts.org, National Quality Forum, www.qualityforum.org

Category II Codes

● **4300F**   Patient receiving warfarin therapy for nonvalvular atrial fibrillation or atrial flutter (AFIB)[1]

● **4301F**   Patient not receiving warfarin therapy for nonvalvular atrial fibrillation or atrial flutter (AFIB)[1]

● **4305F**   Patient education regarding appropriate foot care AND daily inspection of the feet received (CWC)[5]

● **4306F**   Patient counseled regarding psychosocial AND pharmacologic treatment options for opioid addiction (SUD)[1]

● **4320F**   Patient counseled regarding psychosocial AND pharmacologic treatment options for alcohol dependence (SUD)[5]

Follow-up or Other Outcomes

Follow-up or other outcomes codes describe review and communication of test results to patients, patient satisfaction or experience with care, patient functional status, and patient morbidity and mortality.

5005F   Patient counseled on self-examination for new or changing moles (ML)[5]

5010F   Findings of dilated macular or fundus exam communicated to the physician managing the diabetes care (EC)[5]

5015F   Documentation of communication that a fracture occurred and that the patient was or should be tested or treated for osteoporosis (OP)[5]

▲ **5020F**   Treatment summary report communicated to physician(s) managing continuing care and to the patient within 1 month of completing treatment (ONC)[1]

5050F   Treatment plan communicated to provider(s) managing continuing care within 1 month of diagnosis (ML)[5]

5060F   Findings from diagnostic mammogram communicated to practice managing patient's on-going care within 3 business days of exam interpretation (RAD)[5]

5062F   Findings from diagnostic mammogram communicated to the patient within 5 days of exam interpretation (RAD)[5]

● **5100F**   Potential risk for fracture communicated to the referring physician within 24 hours of completion of the imaging study (NUC_MED)[1]

Patient Safety

Patient safety codes that describe patient safety practices.

6005F   Rationale (eg, severity of illness and safety) for level of care (eg, home, hospital) documented (CAP)[1]

6010F   Dysphagia screening conducted prior to order for or receipt of any foods, fluids, or medication by mouth (STR)[5]

6015F   Patient receiving or eligible to receive foods, fluids, or medication by mouth (STR)[5]

6020F   NPO (nothing by mouth) ordered (STR)[5]

▲ **6030F**   All elements of maximal sterile barrier technique followed including: cap AND mask AND sterile gown AND sterile gloves AND a large sterile sheet AND hand hygiene AND 2% chlorhexidine for cutaneous antisepsis (or acceptable alternative antiseptics, per current guideline) (CRIT)[1]

6040F   Use of appropriate radiation dose reduction devices OR manual techniques for appropriate moderation of exposure, documented (RAD)[5]

6045F   Radiation exposure or exposure time in final report for procedure using fluoroscopy, documented (RAD)[5]

Structural Measures

Structural measures codes are used to identify measures that address the setting or system of the delivered care. These codes also address aspects of the capabilities of the organization or health care professional providing the care.

7010F   Patient information entered into a recall system with the target date for the next exam specified (ML)[5]

7020F   Mammogram assessment category (eg, Mammography Quality Standards Act [MQSA], Breast Imaging Reporting and Data System [BI-RADS®], or FDA approved equivalent categories) entered into an internal database to allow for analysis of abnormal interpretation (recall) rate (RAD)[5]

7025F   Patient information entered into a reminder system with a target due date for the next mammogram (RAD)[5]

Footnotes
[1] Physician Consortium for Performance Improvement® (PCPI), www.physicianconsortium.org
[2] National Committee on Quality Assurance (NCQA), Health Employer Data Information Set (HEDIS®), www.ncqa.org
[3] The Joint Commission (TJC) ORYX Initiative Performance Measures, www.thejointcommission.org
[4] National Diabetes Quality Improvement Alliance (NDQIA), www.nationaldiabetesalliance.org
[5] Joint measure from the Physician Consortium for Performance Improvement, www.physicianconsortium.org and National Committee on Quality Assurance (NCQA), www.ncqa.org
[6] The Society of Thoracic Surgeons, www.sts.org, National Quality Forum, www.qualityforum.org

Category II Codes

▲=Revised code   ●=New code   ►◄=Contains new or revised text   ⊘=Modifier 51 exempt

Notes

⊙=Moderate sedation ✚=Add-on code ✎=FDA approval pending #=Resequenced code

Category II Codes

Category III Codes

The following section contains a set of temporary codes for emerging technology, services, and procedures. Category III codes allow data collection for these services/procedures. Use of unlisted codes does not offer the opportunity for the collection of specific data. If a Category III code is available, this code must be reported instead of a Category I unlisted code. This is an activity that is critically important in the evaluation of health care delivery and the formation of public and private policy. The use of the codes in this section allow physicians and other qualified health care professionals, insurers, health services researchers, and health policy experts to identify emerging technology, services, and procedures for clinical efficacy, utilization and outcomes.

The inclusion of a service or procedure in this section neither implies nor endorses clinical efficacy, safety or the applicability to clinical practice. The codes in this section may not conform to the usual requirements for CPT Category I codes established by the Editorial Panel. For Category I codes, the Panel requires that the service/procedure be performed by many health care professionals in clinical practice in multiple locations and that FDA approval, as appropriate, has already been received. The nature of emerging technology, services, and procedures is such that these requirements may not be met. For these reasons, temporary codes for emerging technology, services, and procedures have been placed in a separate section of the CPT codebook and the codes are differentiated from Category I CPT codes by the use of alphanumeric characters.

▶Services/procedures described in this section make use of alphanumeric characters. These codes have an alpha character as the 5th character in the string, preceded by four digits. The digits are not intended to reflect the placement of the code in the Category I section of CPT nomenclature. Codes in this section may or may not eventually receive a Category I CPT code. In either case, in general, a given Category III code will be archived five years from its date of publication or revision in the CPT code book unless it is demonstrated that a temporary code is still needed. Services/procedures described by Category III codes which have been archived after five years, without conversion, may be reported using the Category I unlisted code. New codes in this section are released semi-annually via the AMA/CPT internet site, to expedite dissemination for reporting. The full set of temporary codes for emerging technology, services, and procedures are published annually in the CPT codebook. Go to www.ama-assn.org/go/cpt for the most current listing.◀

0016T   Destruction of localized lesion of choroid (eg, choroidal neovascularization), transpupillary thermotherapy

0017T   Destruction of macular drusen, photocoagulation

0019T   Extracorporeal shock wave involving musculoskeletal system, not otherwise specified, low energy

(For application of high energy extracorporeal shock wave involving musculoskeletal system not otherwise specified, use 0101T)

(For application of high energy extracorporeal shock wave involving lateral humeral epicondyle, use 0102T)

(0024T has been deleted)

(For non-surgical septal reduction therapy, use 93799)

(0026T has been deleted)

(For lipoprotein, direct measurement, intermediate density lipoproteins [IDL] [remnant lipoprotein], use 84999)

(0027T has been deleted)

(For endoscopic lysis of epidural adhesions with direct visualization using mechnical means or solution injection [eg, normal saline], use 64999)

(0028T has been deleted)

(For dual energy x-ray absorptiometry [DXA] body composition study, use 76499)

(0029T has been deleted)

(For pulsed magnetic neuromodulation incontinence treatment, use 53899)

0030T   Antiprothrombin (phospholipid cofactor) antibody, each Ig class

(0031T, 0032T have been deleted)

(For speculoscopy, including sampling, use 58999)

(0041T has been deleted)

(For urinalysis infectious agent detection, semi-quantitative analysis of volatile compounds, use 81099)

0042T   Cerebral perfusion analysis using computed tomography with contrast administration, including post-processing of parametric maps with determination of cerebral blood flow, cerebral blood volume, and mean transit time

(0043T has been deleted)

(For carbon monoxide, expired gas analysis [eg, $ETCO_c$/hemolysis breath test], use 84999)

(0046T, 0047T have been deleted)

(For mammary duct[s] catheter lavage, use 19499)

Category III Codes

0048T   Implantation of a ventricular assist device, extracorporeal, percutaneous transseptal access, single or dual cannulation

(0049T has been deleted)

(For prolonged extracorporeal percutaneous transseptal ventricular assist device, use 33999)

0050T   Removal of a ventricular assist device, extracorporeal, percutaneous transseptal access, single or dual cannulation

►(For replacement of a ventricular assist device, extracorporeal, percutaneous transseptal access, use 33999)◄

0051T   Implantation of a total replacement heart system (artificial heart) with recipient cardiectomy

(For implantation of heart assist or ventricular assist device, see 33975, 33976)

0052T   Replacement or repair of thoracic unit of a total replacement heart system (artificial heart)

(For replacement or repair of other implantable components in a total replacement heart system (artificial heart), use 0053T)

0053T   Replacement or repair of implantable component or components of total replacement heart system (artificial heart), excluding thoracic unit

(For replacement or repair of a thoracic unit of a total replacement heart system (artificial heart), use 0052T)

+ 0054T   Computer-assisted musculoskeletal surgical navigational orthopedic procedure, with image-guidance based on fluoroscopic images (List separately in addition to code for primary procedure)

+ 0055T   Computer-assisted musculoskeletal surgical navigational orthopedic procedure, with image-guidance based on CT/MRI images (List separately in addition to code for primary procedure)

(When CT and MRI are both performed, report 0055T only once)

(0056T has been deleted. To report, use 20985)

(0058T, 0059T have been deleted)

(For cryopreservation, ovarian reproductive tissue, oocytes, use 89240)

(0060T has been deleted)

(For electrical impedance breast scan, use 76499)

(0061T has been deleted)

(For destruction/reduction of malignant breast tumor, microwave phased array thermotherapy, use 19499)

►(0062T, 0063T have been deleted)◄

►(For percutaneous intradiscal annuloplasty, any method other than electrothermal, use 22899)◄

(For intradiscal electrothermal annuloplasty, see 22526, 22527)

►(0064T has been deleted. To report, use 94799)◄

(0065T has been deleted. To report, use 99174)

►(0066T has been deleted)◄

►(To report CT colon, screening, use 74263)◄

►(0067T has been deleted)◄

►(To report CT colon, diagnostic, see 74261-74262)◄

►(0068T-0070T have been deleted)◄

►(For acoustic heart sound recording and computer analysis, use 93799)◄

0071T   Focused ultrasound ablation of uterine leiomyomata, including MR guidance; total leiomyomata volume less than 200 cc of tissue

0072T   total leiomyomata volume greater or equal to 200 cc of tissue

(Do not report 0071T, 0072T in conjunction with 51702 or 77022)

0073T   Compensator-based beam modulation treatment delivery of inverse planned treatment using 3 or more high resolution (milled or cast) compensator convergent beam modulated fields, per treatment session

(For treatment planning, use 77301)

(Do not report 0073T in conjunction with 77401-77416, 77418)

(0074T has been deleted. To report, see 98969, 99444)

0075T   Transcatheter placement of extracranial vertebral or intrathoracic carotid artery stent(s), including radiologic supervision and interpretation, percutaneous; initial vessel

+ 0076T   each additional vessel (List separately in addition to code for primary procedure)

(Use 0076T in conjunction with 0075T)

(When the ipsilateral extracranial vertebral or intrathoracic carotid arteriogram (including imaging and selective catheterization) confirms the need for stenting, then 0075T and 0076T include all ipsilateral extracranial vertebral or intrathoracic selective carotid catheterization, all diagnostic imaging for ipsilateral extracranial vertebral or intrathoracic carotid artery stenting, and all related radiologic supervision and interpretation. If stenting is not indicated, then the appropriate codes for selective catheterization and imaging should be reported in lieu of code 0075T or 0076T.)

►(0077T has been deleted. To report, see 61107, 61210)◄

(0078T-0081T should be reported in accordance with the Endovascular Abdominal Aneurysm Repair guidelines established for 34800-34826)

0078T   Endovascular repair using prosthesis of abdominal aortic aneurysm, pseudoaneurysm or dissection, abdominal aorta involving visceral branches (superior mesenteric, celiac and/or renal artery[s])

(Do not report 0078T in conjunction with 34800-34805, 35081, 35102, 35452, 35454, 35472, 37205-37208)

(Report 0078T in conjunction with 35454, 37205-37208 when these procedures are performed outside the target zone of the endoprosthesis)

+ 0079T   Placement of visceral extension prosthesis for endovascular repair of abdominal aortic aneurysm involving visceral vessels, each visceral branch (List separately in addition to code for primary procedure)

(Use 0079T in conjunction with 0078T)

(Do not report 0079T in conjunction with 34800-34805, 35081, 35102, 35452, 35454, 35472, 37205-37208)

(Report 0079T in conjunction with 35454, 37205-37208 when these procedures are performed outside the target zone of the endoprosthesis)

0080T   Endovascular repair of abdominal aortic aneurysm, pseudoaneurysm or dissection, abdominal aorta involving visceral vessels (superior mesenteric, celiac or renal), using fenestrated modular bifurcated prosthesis (2 docking limbs), radiological supervision and interpretation

(Do not report 0080T in conjunction with 34800-34805, 35081, 35102, 35452, 35454, 35472, 37205-37208)

(Report 0080T in conjunction with 35454, 37205-37208 when these procedures are performed outside the target zone of the endoprosthesis)

+ 0081T   Placement of visceral extension prosthesis for endovascular repair of abdominal aortic aneurysm involving visceral vessels, each visceral branch, radiological supervision and interpretation (List separately in addition to code for primary procedure)

(Use 0081T in conjunction with 0080T)

(Do not report 0081T in conjunction with 34800-34805, 35081, 35102, 35452, 35454, 35472, 37205-37208)

(Report 0081T in conjunction with 35454, 37205-37208 when these procedures are performed outside the target zone of the endoprosthesis)

(0082T, 0083T have been deleted. To report, see 77373, 77435)

▶(0084T has been deleted. To report, use 53855)◀

0085T   Breath test for heart transplant rejection

▶(0086T has been deleted. To report use, 93799)◀

▶(0087T has been deleted. To report, use 89398)◀

(0088T has been deleted. To report, use 41530)

(0089T has been deleted. For actigraphy testing, use 95803)

(0090T has been deleted. To report total disc cervical arthroplasty, use 22856)

(To report total disc lumbar arthroplasty, use 22857)

+ 0092T   Total disc arthroplasty (artificial disc), anterior approach, including discectomy with end plate preparation (includes osteophytectomy for nerve root or spinal cord decompression and microdissection), each additional interspace, cervical (List separately in addition to code for primary procedure)

(Use 0092T in conjunction with 22856)

(Do not report 0092T in conjunction with 22851 when performed at the same level)

(0093T has been deleted. To report removal of total disc cervical arthroplasty, use 22864)

(To report removal of total disc lumbar arthroplasty, use 22865)

+ 0095T   Removal of total disc arthroplasty (artificial disc), anterior approach, each additional interspace, cervical (List separately in addition to code for primary procedure)

(Use 0095T in conjunction with 22864)

(0096T has been deleted. To report revision of total disc cervical arthroplasty, use 22861)

(To report revision of total disc lumbar arthroplasty, use 22862)

+ 0098T   Revision including replacement of total disc arthroplasty (artificial disc), anterior approach, each additional interspace, cervical (List separately in addition to code for primary procedure)

(Use 0098T in conjunction with 22861)

(Do not report 0098T in conjunction with 0095T)

(Do not report 0098T in conjunction with 22851 when performed at the same level)

(For decompression, see 63001-63048)

0099T   Implantation of intrastromal corneal ring segments

0100T   Placement of a subconjunctival retinal prosthesis receiver and pulse generator, and implantation of intra-ocular retinal electrode array, with vitrectomy

0101T   Extracorporeal shock wave involving musculoskeletal system, not otherwise specified, high energy

(For application of low energy musculoskeletal system extracorporeal shock wave, use 0019T)

0102T   Extracorporeal shock wave, high energy, performed by a physician, requiring anesthesia other than local, involving lateral humeral epicondyle

(For application of low energy musculoskeletal system extracorporeal shock wave, use 0019T)

0103T   Holotranscobalamin, quantitative

0104T   Inert gas rebreathing for cardiac output measurement; during rest

Category III Codes

0105T   during exercise

0106T   Quantitative sensory testing (QST), testing and interpretation per extremity; using touch pressure stimuli to assess large diameter sensation

0107T   using vibration stimuli to assess large diameter fiber sensation

0108T   using cooling stimuli to assess small nerve fiber sensation and hyperalgesia

0109T   using heat-pain stimuli to assess small nerve fiber sensation and hyperalgesia

0110T   using other stimuli to assess sensation

0111T   Long-chain (C20-22) omega-3 fatty acids in red blood cell (RBC) membranes

      (For very long chain fatty acids, use 82726)

      (0115T-0117T have been deleted. To report, see 99605-99607)

0123T   Fistulization of sclera for glaucoma, through ciliary body

0124T   Conjunctival incision with posterior extrascleral placement of pharmacological agent (does not include supply of medication)

      (For suprachoroidal delivery of pharmacologic agent, use 0186T)

0126T   Common carotid intima-media thickness (IMT) study for evaluation of atherosclerotic burden or coronary heart disease risk factor assessment

0130T   Validated, statistically reliable, randomized, controlled, single-patient clinical investigation of FDA approved chronic care drugs, provided by a pharmacist, interpretation and report to the prescribing health care professional

      (0133T has been deleted)

      (0135T has been deleted. To report, use 50593)

      (0137T has been deleted. For transperineal stereotactic template guided saturation prostate biopsies, use 55706)

0140T   Exhaled breath condensate pH

Pancreatic islet cells are transplanted by infusion into the portal vein. The portal vein may be cannulated percutaneously with imaging guidance, by laparoscopy, or by laparotomy. Codes 0141T-0143T include infusion of islet cells with monitoring and management of portal and systemic hemodynamics, monitoring and management of blood glucose and insulin therapy, immunotherapy infusion, antibiotic infusion, analgesic and sedative administration and monitoring, and all other therapeutic injections and infusions administered during the islet infusion. Codes 0141T-0143T also include typical postprocedural care. When reporting 0141T, percutaneous portal vein catheterization is reported separately (see codes 36481, 75887). Code 0142T includes diagnostic laparotomy (49000, 49002). Code 0143T includes diagnostic laparoscopy (49320).

0141T   Pancreatic islet cell transplantation through portal vein, percutaneous

      (For open approach, use 0142T)

      (For laparoscopic approach, use 0143T)

      (For percutaneous portal vein catheterization, use 36481)

      (For radiological supervision and interpretation, use 75887)

0142T   Pancreatic islet cell transplantation through portal vein, open

      (For percutaneous approach, use 0141T)

      (For laparoscopic approach, use 0143T)

      (Do not report 0142T in conjunction with 49000, 49002)

0143T   Laparoscopy, surgical, pancreatic islet cell transplantation through portal vein

      (For percutaneous approach, use 0141T)

      (For open approach, use 0142T)

      (Do not report 0143T in conjunction with 49320)

      ▶(0144T-0151T have been deleted. To report, see 75571-75574)◀

      (0152T has been deleted. To report, see 0174T, 0175T)

      (0153T has been deleted. To report, use 34806)

      (0154T has been deleted. To report, use 93982)

0155T   Laparoscopy, surgical; implantation or replacement of gastric stimulation electrodes, lesser curvature (ie, morbid obesity)

0156T   revision or removal of gastric stimulation electrodes, lesser curvature (ie, morbid obesity)

      (For open approach, see 0157T, 0158T)

      For laparoscopic or open insertion, revision or removal of antral gastric neurostimulator electrodes, see 43647, 43648, 43881, 43882)

      (For insertion, revision or removal of gastric neurostimulator pulse generator, see 64590, 64595)

      (For electronic analysis and programming of antral gastric neurostimulator pulse generator, see 95980-95982)

      (For electronic analysis and programming of a gastric neurostimulator, lesser curvature, use 0162T)

0157T   Laparotomy, implantation or replacement of gastric stimulation electrodes, lesser curvature (ie, morbid obesity)

0158T   Laparotomy, revision or removal of gastric stimulation electrodes, lesser curvature (ie, morbid obesity)

      (For laparoscopic approach, see 0155T, 0156T)

      (For insertion of gastric neurostimulator pulse generator, use 64590)

      (For revision or removal of gastric neurostimulator pulse generator, use 64595)

(For electronic analysis and programming of antral gastric neurostimulator pulse generator, see 95980-95982)

(For electronic analysis and programming of a gastric neurostimulator, lesser curvature, use 0162T)

+ 0159T Computer-aided detection, including computer algorithm analysis of MRI image data for lesion detection/characterization, pharmacokinetic analysis, with further physician review for interpretation, breast MRI (List separately in addition to code for primary procedure)

(Use 0159T in conjunction with 77058, 77059)

(Do not report 0159T in conjunction with 76376, 76377)

0160T Therapeutic repetitive transcranial magnetic stimulation treatment planning

(Pre-treatment determination of optimal magnetic field strength via titration, treatment location determination and stimulation parameter and protocol programming in the therapeutic use of high power, focal magnetic pulses for the direct, noninvasive modulation of cortical neurons)

0161T Therapeutic repetitive transcranial magnetic stimulation treatment delivery and management, per session

(Treatment session using high power, focal magnetic pulses for the direct, noninvasive modulation of cortical neurons. Clinical evaluation, safety monitoring and treatment parameter review in the therapeutic use of high power, focal magnetic pulses for the direct, noninvasive modulation of cortical neurons)

(0162T has been deleted. To report, see 95980–95982)

+ 0163T Total disc arthroplasty (artificial disc), anterior approach, including discectomy to prepare interspace (other than for decompression), each additional interspace, lumbar (List separately in addition to code for primary procedure)

(Use 0163T in conjunction with 22857)

+ 0164T Removal of total disc arthroplasty, (artificial disc), anterior approach, each additional interspace, lumbar (List separately in addition to code for primary procedure)

(Use 0164T in conjunction with 22865)

+ 0165T Revision including replacement of total disc arthroplasty (artificial disc), anterior approach, each additional interspace, lumbar (List separately in addition to code for primary procedure)

(Use 0165T in conjunction with 22862)

(Do not report 0163T-0165T in conjunction with 22851, 49010, when performed at the same level)

(For decompression, see 63001-63048)

0166T Transmyocardial transcatheter closure of ventricular septal defect, with implant; without cardiopulmonary bypass

0167T   with cardiopulmonary bypass

(Do not report 0166T, 0167T in conjunction with 32551, 33210, 33211)

(For ventricular septal defect closure via percutaneous transcatheter implant delivery, use 93581)

0168T Rhinophototherapy, intranasal application of ultraviolet and visible light, bilateral

0169T Stereotactic placement of infusion catheter(s) in the brain for delivery of therapeutic agent(s), including computerized stereotactic planning and burr hole(s)

(Do not report code 0169T in conjunction with 20660, 61107, 61795)

►(0170T has been deleted. To report, use 46707)◄

0171T Insertion of posterior spinous process distraction device (including necessary removal of bone or ligament for insertion and imaging guidance), lumbar; single level

+ 0172T   each additional level (List separately in addition to code for primary procedure)

(Use 0172T in conjunction with 0171T)

+ 0173T Monitoring of intraocular pressure during vitrectomy surgery (List separately in addition to code for primary procedure)

►(Use 0173T in conjunction with 67036, 67039-67043, 67108, 67112, 67113)◄

+ 0174T Computer-aided detection (CAD) (computer algorithm analysis of digital image data for lesion detection) with further physician review for interpretation and report, with or without digitization of film radiographic images, chest radiograph(s), performed concurrent with primary interpretation (List separately in addition to code for primary procedure)

(Use 0174T in conjunction with 71010, 71020, 71021, 71022, 71030)

0175T Computer-aided detection (CAD) (computer algorithm analysis of digital image data for lesion detection) with further physician review for interpretation and report, with or without digitization of film radiographic images, chest radiograph(s), performed remote from primary interpretation

(Do not report 0175T in conjunction with 71010, 71020, 71021, 71022, 71030)

0176T Transluminal dilation of aqueous outflow canal; without retention of device or stent

0177T   with retention of device or stent

0178T Electrocardiogram, 64 leads or greater, with graphic presentation and analysis; with interpretation and report

0179T   tracing and graphics only, without interpretation and report

0180T   interpretation and report only

(For electrocardiogram, routine, with at least 12 leads separately performed, see 93000-93010)

0181T Corneal hysteresis determination, by air impulse stimulation, bilateral, with interpretation and report

Category III Codes

0182T High dose rate electronic brachytherapy, per fraction

►(Do not report 0182T in conjunction with 77761-77763, 77776-77778, 77785-77787, 77789)◄

0183T Low frequency, non-contact, non-thermal ultrasound, including topical application(s), when performed, wound assessment, and instruction(s) for ongoing care, per day

0184T Excision of rectal tumor, transanal endoscopic microsurgical approach (ie, TEMS)

►(For non-endoscopic excision of rectal tumor, see 45160, 45171, 45172)◄

(Do not report 0184T in conjunction with 45300-45327, 69990)

0185T Multivariate analysis of patient-specific findings with quantifiable computer probability assessment, including report

(Do not report 0185T in conjunction with 99090)

0186T Suprachoroidal delivery of pharmacologic agent (does not include supply of medication)

0187T Scanning computerized ophthalmic diagnostic imaging, anterior segment, with interpretation and report, unilateral

Remote Real-Time Interactive Videoconferenced Critical Care Services

Remote real-time interactive video-conferenced critical care is the direct delivery by a physician(s) of medical care for a critically ill or critically injured patient from an off-site location. Remote real-time interactive video-conferenced critical care is intended to supplement on-site critical care services at times when a critically ill or injured patient requires additional critical care resources than are available on-site. (For definitions of critical illness or injury and critical care services, see **Critical Care Services** section).

In order to report remote real-time interactive video-conferenced critical care, the physician(s) in the remote location must have real-time access to the patient's medical record including progress notes, nursing notes, current medications, vital signs, clinical laboratory test results, other diagnostic test results, and radiographic images. The physician must have real-time capability to enter electronic orders; document the remote care services provided in the hospital medical record; videoconference with the on-site health care team in the patient room; assess patients in their individual rooms, using high fidelity audio and video capabilities, including clear observation of the patient, monitors, ventilators, and infusion pumps; and speak to patients and family members.

The review and/or interpretation of all diagnostic information is included in reporting remote real-time interactive video-conferenced critical care when performed during the critical period by the physician(s) providing remote real-time interactive video-conferenced critical care and should not be reported separately.

The remote real-time interactive video-conferenced critical care codes 0188T and 0189T are used to report the total duration of time spent by a physician providing remote real-time interactive video-conferenced critical care services to a critically ill or critically injured patient, even if the time spent by the physician on that date is not continuous. For any given period of time spent providing remote real-time interactive video-conferenced critical care services, the physician must devote his or her full attention to the patient and, therefore, cannot provide services to any other patient during the same period of time.

Time spent with the individual patient should be recorded in the patient's record. The time that can be reported as remote real-time interactive video-conferenced critical care is the time spent engaged in work directly related to the individual patient's care. For example, time spent reviewing test results or imaging studies, discussing the critically ill patient's care with other medical staff or documenting remote real-time interactive video-conferenced critical care services in the medical record would be reported as remote real-time interactive video-conferenced critical care, even though it does not occur at the bedside. Also, when the patient is unable or lacks capacity to participate in discussions, time spent from the remote site with family members or surrogate decision makers obtaining a medical history, reviewing the patient's condition or prognosis, or discussing treatment or limitation(s) of treatment may be reported as remote real-time interactive video-conferenced critical care, provided that the conversation bears directly on the management of the patient.

Time spent in activities that occur away from the bedside when the physician does not have the real-time capabilities described above may not be reported as remote real-time interactive video-conferenced critical care because the physician is not immediately available to the patient. Time spent in activities that do not directly contribute to the treatment of the patient may not be reported as remote real-time interactive video-conferenced critical care, even if they are performed in the remote site (eg, participation in administrative meetings or telephone calls to discuss other patients). Only one physician may report either Critical Care Services (99291, 99292) or remote real-time interactive video-conferenced Critical Care for the same period of time. Do not report remote real-time interactive video-conferenced critical care if another physician reports Pediatric or Neonatal Critical Care or Intensive Care services (99468-99476).

Code 0188T is used to report the first 30 to 74 minutes of remote real-time interactive video-conferenced, critical care on a given date. It should be used only once per date even if the time spent by the physician is not continuous on that date. Remote real-time interactive video-conferenced, critical care of less than 30 minutes total duration on a given date should not be reported.

Code 0189T is used to report additional block(s) of time, of up to 30 minutes each, beyond the first 74 minutes (see table below).

The following examples illustrate the correct reporting of remote critical care services:

Total Duration of Critical Care	Codes
less than 30 minutes (less than 1/2 hour)	Do not report
30-74 minutes (1/2 hr. - 1 hr. 14 min.)	0188T X 1
75-104 minutes (1 hr. 15 min. - 1 hr. 44 min.)	0188T X 1 AND 0189T X 1
105-134 minutes (1 hr. 45 min. - 2 hr. 14 min.)	0188T X 1 AND 0189T X 2

0188T   Remote real-time interactive video-conferenced critical care, evaluation and management of the critically ill or critically injured patient; first 30-74 minutes

+ 0189T   each additional 30 minutes (List separately in addition to code for primary service)

(Use 0189T in conjunction with 0188T)

+ 0190T   Placement of intraocular radiation source applicator (List separately in addition to primary procedure)

(Use 0190T in conjunction with 67036)

(For application of the source by radiation oncologist, see Clinical Brachytherapy section)

0191T   Insertion of anterior segment aqueous drainage device, without extraocular reservoir; internal approach

0192T   external approach

0193T   Transurethral, radiofrequency micro-remodeling of the female bladder neck and proximal urethra for stress urinary incontinence

(Do not report 0193T in conjunction with 51701)

▶(0194T has been deleted. To report procalcitonin, use 84145)◀

0195T   Arthrodesis, pre-sacral interbody technique, including instrumentation, imaging (when performed), and discectomy to prepare interspace, lumbar; single interspace

+ 0196T   each additional interspace (List separately in addition to code for primary procedure)

(Use 0196T in conjunction with 0195T)

(Do not report 0195T, 0196T in conjunction with 22558, 22845, 22851, 76000, 76380, 76496, 76497)

● **0197T**   Intra-fraction localization and tracking of target or patient motion during delivery of radiation therapy (eg, 3D positional tracking, gating, 3D surface tracking), each fraction of treatment

● **0198T**   Measurement of ocular blood flow by repetitive intraocular pressure sampling, with interpretation and report

● **0199T**   Physiologic recording of tremor using accelerometer(s) and/or gyroscope(s) (including frequency and amplitude), including interpretation and report

⊙● **0200T**   Percutaneous sacral augmentation (sacroplasty), unilateral injection(s), including the use of a balloon or mechanical device, when used, 1 or more needles

⊙● **0201T**   Percutaneous sacral augmentation (sacroplasty), bilateral injections, including the use of a balloon or mechanical device, when used, 2 or more needles

▶(For radiological supervision and interpretation, see 72291, 72292)◀

▶(If bone biopsy is performed, see 20220, 20225)◀

● **0202T**   Posterior vertebral joint(s) arthroplasty (eg, facet joint[s] replacement), including facetectomy, laminectomy, foraminotomy, and vertebral column fixation, injection of bone cement, when performed, including fluoroscopy, single level, lumbar spine

▶(Do not report 0202T in conjunction with 22521, 22524, 22840, 22851, 22857, 63005, 63012, 63017, 63030, 63042, 63047, 63056 at the same level)◀

● **0203T**   Sleep study, unattended, simultaneous recording; heart rate, oxygen saturation, respiratory analysis (eg, by airflow or peripheral arterial tone) and sleep time

▶(Do not report 0203T in conjunction with 93012, 93014, 93041-93227, 93228, 93229, 93230-93272, 95803, 95806, 0204T)◀

▶(For unattended sleep study that measures a minimum of heart rate, oxygen saturation, and respiratory analysis, use 0204T)◀

▶(For unattended sleep study that measures heart rate, oxygen saturation, respiratory airflow, and respiratory effort, use 95806)◀

Category III Codes

● **0204T**   minimum of heart rate, oxygen saturation, and respiratory analysis (eg, by airflow or peripheral arterial tone)

►(Do not report 0204T in conjunction with 93012, 93014, 93041-93227, 93228, 93229, 93230-93272, 95806, 0203T)◄

►(For unattended sleep study that measures heart rate, oxygen saturation, respiratory analysis and sleep time, use 0203T)◄

►(For unattended sleep study that measures heart rate, oxygen saturation, respiratory airflow, and respiratory effort, use 95806)◄

+● **0205T**   Intravascular catheter-based coronary vessel or graft spectroscopy (eg, infrared) during diagnostic evaluation and/or therapeutic intervention including imaging supervision, interpretation, and report, each vessel (List separately in addition to code for primary procedure)

►(Use 0205T in conjunction with 92980, 92982, 92995, 93508, 93510-93533)◄

● **0206T**   Algorithmic analysis, remote, of electrocardiographic-derived data with computer probability assessment, including report

►(When a 12-lead ECG is performed, 93000-93010 may be reported, as appropriate)◄

● **0207T**   Evacuation of meibomian glands, automated, using heat and intermittent pressure, unilateral

Appendix A

Modifiers

This list includes all of the modifiers applicable to *CPT 2010* codes.

A modifier provides the means to report or indicate that a service or procedure that has been performed has been altered by some specific circumstance but not changed in its definition or code. Modifiers also enable health care professionals to effectively respond to payment policy requirements established by other entities.

(Modifier 21 has been deleted. To report prolonged physician services, see 99354-99357)

22 **Increased Procedural Services:** When the work required to provide a service is substantially greater than typically required, it may be identified by adding modifier 22 to the usual procedure code. Documentation must support the substantial additional work and the reason for the additional work (ie, increased intensity, time, technical difficulty of procedure, severity of patient's condition, physical and mental effort required). **Note:** This modifier should not be appended to an E/M service.

23 **Unusual Anesthesia:** Occasionally, a procedure, which usually requires either no anesthesia or local anesthesia, because of unusual circumstances must be done under general anesthesia. This circumstance may be reported by adding modifier 23 to the procedure code of the basic service.

24 **Unrelated Evaluation and Management Service by the Same Physician During a Postoperative Period:** The physician may need to indicate that an evaluation and management service was performed during a postoperative period for a reason(s) unrelated to the original procedure. This circumstance may be reported by adding modifier 24 to the appropriate level of E/M service.

25 **Significant, Separately Identifiable Evaluation and Management Service by the Same Physician on the Same Day of the Procedure or Other Service:** It may be necessary to indicate that on the day a procedure or service identified by a CPT code was performed, the patient's condition required a significant, separately identifiable E/M service above and beyond the other service provided or beyond the usual preoperative and postoperative care associated with the procedure that was performed. A significant, separately identifiable E/M service is defined or substantiated by documentation that satisfies the relevant criteria for the respective E/M service to be reported (see **Evaluation and Management Services Guidelines** for instructions on determining level of E/M service). The E/M service may be prompted by the symptom or condition for which the procedure and/or service was provided. As such, different diagnoses are not required for reporting of the E/M services on the same date. This circumstance may be reported by adding modifier 25 to the appropriate level of E/M service. **Note:** This modifier is not used to report an E/M service that resulted in a decision to perform surgery. See modifier 57. For significant, separately identifiable non-E/M services, see modifier 59.

26 **Professional Component:** Certain procedures are a combination of a physician component and a technical component. When the physician component is reported separately, the service may be identified by adding modifier 26 to the usual procedure number.

32 **Mandated Services:** Services related to *mandated* consultation and/or related services (eg, third party payer, governmental, legislative or regulatory requirement) may be identified by adding modifier 32 to the basic procedure.

47 **Anesthesia by Surgeon:** Regional or general anesthesia provided by the surgeon may be reported by adding modifier 47 to the basic service. (This does not include local anesthesia.) **Note:** Modifier 47 would not be used as a modifier for the anesthesia procedures.

50 **Bilateral Procedure:** Unless otherwise identified in the listings, bilateral procedures that are performed at the same operative session, should be identified by adding modifier 50 to the appropriate 5 digit code.

51 **Multiple Procedures:** When multiple procedures, other than E/M services, Physical Medicine and Rehabilitation services or provision of supplies (eg, vaccines), are performed at the same session by the same provider, the primary procedure or service may be reported as listed. The additional procedure(s) or service(s) may be identified by appending modifier 51 to the additional procedure or service code(s). **Note:** This modifier should not be appended to designated "add-on" codes (see Appendix D).

52 **Reduced Services:** Under certain circumstances a service or procedure is partially reduced or eliminated at the physician's discretion. Under these circumstances the service provided can be identified by its usual procedure number and the addition of modifier 52, signifying that the service is reduced. This provides a means of reporting reduced services without disturbing the identification of the basic service. **Note:** For hospital outpatient reporting of a previously scheduled procedure/service that is partially reduced or cancelled as a result of extenuating circumstances or those that threaten the well-being of the patient prior to or after administration of anesthesia, see modifiers 73 and 74 (see modifiers approved for ASC hospital outpatient use).

53 **Discontinued Procedure:** Under certain circumstances, the physician may elect to terminate a surgical or diagnostic procedure. Due to extenuating circumstances or those that threaten the well being of the patient, it may be necessary to indicate that a surgical or diagnostic procedure was started but discontinued. This circumstance may be reported by adding modifier 53 to the code reported by the physician for the discontinued procedure. **Note:** This modifier is not used to report the elective cancellation of a procedure prior to the patient's anesthesia induction and/or surgical preparation in the operating suite. For outpatient hospital/ambulatory surgery center (ASC) reporting of a previously scheduled procedure/service that is partially reduced or cancelled as a result of extenuating circumstances or those that threaten the well being of the patient prior to or after administration of anesthesia, see modifiers 73 and 74 (see modifiers approved for ASC hospital outpatient use).

54 Surgical Care Only: When 1 physician performs a surgical procedure and another provides preoperative and/or postoperative management, surgical services may be identified by adding modifier 54 to the usual procedure number.

55 Postoperative Management Only: When 1 physician performed the postoperative management and another physician performed the surgical procedure, the postoperative component may be identified by adding modifier 55 to the usual procedure number.

56 Preoperative Management Only: When 1 physician performed the preoperative care and evaluation and another physician performed the surgical procedure, the preoperative component may be identified by adding modifier 56 to the usual procedure number.

57 Decision for Surgery: An evaluation and management service that resulted in the initial decision to perform the surgery may be identified by adding modifier 57 to the appropriate level of E/M service.

58 Staged or Related Procedure or Service by the Same Physician During the Postoperative Period: It may be necessary to indicate that the performance of a procedure or service during the postoperative period was: (a) planned or anticipated (staged); (b) more extensive than the original procedure; or (c) for therapy following a surgical procedure. This circumstance may be reported by adding modifier 58 to the staged or related procedure. **Note:** For treatment of a problem that requires a return to the operating/procedure room (eg, unanticipated clinical condition), see modifier 78.

59 Distinct Procedural Service: Under certain circumstances, it may be necessary to indicate that a procedure or service was distinct or independent from other non-E/M services performed on the same day. Modifier 59 is used to identify procedures/services, other than E/M services, that are not normally reported together, but are appropriate under the circumstances. Documentation must support a different session, different procedure or surgery, different site or organ system, separate incision/excision, separate lesion, or separate injury (or area of injury in extensive injuries) not ordinarily encountered or performed on the same day by the same individual. However, when another already established modifier is appropriate it should be used rather than modifier 59. Only if no more descriptive modifier is available, and the use of modifier 59 best explains the circumstances, should modifier 59 be used. **Note:** Modifier 59 should not be appended to an E/M service. To report a separate and distinct E/M service with a non-E/M service performed on the same date, see modifier 25.

62 Two Surgeons: When 2 surgeons work together as primary surgeons performing distinct part(s) of a procedure, each surgeon should report his/her distinct operative work by adding modifier 62 to the procedure code and any associated add-on code(s) for that procedure as long as both surgeons continue to work together as primary surgeons. Each surgeon should report the co-surgery once using the same procedure code. If additional procedure(s) (including add-on procedure(s) are performed during the same surgical session, separate code(s) may also be reported with modifier 62 added. **Note:** If a co-surgeon acts as an assistant in the performance of additional procedure(s) during the same surgical session, those services may be reported using separate procedure code(s) with modifier 80 or modifier 82 added, as appropriate.

63 Procedure Performed on Infants less than 4 kg: Procedures performed on neonates and infants up to a present body weight of 4 kg may involve significantly increased complexity and physician work commonly associated with these patients. This circumstance may be reported by adding modifier 63 to the procedure number. **Note:** Unless otherwise designated, this modifier may only be appended to procedures/services listed in the 20000-69990 code series. Modifier 63 should not be appended to any CPT codes listed in the **Evaluation and Management Services, Anesthesia, Radiology, Pathology/Laboratory, or Medicine** sections.

66 Surgical Team: Under some circumstances, highly complex procedures (requiring the concomitant services of several physicians, often of different specialties, plus other highly skilled, specially trained personnel, various types of complex equipment) are carried out under the "surgical team" concept. Such circumstances may be identified by each participating physician with the addition of modifier 66 to the basic procedure number used for reporting services.

76 Repeat Procedure or Service by Same Physician: It may be necessary to indicate that a procedure or service was repeated subsequent to the original procedure or service. This circumstance may be reported by adding modifier 76 to the repeated procedure/service.

77 Repeat Procedure by Another Physician: The physician may need to indicate that a basic procedure or service performed by another physician had to be repeated. This situation may be reported by adding modifier 77 to the repeated procedure/service.

78 Unplanned Return to the Operating/Procedure Room by the Same Physician Following Initial Procedure for a Related Procedure During the Postoperative Period: It may be necessary to indicate that another procedure was performed during the postoperative period of the initial procedure (unplanned procedure following initial procedure). When this procedure is related to the first, and requires the use of an operating/procedure room, it may be reported by adding modifier 78 to the related procedure. (For repeat procedures, see modifier 76.)

79 Unrelated Procedure or Service by the Same Physician During the Postoperative Period: The physician may need to indicate that the performance of a procedure or service during the postoperative period was unrelated to the original procedure. This circumstance may be reported by using modifier 79. (For repeat procedures on the same day, see modifier 76.)

80 Assistant Surgeon: Surgical assistant services may be identified by adding modifier 80 to the usual procedure number(s).

81 Minimum Assistant Surgeon: Minimum surgical assistant services are identified by adding modifier 81 to the usual procedure number.

82 Assistant Surgeon (when qualified resident surgeon not available): The unavailability of a qualified resident surgeon is a prerequisite for use of modifier 82 appended to the usual procedure code number(s).

90 Reference (Outside) Laboratory: When laboratory procedures are performed by a party other than the treating or reporting physician, the procedure may be identified by adding modifier 90 to the usual procedure number.

91 Repeat Clinical Diagnostic Laboratory Test: In the course of treatment of the patient, it may be necessary to repeat the same laboratory test on the same day to obtain subsequent (multiple) test results. Under these circumstances, the laboratory test performed can be identified by its usual procedure number and the addition of modifier 91. **Note:** This modifier may not be used when tests are rerun to confirm initial results; due to testing problems with specimens or equipment; or for any other reason when a normal, one-time, reportable result is all that is required. This modifier may not be used when other code(s) describe a series of test results (eg, glucose tolerance tests, evocative/suppression testing). This modifier may only be used for laboratory test(s) performed more than once on the same day on the same patient.

92 Alternative Laboratory Platform Testing: When laboratory testing is being performed using a kit or transportable instrument that wholly or in part consists of a single use, disposable analytical chamber, the service may be identified by adding modifier 92 to the usual laboratory procedure code (HIV testing 86701-86703). The test does not require permanent dedicated space, hence by its design may be hand carried or transported to the vicinity of the patient for immediate testing at that site, although location of the testing is not in itself determinative of the use of this modifier.

99 Multiple Modifiers: Under certain circumstances 2 or more modifiers may be necessary to completely delineate a service. In such situations modifier 99 should be added to the basic procedure, and other applicable modifiers may be listed as part of the description of the service.

Anesthesia Physical Status Modifiers

The Physical Status modifiers are consistent with the American Society of Anesthesiologists ranking of patient physical status, and distinguishing various levels of complexity of the anesthesia service provided. All anesthesia services are reported by use of the anesthesia five-digit procedure code (00100-01999) with the appropriate physical status modifier appended.

Example: 00100-P1

Under certain circumstances, when another established modifier(s) is appropriate, it should be used in addition to the physical status modifier.

Example: 00100-P4-53

Physical Status Modifier P1: A normal healthy patient

Physical Status Modifier P2: A patient with mild systemic disease

Physical Status Modifier P3: A patient with severe systemic disease

Physical Status Modifier P4: A patient with severe systemic disease that is a constant threat to life

Physical Status Modifier P5: A moribund patient who is not expected to survive without the operation

Physical Status Modifier P6: A declared brain-dead patient whose organs are being removed for donor purposes

Modifiers Approved for Ambulatory Surgery Center (ASC) Hospital Outpatient Use

CPT Level I Modifiers

25 Significant, Separately Identifiable Evaluation and Management Service by the Same Physician on the Same Day of the Procedure or Other Service: It may be necessary to indicate that on the day a procedure or service identified by a CPT code was performed, the patient's condition required a significant, separately identifiable E/M service above and beyond the other service provided or beyond the usual preoperative and postoperative care associated with the procedure that was performed. A significant, separately identifiable E/M service is defined or substantiated by documentation that satisfies the relevant criteria for the respective E/M service to be reported (see **Evaluation and Management Services Guidelines** for instructions on determining level of E/M service). The E/M service may be prompted by the symptom or condition for which the procedure and/or service was provided. As such, different diagnoses are not required for reporting of the E/M services on the same date. This circumstance may be reported by adding modifier 25 to the appropriate level of E/M service. **Note:** This modifier is not used to report an E/M service that resulted in a decision to perform surgery. See modifier 57. For significant, separately identifiable non-E/M services, see modifier 59.

27 Multiple Outpatient Hospital E/M Encounters on the Same Date: For hospital outpatient reporting purposes, utilization of hospital resources related to separate and distinct E/M encounters performed in multiple outpatient hospital settings on the same date may be reported by adding modifier 27 to each appropriate level outpatient and/or emergency department E/M code(s). This modifier provides a means of reporting circumstances involving evaluation and management services provided by physician(s) in more than one (multiple) outpatient hospital setting(s) (eg, hospital emergency department, clinic). **Note:** This modifier is not to be used for physician reporting of multiple E/M services performed by the same physician on the same date. For physician reporting of all outpatient evaluation and management services provided by the same physician on the same date and performed in multiple outpatient setting(s) (eg, hospital emergency department, clinic), see **Evaluation and Management, Emergency Department, or Preventive Medicine Services** codes.

50 Bilateral Procedure: Unless otherwise identified in the listings, bilateral procedures that are performed at the same operative session should be identified by adding modifier 50 to the appropriate 5 digit code.

52 Reduced Services: Under certain circumstances a service or procedure is partially reduced or eliminated at the physician's discretion. Under these circumstances the service provided can be identified by its usual procedure number and the addition of modifier 52, signifying that the service is reduced. This provides a means of reporting reduced services without disturbing the identification of the basic service. **Note:** For hospital outpatient reporting of a previously scheduled procedure/service that is partially reduced or cancelled as a result of extenuating circumstances or those that threaten the well-being of the patient prior to or after administration of anesthesia, see modifiers 73 and 74.

58 Staged or Related Procedure or Service by the Same Physician During the Postoperative Period: It may be necessary to indicate that the performance of a procedure or service during the postoperative period was: (a) planned or anticipated (staged); (b) more extensive than the original procedure; or (c) for therapy following a surgical procedure. This circumstance may be reported by adding modifier 58 to the staged or related procedure. **Note:** For treatment of a problem that requires a return to the operating/procedure room (eg, unanticipated clinical condition), see modifier 78.

59 Distinct Procedural Service: Under certain circumstances, it may be necessary to indicate that a procedure or service was distinct or independent from other non-E/M services performed on the same day. Modifier 59 is used to identify procedures/services, other than E/M services, that are not normally reported together, but are appropriate under the circumstances. Documentation must support a different session, different procedure or surgery, different site or organ system, separate incision/excision, separate lesion, or separate injury (or area of injury in extensive injuries) not ordinarily encountered or performed on the same day by the same individual. However, when another already established modifier is appropriate it should be used rather than modifier 59. Only if no more descriptive modifier is available, and the use of modifier 59 best explains the circumstances, should modifier 59 be used. **Note:** Modifier 59 should not be appended to an E/M service. To report a separate and distinct E/M service with a non-E/M service performed on the same date, see modifier 25.

73 Discontinued Out-Patient Hospital/Ambulatory Surgery Center (ASC) Procedure Prior to the Administration of Anesthesia: Due to extenuating circumstances or those that threaten the well being of the patient, the physician may cancel a surgical or diagnostic procedure subsequent to the patient's surgical preparation (including sedation when provided, and being taken to the room where the procedure is to be performed), but prior to the administration of anesthesia (local, regional block(s) or general). Under these circumstances, the intended service that is prepared for but cancelled can be reported by its usual procedure number and the addition of modifier 73. **Note:** The elective cancellation of a service prior to the administration of anesthesia and/or surgical preparation of the patient should not be reported. For physician reporting of a discontinued procedure, see modifier 53.

74 Discontinued Out-Patient Hospital/Ambulatory Surgery Center (ASC) Procedure After Administration of Anesthesia: Due to extenuating circumstances or those that threaten the well being of the patient, the physician may terminate a surgical or diagnostic procedure after the administration of anesthesia (local, regional block(s), general) or after the procedure was started (incision made, intubation started, scope inserted, etc). Under these circumstances, the procedure started but terminated can be reported by its usual procedure number and the addition of modifier 74. **Note:** The elective cancellation of a service prior to the administration of anesthesia and/or surgical preparation of the patient should not be reported. For physician reporting of a discontinued procedure, see modifier 53.

76 Repeat Procedure or Service by Same Physician: It may be necessary to indicate that a procedure or service was repeated subsequent to the original procedure or service. This circumstance may be reported by adding modifier 76 to the repeated procedure/service.

77 Repeat Procedure by Another Physician: The physician may need to indicate that a basic procedure or service performed by another physician had to be repeated. This situation may be reported by adding modifier 77 to the repeated procedure/service.

78 Unplanned Return to the Operating/Procedure Room by the Same Physician Following Initial Procedure for a Related Procedure During the Postoperative Period: It may be necessary to indicate that another procedure was performed during the postoperative period of the initial procedure (unplanned procedure following initial procedure). When this procedure is related to the first, and requires the use of an operating/procedure room, it may be reported by adding modifier 78 to the related procedure. (For repeat procedures, see modifier 76.)

79 Unrelated Procedure or Service by the Same Physician During the Postoperative Period: The physician may need to indicate that the performance of a procedure or service during the postoperative period was unrelated to the original procedure. This circumstance may be reported by using modifier 79. (For repeat procedures on the same day, see 76.)

91 Repeat Clinical Diagnostic Laboratory Test: In the course of treatment of the patient, it may be necessary to repeat the same laboratory test on the same day to obtain subsequent (multiple) test results. Under these circumstances, the laboratory test performed can be identified by its usual procedure number and the addition of modifier 91. **Note:** This modifier may not be used when tests are rerun to confirm initial results; due to testing problems with specimens or equipment; or for any other reason when a normal, one-time, reportable result is all that is required. This modifier may not be used when other code(s) describe a series of test results (eg, glucose tolerance tests, evocative/suppression testing). This modifier may only be used for laboratory test(s) performed more than once on the same day on the same patient.

Level II (HCPCS/National) Modifiers
E1 Upper left, eyelid

E2 Lower left, eyelid

E3 Upper right, eyelid

E4 Lower right, eyelid

F1 Left hand, second digit

F2 Left hand, third digit

F3 Left hand, fourth digit

F4 Left hand, fifth digit

F5 Right hand, thumb

F6 Right hand, second digit

F7 Right hand, third digit

F8 Right hand, fourth digit

F9 Right hand, fifth digit

FA Left hand, thumb

GG Performance and payment of a screening mammogram and diagnostic mammogram on the same patient, same day

GH Diagnostic mammogram converted from screening mammogram on same day

LC Left circumflex coronary artery

LD Left anterior descending coronary artery

LT Left side (used to identify procedures performed on the left side of the body)

QM Ambulance service provided under arrangement by a provider of services

QN Ambulance service furnished directly by a provider of services

RC Right coronary artery

RT Right side (used to identify procedures performed on the right side of the body)

T1 Left foot, second digit

T2 Left foot, third digit

T3 Left foot, fourth digit

T4 Left foot, fifth digit

T5 Right foot, great toe

T6 Right foot, second digit

T7 Right foot, third digit

T8 Right foot, fourth digit

T9 Right foot, fifth digit

TA Left foot, great toe

Appendix B

Summary of Additions, Deletions, and Revisions

▶Appendix B shows the actual changes that were made to the code descriptors. New codes appear with a bullet (●) and are indicated as "Code Added." Revised codes are preceded with a triangle (▲). Within revised codes, the deleted language appears with a ~~strikethrough~~, while new text appears <u>underlined</u>. Codes with which conscious sedation would not be separately reported when performed at the same session by the same provider are denoted with the bullseye (⊙). The symbol (✔) is used to identify codes for vaccines that are pending FDA approval (see **Appendix K**). The symbol (#) is used to identify codes that have been resequenced (see **Appendix N**). CPT add-on codes are annotated by the symbol (✚) (see **Appendix D**). The symbol (⊘) is used to identify codes that are exempt from the use of modifier 51 (see **Appendix E**).◀

Evaluation and Management

▲ 99304   Initial nursing facility care, per day, for the evaluation and management of a patient, which requires these 3 key components:

- ■ A detailed or comprehensive history;

- ■ A detailed or comprehensive examination; and

- ■ Medical decision making that is straightforward or of low complexity.

Counseling and/or coordination of care with other providers or agencies are provided consistent with the nature of the problem(s) and the patientís and/or familyís needs.

Usually, the problem(s) requiring admission are of low severity. Physicians typically spend 25 minutes <u>at the bedside and on the patient's facility floor or unit.</u> ~~with the patient and/or family or caregiver.~~

▲ 99305   Initial nursing facility care, per day, for the evaluation and management of a patient, which requires these 3 key components:

- ■ A comprehensive history;

- ■ A comprehensive examination; and

- ■ Medical decision making of moderate complexity.

Counseling and/or coordination of care with other providers or agencies are provided consistent with the nature of the problem(s) and the patientís and/or familyís needs.

Usually, the problem(s) requiring admission are of moderate severity. Physicians typically spend 35 minutes <u>at the bedside and on the patient's facility floor or unit.</u> ~~with the patient and/or family or caregiver.~~

▲ 99306   Initial nursing facility care, per day, for the evaluation and management of a patient, which requires these 3 key components:

- ■ A comprehensive history;

- ■ A comprehensive examination; and

- ■ Medical decision making of high complexity.

Counseling and/or coordination of care with other providers or agencies are provided consistent with the nature of the problem(s) and the patientís and/or familyís needs.

Usually, the problem(s) requiring admission are of high severity. Physicians typically spend 45 minutes <u>at the bedside and on the patient's facility floor or unit.</u> ~~with the patient and/or family or caregiver.~~

▲ 99307   Subsequent nursing facility care, per day, for the evaluation and management of a patient, which requires at least 2 of these 3 key components:

- ■ A problem focused interval history;

- ■ A problem focused examination;

- ■ Straightforward medical decision making.

Counseling and/or coordination of care with other providers or agencies are provided consistent with the nature of the problem(s) and the patientís and/or familyís needs.

Usually, the patient is stable, recovering, or improving. Physicians typically spend 10 minutes <u>at the bedside and on the patient's facility floor or unit.</u> ~~with the patient and/or family or caregiver.~~

▲ 99308   Subsequent nursing facility care, per day, for the evaluation and management of a patient, which requires at least 2 of these 3 key components:

- ■ An expanded problem focused interval history;

- ■ An expanded problem focused examination;

- ■ Medical decision making of low complexity.

Counseling and/or coordination of care with other providers or agencies are provided consistent with the nature of the problem(s) and the patientís and/or familyís needs.

Usually, the patient is responding inadequately to therapy or has developed a minor complication. Physicians typically spend 15 minutes <u>at the bedside and on the patient's facility floor or unit.</u> ~~with the patient and/or family or caregiver.~~

▲ 99309   Subsequent nursing facility care, per day, for the evaluation and management of a patient, which requires at least 2 of these 3 key components:

- ■ A detailed interval history;

- ■ A detailed examination;

- ■ Medical decision making of moderate complexity.

Counseling and/or coordination of care with other providers or agencies are provided consistent with the nature of the problem(s) and the patientís and/or familyís needs.

Usually, the patient has developed a significant complication or a significant new problem. Physicians typically spend 25 minutes <u>at the bedside and on the patient's facility floor or unit.</u> ~~with the patient and/or family or caregiver.~~

▲ **99310** Subsequent nursing facility care, per day, for the evaluation and management of a patient, which requires at least 2 of these 3 key components:

■ **A comprehensive interval history;**

■ **A comprehensive examination;**

■ **Medical decision making of high complexity.**

Counseling and/or coordination of care with other providers or agencies are provided consistent with the nature of the problem(s) and the patientís and/or familyís needs.

The patient may be unstable or may have developed a significant new problem requiring immediate physician attention. Physicians typically spend 35 minutes <u>at the bedside and on the patient's facility floor or unit.</u> ~~with the patient and/or family or caregiver.~~

▲ **99318** Evaluation and management of a patient involving an annual nursing facility assessment, which requires these 3 key components:

■ **A detailed interval history;**

■ **A comprehensive examination; and**

■ **Medical decision making that is of low to moderate complexity.**

Counseling and/or coordination of care with other providers or agencies are provided consistent with the nature of the problem(s) and the patientís and/or familyís needs.

Usually, the patient is stable, recovering, or improving. Physicians typically spend 30 minutes <u>at the bedside and on the patient's facility floor or unit.</u> ~~with the patient and/or family or caregiver.~~

+ **99356** Grammatical Change

▲ **99358** **Prolonged evaluation and management service** before and/or after direct (face-to-face) patient care ~~(eg, review of extensive records and tests, communication with other professionals and/or the patient/family)~~; first hour ~~(List separately in addition to code(s) for other physician service(s) and/or inpatient or outpatient Evaluation and Management service)~~

+▲ **99359** each additional 30 minutes (List separately in addition to code for prolonged physician service)

99466 Grammatical Change

99468 Grammatical Change

99469 Grammatical Change

99477 Grammatical Change

Anesthesia

00528 Grammatical Change

00529 Grammatical Change

00541 Grammatical Change

00625 Grammatical Change

00626 Grammatical Change

~~01632~~ ~~radical resection~~

Surgery

~~14300~~ ~~Adjacent tissue transfer or rearrangement, more than 30 sq cm, unusual or complicated, any area~~

● **14301** Code added

+● **14302** Code added

+ **15787** Grammatical Change

16030 Grammatical Change

19120 Grammatical Change

+▲ **19295** Image guided placement, metallic localization clip, percutaneous, during breast biopsy<u>/aspiration</u> (List separately in addition to code for primary procedure)

20690 Grammatical Change

20692 Grammatical Change

20696 Grammatical Change

● **21011** Code added

● **21012** Code added

● **21013** Code added

● **21014** Code added

▲ **21015** Radical resection of tumor (eg, malignant neoplasm), soft tissue of face or scalp<u>; less than 2 cm</u>

● **21016** Code added

● **21552** Code added

● **21554** Code added

▲ **21555** Excision<u>,</u> tumor, soft tissue of neck or <u>anterior</u> thorax<u>,</u>~~;~~ subcutaneous<u>; less than 3 cm</u>

▲ **21556** Excision, tumor, soft tissue of neck or anterior thorax~~; deep~~, subfascial~~,~~ <u>(eg, intramuscular); less than 5 cm</u>

▲ **21557** Radical resection of tumor (eg, malignant neoplasm), soft tissue of neck or <u>anterior</u> thorax<u>; less than 5 cm</u>

● **21558** Code added

▲ **21930** Excision, tumor, soft tissue of back or flank<u>, subcutaneous; less than 3 cm</u>

● **21931** Code added

● **21932** Code added

● **21933** Code added

▲ **21935** Radical resection of tumor (eg, malignant neoplasm), soft tissue of back or flank<u>; less than 5 cm</u>

● **21936** Code added

22206 Grammatical Change

22210 Grammatical Change

22325 Grammatical Change

⊙▲ **22520** Percutaneous vertebroplasty, 1 vertebral body, unilateral or bilateral injection; thoracic

⊙▲ **22521** lumbar

22523 Grammatical Change

+⊙ **22527** Grammatical Change

+ **22840** Grammatical Change

▲ **22900** Excision, <u>tumor, soft tissue of</u> abdominal wall ~~tumor~~, subfascial (eg, ~~desmoid~~ <u>intramuscular); less than 5 cm</u>

● **22901** Code added

● **22902** Code added

● **22903** Code added

● **22904**   Code added

● **22905**   Code added

● **23071**   Code added

● **23073**   Code added

▲ **23075**   Excision, <u>tumor,</u> soft tissue ~~tumor,~~ of shoulder area<u>;</u> subcutaneous<u>; less than 3 cm</u>

▲ **23076**   Excision, tumor, soft tissue of shoulder area, ~~deep,~~ subfascial<u>, or</u> <u>(eg,</u> intramuscular)<u>; less than 5 cm</u>

▲ **23077**   Radical resection of tumor (eg, malignant neoplasm), soft tissue of shoulder area<u>; less than 5 cm</u>

● **23078**   Code added

▲ **23200**   Radical resection ~~for~~<u>of</u> tumor; clavicle

▲ **23210**   scapula

▲ **23220**   Radical resection of ~~bone~~ tumor, proximal humerus~~;~~

~~23221~~   ~~with autograft (includes obtaining graft)~~

~~23222~~   ~~with prosthetic replacement~~

● **24071**   Code added

● **24073**   Code added

▲ **24075**   Excision, tumor, soft tissue of upper arm or elbow area<u>;</u> subcutaneous<u>; less than 3 cm</u>

▲ **24076**   Excision, tumor, soft tissue of upper arm or elbow area, ~~deep~~ ~~(~~subfascial ~~or~~ <u>(eg,</u> intramuscular)<u>; less than 5 cm</u>

▲ **24077**   Radical resection of tumor (eg, malignant neoplasm), soft tissue of upper arm or elbow area<u>; less than 5 cm</u>

● **24079**   Code added

▲ **24150**   Radical resection ~~for~~<u>of</u> tumor, shaft or distal humerus~~;~~

~~24151~~   ~~with autograft (includes obtaining graft)~~

▲ **24152**   Radical resection ~~for~~<u>of</u> tumor, radial head or neck~~;~~

~~24153~~   ~~with autograft (includes obtaining graft)~~

● **25071**   Code added

● **25073**   Code added

▲ **25075**   Excision, tumor, soft tissue of forearm and/or wrist area<u>;</u> subcutaneous<u>; less than 3 cm</u>

▲ **25076**   Excision, tumor, soft tissue of forearm and/or wrist area, ~~deep~~ ~~(~~subfascial ~~or~~ <u>(eg,</u> intramuscular)<u>; less than 3 cm</u>

▲ **25077**   Radical resection of tumor (eg, malignant neoplasm), soft tissue of forearm and/or wrist area<u>; less than 3 cm</u>

● **25078**   Code added

▲ **25170**   Radical resection ~~for~~<u>of</u> tumor, radius or ulna

25210   Grammatical Change

25660   Grammatical Change

25670   Grammatical Change

● **26111**   Code added

● **26113**   Code added

▲ **26115**   Excision, tumor or vascular malformation, soft tissue of hand or finger<u>;</u> subcutaneous<u>; less than 1.5 cm</u>

▲ **26116**   Excision, tumor, soft tissue, or vascular malformation, of hand or finger, ~~deep~~ ~~(~~subfascial ~~or~~ <u>(eg,</u> intramuscular)<u>; less than 1.5 cm</u>

▲ **26117**   Radical resection of tumor (eg, malignant neoplasm), soft tissue of hand or finger<u>; less than 3 cm</u>

● **26118**   Code added

▲ **26250**   Radical resection <u>of tumor,</u> metacarpal ~~(eg, tumor);~~

~~26255~~   ~~with autograft (includes obtaining graft)~~

▲ **26260**   Radical resection <u>of tumor,</u> proximal or middle phalanx of finger ~~(eg, tumor);~~

~~26261~~   ~~with autograft (includes obtaining graft)~~

▲ **26262**   Radical resection <u>of tumor,</u> distal phalanx of finger ~~(eg, tumor)~~

26498   Grammatical Change

● **27043**   Code added

● **27045**   Code added

▲ **27047**   Excision, tumor, <u>soft tissue of</u> pelvis and hip area<u>;</u> subcutaneous ~~tissue~~<u>; less than 3 cm</u>

▲ **27048**   Excision, tumor, soft tissue of pelvis and hip area, ~~deep,~~ subfascial<u>, (eg,</u> intramuscular)<u>; less than 5 cm</u>

▲ **27049**   Radical resection of tumor <u>(eg, malignant neoplasm),</u> soft tissue of pelvis and hip area ~~(eg, malignant neoplasm);~~ <u>less than 5 cm</u>

● **27059**   Code added

▲ **27075**   Radical resection of tumor ~~or infection~~; wing of ilium, 1 pubic or ischial ramus or symphysis pubis

▲ **27076**   ilium, including acetabulum, both pubic rami, or ischium and acetabulum

▲ **27077**   innominate bone, total

▲ **27078**   ischial tuberosity and greater trochanter of femur

~~27079~~   ~~ischial tuberosity and greater trochanter of femur, with skin flaps~~

▲ **27327**   Excision, tumor, <u>soft tissue of</u> thigh or knee area<u>;</u> subcutaneous<u>; less than 3 cm</u>

▲ **27328**   Excision, tumor, soft tissue of thigh or knee area, ~~deep,~~ subfascial, ~~or~~ <u>(eg,</u> intramuscular)<u>; less than 5 cm</u>

▲ **27329**   Radical resection of tumor (eg, malignant neoplasm), soft tissue of thigh or knee area<u>; less than 5 cm</u>

● **27337**   Code added

● **27339**   Code added

● **27364**   Code added

▲ **27365**   Radical resection of tumor, ~~bone,~~ femur or knee

27391   Grammatical Change

27394   Grammatical Change

27486   Grammatical Change

27496   Grammatical Change

▲ **27615**   Radical resection of tumor (eg, malignant neoplasm), soft tissue of leg or ankle area<u>; less than 5 cm</u>

● **27616**   Code added

▲ **27618**   Excision, tumor, <u>soft tissue of</u> leg or ankle area<u>;</u> subcutaneous ~~tissue~~<u>; less than 3 cm</u>

▲ **27619**   Excision, tumor, soft tissue of leg or ankle area, ~~deep~~ ~~(~~subfascial ~~or~~ <u>(eg,</u> intramuscular)<u>; less than 5 cm</u>

● **27632**   Code added

● **27634**   Code added

▲ 27640 Partial excision (craterization, saucerization, or diaphysectomy), bone (eg, osteomyelitis ~~or exostosis~~); tibia

▲ 27641 fibula

▲ 27645 Radical resection of tumor~~, bone~~; tibia

▲ 27646 fibula

▲ 27647 talus or calcaneus

● 28039 Code added

● 28041 Code added

▲ 28043 Excision, tumor, soft tissue of foot or toe~~.~~; subcutaneous ~~tissue~~; less than 1.5 cm

▲ 28045 Excision, tumor, soft tissue of foot or toe, ~~deep,~~ subfascial~~,~~ (eg, intramuscular); less than 1.5 cm

▲ 28046 Radical resection of tumor (eg, malignant neoplasm), soft tissue of foot or toe; less than 3 cm

● 28047 Code added

▲ 28171 Radical resection of tumor~~, bone~~; tarsal (except talus or calcaneus)

▲ 28173 metatarsal

▲ 28175 phalanx of toe

   29044 Grammatical Change

~~29220~~ ~~low back~~

   29305 Grammatical Change

   29325 Grammatical Change

● 29581 Code added

   29876 Grammatical Change

▲ 30801 ~~Cautery and/or a~~Ablation, soft tissue~~mucosa~~ of inferior turbinates, unilateral or bilateral, any method (eg, electrocautery, radiofrequency ablation, or tissue volume reduction); superficial

▲ 30802 intramural (ie, submucosal)

   31090 Grammatical Change

   31580 Grammatical Change

   31601 Grammatical Change

⊙▲ 31622 Bronchoscopy, rigid or flexible, including~~with or without~~ fluoroscopic guidance, when performed; diagnostic, with ~~or without~~ cell washing, when performed (separate procedure)

⊙● 31626 Code added

+⊙● 31627 Code added

▲ 31641 ~~Bronchoscopy (rigid or flexible);~~ with destruction of tumor or relief of stenosis by any method other than excision (eg, laser therapy, cryotherapy)

▲ 31643 with placement of catheter(s) for intracavitary radioelement application

⊙▲ 31645 with therapeutic aspiration of tracheobronchial tree, initial (eg, drainage of lung abscess)

⊙▲ 31646 with therapeutic aspiration of tracheobronchial tree, subsequent

⊙▲ 31656 with injection of contrast material for segmental bronchography (fiberscope only)

   32482 Grammatical Change

● 32552 Code added

⊙● 32553 Code added

▲ 32560 Instillation, via chest tube/catheter, ~~Chemical~~ agent for pleurodesis (eg, talc for recurrent or persistent pneumothorax)

● 32561 Code added

● 32562 Code added

   32998 Grammatical Change

⊙▲ 33216 Insertion of a single transvenous electrode, ~~single chamber (1 electrode)~~ permanent pacemaker or ~~single chamber pacing~~ cardioverter-defibrillator

⊙▲ 33217 Insertion of ~~dual chamber (~~2 transvenous electrodes~~,)~~ permanent pacemaker or ~~dual chamber pacing~~ cardioverter-defibrillator

⊙ 33220 Grammatical Change

⊙▲ 33223 Revision of skin pocket for ~~single or dual chamber pacing~~ cardioverter-defibrillator

   33511 Grammatical Change

   33512 Grammatical Change

   33513 Grammatical Change

   33514 Grammatical Change

   33516 Grammatical Change

+ 33518 Grammatical Change

+ 33519 Grammatical Change

+ 33521 Grammatical Change

+ 33522 Grammatical Change

+ 33523 Grammatical Change

+ 33530 Grammatical Change

   33534 Grammatical Change

   33535 Grammatical Change

   33536 Grammatical Change

   33766 Grammatical Change

● 33782 Code added

● 33783 Code added

● 33981 Code added

● 33982 Code added

● 33983 Code added

   34802 Grammatical Change

   34803 Grammatical Change

+ 35390 Grammatical Change

+ 35500 Grammatical Change

+ 35572 Grammatical Change

+ 35600 Grammatical Change

+ 35682 Grammatical Change

+ 35683 Grammatical Change

+ 35700 Grammatical Change

~~36145~~ ~~arteriovenous shunt created for dialysis (cannula, fistula, or graft)~~

⊙● 36147 Code added

+⊙● 36148 Code added

⊙▲ 36481 Percutaneous portal vein catheterization by any method

⊙ 36565 Grammatical Change

36834 ~~Plastic repair of arteriovenous aneurysm (separate procedure)~~

⊙▲ **37183** Revision of transvenous intrahepatic portosystemic shunt(s) (TIPS) (includes venous access, hepatic and portal vein catheterization, portography with hemodynamic evaluation, intrahepatic tract recanulization/dilatation, stent placement and all associated imaging guidance and documentation)

▲ **37760** Ligation of perforator veins, subfascial, radical (Linton type), including~~with or without~~ skin graft, when performed, open,1 leg

● **37761** Code added

37765 Grammatical Change

37785 Grammatical Change

40701 Grammatical Change

40702 Grammatical Change

41530 Grammatical Change

42508 Grammatical Change

▲ **42894** Resection of pharyngeal wall requiring closure with myocutaneous or fasciocutaneous flap or free muscle, skin, or fascial flap with microvascular anastamosis

● **43281** Code added

● **43282** Code added

43600 Grammatical Change

▲ **43761** Repositioning of ~~the~~a naso- or oro-gastric feeding tube, through the duodenum for enteric nutrition

● **43775** Code added

44100 Grammatical Change

44110 Grammatical Change

45170 ~~Excision of rectal tumor, transanal approach~~

● **45171** Code added

● **45172** Code added

▲ **46200** Fissurectomy, including ~~with or without~~ sphincterotomy, when performed

46210 ~~Cryptectomy; single~~

46211 ~~multiple (separate procedure)~~

▲ **46220** ~~Papillectomy or e~~Excision of single external papilla or tag, anus ~~(separate procedure)~~

▲ **46221** Hemorrhoidectomy, internal, by rubber band ligation(s)~~simple ligature (eg, rubber band)~~

▲ **46230** Excision of ~~external hemorrhoid tags and/or~~multiple external papillae or tags, anus

▲ **46250** Hemorrhoidectomy, external, ~~complete~~2 or more columns/groups

▲ **46255** Hemorrhoidectomy, internal and external, ~~simple~~single column/group;

▲ **46258** with fistulectomy, including ~~with or without~~fissurectomy, when performed

▲ **46260** Hemorrhoidectomy, internal and external, ~~complex or extensive~~2 or more columns/groups;

▲ **46262** with fistulectomy, including ~~with or without~~fissurectomy, when performed

▲ **46275** ~~submuscular~~intersphincteric

▲ **46280** ~~complex~~transsphincteric, suprasphincteric, extrasphincteric or multiple, including ~~with or without~~placement of seton, when performed

▲ **46320** ~~Enucleation or e~~Excision of thrombosed hemorrhoid, external ~~thrombotic hemorrhoid~~

● **46707** Code added

46937 ~~Cryosurgery of rectal tumor; benign~~

46938 ~~malignant~~

▲ **46945** Hemorrhoidectomy, internal, by ~~L~~ligation ~~of internal hemorrhoids~~other than rubber band; single hemorrhoid column/group ~~procedure~~

▲ **46946** ~~multiple procedures~~2 or more hemorrhoid columns/groups

47010 Grammatical Change

⊙ **47011** Grammatical Change

47144 Grammatical Change

47145 Grammatical Change

47370 Grammatical Change

47380 Grammatical Change

⊙▲ **47382** Ablation, 1 or more liver tumor(s), percutaneous, radiofrequency

⊙▲ **47525** Change of percutaneous biliary drainage catheter

⊙● **49411** Code added

⊙▲ **50200** Renal biopsy; percutaneous, by trocar or needle

50540 Grammatical Change

▲ **51726** Complex cystometrogram (~~eg~~ie, calibrated electronic equipment);

● **51727** Code added

● **51728** Code added

● **51729** Code added

51772 ~~Urethral pressure profile studies (UPP) (urethral closure pressure profile), any technique~~

51795 ~~Voiding pressure studies (VP); bladder voiding pressure, any technique~~

+▲ **51797** Voiding pressure studies, intra-abdominal ~~voiding pressure (AP)~~ (ie, rectal, gastric, intraperitoneal) (List separately in addition to code for primary procedure)

▲ **52282** Cystourethroscopy, with insertion of permanent urethral stent

● **53855** Code added

54322 Grammatical Change

54332 Grammatical Change

54336 Grammatical Change

▲ **55873** Cryosurgical ablation of the prostate (includes ultrasonic guidance and monitoring~~for interstitial cryosurgical probe placement~~)

▲ **55876** Placement of interstitial device(s) for radiation therapy guidance (eg, fiducial markers, dosimeter), percutaneous, prostate~~(via needle, any approach)~~, single or multiple

56605 Grammatical Change

● **57426** Code added

59850 Grammatical Change

59855 Grammatical Change

▲ 59897   Unlisted fetal invasive procedure, including ultrasound guidance, when performed

61460   Grammatical Change

61531   Grammatical Change

61886   Grammatical Change

63050   Grammatical Change

~~63660~~   ~~Revision or removal of spinal neurostimulator electrode percutaneous array(s) or plate/paddle(s)~~

● 63661   Code added

● 63662   Code added

● 63663   Code added

● 63664   Code added

~~64470~~   ~~Injection, anesthetic agent and/or steroid, paravertebral facet joint or facet joint nerve; cervical or thoracic, single level~~

~~64472~~   ~~cervical or thoracic, each additional level (List separately in addition to code for primary procedure)~~

~~64475~~   ~~lumbar or sacral, single level~~

~~64476~~   ~~lumbar or sacral, each additional level (List separately in addition to code for primary procedure)~~

● 64490   Code added

+● 64491   Code added

+● 64492   Code added

● 64493   Code added

+● 64494   Code added

+● 64495   Code added

64834   Grammatical Change

66982   Grammatical Change

Radiology

70160   Grammatical Change

▲ 72291   Radiological supervision and interpretation, percutaneous vertebroplasty, or vertebral augmentation, or sacral augmentation (sacroplasty), including cavity creation, per vertebral body or sacrum; under fluoroscopic guidance

▲ 72292   under CT guidance

● 74261   Code added

● 74262   Code added

● 74263   Code added

~~75558~~   ~~with flow/velocity quantification~~

~~75560~~   ~~with flow/velocity quantification and stress~~

~~75562~~   ~~with flow/velocity quantification~~

~~75564~~   ~~with flow/velocity quantification and stress~~

+● 75565   Code added

● 75571   Code added

● 75572   Code added

● 75573   Code added

● 75574   Code added

~~75790~~   ~~Angiography, arteriovenous shunt (eg, dialysis patient), radiological supervision and interpretation~~

● 75791   Code added

▲ 77003   Fluoroscopic guidance and localization of needle or catheter tip for spine or paraspinous diagnostic or therapeutic injection procedures (epidural, transforaminal epidural, subarachnoid, ~~paravertebral facet joint, paravertebral facet joint nerve,~~ or sacroiliac joint), including neurolytic agent destruction

● 77338   Code added

⊙▲ 77371   Radiation treatment delivery, stereotactic radiosurgery (SRS), complete course of treatment of cranial lesion(s) consisting of 1 session; multi-source Cobalt 60 based

● 78451   Code added

● 78452   Code added

● 78453   Code added

● 78454   Code added

~~78460~~   ~~Myocardial perfusion imaging; (planar) single study, at rest or stress (exercise and/or pharmacologic), with or without quantification~~

~~78461~~   ~~multiple studies (planar), at rest and/or stress (exercise and/or pharmacologic), and redistribution and/or rest injection, with or without quantification~~

~~78464~~   ~~tomographic (SPECT), single study (including attenuation correction when performed), at rest or stress (exercise and/or pharmacologic), with or without quantification~~

~~78465~~   ~~tomographic (SPECT), multiple studies (including attenuation correction when performed), at rest and/or stress (exercise and/or pharmacologic) and redistribution and/or rest injection, with or without quantification~~

~~78478~~   ~~Myocardial perfusion study with wall motion, qualitative or quantitative study (List separately in addition to code for primary procedure)~~

~~78480~~   ~~Myocardial perfusion study with ejection fraction (List separately in addition to code for primary procedure)~~

78483   Grammatical Change

Pathology and Laboratory

▲ 80055   Obstetric panel

This panel must include the following:

Blood count, complete (CBC), automated and automated differential WBC count (85025 or 85027 and 85004)

OR

Blood count, complete (CBC), automated (85027) and appropriate manual differential WBC count (85007 or 85009)

Hepatitis B surface antigen (HBsAg) (87340)

Antibody, rubella (86762)

Syphilis test, non-treponemal antibody; qualitative (eg, VDRL, RPR, ART) (86592)

Antibody screen, RBC, each serum technique (86850)

Blood typing, ABO (86900) AND

Blood typing, Rh (D) (86901)

▲ 82306   ~~Calcifediol (25-OH~~ Vitamin D~~-3)~~; 25 hydroxy, includes fraction(s), if performed

~~82307~~   ~~Calciferol (Vitamin D)~~

▲ 82652   ~~Dihydroxyvitamin D,~~ 1, 25- dihydroxy, includes fraction(s), if performed

▲ 82784   Gammaglobulin (immunoglobulin); IgA, IgD, IgG, IgM, each

▲ 82785   IgE

▲ 82787   immunoglobulin subclasses (eg, IgG1, 2, 3, or 4), each

82951   Grammatical Change

82952   Grammatical Change

▲ 83516   Immunoassay for analyte other than infectious agent antibody or infectious agent antigen~~;~~ qualitative or semiquantitative~~;~~ multiple step method

▲ 83518   qualitative or semiquantitative, single step method (eg, reagent strip)

▲ 83519   ~~Immunoassay, analyte,~~ quantitative~~;~~ by ~~radiopharmaceutical technique~~ radioimmunoassay (eg, RIA)

▲ 83520   quantitative, not otherwise specified

▲ 83986   pH~~;~~ body fluid, ~~except blood~~not otherwise specified

● 83987   Code added

● 84145   Code added

● 84431   Code added

85046   Grammatical Change

85240   Grammatical Change

● 86305   Code added

● 86352   Code added

▲ 86592   Syphilis test, non-treponemal antibody; qualitative (eg, VDRL, RPR, ART)

▲ 86593   quantitative

● 86780   Code added

~~86781~~   ~~Treponema pallidum, confirmatory test (eg, FTA-abs)~~

● 86825   Code added

+● 86826   Code added

▲ 87149   identification by nucleic acid (DNA or RNA) probe, direct probe technique, per culture or isolate, each organism probed

● 87150   Code added

● 87153   Code added

● 87493   Code added

▲ 88312   Special stains ~~(List separately in addition to code for primary service)~~; Group I for microorganisms (eg, Gridley, acid fast, methenamine silver), including interpretation and report, each

▲ 88313   Group II, all other (eg, iron, trichrome), except immunocytochemistry and immunoperoxidase stains, including interpretation and report, each

+▲ 88314   histochemical staining with frozen section(s), including interpretation and report (List separately in addition to code for primary procedure)

● 88387   Code added

+● 88388   Code added

● 88738   Code added

● 89398   Code added

Medicine

▲ 90378   Respiratory syncytial virus ~~immune globulin (RSV IgIM)~~, monoclonal antibody, recombinant, for intramuscular use, 50 mg, each

~~90379~~   ~~Respiratory syncytial virus immune globulin (RSV IgIV), human, for intravenous use~~

90471   Grammatical Change

90473   Grammatical Change

▲ 90669   Pneumococcal conjugate vaccine, ~~polyvalent~~7 valent, ~~when administered to children younger than 5 years,~~ for intramuscular use

↗● 90670   Code added

▲ 90738   Japanese encephalitis virus vaccine, inactivated, for intramuscular use

92533   Grammatical Change

● 92540   Code added

92543   Grammatical Change

● 92550   Code added

~~92569~~   ~~decay~~

● 92570   Code added

▲ 93279   Programming device evaluation (in person) with iterative adjustment of the implantable device to test the function of the device and select optimal permanent programmed values with physician analysis, review and report; single lead pacemaker system

▲ 93280   dual lead pacemaker system

▲ 93281   multiple lead pacemaker system

▲ 93282   single lead implantable cardioverter-defibrillator system

▲ 93283   dual lead implantable cardioverter-defibrillator system

▲ 93284   multiple lead implantable cardioverter-defibrillator system

▲ 93285   implantable loop recorder system

▲ 93286   Peri-procedural device evaluation (in person) and programming of device system parameters before or after a surgery, procedure, or test with physician analysis, review and report; single, dual, or multiple lead pacemaker system

▲ 93287   single, dual, or multiple lead implantable cardioverter-defibrillator system

⊘⊙ 93540   Grammatical Change

▲ 93701   Bioimpedance-derived physiologic cardiovascular analysis~~, thoracic, electrical~~

● 93750   Code added

⊙● 94011   Code added

⊙● 94012   Code added

⊙● 94013   Code added

▲ 95806   Sleep study, unattended, simultaneous recording of, ~~ventilation~~ heart rate, oxygen saturation, respiratory airflow, and respiratory effort~~, ECG~~ (eg, thoracoabdominal movement)~~or heart rate, and oxygen saturation, unattended by a technologist~~

95860   Grammatical Change

95870   Grammatical Change

⊘● 95905   Code added

95921	Grammatical Change	
95923	Grammatical Change	
95937	Grammatical Change	
+▲ 96570	Photodynamic therapy by endoscopic application of light to ablate abnormal tissue via activation of photosensitive drug(s); first 30 minutes (List separately in addition to code for endoscopy or bronchoscopy procedures of lung and ~~esophagus~~gastrointestinal tract)	
+▲ 96571	each additional 15 minutes (List separately in addition to code for endoscopy or bronchoscopy procedures of lung and ~~esophagus~~gastrointestinal tract)	
96913	Grammatical Change	
97032	Grammatical Change	
97110	Grammatical Change	
97140	Grammatical Change	
~~99185~~	~~Hypothermia; regional~~	
~~99186~~	~~total body~~	

Category II Codes

0500F	Grammatical Change
0501F	Grammatical Change
▲ 0519F	Planned chemotherapy regimen, including at a minimum: drug(s) prescribed, dose, and duration, documented prior to initiation of ~~course of treatment~~a new treatment regimen (ONC)[1]
▲ 0520F	~~Normal tissue dose constraints~~Radiation dose limits to normal tissues established ~~within 5 treatment days from~~prior to the initiation of a course of 3D conformal radiation for a minimum of ~~one~~2 tissue/organ (ONC)[1]
▲ 0521F	Plan of care to address pain documented (COA)[2] (ONC)[1]
● 0528F	Code added
● 0529F	Code added
● 0535F	Code added
● 0540F	Code added
● 0575F	Code added
1100F	Grammatical Change
1101F	Grammatical Change
1110F	Grammatical Change
1111F	Grammatical Change
1123F	Grammatical Change
1124F	Grammatical Change
1125F	Grammatical Change
1126F	Grammatical Change
1136F	Grammatical Change
● 1150F	Code added
● 1151F	Code added
● 1152F	Code added
● 1153F	Code added
● 1157F	Code added
● 1158F	Code added

● 1159F	Code added
● 1160F	Code added
● 1170F	Code added
● 1180F	Code added
● 1220F	Code added
2024F	Grammatical Change
● 2050F	Code added
● 3016F	Code added
● 3018F	Code added
3082F	Grammatical Change
3083F	Grammatical Change
3084F	Grammatical Change
3095F	Grammatical Change
3096F	Grammatical Change
● 3250F	Code added
3290F	Grammatical Change
3291F	Grammatical Change
3292F	Grammatical Change
~~3302F~~	~~AJCC Cancer Stage 0, documented (ONC)³, (ML)⁶~~
~~3303F~~	~~AJCC Cancer Stage IA, documented (ONC)³, (ML)⁶~~
~~3304F~~	~~AJCC Cancer Stage IB, documented (ONC)³, (ML)⁶~~
~~3305F~~	~~AJCC Cancer Stage IC, documented (ONC)³, (ML)⁶~~
~~3306F~~	~~AJCC Cancer Stage IIA, documented (ONC)³, (ML)⁶~~
~~3307F~~	~~AJCC Cancer Stage IIB, documented (ONC)³, (ML)⁶~~
~~3308F~~	~~AJCC Cancer Stage IIC, documented (ONC)³, (ML)⁶~~
~~3309F~~	~~AJCC Cancer Stage IIIA, documented (ONC)³, (ML)⁶~~
~~3310F~~	~~AJCC Cancer Stage IIIB, documented (ONC)³, (ML)⁶~~
~~3311F~~	~~AJCC Cancer Stage IIIC, documented (ONC)³, (ML)⁶~~
~~3312F~~	~~AJCC Cancer Stage IV, documented (ONC)³, (ML)⁶~~
▲ 3319F	1 of the following diagnostic imaging studies ordered: chest x-ray, CT, Ultrasound, MRI, PET, or nuclear medicine scans (ML)[5]
● 3321F	Code added
● 3322F	Code added
3325F	Grammatical Change
3341F	Grammatical Change
● 3370F	Code added
● 3372F	Code added
● 3374F	Code added
● 3376F	Code added
● 3378F	Code added
● 3380F	Code added
● 3382F	Code added
● 3384F	Code added
● 3386F	Code added
● 3388F	Code added

● 3390F   Code added

● 3450F   Code added

● 3451F   Code added

● 3452F   Code added

● 3455F   Code added

● 3470F   Code added

● 3471F   Code added

● 3472F   Code added

● 3475F   Code added

● 3476F   Code added

● 3490F   Code added

● 3491F   Code added

● 3492F   Code added

● 3493F   Code added

● 3494F   Code added

● 3495F   Code added

● 3496F   Code added

● 3497F   Code added

● 3498F   Code added

● 3500F   Code added

● 3502F   Code added

● 3503F   Code added

● 3510F   Code added

● 3511F   Code added

● 3512F   Code added

● 3513F   Code added

● 3514F   Code added

● 3515F   Code added

● 3550F   Code added

● 3551F   Code added

● 3552F   Code added

● 3555F   Code added

● 3570F   Code added

● 3572F   Code added

● 3573F   Code added

▲ 4011F   Oral antiplatelet therapy prescribed (~~eg, aspirin, clopidogrel/Plavix, or combination of aspirin and dipyridamole/Aggrenox~~) (CAD)[1]

4014F   Grammatical Change

4058F   Grammatical Change

4066F   Grammatical Change

● 4148F   Code added

● 4149F   Code added

~~4152F~~   ~~Documentation that combination peginterferon and ribavirin therapy considered (HEP-C)[1]~~

~~4154F~~   ~~Hepatitis A vaccine series recommended (HEP-C)[1]~~

~~4156F~~   ~~Hepatitis B vaccine series recommended (HEP-C)[1]~~

▲ 4158F   Patient ~~education regarding risk of alcohol consumption performed~~ counseled about risks of alcohol use (HEP-C)[1]

4176F   Grammatical Change

4178F   Grammatical Change

▲ 4180F   Adjuvant chemotherapy referred, prescribed, or previously received for Stage III~~A through Stage IIIC~~ colon cancer (ONC)[1]

● 4192F   Code added

● 4193F   Code added

● 4194F   Code added

● 4195F   Code added

● 4196F   Code added

▲ 4200F   External beam radiotherapy as primary therapy to prostate ~~only~~with or without nodal irradiation (PRCA)[1]

▲ 4201F   External beam radiotherapy with or without nodal irradiation as adjuvant or salvage therapy for prostate cancer ~~to region(s) other than prostate only~~patient (PRCA)[1]

▲ 4250F   Active warming used intraoperatively for the purpose of maintaining normothermia, OR at least 1 body temperature equal to or greater than 36 degrees Centigrade (or 96.8 degrees Fahrenheit) recorded within the 30 minutes immediately before or the ~~30~~15 minutes immediately after anesthesia end time (CRIT)[1]

● 4260F   Code added

● 4261F   Code added

● 4265F   Code added

● 4266F   Code added

● 4267F   Code added

● 4268F   Code added

● 4269F   Code added

● 4270F   Code added

● 4271F   Code added

● 4274F   Code added

● 4275F   Code added

● 4276F   Code added

● 4279F   Code added

● 4280F   Code added

● 4290F   Code added

● 4293F   Code added

● 4300F   Code added

● 4301F   Code added

● 4305F   Code added

● 4306F   Code added

● 4320F   Code added

▲ 5020F   Treatment summary report communicated to physician(s) managing continuing care and to the patient within 1 month of completing treatment (ONC)[1]

5060F   Grammatical Change

5062F   Grammatical Change

● **5100F**   Code added

▲ **6030F**   All elements of maximal sterile barrier technique <u>followed</u> including: cap AND mask AND sterile gown AND sterile gloves AND a large sterile sheet AND hand hygiene AND 2% chlorhexidine for cutaneous antisepsis~~, followed~~ <u>(or acceptable alternative antiseptics, per current guideline)</u> (CRIT)[1]

Category III Codes

~~0062T~~   ~~Percutaneous intradiscal annuloplasty, any method except electrothermal, unilateral or bilateral including fluoroscopic guidance; single level~~

~~0063T~~   ~~1 or more additional levels (List separately in addition to 0062T for primary procedure)~~

~~0064T~~   ~~Spectroscopy, expired gas analysis (eg, nitric oxide/carbon dioxide test)~~

~~0066T~~   ~~Computed tomographic (CT) colonography (ie, virtual colonoscopy); screening~~

~~0067T~~   ~~diagnostic~~

~~0068T~~   ~~Acoustic heart sound recording and computer analysis; with interpretation and report~~

~~0069T~~   ~~acoustic heart sound recording and computer analysis only~~

~~0070T~~   ~~interpretation and report only~~

~~0077T~~   ~~Implanting and securing cerebral thermal perfusion probe, including twist drill or burr hole, to measure absolute cerebral tissue perfusion~~

~~0084T~~   ~~Insertion of a temporary prostatic urethral stent~~

~~0086T~~   ~~Left ventricular filling pressure indirect measurement by computerized calibration of the arterial waveform response to Valsalva maneuver~~

~~0087T~~   ~~Sperm evaluation, Hyaluronan sperm binding test~~

~~0144T~~   ~~Computed tomography, heart, without contrast material, including image postprocessing and quantitative evaluation of coronary calcium~~

~~0145T~~   ~~Computed tomography, heart, with contrast material(s), including noncontrast images, if performed, cardiac gating and 3D image postprocessing; cardiac structure and morphology~~

~~0146T~~   ~~computed tomographic angiography of coronary arteries (including native and anomalous coronary arteries, coronary bypass grafts), without quantitative evaluation of coronary calcium~~

~~0147T~~   ~~computed tomographic angiography of coronary arteries (including native and anomalous coronary arteries, coronary bypass grafts), with quantitative evaluation of coronary calcium~~

~~0148T~~   ~~cardiac structure and morphology and computed tomographic angiography of coronary arteries (including native and anomalous coronary arteries, coronary bypass grafts), without quantitative evaluation of coronary calcium~~

~~0149T~~   ~~cardiac structure and morphology and computed tomographic angiography of coronary arteries (including native and anomalous coronary arteries, coronary bypass grafts), with quantitative evaluation of coronary calcium~~

~~0150T~~   ~~cardiac structure and morphology in congenital heart disease~~

~~0151T~~   ~~Computed tomography, heart, with contrast material(s), including noncontrast images, if performed, cardiac gating and 3D image postprocessing, function evaluation (left and right ventricular function, ejection fraction and segmental wall motion) (List separately in addition to code for primary procedure)~~

~~0170T~~   ~~Repair of anorectal fistula with plug (eg, porcine small intestine submucosa [SIS])~~

0188T   Grammatical Change

~~0194T~~   ~~Procalcitonin (PCT)~~

● 0197T   Code added

● 0198T   Code added

● 0199T   Code added

⊙● 0200T   Code added

⊙● 0201T   Code added

● 0202T   Code added

● 0203T   Code added

● 0204T   Code added

+● 0205T   Code added

● 0206T   Code added

● 0207T   Code added

Appendix C

Clinical Examples

As described in *CPT 2010*, clinical examples of the CPT codes for Evaluation and Management (E/M) services are intended to be an important element of the coding system. The clinical examples, when used with the E/M descriptors contained in the full text of *CPT*, provide a comprehensive and powerful tool for physicians to report the services provided to their patients.

The American Medical Association is pleased to provide you with these clinical examples for *CPT 2010*. The clinical examples that are provided in this supplement are limited to Office or Other Outpatient Services, Hospital Inpatient Services, Consultations, Critical Care, Prolonged Services and Care Plan Oversight.

These clinical examples do not encompass the entire scope of medical practice. Inclusion or exclusion of any particular specialty group does not infer any judgment of importance or lack thereof; nor does it limit the applicability of the example to any particular specialty.

Of utmost importance is that these clinical examples are just that: examples. A particular patient encounter, depending on the specific circumstances, must be judged by the services provided by the physician for that particular patient. Simply because the patient's complaints, symptoms, or diagnoses match those of a particular clinical example, does not automatically assign that patient encounter to that particular level of service. The three components (history, examination, and medical decision making) must be met and documented in the medical record to report a particular level of service.

New Patient

Office or Other Outpatient Service

99201 Initial office visit for a 50-year-old male from out-of-town who needs a prescription refill for a nonsteroidal anti-inflammatory drug. (Anesthesiology)

Initial office visit for a 40-year-old female, new patient, requesting information about local pain clinics. (Anesthesiology/Pain Medicine)

Initial office visit for a 10-year-old girl for determination of visual acuity as part of a summer camp physical (does not include determination of refractive error). (Ophthalmology)

Initial office visit for an out-of-town patient requiring topical refill. (Dermatology)

Initial office visit for a 65-year-old male for reassurance about an isolated seborrheic keratosis on upper back. (Plastic Surgery)

Initial office visit for an out-of-state visitor who needs refill of topical steroid to treat lichen planus. (Dermatology)

Initial office visit for an 86-year-old male, out-of-town visitor, who needs prescription refilled for an anal skin preparation that he forgot. (General Surgery/Colon & Rectal Surgery)

Initial office visit for a patient with alveolar osteitis for repacking. (Oral & Maxillofacial Surgery)

Initial office visit for a patient with a pedunculated lesion of the neck which is unsightly. (Dermatology)

Initial office visit for a 10-year-old male, for limited subungual hematoma not requiring drainage. (Internal Medicine)

Initial office visit with an out-of-town visitor who needs a prescription refilled because she forgot her hay fever medication. (Allergy & Immunology/Internal Medicine)

Initial office visit with a 9-month-old female with diaper rash. (Pediatrics)

Initial office visit with a 10-year-old male with severe rash and itching for the past 24 hours, positive history for contact with poison oak 48 hours prior to the visit. (Family Medicine)

Initial office visit with a 5-year-old female to remove sutures from simple wound placed by another physician. (Plastic Surgery)

Initial office visit for a 22-year-old male with a small area of sunburn requiring first aid. (Dermatology/Family Medicine/Internal Medicine)

Initial office visit for the evaluation and management of a contusion of a finger. (Orthopaedic Surgery)

99202 Initial office visit for a 13-year-old patient with comedopapular acne of the face unresponsive to over-the-counter medications. (Family Medicine)

Initial office visit for a patient with a clinically benign lesion or nodule of the lower leg which has been present for many years. (Dermatology)

Initial office visit for a patient with a circumscribed patch of dermatitis of the leg. (Dermatology)

Initial office visit for a patient with papulosquamous eruption of elbows. (Dermatology)

Initial office visit for a 9-year-old patient with erythematous grouped, vesicular eruption of the lip of three day's duration. (Pediatrics)

Initial office visit for an 18-year-old male referred by an orthodontist for advice regarding removal of four wisdom teeth. (Oral & Maxillofacial Surgery)

Initial office visit for a 14-year-old male, who was referred by his orthodontist, for advice on the exposure of impacted maxillary cuspids. (Oral & Maxillofacial Surgery)

Initial office visit for a patient presenting with itching patches on the wrists and ankles. (Dermatology)

Initial office visit for a 30-year-old male for evaluation and discussion of treatment of rhinophyma. (Plastic Surgery)

Initial office visit for a 16-year-old male with severe cystic acne, new patient. (Dermatology)

Initial office evaluation for gradual hearing loss, 58-year-old male, history and physical examination, with interpretation of complete audiogram, air bone, etc. (Otolaryngology)

Initial evaluation and management of recurrent urinary infection in female. (Internal Medicine)

Initial office visit with a 10-year-old girl with history of chronic otitis media and a draining ear. (Pediatrics)

Initial office visit for a 10-year-old female with acute maxillary sinusitis. (Family Medicine)

Initial office visit for a patient with recurring episodes of herpes simplex who has developed a clustering of vesicles on the upper lip. (Internal Medicine)

Initial office visit for a 25-year-old patient with a single season allergic rhinitis. (Allergy & Immunology)

99203   Initial office visit of a 76-year-old male with a stasis ulcer of three month's duration. (Dermatology)

Initial office visit for a 30-year-old female with pain in the lateral aspect of the forearm. (Physical Medicine & Rehabilitation)

Initial office visit for a 15-year-old patient with a four-year history of moderate comedopapular acne of the face, chest, and back with early scarring. Discussion of use of systemic medication. (Dermatology)

Initial office visit for a patient with papulosquamous eruption of the elbow with pitting of nails and itchy scalp. (Dermatology)

Initial office visit for a 57-year-old female who complains of painful parotid swelling for one week's duration. (Oral & Maxillofacial Surgery)

Initial office visit for a patient with an ulcerated non-healing lesion or nodule on the tip of the nose. (Dermatology)

Initial office visit for a patient with dermatitis of the antecubital and popliteal fossae. (Dermatology)

Initial office visit for a 22-year-old female with irregular menses. (Family Medicine)

Initial office visit for a 50-year-old female with dyspepsia and nausea. (Family Medicine)

Initial office visit for a 53-year-old laborer with degenerative joint disease of the knee with no prior treatment. (Orthopaedic Surgery)

Initial office visit for a 60-year-old male with Dupuytren's contracture of one hand with multiple digit involvement. (Orthopaedic Surgery)

Initial office visit for a 33-year-old male with painless gross hematuria without cystoscopy. (Internal Medicine)

Initial office visit for a 55-year-old female with chronic blepharitis. There is a history of use of many medications. (Ophthalmology)

Initial office visit for an 18-year-old female with a two-day history of acute conjunctivitis. Extensive history of possible exposures, prior normal ocular history, and medication use is obtained. (Ophthalmology)

Initial office visit for a 14-year-old male with unilateral anterior knee pain. (Physical Medicine & Rehabilitation)

Initial office visit of an adult who presents with symptoms of an upper-respiratory infection that has progressed to unilateral purulent nasal discharge and discomfort in the right maxillary teeth. (Otolaryngology, Head & Neck Surgery)

Initial office visit of a 40-year-old female with symptoms of atopic allergies including eye and sinus congestion, often associated with infections. She would like to be tested for allergies. (Otolaryngology, Head & Neck Surgery)

Initial office visit of a 65-year-old with nasal stuffiness. (Otolaryngology, Head & Neck Surgery)

Initial office visit for initial evaluation of a 48-year-old man with recurrent low back pain radiating to the leg. (General Surgery)

Initial office visit for evaluation, diagnosis, and management of painless gross hematuria in a new patient, without cystoscopy. (Internal Medicine)

Initial office visit with couple for counseling concerning voluntary vasectomy for sterility. Spent 30 minutes discussing procedure, risks and benefits, and answering questions. (Urology)

Initial office visit of a 49-year-old male with nasal obstruction. Detailed exam with topical anesthesia. (Plastic Surgery)

Initial office visit for evaluation of a 13-year-old female with progressive scoliosis. (Physical Medicine & Rehabilitation)

Initial office visit for a 21-year-old female desiring counseling and evaluation of initiation of contraception. (Family Practice/Internal Medicine/Obstetrics & Gynecology)

Initial office visit for a 49-year-old male presenting with painless blood per rectum associated with bowel movement. (Colon & Rectal Surgery)

Initial office visit for a 19-year-old football player with three-day-old acute knee injury; now with swelling and pain. (Orthopaedic Surgery)

99204   Initial office visit for a 13-year-old female with progressive scoliosis. (Orthopaedic Surgery)

Initial office visit for a 34-year-old female with primary infertility for evaluation and counseling. (Obstetrics & Gynecology)

Initial office visit for a 6-year-old male with multiple upper respiratory infections. (Allergy & Immunology)

Initial office visit for a patient with generalized dermatitis of 80 percent of the body surface area. (Dermatology)

Initial office visit for an adolescent who was referred by school counselor because of repeated skipping school. (Psychiatry)

Initial office visit for a 50-year-old machinist with a generalized eruption. (Dermatology)

Initial office visit for a 45-year-old female who has been abstinent from alcohol and benzodiazepines for three months but complains of headaches, insomnia, and anxiety. (Psychiatry)

Initial office visit for a 60-year-old male with recent change in bowel habits, weight loss, and abdominal pain. (Abdominal Surgery/General Surgery)

Initial office visit for a 50-year-old male with an aortic aneurysm who is considering surgery. (General Surgery)

Initial office visit for a 17-year-old female with depression. (Internal Medicine)

Initial office visit of a 40-year-old with chronic draining ear, imbalance, and probable cholesteatoma. (Otolaryngology, Head & Neck Surgery)

Initial office visit for initial evaluation of a 63-year-old male with chest pain on exertion. (Cardiology/Internal Medicine)

Initial office visit for evaluation of a 70-year-old patient with recent onset of episodic confusion. (Internal Medicine)

Initial office visit for a 7-year-old female with juvenile diabetes mellitus, new to area, past history of hospitalization times three. (Pediatrics)

Initial office visit of a 50-year-old female with progressive solid food dysphagia. (Gastroenterology)

Initial office visit for a 34-year-old patient with primary infertility, including counseling. (Obstetrics & Gynecology)

Initial office visit for evaluation of a 70-year-old female with polyarthralgia. (Rheumatology)

Initial office visit for a patient with papulosquamous eruption involving 60 percent of the cutaneous surface with joint pain. Combinations of topical and systemic treatments discussed. (Dermatology)

99205 Initial office visit for a patient with disseminated lupus erythematosus with kidney disease, edema, purpura, and scarring lesions on the extremities plus cardiac symptoms. (Dermatology/General Surgery/Internal Medicine)

Initial office visit for a 25-year-old female with systemic lupus erythematosus, fever, seizures, and profound thrombocytopenia. (Rheumatology/Allergy & Immunology)

Initial office visit for an adult with multiple cutaneous blisters, denuded secondarily infected ulcerations, oral lesions, weight loss, and increasing weakness refractory to high dose corticosteroid. Initiation of new immunosuppressive therapy. (Dermatology)

Initial office visit for a 28-year-old male with systemic vasculitis and compromised circulation to the limbs. (Rheumatology)

Initial office visit for a 41-year-old female new to the area requesting rheumatologic care, on disability due to scleroderma and recent hospitalization for malignant hypertension. (Rheumatology)

Initial office visit for a 52-year-old female with acute four extremity weakness and shortness of breath one week post-flu vaccination. (Physical Medicine & Rehabilitation)

Initial office visit for a 60-year-old male with previous back surgery; now presents with back and pelvic pain, two-month history of bilateral progressive calf and thigh tightness and weakness when walking, causing several falls. (Orthopaedic Surgery)

Initial office visit for an adolescent referred from emergency department after making suicide gesture. (Psychiatry)

Initial office visit for a 49-year-old female with a history of headaches and dependence on opioids. She reports weight loss, progressive headache, and depression. (Psychiatry)

Initial office visit for a 50-year-old female with symptoms of rash, swellings, recurrent arthritic complaints, and diarrhea and lymphadenopathy. Patient has had a 25 lb weight loss and was recently camping in the Amazon. (Allergy & Immunology)

Initial office visit for a 34-year-old uremic Type I diabetic patient referred for ESRD modality assessment and planning. (Nephrology)

Initial office visit for a 75-year-old female with neck and bilateral shoulder pain, brisk deep tendon reflexes, and stress incontinence. (Physical Medicine & Rehabilitation)

Initial office visit for an 8-year-old male with cerebral palsy and spastic quadriparesis. (Physical Medicine & Rehabilitation)

Initial office visit for a 73-year-old male with known prostate malignancy, who presents with severe back pain and a recent onset of lower extremity weakness. (Physical Medicine & Rehabilitation)

Initial office visit for a 38-year-old male with paranoid delusions and a history of alcohol abuse. (Psychiatry)

Initial office visit for a 12-week-old with bilateral hip dislocations and bilateral club feet. (Orthopaedic Surgery)

Initial office visit for a 29-year-old female with acute orbital congestion, eyelid retraction, and bilateral visual loss from optic neuropathy. (Ophthalmology)

Initial office visit for a 70-year-old diabetic patient with progressive visual field loss, advanced optic disc cupping and neovascularization of retina. (Ophthalmology)

Initial office visit for a newly diagnosed Type I diabetic patient. (Endocrinology)

Initial office evaluation of a 65-year-old female with exertional chest pain, intermittent claudication, syncope and a murmur of aortic stenosis. (Cardiology)

Initial office visit for a 73-year-old male with an unexplained 20 lb weight loss. (Hematology/Oncology)

Initial office evaluation, patient with systemic lupus erythematosus, fever, seizures and profound thrombocytopenia. (Allergy & Immunology/Internal Medicine/Rheumatology)

Initial office evaluation and management of patient with systemic vasculitis and compromised circulation to the limbs. (Rheumatology)

Initial office visit for a 24-year-old homosexual male who has a fever, a cough, and shortness of breath. (Infectious Disease)

Initial outpatient evaluation of a 69-year-old male with severe chronic obstructive pulmonary disease, congestive heart failure, and hypertension. (Family Medicine)

Initial office visit for a 17-year-old female, who is having school problems and has told a friend that she is considering suicide. The patient and her family are consulted in regard to treatment options. (Psychiatry)

Initial office visit for a female with severe hirsutism, amenorrhea, weight loss and a desire to have children. (Endocrinology/Obstetrics & Gynecology)

Initial office visit for a 42-year-old male on hypertensive medication, newly arrived to the area, with diastolic blood pressure of 110, history of recurrent calculi, episodic headaches, intermittent chest pain and orthopnea. (Internal Medicine)

Established Patient

99211 Office visit for an 82-year-old female, established patient, for a monthly B12 injection with documented Vitamin B12 deficiency. (Geriatrics/Internal Medicine/Family Medicine)

Office visit for a 50-year-old male, established patient, for removal of uncomplicated facial sutures. (Plastic Surgery)

Office visit for an established patient who lost prescription for lichen planus. Returned for new copy. (Dermatology)

Office visit for an established patient undergoing orthodontics who complains of a wire which is irritating his/her cheek and asks you to check it. (Oral & Maxillofacial Surgery)

Office visit for a 50-year-old female, established patient, seen for her gold injection by the nurse. (Rheumatology)

Office visit for a 73-year-old female, established patient, with pernicious anemia for weekly B12 injection. (Gastroenterology)

Office visit for an established patient for dressing change on a skin biopsy. (Dermatology)

Office visit for a 19-year-old, established patient, for removal of sutures from a 2-cm laceration of forehead, which you placed four days ago in ER. (Plastic Surgery)

Office visit of a 20-year-old female, established patient, who receives an allergy vaccine injection and is observed for a reaction by the nurse. (Otolaryngology, Head & Neck Surgery)

Office visit for a 45-year-old male, established patient, with chronic renal failure for the administration of erythropoietin. (Nephrology)

Office visit for an established patient, a Peace Corps enlistee, who requests documentation that third molars have been removed. (Oral & Maxillofacial Surgery)

Office visit for a 69-year-old female, established patient, for partial removal of antibiotic gauze from an infected wound site. (Plastic Surgery)

Office visit for a 9-year-old, established patient, successfully treated for impetigo, requiring release to return to school. (Dermatology/Pediatrics)

Office visit for an established patient requesting a return-to-work certificate for resolving contact dermatitis. (Dermatology)

Office visit for an established patient who is performing glucose monitoring and wants to check accuracy of machine with lab blood glucose by technician who checks accuracy and function of patient machine. (Endocrinology)

Follow-up office visit for a 65-year-old female with a chronic indwelling percutaneous nephrostomy catheter seen for routine pericatheter skin care and dressing change. (Interventional Radiology)

Outpatient visit with 19-year-old male, established patient, for supervised drug screen. (Addiction Medicine)

Office visit with 12-year-old male, established patient, for cursory check of hematoma one day after venipuncture. (Internal Medicine)

Office visit with 31-year-old female, established patient, for return to work certificate. (Anesthesiology)

Office visit for a 42-year-old, established patient, to read tuberculin test results. (Allergy & Immunology)

Office visit for 14-year-old, established patient, to re-dress an abrasion. (Orthopaedic Surgery)

Office visit for a 45-year-old female, established patient, for a blood pressure check. (Obstetrics & Gynecology)

Office visit for a 23-year-old, established patient, for instruction in use of peak flow meter. (Allergy & Immunology)

Office visit for prescription refill for a 35-year-old female, established patient, with schizophrenia who is stable but has run out of neuroleptic and is scheduled to be seen in a week. (Psychiatry)

99212 Office visit for an 11-year-old, established patient, seen in follow-up for mild comedonal acne of the cheeks on topical desquamating agents. (Dermatology/Family Medicine/Pediatrics)

Office visit for a 10-year-old female, established patient, who has been swimming in a lake, now presents with a one-day history of left ear pain with purulent drainage. (Family Medicine)

Office visit for a child, established patient, with chronic secretory otitis media. (Otolaryngology, Head & Neck Surgery)

Office visit for an established patient seen in follow-up of clearing patch of localized contact dermatitis. (Family Medicine/Dermatology)

Office visit for an established patient returning for evaluation of response to treatment of lichen planus on wrists and ankles. (Dermatology)

Office visit for an established patient with tinea pedis being treated with topical therapy. (Dermatology)

Office visit for an established patient with localized erythematous plaque of psoriasis with topical hydration. (Dermatology)

Office visit for a 50-year-old male, established patient, recently seen for acute neck pain, diagnosis of spondylosis, responding to physical therapy and intermittent cervical traction. Returns for evaluation for return to work. (Neurology)

Office visit for an established patient with recurring episodes of herpes simplex who has developed a clustering of vesicles on the upper lip. (Oral & Maxillofacial Surgery)

Evaluation of a 50-year-old male, established patient, who has experienced a recurrence of knee pain after he discontinued NSAID. (Anesthesiology/Pain Medicine)

Office visit for an established patient with an irritated skin tag for reassurance. (Dermatology)

Office visit for a 40-year-old, established patient, who has experienced a systemic allergic reaction following administration of immunotherapy. The dose must be readjusted. (Allergy & Immunology)

Office visit for a 33-year-old, established patient, for contusion and abrasion of lower extremity. (Orthopaedic Surgery)

Office visit for a 22-year-old male, established patient, one month after I & D of "wrestler's ear." (Plastic Surgery)

Office visit for a 21-year-old, established patient, who is seen in follow-up after antibiotic therapy for acute bacterial tonsillitis. (Otolaryngology, Head & Neck Surgery)

Office visit for a 4-year-old, established patient, with tympanostomy tubes, check-up. (Otolaryngology, Head & Neck Surgery)

Office visit for an established patient who has had needle aspiration of a peritonsillar abscess. (Otolaryngology, Head & Neck Surgery)

Follow-up office examination for evaluation and treatment of acute draining ear in a 5-year-old with tympanotomy tubes. (Otolaryngology, Head & Neck Surgery)

Office visit, established patient, 6-year-old with sore throat and headache. (Family Medicine/Pediatrics)

Office evaluation for possible purulent bacterial conjunctivitis with one- to two-day history of redness and discharge, 16-year-old female, established patient. (Pediatrics/Internal Medicine/Family Medicine)

Office visit for a 65-year-old female, established patient, returns for three-week follow-up for resolving severe ankle sprain. (Orthopaedic Surgery)

Office visit, sore throat, fever, and fatigue in a 19-year-old college student, established patient. (Internal Medicine)

Office visit with a 33-year-old female, established patient, recently started on treatment for hemorrhoidal complaints, for re-evaluation. (Colon & Rectal Surgery)

Office visit with a 36-year-old male, established patient, for follow-up on effectiveness of medicine management of oral candidiasis. (Oral & Maxillofacial Surgery)

Office visit for a 27-year-old female, established patient, with complaints of vaginal itching. (Obstetrics & Gynecology)

Office visit for a 65-year-old, established patient, with eruptions on both arms from poison oak exposure. (Allergy & Immunology/Internal Medicine)

99213 Office visit for an established patient with new lesions of lichen planus in spite of topical therapies. (Dermatology)

Office visit for the quarterly follow-up of a 45-year-old male with stable chronic asthma requiring regular drug therapy. (Allergy & Immunology)

Office visit for a 13-year-old, established patient, with comedopapular acne of the face which has shown poor response to topical medication. Discussion of use of systemic medication. (Dermatology)

Office visit for a 62-year-old female, established patient, for follow-up for stable cirrhosis of the liver. (Internal Medicine/Family Medicine)

Office visit for a 3-year-old, established patient, with atopic dermatitis and food hypersensitivity for quarterly follow-up evaluation. The patient is on topical lotions and steroid creams as well as oral antihistamines. (Allergy & Immunology)

Office visit for an 80-year-old female, established patient, to evaluate medical management of osteoarthritis of the temporomandibular joint. (Rheumatology)

Office visit for a 70-year-old female, established patient, one year post excision of basal cell carcinoma of nose with nasolabial flap. Now presents with new suspicious recurrent lesion and suspicious lesion of the back. (Plastic Surgery)

Office visit for a 68-year-old female, established patient, with polymyalgia rheumatic, maintained on chronic low-dose corticosteroid, with no new complaints. (Rheumatology)

Office visit for a 3-year-old female, established patient, for earache and dyshidrosis of feet. (Pediatrics/Family Medicine)

Office visit for an established patient for 18-months post-operative follow-up of TMJ repair. (Oral & Maxillofacial Surgery)

Office visit for a 45-year-old male, established patient, being re-evaluated for recurrent acute prostatitis. (Urology)

Office visit for a 43-year-old male, established patient, with known reflex sympathetic dystrophy. (Anesthesiology)

Office visit for an established patient with an evenly pigmented superficial nodule of leg which is symptomatic. (Dermatology)

Office visit for an established patient with psoriasis involvement of the elbows, pitting of the nails, and itchy scalp. (Dermatology)

Office visit for a 27-year-old male, established patient, with deep follicular and perifollicular inflammation unable to tolerate systemic antibiotics due to GI upset, requires change of systemic medication. (Dermatology)

Office visit for a 16-year-old male, established patient, who is on medication for exercise-induced bronchospasm. (Allergy & Immunology)

Office visit for a 60-year-old, established patient, with chronic essential hypertension on multiple drug regimen, for blood pressure check. (Family Medicine)

Office visit for a 20-year-old male, established patient, for removal of sutures in hand. (Family Medicine)

Office visit for a 58-year-old female, established patient, with unilateral painful bunion. (Orthopaedic Surgery)

Office visit for a 45-year-old female, established patient, with known osteoarthritis and painful swollen knees. (Rheumatology)

Office visit for a 25-year-old female, established patient, complaining of bleeding and heavy menses. (Obstetrics & Gynecology)

Office visit for a 55-year-old male, established patient, with hypertension managed by a beta blocker/thiazide regime; now experiencing mild fatigue. (Nephrology)

Office visit for a 65-year-old female, established patient, with primary glaucoma for interval determination of intraocular pressure and possible adjustment of medication. (Ophthalmology)

Office visit for a 56-year-old male, established patient, with stable exertional angina who complains of new onset of calf pain while walking. (Cardiology)

Office visit for a 63-year-old female, established patient, with rheumatoid arthritis on auranofin and ibuprofen, seen for routine follow-up visit. (Rheumatology)

Office visit for an established patient with Graves' disease, three months post I-131 therapy, who presents with lassitude and malaise. (Endocrinology)

Office visit for the quarterly follow-up of a 63-year-old male, established patient, with chronic myofascial pain syndrome, effectively managed by doxepin, who presents with new onset urinary hesitancy. (Pain Medicine)

Office visit for the biannual follow-up of an established patient with migraine variant having infrequent, intermittent, moderate to severe headaches with nausea and vomiting, which are sometimes effectively managed by ergotamine tartrate and an antiemetic, but occasionally requiring visits to an emergency department. (Pain Medicine)

Office visit for an established patient after discharge from a pain rehabilitation program to review and adjust medication dosage. (Pain Medicine)

Office visit with 55-year-old male, established patient, for management of hypertension, mild fatigue, on beta blocker/thiazide regimen. (Family Medicine/Internal Medicine)

Outpatient visit with 37-year-old male, established patient, who is three years post total colectomy for chronic ulcerative colitis, presents for increased irritation at his stoma. (General Surgery)

Office visit for a 70-year-old diabetic hypertensive established patient with recent change in insulin requirement. (Internal Medicine/Nephrology)

Office visit with 80-year-old female, established patient, for follow-up osteoporosis, status-post compression fractures. (Rheumatology)

Office visit for an established patient with stable cirrhosis of the liver. (Gastroenterology)

Routine, follow-up office evaluation at a three-month interval for a 77-year-old female, established patient, with nodular small cleaved-cell lymphoma. (Hematology/Oncology)

Quarterly follow-up office visit for a 45-year-old male, established patient, with stable chronic asthma, on steroid and bronchodilator therapy. (Pulmonary Medicine)

Office visit for a 50-year-old female, established patient, with insulin-dependent diabetes mellitus and stable coronary artery disease, for monitoring. (Family Medicine/Internal Medicine)

99214 Office visit for an established patient now presenting with generalized dermatitis of 80% of the body surface area. (Dermatology)

Office visit for a 32-year-old female, established patient, with new onset right lower quadrant pain. (Family Medicine)

Office visit for reassessment and reassurance/counseling of a 40-year-old female, established patient, who is experiencing increased symptoms while on a pain management treatment program. (Pain Medicine)

Office visit for a 30-year-old, established patient, under management for intractable low back pain, who now presents with new onset right posterior thigh pain. (Pain Medicine)

Office visit for an established patient with frequent intermittent, moderate to severe headaches requiring beta blocker or tricyclic antidepressant prophylaxis, as well as four symptomatic treatments, but who is still experiencing headaches at a frequency of several times a month that are unresponsive to treatment. (Pain Medicine)

Office visit for an established patient with psoriasis with extensive involvement of scalp, trunk, palms, and soles with joint pain. Combinations of topical and systemic treatments discussed and instituted. (Dermatology)

Office visit for a 55-year-old male, established patient, with increasing night pain, limp, and progressive varus of both knees. (Orthopaedic Surgery)

Follow-up visit for a 15-year-old withdrawn patient with four-year history of papulocystic acne of the face, chest, and back with early scarring and poor response to past treatment. Discussion of use of systemic medication. (Dermatology)

Office visit for a 28-year-old male, established patient, with regional enteritis, diarrhea, and low-grade fever. (Internal Medicine)

Office visit for a 25-year-old female, established patient, following recent arthrogram and MR imaging for TMJ pain. (Oral & Maxillofacial Surgery)

Office visit for a 32-year-old female, established patient, with large obstructing stone in left mid-ureter, to discuss management options including urethroscopy with extraction or ESWL. (Urology)

Evaluation for a 28-year-old male, established patient, with new onset of low back pain. (Anesthesiology/Pain Medicine)

Office visit for a 28-year-old female, established patient, with right lower quadrant abdominal pain, fever, and anorexia. (Internal Medicine/Family Medicine)

Office visit for a 45-year-old male, established patient, four months follow-up of L4-5 discectomy, with persistent incapacitating low back and leg pain. (Orthopaedic Surgery)

Outpatient visit for a 77-year-old male, established patient, with hypertension, presenting with a three-month history of episodic substernal chest pain on exertion. (Cardiology)

Office visit for a 25-year-old female, established patient, for evaluation of progressive saddle nose deformity of unknown etiology. (Plastic Surgery)

Office visit for a 65-year-old male, established patient, with BPH and severe bladder outlet obstruction, to discuss management options such as TURP. (Urology)

Office visit for an adult diabetic established patient with a past history of recurrent sinusitis who presents with a one-week history of double vision. (Otolaryngology, Head & Neck Surgery)

Office visit for an established patient with lichen planus and 60% of the cutaneous surface involved, not responsive to systemic steroids, as well as developing symptoms of progressive heartburn and paranoid ideation. (Dermatology)

Office visit for a 52-year-old male, established patient, with a 12-year history of bipolar disorder responding to lithium carbonate and brief psychotherapy. Psychotherapy and prescription provided. (Psychiatry)

Office visit for a 63-year-old female, established patient, with a history of familial polyposis, status post-colectomy with sphincter sparing procedure, who now presents with rectal bleeding and increase in stooling frequency. (General Surgery)

Office visit for a 68-year-old male, established patient, with the sudden onset of multiple flashes and floaters in the right eye due to a posterior vitreous detachment. (Ophthalmology)

Office visit for a 55-year-old female, established patient, on cyclosporin for treatment of resistant, small vessel vasculitis. (Rheumatology)

Follow-up office visit for a 55-year-old male, two months after iliac angioplasty with new onset of contralateral extremity claudication. (Interventional Radiology)

Office visit for a 68-year-old male, established patient, with stable angina, two months post myocardial infarction, who is not tolerating one of his medications. (Cardiology)

Weekly office visit for 5FU therapy for an ambulatory established patient with metastatic colon cancer and increasing shortness of breath. (Hematology/Oncology)

Follow-up office visit for a 60-year-old male, established patient, whose post-traumatic seizures have disappeared on medication and who now raises the question of stopping the medication. (Neurology)

Office evaluation on new onset RLQ pain in a 32-year-old female, established patient. (Urology/General Surgery/Internal Medicine/Family Medicine)

Office evaluation of 28-year-old, established patient, with regional enteritis, diarrhea, and low-grade fever. (Family Medicine/Internal Medicine)

Office visit with 50-year-old female, established patient, diabetic, blood sugar controlled by diet. She now complains of frequency of urination and weight loss, blood sugar of 320, and negative ketones on dipstick. (Internal Medicine)

Follow-up office visit for a 45-year-old, established patient, with rheumatoid arthritis on gold, methotrexate, or immunosuppressive therapy. (Rheumatology)

Office visit for a 60-year-old male, established patient, two years post-removal of intracranial meningioma, now with new headaches and visual disturbance. (Neurosurgery)

Office visit for a 68-year-old female, established patient, for routine review and follow-up of non-insulin dependent diabetes, obesity, hypertension, and congestive heart failure. Complains of vision difficulties and admits dietary noncompliance. Patient is counseled concerning diet and current medications adjusted. (Family Medicine)

99215 Office visit for an established patient who developed persistent cough, rectal bleeding, weakness, and diarrhea plus pustular infection on skin. Patient on immunosuppressive therapy. (Dermatology)

Office visit for an established patient with disseminated lupus erythematosus, extensive edema of extremities, kidney disease, and weakness requiring monitored course on azathioprene, corticosteroid and complicated by acute depression. (Dermatology/Internal Medicine/Rheumatology)

Office visit for an established patient with progressive dermatomyositis and recent onset of fever, nasal speech, and regurgitation of fluids through the nose. (Dermatology)

Office visit for a 28-year-old female, established patient, who is abstinent from previous cocaine dependence, but reports progressive panic attacks and chest pains. (Psychiatry)

Office visit for an established adolescent patient with history of bipolar disorder treated with lithium; seen on urgent basis at family's request because of severe depressive symptoms. (Psychiatry)

Office visit for an established patient having acute migraine with new onset neurological symptoms and whose headaches are unresponsive to previous attempts at management with a combination of preventive and abortive medication. (Pain Medicine)

Office visit for an established patient with exfoliative lichen planus with daily fever spikes, disorientation, and shortness of breath. (Dermatology)

Office visit for a 25-year-old, established patient, two years post-burn with bilateral ectropion, hypertrophic facial burn scars, near absence of left breast, and burn syndactyly of both hands. Discussion of treatment options following examination. (Plastic Surgery)

Office visit for a 6-year-old, established patient, to review newly diagnosed immune deficiency with recommendations for therapy including IV immunoglobulin and chronic antibiotics. (Allergy & Immunology)

Office visit for a 36-year-old, established patient, three months status post-transplant, with new onset of peripheral edema, increased blood pressure, and progressive fatigue. (Nephrology)

Office visit for an established patient with Kaposi's sarcoma who presents with fever and widespread vesicles. (Dermatology)

Office visit for a 27-year-old female, established patient, with bipolar disorder who was stable on lithium carbonate and monthly supportive psychotherapy but now has developed symptoms of hypomania. (Psychiatry)

Office visit for a 25-year-old male, established patient with a history of schizophrenia who has been seen bi-monthly but is complaining of auditory hallucinations. (Psychiatry)

Office visit for a 62-year-old male, established patient, three years postoperative abdominal perineal resection, now with a rising carcinoembryonic antigen, weight loss, and pelvic pain. (Abdominal Surgery)

Office visit for a 42-year-old male, established patient, nine months postoperative emergency vena cava shunt for variceal bleeding, now presents with complaints of one episode of "dark" bowel movement, weight gain, tightness in abdomen, whites of eyes seem "yellow" and occasional drowsiness after eating hamburgers. (Abdominal Surgery)

Office visit for a 68-year-old male, established patient, with biopsy-proven rectal carcinoma, for evaluation and discussion of treatment options. (General Surgery)

Office visit for a 60-year-old, established patient, with diabetic nephropathy with increasing edema and dyspnea. (Endocrinology)

Office visit with 30-year-old male, established patient for three-month history of fatigue, weight loss, intermittent fever, and presenting with diffuse adenopathy and splenomegaly. (Family Medicine)

Office visit for restaging of an established patient with new lymphadenopathy one year post-therapy for lymphoma. (Hematology/Oncology)

Office visit for evaluation of recent onset syncopal attacks in a 70-year-old female, established patient. (Internal Medicine)

Follow-up visit, 40-year-old mother of three, established patient, with acute rheumatoid arthritis, anatomical Stage 3, ARA function Class 3 rheumatoid arthritis, and deteriorating function. (Rheumatology)

Follow-up office visit for a 65-year-old male, established patient, with a fever of recent onset while on outpatient antibiotic therapy for endocarditis. (Infectious Disease)

Office visit for a 75-year-old, established patient, with ALS (amyotrophic lateral sclerosis), who is no longer able to swallow. (Neurology)

Office visit for a 70-year-old female, established patient, with diabetes mellitus and hypertension, presenting with a two-month history of increasing confusion, agitation and short-term memory loss. (Family Medicine/Internal Medicine)

Hospital Inpatient Services

Initial Hospital Care

New or Established Patient

99221 Initial hospital visit following admission for a 42-year-old male for observation following an uncomplicated mandible fracture. (Plastic Surgery/Oral & Maxillofacial Surgery)

Initial hospital visit for a 40-year-old patient with a thrombosed synthetic arteriovenous conduit. (Nephrology)

Initial hospital visit for a healthy 24-year-old male with an acute onset of low back pain following a lifting injury. (Internal Medicine/Anesthesiology/Pain Medicine)

Initial hospital visit for a 69-year-old female with controlled hypertension, scheduled for surgery. (Internal Medicine/Cardiology)

Initial hospital visit for a 24-year-old healthy female with benign tumor of palate. (Oral & Maxillofacial Surgery)

Initial hospital visit for a 14-year-old female with infectious mononucleosis and dehydration. (Internal Medicine)

Initial hospital visit for a 62-year-old female with stable rheumatoid arthritis, admitted for total joint replacement. (Rheumatology)

Initial hospital visit for a 12-year-old patient with a laceration of the upper eyelid, involving the lid margin and superior canaliculus, admitted prior to surgery for IV antibiotic therapy. (Plastic Surgery)

Initial hospital visit for a 69-year-old female with controlled hypertension, scheduled for surgery. (Cardiology)

Hospital admission, examination, and initiation of treatment program for a 67-year-old male with uncomplicated pneumonia who requires IV antibiotic therapy. (Internal Medicine)

Hospital admission for an 18-month-old with 10% dehydration. (Pediatrics)

Hospital admission for a 12-year-old with a laceration of the upper eyelid involving the lid margin and superior canaliculus, admitted prior to surgery for IV antibiotic therapy. (Ophthalmology)

Hospital admission for a 32-year-old female with severe flank pain, hematuria and presumed diagnosis of ureteral calculus as determined by Emergency Department physician. (Urology)

Initial hospital visit for a patient with several large venous stasis ulcers not responding to outpatient therapy. (Dermatology)

Initial hospital visit for 21-year-old pregnant patient (nine-weeks gestation) with hyperemesis gravidarum. (Obstetrics & Gynecology)

Initial hospital visit for a 73-year-old female with acute pyelonephritis who is otherwise generally healthy. (Geriatrics)

Initial hospital visit for 62-year-old patient with cellulitis of the foot requiring bedrest and intravenous antibiotics. (Orthopaedic Surgery)

99222   Initial hospital visit for a 50-year-old patient with lower quadrant abdominal pain and increased temperature, but without septic picture. (General Surgery/Abdominal Surgery/Colon & Rectal Surgery)

Initial hospital visit for airway management, due to a benign laryngeal mass. (Otolaryngology, Head & Neck Surgery)

Initial hospital visit for a 66-year-old female with an L-2 vertebral compression fracture with acute onset of paralytic ileus; seen in the office two days previously. (Orthopaedic Surgery)

Initial hospital visit and evaluation of a 15-year-old male admitted with peritonsillar abscess or cellulitis requiring intravenous antibiotic therapy. (Otolaryngology, Head & Neck Surgery)

Initial hospital visit for a 42-year-old male with vertebral compression fracture following a motor vehicle accident. (Orthopaedic Surgery)

Initial hospital visit for a patient with generalized atopic dermatitis and secondary infection. (Dermatology)

Initial hospital visit for a 3-year-old patient with high temperature, limp, and painful hip motion of 18 hours' duration. (Pediatrics/Orthopaedic Surgery)

Initial hospital visit for a young adult, presenting with an acute asthma attack unresponsive to outpatient therapy. (Allergy & Immunology)

Initial hospital visit for an 18-year-old male who has suppurative sialoadenitis and dehydration. (Oral & Maxillofacial Surgery)

Initial hospital visit for a 65-year-old female for acute onset of thrombotic cerebrovascular accident with contralateral paralysis and aphasia. (Neurology)

Initial hospital visit for a 50-year-old male chronic paraplegic patient with pain and spasm below the lesion. (Anesthesiology)

Partial hospital admission for an adolescent patient from chaotic blended family, transferred from inpatient setting, for continued treatment to control symptomatic expressions of hostility and depression. (Psychiatry)

Initial hospital visit for a 15-year-old male with acute status asthmaticus, unresponsive to outpatient therapy. (Internal Medicine)

Initial hospital visit for a 61-year-old male with history of previous myocardial infarction, who now complains of chest pain. (Internal Medicine)

Initial hospital visit of a 15-year-old on medications for a sore throat over the last two weeks. The sore throat has worsened and patient now has dysphagia. The exam shows large necrotic tonsils with an adequate airway and small palpable nodes. The initial mono test was negative. (Otolaryngology, Head & Neck Surgery)

Initial hospital evaluation of a 23-year-old allergy patient admitted with eyelid edema and pain on fifth day of oral antibiotic therapy. (Otolaryngology, Head & Neck Surgery)

Hospital admission, young adult patient, failed previous therapy and now presents in acute asthmatic attack. (Family Medicine/Allergy & Immunology)

Hospital admission of a 62-year-old smoker, established patient, with bronchitis in acute respiratory distress. (Internal Medicine/Pulmonary Medicine)

Hospital admission, examination, and initiation of a treatment program for a 65-year-old female with new onset of right-sided paralysis and aphasia. (Neurology)

Hospital admission, examination, and initiation of treatment program for a 66-year-old chronic hemodialysis patient with fever and a new pulmonary infiltrate. (Nephrology)

Hospital admission for an 8-year-old febrile patient with chronic sinusitis and severe headache, unresponsive to oral antibiotics. (Allergy & Immunology)

Hospital admission for a 40-year-old male with submaxillary cellulitis and trismus from infected lower molar. (Oral & Maxillofacial Surgery)

99223   Initial hospital visit for a 45-year-old female, who has a history of rheumatic fever as a child and now has anemia, fever, and congestive heart failure. (Cardiology)

Initial hospital visit for a 50-year-old male with acute chest pain and diagnostic electrocardiographic changes of an acute anterior myocardial infarction. (Cardiology/Family Medicine/Internal Medicine)

Initial hospital visit of a 75-year-old with progressive stridor and dysphagia with history of cancer of the larynx treated by radiation therapy in the past. Exam shows a large recurrent tumor of the glottis with a mass in the neck. (Otolaryngology, Head & Neck Surgery)

Initial hospital visit for a 70-year-old male admitted with chest pain, complete heart block, and congestive heart failure. (Cardiology)

Initial hospital visit for an 82-year-old male who presents with syncope, chest pain, and ventricular arrhythmias. (Cardiology)

Initial hospital visit for a 75-year-old male with history of arteriosclerotic coronary vascular disease, who is severely dehydrated, disoriented, and experiencing auditory hallucinations. (Psychiatry)

Initial hospital visit for a 70-year-old male with alcohol and sedative-hypnotic dependence, admitted by family for severe withdrawal, hypertension, and diabetes mellitus. (Psychiatry)

Initial hospital visit for a persistently suicidal latency-aged child whose parents have requested admission to provide safety during evaluation, but are anxious about separation from her. (Psychiatry)

Initial psychiatric visit for an adolescent patient without previous psychiatric history, who was transferred from the medical ICU after a significant overdose. (Psychiatry)

Initial hospital visit for a 35-year-old female with severe systemic lupus erythematosus on corticosteroid and cyclophosphamide, with new onset of fever, chills, rash, and chest pain. (Rheumatology)

Initial hospital visit for a 52-year-old male with known rheumatic heart disease who presents with anasarca, hypertension, and history of alcohol abuse. (Cardiology)

Initial hospital visit for a 55-year-old female with a history of congenital heart disease; now presents with cyanosis. (Cardiology)

Initial hospital visit for a psychotic, hostile, violently combative adolescent, involuntarily committed, for seclusion and restraint in order to provide for safety on unit. (Psychiatry)

Initial hospital visit for a now subdued and sullen teenage male with six-month history of declining school performance, increasing self-endangerment, and resistance of parental expectations, including running away past weekend after physical fight with father. (Psychiatry)

Initial partial hospital admission for a 17-year-old female with history of borderline mental retardation who has developed auditory hallucinations. Parents are known to abuse alcohol, and Child Protective Services is investigating allegations of sexual abuse of a younger sibling. (Psychiatry)

Initial hospital visit of a 67-year-old male admitted with a large neck mass, dysphagia, and history of myocardial infarction three months before. (Otolaryngology, Head & Neck Surgery)

Initial hospital visit for a patient with suspected cerebrospinal fluid rhinorrhea which developed two weeks after head injury. (Otolaryngology, Head & Neck Surgery)

Initial hospital visit for a 25-year-old female with history of poly-substance abuse and psychiatric disorder. The patient appears to be psychotic with markedly elevated vital signs. (Psychiatry)

Initial hospital visit for a 70-year-old male with cutaneous T-cell lymphoma who has developed fever and lymphadenopathy. (Internal Medicine)

Initial hospital visit for a 62-year-old female with known coronary artery disease, for evaluation of increasing edema, dyspnea on exertion, confusion, and sudden onset of fever with productive cough. (Internal Medicine)

Initial hospital visit for a 3-year-old female with 36-hour history of sore throat and high fever; now with sudden onset of lethargy, irritability, photophobia, and nuchal rigidity. (Pediatrics)

Initial hospital visit for a 26-year-old female for evaluation of severe facial fractures (LeFort's II/III). (Plastic Surgery)

Initial hospital visit for a 55-year-old female for bilateral mandibular fractures resulting in flail mandible and airway obstruction. (Plastic Surgery)

Initial hospital visit for a 71-year-old patient with a red painful eye four days following uncomplicated cataract surgery due to endophthalmitis. (Ophthalmology)

Initial hospital visit for a 45-year-old patient involved in a motor vehicle accident who suffered a perforating corneoscleral laceration with loss of vision. (Ophthalmology)

Initial hospital visit for a 58-year-old male who has Ludwig's angina and progressive airway compromise. (Oral & Maxillofacial Surgery)

Initial hospital visit for a patient with generalized systemic sclerosis, receiving immunosuppressive therapy because of recent onset of cough, fever, and inability to swallow. (Dermatology)

Initial hospital visit for an 82-year-old male who presents with syncope, chest pain, and ventricular arrhythmias. (Cardiology)

Initial hospital visit for a 62-year-old male with history of previous myocardial infarction, comes in with recurrent, sustained ventricular tachycardia. (Cardiology)

Initial hospital visit for a chronic dialysis patient with infected PTFE fistula, septicemia, and shock. (Nephrology)

Initial hospital visit for a 1-year-old male, victim of child abuse, with central nervous system depression, skull fracture, and retinal hemorrhage. (Family Medicine/Neurology)

Initial hospital visit for a 25-year-old female with recent C4-5 quadriplegia, admitted for rehabilitation. (Physical Medicine & Rehabilitation)

Initial hospital visit for an 18-year-old male, post-traumatic brain injury with multiple impairment. (Physical Medicine & Rehabilitation)

Initial partial hospital admission for 16-year-old male, sullen and subdued, with six-month history of declining school performance, increasing self-endangerment, and resistance to parental expectations. (Psychiatry)

Initial hospital visit for a 16-year-old primigravida at 32-weeks gestation with severe hypertension (200/110), thrombocytopenia, and headache. (Obstetrics & Gynecology)

Initial hospital visit for a 49-year-old male with cirrhosis of liver with hematemesis, hepatic encephalopathy, and fever. (Gastroenterology)

Initial hospital visit for a 55-year-old female in chronic pain who has attempted suicide. (Psychiatry)

Initial hospital visit for a 70-year-old male, with multiple organ system disease, admitted with history of being aneuric and septic for 24 hours prior to admission. (Urology)

Initial hospital visit for a 3-year-old female with 36-hour history of sore throat and high fever, now with sudden onset of lethargy, irritability, photophobia, and nuchal rigidity. (Internal Medicine)

Initial hospital visit for a 78-year-old male, transfers from nursing home with dysuria and pyuria, increasing confusion, and high fever. (Internal Medicine)

Initial hospital visit for a 1-day-old male with cyanosis, respiratory distress, and tachypnea. (Cardiology)

Initial hospital visit for a 3-year-old female with recurrent tachycardia and syncope. (Cardiology)

Initial hospital visit for a thyrotoxic patient who presents with fever, atrial fibrillation, and delirium. (Endocrinology)

Initial hospital visit for a 50-year-old Type I diabetic who presents with diabetic ketoacidosis with fever and obtundation. (Endocrinology)

Initial hospital visit for a 40-year-old female with anatomical stage 3, ARA functional class 3 rheumatoid arthritis on methotrexate, corticosteroid, and nonsteroidal anti-inflammatory drugs. Patient presents with severe arthritis flare, new oral ulcers, abdominal pain, and leukopenia. (Rheumatology)

Initial hospital exam of a pediatric patient with high fever and proptosis. (Otolaryngology, Head & Neck Surgery)

Initial hospital visit for a 25-year-old patient admitted for the first time to the rehab unit, with recent C4-C5 quadriplegia. (Physical Medicine & Rehabilitation)

Hospital admission, examination, and initiation of treatment program for a previously unknown 58-year-old male who presents with acute chest pain. (Cardiology)

Hospital admission, examination, and initiation of induction chemotherapy for a 42-year-old patient with newly diagnosed acute myelogenous leukemia. (Hematology/Oncology)

Hospital admission following a motor vehicle accident of a 24-year-old male with fracture dislocation of C5-C6; neurologically intact. (Neurosurgery)

Hospital admission for a 78-year-old female with left lower lobe pneumonia and a history of coronary artery disease, congestive heart failure, osteoarthritis and gout. (Family Medicine)

Hospital admission, examination, and initiation of treatment program for a 65-year-old immunosuppressed male with confusion, fever, and a headache. (Infectious Disease)

Hospital admission for a 9-year-old with vomiting, dehydration, fever, tachypnea, and an admitting diagnosis of diabetic ketoacidosis. (Pediatrics)

Initial hospital visit for a 65-year-old male who presents with acute myocardial infarction, oliguria, hypotension, and altered state of consciousness. (Cardiology)

Initial hospital visit for a hostile/resistant adolescent patient who is severely depressed and involved in poly-substance abuse. Patient is experiencing significant conflict in his chaotic family situation and was suspended from school following an attack on a teacher with a baseball bat. (Psychiatry)

Initial hospital visit for 89-year-old female with fulminant hepatic failure and encephalopathy. (Gastroenterology)

Initial hospital visit for a 42-year-old female with rapidly progressing scleroderma, malignant hypertension, digital infarcts, and oligurea. (Rheumatology)

Subsequent Hospital Care

99231   Subsequent hospital visit for a 65-year-old female, post-open reduction and internal fixation of a fracture. (Physical Medicine & Rehabilitation)

Subsequent hospital visit for a 33-year-old patient with pelvic pain who is responding to pain medication and observation. (Obstetrics & Gynecology)

Subsequent hospital visit for a 21-year-old female with hyperemesis who has responded well to intravenous fluids. (Obstetrics & Gynecology)

Subsequent hospital visit to re-evaluate postoperative pain and titrate patient-controlled analgesia for a 27-year-old female. (Anesthesiology)

Follow-up hospital visit for a 35-year-old female, status post-epidural analgesia. (Anesthesiology/Pain Medicine)

Subsequent hospital visit for a 56-year-old male, post-gastrectomy, for maintenance of analgesia using an intravenous dilaudid infusion. (Anesthesiology)

Subsequent hospital visit for a 4-year-old on day three receiving medication for uncomplicated pneumonia. (Allergy & Immunology)

Subsequent hospital visit for a 30-year-old female with urticaria which has stabilized with medication. (Allergy & Immunology)

Subsequent hospital visit for a 76-year-old male with venous stasis ulcers. (Dermatology)

Subsequent hospital visit for a 24-year-old female with otitis externa, seen two days before in consultation, now to have otic wick removal. (Otolaryngology, Head & Neck Surgery)

Subsequent hospital visit for a 27-year-old with acute labyrinthitis. (Otolaryngology, Head & Neck Surgery)

Subsequent hospital visit for a 10-year-old male admitted for lobar pneumonia with vomiting and dehydration; is becoming afebrile and tolerating oral fluids. (Family Medicine/Pediatrics)

Subsequent hospital visit for a 62-year-old patient with resolving cellulitis of the foot. (Orthopaedic Surgery)

Subsequent hospital visit for a 25-year-old male admitted for supra-ventricular tachycardia and converted on medical therapy. (Cardiology)

Subsequent hospital visit for a 27-year-old male two days after open reduction and internal fixation for malar complex fracture. (Plastic Surgery)

Subsequent hospital visit for a 76-year-old male with venous stasis ulcers. (Geriatrics)

Subsequent hospital visit for a 67-year-old female admitted three days ago with bleeding gastric ulcer; now stable. (Gastroenterology)

Subsequent hospital visit for stable 33-year-old male, status post-lower gastrointestinal bleeding. (General Surgery/Gastroenterology)

Subsequent hospital visit for a 29-year-old auto mechanic with effort thrombosis of left upper extremity. (General Surgery)

Subsequent hospital visit for a 14-year-old female in middle phase of inpatient treatment, who is now behaviorally stable and making satisfactory progress in treatment. (Psychiatry)

Subsequent hospital visit for an 18-year-old male with uncomplicated asthma who is clinically stable. (Allergy & Immunology)

Subsequent hospital visit for a 55-year-old male with rheumatoid arthritis, two days following an uncomplicated total joint replacement. (Rheumatology)

Subsequent hospital visit for a 60-year-old dialysis patient with an access infection, now afebrile on antibiotic. (Nephrology)

Subsequent hospital visit for a 36-year-old female with stable post-rhinoplasty epistaxis. (Plastic Surgery)

Subsequent hospital visit for a 66-year-old female with L-2 vertebral compression fracture with resolving ileus. (Orthopaedic Surgery)

Subsequent hospital visit for a patient with peritonsillar abscess. (Otolaryngology, Head & Neck Surgery)

Subsequent hospital visit for an 18-year-old female responding to intravenous antibiotic therapy for ear or sinus infection. (Otolaryngology, Head & Neck Surgery)

Subsequent hospital visit for a 70-year-old male admitted with congestive heart failure who has responded to therapy. (Cardiology)

Follow-up hospital visit for a 32-year-old female with left ureteral calculus; being followed in anticipation of spontaneous passage. (Urology)

Subsequent hospital visit for a 4-year-old female, admitted for acute gastroenteritis and dehydration, requiring IV hydration; now stable. (Family Medicine)

Subsequent hospital visit for a 50-year-old Type II diabetic who is clinically stable and without complications requiring regulation of a single dose of insulin daily. (Endocrinology)

Subsequent hospital visit to reassesses the status of a 65-year-old patient post-open reduction and internal fixation of hip fracture, on the rehab unit. (Physical Medicine & Rehabilitation)

Subsequent hospital visit for a 78-year-old male with cholangiocarcinoma managed by biliary drainage. (Interventional Radiology)

Subsequent hospital visit for a 50-year-old male with uncomplicated myocardial infarction who is clinically stable and without chest pain. (Family Medicine/Cardiology/Internal Medicine)

Subsequent hospital visit for a stable 72-year-old lung cancer patient undergoing a five-day course of infusion chemotherapy. (Hematology/Oncology)

Subsequent hospital visit, two days post admission for a 65-year-old male with a CVA (cerebral vascular accident) and left hemiparesis, who is clinically stable. (Neurology/Physical Medicine and Rehabilitation)

Subsequent hospital visit for now stable, 33-year-old male, status post lower gastrointestinal bleeding. (General Surgery)

Subsequent visit on third day of hospitalization for a 60-year-old female recovering from an uncomplicated pneumonia. (Infectious Disease/Internal Medicine/Pulmonary Medicine)

Subsequent hospital visit for a 3-year-old patient in traction for a congenital dislocation of the hip. (Orthopaedic Surgery)

Subsequent hospital visit for a 4-year-old female, admitted for acute gastroenteritis and dehydration, requiring IV hydration; now stable. (Family Medicine/Internal Medicine)

Subsequent hospital visit for 50-year-old female with resolving uncomplicated acute pancreatitis. (Gastroenterology)

99232 Subsequent hospital visit for a patient with venous stasis ulcers who developed fever and red streaks adjacent to the ulcer. (Dermatology/Internal Medicine/Family Medicine)

Subsequent hospital visit for a 66-year-old male for dressing changes and observation. Patient has had a myocutaneous flap to close a pharyngeal fistula and now has a low-grade fever. (Plastic Surgery)

Subsequent hospital visit for a 54-year-old female admitted for myocardial infarction, but who is now having frequent premature ventricular contractions. (Internal Medicine)

Subsequent hospital visit for an 80-year-old patient with a pelvic rim fracture, inability to walk, and severe pain; now 36 hours post-injury, experiencing urinary retention. (Orthopaedic Surgery)

Subsequent hospital visit for a 17-year-old female with fever, pharyngitis, and airway obstruction, who after 48 hours develops a maculopapular rash. (Pediatrics/Family Medicine)

Follow-up hospital visit for a 32-year-old patient admitted the previous day for corneal ulcer. (Dermatology)

Follow-up visit for a 67-year-old male with congestive heart failure who has responded to antibiotics and diuretics, and has now developed a monoarthropathy. (Internal Medicine)

Follow-up hospital visit for a 58-year-old male receiving continuous opioids who is experiencing severe nausea and vomiting. (Pain Medicine)

Subsequent hospital visit for a patient after an auto accident who is slow to respond to ambulation training. (Physical Medicine & Rehabilitation)

Subsequent hospital visit for a 14-year-old with unstable bronchial asthma complicated by pneumonia. (Allergy & Immunology)

Subsequent hospital visit for a 50-year-old diabetic, hypertensive male with back pain not responding to conservative inpatient management with continued radiation of pain to the lower left extremity. (Orthopaedic Surgery)

Subsequent hospital visit for a 37-year-old female on day five of antibiotics for bacterial endocarditis, who still has low-grade fever. (Cardiology)

Subsequent hospital visit for a 54-year-old patient, post MI (myocardial infarction), who is out of the CCU (coronary care unit) but is now having frequent premature ventricular contractions on telemetry. (Cardiology/Internal Medicine)

Subsequent hospital visit for a patient with neutropenia, a fever responding to antibiotics, and continued slow gastrointestinal bleeding on platelet support. (Hematology/Oncology)

Subsequent hospital visit for a 50-year-old male admitted two days ago for sub-acute renal allograft rejection. (Nephrology)

Subsequent hospital visit for a 35-year-old drug addict, not responding to initial antibiotic therapy for pyelonephritis. (Urology)

Subsequent hospital visit of an 81-year-old male with abdominal distention, nausea, and vomiting. (General Surgery)

Subsequent hospital care for a 62-year-old female with congestive heart failure, who remains dyspneic and febrile. (Internal Medicine)

Subsequent hospital visit for a 73-year-old female with recently diagnosed lung cancer, who complains of unsteady gait. (Pulmonary Medicine)

Subsequent hospital visit for a 20-month-old male with bacterial meningitis treated one week with antibiotic therapy; has now developed a temperature of 101.0 degrees. (Pediatrics)

Subsequent hospital visit for 13-year-old male admitted with left lower quadrant abdominal pain and fever, not responding to therapy. (General Surgery)

Subsequent hospital visit for a 65-year-old male with hemiplegia and painful paretic shoulder. (Physical Medicine & Rehabilitation)

99233 Subsequent hospital visit for a 38-year-old male, quadriplegic with acute autonomic hyperreflexia, who is not responsive to initial care. (Physical Medicine & Rehabilitation)

Follow-up hospital visit for a teenage female who continues to experience severely disruptive, violent and life-threatening symptoms in a complicated multi-system illness. Family/social circumstances also a contributing factor. (Psychiatry)

Subsequent hospital visit for a 42-year-old female with progressive systemic sclerosis (scleroderma), renal failure on dialysis, congestive heart failure, cardiac arrhythmias, and digital ulcers. (Allergy & Immunology)

Subsequent hospital visit for a 50-year-old diabetic, hypertensive male with nonresponding back pain and radiating pain to the lower left extremity, who develops chest pain, cough, and bloody sputum. (Orthopaedic Surgery)

Subsequent hospital visit for a 64-year-old female, status post-abdominal aortic aneurysm resection, with non-responsive coagulopathy, who has now developed lower GI bleeding. (Abdominal Surgery/Colon & Rectal Surgery/General Surgery)

Follow-up hospital care of a patient with pansinusitis infection complicated by a brain abscess and asthma; no response to current treatment. (Otolaryngology, Head & Neck Surgery)

Subsequent hospital visit for a patient with a laryngeal neoplasm who develops airway compromise, suspected metastasis. (Otolaryngology, Head & Neck Surgery)

Subsequent hospital visit for a 49-year-old male with significant rectal bleeding, etiology undetermined, not responding to treatment. (Abdominal Surgery/General Surgery/Colon & Rectal Surgery)

Subsequent hospital visit for a 50-year-old male, post-aortocoronary bypass surgery; now develops hypotension and oliguria. (Cardiology)

Subsequent hospital visit for an adolescent patient who is violent, unsafe, and noncompliant, with multiple expectations for participation in treatment plan and behavior on the treatment unit. (Psychiatry)

Subsequent hospital visit for an 18-year-old male being treated for presumed PCP psychosis. Patient is still moderately symptomatic with auditory hallucinations and is insisting on signing out against medical advice. (Psychiatry)

Subsequent hospital visit for an 8-year-old female with caustic ingestion, who now has fever, dyspnea, and dropping hemoglobin. (Gastroenterology)

Follow-up hospital visit for a chronic renal failure patient on dialysis who develops chest pain and shortness of breath and a new onset pericardial friction rub. (Nephrology)

Subsequent hospital visit for a 44-year-old patient with electrical burns to the left arm with ascending infection. (Orthopaedic Surgery)

Subsequent hospital visit for a patient with systemic sclerosis who has aspirated and is short of breath. (Dermatology)

Subsequent hospital visit for a 65-year-old female, status postoperative resection of abdominal aortic aneurysm, with suspected ischemic bowel. (General Surgery)

Subsequent hospital visit for a 50-year-old male, post-aortocoronary bypass surgery, now develops hypotension and oliguria. (Cardiology)

Subsequent hospital visit for a 65-year-old male, following an acute myocardial infarction, who complains of shortness of breath and new chest pain. (Cardiology)

Subsequent hospital visit for a 65-year-old female with rheumatoid arthritis (stage 3, class 3) admitted for urosepsis. On the third hospital day, chest pain, dyspnea and fever develop. (Rheumatology)

Follow-up hospital care of a pediatric case with stridor, laryngomalacia, established tracheostomy, complicated by multiple medical problems in PICU. (Otolaryngology, Head & Neck Surgery)

Subsequent hospital visit for a 60-year-old female, four days post uncomplicated inferior myocardial infarction who has developed severe chest pain, dyspnea, diaphoresis and nausea. (Family Medicine)

Subsequent hospital visit for a patient with AML (acute myelogenous leukemia), fever, elevated white count and uric acid undergoing induction chemotherapy. (Hematology/Oncology)

Subsequent hospital visit for a 38-year-old quadriplegic male with acute autonomic hyperreflexia, who is not responsive to initial care. (Physical Medicine & Rehabilitation)

Subsequent hospital visit for a 65-year-old female postoperative resection of abdominal aortic aneurysm, with suspected ischemic bowel. (General Surgery)

Subsequent hospital visit for a 60-year-old female with persistent leukocytosis and a fever seven days after a sigmoid colon resection for carcinoma. (Infectious Disease)

Subsequent hospital visit for a chronic renal failure patient on dialysis, who develops chest pain, shortness of breath and new onset of pericardial friction rub. (Nephrology)

Subsequent hospital visit for a 65-year-old male with acute myocardial infarction who now demonstrates complete heart block and congestive heart failure. (Cardiology)

Subsequent hospital visit for a 25-year-old female with hypertension and systemic lupus erythematosus, admitted for fever and respiratory distress. On the third hospital day, the patient presented with purpuric skin lesions and acute renal failure. (Allergy & Immunology)

Subsequent hospital visit for a 55-year-old male with severe chronic obstructive pulmonary disease and bronchospasm; initially admitted for acute respiratory distress requiring ventilatory support in the ICU. The patient was stabilized, extubated and transferred to the floor, but has now developed acute fever, dyspnea, left lower lobe rhonchi and laboratory evidence of carbon dioxide retention and hypoxemia. (Family Medicine/Internal Medicine)

Subsequent hospital visit for 46-year-old female, known liver cirrhosis patient, with recent upper gastrointestinal hemorrhage from varices; now with worsening ascites and encephalopathy. (Gastroenterology)

Subsequent hospital visit for 62-year-old female admitted with acute subarachnoid hemorrhage, negative cerebral arteriogram, increased lethargy and hemiparesis with fever. (Neurosurgery)

Consultations

Office or Other Outpatient Consultations

New or Established Patient

99241   Initial office consultation for a 40-year-old female in pain from blister on lip following a cold. (Oral & Maxillofacial Surgery)

Initial office consultation for a 62-year-old construction worker with olecranon bursitis. (Orthopaedic Surgery)

Office consultation with 25-year-old postpartum female with severe symptomatic hemorrhoids. (Colon & Rectal Surgery)

Office consultation with 58-year-old male, referred for follow-up of creatinine level and evaluation of obstructive uropathy, relieved two months ago. (Nephrology)

Office consultation for 30-year-old female tennis player with sprain or contusion of the forearm. (Orthopaedic Surgery)

Office consultation for a 45-year-old male, requested by his internist, with asymptomatic torus palatinus requiring no further treatment. (Oral & Maxillofacial Surgery)

99242   Initial office consultation for a 20-year-old male with acute upper respiratory tract symptoms. (Allergy & Immunology)

Initial office consultation for a 29-year-old soccer player with painful proximal thigh/groin injury. (Orthopaedic Surgery)

Initial office consultation for a 66-year-old female with wrist and hand pain, numbness of finger tips, suspected median nerve compression by carpal tunnel syndrome. (Plastic Surgery)

Initial office consultation for a patient with a solitary lesion of discoid lupus erythematosus on left cheek to rule out malignancy or self-induced lesion. (Dermatology)

Office consultation for management of systolic hypertension in a 70-year-old male scheduled for elective prostate resection. (Geriatrics)

Office consultation with 27-year-old female, with old amputation, for evaluation of existing above-knee prosthesis. (Physical Medicine & Rehabilitation)

Office consultation with 66-year-old female with wrist and hand pain, and finger numbness, secondary to suspected carpal tunnel syndrome. (Orthopaedic Surgery)

Office consultation for 61-year-old female, recently on antibiotic therapy, now with diarrhea and leukocytosis. (Abdominal Surgery)

Office consultation for a patient with papulosquamous eruption of elbow with pitting of nails and itchy scalp. (Dermatology)

Office consultation for a 30-year-old female with single season allergic rhinitis. (Allergy & Immunology)

99243   Initial office consultation for a 60-year-old male with avascular necrosis of the left femoral head with increasing pain. (Orthopaedic Surgery)

Office consultation for a 31-year-old woman complaining of palpitations and chest pains. Her internist had described a mild systolic click. (Cardiology)

Office consultation for a 65-year-old female with persistent bronchitis. (Infectious Disease)

Office consultation for a 65-year-old man with chronic low-back pain radiating to the leg. (Neurosurgery)

Office consultation for 23-year-old female with Crohn's disease not responding to therapy. (Abdominal Surgery/Colon & Rectal Surgery)

Office consultation for 25-year-old patient with symptomatic knee pain and swelling, with torn anterior cruciate ligament and/or torn meniscus. (Orthopaedic Surgery)

Office consultation for a 67-year-old patient with osteoporosis and mandibular atrophy with regard to reconstructive alternatives. (Oral & Maxillofacial Surgery)

Office consultation for 39-year-old patient referred at a perimenopausal age for irregular menses and menopausal symptoms. (Obstetrics & Gynecology)

99244   Initial office consultation for a 28-year-old male, HIV+, with a recent change in visual acuity. (Ophthalmology)

Initial office consultation for a 15-year-old male with failing grades, suspected drug abuse. (Pediatrics)

Initial office consultation for a 36-year-old factory worker, status four months post-occupational low back injury and requires management of intractable low back pain. (Pain Medicine)

Initial office consultation for a 45-year-old female with a history of chronic arthralgia of TMJ and associated myalgia and sudden progressive symptomatology over last two to three months. (Oral & Maxillofacial Surgery)

Initial office consultation for evaluation of a 70-year-old male with appetite loss and diminished energy. (Psychiatry)

Initial office consultation for an elementary school-aged patient, referred by pediatrician, with multiple systematic complaints and recent onset of behavioral discontrol. (Psychiatry)

Initial office consultation for a 23-year-old female with developmental facial skeletal anomaly and subsequent abnormal relationship of jaw(s) to cranial base. (Oral & Maxillofacial Surgery)

Initial office consultation for a 45-year-old myopic patient with a one-week history of floaters and a partial retinal detachment. (Ophthalmology)

Initial office consultation for a 65-year-old female with moderate dementia, mild unsteadiness, back pain fatigue on ambulation, intermittent urinary incontinence. (Neurosurgery)

Initial office consultation for a 33-year-old female referred by endocrinologist with amenorrhea and galactorrhea, for evaluation of pituitary tumor. (Neurosurgery)

Initial office consultation for a 34-year-old male with new onset nephrotic syndrome. (Nephrology)

Initial office consultation for a 39-year-old female with intractable chest wall pain secondary to metastatic breast cancer. (Anesthesiology/Pain Medicine)

Initial office consultation for a patient with multiple giant tumors of jaws. (Oral & Maxillofacial Surgery)

Initial office consultation for a patient with a failed total hip replacement with loosening and pain upon walking. (Orthopaedic Surgery)

Initial office consultation for a 60-year-old female with three-year history of intermittent tic-like unilateral facial pain; now constant pain for six weeks without relief by adequate carbamazepine dosage. (Neurosurgery)

Initial office consultation for a 45-year-old male heavy construction worker with prior lumbar disc surgery two years earlier; now gradually recurring low back and unilateral leg pain for three months, unable to work for two weeks. (Neurosurgery)

Initial office consultation of a patient who presents with a 30-year history of smoking and right neck mass. (Otolaryngology, Head & Neck Surgery)

Office consultation with 38-year-old female, with inflammatory bowel disease, who now presents with right lower quadrant pain and suspected intra-abdominal abscess. (General Surgery/Colon & Rectal Surgery)

Office consultation with 72-year-old male with esophageal carcinoma, symptoms of dysphagia, and reflux. (Thoracic Surgery)

Office consultation for discussion of treatment options for a 40-year-old female with a 2-cm adenocarcinoma of the breast. (Radiation Oncology)

Office consultation for young patient referred by pediatrician because of patient's short attention span, easy distractibility, and hyperactivity. (Psychiatry)

Office consultation for 66-year-old female, history of colon resection for adenocarcinoma six years earlier, now with severe mid-back pain; X rays showing osteoporosis and multiple vertebral compression fractures. (Neurosurgery)

Office consultation for a patient with chronic pelvic inflammatory disease who now has left lower quadrant pain with a palpable pelvic mass. (Obstetrics & Gynecology)

Office consultation for a patient with long-standing psoriasis with acute onset of erythroderma, pustular lesions, chills, and fever. Combinations of topical and systemic treatments discussed and instituted. (Dermatology)

99245 Initial office consultation for a 35-year-old multiple-trauma male patient with complex pelvic fractures, for evaluation and formulation of management plan. (Orthopaedic Surgery)

Initial emergency room consultation for 10-year-old male in status epilepticus, recent closed head injury, information about medication not available. (Neurosurgery)

Initial emergency room consultation for a 23-year-old patient with severe abdominal pain, guarding, febrile, and unstable vital signs. (Obstetrics & Gynecology)

Office consultation for a 67-year-old female longstanding uncontrolled diabetic who presents with retinopathy, nephropathy, and a foot ulcer. (Endocrinology)

Office consultation for a 37-year-old male for initial evaluation and management of Cushing's disease. (Endocrinology)

Office consultation for a 60-year-old male who presents with thyrotoxicosis, exophthalmos, frequent premature ventricular contractions and congestive heart failure. (Endocrinology)

Initial office consultation for a 36-year-old patient, one year status post occupational herniated cervical disk treated by laminectomy, requiring management of multiple sites of intractable pain, depression, and narcotic dependence. (Pain Medicine)

Office consultation for a 58-year-old man with a history of MI and CHF who complains of the recent onset of rest angina and shortness of breath. The patient has a systolic blood pressure of 90 mmHG and is in Class IV heart failure. (Cardiology)

Emergency department consultation for a 1-year-old with a three-day history of fever with increasing respiratory distress who is thought to have cardiac tamponade by the ER physician. (Cardiology)

Office consultation in the emergency department for a 25-year-old male with severe, acute, closed head injury. (Neurosurgery)

Office consultation for a 23-year-old female with Stage II A Hodgkins disease with positive supraclavicular and mediastinal nodes. (Radiation Oncology)

Office consultation for a 27-year-old juvenile diabetic patient with severe diabetic retinopathy, gastric atony, nephrotic syndrome and progressive renal failure, now with a serum creatinine of 2.7, and a blood pressure of 170/114. (Nephrology)

Office consultation for independent medical evaluation of a patient with a history of complicated low back and neck problems with previous multiple failed back surgeries. (Orthopaedic Surgery)

Office consultation for an adolescent referred by pediatrician for recent onset of violent and self-injurious behavior. (Psychiatry)

Office consultation for a 6-year-old male for evaluation of severe muscle and joint pain and a diffuse rash. Patient was feeling well until 4 to 6 weeks earlier, when he developed arthralgia, myalgias, and a fever of 102 degrees for one week. (Rheumatology)

Inpatient Consultations

New or Established Patient

99251 Initial hospital consultation for a 27-year-old female with fractured incisor post-intubation. (Oral & Maxillofacial Surgery)

Initial hospital consultation for an orthopaedic patient on IV antibiotics who has developed an apparent candida infection of the oral cavity. (Oral & Maxillofacial Surgery)

Initial inpatient consultation for a 30-year-old female complaining of vaginal itching, post orthopaedic surgery. (Obstetrics & Gynecology)

Initial inpatient consultation for a 36-year-old male on orthopaedic service with complaint of localized dental pain. (Oral & Maxillofacial Surgery)

99252 Initial hospital consultation for a 45-year-old male, previously abstinent alcoholic, who relapsed and was admitted for management of gastritis. The patient readily accepts the need for further treatment. (Addiction Medicine)

Initial hospital consultation for a 35-year-old dialysis patient with episodic oral ulcerations. (Oral & Maxillofacial Surgery)

Initial inpatient preoperative consultation for a 43-year-old female with cholecystitis and well-controlled hypertension. (Cardiology)

Initial inpatient consultation for recommendation of antibiotic prophylaxis for a patient with a synthetic heart valve who will undergo urologic surgery. (Internal Medicine)

Initial inpatient consultation for possible drug induced skin eruption in 50-year-old male. (Dermatology)

Preoperative inpatient consultation for evaluation of hypertension in a 60-year-old male who will undergo a cholecystectomy. Patient had a normal annual check-up in your office four months ago. (Internal Medicine)

Initial inpatient consultation for 66-year-old patient with wrist and hand pain and finger numbness, secondary to carpal tunnel syndrome. (Orthopaedic Surgery/Plastic Surgery)

Initial inpatient consultation for a 66-year-old male smoker referred for pain management immediately status post-biliary tract surgery done via sub-costal incision. (Anesthesiology/Pain Medicine)

99253 Initial hospital consultation for a 50-year-old female with incapacitating knee pain due to generalized rheumatoid arthritis. (Orthopaedic Surgery)

Initial hospital consultation for a 60-year-old male with avascular necrosis of the left femoral heel with increasing pain. (Orthopaedic Surgery)

Initial hospital consultation for a 45-year-old female with compound mandibular fracture and concurrent head, abdominal and/or orthopaedic injuries. (Oral & Maxillofacial Surgery)

Initial hospital consultation for a 22-year-old female, paraplegic, to evaluate wrist and hand pain. (Orthopaedic Surgery)

Initial hospital consultation for a 40-year-old male with 10-day history of incapacitating unilateral sciatica, unable to walk now, not improved by bed rest. (Neurosurgery)

Initial hospital consultation, requested by pediatrician, for treatment recommendations for a patient admitted with persistent inability to walk following soft tissue injury to ankle. (Physiatry)

Initial hospital consultation for a 27-year-old previously healthy male who vomited during IV sedation and may have aspirated gastric contents. (Anesthesiology)

Initial hospital consultation for a 33-year-old female, post-abdominal surgery, who now has a fever. (Internal Medicine)

Initial inpatient consultation for a 57-year-old male, post lower endoscopy, for evaluation of abdominal pain and fever. (General Surgery)

Initial inpatient consultation for rehabilitation of a 73-year-old female one week after surgical management of a hip fracture. (Physical Medicine & Rehabilitation)

Initial inpatient consultation for diagnosis/management of fever following abdominal surgery. (Internal Medicine)

Initial inpatient consultation for a 35-year-old female with a fever and pulmonary infiltrate following cesarean section. (Pulmonary Medicine)

Initial inpatient consultation for a 42-year-old nondiabetic patient, postop cholecystectomy, now with an acute urinary tract infection. (Nephrology)

Initial inpatient consultation for 53-year-old female with moderate uncomplicated pancreatitis. (Gastroenterology)

Initial inpatient consultation for 45-year-old patient with chronic neck pain with radicular pain of the left arm. (Orthopaedic Surgery)

Initial inpatient consultation for 8-year-old patient with new onset of seizures who has a normal examination and previous history. (Neurology)

99254 Initial hospital consultation for a 15-year-old patient with painless swelling of proximal humerus with lytic lesion by X ray. (Orthopaedic Surgery)

Initial hospital consultation for evaluation of a 29-year-old female with a diffusely positive medical review of systems and history of multiple surgeries. (Psychiatry)

Initial hospital consultation for a 70-year-old diabetic female with gangrene of the foot. (Orthopaedic Surgery)

Initial inpatient consultation for a 47-year-old female with progressive pulmonary infiltrate, hypoxemia, and diminished urine output. (Anesthesiology)

Initial hospital consultation for a 13-month-old with spasmodic cough, respiratory distress, and fever. (Allergy & Immunology)

Initial hospital consultation for a patient with failed total hip replacement with loosening and pain upon walking. (Orthopaedic Surgery)

Initial hospital consultation for a 62-year-old female with metastatic breast cancer to the femoral neck and thoracic vertebra. (Orthopaedic Surgery)

Initial hospital consultation for a 39-year-old female with nephrolithiasis requiring extensive opioid analgesics, whose vital signs are now elevated. She initially denied any drug use, but today gives history of multiple substance abuse, including opioids and prior treatment for a personality disorder. (Psychiatry)

Initial hospital consultation for a 70-year-old female without previous psychiatric history, who is now experiencing nocturnal confusion and visual hallucinations following hip replacement surgery. (Psychiatry)

Initial inpatient consultation for evaluation of a 63-year-old in the ICU with diabetes and chronic renal failure who develops acute respiratory distress syndrome 36 hours after a mitral valve replacement. (Anesthesiology)

Initial inpatient consultation for a 66-year-old female with enlarged supraclavicular lymph nodes, found on biopsy to be malignant. (Hematology/Oncology)

Initial inpatient consultation for a 43-year-old female for evaluation of sudden painful visual loss, optic neuritis and episodic paresthesia. (Ophthalmology)

Initial inpatient consultation for evaluation of a 71-year-old male with hyponatremia (serum sodium 114) who was admitted to the hospital with pneumonia. (Nephrology)

Initial inpatient consultation for a 72-year-old male with emergency admission for possible bowel obstruction. (Internal Medicine/General Surgery)

Initial inpatient consultation for a 35-year-old female with fever, swollen joints, and rash of one-week duration. (Rheumatology)

99255 Initial inpatient consultation for a 76-year-old female with massive, life-threatening gastrointestinal hemorrhage and chest pain. (Gastroenterology)

Initial inpatient consultation for a 75-year-old female, admitted to intensive care with acute respiratory distress syndrome, who is hypersensitive, has a moderate metabolic acidosis, and a rising serum creatinine. (Nephrology)

Initial hospital consultation for patient with a history of complicated low back pain and neck problems with previous multiple failed back surgeries. (Orthopaedic Surgery/Neurosurgery)

Initial hospital consultation for a 66-year-old female, two days post-abdominal aneurysm repair, with oliguria and hypertension of one-day duration. (Nephrology/Internal Medicine)

Initial hospital consultation for a patient with shotgun wound to face with massive facial trauma and airway obstruction. (Oral & Maxillofacial Surgery)

Initial hospital consultation for patient with severe pancreatitis complicated by respiratory insufficiency, acute renal failure, and abscess formation. (General Surgery/Colon & Rectal Surgery)

Initial hospital consultation for a 35-year-old multiple-trauma male patient with complex pelvic fractures to evaluate and formulate management plan. (Orthopaedic Surgery)

Initial inpatient consultation for adolescent patient with fractured femur and pelvis who pulled out IVs and disconnected traction in attempt to elope from hospital. (Psychiatry)

Initial hospital consultation for a 16-year-old primigravida at 32-weeks gestation requested by a family practitioner for evaluation of severe hypertension, thrombocytopenia, and headache. (Obstetrics & Gynecology)

Initial hospital consultation for a 58-year-old insulin-dependent diabetic with multiple antibiotic allergies, now with multiple fascial plane abscesses and airway obstruction. (Oral & Maxillofacial Surgery)

Initial inpatient consultation for a 55-year-old male with known cirrhosis and ascites, now with jaundice, encephalopathy, and massive hematemesis. (Gastroenterology)

Initial hospital consultation for a 25-year-old male, seen in emergency room with severe, closed head injury. (Neurosurgery)

Initial hospital consultation for a 2-day-old male with single ventricle physiology and subaortic obstruction. Family counseling following evaluation for multiple, staged surgical procedures. (Thoracic Surgery)

Initial hospital consultation for a 45-year-old male admitted with subarachnoid hemorrhage and intracranial aneurysm on angiogram. (Neurosurgery)

Initial inpatient consultation for myxedematous patient who is hypoventilating and obtunded. (Endocrinology)

Initial hospital consultation for a 45-year-old patient with widely metastatic lung carcinoma, intractable back pain, and a history that includes substance dependence, NSAID allergy, and two prior laminectomies with fusion for low back pain. (Pain Medicine)

Initial hospital consultation for evaluation of treatment options in a 50-year-old patient with cirrhosis, known peptic ulcer disease, hypotension, encephalopathy, and massive acute upper gastrointestinal bleeding which cannot be localized by endoscopy. (Interventional Radiology)

Initial inpatient consultation in the ICU for a 70-year-old male who experienced a cardiac arrest during surgery and was resuscitated. (Cardiology)

Initial inpatient consultation for a patient with severe pancreatitis complicated by respiratory insufficiency, acute renal failure and abscess formation. (Gastroenterology)

Initial inpatient consultation for a 70-year-old cirrhotic male admitted with ascites, jaundice, encephalopathy, and massive hematemesis. (Gastroenterology)

Initial inpatient consultation in the ICU for a 51-year-old patient who is on a ventilator and has a fever two weeks after a renal transplantation. (Infectious Disease)

Initial inpatient consultation for evaluation and formulation of plan for management of multiple trauma patient with complex pelvic fracture, 35-year-old male. (General Surgery/Orthopaedic Surgery)

Initial inpatient consultation for a 50-year-old male with a history of previous myocardial infarction, now with acute pulmonary edema and hypotension. (Cardiology)

Initial inpatient consultation for 45-year-old male with recent, acute subarachnoid hemorrhage, hesitant speech, mildly confused, drowsy. High risk group for HIV+ status. (Neurosurgery)

Initial inpatient consultation for 36-year-old female referred by her internist to evaluate a patient being followed for abdominal pain and fever. The patient has developed diffuse abdominal pain, guarding, rigidity and increased fever. (Obstetrics & Gynecology)

Emergency Department Services

New or Established Patient

99281 Emergency department visit for a patient for removal of sutures from a well-healed, uncomplicated laceration. (Emergency Medicine)

Emergency department visit for a patient for tetanus toxoid immunization. (Emergency Medicine)

Emergency department visit for a patient with several uncomplicated insect bites. (Emergency Medicine)

99282 Emergency department visit for a 20-year-old student who presents with a painful sunburn with blister formation on the back. (Emergency Medicine)

Emergency department visit for a child presenting with impetigo localized to the face. (Emergency Medicine)

Emergency department visit for a patient with a minor traumatic injury of an extremity with localized pain, swelling, and bruising. (Emergency Medicine)

Emergency department visit for an otherwise healthy patient whose chief complaint is a red, swollen cystic lesion on his/her back. (Emergency Medicine)

Emergency department visit for a patient presenting with a rash on both legs after exposure to poison ivy. (Emergency Medicine)

Emergency department visit for a young adult patient with infected sclera and purulent discharge from both eyes without pain, visual disturbance or history of foreign body in either eye. (Emergency Medicine)

99283 Emergency department visit for a sexually active female complaining of vaginal discharge who is afebrile and denies experiencing abdominal or back pain. (Emergency Medicine)

Emergency department visit for a well-appearing 8-year-old who has a fever, diarrhea, and abdominal cramps, is tolerating oral fluids and is not vomiting. (Emergency Medicine)

Emergency department visit for a patient with an inversion ankle injury, who is unable to bear weight on the injured foot and ankle. (Emergency Medicine)

Emergency department visit for a patient who has a complaint of acute pain associated with a suspected foreign body in the painful eye. (Emergency Medicine)

Emergency department visit for a healthy, young adult patient who sustained a blunt head injury with local swelling and bruising without subsequent confusion, loss of consciousness or memory deficit. (Emergency Medicine)

99284 Emergency department visit for a 4-year-old who fell off a bike sustaining a head injury with brief loss of consciousness. (Emergency Medicine)

Emergency department visit for an elderly female who has fallen and is now complaining of pain in her right hip and is unable to walk. (Emergency Medicine)

Emergency department visit for a patient with flank pain and hematuria. (Emergency Medicine)

Emergency department visit for a female presenting with lower abdominal pain and a vaginal discharge. (Emergency Medicine)

99285 Emergency department visit for a patient with a complicated overdose requiring aggressive management to prevent side effects from the ingested materials. (Emergency Medicine)

Emergency department visit for a patient with a new onset of rapid heart rate requiring IV drugs. (Emergency Medicine)

Emergency department visit for a patient exhibiting active, upper gastrointestinal bleeding. (Emergency Medicine)

Emergency department visit for a previously healthy young adult patient who is injured in an automobile accident and is brought to the emergency department immobilized and has symptoms compatible with intra-abdominal injuries or multiple extremity injuries. (Emergency Medicine)

Emergency department visit for a patient with an acute onset of chest pain compatible with symptoms of cardiac ischemia and/or pulmonary embolus. (Emergency Medicine)

Emergency department visit for a patient who presents with a sudden onset of "the worst headache of her life," and complains of a stiff neck, nausea, and inability to concentrate. (Emergency Medicine)

Emergency department visit for a patient with a new onset of a cerebral vascular accident. (Emergency Medicine)

Emergency department visit for acute febrile illness in an adult, associated with shortness of breath and an altered level of alertness. (Emergency Medicine)

Critical Care Services

99291 First hour of critical care of a 65-year-old male with septic shock following relief of ureteral obstruction caused by a stone.

First hour of critical care of a 15-year-old with acute respiratory failure from asthma.

First hour of critical care of a 45-year-old who sustained a liver laceration, cerebral hematoma, flailed chest, and pulmonary contusion after being struck by an automobile.

First hour of critical care of a 65-year-old female who, following a hysterectomy, suffered a cardiac arrest associated with a pulmonary embolus.

First hour of critical care of a 6-month-old with hypovolemic shock secondary to diarrhea and dehydration.

First hour of critical care of a 3-year-old with respiratory failure secondary to pneumocystis carinii pneumonia.

Prolonged Services

Prolonged Physician Service With Direct (Face-to-Face) Patient Contact

Office or Other Outpatient

99354/ 99355 A 20-year-old female with history of asthma presents with acute bronchospasm and moderate respiratory distress. Initial evaluation shows respiratory rate 30, labored breathing and wheezing heard in all lung fields. Office treatment is initiated, which includes intermittent bronchial dilation and subcutaneous epinephrine. Requires intermittent physician face-to-face time with patient over a period of 2 to 3 hours. (Family Medicine/Internal Medicine)

Inpatient

99356 A 34-year-old primigravida presents to hospital in early labor. Admission history and physical reveals severe preeclampsia. Physician supervises management of preeclampsia, IV magnesium initiation and maintenance, labor augmentation with pitocin, and close maternal-fetal monitoring. Physician face-to-face involvement includes 40 minutes of continuous bedside care until the patient is stable, then is intermittent over several hours until the delivery. (Family Medicine/Internal Medicine/Obstetrics & Gynecology)

Prolonged Physician Service Without Direct Patient (Face-to-Face) Contact

99358/ 99359 An 85-year-old new patient with multiple complicated medical problems has moved to the area to live closer to her daughter. She is brought to the primary care office by her daughter and has been seen and examined by the physician. The physician indicated that past medical records would be obtained from the patient's prior physicians' and that he will communicate further with the daughter upon review of them.

Physician Standby Services

99360   A 24-year-old patient is admitted to OB unit attempting VBAC. Fetal monitoring shows increasing fetal distress. Patient's blood pressure is rising and labor progressing slowly. A primary care physician is requested by the OB/GYN to standby in the unit for possible cesarean delivery and neonatal resuscitation. (Family Medicine/Internal Medicine)

Care Plan Oversight Services

99375   First month of care plan oversight for terminal care of a 58-year-old female with advanced intraabdominal ovarian cancer. Care plan includes home oxygen, diuretics IV for edema and ascites control and pain control management involving IV morphine infusion when progressive ileus occurred. Physician phone contacts with nurse, family, and MSW. Discussion with MSW concerning plans to withdraw supportive measures per patient wishes. Documentation includes review and modification of care plan and certifications from nursing, MSW, pharmacy, and DME. (Family Medicine/Internal Medicine)

Appendix D

Summary of CPT Add-on Codes

This listing is a summary of CPT add-on codes for *CPT 2010*. The codes listed below are identified in *CPT 2010* with a + symbol.

01953	15361	22841	33961
01968	15366	22842	34806
01969	15401	22843	34808
11001	15421	22844	34813
11008	15431	22845	34826
11101	15787	22846	35306
11201	15847	22847	35390
11732	16036	22848	35400
11922	17003	22851	35500
13102	17312	26125	35572
13122	17314	26861	35600
13133	17315	26863	35681
13153	19001	27358	35682
14302	19126	27692	35683
15003	19291	31620	35685
15005	19295	31627	35686
15101	19297	31632	35697
15111	20930	31633	35700
15116	20931	31637	36148
15121	20936	32501	36218
15131	20937	33141	36248
15136	20938	33225	36476
15151	20985	33257	36479
15152	22103	33258	37185
15156	22116	33259	37186
15157	22208	33508	37206
15171	22216	33517	37208
15176	22226	33518	37250
15201	22328	33519	37251
15221	22522	33521	38102
15241	22525	33522	38746
15261	22527	33523	38747
15301	22534	33530	43273
15321	22585	33572	43635
15331	22614	33768	44015
15336	22632	33884	44121
15341	22840	33924	44128

44139	63295	77051
44203	63308	77052
44213	63621	78020
44701	64480	78496
44955	64484	78730
47001	64491	83901
47550	64492	86826
48400	64494	87187
49326	64495	87904
49435	64623	88155
49568	64627	88185
49905	64727	88311
51797	64778	88314
56606	64783	88388
57267	64787	90466
58110	64832	90468
58611	64837	90472
59525	64859	90474
60512	64872	92547
61316	64874	92608
61517	64876	92627
61609	64901	92973
61610	64902	92974
61611	65757	92978
61612	66990	92979
61641	67225	92981
61642	67320	92984
61795	67331	92996
61797	67332	92998
61799	67334	93320
61800	67335	93321
61864	67340	93325
61868	69990	93352
62148	74301	93571
62160	75565	93572
63035	75774	93609
63043	75946	93613
63044	75964	93621
63048	75968	93622
63057	75993	93623
63066	75996	93662
63076	76125	94645
63078	76802	95873
63082	76810	95874
63086	76812	95920
63088	76814	95962
63091	76937	95967
63103	77001	95973

95975	0174T
95979	0189T
96361	0190T
96366	0196T
96367	0205T
96368	
96370	
96371	
96375	
96376	
96411	
96415	
96417	
96423	
96570	
96571	
97546	
97811	
97814	
99100	
99116	
99135	
99140	
99145	
99150	
99292	
99354	
99355	
99356	
99357	
99359	
99467	
99602	
99607	
0054T	
0055T	
0076T	
0079T	
0081T	
0092T	
0095T	
0098T	
0159T	
0163T	
0164T	
0165T	
0172T	
0173T	

Appendix E

Summary of CPT Codes Exempt from Modifier 51

This listing is a summary of CPT codes that are exempt from the use of modifier 51. Procedures on this list are typically performed with another procedure but may be a stand alone procedure and not always be performed with other specified procedures. For add-on codes see Appendix D. This is not an exhaustive list of procedures that are typically exempt from multiple procedure reductions. The codes listed below are identified in *CPT 2010* with a ⊘ symbol.

17004

20697

20974

20975

31500

36620

44500

61107

93503

93539

93540

93544

93545

93555

93556

93600

93602

93603

93610

93612

93615

93616

93618

93631

94610

95900

95903

95904

95905

95992

99143

99144

Appendix F

Summary of CPT Codes Exempt from Modifier 63

The listing is a summary of CPT codes that are exempt from the use of modifier 63. The codes listed below are additionally identified in *CPT 2010* with the parenthetical instruction "(Do not report modifier 63 in conjunction with...)"

30540	36660	63700
30545	39503	63702
31520	43313	63704
33401	43314	63706
33403	43520	65820
33470	43831	
33472	44055	
33502	44126	
33503	44127	
33505	44128	
33506	46070	
33610	46705	
33611	46715	
33619	46716	
33647	46730	
33670	46735	
33690	46740	
33694	46742	
33730	46744	
33732	47700	
33735	47701	
33736	49215	
33750	49491	
33755	49492	
33762	49495	
33778	49496	
33786	49600	
33922	49605	
33960	49606	
33961	49610	
36415	49611	
36420	53025	
36450	54000	
36460	54150	
36510	54160	

Appendix G

Summary of CPT Codes That Include Moderate (Conscious) Sedation

The following list of procedures includes conscious sedation as an inherent part of providing the procedure. These codes are identified in the CPT codebook with a ⊙ symbol.

Since these services include moderate sedation, it is not appropriate for the same physician to report both the service and the sedation codes 99143-99145. It is expected that if conscious sedation is provided to the patient as part of one of these services, it is provided by the same physician who is providing the service.

In the unusual event when a second physician other than the health care professional performing the diagnostic or therapeutic services provides moderate sedation in the facility setting (eg, hospital, outpatient hospital/ambulatory surgery center, skilled nursing facility) for the procedures listed in Appendix G, the second physician can report 99148-99150. However, for the circumstance in which these services are performed by the second physician in the nonfacility setting (eg, physician office, freestanding imaging center), codes 99148-99150 would not be reported. Moderate sedation does not include minimal sedation (anxiolysis), deep sedation, or monitored anesthesia care (00100-01999).

The inclusion of a procedure on this list does not prevent separate reporting of an associated anesthesia procedure/service (CPT codes 00100-01999) when performed by a physician other than the health care professional performing the diagnostic or therapeutic procedure. In such cases the person providing anesthesia services shall be present for the purpose of continuously monitoring the patient and shall not act as a surgical assistant. When clinical conditions of the patient require such anesthesia services, or in the circumstances when the patient does not require sedation, the operating physician is not required to report the procedure as a reduced service using modifier 52.

19298	31622	31635	32553	33212	37186	43263
20982	31623	31645	33010	33213	37187	43264
22520	31624	31646	33011	33214	37188	43265
22521	31625	31656	33206	33216	37203	43267
22526	31626	31725	33207	33217	37210	43268
22527	31627	32201	33208	33218	37215	43269
31615	31628	32550	33210	33220	37216	43271
31620	31629	32551	33211	33222	43200	43272
				33223	43201	43273
				33233	43202	43453
				33234	43204	43456
				33235	43205	43458
				33240	43215	44360
				33241	43216	44361
				33244	43217	44363
				33249	43219	44364
				35470	43220	44365
				35471	43226	44366
				35472	43227	44369
				35473	43228	44370
				35474	43231	44372
				35475	43232	44373
				35476	43234	44376
				36147	43235	44377
				36148	43236	44378
				36481	43237	44379
				36555	43238	44380
				36557	43239	44382
				36558	43240	44383
				36560	43241	44385
				36561	43242	44386
				36563	43243	44388
				36565	43244	44389
				36566	43245	44390
				36568	43246	44391
				36570	43247	44392
				36571	43248	44393
				36576	43249	44394
				36578	43250	44397
				36581	43251	44500
				36582	43255	44901
				36583	43256	45303
				36585	43257	45305
				36590	43258	45307
				36870	43259	45308
				37183	43260	45309
				37184	43261	45315
				37185	43262	45317

45320	58823	93544
45321	66720	93545
45327	69300	93555
45332	77371	93556
45333	77600	93561
45334	77605	93562
45335	77610	93571
45337	77615	93572
45338	92953	93609
45339	92960	93613
45340	92961	93615
45341	92973	93616
45342	92974	93618
45345	92975	93619
45355	92978	93620
45378	92979	93621
45379	92980	93622
45380	92981	93624
45381	92982	93640
45382	92984	93641
45383	92986	93642
45384	92987	93650
45385	92995	93651
45386	92996	93652
45387	93312	94011
45391	93313	94012
45392	93314	94013
47011	93315	0200T
47382	93316	0201T
47525	93317	
48511	93318	
49021	93501	
49041	93505	
49061	93508	
49411	93510	
49440	93511	
49441	93514	
49442	93524	
49446	93526	
50021	93527	
50200	93528	
50382	93529	
50384	93530	
50385	93539	
50386	93540	
50387	93541	
50592	93542	
50593	93543	

Appendix H

Alphabetic Index of Performance Measures by Clinical Condition or Topic

The Alphabetic Index of Performance Measures by Clinical Condition/Topic (ie, Appendix H) has been removed from the CPT Codebook. Since this document is a dynamic, rapidly expanding source of information, the Alphabetic Index of Performance Measures by Clinical Topic has been transferred to be accessed solely on the AMA web site at www.ama-assn.org/go/cpt.

In addition, the revised codes for the publication cycle (ie, **the Update to List of Category II Codes**) will continue to be located on the AMA web site and also in the CPT Codebook for the following publication cycle (subsequent to its listing to the web).

Appendix I

Genetic Testing Code Modifiers

This listing of modifiers is intended for reporting with molecular laboratory procedures related to genetic testing. Genetic testing modifiers should be used in conjunction with CPT and HCPCS codes to provide diagnostic granularity of service to enable providers to submit complete and precise genetic testing information without altering test descriptors. These two-character modifiers are categorized by mutation. The first (numeric) character indicates the disease category and the second (alpha) character denotes gene type. Introductory guidelines in the molecular diagnostic and molecular cytogenetic code sections of the CPT codebook provide further guidance in interpretation and application of genetic testing modifiers.

Neoplasia (Solid Tumor, Excluding Sarcoma and Lymphoma)

0A   BRCA1 (hereditary breast/ovarian cancer)

0B   BRCA2 (hereditary breast cancer)

0C   Neurofibromin (neurofibromatosis, type 1)

0D   Merlin (neurofibromatosis, type 2)

0E   c-RET (multiple endocrine neoplasia, types 2A/B, familial medullary thyroid carcinoma)

0F   VHL (Von Hippel Lindau disease, renal carcinoma)

0G   SDHD (hereditary paraganglioma)

0H   SDHB (hereditary paraganglioma)

0I   ERRB2, commonly called Her-2/neu

0J   MLH1 (HNPCC, mismatch repair genes)

0K   MSH2, MSH6, or PMS2 (HNPCC, mismatch repair genes)

0L   APC (hereditary polyposis coli)

0M   Rb (retinoblastoma)

0N   TP53, commonly called p53

0O   PTEN (Cowden's syndrome)

0P   KIT, also called CD117 (gastrointestinal stromal tumor)

0Z   Solid tumor gene, not otherwise specified

Neoplasia (Sarcoma)

1A   WT1 or WT2 (Wilm's tumor)

1B   PAX3, PAX7, or FOXO1A (alveolar rhabdomyosarcoma)

1C   FLI1, ERG, ETV1, or EWSR1 (Ewing's sarcoma, desmoplastic round cell)

1D   DDIT3 or FUS (myxoid liposarcoma)

1E   NR4A3, RBF56, or TCF12 (myxoid chondrosarcoma)

1F   SSX1, SSX2, or SYT (synovial sarcoma)

1G   MYCN (neuroblastoma)

1H   COL1A1 or PDGFB (dermatofibrosarcoma protruberans)

1I   TFE3 or ASPSCR1 (alveolar soft parts sarcoma)

1J   JAZF1 or JJAZ1 (endometrial stromal sarcoma)

1Z   Sarcoma gene, not otherwise specified

Neoplasia (Lymphoid/Hematopoietic)

2A   RUNX1 or CBFA2T1, commonly called AML1 or ETO, genes associated with t(8;21) AML1—also ETO (acute myelogenous leukemia)

2B   BCR or ABL1, genes associated with t(9;22) (chronic myelogenous or acute leukemia) BCR— also ABL (chronic myeloid, acute lymphoid leukemia)

2C   PBX1 or TCF3, genes associated with t(1;19) (acute lymphoblastic leukemia) CGF1

2D   CBFB or MYH11, genes associated with inv 16 (acute myelogenous leukemia) CBF beta (leukemia)

2E   MLL (acute leukemia)

2F   PML or RARA, genes associated with t(15;17) (acute promyelocytic leukemia) PML/RAR alpha (promyelocytic leukemia)

2G   ETV6, commonly called TEL, gene associated with t(12;21) (acute leukemia) TEL (Leukemia)

2H   BCL2 (B cell lymphoma, follicle center cell origin) bcl-2 (Lymphoma)

2I   CCND1, commonly called BCL1, cyclin D1 (Mantle cell lymphoma, myeloma) bcl-1 (lymphoma)

2J   MYC (Burkitt lymphoma) c-myc (lymphoma)

2K   IgH (lymphoma/leukemia)

2L   IGK (lymphoma/leukemia)

2M   TRB, T cell receptor beta (lymphoma/leukemia)

2N   TRG, T cell receptor gamma (lymphoma/leukemia)

2O SIL or TAL1 (T cell leukemia)

2T BCL6 (B cell lymphoma)

2Q API1 or MALT1 (MALT lymphoma)

2R NPM or ALK, genes associated with t(2;5) (anaplastic large cell lymphoma)

2S FLT3 (Acute myelogenous leukemia)

2Z Lymphoid/hematopoietic neoplasia, not otherwise specified

Non-Neoplastic Hematology/Coagulation

3A F5, commonly called Factor V (Leiden, others) (hypercoagulable state)

3B FACC (Fanconi anemia)

3C FACD (Fanconi anemia)

3D HBB, beta globin (thalassemia, sickle cell anemia, other hemoglobinopathies)

3E HBA, commonly called alpha globin (thalassemia)

3F MTHFR (elevated homocystinemia)

3G F2, commonly called prothrombin (20210, others) (hypercoagulable state) prothrombin (factor II, 20210A) (hypercoagulable state)

3H F8, commonly called factor VIII (hemophilia A/VWF)

3I F9, commonly called factor IX (hemophilia B)

3K F13, commonly called factor XIII (bleeding or hypercoagulable state) beta globin

3Z Non-neoplastic hematology/coagulation, not otherwise specified

Histocompatiblity/Blood Typing/Identity/Microsatellite

4A HLA-A

4B HLA-B

4C HLA-C

4D HLA-D

4E HLA-DR

4F HLA-DQ

4G HLA-DP

4H Kell

4I Fingerprint for engraftment (post allogeneic progenitor cell transplant)

4J Fingerprint for donor allelotype (allogeneic transplant)

4K Fingerprint for recipient allelotype (allogeneic transplant)

4L Fingerprint for leukocyte chimerism (allogeneic solid organ transplant)

4M Fingerprint for maternal versus fetal origin

4N Microsatellite instability

4O Microsatellite loss (loss of heterozygosity)

4Z Histocompatiblity/blood typing, not otherwise specified

Neurologic, Non-Neoplastic

5A ASPA, commonly called Aspartoacylase A (Canavan disease)

5B FMR-1 (fragile X, FRAXA, syndrome)

5C FRDA, commonly called Frataxin (Freidreich ataxia)

5D HD, commonly called Huntington (Huntington's disease)

5E GABRA5, NIPA1, UBE3A, or ANCR GABRA (Prader Willi-Angelman syndrome)

5F GJB2, commonly called Connexin-26 (hereditary hearing loss) Connexin-32 (GJB2) (hereditary deafness)

5G GJB1, commonly called Connexin-32 (X-linked Charcot-Marie-Tooth disease)

5H SNRPN (Prader Willi-Angelman syndrome)

5I SCA1, commonly called Ataxin-1 (spinocerebellar ataxia, type 1)

5J SCA2, commonly called Ataxin-2 (spinocerebellar ataxia, type 2)

5K MJD, commonly called Ataxin-3 (spinocerebellar ataxia, type 3, Machado-Joseph disease)

5L CACNA1A (spinocerebellar ataxia, type 6)

5M ATXN7 Ataxin-7 (spinocerebellar ataxia, type 7)

5N PMP-22 (Charcot-Marie-Tooth disease, type 1A)

5O MECP2 (Rett syndrome)

5Z Neurologic, non-neoplastic, not otherwise specified

Muscular, Non-Neoplastic

6A DMD, commonly called dystrophin (Duchenne/Becker muscular dystrophy)

6B DMPK (myotonic dystrophy, type 1)

6C ZNF-9 (myotonic dystrophy, type 2)

6D SMN1/SMN2 (autosomal recessive spinal muscular atrophy)

6E MTTK, commonly called tRNAlys (myotonic epilepsy, MERRF)

6F MTTL1, commonly called tRNAleu (mitochondrial encephalomyopathy, MELAS)

6Z Muscular, not otherwise specified

Metabolic, Other

7A APOE, commonly called apolipoprotein E (cardiovascular disease or Alzheimer's disease)

7B NPC1 or NPC2, commonly called sphingomyelin phosphodiesterase (Nieman-Pick disease)

7C GBA, commonly called acid beta glucosidase (Gaucher disease)

7D HFE (hemochromatosis)

7E HEXA, commonly called hexosaminidase A (Tay-Sachs disease)

7F ACADM (medium chain acyl CoA dehydrogenase deficiency)

7Z Metabolic, other, not otherwise specified

Metabolic, Transport

8A CFTR (cystic fibrosis)

8B PRSS1 (hereditary pancreatitis)

8C Long QT syndrome, KCN (Jervell and Lange-Nielsen syndromes, types 1, 2, 5, and 6) and SCN (Brugada syndrome, SIDS and type 3)

8Z Metabolic, transport, not otherwise specified

Metabolic-Pharmacogenetics

9A TPMT, commonly called (thiopurine methyltransferase) (patients on antimetabolite therapy)

9B CYP2 genes, commonly called cytochrome p450 (drug metabolism)

9C ABCB1, commonly called MDR1 or p-glycoprotein (drug transport)

9D NAT2 (drug metabolism)

9L Metabolic-pharmacogenetics, not otherwise specified

Dysmorphology

9M FGFR1 (Pfeiffer and Kallman syndromes)

9N FGFR2 (Crouzon, Jackson-Weiss, Apert, Saethre-Chotzen syndromes)

9O FGFR3 (achondroplasia, hypochondroplasia, thanatophoric dysplasia, types I and II, Crouzon syndrome with acanthosis nigricans, Muencke syndromes)

9P TWIST (Saethre-Chotzen syndrome)

9Q DGCR, commonly called CATCH-22 (DiGeorge and 22q11 deletion syndromes)

9Z Dysmorphology, not otherwise specified

Appendix J

Electrodiagnostic Medicine Listing of Sensory, Motor, and Mixed Nerves

This summary assigns each sensory, motor, and mixed nerve with its appropriate nerve conduction study code in order to enhance accurate reporting of codes 95900, 95903, and 95904. Each nerve constitutes one unit of service.

Motor Nerves Assigned to Codes 95900 and 95903

I. Upper extremity, cervical plexus, and brachial plexus motor nerves
- A. Axillary motor nerve to the deltoid
- B. Long thoracic motor nerve to the serratus anterior
- C. Median nerve
    1. Median motor nerve to the abductor pollicis brevis
    2. Median motor nerve, anterior interosseous branch, to the flexor pollicis longus
    3. Median motor nerve, anterior interosseous branch, to the pronator quadratus
    4. Median motor nerve to the first lumbrical
    5. Median motor nerve to the second lumbrical
- D. Musculocutaneous motor nerve to the biceps brachii
- E. Radial nerve
    1. Radial motor nerve to the extensor carpi ulnaris
    2. Radial motor nerve to the extensor digitorum communis
    3. Radial motor nerve to the extensor indicis proprius
    4. Radial motor nerve to the brachioradialis
- F. Suprascapular nerve
    1. Suprascapular motor nerve to the supraspinatus
    2. Suprascapular motor nerve to the infraspinatus
- G. Thoracodorsal motor nerve to the latissimus dorsi
- H. Ulnar nerve
    1. Ulnar motor nerve to the abductor digiti minimi
    2. Ulnar motor nerve to the palmar interosseous
    3. Ulnar motor nerve to the first dorsal interosseous
    4. Ulnar motor nerve to the flexor carpi ulnaris
- I. Other

II. Lower extremity motor nerves
- A. Femoral motor nerve to the quadriceps
    1. Femoral motor nerve to vastus medialis
    2. Femoral motor nerve to vastus lateralis
    3. Femoral motor nerve to vastus intermedialis
    4. Femoral motor nerve to rectus femoris
- B. Ilioinguinal motor nerve
- C. Peroneal (fibular) nerve
    1. Peroneal motor nerve to the extensor digitorum brevis
    2. Peroneal motor nerve to the peroneus brevis
    3. Peroneal motor nerve to the peroneus longus
    4. Peroneal motor nerve to the tibialis anterior
- D. Plantar motor nerve
- E. Sciatic nerve
- F. Tibial nerve
    1. Tibial motor nerve, inferior calcaneal branch, to the abductor digiti minimi
    2. Tibial motor nerve, medial plantar branch, to the abductor hallucis
    3. Tibial motor nerve, lateral plantar branch, to the flexor digiti minimi brevis
- G. Other

III. Cranial nerves and trunk
- A. Cranial nerve VII (facial motor nerve)
    1. Facial nerve to the frontalis
    2. Facial nerve to the nasalis
    3. Facial nerve to the orbicularis oculi
    4. Facial nerve to the orbicularis oris
- B. Cranial nerve XI (spinal accessory motor nerve)
- C. Cranial nerve XII (hypoglossal motor nerve)
- D. Intercostal motor nerve
- E. Phrenic motor nerve to the diaphragm
- F. Recurrent laryngeal nerve
- G. Other

IV. Nerve Roots
- A. Cervical nerve root stimulation
    1. Cervical level 5 (CT)
    2. Cervical level 6 (C6)
    3. Cervical level 7 (C7)
    4. Cervical level 8 (C8)

B. Thoracic nerve root stimulation
1. Thoracic level 1 (T1)
2. Thoracic level 2 (T2)
3. Thoracic level 3 (T3)
4. Thoracic level 4 (T4)
5. Thoracic level 5 (T5)
6. Thoracic level 6 (T6)
7. Thoracic level 7 (T7)
8. Thoracic level 8 (T8)
9. Thoracic level 9 (T9)
10. Thoracic level 10 (T10)
11. Thoracic level 11 (T11)
12. Thoracic level 12 (T12)
C. Lumbar nerve root stimulation
1. Lumbar level 1 (L1)
2. Lumbar level 2 (L2)
3. Lumbar level 3 (L3)
4. Lumbar level 4 (L4)
5. Lumbar level 5 (L5)
D. Sacral nerve root stimulation
1. Sacral level 1 (S1)
2. Sacral level 2 (S2)
3. Sacral level 3 (S3)
4. Sacral level 4 (S4)

Sensory and Mixed Nerves Assigned to Code 95904

I. Upper extremity sensory and mixed nerves
A. Lateral antebrachial cutaneous sensory nerve
B. Medial antebrachial cutaneous sensory nerve
C. Medial brachial cutaneous sensory nerve
D. Median nerve
1. Median sensory nerve to the first digit
2. Median sensory nerve to the second digit
3. Median sensory nerve to the third digit
4. Median sensory nerve to the fourth digit
5. Median palmar cutaneous sensory nerve
6. Median palmar mixed nerve
E. Posterior antebrachial cutaneous sensory nerve
F. Radial sensory nerve
1. Radial sensory nerve to the base of the thumb
2. Radial sensory nerve to digit 1
G. Ulnar nerve
1. Ulnar dorsal cutaneous sensory nerve
2. Ulnar sensory nerve to the fourth digit
3. Ulnar sensory nerve to the fifth digit
4. Ulnar palmar mixed nerve
H. Intercostal sensory nerve
I. Other

II. Lower extremity sensory and mixed nerves
A. Lateral femoral cutaneous sensory nerve
B. Medial calcaneal sensory nerve
C. Medial femoral cutaneous sensory nerve
D. Peroneal nerve
1. Deep peroneal sensory nerve
2. Superficial peroneal sensory nerve, medial dorsal cutaneous branch
3. Superficial peroneal sensory nerve, intermediate dorsal cutaneous branch
E. Posterior femoral cutaneous sensory nerve
F. Saphenous nerve
1. Saphenous sensory nerve (distal technique)
2. Saphenous sensory nerve (proximal technique)
G. Sural nerve
1. Sural sensory nerve, lateral dorsal cutaneous branch
2. Sural sensory nerve
H. Tibial sensory nerve (digital nerve to toe 1)
I. Tibial sensory nerve (medial plantar nerve)
J. Tibial sensory nerve (lateral plantar nerve)
K. Other
III. Head and trunk sensory nerves
A. Dorsal nerve of the penis
B. Greater auricular nerve
C. Ophthalmic branch of the trigeminal nerve
D. Pudendal sensory nerve
E. Suprascapular sensory nerves
F. Other

The following table provides a reasonable maximum number of studies performed per diagnostic category necessary for a physician to arrive at a diagnosis in 90% of patients with that final diagnosis. The numbers in each column represent the number of studies recommended. The appropriate number of studies to be performed is based upon the physician's discretion.

Indication	Needle EMG (95860-95864, 95867-95870)	Nerve Conduction Studies (95900, 95903, 95904)		Other EMG Studies (95934, 95936, 95937)	
		Motor NCS With and/or Without F wave	Sensory NCS	H-Reflex	Neuromuscular Junction Testing (Repetitive Stimulation)
Carpal Tunnel (Unilateral)	1	3	4	—	—
Carpal Tunnel (Bilateral)	2	4	6	—	—
Radiculopathy	2	3	2	2	—
Mononeuropathy	1	3	3	2	—
Polyneuropathy/Mononeuropathy Multiplex	3	4	4	2	—
Myopathy	2	2	2	—	2
Motor Neuronopathy (eg, ALS)	4	4	2	—	2
Plexopathy	2	4	6	2	—
Neuromuscular Junction	2	2	2	—	3
Tarsal Tunnel Syndrome (Unilateral)	1	4	4	—	—
Tarsal Tunnel Syndrome (Bilateral)	2	5	6	—	—
Weakness, Fatigue, Cramps, or Twitching (Focal)	2	3	4	—	2
Weakness, Fatigue, Cramps, or Twitching (General)	4	4	4	—	2
Pain, Numbness, or Tingling (Unilateral)	1	3	4	2	—
Pain, Numbness, or Tingling (Bilateral)	2	4	6	2	—

Appendix K

Product Pending FDA Approval

Some vaccine products have been assigned a CPT Category I code in anticipation of future approval from the Food and Drug Administration (FDA). Following is a list of the vaccine product codes pending FDA approval status that are identified in the CPT codebook with the (⊮) symbol. Upon revision of the approval status by the FDA, notation of this revision will be provided via the AMA CPT "Category I Vaccine Codes" Internet listing (www.ama-assn.org/ama/pub/category/10902.html) and in subsequent publications of the CPT codebook.

90650

90661

90662

90663

90670

Appendix L

Vascular Families

Assignment of branches to first, second, and third order in this table makes the assumption that the starting point is catheterization of the aorta. This categorization would not be accurate, for instance, if a femoral or carotid artery were catheterized directly in an antegrade direction. Arteries highlighted in bold are those more commonly reported during arteriographic procedures.

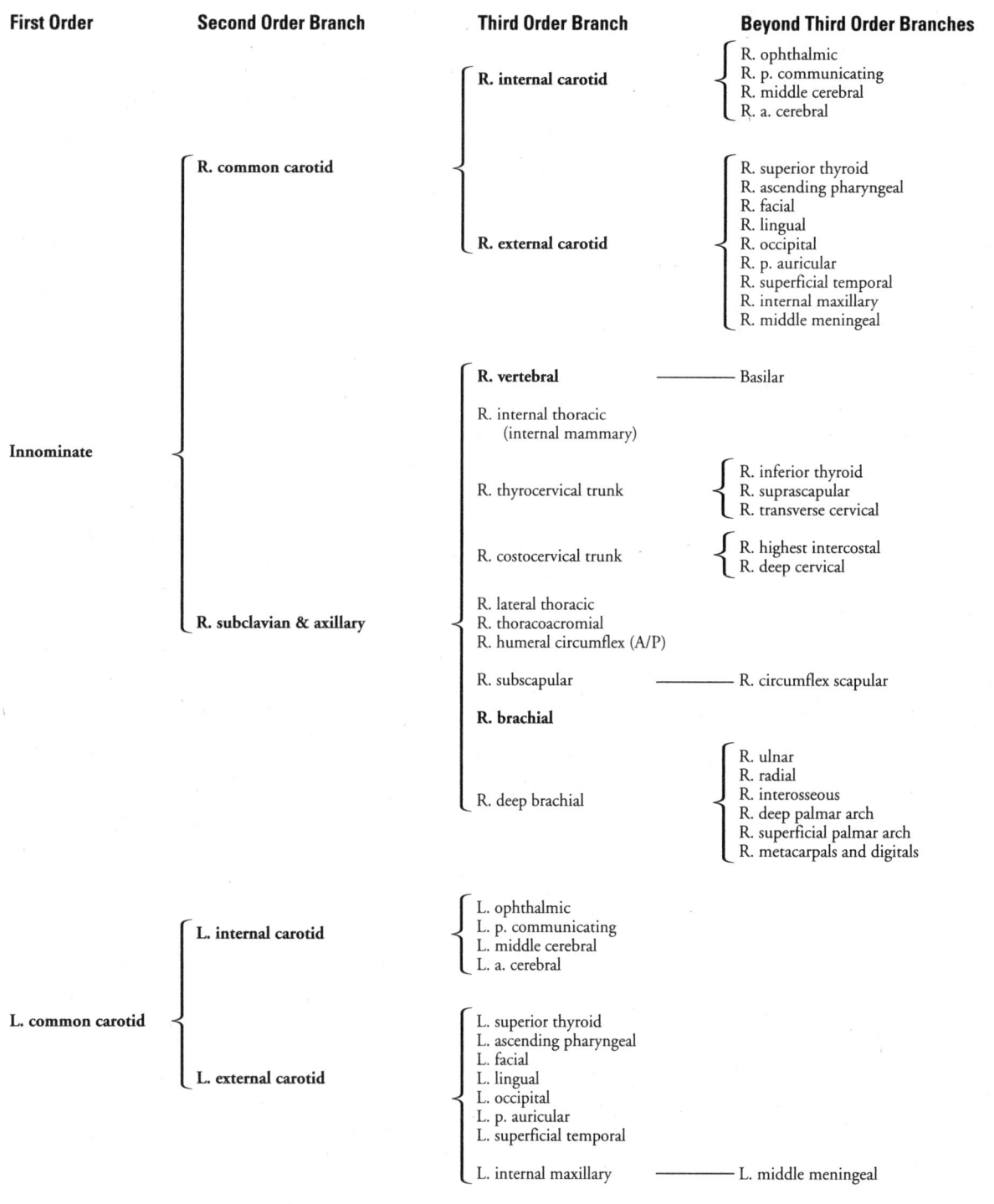

First Order	Second Order Branch	Third Order Branch	Beyond Third Order Branches
		R. internal carotid	R. ophthalmic R. p. communicating R. middle cerebral R. a. cerebral
	R. common carotid	**R. external carotid**	R. superior thyroid R. ascending pharyngeal R. facial R. lingual R. occipital R. p. auricular R. superficial temporal R. internal maxillary R. middle meningeal
Innominate		**R. vertebral**	—— Basilar
		R. internal thoracic (internal mammary)	
		R. thyrocervical trunk	R. inferior thyroid R. suprascapular R. transverse cervical
		R. costocervical trunk	R. highest intercostal R. deep cervical
	R. subclavian & axillary	R. lateral thoracic R. thoracoacromial R. humeral circumflex (A/P)	
		R. subscapular	—— R. circumflex scapular
		R. brachial	
		R. deep brachial	R. ulnar R. radial R. interosseous R. deep palmar arch R. superficial palmar arch R. metacarpals and digitals
	L. internal carotid	L. ophthalmic L. p. communicating L. middle cerebral L. a. cerebral	
L. common carotid	**L. external carotid**	L. superior thyroid L. ascending pharyngeal L. facial L. lingual L. occipital L. p. auricular L. superficial temporal	
		L. internal maxillary	—— L. middle meningeal

R = right, L = left, A = anterior, P = posterior

First Order	Second Order Branch	Third Order Branch	Beyond Third Order Branches

L. vertebral
L. internal thoracic (internal mammary)

L. thyrocervical trunk
{ L. inferior thyroid
L. suprascapular
L. transverse cervical

L. costocervical trunk
{ L. highest intercostal
L. deep cervical

L. subclavian & axillary
L. lateral thoracic
L. thoracoacromial
L. humeral circumflex (A/P)
L. subscapular ——— L. circumflex scapular
L. brachial

L. deep brachial
{ L. ulnar
L. radial
L. interosseous
{ L. deep palmar arch
L. superficial palmar arch
L. metacarpals and digitals

Intercostals

Bronchials

Recurrent esophageal

Inferior phrenic ——— Superior suprarenal

L. gastric ——— Esophageal branch

Splenic
{ Dorsal pancreatic ——— Inferior transverse pancreatic
Great pancreatic
Caudal pancreatic
Gastroepiploic
Short gastrics

Celiac trunk

Common hepatic
{ Gastroduodenal
{ P. superior pancreaticoduodenal
A. superior pancreaticoduodenal

Proper Hepatic
{ L. hepatic
R. hepatic
Cystic
Gastroepiploic
Supraduodenal
Intermediate hepatic

Middle suprarenal

Middle colic

Inferior pancreaticoduodenal
{ P. inferior pancreaticoduodenal
A. inferior pancreaticoduodenal

Superior mesenteric
Jejunal
Ileocolic
Appendicular
P. cecal
A. cecal
Marginal
R. colic

R = right, L = left, A = anterior, P = posterior

First Order	Second Order Branch	Third Order Branch	Beyond Third Order Branches

Renal ———————— Inferior suprarenal

Testicular / Ovarian

Lumbar

Inferior mesenteric { L. colic

Sigmoid { Rectosigmoid / Superior rectal

Middle sacral

Common Iliac

Internal iliac { Iliolumbar / Lateral sacral / Superior gluteal / Umbilical / Superior vesical / Obturator / Inferior vesical / Middle rectal / Inferior rectal / Internal pudendal / Inferior gluteal

External iliac { Inferior epigastric { Cremasteric / Pubic

Deep circumflex iliac ———— Ascending deep circumflex iliac

Common femoral

Profunda femoris { Medial descending / Perforating branches / Lateral descending / Lateral circumflex

Deep external pudendal / Superficial external pudendal / Ascending lateral circumflex femoral / Descending lateral circumflex femoral / Transverse lateral circumflex femoral

Superficial femoral { Geniculate / **Popliteal** / **A. tibial** / **Peroneal** / **P. tibial**

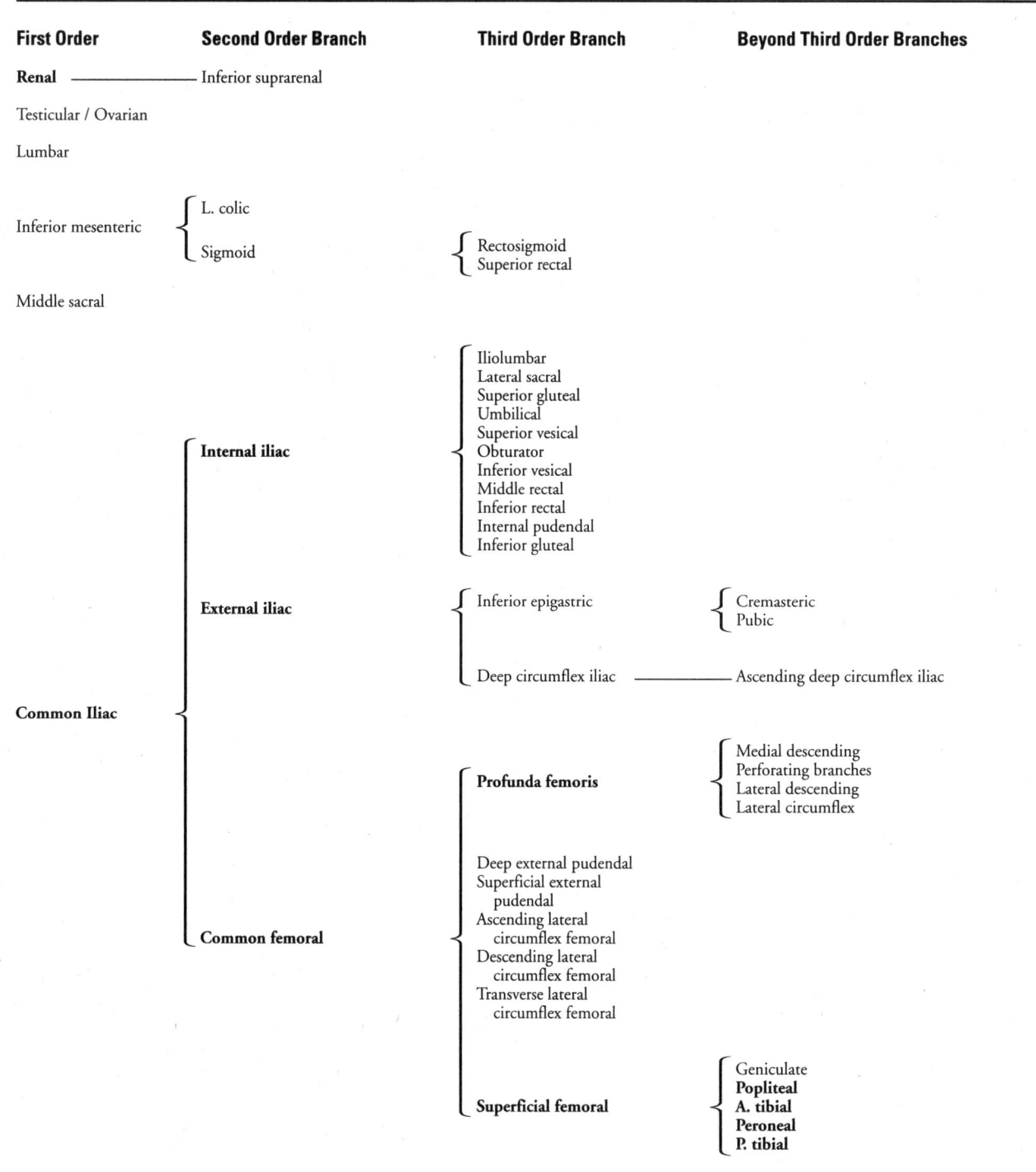

R. & L. main pulmonary arteries
(venous selective)

Reference: Kadir S. *Atlas of Normal and Variant Angiographic Anatomy.* Philadephia, Pa: WB Saunders Co; 1991.
R = right, L = left, A = anterior, P = posterior

Appendix M

Summary of Crosswalked Deleted CPT Codes

This listing is a summary of crosswalked deleted and renumbered codes and descriptors with the associated CPT Assistant references for the deleted codes

Current Code(s)	Deleted/Former Code	Year Code Deleted	Citations Referencing Former Code—Applicable To Current Code(s)
89240	0058T	2009	Jun 04:8 CPT Changes: An Insider's View 2004
89240	0059T	2009	CPT Changes: An Insider's View 2004
41530	0088T	2009	May 05:7, Sep 05:9 CPT Changes: An Insider's View 2005
95803	0089T	2009	Jun 05:6, Feb 06:1 CPT Changes: An Insider's View 2006
22856	0090T	2009	Jun 05:6, Feb 06:1 CPT Changes: An Insider's View 2006, 2007
22864	0093T	2009	Jun 05:6, Feb 06:1 CPT Changes: An Insider's View 2006, 2007
22861	0096T	2009	Jun 05:6, Feb 06:1 CPT Changes: An Insider's View 2006, 2007
55706	0137T	2009	CPT Changes: An Insider's View 2006
95980-95982	0162T	2009	CPT Changes: An Insider's View 2007
1123F, 1124F	1080F	2009	CPT Changes: An Insider's View 2008
0054T, 0055T	20986	2009	CPT Changes: An Insider's View 2008
0054T, 0055T	20987	2009	CPT Changes: An Insider's View 2008
4177F	4007F	2009	CPT Changes: An Insider's View 2008
52214	52606	2009	Apr 01:4
52601	52612	2009	Apr 01:4
52601	52614	2009	Apr 01:4
52630	52620	2009	Apr 01:4
61796-61800, 63620, 63621	61793	2009	Nov 97:23, May 03:19, Apr 04:15, Jan 06:46
77785, 77786	77781	2009	Winter 90:10, Winter 91:23, Mar 99:3, Feb 02:7, Mar 02:2, Sep 05:1, Nov 05:15
77785-77787	77782	2009	Winter 90:10, Winter 91:23, Mar 99:3, Feb 02:7, Mar 02:2, Sep 05:1, Nov 05:15
77785-77787	77783	2009	Winter 90:10, Winter 91:23, Mar 99:3, Feb 02:7, Mar 02:2, Sep 05:1, Nov 05:15
77785-77787	77784	2009	Winter 90:10, Winter 91:23, Mar 99:3, Feb 02:7, Mar 02:2, Sep 05:1, Nov 05:15
88720	88400	2009	Aug 05:9
96360	90760	2009	Nov 05:1, Jul 06:4, Sep 06:14, Dec 06:14 CPT Changes: An Insider's View 2006, 2008
96361	90761	2009	Nov 05:1, Jul 06:4, Sep 06:14, Dec 06:14, Mar 07:10 CPT Changes: An Insider's View 2006, 2007
96365	90765	2009	Nov 05:1, Sep 06:14, Nov 06:22, Dec 06:14 CPT Changes: An Insider's View 2006
96366	90766	2009	Nov 05:1, Sep 06:14, Dec 06:14, Mar 07:10 CPT Changes: An Insider's View 2006, 2007
96367	90767	2009	Nov 05:1, Sep 06:14, Nov 06:22, Dec 06:14 CPT Changes: An Insider's View 2006
96368	90768	2009	Nov 05:1, Aug 06:11, Sep 06:14, Nov 06:22, Dec 06:14 CPT Changes: An Insider's View 2006
96369	90769	2009	CPT Changes: An Insider's View 2008
96370	90770	2009	CPT Changes: An Insider's View 2008
96371	90771	2009	CPT Changes: An Insider's View 2008
96372	90772	2009	Nov 05:1, Sep 06:14, Dec 06:14 CPT Changes: An Insider's View 2006
96373	90773	2009	Nov 05:1, Sep 06:14, Dec 06:14 CPT Changes: An Insider's View 2006
96374	90774	2009	Nov 05:1, Sep 06:14, Dec 06:14 CPT Changes: An Insider's View 2006

Current Code(s)	Deleted/Former Code	Year Code Deleted	Citations Referencing Former Code—Applicable To Current Code(s)
96375	90775	2009	Nov 05:1, Sep 06:14, Dec 06:14 CPT Changes: An Insider's View 2006
96376	90776	2009	CPT Changes: An Insider's View 2008
96379	90779	2009	Nov 05:1, Sep 06:14, Dec 06:14 CPT Changes: An Insider's View 2006
90951-90953, 90963, 90967	90918	2009	Fall 93:5, May 96:4, May 02:17, Jan 03:22
90954-90956, 90964, 90968	90919	2009	Fall 93:5, May 96:5, May 02:17, Jan 03:22
90957-90959, 90965, 90969	90920	2009	Fall 93:5, May 96:5, May 02:17, Jan 03:22
90960-90962, 90966, 90970	90921	2009	Fall 93:5, May 96:5, May 02:17, Jan 03:22
90951-90953, 90963, 90967	90922	2009	Fall 93:5, May 96:5, May 02:17, Jan 03:22
90954-90956, 90964, 90968	90923	2009	May 96:5, May 02:17, Jan 03:22
90957-90959, 90965, 90969	90924	2009	May 96:5, May 02:17, Jan 03:22
90960-90962, 90966, 90970	90925	2009	May 96:5, May 02:17, Jan 03:22
93285, 93291, 93298	93727	2009	Nov 99:50, Jul 00:5 CPT Changes: An Insider's View 2000
93280, 93288, 93294	93731	2009	Summer 94:23, Feb 98:11
93280, 93288, 93294	93732	2009	Summer 94:23, Feb 98:11, Mar 00:10
93293	93733	2009	Summer 94:23
93279, 93288, 93294	93734	2009	Summer 94:23, Feb 98:11
93279, 93288, 93294	93735	2009	Summer 94:23, Feb 98:11
93293	93736	2009	Summer 94:23
93282, 93289, 93292, 93295	93741	2009	Nov 99:50-51, Jul 00:5, Nov 00:9, Sep 05:8 CPT Changes: An Insider's View 2000, 2005
93282, 93289, 93292, 93295	93742	2009	Nov 99:50-51, Jul 00:5, Nov 00:9 CPT Changes: An Insider's View 2000, 2005
93283, 93289, 93295	93743	2009	Nov 99:50-51, Jul 00:5, Nov 00:9, Sep 05:8 CPT Changes: An Insider's View 2000
93283, 93289, 93295	93744	2009	Nov 99:50-51, Jul 00:5, Nov 00:9 CPT Changes: An Insider's View 2000
99466	99289	2009	May 05:1, Jul 06:4 CPT Changes: An Insider's View 2002, 2003
99467	99290	2009	CPT Changes: An Insider's View 2002
99471	99293	2009	Feb 03:15, Oct 03:2, Aug 04:7, 10, May 05:1, Nov 05:10, Jul 06:4, Apr 07:3 CPT Changes: An Insider's View 2003, 2004, 2005
99472	99294	2009	Feb 03:15, Oct 03:2, Aug 04:7, Nov 05:10, Jul 06:4, Apr 07:3 CPT Changes: An Insider's View 2003, 2004, 2005
99468	99295	2009	Summer 93:1, Nov 97:4-5, Mar 98:11, Nov 99:5-6, Dec 00:14, Feb 03:15, Oct 03:1, May 05:1, Nov 05:10, CPT Changes: An Insider's View 2000, 2003, 2004, 2005
99469	99296	2009	Summer 93:1, Nov 97:4-5, Mar 98:11, Nov 99:5-6, Dec 00:14, Feb 03:15, Oct 03:1, Nov 05:10, CPT Changes: An Insider's View 2000, 2003, 2004, 2005, 2008

Current Code(s)	Deleted/Former Code	Year Code Deleted	Citations Referencing Former Code— Applicable To Current Code(s)
99478	99298	2009	Nov 98:2-3, Nov 99:5-6, Aug 00:4, Dec 00:15, Oct 03:2, May 05:1, Nov 05:10; CPT Changes: An Insider's View 2000, 2003
99479	99299	2009	Oct 03:2, Nov 05:10; CPT Changes: An Insider's View 2003
99480	99300	2009	CPT Changes: An Insider's View 2006
99460	99431	2009	Apr 97:10, Nov 97:9, Sep 98:5, Apr 04:14, May 05:1
99461	99432	2009	Sep 98:5, May 99:11, Apr 04:14
99462	99433	2009	Sep 98:5, Apr 03:27
99463	99435	2009	Sep 98:5, Apr 04:14
99464	99436	2009	Nov 97:9-10, Sep 98:5, Nov 99:5-6, Aug 00:3, Aug 04:9, Nov 05:15
99465	99440	2009	Summer 93:3, Mar 96:10, Nov 97:9, Sep 98:5, Nov 99:5-6, Aug 00:3, Oct 03:3, Aug 04:9, Apr 07:3
20985-20987	0054T	2008	May 04:14, Jun 04:8 CPT Changes: An Insider's View 2004
20985-20987	0055T	2008	May 04:14, Jun 04:8 CPT Changes: An Insider's View 2004, 2005
20985-20987	0056T	2008	May 04:14, Jun 04:8 CPT Changes: An Insider's View 2004
99174	0065T	2008	Mar 05:1, 3-4 CPT Changes: An Insider's View 2005
99444	0074T	2008	May 05:7, Sep 05:6 CPT Changes: An Insider's View 2005
99605-99607	0115T	2008	CPT Changes: An Insider's View 2006
99605-99607	0116T	2008	CPT Changes: An Insider's View 2006
99605-99607	0117T	2008	CPT Changes: An Insider's View 2006
50593	0135T	2008	CPT Changes: An Insider's View 2006, Clinical Examples in Radiology Winter 06:18
34806	0153T	2008	CPT Changes: An Insider's View 2007, Clinical Examples in Radiology Winter 06:19
93982	0154T	2008	CPT Changes: An Insider's View 2007, Clinical Examples in Radiology Winter 06:19
01935, 01936	01905	2008	Mar 06:15 CPT Changes: An Insider's View 2002
24357-24359	24350	2008	
24357-24359	24351	2008	
24357-24359	24352	2008	
24357-24359	24354	2008	
24357-24359	24356	2008	
3044F-3045F	3047F	2008	CPT Changes: An Insider's View 2007
3074F-3075F	3076F	2008	CPT Changes: An Insider's View 2007
32421	32000	2008	Spring 91:4, Winter 92:20
32422	32002	2008	Nov 03:14
32560	32005	2008	
32550	32019	2008	CPT Changes: An Insider's View 2005
32551	32020	2008	Fall 92:13, Nov 03:14
36591	36540	2008	Jan 02:11, Nov 02:3, Apr 03:26, Nov 05:1 CPT Changes: An Insider's View 2001, 2003
36593	36550	2008	Nov 99:20, Nov 05:1 CPT Changes: An Insider's View 2000
49203-49205, 58957, 58958	49200	2008	CPT Changes: An Insider's View 2003
49203-49205, 58957, 58958	49201	2008	
51100	51000	2008	Nov 99:32-33, Aug 00:3, Oct 03:2
51101	51005	2008	
51102	51010	2008	
60300	60001	2008	

Current Code(s)	Deleted/Former Code	Year Code Deleted	Citations Referencing Former Code—Applicable To Current Code(s)
67041, 67042, 67043	67038	2008	Aug 03:15, Sep 05:12
75557-75564	75552	2008	Fall 95:2
75557-75564	75553	2008	Fall 95:2
75557-75564	75554	2008	Fall 95:2
75557-75564	75555	2008	Fall 95:2
75557-75564	75556	2008	Fall 95:2
78610	78615	2008	CPT Changes: An Insider's View 2002
86356, 86486	86586	2008	Jul 98:11
99365-99368	99361	2008	May 05:1
99365-99368	99362	2008	
99441-99443	99371	2008	Spring 94:34, May 00:11, May 05:1, Nov 05:10
99441-99443	99372	2008	Spring 94:34, May 00:11, Nov 05:10
99441-99443	99373	2008	Spring 94:34, May 00:11, Nov 05:10
0160T, 0161T	0018T	2007	CPT Changes: An Insider's View 2002
96904	0044T	2007	CPT Changes: An Insider's View 2003, 2004
96904	0045T	2007	Jul 04:7 CPT Changes: An Insider's View 2004
77371-77373	0082T	2007	CPT Changes: An Insider's View 2005
77371-77373	0083T	2007	CPT Changes: An Insider's View 2005
22857	0091T	2007	CPT Changes: An Insider's View 2006
22865	0094T	2007	CPT Changes: An Insider's View 2006
22862	0097T	2007	CPT Changes: An Insider's View 2006
19105	0120T	2007	CPT Changes: An Insider's View 2006
15002, 15004	15000	2007	Fall 93:7, Apr 97:4, Aug 97:6, Sep 97:2, Nov 98:5, Jan 99:4, Apr 99:10, May 99:10, Nov 02:7, Aug 03:14 CPT Changes: An Insider's View 2001, 2006
15003, 15005	15001	2007	Nov 98:5-6, Jan 99:4, May 99:10, Aug 03:14
15830, 15847, 17999	15831	2007	May 01:11 CPT Changes: An Insider's View 2007
17311	17304	2007	Winter 94:19, Mar 99:11, Jun 99:10, Nov 02:7, Nov 03:15, Feb 04:11, Jul 04:2 CPT Changes: An Insider's View 2003
17312, 17314	17305	2007	Winter 94:19, Mar 99:11, Jun 99:10, Nov 02:7, Feb 04:11, Jul 04:3
17312, 17314	17306	2007	Winter 94:19, Mar 99:11, Jun 99:10, Nov 02:7, Feb 04:11, Jul 04:4
17312, 17314	17307	2007	Winter 94:19, Mar 99:11, Jun 99:10, Nov 02:7, Nov 03:15, Feb 04:11, Jul 04:4
17315	17310	2007	Winter 94:19, Mar 99:11, Jun 99:10, Nov 02:7, Feb 04:11, May 04:14, Jul 04:4 CPT Changes: An Insider's View 2003
19300	19140	2007	Feb 96:9, Apr 05:13
19301	19160	2007	Apr 05:7 CPT Changes: An Insider's View 2005
19302	19162	2007	Jun 00:11, Apr 05:7
19303	19180	2007	Apr 05:7
19304	19182	2007	Apr 05:7
19305	19200	2007	Apr 05:7
19306	19220	2007	Apr 05:7
19307	19240	2007	Apr 05:7
25606	25611	2007	Fall 93:23, Oct 99:5
25607-25609	25620	2007	
26390	26504	2007	

Current Code(s)	Deleted/Former Code	Year Code Deleted	Citations Referencing Former Code— Applicable To Current Code(s)
27325	27315	2007	
27326	27320	2007	
28055	28030	2007	
33254-33256	33253	2007	
35302-35306	35381	2007	
35506	35507	2007	
35537, 35538	35541	2007	
35539, 35540	35546	2007	
35637, 35638	35641	2007	Dec 01:7
44799	44152	2007	
44799	44153	2007	
47719	47716	2007	
48105	48005	2007	
48548	48180	2007	
49402	49085	2007	
54150	54152	2007	Sep 96:11, Dec 96:10, May 98:11, Apr 03:27 CPT Changes: An Insider's View 2007
54865	54820	2007	Oct 01:8
55875	55859	2007	Apr 04:6
56442	56720	2007	
57558	57820	2007	
67346	67350	2007	
77001	75998	2007	Dec 04:12-13 CPT Changes: An Insider's View 2004 Clinical Examples in Radiology Inaugural 04:1-2, Winter 05:9
77002	76003	2007	Fall 93:14, Jul 01:7 CPT Changes: An Insider's View 2001 Clinical Examples in Radiology Spring 05:5-6
77003	76005	2007	Nov 99:32, 34, 41, Jan 00:2, Feb 00:6, Aug 00:8, Sep 02:11, Sep 04:5 CPT Changes: An Insider's View 2000
77071	76006	2007	Nov 98:21 CPT Changes: An Insider's View 2003
72291	76012	2007	Mar 01:2 CPT Changes: An Insider's View 2001, 2006
72292	76013	2007	Mar 01:2 CPT Changes: An Insider's View 2001
77072	76020	2007	
77073	76040	2007	
77074	76061	2007	
77075	76062	2007	
77076	76065	2007	
77077	76066	2007	CPT Changes: An Insider's View 2002
77078	76070	2007	Nov 97:24 CPT Changes: An Insider's View 2002, 2003
77079	76071	2007	CPT Changes: An Insider's View 2003
77080	76075	2007	Nov 97:24, Jun 03:11 CPT Changes: An Insider's View 2005
77081	76076	2007	Nov 97:24
77082	76077	2007	CPT Changes: An Insider's View 2005
77083	76078	2007	Nov 97:24 CPT Changes: An Insider's View 2002
77051	76082	2007	CPT Changes: An Insider's View 2004
77052	76083	2007	CPT Changes: An Insider's View 2004
77053	76086	2007	

Current Code(s)	Deleted/Former Code	Year Code Deleted	Citations Referencing Former Code—Applicable To Current Code(s)
77054	76088	2007	
77055	76090	2007	Jul 96:6, Jun 99:10 CPT Changes: An Insider's View 2004
77056	76091	2007	Jul 96:6 CPT Changes: An Insider's View 2004
77057	76092	2007	Jul 96:6, Jun 99:10 CPT Changes: An Insider's View 2004
77058	76093	2007	
77059	76094	2007	
77031	76095	2007	Apr 96:9, Nov 97:24, Jan 01:9 CPT Changes: An Insider's View 2001
77032	76096	2007	Jan 01:10 CPT Changes: An Insider's View 2001
77011	76355	2007	CPT Changes: An Insider's View 2002, 2003
77012	76360	2007	Fall 93:12, Fall 94:2, Jan 01:9-10, Mar 05:2 CPT Changes: An Insider's View 2001, 2002, 2003
77013	76362	2007	Oct 02:4 CPT Changes: An Insider's View 2002, 2004
77014	76370	2007	Fall 91:12 CPT Changes: An Insider's View 2002, 2003
77021	76393	2007	Jan 01:10, Mar 05:2 CPT Changes: An Insider's View 2001, 2002
77022	76394	2007	Oct 02:4, Mar 05:5 CPT Changes: An Insider's View 2002, 2004
77084	76400	2007	
76775, 76776	76778	2007	CPT Changes: An Insider's View 2002
76998	76986	2007	CPT Changes: An Insider's View 2001
78707-78709	78704	2007	
78701-78709	78715	2007	
78761	78760	2007	
92700	92573	2007	
94002, 94004	94656	2007	Fall 92:30, Spring 95:4, Summer 95:4, Feb 96:9, Aug 00:2, Oct 03:2
94003, 94004	94657	2007	Fall 92:30, Spring 95:4, Summer 95:4, Feb 96:9, Aug 00:2, Oct 03:2

Appendix N

Summary of Resequenced CPT Codes

This is a summary of CPT codes that do not appear in numeric sequence in the listing of CPT codes. Rather than deleting and renumbering, resequencing allows existing codes to be relocated to an appropriate location for the code concept, regardless of the numeric sequence. The codes listed below are identified in *CPT 2010* with a # symbol for location of the resequenced number within the family of related concepts. Numerically placed references (eg, **Code is out of numerical sequence. See...**) are used as navigational alerts to direct the user to the location of the out-of-sequence code.

21552	27337
21554	27339
23071	27632
23073	27634
24071	28039
24073	28041
25071	46220
25073	46320
26111	46945
26113	46946
27043	46947
27045	51797
27059	82652
27329	

Notes

Index

Instructions for the Use of the CPT Index

Main Terms

The index is organized by main terms. Each main term can stand alone, or be followed by up to three modifying terms. There are four primary classes of main entries:

1. Procedure or service.
   For example: Endoscopy; Anastomosis; Splint

2. Organ or other anatomic site.
   For example: Tibia; Colon; Salivary Gland

3. Condition.
   For example: Abscess; Entropion; Tetralogy of Fallot

4. Synonyms, Eponyms, and Abbreviations.
   For example: EEG; Bricker Operation; Clagett Procedure

Modifying Terms

A main term may be followed by a series of up to three indented terms that modify the main term. When modifying terms appear, one should review the list, as these subterms do have an effect on the selection of the appropriate code for the procedure.

Code Ranges

Whenever more than one code applies to a given index entry, a code range is listed. If several non-sequential codes apply, they will be separated by a comma. For example:

Esophagus
    Reconstruction 43300, 43310, 43313

If two or more sequential codes apply, they will be separated by a hyphen. For example:

Debridement
    Burns 01951-01953, 16020-16030

Conventions

As a space saving convention, certain words infer some meaning. This convention is primarily used when a procedure or service is listed as a subterm. For example:

Knee
    Incision (of)

In this example, the word in parentheses (of) does not appear in the index, but it is inferred. As another example:

Pancreas
    Anesthesia (for procedures on)

In this example, as there is no such entity as pancreas anesthesia, the words in parentheses are inferred. That is, anesthesia for procedures on the pancreas.

The alphabetic index is NOT a substitute for the main text of the CPT codebook. Even if only one code appears, the user must refer to the main text to ensure that the code selection is accurate.

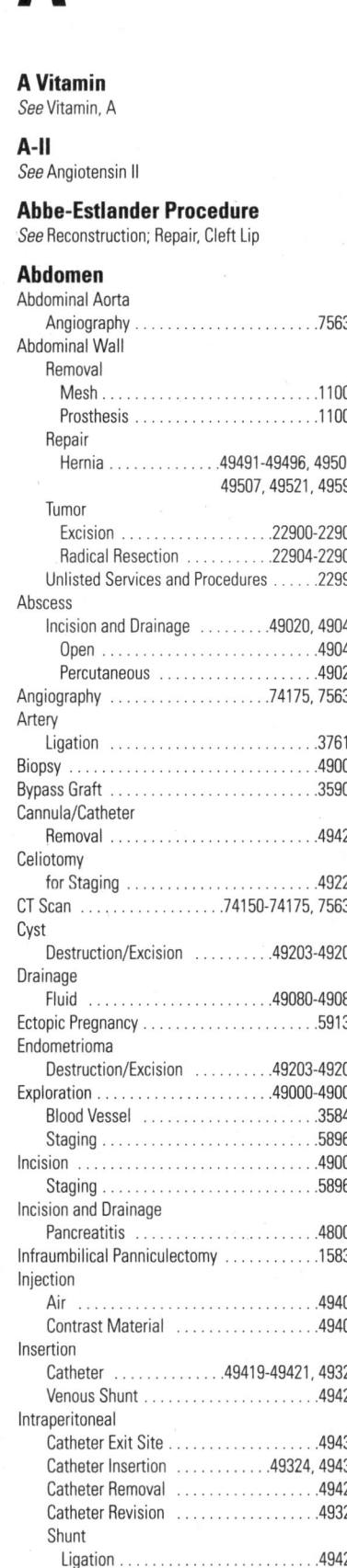

A

A Vitamin
See Vitamin, A

A-II
See Angiotensin II

Abbe-Estlander Procedure
See Reconstruction; Repair, Cleft Lip

Abdomen
Abdominal Aorta
   Angiography 75635
Abdominal Wall
   Removal
      Mesh 11008
      Prosthesis 11008
   Repair
      Hernia 49491-49496, 49501,
               49507, 49521, 49590
   Tumor
      Excision 22900-22903
      Radical Resection 22904-22905
   Unlisted Services and Procedures 22999
Abscess
   Incision and Drainage 49020, 49040
      Open 49040
      Percutaneous 49021
Angiography 74175, 75635
Artery
   Ligation 37617
Biopsy 49000
Bypass Graft 35907
Cannula/Catheter
   Removal 49422
Celiotomy
   for Staging 49220
CT Scan 74150-74175, 75635
Cyst
   Destruction/Excision 49203-49205
Drainage
   Fluid 49080-49081
Ectopic Pregnancy 59130
Endometrioma
   Destruction/Excision 49203-49205
Exploration 49000-49002
   Blood Vessel 35840
   Staging 58960
Incision 49000
   Staging 58960
Incision and Drainage
   Pancreatitis 48000
Infraumbilical Panniculectomy 15830
Injection
   Air 49400
   Contrast Material 49400
Insertion
   Catheter 49419-49421, 49324
   Venous Shunt 49425
Intraperitoneal
   Catheter Exit Site 49436
   Catheter Insertion 49324, 49435
   Catheter Removal 49422
   Catheter Revision 49325
   Shunt
      Ligation 49428
      Removal 49429

Laparotomy
   Staging 49220
Magnetic Resonance Imaging
(MRI) 74181-74183
Needle Biopsy
   Mass 49180
Peritoneocentesis 49080-49081
Radical Resection 51597
Radiation Therapy
   Placement of Guidance
   Devices 49410-49411
Repair
   Blood Vessel 35221
      with Other Graft 35281
      with Vein Graft 35251
   Hernia 49491-49525, 49560-49587
   Suture 49900
Revision
   Venous Shunt 49426
Suture 49900
Tumor
   Destruction/Excision 49203-49205
Ultrasound 76700-76705
Unlisted Services and Procedures 49999
Wound Exploration
   Penetrating 20102
X-ray 74000-74022

Abdominal
Aorta
   See Abdomen, Abdominal Aorta; Aorta,
   Abdominal
Aortic Aneurysm
   See Aorta, Abdominal, Aneurysm
Deliveries
   See Caesarean Delivery
Hysterectomy
   See Hysterectomy, Abdominal
Lymphangiogram
   See Lymphangiography, Abdomen
Paracentesis
   See Abdomen, Drainage
Radiographies
   See Abdomen, X-ray
Wall
   See Abdomen, Abdominal Wall
   Debridement
      Infected 11005-11006
   Reconstruction 49905
   Removal
      Mesh 11008
      Prosthesis 11008
   Surgery 22999
   Tumor
      Excision 22900-22903

Abdominohysterectomy
See Hysterectomy, Abdominal

Abdominopelvic Amputation
See Amputation, Interpelviabdominal

Abdominoplasty
See Panniculectomy
Excision 15830, 15847

Ablation
Anal
   Polyp 46615
   Tumor 46615
Bone
   Tumor 20982

Colon
   Tumor 45339
Cryosurgical
   Fibroadenoma 19105
   Renal Mass 50250
   Renal Tumor
      Percutaneous 50593
CT Scan Guidance 77013
Endometrial 58353-58356, 58563
Endometrium
   Ultrasound Guidance 58356
Heart
   Arrhythmogenic Focus 93650-93652
      See Cardiology; Diagnostic, Intracardiac
      Pacing and Mapping
   Atrioventricular Node Function 93650
Liver
   Tumor
      Laparoscopic 47370-47371
      Open 47380-47382
Lung
   Tumor
      Radiofrequency 32998
Magnetic Resonance Guidance 77022
Parenchymal Tissue
   CT Scan Guidance 77013
Prostate 55873
Pulmonary Tumor 32998
Radiofrequency 32998
Renal Cyst 50541
Renal Mass 50542
   Radiofrequency 50592
Renal Tumor
   Cryotherapy
      Percutaneous 50593
Tongue Base
   Radiofrequency 41530
Turbinate Mucosa 30801-30802
Ultrasound
   Guidance 76940
   Uterine Tumor 0071T-0072T
Uterine Tumor
   Ultrasound, Focused 0071T-0072T
Vein
   Endovenous 36475-36479

Abortion
See Obstetrical Care
Incomplete 59812
Induced
   by Dilation and Curettage 59840
   by Dilation and Evacuation 59841
   by Saline 59850-59851
   by Vaginal Suppositories 59855-59856
   with Hysterectomy 59100, 59852, 59857
Missed
   First Trimester 59820
   Second Trimester 59821
Septic 59830
Spontaneous 59812
Therapeutic
   by Saline 59850
      with Dilation and Curettage 59851
      with Hysterectomy 59852

Abrasion
Skin
   Chemical Peel 15788-15793
   Dermabrasion 15780-15783
   Lesion 15786-15787

Abscess

Abdomen 49040-49041
  Incision and Drainage
    Open 49040
    Percutaneous 49021
Anal
  Incision and Drainage 46045-46050
Ankle 27603
Appendix
  Incision and Drainage 44900
    Open 44900
    Percutaneous 44901
Arm, Lower 25028
  Excision 25145
  Incision and Drainage 25035
Arm, Upper
  Incision and Drainage 23930-23935
Auditory Canal, External 69020
Bartholin's Gland
  Incision and Drainage 56420
Bladder
  Incision and Drainage 51080
Brain
  Drainage 61150-61151
  Excision 61514, 61522
  Incision and Drainage 61320-61321
Breast
  Incision and Drainage 19020
Carpals
  Incision, Deep 25035
Clavicle
  Sequestrectomy 23170
Drainage
  with X-ray 75989
Ear, External
  Complicated 69005
  Simple 69000
Elbow
  Incision and Drainage 23930-23935
Epididymis
  Incision and Drainage 54700
Excision
  Olecranon Process 24138
  Radius 24136
  Ulna 24138
Eyelid
  Incision and Drainage 67700
Facial Bones
  Excision 21026
Finger 26010-26011
  Incision and Drainage 26034
Foot
  Incision 28005
Gums
  Incision and Drainage 41800
Hand
  Incision and Drainage 26034
Hematoma
  Incision and Drainage 27603
Hip
  Incision and Drainage 26990-26992
Humeral Head 23174
Humerus
  Excision 24134
  Incision and Drainage 23935
Kidney
  Incision and Drainage 50020
  Open 50020
  Percutaneous 50021
Leg, Lower
  Incision and Drainage 27603

Liver 47010
  Drainage
    Open 47010
  Injection 47015
  Repair 47300
Localization
  Nuclear Medicine 78806-78807
Lung
  Percutaneous Drainage 32200-32201
Lymph Node
  Incision and Drainage 38300-38305
Lymphocele Drainage 49062
Mandible
  Excision 21025
Mouth
  Incision and Drainage 40800-40801,
      41005-41009, 41015-41018
Nasal Septum
  Incision and Drainage 30020
Neck
  Incision and Drainage 21501-21502
Ovarian
  Incision and Drainage 58820-58822
    Abdominal Approach 58822
    Vaginal Approach 58820
Ovary
  Drainage
    Percutaneous 58823
Palate
  Incision and Drainage 42000
Paraurethral Gland
  Incision and Drainage 53060
Parotid Gland Drainage 42300-42305
Pelvic
  Drainage
    Percutaneous 58823
Pelvis
  Incision and Drainage 26990-26992, 45000
Pericolic
  Drainage
    Percutaneous 58823
Perineum
  Incision and Drainage 56405
Perirenal or Renal
  Drainage 50020-50021
  Percutaneous 50021
Peritoneum
  Incision and Drainage
    Open 49020
    Percutaneous 49021
Prostate
  Incision and Drainage 55720-55725
  Transurethral Drainage 52700
Radius
  Incision, Deep 25035
Rectum
  Incision and Drainage 45005-45020,
      46040, 46060
Retroperitoneal 49060-49061
  Drainage
    Open 49060
    Percutaneous 49061
Salivary Gland
  Drainage 42300-42320
Scapula
  Sequestrectomy 23172
Scrotum
  Incision and Drainage 54700, 55100
Shoulder
  Drainage 23030
Skene's Gland
  Incision and Drainage 53060

Skin
  Incision and Drainage 10060-10061
  Puncture Aspiration 10160
Soft Tissue
  Incision 20000-20005
Spine
  Incision and Drainage 22010-22015
Subdiaphragmatic 49040-49041
Sublingual Gland
  Drainage 42310-42320
Submaxillary Gland
  Drainage 42310-42320
Subphrenic 49040-49041
Testis
  Incision and Drainage 54700
Thoracostomy 32551
Thorax
  Incision and Drainage 21501-21502
Throat
  Incision and Drainage 42700-42725
Tongue
  Incision and Drainage 41000-41006
Tonsil
  Incision and Drainage 42700
Ulna
  Incision, Deep 25035
Urethra
  Incision and Drainage 53040
Uvula
  Incision and Drainage 42000
Vagina
  Incision and Drainage 57010
Vulva
  Incision and Drainage 56405
Wrist
  Excision 25145
  Incision and Drainage 25028, 25035
X-ray 76080

Abscess, Nasal
See Nose, Abscess

Abscess, Parotid Gland
See Parotid Gland, Abscess

Absorptiometry
Dual Energy 3095F-3096F
  Bone
    Appendicular 77081
    Axial Skeleton 77080
    Vertebral 77082
Dual Photon
  Bone 78351
Radiographic
  Photodensity 77083
Single Photon
  Bone 78350

Absorption Spectrophotometry, Atomic
See Atomic Absorption Spectroscopy

Accessory Nerve, Spinal
See Nerves, Spinal Accessory

Accessory, Toes
See Polydactyly, Toes

ACE
See Angiotensin Converting Enzyme (ACE), Performance Measures

Acetabuloplasty 27120-27122

Adenosine Diphosphate
Blood 82030

Adenosine Monophosphate (AMP)
Blood 82030

Adenovirus
Antibody 86603
Antigen Detection
    Enzyme Immunoassay 87301
    Immunofluorescense 87260

Adenovirus Vaccine
See Vaccines

Adenylic Acid
See Adenosine Monophosphate (AMP)

ADH
See Antidiuretic Hormone

Adhesions
Epidural 62263-62264
Eye
    Corneovitreal 65880
    Incision
        Anterior Segment 65860-65870
        Posterior Segment 65875
Intermarginal
    Construction .67880
        Transposition of Tarsal Plate 67882
Intestinal
    Enterolysis .44005
        Laparoscopic 44180
Intracranial
    Lysis 62161
Intrauterine
    Lysis 58559
Labial
    Lysis 56441
Lungs
    Lysis 32124
Pelvic
    Lysis 58660, 58662, 58740
Penile
    Lysis
        Post-circumcision 54162
Preputial
    Lysis 54450
Urethral
    Lysis 53500

Adipectomy
See Lipectomy

ADL
See Activities of Daily Living

Administration
Immunization
    Each Additional
        Vaccine/Toxoid 90472, 90474
            with Counseling 90466, 90468
        One Vaccine/Toxoid 90471, 90473
            with Counseling 90465, 90467

ADP
See Adenosine Diphosphate

**ADP Phosphocreatine
Phosphotransferase**
See CPK

Adrenal Cortex Hormone
See Corticosteroids

Adrenal Gland
Biopsy .60540-60545
Excision
    Laparoscopy 60650
    Retroperitoneal Tumor 60545
Exploration 60540-60545
Nuclear Medicine
    Imaging 78075

Adrenal Medulla
See Medulla

Adrenalectomy 60540
Anesthesia 00866
Laparoscopic .50545

Adrenalin
See Catecholamines
Blood 82383
Urine 82384

Adrenaline-Noradrenaline
Testing .82382-82384

**Adrenocorticotropic Hormone
(ACTH)** 80400-80406, 80412, 80418, 82024
Blood or Urine .82024
Stimulation Panel 80400-80406

Adrenogenital Syndrome 56805, 57335

**Adult T Cell Leukemia Lymphoma
Virus I**
See HTLV I

Advanced Life Support
See Emergency Department Services
Physician Direction 99288

Advancement
Genioglossus 21199
Tendon
    Foot 28238

Advancement Flap
See Skin, Adjacent Tissue Transfer

Aerosol Inhalation
See Pulmonology, Therapeutic
Pentamidine .94642

AFB
See Acid Fast Bacilli (AFB)

Afferent Nerve
See Sensory Nerve

AFP
See Alpha-Fetoprotein

After Hours Medical Services 99050

Agents, Anticoagulant
See Clotting Inhibitors

Agglutinin
Cold 86156-86157
Febrile 86000

Aggregation
Platelet 85576

AHG
See Clotting Factor

**AICD (Pacing Cardioverter-
Defibrillator)**
See Defibrillator, Heart; Pacemaker, Heart

Aid, Hearing
See Hearing Aid

AIDS Antibodies
See Antibody, HIV

AIDS Virus
See HIV-1

Akin Operation
See Bunion Repair

ALA
See Aminolevulinic Acid (ALA)

**Alanine 2 Oxoglutarate
Aminotransferase**
See Transaminase, Glutamic Pyruvic

Alanine Amino (ALT) 84460

Alanine Transaminase
See Transaminase, Glutamic Pyruvic

Albarran Test
See Water Load Test

Albumin
Ischemia modified 82045
Serum, Plasma or Whole Blood 82040
Urine 82042-82044

Alcohol
Breath 82075
Ethyl
    Blood 82055
    Urine 82055
Ethylene Glycol 82693
Use–See Performance Measures–Preventive
Care & Screening–Interventions–Unhealthy
Alcohol Use: Sceening

Alcohol Dehydrogenase
See Antidiuretic Hormone

Alcohol, Isopropyl
See Isopropyl Alcohol

Alcohol, Methyl
See Methanol

Aldolase
Blood 82085

Aldosterone
Blood 82088
Suppression Evaluation 80408
Urine 82088

Alimentary Canal
See Gastrointestinal Tract

Alkaline Phosphatase 84075-84080
Leukocyte 85540
WBC 85540

Alkaloids
See Specific Drug
Urine 82101

Leg, Upper 27590-27592
    at Hip 27290-27295
    Revision 27594-27596
Metacarpal 26910
Metatarsal 28810
Penis
    Partial 54120
    Radical 54130-54135
    Total 54125
Thumb 26910-26952
Toe 28810-28825
Tuft of Distal Phalanx 11752
Upper Extremity 24940
    Cineplasty 24940

Amputation through Hand
See Hand, Amputation

Amputation, Nose
See Resection, Nose

Amylase
Blood 82150
Urine 82150

ANA
See Antinuclear Antibodies (ANA)

Anabolic Steroid
See Androstenedione

Anal Abscess
See Abscess, Anal

Anal Bleeding
See Anus, Hemorrhage

Anal Fistula
See Fistula, Anal

Anal Fistulectomy
See Excision, Fistula, Anal

Anal Fistulotomy
See Fistulotomy, Anal

Anal Sphincter
Dilation 45905
Incision 46080

Anal Ulceration
See Anus, Fissure

Analgesia
See Anesthesia; Sedation

Analgesic Cutaneous Electrostimulation
See Application, Neurostimulation

Analysis
Computer Data 99090
    Cardiovascular Monitoring 93290, 93297,
                           93299
    Device Evaluation and Programming
        Cardioverter-Defibrillator ...93282-93284,
                93287, 93289-93290, 93292,
                       93295, 93296
        Loop Recorder 93285, 93291,
                          93298-93299
        Pacemaker ...93279-93281, 93293-93294
    Electrocardiograph
        Data Analysis 0206T
    Multivariate Probability Assessment ...0185T
    Pacemaker 93288, 93293-93294

Electroencephalogram
    Digital 95957
Electronic
    Drug Infusion Pump 62367-62368
    Pacing Cardioverter-Defibrillator
        Data Analysis 93289, 93295-93296
        Initial Evaluation 93640
        See Pacemaker, Heart
    Pulse Generator ...95970-95971, 95980-95982
Physiologic Data, Remote 99091
Protein
    Tissue
        Western Blot 88372
Semen 89320-89322
    Sperm Isolation 89260-89261

Analysis, Spectrum
See Spectrophotometry

Anaspadias
See Epispadias

Anastomosis
Arteriovenous Fistula
    Direct 36821
    with Bypass Graft 35686
    with Graft 36825-36830, 36832
Artery
    to Aorta 33606
    to Artery
        Cranial 61711
Bile Duct
    to Bile Duct 47800
    to Intestines 47760, 47780
Bile Duct to Gastrointestinal 47785
Broncho-Bronchial 32486
Caval to Mesenteric 37160
Cavopulmonary 33768
Colorectal 44620
Epididymis
    to Vas Deferens
        Bilateral 54901
        Unilateral 54900
Excision
    Trachea 31780-31781
Fallopian Tube 58750
Gallbladder to Intestines 47720-47740
Hepatic Duct to Intestines 47765, 47802
Ileo-Anal 45113
Intestine to Intestine 44130
Intestines
    Colo-anal 45119
    Cystectomy 51590
    Enterocystoplasty 51960
    Ileoanal 44157-44158
    Resection
        Laparoscopic 44202-44205
Intrahepatic Portosystemic 37182-37183
Jejunum 43825
Microvascular
    Free Transfer
        Jejunum 43496
Nerve
    Facial to Hypoglossal 64868
    Facial to Phrenic 64870
Oviduct 58750
Pancreas to Intestines 48520-48540, 48548
Portocaval 37140
Pulmonary 33606
Renoportal 37145
Splenorenal 37180-37181

Stomach 43825
    to Duodenum 43810, 43855
    Revision 43850
    to Jejunum 43820, 43860-43865
Tubotubal 58750
Ureter
    to Bladder 50780-50785
    to Colon 50810-50815
    Removal 50830
    to Intestine 50800, 50820-50825
    Removal 50830
    to Kidney 50727-50750
    to Ureter 50727, 50760-50770
Vein
    Saphenopopliteal 34530
Vein to Vein 37140-37160, 37182-37183

Anastomosis of Lacrimal Sac to Conjunctival Sac
See Conjunctivorhinostomy

Anastomosis of Pancreas
See Pancreas, Anastomosis

Anastomosis, Aorta-Pulmonary Artery
See Aorta, Anastomosis, to Pulmonary Artery

Anastomosis, Bladder, to Intestine
See Enterocystoplasty

Anastomosis, Hepatic Duct
See Hepatic Duct, Anastomosis

Anderson Tibial Lengthening 27715
See Ankle; Tibia, Osteoplasty, Lengthening

Androstanediol Glucuronide 82154

Androstanolone
See Dihydrotestosterone

Androstenedione
Blood or Urine 82157

Androstenolone
See Dehydroepiandrosterone

Androsterone
Blood or Urine 82160

Anesthesia
See Analgesia
Abbe-Estlander Procedure 00102
Abdomen
    Abdominal Wall 00700, 00730,
               00800-00802, 00820, 00836
        Halsted Repair 00750-00756
    Blood Vessels 00770, 00880-00882
    Endoscopy 00740, 00810
    Extraperitoneal 00860-00862,
                  00866-00868, 00870
    Hernia Repair 00830-00836
        Halsted Repair 00750-00756
    Intraperitoneal 00790-00797, 00840-00842
Abdominoperineal Resection 00844
Abortion
    Incomplete 01965
    Induced 01966
Achilles Tendon Repair 01472
Acromioclavicular Joint 01620
Adrenalectomy 00866
Amniocentesis 00842

Anesthesia Local

See Anesthesia, Local

Repair

Achilles Tendon 27650-27654
Ligament 27695-27698
Tendon 27612, 27680-27687
Strapping 29540
Synovium
Excision 27625-27626
Tenotomy 27605-27606
Tumor
Excision 27618-27619, 27630-27634
Radical Resection 27615-27616
Unlisted Services and Procedures 27899
X-ray 73600-73610
with Contrast 73615

Ankylosis (Surgical)
See Arthrodesis

Annuloplasty
Percutaneous, Intradiscal 22526-22527

Anogenital Region
See Perineum

Anoplasty
Stricture 46700-46705

Anorectal
Biofeedback 90911
Repair
Fistula 46706-46707

Anorectal Exam (Surgical) 45990

Anorectal Myectomy
See Myomectomy, Anorectal

Anorectovaginoplasty 46744-46746

Anoscopy
Ablation
Polyp 46615
Tumor 46615
Biopsy 46606
Dilation 46604
Exploration 46600
Hemorrhage 46614
Removal
Foreign Body 46608
Polyp 46610-46612
Tumor 46610-46612

Antebrachium
See Forearm

Antecedent, Plasma Thromboplastin
See Plasma Thromboplastin, Antecedent

Antepartum Care
Cesarean Delivery 59510
Previous 59610, 59618
Vaginal Delivery 59425-59426

Anterior Ramus of Thoracic Nerve
See Intercostal Nerve

Anthrax Vaccine
See Vaccines

Anthrogon
See Follicle Stimulating Hormone (FSH)

Anti Australia Antigens
See Antibody, Hepatitis B

Anti D Immunoglobulin
See Immune Globulins, Rho (D)

Anti-Human Globulin Consumption Test
See Coombs Test

Anti-Phospholipid Antibody
See Antibody, Phospholipid

Antiactivator, Plasmin
See Alpha-2 Antiplasmin

Antibiotic Administration
Injection 96372-96379
Prescribed or Dispensed 4120F-4124F

Antibiotic Sensitivity 87181-87184, 87188
Enzyme Detection 87185
Minimum Bactericidal Concentration 87187
Minimum Inhibitory Concentration 87186

Antibodies, Thyroid-Stimulating
See Immunoglobulin, Thyroid Stimulating

Antibodies, Viral
See Viral Antibodies

Antibody
See Antibody Identification; Microsomal Antibody
Actinomyces 86602
Adenovirus 86603
Antinuclear 86038-86039
Antiphosphatidylserine (Phospholipid) 86148
Antiprothrombin 0030T
Antistreptolysin O 86060-86063
Aspergillus 86606
Bacterium 86609
Bartonella 86611
Beta 2 Glycoprotein I 86146
Blastomyces 86612
Blood Crossmatch 86920-86923
Bordetella 86615
Borrelia 86618-86619
Brucella 86622
Campylobacter 86625
Candida 86628
Cardiolipin 86147
Chlamydia 86631-86632
Coccidioides 86635
Coxiella Burnetii 86638
Cryptococcus 86641
Cyclic Citrullinated Peptide (CCP) 86200
Cytomegalovirus 86644-86645
Cytotoxic Screen 86807-86808
Deoxyribonuclease 86215
Deoxyribonucleic Acid (DNA) 86225-86226
Diphtheria 86648
Ehrlichia 86666
Encephalitis 86651-86654
Enterovirus 86658
Epstein-Barr Virus 86663-86665
Fluorescent 86255-86256
Francisella Tularensis 86668
Fungus 86671
Giardia Lamblia 86674
Growth Hormone 86277
Helicobacter Pylori 86677
Helminth 86682
Hemophilus Influenza 86684
Hepatitis
Delta Agent 86692

Hepatitis A 86708-86709
Hepatitis B
Core 86704
IgM 86705
Surface 86706
Hepatitis Be 86707
Hepatitis C 86803-86804
Herpes Simplex 86694-86696
Heterophile 86308-86310
Histoplasma 86698
HIV 86689, 86701-86703
HIV-1 ....86701, 86703
HIV-2 86702-86703
HTLV-I 86687, 86689
HTLV-II 86688
Influenza Virus 86710
Insulin 86337
Intrinsic Factor 86340
Islet Cell 86341
Legionella 86713
Leishmania 86717
Leptospira 86720
Listeria Monocytogenes 86723
Lyme Disease 86617
Lymphocytic Choriomeningitis 86727
Lymphogranuloma Venereum 86729
Microsomal 86376
Mucormycosis 86732
Mumps 86735
Mycoplasma 86738
Neisseria Meningitidis 86741
Nocardia 86744
Nuclear Antigen 86235
Other Virus 86790
Parvovirus 86747
Phospholipid 86147
Phospholipid Cofactor 0030T
Plasmodium 86750
Platelet 86022-86023
Protozoa 86753
Red Blood Cell 86850-86870
Respiratory Syncytial Virus 86756
Rickettsia 86757
Rotavirus 86759
Rubella 86762
Rubeola 86765
Salmonella 86768
Shigella 86771
Sperm 89325
Streptokinase 86590
Tetanus 86774
Thyroglobulin 86800
Toxoplasma 86777-86778
Treponema Pallidum 86780
Trichinella 86784
Varicella-Zoster 86787
West Nile Virus 86788-86789
White Blood Cell 86021
Yersinia 86793

Antibody Identification
Leukocyte Antibodies 86021
Platelet 86022-86023
Red Blood Cell
Pretreatment 86970-86972
Serum
Pretreatment 86975-86978

Antibody Neutralization Test
See Neutralization Test

Lesion
- Destruction 46900-46917, 46924
- Excision .... .45108, 46922

Manometry 91122

Placement
- Seton 46020

Reconstruction 46742
- Congenital Absence 46730-46740
- Sphincter 46750-46751, 46760-46762
- with Graft 46753
- with Implant 46762

Removal
- Foreign Body 46608
- Seton 46030
- Suture 46754
- Wire 46754

Repair
- Anovaginal Fistula 46715-46716
- Cloacal Anomaly 46748
- Fistula 46706
- Stricture 46700-46705

Sphincter
- Chemodenervation 46505
- Electromyography 51784-51785
- Needle 51785
- Sphincterotomy 46200

Unlisted Services and Procedures 46999

Aorta

Abdominal
- Aneurysm ...... .0078T, 0079T, 0080T, 0081T, 34800-34805, 34825-34832, 35081-35103, 75952-75953
- Thromboendarterectomy 35331

Anastomosis
- to Pulmonary Artery 33606

Angiogram
- Radiologic Injection 93544
  - *See* Cardiac Catheterization, Injection

Angioplasty 35452

Aortography 75600-75630

Ascending
- Graft 33864

Balloon .... .33967, 33970

Catheterization
- Catheter 36200
- Intracatheter/Needle 36160

Circulation Assist .... .33967, 33970

Conduit to Heart 33404

Excision
- Coarctation 33840-33851

Insertion
- Balloon Device 33967
- Graft 33330-33335, 33864
- Intracatheter/Needle 36160

Removal
- Balloon Assist Device .... .33968, 33971

Repair 33320-33322, 33802-33803
- Coarctation 33840-33851
- Graft 33860-33877
  - Ascending 33864
- Hypoplastic or Interrupted
  - Aortic Arch 33852-33853
  - Sinus of Valsalva 33702-33720
- Suspension 33800
- Suture 33320-33322

Thoracic
- Repair 75956-75959
  - Endovascular 33880-33891

Translocation
- Aortic Root 33782-33783

Valve
- Incision 33415
- Repair 33400-33403
  - Left Ventricle 33414
  - Supravalvular Stenosis .... .33417
  - Replacement 33405-33413

X-ray with Contrast 75600-75630

Aorta-Pulmonary ART Transposition
See Transposition, Great Arteries

Aortic Sinus
See Sinus of Valsalva

Aortic Stenosis

Repair 33415
- Nikaidoh Procedure 33782-33783
- Supravalvular 33417

Aortic Valve
See Heart, Aortic Valve

Aortic Valve Replacement
See Replacement, Aortic Valve

Aortocoronary Bypass
See Coronary Artery Bypass Graft (CABG)

Aortocoronary Bypass for Heart Revascularization
See Artery, Coronary, Bypass

Aortography 75600-75605, 75630, 93544
See Angiography
- Serial 75625
- with Iliofemoral Artery 75630

Aortoiliac
- Embolectomy 34151-34201
- Thrombectomy 34151-34201

Aortopexy 33800

Aortoplasty
- Supravalvular Stenosis .... .33417

AP
See Voiding Pressure Studies

Apert-Gallais Syndrome
See Adrenogenital Syndrome

Aphasia Testing 96105
See Neurology, Diagnostic

Apheresis
- Therapeutic 36511-36516

Apical-Aortic Conduit .... .33404

Apicectomy
- with Mastoidectomy 69605
- Petrous 69530

Apoaminotransferase, Aspartate
See Transaminase, Glutamic Oxaloacetic

Apolipoprotein
- Blood or Urine 82172

Appendectomy 44950-44960
- Laparoscopic 44970

Appendiceal Abscess
See Abscess, Appendix

Appendico-Vesicostomy
- Cutaneous 50845

Appendix

Abscess
- Incision and Drainage
  - Open 44900
  - Percutaneous 44901
- Excision 44950-44960

Application

Allergy Tests 95044

Bone Fixation Device
- Multiplane 20692
  - Stereotactic Computer
    - Assisted 20696-20697
  - Uniplane 20690

Caliper 20660

Cranial Tongs 20660

Fixation Device
- Shoulder 23700

Halo
- Cranial 20661
  - Thin Skull Osteology 20664
- Femoral 20663
- Maxillofacial Fixation 21100
- Pelvic 20662

Interdental Fixation Device 21110

Intervertebral Device 22851

Neurostimulation 64550

Radioelement 77761-77778
- Surface 77789
- with Ultrasound 76965

Stereotactic Frame 20660
- Headframe 61800

Application of External Fixation Device
See Fixation Device, Application, External

APPT
See Thromboplastin, Partial, Time

Aquatic Therapy
See Physical Medicine/Therapy/Occupational Therapy

Aqueous Shunt
- to Extraocular Reservoir 66180
  - Revision 66185

Arch, Zygomatic
See Zygomatic Arch

Arm
See Radius; Ulna; Wrist

Lower
- Abscess 25028
- Amputation 24900-24920, 25900-25905, 25915
  - Cineplasty 24940
  - Revision 25907-25909
- Angiography 73206
- Artery
  - Ligation 37618
- Biopsy 25065-25066
- Bursa
  - Incision and Drainage 25031
- Bypass Graft 35903
- Cast 29075
- CT Scan 73200-73206
- Decompression 25020-25025

Catheterization 36120
Embolectomy 34101
Exploration 24495
Exposure 34834
Thrombectomy 34101
Thromboendarterectomy 35321
Brachiocephalic
   Angioplasty 35458
   Atherectomy 35484, 35494
   Catheterization 36215-36218
Bypass Graft
   with Composite Graft 35681-35683
Cannulization
   for Extra Corporeal Circulation 36823
   to Vein 36810-36815
Carotid
   Aneurysm 35001-35002, 61697-61705
     Vascular Malformation or Carotid
     Cavernous Fistula 61705-61710
   Angiography 75660-75680
   Bypass Graft 33891, 35501-35510, 35526,
                  35601-35606, 35626, 35642
   Catheterization 36100
   Decompression ..61590-61591, 61595-61596
   Embolectomy 34001
   Exploration 35701
   Ligation 37600-37606, 61611-61612
   Stenosis
     Imaging Study Measurement 3100F
   Thrombectomy 34001
   Thromboendarterectomy 35301, 35390
   Transection 61611-61612
   Transposition 33889
Carotid, Common
   Intima-Media Thickness (IMT) Study ...0126T
Celiac
   Aneurysm 35121-35122
   Bypass Graft 35531, 35631
   Embolectomy 34151
   Thrombectomy 34151
   Thromboendarterectomy 35341
Chest
   Ligation 37616
Coronary
   Angiography 93556
   Atherectomy 92995-92996
   Bypass 33517-33519
     Arterial 33533-33536
   Bypass Venous Graft 33510-33517, 35523
     Internal Mammary Artery Graft 4110F
   Graft 33503-33505
   Ligation 33502
   Repair 33500-33507
   Thrombectomy
     Percutaneous 92973
Digital
   Sympathectomy 64820
Ethmoidal
   Ligation 30915
Extra Corporeal Circulation
   for Regional Chemotherapy
   of Extremity 36823
Extracranial
   Vascular Studies
     Non-Invasive, Physiologic 93875
Extremities
   Vascular Studies 93922-93923
Extremity
   Bypass Graft Revision 35879-35884
   Catheterization 36140
   Ligation 37618

Femoral
   Aneurysm 35141-35142
   Angioplasty 35456
   Atherectomy 35483, 35493
   Bypass Graft 35521, 35533, 35551-35558,
             35566, 35621, 35646-35647,
             35651-35661, 35666, 35700
   Bypass Graft Revision 35883-35884
   Bypass In-Situ 35583-35585
   Embolectomy 34201
   Exploration 35721
   Exposure 34812-34813
   Thrombectomy 34201
   Thromboendarterectomy 35371-35372
Great Vessel
   Repair 33770-33781
Head
   Angiography 75650
Hepatic
   Aneurysm 35121-35122
Iliac
   Aneurysm 35131-35132, 75954
   Angioplasty 35454
   Atherectomy 35482, 35492
   Bypass Graft 35563, 35632-35634, 35663
   Embolectomy 34151-34201
   Exposure 34820, 34833
   Graft 34900
   Occlusion Device 34808
   Thrombectomy 34151-34201
   Thromboendarterectomy 35351,
                      35361-35363
Ilio-celiac
   Bypass Graft 35632
Iliofemoral
   Bypass Graft 35548-35549, 35565
   Thromboendarterectomy 35355, 35363
   X-ray with Contrast 75630
Ilio-mesenteric
   Bypass Graft 35633
Iliorenal
   Bypass Graft 35634
Innominate
   Aneurysm 35021-35022
   Embolectomy 34001-34101
   Thrombectomy 34001-34101
   Thromboendarterectomy 35311
Leg
   Angiography 75710-75716
   Catheterization 36245-36248
Mammary
   Angiography 75756
Maxillary
   Ligation 30920
Mesenteric
   Aneurysm 35121-35122
   Bypass Graft 35531, 35631
   Embolectomy 34151
   Thrombectomy 34151
   Thromboendarterectomy 35341
Middle Cerebral Artery, Fetal
   Vascular Studies 76821
Neck
   Angiography 75650
   Ligation 37615
Nose
   Incision 30915-30920
Other Angiography 75774
Other Artery
   Exploration 35761

Pelvic
   Angiography 75736
   Catheterization 36245-36248
Peripheral Arterial Rehabilitation 93668
Peroneal
   Bypass Graft 35566-35571, 35666-35671
   Bypass In-Situ 35585-35587
   Embolectomy 34203
   Thrombectomy 34203
   Thromboendarterectomy 35305-35306
Popliteal
   Aneurysm 35151-35152
   Angioplasty 35456
   Atherectomy 35483, 35493
   Bypass Graft 35551-35556, 35571, 35623,
             35651, 35656, 35671, 35700
   Bypass In-Situ 35583, 35587
   Embolectomy 34203
   Exploration 35741
   Thrombectomy 34203
   Thromboendarterectomy 35303
Pulmonary
   Anastomosis 33606
   Angiography 75741-75746
   Repair 33690, 33925-33926
Radial
   Aneurysm 35045
   Embolectomy 34111
   Sympathectomy 64821
   Thrombectomy 34111
Rehabilitation 93668
Reimplantation
   Carotid 35691, 35694-35695
   Subclavian 35693-35695
   Vertebral 35691-35693
   Visceral 35697
Renal
   Aneurysm 35121-35122
   Angiography 75722-75724
   Angioplasty 35450
   Atherectomy 35480, 35490
   Bypass Graft 35535-35536, 35560,
                    35631-35636
   Embolectomy 34151
   Thrombectomy 34151
   Thromboendarterectomy 35341
Repair
   Aneurysm 61697-61708
   Angioplasty 75962-75968
Revision
   Hemodialysis Graft or Fistula
     with Thrombectomy 36833
     without Thrombectomy 36832
Spine
   Angiography 75705
Splenic
   Aneurysm 35111-35112
   Bypass Graft 35536, 35636
Subclavian
   Aneurysm 35001-35002, 35021-35022
   Angioplasty 35458
   Bypass Graft 35506, 35511-35516, 35526,
             35606-35616, 35626, 35645
   Embolectomy 34001-34101
   Thrombectomy 34001-34101
   Thromboendarterectomy 35301, 35311
   Transposition 33889
   Unlisted Services and Procedures 37799
Superficial Femoral
   Thromboendarterectomy 35302
Superficial Palmar Arch
   Sympathectomy 64823

Artery Catheterization, Pulmonary

Arthrectomy

Arthrocentesis

Arthrodeses

Arthrodesis

Arthrography

Arthroplasties, Knee Replacement

Arthroplasty

Arthroplasty, Hip, Total

Arthroplasty, Shoulder

Arthropods

Arthroscopy

Diagnostic
　Elbow 29830
　Hip 29860
　Knee 29870
　Metacarpophalangeal Joint 29900
　Shoulder 29805
　Temporomandibular Joint 29800
　Wrist 29840
Surgical
　Ankle .29891-29899
　Elbow .29834-29838
　Hip 29861-29863
　Knee 29871-29889
　　Cartilage Allograft 29867
　　Osteochondral Autograft 29866
　　Meniscal Transplantation 29868
　Metacarpophalangeal Joint 29901-29902
　Shoulder 29806-29828
　　Biceps Tenodesis 29828
　Subtalar Joint
　　Arthrodesis 29907
　　Debridement 29906
　　Removal of Loose or Foreign Body 29904
　　Synovectomy 29905
　Temporomandibular Joint 29804
　Wrist 29843-29848
Unlisted Services and Procedures 29999

Arthroscopy of Ankle
See Ankle, Arthroscopy

Arthrotomy

Acromioclavicular Joint 23044
Ankle 27610-27612, 27620
Ankle Joint 27625-27626
Carpometacarpal Joint 26070
　with Biopsy, Synovium
　　with Synovial Biopsy 26100
Elbow 24000
　Capsular Release 24006
　with Joint Exploration 24101
　with Synovectomy 24102
　with Synovial Biopsy 24100
Finger Joint 26075
　Interphalangeal
　　with Synovial Biopsy 26110
　Metacarpophalangeal
　　with Biopsy, Synovium 26105
Glenohumeral Joint 23040
Hip 27033
　for Infection
　　with Drainage 27030
　with Synovectomy 27054
Interphalangeal Joint 26080, 26110
　Toe 28024, 28054
Intertarsal Joint 28020, 28050
Knee 27310, 27330-27335, 27403, 29868
Metacarpophalangeal Joint 26075, 26105
Metatarsophalangeal Joint 28022, 28052
Shoulder 23044, 23105-23107
Shoulder Joint 23100-23101
　Exploration and/or Removal of Loose or
　　Foreign Body 23107
Sternoclavicular Joint 23044
Tarsometatarsal Joint 28020, 28050
Temporomandibular Joint 21010
　with Biopsy
　　Acromioclavicular Joint 23101
　　Glenohumeral Joint 23100
　　Hip Joint 27052

Knee Joint 27330
Sacroiliac Joint
　Hip Joint 27050
Sternoclavicular Joint 23101
with Synovectomy
　Glenohumeral Joint 23105
　Sternoclavicular Joint 23106
Wrist 25040, 25100-25107

Arthrotomy for Removal of Prosthesis of Ankle
See Ankle, Removal, Implant

Arthrotomy for Removal of Prosthesis of Hip
See Hip, Removal, Prosthesis

Arthrotomy for Removal of Prosthesis of Wrist
See Prosthesis, Wrist, Removal

Articular Ligament
See Ligament

Artificial Abortion
See Abortion

Artificial Cardiac Pacemaker
See Heart, Pacemaker

Artificial Eye
See Prosthesis

Artificial Genitourinary Sphincter
See Prosthesis, Urethral Sphincter

Artificial Insemination 58976
See In Vitro Fertilization
Intra-Cervical 58321
Intra-Uterine 58322
Sperm Washing .58323

Artificial Knee Joints
See Prosthesis, Knee

Artificial Penis
See Penile Prosthesis

Artificial Pneumothorax
See Pneumothorax, Therapeutic

Arytenoid

Excision
　Endoscopic 31560-31561

Arytenoid Cartilage
Excision 31400
Repair 31400

Arytenoidectomy 31400
Endoscopic 31560

Arytenoidopexy 31400

Ascorbic Acid
Blood 82180

Aspartate Aminotransferase
See Transaminase, Glutamic Oxaloacetic

Aspergillus
Antibody 86606
Antigen Detection
　Enzyme Immunoassay 87305

Aspiration
See Puncture Aspiration
Amniotic Fluid
　Diagnostic 59000
　Therapeutic 59001
Bladder .51100-51102
Bone Marrow 38220
Brain Lesion
　Stereotactic 61750-61751
Breast
　Metallic Localization Clip Placement . . .19295
Bronchi
　Endoscopy 31645-31646
Bursa 20600-20610
Catheter
　Nasotracheal .31720
　Tracheobronchial 31725
Cyst
　Bone 20615
　Kidney 50390
　Pelvis 50390
　Spinal Cord 62268
　Thyroid 60300
Disc 62267
Duodenal 89100-89105
Fetal Fluid 59074
Ganglion Cyst 20612
Hydrocele
　Tunica Vaginalis 55000
Joint 20600-20610
Laryngoscopy
　Direct 31515
Lens Material 66840
Liver 47015
Lung 32420
Orbital Contents .67415
Pelvis
　Endoscopy 49322
Pericardium 33010-33011
Pleural Cavity 32421-32422
Puncture
　Cyst
　　Breast 19000-19001
Spinal Cord
　Stereotaxis 63615
Syrinx
　Spinal Cord 62268
Thyroid 60300
Trachea
　Nasotracheal .31720
　Puncture 31612
Tunica Vaginalis
　Hydrocele 55000
Vitreous 67015

Aspiration Lipectomies
See Liposuction

Aspiration of Bone Marrow from Donor for Transplant
See Bone Marrow, Harvesting

Aspiration, Chest
See Thoracentesis

Aspiration, Lung Puncture
See Pneumocentesis

Aspiration, Nail
See Evacuation, Hematoma, Subungual

Aspiration, Spinal Puncture
See Spinal Tap

BCG Vaccine 90585-90586
See Vaccines

Be Antigens, Hepatitis
See Hepatitis Antigen, Be

Bed Sores
See Debridement; Pressure Ulcer (Decubitus);
Skin Graft and Flap

Bekesy Audiometry
See Audiometry, Bekesy

Belsey IV Procedure
See Fundoplasty

Bender-Gestalt Test 96101-96103

Benedict Test for Urea
See Urinalysis, Qualitative

Benign Cystic Mucinous Tumor
See Ganglion

Benign Neoplasm of Cranial Nerves
See Cranial Nerve

Bennett Fracture
See Phalanx; Thumb, Fracture

Bennett Procedure
See Repair, Leg, Upper, Muscle; Revision

Benzidine Test
See Blood, Feces

Benzodiazepine
Assay 80154

Benzoyl Cholinesterase
See Cholinesterase

Bernstein Test
See Acid Perfusion Test, Esophagus

Beryllium 83015

Beta 2 Glycoprotein I Antibody . .86146

Beta Blocker Therapy
See Performance Measures

Beta Glucosidase 82963

Beta Hypophamine
See Antidiuretic Hormone

Beta Lipoproteins
See Lipoprotein, LDL

Beta Test
See Psychiatric Diagnosis

Beta-2-Microglobulin
Blood 82232
Urine 82232

Beta-hydroxydehydrogenase 80406

Bethesda System 88164-88167

Bicarbonate 82374

Biceps Tendon
Insertion 24342

Bichloride, Methylene
See Dichloromethane

Bicuspid Valve
See Mitral Valve

Bifrontal Craniotomy 61557

**Bilaminate Skin
Substitute/Neodermis**
See Tissue
Repair
  See Tissue, Culture
  Repair; Tissue, Culture, Skin Grafts

Bile Acids 82239
Blood 82240

Bile Duct
See Gallbladder
Anastomosis
  with Intestines 47760, 47780-47785
Biopsy
  Endoscopy 47553
Catheterization .75982
Change Catheter Tube 75984
Cyst
  Excision 47715
Destruction
  Calculi (Stone) 43265
Dilation
  Endoscopy 43271, 47555-47556
Drainage
  Transhepatic .75980
Endoscopy
  Biopsy 47553
  Cannulation .43273
  Destruction
    Calculi (Stone) 43265
    Tumor 43272
  Dilation 43271, 47555-47556
  Exploration 47552
  Intraoperative 47550
  Removal
    Calculi (Stone) 43264, 47554
    Foreign Body 43269
    Stent 43269
  Specimen Collection 43260
  Sphincter Pressure 43263
  Sphincterotomy 43262
  Tube Placement 43267-43268
Exploration
  Atresia 47700
  Endoscopy 47552
Incision
  Sphincter 43262, 47460
Incision and Drainage 47420-47425
Insertion
  Catheter 47510, 47525, 75982
    Revision 47530
  Stent 47511, 47801
Nuclear Medicine
  Imaging 78223
Reconstruction
  Anastomosis .47800
Removal
  Calculi (Stone) 43264, 47420-47425
  Percutaneous 47630
  Foreign Body 43269
  Stent 43269
Repair 47701
  Gastrointestinal Tract 47785
  with Intestines 47760, 47780
Tube Placement
  Nasobiliary 43267
  Stent 43268

Tumor
  Destruction 43271
  Excision 47711-47712
Unlisted Services and Procedures 47999
X-ray
  Guide Dilation 74360
  with Contrast 74300-74320
    Calculus Removal 74327
    Guide Catheter 74328, 74330

Bile Duct, Common, Cystic Dilatation
See Cyst, Choledochal

Bilirubin
Blood 82247-82248
Feces 82252
Total
  Direct 82247-82248
  Transcutaneous 88720

Billroth I or II
See Gastrectomy, Partial

Bilobectomy .32482

Bimone
See Testosterone

**Binding Globulin, Testosterone-
Estradiol**
See Globulin, Sex Hormone Binding

Binet Test 96101-96103

Binet-Simon Test 96101-96103

Binocular Microscopy 92504

Biofeedback
See Training, Biofeedback
Anorectal 90911
Psychiatric Treatment 90875-90876

Biofeedback Training
See Training, Biofeedback

Bioimpedance
Cardiovascular Analysis 93701

Biological Skin Grafts
See Allograft, Skin

Biometry
Eye 76516-76519, 92136

Biopsies, Needle
See Needle Biopsy

Biopsy
See Brush Biopsy; Needle Biopsy
Abdomen 49000
Adrenal Gland 60540-60545
Anal
  Endoscopy 46606
Ankle 27613-27614, 27620
Arm, Lower 25065-25066
Arm, Upper 24065-24066
Artery
  Temporal 37609
Auditory Canal, External 69105
Back/Flank 21920-21925
Bile Duct
  Endoscopy 47553
Bladder 52354
  Cystourethroscope 52204
  Cystourethroscopy 52224, 52250

Blood Vessel
   Transcatheter .75970
Bone 20220-20245
Bone Marrow 38221
Brain 61140
   Stereotactic 61750-61751
Brainstem 61575-61576
Breast 19100-19103
Metallic Localization Clip Placement 19295
   Stereotactic Localization 77031
Bronchi
   Catheterization 31717
   Endoscopic 31625-31629, 31632-31633
Brush
   Bronchi 31717
   Renal Pelvis .52007
   Ureter 52007
   with Cystourethroscopy 52204
Carpometacarpal Joint
   Synovium 26100
Cervix 57454-57455, 57460, 57500, 57520
Chorionic Villus 59015
Colon 44025, 44100
   Endoscopy 44389, 45380, 45391-45392
   Multiple
     with Colostomy, Cecostomy 44322
Colon-Sigmoid
   Endoscopy 45305, 45331
Conjunctiva 68100
Cornea 65410
Duodenum 44010
Ear
   External 69100
Elbow 24065-24066, 24101
   Synovium 24100
Embryo Blastomere 89290-89291
Endometrium 58100-58110, 58558
Epididymis 54800, 54865
Esophagus
   Endoscopy .43202
   Forceps 3150F
Eye Muscle 67346
Eyelid 67810
Forearm
   Soft Tissue 25065-25066
Gallbladder
   Endoscopy .43261
Gastrointestinal, Upper
   Endoscopy .43239
Hand Joint
   Synovium 26100
Heart 93505
Hip .27040-27041
   Joint 27052
Hypopharynx .42802
Ileum
   Endoscopy .44382
Interphalangeal Joint
   Finger 26110
   Toe 28054
Intertarsal Joint
   Toe 28050
Intestines, Small 44020, 44100
   Endoscopy 44361, 44377
Kidney 50200-50205
   Endoscopic 50555-50557,
                   50574-50576, 52354
Knee .27323-27324
   Synovium 27330
Knee Joint
   Synovium 27330
Lacrimal Gland 68510

Lacrimal Sac .68525
Larynx
   Endoscopy 31510, 31576
Leg
   Lower 27613-27614
   Upper 27323-27324
Lip 40490
Liver 47000-47001, 47100
Lung
   Needle 32405
   Thoracotomy 32095-32100
Lymph Nodes 38500-38530
   Injection Procedure
     for Identification of Sentinel Node . . .38792
   Laparoscopic 38570-38572
   Needle 38505
   Open 38500, 38510-38530
     Superficial 38500
Mediastinum .39400
   Needle 32405
Metacarpophalangeal Joint 26105
Metatarsophalangeal Joint 28052
Mouth 40808, 41108
Muscle 20200-20206
Nail 11755
Nasopharynx 42804-42806
Neck 21550
Nerve 64795
Nose
   Endoscopic .31237
   Intranasal 30100
Oocyte Polar Body 89290-89291
Orbit 61332
   Exploration 67400, 67450
   Fine Needle Aspiration 67415
Oropharynx 42800
Ovary 58900
Palate 42100
Pancreas 48100
Pelvis 27040-27041
Penis 54100
   Deep Structures 54105
Percutaneous Needle
   Spinal Cord 62269
Perineum 56605-56606
Peritoneum
   Endoscopic .47561
Pharynx 42800-42806
Pleura
   Needle 32400-32402
   Thoracotomy 32095-32100
Pleural
   Open 32402
Prostate 55700-55706
Rectum 45100
Retroperitoneal Area 49010
Sacroiliac Joint 27050
Salivary Gland 42405
Shoulder
   Deep 23066
   Soft Tissue .23065
Shoulder Joint 23100-23101
Sinus
   Sphenoid 31050-31051
Skin Lesion 11100-11101
Spinal Cord 63275-63290
   Percutaneous 62269
   Stereotaxis .63615
Stomach 43600-43605
Tarsometatarsal Joint
   Synovial 28050
Testis 54500-54505

Thorax 21550
Throat 42800-42806
Tongue 41100-41105
Transcatheter .37200
Ureter 52354
   Endoscopic 50955-50957, 50974-50976
Urethra 52204, 52354, 53200
Uterus
   Endometrial 58100-58110
   Endoscopic .58558
Uvula 42100
Vagina 57100-57105, 57421
Vertebral Body 20250-20251
Vulva 56605-56606, 56821
with Arthrotomy
   Acromioclavicular Joint 23101
   Glenohumeral Joint 23100
   Sternoclavicular Joint 23101
with Cystourethroscopy 52354
Wrist 25065-25066, 25100-25101

Biopsy, Skin
See Skin, Biopsy

Biopsy, Vein
See Vein, Biopsy

Biostatistics
See Biometry

Biosterol
See Vitamin, A

Biotinidase .82261

Birthing Room
Newborn Care 99460, 99463
   Attendance at Delivery 99464
   Resuscitation 99465

Bischof Procedure
See Laminectomy, Surgical

Bismuth 83015

Bizzozero's Corpuscle/Cell
See Blood, Platelet

Bladder
Abscess
   Incision and Drainage 51080
Anastomosis .51960
Aspiration 51100-51102
Biopsy 52204
Catheterization 51045, 51701-51703
Change Tube 51705-51710
Creation
   Stoma 51980
Cyst
   Urachal
     Excision .51500
Destruction
   Endoscopic 52214-52224, 52354
Dilation
   Ureter 52260-52265, 52341-52342,
                    52344-52345
Diverticulum
   Excision 51525
   Incision 52305
   Resection 52305
Endoscopy 52000
   Biopsy 52204, 52354
   Catheterization 52005, 52010
   Destruction 52214-52224, 52400

Blood Banking

Frozen Blood Preparation	.86930-86932
Frozen Plasma Preparation	.86927
Physician Services	.86077-86079

Blood Cell

CD4 and CD8
Including Ratio	.86360
Enzyme Activity	.82657
Exchange	.36511-36513

Sedimentation Rate
Automated	.85652
Manual	.85651

Blood Cell Count

Automated	.85049
B-Cells	.86355
Blood Smear	.85007-85008
Differential WBC Count	.85004-85007, 85009
Hematocrit	.85014
Hemoglobin	.85018

Hemogram
Added Indices	.85025-85027
Automated	.85025-85027
Manual	.85032
Microhematocrit	.85013
Natural Killer (NK) Cells	.86357
Red Blood Cells	.85032-85041
Reticulocyte	.85044-85046
Stem Cells	.86367
T-Cells	.86359-86361
White Blood Cells	.85032, 85048, 89055

Blood Cell Count, Red

See Red Blood Cell (RBC), Count

Blood Cell Count, White

See White Blood Cell, Count

Blood Cell, Red

See Red Blood Cell (RBC)

Blood Cell, White

See Leukocyte

Blood Coagulation

Defect
   See Coagulopathy
Disorders
   See Clot
Factor
   See Clotting Factor
   Factor I
     See Fibrinogen
   Factor II
     See Prothrombin
   Factor III
     See Thromboplastin
   Factor IV
     See Calcium
   Factor VII
     See Proconvertin
   Factor VIII
     See Clotting Factor
   Factor IX
     See Christmas Factor
   Factor X
     See Stuart-Prower Factor
   Factor X, Activated
     See Thrombokinase
   Factor XI
     See Plasma Thromboplastin, Antecedent

Factor XIII
   See Fibrin Stabilizing Factor
Test
   See Coagulation

Blood Component Removal

See Apheresis

Blood Count, Complete

See Complete Blood Count (CBC)

Blood Flow Check, Graft .... .15860, 90940

Blood Gases

CO_2	.82803
HCO_3	.82803
O_2 Saturation	.82805-82810
pCO_2	.82803
pH	.82800-82803
pO_2	.82803

Blood Letting

See Phlebotomy

Blood Lipoprotein

See Lipoprotein

Blood Occult

See Occult, Blood

Blood Pool Imaging 78472-78473, 78481-78483, 78494-78496

Blood Pressure

See Performance Measures
Monitoring, 24 Hour	.93784-93790

Ocular
Measurement	.0198T
Systolic	.3074F-3075F
Venous	.93770

Blood Products

Irradiation	.86945
Pooling	.86965
Splitting	.86985
Volume Reduction	.86960

Blood Sample

Fetal	.59030

Blood Serum

See Serum

Blood Smear .... .85060

Blood Syndrome

Chromosome Analysis	.88245-88248

Blood Tests

Iron Stores	.3160F
Kt/V	.3082F-3084F

Nuclear Medicine
Plasma Volume	.78110-78111
Platelet Survival	.78190-78191
Red Cell Volume	.78120-78121
Whole Blood Volume	.78122

Panels
Electrolyte	.80051
General Health Panel	.80050
Hepatic Function	.80076
Hepatitis, Acute	.80074
Lipid Panel	.80061
Metabolic Panel, Basic	
Ionized Calcium	.80047
Total Calcium	.80048
Comprehensive	.80053

Obstetric Panel	.80055
Renal Function	.80069
Volume Determination	.78122

Blood Transfusion, Autologous

See Autotransfusion

Blood Typing

ABO Only	.86900
Antigen Screen	.86903-86904
Crossmatch	.86920-86923
Other RBC Antigens	.86905
Paternity Testing	.86910-86911
Rh (D)	.86901
Rh Phenotype	.86906

Blood Urea Nitrogen 84520-84525

Blood Vessels

See Artery; Vein
Angioscopy
Non-Coronary	.35400

Endoscopy
Surgical	.37500

Excision
Arteriovenous Malformation	.63250-63252

Exploration
Abdomen	.35840
Chest	.35820
Extremity	.35860
Neck	.35800

Great
Suture	.33320-33322

Harvest
Endoscopic	.33508
Lower Extremity Vein	.35572
Upper Extremity Artery	.35600
Upper Extremity Vein	.35500

Kidney
Repair	.50100

Repair
   Abdomen
     See Aneurysm Repair; Fistula, Repair
with Composite Graft	.35681-35683
with Other Graft	.35281
with Vein Graft	.35251
Aneurysm	.61705-61708
Arteriovenous Malformation	.61680-61692, 61705-61710, 63250-63252

Chest
with Composite Graft	.35681-35683
with Other Graft	.35271-35276
with Vein Graft	.35241-35246
Direct	.35201-35226
Finger	.35207
Graft Defect	.35870
Hand	.35207
Lower Extremity	.35226
with Composite Graft	.35681-35683
with Other Graft	.35281
with Vein Graft	.35251

Neck
with Composite Graft	.35681-35683
with Other Graft	.35261
with Vein Graft	.35231
Upper Extremity	.35206
with Composite Graft	.35681-35683
with Other Graft	.35266
with Vein Graft	.35236

Shunt Creation
Direct	.36818, 36821
Thomas Shunt	.36835

with Bypass Graft 35686
with Graft 36825-36830
Shunt Revision
with Graft 36832

Blood, Occult
See Occult Blood

Bloom Syndrome
Chromosome Analysis 88245

Blot Test, Ink
See Inkblot Test

Blotting, Western
See Western Blot

Blow-Out Fracture
Orbital Floor 21385-21395

Blue, Dome Cyst
See Breast, Cyst

BMT
See Bone Marrow, Transplantation

Boarding Home Care 99324-99337

Bodies
Acetone
See Acetone Body
Barr
See Barr Bodies
Carotid
See Carotid Body
Ciliary
See Ciliary Body
Heinz
See Heinz Bodies
Inclusion
See Inclusion Bodies
Ketone
See Ketone Body

Body Cast
Halo 29000
Removal 29700, 29710-29715
Repair 29720
Risser Jacket 29010-29015
Turnbuckle Jacket 29020-29025
Upper Body and Head 29040
Upper Body and Legs 29046
Upper Body and One Leg 29044
Upper Body Only 29035

Body Fluid
Crystal Identification 89060

Body of Vertebra
See Vertebral Body

Body Section
X-ray 76100
Motion 76101-76102

Body System, Neurologic
See Nervous System

Boil
See Furuncle

Boil, Vulva
See Abscess, Vulva

Bone
See Specific Bone

Ablation
Tumor 20982
Biopsy 20220-20245
Carpal
See Carpal Bone
Cheek
See Cheekbone
CT Scan
Density Study 77078-77079
Cyst
Drainage 20615
Injection 20615
Dual Energy X-ray Absorptiometry ...77080-77081
Excision
Epyphyseal Bar 20150
Facial Bones 21026
Mandible 21025
Facial
See Facial Bone
Fixation
Caliper 20660
Cranial Tong 20660
Halo 20661-20663, 21100
Interdental 21110
Multiplane 20692
Stereotactic Computer
Assisted 20696-20697
Pin/Wire 20650
Skeletal
Humeral Epicondyle
Percutaneous 24566
Stereotactic Frame 20660
Uniplane 20690
Vertebral with Arthroplasty 0202T
Fracture
Osteoporosis Screening 5015F
Hyoid
See Hyoid Bone
Insertion
Needle 36680
Osseointegrated Implant
for External Speech Processor/Cochlear
Stimulator 69714-69718
Marrow
Cytogenic Testing 3155F
Metatarsal
See Metatarsal Bone
Nasal
See Nasal Bone
Navicular
See Navicular
Nuclear Medicine
Density Study 78350-78351
Imaging 78300-78320
SPECT 78320
Unlisted Services and Procedures 78399
Osteoporosis
Pharmacologic Therapy 4005F
Protein 83937
Removal
Fixation Device 20670-20680
Replacement
Osseointegrated Implant
for External Speech Processor/Cochlear
Stimulator 69717-69718
Scan
See Bone, Nuclear Medicine; Nuclear Medicine
Imaging
Semilunar
See Lunate
Sesamoid
See Sesamoid Bone

Spur
See Exostosis
Tarsal
See Ankle Bone
Temporal
See Temporal Bone
X-ray
Age Study 77072
Dual Energy Absorptiometry 77080-77081
Length Study 77073
Osseous Survey 77074-77077

Bone 4-Carboxyglutamic Protein
See Osteocalcin

Bone Conduction Hearing Device, Electromagnetic
Implantation/Replacement 69710
Removal/Repair 69711

Bone Density Study
Appendicular Skeleton 77079, 77081
Axial Skeleton 77078, 77080
Ultrasound 76977
Vertebral Fracture Assessment 77082

Bone Graft
Any Donor Area 20900-20902
Augmentation
Mandibular Body 21127
Femur 27170
Fracture
Orbit 21408
Harvesting 20900-20902
Malar Area 21210
Mandible 21215
Mandibular Ramus 21194
Maxilla 21210
Microvascular Anastomosis
Fibula 20955
Other 20962
Nasal Area 21210
Nasomaxillary Complex Fracture 21348
Open Treatment
Craniofacial Separation 21436
Osteocutaneous Flap 20969-20973
Reconstruction
Mandibular Rami 21194
Midface 21145-21160
Skull 61316
Excision 62148
Spine Surgery
Allograft
Morselized 20930
Structural 20931
Autograft
Local 20936
Morselized 20937
Structural 20938
Vascular Pedicle 25430

Bone Healing
Electrical Stimulation
Invasive 20975
Noninvasive 20974
Ultrasound Stimulation 20979

Bone Infection
See Osteomyelitis

Bone Marrow
Aspiration 38220
Harvesting 38230

Magnetic Resonance Imaging (MRI) 77084
Needle Biopsy 38221
Nuclear Medicine
　　Imaging 78102-78104
Smear 85097
T-Cell Transplantation 38240-38242
Trocar Biopsy 38221

Bone Plate
Mandible 21244

Bone Wedge Reversal
Osteotomy 21122

Bordetella
Antibody 86615
Antigen Detection
　　Direct Fluorescence 87265

Borrelia
Antibody .86618-86619

Borrelia burgdorferi ab
See Antibody, Lyme Disease

Borreliosis, Lyme
See Lyme Disease

Bost Fusion
See Arthrodesis, Wrist

Bosworth Operation
See Acromioclavicular Joint, Dislocation;
Arthrodesis, Vertebrae; Fasciotomy

Bottle Type Procedure 55060

Botulinum Toxin
See Chemodenervation

Boutonniere Deformity 26426-26428

Bowel
See Intestine

Bowleg Repair 27455-27457

Boyd Hip Disarticulation
See Amputation, Leg, Upper; Radical Resection;
Replantation

Brace
See Cast
for Leg Cast 29358

Brachial Arteries
See Artery, Brachial

Brachial Plexus
Decompression .64713
Injection
　Anesthetic 64415-64416
Neuroplasty 64713
Release 64713
Repair/Suture 64861

Brachiocephalic Artery
See Artery, Brachiocephalic

Brachycephaly 21175

Brachytherapy 77761-77778, 77789
Dose Plan 77326-77328
　　High Dose Electronic 0182T
Remote Afterloading
　1 Channel 77785
　2-12 Channels 77786

More Than 1 Channel 77786-77787
More Than 12 Channels 77787
Unlisted Services and Procedures 77799

Bradykinin
Blood or Urine 82286

Brain
See Brainstem; Mesencephalon; Skull Base Surgery
Abscess
　Drainage 61150-61151
　Excision 61514, 61522
　Incision and Drainage 61320-61321
Adhesions
　Lysis 62161
Anesthesia 00210-00218, 00220-00222
Angiography 70496
Biopsy 61140
　Stereotactic 61750-61751
Catheter
　Irrigation 62194, 62225
　Replacement 62160, 62194, 62225
Catheter Placement
　for Chemotherapy 0169T
Cisternography .70015
Computer Assisted
　Surgery 61795
Cortex
　Magnetic Stimulation 0160T-0161T
Craniopharyngioma
　Excision 61545
CT Scan 0042T, 70450-70470, 70496
Cyst
　Drainage 61150-61151, 62161-62162
　Excision 61516, 61524, 62162
Doppler, Transcranial 93886-93893
Epileptogenic Focus
　Excision 61534, 61536
Excision
　Amygdala 61566
　Choroid Plexus 61544
　Hemisphere 61542-61543
　Hippocampus 61566
　Other Lobe 61323, 61539-61540
　Temporal Lobe 61537-61538
Exploration
　Infratentorial .61305
　Supratentorial 61304
Hematoma
　Drainage 61154
　Incision and Drainage 61312-61315
Implantation
　Chemotherapy Agent 61517
　Electrode 61850-61875
　Pulse Generator 61885-61886
　Receiver 61885-61886
Incision
　Corpus Callosum 61541
　Frontal Lobe .61490
　Mesencephalic Tract 61480
　Subpial 61567
Infusion 0169T
Insertion
　Catheter 61210
　Electrode 61531-61533, 61850-61875
　Pulse Generator 61885-61886
　Receiver 61885-61886
　Reservoir 61210-61215
Lesion
　Aspiration, Stereotactic 61750-61751
　Excision 61534, 61536, 61600-61608,
　　　　　　　　　　　　　　　　　61615-61616

Magnetic Resonance Imaging
(MRI) 70551-70555
　Intraoperative 70557-70559
Magnetic Stimulation
　Transcranial 0160T, 0161T
Meningioma
　Excision 61512, 61519
Myelography 70010
Nuclear Medicine
　Blood Flow 78610
　Cerebrospinal Fluid 78630-78650
　Imaging 78600-78607
　　Vascular Flow 78610
Positron Emission Tomography 78608-78609
Removal
　Electrode 61535, 61880
　Foreign Body 61570, 62163
　Pulse Generator 61888
　Receiver 61888
　Shunt .62256-62258
Repair
　Dura 61618
　Wound 61571
Shunt
　Creation 62180-62192, 62200-62223
　Removal 62256-62258
　Replacement 62160, 62194, 62225-62230,
　　　　　　　　　　　　　　　　　62256-62258
　Reprogramming 62252
Skull
　Transcochlear Approach 61596
　Transcondylar Approach 61597
　Transpetrosal Approach 61598
　Transtemporal Approach 61595
Skull Base
　Craniofacial Approach 61580-61585
　Infratemporal Approach 61590-61591
　Orbitocranial Zygomatic Approach 61592
Stereotactic
　Aspiration 61750-61751
　Biopsy 61750-61751
　Catheter Placement 0169T
　Create Lesion 61720-61735, 61790-61791
　Localization for Placement Therapy
　　Fields 61770
　Radiation Treatment 77432
　Radiosurgery 61796-61800,
　　　　　　　　　　　　　　77371-77373, 77435
　Surgery 61795
　Trigeminal Tract 61791
Transection
　Subpial 61567
Tumor
　Excision 61510, 61518, 61520-61521,
　　　　　　　　　　61526-61530, 61545, 62164
X-ray
　with Contrast 70010-70015

Brain Coverings
See Meninges

Brain Death
Determination 95824

Brain Stem
See Brainstem

Brain Stem Auditory Evoked Potential
See Evoked Potential, Auditory Brainstem

Brain Surface Electrode
Stimulation 95961-95962

Bronchopulmonary Lavage
See Lung, Lavage

Bronchoscopy
Ablation
　　Photodynamic Therapy 96570-96571
Alveolar Lavage 31624
Aspiration 31645-31646
Biopsy 31625-31629, 31632-31633
Brushing/Protected Brushing 31623
Catheter Placement
　　Intracavitary Radioelement 31643
Computer-assisted Navigation 31627
Dilation 31630-31631, 31636-31638
Exploration 31622
Fiducial Marker Placement 31626
Fracture 31630
Injection 31656
Needle Biopsy 31629, 31633
Removal
　　Foreign Body .31635
　　Tumor 31640, 31641
Stenosis 31641
Stent Placement 31631, 31636-31637
Stent Revision 31638
Ultrasound 31620
X-ray, Contrast 31656

Bronchospasm Evaluation
See Pulmonology, Diagnostic, Spirometry

Bronkodyl
See Theophylline

Brow Ptosis
Repair 67900

Brucella 86000
Antibody 86622

Bruise
See Hematoma

Brunschwig Operation 58240
See Hip; Pelvis, Exenteration

Brush Biopsy
See Biopsy; Needle Biopsy
Bronchi 31717

Brush Border ab
See Antibody, Heterophile

Bucca
See Cheek

Buccal Mucosa
See Mouth, Mucosa

Bulbourethral Gland
Excision 53250

Bulla
Incision and Drainage
　　Puncture Aspiration 10160
Lung
　　Excision-Plication 32141
　　　Endoscopic .32655

BUN
See Blood Urea Nitrogen; Urea Nitrogen

Bunion Repair 28296-28299
Chevron Procedure .28296
Concentric Procedure 28296

Joplin Procedure 28294
Keller Procedure 28292
Lapidus Procedure .28297
Mayo Procedure 28292
McBride Procedure .28292
Mitchell Procedure .28296
Silver Procedure 28290
with Implant 28293

Burgess Amputation
See Disarticulation, Ankle

Burkitt Herpesvirus
See Epstein-Barr Virus

Burns
Allograft 15300-15336
Debridement 01951-01953, 15002-15005,
　　　　　　　　　　　　　　　　　16020-16030
Dressings 16020-16030
Escharotomy 16035-16036
Excision 01951-01953
Initial Treatment 16000
Tissue Culture Skin Grafts 15100-15157
Xenograft 15400-15431

Burr Hole
Anesthesia 00214
Skull
　　Biopsy, Brain .61140
　　Catheterization 61210
　　Drainage
　　　Abscess 61150-61151
　　　Cyst 61150-61151
　　　Hematoma 61154-61156
　　Exploration
　　　Infratentorial 61253
　　　Supratentorial 61250
　　for Implant of Neurostimulator
　　Array 61863-61868
　　Injection, Contrast Media 61120
　　Insertion
　　　Catheter 61210
　　　Reservoir 61210

Burrow's Operation
See Skin, Adjacent Tissue Transfer

Bursa
Ankle 27604
Arm, Lower 25031
Elbow
　　Excision 24105
　　Incision and Drainage 23931
Femur
　　Excision 27062
Foot
　　Incision and Drainage 28001
Hip
　　Incision and Drainage 26991
Injection 20600-20610
Ischial
　　Excision 27060
Joint
　　Aspiration 20600-20610
　　Drainage 20600-20610
　　Injection 20600-20610
Knee
　　Excision 27340
Leg, Lower 27604
Palm
　　Incision and Drainage 26025-26030

Pelvis
　　Incision and Drainage 26991
Shoulder
　　Drainage 23031
Wrist 25031
　　Excision 25115-25116

Bursectomy
See Excision, Bursa

Bursitis, Radiohumeral
See Tennis Elbow

Bursocentesis
See Aspiration, Bursa

Button
Nasal Septal Prosthesis
　　Insertion 30220

Butyrylcholine Esterase
See Cholinesterase

Bypass Graft
Aortobi-iliac 35538, 35638
Aortobifemoral 35540
Aortofemoral 35539
Aortoiliac 35537, 35637
Axillary Artery 35516-35522, 35533,
　　　　　　　　　　35616-35623, 35650, 35654
Brachial Artery 35510, 35512, 35522-35525
Carotid Artery 33891, 35501-35510, 35526,
　　　　　　　　　　35601-35606, 35626, 35642
Celiac Artery 35531, 35631
Coronary Artery
　　Angiography 93556
　　Arterial 33533-33536
　　Venous Graft 33510-33516
Excision
　　Abdomen 35907
　　Extremity 35903
　　Neck 35901
　　Thorax 35905
Femoral Artery 35521, 35533, 35551-35558,
　　　　　　　　　　35566, 35621, 35646-35647,
　　　　　　　　　　35651-35661, 35666, 35700
Harvest
　　Endoscopic 33508
　　Upper Extremity Vein 35500
Hepatorenal
　　Venous Graft .35535
Iliac Artery 35563
Ilio-celiac Artery 35632
Iliofemoral Artery 35548-35549, 35565, 35665
Ilio-mesenteric Artery 35633
Iliorenal Artery 35634
Mesenteric Artery 35531, 35631
Peroneal Artery 35566-35571, 35666-35671
Peroneal-Tibial
　　Venous Graft .35570
Placement
　　Vein Patch 35685
Popliteal Artery 35551-35558, 35571, 35623,
　　　　　　　　　　35651, 35656, 35671, 35700
Renal Artery 35536, 35560, 35631-35636
Reoperation 35700
Repair
　　Abdomen 35907
　　Extremity 35903
　　Lower Extremity
　　　with Composite Graft 35681-35683
　　Neck 35901
　　Thorax 35905

C

Canthopexy
Lateral 21282
Medial 21280

Canthoplasty 67950

Canthorrhaphy 67880-67882

Canthotomy .67715

Canthus
Reconstruction 67950

Cap, Cervical
See Cervical Cap

Capsule
See Capsulodesis
Elbow
    Arthrotomy .24006
    Excision 24006
Foot 28264
Interphalangeal Joint
    Excision 26525
    Incision 26525
Knee 27435
Metacarpophalangeal Joint
    Excision 26520
    Incision 26520
Metatarsophalangeal Joint
    Release 28289
Shoulder
    Incision 23020
Wrist
    Excision 25320

Capsulectomy
Breast
    Periprosthetic 19371

Capsulodesis
Metacarpophalangeal Joint 26516-26518

Capsulorrhaphy
Anterior 23450-23462
Multi-Directional Instability 23466
Posterior 23465
Wrist 25320

Capsulotomy
Breast
    Periprosthetic 19370
Foot 28260-28262
Hip
    with Release, Flexor Muscles 27036
Interphalangeal Joint 28272
Knee 27435
Metacarpophalangeal Joint 26520
Metatarsophalangeal Joint 28270
Toe 28270-28272
Wrist 25085

Captopril 80416-80417

Carbamazepine
Assay 80156-80157

Carbazepin
See Carbamazepine

Carbinol
See Methanol

Carbohydrate Deficient Transferrin 82373

Carbon Dioxide
Blood or Urine .82374

Carbon Tetrachloride 84600

Carboxycathepsin
See Angiotensin Converting Enzyme (ACE)

Carboxyhemoglobin . . .82375-82376, 88740

Carbuncle
Incision and Drainage 10060-10061

Carcinoembryonal Antigen
See Antigen, Carcinoembryonic

Carcinoembryonic Antigen 82378

Cardiac
See Coronary
Muscle
    See Myocardium
Neoplasm
    See Heart, Tumor
Pacemaker
    See Heart, Pacemaker
Septal Defect
    See Septal Defect

Cardiac Arrhythmia, Tachycardia
See Tachycardia

Cardiac Atria
See Atria

Cardiac Catheterization
Combined Left and Right Heart 93526-93529
Combined Right and Retrograde Left
    Congenital Cardiac Anomalies 93531
Combined Right and Transseptal Left
    Congenital Cardiac Anomalies . . .93532-93533
for Angiography 93508, 93541-93543
for Biopsy 93505
for Dilution Studies 93561-93562
Imaging .93555-93556
Injection .93539-93545
    See Catheterization, Cardiac
Left Heart 93510-93524
Pacemaker 33210
Right
    Congenital Cardiac Anomalies 93530
Right Heart 93501-93503

Cardiac Electroversion
See Cardioversion

Cardiac Event Recorder
Implantation .33282
Removal 33284

Cardiac Magnetic Resonance Imaging (CMRI)
Complete Study 75554
Limited Study 75555
Morphology 75553
Velocity Flow Mapping 75556

Cardiac Massage
Thoracotomy .32160

Cardiac Output
Indicator Dilution 93561-93562
Inert Gas Rebreathing 0104T-0105T

Cardiac Rehabilitation 93797-93798

Cardiac Transplantation
See Heart, Transplantation

Cardiectomy
Donor 33930, 33940

Cardioassist 92970-92971

Cardiolipin Antibody 86147

Cardiology
See Defibrillator, Heart; Electrocardiography;
Pacemaker, Heart
Diagnostic
    Acoustic Recording with Computer Analysis
    Atrial Electrogram
        Esophageal Recording 93615-93616
    Bioimpedance Analysis 93701
    Cardiovascular Monitor, Implantable
        Data Analysis 93290, 93297, 93299
    Cardioverter-Defibrillator, Implantable
        Data Analysis 93289, 93295-93296
        Evaluation of Programming . . .93282-93284,
            93287, 93289, 93292, 93295-93296,
                93640-93642
    Echocardiography
        Doppler 93303-93321, 93662
        Intracardiac 93662
        Transesophageal 93318
        Transthoracic . . .93303-93317, 93350-93352
    Electrocardiogram
        Evaluation 0178T-0180T, 93000, 93010,
                93014, 93660
        Microvolt T-wave Alternans 93025
        Monitoring 93224-93237
        Rhythm 93040-93042
        Tracing 93005
        Transmission 93012
        Patient-Activated 93268, 93272
    Ergonovine Provocation Test 93024
    Intracardiac Pacing and Mapping 93631
        3-D Mapping 93613
        Follow-up Study 93624
        Stimulation and Pacing 93623
    Intracardiac Pacing and Recording
        Arrhythmia Induction 93618-93624
        Bundle of His 93600, 93619-93620
        Comprehensive 93619-93622
        Intra-Atrial 93602, 93610
        Right Ventricle 93603
        Tachycardia Sites 93609
        Ventricular 93612
    Intravascular Ultrasound 92978-92979
    Loop Recorder, Implantable
        Data Analysis 93291, 93298-93299
        Evaluation of Device Programming . . .93285,
                93291, 93298-93299
    Pacemaker Testing 93642
        Antitachycardia System 93724
        Data Analysis 93288, 93293-93294
        Evaluation of Device
            Programming 93279-93281, 93286,
                93288, 93290, 93293-93294, 93296
    Perfusion Imaging 78460-78461
        See Nuclear Medicine
    Stress Tests
        Cardiovascular 93015-93018
        Drug Induced 93024
        Multiple Gated Acquisition (MUGA) . .78473
    Tilt Table Evaluation 93660

Bladder 51701-51703
   Irrigation 51700
Declotting 36593
Exchange
   Intravascular 37209, 75900
   Peritoneal 49423
Intracatheter
   Irrigation 99507
   Obstruction Clearance 36596
Pericatheter
   Obstruction
     Clearance 36595
Placement
   Brain
     Stereotactic 0169T
   Breast
     for Interstitial Radioelement
     Application 19296-19298, 20555, 41019
   Bronchus
     for Intracavitary Radioelement
     Application 31643
Removal
   Central Venous 36589
   Peritoneum 49422
   Spinal Cord 62355
Repair
   Central Venous 36575
Replacement
   Central Venous 36580-36581, 36584
Repositioning 36597

Catheterization
See Catheter
Abdomen 49420-49421
Abdominal Artery 36245-36248
Aorta 36160-36215
Arterial
   Cutdown 36625
   Intracatheter/Needle 36100-36140
   Percutaneous 36620
Arteriovenous Shunt 36147-36148
Bile Duct 47530
   Change 47525
   Percutaneous 47510
Bladder 51010, 51045
Brachiocephalic Artery 36215-36218
Brain 61210
   Replacement 62160, 62194, 62225
   Stereotactic 0169T
Bronchography 31710
Cardiac
   Combined Left and Right Heart ..93526-93529
   Combined Right and Retrograde Left for
   Congenital Cardiac Anomalies 93531
   Combined Right and Transseptal Left for
   Congenital Cardiac Anomalies ...93532-93533
   Flow Directed 93503
   for Biopsy 93505
   for Dilution Studies 93561-93562
   Imaging 93555-93556
   Injection 93539-93545
   Left Heart 93510-93524
   Pacemaker 33210
   Right Heart 36013, 93501
     for Congenital Cardiac Anomalies 93530
Central 36555-36566
Cerebral Artery 36215
Cystourethroscopy
   Ejaculatory Duct 52010
   Ureteral 52005
Ear, Middle 69405
Eustachian Tube 69405

Fallopian Tube 58345, 74742
Intracardiac
   Ablation 93650-93652
Jejunum
   for Enteral 44015
Kidney
   Drainage 50392
   with Ureter 50393
Legs 36245-36248
Nasotracheal 31720
Newborn
   Umbilical Vein 36510
Pelvic Artery 36245-36248
Peripheral 36568-36571
Placement
   Arterial Coronary Conduit
     without Concomitant Left Heart
     Catheterization 93508
   Coronary Artery
     without Concomitant Left Heart
     Catheterization 93508
   Venous Coronary Bypass Graft
     without Concomitant Left Heart
     Catheterization 93508
Pleural Cavity 32550-32552
Portal Vein 36481
Pulmonary Artery 36013-36015
Radioelement Application 55875
Removal
   Fractured Catheter 75961
   Obstructive Material
     Intracatheter 36596
     Pericatheter 36595
Salivary Duct 42660
Skull 61107
Spinal Cord 62350-62351
Thoracic Artery 36215-36218
Tracheobronchi 31725
Umbilical Artery 36660
Umbilical Vein 36510
Ureter
   Endoscopic 50553, 50572, 50953,
               50972, 52005
   Injection 50394, 50684
   Manometric Studies 50396, 50686
Uterus
   Radiology 58340
Vena Cava 36010
Venous
   Central Line 36555-36556, 36568-36569,
               36580, 36584
   First Order 36011
   Intracatheter/Needle 36000
   Organ Blood 36500
   Second Order 36012
   Umbilical Vein 36510
Ventricular 61020-61026, 61210-61215

Cauda Equina
See Spinal Cord
Decompression 63005-63011, 63017,
      63047-63048, 63055-63057, 63087-63091
Exploration 63005-63011, 63017

Cauterization
Anal Fissure 46940-46942
Cervix 57522
   Cryocautery 57511
   Electro or Thermal 57510
   Laser Ablation 57513
Chemical
   Granulation Tissue 17250

Everted Punctum 68705
Nasopharyngeal Hemorrhage 42970
Nose
   Hemorrhage 30901-30906
Skin Lesion 11055-11057, 17000-17004
Skin Tags 11200-11201
Turbinate Mucosa
   Electrocautery 30801-30802

Cavernitides, Fibrous
See Peyronie Disease

Cavernosography
Corpora 54230

Cavernosometry 54231

Cavities, Pleural
See Pleural Cavity

Cavus Foot Correction 28309

CBC
See Blood Cell Count; Complete Blood Count (CBC)

CCL4
See Carbon Tetrachloride

CCU Visit
See Critical Care Services

CD142 Antigens
See Thromboplastin

CD143 Antigens
See Angiotensin Converting Enzyme (ACE)

CD4 86360

CD8 86360

CEA
See Carcinoembryonic Antigen

Cecil Repair
See Urethroplasty

Cecostomy 44300
Contrast 49465
Insertion of Tube 49442
Laparoscopic 44188
Obstructive Material Removal 49460
Radiological Evaluation of Tube 49465
Tube Replacement 49450

Celiac Plexus
Destruction 64680
Injection
   Anesthetic 64530
   Neurolytic 64680

Celiac Trunk Artery
See Artery, Celiac

Celioscopy
See Endoscopy, Peritoneum

Celiotomy 49000
Abdomen
   for Staging 49220

Cell Count
Body Fluid 89050-89051

Cell, Blood
See Blood Cell

Open Treatment 21360-21366
Reconstruction .21270
Fascia Graft 15840
Muscle Graft 15841-15845
Muscle Transfer 15845

Cheilectomy
Metatarsophalangeal Joint Release 28289

Cheiloplasty
See Lip, Repair

Cheiloschisis
See Cleft Lip

Cheilotomy
See Incision, Lip

Chemical Cauterization
Granulation Tissue .17250

Chemical Exfoliation 17360

Chemical Peel 15788-15793

Chemiluminescent Assay 82397

Chemistry Tests
Clinical
Unlisted Services and Procedures 84999

Chemocauterization
Corneal Epithelium .65435
with Chelating Agent 65436

Chemodenervation
Anal Sphincter 46505
Eccrine Glands
Axillae 64650
Other Area 64653
Electrical Stimulation for Guidance 95873
Extraocular Muscle 67345
Extremity Muscle .64614
Facial Muscle 64612
Neck Muscle 64613
Needle Electromyography for Guidance 95874
Trunk Muscle 64614

Chemonucleolysis 62292

Chemosurgery
Destruction of Benign Lesions 17110-17111
Skin Lesion 17000-17004, 17110-17111,
17270, 17280

Chemotaxis Assay 86155

Chemotherapy
Arterial Catheterization 36640
Bladder Instillation 51720
CNS 61517, 96450
Extracorporeal Circulation
Extremity 36823
Home Infusion Procedures 99601-99602
Intra-Arterial 96420-96425
Intralesional 96405-96406
Intramuscular 96401-96402
Intravenous 96409-96415, 96417
Infusion Pump 96416
Kidney Instillation 50391
Peritoneal Cavity .96445
Pleural Cavity 96440
Pump Services
Implantable 96522
Maintenance 95990-95991
Portable 96521

Reservoir Filling 96542
Subcutaneous 96401-96402
Unlisted Services and Procedures 96549
Ureteral Instillation 50391

Chest
See Mediastinum; Thorax
Angiography 71275
Artery
Ligation 37616
CT Scan .71250-71275
Exploration
Blood Vessel .35820
Magnetic Resonance Imaging
(MRI) 71550-71552
Repair
Blood Vessel 35211-35216
with Other Graft 35271-35276
with Vein Graft 35241-35246
Ultrasound 76604
Wound Exploration
Penetrating 20101
X-ray 71010-71035
Complete (Four Views)
with Fluoroscopy 71034
Insertion Pacemaker 71090
Partial (Two Views)
with Fluoroscopy 71023
Stereo 71015
with Computer-aided Detection . . .0174T-0175T
with Fluoroscopy 71090

Chest Cavity
Bypass Graft 35905
Endoscopy
Exploration 32601-32606
Surgical 32650-32665

Chest Wall
See Pulmonology, Therapeutic
Manipulation 94667-94668
Reconstruction 49904
Trauma 32820
Repair 32905
Closure 32810
Fistula 32906
Tumor
Excision 19260-19272
Unlisted Services and Procedures 32999

Chest Wall Fistula
See Fistula, Chest Wall

Chest, Funnel
See Pectus Excavatum

Chevron Procedure 28296

Chiari Osteotomy of the Pelvis
See Osteotomy, Pelvis

Chicken Pox Vaccine 90716

Child Procedure
See Excision, Pancreas, Partial

Chin
Repair
Augmentation 21120
Osteotomy 21121-21123

Chinidin
See Quinidine

Chiropractic Manipulation
See Manipulation, Chiropractic

Chiropractic Treatment
Spinal
Extraspinal 98940-98943

Chlamydia
Antibody 86631-86632
Antigen Detection
Direct Fluorescence 87270
Direct Optical 87810
Enzyme Immunoassay 87320
Culture 87110

Chloramphenicol 82415

Chloride
Blood 82435
Other Source 82438
Spinal Fluid 82438
Urine 82436

Chloride, Methylene
See Dichloromethane

Chlorinated Hydrocarbons 82441

Chlorohydrocarbon
See Chlorinated Hydrocarbons

Chlorpromazine 84022

Choanal Atresia
Repair 30540-30545

Cholangiography
Injection 47500-47505
Intraoperative 74300-74301
Percutaneous 74320
with Laparoscopy 47560-47561
Postoperative 74305
Repair
with Bile Duct Exploration 47700
with Cholecystectomy . . .47563, 47605, 47620

Cholangiopancreatography 43260
See Bile Duct; Pancreatic Duct
Repair
See Bile Duct; Pancreatic Duct
with Biopsy 43261
with Surgery 43262-43267, 43269

Cholangiostomy
See Hepaticostomy

Cholangiotomy
See Hepaticostomy

Cholecalciferol
See Vitamin, D-3

Cholecystectomy 47562-47564,
47600-47620
Any Method 47562-47564
with Cholangiography . . .47563, 47605, 47620
with Exploration Common
Duct 47564, 47610

Cholecystenterostomy 47570,
47720-47741

Cholecystography 74290-74291

Cholecystotomy 47480, 48001
Percutaneous 47490

Choledochoplasty
See Bile Duct, Repair

Choledochoscopy 47550

Choledochostomy 47420-47425

Choledochotomy 47420-47425

Choledochus, Cyst
See Cyst, Choledochal

Cholera Vaccine
Injectable 90725

Cholesterol
Measurement 83721
Serum 82465
Testing 83718-83719

Choline Esterase I
See Acetylcholinesterase

Choline Esterase II
See Cholinesterase

Cholinesterase
Blood 82480-82482

Cholylglycine
Blood 82240

Chondroitin Sulfate 82485

Chondromalacia Patella
Repair 27418

Chondropathia Patellae
See Chondromalacia Patella

Chondrosteoma
See Exostosis

Chopart Procedure 28800-28805
See Amputation, Foot; Radical Resection;
Replantation

Chordotomies
See Cordotomy

Chorioangioma
See Lesion, Skin

Choriogonadotropin
See Chorionic Gonadotropin

Choriomeningitides, Lymphocytic
See Lymphocytic Choriomeningitis

Chorionic Gonadotropin 80414,
84702-84703
Stimulation 80414-80415

Chorionic Growth Hormone
See Lactogen, Human Placental

Chorionic Tumor
See Hydatidiform Mole

Chorionic Villi
See Biopsy, Chorionic Villus

Chorionic Villus
Biopsy 59015

Choroid
Destruction
Lesion 0016T, 67220-67225

Choroid Plexus
Excision 61544

Christmas Factor 85250

Chromaffinoma, Medullary
See Pheochromocytoma

Chromatin, Sex
See Barr Bodies

Chromatography
Column/Mass Spectrometry 82541-82544
Gas Liquid or HPLC 82486, 82491-82492
Paper 82487-82488
Thin-Layer 82489

Chromium 82495

Chromogenic Substrate Assay ... 85130

Chromosome Analysis
See Amniocentesis
Added Study 88280-88289
Amniotic Fluid 88267-88269
Culture 88235
Biopsy Culture
Tissue 88233
Bone Marrow Culture 88237
Chorionic Villus 88267
5 Cells 88261
15-20 Cells 88262
20-25 Cells 88264
45 Cells 88263
Culture 88235
for Breakage Syndromes 88245-88249
Fragile-X 88248
Lymphocyte Culture 88230
Pregnancy Associated Plasma Protein-A ... 84163
Skin Culture
Tissue 88233
Tissue Culture 88239
Unlisted Services and Procedures 88299

Chromotubation 58350
Oviduct 58350

Chronic Erection
See Priapism

Chronic Interstitial Cystitides
See Cystitis, Interstitial

Ciliary Body
Cyst
Destruction
Cryotherapy 66720
Cyclodialysis 66740
Cyclophotocoagulation 66710-66711
Diathermy 66700
Nonexcisional 66770
Destruction
Cyclophotocoagulation 66710-66711
Endoscopic 66711
Lesion
Destruction 66770
Repair 66680

Cimino Type Procedure 36821

Cinefluorographies
See Cineradiography

Cineplasty
Arm, Lower or Upper 24940

Cineradiography
Esophagus 74230
Pharynx 70371, 74230
Speech Evaluation 70371
Swallowing Evaluation 74230
Unlisted Services and Procedures 76120-76125

Circulation Assist
Aortic 33967, 33970
Balloon 33967, 33970
External 33960-33961

Circulation, Extracorporeal
See Extracorporeal Circulation

Circulatory Assist
See Circulation Assist

Circumcision
Repair 54163
Surgical Excision 54161
Newborn 54150, 54160

Cisternal Puncture 61050-61055

Cisternography 70015
Nuclear 78630

Citrate
Blood or Urine 82507

Clagett Procedure
See Chest Wall, Repair, Closure

Clavicle
Craterization 23180
Cyst
Excision 23140
with Allograft 23146
with Autograft 23145
Diaphysectomy 23180
Dislocation
Acromioclavicular Joint
Closed Treatment 23540-23545
Open Treatment 23550-23552
Sternoclavicular Joint
Closed Treatment 23520-23525
Open Treatment 23530-23532
without Manipulation 23540
Excision 23170
Partial 23120, 23180
Total 23125
Fracture
Closed Treatment
with Manipulation 23505
without Manipulation 23500
Open Treatment 23515
Pinning, Wiring 23490
Prophylactic Treatment 23490
Repair Osteotomy 23480-23485
Saucerization 23180
Sequestrectomy 23170
Tumor
Excision 23140, 23146, 23200
with Autograft 23145
Radical Resection 23200
X-ray 73000

Clavicula
See Clavicle

Claviculectomy
Partial 23120
Total 23125

Claw Finger Repair 26499

Cleft Cyst, Branchial
See Branchial Cleft, Cyst

Cleft Foot
Reconstruction 28360

Cleft Hand
Repair 26580

Cleft Lip
Repair 40700-40761
Rhinoplasty .30460-30462

Cleft Palate
Repair .42200-42225
Rhinoplasty .30460-30462

Cleft, Branchial
See Branchial Cleft

Clinical Act of Insertion
See Insertion

Clinical Chemistry Test
See Chemistry Tests, Clinical

Clinical Investigation
FDA-approved Drugs
  Single Patient
    by Pharmacist 0130T

Clinical Pathology
See Pathology, Clinical

Clitoroplasty
Intersex State 56805

Closed [Transurethral] Biopsy of Bladder
See Biopsy, Bladder, Cystourethroscopy

Clostridial Tetanus
See Tetanus

Clostridium Botulinum Toxin
See Chemodenervation

Clostridium Difficile
Antigen Detection
  Enzyme Immunoassay 87324
by Immunoassay
  with Direct Optical Observation 87803

Clostridium Tetani ab
See Antibody, Tetanus

Closure 12001-13160
Anal Fistula 46288
Atrioventricular Valve 33600
Cystostomy 51880
Enterostomy 44625-44626
  Laparoscopic 44227
Lacrimal Fistula 68770
Lacrimal Punctum
  Plug 68761
  Thermocauterization, Ligation or
  Laser Surgery 68760
Rectovaginal Fistula 57300-57308
Semilunar Valve 33602
Septal Defect 33615
  Ventricular 33675-33677,
                                  0166T-0167T, 93581
Sternotomy 21750
Ventricular Tunnel 33722

Closure of Esophagostomy
See Esophagostomy, Closure

Closure of Gastrostomy
See Gastrostomy, Closure

Closure, Atrial Septal Defect
See Heart, Repair, Atrial Septum

Closure, Cranial Sutures, Premature
See Craniosynostosis

Closure, Fistula, Vesicouterine
See Fistula, Vesicouterine, Closure

Closure, Meningocele Spinal
See Meningocele Repair

Closure, Vagina
See Vagina, Closure

Clot 34401-34490, 35875-35876, 50230
See Thrombectomy; Thromboendarterectomy

Clot Lysis Time 85175

Clot Retraction 85170

Clotting Disorder
See Coagulopathy

Clotting Factor 85210-85293

Clotting Inhibitors 85300-85305, 85307

Clotting Operation
See Excision, Nail Fold

Clotting Test
Protein C 85303, 85307
Protein S 85306

Clotting Time
See Coagulation Time

Clubfoot Cast 29450
Wedging 29750

CMG
See Cystometrogram

CMRI
See Cardiac Magnetic Resonance Imaging

CMV
See Cytomegalovirus

CNPB
See Continuous Negative Pressure Breathing
(CNPB); Pulmonology, Therapeutic

Co-Factor I, Heparin
See Antithrombin III

CO$_2$
See Carbon Dioxide

Coagulation
Unlisted Services and Procedures 85999

Coagulation Defect
See Coagulopathy

Coagulation Factor
See Clotting Factor
Factor I
  See Fibrinogen

Factor II
  See Prothrombin
Factor III
  See Thromboplastin
Factor IV
  See Calcium
Factor VII
  See Proconvertin
Factor VIII
  See Clotting Factor
Factor IX
  See Christmas Factor
Factor X
  See Stuart-Prower Factor
Factor Xa
  See Thrombokinase
Factor XI
  See Plasma Thromboplastin, Antecedent
Factor XII
  See Hageman Factor
Factor XIII
  See Fibrin Stabilizing Factor

Coagulation Time 85345-85348

Coagulation, Blood
See Blood Clot

Coagulation, Light
See Photocoagulation

Coagulin
See Thromboplastin

Coagulopathy .85390
Assay 85130

Cocaine
Blood or Urine 82520
Screen 82486

Coccidioides
Antibody 86635

Coccidioidin Test
See Streptokinase, Antibody

Coccidioidomycosis
Skin Test 86490

Coccygeal Spine Fracture
See Coccyx, Fracture

Coccygectomy 15920-15922, 27080

Coccyx
Excision 27080
Fracture
  Closed Treatment 27200
  Open Treatment 27202
Tumor
  Excision 49215
X-ray 72220

Cochlear Device
Insertion 69930
Programming 92601-92604

Codeine
Alkaloid Screening 82101

Codeine Screen 82486

Cofactor Protein S
See Protein S

Colonography
CT Scan
    Diagnostic 74261-74262
    Screening 74263

Colonoscopy
Biopsy 45380, 45392
Collection Specimen 45380
    via Colotomy 45355
Destruction
    Lesion 45383
    Tumor 45383
Dilation 45386
Hemorrhage Control 45382
Injection
    Submucosal 45381
Placement
    Stent 45387
Removal
    Foreign Body 45379
    Polyp 45384-45385
    Tumor 45384-45385
Surveillance Intervals 0528F-0529F
Ultrasound 45391-45392
via Stoma .44388-44390
    Biopsy 44389
    Destruction
        of Lesion .44393
        of Tumor .44393
    Exploration .44388
    Hemorrhage 44391
    Placement
        Stent 44397
    Removal
        Foreign Body 44390
        Polyp 44392, 44394
        Tumor 44392, 44394

Color Vision Examination 92283

Colorrhaphy .44604

Colostomy 44320, 45563
Abdominal
    Establishment 50810
Colostomy 44188
Home Visit 99505
Intestine, Large
    with Suture 44605
Laparoscopic 44188
Perineal
    Establishment 50810
Revision 44340
    Paracolostomy Hernia 44345-44346

Colotomy 44025

Colpectomy
Partial 57106
Total 57110
with Hysterectomy 58275-58280
    with Repair of Enterocele 58280

Colpo-Urethrocystopexy 58152,
                         58267, 58293
Marshall-Marchetti-Krantz Procedure 58152, 58267,
                            58293
Pereyra Procedure 58267, 58293

Colpoceliocentesis
See Colpocentesis

Colpocentesis 57020

Colpocleisis 57120

Colpocleisis Complete
See Vagina, Closure

Colpohysterectomies
See Excision, Uterus, Vaginal

Colpoperineorrhaphy 57210

Colpopexy
Extra-Peritoneal 57282
Intra-Peritoneal 57283
Laparoscopic 57425
Open 57280

Colpoplasty
See Repair, Vagina

Colporrhaphy
Anterior 57240, 57289
    with Insertion of Mesh 57267
    with Insertion of Prosthesis 57267
Anteroposterior 57260-57265
    with Enterocele Repair 57265
    with Insertion of Mesh 57267
    with Insertion of Prosthesis 57267
Nonobstetrical 57200
Posterior 57250
    with Insertion of Mesh 57267
    with Insertion of Prosthesis 57267

Colposcopy
Biopsy 56821, 57421, 57454-57455, 57460
    Endometrium 58110
Cervix 57421, 57452-57461
Exploration .57452
Loop Electrode Biopsy 57460
Loop Electrode Conization 57461
Perineum 99170
Vagina 57420-57421
Vulva 56820
    Biopsy 56821

Colpotomy
Drainage
    Abscess .57010
Exploration .57000

Colprosterone
See Progesterone

Column Chromatography/Mass Spectrometry 82541-82544

Columna Vertebralis
See Spine

Combined Heart-Lung Transplantation
See Transplantation, Heart-Lung

Combined Right and Left Heart Cardiac Catheterization
See Cardiac Catheterization, Combined Left and Right Heart

Comedones
Removal 10040

Commissurotomy
Right Ventricle 33476-33478

Common Sensory Nerve
Repair/Suture 64834

Common Truncus
See Truncus Arteriosus

Communication Device
Non-Speech-Generating 92605-92606
Speech-Generating 92606-92609

Community/Work Reintegration
Training 97537
    See Physical Medicine/Therapy/Occupational Therapy

Compatibility Test
Blood 86920, 86923

Complement
Antigen 86160
Fixation Test 86171
Functional Activity 86161
Hemolytic
    Total 86162
Total 86162

Complete Blood Count (CBC) 85025-85027
See Blood Cell Count

Complete Colectomy
See Colectomy, Total

Complete Pneumonectomy
See Pneumonectomy, Completion

Complete Transposition of Great Vessels
See Transposition, Great Arteries

Complex, Factor IX
See Christmas Factor

Complex, Vitamin B
See B Complex Vitamins

Component Removal, Blood
See Apheresis

Composite Graft 15760-15770,
                         35681-35683

Compound B
See Corticosterone

Compound F
See Cortisol

Compression, Nerve, Median
See Carpal Tunnel Syndrome

Computed Tomographic Scintigraphy
See Emission Computerized Tomography

Computed Tomography (CT)
See CT Scan; Specific Anatomic Site

Computer Analysis
Acoustic Recording
    Heart Sounds
Probability Assessment 0185T

Computer-Aided Detection
Chest X-ray .0152T
Lesion
    Chest Radiograph 0174T-0175T
    Mammography 77051-77052
        Magnetic Resonance Imaging (MRI) 0159T

Contracture of Palmar Fascia
See Dupuytren's Contracture

Contralateral Ligament
Repair
  Knee 27405

Contrast Aortogram
See Aortography

Contrast Bath Therapy 97034
See Physical Medicine/Therapy/Occupational Therapy

Contrast Material
Injection
  via Peritoneal Catheter 49424

Contrast Phlebogram
See Venography

Contusion
See Hematoma

Converting Enzyme, Angiotensin
See Angiotensin Converting Enzyme (ACE)

Coombs Test 86880, 86885-86886

Copper 82525

Coprobilinogen
Feces 84577

Coproporphyrin 84120

Coracoacromial Ligament Release 23415

Coracoid Process Transfer 23462

Cord, Spermatic
See Spermatic Cord

Cord, Spinal
See Spinal Cord

Cord, Vocal
See Vocal Cords

Cordectomy 31300

Cordocenteses
See Cordocentesis

Cordocentesis 59012

Cordotomy 63194-63199

Corectomy
See Excision, Iris

Coreoplasty 66762

Cornea
Biopsy 65410
Curettage 65435-65436
  with Chelating Agent 65436
Epithelium
  Excision 65435-65436
    with Chelating Agent 65436
Hysteresis Determination 0181T
Lesion
  Destruction 65450
  Excision 65400
    with Graft .65426
    without Graft 65420

Pachymetry 76514
Prosthesis 65770
Pterygium
  Excision 65420
Puncture 65600
Relaxing Incisions 65772-65775
Repair
  Astigmatism 65772-65775
  Wedge Resection 65775
  with Glue 65286
  Wound
    Nonperforating 65275
    Perforating 65280-65285
    Tissue Glue 65286
Reshape
  Epikeratoplasty 65765
  Keratomileusis 65760
  Keratoprosthesis 65767
Scraping
  Smear 65430
Tattoo 65600
Thickness Measurement 76514
Transplantation
  Autograft or Homograft
    Allograft Preparation 65757
    Endothelial 65756
    Lamellar .65710
    Penetrating 65730-65755
  for Aphakia .65750

Coronary
Atherectomy
  Percutaneous 92995-92996
Thrombectomy
  Percutaneous 92973

Coronary Angioplasty, Transluminal Balloon
See Percutaneous Transluminal Angioplasty

Coronary Artery
Insertion
  Stent .92980-92981
Ligation 33502
Placement
  Radiation Delivery Device 92974
Repair .33500-33507

Coronary Artery Bypass Graft (CABG) 33503-33505, 33510-33516
Arterial .33533-33536
Arterial Graft .33548
Spectroscopy
  Catheter Based 0205T
Arterial-Venous 33517-33523
Beta Blocker Administered 4115F
Harvest
  Upper Extremity Artery 35600
Internal Mammary Artery Graft 4110F
Reoperation 33530
Venous .33510-33516

Coronary Endarterectomy 33572

Coroner's Exam 88045

Coronoidectomy
Temporomandibular Joint 21070

Corpectomy 63101-63103

Corpora Cavernosa
Corpus Spongiosum Shunt 54430
Glans Penis Fistulization 54435

Injection 54235
Irrigation
  Priapism 54220
Saphenous Vein Shunt 54420
X-ray with Contrast 74445

Corpora Cavernosa, Plastic Induration
See Peyronie Disease

Corpora Cavernosography 74445

Corpus Callosum
Transection 61541

Corpus Vertebrae (Vertebrale)
See Vertebral Body

Correction of Cleft Palate
See Cleft Palate, Repair

Correction of Lid Retraction
See Repair, Eyelid, Retraction

Correction of Malrotation of Duodenum
See Ladd Procedure

Correction of Syndactyly
See Syndactyly, Repair

Correction of Ureteropelvic Junction
See Pyeloplasty

Cortex Decortication, Cerebral
See Decortication

Cortical Mapping
Transection
  by Electric Stimulation 95961-95962

Corticoids
See Corticosteroids

Corticoliberin
See Corticotropic Releasing Hormone (CRH)

Corticosteroid Binding Globulin
See Transcortin

Corticosteroid Binding Protein
See Transcortin

Corticosteroids
Blood 83491
Urine 83491

Corticosterone
Blood or Urine .82528

Corticotropic Releasing Hormone (CRH) 80412

Cortisol 80400-80406, 80418-80420,
                        80436, 82530
Stimulation 80412
Total 82533

Cortisol Binding Globulin 84449

Costectomy
See Resection, Ribs

Costen Syndrome
See Temporomandibular Joint (TMJ)

Costotransversectomy 21610

Cothromboplastin
See Proconvertin

Cotte Operation 58400-58410
See Repair, Uterus, Suspension; Revision

Cotton Procedure
Bohler Procedure 28405

Counseling
See Preventive Medicine
Smoking and Tobacco Use
Cessation 99406-99407

Counseling and/or Risk Factor Reduction Intervention, Preventive Medicine, Individual Counseling
See Preventive Medicine, Counseling and/or Risk Factor Reduction Intervention, Individual Counseling

Count
Blood Cell
   See Blood Cell Count
Blood Platelet
   See Blood, Platelet, Count
Cell
   See Cell Count
Complete Blood
   See Complete Blood Count (CBC)
Erythrocyte
   See Red Blood Cell (RBC), Count
Leukocyte
   See White Blood Cell, Count
Reticulocyte
   See Reticulocyte, Count

Counterimmuno-electrophoresis 86185

Counters, Cell
See Cell Count

Countershock, Electric
See Cardioversion

Coventry Tibial Wedge Osteotomy
See Osteotomy, Tibia

Cowper's Gland
Excision 53250

Coxa
See Hip

Coxiella Burnetii
Antibody 86638

Coxsackie
Antibody 86658

CPAP
See Continuous Positive Airway Pressure

CPK
Blood 82550-82552

CPR (Cardiopulmonary Resuscitation) 92950

Cranial Bone
Halo
   Thin Skull Osteology 20664
Reconstruction
   Extracranial 21181-21184

Tumor
   Excision 61563-61564

Cranial Halo 20661

Cranial Nerve
Avulsion 64732-64760, 64771
Cranial Nerve II
   See Optic Nerve
Cranial Nerve V
   See Trigeminal Nerve
Cranial Nerve VII
   See Facial Nerve
Cranial Nerve X
   See Vagus Nerve
Cranial Nerve XI
   See Accessory Nerve
Cranial Nerve XII
   See Hypoglossal Nerve
Decompression 61458, 64716
Implantation
   Electrode 64553, 64573
Incision 64732-64752, 64760, 65771
Injection
   Anesthetic 64400-64408, 64412
   Neurolytic 64600-64610
Insertion
   Electrode 64553, 64573
Neuroplasty 64716
Release 64716
Repair
   Suture, with or without Graft 64864-64865
Section 61460
Transection 64732-64760, 64771
Transposition 64716

Cranial Tongs
Application/Removal 20660
Removal 20665

Craniectomy 61501
See Craniotomy
Anesthesia 00225
Decompression 61322-61323, 61340-61343
Exploratory 61304-61305
Extensive, for Multiple Suture
Craniosynostosis 61558-61559
for Electrode 61860-61875
Release Stenosis 61550-61552
Surgical 61312-61315, 61320-61323,
      61440-61480, 61500-61516, 61518-61522

Craniofacial Procedures
Unlisted Services and Procedures 21299

Craniofacial Separation
Closed Treatment 21431
Open Treatment 21432-21436
Wire Fixation 21431

Craniomegalic Skull
Reduction 62115-62117

Craniopharyngioma
Excision 61545

Cranioplasty 62120
Encephalocele Repair 62120
for Defect 62140-62141, 62145
with Autograft 62146-62147
with Bone Graft 61316, 62146-62147

Craniostenosis
See Craniosynostosis

Craniosynostosis
Bifrontal Craniotomy 61557
Extensive Craniectomy 61558-61559

Craniotomy
See Burr Hole; Craniectomy; Drill Hole; Puncture
Anesthesia 00211
Bifrontal 61557
Decompression 61322-61323
Exploratory 61304-61305
for Craniosynostosis 61556-61557
for Encephalocele 62121
for Implant of Neurostimulators 61850-61875
Frontal 61556
Parietal 61556
Surgery 61312-61315, 61320-61323, 61440,
     61490, 61546, 61570-61571, 61582-61583,
        61590, 61592, 61760, 62120
with Bone Flap 61510-61516, 61526-61530,
        61533-61545, 61566-61567

Cranium
See Skull

Craterization
Calcaneus 28120
Clavicle 23180
Femur 27070-27071, 27360
Fibula 27360, 27641
Hip 27070
Humerus 23184, 24140
Ileum 27070
Metacarpal 26230
Metatarsal 28122
Olecranon Process 24147
Phalanges
   Finger 26235-26236
   Toe 28124
Pubis 27070
Radius 24145, 25151
Scapula 23182
Talus 28120
Tarsal 28122
Tibia 27360, 27640
Ulna 24147, 25150

Creatine 82553-82554
Blood or Urine 82540

Creatine Kinase
Total 82550

Creatine Phosphokinase
Blood 82552
Total 82550

Creatinine
Blood 82565
Clearance 82575
Other Source 82570
Urine 82570-82575

Creation
Arteriovenous
   Fistula/Autogenous Graft 36825
Catheter Exit Site 49436
Colonic Reservoir 45119
Complete Heart Block 93650
Defect 40720
Ileal Reservoir 44158, 45113
Lesion 61790, 63600
Mucofistula 44144
Pericardial Window 32659
Recipient Site 15002-15005

Shunt
  Cerebrospinal Fluid 62200
  Subarachnoid
    Lumbar-Peritoneal 63740
    Subarachnoid-Subdural 62190
    Ventriculo 62220
Sigmoid Bladder 50810
Speech Prosthesis 31611
Stoma
  Bladder 51980
  Kidney 50395
  Renal Pelvis 50395
  Tympanic Membrane 69433-69436
  Ureter 50860
Ventral Hernia 39503

CRF
See Corticotropic Releasing Hormone (CRH)

CRH
See Corticotropic Releasing Hormone (CRH)

Cricoid Cartilage Split
Larynx 31587

Cricothyroid Membrane
Incision 31605

Cristobalite
See Silica

Critical Care Services 99291-99292
See Emergency Department Services; Prolonged Attendance
Evaluation and Management 99291-99292
Gastric Intubation 91105
Interfacility Transport 99466-99467
Ipecac Administration for Poison 99175
Neonatal
  Initial 99468
  Low Birth Weight Infant 99478-99479
  Subsequent 99469
Pediatric
  Initial 99471, 99475
  Interfacility Transport 99466-99467
  Subsequent 99472, 99476
Remote
  Video-Conferenced Evaluation and
  Management 0188T-0189T

Cross Finger Flap 15574

Crossmatch 86825-86826, 86920-86923

Crossmatching, Tissue
See Tissue, Typing

Cruciate Ligament
Arthroscopic Repair 29888-29889
Repair 27407-27409
  Knee
    with Collateral Ligament 27409

Cryoablation
See Cryosurgery

Cryofibrinogen 82585

Cryofixation
See Cryopreservation

Cryoglobulin 82595

Cryopreservation
Cells 38207-38209, 88240-88241
Embryo 89258

for Transplantation 32850, 33930, 33940,
  44132, 47133, 47140, 48550, 50300-50320, 50547
Freezing and Storage 38207, 88240
Sperm 89259
Testes 89335
Thawing
  Embryo 89352
  Oocytes 89353
  Reproductive Tissue 89354
  Sperm 89356

Cryosurgery 17000-17286, 47371, 47381
See Cryotherapy; Destruction
Fibroadenoma 0120T
  Breast 19105
Labyrinthotomy 69801
Lesion
  Kidney 50250
  Mouth 40820
  Penis 54056, 54065
  Vagina 57061-57065
  Vulva 56501-56515

Cryotherapy
Ablation
  Renal Tumor 50593
Acne 17340
Destruction
  Ciliary Body 66720
Lesion
  Cornea 65450
  Retina 67208, 67227
Retinal Detachment
  Prophylaxis 67141
  Repair 67101, 67113
Trichiasis
  Correction 67825

Cryptectomy 46999

Cryptococcus
Antibody 86641
Antigen Detection
  Enzyme Immunoassay 87327

Cryptococcus Neoformans
Antigen Detection
  Enzyme Immunoassay 87327

Cryptorchism
See Testis, Undescended

Cryptosporidium
Antigen Detection
  Direct Fluorescence 87272
  Enzyme Immunoassay 87328

Crystal Identification
Any Body Fluid 89060
Tissue 89060

CSF
See Cerebrospinal Fluid Leak

CT Scan
3-D Rendering 76376-76377
Bone
  Density Study 77078-77079
Brain 3111F-3112F
Drainage 75989
Follow-up Study 76380
Guidance
  Localization 77011
  Needle Placement 77012

  Parenchymal Tissue Ablation 77013
  Radiation Therapy 77014
  Vertebroplasty 72292
  Visceral Tissue Ablation 76362
Heart
  Evaluation
    Angiography 75574
    for Coronary Calcium 75571
    for Structure and
    Morphology 75572-75573
  Hemorrhage Documented 3110F
  Infarction Documented 3110F
  Lesion Documented 3110F
Unlisted Services and Procedures 76497
with Contrast 70460
  Abdomen 74160
  Arm 73201
  Brain 0042T, 70460
  Cerebral Blood Flow/Volume 0042T
  Ear 70481
  Face 70487
  Head 70460
  Leg 73701
  Maxilla 70487
  Neck 70491
  Orbit 70481
  Pelvis 72193
  Sella Turcica 70481
  Spine
    Cervical 72126
    Lumbar 72132
    Thoracic 72129
  Thorax 71260
without and with Contrast
  Abdomen 74170-74175, 75635
  Arm 73202-73206
  Brain 70470, 70496
  Chest 71275
  Ear 70482
  Face 70488
  Head 70470, 70496
  Leg 73702-73706, 75635
  Maxilla 70488
  Neck 70492, 70498
  Orbit 70482
  Pelvis 72191, 72194
  Sella Turcica 70482
  Spine
    Cervical 72127
    Lumbar 72133
    Thoracic 72130
  Thorax 71270-71275
without Contrast 70450
  Abdomen 74150
  Arm 73200
  Brain 70450
  Colon
    Colonography 74261-74263
  Ear 70480
  Face 70486
  Head 70450
  Leg 73700
  Maxilla 70486
  Neck 70490
  Orbit 70480
  Pelvis 72192
  Sella Turcica 70480
  Spine
    Cervical 72125
    Lumbar 72131
    Thoracic 72128
  Thorax 71250

Iris
  Destruction 66770
Kidney
  Ablation 50541
  Aspiration 50390
  Excision 50280-50290
  Injection 50390
  X-ray 74470
Knee
  Baker's 27345
  Excision 27347
Leg, Lower
  Capsule 27630
  Tendon Sheath 27630
Liver 47010
  Drainage 47010
    Open 47010
  Repair 47300
Lung
  Incision and Drainage 32200
  Removal 32140
Lymph Node
  Axillary/Cervical
    Excision 38550-38555
Mandible
  Excision 21040, 21046-21047
Maxilla
  Excision 21030, 21048-21049
Mediastinal
  Excision 39200
Metacarpal 26200-26205
Metatarsal 28104-28107
Mouth 41005-41009, 41015-41018
  Incision and Drainage 40800-40801
Mullerian Duct
  Excision 55680
Nose
  Excision 30124-30125
Olecranon 24120
Ovarian
  Excision 58925
  Incision and Drainage 58800-58805
Pancreas 48500
  Anastomosis 48520-48540
  Excision 48120
Pelvis
  Aspiration 50390
  Injection 50390
Pericardial
  Excision 33050
Phalanges
  Finger 26210-26215
  Toe 28108
Pilonidal
  Excision 11770-11772
  Incision and Drainage 10080-10081
Pubis 27065-27067
Radius 24120, 25120-25126
Rathke's Pouch
  See Craniopharyngioma
Removal
  Skin 10040
Retroperitoneal
  Destruction/Excision 49203-49205
Salivary Gland Creation
  Destruction/Excision
    Drainage 42409
    Excision 42408
Scapula
  Excision 23140-23146
Seminal Vesicle
  Excision 55680

Skin
  Puncture Aspiration 10160
Spinal Cord
  Aspiration 62268
  Incision and Drainage 63172-63173
Sublingual Gland Drainage 42409
  Excision 42408
Talus 28100-28103
Tarsal 28104-28107
Thyroglossal Duct
  Excision 60280-60281
  Incision and Drainage 60000
Thyroid Gland Aspiration 60300
  Excision 60200
  Injection 60300
Tibia 27635-27638
Tongue 41000-41006, 41015
Ulna 24120, 25120-25126
Urachal
  Bladder
    Excision 51500
Vaginal
  Excision 57135
Wrist 25130-25136
  Excision 25111-25112
Zygoma
  Excision 21030

Cyst, Ovary
See Ovary, Cyst

Cystatin C
Blood 82610

Cystatins, Kininogen
See Kininogen

Cystectomy
Complete 51570
  with Bilateral Pelvic
    Lymphadenectomy 51575, 51585, 51595
  with Continent Diversion 51596
  with Ureteroileal Conduit 51590
  with Ureterosigmoidostomy 51580
Ovarian 58925
  Laparoscopic 58661
Partial
  Complicated 51555
  Reimplantation of Ureters 51565
  Simple 51550

Cystic Hygroma
See Hygroma

Cystine
Urine 82615

Cystitis
Interstitial 52260-52265

Cystography 74430
Injection 52281
  Radiologic 51600

Cystolithotomy 51050

Cystometrogram 51725-51729

Cystoplasty 51800

Cystorrhaphy 51860-51865

Cystoscopy 52000

Cystoscopy, with Biopsy
See Biopsy, Bladder, Cystourethroscopy

Cystostomy
Change Tube 51705-51710
Closure 51880
Home Visit 99505
with Fulguration 51020
with Insertion Radioactive Material 51020
with Urethrectomy
  Female 53210
  Male 53215

Cystotomy
Excision
  Bladder Diverticulum 51525
  Bladder Tumor 51530
  Repair of Ureterocele 51535
  Vesical Neck 51520
Repair Ureterocele 51535
with Calculus Basket Extraction 51065
with Destruction Intravesical Lesion 51030
with Drainage 51040
with Fulguration 51020
with Insertion
  Radioactive Material 51020
  Ureteral Catheter 51045
with Removal Calculus 51050, 51065

Cystourethrogram, Retrograde
See Urethrocystography, Retrograde

Cystourethropexy
See Vesicourethropexy

Cystourethroplasty 51800-51820
Radiofrequency Micro-Remodeling 0193T

Cystourethroscopy 52000, 52351,
                          52601, 52647-52648, 53500
Biopsy 52204, 52354
  Brush 52007
Calibration and/or Dilation Urethral Stricture
  or Stenosis 52281
Catheterization
  Ejaculatory Duct 52010
  Ureteral 52005
Destruction
  Lesion 52400
Dilation
  Bladder 52260-52265
  Intra-Renal Stricture 52343, 52346
  Ureter 52341-52342, 52344-52345
  Urethra 52281
Evacuation
  Clot 52001
Female Urethral Syndrome 52285
Incision
  Ejaculatory Duct 52402
Injection of Implant Material 52327
Insertion
  Indwelling Ureteral Stent 50947, 52332
  Radioactive Substance 52250
  Ureteral Guide Wire 52334
  Urethral Stent 52282
Lithotripsy 52353
Manipulation of Ureteral Calculus 52330
Meatotomy
  Ureteral 52290-52305
Removal
  Calculus ...52310-52315, 52320-52325, 52352
  Foreign Body 52310-52315
  Urethral Stent 52310-52315

D

Dialyses, Peritoneal
See Dialysis, Peritoneal
Plan of Care Documented .... .0507F

Dialysis
Arteriovenous Fistula
   Revision
     without Thrombectomy .... .36832
Arteriovenous Shunt 36147-36148
   Revision
     with Thrombectomy .... .36833
   Thrombectomy .... .36831
End Stage Renal Disease 90951-90970
Hemodialysis 90935-90937, 4051F-4054F
   Blood Flow Study .... .90940
   Plan of Care Documented .... .0505F
Hemoperfusion .... .90997
Kt/V Level .... .3082F-3084F
Patient Training
   Completed Course .... .90989
   Per Session .... .90993
Peritoneal 90945-90947, 4055F
   Plan of Care Documented .... .0507F
Unlisted Services and Procedures .... .90999

Dialysis, Extracorporeal
See Hemodialysis

Diaphragm
Repair
   for Eventration .... .39545
   Hernia 39502-39541
   Laceration .... .39501
Resection 39560-39561
Unlisted Procedures .... .39599
Vagina
   Fitting .... .57170

Diaphragm Contraception
See Contraception, Diaphragm

Diaphysectomy
Calcaneus .... .28120
Clavicle .... .23180
Femur .... .27360
Fibula .... .27360, 27641
Humerus .... .23184, 24140
Metacarpal .... .26230
Metatarsal .... .28122
Olecranon Process .... .24147
Phalanges
   Finger 26235-26236
   Toe .... .28124
Radius .... .24145, 25151
Scapula .... .23182
Talus .... .28120
Tarsal .... .28122
Tibia .... .27360, 27640
Ulna .... .24147, 25150

Diastase
See Amylase

Diastasis
See Separation

Diathermy .... .97024
See Physical Medicine/Therapy/Occupational
Therapy
Destruction
   Ciliary Body .... .66700
Lesion
   Retina .... .67208, 67227

Retinal Detachment
   Prophylaxis .... .67141
   Repair .... .67101

Diathermy, Surgical
See Electrocautery

Dibucaine Number .... .82638

Dichloride, Methylene
See Dichloromethane

Dichlorides, Ethylene
See Dichloroethane

Dichloroethane .... .84600

Dichloromethane .... .84600

Diethylamide, Lysergic Acid
See Lysergic Acid Diethylamide

Diethylether .... .84600

Differential Count
See White Blood Cell Count

Differentiation Reversal Factor
See Prothrombin

Diffusion Test, Gel
See Immunodiffusion

Digestive Tract
See Gastrointestinal Tract

Digit
See Finger; Toe
Destruction .... .64632
Injection .... .64455
Replantation 20816-20822

Digital Artery Sympathectomy .... .64820

Digital Slit-Beam Radiograph
See Scanogram

Digits
Pinch Graft .... .15050

Digoxin
Assay .... .80162

Dihydrocodeinone .... .82646

Dihydrocodeinone Screen ...... .82486

Dihydroepitestosterone
See Dihydrotestosterone

Dihydrohydroxycodeinone
See Oxycodinone

Dihydromorphinone .... .82486, 82649

Dihydrotestosterone .... .82651

Dihydroxyethanes
See Ethylene Glycol

Dihydroxyvitamin D .... .82652

Dilatation, Transluminal Arterial
See Angioplasty, Transluminal

Dilation
See Dilation and Curettage
Anal
   Endoscopy .... .46604

Sphincter .... .45905
Bile Duct
   Endoscopy .... .43271, 47555-47556
   Stricture .... .74363
Bladder
   Cystourethroscopy 52260-52265
Bronchi
   Endoscopy .... .31630, 31636-31638
Cerebral Vessels
   Intracranial Vasospasm 61640-61642
Cervix
   Canal .... .57800
   Stump .... .57558
Colon
   Endoscopy .... .45386
Colon-Sigmoid
   Endoscopy .... .45340
Esophagus 43450-43458
   Balloon .... .43220, 43249
   Endoscopy 43220-43226, 43249
   Surgical .... .43510
Intestines, Small
   Endoscopy .... .44370
Kidney .... .50395
   Intra-Renal Stricture .... .52343, 52346
Lacrimal Punctum .... .68801
Larynx
   Endoscopy 31528-31529
Nasolacrimal Duct
   Balloon Catheter .... .68816
Pancreatic Duct
   Endoscopy .... .43271
Rectum
   Endoscopy .... .45303
   Sphincter .... .45910
Salivary Duct 42650-42660
Trachea
   Endoscopy 31630-31631, 31636-31638
Transluminal
   Aqueous Outflow Canal .... .0176T-0177T
Ureter .... .50395, 52341-52342, 52344-52345
   Endoscopy ..... .50553, 50572, 50953, 50972
Urethra 52260-52265
   General .... .53665
   Suppository and/or Instillation 53660-53661
Urethral
   Stenosis .... .52281
   Stricture .... .52281, 53600-53621
Vagina .... .57400

Dilation and Curettage .... .59840
See Curettage; Dilation
Cervical Stump .... .57558
Cervix .... .57558, 57800
Corpus Uteri .... .58120
Hysteroscopy .... .58558
Postpartum .... .59160
with Amniotic Injections .... .59851
with Vaginal Suppositories .... .59856

Dilation and Evacuation .... .59841
with Amniotic Injections .... .59851

Dimethadione .... .82654

Dioxide, Carbon
See Carbon Dioxide

Dioxide, Silicon
See Silica

Dipeptidyl Peptidase A
See Angiotensin Converting Enzyme (ACE)

Open Treatment 28615
Percutaneous Fixation 28606
Temporomandibular Joint
    Closed Treatment 21480-21485
    Open Treatment 21490
Thumb
    Closed Treatment 26641-26645
    Open Treatment 26665
    Percutaneous Fixation 26650
    with Fracture 26645
        Open Treatment 26665
        Percutaneous Fixation 26650
    with Manipulation 26641-26650
Tibiofibular Joint
    Closed Treatment 27830-27831
    Open Treatment 27832
Vertebra
    Additional Segment
        Open Treatment 22328
    Cervical
        Open Treatment 22326
        Closed Treatment 22305
        with Manipulation, Casting and/or
        Bracing 22315
        without Manipulation 22310
    Lumbar
        Open Treatment 22325
    Thoracic
        Open Treatment 22327
Wrist
    Closed Treatment 25660, 25675, 25680
    Intercarpal 25660
        Open Treatment 25670
    Open Treatment 25670, 25685
    Percutaneous Fixation 25671
    Radiocarpal 25660
        Open Treatment 25670
    Radioulnar
        Closed Treatment 25675
        Open Treatment 25676
        Percutaneous Fixation 25671
    with Fracture
        Closed Treatment 25680
        Open Treatment 25685
    with Manipulation 25660, 25675, 25680

Dislocation, Radiocarpal Joint
See Radiocarpal Joint, Dislocation

Disorder
Blood Coagulation
    See Coagulopathy
Penis
    See Penis
Retinal
    See Retina

Displacement Therapy
Nose 30210

Dissection
Hygroma, Cystic
    Axillary/Cervical 38550-38555
Lymph Nodes 38542

Dissection, Neck, Radical
See Radical Neck Dissection

Distention
See Dilation

Diverticula, Meckel's
See Diverticulum, Meckel's

Diverticulectomy 44800
Esophagus 43130-43135

Diverticulectomy, Meckel's
See Meckel's Diverticulum, Excision

Diverticulum
Bladder
    See Bladder, Diverticulum
Meckel's
    Excision 44800
Repair
    Urethra 53400-53405

Division
Muscle
    Foot 28250
Plantar Fascia
    Foot 28250

Division, Isthmus, Horseshoe Kidney
See Symphysiotomy, Horseshoe Kidney

Division, Scalenus Anticus Muscle
See Muscle Division, Scalenus Anticus

Dl-Amphetamine
See Amphetamine

DMO
See Dimethadione

DNA
Antibody 86225-86226

DNA Endonuclease
See DNAse

DNA Probe
See Cytogenetics Studies; Nucleic Acid Probe

DNAse
Antibody 86215

Domiciliary Services
See Nursing Facility Services
Assisted Living 99339-99340
Discharge Services 99315-99316
Established Patient 99334-99337
New Patient 99324-99328

Donor Procedures
Conjunctival Graft 68371
Heart Excision 33940
Heart/Lung Excision 33930
Liver Segment 47140-47142
Stem Cells
    Donor Search 38204

Dopamine
See Catecholamines
Blood 82383-82384
Urine 82382, 82384

Doppler
Doppler Echocardiography 76827-76828,
            93306-93308, 93320-93350
Extracranial 93875
Intracardiac 93662
Transesophageal 93318
Transthoracic 93303-93317

Doppler Scan
Arterial Studies
    Extremities 93922-93924

Fetal
    Middle Cerebral Artery 76821
    Umbilical Artery 76820
Extremities 93965
Intracranial Arteries 93886-93893

Dorsal Vertebra
See Vertebra, Thoracic

Dose Plan
See Dosimetry

Dosimetry
Radiation Therapy 77300, 77331
    Brachytherapy 77326-77328
    Intensity Modulation 77301, 77338
    Teletherapy 77305-77321

Double-Stranded DNA
See Deoxyribonucleic Acid

Doxepin
Assay 80166

DPH
See Phenytoin

Drainage
See Excision; Incision; Incision and Drainage;
Paracentesis
Abdomen
    Abdomen Fluid 49080-49081
Abscess
    Appendix 44900-44901
        Percutaneous 44901
    Brain 61150-61151
    Eyelid 67700
    Liver 47010-47011
    Ovary
        Percutaneous 58823
    Pelvic
        Percutaneous 58823
    Pericolic
        Percutaneous 58823
    Perirenal or Renal 50020-50021
        Percutaneous 50021
    Prostate 52700
    Retroperitoneal 49060-49061
        Percutaneous 49061
    Subdiaphragmatic or
        Subphrenic 49040-49041
        Percutaneous 49040-49041
    with X-ray 75989
Amniotic Fluid
    Diagnostic Aspiration 59000
    Therapeutic Aspiration 59001
Bile Duct
    Transhepatic 75980
Brain Fluid 61070
Bursa 20600-20610
Cerebrospinal Fluid 61000-61020, 61050,
                  61070, 62272
Cervical Fluid 61050
Cisternal Fluid 61050
Cyst
    Bone 20615
    Brain 61150-61151, 62161-62162
    Breast 19000-19001
    Ganglion 20612
    Liver 47010-47011
        Percutaneous 47011
    Salivary Gland 42409
    Sublingual Gland 42409

Physical Therapy
  Attended, Manual 97032
  Unattended 97014

Electro-Hydraulic Procedure 52325

Electro-Oculography 92270

Electroanalgesia
See Application, Neurostimulation

Electrocardiography
12 Lead 3120F
24 Hour Monitoring 93224-93237
Evaluation 93000, 93010, 93014, 93660
Rhythm
  Evaluation .93042
  Microvolt T-wave Alternans 93025
  Tracing 93041
  Tracing and Evaluation 93040
Signal Averaged 93278
Transmission 93012
Wearable Patient-Activated Recording
  Transmission and Evaluation 93268, 93270
    Interpretation 93272
    Monitoring 93271

Electrocautery 17000-17286
See Destruction

Electrochemistry
See Electrolysis

Electroconvulsive Therapy 90870

Electrocorticogram
Intraoperative .95829

Electrode, Depth
See Depth Electrode
Electrode Array Intracranial 61850-61868,
                                              61885-61886
Peripheral Nerve 64555, 64575
Retinal 0100T
Spinal 63650-63655

Electrodesiccation 17000-17286
Lesion
  Penis 54055

Electroejaculation 55870

Electroencephalography (EEG) 95816
Brain Death 95824
Coma 95822
Digital Analysis 95957
Electrode Placement 95830
Intraoperative .95955
Monitoring 95812-95813, 95950-95953, 95956
  with Drug Activation 95954
  with Physical Activation 95954
  with WADA Activation 95958
Sleep 95822, 95827
Standard 95819

Electrogastrography 91132-91133

Electrogram, Atrial
Esophageal Recording 93615-93616

Electrolysis .17380

Electromyographs
See Electromyography, Needle

Electromyography
Anorectal with Biofeedback 90911
Fine Wire
  Dynamic 96004
Needle
  Extremities 95861-95864
  Extremity 95860
  Face and Neck Muscles 95867-95868
  Guidance
    for Chemodenervation 95874
  Hemidiaphragm 95866
  Larynx 95865
  Ocular 92265
  Other than Thoracic Paraspinal 95870
  Single Fiber Electrode 95872
  Thoracic Paraspinal Muscles 95869
Sphincter Muscles
  Anus 51784-51785
    Needle 51785
  Urethra 51784-51785
    Needle 51785
Surface
  Dynamic 96002-96004

Electron Microscopy 88348-88349

Electronic Analysis
Cardioverter-Defibrillator, Implantable
  Data Analysis 93289, 93295-93296
  Evaluation of Programming
    In Person 93282-93284, 93287,
                                    93640, 93642
    Remote 93295-93296
Drug Infusion Pump 62367-62368
Neurostimulator Pulse Generator . . .95970-95982
Loop Recorder, Implantable
  Data Analysis 93291, 93298-93299
  Evaluation of Programming 93285, 93291,
                                    93298-93299

Electrophoresis
Counterimmuno- 86185
Immuno- 86320-86327
Immunofixation 86334-86335
Protein .84165-84166
Unlisted Services and Procedures 82664

**Electrophysiology
Procedure** 93600-93660

Electroretinogram
See Electroretinography

Electroretinography 92275

**Electrostimulation, Analgesic
Cutaneous**
See Application, Neurostimulation

Electrosurgery
Benign Lesions 17110-17111
Trichiasis
  Correction 67825

Electroversion, Cardiac
See Cardioversion

Elevation, Scapula, Congenital
See Sprengel's Deformity

Elliot Operation
See Excision, Lesion, Sclera

Eloesser Procedure
See Thoracostomy, Empyema

Eloesser Thoracoplasty
See Thoracoplasty

Embolectomy
Aortoiliac Artery 34151-34201
Axillary Artery 34101
Brachial Artery 34101
Carotid Artery 34001
Celiac Artery .34151
Femoral 34201
Iliac 34151-34201
Innominate Artery 34001-34101
Mesentery Artery 34151
Peroneal Artery 34203
Popliteal Artery 34203
Pulmonary Artery 33910-33916
Radial Artery 34111
Renal Artery .34151
Subclavian Artery 34001-34101
Tibial Artery .34203
Ulnar Artery .34111

Embolization
Leiomyomata. .37210

Embryo
Biopsy .89290-89291
Cryopreservation 89258
Cryopreserved
  Preparation
    Thawing 89352
Culture 89250
  with Co-Culture Oocyte 89251
Hatching
  Assisted
    Microtechnique 89253
Preparation
  for Transfer 89255
Storage 89342

Embryo Implantation
See Implantation

Embryo Transfer
In Vitro Fertilization 58974-58976
  Intrafallopian Transfer 58976
  Intrauterine Transfer 58974

Embryo/Fetus Monitoring
See Monitoring, Fetal

Embryonated Eggs
Inoculation 87250

**Emergency Department
Services** 99281-99288
See Critical Care; Emergency Department Services
Anesthesia 99140
Physician Direction of Advanced Life
Support 99288

Emesis Induction 99175

EMG
See Electromyography, Needle

EMI Scan
See CT Scan

**Emission Computerized
Tomography** 78607

Removal
  Foreign Body 43215
  Polyp 43216-43217, 43228
  Tumor 43216, 43228
Ultrasound 43231-43232
Vein Ligation 43205
Eye 66990
Foot
  Plantar Fasciotomy 29893
Gastrointestinal
  Ablation
    Photodynamic Therapy 96570-96571
  Upper 3130F-3132F, 3140F-3141F
    Biopsy 43239
    Catheterization 43241
    Destruction of Lesion 43258
    Dilation 43245, 43248-43249
    Drainage of Pseudocyst 43240
    Exploration 43234-43235
    Foreign Body 43247
    Gastric Bypass 43644-43645
    Gastroenterostomy 43644-43645
    Hemorrhage 43255
    Inject Varices 43243
    Injection ...., 43236
    Needle Biopsy 43238, 43242
    Referral 3132F
    Removal 43247, 43250-43251
    Roux-En-Y 43644
    Stent Placement 43256
    Thermal Radiation 43257
    Tube Placement 43246
    Ultrasound 43237-43242, 43259, 76975
    Vein Ligation 43244
Heart
  Atria 33265-33266
Ileum
  via Stoma 44383
Intestines, Small
  Biopsy 44361, 44377
  Destruction
    Lesion 44369
    Tumor 44369
  Diagnostic 44376
  Exploration 44360
  Hemorrhage 44366, 44378
  Insertion
    Stent 44370, 44379
    Tube 44379
  Pelvic Pouch 44385-44386
  Removal
    Foreign Body 44363
    Lesion 44365
    Polyp 44364-44365
  Tube Placement 44372
  Tube Revision 44373
  via Stoma 44380-44383
  Tumor 44364-44365
Intracranial 62160-62165
Kidney
  Biopsy 50555, 50574-50576, 52354
  Catheterization 50553, 50572
  Destruction 50557, 50576, 52354
  Dilation of Ureter 50553
  Excision
    Tumor 52355
  Exploration 52351
  Lithotripsy 52353
  Removal
    Calculus 50561, 50580, 52352
    Foreign Body 50561, 50580

via Incision 50562-50580
via Stoma 50551-50561
Larynx
  Biopsy 31510, 31535-31536
  Direct 31515-31571
  Exploration 31505, 31520-31526, 31575
  Fiberoptic 31575-31579
  Indirect 31505-31513
  Operative 31530-31561
  Removal
    Foreign Body 31530-31531
    Lesion 31511, 31545-31546
    See Endoscopic
Mediastinoscopy
  Biopsy 39400
  Exploration 39400
Nose
  Diagnostic 31231-31235
  Surgical 31237-31294
  Unlisted Services and Procedures 31299
Pancreatic Duct
  Cannulation 43273
  Destruction
    Calculi (Stone) 43265
    Tumor 43272
  Dilation 43271
  Removal
    Calculi (Stone) 43264
    Foreign Body 43269
    Stent 43269
  Specimen Collection 43260
  Sphincter Pressure 43263
  Sphincterotomy 43262
  Tube Placement 43267-43268
Pelvis
  Aspiration 49322
  Destruction of Lesion 58662
  Lysis of Adhesions 58660
  Oviduct Surgery 58670-58671
  Removal of Adnexal Structures 58661
Peritoneum
  Biopsy 47561
  Drainage
    Lymphocele 49323, 54690
    Radiologic 47560
Pleural Cavity
  Ablation
    Photodynamic Therapy 96570-96571
Rectum
  Biopsy 45305
  Destruction
    Tumor 45320
  Dilation 45303
  Exploration 45300
  Hemorrhage 45317
  Removal
    Foreign Body 45307
    Polyp 45308-45315
    Tumor 45308-45315
  Volvulus 45321
Spleen
  Removal 38120
Testis
  Removal 54690
Trachea
  Dilation 31630-31631, 31636-31638
  via Tracheostomy 31615
Ureter
  Biopsy ...50955-50957, 50974-50976, 52354
  Catheterize 50953, 50972
  Destruction 50957, 50976, 52354

Excision
  Tumor 52355
  Exploration 52351
  Injection of Implant Material 52327
  Lithotripsy 52353
  Manipulation of Ureteral Calculus 52330
  Placement
    Stent 50947
  Removal
    Calculus 50961, 50980, 52352
    Foreign Body 50961, 50980
  Resection 52355
  via Incision 50970-50980
  via Stoma 50951-50961
Ureteral
  Biopsy 52007
  Catheterization 52005
Urethra 52000
  Biopsy 52204, 52354
  Catheterization 52010
  Destruction 52354
    Lesion 52400
  Evacuation
    Clot 52001
  Excision
    Tumor 52355
  Exploration 52351
  Incision
    Ejaculatory Duct 52402
  Injection of Implant Material 51715
  Lithotripsy 52353
  Removal
    Calculus 52352
  Resection
    Ejaculatory Duct 52402
  Vasectomy 52402
  Vasotomy 52402
Uterus
  Anesthesia 00952
  Hysteroscopy
    Diagnostic 58555
    with Division/Resection Intrauterine
      Septum 58560
    with Lysis of Intrauterine Adhesions ...58559
  Placement
    Fallopian Tube 58565
  Removal
    Endometrial 58563
    Impacted Foreign Body 58562
    Leiomyomata 58561
  Surgical with Biopsy 58558
Vagina
  Anesthesia 00950
  Biopsy 57454
  Exploration 57452
Vascular
  Surgical 33508, 37500-37501

Endosteal Implant
Reconstruction
  Mandible 21248-21249
  Maxilla 21248-21249

Endothelioma, Dural
See Meningioma

Endotracheal Intubation
See Insertion, Endotracheal Tube

Endotracheal Tube
Intubation 31500

ERCP
See Bile Duct; Cholangiopancreatography; Pancreatic Duct

ERG
See Electroretinography

Ergocalciferol
See Vitamin D

Ergocalciferols
See Vitamin D

Ergonovine Provocation Test 93024

Erythrocyte
See Red Blood Cell (RBC)

Erythrocyte ab
See Antibody, Red Blood Cell

Erythrocyte Count
See Red Blood Cell (RBC), Count

Erythropoietin 82668

Escharotomy
Burns 16035-16036

Escherichia coli 0157
Antigen Detection
    Enzyme Immunoassay 87335

ESD
See Endoscopy, Gastrointestinal, Upper

Esophageal Acid Infusion Test
See Acid Perfusion Test

Esophageal Polyp
See Polyp, Esophagus

Esophageal Tumor
See Tumor, Esophagus

Esophageal Varices
Ligation 43205, 43400
Transection/Repair 43401

Esophagectomy
Partial 43116-43124
Total 43107-43113, 43124

Esophagoenterostomy
with Total Gastrectomy.................43620

Esophagogastroduodenoscopies
See Endoscopy, Gastrointestinal, Upper

Esophagogastromyotomy
See Esophagomyotomy

Esophagogastrostomy 43320

Esophagojejunostomy 43340-43341

Esophagomyotomy 32665, 43330-43331
with Fundoplasty 43279

Esophagorrhaphy
See Esophagus, Suture

Esophagoscopies
See Endoscopy, Esophagus

Esophagostomy 43350-43352
Closure 43420-43425

Esophagotomy 43020, 43045

Esophagotracheal Fistula
See Fistula, Tracheoesophageal

Esophagus
Acid Perfusion Test 91030
Acid Reflux Tests 91034-91038
Balloon Distension
    Provocation Study 91040
Biopsy
    Endoscopy 43202
    Forceps 3150F
Cineradiography 74230
Dilation 43450-43458
    Endoscopic 43220-43226, 43248-43249
    Surgical 43510
Endoscopy
    Biopsy 43202
    Dilation 43220-43226
    Exploration 43200
    Hemorrhage 43227
    Injection 43201, 43204
    Insertion Stent 43219
    Needle Biopsy 43232
    Removal
      Foreign Body 43215
      Polyp 43216-43217, 43228
      Tumor 43216, 43228
    Ultrasound 43231-43232
    Vein Ligation 43205
Excision
    Diverticula 43130-43135
    Partial 43116-43124
    Total 43107-43113, 43124
Exploration
    Endoscopy 43200
Hemorrhage 43227
Incision 43020, 43045
    Muscle 43030
Injection
    Sclerosing Agent 43204
    Submucosal 43201
Insertion
    Stent 43219
    Tamponade 43460
    Tube 43510
Intubation with Specimen Collection 91000
Lesion
    Excision 43100-43101
Ligation 43405
Motility Study 78258, 91010-91012
Needle Biopsy
    Endoscopy 43232
Nuclear Medicine
    Imaging (Motility) 78258
    Reflux Study 78262
Reconstruction 43300, 43310, 43313
    Creation
      Stoma 43350-43352
    Esophagostomy 43350
    Fistula 43305, 43312, 43314
    Gastrointestinal 43360-43361
Removal
    Foreign Bodies ...43020, 43045, 43215, 74235
    Lesion 43216
    Polyp 43216-43217, 43228
Repair 43300, 43310, 43313
    Esophagogastric Fundoplasty 43324-43325
      Laparoscopic 43280
    Esophagogastrostomy 43320
    Esophagojejunostomy 43340-43341

Fistula 43305, 43312, 43314, 43420-43425
Muscle 43330-43331
Paraesophageal Hernia
    Laparascopic 43281-43282
Pre-existing Perforation 43405
Varices 43401
Wound 43410-43415
Suture 43405
    Wound 43410-43415
Ultrasound
    Endoscopy 43231-43232
Unlisted Services and Procedures ...43289, 43499
Vein
    Ligation 43205, 43400
Video 74230
X-ray 74220

Esophagus Neoplasm
See Tumor, Esophagus

Esophagus, Varix
See Esophageal Varices

Established Patient
Domiciliary or Rest Home Visit 99334-99337
Emergency Department Services 99281-99285
Home Services 99347-99350
Hospital Inpatient Services 99221-99239
Hospital Observation Services 99217-99220
Inpatient Consultations 99251-99255
Office and/or Other Outpatient
    Consultations 99241-99245
Office Visit 99211-99215
Online Medical Evaluation 98969, 99444
Outpatient Visit 99211-99215
Telephone Services ...98966-98968, 99441-99443

Establishment
Colostomy
    Abdominal 50810
    Perineal 50810

Estes Operation
See Ovary, Transposition

Estlander Procedure 40525

Estradiol 82670
Response 80414

Estriol
Blood or Urine 82677

Estrogen
Blood or Urine 82671-82672
Receptor 84233

Estrone
Blood or Urine 82679

Ethanediols
See Ethylene Glycol

Ethanol
Blood 82055
Breath 82075
Urine 82055

Ethchlorovynol
See Ethchlorvynol

Ethchlorvinol
See Ethchlorvynol

Suprahyoid	38700
Retroperitoneal Transabdominal	38780
Thoracic	38746

Mandibular
Exostosis	21031

Mastoid
Complete	69502
Radical	69511
Modified	69505
Petrous Apicectomy	69530
Simple	69501

Maxilla
Exostosis	21032

Maxillary Torus Palatinus ... 21032

Meningioma
Brain	61512, 61519

Meniscectomy
Temporomandibular Joint	21060

Metacarpal ... 26230
Metatarsal ... 28110-28114, 28122, 28140
Condyle	28288

Mouth
Frenum	40819

Mucosa
Gums	41828
Mouth	40818

Nail Fold ... 11765
Nails ... 11750-11752

Nerve
Foot	28055
Leg, Lower	27326
Leg, Upper	27325
Sympathetic	64802-64818

Neurofibroma ... 64788-64790
Neurolemmoma ... 64788-64792
Neuroma ... 64774-64786

Nose
Dermoid Cyst
Complex	30125
Simple	30124
Polyp	30110-30115
Rhinectomy	30150-30160
Skin	30120

Submucous Resection
Nasal Septum	30520
Turbinate	30140
Turbinate	30130-30140

Odontoid Process ... 22548
Olecranon Process ... 24147
Omentum ... 49255
Ovary ... 58720
Partial
Oophorectomy	58940
Ovarian Malignancy	58943
Peritoneal Malignancy	58943
Tubal Malignancy	58943
Wedge Resection	58920
Total	58940-58943

Oviduct ... 58720
Palate ... 42120, 42145
Pancreas
Ampulla of Vater	48148
Duct	48148
Partial	48140-48146, 48150, 48153-48154, 48160
Peripancreatic Tissue	48105
Total	48155-48160

Parathyroid Gland ... 60500-60502
Parotid Gland ... 42340
Partial	42410-42415
Total	42420-42426

Patella	27350
See Patellectomy

Penile Adhesions
Post-circumcision	54162

Penis
Frenulum	54164
Partial	54120
Prepuce	54150-54161, 54163
Radical	54130-54135
Total	54125

Pericardium ... 33030-33031
Endoscopic	32659

Petrous Temporal
Apex	69530

Phalanges
Finger	26235-26236
Toe	28124-28126, 28150-28160

Pharynx ... 42145
Partial	42890
Resection	42892-42894
with Larynx	31390-31395

Pituitary Gland ... 61546-61548
Pleura ... 32310-32320
Endoscopic	32656

Polyp
Intestines ... 43250
Nose
Extensive	30115
Simple	30110
Sinus	31032
Urethra	53260

Pressure Ulcers ... 15920-15999
See Skin Graft and Flap

Prostate
Abdominoperineal	45119
Partial	55801, 55821-55831
Perineal	55801-55815
Radical	55810-55815, 55840-55845
Regrowth	52630
Residual Obstructive Tissue	52630
Retropubic	55831-55845
Suprapubic	55821
Transurethral	52601, 52630

Pterygium
with Graft	65426

Pubis
Partial	27070-27071

Radical Synovium Wrist ... 25115-25116
Radius ... 24130, 24136, 24145, 24152, 25145
Styloid Process	25230

Rectum
Partial	45111, 45113-45116, 45123
Prolapse	45130-45135
Stricture	45150
Total	45119-45120
with Colon	45121

Redundant Skin of Eyelid
See Blepharoplasty
Ribs ... 21600-21616, 32900

Scapula
Ostectomy	23190
Partial	23182
Sequestrectomy	23172
Tumor
Radical Resection	23210

Sclera ... 66160
Scrotum ... 55150
Semilunar Cartilage of Knee
See Knee, Meniscectomy
Seminal Vesicle ... 55650
Sesamoid Bone
Foot	28315

Sinus
Ethmoid	31200-31205
Maxillary	31225-31230

Skene's Gland ... 53270
Skin
Excess	15830-15839, 15847
Lesion
Benign	11400-11471
Malignant	11600-11646
Nose	30120

Skin Graft
Preparation of Site	15002-15005

Skull ... 61501
Spermatic Veins ... 55530-55540
Abdominal Approach	55535
Hernia Repair	55540

Spleen ... 38100-38102
Laparoscopic	38120

Stapes
with Footplate Drill Out	69661
without Foreign Material	69660

Sternum ... 21620, 21630-21632
Stomach
Partial	43631-43635, 43845
Total	43620-43622

Sublingual Gland ... 42450
Submandibular Gland ... 42440, 42508
Sweat Glands
Axillary	11450-11451
Inguinal	11462-11463
Perianal	11470-11471
Perineal	11470-11471
Umbilical	11470-11471

Synovium
Ankle	27625-27626
Carpometacarpal Joint	26130
Elbow	24102
Hip Joint	27054
Interphalangeal Joint	26140
Intertarsal Joint	28070
Knee Joint	27334-27335
Metacarpophalangeal Joint	26135
Metatarsophalangeal Joint	28072
Shoulder	23105-23106
Tarsometatarsal Joint	28070
Wrist	25105, 25118-25119

Talus ... 28120, 28130
Tarsal ... 28116, 28122
Temporal Bone ... 69535
Temporal, Petrous
Apex	69530

Tendon
Arm
Lower	25109
Finger	26180, 26390, 26415
Hand	26390, 26415
Palm	26170

Tendon Sheath
Finger	26145
Foot	28086-28088
Palm	26145
Wrist	25115-25116

Testis
Laparoscopic	54690
Partial	54522
Radical	54530-54535
Simple	54520
Tumor	54530-54535

Thrombectomy
Axillary Vein	34490
Bypass Graft	35875-35876
Femoropopliteal Vein	34401-34451

Skeletal
    Humeral Epycondyle
       Percutaneous 24566
Spinal
    Insertion 22841-22847
    Prosthetic 22851
    Reinsertion 22849

Fixation Test, Complement
See Complement, Fixation Test

Fixation, External
See External Fixation

Fixation, Kidney
See Nephropexy

Fixation, Rectum
See Proctopexy

Fixation, Tongue
See Tongue, Fixation

Flank
See Back/Flank

Flap
See Skin Graft and Flap
Free
    Breast Reconstruction 19364
Grafts 15570-15738, 15842
Latissimus Dorsi
    Breast Reconstruction 19361
Omentum 49905
    Free
       with Microvascular Anastomosis 49906
Transverse Rectus Abdominis Myocutaneous
    Breast Reconstruction 19367-19369

Flatfoot Correction 28735

Flea Typhus
See Murine Typhus

Fletcher Factor 85292

Flow Cytometry 88182-88189
Diagnostic/Pretreatment 3170F

Flow-Volume Loop
See Pulmonology, Diagnostic
Pulmonary 94375

Flu Vaccines 90645-90648, 90655-90663

Fluid Collection
Incision and Drainage
    Skin 10140

Fluid, Amniotic
See Amniotic Fluid

Fluid, Body
See Body Fluid

Fluid, Cerebrospinal
See Cerebrospinal Fluid

Fluorescein
Angiography, Ocular 92287
Intravenous Injection
    Vascular Flow Check, Graft 15860

Fluorescein Angiography
See Angiography, Fluorescein

**Fluorescent In Situ
Hybridization** 88365

Fluoride
Blood 82735
Urine 82735

Fluoroscopy
Bile Duct
    Calculus Removal 74327
    Guide Catheter 74328, 74330
Chest
    Bronchoscopy 31622-31646
    Complete (Four Views) 71034
    Partial (Two Views) 71023
Drain Abscess 75989
GI Tract
    Guide Intubation 74340
Hourly 76000-76001
Introduction
    GI Tube 74340
Larynx 70370
Nasogastric 43752
Needle Biopsy 77002
Orogastric 43752
Pancreatic Duct
    Guide Catheter 74329-74330
Pharynx 70370
Renal
    Guide Catheter 74475
Spine/Paraspinous
    Guide Catheter/Needle 77003
Unlisted Services and Procedures 76496
Ureter
    Guide Catheter 74480
Venous Access Device 36598, 77001
Vertebra
    Osteoplasty 77291

Flurazepam
Blood or Urine 82742

Flush Aortogram 75722-75724

FNA
See Fine Needle Aspiration

Foam Stability Test 83662

Fold, Vocal
See Vocal Cords

Foley Operation Pyeloplasty
See Pyeloplasty

Foley Y-Pyeloplasty 50400-50405

Folic Acid 82747
Blood 82746

**Follicle Stimulating Hormone
(FSH)** 80418, 80426, 83001

Folliculin
See Estrone

Follitropin
See Follicle Stimulating Hormone (FSH)

Follow-up Inpatient Consultations
See Consultation, Follow-up Inpatient

Follow-up Services
See Hospital Services; Office and/or Other
Outpatient Services
Post-Op 99024

Fontan Procedure
See Repair, Heart, Anomaly; Revision

Food Allergy Test 95075
See Allergy Tests

Foot
See Metatarsal; Tarsal
Amputation 28800-28805
Bursa
    Incision and Drainage 28001
Capsulotomy 28260-28264
Cast 29450
Fasciectomy 28060
    Radical 28060-28062
Fasciotomy 28008
    Endoscopic 29893
Incision 28002-28005
Joint
    See Talotarsal Joint; Tarsometatarsal Joint
    Magnetic Resonance Imaging
    (MRI) 73721-73723
Lesion
    Excision 28080, 28090
Magnetic Resonance Imaging (MRI) ...73718-73720
Nerve
    Destruction
       Neurolytic 64632
    Excision 28055
    Incision 28035
Neurectomy 28055
Neuroma
    Excision 28080
    Injection of Anesthetic or Steroid 64455
    Morton's
       Destruction 64632
       Injection 64455
Reconstruction
    Cleft Foot 28360
Removal
    Foreign Body 28190-28193
Repair
    Muscle 28250
    Tendon 28200-28230, 28234-28238
Replantation 20838
Sesamoid
    Excision 28315
Splint 29590
Strapping 29540, 29590
Suture
    Tendon 28200-28210
Tendon Sheath
    Excision 28086-28088
Tenotomy 28230, 28234
Tumor
    Excision 28039-28045
    Radical Resection 28046-28047
Unlisted Services and Procedures 28899
X-ray 73620-73630

Foot Abscess
See Abscess, Foot

Foot Navicular Bone
See Navicular

Forearm 20805
See Arm, Lower

G

Gall Bladder
See Gallbladder

Gallbladder
See Bile Duct
Anastomosis
    with Intestines 47720-47741
Excision 47562-47564, 47600-47620
Exploration 47480
Incision 47490
Incision and Drainage 47480
Nuclear Medicine
    Imaging 78223
Removal
    Calculi (Stone) 47480
Repair
    with Gastroenterostomy 47741
    with Intestines 47720-47740
Unlisted Services and Procedures 47999
X-ray with Contrast 74290-74291

Galvanocautery
See Electrocautery

Galvanoionization
See Iontophoresis

Gamete Intrafallopian Transfer (GIFT) 58976

Gamete Transfer
In Vitro Fertilization 58976

Gamma Camera Imaging
See Nuclear Medicine

Gamma Glutamyl Transferase 82977

Gamma Seminoprotein
See Antigen, Prostate Specific

Gammacorten
See Dexamethasone

Gammaglobulin
Blood 82784-82787

Gamulin Rh
See Immune Globulins, Rho (D)

Ganglia, Trigeminal
See Gasserian Ganglion

Ganglion
See Gasserian Ganglion
Cyst
    Aspiration/Injection 20612
    Drainage 20612
    Wrist
      Excision 25111-25112
Injection
    Anesthetic 64505, 64510

Ganglion Cervicothoracicum
See Stellate Ganglion

Ganglion Pterygopalatinum
See Sphenopalatine Ganglion

Ganglion, Gasser's
See Gasserian Ganglion

Gardner Operation
See Meningocele Repair

Gardnerella Vaginalis Detection 87510-87512

Gasser Ganglion
See Gasserian Ganglion

Gasserian Ganglion
Sensory Root
    Decompression 61450
    Section 61450
Stereotactic 61790

Gastrectomy
Longitudinal 43775
Partial 43631-43635, 43845
    with Gastrojejunostomy 43632
Sleeve 43775
Total 43621-43622
    with Esophagoenterostomy 43620
with Gastroduodenostomy 43631

Gastric Acid 82926-82928

Gastric Analysis Test 91052

Gastric Electrodes
Implantation
    Laparoscopic
      Neurostimulator 43647
      Stimulation 0155T
    Open
      Neurostimulator 43881
      Stimulation 0157T
Removal
    Laparoscopic
      Neurostimulator 43648
      Stimulation 0156T
    Open
      Neurostimulator 43882
      Stimulation 0158T
Replacement
    Laparoscopic
      Neurostimulator 43647
      Stimulation 0155T
    Open
      Neurostimulator 43881
      Stimulation 0157T
Revision
    Laparoscopic
      Neurostimulator 43648
      Stimulation 0156T
    Open
      Neurostimulator 43882
      Stimulation 0158T

Gastric Intubation 89130-89141, 91105

Gastric Lavage, Therapeutic 91105

Gastric Tests
Manometry 91020

Gastric Ulcer Disease
See Stomach, Ulcer

Gastrin 82938-82941

Gastrocnemius Recession
Leg, Lower 27687

Gastroduodenostomy 43810,
                         43850-43855

Gastroenterology, Diagnostic
Breath Hydrogen Test 91065
Esophagus Tests
    Acid Perfusion 91030
    Acid Reflux 91034-91038
    Balloon Distension Provocation Study ..91040
    Intubation with Specimen Collection ...91000
    Motility Study 91010-91012
Gastric Tests
    Manometry 91020
Gastroesophageal Reflux Test
    See Acid Reflux
Intestine
    Bleeding Tube 91100
Manometry 91020
Rectum
    Sensation, Tone, and Compliance Test ...91120
Rectum/Anus
    Manometry 91122
Stomach
    Intubation with Specimen Prep 91055
    Stimulation of Secretion 91052
Unlisted Services and Procedures 91299

Gastroenterostomy
for Obesity 43644-43645, 43842-43848

Gastroesophageal Reflux Test 91034-91038

Gastrointestinal Endoscopies
See Endoscopy, Gastrointestinal

Gastrointestinal Exam
Nuclear Medicine
    Blood Loss Study 78278
    Protein Loss Study 78282
    Shunt Testing 78291
    Unlisted Services and Procedures 78299

Gastrointestinal Tract
Imaging
    Intraluminal 91110-91111
Reconstruction 43360-43361
Upper
    Dilation 43249
X-ray 74240-74245
    Guide Dilator 74360
    Guide Intubation 74340
    with Contrast 74246-74249

Gastrointestinal, Upper
Biopsy
    Endoscopy 43239
Dilation
    Endoscopy 43245
    Esophagus 43248
Endoscopy
    Catheterization 43241
    Destruction
      Lesion 43258
    Dilation 43245
    Drainage
      Pseudocyst 43240
    Exploration 43234-43235
    Hemorrhage 43255
    Inject Varices 43243
    Injection 43236
    Needle Biopsy 43238, 43242
    Removal
      Foreign Body 43247
      Lesion 43251

Glaucoma
Cryotherapy 66720
Cyclophotocoagulation 66710-66711
Diathermy 66700
Fistulization of Sclera 66150
Provocative Test 92140

Glaucoma Drainage Implant
See Aqueous Shunt

Glenn Procedure 33766-33767

Glenohumeral Joint
Arthrotomy 23040
   with Biopsy 23100
   with Synovectomy 23105
Exploration 23107
Removal
   Foreign or Loose Body 23107

Glenoid Fossa
Reconstruction 21255

GLN
See Glutamine

Globulin
Antihuman 86880-86886
Immune 90281-90399
Sex Hormone Binding 84270

Globulin, Corticosteroid-Binding
See Transcortin

Globulin, Rh Immune
See Immune Globulins, Rho (D)

Globulin, Thyroxine-Binding
See Thyroxine Binding Globulin

Glomerular Procoagulant Activity
See Thromboplastin

Glomus Caroticum
See Carotid Body

Glossectomies
See Excision, Tongue

Glossopexy
See Tongue, Fixation

Glossorrhaphy
See Suture, Tongue

Glucagon 82943
Tolerance Panel 80422-80424
Tolerance Test 82946

Glucose 80422-80424, 80430-80435,
            95250-95251
Blood Test 82947-82950, 82962
Body Fluid 82945
Interstitial Fluid
   Continuous Monitoring 95250-95251
Tolerance Test 82951-82952
   with Tolbutamide 82953

Glucose Phosphate Isomerase
See Phosphohexose Isomerase

Glucose Phosphate Isomerase Measurement
See Phosphohexose Isomerase

Glucose-6-Phosphate
Dehydrogenase 82955-82960

Glucosidase 82963

Glucuronide Androstanediol 82154

Glue
Cornea Wound 65286
Sclera Wound 65286

Glukagon
See Glucagon

Glutamate Dehydrogenase
Blood 82965

Glutamate Pyruvate Transaminase
See Transaminase, Glutamic Pyruvic

Glutamic Alanine Transaminase
See Transaminase, Glutamic Pyruvic

Glutamic Aspartic Transaminase
See Transaminase, Glutamic Oxaloacetic

Glutamic Dehydrogenase
See Glutamate Dehydrogenase

Glutamine 82975

Glutamyltransferase, Gamma 82977

Glutathione 82978

Glutathione Reductase 82979

Glutethimide 82980

Glycanhydrolase, N-Acetylmuramide
See Lysozyme

Glycated Hemoglobins
See Glycohemoglobin

Glycated Protein 82985

Glycerol Phosphoglycerides
See Phosphatidylglycerol

Glycerol, Phosphatidyl
See Phosphatidylglycerol

Glycerophosphatase
See Alkaline Phosphatase

Glycinate, Theophylline Sodium
See Theophylline

Glycocholic Acid
See Cholylglycine

Glycohemoglobin 83036

Glycol, Ethylene
See Ethylene Glycol

Glycols, Ethylene
See Ethylene Glycol

Glycosaminoglycan
See Mucopolysaccharides

GMP
See Guanosine Monophosphate

GMP, Cyclic
See Cyclic GMP

Goeckerman Treatment 96910-96913

Gol-Vernet Operation
See Pyelotomy, Exploration

Gold
Assay 80172

Goldwaite Procedure 27422

Golfer's Elbow
See Tennis Elbow

Gonadectomy, Female
See Oophorectomy

Gonadectomy, Male
See Excision, Testis

Gonadotropin
Chorionic 84702-84704
FSH 83001
ICSH 83002
LH 83002

Gonadotropin Panel 80426

Gonioscopy 92020

Goniotomy 65820

Gonococcus
See Neisseria Gonorrhoeae

Goodenough Harris Drawing
Test 96101-96103

GOTT
See Transaminase, Glutamic Oxaloacetic

GPUT
See Galactose-1-Phosphate, Uridyl Transferase

Graft
See Bone Graft; Bypass Graft
Anal 46753
Aorta 33840-33851, 33860-33877
Artery
   Coronary 33503-33505
Bone
   See Bone Marrow, Transplantation
   Harvesting 20900-20902
   Microvascular/Anastomosis 20955-20962
   Osteocutaneous Flap with
   Microvascular Anastomosis 20969-20973
   Vascular Pedicle 25430
Bone and Skin 20969-20973
Cartilage
   Costochondral 20910
   Ear to Face 21235
   Harvesting 20910-20912
      See Cartilage Graft
   Rib to Face 21230
Conjunctiva 65782
   Harvesting 68371
Cornea
   with Lesion Excision 65426
Cornea Transplant
   Allograft Preparation 65757
   Endothelial 65756
   in Aphakia 65750
   in Pseudophakia 65755
   Lamellar
      Anterior 65710
      Penetrating 65730

Dura
Spinal Cord 63710
Endovascular 34900
Eye
Amniotic Membrane 65780
Conjunctiva 65782
Stem Cell 65781
Facial Nerve Paralysis 15840-15845
Fascia
Cheek 15840
Fascia Lata
Harvesting 20920-20922
Gum Mucosa 41870
Heart
See Heart, Transplantation
Heart Lung
See Transplantation, Heart-Lung
Kidney
See Kidney, Transplantation
Liver
See Liver, Transplantation
Lung
See Lung, Transplantation
Muscle
Cheek 15841-15845
Nail Bed
Reconstruction 11762
Nerve 64885-64907
Oral Mucosa 40818
Organ
See Transplantation
Pancreas
See Pancreas, Transplantation
Skin
Biological
See Allograft, Skin
Blood Flow Check, Graft 15860
See Skin Graft and Flap
Harvesting
for Tissue Culture 15040
Vascular Flow Check, Graft 15860
Tendon
Finger 26392
Hand 26392
Harvesting 20924
Tissue
Harvesting 20926
Vein
Cross-Over 34520

Grain Alcohol
See Alcohol, Ethyl

Granulation Tissue
Cauterization, Chemical 17250

Gravi, Myasthenia
See Myasthenia Gravis

Gravities, Specific
See Specific Gravity

Great Toe
Free Osteocutaneous Flap with Microvascular
Anastomosis 20973

Great Vessels
Shunt
Aorta to Pulmonary Artery
Ascending 33755
Descending 33762
Central 33764
Subclavian to Pulmonary Artery 33750

Vena Cava to Pulmonary Artery ...33766-33767
Unlisted Services and Procedures 33999

Great Vessels Transposition
See Transposition, Great Arteries

Greater Tuberosity Fracture
with Shoulder Dislocation
Closed Treatment 23665
Open Treatment 23670

Greater Vestibular Gland
See Bartholin's Gland

Green Operation
See Scapulopexy

Gridley Stain 88312

Grippe, Balkan
See Q Fever

Gritti Operation
See Amputation, Leg, Upper; Radical Resection;
Replantation

Groin Area
Repair
Hernia 49550-49557

Group Health Education 98961-98962,
99078

Grouping, Blood
See Blood Typing

Growth Factors, Insulin-Like
See Somatomedin

Growth Hormone 83003
Human 80418, 80428-80430, 86277

Growth Hormone Release Inhibiting Factor
See Somatostatin

GTT
See Hydatidiform Mole

Guaiac Test
See Blood, Feces

Guanosine Monophosphate 83008

Guanosine Monophosphate, Cyclic
See Cyclic GMP

Guanylic Acids
See Guanosine Monophosphate

Guard Stain 88313

Gullet
See Esophagus

Gums
Abscess
Incision and Drainage 41800
Alveolus
Excision 41830
Cyst
Incision and Drainage 41800
Excision
Gingiva 41820
Operculum 41821
Graft
Mucosa 41870

Hematoma
Incision and Drainage 41800
Lesion
Destruction 41850
Excision 41822-41828
Mucosa
Excision 41828
Reconstruction
Alveolus 41874
Gingiva 41872
Removal
Foreign Body 41805
Tumor
Excision 41825-41827
Unlisted Services and Procedures 41899

Gunning-Lieben Test
See Acetone, Blood or Urine

Guthrie Test 84030

H

H Flu
See Hemophilus Influenza

H-Reflex Study 95934-95936

HAA (Hepatitis Associated Antigen)
See Hepatitis Antigen, B Surface

HAAb
See Antibody, Hepatitis

Haemoglobin F
See Fetal Hemoglobin

Haemorrhage
See Hemorrhage

Haemorrhage Rectum
See Hemorrhage, Rectum

Hageman Factor 85280

HAI Test
See Hemagglutination Inhibition Test

Hair
Electrolysis 17380
KOH Examination 87220
Microscopic Evaluation 96902
Transplant
Punch Graft 15775-15776
Strip Graft 15220-15221

Hair Removal
See Removal, Hair

Hallux
See Great Toe

Halo
Body Cast 29000
Cranial 20661
for Thin Skull Osteology 20664
Femur 20663
Maxillofacial 21100
Pelvic 20662
Removal 20665

Tricuspid Valve .33465
Ventricular Assist Device 33981-33983
Repositioning
　Electrode 33215, 33217, 33226
　Tricuspid Valve .33468
Resuscitation 92950
Septal Defect
　See Septal Defect
Stimulation and Pacing 93623
Thrombectomy 33310-33315
Transplantation 33935, 33945
　Allograft Preparation 33933, 33944
Tricuspid Valve
　See Tricuspid Valve
Tumor
　Excision 33120-33130
Unlisted Services and Procedures 33999
Ventricular Assist Device (VAD)
　Interrogation and Programming 93750
Ventriculography
　See Ventriculography
Ventriculomyectomy 33416
Wound
　Repair .33300-33305

Heart Sounds
Acoustic Recording
　with Computer Analysis 93799

Heart Vessels
Angioplasty
　Percutaneous 92982-92984
　　See Angioplasty; Percutaneous
　　Transluminal Angioplasty
Insertion
　Graft 33330-33335
Thrombolysis 92975-92977
Valvuloplasty
　See Valvuloplasty
　Percutaneous 92986-92990

Heat Unstable Haemoglobin
See Hemoglobin, Thermolabile

Heavy Lipoproteins
See Lipoprotein

Heavy Metal 83015-83018

Heel
See Calcaneus
Collection of Blood 36415-36416
X-ray 73650

Heel Bone
See Calcaneus

Heel Fracture
See Calcaneus, Fracture

Heel Spur
Excision 28119

Heine-Medin Disease
See Polio

Heinz Bodies 85441-85445

Helicobacter Pylori
Antibody 86677
Antigen Detection
　Enzyme Immunoassay 87338-87339
Blood Test 83009
Breath Test 78267-78268, 83013-83014

Stool 87338
Urease Activity 83009, 83013-83014

Heller Operation
See Esophagomyotomy

Heller Procedure 32665, 43279,
　　　　　　　　　　　　　　　　　43330-43331

Helminth
Antibody 86682

Hemagglutination Inhibition
Test 86280

Hemangioma
See Lesion, Skin; Tumor

Hemapheresis
See Apheresis

Hematochezia
See Blood, Feces

Hematologic Test
See Blood Tests

Hematology
Unlisted Services and Procedures 85999

Hematoma
Ankle 27603
Arm, Lower 25028
Arm, Upper
　Incision and Drainage 23930
Brain
　Drainage 61154-61156
　Evacuation 61312-61315
　Incision and Drainage 61312-61315
Drain 61108
Ear, External
　Complicated 69005
　Simple 69000
Elbow
　Incision and Drainage 23930
Epididymis
　Incision and Drainage 54700
Gums
　Incision and Drainage 41800
Hip 26990
Incision and Drainage
　Neck 21501-21502
　Skin 10140
　Thorax 21501-21502
Knee 27301
Leg, Lower 27603
Leg, Upper 27301
Mouth 41005-41009, 41015-41018
　Incision and Drainage 40800-40801
Nasal Septum
　Incision and Drainage 30020
Nose
　Incision and Drainage 30000-30020
Pelvis 26990
Scrotum
　Incision and Drainage 54700
Shoulder
　Drainage 23030
Skin
　Incision and Drainage 10140
　Puncture Aspiration 10160
Subdural 61108
Subungual
　Evacuation 11740

Testis
　Incision and Drainage 54700
Tongue 41000-41006, 41015
Vagina
　Incision and Drainage 57022-57023
Wrist 25028

Hematopoietic Stem Cell
Transplantation
See Stem Cell, Transplantation

Hematopoietin
See Erythropoietin

Hematuria
See Blood, Urine

Hemic System
Unlisted Procedure 38999

Hemiepiphyseal Arrest
Elbow 24470

Hemifacial Microsomia
Reconstruction
　Mandibular Condyle 21247

Hemilaminectomy 63020-63044

Hemilaryngectomy 31370-31382

Hemipelvectomies
See Amputation, Interpelviabdominal

Hemiphalangectomy
Toe 28160

Hemispherectomy
Partial 61543
Total 61542

Hemocytoblast
See Stem Cell

Hemodialyses
See Hemodialysis

Hemodialysis 90935-90937
Blood Flow Study 90940
Duplex Scan of Access 93990
Kt/V Level .3082F-3084F
Plan of Care Documented 0505F
via Catheter 4054F
via Functioning Arteriovenous Fistula 4052F
via Functioning Arteriovenous Graft 4053F

Hemofiltration 90945-90947

Hemoglobin
A1c (HbA1c) Level 3044F-3045F
Analysis
　O_2 Affinity 82820
Carboxyhemoglobin 82375-82376, 88740
Chromatography .83021
Concentration 85046
Electrophoresis .83020
Fetal 83030-83033, 85460-85461
Fractionation and Quantitation 83020
Glycosylated (A1C) 83036-83037
Hgb
　Transcutaneous Testing 88738
Methemoglobin 83045-83050
　Transcutaneous 88741
Non-Automated .83026
Plasma 83051
Sulfhemoglobin 83055-83060

Huggin Operation
See Orchiectomy, Simple

Huhner Test 89300, 89320

Human Chorionic Gonadotropin
See Chorionic Gonadotropin

Human Chorionic Somatomammotropin
See Lactogen, Human Placental

Human Cytomegalovirus Group
See Cytomegalovirus

Human Epididymis Protein 86305

Human Growth Hormone (HGH) 80418, 80428-80430

Human Herpes Virus 4
See Epstein-Barr Virus

Human Immunodeficiency Virus
See HIV

Human Immunodeficiency Virus 1
See HIV-1

Human Immunodeficiency Virus 2
See HIV-2

Human Papillomavirus
See Vaccine

Human Papillomavirus Detection 87620-87622

Human Placental Lactogen
See Lactogen, Human Placental

Human T Cell Leukemia Virus I
See HTLV I

Human T Cell Leukemia Virus I Antibodies
See Antibody, HTLV I

Human T Cell Leukemia Virus II
See HTLV II

Human T Cell Leukemia Virus II Antibodies
See Antibody, HTLV II

Humeral Epicondylitides, Lateral
See Tennis Elbow

Humeral Fracture
See Fracture, Humerus

Humerus
See Arm, Upper; Shoulder
Abscess
　Incision and Drainage 23935
Craterization 23184, 24140
Cyst
　Excision 23150, 24110
　　with Allograft 23156, 24116
　　with Autograft 23155, 24115
Diaphysectomy 23184, 24140
Excision 23174, 23184, 23195,
　　　　　　　　　　24134, 24140, 24150

Fracture
　Closed Treatment 24500-24505
　　with Manipulation 23605
　　without Manipulation 23600
　Condyle
　　Closed Treatment 24576-24577
　　Open Treatment 24579
　　Percutaneous Fixation 24582
　Epicondyle
　　Closed Treatment 24560-24565
　　Open Treatment 24575
　　Skeletal Fixation
　　　Percutaneous 24566
　Greater Tuberosity Fracture
　　Closed Treatment with
　　　Manipulation 23625
　　Closed Treatment without
　　　Manipulation 23620
　　Open Treatment 23630
　Open Treatment 23615-23616
　Shaft 24500-24505, 24516
　　Open Treatment 24515
　Supracondylar
　　Closed Treatment 24530-24535
　　Open Treatment 24545-24546
　　Percutaneous Fixation 24538
　Transcondylar
　　Closed Treatment 24530-24535
　　Open Treatment 24545-24546
　　Percutaneous Fixation 24538
　with Dislocation 23665-23670
Osteomyelitis 24134
Pinning, Wiring 23491, 24498
Prophylactic Treatment 23491, 24498
Radical Resection 23220, 24150, 24152
Repair 24430
　Nonunion, Malunion 24430-24435
　Osteoplasty 24420
　Osteotomy 24400-24410
　with Graft 24435
Resection Head 23195
Saucerization 23184, 24140
Sequestrectomy 23174, 24134
Tumor
　Excision 23150, 23220, 24110,
　　　　　　　　　　　24071-24076
　　with Allograft 23156, 24116
　　with Autograft 23155, 24115
X-ray 73060

Hummelshein Operation
See Strabismus, Repair

Humor Shunt, Aqueous
See Aqueous Shunt

HVA
See Homovanillic Acid

Hybridization Probes, DNA
See Nucleic Acid Probe

Hydatid Disease
See Echinococcosis

Hydatid Mole
See Hydatidiform Mole

Hydatidiform Mole
Evacuation and Curettage 59870
Excision 59100

Hydration 96360-96361
Rehydration Oral Solution 4056F
Status 2030F-2031F

Hydrocarbons, Chlorinated
See Chlorinated Hydrocarbons

Hydrocele
Aspiration 55000
Excision
　Bilateral
　　Tunica Vaginalis 55041
　Unilateral
　　Spermatic Cord 55500
　　Tunica Vaginalis 55040
Repair 55060

Hydrochloric Acid, Gastric
See Acid, Gastric

Hydrochloride, Vancomycin
See Vancomycin

Hydrocodon
See Dihydrocodeinone

Hydrogen Ion Concentration
See pH

Hydrolase, Acetylcholine
See Acetylcholinesterase

Hydrolase, Triacylglycerol
See Lipase

Hydrolases, Phosphoric Monoester
See Phosphatase

Hydrotherapy (Hubbard Tank) 97036
See Physical Medicine/Therapy/Occupational Therapy

Hydrotubation 58350

Hydroxyacetanilide
See Acetaminophen

Hydroxycorticosteroid 83491

Hydroxyindolacetic Acid 83497
Urine 83497

Hydroxypregnenolone 80406, 84143

Hydroxyprogesterone 80402-80406,
　　　　　　　　　　　　83498-83499

Hydroxyproline 83500-83505

Hydroxytyramine
See Dopamine

Hygroma
Cystic
　Axillary/Cervical
　　Excision 38550-38555

Hymen
Excision 56700
Incision 56442

Hymenal Ring
Revision 56700

Hymenectomy 56700

Hymenotomy 56442

Hyoid
Bone
  Fracture
    Open Treatment 21495
Muscle
  Incision and Suspension 21685

Hyperbaric Oxygen Pressurization .99183

Hypercycloidal X-ray 76101-76102

Hyperdactylies
See Supernumerary Digit

Hyperglycemic Glycogenolytic Factor
See Glucagon

Hyperhidrosis 64650-64653

Hypertelorism of Orbit
See Orbital Hypertelorism

Hyperthermia Therapy
See Thermotherapy

Hyperthermia Treatment 77600-77620

Hypnotherapy 90880

Hypodermis
See Subcutaneous Tissue

Hypogastric Plexus
Destruction 64681
Injection
  Anesthetic 64517
  Neurolytic 64681

Hypoglossal Nerve
Anastomosis
  to Facial Nerve 64868

Hypoglossal-Facial Anastomosis
See Anastomosis, Nerve, Facial to Hypoglossal

Hypopharynges
See Hypopharynx

Hypopharynx
Biopsy 42802

Hypophysectomy 61546-61548, 62165

Hypophysis
See Pituitary Gland

Hypopyrexia
See Hypothermia

Hypospadias
Repair 54300, 54352
  Complications 54340-54348
  First Stage 54304
    Proximal Penile or Penoscrotal 54332
  One Stage
    Meatal Advancement 54322
    Perineal 54336
  Urethroplasty
    Local Skin Flaps 54324
    Local Skin Flaps and Mobilization of
    Urethra 54326
    Local Skin Flaps, Skin Graft Patch
    and/or Island Flap 54328

    Urethroplasty for Second Stage . . .54308-54316
      Free Skin Graft 54316
    Urethroplasty for Third Stage 54318

Hypoxia
Breathing Response 94450
High Altitude Simulation Test 94452-94453

Hysterectomy
Abdominal
  Radical 58210
  Resection of Ovarian Malignancy 58951,
                        58953-58956
  Supracervical 58180
  Total 58150, 58200, 58956
    with Colpo-Urethrocystopexy 58152
    with Omentectomy 58956
    with Partial Vaginectomy 58200
Cesarean
  after Cesarean Delivery 59525
  with Closure of Vesicouterine Fistula . . .51925
Laparoscopic 58541-58544
  Radical 58548
  Total 58570-58573
Removal
  Lesion 59100
Supracervical
  Laparoscopic 58541-58544
Vaginal 58260-58270, 58290-58294,
                        58550-58554
  Laparoscopic 58550, 58570-58573
  Radical 58285
  Removal Tubes/Ovaries 58262-58263,
               58291-58292, 58552, 58554
    Repair of Enterocele . . .58263, 58292, 58294
  with Colpectomy 58275-58280
  with Colpo-Urethrocystopexy . . .58267, 58293

Hysterolysis
See Lysis, Adhesions, Uterus

Hysteroplasty .58540

Hysterorrhaphy 58520, 59350

Hysterosalpingography 74740
Catheterization 58345
Injection Procedure 58340

Hysterosalpingostomy
See Implantation, Tubouterine

Hysteroscopy
Ablation
  Endometrial .58563
Diagnostic 58555
Lysis
  Adhesions 58559
Placement
  Fallopian Tube Implants 58565
Removal
  Impacted Foreign Body 58562
  Leiomyomata 58561
Resection
  of Intrauterine Septum 58560
Surgical with Biopsy 58558
Unlisted Services and Procedures 58578-58579

Hysterosonography
See Ultrasound; Sonohysterography

Hysterotomy 59100
See Ligation, Uterus
Induced Abortion
  with Amniotic Injections 59852
  with Vaginal Suppositories 59857

Hysterotrachelectomy
See Amputation, Cervix

I

I Antibodies, HTLV
See Antibody, HTLV-I

I, Angiotensin
See Angiotensin I

I, Coagulation Factor
See Fibrinogen

I, Heparin Co-Factor
See Antithrombin III

ICCE
See Extraction, Lens, Intracapsular

Ichthyosis, Sex Linked
See Syphilis Test

ICSH
See Luteinizing Hormone (LH)

Identification
Oocyte
  from Follicular Fluid 89254
Sperm
  from Aspiration 89257
  from Tissue 89264

IDH
See Isocitric Dehydrogenase, Blood

IG
See Immune Globulins

IgA 82784

IgD 82784

IgE 82785, 86003-86005

IgG 82784, 82787, 86001

IgM 82784

II, Coagulation Factor
See Prothrombin

II, Cranial Nerve
See Optic Nerve

Ileal Conduit
Visualization 50690

Ileoscopy
via Stoma 44383

Ileostomy 44310, 45136
Continent (Kock Procedure) 44316
Laparoscopic 44186-44187

Non-Tube 44187
Revision 44312-44314

Iliac Arteries
See Artery, Iliac

Iliac Crest
Free Osteocutaneous Flap with Microvascular
Anastomosis 20970

Iliohypogastric Nerve
Injection
    Anesthetic 64425

Ilioinguinal Nerve
Injection
    Anesthetic .64425

Ilium
Craterization 27070
Cyst
    Excision .27065-27067
Excision 27070
Fracture
    Open Treatment 27215, 27218
Saucerization 27070
Tumor
    Excision 27065-27067, 27075, 27076

Ilizarov Procedure
Monticelli Type 20692
    See Application, Bone Fixation Device

IM Injection
See Injection, Intramuscular

Imaging
See Vascular Studies

Imaging, Gamma Camera
See Nuclear Medicine

Imaging, Magnetic Resonance
See Magnetic Resonance Imaging (MRI)

Imaging, Ultrasonic
See Echography

Imbrication
Diaphragm 39545

Imidobenzyle
See Imipramine

Imipramine
Assay 80174

Immune Complex Assay 86332

Immune Globulin
Administration 96365-96368,
                    96372, 96374-96375

Immune Globulin E
See IgE

Immune Globulins
Antitoxin
    Botulinum 90287
    Diphtheria 90296
Botulism 90288
Cytomegalovirus .90291
Hepatitis B 90371
Human 90281-90284
Rabies 90375-90376
Respiratory Syncytial Virus 90378

Rho (D) 90384-90386
Tetanus 90389
Unlisted Immune Globulin 90399
Vaccinia 90393
Varicella-Zoster 90396

Immunization Administration
Each Additional Vaccine/Toxoid 90472, 90474
    with Counseling 90466, 90468
One Vaccine/Toxoid 90471, 90473
    with Counseling 90465, 90467

Immunization, Mumps
See Mumps, Immunization

Immunoassay
Analyte 83516-83520
    Calprotectin, Fecal 83993
Cellular Function
    Detection of Biomarker 86352
Infectious Agent 86317-86318,
                  87449-87451, 87809
Nonantibody 83516-83519
Tumor Antigen 86294, 86316
    CA 125 86304
    CA 15-3 86300
    CA 19-9 86301
    Human Epididymis Protein 4 (HE4) 86305

Immunoblotting, Western
See Western Blot

Immunochemical, Lysozyme (Muramidase)
See Lysozyme

Immunocytochemistry 88342

Immunodeficiency Virus Type 1, Human
See HIV 1

Immunodeficiency Virus Type 2, Human
See HIV 2

Immunodeficiency Virus, Human
See HIV

Immunodiffusion 86329-86331

Immunoelectrophoresis 86320-86327,
                     86334-86335

Immunofixation Electrophoresis 86334-86335

Immunofluorescent Study .88346-88347

Immunogen
See Antigen

Immunoglobulin 82784-82787
Platelet Associated 86023
Thyroid Stimulating 84445

Immunoglobulin E
See IgE

Immunoglobulin Receptor Assay 86243

Immunologic Skin Test
See Skin, Tests

Immunology
Unlisted Services and Procedures 86849

Immunotherapies, Allergen
See Allergen Immunotherapy

Impedance Testing 92567, 92570
See Audiologic Function Tests

Imperfectly Descended Testis
See Testis, Undescended

Implant Removal
See Specific Anatomical Site

Implant, Breast
See Breast, Implants

Implant, Glaucoma Drainage
See Aqueous Shunt

Implant, Orbital
See Orbital Implant

Implant, Penile
See Penile Prosthesis

Implant, Penile Prosthesis, Inflatable
See Penile Prosthesis, Insertion, Inflatable

Implant, Subperiosteal
See Subperiosteal Implant

Implant, Ureters into, Bladder
See Anastomosis, Ureter, to Bladder

Implantation
Artificial Heart
    Intracorporeal .0051T
Bone
    for External Speech Processor/Cochlear
        Stimulator 69714-69718
Brain
    Chemotherapy 61517
Cardiac Event Recorder 33282
Contraceptive Capsules 11975, 11977
Drug Delivery Device 11981, 11983, 61517
Electrode
    Brain 61850-61875
    Gastric 43647-43648
    Nerve 64553-64581
    Spinal Cord 63650-63655
    Stomach 0155T, 0157T
Eye
    Anterior Segment 65920
    Aqueous Shunt to Extracular Placement or
        Replacement of Pegs 65125
    Corneal Ring Segments 0099T
    Posterior Segment
        Extraocular 67120
        Intraocular 67121
    Reservoir 66180
    Vitreous
        Drug Delivery System 67027
Fallopian Tube 58565
Hearing Aid Hormone Pellet(s)
    Bone Conduction 69710
Hip Prosthesis
    See Arthroplasty, Hip
Hormone Pellet 11980
Intraocular Lens
    See Insertion, Intraocular Lens
Joint
    See Arthroplasty

Incision and Drainage

Incisional Hernia Repair

See Hernia, Repair, Incisional

Incomplete Abortion
See Abortion, Incomplete

Indicator Dilution Studies 93561-93562

Induced Abortion
See Abortion

Induced Hyperthermia
See Thermotherapy

Induced Hypothermia
See Hypothermia

Induratio Penis Plastica
See Peyronie Disease

Infant, Newborn, Intensive Care
See Intensive Care, Neonatal

Infantile Paralysis
See Polio

Infection, Actinomyces
See Actinomycosis

Infection, Bone
See Osteomyelitis

Infection, Filarioidea
See Filariasis

Infection, Postoperative Wound
See Postoperative Wound Infection

Infection, Wound
See Wound, Infection

Infectious Mononucleosis Virus

Inflammatory Process

Inflation

Influenza A

Influenza B

Influenza Vaccine

Influenza Virus

Infraorbital Nerve

Infrared Light Treatment 97026

**Infratentorial
Craniectomy** 61520-61521

Infusion

Infusion Pump

Infusion Therapy 62350-62351,
62360-62362

Ingestion Challenge Test 95075

Inguinal Hernia Repair

INH

Inhalation

Inhalation Provocation Tests

Inhalation Treatment 94640,
94644-94645, 94664, 99503

Inhibin A 86336

Inhibition Test, Hemagglutination

Inhibition, Fertilization

Inhibitor, Alpha 1-Protease

Inhibitor, Alpha 2-Plasmin

Inhibitory Concentration, Minimum

Initial Inpatient Consultations

Inorganic Sulfates
See Sulfate

Inpatient Consultations
See Consultation, Initial Inpatient

INR Test Review 99363-99364

Insemination
Artificial 58321-58322, 89268

Insertion
See Implantation; Intubation; Transplantation
Balloon
    Intra-Aortic 33967, 33973
Breast
    Implants 19340-19342
Cannula
    Arteriovenous 36810-36815
    ECMO 36822
    Extra Corporeal Circulation
      for Regional Chemotherapy of
      Extremity 36823
    Thoracic Duct 38794
    Vein to Vein 36800
Catheter
    Abdomen 49324, 49419-49421, 49435
    Abdominal Artery 36245-36248
    Aorta 36200
    Bile Duct 47525-47530, 75982
    Percutaneous 47510
    Bladder 51045, 51701-51703
    Brachiocephalic Artery 36215-36218
    Brain 0169T, 61210, 61770
    Breast 0169T
      for Interstitial Radioelement
      Application 19296-19298, 20555, 41019
    Bronchi 31717
    Bronchus
      for Intracavitary Radioelement
      Application 31643
    Cardiac
      See Catheterization, Cardiac
      Flow Directed 93503
    Ear, Middle 69405
    Eustachian Tube 69405
    Gastrointestinal, Upper 43241
    Jejunum 44015
    Kidney 50392
    Lower Extremity Artery 36245-36248
    Nasotracheal 31720
    Pelvic Artery 36245-36248
    Pleural Cavity 32550
    Portal Vein 36481
    Prostate 55875
    Pulmonary Artery 36013-36015
    Right Heart 36013
    Skull 61107
    Spinal Cord 62350-62351
    Suprapubic 51010
    Thoracic Artery 36215-36218
    Trachea 31700
    Tracheobronchial 31725
    Ureter via Kidney 50393
    Urethra 51701-51703
    Vena Cava 36010
    Venous 36011-36012, 36400-36410,
              36420-36425, 36500-36510,
              36555-36558, 36568-36569
Cecostomy Tube 49442
Cervical Dilation 59200
Cochlear Device 69930
Colonic Tube 49442

Contraceptive Capsules 11975, 11977
Distraction Device
    Posterior Spinous Process,
    Lumbar 0171T-0172T
Drug Delivery Implant 11981, 11983
Duodenostomy Tube 49441
Electrode
    Brain 61531-61533, 61760, 61850-61875
    Heart 33202-33203, 33210-33211,
      33216-33217, 33224-33225, 93620-93622
    Nerve 64553-64581
    Retina 0100T
    Sphenoidal 95830
    Spinal Cord 63650-63655
    Stomach
      Laparoscopic
        Neurostimulator 43647
        Stimulation 0155T
      Open
        Neurostimulator 43881
        Stimulation 00157T
Endotracheal Tube
    Emergency Intubation 31500
Gastrostomy Tube
    Laparoscopic 43653
    Percutaneous 43246
Graft
    Aorta 33330-33335
    Heart Vessel 33330-33335
Guide
    Kidney Pelvis 50395
Guide Wire
    Endoscopy 43248
    Esophagoscopy 43248
    with Dilation 43226
Heyman Capsule
    Uterus
      for Brachytherapy 58346
Iliac Artery
    Occlusion Device 34808
Implant
    Bone
      for External Speech Processor/
      Cochlear Stimulator 69714-69718
Infusion Pump
    Intra-Arterial 36260
    Intravenous 36563
    Spinal Cord 62361-62362
Intracatheter/Needle
    Aorta 36160
    Arteriovenous Shunt 36147-36148
    Intra-Arterial 36100-36140
    Intravenous 36000
    Kidney 50392
Intraocular Lens 66983
    Manual or Mechanical Technique 66982, 66984
    Not Associated with Concurrent Cataract
    Removal 66985
Intrauterine Device (IUD) 58300
IVC Filter 75940
Jejunostomy Tube
    Endoscopy 44372
    Percutaneous 49441
Keel
    Laryngoplasty 31580
Laminaria 59200
Mesh
    Pelvic Floor 57267
Nasobiliary Tube
    Endoscopy 43267
Nasopancreatic Tube
    Endoscopy 43267

Needle
    Bone 36680
    Intraosseous 36680
    Prostate 55875
Needle Wire
    Trachea 31730
Neurostimulator
    Pulse Generator 64590
    Receiver 64590
Nose
    Septal Prosthesis 30220
Obturator
    Larynx 31527
Ocular Implant
    in Scleral Shell 65130
    Muscles, Attached 65140
    Muscles, Not Attached 65135
    with Foreign Material 65155
    with/without Conjunctival Graft 65150
Orbital Transplant 67550
Oviduct
    Chromotubation 58350
    Hydrotubation 58350
Ovoid
    Vagina
      for Brachytherapy 57155
Pacemaker
    Fluoroscopy/Radiography 71090
    Heart 33206-33208, 33212-33213
Pacing Cardio-Defibrillator
    Leads 33216-33220, 33224-33225,
               33243-33244
    Pulse Generator Only 33240-33241
Packing
    Vagina 57180
Penile Prosthesis, Inflatable
    See Penile Prosthesis, Insertion, Inflatable
Pessary
    Vagina 57160
Pin
    Skeletal Traction 20650
Probe
    Brain 61770
Prostaglandin 59200
Prostate
    Radioactive Substance 55860
Prosthesis
    Knee 27438, 27445
    Nasal Septal 30220
    Palate 42281
    Pelvic Floor 57267
    Penis
      Inflatable 54401-54405
      Noninflatable 54400
    Speech 31611
    Testis 54660
    Urethral Sphincter 53444-53445
Pulse Generator
    Brain 61885-61886
    Heart 33212-33213
    Spinal Cord 63685
Radioactive Material
    Bladder 51020
    Cystourethroscopy 52250
Receiver
    Brain 61885-61886
    Spinal Cord 63685
Reservoir
    Brain 61210-61215
    Spinal Cord 62360
    Subcutaneous 49419

Inspiratory Positive Pressure Breathing

Instillation

Instillation, Bladder

Instrumentation

Insufflation, Eustachian Tube

Insulin

Insulin C-Peptide Measurement

Insulin Like Growth Factors

Insurance

Integumentary System

Integumentum Commune

Intelligence Test

Intensive Care

Intercarpal Joint

Intercostal Nerve

Interdental Fixation

Interdental Papilla

Interdental Wire Fixation
Closed Treatment
    Craniofacial Separation 21431

Interferometry
Eye
    Biometry 92136

Intermediate Care Facilities (ICFs)
See Nursing Facility Services

Intermittent Positive Pressure Breathing (IPPB)
See Continuous Negative Pressure Breathing (CNPB); Continuous Positive Airway Pressure (CPAP)

Internal Breast Prostheses
See Breast, Implants

Internal Ear
See Ear, Inner

Internal Rigid Fixation
Reconstruction
    Mandibular Rami 21196

International Normalized Ratio
Test Review .99363-99364

Internet E/M Service 98969, 99444

Interphalangeal Joint
Arthrodesis 26860-26863
Arthroplasty 26535-26536
Arthrotomy 26080, 26054
Biopsy
    Synovium 26110
Capsule
    Excision 26525
    Incision 26525
Dislocation
    Closed Treatment 26770
    Open Treatment 26785
    Percutaneous Fixation 26776
    with Manipulation 26340
Exploration 26080
Fracture
    Closed Treatment 26740
    Open Treatment 26746
    with Manipulation 26742
Fusion .26860-26863
Great Toe
    Arthrodesis .28755
        with Tendon Transfer 28760
    Fusion 28755
        with Tendon Transfer 28760
Removal of Foreign Body 26080
Repair
    Collateral Ligament 26545
    Volar Plate .26548
Synovectomy 26140
Toe 28272
    Arthrotomy .28024
    Dislocation 28660-28665, 28675
        Percutaneous Fixation 28666
    Excision 28160
    Exploration .28024
    Removal
        Foreign Body 28024
        Loose Body 28024
    Synovial
        Biopsy 28054

Interruption
Vein
    Femoral 37650
    Iliac 37660
    Vena Cava 37620

Intersex State
Clitoroplasty 56805
Vaginoplasty 57335

Intersex Surgery
Female to Male .55980
Male to Female .55970

Interstitial Cell Stimulating Hormone
See Luteinizing Hormone (LH)

Interstitial Cystitides, Chronic
See Cystitis, Interstitial

Interstitial Cystitis
See Cystitis, Interstitial

Interstitial Fluid Pressure
Monitoring 20950

Interstitial Cell Stimulating Hormone
See Luteinizing Hormone (LH)

Intertarsal Joint
Arthrotomy 28020, 28050
Exploration 28020
Removal
    Foreign Body 28020
    Loose Body .28020
Synovial
    Biopsy 28050
    Excision 28070

Interthoracoscapular Amputation
See Amputation, Interthoracoscapular

Intertrochanteric Femur Fracture
See Femur, Fracture, Intertrochanteric

Intervertebral Chemonucleolysis
See Chemonucleolysis

Intervertebral Disc
Annuloplasty 22526-22527
Arthroplasty 0092T, 0163T, 22856-22857
Discography
    Cervical 72285
    Lumbar 72295
    Thoracic 72285
Excision
    Decompression 63075-63078
    Herniated 63020-63044, 63055-63066
Injection
    Chemonucleolysis Agent 62292
    X-ray 62290-62291
Removal 0095T, 0164T, 22864-22865
Revision 0098T, 0165T, 22861-22862

Intestinal Anastomosis
See Anastomosis, Intestines

Intestinal Invagination
See Intussusception

Intestinal Peptide, Vasoactive
See Vasoactive Intestinal Peptide

Intestine
Biopsy 44100

Lesion
    Excision 44110-44111
Unlisted Services and Procedures . . .44238, 44799

Intestines
Allotransplantation 44135-44136
    Removal 44137
Anastomosis 44625-44626
    Laparoscopic 44227
Bleeding Tube .91100
Closure
    Enterostomy
        Large or Small 44625-44626
        Stoma 44620-44625
Excision
    Donor 44132-44133
Exclusion 44700
Laparoscopic Resection
    with Anastomosis 44202-44208
Lysis of Adhesions
    Laparoscopic 44180
Nuclear Medicine
    Imaging 78290
Reconstruction
    Bladder 50820
    Colonic Reservoir 45119
Repair
    Diverticula .44605
    Obstruction 44615
    Ulcer 44605
    Wound 44605
Resection
    Laparoscopic 44227
Suture
    Diverticula .44605
    Stoma 44620-44625
    Ulcer 44605
    Wound 44605
Transplantation
    Allograft Preparation 44715-44721
    Donor Enterectomy 44132-44133
    Removal of Allograft 44137

Intestines, Large
See Anus; Colon; Rectum

Intestines, Small
Anastomosis 43845, 44130
Biopsy 44020
    Endoscopy .44361
Catheterization
    Jejunum 44015
Decompression 44021
Destruction
    Lesion 44369
    Tumor 44369
Endoscopy 44364
    Biopsy 44361, 44377
    Control of Bleeding 44366, 44378
        via Stoma 44382
    Destruction
        Lesion .44369
        Tumor .44369
    Diagnostic .44376
    Exploration .44360
    Hemorrhage 44366
    Insertion
        Stent 44370, 44379
        Tube 44379
    Pelvic Pouch 44385-44386
    Removal
        Foreign Body 44363

Iridectomy

by Laser Surgery 66761
Peripheral for Glaucoma 66625
with Corneoscleral or Corneal Section 66600
with Sclerectomy with Punch or Scissors ...66160
with Thermocauterization 66155
with Transfixion as for Iris Bombe 66605
with Trephination 66150

Iridencleisis 66165

Iridodialysis 66680

Iridoplasty 66762

Iridotasis 66165

Iridotomy

by Laser Surgery 66761
by Stab Incision 66500
Excision
    Optical 66635
    Peripheral 66625
    with Corneoscleral or Corneal Section ...66600
    with Cyclectomy 66605
Incision
    Stab 66500
    with Transfixion as for Iris Bombe 66505
Optical 66635
Peripheral 66625
Sector 66630

Iris

Cyst
    Destruction 66770
Excision
    Iridectomy
        Optical 66635
        Peripheral 66625
        Sector 66630
        with Corneoscleral or Corneal
        Section 66600
        with Cyclectomy 66605
Incision
    Iridotomy
        Stab 66500
        with Transfixion as for Iris Bombe ...66505
Lesion
    Destruction 66770
Repair
    with Ciliary Body 66680
        Suture 66682
Revision
    Laser Surgery 66761
    Photocoagulation 66762
Suture
    with Ciliary Body 66682

Iron 83540

Iron Binding Capacity 83550

Iron Hematoxylin Stain 88312

Iron Stain 85536, 88313

Irradiation

Blood Products 86945

Irrigation

Bladder 51700
Catheter
    Brain 62194, 62225
Corpora Cavernosa
    Priapism 54220

Penis
    Priapism 54220
Peritoneal
    See Peritoneal Lavage
Rectum
    for Fecal Impaction 91123
Shunt
    Spinal Cord 63744
Sinus
    Maxillary 31000
    Sphenoid 31002
Vagina 57150
Venous Access Device 96523

Irving Sterilization

See Ligation, Fallopian Tube, Oviduct

Ischemic Stroke

Onset 1065F-1066F
Tissue Plasminogen Activator (tPA)
    Documentation That Administration
    Was Considered 4077F

Ischial

Bursa
    Excision 27060
Tumor
    Radical Resection 27075, 27078

Ischiectomy 15941

Island Pedicle Flaps 15740

Islands of Langerhans

See Islet Cell

Islet Cell

Antibody 86341
Transplantation 0141T-0143T

Isocitrate Dehydrogenase

See Isocitric Dehydrogenase

Isocitric Dehydrogenase

Blood 83570

Isolation

Sperm 89260-89261

Isomerase, Glucose 6 Phosphate

See Phosphohexose Isomerase

Isopropanol

See Isopropyl Alcohol

Isopropyl Alcohol 84600

Isthmusectomy

Thyroid Gland 60210-60225

IUD

See Intrauterine Device (IUD)

IV

See Injection, Chemotherapy; Intravenous Therapy

IV Infusion Therapy

See Allergen Immunotherapy; Chemotherapy;
Infusion; Injection, Chemotherapy

IV Injection

See Injection, Intravenous

IV, Coagulation Factor

See Calcium

IVC Filter

Placement 75940

IVF

See Artificial Insemination; In Vitro Fertilization

Ivy Bleeding Time 85002

IX Complex, Factor

See Christmas Factor

J

Jaboulay Operation

See Gastroduodenostomy

Jaboulay Operation Gastroduodenostomy

See Gastroduodenostomy

Jannetta Procedure

See Decompression, Cranial Nerve; Section

Japanese Encephalitis Virus

See Vaccine

Japanese, River Fever

See Scrub Typhus

Jatene Type 33770-33781

Jaw Joint

See Facial Bones; Mandible; Maxilla

Jaws

Muscle Reduction 21295-21296
X-ray
    for Orthodontics 70355

Jejunostomy

Catheterization 44015
Contrast 49465
Insertion
    Catheter 44015
    Percutaneous 49441
Laparoscopic 44186-44187
Non-Tube 44187, 44310
Obstructive Material Removal 49460
Replacement 49451
with Pancreatic Drain 48001

Jejunum

Creation
    Stoma
Laparoscopic 44186
Transfer
    with Microvascular Anastomosis
        Free 43496

Johannsen Procedure 53400

Joint

See Specific Joint
Acromioclavicular
    See Acromioclavicular Joint
Arthrocentesis 20600-20610
Aspiration 20600-20610
Dislocation
    See Dislocation

K

Reimplantation Kidney 50380
Removal Transplant Renal Autograft 50370
Tumor
  Ablation
    Cryotherapy 0135T, 50593
Ultrasound 76770-76776
X-ray with Contrast
  Guide Catheter 74475

Kidney Stone
See Calculus, Removal, Kidney

Killian Operation
See Sinusotomy, Frontal

Kinase, Creatine
See CPK

Kineplasty
See Cineplasty

Kinetic Therapy 97530
See Physical Medicine/Therapy/Occupational
Therapy

Kininase A
See Angiotensin Converting Enzyme (ACE)

Kininogen 85293

Kininogen, High Molecular Weight
See Fitzgerald Factor

Kleihauer-Betke Test 85460

Kloramfenikol
See Chloramphenicol

Knee
See Femur; Fibula; Patella; Tibia
Abscess 27301
Arthrocentesis 20610
Arthrodesis 27580
Arthroplasty 27440-27445, 27447
  Revision 27486-27487
Arthroscopy
  Diagnostic 29870
  Surgical 29866-29868, 29871-29889
Arthrotomy 27310, 27330-27335, 27403
Autogaft, Osteochondral, Open 27416
Biopsy 27323-27324, 27330-27331
  Synovium 27330
Bone
  Drainage 27303
Bursa 27301
  Excision 27340
Cyst
  Excision 27345-27347
Disarticulation 27598
Dislocation 27550-27552, 27560-27562
  Open Treatment 27556-27558, 27566
Drainage 27310
Excision
  Cartilage 27332-27333
  Ganglion 27347
  Lesion 27347
  Synovium 27334-27335
Exploration 27310, 27331
Fasciotomy 27305, 27496-27499
Fracture 27520-27524
  Arthroscopic Treatment 29850-29851
Fusion 27580
Hematoma 27301
Incision
  Capsule 27435

Injection
  X-ray 27370
Magnetic Resonance Imaging (MRI) . . .73721-73723
Manipulation 27570
Meniscectomy 27332-27333
Reconstruction 27437-27438
  Ligament 27427-27429
  with Prosthesis 27445
Removal
  Foreign Body 27310, 27331, 27372
  Loose Body .27331
  Prosthesis 27488
Repair
  Ligament 27405-27409
    Collateral 27405
    Collateral and Cruciate 27409
    Cruciate 27407-27409
    Meniscus 27403
    Tendon 27380-27381
Replacement 27447
Retinacular
  Release 27425
Strapping 29530
Suture
  Tendon 27380-27381
Transplantation
  Chondrocytes 27412
  Meniscus 29868
  Osteochondral
    Allograft 27415, 29867
    Autograft 27412, 29866
Tumor
  Excision 27327-27328, 27337-27339
  Radical Resection 27329, 27364-27365
Unlisted Services and Procedures 27599
X-ray 73560-73564
  Arthrography 73580
  Bilateral 73565
X-ray with Contrast
  Arthrography 73580

Knee Joint
Arthroplasty 27446

Knee Prosthesis
See Prosthesis, Knee

Kneecap
Excision 27350
Repair
  Instability 27420-27424

Knock-Knee Repair 27455-27457

Kocher Operation 23650-23680
See Clavicle; Scapula; Shoulder, Dislocation,
Closed Treatment

Kocher Pylorectomy
See Gastrectomy, Partial

Kock Pouch 44316
Formation 50825

Kock Procedure 44316

KOH
See Hair, Nails, Tissue, Examination for Fungi

Kraske Procedure 45116

Kroenlein Procedure 67420

Krukenberg Procedure 25915

Kuhlmann Test 96101-96103

Kyphectomy
More than Two Segments 22819
Up to Two Segments 22818

Kyphoplasty 22523-22525

L

L Ascorbic Acid
See Ascorbic Acid

L Aspartate 2 Oxoglutarate Aminotransferase
See Transaminase, Glutamic Oxaloacetic

L Glutamine
See Glutamine

L-Alanine
See Aminolevulinic Acid (ALA)

L-Leucylnaphthylamidase
See Leucine Aminopeptidase

L/S Ratio
Amniotic Fluid 83661

Labial Adhesions
Lysis 56441

Labyrinth
See Ear, Inner

Labyrinthectomy 69905
with Mastoidectomy 69910
with Skull Base Surgery 61596

Labyrinthotomy
with Mastoidectomy 69802
with/without Cryosurgery 69801

Laceration Repair
See Specific Site

Lacrimal Duct
Balloon 68816
Canaliculi
  Repair 68700
Dilation 68816
Exploration 68810
  Canaliculi 68840
  Stent 68815
  with Anesthesia 68811
Insertion
  Stent 68815
Nasolacrimal Duct Probing 68816
Removal
  Dacryolith 68530
  Foreign Body 68530
X-ray with Contrast 70170

Lacrimal Gland
Biopsy 68510
Close Fistula 68770
Excision
  Partial 68505
  Total 68500

Proctectomy
  Complete 45395
    with Creation of Colonic Reservoir 45397
Proctopexy
  for Prolapse 45400-45402
Prostatectomy 55866
Pyeloplasty 50544
Rectum
  Resection 45395-45397
  Unlisted 45499
Removal
  Fallopian Tube 58661
  Leiomyomata 58545-58546
  Ovaries 58661
  Spleen .38120
  Testis .54690
Resection
  Intestines
    with Anastomosis 44202-44203
  Rectum 45395-45397
Salpingostomy .58673
Splenectomy 38120-38129
Splenic Flexure
  Mobilization 44213
Stomach 43647-43659
  Gastric Bypass 43644-43645
  Gastric Restrictive Procedures . . .43770-43775,
                              43848, 43886-43888
  Gastroenterostomy 43644-43645
  Roux-En-Y 43644
Transplantation
  Islet Cell .0143T
Unlisted Services and Procedures
  Abdomen, Omentum, and Peritoneum . . .49329
  Appendix 44979
  Biliary Tract 47579
  Bladder 51999
  Esophagus 43289
  Hernioplasty, Herniorrhaphy,
  Herniotomy 49659
  Intestine .44238
  Liver 47379
  Lymphatic System 38589
  Maternity Care and Delivery 59898-59899
  Oviduct, Ovary 58679
  Rectum 45499
  Renal 50549
  Spermatic Cord 55559
  Spleen 38129
  Stomach .43659
  Testis 54699
  Ureter 50949
  Uterus 58578-58579
Ureterolithotomy 50945
Ureteroneocystostomy 50947-50948
Urethral Suspension 51990
Vaginal Hysterectomy 58550-58554
Vaginal Suspension 57425
Vagus Nerves
  Transection 43651-43652
with X-ray 47560

Laparotomy
Electrode Implantation
  Gastric 43881, 0157T
Electrode Removal
  Gastric 43882, 0158T
Electrode Replacement
  Gastric 43881, 0157T
Electrode Revision
  Gastric 43882, 0158T
Exploration 47015, 49000-49002

Hemorrhage Control 49002
Second Look .58960
Staging 49220, 58960
with Biopsy .49000

Laparotomy, Exploratory
See Abdomen, Exploration

Lapidus Procedure 28297

Large Bowel
See Anus; Rectum

Laroyenne Operation
See Vagina, Abscess, Incision and Drainage

Laryngeal Function Study 92520

**Laryngeal Sensory
Testing** 92614-92617

Laryngectomy 31360-31382
Partial 31367-31382
Subtotal 31367-31368

Laryngocele
Removal 31300

Laryngofissure 31300

Laryngography 70373
Instillation

Laryngopharyngectomy
See Excision, Larynx, with Pharynx

Laryngopharynx
See Hypopharynx

Laryngoplasty
Burns 31588
Cricoid Split .31587
Laryngeal Stenosis 31582
Laryngeal Web 31580
Open Reduction of Fracture 31584

Laryngoscopy
Diagnostic 31505
Direct 31515-31571
Exploration 31505, 31520-31526, 31575
Fiberoptic 31575-31579
  with Stroboscopy 31579
Indirect 31505-31513
Newborn 31520
Operative 31530-31561

Laryngotomy 31300
Diagnostic 31320

Larynx
Aspiration
  Endoscopy .31515
Biopsy
  Endoscopy 31510, 31535-31536, 31576
Dilation
  Endoscopic 31528-31529
Electromyography
  Needle 95865
Endoscopy
  Direct 31515-31571
  Excision 31545-31546
  Exploration 31505, 31520-31526, 31575
  Fiberoptic 31575-31579
    with Stroboscopy 31579
  Indirect 31505-31513
  Operative 31530-31561

Excision
  Lesion 31512, 31578
    Endoscopic 31545-31546
  Partial 31367-31382
  Total 31360-31365
  with Pharynx 31390-31395
Exploration
  Endoscopic 31505, 31520-31526, 31575
Fracture 31584
Insertion
  Obturator .31527
Nerve
  Destruction 31595
Reconstruction
  Burns 31588
  Cricoid Split 31587
  Other 31588
  Stenosis .31582
  Web 31580
Removal
  Foreign Body
    Endoscopic 31511, 31530-31531, 31577
  Lesion
    Endoscopic 31512, 31545-31546, 31578
Repair
  Reinnervation Neuromuscular Pedicle . . .31590
Stroboscopy .31579
Tumor
  Excision 31300
    Endoscopic 31540-31541
Unlisted Services and Procedures 31599
Vocal Cord(s)
  Injection 31513, 31570-31571
X-ray 70370
  with Contrast 70373

Laser Surgery
Anus 46614, 46917
Cautery
  Esophagus .43227
  Hemorrhoids 46930
Lacrimal Punctum 68760
Lens, Posterior 66821
Lesion
  Mouth 40820
  Nose 30117-30118
  Penis 54057
  Skin 17000-17111, 17260-17286
Myocardium 33140-33141
Prostate 52647-52648
Spine
  Discectomy 62287
Tumors
  Urethra and Bladder 52234
Urethra and Bladder 52214

Laser Treatment 17000-17286,
                                       96920-96922

See Destruction

Lateral Epicondylitis
See Tennis Elbow

Latex Fixation 86403-86406

LATS
See Thyrotropin Releasing Hormone (TRH)

Latzko Operation
See Repair, Vagina, Fistula; Revision

LAV
See HIV

Arm, Lower
  Tendon Sheath
    Excision 25110
Auditory Canal, External
  Excision
    Exostosis 69140
    Radical with Neck Dissection 69155
    Radical without Neck Dissection ...69150
    Soft Tissue 69145
Bladder
  Destruction 51030
Brain
  Excision 61534, 61536,
            61600-61608, 61615-61616
Brainstem
  Excision 61575-61576
Breast
  Excision 19120-19126
Carotid Body
  Excision 60600-60605
Chemotherapy 96405-96406
  Destruction 67220-67225
Choroid
  Destruction 0016T
Ciliary Body
  Destruction 66770
Colon
  Destruction 44393, 45383
  Excision 44110-44111
Conjunctiva
  Destruction 68135
  Excision 68110-68130
    Over 1 cm 68115
    with Adjacent Sclera 68130
  Expression 68040
Cornea
  Destruction 65450
  Excision 65400
    of Pterygium 65420-65426
Cranium 77432
Destruction
  Ureter 52341-52342, 52344-52345, 52354
Ear, Middle
  Excision 69540
Epididymis
  Excision 54830
Esophagus
  Ablation 43228
  Excision 43100-43101
  Removal 43216
Excision 59100
  Bladder 52224
  Urethra 52224, 53265
Eye
  Excision 65900
Eyelid
  Destruction 67850
  Excision
    Multiple, Different Lids 67805
    Multiple, Same Lid 67801
    Single 67800
    Under Anesthesia 67808
    without Closure 67840
Facial
  Destruction 17000-17004, 17280-17286
Femur
  Excision 27062
Finger
  Tendon Sheath 26160
Foot
  Excision 28080, 28090

Gums
  Destruction 41850
  Excision 41822-41828
Hand Tendon Sheath 26160
Intestines
  Excision 44110
Intestines, Small
  Destruction 44369
  Excision 44111
Iris
  Destruction 66770
Larynx
  Excision 31545-31546
Leg, Lower
  Tendon Sheath 27630
Lymph Node
  Incision and Drainage 38300-38305
Mesentery
  Excision 44820
Mouth
  Destruction 40820
  Excision 40810-40816, 41116
  Vestibule
    Destruction 40820
    Repair 40830
Nerve
  Excision 64774-64792
Nose
  Intranasal
    External Approach 30118
    Internal Approach 30117
Orbit
  Excision 61333, 67412
Palate
  Destruction 42160
  Excision 42104-42120
Pancreas
  Excision 48120
Pelvis
  Destruction 58662
Penis
  Destruction
    Cryosurgery 54056
    Electrodesiccation 54055
    Extensive 54065
    Laser Surgery 54057
    Simple 54050-54060
    Surgical Excision 54060
  Excision 54060
    Penile Plaque 54110-54112
Pharynx
  Destruction 42808
  Excision 42808
Radiosurgery
  Cranial 61796-61800
Rectum
  Excision 45108
Removal
  Larynx 31512, 31578
  Resection 52354
Retina
  Destruction
    Extensive 67227-67228
    Localized 0017T, 67208-67210
    Radiation by Implantation of Source 67218
Sciatic Nerve
  Excision 64786
Sclera
  Excision 66130
Skin
  Abrasion 15786-15787
  Biopsy 11100-11101

Destruction
  Benign 17110-17111, 17250
  Malignant 17260-17286
  Premalignant 17000-17004
Excision
  Benign 11400-11471
  Malignant 11600-11646
  Injection 11900-11901
  Paring or Curettement 11055-11057
  Shaving 11300-11313
Skin Tags
  Removal 11200-11201
Skull
  Excision ...61500, 61600-61608, 61615-61616
Spermatic Cord
  Excision 55520
Spinal Cord
  Destruction 62280-62282
  Excision 63265-63273
Stomach
  Excision 43611
Testis
  Excision 54512
Toe
  Excision 28092
Tongue
  Excision 41110-41114
Uvula
  Destruction 42145
  Excision 42104-42107
Vagina
  Destruction 57061-57065
Vulva
  Destruction
    Extensive 56515
    Simple 56501
Wrist Tendon
  Excision 25110

Leu 2 Antigens
See CD8

Leucine Aminopeptidase 83670

**Leukemia Lymphoma Virus I
Antibodies, Human T Cell**
See Antibody, HTLV-I

**Leukemia Lymphoma Virus I,
Adult T Cell**
See HTLV I

**Leukemia Lymphoma Virus II
Antibodies, Human T Cell**
See Antibody, HTLV-II

**Leukemia Virus II, Hairy Cell
Associated, Human T Cell**
See HTLV II

Leukoagglutinins 86021

Leukocyte
See White Blood Cell
Alkaline Phosphatase 85540
Antibody 86021
Count 85032, 85048, 89055
Histamine Release Test 86343
Phagocytosis 86344
Transfusion 86950

Levarterenol
See Noradrenalin

Excision
Extensive 47122
Partial 47120, 47125-47130, 47140-47142
Total 47133
Injection 47015
Radiologic 47505
X-ray 47500
Lobectomy 47125-47130
Partial 47120
Needle Biopsy 47000-47001
Nuclear Medicine
Function Study 78220
Imaging 78201-78216
Vascular Flow 78206
Repair
Abscess 47300
Cyst 47300
Wound 47350-47362
Suture
Wound 47350-47362
Transplantation 47135-47136
Allograft Preparation 47143-47147
Trisegmentectomy 47122
Unlisted Services and Procedures ...47379, 47399

Living Activities, Daily
See Activities of Daily Living

Lobectomy
Brain 61323, 61537-61540
Contralateral Subtotal
Thyroid Gland 60212, 60225
Liver 47120-47130
Lung 32480-32482
Sleeve 32486
Parotid Gland 42410-42415
Segmental 32663
Sleeve 32486
Temporal Lobe 61537-61538
Thyroid Gland Partial 60210-60212
Total 60220-60225
Total 32663

Lobotomy
Frontal 61490

Local Excision Mastectomies
See Breast, Excision, Lesion

Local Excision of Lesion or Tissue of Femur
See Excision, Lesion, Femur

Localization of Nodule
Radiographic
Breast 77032

Log Hydrogen Ion Concentration
See pH

Long Acting Thyroid Stimulator
See Thyrotropin Releasing Hormone (TRH)

Long-Term Care Facility Visits
See Nursing Facility Services

Longmire Operation
See Anastomosis, Hepatic Duct to Intestines

Loopogram
See Urography, Antegrade

Loose Body
Removal

Ankle 27620
Carpometacarpal Joint 26070
Elbow 24101
Interphalangeal Joint 28020
Toe 28024
Knee Joint 27331
Metatarsophalangeal Joint 28022
Tarsometatarsal Joint 28020
Toe 28022
Wrist 25101

Lord Procedure
See Anal Sphincter, Dilation

Louis Bar Syndrome
See Ataxia Telangiectasia

Low Birth Weight Intensive Care Services 99478-99480

Low Density Lipoprotein
See Lipoprotein, LDL

Low Frequency Ultrasound 0183T

Low Vision Aids
See Spectacle Services
Fitting 92354-92355

Lower Extremities
See Extremity, Lower

Lower GI Series
See Barium Enema

LRH
See Luteinizing Releasing Factor

LSD
See Lysergic Acid Diethylamide

LTH
See Prolactin

Lumbar
See Spine
Decompression, Disc
Percutaneous 62287

Lumbar Plexus
Decompression 64714
Injection
Anesthetic 64449
Neuroplasty 64714
Release 64714
Repair/Suture 64862

Lumbar Puncture
See Spinal Tap

Lumbar Spine Fracture
See Fracture, Vertebra, Lumbar

Lumbar Sympathectomy
See Sympathectomy, Lumbar

Lumbar Vertebra
See Vertebra, Lumbar

Lumen Dilation 74360

Lumpectomy 19301-19302

Lunate
Arthroplasty
with Implant 25444

Dislocation
Closed Treatment 25690
Open Treatment 25695

Lung
Ablation 32998
Abscess
Incision and Drainage
Open 32200
Percutaneous 32200-32201
Aspiration 32420
Biopsy 32095-32100
Bullae
Excision 32141
Endoscopic 32655
Cyst
Incision and Drainage
Open 32200
Removal 32140
Decortication
Endoscopic 32651-32652
Partial 32225
Total 32220
with Parietal Pleurectomy 32320
Empyema
Excision 32540
Excision
Bronchus Resection 32486
Completion 32488
Donor
Heart-Lung 33930
Lung 32850
Emphysematous 32491
Empyema 32540
Lobe 32480-32482
Segment 32484
Total 32440-32445
Tumor 32503-32504
Wedge Resection 32500
Endoscopic 32657
Foreign Body
Removal 32151
Hemorrhage 32110
Lavage
Bronchial 31624
Total 32997
Lysis
Adhesions 32124
Needle Biopsy 32405
Nuclear Medicine
Imaging, Perfusion 78580-78585
Imaging, Ventilation 78586-78594
Unlisted Services and Procedures 78599
Placement
Interstitial Device 32553
Pneumocentesis 32420
Pneumolysis 32940
Pneumothorax 32960
Puncture 32420
Removal
Bronchoplasty 32501
Completion Pneumonectomy 32488
Extrapleural 32445
Single Lobe 32480
Single Segment 32484
Sleeve Lobectomy 32486
Sleeve Pneumonectomy 32442
Total Pneumonectomy 32440-32445
Two Lobes 32482
Volume Reduction 32491
Wedge Resection 32500

Labial 56441
Lung 32124
Nose 30560
Ovary 58740
Oviduct 58740
Penile
    Post-Circumcision 54162
Ureter 50715-50725
Urethra 53500
Uterus 58559
Euglobulin 85360
Labial
    Adhesions 56441
Nose
    Intranasal Synechia 30560

Lysozyme 85549

M

Macrodactylia
Repair 26590

Macroscopic Evaluation ...88387-88388

Magnesium 83735

Magnet Operation
See Ciliary Body; Cornea; Eye, Removal, Foreign
Body; Iris; Lens; Retina; Sclera; Vitreous

Magnetic Resonance
Unlisted Services and Procedures 76498

**Magnetic Resonance Angiography
(MRA)**
Abdomen 74185
Arm 73225
Chest 71555
Head 70544-70546
Leg 73725
Neck 70547-70549
Pelvis 72198
Spine 72159

Magnetic Resonance Imaging (MRI)
3-D Rendering 76376-76377
Abdomen 74181-74183
Ankle 73721-73723
Arm 73218-73220, 73223
Bone Marrow Study 77084
Brain 70551-70555
    Intraoperative 70557-70559
Breast 77058-77059
    with Computer-aided Detection 0159T
Chest 71550-71552
Elbow 73221
Face 70540-70543
Finger Joint 73221
Foot 73718-73719
Foot Joints 73721-73723
Guidance
    Needle Placement 77021
    Parenchymal Tissue Ablation 77022
Hand 73218-73220, 73223
Heart 75557-75565

Joint
    Lower Extremity 73721-73723
    Upper Extremity 73221-73223
Knee 73721-73723
Leg 73718-73720
Neck 70540-70543
Orbit 70540-70543
Pelvis 72195-72197
Spectroscopy 76390
Spine
    Cervical 72141-72142, 72156-72158
    Lumbar 72148-72158
    Thoracic 72146-72147, 72156-72158
Temporomandibular Joint (TMJ) 70336
Toe 73721-73723
Unlisted 76498
Wrist 73221

**Magnetic Resonance
Spectroscopy** 76390

Magnetic Stimulation
Transcranial 0160T, 0161T

**Magnetoencephalography
(MEG)** 95965-95967

Magnuson Procedure 23450

MAGPI Operation 54322

MAGPI Procedure
See Hypospadias, Repair

Major Vestibular Gland
See Bartholin's Gland

Malar Area
Augmentation 21270
Bone Graft 21210
Fracture
    Open Treatment 21360-21366
    with Bone Graft 21366
    with Manipulation 21355
Reconstruction 21270

Malar Bone
See Cheekbone

Malaria Antibody 86750

Malaria Smear 87207

Malate Dehydrogenase 83775

Maldescent, Testis
See Testis, Undescended

Male Circumcision
See Circumcision

Malformation, Arteriovenous
See Arteriovenous Malformation

Malic Dehydrogenase
See Malate Dehydrogenase

**Malignant Hyperthermia
Susceptibility**
Caffeine Halothane Contracture
Test (CHCT) 89049

Malleolus
See Ankle; Fibula; Leg, Lower; Tibia; Tibiofibular
Joint

Mallet Finger Repair 26432

Maltose
Tolerance Test 82951-82952

Malunion Repair
Femur
    with Graft 27472
    without Graft 27470
Metatarsal 28322
Tarsal Joint 28320

Mammalian Oviduct
See Fallopian Tube

Mammaplasty
See Breast, Reconstruction; Mammoplasty

Mammary Abscess
See Abscess, Breast

Mammary Arteries
See Artery, Mammary

Mammary Duct
X-ray with Contrast 77053-77054

Mammary Ductogram
Injection 19030

Mammary Stimulating Hormone
See Prolactin

Mammillaplasty
See Nipples, Reconstruction

Mammogram
Breast
    Localization Nodule 77032

Mammography 77055-77057
Magnetic Resonance Imaging (MRI)
    with Computer-Aided Detection 0159T
Screening 77057
with Computer-Aided Detection 77051-77052

Mammoplasty
Augmentation 19324-19325
Reduction 19318

Mammotomy
See Incision, Breast; Incision and Drainage, Breast;
Mastotomy

Mammotropic Hormone, Pituitary
See Prolactin

Mammotropic Hormone, Placental
See Lactogen, Human Placental

Mammotropin
See Prolactin

Mandated Services
On Call Services 99027

Mandible
See Facial Bones; Maxilla; Temporomandibular
Joint (TMJ)
Abscess
    Excision 21025
Bone Graft 21215
Cyst
    Excision 21040, 21046-21047

with Tympanoplasty 69604, 69641-69646
   Cochlear Device Implantation 69930
   Complete 69502
     Revision .69601
   Ossicular Chain Reconstruction 69605
   Radical 69511
     Modified .69505
     Revision 69602-69603
   Simple 69501
   with Labyrinthectomy 69910
   with Labyrinthotomy 69802
   with Petrous Apicectomy 69530

Mastoidotomy 69635-69637
with Tympanoplasty 69635
   Ossicular Chain Reconstruction 69636
     and Synthetic Prosthesis 69636

Mastoids
Polytomography 76101-76102
X-ray 70120-70130

Mastopexy 19316

Mastotomy 19020

Maternity Care
See Abortion; Cesarean Delivery; Ectopic
Pregnancy; Obstetrical Care

**Maternity Care and
Delivery** 59612-59622, 59898

Maxilla
See Facial Bones; Mandible
Bone Graft 21210
CT Scan .70486-70488
Cyst
   Excision 21048-21049
Excision 21030, 21032-21034
Fracture
   Closed Treatment 21345, 21421
   Open Treatment . . .21346-21348, 21422-21423
   with Fixation 21345-21347
Osteotomy 21206
Reconstruction
   with Implant 21245-21246, 21248-21249
Tumor
   Excision 21048-21049

Maxillary Arteries
See Artery, Maxillary

Maxillary Sinus
See Sinus/Sinuses, Maxillary

Maxillary Torus Palatinus
Tumor Excision 21032

Maxillectomy 31225-31230

Maxillofacial Fixation
Application
   Halo Type Appliance 21100

Maxillofacial Impressions
Auricular Prosthesis 21086
Definitive Obturator Prosthesis 21080
Facial Prosthesis 21088
Interim Obturator Prosthesis 21079
Mandibular Resection Prosthesis 21081
Nasal Prosthesis 21087
Oral Surgical Splint 21085
Orbital Prosthesis 21077
Palatal Augmentation Prosthesis 21082

Palatal Lift Prosthesis 21083
Speech Aid Prosthesis 21084
Surgical Obturator Prosthesis 21076

Maxillofacial Procedures
Unlisted Services and Procedures 21299

Maxillofacial Prosthetics 21076-21089
Unlisted Services and Procedures 21089

Maydl Operation 45563, 50810
See Colostomy

Mayo Hernia Repair
See Hernia, Repair, Umbilicus

Mayo Procedure 28292

Maze Procedure
   Endoscopic 33265-33266
   Open 33254-33256

McBride Procedure 28292

McBurney Operation
See Hernia, Repair, Inguinal

McCannel Procedure 66682

McKissock Surgery
See Breast, Reduction

McVay Operation
See Hernia, Repair, Inguinal

Measles Uncomplicated
See Rubeola

Measles Vaccine
See Vaccines

Measles, German
See Rubella

Meat Fibers
Feces 89160

Meatoplasty 69310

Meatotomy 53020-53025
Cystourethroscopy 52281
Infant 53025
Prostate
   Laser Coagulation 52647
   Laser Vaporization 52648
Transurethral Electrosurgical Resection
   Prostate 52601
Ureter 52290
Ureteral
   Cystourethroscopy 52290-52305

Meckel's Diverticulum
Excision 44800
Unlisted Services and Procedures 44899

Median Nerve
Decompression 64721
Neuroplasty 64721
Release 64721
Repair/Suture
   Motor Thenar 64835
Transposition .64721

Median Nerve Compression
See Carpal Tunnel Syndrome

Mediastinal Cyst
See Cyst, Mediastinal; Mediastinum, Cyst

Mediastinoscopy 39400

Mediastinotomy
Cervical Approach 39000
Transthoracic Approach 39010

Mediastinum
See Chest; Thorax
Cyst
   Excision 32662, 39200
Endoscopy
   Biopsy 39400
   Exploration 39400
Exploration 39000-39010
Incision and Drainage 39000-39010
Needle Biopsy 32405
Removal
   Foreign Body 39000-39010
Tumor
   Excision 32662, 39220
Unlisted Procedures 39499

**Medical Disability Evaluation
Services** 99455-99456

Medical Genetics 96040
Genetic Counseling 96040

**Medical Team
Conference** 99366-99368

Medical Testimony 99075

Medication Therapy Management
Pharmacist Provided 99605-99607

Medicine, Preventive
See Preventive Medicine

Medicine, Pulmonary
See Pulmonology

Medulla
Tractotomy 61470

Medullary Tract
Incision 61470
Section 61470

Meibomian Cyst
See Chalazion

**Membrane Oxygenation,
Extracorporeal**
See Extracorporeal Membrane Oxygenation

Membrane, Mucous
See Mucosa

Membrane, Tympanic
See Ear, Drum

Meninges
Tumor
   Excision 61512, 61519

Meningioma
Excision 61512, 61519
Tumor
   Excision 61512, 61519

Meningitis, Lymphocytic Benign
See Lymphocytic Choriomeningitis

Micro-Ophthalmia
Orbit Reconstruction 21256

Microalbumin
Urine 82043-82044

Microbiology 87001-87999

Microdissection 88380-88381

Microfluorometries, Flow
See Flow Cytometry

Microglobulin, Beta 2
Blood 82232
Urine 82232

Micrographic Surgery
Mohs Technique 17311-17315

Micrographic Surgery, Mohs
See Mohs Micrographic Surgery

Micropigmentation
Correction .11920-11922

Microscope, Surgical
See Operating Microscope

Microscopic Evaluation
Hair 96902

Microscopies, Electron
See Electron Microscopy

Microscopy
Ear Exam 92504

Microsomal Antibody 86376

Microsomia, Hemifacial
See Hemifacial Microsomia

Microsurgery
Operating Microscope 69990

Microvascular Anastomosis
Bone Graft
　Fibula 20955
　Other 20962
Fascial Flap, Free 15758
Muscle Flap, Free 15756
Osteocutaneous Flap with 20969-20973
Skin Flap, Free 15757

Microvite A
See Vitamin, A

Microwave Therapy 97024
See Physical Medicine/Therapy/Occupational Therapy

Midbrain
See Brain; Brainstem; Mesencephalon; Skull Base Surgery

Midcarpal Medioccipital Joint
Arthrotomy 25040

Middle Cerebral Artery Velocimetry .76821

Middle Ear
See Ear, Middle

Midface
Reconstruction
　Forehead Advancement 21159-21160
　with Bone Graft 21145-21160, 21188
　without Bone Graft 21141-21143

Migration Inhibitory Factor (MIF) 86378

Mile Operation
See Colectomy, Total, with Proctectomy

Milia, Multiple
Removal 10040

Miller Procedure 28737

Miller-Abbott Intubation . . .44500, 74340

Minerva Cast 29035
Removal 29710

Minimum Inhibitory Concentration 87186

Minimum Lethal Concentration 87187

Minnesota Multiphasic Personality Inventory
See MMPI

Miscarriage
Incomplete Abortion 59812
Missed Abortion
　First Trimester 59820
　Second Trimester 59821
Septic Abortion 59830

Missed Abortion
See Abortion

Mitchell Procedure 28296

Mitogen Blastogenesis 86353

Mitral Valve
Incision .33420-33422
Repair .33420-33427
　Incision 33420-33422
Replacement .33430

Mitrofanoff Operation 50845
See Appendico-Vesicostomy

Miyagawanella
See Chlamydia

MLC
See Lymphocyte, Culture

MMPI 96101-96103
Computer-Assisted 96103

MMR Shots 90707
See Vaccines

Mobilization
Splenic Flexure 44139
　Laparoscopic 44213
Stapes 69650

Moderate Sedation
See Sedation

Modified Radical Mastectomy
See Mastectomy, Modified Radical

Mohs Micrographic Surgery 17311-17315

Molar Pregnancy
See Hydatidiform Mole

Mold
Culture 87107

Mole, Carneous
See Abortion

Mole, Hydatid
See Hydatidiform Mole

Molecular Cytogenetics 88271-88275
Interpretation and Report 88291

Molecular Diagnostics 83890-83914
Amplification 83898-83901, 83908
Cell Lysis 83907
Dot/Slot Production 83893
Enzymatic Digestion 83892
Extraction 83890-83891
Interpretation .83912
Macroscopic Evaluation 88387-88388
Molecular Isolation (Extraction) 83890
Mutation Identification 83904-83906
　Enzymatic Ligation 83914
Mutation Scanning 83903
Nucleic Acid Amplification . . .83900-83901, 83908
Nucleic Acid Extraction 83890-83891, 83907
Nucleic Acid Probe 83896
Nucleic Acid Transfer 83897
Polymerase Reaction Chain 83898
Reverse Transcription 83902
RNA Stabilization 83913
Separation 83894
Separation and Identification
　High Resolution Technique 83909

Molecular Oxygen Saturation
See Oxygen Saturation

Molecular Probes 88384-88386
Multiple
　Array-Based Evaluation 88384-88386

Molluscum Contagiosum
Destruction 17110-17111, 54050-54065

Molteno Procedure 66180

Monilia
See Candida

Monitoring
Blood Pressure, 24 Hour 93784-93790
Cardiovascular Device
　Evaluation and Programming
　　Cardioverter-Defibrillator 93282-93284,
　　　　　93287, 93289-93290, 93292,
　　　　　　　　　　93295, 93296
　　Loop Recorder . . .93285, 93291, 93298-93299
　　Pacemaker 93279-93281, 93294, 93296
Electrocardiogram 93224-93237, 93268-93272
　See Electrocardiography
Electroencephalogram 95812-95813,
　　　　　95950-95953, 95956
　with Drug Activation 95954
　with Physical Activation 95954
　with WADA Activation 95958

Muscle
See Specific Muscle
Abdomen
　See Abdominal Wall
Biopsy 20200-20206
Debridement
　Infected 11004-11006
　Nonviable 27057
Heart
　See Myocardium
Neck
　See Neck Muscle
Removal
　Foreign Body 20520-20525
Repair
　Extraocular 67346
　Forearm 25260-25274
　Wrist 25260-25274
Revision
　Arm, Upper 24330-24331
Transfer
　Arm, Upper 24301, 24320
　Elbow 24301
　Femur 27110
　Hip 27100-27105, 27111
　Shoulder 23395-23397, 24301, 24320

Muscle Compartment Syndrome
Detection 20950

Muscle Denervation
See Denervation

Muscle Division
Scalenus Anticus 21700-21705
Sternocleidomastoid 21720-21725

Muscle Flaps 15731-15738
Free 15756

Muscle Grafts 15841-15845

Muscle Testing
Dynamometry, Eye 92260
Extraocular Multiple Muscles 92265
Manual 95831-95834

Muscle, Oculomotor
See Eye Muscles

Muscles
Repair
　Extraocular 65290, 67346

Musculo-Skeletal System
See Musculoskeletal System

Musculoplasty
See Muscle, Repair

Musculoskeletal System
Computer-Assisted Surgical
Navigation 0054T-0055T, 20985
Unlisted Services and Procedures 20999,
　24999, 25999, 26989, 27299, 27599, 27899
Unlisted Services and Procedures, Head 21499

Musculotendinous (Rotator) Cuff
Repair 23410-23412

Mustard Procedure
See Repair, Great Arteries; Revision

Myasthenia Gravis
Tensilon Test 95857

Myasthenic, Gravis
See Myasthenia Gravis

Mycobacteria
Culture 87116
　Identification 87118
Detection 87550-87562
Sensitivity Studies 87190

Mycoplasma
Antibody 86738
Culture 87109
Detection 87580-87582

Mycota
See Fungus

Myectomy, Anorectal
See Myomectomy, Anorectal

Myelencephalon
See Medulla

Myelin Basic Protein
Cerebrospinal Fluid 83873

Myelography
Brain 70010
Spine
　Cervical 72240
　Lumbosacral 72265
　Thoracic 72255
　Total 72270

Myelomeningocele
Repair 63704-63706

Myeloperoxidase (MPO) 83876

Myelotomy 63170

Myocardial
Perfusion Imaging 78451-78454
　See Nuclear Medicine
Positron Emission Tomography (PET) 78459

Myocardial Imaging 78466-78469
Perfusion Study
　Positron Emission Tomography
　　(PET) 78491-78492
　Single Photon Emission Computed
　　Tomography (SPECT) 78451-78452
Repair
　Postinfarction 33542

Myocutaneous
Flaps 15731-15738, 15756

Myofascial Pain Dysfunction Syndrome
See Temporomandibular Joint (TMJ)

Myofibroma
See Leiomyomata

Myoglobin 83874

Myomectomy
Anorectal 45108
Uterus 58140-58146, 58545-58546

Myoplasty
See Muscle, Repair

Myotomy
Esophagus 43030
Hyoid 21685

Myringoplasty 69620

Myringostomy
See Myringotomy

Myringotomy 69420-69421

Myxoid Cyst
See Ganglion

N

N. Meningitidis
See Neisseria Meningitidis

Naffziger Operation
See Decompression, Orbit; Section

Nagel Test
See Color Vision Examination

Nail Bed
Reconstruction 11762
Repair 11760

Nail Fold
Excision
　Wedge 11765

Nail Plate Separation
See Nails, Avulsion

Nails
Avulsion 11730-11732
Biopsy 11755
Debridement 11720-11721
Drainage 10060-10061
Evacuation
　Hematoma, Subungual 11740
Excision 11750-11752
KOH Examination 87220
Removal 11730-11732, 11750-11752
Trimming 11719

Narcosynthesis
Diagnostic and Therapeutic 90865

Nasal Abscess
See Nose, Abscess

Nasal Area
Bone Graft 21210

Nasal Bleeding
See Epistaxis

Nasal Bone
Fracture
　Closed Treatment 21310-21320
　Open Treatment 21325-21335
　with Manipulation 21315-21320
　without Manipulation 21310
X-ray 70160

Nasal Deformity
Repair 40700-40761

Neoplastic Growth
See Tumor

Nephelometry 83883

Nephrectomy
Donor 50300-50320, 50547
Laparoscopic 50545-50548
Partial 50240
    Laparoscopic 50543
Recipient 50340
with Ureters 50220-50236, 50546, 50548

Nephrolith
See Calculus, Removal, Kidney

Nephrolithotomy 50060-50075

Nephropexy 50400-50405

Nephroplasty
See Kidney, Repair

Nephropyeloplasty
See Pyeloplasty

Nephrorrhaphy 50500

Nephroscopy
See Endoscopy, Kidney

Nephrostogram 50394

Nephrostolithotomy
Percutaneous 50080-50081

Nephrostomy 50040
Change Tube 50398
Endoscopic.................50562-50570
Percutaneous 52334
with Drainage 50040
X-ray with Contrast
    Guide Dilation 74485

Nephrostomy Tract
Establishment 50395

Nephrotomogram
See Nephrotomography

Nephrotomography 74415

Nephrotomy 50040-50045
with Exploration 50045

Nerve
Cranial
    See Cranial Nerve
Facial
    See Facial Nerve
Intercostal
    See Intercostal Nerve
Lingual
    See Lingual Nerve
Median
    See Median Nerve
Obturator
    See Obturator Nerve
Peripheral
    See Peripheral Nerve
Phrenic
    See Phrenic Nerve
Sciatic
    See Sciatic Nerve
Spinal
    See Spinal Nerve

Tibial
    See Tibial Nerve
Ulnar
    See Ulnar Nerve
Vestibular
    See Vestibular Nerve

Nerve Conduction
Motor Nerve 95900-95903
Preconfigured Electrode Array 0197T
Sensory Nerve or Mixed 95904-95905

Nerve Root
See Cauda Equina; Spinal Cord
Decompression 22856, 63020-63048,
                              63055-63103
Incision 63185-63190
Section 63185-63190

Nerve Stimulation, Transcutaneous
See Application, Neurostimulation

Nerve Teasing 88362

Nerve II, Cranial
See Optic Nerve

Nerve V, Cranial
See Trigeminal Nerve

Nerve VII, Cranial
See Facial Nerve

Nerve X, Cranial
See Vagus Nerve

Nerve XI, Cranial
See Accessory Nerve

Nerve XII, Cranial
See Hypoglossal Nerve

Nerves
Anastomosis
    Facial to Hypoglossal 64868
    Facial to Phrenic 64870
    Facial to Spinal Accessory 64866
Avulsion 64732-64772
Biopsy 64795
Decompression 64702-64727
Destruction 64600-64681
    Laryngeal, Recurrent 31595
Foot
    Excision 28055
    Incision 28035
Graft.........................64885-64907
Implantation
    Electrode 64553-64581
    to Bone 64787
    to Muscle 64787
Incision 43640-43641, 64732-64772
Injection
    Anesthetic 01991-01992, 64400-64530
    Neurolytic Agent 64600-64681
Insertion
    Electrode 64553-64581
Lesion
    Excision 64774-64792
Neurofibroma
    Excision 64788-64792
Neurolemmoma
    Excision 64788-64792
Neurolytic
    Internal 64727

Neuroma
    Destruction 64632
    Excision 64774-64786
    Injection 64455
Neuroplasty 64702-64721
Removal
    Electrode 64585
Repair
    Graft 64885-64911
    Microdissection 69990
    Suture 64831-64876
Spinal Accessory
    Incision 63191
    Section 63191
Suture 64831-64876
Sympathectomy
    Excision 64802-64818
Transection 43640-43641, 64732-64772
Transposition 64718-64721
Unlisted Services and Procedures 64999

Nervous System
Nuclear Medicine
    Unlisted Services and Procedures 78699

Nesidioblast
See Islet Cell

Neural Conduction
See Nerve Conduction

Neural Ganglion
See Ganglion

Neurectomy
Foot 28055
Gastrocnemius 27326
Hamstring Muscle 27325
Leg, Lower 27326
Leg, Upper 27325
Popliteal 27326
Tympanic 69676

Neuroendoscopy
Intracranial 62160-62165

Neurofibroma
Cutaneous Nerve
    Excision 64788
Extensive
    Excision 64792
Peripheral Nerve
    Excision 64790

Neurolemmoma
Cutaneous Nerve
    Excision 64788
Extensive
    Excision 64792
Peripheral Nerve
    Excision 64790

Neurologic System
See Nervous System

Neurology
Brain Cortex Magnetic Stimulation ...0160T-0161T
Brain Mapping 96020
Brain Surface Electrode Stimulation ...95961-95962
Central Motor
    Transcranial Motor Stimulation ...95928-95929
Cognitive Performance 96125

Orbitotomy
with Bone Flap
  for Exploration 67450
  Lateral Approach 67420
  with Drainage 67440
  with Removal Foreign Body 67430
  with Removal of Bone for
    Decompression 67445
  with Removal Foreign Body 67413
  with Removal of Bone for Decompression ...67414
without Bone Flap
  for Exploration 67400
  with Drainage Only 67405
  with Removal Lesion 67412

Orchidectomies
See Excision, Testis

Orchidopexy
See Orchiopexy

Orchidoplasty
See Repair, Testis

Orchiectomy
Laparoscopic 54690
Partial 54522
Radical
  Abdominal Exploration 54535
    Inguinal Approach 54530
Simple 54520

Orchiopexy
Abdominal Approach 54650
Inguinal Approach 54640
Intra-Abdominal Testis 54692

Orchioplasty
See Repair, Testis

Organ Grafting
See Transplantation

Organ or Disease-Oriented Panel
Electrolyte 80051
General Health Panel 80050
Hepatic Function Panel 80076
Hepatitis Panel 80074
Lipid Panel 80061
Metabolic
  Basic 80047, 80048
  Comprehensive 80053
Obstetric Panel 80055
Renal Function 80069

Organ System, Neurologic
See Nervous System

Organic Acids 83918-83921

Ormond Disease
See Retroperitoneal Fibrosis

Orogastric Tube
Placement 43752

Oropharynx
Biopsy 42800

Orthodontic Cephalogram 70350

Orthomyxoviridae
See Influenza Virus

Orthomyxovirus
See Influenza Virus

Orthopantogram 70355

Orthopedic Cast
See Cast

Orthopedic Surgery
Computer Assisted Navigation 20985-20987
Stereotaxis
  Computer Assisted 20985-20987

Orthoptic Training 92065

Orthoroentgenogram 77073

Orthosis
See Orthotics

Orthotics
Check-Out 97762
Management and Training 97760

Os Calcis Fracture
See Calcaneus, Fracture

Osmolality
Blood 83930
Urine 83935

Osseous Survey 77074-77076

Osseous Tissue
See Bone

Ossicles
Excision
  Stapes
    with Footplate Drill Out 69661
    without Foreign Material 69660-69661
Reconstruction
  Ossicular Chain
    Tympanoplasty with Antrotomy or
      Mastoidotomy 69636-69637
    Tympanoplasty with
      Mastoidectomy 69642, 69644, 69646
    Tympanoplasty without
      Mastoidectomy 69632-69633
Release
  Stapes 69650
Replacement
  with Prosthesis 69633, 69637

Ostectomy
Metacarpal 26250
Metatarsal 28288
Phalanges
  Finger 26260-26262
Pressure Ulcer
  Ischial 15941, 15945
  Sacral 15933, 15935, 15937
  Trochanteric 15951, 15953, 15958
Scapula 23190
Sternum 21620

Osteocalcin 83937

Osteocartilaginous Exostoses
See Exostosis

Osteochondroma
See Exostosis

Osteocutaneous Flap
with Microvascular Anastomosis 20969-20973

Osteoma
Sinusotomy
  Frontal 31075

Osteomyelitis 20000-20005
Elbow
  Incision and Drainage 23935
Excision
  Clavicle 23180
  Facial 21026
  Humerus, Proximal 23184
  Mandible 21025
  Scapula 23182
Femur/Knee
  Incision and Drainage 27303
Finger
  Incision 26034
Hand Incision 26034
Hip
  Incision, Deep 26992
Humerus 24134
  Incision and Drainage 23935
Incision
  Foot 28005
  Shoulder 23035
  Thorax 21510
Olecranon Process 24138, 24147
Pelvis
  Incision, Deep 26992
Radius 24136, 24145
Sequestrectomy
  Clavicle 23170
  Humeral Head 23174
  Scapula 23172
  Skull 61501

**Osteopathic
Manipulation** 98925-98929

Osteoplasty
Carpal Bone 25394
Facial Bones
  Augmentation 21208
  Reduction 21209
Femoral Neck 27179
Femur 27179
  Lengthening 27466-27468
  Shortening 27465, 27468
Fibula
  Lengthening 27715
Humerus 24420
Metacarpal 26568
Phalanges, Finger 26568
Radius 25390-25393
Tibia
  Lengthening 27715
Ulna 25390-25393
Vertebra 72291-72292
  Lumbar 22521-22522
  Thoracic 22520, 22522

Osteotomy
Calcaneus 28300
Chin 21121-21123
Clavicle 23480-23485
Femur 27140, 27151
  Femoral Neck 27161
  for Slipped Epiphysis 27181
  with Fixation 27165
  with Open Reduction of Hip 27156
  with Realignment 27454
  without Fixation 27448-27450

Neurovascular 15750
Transfer 15650

PEEP
See Pressure Breathing, Positive

Pelvi-Ureteroplasty
See Pyeloplasty

Pelvic Adhesions
See Adhesions, Pelvic

Pelvic Exam 57410

Pelvic Exenteration 51597

Pelvic Fixation
Insertion 22848

Pelvic Lymphadenectomy 58210, 58958

Pelvimetry 74710

Pelviolithotomy 50130

Pelvis
See Hip
Abscess
    Incision and Drainage 26990, 45000
Angiography 72191
Biopsy 27040-27041
Bone
    Drainage 26992
Brace Application 20662
Bursa
    Incision and Drainage 26991
CT Scan 72191-72194
Cyst
    Aspiration 50390
    Injection 50390
Destruction
    Lesion 58662
Endoscopy
    Destruction of Lesion 58662
    Lysis of Adhesions 58660
    Oviduct Surgery 58670-58671
Exclusion
    Small Intestine 44700
Exenteration 45126, 58240
Fasciotomy
    Decompression 27027
       with Debridement 27057
Halo 20662
Hematoma
    Incision and Drainage 26990
Lysis
    Adhesions 58660
Magnetic Resonance Angiography 72198
Magnetic Resonance Imaging
(MRI) 72195-72197
Removal
    Foreign Body 27086-27087
Repair
    Osteotomy 27158
    Tendon 27098
Ring
    Dislocation 27193-27194, 27216-27218
    Fracture 27216-27218
       Closed Treatment 27193-27194
Tumor
    Excision 27043-27048
    Radical Resection 27049, 27059
Ultrasound 76856-76857

Unlisted Services and Procedures for Hips
and Hip Joint 27299
X-ray 72170-72190, 73540
    Manometry 74710

Pemberton Osteotomy of Pelvis
See Osteotomy, Pelvis

Penectomy
See Amputation, Penis

Penetrating Keratoplasties
See Keratoplasty, Penetrating

Penile Induration
See Peyronie Disease

Penile Prosthesis
Insertion
    Inflatable 54401-54405
    Noninflatable 54400
Removal
    Inflatable 54406, 54410-54417
    Semi-Rigid 54415-54417
Repair
    Inflatable 54408
Replacement
    Inflatable 54410-54411, 54416-54417
    Semi-Rigid 54416-54417

Penile Rigidity Test 54250

Penile Tumescence Test 54250

Penis
Amputation
    Partial 54120
    Radical 54130-54135
    Total 54125
Biopsy 54100-54105
Circumcision
    Repair 54163
    Surgical Excision
       Newborn 54150, 54160
Excision
    Partial 54120
    Prepuce 54150-54161, 54163
    Total 54125-54135
Frenulum
    Excision 54164
Incision
    Prepuce 54000-54001
Incision and Drainage 54015
Injection
    for Erection 54235
    Peyronie Disease 54200
       Surgical Exposure Plague 54205
    Vasoactive Drugs 54231
    X-ray 54230
Insertion
    Prosthesis
       Inflatable 54401-54405
       Noninflatable 54400
Irrigation
    Priapism 54220
Lesion
    Destruction
       Cryosurgery 54056
       Electrodesiccation 54055
       Extensive 54065
       Laser Surgery 54057
       Simple 54050-54060
       Surgical Excision 54060

       Excision 54060
       Penile Plaque 54110-54112
Nocturnal Penile Tumescence Test 54250
Occlusion
    Vein 37790
Plaque
    Excision 54110-54112
Plethysmography 54240
Prepuce
    Stretch 54450
Reconstruction
    Angulation 54360
    Chordee 54300-54304, 54328
    Complications 54340-54348
    Epispadias 54380-54390
    Hypospadias 54328-54352
    Injury 54440
Removal
    Foreign Body 54115
    Prosthesis
       Inflatable 54406, 54410-54417
       Semi-Rigid 54415-54417
Repair
    Fistulization 54435
    Priapism with Shunt 54420-54430
    Prosthesis
       Inflatable 54408
Replacement
    Prosthesis
       Inflatable 54410-54411, 54416-54417
       Semi-Rigid 54416-54417
Revascularization 37788
Rigidity Test 54250
Test Erection 54250
Unlisted Services and Procedures 55899
Venous Studies 93980-93981

Penis Adhesions
Lysis
    Post-circumcision 54162

Penis Prostheses
See Penile Prosthesis

Pentagastrin Test
See Gastric Analysis Test

Pentamidine
See Inhalation Treatment

Peptidase P
See Angiotensin Converting Enzyme (ACE)

Peptidase S
See Leucine Aminopeptidase

Peptide, Connecting
See C-Peptide

Peptide, Vasoactive Intestinal
See Vasoactive Intestinal Peptide

Peptidyl Dipeptidase A
See Angiotensin Converting Enzyme (ACE)

Percutaneous Abdominal Paracentesis
See Abdomen, Drainage

Percutaneous Atherectomies
See Artery, Atherectomy

Percutaneous Biopsy, Gallbladder/Bile Ducts
See Bile Duct, Biopsy

Persistent, Omphalomesenteric Duct
See Diverticulum, Meckel's

Personal Care
See Self Care

Personality Test 96101-96103
Computer-Assisted 96103

Pessary
Insertion 57160

Pesticides
Chlorinated Hydrocarbons 82441

PET
See Positron Emission Tomography

Petrous Temporal
Excision
    Apex 69530

Peyronie Disease
Injection 54200
Surgical Exposure 54205
with Graft 54110-54112

pH
See Blood
Exhaled Breath Condensate 0140T, 83987
Other Fluid 83986
Urine 83986

Phacoemulsification
Removal
    Extracapsular Cataract 66982, 66984
    Secondary Membranous Cataract 66850

Phagocytosis
White Blood Cells 86344

Phalangectomy
Toe 28150
    Partial 28160

Phalanges (Hand)
See Finger, Bone

Phalanx, Finger
Craterization 26235-26236
Cyst
    Excision 26210-26215
Diaphysectomy 26235-26236
Excision 26235-26236
    Radical
        for Tumor 26260-26262
Fracture
    Articular
        Closed Treatment 26740
        Open Treatment 26746
        with Manipulation 26742
    Distal 26755-26756
        Closed Treatment 26750
        Open Treatment 26765
        Percutaneous Fixation 26756
    Open Treatment 26735
        Distal 26765
    Shaft 26720-26727
        Open Treatment 26735
Incision and Drainage 26034
Ostectomy
    Radical
        for Tumor 26260-26262
Repair
    Lengthening 26568

Nonunion 26546
Osteotomy 26567
Saucerization 26235-26236
Thumb
    Fracture
        Shaft 26720-26727
Tumor
    Excision 26210-26215

Phalanx, Great Toe
See Phalanx, Toe
Fracture 28490
    Open Treatment 28505
    with Manipulation 28495-28496
Percutaneous Fixation 28496
without Manipulation 28490

Phalanx, Toe
Condyle
    Excision 28126
Craterization 28124
Cyst
    Excision 28108
Diaphysectomy 28124
Excision 28124, 28150-28160
Fracture
    Open Treatment 28525
    with Manipulation 28515
    without Manipulation 28510
Repair
    Osteotomy 28310-28312
Saucerization 28124
Tumor
    Excision 28108
    Radical Resection 28175

Pharmaceutic Preparations
See Drug

Pharmacotherapies
See Chemotherapy

Pharyngeal Tonsil
See Adenoids

Pharyngectomy
Partial 42890

Pharyngolaryngectomy 31390-31395

Pharyngoplasty 42950

Pharyngorrhaphy
See Suture, Pharynx

Pharyngostomy 42955

Pharyngotomy
See Incision, Pharynx

Pharyngotympanic Tube
See Eustachian Tube

Pharynx
See Nasopharynx; Throat
Biopsy 42800-42806
Cineradiography 70371, 74230
Creation
    Stoma 42955
Excision 42145
    Partial 42890
    Resection 42892-42894
    with Larynx 31390-31395
Hemorrhage 42960-42962

Lesion
    Destruction 42808
    Excision 42808
Reconstruction 42950
Removal
    Foreign Body 42809
Repair
    with Esophagus 42953
Unlisted Services and Procedures 42999
Video Study 70371, 74230
X-ray 70370, 74210

Phencyclidine 83992

Phenobarbital 82205
Assay 80184

Phenothiazine 84022

Phenotype Analysis
by Nucleic Acid
    Infectious Agent
        HIV-1 Drug Resistance 87903-87904

Phenotype Prediction
by Genetic Database
    HIV-1 Drug Susceptibility 87900

Phenylalanine 84030

Phenylalanine-Tyrosine Ratio ...84030

Phenylketones 84035

Phenylketonuria
See Phenylalanine

Phenytoin
Assay 80185-80186

Pheochromocytoma 80424

Pheresis
See Apheresis

Phlebectasia
See Varicose Vein

Phlebectomy
Varicose Veins 37765-37766

Phlebographies
See Venography

Phleborrhaphy
See Suture, Vein

Phlebotomy
Therapeutic 99195

Phoria
See Strabismus

Phosphatase
Alkaline 84075, 84080
    Blood 84078
Forensic Examination 84061

Phosphatase Acid 84060
Blood 84066

Phosphate, Pyridoxal
See Pyridoxal Phosphate

Phosphatidyl Glycerol
See Phosphatidylglycerol

Pituitary Gland
Excision 61546-61548
Tumor
    Excision 61546-61548, 62165

Pituitary Growth Hormone
See Growth Hormone

Pituitary Lactogenic Hormone
See Prolactin

Pituitectomy
See Excision, Pituitary Gland

PKU
See Phenylalanine

Placement
Adjustable Gastric Restrictive Device 43770
Broncheal Stent 31636-31637
Catheter
    Aneurysm Sac
        Pressure Sensor 34806
            Complete Study 93982
    Brain
        for Chemotherapy 0169T
    Breast
        for Interstitial Radioelement
        Application 19296-19298, 20555, 41019
    Bronchus
        for Intracavitary Radioelement
        Application 31643
            See Catheterization
    Head
        Interstitial Radioelement Application ...41019
    Neck
        Interstitial Radioelement Application ...41019
    Pelvic Organs
        Interstitial Radioelement Application ...55920
    Prostate 55875
Catheter, Cardiac 93503
    See Catheterization, Cardiac
Cecostomy Tube 44300, 49442
Colonic Stent 44397, 45327, 45345, 45387
Dosimeter
    Prostate 55876
Drainage
    Pancreas 48001
Duodenostomy Tube 49441
Endovascular Prosthesis
    Aorta 33883-33886
Enterostomy Tube 44300
Fiducial Markers
    Bronchus 31626
    Prostate 55876
Gastrostomy Tube 43246, 49440
Guidance
    Catheter
        Abscess 75989
        Bile 75982
        Specimen 75989
    Prosthesis
        Thoracic Aorta 75958-75959
Interstitial Device
    Abdomen 49410
    Lungs 32553
    Omentum 49410
    Pelvis 49410
    Pleura 32553
    Peritoneum 49410
    Prostate 55876
    Retroperitoneum 49410

Intravascular Stent
    Coronary 92980-92981
    Intracranial 61635
IVC Filter 75940
Jejunostomy Tube
    Endoscopic 44372
    Percutaneous 49441
Metallic Localization Clip
    Breast 19295
Nasogastric Tube 43752
Needle
    Bone 36680
    Interstitial Radioelement Application
        Genitalia 55920
        Head 41019
        Muscle 20555
        Neck 41019
        Pelvic Organs 55920
        Soft Tissue 20555
        Prostate 55875
Needle Wire
    Breast 19290-19291
Orogastric Tube 43752
Pressure Sensor 34806
Radiation Delivery Device
    Intracoronary Artery 92974
    Pleural Cavity 32553
Sensor, Wireless
    Endovascular Repair 34806
Seton
    Anal 46020
Subconjuntival Retinal Prosthesis 0100T
Tracheal Stent 31631
Transcatheter
    Pressure Sensor 34806
Ureteral Stent 50947

Placenta
Delivery 59414

Placental Lactogen
See Lactogen, Human Placental

Placental Villi
See Chorionic Villus

Plagiocephaly 21175

Plague Vaccine 90727

Planing
Nose
    Skin 30120

Plantar Common Digital Nerve
Destruction
    Neurolytic 64632

Plantar Digital Nerve
Decompression 64726

Plantar Pressure Measurements
Dynamic 96001, 96004

Plasma
Frozen Preparation 86927

Plasma Prokallikrein
See Fletcher Factor

Plasma Protein-A, Pregnancy-Associated (PAPP-A) 84163

Plasma Test
Volume Determination 78110-78111

Plasma Thromboplastin
Antecedent 85270
Component 85250

Plasmin 85400

Plasmin Antiactivator
See Alpha-2 Antiplasmin

Plasminogen 85420-85421

Plasmodium
Antibody 86750

Plastic Repair of Mouth
See Mouth, Repair

Plate, Bone
See Bone Plate

Platelet
See Blood Cell Count, Complete Blood Count
Aggregation 85576
Antibody 86022-86023
Assay 85055
Blood 85025
Count 85032, 85049
Neutralization 85597

Platelet Cofactor I
See Clotting Factor

Platelet Test
Survival Test 78190-78191

Platysmal Flap 15825

PLC
See Lymphocyte, Culture; Tissue, Typing

Pleoptic Training 92065

Plethysmography
See Vascular Studies
Extremities 93922-93923
    Veins 93965
Penis 54240
Total Body 93720-93722

Pleura
Biopsy 32095-32100, 32400-32402
Decortication 32320
Empyema
    Excision 32540
Excision 32310-32320
    Endoscopic 32656
Foreign Body
    Removal 32150-32151
Needle Biopsy 32400
Placement
    Interstitial Device 32553
Removal
    Foreign Body 32653
Repair 32215
Thoracotomy 32095-32100
Unlisted Services and Procedures 32999

Pleural Cavity
Ablation
    Photodynamic Therapy 96570-96571
Aspiration 32421-32422
Catheterization 32550-32552
Chemotherapy Administration 96440
    See Chemotherapy

Postpartum Care
Cesarean Delivery .59515
    after Attempted Vaginal Delivery 59622
    Previous 59610, 59614-59618, 59622
Vaginal Delivery 59430
    after Previous Cesarean Delivery 59614

Potassium 84132
Urine 84133

Potential, Auditory Evoked
See Auditory Evoked Potentials

Potential, Evoked
See Evoked Potential

Potts-Smith Procedure 33762

Pouch, Kock
See Kock Pouch

PPP
See Fibrin Degradation Products

PRA
See Cytotoxic Screen

Prealbumin .84134

Prebeta Lipoproteins
See Lipoprotein, Blood

Pregnancy
Abortion
    Induced .59855-59857
      by Amniocentesis Injection 59850-59852
      by Dilation and Curettage 59840
      by Dilation and Evaluation 59841
    Septic 59830
    Therapeutic
      by Dilation and Curettage 59851
      by Hysterectomy 59852
      by Saline 59850
Cesarean Delivery 59618-59622
    Only 59514
    Postpartum Care 59514-59515
    Routine Care .59510
    Vaginal Birth After 59610-59614
    with Hysterectomy 59525
Ectopic
    Abdominal 59130
    Cervix 59140
    Interstitial
      Partial Resection Uterus 59136
      Total Hysterectomy 59135
    Laparoscopy
      with Salpingectomy and/or
      Oophorectomy 59151
      without Salpingectomy and/or
      Oophorectomy 59150
    Tubal 59121
      with Salpingectomy and/or
      Oophorectomy 59120
Miscarriage
    Surgical Completion
      Any Trimester 59812
      First Trimester 59820
      Second Trimester 59821
Molar
    See Hydatidiform Mole
Multifetal Reduction 59866
Placenta Delivery 59414
Vaginal Delivery 59409-59410
    after Cesarean Delivery 59610-59614

Antepartum Care 59425-59426
Postpartum Care 59430
Total Obstetrical Care . . .59400, 59610, 59618

Pregnancy Test 84702-84703, 84704
Urinalysis 81025

Pregnanediol 84135

Pregnanetriol 84138

Pregnenolone 84140

Prekallikrein
See Fletcher Factor

Prekallikrein Factor 85292

Premature, Closure, Cranial Suture
See Craniosynostosis

Prenatal Procedure 59897
Amnioinfusion
    Transabdominal 59070
Drainage
    Fluid 59074
Occlusion
    Umbilical Cord 59072
Shunt 59076

Prenatal Testing
Amniocentesis 59000
    with Amniotic Fluid Reduction 59001
Chorionic Villus Sampling 59015
Cordocentesis 59012
Fetal Blood Sample 59030
Fetal Monitoring .59050
    Interpretation Only 59051
Non-Stress Test, Fetal 59025, 99500
Oxytocin Stress Test 59020
Stress Test
    Oxytocin 59020
Ultrasound 76801-76817
    Fetal Biophysical Profile 76818-76819
    Fetal Heart 76825

Preparation
for Transfer
    Embryo 89255
for Transplantation
    Heart 33933, 33944
    Heart/Lung 33933
    Intestines 44715-44721
    Kidney 50323-50329
    Liver .47143-47147
    Lung 32855-32856, 33933
    Pancreas 48551-48552
    Renal 50323-50329
Thawing
    Embryo
      Cryopreserved 89352
    Oocytes
      Cryopreserved 89356
    Reproductive Tissue
      Cryopreserved 89354
    Sperm
      Cryopreserved 89353

Presacral Sympathectomy
See Sympathectomy, Presacral

Prescription
Contact Lens 92310-92317
    See Contact Lens Services

Pressure Breathing
See Pulmonology, Therapeutic
Negative
    Continuous (CNP) 94662
Positive
    Continuous (CPAP) 94660

Pressure
Blood
    See Blood Pressure
Measurement of Sphincter of Oddi
    See Sphincter of Oddi, Pressure Measurement
Sensor, Aneurysm
    Placement 34806
Ulcer (Decubitus)
    See Debridement; Skin Graft and Flap
    Excision 15920-15999
Venous
    See Blood Pressure, Venous

Pretreatment
Red Blood Cell
    Antibody Identification 86970-86972
Serum
    Antibody Identification 86975-86978

Prevention & Control
See Prophylaxis

Preventive Medicine 99381-99397
See Immunization; Newborn Care, Normal; Office
and/or Other Outpatient Services; Performance
Measures, Prophylatic Treatment
Administration/Interpretation of Health Risk
Assessment 99420
Counseling and/or Risk Factor Reduction
Intervention 99401-99429
    Behavior Change 99406-99408
    Calcium/Vitamin D Use 4019F
    Exercise 4019F
    Group Counseling 99411-99412
    Individual Counseling 99401-99404
      Self-Examination for Moles 5005F
Established Patient 99382-99397
New Patient 99381-99387
Newborn Care 99432
Respiratory Pattern Recording 94772
Unlisted Services and Procedures 99429

Priapism
Repair
    Fistulization .54435
    with Shunt 54420-54430

Primidone
Assay 80188

PRL
See Prolactin

Proalbumin
See Prealbumin

Probes, DNA
See Nucleic Acid Probe

Probes, Nucleic Acid
See Nucleic Acid Probe

Procainamide
Assay 80190-80192

Procalcitonin (PCT) 84145

Puncturing
See Puncture

Pure-Tone Audiometry
See Audiometry, Pure Tone

Pustules
Removal 10040

Putti-Platt Procedure 23450

PUVA
See Dermatology; Photochemotherapy; Ultraviolet Light Therapy

Pyelogram
See Urography, Intravenous; Urography, Retrograde

Pyelography 74400, 74425
Injection 50394

Pyelolithotomy 50130
Anatrophic 50075
Coagulum 50130

Pyeloplasty 50400-50405, 50544
Repair
    Horseshoe Kidney 50540
Secondary 50405

Pyeloscopy
with Cystourethroscopy 52351
    Biopsy 52354
    Destruction 52354
    Lithotripsy 52353
    Removal
        Calculus 52352
    Tumor Excision 52355

Pyelostogram 50394

Pyelostolithotomy
Percutaneous 50080-50081

Pyelostomy 50125, 50400-50405
Change Tube 50398

Pyelotomy
Complicated 50135
Endoscopic 50570
Exploration 50120
with Drainage 50125
with Removal Calculus 50130

Pyeloureterogram
Antegrade 50394

Pyeloureteroplasty
See Pyeloplasty

Pyloric Sphincter
Incision 43520
Reconstruction 43800

Pyloromyotomy 43520

Pyloroplasty 43800
with Vagotomy 43640

Pyothorax
See Abscess, Thorax

Pyridoxal Phosphate 84207

Pyrophosphate, Adenosine
See Adenosine Diphosphate

Pyrophosphorylase, Udp Galactose
See Galactose-1-Phosphate, Uridyl Transferase

Pyruvate 84210-84220

Q

Q Fever 86000, 86638

Q Fever ab
See Antibody, Coxiella Burnetii

QST
See Quantitative Sensory Testing

Quadrantectomy 19301-19302

Quadriceps Repair 27430

Quantitative Sensory Testing (QST)
Cooling Stimuli 0108T
Heat-Pain Stimuli 0109T
Other Stimuli 0110T
Touch Pressure Stimuli 0106T
Vibration Stimuli 0107T

Quick Test
See Prothrombin Time

Quinidine
Assay 80194

Quinine 84228

R

Rabies Vaccine
See Vaccines

Rachicentesis
See Spinal Tap

Radial Artery
See Artery, Radial

Radial Head, Subluxation
See Nursemaid Elbow

Radial Keratotomy 65771

Radiation
See Irradiation

Radiation Physics
Consultation 77336-77370
Unlisted Services and Procedures 77399

Radiation Therapy 77280-77295
Consultation
    Radiation Physics 77336-77370
Dose Plan 77300, 77305-77331
    Brachytherapy 77326-77328, 0182T
    Intensity Modulation 77301
        Multi-leaf Collimator (MLC) Device ...77338
    Teletherapy 77305-77321

Field Set-up 77280-77295
Guidance
    CT 77014
    Interstitial Devices, Placement ...49410-49411
Planning 77261-77263, 77299
Radiosurgery 77371-77373
Special 77470
Stereotactic
    Body 77373
    Cerebral Lesions 77371-77372
    Guidance 77421
Treatment Delivery 77371-77373
    2 Areas 77407-77411
    3 or More Areas 77412-77416
    Beam Modulation 0073T
    High Energy Neutron Radiation ...77422-77423
    Intensity Modulation 77418
    Localization 0197T
    Proton Beam 77520-77525
    Single Area 77402-77406, 77422
    Stereotactic 77371-77373
        Body 77373
    Superficial 77401
    Tracking 0197T
    Weekly 77427
Treatment Device 77332-77334
Treatment Management
    1 or 2 Fractions Only 77431
    Stereotactic
        Body 77435
        Cerebral 77432
    Unlisted Services and Procedures 77499
    Weekly 77427

Radiation, X
See X-ray

Radical Excision of Lymph Nodes
See Excision, Lymph Nodes, Radical

Radical Mastectomies, Modified
See Mastectomy, Modified Radical

Radical Neck Dissection
Laryngectomy 31365-31368
Pharyngolaryngectomy 31390-31395
with Auditory Canal Surgery 69155
with Thyroidectomy 60254
with Tongue Excision 41135, 41145,
                      41153-41155

Radical Resection
See Resection, Radical
Abdomen 51597
Acetabulum 27076
Arm, Lower 25077
Elbow
    Capsule, Soft Tissue, Bone
        with Contracture Release 24149
Forearm 25077
Hip
    Soft Tissue 27049
Humerus 23220-23222
Innominate 27077
Ischial 27078, 27079
Metatarsal 28173
Ovarian Tumor
    Bilateral Salpingo-Oophorectomy-
    Omentectomy 58950-58956
    with Radical Dissection for
    Debulking 58952-58954
    with Total Abdominal
    Hysterectomy 58953, 58954

Rapid Heart Rate
See Tachycardia

Rapid Plasma Reagin Test 86592, 86593

Rapid Test for Infection 86308, 86403-86406
Monospot Test 86308

Rapoport Test 52005

Raskind Procedure 33735-33737

Rat Typhus
See Murine Typhus

Rathke Pouch Tumor
See Craniopharyngioma

Rays, Roentgen
See X-ray

Raz Procedure 51845
See Repair, Bladder, Neck

RBC
See Red Blood Cell (RBC)

RBC ab
See Antibody, Red Blood Cell

Reaction
Lip
 without Reconstruction 40530

Reaction, Polymerase Chain
See Polymerase Chain Reaction

Realignment
Femur
 with Osteotomy 27454
Knee
 Extensor 27422

Receptor
See CD4; Estrogen, Receptor; FC Receptor; Progesterone Receptors

Receptor Assay
Hormone 84233-84235
Non Hormone 84238

Recession
Gastrocnemius
 Leg, Lower 27687

Reconstruction
See Revision
Abdominal Wall
 Omental Flap 49905
Acetabulum 27120-27122
Anal
 Congenital Absence 46730-46740
 Fistula 46742
 Graft 46753
 Sphincter 46750-46751, 46760-46762
 with Implant 46762
Ankle 27700-27703
Apical-Aortic Conduit 33404
Atrial 33257-33259
 Endoscopic 33265-33266
 Open 33254-33259
Auditory Canal, External 69310-69320
Bile Duct
 Anastomosis 47800

Bladder
 and Urethra 51800-51820
  Radiofrequency Micro-Remodeling ...0193T
 from Colon 50810
 from Intestines 50820, 51960
Breast 19357-19369
 Augmentation 19324-19325
 Mammoplasty 19318-19325
 Nipple 19350-19355
 Revision 19380
 Transverse Rectus Abdominis
  Myocutaneous Flap 19367-19369
  with Free Flap 19364
  with Latissimus Dorsi Flap 19361
  with Other Techniques 19366
  with Tissue Expander 19357
Bronchi 32501
 Graft Repair 31770
 Stenosis 31775
Canthus 67950
Carpal 25443
Carpal Bone 25394, 25430
Cheekbone 21270
Chest Wall 32504
 Omental Flap 49904
 Trauma 32820
Cleft Palate 42200-42225
Conduit
 Apical-Aortic 33404
Conjunctiva 68320-68335
 with Flap
  Bridge or Partial 68360
  Total 68362
Cranial Bone
 Extracranial 21181-21184
Ear, Middle
 Tympanoplasty with Antrotomy or Mastoidotomy
  with Ossicular Chain
   Reconstruction 69636-69637
 Tympanoplasty with Mastoidectomy ...69641
  Radical or Complete 69644-69645
  with Intact or Reconstructed
   Wall 69643-69644
  with Ossicular Chain Reconstruction ..69642
 Tympanoplasty without Mastoidectomy 69631
  with Ossicular Chain
   Reconstruction 69632-69633
Elbow 24360
 Total Replacement 24363
 with Implant 24361-24362
Esophagus 43300, 43310, 43313
 Creation
  Stoma 43350-43352
 Esophagostomy 43350
 Fistula 43305, 43312, 43314
 Gastrointestinal 43360-43361
Eye
 Graft
  Conjunctiva 65782
  Stem Cell 65781
 Transplantation
  Amniotic Membrane 65780
Eyelid
 Canthus 67950
 Second Stage 67975
 Total 67973-67975
 Total Eyelid
  Lower, One Stage 67973
  Upper, One Stage 67974

 Transfer Tarsoconjunctival Flap from
  Opposing Eyelid 67971
Facial Bones
 Secondary 21275
Fallopian Tube
 See Repair
Femur
 Lengthening 27466-27468
 Shortening 27465, 27468
Fibula
 Lengthening 27715
Finger
 Polydactylous 26587
Foot
 Cleft 28360
Forehead 21172-21180, 21182-21184
Glenoid Fossa 21255
Gums
 Alveolus 41874
 Gingiva 41872
Hand
 Tendon Pulley 26390, 26500-26502
 Toe to Finger Transfer 26551-26556
Heart
 Atrial 33257-33259
  Endoscopic 33265-33266
  Open 33254-33256
 Atrial Septum 33735-33737
 Pulmonary Artery Shunt 33924
 Vena Cava 34502
Hip
 Replacement 27130-27132
 Secondary 27134-27138
Hip Joint
 with Prosthesis 27125
Interphalangeal Joint 26535-26536
 Collateral Ligament 26545
Intestines, Small
 Anastomosis 43845, 44130
Knee 27437-27438
 Femur 27442-27443, 27446
 Ligament 27427-27429
 Replacement 27447
 Revision 27486-27487
 Tibia 27440-27443, 27446
 with Prosthesis 27438, 27445
Kneecap
 Instability 27420-27424
Larynx
 Burns 31588
 Cricoid Split 31587
 Other 31545-31546, 31588
 Stenosis 31582
 Web 31580
Lip 40525-40527, 40761
Lunate 25444
Malar Augmentation
 Prosthetic Material 21270
 with Bone Graft 21210
Mandible
 with Implant 21244-21246, 21248-21249
Mandibular Condyle 21247
Mandibular Rami
 with Bone Graft 21194
 with Internal Rigid Fixation 21196
 without Bone Graft 21193
 without Internal Rigid Fixation 21195
Maxilla
 with Implant 21245-21246, 21248-21249
Metacarpophalangeal Joint 26530-26531

Sedimentation Rate
Automated 85652
Manual 85651
Sequestration 78140
Sickling 85660
Survival Test 78130-78135
Volume Determination 78120-78121

Red Blood Cell ab
See Antibody, Red Blood Cell

Reductase, Glutathione
See Glutathione Reductase

Reductase, Lactic Cytochrome
See Lactic Dehydrogenase

Reduction
Forehead 21137-21139
Lung Volume 32491
Mammoplasty 19318
Masseter Muscle/Bone 21295-21296
Osteoplasty
  Facial Bones 21209
Pregnancy
  Multifetal 59866
Skull
  Craniomegalic 62115-62117
Ventricular Septum
  Non-Surgical 93733

Reflex Test
Blink Reflex 95933
H-Reflex 95934-95936

Reflux Study 78262
Gastroesophageal 91034-91038

Refraction 92015

Rehabilitation
Artery
  Occlusive Disease 93668
Auditory
  Post-Lingual Hearing Loss 92633
  Pre-Lingual Hearing Loss 92630
  Status Evaluation 92626-92627
Cardiac 93797-93798
Services Considered
  Documentation 4079F

Rehabilitation Facility
Discharge Services 1110F-1111F

Rehabilitative
See Rehabilitation

Reimplantation
Arteries
  Aorta
    Prosthesis 35697
  Carotid 35691, 35694-35695
  Subclavian 35693-35695
  Vertebral 35691-35693
  Visceral 35697
Kidney 50380
Ovary 58825
Pulmonary Artery 33788
Ureter, to Bladder 50780-50785
Ureters 51565

Reinnervation
Larynx
  Neuromuscular Pedicle 31590

Reinsch Test 83015

Reinsertion
Drug Delivery Implant 11983
Implantable Contraceptive Capsules 11977
Spinal Fixation Device 22849

Relative Density
See Specific Gravity

Release
Carpal Tunnel 64721
Elbow Contracture
  with Radical Release of Capsule 24149
Flexor Muscles
  Hip 27036
Muscle
  Knee 27422
Nerve 64702-64726
  Neurolytic 64727
Retina
  Encircling Material 67115
Spinal Cord 63200
Stapes 69650
Tarsal Tunnel 28035
Tendon 24332, 25295

Release-Inhibiting Hormone, Somatotropin
See Somatostatin

Removal
Adjustable Gastric Restrictive
Device 43772-43774
Allograft
  Intestinal 44137
Artificial Intervertebral Disc
  Cervical Interspace 0095T, 22864
  Lumbar Interspace 0164T, 22865
Balloon
  Intra-Aortic 33974
Balloon Assist Device
  Intra-Aortic 33968, 33971
Blood Clot
  Eye 65930
Blood Component
  Apheresis 36511-36516
Breast
  Capsules 19371
  Implants 19328-19330
  Modified Radical 19307
  Partial 19300-19302
  Radical 19305-19306
  Simple, Complete 19303
  Subcutaneous 19304
Calcareous Deposits
  Subdeltoid 23000
Calculi (Stone)
  Bile Duct 43264, 47420-47425
    Percutaneous 47554, 47630
  Bladder 51050, 52310-52318, 52352
  Gallbladder 47480
  Hepatic Duct 47400
  Kidney 50060-50081, 50130,
                50561, 50580, 52352
  Pancreas 48020
  Pancreatic Duct 43264
  Salivary Gland 42330-42340
  Ureter 50610-50630, 50961, 50980,
        51060-51065, 52320-52330, 52352
  Urethra 52310-52315, 52352
Cardiac Event Recorder 33284
Cast 29700-29715

Cataract
Dilated Fundus Evaluation 2021F
with Replacement
  Extracapsular 66982, 66984
  Intracapsular 66983
  Not Associated with Concurrent 66983
Catheter
  Central Venous 36589
  Fractured 75961
  Peritoneum 49422
  Pleural Cavity 32552
  Spinal Cord 62355
Cerclage
  Cervix 59871
Cerumen
  Auditory Canal, External 69210
Clot
  Pericardium 33020
    Endoscopic 32658
Comedones 10040
Contraceptive Capsules 11976-11977
Cranial Tongs 20665
Cyst 10040
Dacryolith
  Lacrimal Duct 68530
  Lacrimal Gland 68530
Defibrillator
  Heart 33244
    Pulse Generator Only 33241
    via Thoracotomy 33243
Drug Delivery Implant 11982-11983
Ear Wax
  Auditory Canal, External 69210
Electrode
  Brain 61535, 61880
  Heart 33238
  Nerve 64585
  Spinal Cord 63661-63664
  Stomach 0156T, 0158T, 43648, 43882
Embolus
  See Embolectomy
External Fixation System 20694
Eye
  Bone 67414, 67445
  Ocular Contents
    with Implant 65093
    without Implant 65091
  Orbital Contents Only 65110
    with Bone 65112
  with Implant
    Muscles Attached 65105
    Muscles, Not Attached 65103
  with Muscle or Myocutaneous Flap 65114
  without Implant 65101
Fallopian Tube
  Laparoscopy 58661
  with Hysterectomy 58542, 58544, 58548
Fat
  Lipectomy 15876-15879
Fecal Impaction
  Rectum 45915
Fibrin Deposit 32150
Fixation Device 20670-20680
Foreign Body 65205-65265
  Anal 46608
  Ankle Joint 27610, 27620
  Arm
    Lower 25248
    Upper 24200-24201
  Auditory Canal, External 69200
    with Anesthesia 69205
  Bile Duct 43269

Posterior Nonsegmental
   Harrington Rod 22850
Posterior Segmental 22852
Stent
   Bile Duct 43269
   Pancreatic Duct 43269
   Ureteral 50382-50387
Subcutaneous Port
  for Gastric Restrictive
  Procedure 43887-43888
Suture
   Anal 46754
   Anesthesia 15850-15851
Thrombus
   See Thrombectomy
Tissue Expanders
   Skin 11971
Transplant
   Intestines 44137
   Kidney 50370
Tube
   Ear, Middle .69424
   Finger 26392, 26416
   Hand 26392, 26416
   Nephrostomy 50389
Tumor
   Temporal Bone 69970
Ureter
   Ligature 50940
Urethral Stent
   Bladder 52310-52315
   Urethra 52310-52315
Uterus
   Laparoscopy 58541, 58543, 58548
Vein
   Clusters 37785
   Perforation 37760-37761
   Saphenous 37718-37735, 37780
   Varicose 37765-37766
Venous Access Device 36590
   Obstruction 75901-75902
Ventilating Tube
   Ear, Middle .69424
Ventricular Assist Device 33977-33978
   Extracorporeal 0050T
   Intracorporeal 33980
Vitreous
   Anterior Approach 67005-67010
Wire
   Anal 46754

Renal Abscess
See Abscess, Kidney

Renal Arteries
See Artery, Renal

Renal Autotransplantation
See Autotransplantation, Renal

Renal Calculus
See Calculus, Removal, Kidney

Renal Cyst
See Cyst, Kidney

Renal Dialyses
See Hemodialysis

Renal Disease Services
See Dialysis

Renal Transplantation
See Kidney, Transplantation

Renin 80408, 80416, 84244
Peripheral Vein 80417

Renin-Converting Enzyme 82164

Reoperation
Carotid
   Thromboendarterectomy 35390
Coronary Artery Bypass
   Valve Procedure 33530
Distal Vessel Bypass 35700

Repair
See Revision
Abdomen 49900
   Hernia 49491-49525, 49565,
               49570, 49582-49590
   Omphalocele 49600-49611
   Suture 49900
Abdominal Wall 15830, 15847
Anal
   Anomaly 46744-46748
   Fistula 46288, 46706, 46715-46716
   Stricture 46700-46705
Aneurysm
   Aorta
      Abdominal 0078T-0081T
      Infrarenal 34800-34805, 34825-34832
        Imaging 75952-75953
      Thoracic 33877-33886
   Iliac Artery .75954
   Intracranial Artery 61697-61708
Ankle
   Ligament 27695-27698
   Tendon 27612, 27650-27654, 27680-27687
Anorectum
   Fistula 46707
Aorta 33320-33322, 33802-33803
   Coarctation 33840-33851
   Graft 33860-33877
   Sinus of Valsalva 33702-33720
   Thoracic 75956-75959
      Endovascular 33880-33891
Aortic Arch
  with Cardiopulmonary Bypass 33853
  without Cardiopulmonary Bypass 33852
Aortic Valve 33400-33403
   Obstruction
      Outflow Tract 33414
      Septic Hypertrophy 33416
      Stenosis .33415
Arm
   Lower 25260-25263, 25270
      Fasciotomy 24495
      Secondary 25265, 25272-25274
      Tendon 25290
      Tendon Sheath 25275
   Muscle 24341
   Tendon 24332, 24341, 25280, 25295,
                  25310-25316
   Upper
      Muscle Revision 24330-24331
      Muscle Transfer 24301, 24320
      Tendon Lengthening 24305
      Tendon Revision 24320
      Tendon Transfer 24301
      Tenotomy 24310
Arteriovenous Fistula
   Abdomen 35182
      Acquired or Traumatic 35189
   Head 35180
      Acquired or Traumatic 35188

Lower Extremity 35184
   Acquired or Traumatic 35190
Neck 35180
   Acquired or Traumatic 35188
Thorax 35182
   Acquired or Traumatic 35189
Upper Extremity 35184
   Acquired or Traumatic 35190
Arteriovenous Malformation
   Intracranial 61680-61692
   Intracranial Artery 61705-61708
   Spinal Artery 62294
   Spinal Cord 63250-63252
Artery
   Angioplasty 75962-75968
   Aorta 35452, 35472
   Axillary 35458
   Brachiocephalic 35458, 35475
   Bypass Graft 35501-35571, 35601-35683,
                35691-35695, 35700
   Bypass In-Situ 35583-35587
   Bypass Venous Graft 33510-33516,
                  35510-35525
   Coronary 33507
   Femoral 35456, 35474
   Iliac 34900, 35454, 35473
   Occlusive Disease 35001, 35005-35021, 35045-
        35081, 35091, 35102, 35111,
        35121, 35131, 35141, 35151
   Popliteal 35456, 35474
   Pulmonary .33690
   Renal 35450
   Renal or Visceral 35471
   Subclavian .35458
   Thromboendarterectomy 35301-35321,
                  35341-35390
   Tibioperoneal 35459, 35470
   Viscera 35450, 35471
Arytenoid Cartilage 31400
Atria
   Laparoscopic 33265-33266
   Open 33254-33256
Bile Duct 47701
   with Intestines 47760, 47780-47785
   Wound 47900
Bladder
   Exstrophy .51940
   Fistula 44660-44661, 45800-45805,
                  51880-51925
   Neck 51845
   Resection .52500
   Wound 51860-51865
Blepharoptosis
   Frontalis Muscle Technique with
      Fascial Sling 67902
Blood Vessel
   Abdomen 35221
      with Other Graft 35281
      with Vein Graft 35251
   Chest 35211-35216
      with Other Graft 35271-35276
      with Vein Graft 35241-35246
   Finger 35207
   Graft Defect 35870
   Hand 35207
   Kidney 50100
   Lower Extremity 35226
      with Other Graft 35286
      with Vein Graft 35256
   Neck 35201
      with Other Graft 35261
      with Vein Graft 35231

Electrode
　　Stomach 0156T, 0158T
External Fixation System 20693
Eye
　　Aqueous Shunt 66185
Gastric Restrictive Procedure
　　Other than Adjustable Gastric Restrictive
　　Device 43848
Gastrostomy Tube 44373
Hip Replacement
　　See Replacement, Hip, Revision
Hymenal Ring 56700
Ileostomy
　　See Ileostomy, Revision
Infusion Pump
　　Intraarterial 36261
　　Intravenous 36576-36578, 36582-36583
Iris
　　Iridoplasty 66762
　　Iridotomy 66761
Jejunostomy Tube 44373
Lower Extremity Arterial Bypass 35879-35881
Pacemaker Site
　　Chest 33222
Rhytidectomy 15824-15829
Semicircular Canal
　　Fenestration 69840
Shunt
　　Intrahepatic Portosystemic 37183
Sling 53442
Stapedectomy
　　See Stapedectomy, Revision
Stomach
　　for Obesity 43848
Subcutaneous Port
　　for Gastric Restrictive Procedure 43886
Tracheostomy
　　Scar 31830
Urinary-Cutaneous Anastomosis 50727-50728
Vagina
　　Prosthetic Graft 57295-57296, 57426
　　Sling
　　　　Stress Incontinence 57287
Venous Access Device 36576-36578,
　　　　　　　　　　　　　　36582, 36583, 36585
Ventricle
　　Ventriculomyectomy 33416
　　Ventriculomyotomy 33416

Rh (D)
See Blood Typing

Rh Immune Globulin
See Immune Globulins, Rho (D)

Rheumatoid Factor 86430-86431

Rhinectomy
Partial 30150
Total 30160

Rhinomanometry 92512

Rhinopharynx
See Nasopharynx

Rhinophototherapy 0168T

Rhinophyma
Repair 30120

Rhinoplasty
Cleft Lip/Cleft Palate 30460-30462

Primary 30400-30420
Secondary 30430-30450

Rhinoscopy
See Endoscopy, Nose

Rhinotomy
Lateral 30118, 30320

Rhizotomy 63185-63190

Rho Variant Du 86905

Rhytidectomy 15824-15829

Rhytidoplasties
See Face Lift

Rib
Antibody 86756
Antigen Detection
　　by Immunoassay
　　　　with Direct Optical Observation
　　Direct Fluorescense 87280
　　Enzyme Immunoassay 87420
Excision 21600-21616, 32900
Fracture
　　Closed Treatment 21800
　　External Fixation 21810
　　Open Treatment 21805
Graft
　　to Face 21230
Resection 19260-19272, 32900
X-ray 71100-71111

Riboflavin 84252

Richardson Operation Hysterectomy
See Hysterectomy, Abdominal, Total

Richardson Procedure 53460

Rickettsia
Antibody 86757

Ridell Operation
See Sinusotomy, Frontal

Ridge, Alveolar
See Alveolar Ridge

Right Atrioventricular Valve
See Tricuspid Valve

Right Heart Cardiac Catheterization
See Cardiac Catheterization, Right Heart

Ripstein Operation
See Proctopexy

Risk Factor Reduction Intervention
See Performance Measures, Preventive Medicine

Risser Jacket 29010-29015
Removal 29710

Rocky Mountain Spotted Fever 86000

Roentgen Rays
See X-ray

Roentgenographic
See X-ray

Roentgenography
See Radiology, Diagnostic

Ropes Test 83872

Rorschach Test 96101

**Ross Information Processing
Assessment** 96125

Ross Procedure 33413

Rotation Flap
See Skin, Adjacent Tissue Transfer

Rotator Cuff
Repair 23410-23420

Rotavirus
Antibody 86759
Antigen Detection
　　Enzyme Immunoassay 87425

Rotavirus Vaccine
3 Dose 90680
2 Dose 90681

Round Window
Repair Fistula 69667

Round Window Fistula
See Fistula, Round Window

Roux-En-Y Procedure 43621,
　　　　　　　43633-43634, 43644, 43846,
　　　　　　47740-47741, 47780-47785, 48540

RPR 86592-86593

RSV
See Immune Globulins; Respiratory Syncytial Virus

RT3
See Triiodothyronine, Reverse

Rubbing Alcohol
See Isopropyl Alcohol

Rubella
Antibody 86762
Vaccine 90706-90710

Rubella HI Test
See Hemagglutination Inhibition Test

Rubella/Mumps
See Vaccines

Rubeola
Antibody 86765
Antigen Detection
　　Immunofluorescence 87283

Rubeolla
See Rubeola

**Russell Viper Venom
Time** 85612-85613

S

Sac, Endolymphatic
See Endolymphatic Sac

Saccomanno Technique 88108

Schlatter Operation Total Gastrectomy
See Excision, Stomach, Total

Schlicter Test 87197
See Bactericidal Titer, Serum

Schocket Procedure 66180
See Aqueous Shunt

Schuchard Procedure
Osteotomy
    Maxilla 21206

Schwannoma, Acoustic
See Brain, Tumor, Excision

Sciatic Nerve
Decompression 64712
Injection
    Anesthetic 64445-64446
Lesion
    Excision 64786
Neuroma
    Excision 64786
Neuroplasty 64712
Release 64712
Repair/Suture 64858

Scintigraphy
See Nuclear Medicine
Computed Tomographic
    See Emission Computerized Tomography

Scissoring
Skin Tags 11200-11201

Sclera
Excision
    Sclerectomy with Punch or Scissors 66160
Fistulization
    for Glaucoma 0123T
    Iridencleisis or Iridotasis 66165
    Sclerectomy with Punch or Scissors with
    Iridectomy 66160
    Thermocauterization with Iridectomy ...66155
    Trabeculectomy ab Externo in Absence of
    Previous Surgery 66170
    Trephination with Iridectomy 66150
Incision
    Fistulization
        Iridencleisis or Iridotasis 66165
        Sclerectomy with Punch or Scissors
        with Iridectomy 66160
        Thermocauterization with
        Iridectomy 66155
        Trabeculectomy ab Externo in Absence
        of Previous Surgery 66170
        Trephination with Iridectomy 66150
Lesion
    Excision 66130
Repair
    Reinforcement
        with Graft 67255
        without Graft 67250
    Staphyloma
        with Graft 66225
        without Graft 66220
    with Glue 65286
    Wound
        Operative 66250
        Tissue Glue 65286

Scleral Buckling Operation
See Retina, Repair, Detachment

Scleral Ectasia
See Staphyloma, Sclera

Sclerectomy 66160

Sclerotherapy
Venous 36468-36471

Sclerotomy
See Incision, Sclera

Screening, Drug
See Drug Screen
Alcohol and/or Substance Abuse 99408-99409

Scribner Cannulization 36810

Scrotal Varices
See Varicocele

Scrotoplasty 55175-55180

Scrotum
Abscess
    Incision and Drainage 54700, 55100
Excision 55150
Exploration 55110
Hematoma
    Incision and Drainage 54700
Removal
    Foreign Body 55120
Repair 55175-55180
Ultrasound 76870
Unlisted Services and Procedures 55899

Scrub Typhus 86000

Second Look Surgery
See Reoperation

Section
See Decompression
Cesarean
    See Cesarean Delivery
Cranial Nerve 61460
    Spinal Access 63191
Dentate Ligament 63180-63182
Gasserian Ganglion
    Sensory Root 61450
Medullary Tract 61470
Mesencephalic Tract 61480
Nerve Root 63185-63190
Spinal Accessory Nerve 63191
Spinal Cord Tract 63194-63199
Tentorium Cerebelli 61440
Vestibular Nerve
    Transcranial Approach 69950
    Translabyrinthine Approach 69915

Sedation
Moderate 99143-99150
    with Independent Observation ...99143-99145

Seddon-Brookes Procedure 24320

Sedimentation Rate
Blood Cell
    Automated 85652
    Manual 85651

Segmentectomy
Breast 19301-19302
Lung 32484

Seidlitz Powder Test
See X-ray, with Contrast

Selective Cellular Enhancement Technique 88112

Selenium 84255

Self Care
See Physical Medicine/Therapy/Occupational Therapy
Training 97535, 98960-98962, 99509

Sella Turcica
CT Scan 70480-70482
X-ray 70240

Semen
See Sperm

Semen Analysis 89300-89322
Sperm Analysis 89331
    Antibodies 89325
with Sperm Isolation 89260-89261

Semenogelase
See Antigen, Prostate Specific

Semicircular Canal
Incision
    Fenestration 69820
    Revised 69840

Semilunar
Bone
    See Lunate
Ganglion
    See Gasserian Ganglion

Seminal Vesicle
Cyst
    Excision 55680
Excision 55650
Incision 55600-55605
Mullerian Duct
    Excision 55680
Unlisted Services and Procedures 55899

Seminal Vesicles
Vesiculography 74440
X-ray with Contrast 74440

Seminin
See Antigen, Prostate Specific

Semiquantitative 81005

Sengstaken Tamponade
Esophagus 43460

Senning Procedure 33774-33777
See Repair, Great Arteries; Revision

Senning Type 33774-33777

Sensitivity Study
Antibiotic
    Agar 87181
    Disc 87184
    Enzyme Detection 87185
    Macrobroth 87188
    MIC 87186
    Microtiter 87186
    MLC 87187
    Mycobacteria 87190

Shoulder Joint
See Clavicle; Scapula
Arthroplasty
    with Implant 23470-23472
Arthrotomy
    with Biopsy 23100-23101
    with Synovectomy 23105-23106
Dislocation
    Open Treatment 23660
    with Greater Tuberosity Fracture
       Closed Treatment 23665
       Open Treatment 23670
    with Surgical or Anatomical Neck Fracture
       Closed Treatment with
       Manipulation 23675
       Open Treatment 23680
Excision
    Torn Cartilage 23101
Exploration 23040-23044
Incision and Drainage 23040-23044
Removal
    Foreign Body 23040-23044
X-ray 73050

Shunt(s)
Aqueous
    to Extraocular Reservoir 66180
    Revision 66185
Arteriovenous
    See Arteriovenous Shunt
Brain
    Creation 62180-62223
    Removal 62256-62258
    Replacement 62160, 62194,
               62225-62230, 62258
    Reprogramming 62252
Cerebrospinal Fluid
    See Cerebrospinal Fluid Shunt
Creation
    Arteriovenous
       Direct 36821
       ECMO 36822
       Thomas Shunt 36835
       Transposition 36818-36820
       with Bypass Graft 35686
       with Graft 36825-36830
    Cerebrospinal Fluid 62200
    Thomas Shunt 36835
Fetal 59076
Great Vessel
    Aorta
       Pulmonary 33924
    Aorta to Pulmonary Artery
       Ascending 33755
       Descending 33762
    Central 33764
    Subclavian Pulmonary Artery 33750
    Vena Cava to Pulmonary Artery ...33766-33768
Intra-Atrial 33735-33737
LeVeen
    See LeVeen Shunt
Nonvascular
    X-ray 75809
Peritoneal
    Venous
       Injection 49427
       Ligation 49428
       Removal 49429
       X-ray 75809
Pulmonary Artery
    See Pulmonary Artery, Shunt

Revision
    Arteriovenous 36832
Spinal Cord
    Creation 63740-63741
    Irrigation 63744
    Removal 63746
    Replacement 63744
Superior Mesenteric-Caval
    See Anastomosis, Caval to Mesenteric
Ureter to Colon 50815
Ventriculocisternal with Valve
    See Ventriculocisternostomy

Shuntogram 75809

Sialic Acid 84275

Sialodochoplasty 42500-42505

Sialogram
See Sialography

Sialography 70390

Sickling
Electrophoresis 83020

Siderocytes 85536

Siderophilin
See Transferrin

Sigmoid
See Colon-Sigmoid

Sigmoid Bladder
Cystectomy 51590

Sigmoidoscopy
Ablation
    Polyp 45339
    Tumor 45339
Biopsy 45331
Collection
    Specimen 45331
Exploration 45330, 45335
Hemorrhage Control 45334
Injection
    Submucosal 45335
Needle Biopsy 45342
Placement
    Stent 45345
Removal
    Foreign Body 45332
    Polyp 45333, 45338
    Tumor 45333, 45338
Repair
    Volvulus 45337
Ultrasound 45341-45342

**Signal-Averaged
Electrocardiography**
See Electrocardiogram

Silica 84285

Silicon Dioxide
See Silica

Silicone
Contouring Injections 11950-11954

Silver Operation
See Keller Procedure

Silver Procedure 28290

Simple Mastectomies
See Mastectomy

Single Photon Absorptiometry
See Absorptiometry, Single Photon

**Single Photon Emission Computed
Tomography**
See SPECT

Sinu, Sphenoid
See Sinus/Sinuses, Sphenoid

Sinus/Sinuses
Ethmoid
    Excision 31200-31205
       with Nasal/Sinus Endoscopy ...31254-31255
    Repair of Cerebrospinal Leak 31290
Ethmoidectomy
    Excision 31254
Frontal
    Destruction 31080-31085
    Exploration 31070-31075
       with Nasal/Sinus Endoscopy 31276
    Fracture
       Open Treatment 21343-21344
    Incision 31070-31087
Injection 20500
    Diagnostic 20501
Maxillary
    Antrostomy 31256-31267
    Excision 31225-31230
    Exploration 31020-31032
       with Nasal/Sinus Endoscopy 31233
    Incision 31020-31032, 31256-31267
    Irrigation 31000
    Skull Base 61581
    Surgery 61581
Multiple
    Incision 31090
Paranasal
    Incision 31090
Pilonidal
    See Cyst, Pilonidal
Sinus of Valsalva
    Repair 33702-33722
Sinus Venosus
    Repair 33645
Sphenoid
    Biopsy 31050-31051
    Exploration 31050-31051
       with Nasal/Sinus Endoscopy 31235
    Incision 31050-31051
       with Nasal/Sinus Endoscopy ..31287-31288
    Irrigation 31002
    Repair of Cerebrospinal Leak 31291
    Sinusotomy 31050-31051
    Skull Base Surgery 61580-61581
Unlisted Services and Procedures 31299
X-ray 70210-70220

Sinusectomy, Ethmoid
See Sinus/Sinuses; Ethmoidectomy

Sinusoidal Rotational Testing
See Ear, Nose, and Throat

Sinusoscopy
Sinus
    Maxillary 31233
    Sphenoid 31235

Spinal Instrumentation

Anterior 22845-22847
    Removal 22855
Internal Fixation 22841
Pelvic Fixation 22848
Posterior Nonsegmental 22840
    Harrington Rod Technique
    Removal 22850
Posterior Segmental 22842-22844
    Removal 22852
Prosthetic Device 22851
Reinsertion of Spinal Fixation Device 22849

Spinal Manipulation

See Manipulation, Chiropractic

Spinal Nerve

Avulsion 64772
Transection 64772

Spinal Tap

See Cervical Puncture; Cisternal Puncture;
Subdural Tap; Ventricular Puncture
Drainage Fluid 62272
Lumbar 62270

Spine

See Intervertebral Disc; Spinal Cord; Vertebra;
Vertebral Body; Vertebral Process
Allograft
    Morselized 20930
    Structural 20931
Arthroplasty
    Lumbar 22856-22865
Aspiration 62267
Augmentation
    Lumbar Vertebra 22524-22525
    Thoracic Vertebra 22523, 22525
Autograft
    Local 20936
    Morselized 20937
    Structural 20938
Biopsy 20250-20251
CT Scan
    Cervical 72125-72127
    Lumbar 72131-72133
    Thoracic 72128-72130
Decompression 62287
Fixation 22842
Foraminotomy 0202T
Fusion
    Anterior 22808-22812
    Anterior Approach 22548-22585, 22812
    Exploration 22830
    Lateral Extracavitary 22532-22534
    Posterior Approach 22590-22802
Incision and Drainage
    Abscess 22010-22015
Insertion
    Instrumentation 22840-22848, 22851
Kyphectomy 22818-22819
Magnetic Resonance Angiography 72159
Magnetic Resonance Imaging
    Cervical 72141-72142, 72156-72158
    Lumbar 72148-72158
    Thoracic 72146-72147, 72156-72158
Manipulation
    with Anesthesia 22505
Myelography
    Cervical 72240
    Lumbosacral 72265
    Thoracic 72255
    Total 72270

Radiosurgery
    Stereotactic 63620-63621
Reconstruction
    Dorsal Spine Elements 63295
Reinsertion
    Instrumentation 22849
Removal
    Instrumentation 22850, 22852-22855
Repair, Osteotomy
    Anterior 22220-22226
    Posterior 22210-22214
      Cervical Laminoplasty 63050-63051
      Posterolateral 22216
Ultrasound 76800
Unlisted Services and Procedures,
Surgery 22899
X-ray 72020, 72090
    Absorptiometry 77080-77082
    Cervical 72040-72052
    Lumbosacral 72100-72120
    Standing 72069
    Thoracic 72070-72074
    Thoracolumbar 72080
    Total 72010
    with Contrast
      Cervical 72240
      Lumbosacral 72265
      Thoracic 72255
      Total 72270

Spine Chemotherapy

Administration 96450
    See Chemotherapy

Spirometry 94010-94070

See Pulmonology, Diagnostic
Patient Initiated 94014-94016

Splanchnicectomy

See Nerves, Sympathectomy, Excision

Spleen

Excision 38100-38102
    Laparoscopic 38120
Injection
    Radiologic 38200
Nuclear Medicine
    Imaging 78185, 78215-78216
Repair 38115

Splenectomy

Laparoscopic 38120
Partial 38101
Partial with Repair, Ruptured Spleen 38115
Total 38100
    En bloc 38102

Splenoplasty

See Repair, Spleen

Splenoportography 75810

Injection Procedures 38200

Splenorrhaphy 38115

Splint

See Casting; Strapping
Arm
    Long 29105
    Short 29125-29126
Finger 29130-29131
Foot 29590

Leg
    Long 29505
    Short 29515
Oral Surgical 21085
Ureteral
    See Ureteral Splinting

Split Grafts 15100-15101, 15120-15121

Split Renal Function Test

See Cystourethroscopy, Catheterization, Ureteral

Splitting

Blood Products 86985

Spontaneous Abortion

See Abortion

Sprengel's Deformity 23400

Spring Water Cyst

See Cyst, Pericardial

Spur, Bone

See Exostosis
Calcaneal
    See Heel Spur

Sputum Analysis 89220

SRIH

See Somatostatin

Ssabanejew-Frank Operation

See Incision, Stomach, Creation, Stoma; Incision
and Drainage

Stabilizing Factor, Fibrin

See Fibrin Stabilizing Factor

Stable Factor 85230

Stallard Procedure

See Conjunctivorhinostomy

Stamey Procedure 51845

See Repair, Bladder, Neck

Standby Services

Physician 99360

Stanford-Binet Test

See Psychiatric Diagnosis

Stanftan

See Binet Test

Stapedectomy

Revision 69662
with Footplate Drill Out 69661
without Foreign Material 69660

Stapedotomy

Revision 69662
with Footplate Drill Out 69661
without Foreign Material 69660

Stapes

Excision
    with Footplate Drill Out 69661
    without Foreign Material 69660
Mobilization
    See Mobilization, Stapes
Release 69650
Revision 69662

Staphyloma
Sclera
  Repair
    with Graft 66225
    without Graft 66220

Starch Granules
Feces 89225

Statin Therapy
See Performance Measures

Statistics/Biometry
See Biometry

Steindler Stripping 28250

Stellate Ganglion
Injection
  Anesthetic 64510

Stem Cell
Cell Concentration 38215
Count 86367
Cryopreservation 38207, 88240
Donor Search 38204
Harvesting 38205-38206
Limbal
  Allograft 65781
Plasma Depletion 38214
Platelet Depletion 38213
Red Blood Cell Depletion 38212
T-Cell Depletion 38210
Thawing 38208-38209, 88241
Transplantation 38240-38242
Tumor Cell Depletion 38211
Washing 38209

Stem, Brain
See Brainstem

Stenger Test 92565, 92577
See Audiologic Function Test; Ear, Nose, and Throat

Stenosis
Aortic
  See Aortic Stenosis
Bronchi 31641, 96570-96571
  Reconstruction 31775
Excision
  Trachea 31780-31781
Laryngoplasty 31582
Reconstruction
  Auditory Canal, External 69310
Repair
  Trachea 31780-31781
Tracheal
  See Trachea Stenosis
Urethral
  See Urethral Stenosis

Stensen Duct
See Parotid Duct

Stent
Indwelling
  Insertion
    Ureter 50605, 52282, 53855
Placement
  Bronchoscopy 31631, 31636-31637
  Colonoscopy 45387
    via Stoma 44397

Endoscopy
  Gastrointestinal, Upper 43256
Enteroscopy 44370
Proctosigmoidoscopy 45327
Sigmoidoscopy 45345
Transcatheter
  Intravascular ...37205-37208, 37215-37216
    Extracranial 0075T-0076T
Ureteroneocystomy 50947-50948
Removal
  Ureteral 50382-50387
Replacement
  Ureteral 50382, 50387
Revision
  Bronchoscopy 31638
Transcatheter
  Intravascular
    Intracranial 61635
Urethra 52282

Stent, Intravascular
See Transcatheter, Placement, Intravascular Stents

Stents, Tracheal
See Tracheal Stent

Stereotactic Frame
Application/Removal 20660

Stereotaxis
Aspiration
  Brain Lesion 61750
    with CT Scan and/or MRI 61751
  Spinal Cord 63615
Biopsy
  Aspiration
    Brain Lesion 61750
  Brain 61750
    with CT Scan and/or MRI 61751
  Breast 77031
  Prostate 55706
  Spinal Cord 63615
Catheter Placement
  Brain
    Infusion 0169T
    Radiation Source 61770
Computer Assisted
  Brain Surgery 61795
  Orthopedic Surgery 20985-20987
Creation Lesion
  Brain
    Deep 61720-61735
    Percutaneous 61790
    Gasserian Ganglion 61790
    Spinal Cord 63600
    Trigeminal Tract 61791
CT Scan
  Aspiration 61751
  Biopsy 61751
Excision Lesion
  Brain 61750
  Spinal Cord 63615
Focus Beam
  Radiosurgery 77371-77373
    Cranial 61796-61799
    Spinal 63620-63621
  Stereotactic Frame Application 20660, 61800
Radiation Therapy 77421, 77432-77435
Stimulation
  Spinal Cord 63610
Target Volume Guidance 77421

Sterile Coverings
See Dressings

Sternal Fracture
See Fracture, Sternum

Sternoclavicular Joint
Arthrotomy 23044
  with Biopsy 23101
  with Synovectomy 23106
Dislocation
  Closed Treatment
    with Manipulation 23525
    without Manipulation 23520
  Open Treatment 23530-23532
    with Fascial Graft 23532

Sternocleidomastoid
Division 21720-21725

Sternotomy
Closure 21750

Sternum
Debridement 21627
Excision 21620, 21630-21632
Fracture
  Closed Treatment 21820
  Open Treatment 21825
Ostectomy 21620
Radical Resection 21630-21632
Reconstruction 21740-21742, 21750
  with Thoracoscopy 21743
X-ray 71120-71130

Steroid-Binding Protein, Sex
See Globulin, Sex Hormone Binding

Steroids
Anabolic
  See Androstenedione
Injection
  Foot Neuroma 64455, 64632
  Urethral Stricture 52283
Ketogenic
  Urine 83582

STH (Somatotropic Hormone)
See Growth Hormone

Stimulating Antibody, Thyroid
See Immunoglobulin, Thyroid Stimulating

Stimulation
Electric
  See ElectricalStimulation
Lymphocyte
  See Blastogenesis
Spinal Cord
  Stereotaxis 63610
Transcutaneous Electric
  See Application, Neurostimulation

Stimulator, Long-Acting Thyroid
See Thyrotropin Releasing Hormone (TRH)

Stimulators, Cardiac
See Heart, Pacemaker

Stimulus Evoked Response 51792

Stoffel Operation
See Rhizotomy

Stoma
Creation
- Bladder 51980
- Kidney 50551-50561
- Stomach
  - Neonatal 43831
  - Temporary 43830-43831
- Ureter 50860
Ureter
- Endoscopy via 50951-50961

Stomach
Anastomosis
- with Duodenum 43810, 43850-43855
- with Jejunum 43820-43825, 43860-43865
Biopsy 43600-43605
Creation
- Stoma
  - Temporary 43830-43831
  - Temporary Stoma
    - Laparoscopic 43653
Electrode
- Removal 0156T, 0158T, 43882
Electrogastrography 91132-91133
Excision
- Partial 43631-43635, 43845
- Total 43620-43622
Exploration 43500
Gastric Bypass 43644-43645, 43846
- Revision 43848
Gastric Restrictive Procedures 43770-43775, 43848, 43886-43888
Implantation
- Electrodes 0155T, 0157T, 43647, 43881
Incision 43830-43832
- Exploration 43500
- Pyloric Sphincter 43520
- Removal
  - Foreign Body 43500
Intubation with Specimen Prep 91055
Laparoscopy 0155T-0156T, 43647-43648
Nuclear Medicine
- Blood Loss Study 78278
- Emptying Study 78264
- Imaging 78261
- Protein Loss Study 78282
- Reflux Study 78262
- Vitamin B-12 Absorption 78270-78272
Reconstruction
- for Obesity 43644-43645, 43842-43847
- Roux-En-Y 43644, 43846
Removal
- Foreign Body 43500
Repair 48547
- Fistula 43880
- Fundoplasty 43324-43325
  - Laparoscopic 43280-43282
- Laceration 43501-43502
- Stoma 43870
- Ulcer 43501
Replacement
- Electrodes 0155T, 0157T, 43647, 43881
Specimen Collection 89130-89141
Stimulation of Secretion 91052
Suture
- Fistula 43880
- for Obesity 43842-43843
- Stoma 43870
- Ulcer 43840
- Wound 43840
Tumor
- Excision 43610-43611

Ulcer
- Excision 43610
Unlisted Services and Procedures ...43659, 43999

Stomatoplasty
See Mouth, Repair

Stone, Kidney
See Calculus, Removal, Kidney

Stookey-Scarff Procedure
See Ventriculocisternostomy

Stool Blood
See Blood, Feces

Storage
Embryo 89342
Oocyte 89346
Reproductive Tissue 89344
Sperm 89343

Strabismus
Chemodenervation 67345
Repair
- Adjustable Sutures 67335
- Extraocular Muscles 67340
- One Horizontal Muscle 67311
- One Vertical Muscle 67314
- Posterior Fixation Suture
  - Technique 67334, 67335
- Previous Surgery, Not Involving Extraocular
  - Muscles 67331
- Release Extensive Scar Tissue 67343
- Superior Oblique Muscle 67318
- Transposition 67320
- Two Horizontal Muscles 67312
- Two or More Vertical Muscles 67316

Strapping
See Cast; Splint
Ankle 29540
Chest 29200
Elbow 29260
Finger 29280
Foot 29540, 29590
Hand 29280
Hip 29520
Knee 29530
Leg, Lower
- Venous Wound Compression 29581
Shoulder 29240
Thorax 29200
Toes 29550
Unlisted Services and Procedures 29799
Unna Boot 29580
Wrist 29260

Strassman Procedure 58540

Strayer Procedure
Leg, Lower 27687

Streptococcus pneumoniae Vaccine
See Vaccines

Streptococcus, Group A
Antigen Detection
- Enzyme Immunoassay 87430
- Nucleic Acid 87650-87652
Direct Optical Observation 87880

Streptococcus, Group B
by Immunoassay
- with Direct Optical Observation 87802

Streptokinase, Antibody 86590

Stress Tests
Cardiovascular 93015-93024
Multiple Gated Acquisition
(MUGA) 78472-78473
Myocardial Perfusion Imaging 78451-78454
Pulmonary 94620-94621
- See Pulmonology, Diagnostic

Stricture
Repair
- Urethra 53400-53405
Urethra
- See Urethral Stenosis

Stricturoplasty
Intestines 44615

Stroboscopy
Larynx 31579

STS 86592-86593
See Syphilis Test

Stuart-Power Factor 85260

Study, Color Vision
See Color Vision Examination

Sturmdorf Procedure 57520

Styloid Process
Radial
- Excision 25230

Styloidectomy
Radial 25230

Stypven Time
See Russell Viper Venom Time

Subacromial Bursa
Arthrocentesis 20610

Subclavian Arteries
See Artery, Subclavian

Subcutaneous Infusion
See Infusion, Subcutaneous

Subcutaneous Injection
See Injection, Subcutaneous

Subcutaneous Mastectomies
See Mastectomy, Subcutaneous

Subcutaneous Tissue
Excision 15830-15839, 15847

Subdiaphragmatic Abscess
See Abscess, Subdiaphragmatic

Subdural Electrode
Insertion 61531-61533
Removal 61535

Subdural Hematonia
See Hematoma, Subdural

Subdural Puncture 61105-61108

Subdural Tap 61000-61001

Sublingual Gland
Abscess
- Incision and Drainage 42310-42320

Intestine
  Large
    Diverticula 44605
    Ulcer 44605
    Wound 44605
Intestines
  Large
    Diverticula 44604
    Ulcer 44604
    Wound 44604
  Small
    Diverticula 44602-44603
    Fistula 44640-44661
    Plication 44680
    Ulcer 44602-44603
    Wound 44602-44603
    Stoma 44620-44625
Iris
  with Ciliary Body 66682
Kidney
  Fistula 50520-50526
  Horseshoe 50540
  Wound 50500
Leg, Lower
  Tendon 27658-27665
Leg, Upper
  Muscle 27385-27386
Liver
  Wound 47350-47361
Mesentery 44850
Nerve 64831-64876
Pancreas 48545
Pharynx
  Wound 42900
Rectum
  Fistula 45800-45825
  Prolapse 45540-45541
Removal
  Anesthesia 15850-15851
Spleen
  See Splenorrhapy
Stomach
  Fistula 43880
  Laceration 43501-43502
  Stoma 43870
  Ulcer 43501, 43840
  Wound 43840
Tendon
  Foot 28200-28210
  Knee 27380-27381
Testis
  Injury 54670
  Suspension 54620-54640
Thoracic Duct
  Abdominal Approach 38382
  Cervical Approach 38380
  Thoracic Approach 38381
Throat
  Wound 42900
Tongue
  Base Suspension 41512
  to Lip 41510
Trachea
  Fistula
    with Plastic Repair 31825
    without Plastic Repair 31820
  Stoma
    with Plastic Repair 31825
    without Plastic Repair 31820
  Wound
    Cervical 31800
    Intrathoracic 31805

Ulcer 44604-44605
Ureter 50900
  Deligation 50940
  Fistula 50920-50930
Urethra
  Fistula 45820-45825, 53520
  Stoma 53520
  to Bladder 51840-51841
  Wound 53502-53515
Uterus
  Fistula 51920-51925
  Rupture 58520, 59350
  Suspension 58400-58410
Vagina
  Cystocele 57240, 57260
  Enterocele 57265
  Fistula
    Rectovaginal 57300-57307
    Transvesical and Vaginal Approach ...57330
    Urethrovaginal 57310-57311
    Vesicovaginal 51900, 57320-57330
  Rectocele 57250-57260
  Suspension 57280, 57283
  Wound 57200-57210
Vas Deferens 55400
Vein
  Femoral 37650
  Iliac 37660
  Vena Cava 37620
Wound 44604-44605

Swallowing
  Evaluation 92610-92613, 92616-92617
  Imaging 74230
  Treatment 92526

Swanson Procedure 28309

Sweat Collection
Iontophoresis 89230

Sweat Glands
Excision
  Axillary 11450-11451
  Inguinal 11462-11463
  Perianal 11470-11471
  Perineal 11470-11471
  Umbilical 11470-11471

Sweat Test 82435
See Chloride, Blood

Swenson Procedure 45120

Syme Procedure 27888

Sympathectomy
Artery
  Digital 64820
  Radial 64821
  Superficial Palmar Arch 64823
  Ulnar 64822
Cervical 64802
Cervicothoracic 64804
Digital Artery
  with Magnification 64820
Lumbar 64818
Presacral 58410
Thoracic 32664
Thoracolumbar 64809
with Rib Excision 21616

Sympathetic Nerve
Excision 64802-64818
Injection
  Anesthetic 64508, 64520-64530

Sympathins
See Catecholamines

Symphysiotomy
Horseshoe Kidney 50540

Symphysis, Pubic
See Pubic Symphysis

Syncytial Virus, Respiratory
See Respiratory Syncytial Virus

Syndactylism, Toes
See Webbed, Toe

Syndactyly
Repair 26560-26562

Syndesmotomy
See Ligament, Release

Syndrome
Adrenogenital
  See Adrenogenital Syndrome
Ataxia-Telangiectasia
  See Ataxia Telangiectasia
Bloom
  See Bloom Syndrome
Carpal Tunnel
  See Carpal Tunnel Syndrome
Costen's
  See Temporomandibular Joint (TMJ)
Erb -Goldflam
  See Myasthenia Gravis
Ovarian Vein
  See Ovarian Vein Syndrome
Synechiae, Intrauterine
  See Adhesions, Intrauterine
Treacher Collins
  See Treacher-Collins Syndrome
Urethral
  See Urethral Syndrome

Syngesterone
See Progesterone

Synostosis (Cranial)
See Craniosynostosis

Synovectomy
Arthrotomy with
  Glenohumeral Joint 23105
  Sternoclavicular Joint 23106
Elbow 24102
Excision
  Carpometacarpal Joint 26130
  Finger Joint 26135-26140
  Hip Joint 27054
  Interphalangeal Joint 26140
  Knee Joint 27334-27335
  Metacarpophalangeal Joint 26135
  Palm 26145
Wrist 25105, 25118-25119
  Radical 25115-25116

Synovial

Bursa
  See Bursa
Cyst
  See Ganglion
Membrane
  See Synovium
Popliteal Space
  See Baker's Cyst

Synovium

Biopsy
  Carpometacarpal Joint 26100
  Interphalangeal Joint 26110
  Knee Joint 27330
  Metacarpophalangeal Joint
    with Synovial Biopsy 26105
Excision
  Carpometacarpal Joint 26130
  Finger Joint 26135-26140
  Hip Joint 27054
  Interphalangeal Joint 26140
  Knee Joint 27334-27335

Syphilis ab

See Antibody, Treponema Pallidum

Syphilis Test 86592-86593

Syrinx

Spinal Cord
  Aspiration 62268

System

Endocrine
  See Endocrine System
Hemic
  See Hemic System
Lymphatic
  See Lymphatic System
Musculoskeletal
  See MusculoskeletalSystem
Nervous
  See Nervous System

T

T Cell Leukemia Virus I Antibodies, Adult

See Antibody, HTLV-I

T Cell Leukemia Virus I, Human

See HTLV I

T Cell Leukemia Virus II Antibodies, Human

See Antibody, HTLV-II

T Cell Leukemia Virus II, Human

See HTLV II

T-Cells

CD4
  Absolute 86361
Count 86359
Ratio 86360

T Lymphotropic Virus Type III Antibodies, Human

See Antibody, HIV

T-3

See Triiodothyronine

T3 Free

See Triiodothyronine, Free

T-4 ....84436-84439, 86360

T4 Molecule

See CD4

T4 Total

See Thyroxine, Total

T-7 Index

See Thyroxine, Total

T-8

See CD8; T-Cells, Ratio

T-Cell T8 Antigens

See CD8

T-Phyl

See Theophylline

Taarnhoj Procedure

See Decompression, Gasserian Ganglion, Sensory Root; Section

Tachycardia

Heart
  Recording 93609

Tacrolimus

Drug Assay 80197

Tag, Skin

See Skin, Tags

Tail Bone

Excision 27080
Fracture 27200-27202

Takeuchi Procedure 33505

Talectomy

See Astragalectomy

Talotarsal Joint

Dislocation 28570-28575, 28585
  Percutaneous Fixation 28576

Talus

Arthrodesis
  Pantalar 28705
  Subtalar 28725
  Triple 28715
Arthroscopy
  Surgical 29891-29892
    Subtalar 29904-29907
Autograft, Osteochondral 28446
Craterization 28120
Cyst
  Excision 28100-28103
Diaphysectomy 28120
Excision 28120, 28130
Fracture
  Open Treatment 28445
  Percutaneous Fixation 28436
  with Manipulation 28435-28436
  without Manipulation 28430

Repair

Osteochondritis Dissecans 29892
Osteotomy 28302
Saucerization 28120
Tumor
  Excision 28100-28103
  Radical Resection 27647

Tap

Cisternal
  See Cisternal Puncture
Lumbar Diagnostic
  See Spinal Tap

Tarsal

Fracture
  Percutaneous Fixation 28456

Tarsal Bone

See Ankle Bone

Tarsal Joint

See Foot
Arthrodesis 28730-28735, 28740
  with Advancement 28737
  with Lengthening 28737
Craterization 28122
Cyst
  Excision 28104-28107
Diaphysectomy 28122
Dislocation 28540-28545, 28555
  Percutaneous Fixation 28545-28546
Excision 28116, 28122
Fracture
  Open Treatment 28465
  with Manipulation 28455-28456
  without Manipulation 28450
Fusion 28730-28735, 28740
  with Advancement 28737
  with Lengthening 28737
Repair 28320
  Osteotomy 28304-28305
Saucerization 28122
Tumor
  Excision 28104-28107
  Radical Resection 28171

Tarsal Strip Procedure 67917-67924

Tarsal Tunnel Release 28035

Tarsal Wedge Procedure 67916, 67923

Tarsometatarsal Joint

Arthrodesis 28730-28735, 28740
Arthrotomy 28020, 28050
Dislocation 28600-28605, 28615
  Percutaneous Fixation 28606
Exploration 28020
Fusion 28730-28735, 28740
Removal
  Foreign Body 28020
  Loose Body 28020
Synovial
  Biopsy 28050
  Excision 28070

Tarsorrhaphy 67875

Median 67880
Severing 67710
  with Transposition of Tarsal Plate 67882

Tattoo
Cornea 65600
Skin 11920-11922

TB Test
Antigen Response 86480
Skin Test 86580

TBG
See Thyroxine Binding Globulin

TBS
See Bethesda System

TCT
See Thrombin Time

Td Shots
See Tetanus Immunization; Vaccines

Team Conference
Case Management Services 99366-99368

Tear Duct
See Lacrimal Duct

Tear Gland
See Lacrimal Gland

Technique
Pericardial Window
    See Pericardiostomy
Projective
    See Projective Test

Teeth
X-ray 70300-70320

Telangiectasia
Chromosome Analysis 88248
Injection 36468

Telangiectasia, Cerebello-Oculocutaneous
See Ataxia Telangiectasia

Telephone
Evaluation and Management
    Nonphysician 98966-98968
    Physician 99441-99443
Pacemaker Analysis 93293
Transmission of ECG 93012

Teletherapy
Dose Plan 77305-77321

Temperature Gradient Studies 93740

Temporal Arteries
See Artery, Temporal

Temporal Bone
Electromagnetic Bone Conduction Hearing Device
    Implantation/Replacement 69710
    Removal/Repair 69711
Excision 69535
Resection 69535
Tumor
    Removal 69970
Unlisted Services and Procedures 69979

Temporal, Petrous
Excision
    Apex 69530

Temporomandibular Joint (TMJ)
Arthrocentesis 20605
Arthrography 70328-70332
    Injection 21116
Arthroplasty 21240-21243
Arthroscopy
    Diagnostic 29800
    Surgical 29804
Arthrotomy 21010
Cartilage
    Excision 21060
Condylectomy 21050
Coronoidectomy 21070
Dislocation
    Closed Treatment 21480-21485
    Open Treatment 21490
Injection
    Radiologic 21116
Magnetic Resonance Imaging (MRI) 70336
Manipulation 21073
Meniscectomy 21060
Prostheses
    See Prosthesis, Temporomandibular Joint
Reconstruction
    See Reconstruction, Temporomandibular Joint
X-ray with Contrast 70328-70332

Tenago Procedure 53431

Tendinosuture
See Suture, Tendon

Tendon
Achilles
    See Achilles Tendon
Arm, Upper
    Revision 24320
Excision
    Finger 26180
    Forearm 25109
    Palm 26170
    Wrist 25109
Finger
    Excision 26180
Forearm
    Excision 25109
    Repair 25260-25274
Graft
    Harvesting 20924
Insertion
    Biceps Tendon 24342
Lengthening
    Ankle 27685-27686
    Arm, Upper 24305
    Elbow 24305
    Finger 26476, 26478
    Forearm 25280
    Hand 26476, 26478
    Leg, Lower 27685-27686
    Leg, Upper 27393-27395
    Toe 28240
    Wrist 25280
Palm
    Excision 26170
Release
    Arm, Lower 25295
    Arm, Upper 24332
    Wrist 25295
Shortening
    Ankle 27685-27686
    Finger 26477, 26479

Hand 26477, 26479
Leg, Lower 27685-27686
Transfer
    Arm, Lower 25310-25312, 25316
    Arm, Upper 24301
    Elbow 24301
    Finger 26497-26498
    Hand 26480-26489
    Leg, Lower 27690-27692
    Leg, Upper 27400
    Pelvis 27098
    Thumb 26490-26492, 26510
    Wrist 25310-25312, 25316
Transplant
    Leg, Upper 27396-27397
Wrist
    Excision 25109
    Repair 25260-25274

Tendon Origin
Insertion
    Injection 20551

Tendon Pulley Reconstruction of Hand
See Hand, Reconstruction, Tendon Pulley

Tendon Sheath
Arm
    Lower
        Repair 25275
Finger
    Incision 26055
    Incision and Drainage 26020
    Lesion 26160
Foot
    Excision 28086-28088
Hand Lesion 26160
Injection 20550
Palm
    Incision and Drainage 26020
Removal
    Foreign Body 20520-20525
Wrist
    Excision, Radical 25115-25116
    Incision 25000-25001
    Repair 25275

Tenectomy, Tendon Sheath
See Excision, Lesion, Tendon Sheath

Tennis Elbow
Tenotomy 24357-24359

Tenodesis
Biceps Tendon
    Arthroscopic 29828
    at Elbow 24340
    Shoulder 23430
Finger 26471-26474
Wrist 25300-25301

Tenolysis
Ankle 27680-27681
Arm, Lower 25295
Arm, Upper 24332
Finger
    Extensor 26445-26449
    Flexor 26440-26442
Foot 28220-28226
Hand Extensor 26445-26449
    Flexor 26440-26442
Leg, Lower 27680-27681
Wrist 25295

Therapeutic

Abortion
  See Abortion, Therapeutic
Apheresis
  See Apheresis, Therapeutic
Drug Assay
  See Drug Assay
Mobilization
  See Mobilization
Photopheresis
  See Photopheresis
Radiology
  See Radiology, Therapeutic

Therapies

Cold
  See Cryotherapy
Exercise
  See Exercise Therapy
Family
  See Psychotherapy, Family
Language
  See Language Therapy
Milieu
  See Environmental Intervention
Occupational
  See Occupational Therapy
Photodynamic
  See Photochemotherapy
Photoradiation
  See Actinotherapy
Physical
  See Physical Medicine/Therapy/Occupational
  Therapy
Speech
  See Speech Therapy
Tocolytic
  See Tocolysis
Ultraviolet
  See Actinotherapy

Therapy

ACE Inhibitor Therapy
  See Performance Measures
Beta Blocker Therapy
  See Performance Measures
Desensitization
  See Allergen Immunotherapy
Hemodialysis
  See Hemodialysis
Hot Pack
  See Hot Pack Treatment
Pharmacologic; for Cessation of Tobacco Use
  See Performance Measures
Radiation
  Brachytherapy 0182T
    See Irradiation
Speech
  See Speech Therapy
Statin Therapy, Prescribed
  See Performance Measures.

Thermocauterization

Ectropion
  Repair 67922
Lesion
  Cornea 65450

Thermocoagulation

See Electrocautery

Thermographies

See Thermogram

Thermography, Cerebral

See Thermogram, Cephalic

Thermotherapy

Prostate 53850-53852
  Microwave 53850
  Radiofrequency 53852

Thiamine 84425

Thiersch Operation 15050
See Pinch Graft

Thiersch Procedure 46753

Thigh

Fasciotomy 27025
  See Femur; Leg, Upper

Thin Layer Chromatographies
See Chromatography, Thin-Layer

Thiocyanate 84430

Third Disease
See Rubella

Thompson Procedure 27430

Thoracectomy
See Thoracoplasty

Thoracentesis 32421-32422

Thoracic

Anterior Ramus
  See Intercostal Nerve
Arteries
  See Artery, Thoracic
Cavity
  See Chest Cavity
Duct
  See Lymphatics
  Cannulation 38794
  Ligation 38380
    Abdominal Approach 38382
    Thoracic Approach 38381
  Suture
    Abdominal Approach 38382
    Cervical Approach 38380
    Thoracic Approach 38381
Empyema
  See Abscess, Thorax
Surgery
  Video-Assisted
    See Thoracoscopy
Vertebra
  See Vertebra, Thoracic
Wall
  See Chest Wall

Thoracocentesis
See Thoracentesis

Thoracoplasty 32905
with Closure Bronchopleural Fistula 32906

Thoracoscopy

Diagnostic 32601-32606
  with Biopsy 32602, 32604, 32606
  without Biopsy 32601, 32603, 32605
Surgical 32650-32665
  with Control Traumatic Hemorrhage 32654
  with Creation Pericardial Window 32659
  with Esophagomyotomy 32665

  with Excision Mediastinal Cyst, Tumor
    and/or Mass 32662
  with Excision Pericardial Cyst, Tumor
    and/or Mass 32661
  with Excision-Plication of Bullae 32655
  with Lobectomy 32663
  with Parietal Pleurectomy 32656
  with Partial Pulmonary Decortication ..32651
  with Pleurodesis 32650
  with Removal Intrapleural Foreign
    Body 32653
  with Removal of Clot/Foreign Body 32658
  with Sternum Reconstruction 21743
  with Thoracic Sympathectomy 32664
  with Total Pericardiectomy 32660
  with Total Pulmonary Decortication ...32652
  with Wedge Resection of Lung 32657

Thoracostomy

Empyema 32035-32036
Tube, with/without Water Seal 32551

Thoracotomy

Cardiac Massage 32160
for Post-Op Complications 32120
Hemorrhage 32110
Removal
  Bullae 32141
  Cyst 32140
  Defibrillator 33243
  Electrodes 33238
  Foreign Body
    Intrapleural 32150
    Intrapulmonary 32151
  Pacemaker 33236-33237
  with Biopsy 32095-32100
  with Excision-Plication of Bullae 32141
  with Lung Repair 32110
  with Open Intrapleural Pneumolysis ...32124
Transmyocardial Laser
Revascularization 33140, 33141

Thorax

See Chest; Chest Cavity; Mediastinum
Angiography 71275
Biopsy 21550
CT Scan 71250-71275
Incision
  Empyema 32035-32036
Incision and Drainage
  Abscess 21501-21502
  Deep 21510
  Hematoma 21501-21502
Strapping 29200
Tube Thoracostomy 32551
Tumor
  Excision 21552-21558
  Excision/Resection 21557-21558
Unlisted Services and Procedures, Surgery ...21899

Three Glass Test
See Urinalysis, Glass Test

Three-Day Measles
See Rubella

Throat

See Pharynx
Abscess
  Incision and Drainage 42700-42725
Biopsy 42800-42806
Hemorrhage 42960-42962
Reconstruction 42950

Removal
　Foreign Body 42809
Repair
　Pharyngoesophageal 42953
　Wound 42900
Suture
　Wound 42900
Unlisted Services and Procedures 42999

Thrombectomy
See Thromboendarterectomy
Aortoiliac Artery 34151-34201
Arteriovenous Fistula
　Graft 36870
Axillary Artery 34101
Axillary Vein 34490
Brachial Artery 34101
Bypass Graft
　Other than Hemodialysis Graft or
　Fistula .35875-35876
Carotid Artery 34001
Celiac Artery 34151
Dialysis Graft
　without Revision 36831
Femoral 34201
Femoropopliteal Vein 34421-34451
Iliac 34151-34201
Iliac Vein 34401-34451
Innominate Artery 34001-34101
Mesentery Artery 34151
Percutaneous
　Coronary Artery 92973
　Fluoroscopic Guidance 37184-37188
　Mechanical Arterial 37184-37186
　Mechanical Venous 37187-37188
Peroneal Artery .34203
Popliteal Artery .34203
Radial Artery 34111
Renal Artery 34151
Subclavian Artery 34001-34101
Subclavian Vein 34471-34490
Tibial Artery 34203
Ulnar Artery 34111
Vena Cava 34401-34451
Vena Caval 50230

Thrombin Inhibitor I
See Antithrombin III

Thrombin Time 85670-85675

Thrombocyte (Platelet)
See Blood, Platelet

Thrombocyte ab
See Antibody, Platelet

Thromboendarterectomy
See Thrombectomy
Aorta, Abdominal 35331
Aortoiliofemoral Artery 35363
Axillary Artery 35321
Brachial Artery 35321
Carotid Artery 35301, 35390
Celiac Artery 35341
Femoral Artery 35371-35372
Iliac Artery 35351, 35361-35363
Iliofemoral Artery 35355, 35363
Innominate Artery 35311
Mesenteric Artery 35341
Peroneal Artery 35305-35306
Popliteal Artery .35303
Renal Artery 35341

Subclavian Artery 35301, 35311
Superficial Femoral Artery 35302
Tibial Artery 35305-35306
Tibioperoneal Trunk Artery 35304
Vertebral Artery 35301

Thrombokinase 85260

Thrombolysin
See Plasmin

Thrombolysis
Catheter Exchange
　Intravascular 37209, 75900
Cerebral
　Intravenous Infusion 37195
Coronary Vessels 92975-92977
Cranial Vessels .37195

Thrombolysis Biopsy Intracranial
Arterial Perfusion 61624

Thrombolysis Intracranial 65205
See Ciliary Body; Cornea; Eye, Removal, Foreign
Body; Iris; Lens; Retina; Sclera; Vitreous

Thrombomodulin 85337

Thromboplastin
Inhibition 85705
Inhibition Test .85347
Partial Time 85730-85732

Thromboplastin Antecedent, Plasma
See Plasma Thromboplastin, Antecedent

Thromboplastinogen
See Clotting Factor

Thromboplastinogen B
See Christmas Factor

Thromboxane
Urine 84431

Thumb
See Phalanx
Amputation 26910-26952
Arthrodesis
　Carpometacarpal Joint 26841-26842
Dislocation
　with Fracture 26645-26650
　　Open Treatment 26665
Fracture
　with Dislocation 26645-26650
　　Open Treatment 26665
Fusion
　in Opposition 26820
Reconstruction
　from Finger .26550
　Opponensplasty 26490-26496
Repair
　Muscle 26508
　Muscle Transfer 26494
　Tendon Transfer 26510
Replantation 20824-20827
Sesamoidectomy 26185
Unlisted Services and Procedures 26989

Thymectomy 60520-60521
Sternal Split/Transthoracic
Approach 60521, 60522
Transcervical Approach 60520

Thymotaxin
See Beta-2-Microglobulin

Thymus Gland 60520
Excision 60520-60521

Thyramine
See Amphetamine

Thyrocalcitonin
See Calcitonin

Thyroglobulin 84432
Antibody 86800

Thyroglossal Duct
Cyst
　Excision 60280-60281

Thyroid Gland
Cyst
　Aspiration 60300
　Excision 60200
　Incision and Drainage 60000
　Injection 60300
Excision
　for Malignancy
　　Limited Neck Dissection 60252
　　Radical Neck Dissection 60254
　Partial 60210-60225
　Secondary .60260
　Total 60240, 60271
　　Cervical Approach 60271
　　Removal All Thyroid Tissue 60260
　　Sternal Split/Transthoracic
　　Approach 60270
　　Transcervical Approach 60520
Metastatic Cancer
　Nuclear Imaging 78015-78018
Needle Biopsy .60100
Nuclear Medicine
　Imaging 78010
　Imaging for Metastases 78015-78018
　Imaging with Flow 78011
　Imaging with Uptake 78006-78007
　Metastases Uptake 78020
　Uptake 78000-78003
Procalcitonin 84145
Tumor
　Excision 60200

**Thyroid Hormone Binding
Ratio** 84479

Thyroid Hormone Uptake 84479

**Thyroid Stimulating Hormone
(TSH)** 80418, 80438-80440, 84443

**Thyroid Stimulating Hormone
Receptor ab**
See Thyrotropin Releasing Hormone (TRH)

**Thyroid Stimulating Immune
Globulins** 84445

Thyroid Stimulator, Long Acting
See Thyrotropin Releasing Hormone (TRH)

Thyroid Suppression Test
See Nuclear Medicine, Thyroid, Uptake

Thyroidectomy
Partial .60210-60225
Secondary 60260

Total 60240, 60271
   Cervical Approach 60271
   for Malignancy
      Limited Neck Dissection 60252
      Radical Neck Dissection 60254
   Removal All Thyroid Tissue 60260
   Sternal Split/Transthoracic Approach ...60270

Thyrolingual Cyst
See Cyst, Thyroglossal Duct

Thyrotomy 31300

Thyrotropin Receptor Ab
See Thyrotropin Releasing Hormone (TRH)

Thyrotropin Releasing Hormone (TRH) 80438-80439

Thyroxine
Free 84439
Neonatal 84437
Total 84436
True 84436

Thyroxine Binding Globulin 84442

Tibia
See Ankle
Arthroscopy Surgical 29891-29892
Craterization 27360, 27640
Cyst
   Excision 27635-27638
Diaphysectomy 27360, 27640
Excision 27360, 27640
   Epiphyseal Bar 20150
Fracture
   Arthroscopic Treatment 29855-29856
      Plafond 29892
   Closed Treatment 27824-27825
   Distal 27824-27828
   Intercondylar 27538-27540
   Malleolus 27760-27766, 27808-27814
   Open Treatment 27535-27536,
                27758-27759, 27826-27828
   Plateau 29855-29856
      Closed Treatment 27530-27536
   Shaft 27752-27759
   with Manipulation 27825
   without Manipulation 27824
Incision 27607
Osteoplasty
   Lengthening 27715
Prophylactic Treatment 27745
Reconstruction 27418
   at Knee 27440-27443, 27446
Repair 27720-27725
   Epiphysis 27477-27485, 27730-27742
   Osteochondritis Dissecans
      Arthroscopy 29892
   Osteotomy 27455-27457, 27705,
                    27709-27712
   Pseudoarthrosis 27727
Saucerization 27360, 27640
Tumor
   Excision 27635-27638
   Radical Resection 27645
X-ray 73590

Tibial
Arteries
   See Artery, Tibial

Nerve
   Repair/Suture
      Posterior 64840

Tibiofibular Joint
Arthrodesis 27871
Dislocation 27830-27832
Disruption
   Open Treatment 27829
Fusion 27871

TIG
See Immune Globulins, Tetanus

Time
Bleeding
   See Bleeding Time
Prothrombin
   See Prothrombin Time
Reptilase
   See Thrombin Time

Tinnitus
Assessment 92625

Tissue
Crystal Identification 89060
Culture
   Chromosome Analysis 88230-88239
   Homogenization 87176
   Non-neoplastic Disorder 88230, 88237
   Skin Grafts 15100-15101, 15120-15121
      Harvesting 15040
   Solid Tumor 88239
   Toxin/Antitoxin 87230
   Virus 87252-87253
Dissection, Macroscopic 88387-88388
Examination, Macroscopic 88387-88388
Enzyme Activity 82657
Examination for Ectoparasites 87220
Examination for Fungi 87220
Expander
   Breast Reconstruction with 19357
   Insertion
      Skin 11960
   Removal
      Skin 11971
   Replacement
      Skin 11970
Grafts
   Harvesting 20926
Granulation
   See Granulation Tissue
Homogenization 87176
Hybridization In Situ 88365-88368
Mucosal
   See Mucosa
Preparation
   Drug Analysis 80103
   Macroscopic 88387-88388
Skin Harvest for Culture 15040
Soft
   Abscess 20000-20005
   Tumor
      See Tumor, Excision
      See Tumor, Radical Resection
Transfer
   Adjacent
      Eyelids 67961
      Skin 14000-14350
   Facial Muscles 15845

Finger Flap 14350
Toe Flap 14350
Typing
   Culture 87140-87158
   Human Leukocyte Antigen (HLA)
      Antibodies 86812-86817
      Crossmatch 86825-86826
   Lymphocyte Culture 86821-86822

Tissue Culture
from Skin Harvest 15040
Skin Grafts 15150-15157, 15340-15366

Tissue Factor
See Thromboplastin

TLC
See Chromatography, Thin-Layer
Screen 84375

TMJ
See Temporomandibular Joint (TMJ)
Manipulation, Therapeutic
   See Manipulation, Temporomandibular Joint
Prostheses
   See Prosthesis, Temporomandibular Joint

Tobacco
See Performance Measures

Tobramycin
Assay 80200

Tocolysis 59412

Tocopherol 84446

Toe
See Interphalangeal Joint, Toe;
Metatarsophalangeal Joint; Phalanx
Amputation 28810-28825
Capsulotomy 28270-28272
Fasciotomy 28008
Fracture
   See Fracture, Phalanges, Toe
Lesion
   Excision 28092
Reconstruction
   Angle Deformity 28313
   Extra Toes 28344
   Hammertoe 28285-28286
   Macrodactyly 28340-28341
   Syndactyly 28345
   Webbed Toe 28345
Repair
   Bunion 28290-28299
   Muscle 28240
   Tendon 28232-28234, 28240
   Webbed 28280
   Webbed Toe 28345
Tenotomy 28010-28011, 28232-28234
Unlisted Services and Procedures 28899

Toe Flap
Tissue Transfer 14350

Toes
Arthrocentesis 20600
Dislocation
   See Specific Joint
Magnetic Resonance Imaging
(MRI) 73721-73723
Reconstruction
   Extra Digit 26587

Wound
  Suture
    Cervical 31800
    Intrathoracic 31805

Tracheal
Stent
  Placement 31631
Tubes
  See Endotracheal Tube

Trachelectomy 57530
Radical 57531

Tracheloplasty
See Cervicoplasty

Trachelorrhaphy 57720

Tracheo-Esophageal Fistula
See Fistula, Tracheoesophageal

Tracheobronchoscopy
through Tracheostomy 31615

Tracheoplasty
Cervical 31750
Intrathoracic 31760
Tracheopharyngeal Fistulization 31755

Tracheostoma
Revision 31613-31614

Tracheostomy
Emergency 31603-31605
Planned 31600-31601
Revision
  Scar 31830
Surgical Closure
  with Plastic Repair 31825
  without Plastic Repair 31820
Tracheobronchoscopy through 31615
with Flaps 31610

Tracheotomy
Tube Change 31502

Tracking Tests (Ocular) 92545
See Ear, Nose, and Throat

Tract, Urinary
See Urinary Tract

Traction Therapy
See Physical Medicine/Therapy/Occupational
Therapy
Manual 97140
Mechanical 97012

Tractotomy
Medulla 61470
Mesencephalon 61480

Training
Activities of Daily Living 97535, 99509
Biofeedback 90901-90911
Cognitive Skills 97532
Community/Work Reintegration 97537
Home Management 97535, 99509
Orthoptic/Pleoptic 92065
Orthotics 97760
Prosthetics 97761
Self Care 97535, 98960-98962, 99509
Sensory Integration 97533
Walking (Physical Therapy) 97116
Wheelchair Management 97542

TRAM Flap
Breast Reconstruction 19367-19369

Trans-Scaphoperilunar
Fracture/Dislocation
  Closed Treatment 25680
  Open Treatment 25685

Transaminase
Glutamic Oxaloacetic 84450
Glutamic Pyruvic 84460

Transanal Endoscopic Microsurgery (TEMS)
See Bladder, Neck

Transcatheter
Biopsy 37200
Closure
  Percutaneous
    Heart 93580-93581
  Transmyocardial
    Heart 0166T, 0167T
Embolization
  Percutaneous 37204
    Cranial 61624-61626
Occlusion
  Percutaneous 37204
    Cranial 61624-61626
Placement
  Intravascular Stents 0075T-0076T,
                          37205-37208, 37215-37216
  Sensor, Aneurysmal Sac 34806
Therapy
  Embolization 75894
  Infusion 37201-37202, 75896-75898
  Perfusion
    Cranial 61624-61626
  Retrieval 75961

Transcatheter Foreign Body
Retrieval 37203

Transcortin 84449

Transcranial
Doppler Study (TCP) 93886-93893
Stimulation, Motor 95928-95929

Transcutaneous Testing
Bilirubin 88720
Carboxyhemoglobin 88740
Hemoglobin (Hgb) 88738
Methemoglobin 88741

Transcutaneous Electric Nerve Stimulation
See Application, Neurostimulation

Transdermal Electrostimulation
See Application, Neurostimulation

Transection
Artery
  Carotid 61610, 61612
Blood Vessel
  Kidney 50100
Brain
  Subpial 61567
Carotid
  with Skull Base Surgery 61609
Nerve 64732-64772
  Vagus 43640-43641
Pulmonary Artery 33922

Transesophageal
Doppler Echocardiography 93312-93318

Transfer
Blastocyst
  See Embryo Transfer
Gamete Intrafallopian
  See GIFT
Jejunum
  with Microvascular Anastomosis
    Free 43496
Preparation
  Embryo 89255
    Cryopreserved 89352
Surgical
  See Transposition
Tendon
  See Tendon, Transfer
Toe to Hand 26551-26556

Transferase
Aspartate Amino 84450
Glutamic Oxaloacetic 84450

Transferrin 84466

Transformation
Lymphocyte 86353

Transfusion
Blood 36430
  Exchange 36450-36455
  Fetal 36460
  Push
    Infant 36440
Blood Parts
  Exchange 36511-36516
Unlisted Services and Procedures 86999
White Blood Cells 86950

Transfusion of, Blood, Autologous
See Autotransfusion

Transluminal
Angioplasty
  Arterial 75962-75968
Atherectomies
  See Artery, Atherectomy
Coronary Balloon Dilatation
  See Percutaneous Transluminal Angioplasty

Transmyocardial Laser Revascularization 33140, 33141

Transosteal Bone Plate
Reconstruction
  Mandible 21244

Transpeptidase, Gamma-Glutamyl
See Gamma Glutamyl Transferase

Transplant
See Graft
Bone
  See Bone Graft
Hair
  See Hair, Transplant

Transplantation
See Graft
Allogenic
  See Homograft
Autologous
  See Autograft

Triolean Hydrolase
See Lipase

Trioxopurine
See Uric Acid

Tripcellim
See Trypsin

Trisegmentectomy 47122

Trocar Biopsy
Bone Marrow 38221

Trochanteric Femur Fracture
See Femur, Fracture, Trochanteric

Trophoblastic Tumor GTT
See Hydatidiform Mole

Troponin 84484
Qualitative 84512
Quantitative 84484

Truncal Vagotomies
See Vagotomy, Truncal

Truncus Arteriosus
Repair 33786

Truncus Brachiocephalicus
See Artery, Brachiocephalic

Trunk, Brachiocephalic
See Artery, Brachiocephalic

Trypanosomiases
See Trypanosomiasis

Trypanosomiasis 86171, 86280

Trypsin
Duodenum 84485
Feces 84488-84490

Trypsin Inhibitor, Alpha 1-Antitrypsin
See Alpha-1 Antitrypsin

Trypure
See Trypsin

Tsalicylate Intoxication
See Salicylate

TSH
See Thyroid Stimulating Hormone

TSI
See Thyroid Stimulating Immunoglobulin

Tsutsugamushi Disease
See Scrub Typhus

TT
See Thrombin Time

TT-3
See Triiodothyronine, True

TT-4
See Thyroxine, True

Tuba Auditoria (Auditiva)
See Eustachian Tube

Tubal Embryo Stage Transfer
See Embryo Transfer

Tubal Ligation 58600
Laparoscopic 58670
with Cesarean Delivery 58611

Tubal Occlusion
See Fallopian Tube, Occlusion; Occlusion
Create Lesion

Tubal Pregnancy 59121
with Salpingectomy and/or Oophorectomy ...59120

Tube Change
Colonic 49450
Duodenostomy 49451
Gastro-Jejunostomy 49452
Gastrostomy 43760, 49446
Jejunostomy 49451
Tracheostomy 31502

Tube Placement
Cecostomy Tube 44300, 49442
Duodenostomy Tube 49441
Endoscopic
    Bile Duct, Pancreatic Duct 43268
    Jejunostomy Tube
        Percutaneous 49441
    Nasobiliary, Nasopancreatic
        for Drainage 43267
Enterostomy Tube 44300
Gastrostomy Tube 43246, 49440
Nasogastric Tube 43752
Orogastric Tube 43752

Tube, Fallopian
See Fallopian Tube

Tubectomy
See Excision, Fallopian Tube

Tubed Pedicle Flap
Formation 15570-15576

Tubercle Bacilli
Culture 87116

Tubercleplasty
Tibia
    Anterior 27418

Tuberculin Test
See Skin, Tests, Tuberculosis

Tuberculosis
Antigen Response Test 86480
Culture 87116
Skin Test 86580

Tuberculosis Vaccine
(BCG) 90585-90586

Tubes
Colonic
    See Colon
Duodenostomy
    See Duodenostomy
Endotracheal
    See Endotracheal Tube
Gastrostomy
    See Gastrostomy Tube
Jejunostomy
    See Jejunostomy

Tudor 'Rabbit Ear'
See Urethra, Repair

Tuffier Vaginal Hysterectomy
See Hysterectomy, Vaginal

Tumor
See Craniopharyngioma
Abdomen
    Destruction/Excision 49203-49205
Abdominal Wall
    Excision 22900-22903
    Radical Resection 22904, 22905
Acetabulum
    Excision 27076
Ankle
    Excision 27618-27619, 27632-27634
    Radical Resection 27615-27616
Arm, Lower
    Excision 25071-25076
    Radical Resection 25077-25078
Arm, Upper
    Excision 24071-24076
    Radical Resection 24077, 24079
Back/Flank
    Excision 21930-21933
    Radical Resection 21935, 21936
Bile Duct
    Destruction 43272
    Extrahepatic 47711
    Intrahepatic 47712
Bladder 52234-52240
    Excision 51530, 52355
Bone
    Ablation 20982
Brain 61510
    Excision 61518, 61520-61521,
                      61526-61530, 61545, 62164
Breast
    Excision 19120-19126
Bronchi
    Excision 31640
Calcaneus
    Excision 28100-28103
    Radical Resection 27647
Carpal 25130-25136
Cheekbone 21030, 21034
Chest Wall
    Excision 19260-19272
Clavicle
    Excision 23140, 23200
    with Allograft 23146
    with Autograft 23145
Coccyx 49215
Colon
    Destruction 44393, 45383
Cranial Bone
    Reconstruction 21181-21184
Destruction
    Chemosurgery 17311-17315
    Urethra 53220
Ear, Middle
    Extended 69554
    Transcanal 69550
    Transmastoid 69552
Elbow
    Excision 24071-24076
    Radical Resection 24077, 24079
Esophagus
    Ablation 43228
Excision
    Femur 27355-27358
Face or Scalp
    Excision 21011-21014
    Radical Resection 21015, 21016

Tunica Vaginalis
Hydrocele
    Aspiration 55000
    Excision 55040-55041
    Repair 55060

Turbinate
Excision 30130-30140
Fracture
    Therapeutic 30930
Injection 30200
Submucous Resection
    Nose Excision 30140

Turbinate Mucosa
Cauterization 30801-30802

Turcica, Sella
See Sella Turcica

Turnbuckle Jacket 29020-29025
Removal 29715

TURP
See Prostatectomy, Transurethral

Tylectomy
See Breast, Excision, Lesion

Tylenol
Urine 82003

Tympanic Membrane
Create Stoma 69433-69436
Incision 69420-69421
Reconstruction 69620
Repair 69450, 69610

Tympanic Nerve
Excision 69676

Tympanolysis 69450

Tympanomastoidectomy
See Tympanoplasty

Tympanometry 92550, 92567, 92570
See Audiologic Function Tests

Tympanoplasty
See Myringoplasty
Radical or Complete 69645
    with Ossicular Chain Reconstruction ...69646
with Antrotomy or Mastoidotomy 69635
    with Ossicular Chain Reconstruction ...69636
        and Synthetic Prosthesis 69637
with Mastoidectomy 69641
    with Intact or Reconstructed Wall 69643
        and Ossicular Chain Reconstruction ...69644
    with Ossicular Chain Reconstruction ...69642
without Mastoidectomy 69631
    with Ossicular Chain Reconstruction ...69632
        and Synthetic Prosthesis 69633

Tympanostomy 69433-69436

Tympanotomy
See Myringotomy

Typhoid Vaccine 90690-90693
AKD 90693
H-P 90692
Oral 90690
Polysaccharide 90691

Typhus
Endemic
    See Murine Typhus
Mite-Borne
    See Scrub Typhus
Sao Paulo
    See Rocky Mountain Spotted Fever
Tropical
    See Scrub Typhus

Typing, Blood
See Blood Typing

Typing, HLA
See HLA Typing

Typing, Tissue
See Tissue, Typing

Tyrosine 84510

Tzank Smear 88160-88161

U

UDP Galactose Pyrophosphorylase
See Galactose-1-Phosphate, Uridyl Transferase

UFR
See Uroflowmetry

Ulcer
Anal
    See Anus, Fissure
Decubitus
    See Debridement; Pressure Ulcer (Decubitus);
    Skin Graft and Flap
Pinch Graft 15050
Pressure 15920-15999
Stomach
    Excision 43610

Ulcerative, Cystitis
See Cystitis, Interstitial

Ulna
See Arm, Lower; Elbow; Humerus; Radius
Arthrodesis
    Radioulnar Joint
        with Resection 25830
Arthroplasty
    with Implant 25442
Centralization or Wrist 25335
Craterization 24147, 25150-25151
Cyst
    Excision 24125-24126, 25120-25126
Diaphysectomy 24147, 25150-25151
Excision 24147
    Abscess 24138
    Complete 25240
    Epiphyseal Bar 20150
    Partial 25145-25151, 25240
Fracture
    Closed Treatment 25530-25535
    Olecranon 24670-24675
    Open Treatment 24685, 25545
    Shaft 25530-25545
        Open Treatment 25574

Styloid
    Closed Treatment 25650
    Open Treatment 25652
    Percutaneous Fixation 25651
with Dislocation
    Closed Treatment 24620
    Open Treatment 24635
with Manipulation 25535
with Radius 25560-25565
    Open Treatment 25575
without Manipulation 25530
Incision and Drainage 25035
Osteoplasty 25390-25393
Prophylactic Treatment 25491-25492
Reconstruction
    Radioulnar 25337
Repair
    Epiphyseal Arrest 25450-25455
    Malunion or Nonunion 25400, 25415
    Osteotomy 25360, 25370-25375
        and Radius 25365
    with Graft 25405, 25420-25426
Saucerization 24147, 25150-25151
Sequestrectomy 24138, 25145
Tumor
    Cyst 24120
    Excision ...24125-24126, 25120-25126, 25170

Ulnar Arteries
See Artery, Ulnar

Ulnar Nerve
Decompression 64718
Neuroplasty 64718-64719
Reconstruction 64718-64719
Release 64718-64719
Repair/Suture
    Motor 64836
Transposition 64718-64719

Ultrasonic
See Ultrasound

Ultrasonic Cardiography
See Echocardiography

Ultrasonic Procedure 52325

Ultrasonography
See Echography

Ultrasound
See Echocardiography; Echography
3-D Rendering 76376-76377
Abdomen 76700-76705
Arm 76880
Artery
    Intracranial 93886-93893
    Middle Cerebral 76821
    Umbilical 76820
Bladder 51798
Bone Density Study 76977
Breast 76645
Bronchi
    Endoscopy 31620
Chest 76604
Colon
    Endoscopic 45391-45392
Colon-Sigmoid
    Endoscopic 45341-45342
Computer-Assisted Surgical Navigation
    Intraoperative 20986
    Preoperative 20987

Nervous System 78699
Therapeutic 79999
Obstetrical Care 59898-59899
Omentum 49329, 49999
Ophthalmology 92499
Orbit 67599
Otorhinolaryngology 92700
Ovary .58679, 58999
Oviduct .58679, 58999
Palate 42299
Pancreas Surgery .48999
Pathology 89240
Pelvis 27299
Penis 55899
Peritoneum 49329, 49999
Pharynx 42999
Physical Therapy 97039, 97139, 97799
Pleura 32999
Pressure Ulcer 15999
Preventive Medicine 99429
Prostate 55899
Psychiatric 90899
Pulmonology 94799
Radiation Physics .77399
Radiation Therapy 77499
Planning 77299
Radiology, Diagnostic 76499
Radionuclide Therapy 79999
Radiopharmaceutical Therapy 79999
Rectum 45499, 45999
Reproductive Medicine
Laboratory Procedure 89398
Salivary Gland 42699
Scrotum 55899
Seminal Vesicle 55899
Shoulder Surgery .23929
Sinuses 31299
Skin 17999
Special Services and Reports 99199
Spine 22899
Stomach 43659, 43999
Strapping 29799
Surgical Pathology 88399
Temporal Bone 69979
Testis 54699, 55899
Throat 42999
Tongue 41599
Tonsil/Adenoid 42999
Toxoid 90749
Trachea 31899
Transfusion 86999
Ultrasound 76999
Ureter 50949
Urinary System 53899
Uterus 58578-58579, 58999
Uvula 42299
Vaccine 90749
Vagina 58999
Vas Deferens 55899
Vascular 37799
Vascular Endoscopy 37501
Vascular Injection .36299
Vascular Studies .93799
Wrist 25999

Unna Paste Boot 29580
Removal 29700

UPP
See Urethra Pressure Profile

Upper
Digestive System Endoscopy
See Endoscopy, Gastrointestinal, Upper
Extremity
See Arm, Upper; Elbow; Humerus
Gastrointestinal Bleeding
See Gastrointestinal, Upper, Hemorrhage
Gastrointestinal Endoscopy, Biopsy
See Biopsy
Planning
See Biopsy, Gastrointestinal, Upper
Endoscopy; Endoscopy, Gastrointestinal
GI Tract
See Gastrointestinal Tract, Upper

Urachal Cyst
See Cyst, Urachal

Urea Breath Test 78267-78268, 83014

Urea Nitrogen
See Blood Urea Nitrogen
Clearance 84545
Quantitative 84520
Semiquantitative 84525
Urine 84540

Urea Nitrogen, Blood
See Blood Urea Nitrogen

Urecholine Supersensitivity Test
See Cystometrogram

Ureter
Anastomosis
to Bladder 50780-50785
to Colon 50810-50815
to Intestine 50800, 50820-50825
to Kidney 50740-50750
to Ureter 50760-50770
Biopsy 50955-50957, 50974-50976, 52007
Catheterization .52005
Continent Diversion 50825
Creation
Stoma 50860
Destruction
Endoscopic 50957, 50976
Dilation 52341-52342, 52344-52345
Endoscopic 50553, 50572, 50953, 50972
Endoscopy
Biopsy 50955-50957, 50974-50976,
52007, 52354
Catheterization 50953, 50972, 52005
Destruction 50957, 50976, 52354
Dilation 52341-52342, 52344-52345
Excision
Tumor 52355
Exploration 52351
Injection of Implant Material 52327
Insertion
Stent . . .50947, 52282, 52332-52334, 53855
Lithotripsy 52353
Manipulation of Ureteral Calculus 52330
Removal
Calculus 50961, 50980,
52320-52325, 52352
Foreign Body 50961, 50980
Resection 52355
via Incision 50970-50980
via Stoma 50951-50961
Exploration 50600
Incision and Drainage 50600

Injection
Drugs 50391
Radiologic 50684, 50690
Insertion
Catheter 50393
Stent 50393, 50688, 50947, 52332-52334
Tube 50688
Instillation
Drugs 50391
Lesion
Destruction 52354
Lithotripsy 52353
Lysis
Adhesions 50715-50725
Manometric Studies
Pressure 50686
Meatotomy 52290
Nuclear Medicine
Reflux Study .78740
Postcaval
See Retrocaval Ureter
Reconstruction .50700
with Intestines 50840
Reflux Study 78740
Reimplantation .51565
Removal
Anastomosis .50830
Calculus 50610-50630, 50961,
51060-51065, 52320-52325
Foreign Body 50961
Stent 50382-50387
Repair 50900
Anastomosis 50740-50825
Continent Diversion 50825
Deligation 50940
Fistula 50920-50930
Lysis Adhesions 50715-50725
Ureterocele .51535
Ectopic 52301
Orthotopic 52300
Urinary Undiversion 50830
Replacement
Stent 50382, 50387
with Intestines 50840
Resection 52355
Revision
Anastomosis 50727-50728
Stent
Change 50688
Insertion 50688
Suture 50900
Deligation 50940
Fistula 50920-50930
Tube
Change 50688
Insertion 50688
Tumor Resection 52355
Unlisted Services and Procedures . . .50949, 53899
X-ray with Contrast
Guide Catheter 74480
Guide Dilation 74485

Ureteral
Catheterization
See Catheterization, Ureter
Guide Wire Insertion 52334
Meatotomy
See Meatotomy, Ureteral
Splinting 50400-50405
Stent Insertion .52332

Urethrocystography 74450-74455
Contrast and/or Chain 51605
Retrograde 51610
Voiding 51600

Urethrocystopexy
See Vesicourethropexy

Urethromeatoplasty 53450-53460

Urethropexy 51840-51841

Urethroplasty 46744-46746
First Stage 53400
One Stage
    Hypospadias 54322-54328
Reconstruction
    Female Urethra 53430
    Male Anterior Urethra 53410
    Prostatic/Membranous Urethra
        First Stage 53420
        One Stage 53415
        Second Stage 53425
Second Stage 53405
    Hypospadias 54308-54316
Third Stage
    Hypospadias 54318

Urethrorrhaphy 53502-53515

Urethroscopy
See Endoscopy, Urethra

Urethrostomy 53000-53010

Urethrotomy 53000-53010
Direct Vision
    with Cystourethroscopy 52276
Internal 52601, 52647-52648
with Cystourethroscopy
    Female 52270
    Male 52275

Uric Acid
Blood 84550
Other Source 84560
Urine 84560

**Uridyltransferase,
Galactose-1-Phosphate**
See Galactose-1-Phosphate, Uridyl Transferase

**Uridylyltransferase,
Galactosephosphate**
See Galactose-1-Phosphate, Uridyl Transferase

Urinalysis 81000-81099
Automated 81001, 81003
Glass Test 81020
Microalbumin 82043-82044
Microscopic 81015
Pregnancy Test 81025
Qualitative 81005
Routine 81002
Screen 81007
Semiquantitative 81005
Unlisted Services and Procedures 81099
Volume Measurement 81050
without Microscopy 81002

Urinary Bladder
See Bladder

Urinary Catheter Irrigation
See Irrigation, Catheter

Urinary Concentration Test
See Water Load Test

Urinary Sphincter, Artificial
See Prosthesis, Urethral Sphincter

Urinary Tract
X-ray with Contrast 74400-74425

Urine
Albumin
    See Albumin, Urine
Blood
    See Blood, Urine
Colony Count 87086
Pregnancy Test 81025
Tests 81001

Urobilinogen
Feces 84577
Urine 84578-84583

Urodynamic Tests
Bladder Capacity
    Ultrasound 51798
Cystometrogram 51725-51729
Electromyography Studies
    Needle 51785
Residual Urine
    Ultrasound 51798
Stimulus Evoked Response 51792
Urethra Pressure Profile 51772
Uroflowmetry 51736-51741
Voiding Pressure Studies
    Bladder 51728-51729
    Intra-Abdominal 51797
    Rectal 51797

Uroflowmetry 51736-51741

Urography
Antegrade 74425
Infusion 74410-74415
Intravenous 74400-74415
Retrograde 74420

Uroporphyrin 84120

Urothromboplastin
See Thromboplastin

Uterine
Adhesion
    See Adhesions, Intrauterine
Cervix
    See Cervix
Endoscopies
    See Endoscopy, Uterus
Haemorrhage
    See Hemorrhage, Uterus

Uterus
Ablation
    Endometrium 58353-58356
    Tumor
        Ultrasound, Focused 0071T-0072T
Biopsy
    Endometrium 58100-58110
    Endoscopic 58558
Catheterization
    X-ray 58340
Chromotubation 58350
Curettage 58356
    Postpartum 59160

Dilation and Curettage 58120
    Postpartum 59160
Ectopic Pregnancy
    Interstitial
        Partial Resection Uterus 59136
        Total Hysterectomy 59135
Endoscopy
    Endometrial Ablation 58563
    Exploration 58555
    Surgery 58558-58565
    Treatment 58558-58565
Excision
    Laparoscopic 58541-58544, 58550
        with Removal of Ovaries 58262-58263,
                        58291-58293, 58552, 58554
    Total 58570-58573
    Partial 58180
    Radical
        Laparoscopic 58548
        Open 58210, 58285
    Removal of Tubes and/or
        Total 58150-58152, 58200,
                    58570-58573, 58953-58956
    Vaginal 58260-58270, 58290-58294,
                            58550-58554
        with Colpectomy 58275-58280
        with Colpo-Urethrocystopexy 58267
        with Repair of Enterocele 58270, 58294
Hemorrhage
    Postpartum 59160
Hydatidiform Mole
    Excision 59100
Hydrotubation 58350
Hysterosalpingography 74740
Incision
    Remove Lesion 59100
Insertion
    Heyman Capsule
        for Brachytherapy 58346
    Intrauterine Device (IUD) 58300
    Tandem
        for Brachytherapy 57155
Laparoscopy 58578
Lesion
    Excision 58545-58546, 59100
    Reconstruction 58540
Removal
    Intrauterine Device (IUD) 58301
Repair
    Fistula 51920-51925
    Rupture 58520, 59350
    Suspension 58400
        with Presacral Sympathectomy 58410
Sonohysterography 76831
Suture
    Rupture 59350
Tumor
    Ablation
        Ultrasound, Focused 0071T-0072T
        Embolization 37210
    Excision
        Abdominal Approach 58140, 58146
        Vaginal Approach 58145
Unlisted Services and Procedures ...58578, 58999
X-ray with Contrast 74740

**UTP Hexose 1 Phosphate
Uridylyltransferase**
See Galactose-1-Phosphate, Uridyl Transferase

UV Light Therapy
See Actinotherapy

Vaginal Delivery 59400, 59610-59614
after Previous Cesarean Delivery 59610-59612
    Attempted 59618-59622
Antepartum Care 59400
Cesarean Delivery after Attempted 59618
    Delivery Only 59620
    Postpartum Care 59622
Delivery after Previous
    Vaginal Delivery Only
       Postpartum Care 59614
Delivery Only 59409
External Cephalic Version 59412
Placenta 59414
Postpartum Care 59410
Routine Care 59400

Vaginal Hysterectomy 58552-58554

Vaginal Smear
See Pap Smears

Vaginal Suppositories
Induced Abortion 59855
    with Dilation and Curettage 59856
    with Hysterectomy 59857

Vaginectomy
See Colpectomy

Vaginoplasty
Intersex State 57335

Vaginorrhaphy
See Colporrhaphy

Vaginoscopy
Biopsy 57454
Exploration 57452

Vaginotomy
See Colpotomy

Vagotomy
Abdominal 64760
Highly Selective 43641
Parietal Cell 43641, 64755
Selective 43640
Transthoracic 64752
Truncal 43640
with Gastroduodenostomy Revision,
Reconstruction 43855
with Gastrojejunostomy Revision,
Reconstruction 43865
with Partial Distal Gastrectomy 43635

Vagus Nerve
Avulsion
    Abdominal 64760
    Selective 64755
    Thoracic 64752
Incision 43640-43641
    Abdominal 64760
    Selective 64755
    Thoracic 64752
Injection
    Anesthetic 64408
Transection 43640-43641
    Abdominal 64760
    Selective 43652, 64755
    Thoracic 64752
    Truncal 43651

Valproic Acid
See Dipropylacetic Acid

Valproic Acid Measurement
See Dipropylacetic Acid

Valsalva Sinus
See Sinus of Valsalva

**Valva Atrioventricularis Sinistra
(Valva Mitralis)**
See Mitral Valve

Valve
Aortic
    See Heart, Aortic Valve
Bicuspid
    See Mitral Valve
Mitral
    See Mitral Valve
Pulmonary
    See Pulmonary Valve
Tricuspid
    See Tricuspid Valve

Valve Stenoses, Aortic
See Aortic Stenosis

Valvectomy
Tricuspid Valve 33460

Valvotomy
Mitral Valve 33420-33422
Pulmonary Valve 33470-33474
Reoperation 33530

Valvuloplasty
Aortic Valve 33400-33403
Femoral Vein 34501
Mitral Valve 33425-33427
Percutaneous Balloon
    Aortic Valve 92986
    Mitral Valve 92987
    Pulmonary Valve 92990
Prosthetic Valve 33496
Reoperation 33530
Tricuspid Valve 33463-33465

Van Den Bergh Test
See Bilirubin, Blood

Vancomycin
Assay 80202
Resistance 87500

Vanillylmandelic Acid
Urine 84585

Vanilmandelic Acid
See Vanillylmandelic Acid

Varicella (Chicken Pox)
See Vaccines

Varicella-Zoster
Antibody 86787
Antigen Detection
    Direct Fluorescence 87290

Varices Esophageal
See Esophageal Varices

Varicocele
Spermatic Cord
    Excision 55530-55540

Varicose Vein
Ablation 36475-36479
Removal 37765-37785

Secondary Varicosity 37785
with Tissue Excision 37735-37761

Vas Deferens
Anastomosis
    to Epididymis 54900-54901
Excision 55250
Incision 55200
    for X-ray 55300
Ligation 55450
Repair
    Suture 55400
Unlisted Services and Procedures 55899
Vasography 74440
X-ray with Contrast 74440

Vascular Flow Check, Graft 15860

Vascular Injection
Unlisted Services and Procedures 36299

Vascular Lesion
Cranial
    Excision 61600-61608, 61615-61616
Cutaneous
    Destruction 17106-17108

Vascular Malformation
Cerebral
    Repair 61710
Finger
    Excision 26111-26116
Hand
    Excision 26111-26116

Vascular Procedures
Angioscopy
    Non-Coronary Vessels 35400
Brachytherapy
    Intracoronary Artery 92974
Endoscopy
    Surgical 37500
Harvest
    Lower Extremity Vein 35572
Intravascular Ultrasound
    Coronary Vessels 92978-92979
    Non-Coronary Vessels 75945-75946
Spectroscopy
    Catheter Based 0205T
Stent
    Intracoronary 92980-92981
Thrombolysis
    Coronary Vessels 92975-92977
    Cranial Vessels 37195

Vascular Rehabilitation
See Peripheral Artery Disease Rehabilitation (PAD)

Vascular Studies
See Doppler Scan, Duplex, Plethysmography
Angioscopy
    Non-Coronary Vessels 35400
Aorta 93978-93979
Arterial Studies (Non-Invasive)
    Extracranial 93875-93882
    Extremities 93922-93924
    Intracranial 93886-93890
    Lower Extremity 93925-93926
    Middle Cerebral Artery, Fetal 76821
    Umbilical Artery, Fetal 76820
Artery Studies
    Upper Extremity 93930-93931
Bioimpedance Cardiovascular Analysis 93701

Infant
    Cutdown 36420
    Percutaneous 36400-36406
Routine 36415

Venography
Adrenal 75840-75842
Arm 75820-75822
Epidural 75872
Hepatic Portal 75885-75887
Injection 36005
Jugular 75860
Leg 75820-75822
Liver 75889-75891
Neck 75860
Nuclear Medicine 78445, 78457-78458
Orbit 75880
Renal 75831-75833
Sagittal Sinus 75870
Vena Cava 75825-75827
Venous Sampling 75893

Venorrhaphy
See Suture, Vein

Venotomy
See Phlebotomy

Venous Access Device
Blood Collection 36591-36592
Declotting 36593
Fluoroscopic Guidance 77001
Insertion
    Central 36560-36566
    Peripheral 36570-36571
Irrigation 96523
Obstruction Clearance 36595-36596
    Guidance 75901-75902
Removal 36590
Repair 36576
Replacement 36582-36583, 36585
    Catheter Only 36578

Venous Blood Pressure
See Blood Pressure, Venous

Venovenostomy
See Anastomosis, Vein

Ventilating Tube
Insertion 69433
Removal 69424

Ventilation Assist 94002-94005, 99504
See Pulmonology, Therapeutic

Ventricular Puncture .61020-61026, 61105-
61120

Ventriculocisternostomy 62180,
62200-62201

Ventriculography
Anesthesia
    Brain 00214
    Cardiac 01920
Nuclear Imaging 78635

Ventriculomyectomy 33416

Ventriculomyotomy 33416

Vermiform Appendix
See Appendix

Vermilionectomy 40500

Verruca Plana
See Warts, Flat

Verruca(e)
See Warts

Version, Cephalic
See Cephalic Version

Vertebra
See Intervertebral Disc; Spinal Cord; Spine;
Vertebral Body; Vertebral Process
Additional Segment
    Excision 22103, 22116
Arthrodesis
    Anterior 22548-22585
    Exploration 22830
    Lateral Extracavitary 22532-22534
    Posterior 22590-22802
    Spinal Deformity
        Anterior Approach 22808-22812
        Posterior Approach 22800-22804
Aspiration 62267
Cervical
    Excision
        for Tumor 22100, 22110
    Fracture 23675-23680
Decompression 62287
Fracture/Dislocation
    Additional Segment
        Open Treatment 22328
    Cervical
        Open Treatment 22326
    Lumbar
        Open Treatment 22325
    Thoracic
        Open Treatment 22327
Kyphectomy 22818-22819
Lumbar
    Distraction Device 0171T-0172T
    Excision
        for Tumor 22102, 22114
    Foraminotomy 0202T
Osteoplasty
    CT Scan 72292
    Fluoroscopy 72291
    Lumbar 22521-22522
    Thoracic 22520-22522
Osteotomy
    Additional Segment
        Anterior Approach 22226
        Posterior/Posterolateral Approach ...22216
    Cervical
        Anterior Approach 22220
        Posterior/Posterolateral Approach ...22210
    Lumbar
        Anterior Approach 22224
        Posterior/Posterolateral Approach ...22214
    Thoracic
        Anterior Approach 22222
        Posterior/Posterolateral Approach ...22212
Thoracic
    Excision
        for Tumor 22101, 22112

Vertebrae
See Vertebra
Arthrodesis
    Anterior 22548-22585
    Lateral Extracavitary 22532-22534
    Spinal Deformity 22818-22819

Vertebral
Arteries
    See Artery, Vertebral
Body
    Biopsy 20250-20251
    Excision
        Decompression 63081-63103
        Lesion 63300-63308
        with Skull Base Surgery 61597
    Fracture/Dislocation
        Closed Treatment 22305
        without Manipulation 22310
    Kyphectomy 22818-22819
    Repair
        Injection
            Lumbar 22521
            Thoracic 22520
Column
    See Spine
Corpectomy 63081-63103, 63300-63308
Fracture
    See Fracture, Vertebra
Joint Replacement
    Lumbar Spine 0202T
Process
    Fracture/Dislocation
        Closed Treatment
        with Manipulation, Casting and/or
        Bracing 22315

Very Low Density Lipoprotein
See Lipoprotein, Blood

Vesication
See Bulla

Vesicle, Seminal
See Seminal Vesicle

Vesico-Psoas Hitch 50785

Vesicostomy
Cutaneous 51980

Vesicourethropexy 51840-51841

Vesicovaginal Fistula
See Fistula, Vesicovaginal

Vesiculectomy 55650

Vesiculogram, Seminal
See Vesiculography

Vesiculography 55300, 74440

Vesiculotomy 55600-55605
Complicated 55605

Vessel, Blood
See Blood Vessels

Vessels Transposition, Great
See Transposition, Great Arteries

Vestibular Function Tests
See Ear, Nose, and Throat
Additional Electrodes 92547
Caloric Test 92533
Caloric Vestibular Tests 92543
Foveal Stimulation 92540
Nystagmus
    Optokinetic 92534, 92540, 92544
    Positional 92532, 92540, 92542
    Spontaneous 92531, 92540-92541

Perineum
    Biopsy 56605-56606
    Incision and Drainage 56405
Repair
    Obstetric 59300

Vulvectomy
Complete 56625, 56633-56640
Partial 56620, 56630-56632
Radical 56630-56631, 56633-56640
    Complete
        with Bilateral Inguinofemoral
        Lymphadenectomy 56637
        with Inguinofemoral, Iliac, and Pelvic
        Lymphadenectomy 56640
        with Unilateral Inguinofemoral
        Lymphadenectomy 56634
    Partial
        with Bilateral Inguinofemoral
        Lymphadenectomy 56632
        with Unilateral Inguinofemoral
        Lymphadenectomy 56631
Simple
    Complete 56625
    Partial 56620

VZIG
See Immune Globulins, Varicella-Zoster

W

W-Plasty
See Skin, Adjacent Tissue Transfer

WADA Activation Test 95958
See Electroencephalography

WAIS 96101-96102

Waldius Procedure 27445

Wall, Abdominal
See Abdominal Wall

Walsh Modified Radical
Prostatectomy
See Prostatectomy

Warts
Flat
    Destruction 17110-17111

Washing
Sperm 58323

Wassmund Procedure
Osteotomy
    Maxilla 21206

Water Load Test 89235

Water Wart
See Molluscum Contagiosum

Waterston Procedure 33755

Watson-Jones Procedure ... 27695-27698

Wave, Ultrasonic Shock
See Ultrasound

WBC
See White Blood Cell

Webbed
Toe
    Repair 28280

Wechsler Memory Scales
See Neuropsychological Testing

Wedge Excision
Osteotomy 21122

Wedge Resection
Ovary 58920

Well-Baby Care 99381, 99391, 99432

Wellness Behavior
See Evaluation and Management, Health Behavior

West Nile Virus
Antibody 86788-86789

Westergren Test
See Sedimentation Rate, Blood Cell

Western Blot
HIV 86689
Protein 84181-84182
Tissue Analysis 88371-88372

Wheelchair Management
Training 97542

Wheelchair Management/Propulsion
See Physical Medicine/Therapy/Occupational
Therapy

Wheeler Procedure
See Blepharoplasty, Entropion
Discission Secondary Membranous
Cataract 66820

Whipple Procedure 48150

Whirlpool Therapy 97022
See Physical Medicine/Therapy/Occupational
Therapy

White Blood Cell
Alkaline Phosphatase 85540
Antibody 86021
Count 85032, 85048, 89055
Differential 85004-85007, 85009
Histamine Release Test 86343
Phagocytosis 86344
Transfusion
    See Leukocyte, Transfusion

Whitman Astragalectomy
See Talus, Excision

Whitman Procedure 27120

Wick Catheter Technique 20950

Window
Oval
    See Oval Window
Round
    See Round Window

Window Technic, Pericardial
See Pericardiostomy

Windpipe
See Trachea

Winiwarter Operation
See Anastomosis, Gallbladder to Intestines

Winter Procedure 54435

Wintrobe Test
See Sedimentation Rate, Blood Cell

Wire
See Pin
Insertion/Removal
    Skeletal Traction 20650
Interdental
    without Fracture 21497

Wiring
Prophylactic Treatment
    Humerus 24498

Wirsung Duct
See Pancreatic Duct

Wisconsin Card Sorting Test
See Neuropsychological Tests

Witzel Operation 43500, 43520,
                  43830-43832
See Incision, Stomach, Creation, Stoma; Incision
and Drainage

Womb
See Uterus

Wood Alcohol
See Methanol

Work Hardening 97545-97546
See Physical Medicine/Therapy/Occupational
Therapy

Work Related Evaluation
Services 99455-99456

Worm
See Helminth

Wound
Closure
    Temporary
        Skin Allograft 15300-15321
        Skin Xenograft 15420-15421
Debridement
    Non-Selective 97602
    Selective 97597-97598
Dehiscence
    Repair 12020-12021, 13160
Exploration
    Penetrating
        Abdomen/Flank/Back 20102
        Chest 20101
        Extremity 20103
        Neck 20100
        Penetrating Trauma 20100-20103
Infection
    Incision and Drainage
        Postoperative 10180
Negative Pressure Therapy 97605-97606
Repair
    Complex 13100-13160
    Intermediate 12031-12057
    Simple 12001-12021
    Urethra 53502-53515

X-ray Tomography, Computed
See CT Scan

Xa, Coagulation Factor
See Thrombokinase

Xenoantibodies
See Antibody, Heterophile

Xenografts, Skin
See Heterograft, Skin

Xenotransplantation
See Heterograft

Xerography
See Xeroradiography

XI, Coagulation Factor
See Plasma Thromboplastin, Antecedent

XI, Cranial Nerve
See Accessory Nerve

XII, Coagulation Factor
See Hageman Factor

XII, Cranial Nerve
See Hypoglossal Nerve

XIII, Coagulation Factor
See Fibrin Stabilizing Factor

Xylose Absorption Test

Y

Yacoub Procedure
See Ascending Aorta Graft

Yeast

Yersinia

YHrium-Aluminum-Garnet (YAG) Laser
See Eye, Incision

Z

Ziegler Procedure
Discission Secondary Membranous Cataract 66820

Zinc Manganese Leucine Aminopeptidase
See Leucine Aminopeptidase

Zygoma
See Cheekbone

Zygomatic Arch
Fracture